THE
unofficial GUIDE®
ᴛᴏIreland

STEPHEN BREWER

Please note that prices fluctuate in the course of time and that travel information changes under the impact of many factors that influence the travel industry. We therefore suggest that you write or call ahead for confirmation when making your travel plans. Every effort has been made to ensure the accuracy of information throughout this book, and the contents of this publication are believed to be correct at the time of printing. Nevertheless, the publishers cannot accept responsibility for errors or omissions, for changes in details given in this guide, or for the consequences of any reliance on the information provided by the same. Assessments of attractions and so forth are based upon the author's own experience; therefore, descriptions given in this guide necessarily contain an element of subjective opinion, which may not reflect the publisher's opinion or dictate a reader's own experience on another occasion. Readers are invited to write the publisher with ideas, comments, and suggestions for future editions.

Published by:
John Wiley & Sons, Inc.
111 River Street
Hoboken, NJ 07030-5774

Produced by Menasha Ridge Press

Cover design by Michael J. Freeland

Interior design by Vertigo Design

For information on our other products and services or to obtain technical support, please contact our Customer Care Department within the United States at 800-762-2974, outside the United States at 317-572-3993, or by fax at 317-572-4002.

John Wiley & Sons, Inc., also publishes its books in a variety of electronic formats. Some content that appears in print may not be available in electronic formats.

ISBN 0-7645-9892-9

Manufactured in the United States of America

5 4 3 2 1

CONTENTS

LIST *of* MAPS

ACKNOWLEDGMENTS

I WISH TO THANK ALL MY IRISH FRIENDS AND RELATIVES who shared stories, advice, and inspiration: Gerry Madigan and Hal Erbe, wise and always ready to talk about home; Anna Callan, a fine poet and advisor; Emmet Kelleher and Suzanne Rowan Kelleher, warm, charming, and first-rate conversationalists; and my Coyne cousins, a pleasure to be with and dispensers of good advice on what to say and not to say in a pub. Thanks, too, to the many, many fine folks I met along the way and were on hand with help, humor, and hospitality. Here in America, I am deeply grateful to Molly Merkle, Holly Cross, Ritchey Halphen, and the rest of the crew at Menasha Ridge Press for their skill, professionalism, and patience.

This book is dedicated to the Leonard sisters, Mary and Patricia, who never lost the lilt and magic of the old country and whom I will always miss.

—*Stephen Brewer*

ABOUT *the* AUTHOR

STEPHEN BREWER is a writer and editor who loves his home and friends in New York City but is just as happy traveling. He is the author of several other guidebooks, including *The Unofficial Guide to England*, *Frommer's Best Day Trips from London*, and *Frommer's Venice Day by Day*.

THE
unofficial GUIDE®
ᵀᴼIreland

INTRODUCTION

WELCOME *to* IRELAND

TALK. THE IRISH HAVE A NAME FOR IT—*craic*—and these days the craic is often about the new prosperity that's falling over Ireland. Yes, Ireland's doing well these days, and the unprecedented wealth, as well as the newness that comes with it, may bring to mind the lines of the Irish poet William Butler Yeats: "All changed, changed utterly."

It's not, though—changed, that is. Not really. The essence of being in Ireland is still about taking the first sip of a freshly poured Guinness and wondering how beer could be so much better here than it is back home. Or noticing that a craggy, purple-shaded, heather-covered landscape looks just like the backdrop of an MGM musical, or trying to determine how many shades of green are contained within one valley. The pleasure of being in Ireland is still about sitting in a pub and listening to a discussion about the Troubles, fishing rights, and road improvements (all mixed into one monologue) out of one ear and the strains of a fiddle out of the other. Or finding a comfortable spot next to a crackling fire at your castle hotel or bed-and-breakfast and feeling that you've come back to a familiar place. Ireland has a way of evoking nostalgia for the old country, even in visitors who don't have a trace of Irish blood coursing through their veins.

Ireland will throw a few surprises your way, too. As you travel round the country, you will sit down to some of the best meals you've ever had. The ingredients aren't necessarily exotic—just good Kerry lamb, for example, or Dublin Bay scallops, prepared with a finesse that should put to rest forever the bad jokes about Irish cuisine. With the peace dividends comes the chance to discover Northern Ireland, where yes, signs of the Troubles are still in evidence, but the Giants Causeway and other natural phenomena have a way of reminding us that nature is going to be a force long after we're gone.

In the *Unofficial Guide to Ireland,* we show you how to get the most out of your visit. We point out what's right and what's wrong about hotels and restaurants, tell you what paintings to look for, and lead you to tours that will give you an insider's view of a city or take you to a patch of wilderness you'd never find on your own. For a highly selective list of our favorite places in Ireland, see the Not to Be Missed lists at the beginning of each chapter. Our advice should make your trip more enjoyable (and save you time and money, too), but follow your own travel instincts as well. Make discoveries, make friends (not hard to do in Ireland), let yourself be drawn into a session of craic. We'll help you with the basics, but only you can embrace the welcome that Ireland will extend to you.

ABOUT *this* GUIDE

WHY "UNOFFICIAL"?

MOST TRAVEL GUIDES TO Ireland follow the usual tracks of the typical tourist—automatically sending everyone to the well-known towns and sights without offering any information about how to get the most out of the visit, recommending restaurants and hotels indiscriminately, and failing to recognize the limits of human endurance in sightseeing. This guide is different: we appreciate the fact that you'll want to be discerning about hotels and restaurants, to spend your time doing what you really want to do, and to see what you want to see.

Accordingly, we help you make choices that will maximize your trip to Ireland. We tell you what we think of certain tourist traps, why you should spend time in one place and not in another, what rooms to ask for in hotels and what to order (and what not to order) in restaurants, what the options are if you want to stay off the beaten track, how to spend a little less money on some meals and hotels so you can splurge a little when you want to (and we give you suggestions of places worthy of a splurge). We complain about rip-offs, advise you on bargains, and steer you out of the madness of the crowds for a break now and then. We also give you the kinds of details—from historical background to juicy tidbits—that will make you appreciate Ireland all the more.

We're well aware of the fact that you probably only have a week or two to spend in Ireland, so we've done the footwork to help you prepare and strategize to get the most out of your time. We lead you to hotels that offer the best deals and the most pleasant surroundings, good restaurants in varying price ranges, the sights you won't want to miss (and tips for visiting them when they are least crowded). In laying out our visits, we take things easy, the way we think you'll want to, and we have gone to considerable effort to ensure that the quality of your travels in Ireland will be high and the irritation quotient low. We've tried to anticipate the special needs of older people, families with young children, families with teenagers, solo travelers, people with disabilities, and those who have a particular passion for literature, sports, architecture, shopping, painting, antiques, or whatever.

Please remember that prices and admission hours change constantly; we have listed the most up-to-date information we can get, but it never hurts to double-check times in particular (if prices of attractions change, it is generally not by much). Most of all, whether you're visiting Ireland for the first time or the twentieth, traveling on pleasure or business, we trust we will help you better enjoy the experience.

ABOUT *UNOFFICIAL GUIDES*

READERS CARE ABOUT AUTHORS' OPINIONS. The authors, after all, are supposed to know what they are talking about. This, coupled with the fact that the traveler wants quick answers (as opposed to endless alternatives), dictates that travel authors should be explicit, prescriptive, and above all, direct. The *Unofficial Guides* try to be just that. We spell out alternatives and recommend specific courses of action. We simplify complicated destinations and attractions to allow the traveler to feel in control in the most unfamiliar environments. Our objective is not to give the most information or all the information, but the most accessible, useful information. Of course, many hotels, restaurants, and attractions are so closely woven into the fabric of Ireland that it would be a disservice to omit them from our guide solely because we can't recommend them. So we've included all the famous haunts, giving our opinion of and experience with them, in the hopes that you will approach (or avoid) these institutions armed with the necessary intelligence.

SPECIAL FEATURES

- Vital information about traveling abroad
- Friendly introductions to Irish towns and cities
- Listings that are keyed to your interests, so you can pick and choose
- Advice on how to avoid the worst crowds, traffic, and excessive costs
- Recommendations for lesser-known sights that are off the well-beaten tourist path but no less worthwhile
- Maps that make it easy to find places you want to visit—and places you want to avoid
- Hotel and restaurant selections that help you narrow down your choices quickly, according to your needs and preferences
- Candid opinions of hotels, sights, and restaurants that are overrated, and those that are especially worthwhile
- A table of contents and detailed index to help you find things fast

---

WHAT YOU WON'T GET

- Long, useless lists where everything looks the same
- Information that gets you to your destination at the worst possible time
- Information without advice on how to use it

An *Unofficial Guide* is a critical reference work; we focus on a travel destination that appears to be especially complex. Our authors and researchers are completely independent from the attractions, restaurants, and hotels we describe. *The Unofficial Guide to Ireland* is designed for individuals and families traveling for fun as well as for business, and it will be especially helpful to those hopping "across the pond" for the first time. The guide is directed at value-conscious, consumer-oriented adults who seek a cost-effective but not Spartan travel style.

HOW THIS GUIDE WAS RESEARCHED AND WRITTEN

IN PREPARING THIS BOOK, we took nothing for granted. Each hotel, restaurant, shop, and attraction was visited by trained observers who conducted detailed evaluations and rated each according to formal criteria. Team members conducted interviews with tourists of all ages to determine what they enjoyed most and least during their visits to Ireland.

Although our observers are independent and impartial, they are otherwise ordinary travelers. Like you, they have visited Ireland as tourists or business travelers, noting their satisfaction or dissatisfaction. The primary difference between the average tourist and the trained evaluator is the evaluator's skills in organization, preparation, and observation. Observer teams use detailed checklists to analyze hotel rooms, restaurants, nightclubs, and attractions. Finally, evaluator ratings and observations are integrated with tourist reactions and the opinions of patrons for a comprehensive profile of each feature and service.

In compiling this guide, we recognize that a tourist's age, background, and interests will strongly influence his or her taste in Ireland's wide array of attractions and will account for a preference for one sight or museum over another. Our sole objective is to provide the reader with sufficient description, critical evaluation, and pertinent data to make knowledgeable decisions according to individual tastes.

LETTERS, COMMENTS, AND QUESTIONS FROM READERS

WE EXPECT TO LEARN FROM our mistakes, as well as from the input of our readers, and to improve with each new book and edition. Many of those who use the *Unofficial Guides* write to us asking questions, making comments, or sharing their own discoveries and lessons learned. New hotels, restaurants, and attractions are opening all the time in Ireland, and if there's something new you'd like us to check out, let us know about it. We appreciate all such input, and we encourage our readers to continue writing. Readers' comments and observations will be frequently incorporated in revised editions of *The Unofficial Guide to Ireland* and will contribute immeasurably to its improvement.

How to Write the Author

Stephen Brewer
The Unofficial Guide to Ireland
P.O. Box 43673
Birmingham, AL 35243

When you write, be sure to put your return address on your letter as well as on the envelope—sometimes envelopes and letters get separated. Remember, our work takes us out of the office for long periods of time, so forgive us if our response is delayed.

HOW THIS GUIDE IS ORGANIZED: BY REGION AND BY SUBJECT

WE HAVE ORGANIZED THIS GUIDE by region—not by any sort of official, government-designated regional organization, but by manageably sized geographic areas that we use to help you plan your travels through Ireland. We then organize each region by the major (and the most appealing) cities and towns that you can use as a base. Within our coverage of each place, you'll find detailed coverage on the following:

PLANNING YOUR VISIT This section includes local informational resources and seasonal events that may or may not help you decide when to visit.

ARRIVING AND GETTING ORIENTED Here we give information on reaching the city by air (when relevant), train, car (including where to park), and bus.

GETTING AROUND In larger destinations where walking is not an option, we give detailed descriptions of how to use the bus network, subway, or other public transportation.

HOTELS This section provides profiles of our hotel picks; you can peruse them and book ahead if you wish.

EXPLORING Here we lead you through a town, city, or region, pointing out the sights (including those of secondary interest but still worth a quick visit), then provide detailed profiles of all the major sightseeing attractions. You'll also find a section on tours, with our choices for the best guided tours to help you become acquainted with a place.

DINING Provides our choices of the most pleasant places to eat.

ENTERTAINMENT AND NIGHTLIFE We lead you to theaters, concert halls, pubs, discos, and other venues.

ireland

ATLANTIC
OCEAN

North Sea

SCOTLAND
Edinburgh

NORTHERN
IRELAND

Irish Sea

REPUBLIC OF
IRELAND

ENGLAND

Dublin ★

WALES

St. George's
Channel

London ★

English Channel

FRANCE

| 0 | 100 mi |
| 0 | 100 km |

SCOTLAND

Campbeltown

ATLANTIC OCEAN

NORTH CHANNEL

Tory Island

Rathlin Island

Arranmore
Island

Creeslough

Lough
Foyle

Portrush

Portstewart

Ballycastle

Letterkenny

Eglinton
Airport

Garron
Point

Gweebarra
Bay

DONEGAL

BLUE STACK MTNS.

Finn

Derry

SPERRIN MTNS.

ANTRIM

Ballymena

Ardara

Donegal

Strabane

DERRY

NORTHERN
IRELAND
(U.K.)

Larne

To
Douglas

Donegal Bay

Ballyshannon

TYRONE

Omagh

BELFAST

Bangor

Lower Lough
Erne

Dungannon

Lough
Neagh

Belfast
Airport

Lagan

Strangford
Lough

Killala
Bay

Sligo
Bay

LEITRIM

Enniskillen

Portadown

FERMANAGH

Upper
Lough
Erne

Armagh

DOWN

Newcastle

Ballina

Sligo

ARMAGH

Blacksod Bay

MAYO

Nephin

Lough
Conn

SLIGO

Lough
Allen

Annagh

MONAGHAN

Newry

Achill Island

CAVAN

Dundalk

Clare Island

Clew
Bay

ROSCOMMON

LONGFORD

LOUTH

Dundalk Bay

Inishturk

Westport

Lough
Mask

Roscommon

Longford

Kells

Ardee

Inishbofin

WESTMEATH

MEATH

Drogheda

Irish Sea

Clifden

CONNEMARA

Tuam

GALWAY

Lough Ree

Mullingar

Trim

Boyne

Lough
Corrib

Athlone

Dublin
Airport

To Holyhead &
Douglas

Inishmore

Galway

REPUBLIC OF IRELAND

Liffey

DUBLIN

DUBLIN

Galway Bay

Inishmaan

Doolin

OFFALY

Kildare

Bray

ARAN ISLANDS

Inisheer

Shannon

Portlaoise

KILDARE

WICKLOW

Wicklow
Head

Kilrush

LAOISE

Lugnaquillia ▲

CLARE

Ennis

Lough
Derg

Carlow

Wicklow

Loop Head

Shannon
Airport

TIPPERARY

CARLOW

Arklow

Mouth of the
Shannon

Limerick

KILKENNY

Slaney

Listowel

Cashel

Kilkenny

WICKLOW MOUNTAINS

LIMERICK

Tipperary

Clonmel

Carrick-
on-Suir

Brandon
Mtn.

Feale

Barrow

Great
Blasket
Island

DINGLE
PENINSULA

Tralee

Galtymore ▲

Suir

WEXFORD

Dingle

KERRY

GALTY MTNS.

WATERFORD

Wexford

Dingle
Bay

Carrauntuo
Hill

Blackwater

Rosslare

To Fishguard &
Pembroke

Valentia
Island

Killarney

CORK

Waterford

IVERAGH
PENINSULA

MACGILLYCUDDY'S
REEKS

Lough Leane

Blarney

Lee

Dungarvan

Waterford
Airport

Kenmare

Cork

Youghal

Kenmare River

CAHA MTNS.

Bandon

Cork Airport

Cobh

ST. GEORGE'S CHANNEL

Bantry

Kinsale

To Swansea

Bantry Bay

Skibbereen

Mizen

To Roscoff

| 0 | 50 mi |
| 0 | 50 km |

N

Some Do's and Don'ts When Visiting Ireland

- **Don't** try to intervene in football (soccer) arguments or those about hurling or Gaelic football—these are very serious subjects, and no one really cares what an outsider thinks about them.

- **Don't** think you'll endear yourself to the Irish by complaining about the rain. They tend to like it.

- **Do** be prepared to talk about the weather, and be prepared for a daily forecast that includes showers, fog, periods of sunshine, spells of daytime darkness, and gales.

- **Don't** tell anyone that his or her accent sounds British.

- **Don't** think British pounds are acceptable as currency in the Republic.

- **Do** listen. Not only do the Irish have a lot to say, but they have a nice way of saying it.

- **Do** read. The Irish are still producing great literature; step into any bookshop and stock up on some volumes to enjoy long after you've left Ireland.

SHOPPING Here we focus on items that are unique to a particular place.

EXERCISE AND RECREATION This section provides ideas on where to exercise—we often lead you to walking and biking trails, of which Ireland has so many.

We discuss these categories in greater depth in Part Two, Arriving and Getting Around in Ireland. Here are the regions that make up our coverage of Ireland.

Dublin

The capital of the Republic is an easy place to be—despite the traffic that clogs the streets and the cranes that pierce the sky these days. Prosperity has brought new shops, restaurants, nightlife, hotels, and a burst of cosmopolitan vitality. But there's no need to sing the lament "Me darlin', Dublin's dead and gone." In many ways, the city is still as mellow as the gray stone of its cathedrals and other landmarks and the verdant hues of its parks and greens. You can get around on foot, stepping in and out of the country's great museums and landmarks, and come time to rest, find a snug corner in one of the city's thousand-odd pubs. We guide you through all the major attractions, as well as our favorite minor ones, and give you a selection of hotels, restaurants, shops, and clubs, making sure you enjoy this lovely city as much as we do.

The South of Ireland

Southern Ireland is surprisingly urbane. **Kilkenny** is one of Ireland's most lovely cities, and **Cork** is one of its most lively. **Cobh** and **Kinsale** have long been linked to the sea and are well steeped in episodes of the Irish past. Even when you think you're deep in the countryside, you'll see a remarkable medieval monument (none more haunting than the **Rock of Cashel**) or two rising above the green landscapes.

The Southwest of Ireland

Kenmare, the **Dingle Peninsula, Killarney National Park,** the **Ring of Kerry**—the place-names here read like a list of the most beautiful spots in Ireland. To get the most out of this scenery-endowed region, settle into the welcoming guest houses of Kenmare and Dingle Town, and from there follow our lead off the beaten path to enjoy cliff-hugging coast roads and mountain trails.

The Lower Shannon

The Shannon, the longest river in the British Isles, flows into the Atlantic Ocean through a wide estuary. The green landscapes that roll away from the river are littered with castles (the most famous is **Bunratty**), pretty towns and villages (the prettiest is **Adare**), some of Ireland's grandest hotels, and one of Ireland's largest cities, **Limerick.**

The West of Ireland

The West of Ireland is a land of rugged seascapes, mountains, bogs, and moors. The region is *Gaeltacht* (Irish speaking) in many parts, cradles some of Ireland's most remarkable landscapes, including the **Burren** and **Connemara,** and is home to one of its most hospitable cities, **Galway.**

The Northwest of Ireland

It's easy to bypass the desolate landscapes of counties **Donegal** and **Sligo.** But to do so would mean missing a lot: places such as **Slieve League,** the tallest, and certainly most dramatic, sea cliffs in Europe; the heather-covered mountains of **Glenveagh National Park;** the **pre-historic tombs** that surround **Sligo Town**; and the dramatic **headlands** where the region dips into the North Sea.

Northern Ireland

Derry and **Belfast** still bear the marks of the Troubles, most visibly in the wall murals that are now attractions in both cities, but things have changed with the peace dividends. The talk in Belfast these days is about revival; the surprise for the visitor is just how appealing these places are. The impression is magnified along the **Antrim Coast,** where nature conjures up magic like the **Giants Causeway.**

AN OVERVIEW *of* IRISH HISTORY

THE FIRST INHABITANTS

SCIENTIFIC OPINION IS INCONSISTENT, but it seems likely that humans first arrived in Ireland around the late 8000s BC. These people were Mesolithic, and the artifacts they left behind (mostly flint) make it clear that they lived a nomadic life, fishing and hunting.

Neolithic people begin to appear in Ireland in about 3000 BC. Unlike the earlier inhabitants, these people farmed. Armed with stone axes, they could easily cut down trees and build dwellings. With tilled fields and crops, permanent settlements grew up, leading to relatively stable communities.

These inhabitants also left behind a remarkable variety of megalithic stone monuments: hundreds of court, portal, and passage tombs. Many of these bear fascinating engraved designs. **Newgrange** and **Knowth,** just north of Dublin (see page 175), are two of the most spectacular and moving examples. Later inhabitants came to think that their creators were faeries, or little people, a belief that is still (to a degree) alive today.

The Bronze Age (1750–500 BC) witnessed the introduction of metalworking, a vast improvement over stone. Bronze, copper, and gold objects were fashioned, and by the late Bronze Age (800 BC) the industry was well established.

- **8000 BC**   Mesolithic people first appear in Ireland
- **3000 BC**   Neolithic people arrive
- **1750–500 BC**   The Bronze Age

THE CELTS ARRIVE

THE CELTS ARRIVED IN IRELAND in successive waves, beginning around 500 BC, and immediately began to plant their culture on the new soil in every possible way. The influence of their most important clan, the **Gaels,** lives on in many ways today, especially in the Gaelic language.

The Celts came to Ireland equipped with the ability to produce iron. They brought with them iron weapons and tools, which gave them an advantage over those who produced bronze, as iron is much stronger and tougher. They also brought with them a lively culture of song and poetry.

The Celts were never interested in a unified government. Many tribes existed, loosely allied to several kings. Despite their casual organization, which would seem to invite invasion, the Romans never conquered the Celts in Ireland.

- **500 BC**   Celt settlements begins
- **55 BC**   Romans conquer the Celts in England
- **AD 100**   The Gaels appear in Ireland

CHRISTIANITY COMES TO IRELAND

TRADITION HAS IT THAT priests came to Ireland before **St. Patrick,** but when we think of the birth of Christianity in Ireland, it is Patrick whom we think of. The saint, whose actual name was Maewyn Succat, was kidnapped from his home in Britain and transported to Ireland, where he spent seven years working as a slave. He escaped, went back to Britain, then returned to Ireland in AD 432 to convert the Irish to Christianity. He preached throughout the country, often at Celtic religious festivals, and he became incredibly popular, even among the Celts. Many legends rose around him, the most familiar contending that he drove the snakes out of Ireland—not literal reptiles, but, rather, pagan religion—and that he used the shamrock to explain the Trinity. Patrick, who died on March 17, AD 461, also helped found many schools and monasteries. He later became the patron saint of Ireland.

Many monasteries existed by the sixth and seventh centuries AD, and Ireland had become a major center of Christianity. Scholars from abroad flocked to the monasteries, where they preserved religious and classical texts. Many devoted themselves to illustrating, or illuminating, manuscripts, especially the initial letters, which were elaborately designed. The **Book of Kells** (see page 131), now at Dublin's Trinity College, is perhaps the most famous example.

- **AD 432**   St. Patrick arrives in Ireland to convert the Celts
- **AD 461**   St. Patrick dies
- **AD 500–800**   Ireland becomes one of Europe's major centers of Christianity

THE VIKING INVASIONS

THE VIKINGS FIRST SWEPT into Ireland in AD 795 and continued to arrive in successive waves. They founded Ireland's first towns along the east coast, among them **Dublin** and **Waterford.** Though the Vikings continued to plunder and pillage, they also began an economic relationship with the Irish. Gradually the two groups became traders, and commercial towns sprang up in the countryside.

The Vikings mercilessly attacked the monasteries; the monks had no means of defending themselves and were easy prey. Unable to read, the Vikings saw nothing of value in the manuscripts the monks had produced, preferring gold altarpieces and the jewel-encrusted covers of the manuscripts. Thus came down to us, almost by mistake, masterpieces of classical literature and religious thought.

The Irish defeated the Vikings' High King, Brian Boru, at the Battle of Clontarf in AD 1014. With the departure of the Vikings, Ireland experienced a period of relative prosperity and peace, though the country was attractive to foreign powers. An Irishman, Dermot MacMurrough, wanted to rule all of Ireland and asked Henry II, the Norman king of England, for aid. He sent Richard de Clare, Earl of Pembroke, known as Strongbow, to MacMurrough's aid. Henry was a hands-on ruler, controlling towns, kings, and churches. For the first time, England took an active interest in Ireland.

- **AD 795**   Viking invasions begin
- **AD 841**   A Viking band settles in Ireland, building Dublin
- **AD 1014** High King of Ireland Brian Boru defeats a Viking army at the Battle of Clontarf near Dublin

THE NORMAN INVASION

FROM 1167 UNTIL 1169, Anglo-Normans swept into Ireland. Henry II arrived in 1171, proclaiming Ireland to be under Anglo-Norman rule and giving his troops land. They built a chain of fortresses to protect their possessions, and they built new towns. Many Anglo-Normans married Irish women and gradually adopted Irish culture. Attempts were made to oust the invaders, but none were successful. By 1250 the Anglo-Normans occupied almost all of Ireland. They had a more sophisticated social system than the Irish did, and they organized cities and government to their liking.

- **1066**   William the Conqueror conquers England in the Battle of Hastings
- **1167–69**   The Anglo-Normans sweep into Ireland
- **1171**   King Henry II proclaims Ireland under Anglo-Norman rule and seizes Dublin
- **1348–1350**   The Black Death arrives, killing a third of Dublin's population

THE FLIGHT OF THE EARLS

EVENTUALLY THE ENGLISH KINGS lost interest in Ireland, being preoccupied with their own wars. Yet in 1366 they passed the Statutes of Kilkenny, outlawing all of Gaelic culture, including the Gaelic language.

The Earls of Kildare rebelled against Henry VIII in 1534. When Henry squashed the revolt, he executed the earls and took their land, giving it to English colonists. This scenario would repeat itself over and over again for centuries, with the Irish fighting against English landowners. At the Battle of Yellow Ford in 1598, the nobleman Hugh O'Neill led a revolt against the English and won, but the Irish were soundly defeated by the British in the Battle of Kinsale in 1601. O'Neill and other Ulster nobles later sailed to the Continent in an exodus known as the Flight of the Earls, abandoning their homes and their culture.

- **1366**   The Statutes of Kilkenny outlaw Gaelic culture
- **1534**   The Earls of Kildare rebel against King Henry VIII; they fail and are executed
- **1558–1603** Ireland is divided into counties
- **1598**   A Gaelic revolt led by Hugh O'Neill is successful
- **1601**   The Battle of Kinsdale squashes the revolt
- **1607**   O'Neill and other nobles leave Ireland behind and sail to the Continent; the old Gaelic order sails with them

ENGLISH COLONIZATION

JAMES I SAW IRELAND as an opportunity for his countrymen, and he sent more than 20,000 English and Scottish planters onto land that had been confiscated.

Although there was disparity between the poor and the gentry, these groups were united by their Catholic faith, and they rallied together in the Confederation of Kilkenny against Oliver Cromwell, the ruler of England, and his Protestant Parliament.

Cromwell savagely retaliated by invading Ireland (1649–1650) with more than 20,000 men. They tortured and murdered, destroyed villages and sent thousands into slavery. By 1652, all Irish resistance had ceased. In 1653, Catholic landowners were exiled to the rocky west coast.

The Irish spirit was never really broken, however. In 1688–89, the Catholic James II came to Ireland and with an army tried to regain his crown. He surrounded Londonderry, but the city withstood a siege of 105 days.

In 1690, in the Battle of the Boyne, James and his army met the troops of the Protestant William III of Orange. James was defeated, and *Orange* became associated with the pro-Protestant, pro-English sentiment.

The Penal Laws closed the century. They made it illegal to take part in anything having to do with Gaelic culture—playing certain musical instruments or speaking the language were punishable offenses. The

> **•1642**   In the Confederation of Kilkenny, Catholics form an alliance to defend their rights and their religion

laws also made it illegal to buy land or hold office, and contact with priests was forbidden, as was Catholic education.

•	**1649–1650**	Oliver Cromwell invades Ireland with 20,000 troops and conquers the country savagely, murdering, plundering, raping, and seizing millions of acres of land
•	**1653**	The Cromwellian Settlement strips landowners of their belongings and forces them to move west of the River Shannon
•	**1660**	King Charles II is restored to the throne and returns land to some landowners
•	**1688–89**	Catholic King James II assembles an army in Ireland to retake the crown; he fails after a standoff in Londonderry
•	**1690**	James II fails again, this time defeated by the army of Protestant King William III of Orange at the Battle of the Boyne
•	**1704**	The English Penal Laws strip Irish Catholics of most of their rights

THE IRISH REBELLION

IN 1798, IRISH REBELS—both Catholic and Protestant—banded together against the British. Their goal was to use the word *Irishman* instead of *Catholic* or *Protestant*. More than 30,000 died before the British ended the revolt.

England found the solution to the problem in the Act of Union in 1801. Ireland became united with Great Britain, the Irish Parliament was dissolved, and Catholics were prohibited from the British Parliament.

•	**1798**	The United Irishmen revolt against Britain, but their rebellion is quashed; more than 30,000 die
•	**1801**	The Act of Union dissolves the Irish Parliament

THE GREAT POTATO FAMINE (1845–49)

IN 1845, RURAL IRELAND'S primary food, the potato, suddenly began to rot in the ground. The cause was the fungus *Phytophthora*. Over the next four years, as the blight became worse and worse, it destroyed the country's entire crop, and more than a million people died of starvation and illness. A huge number fled the country, emigrating to America, England, Canada, and Australia.

The British initially ignored the masses of starving, ill, and dead; the aid that was eventually offered—such as the opening of workhouses, with their savage conditions—was often ineffective. After the Famine ended in 1849, mass emigration continued, mostly to America but to England, Europe, Canada, and Australia as well. By 1921, Ireland's population was half what it had been before the blight.

The effects of the Famine lingered for more than 20 years. Emigration continued unabated, reducing the population still more. The rural poor were poorer than ever, and landowners had trouble collecting rents. Continuing anger at the British spawned a number of movements and organizations aimed at promoting all things Irish and breaking away from English control.

• **1845–49**	The Great Potato Famine devastates Ireland, killing more than a million people and forcing a million-plus to emigrate

REBELLION AND HOME RULE

THE IRISH REPUBLICAN BROTHERHOOD, founded in Dublin in 1858, grew quickly, both at home and abroad (its American counterpart, the Fenian Brotherhood, was formed the next year). Its aim was to promote Ireland's freedom by damaging English interests, and it published newspapers to spread its message. Some groups were formed to promote pride. The Gaelic Athletic Association's goal was to foster pride in Irish sports. The Gaelic League attempted to revive interest in the speaking and study of Irish to bring back pride in the Irish heritage.

• **1858**	The Irish Republican Brotherhood, later to become the Irish Republican Army (IRA), forms in Dublin; its U.S. wing, the Fenian Brotherhood, forms in New York in 1859
• **1879–1882**	Reforms return land to those who work it
• **1884**	To foster pride in Irish sports, the Gaelic Athletic Association is formed
• **1886**	First Home Rule Act, intended to give Ireland some independence, is rejected
• **1893**	The Gaelic League is formed to promote pride in traditional poetry, literature, and music
• **1894**	Second Home Rule Act is rejected
• **1905–08**	Sinn Féin (We Ourselves) is founded
• **1914**	Third Home Rule Act is signed by King George V
• **1914–18**	World War I

The Sinn Féin (We Ourselves) movement was connected to the Irish Republican Brotherhood. Home rule was an ever-present goal.

Two home-rule bills were defeated in 1886 and 1892. When the third was being debated in Parliament, World War I broke out. The bill was passed, but it was not put into effect until the end of the war.

THE EASTER REBELLION

WHEN WORLD WAR I BROKE OUT, revolution was still in the air. An uprising finally took place on Easter Monday in 1916, when Patrick Pearse, James Connolly, and others proclaimed the existence of an Irish Republic and occupied the General Post Office in Dublin. The British acted swiftly, alarmed about a rebellion so close to home while they were fighting a war in Europe, and sent in British troops. A fierce battle went on for six days, and then Pearse, Connolly, and others were captured, tried, and executed.

• **1916**	On Easter Sunday, April 24, 1916, Patrick Pearse and James Connolly proclaim Ireland independent and occupy the General Post Office; the rebels are arrested or killed

THE WAR OF INDEPENDENCE

FOLLOWING THE EASTER REBELLION, Eamon de Valera, an Irish-American teacher, returned to Ireland to establish the Sinn Féin party, and Michael Collins joined the Irish Volunteers (a paramilitary organization that the Irish Republican Brotherhood had gradually commandeered), renamed the Irish Republican Army (IRA) in 1919. The two men continued the nationalist movement.

De Valera's party won a huge victory in 1918 and established the first Dáil (independent Parliament) in Dublin. For two years, Britain tried to quash the Irish nationalists. In 1920, Collins ordered 14 British operatives murdered while they slept. England retaliated by shooting into a football crowd in Dublin, killing 12. A truce was eventually declared. In 1921, King George V opened the Parliament in Belfast, pleading for the end of the strife.

The Anglo-Irish Treaty (1921) partitioned Ireland into two separate nations, with 26 counties forming the Irish Free State and 6 counties

• **1917**	Sinn Féin is reorganized under Eamon de Valera
• **1918**	Sinn Féin candidates win 73 seats in the general election
• **1921**	The Anglo-Irish Treaty partitions Ireland into the Irish Free State and Northern Ireland, both parts of the British Commonwealth
• **1922**	A constitution is written for the Irish Free State

remaining part of the United Kingdom. Many republicans objected to the terms of the treaty. After it was passed in the Dáil, de Valera stepped down as president. Civil war quickly broke out between the government and the republicans. Serious fighting lasted in the capital for a week, until de Valera's supporters were ordered to surrender. De Valera escaped to the southwest; Collins was killed in an ambush.

The Civil War influenced politics in Ireland for decades. De Valera founded Fianna Fáil (Warriors of Ireland). The party won the election of 1932, and de Valera governed for 17 years.

• **1922–23**	Ireland enters a civil war that lasts a year; the IRA bitterly opposes dividing Ireland into two countries
• **1932**	Eamon de Valera leads Fianna Fáil to victory
• **1937**	The Free State forms a new constitution, and the name of the country becomes Éire
• **1948**	The Republic severs constitutional ties to England
• **1949**	Éire becomes the Republic of Ireland
• **1955**	The Republic of Ireland joins the United Nations

THE TROUBLES

THE DISPARITY BETWEEN THE ECONOMIES of the Republic and Northern Ireland became more and more pronounced in the 1960s. Religious and economic tension also mounted in the North: Northern Ireland was 55% Protestant and 45% Catholic, and the Protestant majority was far better off economically. Much of the tension was between those who wanted to remain part of the United Kingdom and those who wanted to be part of a unified Ireland.

In 1967, the Northern Ireland Civil Rights Movement demonstrated for better housing and jobs for the Catholic minority. In response,

• **1967**	The Civil Rights Association of Northern Ireland forms to demand reform in local politics
• **1969**	British troops are sent to Northern Ireland to maintain peace when violence breaks out
• **1972**	Riots take place in Derry on "Bloody Sunday"; England imposes direct rule
• **1994**	Peace talks begin when the IRA announces a cease-fire
• **1996**	The IRA begins shooting and bombing again, and rioting begins, the most violent in 15 years
• **1997**	The IRA announces a new cease-fire
• **1998**	The Good Friday Peace Agreement is reached
• **2000**	The IRA states that it will decommission its arms

Protestants marched through Catholic neighborhoods to show their dominance. Bloody riots followed.

In 1969, when England sent in troops to help maintain peace, the IRA considered them an occupying army, and for the next two decades Northern Ireland was a war zone. About 3,000 people were killed. In 1972, police opened fire on a peaceful gathering in Derry, killing 12 on what has come to be known as Bloody Sunday. In retaliation, the IRA began a bombing campaign in England. Secret negotiations in the 1990s eventually led to the 1994 IRA cease-fire. In 1998, on Good Friday, a peace agreement was signed in Belfast.

- **1990**   Mary Robinson becomes Ireland's first woman president
- **1992**   Ireland becomes a charter member of the new European Union
- **1993**   Homosexuality is decriminalized
- **1995**   Divorce becomes legal, but under very restricted circumstances
- **2000**   Ireland's economy continues to grow
- **2002**   Immigration to Ireland reaches record highs, and many of the "newcomers" are Irish returning home

IRELAND TODAY

MANY OF THE CONFLICTS that have plagued Ireland through the centuries still exist. Some believe that Northern Ireland should be united with the Republic, while others favor the status quo. Sharp divisions also continue between Catholics and Protestants. The big force these days, though, is economic growth and prosperity. For much of the 1990s and into the current millennium, Ireland's economy has been one of the fastest growing in the world. With the boom come new construction, improvements, and enormous fortunes—and, as happens with such growth, a great disparity between the poor and the rich.

THE BEST *of* IRELAND

THE BEST ABBEYS AND OTHER RELIGIOUS SITES

Book of Kells

Location   Dublin
For more information   "Exploring Dublin," page 131
One of the world's most exquisite manuscripts—believed to be the work of ninth-century monks at the great scriptorium of the monastic community of St. Colomba, on the island of Iona off Scotland—resided in the Colomban monastery at Kells, north of Dublin, for most of the Middle Ages. The 680-page book, in which four gospels are illustrated with elaborate designs, now occupies pride of place in the Long Library of Trinity College.

Glendalough Abbey
Location Wicklow Mountains, outside Dublin
For more information "Day Trips from Dublin," page 178
These stone structures on the floor of a peaceful valley alongside a pair of interlocking lakes once composed one of Europe's great centers of learning, founded by St. Kevin. Remains of the churches, tower, and outbuildings present a satisfying look at what monastic communities were like in the days when the faithful and those hungry for sustenance and learning found their way to monasteries like this throughout Ireland.

Jerpoint Abbey
Location Outside Kilkenny
For more information The South of Ireland, page 189
These remains of a 12th-century monastery, built for the Benedictine order but handed over to the Cistercians a century later, are richly evocative and utterly charming, lost in time in a bucolic setting. In the roofless nave and well-preserved cloisters, it is easy to imagine an isolated community working the gardens and fields.

Kilmacduagh
Location Outside Gort
For more information The West of Ireland, page 305
Now in ruin on a plain at the edge of the Burren, Kilmacduagh flourished for almost a thousand years—give or take, that is, a couple of centuries of Viking raids between AD 900 and 1100. A round tower from the 11th century leans a bit but is remarkably intact, as are the walls of the now-roofless cathedral.

Kylemore Abbey and Garden
Location Outside Letterfrack, near Connemara
For more information The West of Ireland, page 325
Now the home of an order of Irish Benedictine nuns and an exclusive boarding school for girls, this faux-Gothic castle, surrounded by lavish grounds, lies at the foot of the craggy Twelve Bens Mountains and is surrounded by lakes and glens. Built in the 19th century as a private retreat for a British industrialist, Kylemore is more secular than religious, though a small chapel that's built like a cathedral in miniature is one of Ireland's most distinctive churches.

Rock of Cashel
Location Near Cashel
For more information The South of Ireland, page 200
This giant rock topped with medieval remains is a spectacular sight, even when swept with clouds and rains, and the ruins are richly evocative and telling of the onetime power of the church. Early Irish kings settled the rock as early as the fourth century AD, and the Catholic Church presided here until the late 18th century, leaving behind some of Ireland's most magnificent Romanesque ruins. The extensive lore attached to the rock includes

a visit from St. Patrick, who allegedly held up a shamrock to explain the mystery of the Trinity, endowing Ireland with its enduring emblem.

St. Patrick's Cathedral

Location Dublin
For more information "Exploring Dublin," page 146
Built on the site where St. Patrick is said to have preached in the fifth century AD, St. Patrick's—the largest church in Ireland and the flagship of the Church of Ireland—is littered with the tombs of some of Ireland's greatest sons and daughters. The most famous tomb here is that of satirist Jonathan Swift, who wrote *Gulliver's Travels* and most of his other great works while he was the dean of the cathedral, from 1713 to 1745.

Skellig Michael

Location County Kerry
For more information The Southwest of Ireland, page 252
Early Christian monks retreated to this conical-shaped island some 13 kilometers (8 miles) off the Iveragh Peninsula some 1,000 years ago, where their church, oratory, and beehive-shaped cells have survived pounding surf and brutal winds. A choppy crossing and a climb up 600 rough stone steps still makes this sanctuary seem a world, or two, apart.

THE BEST OF ANCIENT IRELAND

Carrowmore and Carrowkeel

Location Around Sligo
For more information The Northwest of Ireland, page 344
The 40 or so passage tombs dug into the hillside at Carrowmore predate Stonehenge in England and comprise the largest collection of prehistoric tombs in the British Isles. At Carrowkeel, just to the east, you may find yourself alone among the 14 burial chambers high above the shores of Lough Arrow.

Hill of Tara

Location North of Dublin
For more information "Day Trips from Dublin," page 175
The seat of the High Kings of Ireland, was, from the pre-Christian era to as late as the 11th century, an assembly point for tribal and religious leaders from throughout Ireland.

Newgrange

Location North of Dublin
For more information "Day Trips from Dublin," page 175
These 6,000-year-old passage tombs, covered by a mound 100 meters (330 feet) across and constructed with some 250,000 tons of stones, appear to have done double duty as a burial place and an observatory. On each of five days on and around the winter solstice, the main chamber is brilliantly illuminated by sunlight for 20 minutes.

THE BEST OF IRELAND FOR NATURAL BEAUTY

The Antrim Coast

Location Northeast of Derry
For more information Northern Ireland, page 400

A scenic road, A2, hugs this scenic coastline, where green hills drop down to the rugged shore. The Giants Causeway, a sweep of cylindrical basalt outcroppings that extend far out to sea, enhances the allure of this coast; the Glens of Antrim, nine densely wooded river valleys, are etched out of the surrounding mountains.

The Beara Peninsula

Location Outside Kenmare
For more information The Southwest of Ireland, page 241

One of several craggy peninsulas that stretch into the Atlantic Ocean in Southwest Ireland, the Beara remains relatively remote and unspoiled. In addition to magnificent sea views, there are desolate moors and purple peaks, best viewed on a drive across Healy Pass.

The Burren

Location Western County Clare
For more information The West of Ireland, page 301

The Burren (from *boireann,* Gaelic for "rocky land") is a plain of limestone that covers some 1,600 hectares (4,000 acres). This natural wonderland—home to rare butterflies, puffins and other seabirds, and goats and hare—becomes a sea of color when plants flower in profusion from cracks in the limestone.

Cliffs of Moher

Location West of Ennis
For more information The West of Ireland, page 297

Rising some 230 meters (700 feet) out of the sea, the cliffs provide an eight-kilometer (five-mile) swath of spectacular scenery. Puffins and other seabirds nest and roost on shelves in the cliff face of black shale and sandstone, the Aran Islands float in a cloud of mist in the distance, and the surf rushes ceaselessly ashore.

Connemara

Location North of Galway
For more information The West of Ireland, page 323

Connemara is mountainous in some parts, covered with prairielike moors in others, and dotted with forests of pine and fir that surround rushing streams and glittering lakes. The largest of the lakes—in fact, the second largest lake in Ireland—is 175-square-kilometer (65-square-mile) Lough Corrib. The Twelve Bens rise from the center of the region, and bogs cover a third of the landscape. Some 2,000 hectares (4,942 acres) of this beautiful and evocative landscape are preserved as Connemara National Park.

The Dingle Peninsula

Location The Southwest
For more information The Southwest of Ireland, page 263
Stretching some 50 kilometers (30 miles) from the mainland into the Atlantic surf, the westernmost tip of Ireland is a spine of rugged mountains, rocky cliffs, and soft sands. Outside of the busy summer months especially, a sense of otherworldliness prevails, enhanced by thick mists, good stout, and the ever-present traditional Irish tunes.

Glenveagh National Park

Location Northwest of Letterkenny
For more information The Northwest of Ireland, page 364
Here, heaths and woodlands climb the slopes of the Derryveagh Mountains, presenting some of the most beautiful and dramatic landscapes in Ireland. Capping the park is Errigal Mountain, a pyramid-shaped peak that is covered with snow for much of the year.

Howth Head

Location Outside Dublin
For more information "Day Trips from Dublin," page 171
Though hardly remote and just 20 minutes by train from central Dublin, this rocky headland provides stunning views of the sea, the mountains, and the Eye of Ireland, a rocky islet just offshore, all enjoyed from an 8.5-kilometer (5-mile) path.

Inishowen Peninsula

Location Northeast of Letterkenny
For more information The Northwest of Ireland, page 363
The largest of the northern peninsulas ends at Malin Head, not only scenic but also officially the northernmost tip of Ireland. Views are also spectacular from the Gap of Mamore, a mountain pass that climbs to 250 meters (820 feet).

Killarney National Park

Location Outside Killarney
For more information The Southwest of Ireland, page 243
One of the most beautiful corners of Ireland, this wilderness of heather-covered mountains, lush forests, and shimmering lakes is now protected as a 10,000-hectare (25,000-acre) national park. Some of the park's most enchanting scenery is in the Gap of Dunloe, accessible only on foot, horseback, or bike; here, enormous boulders litter a pass that cuts through MacGillycuddy's Reeks, Ireland's highest mountains.

Slieve League

Location North of Donegal
For more information The Northwest of Ireland, page 360
The tallest sea cliffs in Europe—and one the most dramatic spectacles in all of Ireland—rise some 600 meters (2,000 feet) out of the raging surf.

Wicklow Mountains

Location Outside Dublin
For more information "Day Trips from Dublin," page 177
In these gentle, lovely mountains, dense forests cover the slopes and rushing streams sprint through valleys into clear mountain lakes. The Wicklows are all the more appealing because they cradle one of Ireland's grandest estates, Powerscourt, and one of its most romantic monastic ruins, Glendalough.

THE BEST MUSEUMS

Chester Beatty Library and Gallery of Oriental Art

Location Dublin
For more information "Exploring Dublin," page 132
A remarkable collection of sacred texts, illuminated manuscripts, and miniature paintings from the great religions of the world includes cuneiform clay tablets; ancient Biblical papyri; 270 copies of the Koran, paintings from India's Mughal era; and some of the earliest bound books, dating from the Renaissance.

Crawford Municipal Art Gallery

Location Cork
For more information The South of Ireland, page 210
One of Ireland's best collections of art includes a number of casts of Greek and Roman sculptures and canvases by Irish artists.

Hugh Lane Municipal Gallery of Modern Art

Location Dublin
For more information "Exploring Dublin," page 139
The grandest dwelling on Parnell Square houses an exquisite collection of 19th- to early-20th-century artworks by painters of the French Barbizon and Impressionist schools, works by Jack Yeats and other Irish artists, and stained-glass panels by Irish artisans Harry Clark and Evie Hone.

Hunt Museum

Location Limerick
For more information The Lower Shannon, page 282
Limerick's elegant 18th-century Customs House displays an amazing collection of Celtic and medieval artifacts second only to that on display in the National Museum in Dublin, as well as 18th-century ceramics, 19th- and 20th-century paintings by Renoir and Picasso, and other decorative arts that span the centuries.

National Gallery of Ireland

Location Dublin
For more information "Exploring Dublin," page 141
Ireland's national collection of European art is small but immensely satisfying, not overwhelming but boasting an impressive number of masterpieces.

Caravaggio's *The Taking of Christ,* Vermeer's *Lady Writing a Letter with Her Maid,* and Jack Yeats's *The Liffey Swim* are among the works represented.

National Museum of Ireland
Location Dublin
For more information "Exploring Dublin," page 142
Ireland's treasure trove of artifacts from 6,000 BC to the 20th century includes a cache of Irish gold—scepters, jewelry, crosses, a boat from the first century—as well as remnants of the centuries of Viking occupation and an in-depth and highly evocative collection devoted to the Easter Rebellion of 1916.

Ulster Museum
Location Belfast
For more information Northern Ireland, page 385
The most comprehensive museum in Northern Ireland is devoted to history, the natural sciences, and art. Holdings include one of the world's leading collections of African arts and crafts; an exhibit that takes an unflinching look at the Troubles and the developments that led to the formation of the North as a separate entity; and masterpieces by Gainsborough, Reynolds, and other painters.

THE BEST CASTLES
Blarney Castle
Location Outside Cork
For more information The South of Ireland, page 208
Blarney means, basically, nonsense, and you'll encounter a lot of it in this ruin of the onetime stronghold of the McCarthy clan. The highlight of a tour is the thrill of being held by the legs as you dangle precariously backward to kiss the Stone of Eloquence, aka the Blarney Stone. Just as rewarding is a stroll through the colorful gardens to admire the romantic towers and crumbling walls of the castle.

Bunratty Castle and Folk Park
Location Bunratty, County Clare
For more information The Lower Shannon, page 288
Ireland's most intact medieval castle is also one of the country's most visited tourist attractions. Despite its crowds and commercial buzz, the castle is a pleasure to visit, beautifully restored down to its last medieval timber and filled with stunning 15th- to 17th-century furnishings.

Donegal Castle
Location Donegal Town
For more information The Northwest of Ireland, page 358
Standing mightily in the center of town, Donegal Castle is partly in ruin but incorporates the splendid and beautifully restored 15th-century fortified

house that was the residence of the O'Donnell clan. The turrets and gables that lend the castle its distinctive appearance, along with the grounds, enclosed behind high walls, rise high above Donegal Town.

Dunluce Castle
Location   Antrim Coast
For more information   Northern Ireland, page 402
A 14th-century castle complex clings to the edge of oceanside cliffs, high above the pounding surf. Indeed, much of the castle has fallen into the sea, but this former stronghold of the powerful MacDonnell clan still romantically evokes life in the Middle Ages.

Glenveagh Castle
Location   Glenveagh National Park
For more information   The Northwest of Ireland, page 365
One of the most delightful historic homes in Ireland, Glenveagh looks like a Hollywood stage set and has served as a retreat for Greta Garbo and many other glamorous celebs over the years. Perched on the shores of Lough Beagh and surrounded by formal gardens and heath-covered mountainsides, the castle was the creation of John George Adair, a notorious 19th-century landlord, but owes much of its charm to wealthy and refined American Henry P. McIlhenny of Tabasco fame.

Kilkenny Castle
Location   Kilkenny
For more information   The South of Ireland, page 191
A formidable castle has dominated Kilkenny ever since Strongbow, an Anglo-Norman warrior and settler, built a wooden fortress here in 1172. Most of the stone castle rising from the banks of the Kilkenny River dates to the 14th century, and it was once the seat of the Irish Parliament. Generations of Butlers, who lived in Kilkenny Castle from the Middle Ages well into the 20th century, look down from the walls of the Long Gallery.

King John's Castle
Location   Limerick
For more information   The Lower Shannon, page 284
One of Ireland's most intact medieval monuments, this imposing 13th-century fortress on an island in the heart of the city is especially impressive when viewed from across the rivers that surround it. Costumed craftspeople plying their trades enliven the castle courtyard and enrich a visit.

Malahide Castle
Location   Malahide, outside Dublin
For more information   "Day Trips from Dublin," page 173
The home of the Talbot clan for more than 800 years, Malahide has enough turrets and towers to be solidly medieval, but the well-furnished home shows off the domestic habits of the aristocracy well into the 20th century.

One hundred hectares (250 acres) of parkland shelter the Talbot Botanic Garden, one of Ireland's finest collections of exotic flora.

Parke's Castle

Location Outside Sligo
For more information The Northwest of Ireland, page 354
More of a fortified manor house than a castle per se, this tall, handsome manor of light stone and sturdy timbers is formidable nonetheless. A great hall and other drafty rooms surround a courtyard and overlook Lough Gill, the lake that so inspired poet W. B. Yeats.

Ross Castle

Location Killarney, County Kerry
For more information The Southwest of Ireland, page 250
One of the many natural and man-made attractions in and around Killarney National Park rises from the waters of Lough Leane. The medieval walls glimmer romantically in the lake waters, and a fine collection of splendid 16th- and 17th-century furniture warms up the dank and dark rooms of this mighty stronghold, which has been besieged on more than one occasion.

THE BEST PLACES TO ENCOUNTER IRISH HISTORY

Bogside

Location Derry
For more information Northern Ireland, page 394
The Catholic neighborhood beneath Derry's city walls has been largely rebuilt since the violence of the past decades, but political murals are stunning reminders of the recent turbulence. One of the most poignant symbols from the neighborhood's history is the huge sign painted on the end of a building to announce, "You Are Now Entering Free Derry," capturing the quest for independence that ignited the Troubles.

Charles Fort

Location Kinsale
For more information The South of Ireland, page 228
This mighty star-shaped bastion has been protecting Kinsale Harbor since 1677, with a strategic position and miles of thick walls that seem to make it impregnable.

Cobh, the Queenstown Story

Location Cobh
For more information The South of Ireland, page 223
Cobh was once Ireland's major port for emigration, and millions embarked from here between 1750 and the mid–20th century. Extensive exhibits trace conditions in Ireland and life aboard the outgoing ships, as well as the sinkings of the *Titanic,* which called here in 1912 just days before hitting an iceberg and sinking, and the *Lusitania,* torpedoed off nearby Kinsale Head by the Germans in 1915.

Derrynane House
Location Caherdaniel, County Kerry
For more information The Southwest of Ireland, page 252
Daniel O'Connell, whose estate this was, won for Catholics the full rights of citizenship in 1829 and founded the grassroots Catholic Association to promote education and representation. The so-called Liberator is very much a presence in the old rooms, many of which he remodeled with his own hands.

Falls Road and Shankill Road
Location Belfast
For more information Northern Ireland, page 379
No other city in Western Europe, with the possible exception of Derry, has been as war-torn as Belfast in recent decades, and remnants of the divisiveness are much in evidence. In the Catholic neighborhood around Falls Road you'll pass the Sinn Féin offices and endless murals, then go through the so-called peace wall to Milltown Cemetery, where hunger striker Bobby Sands and other IRA members are buried. In the Protestant Shankill Road neighborhood, murals include Union Jack motifs and even elaborate portrayals of the victory of Protestant William of Orange over Catholic King James II in the Battle of the Boyne in 1690.

Kilmainham Gaol
Location Dublin
For more information "Exploring Dublin," page 140
This formidable prison, opened in 1798 and closed in 1927, today serves as a testament to Irish revolutionary history. Displays and commentaries provide excellent background on 18th- and 19th-century revolutionary heroes such as Robert Emmet and Charles Stewart Parnell, the 19th-century nationalist leader and member of the Irish Parliament. Most gripping are those exhibits recounting the 1916 Easter Rebellion, when the Irish Republican Brotherhood mounted an armed revolt in Dublin, for which the British executed 15 of the leaders, many of them here at Kilmainham.

THE BEST LITERARY AND MUSICAL EXPERIENCES
Doolin
Location County Clare
For more information The West of Ireland, page 299
This small village on the rugged coast of northern County Clare is known throughout the world for traditional Irish music, attracting droves of enthusiasts. You'll hear the tunes that make the village famous in three homey pubs.

Dublin Literary Pub Crawl
Location Dublin
For more information "Exploring Dublin," page 121
At one time or another, most Dublin writers found inspiration at the bottom of a pint glass in the hundreds of pubs around the city, and you can

follow in their footsteps to enjoy the *craic* and literary ambience of four famous writerly haunts.

Dublin Writers Museum
Location Dublin
For more information "Exploring Dublin," page 137
Extensive letters, manuscripts, photos, news clippings, audio recordings, and other fascinating memorabilia honor Oscar Wilde, James Joyce, Samuel Beckett, Jonathan Swift, and scores of other writers who have been both stifled by and inspired by Dublin.

Marsh's Library
Location Dublin
For more information "Exploring Dublin," page 141
Ireland's oldest public library, founded in 1701, is an atmospheric repository of rare manuscripts and books from the 16th through 18th centuries. Many of these are so precious that scholars must be locked into mesh cages to view them.

Music Pub Crawl
Location Dublin
For more information "Exploring Dublin," page 122
Evening expeditions depart from Oliver St. John Gogarty's on Fleet Street and make calls at three pubs, where you'll hear an assortment of instruments, Irish ballads, and discussion about the fine points of Irish music—and enjoy a pint or two, too.

Shaw Birthplace
Location Dublin
For more information "Exploring Dublin," page 146
At the childhood home of George Bernard Shaw, one of the greatest playwrights of the late 19th and early 20th centuries, you can peer into the cramped, overfurnished parlors, the primitive kitchen, and the wee bedroom on the landing where the playwright slept as a youth.

Yeats Country
Location In and around Sligo
For more information The Northwest of Ireland, page 354
Admirers of this most Irish of poets can examine first editions and letters in the Sligo County Museum, gaze upon the Isle of Innisfree from the shores of Lough Gill, and pay homage at Yeats's simple grave in the cemetery at Drumcliff.

kids THE BEST OF IRELAND FOR KIDS

Bunratty Castle and Folk Park
Location Bunratty, County Clare
For more information The Lower Shannon, page 288
The Great Hall, drawbridge, and turrets fulfill just about every kid's fantasy of what a medieval castle should like. In the adjoining Folk Park, young visitors will

enjoy stepping in and out of laborers', farmers', and fishing families' cottages; watching water mills; speaking with blacksmiths and millers; and in other ways partaking in scenes of the Irish life of yesteryear.

Carrick-a-Rede Bridge
Location Antrim Coast
For more information Northern Ireland, page 402
Crossing this concoction of rope and planks that sways a dizzying height above the sea is a heck of a lot of fun, a memorable experience that kids and their parents will long remember.

Church of St. Anne Shandon
Location The South
For more information The South of Ireland, page 209
At Cork's most famous landmark, visitors can climb into the pepper-pot steeple and take turns playing a tune on the famous six-ton Bells of Shandon.

Craggaunowen
Location Near Quin, County Clare
For more information The Lower Shannon, page 289
A prehistoric theme park with re-creations of ring forts, fortified island dwellings, and other fragments of Ireland's long past appeals a lot more to kids than to their parents, but a day among costumed Celts and Iron Age farmers can provide relief from more-serious sightseeing.

Dublin Zoo
Location Phoenix Park, Dublin
For more information "Exploring Dublin," page 147
Recent renovations have made the world's third oldest zoo much more pleasant to visit. The most popular denizens of the many cageless environments are the lions, and frolicking cubs often put on a good show.

Fota Wildlife Park
Location Fota Island, County Cork
For more information The South of Ireland, page 219
Only low electronic fences separate visitors from free-roaming flamingos, giraffes, and 90 other species of creatures exotic to Ireland. Other residents include Irish natives such as the white-tailed sea eagle.

Fungie
Location Dingle
For more information The Southwest of Ireland, page 259
The bottle-nosed dolphin who has dwelled in Dingle Harbor since 1983 never fails to make an appearance for boatloads of admirers.

King John's Castle
Location King's Island, Limerick
For more information The Lower Shannon, page 284
This imposing 13th-century fortress, one of Ireland's most intact medieval monuments, houses extensive archaeological treasures that might bore the

young ones. But they will love the rampart walks and the reconstructed medieval courtyard, where costumed craftspeople and merchants ply their trades.

Malahide Castle

Location Malahide, outside Dublin
For more information "Day Trips from Dublin," page 173
For young visitors, a reward for their patience on the guided tours of the castle is a visit to the Fry Model Railway, where dozens of trains chug through fantasy landscapes, and Tara's Dollhouse, filled with delightful miniatures. Youngsters can run and play to their hearts' content in the extensive parklands.

National Transport Museum of Ireland

Location Grounds of Howth Castle, outside Dublin
For more information "Day Trips from Dublin," page 172
Buses, trucks, and trams—60 vintage vehicles in all—will evoke a sense of wonderment in visitors accustomed to the comparatively mundane-looking vehicles that clog the road today. Even vehicles that look surprisingly like their modern-day descendants, such the generations of double-decker buses and trams, delight young visitors.

Ulster Folk and Transport Museum

Location Outside Belfast
For more information Northern Ireland, page 384
Two fascinating collections await visitors to this vast 70-hectare (176-acre) museum compound, an assemblage of old structures and a showcase of cars, planes, and other modes of transport, all built in Ireland. Youngsters will especially enjoy the folk park, where 20 structures include simple farmhouses, and the costumed staff demonstrates spinning and other crafts.

THE BEST CASTLE HOTELS, GUEST HOUSES, AND INNS

Adare Manor

Location Adare Village, County Limerick
For more information The Lower Shannon, page 270
The neo-Gothic manor house of the Earls of Dunraven, on the banks of the River Maigue, is one of Ireland's finest hotels. Two staff members for every guest ensure top-notch service. The extensive grounds are graced not only with a golf course but also the romantic ruins of a castle and monastery.

Ballymaloe House

Location Shanagarry, Midleton, County Cork
For more information The South of Ireland, page 216
The 160-hectare (400-acre) estate of the Allen family may be the most famous country-house hotel in Ireland. Ballymaloe is known for its dining room, cooking school, and attractive yet comfortably simple accommodations.

Ballynahinch Castle
Location Recess, County Galway
For more information The West of Ireland, page 328
This 18th-century manor on the banks of the Ballynahinch River is surrounded by forests and mountain pastures. Fishing, walking, and many other activities await just outside the front door. Airy and beautifully furnished accommodations are complemented by the best dining room in Connemara.

Bushmills Inn
Location Bushmills, County Antrim
For more information Northern Ireland, page 400
At one of Ireland's most beloved and character-rich inns, turf fires burn beneath old beams, and guests relax in charming lounges and accommodations that are tastefully oriented to solid comfort.

Frewin
Location Ramelton, County Donegal
For more information The Northwest of Ireland, page 362
A Victorian rectory is filled with a collection of antiques, memorabilia, books, Persian carpets, and old prints—all handsomely displayed in warm, uncluttered lounges and commodious guest rooms.

Glenview House
Location Midleton, County Cork
For more information The South of Ireland, page 217
Ken and Beth Sherrard set the gold standard for a stay in an Irish country home, with their Georgian farmhouse set amid lovely grounds. The Sherrards' gracious hospitality includes a bountiful breakfast of eggs from Beth's hens as well as fresh fruit and home-baked breads.

Greenmount House
Location Dingle, County Kerry
For more information The Southwest of Ireland, page 256
This hillside perch overlooking the Dingle and its bay is almost legendary on the Irish B&B circuit, and it seems to improve with each passing year. The suitelike rooms enjoy airy and lovely views, and the day begins with a lavish breakfast in the conservatory.

Killeen House
Location Outside Galway
For more information The West of Ireland, page 313
Catherine Doyle shows off her exquisite taste and a great knack for hospitality in elegantly decorated, well-equipped, spacious rooms that overlook gardens and Lough Corrib.

Markree Castle
Location Collooney, County Sligo
For more information The Northwest of Ireland, page 341
This 1640 castle on a 400-hectare (1,000-acre) estate is delightfully quirky,

with massive staircases, a galleried and paneled great hall, roaring fires, and ample comfort in the guest rooms, no two of which are alike.

Rathmullan House
Location Rathmullan, County Donegal
For more information The Northwest of Ireland, page 362
A fine 19th-century mansion overlooking the sea is quietly luxurious but relaxed, with an inviting drawing room and library and distinctive accommodations in the old house, plus a tasteful and appealing new wing.

Shelburne Lodge
Location Kenmare, County Kerry
For more information The Southwest of Ireland, page 238
An 18th-century stone farmhouse at the edge of town is surrounded by stunning grounds and decorated with taste and style, providing a good base for exploring the Southwest.

Temple House
Location Ballymote, County Sligo
For more information The Northwest of Ireland, page 343
This grand Georgian mansion, one of Ireland's largest homes still in private hands, is a delightful country retreat complete with handsome sitting rooms, huge guest rooms filled with comfy old family furniture, and Wellingtons by the door for those who want to wander through the wooded grounds or down to the dock for a row.

THE BEST CITY LODGINGS

The Clarence
Location Dublin
For more information "Hotels in Dublin," page 114
Who knew? U2, the Irish rock band that owns this refurbished old hostelry on the banks of the River Liffey, runs a first-rate hotel, too. They've created a stylish and soothing retreat with light oak paneling, Shaker-style furnishings, state-of-the-art entertainment systems, and many other amenities.

The Fitzwilliam
Location Dublin
For more information "Hotels in Dublin," page 115
Large, light-filled public areas and guest rooms face either St. Stephen's Green or a roof garden at the rear of the hotel. Clean lines, neutral tones, and natural fabrics create attractive and extremely restful surroundings in the city center.

Hayfield Manor
Location Cork
For more information The South of Ireland, page 204
Built in 1996 in the style of a grand Georgian country house, Hayfield Manor serves up more old-world ambience than the real McCoy ever could. Heavy

paneling, a grand staircase, and plush guest rooms provide the ultimate in traditional comfort.

Merrion Hotel
Location Dublin
For more information "Hotels in Dublin," page 118
Dublin's most luxurious hotel consists of four Georgian townhouses and, beyond the large formal gardens, a stylish contemporary wing. One of the country's most extensive private collections of 19th- and 20th-century Irish art hangs in the public lounges, while large and gracious guest rooms are swathed in yards of luxurious Irish fabrics and outfitted with other comforts geared to spoiling guests.

Number 31
Location Dublin
For more information "Hotels in Dublin," page 119
At one of Dublin's most distinctive hostelries, extremely comfortable rooms occupy a contemporary coach house and Georgian terrace house. A sunken conversation pit surrounds a fireplace where an aromatic peat fire burns, and a memorable breakfast is served in a conservatory overlooking a rooftop garden.

Ten Square
Location Belfast
For more information Northern Ireland, page 374
The first and still the best of Belfast's ever-growing stable of small luxury hotels manages to be both showy and relaxing, with handsome public areas and luxurious guest rooms you won't want to leave.

THE BEST FOOD-AND-DRINK EXPERIENCES

Ballymaloe House
Location Shanagarry, Midleton, County Cork
For more information The South of Ireland, page 216
Ballymaloe, in the capable hands of the Allen family of culinary stars, has a well-deserved reputation for turning the freshest ingredients into master-pieces of modern Irish cuisine and serving them in perfect country-house surroundings.

Chart House
Location Dingle, County Kerry
For more information The Southwest of Ireland, page 259
A handsome stone building near the bay provides sophisticated yet infor-mal surroundings for superb meals created with the bounty of local waters and Kerry farms.

Crown Liquor Saloon
Location Belfast
For more information Northern Ireland, page 388

This wonderfully atmospheric Victorian showcase of mirrors and carved wood is a lovely place to enjoy a pint and a plate of oysters or other light fare.

English Market
Location Cork
For more information The South of Ireland, page 211
You haven't experienced real Cork life until you taken a leisurely stroll through this vast covered hall dating back to 1881. More than 140 stalls brim with Irish produce, fish, and meat, making it easy to see why Cork is one of Ireland's culinary capitals. Grab a bite at one of the bustling counters, or enjoy a meal upstairs in the Farmgate Café, with a bird's-eye view of the proceedings below.

Guinness Storehouse
Location Dublin
For more information "Exploring Dublin," page 138
Dublin's most famous tourist attraction is this shrine to Ireland's favorite beverage. A tour through a renovated fermentation plant, built around a five-story glass atrium shaped like a pint and filled with displays on how Guinness is made, ends with a free sample in the top-floor Gravity Bar.

Jacobs on the Mall
Location Cork
For more information The South of Ireland, page 212
A former Turkish bath is the exotic setting for a memorable meal of innovative modern Irish cuisine, with an emphasis on the freshest local ingredients.

Jacob's Ladder
Location Dublin
For more information "Dining in Dublin," page 156
In this series of upstairs rooms overlooking Trinity College through tall windows, excellent service and Adrian Roche's careful preparations, with an emphasis on seafood, enhance the feeling that you are enjoying a special experience high above the city.

James Street South
Location Belfast
For more information Northern Ireland, page 386
Minimalist environs strike just the right note in suggesting that the emphasis here is on the exquisite preparations of chef Niall McKenna. Expertly served, lunch or dinner in this place is always a special occasion.

Lacken House
Location Kilkenny City, County Kilkenny
For more information The South of Ireland, page 198
The restaurant that helped make Kilkenny famous for its cuisine continues to lead the way and takes pride in using local products; the menu pays due

homage to the suppliers who keep the kitchen stocked with lamb, beef, fish, and other fresh ingredients.

L'Ecrivain
Location Dublin
For more information "Dining in Dublin," page 156
One of Ireland's few restaurants to have earned a Michelin star continually lives up to its reputation with a traditional-yet-innovative approach to meat and seafood classics, served in light and airy surroundings.

Michael Deane
Location Belfast
For more information Northern Ireland, page 386
One of Ireland's finest restaurants—and the only dining room in Northern Ireland to have earned a Michelin star—never fails to deliver a memorable dining experience. Here, Irish staples are enlivened with subtle Asian influences.

Nick's Warehouse
Location Belfast
For more information Northern Ireland, page 387
This warm and welcoming eatery, in a warehouse district on an alley near St. Anne's Cathedral, shows just how satisfying simple modern Irish cuisine can be, especially when complemented by a bottle or glass from the extensive wine list.

Nimmo's
Location Galway
For more information The West of Ireland, page 319
An old stone house on a quay beside the River Corrib provides a romantic setting for a heavily timbered wine bar and a charming candlelit upstairs restaurant, where hearty fish soup and succulent roast lamb do justice to the ambience.

Old Bushmills Distillery
Location Bushmills, County Antrim
For more information Northern Ireland, page 404
What makes a tour of Bushmills more satisfying than a visit to any other Irish distillery is the quality of the product—generally regarded as the best Irish whiskey—and the fact that this is a working plant: you'll actually see workers mashing and bottling, which adds a bit of veracity to the guides' lectures on how whiskey is made.

Out of the Blue
Location Dingle, County Kerry
For more information The Southwest of Ireland, page 261
Boats that dock just outside the door supply the ingredients for delicious

chowders and heavenly sauced fish dishes, served in a crowded little shack on the waterfront.

Owenmore Restaurant
Location Ballynahinch Castle, Recess
For more information The West of Ireland, page 329
Chef Robert Webster, taking his inspiration from the Connemara landscapes that surround him, creates artful preparations focusing on local lamb, seafood, and produce.

Restaurant Patrick Guilbaud
Location Dublin
For more information "Dining in Dublin," page 159
Lovely works by Irish painters enliven this simple and elegant room overlooking the gardens of the Merrion Hotel, where French classics are enlivened with an Irish flair.

PART ONE

PLANNING *your* VISIT *to* IRELAND

HOW FAR *in* ADVANCE SHOULD YOU PLAN?

YOUR ORGANIZED, PDA-DRIVEN FRIENDS ARE RIGHT: advance planning has definite advantages. Airline fares are generally (but not always) lower if you book at least a month in advance, and many lower-priced air-and-hotel packages require advance booking. Advance planning is an especially good idea if you're visiting Ireland in the summer. First of all, airfares are highest then and flights are well booked, so if you wait until the last moment, only the highest-priced seats will be available. Second, hotels in Dublin, Dingle, Galway, and many other popular places in Ireland fill up quickly in the summer— remember, many summer resorts are as popular with vacationing Irish as they are with visitors from America and elsewhere. Hotels, too, will often put last-minute guests in their most expensive rooms.

Of course, even spur-of-the-moment travelers will have to admit that the more time you have to plan your trip before it actually begins, the better prepared you'll be. You'll have more leisure time to read up on the places you want to visit, plan the logistics of your trip, and contact the friends of friends you might want to visit.

But what if you just can't plan in advance or don't want to? Take heart. Advance planning is not as important outside of the busy summer months and at Christmastime, when many Irish return home. In fact, at times waiting to book can have definite advantages. Eager to fill empty seats, airlines often offer extremely low fares during the winter (usually January through March) and sometimes run special flight and hotel packages. Hotels try to lure guests with special weekend

unofficial **TIP**
If you're traveling on short notice, it's especially important to check airline consolidators (see page 39) and hotel Web sites (see page 94), and do other kinds of discount shopping.

rates; three-nights-for-two specials; bed, breakfast, and dinner packages; and many other attractive offers.

WHEN *to* GO

THINK RAIN. WHENEVER YOU GO TO IRELAND. OK, that said, don't think about rain, because the predictably unpredictable Irish weather should not keep you from going to Ireland. Then think about where you want to go.

Dublin doesn't really have a tourist season, so prices do not necessarily come down outside of the summer months. The city's indoor attractions can keep a visitor just as occupied and content in winter as in summer, and the fire-warmed pubs, lively concert halls, and treasure-filled museum galleries seem especially well suited to winter visits. What's more, transatlantic airfares are much lower in winter, putting Dublin within reach for a long weekend from the eastern United States.

> *unofficial* **TIP**
> If you plan on seeing more of Ireland than city life—and you should—think May, September, and October. Long twilights make May especially attractive; the scent of peat fires and the feel of autumn in the air will win you over to Ireland in September and October.

The pleasures of the Irish countryside can wane with the colder months. Outside Dublin, Cork, Galway, and other major cities, many hotels, restaurants, and attractions close "for the season" in late October and don't open again until March or April, when more than flowers begin to bloom. Hotels and restaurants are in full swing from mid-April through September or October; attractions often stay open longer.

Summer days in Ireland are long, especially from late May through late July, giving you hours of extra light for country drives and walks (the lovely Irish gloaming can last well past 11 p.m.). The downside is that the Irish and their visitors alike take advantage of the season to descend on beaches and mountain glades, sometimes taking the bucolic blush off even the most lovely spot.

PRICES

IN GENERAL, DUBLIN HOTEL AND RESTAURANT PRICES are on par with those in New York and other expensive cities in North America and Europe. Hotel rates are less costly outside of Dublin, but a meal in a good restaurant is fairly expensive anywhere in Ireland. You can blame the tax man in part for the high bill: value-added tax, or VAT (see page 51), is 21% on wine and 13.5% on food. Admission prices for the country's top attractions are also fairly steep.

Prices in Dublin don't necessarily vary with the seasons. Elsewhere in Ireland the high season is roughly from Easter to mid-September, with prices hitting highs in July and August. You're likely to find better deals on hotels during the "shoulder seasons" of mid-September to mid-December and January to March, but many hotels, especially in smaller towns and in the countryside, close in November and don't open again until March or April.

To give you a very rough idea of what things cost in Ireland, here's a list of some approximate prices in dollars:

Bus or shuttle to and from airport in Dublin	$10
Double room at a medium-range hotel in Dublin	$150–$200
Meal for one in an upscale Dublin restaurant (without wine)	$35–$50
Pub meal	$15–$20
Admission to top attractions throughout the country	$5–$15

WEATHER

RAIN IS A CONSTANT IN IRELAND—even summer months can be chilly. Extremes of climate are rare, and temperatures don't often fall below freezing or soar to uncomfortable levels.

Dublin's Average Temperatures and Rainfall

TEMPERATURE	(FAHRENHEIT)	(CELSIUS)	RAINFALL (INCHES)	(CENTIMETERS)
January	36–46°	2.2–7.7°	2.6	6.6
February	37–48°	2.7–8.8°	2.2	5.6
March	37–49°	2.7–9.4°	2	5.1
April	38–52°	3.3–11°	1.8	4.6
May	42–57°	5.5–13.8°	2.4	6.1
June	46–62°	7.7–16.6°	2.2	5.6
July	51–66°	10.5–18.8°	2.8	7.1
August	50–65°	10–18.3°	2.9	7.4
September	48–62°	8.8–16.6°	2.8	7.1
October	44–60°	6.6–15.5°	2.8	7.1
November	39–49°	3.6–9.4°	2.9	7.4
December	38–47°	3.3–8.3°	2.9	7.4

AIRFARE DEALS *and* PACKAGE TOURS

START WITH YOUR LOCAL TRAVEL AGENT

THE WEB IS RENDERING THE SERVICES of travel agents redundant, but don't give up on these professionals yet. A good agent can save you time and money by booking your flights, scouting out special package deals, reserving hotels, arranging car rentals, and arranging rail tickets and rail passes. If you don't already have a travel agent, ask your friends if they can recommend one. Or contact the American Society of Travel Agents, 1101 King Street, Suite 200, Alexandria, VA 22314; ☎ 703-739-2782; **www.astanet.com.** Ask the travel agent if he or she has experience with booking trips to Ireland, or has visited the country—if the answer is no, find someone else. One of a travel agent's best assets is his or her firsthand knowledge, so don't settle for an agent who can't provide that.

When you meet with the travel agent, you'll need to provide the dates of your trip and at least a rudimentary budget. With the information you provide, the agent can make suggestions about specific flights and hotels, and make the reservations for you. You are not charged for the travel agent's services—although this could change in the future, now that agents no longer receive the same kind of commissions from airlines and hotels.

CHECK THE TRAVEL SECTION OF YOUR LOCAL NEWSPAPER

ONE OF YOUR BEST SOURCES OF INFORMATION on package tours to Ireland is the travel section of your local paper. Ireland—especially Dublin—is a favorite destination of North Americans, and to serve this lucrative market there are frequently special money-saving deals that combine airfare and hotel costs. The paper may also advertise special cut-rate flights to Dublin or Shannon. Blackout dates and a host of restrictions generally accompany these offers. Do a little research before you book a flight or package. Call the tour operator and ask questions: What is and is not included in the deals they're offering? What restrictions apply? Will you receive a refund if you cancel? What are the hotels included in the package? (Then check out the property on the Web.)

SURF THE WEB

WITH ALL THE INFORMATION AVAILABLE ON THE INTERNET, more and more travelers are acting as their own travel agents. Using the Web you can find and book special airfares, surf for discounted hotel rooms (see page 94 for specific hotel Web sites), order Eurailpasses, and much more.

unofficial **TIP**
Special low prices and seasonal deals are often available only on the Web.

Many travel-related Web sites offer reservations and tickets for airlines, plus reservations and purchase capabilities for hotels and car-rental companies. Some to check out are **Travelocity** (**www.travelocity.com**), **Expedia Travel** (**www.expedia.com**), **Yahoo! Travel** (**www.travel.yahoo.com/destinations**), **Cheap Tickets** (**www.cheaptickets.com**), and **Orbitz** (**www.orbitz.com**). You can find some of the lowest prices on **Hotwire** (**www.hotwire.com**), but there's a catch—you provide the dates you want to travel, Hotwire comes up with a fare, and you purchase the ticket—but you don't know departure times or the airlines until you've finalized the purchase. Similarly, you can get some great deals on **Priceline** (**www.priceline.com**)—you provide the price you want to pay, along with your credit card info, but if your price is accepted, your card is charged before you know your departure times or airlines.

It's also useful to check out the Web sites of airlines that fly to Ireland (see the bottom of this page for a list). Frequently they post special discounts only available through online reservations. Some airlines will send you weekly e-newsletters and special last-minute e-fares, including specials for weekend travel from major North American hubs to Ireland. The airlines are also among your best sources for finding package tours to Ireland.

Check the following for air-and-hotel-package options in Ireland:

- Aer Lingus Vacation Store   (**www.aerlingusvacationstore.com**)
- American Airlines Vacations   (**www.aavacations.com**)
- British Airways Holidays   (**www.baholidays.com**)
- Continental Airlines Vacations   (**continental.covacations.com**)
- Delta Vacations   (**www.deltavacations.com**)
- Northwest Airlines WorldVacations (**www.nwaworldvacations.com**)
- United Airlines Vacations   (**www.unitedvacations.com**)

You can, of course, call an airline directly—but you may get a cheaper deal by using the Web. If you do call the airline, have your travel dates handy and be prepared to ask questions: "Will this flight cost less if I fly on a different day of the week or at a different time?" and "What is the cancellation policy if I can't use the tickets I've already paid for on my credit card?" Your goal is to get the lowest fare to your destination. You can be direct and simply ask what the lowest fare is from your city to Dublin, Shannon, or Belfast, and if

AIRLINE CONTACT INFORMATION FROM NORTH AMERICA

Aer Lingus	☎ 800-474-7424	**www.flyaerlingus.com**
Air Canada	☎ 800-361-5373	**www.aircanada.com**
Air New Zealand	☎ 800-262-2468	**www.airnz.co.uk**
American Airlines	☎ 800-433-7300	**www.aa.com**
British Airways	☎ 800-AIRWAYS	**www.ba.com**
Continental Airlines	☎ 800-625-0280	**www.continental.com**
Delta Air Lines	☎ 800-241-4141	**www.delta.com**
United Airlines	☎ 800-538 2929	**www.united.com**

flying into one is considerably cheaper than flying into another. Chances are that the service representative will tell you; if he or she won't, hang up and try again.

SUGGESTED TOUR OPERATORS

ESCORTED TOURS DIFFER FROM PACKAGE TOURS in several fundamental ways. A package tour generally includes your airfare and hotel, but you are left on your own. Escorted tours offer full-service itineraries that generally include transfers to your hotel(s), some meals, sightseeing, nightlife, and more. Dozens of companies offer escorted tours to Dublin and other destinations in Ireland. Many tours cater to special interests, such as theater or history; others are more general. A good travel agent can help you find a tour that suits your particular interests. It's also a good idea to scan the travel section in your local paper for tour possibilities.

It's important to know the basics of what is and isn't offered on an escorted tour before you sign up. Here are some questions you might want to ask:

- When and how much do you pay?
- Will the trip be canceled if not enough people sign up? If so, what must you do to get a refund?
- How big the group will be? What are the age groups? Singles or couples? Men or women?
- What's the daily schedule? Is it reasonable or so jam-packed that you won't have time to breathe?
- What are the accommodations? (Ask for the names and check these out on your own. Some tour operators use large, anonymous hotels in unappealing parts of town.)

Don't assume that anything not specifically spelled out is included in your fee. For example, you may have to pay to get yourself to or from the airport, or admission to attractions may not be included.

Cosmos (**www.cosmos.com**), **Trafalgar Tours** (**www.trafalgartours .com**), and **Maupintour** (**www.maupintour.com**) all offer escorted tours to Dublin and the rest of Ireland. For more information about specific offerings, check out their Web sites, and call or write with questions. *Remember:* Be a wise consumer.

GATHERING INFORMATION

IRISH TOURIST BOARD OFFICES

FOR GENERAL INFORMATION ABOUT IRELAND, contact an office of the **Irish Tourist Board** at one of the following addresses.

Irish Tourist Board
345 Park Avenue
New York, NY 10154
☎ 800-223-6470 or 212-418-0800
FAX: 212-371-9052
www.tourismireland.com

Northern Ireland Tourist Board
551 Fifth Avenue, Suite 701
New York, NY 10176
☎ 800-326-0036 or 212-922-0101
FAX: 212-922-0099
www.discovernorthernireland.com

IN CANADA
Irish Tourist Board
2 Bloor Street West, Suite 1501
Toronto, ON M4W 3E2
☎ 800-223-6470 or 416-925-6368
FAX: 416-929-6783
www.tourismireland.com

Northern Ireland Tourist Board
2 Bloor Street West, Suite 1501
Toronto, ON M4W 3E2
☎ 800-576-8174 or 416-925-6368
FAX: 416-925-6033
www.discovernorthernireland.com

IN IRELAND
Irish Tourist Board–Bord Fáilte
Baggot Street Bridge
Dublin 2
☎ 1890-525-525
FAX: 01-602-4100
www.ireland.travel.ie

Northern Ireland Tourist Board
16 Nassau Street
Dublin 2
☎ 01-679-1977
FAX: 01-679-1863
www.discovernorthernireland.com

IN NORTHERN IRELAND
Irish Tourist Board
53 Castle Street
Belfast BT1 1GH
☎ 028-9024-0201
www.tourismireland.com

Northern Ireland Tourist Board
St. Anne's Court
59 North Street
Belfast BT1 1NB
☎ 028-9023-1221
FAX: 028-9024-0960
www.discovernorthernireland.com

TOURIST INFORMATION CENTRES

YOUR BEST SOURCE OF UP-TO-DATE INFORMATION in any city or town is the Tourist Information Centre. You'll find addresses for them in every "Planning Your Visit to . . ." section in this guidebook. Tourist Information Centres are always centrally located, usually in the busiest areas of a city or town. In larger cities, you'll often find a branch in the train station. What are they good for? First and foremost, this being Ireland, for the chance to ask the friendly personnel any questions you might have. In general, you'll find that these people are eager to help visitors. Handouts, sometimes free, sometimes costing a few euros, usually include easy-to-use maps and guides to the city or town. You'll also find racks of brochures on local attractions. Something might catch your fancy, but remember that the brochures are advertisements—the fact that they are in a Tourist Information Centre doesn't automatically mean they are worth your time or money. There will often be a currency-exchange window in the center, along with a convenient hotel-booking service. For hotel booking there's usually a fee (10% of

unofficial **TIP**
Many Tourist Information
Centres offer free or
low-cost guided walks of
a city or town; join one
of these informative tours
if you have the time.

room cost) that is refunded when you pay for
your room. Some Tourist Information Centres
have a small bookstore stocked with books of
local interest, regional maps and guides, and
souvenirs.

WEB SITES FOR FURTHER RESEARCH

THE WEB IS AN INVALUABLE TOOL when it
comes to travel research, so even if you don't have Internet access at
home we suggest you arrange to spend some time in front of a computer, perhaps one of those available for free use at local libraries.
Web sites often contain the most up-to-date information (provided
that the site is well maintained)—hotels, for instance, list current
prices and discounts (and provide pictures of their rooms), and
attractions provide current prices and opening and closing times. We
list Web sites whenever possible throughout this guide.

The following Web sites should provide you with enough info,
as well as links to other sites, to keep you glued to your computer
for weeks. We also recommend contacting the Web sites for visitors
centers in cities, towns, national parks, and other places we list
throughout this guide—you'll find a wealth of information specific
to the places you most want to visit.

- **www.dublintouristboard.com** Contains up-to-the-minute info on events, hotels, restaurants, sightseeing, exhibits, and more.
- **www.ireland.com** The online edition of the *Irish Times,* the country's most esteemed newspaper. Try reading it before you go to get a taste of what's happening in Ireland today.
- **www.timeout.com** *Time Out* magazine's Web site posts detailed information on what's happening in Dublin and in Cork.
- **www.ireland.travel.ie** Includes current entertainment listings and attractions throughout Ireland.
- **www.entertainment.ie** Find up-to-date listings of events and exhibitions.
- **www.visitdublin.com** A plethora of information about Dublin can be found here, ranging from news about galleries and concerts to facts about car rentals and tours.
- **www.belfast.world-guides.com** Locate information on most facets of travel to Belfast: accommodations, weather, attractions, and more. An excellent source if you are traveling to Northern Ireland.

WHAT *to* PACK

AS LITTLE AS POSSIBLE. BE BRAVE. Resist the urge to cram your
entire closet into your luggage. Take just *one suitcase,* preferably the
kind with wheels. Augment that with a backpack or some kind of

useful, zippered, waterproof carryall. Add a practical purse or bag that you can sling over your shoulder and use every day.

Keep in mind that not all Irish hotels have elevators or porters. In smaller, less expensive hotels and B&Bs, you're going to be lugging your own bags. Remember, too, that airlines now allow only one carry-on bag plus a purse or briefcase or laptop. They are strict about this, and you will have to go through various security checkpoints before boarding with your personal luggage.

unofficial **TIP**
Leave all your electric and electronic doodads at home; if you lug them with you, they'll have to fit in your luggage, and when in Ireland you will have to get a special adapter plug to use or recharge them.

In the wake of September 11, 2001, airlines now confiscate all sharp objects, no matter how innocuous, if they are in your carry-on luggage. This includes tiny scissors, knitting and hypodermic needles (unless you have a note from your doctor explaining why you need one), corkscrews, any kind of knife, and sporting equipment.

PASSPORTS AND VISAS

IF YOU ARE AN AMERICAN, Canadian, Australian, or New Zealand tourist visiting Ireland for less than three months, a valid passport is the only legal form of identification you'll need to enter the country. Visas are required for any stay longer than three months. The Web site of the **U.S. State Department Bureau of Consular Affairs (www.travel.state.gov)** provides exhaustive

unofficial **TIP**
Make a copy of the information page of your passport, and keep it in your luggage in order to expedite replacement in case the passport gets lost or stolen.

information about passports (including a downloadable application), customs, and other government-regulated aspects of travel for U.S. citizens. Alternatively, call the **National Passport Information Center** at ☎ 900-225-5674.

Irish Consular Offices

Irish consulates abroad can advise you on visas for work or study in Ireland, as well as address many other legal and administrative questions prior to your trip.

IN THE UNITED STATES
Irish Consulate General
Chase Building
535 Boylston Street
Boston, MA 02116
☎ 617-267-6375
FAX: 617-267-6375
irlcons@aol.com

Irish Consulate General
Ireland House
345 Park Avenue, 17th Floor

New York, NY 10154-0037
☎ 212-319-2555
FAX: 202-980-9475
congenny@aol.com

Irish Consulate General
400 North Michigan
    Avenue
Chicago, IL 60611
☎ 312-337-1868
FAX: 312-337-1954
irishconsulate@sbcglobal.net

Irish Consulate General
100 Pine Street, 33rd Floor
San Francisco, CA 94111
☎ 415-392-4214
FAX: 415-392-0885
irishcgsf@earthlink.net

Irish Embassy
2234 Massachusetts Avenue NW
Washington, D.C. 20008-2849
☎ 202-462-3939
FAX: 202-232-5993
washingtonembassy@dfi.ie

Honorary Consul
920 Schellbourne Street
Reno, NV 89511
☎ 775-853-4497
FAX: 775-853-4497
bbrady@nvbell.net

Honorary Consul
222 South Central Avenue, Suite 1101
St. Louis, MO 63105
☎ 314-727-1000
FAX: 314-727-2960

Honorary Consul
2630 Sutton Court
Houston, TX 77027
☎ 713-961-5263
FAX: 970-925-7900

Honorary Consul
751 Seadrift Drive
Huntington Beach, CA 92648-4163
☎ 714-658-9832; FAX: 714-374-8972
icla@ireland.com

Honorary Consul
c/o Silverio & Hall
400 Fifth Avenue South, Suite 301
Naples, FL 34102
☎ 239-649-1001; FAX: 239-649-1972
naples@silveriohall.com

IN CANADA
Embassy of Ireland
130 Albert Street, Suite 1105
Ottawa, ON K1P 5G4
☎ 613-223-6281
FAX: 613-233-5835
embassyofireland@rogers.com

Honorary Consul
100 West Pender Street,
 Tenth Floor
Vancouver, BC V6B 1R8
☎ 604-683-9233
FAX: 604-683-8402
irishconsul@telus.net

Honorary Consul General
45 Harvey Road, Fifth Floor
St. John's, NL A1C 2G1
☎ 709-570-0511
FAX: 709-570-0506

Honorary Consul General
20 Toronto Street, Suite 1210
Toronto, ON M5C 2B8
☎ 416-366-9300
FAX: 416-947-0584

Honorary Consul General
3803-8A Street SW
Calgary, AB T2T 3B6
☎ 403-243-2970
FAX: 403-287-1023

Honorary Consul
13 Glenmeadow Crescent
St. Albert, AB T8N 3AT
☎ 780-458-0810
FAX: 780-458-6483

Honorary Consul General
1590 Dr Penrose Avenue
Montréal, QC H3G 1C5
☎ 514-848-7389
FAX: 514-848-4514

American and Canadian Embassies in Ireland

If your passport is lost or stolen, or you need some other kind of special assistance while you're traveling in Ireland, the following embassies, both located in Dublin, will be able to help or direct you.

THE UNITED STATES
42 Elgin Road
Ballsbridge
Dublin 4
☎ 01-668-8777
FAX: 01-668-9946
webmasterireland@state.gov

CANADA
65–68 St. Stephen's Green,
Fourth Floor
Dublin 2
☎ 01-417-4100
FAX: 01-417-4101
dubln@international.gc.ca

HOW TO DRESS

GIVEN THE UNPREDICTABILITY OF IRISH WEATHER, think layers. Bring mix-and-match coordinates that you can shed or add to as needed. A sweater will be welcome in any season, as will a waterproof coat or jacket with a hood and an umbrella (many hotels supply these to guests). A comfortable and casual pair of waterproof walking shoes is handy for city walks and country treks. If traveling to Ireland in the winter months, bring protection against the damp chill: gloves, a scarf, and a warm coat.

unofficial **TIP**
If you're traveling in winter, don't pack more than one sweater, and wait to buy one of the incredibly warm, mostly waterproof, and very beautiful Aran sweaters you'll see throughout the country (look for "Handmade in Ireland" on the label).

A Word on Tourist Garb

The Irish are pretty casual about their clothes, so wearing a pair of blue jeans while sightseeing will not set you apart as a gauche tourist. In better restaurants and at cultural events, a "smart but casual" dress code generally applies: slacks and footwear other than running shoes are usually the norm for men, a dress or good slacks and a nice blouse for women. (There are still a few places where gentlemen are required to wear a coat and tie, but not many.)

SPECIAL CONSIDERATIONS

TRAVELING WITH CHILDREN

THE RATING SYSTEM IN OUR ATTRACTION PROFILES attempts to gauge suitability for children and adults of various ages, but all children have different interests and differing levels of tolerance for museums and other sights. All in all, though, we find that kids love Ireland—the common language provides a level of comfort, there are enough castles and suits of armor around to satisfy their romantic notions of days of yore, and a ride on a double-decker bus can be sheer heaven.

You'll find kid-friendly amusements throughout Ireland. Audio guides are available at many

unofficial **TIP**
If you're traveling as a family, you can usually buy money-saving family tickets at major attractions. These tickets are available for two adults and two children (three children in some cases).

attractions, making them more fun and interesting for children age 9 and up. Kids under 5 get in free almost everywhere. Finally, remember that kids get jet lag, too, so plan your first day accordingly.

DISABLED ACCESS IN IRELAND

MANY, BUT NOT ALL, IRISH ATTRACTIONS, as well as hotels and restaurants, are accessible to disabled visitors in wheelchairs, but portions of some historic properties cannot be changed to accommodate chairs. Larger and newer hotels, plus many smaller properties, provide special rooms designed for the disabled. We provide information on access for the disabled in our listings, but call ahead to find out what, if any, arrangements have been made for wheelchairs.

To make your trip pleasurable, not a struggle, plan ahead by checking out these resources:

In Ireland and Northern Ireland

- The **Irish Wheelchair Association** (Áras Chuchulainn, Blackheath Drive, Clontarf, Dublin 3; ☎ 01-833-8241; **www.iwa.ie**) has information about holiday destinations for travelers with disabilities, as well as other helpful items.
- The **Irish Rail** Web site, **www.irishrail.ie,** has invaluable information for travelers with disabilities.
- In Northern Ireland, **Disability Action** (Portside Business Park, 189 Airport Road West, Belfast BT3 9ED; **www.disabilityaction.org**) lists facilities for the disabled.
- At any Northern Ireland Tourist Board offices, pick up *Information Guide to Accessible Accommodation.*
- The **National Rehabilitation Board of Ireland** (24–25 Clyde Road, Ballsbridge, Dublin 4; ☎ 01-608-0400) publishes *Guide to Accessible Accommodation in Ireland*, helpful in finding lodging.

In the United States

- **Access-Able Travel Source** (☎ 303-232-2979; **www.accessable.com**) has a wealth of information about traveling with disabilities.
- **Accessible Journeys** (☎ 800-846-4537 or 610-521-0339; **www .disabilitytravel.com**) caters to mature travelers, slow walkers, wheelchair travelers, and their families and friends. The company specializes in accessible travel planning, group tours, and cruises.
- **Flying Wheels Travel** (☎ 507-451-5005; **www.flyingwheelstravel.com**) specializes in travel for persons with physical disabilities. The company offers a range of escorted tours.

SENIOR TRAVELERS

IF YOU'RE A SENIOR WHO GETS AROUND FAIRLY WELL, Ireland won't present any particular problems for you. If you have mobility or health issues, though, be aware that not all hotels, particularly less expensive B&Bs, have elevators. Before reserving a hotel room, ask whether or not you'll have access to an elevator or if other facilities for travelers with disabilities are available.

Being a senior may entitle you to some money-saving travel bargains, such as reduced admission at theaters, museums, and other attractions. Always ask, even if a reduction isn't posted.

The following sources can provide information on discounts and other benefits for seniors:

- **AARP** (601 E Street NW, Washington, DC 20049; ☎ 800-424-3410; **www.aarp.org**) offers member discounts on car rentals and hotels.

- **Elderhostel** (75 Federal Street, Boston, MA 02110-1941; ☎ 877-426-8056; **www.elderhostel.org**) offers people 55 and older a variety of university-based education programs in Dublin and throughout Ireland. These courses are value-packed, hassle-free ways to learn while traveling. Package prices include airfare, accommodations, meals, tuition, tips, and insurance. And you'll be glad to know that there are no grades. Recent programs have included "Definitive Ireland," "Discovering the West of Ireland," "Medieval and Gaelic Ireland: A Celebration," "Walking Southwest Ireland's Coast and Country," "Theater and Art in Dublin," and "Celebrating Irish Mythology."

- **SAGA International Holidays** (222 Berkeley Street, Boston, MA 02116; ☎ 877-265-6862; **www.sagaholidays.com**) offers inclusive tours for those 50 and older.

- **Grand Circle Travel** (347 Congress Street, Boston, MA 02210; ☎ 800-597-3644) provides escorted tours for mature travelers. Call for a copy of the publication, "101 Tips for the Mature Traveler," or order online at **www.gct.com.**

GAY AND LESBIAN TRAVELERS

HOMOSEXUALITY WAS NOT DECRIMINALIZED IN IRELAND until 1993 (in the North, not until 1982), and this largely conservative, predominantly Catholic country is still not terribly gay friendly. Gay and lesbian travelers should keep in mind that public expressions of affection may easily attract unwanted attention—gay bashing is not unheard of, even in Dublin.

That said, there's a growing gay community in Dublin and in other, more-liberal cities such as Galway. You can find gay-oriented activities in the free monthly newspaper *Gay Community News* (**GCN**), available in some bookstores. *In Dublin,* the city's main events guide, devotes several pages to gay information, and two recent Dublin publications, *Free!* and *Scene City,* highlight gay venues. On the Web, **Gay Ireland Online** (**www.gay-ireland.com**) and **Outhouse** (**www.outhouse.ie**) provide listings and contacts for organizations and events, along with discussion forums.

The following resources have knowledgeable staffers who can assist gay and lesbian travelers in Dublin and the rest of Ireland:

- **National Lesbian and Gay Federation (NLGF)** 2 Scarlet Row, Dublin 1; ☎ 01-671-0939; nlgf@tinet.ie
- **Outhouse Community Resource Centre** 105 Capel Street, Dublin 1; ☎ 01-873-4932; **www.outhouse.ie**
- **Gay Switchboard Dublin** Carmichael House, North Brunswick Street, Dublin 7; ☎ 01-872-1055; **www.gayswitchboard.ie**
- **Lesbian Line Dublin** Carmichael Centre, North Brunswick Street, Dublin 7; ☎ 01-872-9911

In America

- **International Gay and Lesbian Travel Association (IGLTA)** ☎ 800-448-8550 or 954-776-2626; iglta@iglta.org; **www.iglta.org.** Provides a wealth of information on gay travel, including tour listings and contacts abroad.
- **Now Voyager** ☎ 800-255-6951; **www.nowvoyager.com.** A gay-owned and -operated travel service.

OTHER TRAVEL CONCERNS

ELECTRICITY

LEAVE ALL BUT THE MOST ESSENTIAL ELECTRIC GADGETS and appliances at home. The electricity supply in Ireland is 220-volt AC, which will blow out any American 110-volt appliance unless it is plugged into a transformer. Irish outlets are made for large three-prong plugs, so in addition to the transformer, you will need to get an adapter, available at any hardware store, chemist (drugstore), supermarket, or gadget store. Don't plug anything in until you've checked the voltage on the transformer! It should be set to "Input AC 110-volt, output AC 220-volt." You'll know by the pop, flash, and smoke if you got it wrong.

HEALTH

CHECK YOUR EXISTING INSURANCE to see if it covers medical services abroad. If it doesn't, consider purchasing a policy from a company that offers health coverage for travelers, such as **Travelex,** ☎ 800-228-9792, **www.travelex.com; MEDEX International,** ☎ 888-MEDEX-00 or 410-453-6300, **www.medexassist.com;** or **Travel Assistance International,** ☎ 800-821-2828, **www.travelassistance.com**.

MONEY

THE CURRENCY OF THE REPUBLIC OF IRELAND is the euro (€). For this book, we've assumed an exchange rate of €1 to $1.25 U.S. Euro notes come in denominations of €5, €10, €50, €100, €200, and €500. A euro is divided into 100 euro cents. Coins come in denominations of €2, €1, €0.50, €0.20, €0.10, €0.05, €0.02, and €0.01.

As part of the United Kingdom, Northern Ireland continues to use British pounds (£), one of which converts to about $1.75. The pound is divided into 100 pence (p).

There are no longer any £1 notes. There are red £50s, purple £20s, brown £10s, and green £5s. Coins are divided into £2, £1, 50p, 20p, 10p, 5p, 2p, and 1p.

Check any major newspaper's business section for current exchange rates, or go to **www.travlang .com** or **www.x-rates.com.**

unofficial **TIP**
Coins cannot be changed into foreign cash, so spend them while you're in Ireland; better still, donate them on your way home to the **UNICEF Change Collection** program sponsored by most airlines.

ATMs, Banks, and Bureaux de Change

There are ATMs all over Dublin and in cities and towns throughout the country, in any place large enough to have a bank branch. This is your best bet for getting the optimum rate when you withdraw money. Remember, you can't access your credit-card funds from an ATM without a PIN (personal identification number).

Weekday hours for banks are generally 9:30 a.m. to 4:30 p.m. All banks are closed on public holidays, but many branches have 24-hour banking lobbies with ATMs and/or ATMs on the street outside. Banks and *bureaux de change* (exchange centers) will exchange money at a competitive rate but charge a commission (typically 1 to 3% of the total transaction). All U.K. bureaux de change and other money-changing establishments are required to clearly display exchange rates as well as full details on any fees and rates of commission. Before exchanging your money, always check to see the exchange rate, how much commission will be charged, and whether additional fees apply.

unofficial **TIP**
Bureaux de change are found in major tourist sections of Dublin (some are open 24 hours). Steer clear of those that offer good exchange rates but charge a heavy commission (up to 8%).

Value-added Tax (VAT)

In the Republic, the VAT is 13.5% for restaurants, hotels, car rentals, and the like; the VAT on wine, gifts, and souvenirs is 21%. In Northern Ireland, the VAT is 17.5%; food, children's clothing, and books are exempt from VAT. If you are not a citizen of a country in the European Union (EU), you can often get a refund on this tax (see page 101). VAT is usually added directly to an item's sticker price, except for some merchandise sold in some small shops and some services. Check before you book a hotel to see if the quoted price includes VAT.

TELEPHONE, E-MAIL, AND POSTAL SERVICES

Telephones

Three types of public pay phones are available: those that take only coins (increasingly rare), those that accept only phone cards, and those that take both. You can buy phone cards from newsstands and post offices. At coin-operated phones, insert your coins before dialing.

LOCAL AND INTERNATIONAL CODES The country code for the Republic is 353; for Northern Ireland it is 44. To call Ireland from the United States, dial 011-353 or 011-44, the area or city code, and then the six-, seven-, or eight-digit phone number. If you're in Ireland and dialing a number within the same area code, the local number is all you need.

To make an international call from Ireland, dial the international access code (00), then the country code, then the area code, and finally the local number. Or call through one of the following long-distance access codes: **AT&T,** ☎ 800-550-000; **Sprint,** ☎ 800-552-001; or **MCI,** ☎ 800-55-1001.

Some Important Numbers

00 International dialing code; that is, if calling outside Ireland, dial 00 + 1 for U.S. and Canada, 61 for Australia, 64 for New Zealand, and the like

IN THE REPUBLIC:

10 General operator

999 Emergency for police, fire, or ambulance

1190 U.K. and Irish directory assistance

1198 International directory assistance

114 International operator

IN NORTHERN IRELAND:

100 General operator

999 Emergency for police, fire, or ambulance

192 U.K. and Irish directory assistance

153 International directory assistance

155 International operator

CELL PHONES Within Ireland you can use any cell phone compatible with the GSM (Global System for Mobile Communications) network. However, you'll pay less in roaming charges by swapping out your phone's SIM (subscriber-information module, or "smart card"), the removable computer chip that stores your phone number, messages, and settings, with a prepaid one that has an Ireland phone number (available at electronics stores or through online retailers such as the ones that follow). Many GSM phones will work with any SIM, but be aware that some wireless providers lock their phones—that is, they configure them to work only with the SIMs they supply—so check whether your phone is locked or unlocked before you buy.

You can also rent a GSM cell phone for use in Ireland, either before you leave home or once you arrive. For more information, contact

Cellular Abroad (☎ 800-287-5072; **www.cellularabroad.com**), (**InTouch USA** (☎ 800-872-7626; **www.intouchglobal.com**), or **RoadPost** (☎ 888-290-1606 or 905-272-5665; **www.roadpost.com**).

E-mail

You'll find Internet cafes in Irish cities, although they can be few and far between in the countryside. If you're in dire need of a computer to check or send e-mail, go to the local library. Even the smallest library should have at least one computer available for public use.

If you have a laptop that can take advantage of it, a wireless connection will provide you with a high-speed connection without cable or a phone line—quite handy when you're on the road. The lobbies of better hotels often provide wireless access for guests.

Post Offices

Mail is called *the post* in Ireland. Mailboxes (postboxes) are green with "Post" lettered on them in the Republic, red and green with "Royal Mail" lettered on them in Northern Ireland. Post offices are generally open Monday through Friday, 9 a.m. to 5:30 p.m., and Saturday, 9 a.m. to 12:30 p.m.

CALENDAR *of* SPECIAL EVENTS

IRELAND HAS A LARGE NUMBER OF SPECIAL TRADITIONAL events and festivals throughout the year. Good resources for checking events and dates before you leave home are **www.ireland.travel.ie** and **www.tourismireland.com.** If you're spending a major portion of your trip in Dublin, log on to the **Dublin Tourist Board**'s Web site, **www.visit dublin.com,** or **www.dublintown.com.** As you're traveling through the rest of Ireland, stop in at Tourist Information Centres to find out what's going on.

January

FUNDERLAND ROYAL Dublin Society, Ballsbridge, Dublin 4; ☎ 061-419988; **www.funfair.ie.** A yearly indoor fair, with carnival stalls, exciting rides, and family entertainment.

YEATS WINTER SCHOOL Sligo Park Hotel, Sligo Town; ☎ 071-42693; **www.yeats-sligo.com.** A relaxing weekend in late January with lectures and a tour of Yeats Country.

February

ALL IRELAND DANCING Championships INEC, Killarney, County Kerry; ☎ 01-475-2220; fax 01-475-1053; cirg@tinet.ie. The winners advance to the World Dancing Championship.

ANTIQUES AND COLLECTIBLES FAIR Newman House, 85 St. Stephen's Green, Dublin 2; fax 01-670-8295; antiquesfairsireland@esatclear.ie. Dealers sell small antiques and collectors' items. Four consecutive Sundays.

SIX NATIONS RUGBY TOURNAMENT Lansdowne Road, Ballsbridge, County Dublin. Athletes from Ireland, England, Scotland, Wales, France, and Italy participate in this annual tourney. Contact Irish Rugby Football Union, 62 Lansdowne Road, Dublin 4; ☎ 01-668-4601, fax 01-660-5640.

March

BRIDGE HOUSE IRISH FESTIVAL Bridge House Hotel and Leisure Centre, Tullamore, County Offaly; ☎ 506-22000; fax 506-25690; **www.bridgehouse.com.** The biggest indoor festival in Ireland, with Irish song and dance.

ST. PATRICK'S DAY PARADES Throughout Ireland, in celebration of Ireland's patron saint.

ST. PATRICK'S DUBLIN FESTIVAL Fireworks, dance, street theater, sports, carnival acts, and music ending in a spectacular parade; ☎ 01-676-3205; fax 01-676-3208; **www.stpatricksday.ie.**

April

DUBLIN FILM FESTIVAL Irish Film Centre, Temple Bar, Dublin 2, and cinemas throughout Dublin; ☎ 01-679-2937; fax 01-679-2939. More than a hundred films from Ireland and around the world are featured, plus lectures and seminars.

PAN CELTIC FESTIVAL Kilkenny, County Kilkenny; ☎ 056-51500; panceltic@eircom.net. Celts (including those from Cornwall, the Isle of Man, Scotland, Wales, and Brittany, as well as Ireland) gather for song, dance, cultural events, and nature walks.

WORLD IRISH DANCING CHAMPIONSHIPS Waterfront Hotel, Belfast; ☎ 01-475-2220; fax 01-475-1053; cirg@tinet.ie. Thousands come from around the world to take part in this competition.

May

BELFAST CITY MARATHON 6,000 runners compete in this 26-mile event, which starts and finishes at Maysfield Leisure Centre; ☎ 028-9027-0345.

COUNTY WICKLOW GARDENS FESTIVAL On certain days, heritage properties and gardens are open to the public; ☎ 0404-66058; fax 0404 66057.

DIVERSIONS Temple Bar, Dublin 2; ☎ 01-677-2255; fax 01-677-2255; **www.temple-bar.ie.** A free outdoor festival featuring theater, music, film, visual arts, and even a circus.

MAY DAY RACES Down Royal Racecourse, Maze, Lisburn, County Antrim; ☎ 028-9262-1256; **www.downroyal.com.** An important event in the horse-racing calendar.

WEXFORD FESTIVAL OPERA Theatre Royal, Wexford City; ☎ 053-22400; fax 053-424289; **www.wexfordopera.com.** A delightfully refreshing informal festival known for its productions of little-known 18th- and 19th-century works, as well as recitals and classical music. Late May to early June.

June

AIB MUSIC FESTIVAL IN GREAT IRISH HOUSES A ten-day festival of classical music performed by Irish and international artists in stately buildings and mansions; ☎ 01-278-1528; fax 01-278-1529.

BLOOMSDAY FESTIVAL A celebration of James Joyce's *Ulysses* and its central character Leopold Bloom, set in Joyce's fictitious Dublin on June 16, 1904. Ceremonies take place throughout the city, and there are guided walks. Contact the James Joyce Centre, 34 North Great George's Street, Dublin 1; ☎ 01-878-8547; fax 01-878-8488; **www.jamesjoyce.ie.** June 16.

BUDWEISER IRISH DERBY The Curragh, County Kildare; ☎ 045-441205; fax 045-441442. This horse race is one of the stars of European racing, the Irish equivalent of the Kentucky Derby. Fans converge from around the world in fancy dress, men in jackets and women in hats (think of the Ascot Day scene in *My Fair Lady*). Buy tickets in advance at **www.curragh.ie.**

KILLARNEY SUMMERFEST Fitzgerald Stadium, Killarney, County Kerry. This rock festival is one of Ireland's summer highlights. The big-name performers have included Sheryl Crow and Bryan Adams. For tickets contact **www.ticketmaster.ie.**

WATERFORD MARITIME FESTIVAL Quays of Waterford City. This four-day celebration takes place over the June bank holiday. The highlight is a powerboat race from Waterford to Swansea, Wales. Boats from the Irish, British, French, and Dutch naval fleets gather in Waterford Harbor. Other highlights are kayak races and concerts.

July

BATTLE OF THE BOYNE COMMEMORATION Belfast and other northern cities. This event, often called Orangeman's Day, commemorates a historic battle between two 17th-century kings. Protestants all over Northern Ireland celebrate and parade. Contact the House of Orange, 65 Dublin Road, Belfast BT2 7HE; ☎ 028-9032-2801. July 12.

GALWAY ARTS FESTIVAL AND RACES Galway City and Racecourse; ☎ 091-566577; fax 091-562655; **www.galwayartsfestival.ie.** This festival celebrates all manner of arts: theater, music, film, and more, with hundreds of participating writers, artists, performers, and musicians. The Galway Races follow, with five more days of racing and entertainment. Mid-July.

LUGHNASA FAIR Carrickfergus Castle, County Antrim; ☎ 028-4336-6455. A 12th-century Norman castle provides the setting for this fair. Enjoy medieval games, observe people dressed in period costumes, and sample traditional food and crafts. Late July.

OXYGEN Punchestown Racecourse, County Kildare. One of the largest and most popular rock festivals. To buy tickets, log on to **www.ticketmaster.ie.** Early July.

August

KERRYGOLD HORSE SHOW RDS Showgrounds, Ballsbridge, Dublin 4; ☎ 01-668-0866; fax 01-660-4014; **www.rds.ie.** This event draws a fashionable crowd and is considered the most important equestrian and social event on Ireland's calendar. Aside from the equestrian events, there are balls in the evening, as well as the awarding of the Aga Khan Trophy and the Nation's Cup. Early August.

KILKENNY ARTS FESTIVAL Kilkenny Town; ☎ 056-52175; fax 056-51704; **www.kilkennyarts.ie.** This festival celebrates all the arts, from classical and traditional music to poetry readings.

PUCK FAIR Killorglin, County Kerry; ☎ 066-976-2366; **www.puck fair.ie.** A wild goat is captured, garlanded, and declared king in this three-day festival, one of Ireland's oldest.

ROSE OF TRALEE INTERNATIONAL FESTIVAL Tralee, County Kerry; ☎ 066-712-1322; fax 066-22654; **www.roseoftralee.ie.** This famous five-day festival includes concerts, horse races, and a talent pageant culminating in the selection of the Rose of Tralee.

September

ALL-IRELAND HURLING AND GAELIC FOOTBALL FINALS Croke Park, Dublin 3; ☎ 01-836-3222; fax 01-836-6420. The finals of hurling and Gaelic football, hugely important in Ireland. Buy tickets at **www.ticket master.ie.**

FLEADH CHEOIL NAH ÉIREANN Listowel, County Kerry; ☎ 01-280-0295; fax 01-280-3759; **www.comhaltas.com.** Since 1951, Ireland's most important celebration of traditional music. Late August.

GALWAY INTERNATIONAL OYSTER FESTIVAL Galway and environs; ☎ 091-522066; fax 091-527282; **www.galwayoysterfest.com.** A true feast for oyster lovers, with an oyster-opening championship, a golf tournament, traditional music, and more. Late September.

IRISH ANTIQUE DEALERS' FAIR RDS Showgrounds, Ballsbridge, Dublin 4; ☎ 01-285-9294. The most important antiques fair in Ireland; hundreds of dealers participate. Late September.

NATIONAL HERITAGE WEEK Throughout the country hundreds of events are held, including lectures, music, walks, and more. ☎ 01-647-2455; **www.heritageireland.ie.** Early September.

October

BABORÓ INTERNATIONAL ARTS FESTIVAL FOR CHILDREN Galway; ☎ 091-509705; fax 091-562655; **www.baboro.ie.** Children ages 3 to 12 can enjoy music, dance, and more. Late October.

BELFAST FESTIVAL AT QUEENS Queens University, Belfast; ☎ 028-9066-7687; fax 028 9066-5577; **www.belfastfestival.com.** An outstanding celebration of the arts—music, film, opera, drama, and more.

DUBLIN CITY MARATHON This popular run takes place on the last Monday in October. More than 5,000 runners compete. ☎ 01-626-3746; **www.dublincitymarathon.ie.**

DUBLIN THEATRE FESTIVAL Theaters throughout Dublin; ☎ 01-677-8439; fax 01-679-7709; **www.dublintheatrefestival.com.** Featuring new plays by major Irish companies plus plays from abroad. Early October.

GUINNESS CORK JAZZ FESTIVAL Cork City; ☎ 021-427-8979; fax 021-427-0463; **www.corkjazzfestival.com.** International acts play around town, in pubs, hotels, and concert halls. Late October.

MURPHY'S CORK INTERNATIONAL FILM FESTIVAL Cinemas in Cork; ☎ 021-427-1711; fax 021-427-5945. Ireland's premier film festival offers features, documentaries, and shorts.

December

LEOPARDSTOWN NATIONAL HUNT FESTIVAL Leopardstown Racecourse, Foxrock, Dublin 18; ☎ 01-289-2888; fax 01-289-2634; **www.leopardstown.com.** Three days of thoroughbred racing. Late December.

WOODFORD MUMMERS FEILE Woodford, County Galway; ☎ 059-49248. A celebration of traditional music, song, dance, and mime performed in period costume. Late December.

PART TWO

ARRIVING

ARRIVING *by* AIR

THE MAIN POINT OF ENTRY for most visitors to Ireland is **Dublin Airport,** although many travelers arrive at **Shannon Airport,** in the west of the country. **Belfast Airport,** in Northern Ireland, also handles international flights. For more about airlines flying from the United States and Canada, see page 60.

PASSPORT CONTROL AND CUSTOMS

ON THE PLANE YOU WILL RECEIVE a landing card on which you'll provide your name, address, passport number, and the address of where you'll be staying. Present this completed form and your passport at Passport Control upon deplaning. When your passport is stamped, proceed on to pick up your luggage. From there you'll wend your way to Customs.

At the Customs area there are two choices: Nothing to Declare (the Green Channel) and Goods to Declare (the Red Channel). Limits on imports for visitors entering Ireland from outside the EU include 200 cigarettes, 50 cigars, or 250 grams (8.8 ounces) of loose tobacco; 2 liters (2.1 quarts) of still table wine, and 1 liter of liquor (more than 22% alcohol content), or 2 liters of liquor (less than 22%); and 2 fluid ounces of perfume. The total value of goods brought in must not exceed €175. You may not bring in controlled drugs (any medication you have should be in its original bottle with your name on it), firearms and/or ammunition, plants and vegetables, fresh meats, or any kind of animal. If you fall within these limits, go through the Nothing to Declare area at Customs. Otherwise, go through the Goods to Declare area, where a Customs official will assess the amount of duty that must be paid.

DUBLIN AIRPORT

THE REPUBLIC'S PRIMARY AIR GATEWAY, **Dublin Airport** (☎ 01-814-1111; **www.dublinairport.com**) is eight miles north of the city. It's served by **Aer Lingus** (with direct flights from Boston, Chicago, Dallas, Denver, Los Angeles, New York, San Diego, San Francisco, and Seattle); **Air Canada** (from major Canadian cities); **American** (flights from Boston, Chicago, and New York); **British Airways** (from Boston, Chicago, Miami, Newark, New York, Philadelphia, San Francisco, Seattle, and Washington D.C., all with a change of planes in London or Manchester, England); **Delta** (flights from Atlanta, Chicago, Los Angeles, New York, and many other American cities); and **Northwest** (flights from Detroit, Memphis, Minneapolis, and New York, all with a change in Amsterdam to Aer Lingus flights).

The airport has a tourist office, shops, bank and currency-exchange facilities including ATMs, a post office, a pharmacy, bars and restaurants, and desks for car rentals.

Getting into Dublin from the Airport

Dublin Bus's **Airlink** coach service will take you from the airport into the city. The 747 route runs from the airport to O'Connell Street (in the center of the city) and the Central Bus Station; Monday through Saturday, 5:45 a.m. to 11:30 p.m.; Sunday, 7:15 a.m. to 11:30 p.m. Buses run every 10 minutes Monday through Saturday and every 20 minutes on Sunday. The 748 runs from the airport to the Center Bus Station, Tara Street (DART station), Aston Quay (in the center of the city), and the Heuston Rail Station; Monday through Saturday, 6:50 a.m. to 9:30 p.m.; Sunday, 7 a.m. to 10:05 p.m. Buses run every 30 minutes. The fare on both routes is €5 for adults, €2 for children; tickets can be purchased from an Airlink desk in the arrivals lounge. You can also get into the city center on **Aircoach,** with service from 4:30 a.m. to midnight; the fare is €7.

Taxis line up outside the Arrivals lounge. A ride into the city will cost about €25.

SHANNON AIRPORT

THE GATEWAY TO THE WEST OF IRELAND is **Shannon Airport** (**www.shannonairport.com**). Nonstop service from North America includes flights on **Aer Lingus** (from Boston, Chicago, Los Angeles, and New York), **American** (from Boston, Chicago, and New York), **Continental** (from Newark), and **Delta** (from Atlanta). Shannon also handles many connecting flights on these airlines from Dublin, as well as flights from London (including **Aer Lingus, British Airways**, and **Ryanair**). Bus service runs from the airport to Ennis, Galway, Cork, and Limerick, with connections to many other towns in the west of Ireland.

BELFAST INTERNATIONAL AIRPORT

THIS AIRPORT (**www.belfastairport.com/en**), in Northern Ireland's capital city, handles nonstop flights from North America, with **Continental** flights from Los Angeles, Newark, San Francisco, and Washington D.C.

All of the above airports also handle flights from the Continent, and travelers from North America can connect to Dublin, Shannon, and Belfast from Paris (**Air France, www.airfrance.com**); Frankfurt (**Lufthansa, www.lufthansa.com**); Amsterdam (**KLM, www.klm.com**), and Madrid (**Iberia, www.iberia.com**), among other cities. **Cork Airport** (**www.cork-airport.com**) also handles flights from the Continent, on Aer Lingus, British Airways, KLM, and Ryanair.

ARRIVING *by* FERRY

CAR AND PASSENGER FERRIES cross the Irish Sea from Great Britain and France to Ireland. Many travelers make the crossing on **Irish Ferries** (☎ 772-563-2856; **www.irishferries.com**), which travels from Holyhead, Wales, to Dún Laoghaire, eight miles south of Dublin, and Pembroke, Wales, to Rosslare, County Wexford. Other lines and routes are:

- The **Isle of Man Steam Packet Company–Sea Cat** (☎ 0870-552-3523 in Great Britain or 01 800-80-50-55 in Ireland; **www.steam-packet .com**) sails from Liverpool to Dublin and from Heysham and Troon in Scotland to Belfast.

- **P&O Irish Sea Ferries** (☎ 561-563-2856 in the United States, 0870-242-4777 in Great Britain, and 01-638-3333 in Ireland; **www.poirishsea.com**) links Cairnryan, Scotland, and Larne, County Antrim, in Northern Ireland. P&O ferries also travel between Liverpool and Dublin.

- **Stena Line** (☎ 01-204-7777; **www.stenaline.com**) travels from Holyhead, Wales, to Dún Laoghaire, eight miles south of Dublin.

GETTING AROUND *in* IRELAND

TRAVELING BY TRAIN

IARNRÓD ÉIREANN (**Irish Rail**, ☎ 1850-366222 or 01-836-6222; **www.irishrail.ie**) runs the rail system in Ireland, while **Northern Ireland Railways** (**NIR**, ☎ 028-9066-6630; **www.nirailways.co.uk**) operates trains in the North. Many rail routes originate in Dublin and depart from Heuston and Connolly stations.

irish rail routes

North Channel

ATLANTIC OCEAN

Portrush
Ballycastle
Coleraine
Larne Harbour
Derry
Ballymoney
Larne
Whitehead
Carrickfergus
Antrim
Bangor
Belfast York Road
BELFAST CENTRAL
Lurgan
Portadown
Lisburn

Enniskillen

Ballina
Sligo
Colooney
Boyle
Carrick-on-Shannon
Newry
Irish Sea
Ballymote
Dromod
Dundalk
Foxford
Castlebar
MANULLA JUNCTION
Longford
Westport
Ballyhaunis
Drogheda
Claremorris
Castlerea
Mosney
Balbriggan
Tuam
Roscommon
Mullingar
Enfield
Malahide
Skerries
Dublin Connolly
Woodlawn
Athlone
Maynooth
DUBLIN
Galway
Athenry
Clara
Kildare
Dublin Pearse
Ballinasloe
Tullamore
Dublin Heuston
Dún Laoghaire
Attymon
PORTARLINGTON
Bray
Greystones
ARAN ISLANDS
Portlaoise
Newbridge
Wicklow
Ennistymon
Roscrea
Athy
Rathdrum
Cloughjordan
Arklow
Ennis
Nenagh
Temple-more
BALLYBROPHY
Carlow
Birdhill
Kilkenny
Muine Bheag
Gorey
Limerick
Castle-connell
Thurles
Thomastown
Enniscorthy
LIMERICK JUNCTION
Clonmel
Campile
Wexford
Mouth of the Shannon
Listowel
Charleville
Tipperary
Cahir
Rosslare Strand
Tralee
Rathmore
MALLOW
Carrick-on-Suir
WATERFORD
Rosslare Harbour
Farranfore
Killarney
Banteer
Ballycullane
Bridgetown
Millstreet
Cork
Fota
Wellington Bridge
Cobh

St. George's Channel

0   30 mi
0   30 km
N

The trip from Dublin to Belfast takes just two hours (on speedy Enterprise service; about €40), while slower service to Cork takes about three hours and costs from €54; to Galway, also about three hours, from €29; to Limerick, two hours, from €41; and Waterford, three hours, from €23.

You can buy tickets at any station window and pay with cash or credit card. A one-way trip is called a *single;* a round trip is called a *return*. Trains are divided into first and second classes. First class costs about one-third more than second-class. What are the advantages? First class offers seats that are larger and more comfortable, and in some cases more-personalized service, with small perks such as free newspapers or free tea and coffee. Both first- and second-class passengers use the same cafe cars or, on longer hauls, restaurant cars. Vendors come through on many trains selling beverages and snacks. Make sure you arrive early when you are traveling, because many trains fill up and you'll be left standing.

TRAVELING BY CAR

DRIVING IN DUBLIN is not easy, nor is it necessary. But traveling by car is the only practical way to see much of the Irish countryside. Before you slide behind the wheel, though, make sure you will be comfortable driving on the "wrong" (left) side of the road, shifting with your left hand, and driving a manual (automatic will cost you considerably more). Remember, too, that Ireland has one of the highest accident rates in Europe—roads are narrow, oncoming traffic is often obscured by hedges and sharp curves, and driving under the influence of alcohol is not uncommon.

Car Rentals

Americans and Canadians renting cars in Ireland will need a driver's license that they've had for at least a year, plus a credit card. Renters usually must be 23 years old (21 in some instances); some companies will not rent to drivers 70 or older. Major rental companies include:

Alamo	☎ 800-462-5266	www.alamo.com
Auto-Europe	☎ 888-223-5555	www.autoeurope.com
Avis	☎ 800-331-1084	www.avis.com
Budget	☎ 800-527-0700	www.budget.com
Dan Dooley–Kenning Rent-a-Car	☎ 800-331-9301	www.dan-dooley.ie
Hertz	☎ 800-654-8881	www.hertz.com
Murphys Europcar	☎ 800-800-6000	www.europcar.ie
National	☎ 800-CAR-RENT	www.nationalcar.com

⚓ Rules of the Road

Here are some general rules of the road you'll need to know if you're going to be driving in Ireland:

- In the Republic, distances and speed limits are shown in kilometers and kilometers per hour; in Northern Ireland, they are given in miles. If you need to translate from the metric system, a kilometer is 0.62 miles, and a mile is 1.62 kilometers. Speed limits are usually 30 miles per hour (48 kilometers per hour) in towns, 40 mph (65 kph) on some town roads where posted, 60 mph (97 kph) on most single carriageways, and 70 mph (113 kph) on dual carriageways and motorways.

Also keep these rules in mind:

- Always drive on the left side of the road.
- Road signs are usually the standard international signs.
- Using seat belts, front and back, is required by law. If you have children, make sure that the correct seat belts or car seats are available before you rent a vehicle.
- Children under the age of 12 may not sit in the front seat.
- At roundabouts (traffic circles), give way to traffic coming from the right.
- You can pass other vehicles only on the right.
- Parking in the center of most big towns is difficult and expensive. Make sure you read all posted restrictions, or park in a lot. Be sure to carry a lot of change.
- You must stop for pedestrians in striped (zebra) crossings. Pedestrians have the right of way.
- Don't drink if you are driving. Drivers with blood-alcohol levels higher than .08% are subject to imprisonment. Police carry Breathalyzers.
- It's illegal to talk on a cell phone while driving.

When you make your reservation, ask if the quoted price includes the VAT (value-added tax) and unlimited mileage. VAT on car rentals in the Republic is 13.5%, 17.5% in Northern Ireland. Then find out what insurance options are included. Many credit-card companies do not automatically cover collision-damage insurance as they do for car rentals in other countries. (MasterCard Platinum is one of the few cards that do include the Collision Damage Waiver, though this is subject to change.) As a result of this policy, you must pay a hefty surcharge (about €15 a day) for collision-damage insurance on top of any personal-liability insurance you choose to purchase. Check with the rental-car company to see which cards cover the collision-damage waiver, and then verify this with the credit-card company. Some

Driving on the Left

With a little practice and common sense, you will soon become used to driving on the left side of the road. After all, the Irish do it every day. Some tips to make the adjustment safer and easier.

- If you are not comfortable driving a car with a manual transmission (with which most cars in Ireland are equipped), pay the extra for an automatic. You'll have enough on your mind adjusting to driving on the left.

- Make sure you are well rested when you get behind the wheel for the first time, as you'll need to keep your wits about you. Rather than picking up a car after flying all night, consider getting a good night's sleep and overcoming jet lag first.

- Once you pick up the car, practice. Even before turning on the ignition, get used to the gearshift—remember, you'll be using your left hand to shift gears, and you're probably used to shifting with your right hand. Take a practice spin around the car park (parking lot), and don't set out until you feel comfortable.

- Be extremely cautious making turns. It's easy to forget that everything here is reversed: oncoming traffic will be coming from your right. Chances are, out of habit you will look left for oncoming traffic, as you're used to doing at home.

- When driving on a two-lane road, make sure the center line is on your left. This way, you'll know you're on the right (as in correct) side of the road.

rental-car agencies in Ireland will charge you for collision-damage insurance unless you can produce a letter from a credit-card company stating that the company includes the collision-damage waiver with the use of its card.

You can rent a car before you go at any of the agencies listed on page 63; in addition, some airlines offer package deals that include car rental. Remember, you'll probably get a better deal if you rent the car at least seven days in advance.

Roads and Roundabouts

What drivers in the United States would call a freeway the Irish call a *motorway* (indicated on maps by *M* plus a number). You needn't get too hung up on this designation, though, because there are very few motorways in Ireland—and fewer in the Republic than in the North. A two-way road is called a *single carriageway,* and a four-lane divided highway (two lanes in each direction) is a *dual carriageway.* Roads in the countryside are full of twists and turns and are often barely wide enough for

unofficial **TIP**
If you plan on starting your trip in Dublin, wait to pick up your car until you have completed the Dublin portion of your trip and you're ready to tour the rest of the country. Driving in Dublin is difficult, and you're much better off traveling on public transportation.

two cars to pass. *Roundabouts* are traffic junctions where several roads meet at one traffic circle. On a roundabout, the cars to your right (i.e., already on the roundabout) always have the right of way.

Drive Times

Traffic can add considerably to travel times, but as a rule of thumb, count on: Dublin to Belfast, 2.5 hours; Dublin to Cork, 4.5 hours; Dublin to Galway, 3 hours; Dublin to Limerick, 2 hours.

Road Emergencies

If you have an accident, you must report this to the Gardaí (police), and you should do this before leaving the scene. You can contact the Gardaí from any telephone by dialing 999, which is the Irish equivalent of 911 and can put you in touch with the fire service, ambulance, and coastal rescue as well. You are also required to notify the rental-car agency of an accident.

Buying Gasoline

Gasoline is called *petrol*. Petrol stations are self-service, and major credit cards are usually accepted; prices rise and fall (they mostly rise these days). Petrol is purchased by the liter (3.78 liters equals 1 U.S. gallon). Expect to pay a little more than a euro or more per liter, or at least €5 (£3.50 in the North) per gallon, for unleaded petrol.

TRAVELING BY BUS AND COACH

THE PRIMARY LONG-DISTANCE COACH company in the Republic is **Bus Éireann** (☎ 091-562000; **www.buseireann.ie**). The company serves all regions, with some service to just about every town and village. Because the Irish bus system is so much more extensive than the train system, you may find yourself traveling by coach more in Ireland than you would in other European countries. Or you may travel by train to a major city—from Dublin to Cork or Galway, for instance—and continue by coach from there. The Bus Éireann Web site provides detailed information on schedules and prices. Also included is information on multiday passes, which provide unlimited travel for a certain number of days—8 days of travel within 15 days for €228, for example. **Ulsterbus** (☎ 028-9033-3000; **www.translink.co.uk**) operates the bus network in Northern Ireland.

Rail and Bus Passes

Several money-saving passes are available, but remember: No pass is going to save you money if you don't use it. Before purchasing any kind of travel pass, think about how much moving around you are going to do, and then do some research to determine how much you will be spending on transportation if you buy individual tickets (the Web sites we list for train and bus travel make it easy to do this).

major irish bus routes

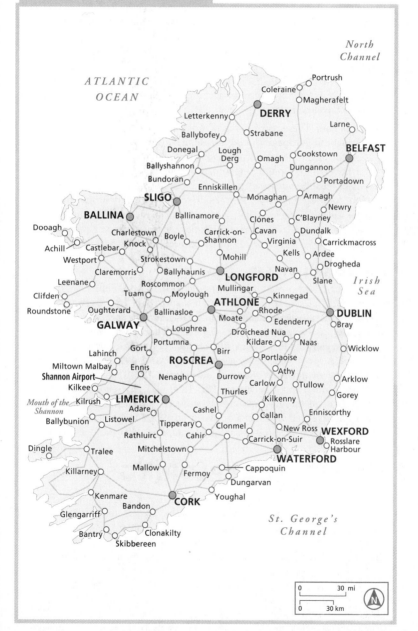

North
Channel

ATLANTIC
OCEAN

Portrush
Coleraine
Magherafelt
Letterkenny
DERRY
Ballybofey
Strabane
Larne
Donegal
Lough
Derg
Omagh
Cookstown
BELFAST
Ballyshannon
Dungannon
Bundoran
Enniskillen
Portadown
Monaghan
Armagh
SLIGO
Ballinamore
Newry
BALLINA
Clones
C'Blayney
Dooagh
Charlestown
Boyle
Carrick-on-
Shannon
Cavan
Dundalk
Achill
Knock
Virginia
Carrickmacross
Castlebar
Mohill
Kells
Ardee
Westport
Strokestown
Ballyhaunis
Navan
Drogheda
Claremorris
Roscommon
LONGFORD
Slane
Irish
Sea
Leenane
Moylough
Mullingar
Tuam
Kinnegad
Clifden
Oughterard
ATHLONE
Rhode
DUBLIN
Roundstone
Ballinasloe
Moate
Edenderry
Bray
GALWAY
Loughrea
Droichead Nua
Gort
Portumna
Kildare
Naas
Lahinch
Birr
Portlaoise
Wicklow
Miltown Malbay
Ennis
ROSCREA
Athy
Shannon Airport
Nenagh
Durrow
Carlow
Tullow
Arklow
Kilkee
Thurles
Gorey
Mouth of the
Shannon
Kilrush
LIMERICK
Kilkenny
Enniscorthy
Ballybunion
Adare
Cashel
Callan
Listowel
Tipperary
Clonmel
New Ross
WEXFORD
Rathluirc
Cahir
Carrick-on-Suir
Rosslare
Harbour
Dingle
Mitchelstown
WATERFORD
Tralee
Mallow
Cappoquin
Killarney
Fermoy
Dungarvan
Kenmare
Youghal
Bandon
CORK
Glengarriff
St. George's
Channel
Bantry
Clonakilty
Skibbereen

0   30 mi
0   30 km

- **BritRail Pass + Ireland** If you're planning on traveling through the United Kingdom and Ireland, this might be just the ticket—it provides unlimited travel in Britain, Northern Ireland, and the Republic of Ireland, plus a round-trip ferry crossing. For more information, contact BritRail, ☎ 800-BRITRAIL; **www.britrail.net.**

- **Emerald Card and Irish Explorer** These passes combine travel on rail and bus services; the Emerald Card covers travel in the Republic and Northern Ireland, while Irish Explorer is good for travel only in the Republic. For more information, contact Bus Éireann, ☎ 091-562000; **www.buseireann.ie.**

- **Eurail Pass** These come in many varieties, including passes good throughout Europe, including the Republic of Ireland, and a pass good only for travel within Ireland. Note that Eurail passes are not good for travel in the United Kingdom, including Northern Ireland, and the passes must be purchased before you leave home. For more information, contact RailEurope, ☎ 877-257-2887; **www.raileurope.com.**

- **Irish Rover** Good for train travel within both the Republic and Northern Ireland. For more information, contact Iarnród Éireann (Irish Rail), ☎ 1850-366222 or 01-836-6222; **www.irishrail.ie.**

TRAVELING BY AIR

IN ADDITION TO THE SIZABLE AIRPORTS in Dublin, Shannon, Cork, and Belfast, some other Irish airports include **Derry Airport** (**www.cityofderryairport.com**), **Donegal Regional Airport** (**www.donegal airport.ie**), **Galway Airport** (**www.galwayairport.com**), **Kerry Airport** (**www.kerryairport.ie**), **Knock Airport** (**www.knockairport.com**), **Sligo Regional Airport** (**www.sligoairport.com**), and **Waterford Regional Airport** (**www.flywaterford.com**). **Aer Lingus** (☎ 01-705-3333; **www .aerlingus.com**) and **Aer Arann** (☎ 1890-462726; **www.aerarann.ie**) service most of these. Keep in mind, though, that Ireland is a relatively small country and distances between cities aren't great, so you can often get to your destination as quickly and easily by land as by air.

TOURS *and* EXPLORING

SO MUCH TO SEE AND DO in Ireland . . . how are you going to fit it all in? You're not. But we're here to help. The secret of successful sightseeing is to be selective. When there's so much to see, it's important to choose wisely where you will spend your sightseeing hours. (And euros and pounds, with admission prices to major attractions in Ireland being pretty expensive.)

In this book, we tell you about the various tours available in a city, town, or region that we think will best help you get a sense of a place. Then we profile what we consider to be the major attractions. We rate each attraction to tell you how appealing we think it is to tourists of all ages. Along with a description that includes advice on what not to miss at an attraction and how best to enjoy it, we also provide all the practical information you need, such as addresses, admission prices, opening hours, and so on. From the information presented you should be able to decide whether or not the attraction is something that interests you or not (some people love visiting Irish country houses; others couldn't care less).

The attraction profiles are found in the Exploring section of each featured city, town, or region. In these sections we also often give you a brief walking tour and some idea of how to get to know a place; plus, we mention secondary sights that are maybe worth a visit or just a glance. If an attraction is not profiled, it's not a major sight. In the Tours sections we provide details on our favorite tours of the cities, towns, and regions we cover.

TOURING ON YOUR OWN OR WITH AN ESCORTED TOUR

THIS IS PURELY A MATTER of individual preference. If you choose not to rent a car, you'll find it difficult to tour the countryside and visit remote sights on your own. Public transportation to many remote parts of Ireland is erratic, even nonexistent. Some major attractions are miles from the nearest train station or bus stop, and bus service to many remote places operates infrequently.

Escorted tours do all the logistical work for you: a coach or mini-van takes you to the attraction, and someone explains it all to you. On page 42 we provide the names of some well-regarded companies that offer escorted tours around Ireland. You can find specific itineraries and other details by visiting their Web sites.

WALKING TOURS

A WALKING TOUR IS ONE of the most enjoyable ways to see a city and learn more about its history. The historic hearts of most Irish cities are compact and full of architectural and historical treasures that add to their charm, character, and fascination. Part of the fun is simply listening to the tour guide. The Irish love to show off their history and usually do so with intelligence, wit, and enthusiasm.

*un*official **TIP**
Most tourist-information offices in Ireland provide information on local walking tours, so take advantage of them.

BUS TOURS

ANOTHER GOOD WAY to introduce yourself to a place is by taking a guided bus tour. All major tourist towns and cities offer bus tours, often by a company called **City Sightseeing** (this company recently acquired **Guide Friday,** which you may have used on previous trips to Ireland). These tours usually make a circuit of all the major sights in about an hour, but the real advantage of them is the "hop on, hop off" service that allows you to get off, visit an attraction, and board another bus. The kind and quality of commentary varies from company to company and is sometimes canned—opt for live commentary if you have a choice.

Bus Éireann (☎ 091-562000; **www.buseireann.ie**) also offers city tours, as well as day tours to nearby sights. Some itineraries include Dublin to Glendalough, Powerscourt Gardens, and Wicklow; Newgrange, the Boyne Valley, and Kilkenny City; Galway to Connemara and the Burren and Cliffs of Moher; and Sligo to Donegal.

Throughout this book, we list what we consider to be the best tours in the Exploring section of each featured city, town, or region.

SIGHTSEEING SAVINGS

THE HERITAGE CARD IS GOOD FOR entry at some 100 properties in the Republic that are maintained by the Irish Office of Public Works. Whether or not the pass will save you money depends on how much touring you plan to do, of course, but chances are it will. Just as a sample of possibilities, **Kilmainham Gaol, Kilkenny Castle,** the **Blasket Centre, Muckross House,** and **Glenveagh Castle** are among our choices for must-see sights in Ireland, and admission to all is included with the card. The cost is €21 adults, €8 children and students, €16 seniors, and €55 families of up to two adults and four children. You can buy the pass at participating sights; by mail from Heritage Card Officer, Visitor Services, Office of Public Works, 6 Upper Ely Place, Dublin 2, Ireland; by calling ☎ 01-647-6587; or online at **www.heritageireland .com,** where you'll also find more information about the card.

EXPLORING IRELAND *on* FOUR WHEELS, TWO WHEELS, *and* TWO FEET

IRELAND IS BEST ENJOYED AT A SLOW PACE—on a country road in a car or, for a real taste of the countryside, on one of the many hiking paths and biking routes that crisscross the country. In addition to the resources below, see the Walks and Drives and Exploring sections included with our coverage of each region. There you will find additional drives, walks, and biking routes.

ESSENTIAL GEAR

HOWEVER YOU PLAN ON GETTING AROUND IRELAND, equip yourself with a good map and, especially if you're walking, a compass. Even the most traveled routes are often poorly and confusingly marked, and walking paths often cross private lands on which signs are few and far between. You'll find a good selection of detailed maps ideal for overland walks and off-the-beaten path drives at **EastWest Mapping,** an online retailer specializing in maps of Ireland, at **homepage .tinet.ie/~eastwest;** EastWest also lists walking routes and provides links to walking resources. **Ordnance Survey Ireland (OSI)** and the **Ordnance Survey of Northern Ireland (OSNI)** compile small- and large-scale maps, 1:50,000 and 1:25,000, that usually indicate walking routes. You can find them at better bookshops throughout Ireland, with especially good selections at the **National Map Centre** (34 Angier Street, Dublin 2; ☎ 01-476-0487; **www.irishmaps.ie**) and the **OSNI** shop (Colby House, Stranmills Road, Belfast BT9 5B1; ☎ 028-9025-5768; **www.osni.gov.uk**).

WALKING AND BIKING IN IRELAND

IRELAND IS A COUNTRY WELL GEARED to hiking and biking, and the Irish are increasingly enthusiastic about both. Hundreds of paths and many resources are available to hikers and bikers. Below and in the regional coverage in this guide you'll find recommendations for routes of particular beauty and interest, but for every one we list there are dozens of others. Check with the tourist office in any region you visit for information on local routes. In addition, browse through the resources of the organizations below.

For Walkers

- **Go Walking Ireland (www.gowalkingireland.com)** lists recommended walks and also provides information on camping and other outdoor activities.

- **Hill-Walking in Ireland (www.simonstewart.ie)**, an excellent Web resource for walks throughout Ireland, provides links to other hiking and climbing organizations.

- The **Irish Ramblers Club (www.theramblers.ie)** and **Wayfarers Association (www.wayfarerassociation.org)** are Dublin-based clubs that organize walks in the surrounding countryside. Both organizations also provide some information on walks throughout the country.

- The **Irish Tourist Board (www.discoverireland.com)** offers a decent overview of opportunities in the Republic in *Walking Ireland*. The **Northern Irish Tourist Board (www.discovernorthernireland.com)** publishes a similar booklet, *An Information Guide to Walking*. Contents are published online as well as in the booklets.

- The **Mountaineering Council of Ireland (☎ 01-450-7376; www.mountaineering.ie)** is an activist organization that promotes the interests of walkers in Ireland. The Web site provides information on paths throughout Ireland, with links to hiking associations and other resources.

- **Walking Ireland (www.walkingireland.com)**, the Web presence of the Walking Centre in Clifden, County Galway, provides detailed information on walks throughout Ireland, with an emphasis on walks in and around Connemara.

- *Walking World Ireland* is a bimonthly magazine that covers all the ins and outs for enthusiasts, with excellent information on routes and events; look for it in bookshops, on newsstands, and at outdoor-equipment shops.

For Cyclists

- Cyclists who don't want to lug their bikes and gear across the Atlantic can rent from outfits that include **Eurotrek Raleigh** (Longmile Road, Dublin 12; ☎ 01-465-9659; **www.raleigh.ie**) and **Rent-A-Bike Ireland** (1 Patrick Street, Limerick, County Limerick; ☎ 061-416983; **www.irelandrentalbike.com**). Both work with a network of dealers who rent bikes throughout Ireland, so you can pick up your bike at one location and drop it off at another; service is readily available. Expect to pay about €20 ($25) per day for a standard rental.

- The **Irish Tourist Board** offers a limited amount of information on cycling in the Republic, with a listing of routes; you can browse the offerings at **www.discoverireland.com.**

- The **Northern Ireland Tourist Board** publishes *Cycling in Northern Ireland,* a fairly comprehensive booklet on biking routes for short- and long-distance rides in Northern Ireland, as well as other resources; contact the office for a copy (see page 43), or find the same information at **www.discovernorthernireland.com.**

WALKING AND BIKING HOLIDAYS

MOST WALKING AND BIKING ROUTES in Ireland are well traveled by groups organized by tour companies specializing in hiking and biking holidays. These outfits can provide an excellent introduction to exploring the country in these ways, and they'll take care of logistics such as transportation to and from routes and accommodations. The outfits offer guided tours, on which one or two guides will accompany you and usually offer plentiful advice and good company, as well as self-guided tours, in which an organization maps out a route and takes care of details such as daily baggage transfer to and from accommodations. The following are based in Ireland, so you can count on the staff knowing the terrain well.

- **Go Ireland** (**www.goactivities.com;** ☎ 066-976-2094) organizes hiking and biking expeditions throughout Ireland.
- **Irish Cycling Safaris** (**www.cyclingsafaris.com;** ☎ 01-260-0749) offers both hiking and biking expeditions, with an emphasis on the Southwest.
- **Irish Ways Walking Holidays** (**www.irishways.com;** ☎ 055-27479) provides guided tours and independent trips through most regions of Ireland, with an emphasis on scenic locales such as Connemara, the Antrim Coast, and the Wicklow Mountains.
- **Michael Gibbons Walking Ireland** (**www.walkingireland.com;** ☎ 095-21492) operates out of the Walking Centre in Clifden, County

Galway, specializing in tours of Connemara and other parts of the West. The Centre offers longer treks as well as daily walks, which provide an excellent introduction to the majestic Connemara landscapes for travelers who have only a day or two to spend in the region.

WALKING FESTIVALS

LEAVE IT TO THE IRISH TO TURN A WALK into a big social event. You'll encounter these festivals throughout the country in all but the dreariest winter months. Lasting one to several days, they usually combine walks through appealing countryside with refreshment, traditional-music sessions, often meals, and always a lot of conversation. Check with local tourist offices for news of upcoming festivals, or contact the Irish Tourist Board (**www.discoverireland.com**) and the Northern Ireland Tourist Board (**www.discovernorthernireland.com**).

GREAT WALKS

IN THE EXPLORING SECTIONS OF THIS GUIDE, you'll find detailed information on walks in each region of Ireland that are particularly scenic and enjoyable. You can travel many of these routes, or at least parts of them, on a bicycle. A sampling of some of the best routes in Ireland would include:

BEARA WAY This 200-kilometer (120-mile) route circumnavigates the Beara Peninsula, one of Ireland's most beautiful coastal spots. Even a short walk along the Beara Way, such as the section around Eyeries Point, will introduce you to stunning views of the coasts and mountains of the Southwest. See page 245.

CAUSEWAY COAST WAY You can walk the northern coast from Portstewart to Ballycastle on this well-maintained path. The most spectacular scenery is around Giants Causeway, a remarkable swath of stone columns stretching into the sea. See page 376.

CROAGH PATRICK A walk up this conical-shaped mountain at the northern edge of Connemara is rewarding not only for the views from the top but also for the human spectacle—pilgrims often make the climb barefoot to pay homage to St. Patrick, who is said to have spent 40 days atop the peak. See page 305.

DINGLE WAY This 150-kilometer (90-mile) route around the Dingle Peninsula affords spectacular scenery at every bend in the path. You need only walk along the section at Slea Head to get a taste of the coastal scenery, or take a much more strenuous walk up Brandon Peak to enjoy wild mountainous terrain. See page 245.

GLENARIFF FOREST PARK Well-maintained trails in this park in the Glens of Antrim—nine forested valleys near the Antrim Coast—follow the Inver and Glenariff rivers. See page 376.

GLENVEAGH NATIONAL PARK You can enjoy the beauty of this remote and spectacularly beautiful park on even a short walk, such as one along the Derrylahan Nature Trail. A more ambitious climb takes you through the moors and bogs on the flanks of Errigal Mountain at the edge of the park. See pages 346 and 348.

HOWTH PENINSULA A walk around the stunning headland would be remarkable, and popular, even if the peninsula and town of the same name weren't so easily accessible from Dublin, via DART. Seabirds, seals, and stunning views of the sea and mountains add to the illusion of remoteness, and the seaside town and fishing port of Howth is a pleasant place to spend time before or after a walk. See page 122.

MUCKROSS Walking the shores of Muckross Lake, in the heart of Killarney National Park, introduces you to the woods, mountain views, streams, and wildlife that are among the delights of one of Ireland's most beautiful national parks. See page 246.

SLIEVE LEAGUE The highest sea cliffs in Europe provide a highly dramatic setting for an unforgettable coastal walk, all the more so when the route comes to landmarks such as One Man's Pass, a narrow passage with steep drops on either side. The biggest thrill, though, is the spectacle of the near-vertical cliff faces that rise some 600 meters (2,000 feet) out of the raging surf. See pages 346 and 360.

THE WICKLOW WAY This well-traveled route traverses forested mountain slopes, mountain valleys, and bogs for some 130 kilometers (78 miles) between the southern suburbs of Dublin and County Wexford. An especially popular and scenic portion of the route leads you past the monastic ruins at Glendalough, along the shores of the two lakes that surround it, and into the surrounding mountains. See page 123.

GREAT DRIVES

SET OUT IN ALMOST ANY DIRECTION ANYWHERE in Ireland, and you're likely to drive through scenery that will awe you, or at least catch your interest. You'll find drives that are especially scenic in the Walks and Drives and Exploring sections in our regional coverage throughout this guide. Here are some routes and driving destinations that are especially worth seeking out.

ACHILL ISLAND Ireland's largest island is also one of its most accessible, reached by a bridge near the town of Westport. Once on the island, follow the Atlantic Drive to golden beaches, craggy sea cliffs, and view-filled summits. See page 336.

THE ANTRIM COAST This spectacular drive along the narrow, winding Antrim Coast Road is filled with scenery and points of interest: green mountainsides, stone coastal villages, the natural wonder of Giants Causeway, and man-made attractions such as medieval Dunluce Castle and the revered Bushmills Distillery are among the sights awaiting you.

THE BEARA PENINSULA Southwestern Ireland meets the sea in a string of long peninsulas on which mountains drop down to the water. The

Beara is relatively unspoiled and, with such spots as moor-clad Healy Pass, one of the most scenic. See page 241.

BLACKWATER VALLEY AND ROCK OF CASHEL   You can visit one of Ireland's most spectacular religious monuments on a drive filled with lovely river views in the Blackwater Valley and the highland scenery of the Knockmealdown Mountains. See page 193.

THE DINGLE PENINSULA   The cliff-top drive west from Dingle Town affords more than stunning sea views—the mysterious Blasket Islands loom just offshore, and the coast is littered with Iron Age and early Christian remains. See page 263.

GLENVEAGH NATIONAL PARK AND SURROUNDINGS   Some of Ireland's wildest scenery is in and around Glenveagh National Park, where some surprisingly sophisticated pleasures, such as the art collection at Glebe House, await you as well. See pages 348 and 364.

LAKES OF CONNEMARA   Lough Corrib and Lough Mask, two of the largest lakes in Ireland, are surrounded by the mountains and the stark moors and mountains of Connemara. You'll find civilization in Cong and other appealing villages. See pages 307 and 324.

THE NORTHERN HEADLANDS   The craggy coast of Northwest Ireland is a string of long bays and peninsulas. You can follow these until you've had your fill of sea views. Mountain slopes, green valleys, and heather-surrounded lakes also contribute to the scenery. See page 347.

WICKLOW MOUNTAINS   A drive through these mountains just south of Dublin takes you through bogs, into valleys glittering with lakes and littered with the ruins of the medieval abbey at Glendalough, and to the highest village in Ireland, Roundwood. See page 125.

YEATS COUNTRY   The poet W. B. Yeats and his brother, the painter Jack Yeats, took inspiration from the mountain, lake, and coastal scenery around Sligo Town. You can enjoy this scenery on a drive around Lough Gill and out to Rosses Point.

THE NATIONAL PARKS

THE REPUBLIC'S SIX NATIONAL PARKS encompass some of Ireland's most beautiful scenery and provide easy access to wilderness regions for hikers and other outdoor enthusiasts. All have visitor centers that offer guided nature tours and provide a wealth of information on activities. For information on these parks, visit the Web site of the National Parks and Wildlife Service, **www.npws.ie.**

THE BURREN NATIONAL PARK   The Burren covers some 1,600 hectares (4,000 acres) of Ireland's most uninhabitable land, a swath of limestone in western County Clare—"a savage land, yielding neither water enough to drown a man, nor tree to hang him, nor soil enough to bury," as Oliver Cromwell put it. Even so, the Burren becomes a sea of color in spring and summer, as plants blown from the Arctic and the Mediterranean flower in profusion from cracks in the limestone.

CONNEMARA NATIONAL PARK Connemara preserves an enchanting landscape of bogs, heather-covered moors, and the slopes of the Twelve Bens Mountains in County Galway. On nature trails and guided walks, visitors encounter the birds, Connemara ponies, and other diverse creatures that add to the charm of this beautiful place.

GLENVEAGH NATIONAL PARK In a remote part of County Donegal, Glenveagh encompasses 10,000 hectares (24,000 acres) of lakes and streams glittering among heaths and woodlands that climb the slopes of the Derryveagh Mountains, presenting some of the most beautiful and dramatic landscapes in Ireland. At the heart of the park is one of Ireland's most appealing historic homes, Glenveagh Castle.

KILLARNEY NATIONAL PARK One of many beautiful spots in County Kerry, Killarney has long and justifiably been admired for its spectacular panoramas of mountains (MacGillycuddy's Reeks, Ireland's tallest, are here), lakes, and forests, all of which can be enjoyed on well-marked walking trails.

BALLYCROY NATIONAL PARK In County Mayo, Ballycroy rises and falls from the Atlantic shorelines up the slopes of the Nephin Beg Mountains. Many trails traverse an eerie and unique landscape of saltwater bogs.

WICKLOW MOUNTAINS NATIONAL PARK Just south of Dublin in County Wicklow, this park provides a quick retreat from city life, with moors and forest-clad mountains. The Wicklow Way, a 132-kilometer-long (80-mile-long) walking path, runs through the park, traversing valleys, skirting lakes, climbing mountains, and passing the ruins of the medieval Glendalough monastery.

OTHER OUTDOOR PURSUITS

Bird-watching

Ireland provides a convenient stopover for migrating birds, with many excellent venues for bird-watching throughout the year. You can keep up with the best places to see what birds when by visiting the Web sites of major Irish birding groups. In the Republic, these are **Irish Birding** (**www.irishbirding.com**) and **Birdwatch Ireland** (**www.bird watchireland.ie**), and in the North, **The Royal Society for the Protection of Birds** (**www.rspb.org.uk/nireland**) and **Birdwatch Northern Ireland** (**www.birdwatch-ni.co.uk**).

Fishing

Irish seas and freshwater lakes and streams provide some of Europe's finest angling. In the Republic, a license is required only for salmon and sea-trout fishing and begins at €15 a day; a rod license, required for all fishing in Northern Ireland, begins at €5 a day. You can usually buy the necessary licenses from angling outfitters. In the Republic, contact the **Central Fisheries Board** (Balnagowan House, Mobhi Boreen, Glasnevin, Dublin 9; ☎ 01-884-2600; **www.cfb.ie**) and the **Irish Tourist Board** (**www.discoverireland.com**), which publishes a booklet, *The Angler's Guide*. In Northern Ireland, contact the **Department of Culture, Arts, and Leisure** (Interpoint Centre, York Street, Belfast BT4 3PW; ☎ 028-9052-3121) and the **Northern Ireland Tourist Board** (**www.discovernorthern ireland.com**), which publishes *An Information Guide to Game Fishing*. These booklets are available at most tourist offices, which can also usually provide a list of local outfitters, guides, deep-sea-fishing excursion operators, and other contacts.

Golf

It's only fitting that in this country where the lush landscapes often resemble a golf green, golfing is a major activity and attraction. In the Exercise and Recreation sections throughout this guide, you will find information on some of Ireland's top courses. You'll also find a wealth of information on golf courses in Ireland at the Web sites of the **Irish Tourist Board** (**www.discoverireland.com**) and the **Northern Ireland Tourist Board** (**www.discovernorthernireland.com**). Companies that offer golf packages, including play on some of Ireland's finest courses, accommodations, and ground transportation from about $2,500 a week, include **Specialty Ireland** (☎ 053-39962; **www.specialty ireland.com**) and **Atlanticgolf** (in the United States, ☎ 800-542-6224 or 203-363-1003).

You'll find that even the finest and most exclusive courses are open to the public at least some days of the week, and that greens fees are relatively reasonable, anywhere from about €50 to €100 for 18 holes at the top courses, depending on the season, the day of the week, and the section of the course you choose to play.

Ireland's top courses include:

ADARE MANOR GOLF COURSE Sprawling across the grounds of the former estate of the Earls of Dunraven, Adare Manor is now one of Ireland's finest manor-house hotels. As if that provenance isn't romantic enough, the Robert Trent Jones course encompasses the ruins of a medieval castle and monastery. Adare, County Limerick; ☎ 061-395-044; **www.adaremanorgolfclub.ie**. 18 holes.

BALLYBUNION GOLF CLUB On the Atlantic at the mouth of the River Shannon, Ballybunion is one of the most beautiful and highly regarded courses in the world, with a section designed by Robert Trent Jones. Sandhill Road, Ballybunion, County Kerry; ☎ 068-27611. 36 holes, open to public only on weekdays.

THE K CLUB Designed by Arnold Palmer, this challenging and beautiful course is on the banks of the River Liffey west of Dublin. Kildare Country Club, Straffan, County Kildare; ☎ 01-627-333; **www.kclub.ie**. 18 holes.

OLD HEAD Old Head occupies, somewhat controversially, a spectacular peninsula in County Cork and is one of the world's most scenic courses. Kinsale, County Cork; ☎ 021-778-444; **www.oldheadgolflinks .com.** 18 holes.

PORTMARNOCK GOLF CLUB This is a legendary course on the sea, only 13 kilometers (8 miles) from the center of Dublin. Portmarnock, County Dublin; ☎ 01-846-2968; **www.portmarnockgolfclub.ie.** 27 holes.

ROYAL COUNTY DOWN This is said to be one of the toughest and most beautiful courses in the world. Golf Links Road, Newcastle, BT33 0AN, County Down, Northern Ireland; ☎ 028-4372-2419; **www.royal countydown.ie.** 36 holes.

ROYAL PORTRUSH Royal Portrush is a favorite of many Irish golfers and host to the British Open. Dunluce Road, Portrush, BT56 8JQ, County Antrim, Northern Ireland; ☎ 028-7082-2311; **www.royalport rushgolfclub.com.** 36 holes.

Horseback Riding

Horse riding, as the Irish call it, is quite popular, and many stables rent to the public for rides along beaches and through other beautiful terrain. The **Irish Tourist Board** (**www.discoverireland.com**) and the **Northern Ireland Tourist Board** (**www.discovernorthernireland.com**) provide information on horseback riding, although you can more easily find local stables through the **Association of Irish Riding Establishments** (☎ 045-431-584), which lists accredited riding facilities throughout the country. For rides in particularly scenic terrain, contact **Horseriding Ireland** (**www.horseridingireland.com**), a network of riding facilities in Connemara, Killarney, Sligo, and Donegal.

Sailing and Kayaking

Ireland's many inlets lend themselves to sea kayaking, and the bays that etch the coast are ideal for sailing. You'll find marinas and leisure ports up and down the coasts, from Malahide and Howth around Dublin to Kinsale, Bantry, Kenmare, Westport, and Sligo on the West Coast. Kayak and sailboat instruction and rentals are available in most ports, and you can get detailed listings, with links to many clubs around the country, from the **Irish Canoe Union** (**www.irishcanoeunion .com**) and the **Irish Sailing Association** (3 Park Road, Dún Laoghaire, County Dublin; ☎ 01-280-0239; **www.sailing.ie**).

GREAT ITINERARIES

DRIVING IN IRELAND IS NOT WITHOUT its perils (see page 63), but traveling by car is nonetheless the best way, and often the only way, to explore the country. Public transportation will get you to the major

itinerary 1: into the south of ireland

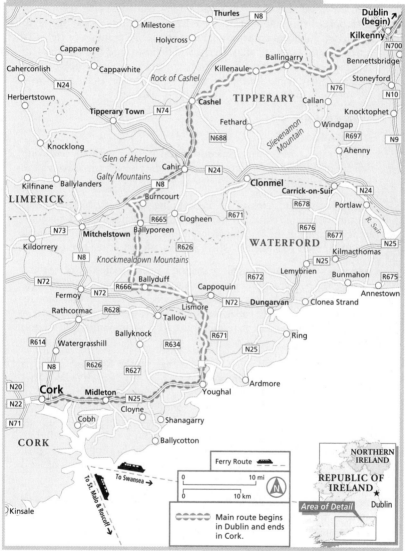

Thurles — N8 — Dublin (begin)

Milestone

Holycross

Kilkenny — N700

Cappamore

Ballingarry — Bennettsbridge

Caherconlish — Cappawhite — Killenaule — Stoneyford

N24 — Rock of Cashel — N76 — N10

Herbertstown — **TIPPERARY** — Callan

Tipperary Town — N74 — **Cashel** — Knocktophet

Fethard — Windgap

N688 — *Slievenamon Mountain* — R697 — N9

Knocklong — Ahenny

Glen of Aherlow — Cahir — N24

Galty Mountains — **Clonmel** — N24

Kilfinane — Ballylanders — N8 — **Carrick-on-Suir**

Burncourt — R678 — Portlaw

LIMERICK — R665 — Clogheen — R671 — R676 — R677 — N25

N73 — **Mitchelstown** — Ballyporeen — **WATERFORD** — Kilmacthomas

Kildorrery — N8 — R626 — N25

Knockmealdown Mountains — R672 — Lemybrien — Bunmahon — R675

N72 — R666 — Ballyduff — Cappoquin — Annestown

Fermoy — N72 — N72 — **Dungarvan** — Clonea Strand

Rathcormac — R628 — Lismore — Ring

Tallow

R614 — Watergrasshill — Ballyknock — R671

N8 — R626 — R627 — R634 — N25

N20 — **Cork** — **Midleton** — N25 — Ardmore

N22 — Cloyne — Youghal

N71 — Cobh — Shanagarry

CORK — Ballycotton

Kinsale

To Swansea →

To St. Malo & Roscoff →

Ferry Route

0 — 10 mi

0 — 10 km

N

Main route begins in Dublin and ends in Cork.

NORTHERN IRELAND

REPUBLIC OF IRELAND — ★ Dublin

Area of Detail

cities, but venturing beyond often leaves you at the whim of infrequent bus service. If you decide to get behind the wheel, here are some routes to follow; see also the Walks and Drives and Exploring sections of each part of this guide for detailed drives and hikes. Should you wish to stick to public transportation, focus on the most vibrant of Ireland's cities—Cork, Galway, Sligo, Derry, and Belfast—and from them piece together excursions on local buses (not always easy to do) or take organized day trips. And however you travel round Ireland, enjoy— the pleasures that await you are almost boundless.

ITINERARY I

Into the South

You can get a nice introduction to rural Ireland without venturing too far from Dublin. In fact, this route begins with a trip through the mountains that begin right at the city's outskirts.

DAY 1 Head south from Dublin, stopping at Powerscourt, an 18th-century house and elaborate gardens, then at Glendalough, a medieval abbey set deep in the Wicklow Mountains. From there it's only about a two-hour drive to Kilkenny, where you'll settle in for two nights.

DAY 2 It's a pleasure to explore Ireland's finest medieval city, with its mighty riverside castle, on foot. In the afternoon, take a short drive south to Jerpoint Abbey, where the remains of a 12th-century monastery are set in a remote valley. Return to Kilkenny in time for a meal at one of the city's excellent restaurants and a traditional-music session in a pub.

DAY 3 A full day of driving takes you east to the Rock of Cashel, a magnificent fortress and church complex set atop a rock overlooking the flat plains of Tipperary. From here, continue through the town of Cahir and through the Vee Gap, a scenic pass over the Knockmealdown Mountains. This brings you to Lismore, dominated by a huge castle that is home to the Duke of Devonshire. Follow the winding waterside route along the Blackwater River to the busy port of Youghal, then along N25 to Midleton; make one of the country hotels around this busy market town your base for two nights.

DAY 4 You won't need to venture too far for a day of memorable sightseeing. Stops include Fota Island, for its beautiful classical-style house and adjoining wildlife park. A very short drive from there south around the estuaries of Cork Harbour brings you to Cobh, where *Cobh, the Queenstown Story* celebrates this port's colorful maritime history, including its role as the point of embarkation for millions of emigrants.

DAY 5 A drive of just half an hour east from Midleton brings you to Cork. Stash the car, settle into a hotel for a two-night stay, and spend

itinerary 2: into the southwest of ireland

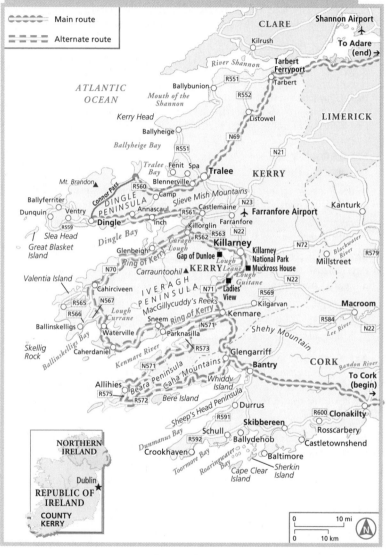

Main route
Alternate route

CLARE
Shannon Airport
To Adare (end) →
Kilrush
River Shannon
Tarbert Ferryport
R551
Tarbert
Ballybunion
R552
Mouth of the Shannon
ATLANTIC OCEAN
Listowel
LIMERICK
Kerry Head
Ballyheige
N69
Ballyheige Bay
R551
N21
Tralee Bay Fenit Spa Tralee
KERRY
Mt. Brandon
R560
Blennerville
Connor Pass DINGLE PENINSULA Camp Slieve Mish Mountains
Ballyferriter
Castlemaine N23
Kanturk
Dunquin Ventry Annascaul R561
Farranfore Airport
R559
Dingle
Inch
Farranfore
Slea Head
Killorglin N22
Dingle Bay
Caragh Lough R562 R563
Killarney
Great Blasket Island
Glenbeigh
Killarney N72 Blackwater River R579
Valentia Island
Gap of Dunloe Lough National Park Millstreet
Carrauntoohil ▲ KERRY Leane Muckross House
N70
Lough Guitane
Cahirciveen
IVERAGH PENINSULA N71 Ladies' N22
R565 N567
MacGillycuddy's Reeks View R569 Macroom
Lough Currane
Kilgarvan
R566
Ring of Kerry Kenmare R584 Lee River N22
Ballinskelligs
Sneem Parknasilla N571
Shehy Mountain
Skellig Rock
Waterville
Kenmare River Shehy Mountain
Ballinskelligs Bay Caherdaniel
N571 Beara Peninsula Caha Mountains R573 Glengarriff CORK Bandon River
Allihies
Bantry To Cork (begin) →
R575 R572 Bere Island Whiddy Island Durrus R600 Clonakilty
Sheep's Head Peninsula R591 Skibbereen Rosscarbery
Dunmanus Bay Schull R592 Ballydehob Castletownshend
Crookhaven Baltimore
Toormore Bay Roaringwater Bay Sherkin Island
Cape Clear Island

NORTHERN IRELAND
Dublin ★
REPUBLIC OF IRELAND
COUNTY KERRY

0   10 mi
0   10 km

the rest of the day exploring this colorful and attractive city on foot. Enjoy an evening meal at one of the many restaurants that have earned the city a reputation as a culinary capital, and attend a concert or other event on the city's lively cultural roster.

DAY 6 Easy excursions can take you to nearby sights such as Blarney Castle, home of the famously kissable stone, and, more worthwhile, to Kinsale, a pleasant port town with seaside walks and a mighty fort.

DAY 7 You can return to Dublin speedily on any number of routes. One option is to begin the trip on N25 north to Waterford, where you can visit the famous crystal factory and shop.

ITINERARY 2
Into the Southwest

In the Southwest, a bounty of magnificent scenery is compressed into a relatively small area. You can either add this itinerary to the one above or simply take the N8 south from Dublin to Cork, a trip of less than four hours, and begin a tour there.

DAY 1 After settling into a hotel in Cork, walk around this delightful city. A stroll through the English Market will whet your appetite for a meal at one of the city's many fine restaurants.

DAY 2 Spend the day exploring Cork and your pick of the nearby sights to the east—the Old Midleton Distillery, Fota House and Wildlife Park, and Cobh.

DAY 3 It's time to move on, but not far, to the pleasant port of Kinsale. En route, stop at Blarney Castle. You'll have the rest of the day and evening to explore Kinsale. Weather permitting, follow the Scilly Walk along the harbor to the Bulman, an atmospheric seaside pub warmed by fires, and to Charles Fort.

DAY 4 Head east to Bantry, paying a visit to one of Ireland's finest historic homes, Bantry House. From there, follow the lovely drive around Bantry Bay to Glengarriff. You have a choice here: you can either make a circuit of the unspoiled Beara Peninsula for some stunning seascapes or cross the peninsula over Healy Pass for a panorama of moors and heather-covered mountains—hands down one of the most gorgeous drives in Ireland. Just beyond is Kenmare, where you'll find a nice selection of appealing guest houses.

DAY 5 You'll want to spend a little time just soaking in the pleasant small-town atmosphere of Kenmare. If you're up for a longish drive, make the circuit of the Iveragh Peninsula, better known as the Ring of Kerry. But if you didn't explore the Beara Peninsula the day before, do that instead—the scenery is just as grand or even grander, and the roads are much less traveled.

itinerary 3: into the west of ireland

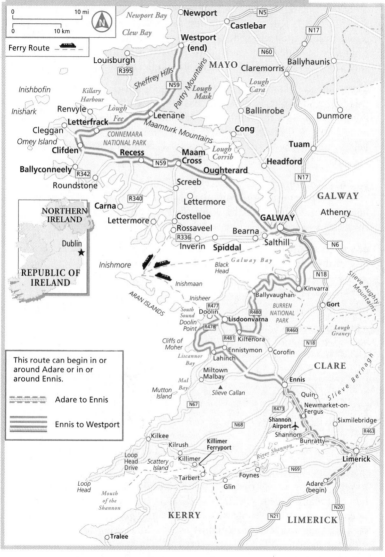

0   10 mi
0   10 km

Ferry Route

Newport Bay
Newport
Clew Bay
Castlebar   N5
N17
Westport
(end)   N60
Louisburgh   Ballyhaunis
R395   MAYO   Claremorris
Sheffrey Hills   N59 Lough   Lough
Mask   Cara
Inishbofin   Killary   Partry Mountains
Harbour
Inishark   Renvyle   Lough   Leenane   Ballinrobe   Dunmore
Letterfrack   Fee   Maamturk Mountains   Cong
Cleggan   CONNEMARA   Tuam
NATIONAL PARK   Lough
Omey Island   Clifden   Recess   Maam   Corrib   Headford
Ballyconneely   R342   Cross   Oughterard   N17
Roundstone   Screeb   GALWAY
R340   Lettermore   Athenry
NORTHERN   Carna   GALWAY
IRELAND   Lettermore   Costelloe
Rossaveel   Bearna   N6
Dublin ★   R336   Inverin   Spiddal   Salthill
REPUBLIC OF   Galway Bay
IRELAND   Inishmore   Black   N18
Head   Kinvarra   Slieve Aughty
Inishmaan   Mountains
Inisheer   Ballyvaughan
South   R477   BURREN   Gort
Sound   Doolin   R480   NATIONAL
Doolin   Lisdoonvarna   PARK   Lough
Point   R478   R460   Graney
Cliffs of   R481   Kilfenora
Moher   N18
Ennistymon   Corofin
Liscannor   Lahinch   CLARE
Bay   Miltown
Mal   Malbay   Ennis
Mutton   Bay   Slieve Callan   Quin
Island   ▲   Newmarket-on-
N67   R473   Fergus
N68   Shannon   Sixmilebridge
Airport
Kilkee   Shannon   R463
Kilrush   Killimer   Bunratty
Loop   Ferryport   River Shannon   Limerick
Head   Scattery   Killimer
Drive   Island   Adare
Tarbert   N69   (begin)
Loop   Foynes   N20
Head   Mouth   Glin
of the
Shannon   KERRY   N21   LIMERICK
Tralee

This route can begin in or
around Adare or in or
around Ennis.

‒ ‒ ‒ ‒   Adare to Ennis

═══════   Ennis to Westport

DAY 6 Follow the scenic route, the so-called "tunnel road," into Killarney National Park, stopping at Ladies View for a panorama of lakes and mountains and sights such as Muckross House and Ross Castle. At Killarney, head west into the Gap of Dunloe, a rocky pass through the tall mountains known as MacGillycuddy's Reeks. This scenery-filled day ends with a drive past the beaches on the south side of the Dingle Peninsula to Dingle Town.

DAY 7 Spend the day exploring the Dingle Peninsula, the westernmost tip of Ireland. Sights include the Blasket Centre, celebrating the life of the inhabitants of the remote Blasket Islands, and Gallus Oratory, a remarkably well-preserved church from the early days of Christianity. Best of all are the views of the rugged scenery and the sea from Slea Head, just to the west of Dingle Town.

DAY 8 Cross the spine of the Dingle Peninsula on Connor Pass, a view-a-minute mountain route that drops down to Tralee. From here, head north to Glin on the banks of the River Shannon, and follow the river east toward Adare, one of the prettiest villages in Ireland.

DAY 9 From Adare, head east back to Dublin, with a stop in Limerick, or continue north into the West, following Itinerary 3.

ITINERARY 3
Into the West

This route begins near Shannon Airport, the point of arrival for many visitors to Ireland. If you are coming from Dublin, follow Route N7 across Ireland to Limerick, a trip of about three hours—but add a couple of hours to the schedule and take the N8 so you can include a stop at the Rock of Cashel.

DAY 1 Ennis and Adare, just north and south of Limerick, respectively, are good bases from which to explore the surrounding region. Both are appealing low-key towns in which you'll enjoy spending time, and from both you can easily visit the city of Limerick and sights such as Bunratty Castle.

DAY 2 An easy drive brings you to the coast and the Cliffs of Moher, one of Ireland's great natural wonders. These cliffs lie at the edge of one of the country's strangest landscapes: the Burren, a stark expanse of limestone riddled with prehistoric remains. Seaside Doolin is a pleasant stopover, all the more so because this small and otherwise un-remarkable village is known around the world for its traditional music.

DAYS 3 AND 4 A short drive around Galway Bay brings you to Galway, one of Ireland's liveliest and most colorful cities. Spend two days here enjoying the pleasant buzz on the streets, the sound of spoken Irish, and some good music, and making several pleasant excursions—a day trip to the Aran Islands, time permitting, or a boat trip into Lough Corrib.

DAYS 5 AND 6 Just north of Galway lies the majestic landscape of the Connemara, mountainous in some parts, covered with prairielike moors in others, and dotted with forests of pine and fir that surround rushing streams and glittering lakes. You might want to treat yourself to stay at a retreat such as Ballynahinch Castle, or use the pleasant seaside town of Clifden or the village of Cong as your base. The best place to experience the wild splendor of this part of the world is in Connemara National Park, which is laced with excellent hiking trails.

DAY 7 You'll encounter more gorgeous scenery as you continue north through the Kylemore Valley, past Kylemore Abbey, and around con-ical-shaped Crough Patrick to the appealing town of Westport.

DAY 8 You can return south to Shannon from Westport in about three hours or continue into the Northwest following Itinerary 4.

ITINERARY 4
Into the Northwest

The Northwest is rugged, bounded by rough seas and desolate moun-tain landscapes. If you're coming from Dublin, plan on a drive of about three hours to Sligo Town.

DAY 1 After settling into Sligo Town or, better yet, into one of the distinctive lodgings in the nearby countryside, take a walk along the animated streets that run down to the River Garavogue. Step into the County Museum, for a look at manuscripts by the poet William Butler Yeats and canvases by his brother, Jack Yeats.

DAY 2 In the near vicinity of Sligo Town are two prehistoric sites: the passage tombs at Carrowmore and Carrowkeel. This is also Yeats country, and you can pay homage to the poet with a drive around Lough Gill, where the Isle of Innisfree inspired the poet's line "I will arise now and go, and go to Innisfree," and with a visit to Drumcliff, where Yeats is buried in the shadow of Ben Bulben mountain.

DAY 3 Break up the drive north with a walk around Donegal Town, dominated by its castle, and then pass through the busy fishing port of Killybegs to Slieve League, a majestic swath of tall cliffs that soar vertically out of the surf. If the weather's good, take time out for a short but hair-raising hike along the top of the cliffs. From here, head east and settle into one of several pleasant hotels in the countryside outside Letterkenny.

DAY 4 A short excursion takes you west into the wonders of Glenveagh National Park, where enchanting Glenveagh Castle is set amid the moor-clad hillsides of the Derryveagh Mountains. You might want to

itinerary 4: into the northwest of ireland

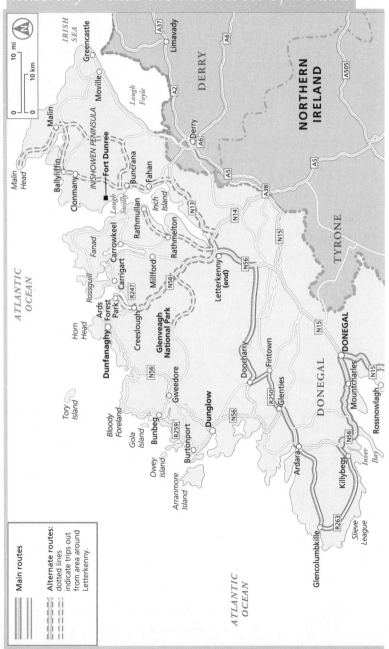

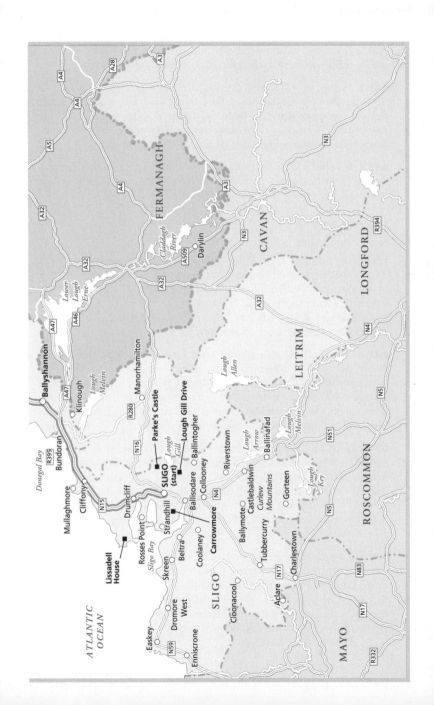

make a stop en route at Glebe House, a Regency manor filled with an outstanding collection of European art. You can explore the rugged North Sea coast on any number of headlands or in Ards Forest Park, whose trails traverse marshes, forested valleys, and the coast.

DAY 5 A day of exploring can include the sights you couldn't fit into the schedule the day before (you might want to spend that entire day in Glenveagh National Park and devote this day to driving along the coast). Venture east from Letterkenny onto the mountainous Inishowen Peninsula, the northernmost point in Ireland.

DAY 6 It's about a five-hour drive south to either Dublin or Shannon. If you're planning to continue east into Northern Ireland, follow Itinerary 5 in reverse, beginning in Derry.

ITINERARY 5
Northern Ireland

Peace has brought with it the chance to discover just how rich in natural beauty and urban pleasures the North is. Belfast is only two hours north of Dublin by car, though you might want to take a bit longer and leave the busy M1 for stops at the Hill of Tara, seat of the ancient kings of Ireland, and Newgrange, one of the world's most impressive prehistoric burial grounds.

DAY 1 After settling into a Belfast hotel for a two-night stay, hit the streets and walk through the city center. Along with the Victorian grandeur of the place, you can't help but notice the upbeat buzz of this city that's moving toward a better future. You'll have a choice of excellent and exciting dinner spots, and you'll enjoy fine entertainment at the Grand Opera House and other venues.

DAY 2 Your explorations of the city should extend south to the pleasant Stranmills neighborhood around the Botanic Gardens, the Ulster Museum, and Queen's University. You should also take a bus or taxi tour of the Falls Road and Shankill Road neighborhoods, epicenters of the Troubles in the recent past. If you have kids in tow, consider a half-day visit to the Ulster Folk and Transport Museum, just northeast of the city.

DAY 3 An incredibly scenic drive takes you north through the forested Glens of Antrim to the Antrim Coast. Slow down the pace for visits to the Dunluce Castle, the Old Bushmills Distillery, the Giants Causeway, and Carrick-a-Rede Bridge. If the weather's good, follow at least a small section of the path that follows the coast. You can press on to Derry at the end of the day, but you might want to settle in for the night in Portrush or Bushmills.

DAY 4 A day in Derry allows you to explore this walled city at your leisure. The first order of business is to walk the walls, a 1.5-kilometer (1-mile) circuit that will provide a bird's-eye views of the sights. Your explorations should take you into Bogside, the Catholic neighborhood beneath the walls where political murals recall the violence of decades past.

DAY 5 You might want to continue into the Northwest (see Itinerary 4) or, if you're heading back south, take in the green hills that surround the Loughs of Erne en route, with stops in the pleasant town of Enniskillen and at Castle Coole.

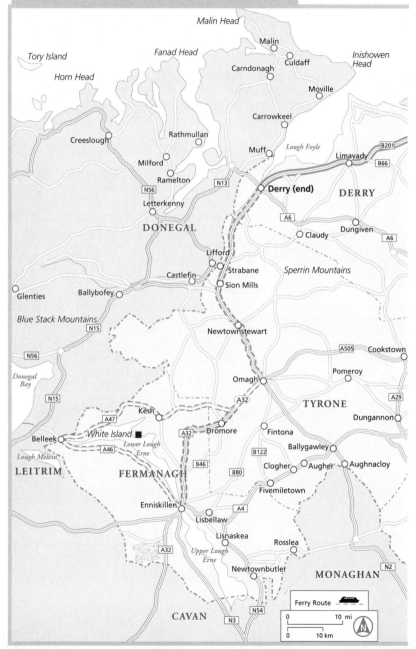

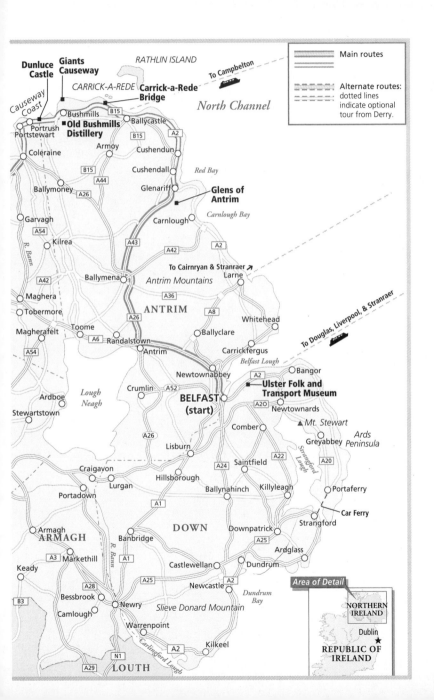

Dunluce Castle
Giants Causeway
RATHLIN ISLAND
To Campbelton
CARRICK-A-REDE
Carrick-a-Rede Bridge
North Channel
Causeway Coast
Bushmills B15
Portrush Ballycastle
Portstewart
Old Bushmills Distillery
B15 A2
Coleraine Armoy Cushendun
B15 Cushendall *Red Bay*
A44
Ballymoney Glenariff **Glens of Antrim**
A26 *Carnlough Bay*
Garvagh Cushendun
A54 Carnlough
R. Bann
Kilrea A43
A42 A2
Maghera A42
Tobermore Ballymena *Antrim Mountains* To Cairnryan & Stranraer
Larne
Magherafelt A36
A54 **ANTRIM** A8 Whitehead
Toome A26 To Douglas, Liverpool, & Stranraer
A6 Randalstown Ballyclare
Antrim Carrickfergus
Ardboe *Lough Neagh* Crumlin A52 Newtownabbey *Belfast Lough* Bangor
Stewartstown **BELFAST (start)** **Ulster Folk and Transport Museum**
A2O Newtownards
A26 Comber ▲*Mt. Stewart*
Greyabbey *Ards Peninsula*
Lisburn
Craigavon A24 Saintfield A22 A20
Hillsborough *Strangford Lough*
Portadown Lurgan Ballynahinch Killyleagh
A1 Portaferry
DOWN Downpatrick **Car Ferry**
Armagh Banbridge A25 Strangford
ARMAGH Ardglass
A3 Markethill *R. Bann* A1 Dundrum
Keady Castlewellan Dundrum
A28 A25 A2 *Dundrum Bay* *Area of Detail*
Bessbrook Newcastle
B3 Newry *Slieve Donard Mountain* **NORTHERN IRELAND**
Camlough
Warrenpoint ★ Dublin
A2 Kilkeel **REPUBLIC OF IRELAND**
N1 *Carlingford Lough*
A29 **LOUTH**

Main routes

Alternate routes: dotted lines indicate optional tour from Derry.

PART THREE

LODGING, DINING, *and* SHOPPING

HOTELS *in* IRELAND

LODGING IN IRELAND comes in many varieties: urban luxury hotels, castles, country houses, country inns, guest houses, and bed-and-breakfasts. However the accommodation chooses to bill itself, chances are you'll receive a friendly welcome, a high level of service, a good degree of cleanliness, and a darned good breakfast. You can also expect to pay a bit for all this—lodging is as expensive as everything else is in Ireland these days.

In general, expect to pay at least €100 to €150 (£60 to £80 in the North) for a double; of course, you can easily pay a lot more than that. Bed-and-breakfasts are often a bit less expensive than that, but just a bit.

WHAT TO EXPECT

LUXURY CITY HOTELS Hoteliers in Dublin, Belfast, and other Irish cities seem to be engaged in a contest to see who can provide the most luxurious, atmospheric lodgings, going overboard to equip rooms and suites with elegant furnishings, palatial bathrooms, state-of-the-art audio/video equipment, and every other amenity.

CHAIN HOTELS Novotel, InterContinental, Best Western, Hilton, and Westin are among the many chains that operate in Ireland. Predictable, yes, but that's a quality some travelers value.

GUEST HOUSES These are often large private homes and other distinctive properties that have been converted to inns, usually providing character-filled and comfortable accommodations but not the full services of a hotel.

 CASTLE HOTELS Converting historic castles into hotels is an Irish specialty, and **Dromoland, Ashford,** and **Adare Manor** set the gold standard for luxury within stone walls. Some castles have forfeited character for standardized comfort, providing a strange hybrid: chain hotels with turrets. Others are charmingly idiosyncratic, right down to the drafts in the hallways. The **Irish Landmark Trust** can put you up in castles around the country, as well as other distinctive properties. Contact the trust at 25 Eustace Street, Dublin 2; ☎ 01-670-4733; **www.irishlandmark.com.**

COUNTRY-HOUSE HOTELS Formerly private estates, often set within landscaped grounds, these places work hard to make guests feel like the lord and lady of the manor. You can usually expect pleasant lounges, and many have well-decorated rooms with private baths.

BED-AND-BREAKFASTS Long the mainstay of the budget-travel circuit, B&Bs are essentially private homes that take in guests—though these days some B&Bs are independent of a home. Some are filled with more chintz than your great-auntie ever dreamed of, but many are quite attractive and increasingly offer amenities such as TV, private bathrooms, and direct-dial telephones. B&Bs are still, however, usually less expensive than hotels and guest houses.

SELF-CATERING ACCOMMODATIONS These range from apartments to cottages, always providing equipped kitchens. Well suited for families and groups, they usually rent by the week. The **Irish Tourist Board** and the **Northern Ireland Tourist Board** (see page 43) list self-catering accommodations.

FARM STAYS Many Irish farmers have learned that catering to city folk who want a rural experience beats a lot of other kinds of farm chores. These are essentially B&Bs in the countryside; some serve meals made from produce grown on the property. For listings, contact Irish Farm Holidays, **www.irishfarmholidays.com.**

SOME OTHER WEB RESOURCES

FOR A COMPREHENSIVE LISTING of Irish lodging, click your way through the following Web resources. But remember that these are just listings, and they do not provide you with critical reviews (for those, see the hotel reviews throughout this book). The **Irish Tourist Board** Web site, **www.ireland.ie,** can help you find any kind of accommodation anywhere in Ireland, from B&Bs to luxury hotels. *Be Our Guest* (**www.irelandhotels.com**), published by the Irish Hotel Federation and available in print from the Irish Tourist Board, provides information on hotels, castles, and other accommodations. **Ireland's Blue Book** (**www.irelands-blue-book.ie**) will introduce you to manor houses, castles, convents, and other significant buildings where you can stay. **Hidden Ireland** (**www.hidden-ireland.com**) lists B&Bs and guest houses that are especially appealing; in fact, you would do well to stay at as many of the places listed as you can.

ROOM RATES

ROOM RATES CHANGE with the seasons and as occupancy rates rise and fall. If a hotel is close to full, don't expect to find any kind of rate reduction; if it's close to empty, though, you may be able to negotiate a discount. Here are some money-saving options to consider:

- Expensive hotels catering to business travelers are most crowded on weekdays and usually offer substantial discounts for weekend stays.
- You may be able to save 20% or more by traveling off season (mid-October to mid-December and January to March).
- Some of the best hotel rates of all, especially in Dublin, are found with air/hotel packages.
- The major travel-booking Web sites listed in Part One, Planning Your Visit to Ireland (see page 40), offer hotel-reservation services. Other Web sites are devoted entirely to lodging, including the following:
  Hotel Reservations Network lists bargain rates at hotels in Dublin, Belfast, Cork, and Limerick; **www.180096hotel.com.**
  InnSite provides B&B listings for inns around the globe, including Ireland; **www.innsite.com.**
  TravelWeb, focusing on chains such as Hyatt and Hilton, offers weekend deals at many leading chains; **www.travelweb.com.**
- Always check out a hotel's Web site to see what deals and packages might be available when you plan to stay. Many city hotels that cater to businesspeople offer reduced rates on weekends. Conversely, a hotel in Kinsale or Dingle that caters to Irish weekenders might offer midweek specials.
- And finally, never be afraid to ask for the lowest rate—call and ask if special rates might apply or if rates are lower for longer stays.

Confirming a Room

Hotels do not consider a room reservation confirmed until they receive partial or full payment. You can almost always confirm your reservations immediately with a credit card; otherwise, you must mail in your payment using an International Money Order, available at most banks. Before you reserve your room, ask about the cancellation policy. At some hotels you can get your money back if you cancel a room with 24 hours' notice; others require you to notify the hotel five or more

unofficial **TIP**
Do not arrive in Dublin without a hotel reservation at any time of year, or anywhere in Ireland if you're traveling from mid-May to September (high season). This is especially important on weekends in popular getaways such as Dingle and Kinsale. In the fall, winter, and early spring, you will probably be able to find rooms on the spot, although many B&Bs and guest houses are closed in winter.

unofficial **TIP**
Some smaller B&Bs, especially those in country villages, do not accept credit cards. If you're going to be choosing small hotels or B&Bs as they strike your fancy, make sure you have enough cash.

days in advance. After you've reserved the room, request a written confirmation by fax, e-mail, or post.

HOTEL RATINGS

PRICES IN OUR LISTINGS include (VAT) value-added tax, 13.5% in the Republic and 17.5% in Northern Ireland, and refer to the starting price for a standard single and a standard double room. Prices for deluxe, executive, triple-occupancy, and family rooms, as well as suites and rooms with special features (such as four-poster beds, fireplaces, and balconies), may be significantly higher, but not necessarily: if the hotel's not full, ask if you can have a room with deluxe features for the price of a standard. Remember that prices are flexible and change all the time; you may find that a hotel charges more than the listed price and, just as often, less. Also keep in mind that these are standard rates; you may be able to get a better price with a Web offer, special package, or weekend rate—or just by asking.

OVERALL RATINGS We have distinguished properties according to the relative quality, tastefulness, state of repair, cleanliness, and size of standard rooms, grouping them into classifications denoted by stars. Overall star ratings in this guide do not correspond to ratings awarded by the Irish Tourist Board, the Northern Ireland Tourist Board, automobile clubs, or other travel critics. Overall ratings are presented to show the difference we perceive between one property and another. They are assigned without regard to location or to whether a property has restaurants, recreational facilities, entertainment, or other extras.

★★★★★	Superior	Tasteful and luxurious by any standard
★★★★	Extremely Nice	Above average in appointments and design; very comfortable
★★★	Nice	Average but quite comfortable
★★	Adequate	Plain but meets all essential needs
★	Budget	Spartan; not aesthetically pleasing, but clean

QUALITY RATINGS In addition to overall ratings (which delineate broad categories), we also employ quality ratings. These apply to room quality only and describe the property's standard accommodations. In addition to standard accommodations, many hotels offer luxury rooms and special suites that are not rated in this guide. Our rating scale is ★ to ★★★★★, with ★★★★★ as the best possible rating and ★ as the worst.

VALUE RATINGS We also provide a value rating to give you some sense of the quality of a room in relation to its cost. As before, the ratings are based on the quality of room for the money and do not take into account location, services, or amenities.

Our scale is as follows:

★★★★★	An exceptional bargain
★★★★	A good deal
★★★	Fairly priced (you get exactly what you pay for)
★★	Somewhat overpriced
★	Significantly overpriced

A ★★½ room at €100 may have the same value rating as a ★★★★★ room at €180, but that does not mean that the rooms will be of comparable quality. Regardless of whether it's a good deal or not, a ★★½ room is still a ★★½ room.

DINING *in* IRELAND

STEREOTYPICAL IRISH FOOD—potatoes accompanied by potatoes with a garnish of cabbage—has been the brunt of jokes for centuries. Well, let's put the ridicule to rest once and for all: you're in for a pleasant surprise, because Irish cooking is more varied and interesting, with an emphasis on fresh ingredients, by the day. In fact, dining in Ireland can be a real treat these days, when even old-fashioned stews are being reinvented as part of modern Irish cuisine.

Fish and seafood are fresh and plentiful, bread is almost always baked on the premises, and Irish cheeses give French *fromages* a run for their money. What you won't find in Ireland—yet, at least—is a great deal of variety. Irish cooking remains straightforward, and delightfully so, relying on farm-raised lamb, pork, and poultry; garden-fresh vegetables; fish just out of the sea; and wild game, among other high-quality ingredients. Ethnic food is scarce, even in Dublin, though many Irish chefs infuse their creations with spices to provide a hint of exoticism.

THE COST FACTOR

A MEAL IN IRELAND IS, on the whole, less expensive than it would be in London or New York, but it probably costs more than you're used to paying if you live elsewhere. It's hard to find a good three-course meal with a bottle of wine for less than €40 a head, and you'll often pay more. There are ways to cut costs, though. Many restaurants offer lunch specials and early-bird dinner specials; if you're willing to dine before 7 p.m., you can enjoy a very nice meal in some of Ireland's better restaurants for about €30 to €35 per person, with wine. Pub meals

---

TIPS AND VAT

A word on tipping: €1 or €2 a bag for bellhops, €3 a night for the housekeeper, and more if service is extraordinary, as it often is in Ireland.

In general, the quoted room rate includes the VAT (value-added tax), 13.5% in the Republic and 17.5% in Northern Ireland. Be sure to ask if the VAT is included so you won't get an unpleasant surprise when you're checking out.

are usually reasonably priced, as are those at casual eateries such as wine bars and cafes. With drinks making up a large part of many bills, look for house wines, or order by the glass if that's all you want—and no one's going to object if you opt for a pint instead of wine. Don't feel obliged to order bottled water (almost always marked up heavily) if tap water will please you just as well. If you're traveling with children but don't see a kids' menu, ask if a child-size portion can be prepared.

Prices usually include the 13.5% VAT. In many restaurants, a service charge of 12 to 15% is added to the bill, so make sure you examine your menu and your bill to see if it has already been added. If service is not included, it will be mentioned in some obvious manner on the bill. The normal range for tipping in restaurants is 12 to 20%, and because service is usually excellent, you probably won't mind paying it.

RATING OUR FAVORITE RESTAURANTS

WE HAVE DEVELOPED detailed profiles for the best and (in our opinion) most interesting restaurants all over Ireland. Each profile features an easily scanned heading that allows you to check out at a glance the restaurant's name and cuisine, the star rating, quality rating, and value rating we've assigned it, and the cost, along with a description of the dining experience you can expect to have.

CUISINE This is actually less straightforward than it sounds. In some cases we've used the broader terms (for example, "French" or "Italian") but added descriptions to give a clearer idea of the fare (for example, "Provençal" or "Southern Italian"). Don't hold us, or the chefs, to too strict a style, but we do ensure that we give you some idea of what type of cuisine to expect. Irish restaurants stick to mainstream cooking—that is, you'll notice that the cuisine in many is labeled as "Irish" or "Modern Irish" cuisine.

OVERALL RATING The overall rating is a rating that encompasses the entire dining experience, including style, service, and ambience, in addition to the taste, presentation, and quality of the food. Five stars is the highest rating possible and denotes the best of everything. Four-star restaurants are exceptional, three-star restaurants well above average. Two-star restaurants are so-so. One star is used to indicate a forgettable restaurant that demonstrates an unusual capability in some area of specialization—for example, an otherwise unmemorable place that serves fresh fish.

COST Our expense description provides a comparative sense of how much a complete meal will cost. A complete meal for our purposes consists of an appetizer, entree, and dessert. Drinks and tips are excluded.

Inexpensive	Less than €20 (£14) per person
Moderate	€20–€35 (£14–£25) per person
Expensive	More than €35 (£25) per person

QUALITY RATING Food quality is rated on a scale of one to five stars, five being the best rating attainable. The quality rating is based on the taste, freshness of ingredients, preparation, presentation, and creativity of food served. There is no consideration of price. If you want the best food available and cost is not an issue, you need look no further than the quality ratings.

VALUE RATING If, on the other hand, you are looking for both quality and value, then you should check the value rating. This rating breaks down as follows:

★★★★★	Exceptional value; a real bargain
★★★★	Good value
★★★	Fair value; you get exactly what you pay for
★★	Somewhat overpriced
★	Significantly overpriced

PAYMENT We've listed the type of payment accepted at each restaurant using the following codes: AE for American Express (and American Express Optima), D for Discover, DC for Diners Club, MC for MasterCard, and V for VISA.

WHO'S INCLUDED Our list is highly selective. We try to include the most noteworthy restaurants, and these needn't be expensive or fancy—we also provide as broad a range of dining experiences as we can. The omission of a particular establishment does not necessarily indicate that the restaurant is bad, only that we felt it didn't rank among the best we wanted to offer our readers in a particular place.

SHOPPING *in* IRELAND

IT'S WORTH NOTING that many Irish are flying to New York these days for weekend shopping sprees. The savings on everything from clothing to housewares more than offsets the airfare. From this you can rightfully conclude that goods in Ireland are expensive. Rather than bargains, you will find high-quality, distinctively Irish goods—especially china, crystal, lace and linen, and woolen goods.

WISE BUYS IN IRELAND

THE FOLLOWING ITEMS are worth buying in Ireland because of their high quality or their unavailability in the United States.

Antiques

You find antiques shops in the old districts of every major city and town, which also usually have a market where vendors sell antiques. See our shopping sections throughout this guide for tips on the places where you are most likely to pick up a bargain. There are fewer bargains to be had in these days of prosperity, but you can still come upon some finds—good china, prints, jewelry, and bric-a-brac are market mainstays and can be quite a find.

Crystal and China

Waterford crystal is widely available throughout Ireland, including the factory shops in Waterford. Prices are set, so you won't find many bargains, but you will find a much greater selection here in Ireland than you will abroad. You'll also encounter fine pieces from **Dublin Crystal** and other Irish manufacturers, as well as china from **Belleek** and other Irish houses.

Books

In general, the Irish are avid readers, and almost every town of any size has one or two excellent bookshops, some selling contemporary editions and others used and rare volumes. Staffs tend to be knowledgeable—they usually know the stock well and, should you be eager to immerse yourself in the depths of Irish literature, are willing to make recommendations.

Designer Clothing

John Rocha, Jen Kelly, and other Irish designers are making names for themselves with distinctive, high-quality fashions. Most are well represented in the better Dublin shops, and also at the **Kilkenny Design Centre** in Kilkenny City.

Knits and Woolens

You'll encounter well-crafted, often handwoven goods throughout Ireland. Some of the names to look for are **Avoca Handweavers** (which branches out from its sumptuous wovens into all things Irish), **Blarney Woollen Mills,** and **Dublin Woollen Mills.** These are the big names, but you will also encounter many shops that sell exceptional sweaters, scarves, and other pieces hand-knit locally, often very well priced. Many shops will knit Aran sweaters to your specifications.

Pottery

Ireland is renowned for its beautifully crafted and glazed pottery, including pieces by internationally acclaimed artisans **Stephen Pearse** and **Louis Mulcahy;** you'll encounter their work, and that of others, in Dublin, and in heavily touristed places such as Dingle and Killarney.

TIME TO SHOP

STORES IN IRELAND TEND to open at 9 a.m. and close at 6 or 6:30 p.m., with one weekly late closing at 8 or 9 p.m. So if you're used to popping round the corner and finding whatever you want at any time, plan accordingly. Sunday is still relatively sacrosanct as a day of rest for shopkeepers, although some stores on the major shopping streets are starting to open for a half day, from noon to 5 or 6 p.m.

Street markets generally come to life on weekends, although you'll find weekday markets in Dublin, Cork, Belfast, and other cities.

PAYING UP

MOST SHOPS TAKE ALL major credit cards (note that some small shops in small towns and villages may not). The credit card is a good way to go, as you'll have a record of your purchases and the exchange rate will be fair. The rate used will be that on the day the purchase clears the credit-card company or bank.

AS FOR VAT

VALUE-ADDED TAX (VAT), which varies in the Republic, is 13.5% on hotel and restaurant bills and car rentals, as well as on many household items, and 21% for gifts and souvenirs. In Northern Ireland, VAT is 17.5% across the board. VAT is usually included in an item's sticker price, but in a few places it may be an add-on.

VAT Refunds

If you do not live in a country in the European Union (EU), you may qualify for a VAT refund, provided you spend at least €155 at any one store. Make sure you keep the invoice; then present it to the VAT desk at the airport (don't pass it—you'll usually come to it before you pass through passport control). Mail the stamped invoice back to the store within 90 days of your purchase, and the store will send you a refund check.

unofficial **TIP**
The **Tax Free for Tourists Network** makes getting a VAT refund a lot easier, but not all stores are part of this scheme (look for a sticker in the window). Stores that do participate will issue you a refund check at the time of purchase. Take this and the invoice to the airport VAT office, which will cash the check on the spot. For more information, visit **www.global refund.com.**

SALESPEOPLE'S ATTITUDES AND BEHAVIOR

YOU'LL PROBABLY BE SURPRISED at just how pleasant and helpful salespeople are in Ireland. A new crop of service workers, many from Eastern Europe and elsewhere in the EU, have adopted Irish courtesy, so shopping or dealing with hotel and restaurant staffs can be a real pleasure.

PART FOUR

DUBLIN

YOU MAY WELL COME TO DUBLIN equipped with few notions of what to expect other than a ditty running through your head ("In Dublin's Fair City, Where the Girls Are So Pretty . . . ") and literary visions of Leopold Bloom and Stephen Daedalus roaming damp streets. You'll leave, though, with many more impressions tucked away, most of them as pleasant as the sight of the slow-moving River Liffey, the first gulp of a really good pint of Guinness, and the sensation of a gentle mist on your face. Dublin, you'll soon learn, is a marvelous place, steeped though it is in sad episodes of a long past and the traffic-induced inconveniences of the present day. Walking across the city center on a leisurely stroll, you'll encounter Celtic crosses, Georgian fanlights, James Joyce's handwritten manuscripts, and Renoir canvases. You'll enjoy the city on less lofty planes, too. You'll have pleasant encounters, pass many pubs, and everywhere you go, hear the lovely lilt of what your grandparents may have always referred to as the old country. As the Irish say, you'll think Dublin is "spot on."

THE NEIGHBORHOODS

DUBLIN POSTAL CODES ARE PRETTY STRAIGHTFORWARD. The two you will encounter most often are **Dublin 1,** the center of town north of the River Liffey (the **North Side**), and **Dublin 2,** the center of town south of the Liffey (the **South Side**). We break Dublin into neighborhoods that take the concept a little further to make getting around the city even easier. To explore each of these neighborhoods on foot, see Dublin Walks, page 127.

CENTRAL DUBLIN, NORTH OF THE LIFFEY

HERE YOU'LL FIND WHAT MANY Dubliners still consider to be the city center, comprising **O'Connell Street** and the streets and squares

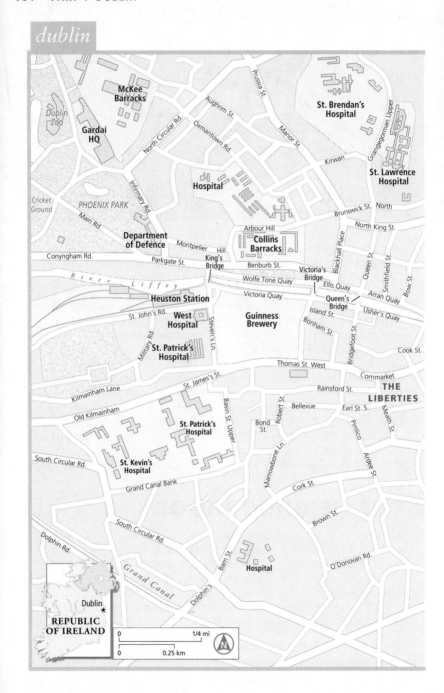

dublin

McKee Barracks

Dublin Zoo

Gardaí HQ

St. Brendan's Hospital

Grangegorman Upper

St. Lawrence Hospital

Prussia St.

Aughrim St.

Oxmantown Rd.

North Circular Rd.

Manor St.

Kirwan

Hospital

Brunswick St. North

Cricket Ground

PHOENIX PARK

Main Rd.

Infirmary Rd.

North King St.

Arbour Hill

Collins Barracks

Blackhall Place

Department of Defence

Montpelier Hill

King's Bridge

Benburb St.

Queen St.

Smithfield St.

Bow St.

Conyngham Rd.

Parkgate St.

Wolfe Tone Quay

Victoria's Bridge

Ellis Quay

Arran Quay

River Liffey

Victoria Quay

Queen's Bridge

Usher's Quay

Heuston Station

West Hospital

St. John's Rd.

Guinness Brewery

Island St.

Bonham St.

Bridgefoot St.

Cook St.

Steven's Ln.

St. Patrick's Hospital

Military Rd.

Thomas St. West

Cornmarket

Kilmainham Lane

St. James's St.

Rainsford St.

THE LIBERTIES

Old Kilmainham

Bellevue

Earl St. S.

Meath St.

Basin St. Upper

Robert St.

Pimlico

St. Patrick's Hospital

Bond St.

St. Kevin's Hospital

South Circular Rd.

Grand Canal Bank

Marrowbone Ln.

Cork St.

Ardee St.

Dolphin Rd.

South Circular Rd.

Brown St.

O'Donovan Rd.

Barn St.

Dolphin's

Grand Canal

Hospital

Dublin

REPUBLIC OF IRELAND

0		1/4 mi
0	0.25 km	

N

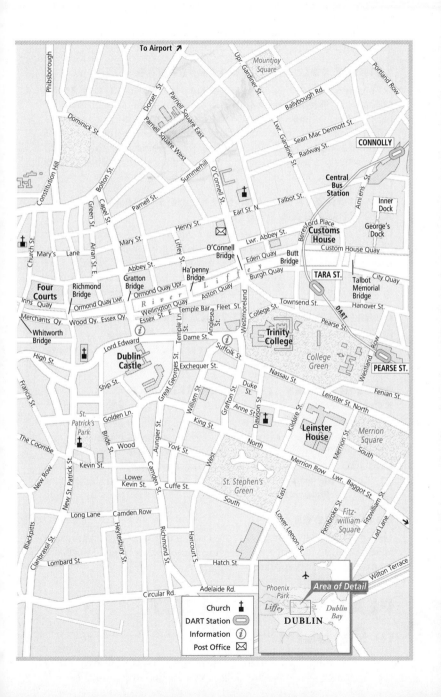

around it. Some of the city's most beloved cultural institutions are here, including the **Abbey** and **Gate theaters,** and the **Hugh Lane Gallery,** as well as the big shops lining O'Connell and Henry streets.

TRINITY COLLEGE AND TEMPLE BAR

IRELAND'S OLDEST AND MOST HALLOWED UNIVERSITY, **Trinity College,** and **Temple Bar,** the city's raucous nightlife quarter, are both near the south banks of the River Liffey. Between the student population in one and the barely-of-age pub crawlers in the other, this neighborhood is decidedly youthful. You'll come here to drink, to dine, and, on a more serious note, to see the exquisite **Book of Kells** (see page 131), on display in the Trinity Library.

GRAFTON STREET, ST. STEPHEN'S GREEN, AND GEORGIAN DUBLIN

STREETS OF EXPENSIVE SHOPS and squares of elegant Georgian houses surround **St. Stephen's Green,** creating what upwardly mobile Dubliners consider to be their center of town—that is, as opposed to the other center of town around O'Connell Street, north of the river. Also in this neighborhood are the **National Gallery** and the **National Museum.**

DUBLIN CASTLE AND THE CATHEDRALS

DUBLIN CASTLE STANDS AT THE EDGE of some of the city's oldest and most sacred ground. Here, the city's two cathedrals, **Christ Church** and **St. Patrick's,** are remnants of Dublin's medieval beginnings.

PHOENIX PARK, THE LIBERTIES, AND KILMAINHAM

IN MEANDERING NEIGHBORHOODS of terrace houses and factories west of the city center are scattered some of the city's most visited attractions. Foremost among these is the **Guinness Storehouse** (see page 138), although places such as the **Royal Hospital Kilmainham** and **Collins Barracks** warrant a trip out here, too, as do the verdant precincts of **Phoenix Park.**

BALLSBRIDGE

THIS IS A LEAFY RESIDENTIAL NEIGHBORHOOD at the southern edge of the city center. Amid the fine houses on tree-lined streets are many embassies, corporate headquarters, and hotels.

PLANNING *your* VISIT *to* DUBLIN

LOCATED AS IT IS IN AN OLD CHURCH on an atmospheric lane in the city center, **Dublin Tourism** itself seems like an attraction. The staff

NOT TO BE MISSED IN DUBLIN
Book of Kells (page 131)
Chester Beatty Library and Gallery of Oriental Art (page 132)
Christ Church Cathedral (page 133)
Dublin Writers Museum (page 137)
Hugh Lane Municipal Gallery of Modern Art (page 139)
Kilmainham Gaol (page 140)
National Gallery of Ireland (page 141)
National Museum of Ireland (page 142)
Number 29 (page 143)
St. Patrick's Cathedral (page 146)

is quite eager to answer any questions visitors might have, and although the place is mainly a souvenir shop, it also distributes some free maps and helpful pamphlets. You'll want the Event Guide, which includes decent coverage of entertainment and activities around town. Especially helpful is the Dublin Bus desk, where you can pick up a route map, buy bus tickets, and ask the staff how to get where you want to go. The center also books hotel rooms (for a fee), provides rail and long-distance bus information, and operates a pleasant cafe. The main office (Suffolk Street, Trinity College and Temple Bar; ☎ 01-605-7700; **www.visitdublin.com**): July to August, Monday through Saturday, 9 a.m. to 7 p.m. and Sunday, 10:30 a.m. to 3 p.m.; September to June, Monday through Saturday, 9 a.m. to 5:30 p.m. and Sunday, 10:30 a.m. to 3 p.m. Dublin Tourism also maintains offices on O'Connell Street (Central Dublin): Monday through Saturday, 9 a.m. to 5 p.m.; Lower Baggot Street (near St. Stephen's Green): Monday through Friday, 9:30 a.m. to noon and 12:30 to 5 p.m.; Dublin Airport: 8 a.m. to 10 p.m. daily; Dún Laoghaire (at the ferry terminal): Monday through Saturday, 10 a.m. to 1 p.m. and 2 to 6 p.m.

THE DUBLIN PASS

THE PRICE OF THIS PASS INCLUDES ADMISSION to many sights in Dublin, plus privilege of going to the head of the line. The pass is available at Dublin Tourism offices. One day: €29 adults, €17 children; two days: €49 adults, €29 children; three days: €59 adults, €34 children; six days: €89 adults, €44 children. If you decide to purchase the pass and are flying into Dublin, buy it when you arrive at Dublin Airport, because airport transfers on Aircoach are also included. For more information, check with Dublin Tourism or go to **www.dublinpass.com.**

unofficial **TIP**
Do some math before plunking down your euros for a Dublin Pass—you might be better off paying for individual admissions. Some of the places that you might want to visit and that are included on the pass, are expensive (such as the **Guinness Storehouse** and the **Old Jameson Distillery**), but others are free. Also, think about how you're going to approach your visits—you might want to consider buying a one-day pass and squeezing visits to all the most expensive places into one day.

GETTING *around* DUBLIN

BY FOOT

THIS IS AN EASY AND PLEASANT WAY to get around Dublin. Most sights within the city center (starting on page 127) are within easy walking distance from one another. Exercise extreme caution when crossing a street, because directions are reversed here—driving is in the left lane—and your instincts are geared to traffic moving on the right. Always look right before stepping into a street (your instinct will be to look left first), and for the greatest safety, cross only at signals or so-called zebra crossings, where diagonal white lines indicate that pedestrians have the right of way.

BY BUS

THE GREEN BUSES OF DUBLIN BUS, the main provider of transportation within Dublin, cover an extensive network serving every corner of the city. Many routes run along O'Connell Street on the North Side and Dame Street on the South Side. A bus that has "An Lar" (Gaelic for "City Center") posted on the sign in front will most likely take you to O'Connell Street and probably to Dame Street and somewhere on or around St. Stephen's Green. Fares vary with distances traveled, beginning at €0.95; pay the driver in exact change. Passes are available for one day of travel (€5), three days (€10.50), five days (€16.50), and seven days (€20).

> *unofficial* **TIP**
> Because you can reach most places in the city center fairly easily on foot, you may want to purchase only a one-day Dublin Bus pass, to use when you venture out to outlying sights such as the Guinness Storehouse and Kilmainham Gaol.

Buses run Monday through Saturday, from 6 a.m. to 11:30 p.m., and on Sunday, 10 a.m. to 6 p.m. For more information and to pick up schedules and route maps, visit the Dublin Bus office at Dublin Tourism; drop into Dublin Bus (59 Upper O'Connell Street, ☎ 01-872-0000); or visit **www.dublinbus.ie.**

BY DART

A SUBURBAN LIGHT-RAIL SERVICE, **Dublin Area Rapid Transit (DART)** follows the shores of Dublin Bay, from Greystone in the south to Malahide in the north. DART also links parts of the city center, with stops at Pearse and Tara streets on the South Side and Connolly Station on the North Side. Service runs Monday through Saturday, 7 a.m. to midnight and Sunday, 9:30 a.m. to 11 p.m. DART is a handy way to make excursions to outlying places such as Howth and Dún Laoghaire (see "Day Trips from Dublin," page 171). For more information, inquire at DART ticket windows at Pearse or Connolly Station, call ☎ 1850-366222, or visit **www.irishrail.ie.**

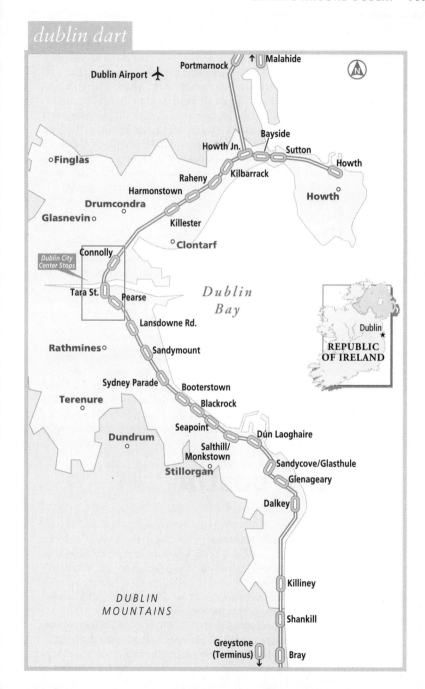

dublin dart

Dublin Airport ✈
Portmarnock
↑ Malahide

Bayside
Howth Jn.
Sutton
Finglas
Raheny
Kilbarrack
Howth
Harmonstown
Howth
Drumcondra
Killester
Glasnevin
Clontarf
Dublin City Center Stops
Connolly
Dublin Bay
Tara St.
Pearse
Lansdowne Rd.
Rathmines
Sandymount
Dublin
Terenure
Sydney Parade
Booterstown
Blackrock
Seapoint
Dún Laoghaire
Dundrum
Salthill/Monkstown
Stillorgan
Sandycove/Glasthule
Glenageary
Dalkey
DUBLIN MOUNTAINS
Killiney
Shankill
Greystone (Terminus)
Bray

REPUBLIC OF IRELAND
Dublin ★

BY LUAS

THIS NEW STREETCAR SYSTEM LINKS central Dublin with surrounding areas, and it also provides a handy way to get from Heuston Station to the O'Connell Street area and Connolly Station. The system is a bit frustrating because it is not citywide. There are two LUAS lines, one from St. Stephen's Green to Sandyford in the southern suburbs and one from Connolly Station to Tallaght in the southwest suburbs, but the two don't intersect—meaning, for instance, that you can't get from Heuston or Connolly Station to St. Stephen's Green on LUAS. Plus, the trams run on city streets, not necessarily alleviating congestion. Fares begin at €1.40 (that's what it costs to travel between Heuston and Connolly stations). For more information, call ☎ 01-703-2029 or go to **www.luas.ie.**

unofficial **TIP**
Traffic in Dublin can make travel by taxi excruciatingly slow and even more expensive, because the meters click to fractions of miles as well as to fractions of minutes.

BY TAXI

YOU'LL FIND TAXI RANKS AROUND the city center, especially near the larger hotels. Fares aren't cheap, though—expect to pay about €10 to get from St. Stephen's Green to O'Connell Street. To call a cab, try **Access** and **Metro** (☎ 01-668-333) or **VIP** (☎ 01-478-3333).

BY CAR

DON'T EVEN THINK OF IT. Traffic is terrible, the one-way grid confounding, parking sometimes hard to find. If for some reason you choose to bring a car into the city center, stash it in a car park and leave it there. You'll find handy facilities at St. Stephen's Green West on the South Side and Abbey Street on the North Side for about €2 an hour, up to about €20 for 24 hours. Some hotels provide garages, as noted in our hotel listings.

HOTELS *in* DUBLIN

GOOD NEWS ON THE DUBLIN HOTEL FRONT: Rooms are plentiful; you have a wide choice of places to stay, from modest bed-and-breakfasts to sophisticated contemporary showcases; and prices have not yet caught up with those in New York, London, and other cities that draw visitors from around the world. That said, here are some do's and don'ts to keep in mind:

- *Do* expect good service and clean surroundings. These are hallmarks of Irish hospitality, so don't settle for less.
- *Do* check weekend packages (often providing a room for two nights and a dinner) and other special rates; hotel Web sites are the best places to find them. Some chain hotels and the more expensive lodgings offer good-value weekend rates; you might consider spending

the weekend in luxury and then moving down a notch or two during the week.

- *Don't* bring a car. Only a few city-center hotels provide parking, fees are high (about €20 a day), traffic is awful, and you can get around easily on foot and via public transportation.

- *Do* make sure breakfast and all taxes and service fees are included in the price you are quoted; these extras can add a lot to your bill.

CHOOSING YOUR LOCALE

CENTRAL DUBLIN IS SMALL ENOUGH that just about any city-center hotel will put you within easy reach of most major attractions. Hotels in the **Central Dublin** vicinity are close to Connolly Station, O'Connell Street shopping, and the Abbey and Gate theaters. Those in the **Trinity College and Temple Bar** neighborhood are in the heart of the action—handy when you want to pop round the corner for a pint, annoying when you have to step around a pile of unconscious, inebriated youths from Northern Europe. Hotels in the **Grafton Street, St. Stephen's Green, and Georgian Dublin** area tend to have the toniest addresses, on and off the streets of Georgian Dublin; many, in fact, occupy charmingly historic houses. This neighborhood is convenient, too: many of Dublin's best restaurants are in this part of town, as are the fashionable Grafton Street shops and sights such as the National Gallery of Ireland. A hotel in the **Dublin Castle and Cathedrals** neighborhood is convenient to Christ Church and other historic landmarks and within close range of Temple Bar, while staying in **Ballsbridge** removes you from the action—you'll have to take a bus or DART to get to most places you want to go.

THE CHAIN GANG

MANY INTERNATIONAL HOTEL GROUPS have followed the clarion call of Dublin's new prosperity and opened up shop in Dublin. To the standard list of comforts and amenities, all add the stamp of Irish hospitality.

CONRAD HOTEL This commanding brick-and-glass presence on a corner of St. Stephen's Green has recently been spiffed up, bringing its small guest rooms up to a high standard of comfort. 191 units, from about €200. Earlsfort Terrace, Dublin 2; ☎ 01-676-5555; fax 01-676-5424; **www.conradhotels.com;** buses 10, 11, 13, 14, 15, 44, 46A, 47, 48, 86.

DAYS INN TALBOT STREET A chain with chic: contemporary furnishings, mellow lighting, lots of blond wood, a patio, and a handy central location near shops and transportation. 60 units, from about €90. 95–98 Talbot Street, Dublin 1; ☎ 01-874-9202; fax 01-874-9672; **www.daysinntalbot.com;** all city-center buses.

HILTON DUBLIN Views over the Grand Canal and a swath of greenery belie the fact that the city center is just minutes away. 189 units, from

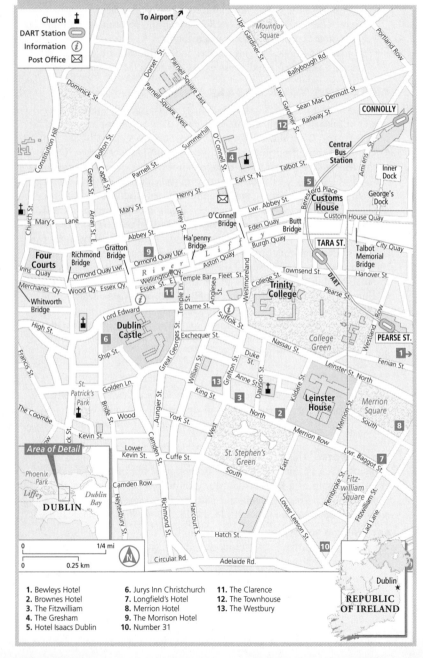

dublin accommodations

Legend:
- Church †
- DART Station ⬭
- Information ⓘ
- Post Office ✉

Landmarks: To Airport, Mountjoy Square, Portland Row, Upr. Gardiner St., Ballybough Rd., Dominick St., Dorset St., Parnell Square East, Parnell Square West, Summerhill, O'Connell St., Sean Mac Dermott St., CONNOLLY, Railway St., Lwr. Gardiner St., Constitution Hill, Bolton St., Green St., Capel St., Parnell St., Henry St., Earl St. N., Talbot St., Central Bus Station, Amiens St., Inner Dock, Church St., Mary's Lane, Arran St. E., Mary St., Lwr. Abbey St., Berresford Place, Customs House, Custom House Quay, George's Dock, O'Connell Bridge, Eden Quay, Butt Bridge, Four Courts, Inns Quay, Richmond Bridge, Gratton Bridge, Ormond Quay Upr., Ha'penny Bridge, Liffey, Burgh Quay, TARA ST., Talbot Memorial Bridge, City Quay, Merchants Qy., Wood Qy., Essex Qy., Ormond Quay Lwr., River, Wellington Qy., Essex St. E., Temple Bar, Fleet St., Aston Quay, Westmoreland, College St., Townsend St., Hanover St., Whitworth Bridge, Lord Edward St., Dame St., Anglesea St., Temple Ln. St., Suffolk St., Trinity College, Pearse St., DART, PEARSE ST., High St., Dublin Castle, Great Georges St., Exchequer St., Nassau St., College Green, Westland Row, Fenian St., Ship St., Francis St., St. Patrick's Park, Golden Ln., Bride St., Wood, William St., King St., Grafton St., Anne St., Dawson St., Duke St., Kildare St., Leinster St. North, Leinster House, Merrion Square North, Merrion Square South, The Coombe, Kevin St., Aungier St., York St., West, North, Merrion Row, Merrion St., Lwr. Baggot St., Lower Kevin St., Cuffe St., St. Stephen's Green, East, South, Pembroke St., Fitzwilliam Square, Fitzwilliam St., Lad Lane, Camden St., Camden Row, Heytesbury St., Richmond St., Harcourt S., Lower Leeson St., Hatch St., Circular Rd., Adelaide Rd.

Area of Detail: Phoenix Park, Liffey, Dublin Bay, DUBLIN

Scale: 0 — 1/4 mi / 0 — 0.25 km

Dublin ★, REPUBLIC OF IRELAND

1. Bewleys Hotel
2. Brownes Hotel
3. The Fitzwilliam
4. The Gresham
5. Hotel Isaacs Dublin
6. Jurys Inn Christchurch
7. Longfield's Hotel
8. Merrion Hotel
9. The Morrison Hotel
10. Number 31
11. The Clarence
12. The Townhouse
13. The Westbury

How Hotels Compare in Dublin

HOTEL	OVERALL	QUALITY	VALUE	PRICE
The Fitzwilliam	★★★★½	★★★★½	★★★★	€215–€450
Merrion Hotel	★★★★½	★★★★½	★★★	€370–€470
The Clarence	★★★★	★★★★½	★★★★	from €340
The Morrison Hotel	★★★★	★★★★½	★★★	from €285
Number 31	★★★★	★★★★	★★★★½	€110–€150
The Westbury	★★★★	★★★★	★★★	€340–€380
Bewleys Hotel	★★★½	★★★½	★★★★½	€99
Brownes Hotel	★★★	★★★★	★★★	€185–€270
Jurys Inn Christchurch	★★★	★★★	★★★★	€98–€140
Hotel Isaacs Dublin	★★★	★★½	★★★★	from €50
Longfield's Hotel	★★★	★★½	★★★	€99–€165
The Townhouse	★★	★★★	★★★★	€60–€102
The Gresham	★★	★–★★★	★★★	€100–€350

about €110. Charlemont Place, Dublin 2; ☎ 01-402-9988; fax 01-402-9966; **www.dublin.hilton.com;** LUAS: Grand Canal.

THE WESTIN DUBLIN An imposing 19th-century bank building lends such features as a grand facade and distinctive public spaces (including the Mint bar, tucked away in the former bank vaults). This is the most grown-up place to stay near Temple Bar. 164 units, from about €215. College Green, Dublin 2; ☎ 01-645-1000; fax 01-645-1234; **www.westin.com/dublin;** buses 5, 7A, 10, 11, 11A, 11B, 13A, 13B.

HOTEL PROFILES

Bewleys Hotel ★ ★ ★ ½

QUALITY ★★★½	VALUE ★★★★½	€99

Merrion Road, Dublin 4, Ballsbridge; ☎ 01-668-1111; fax 01-668-1999; ballsbridge@bewleyshotels.com; www.bewleyshotels.com

Location Ballsbridge. **Buses** 7, 45; DART: Sandymount. **Amenities and services** 304 units; Internet access, hair dryers, in-room safes, in-room tea and coffee facilities, irons and ironing boards, restaurant, trouser press. **Elevator** Yes. **Parking** On property; free for 3 hours, €6.35 per day. **Price** Full Irish breakfast, €8.95; à la carte breakfast also available. **Credit cards** AE, DC, MC, V.

Ballsbridge is an attractive Dublin neighborhood, a bastion of tree-shaded streets lined with swanky homes, embassies, and corporate headquarters. The out-of-city-center location makes the neighborhood less than ideal as a place to stay, but if you're trying to save euros, you may want to make an exception for Bewleys. This snazzy outlet in a small but popular chain occupies an old school to which a new wing has been seamlessly attached, providing comfortable, no-nonsense accommodations at a very good price. Bewleys is an especially good choice for guests traveling with children—family suites have living areas with pullout couches and kitchenettes, and sleep up to two adults and three children; plus, the grounds provide a place where little ones can run off steam. The excellent in-house restaurant, O'Connell's, is run by Tom O'Connell, part of the culinarily inspired clan that operates Ballymaloe, the famous cooking school, restaurant, and hotel. You'll find other Bewleys in Newland's Cross west of the city center (☎ 01-464-0140), in outlying Leopardstown (☎ 01-293-5000), and at Dublin Airport (☎ 01-871-1000); the Ballsbridge Bewleys is the most convenient to the city center.

Brownes Hotel ★ ★ ★

QUALITY ★★★★	VALUE ★★★	€185–€270

22 St. Stephen's Green, Dublin 2, St. Stephen's Green; ☎ 01-638-3939; fax 01-638-3900; info@brownesdublin.com; www.brownesdublin.com

Location On St. Stephen's Green. **Buses** 10, 11A, 11B, 13, 20B; DART: Pearse. **Amenities and services** 11 units; bar, CD players, cable TV, Internet access, restaurant. **Elevator** Yes. **Parking** In nearby car parks, about €25 per day. **Price** Includes full Irish breakfast. **Credit cards** AE, MC, V.

This small, rather quirky hotel in a Georgian mansion has a lot going for it, including the genuine feeling of being in a private home, a handy location on the north side of St. Stephen's Green, and an ornate and charming bistro of the same name. Despite its small size, Brownes takes the hotel side of the business seriously. These luxurious quarters are the most comfortable of the many townhouse hotels in this part of Dublin, and a small but skilled staff adeptly sees to the needs of guests. The hotel has no public lounges aside from a small cocktail lounge adjoining the restaurant, but the spacious rooms adeptly serve as sitting rooms as well as bedrooms, with comfortable reading chairs and writing desks. Retaining marble fireplaces, ornate plasterwork, and other original detailing, they are tastefully and comfortably furnished (if you splurge on the junior suite, you can sleep in a king-size Murphy bed once owned by Marilyn Monroe). Rooms in front overlook the green through double-glazed windows.

kids The Clarence ★ ★ ★ ★

QUALITY ★★★★½	VALUE ★★★★	FROM €340

6–8 Wellington Quay, Dublin 2, Temple Bar; ☎ 01-407-0800; fax 01-407-0820; reservations@theclarence.ie; www.theclarence.ie

Location On the River Liffey, at the edge of Temple Bar. **Buses** 51B, 51C, 68, 69, 79. **Amenities and services** 48 units; bar, bathrobes, DVD/CD players, hair dryers, high-speed Internet access, in-room entertainment, laundry and dry cleaning, minibars, 24-hour room service, 2 telephone lines. **Elevator** Yes. **Parking** Valet, €25 per day. **Price** Includes full Irish breakfast; many special offers available, including dinner and bed-and-breakfast packages. **Credit cards** AE, DC, MC, V.

An old Dublin hostelry that had fallen on hard times by the 1990s, the Clarence is now owned by the Irish rock band U2. One doesn't necessarily equate rockers with sensible comfort, but that is exactly what this lovely hotel achieves. The décor complements the original Arts and Crafts details: light oak paneling, Shaker-style furnishings, and gentle neutral tones create a soothing environment throughout the public areas and guest rooms. Thoughtful lighting, large writing desks, state-of-the-art entertainment systems, and fine towels and bed linens all create a retreat that you will find hard to leave—all the more so given that most rooms have nice outlooks (rooms in front of the hotel overlook the river, while the quieter rear-facing rooms look across the rooftops of old Dublin) and many on the top floor open to small balconies. The Octagon Bar and the Study are popular meeting places, and the Tea Room (see page 159) is one of Dublin's finest restaurants. As adult as the Clarence is, it still welcomes kids, catering to them with milk and cookies, video games, and other amenities.

The Fitzwilliam   ★ ★ ★ ★ ½

QUALITY ★★★★½	VALUE ★★★★	€215–€450

St. Stephen's Green, Dublin 2, St. Stephen's Green; ☎ 01-478-7000; fax 01-478-7878; enq@fitzwilliamhotel.com; www.fitzwilliamhotel.com

Location On St. Stephen's Green. **Buses** 10, 11A, 11B, 13, 20B; DART: Pearse. **Amenities and services** 128 units; bar, beauty salon, CD players, cafe, concierge, in-room entertainment, in-room tea and coffee facilities, Internet access, restaurant, roof garden, spa treatments, 2 telephones. **Elevator** Yes. **Parking** In nearby car parks, about €25 per day. **Price** Breakfast included in some rates; many special offers and packages available. **Credit cards** AE, DC, MC, V.

Sir Terrence Conran, the British purveyor of contemporary good taste, designed the interiors of this attractive hotel, and he had good space to work with—large, light-filled public areas and guest rooms face either St. Stephen's Green or a roof garden at the rear of the hotel. Sir Terrence's stamp is much in evidence where clean lines, neutral tones, and natural fabrics create stylish and restful surroundings. Many amenities and thoughtful touches, such as large tubs, separate showers, fluffy towels and bathrobes, and fresh-cut flowers, ensure a great deal of comfort. While the views over the green are wonderful, those onto the large roof garden are extremely pleasant, too, and provide a sense of escape from the city hubbub. Many rooms take advantage of these outlooks from small balconies. Citron Café serves light meals, Inn on the Green is the snug bar, and Thornton's is one of the city's finest restaurants.

The Gresham   ★ ★

QUALITY ★–★★★	VALUE ★★★	€100–€350

23 Upper O'Connell Street, Dublin 1, Central Dublin; ☎ 01-874-6881; fax 01-878-7175; info@thegresham.com; www.gresham-hotels.com

Location In city center, north of the River Liffey. **Buses** All city-center buses; DART: Tara Street. **Amenities and services** 288 units; bars, fitness center, laundry service, lobby lounge, restaurant, some smoking rooms. **Elevator** Yes. **Parking** On premises, €12.50 per day. **Price** Some rates include full Irish breakfast; special offers available. **Credit cards** AE, DC, MC, V.

Dublin's most famous hotel lives up to its reputation in a series of grand public rooms, especially the sprawling lobby lounge and a stylish restaurant, 23. The lobby lounge is a popular and extremely appealing meeting place in downtown Dublin; here you can sit on plush couches and enjoy tea and light snacks while watching the passersby on busy O'Connell Street. Sadly, the guest rooms are in a rather sorry state. Some have not been updated in what looks to be decades and are about as dreary as rooms in a hostel. Those in the newer Lavery Wing are better cared for and geared to business travelers, but these contain fairly bland décor and furnishings. On the plus side, bathrooms in this wing are new and convenient, and service throughout the hotel is attentive and efficient. Better still, rumors are afoot that the Gresham is on the block and may soon be bought and totally renovated—that would be a welcome turn of events.

Hotel Isaacs Dublin   ★ ★ ★

QUALITY ★ ★ ½	VALUE ★ ★ ★ ★	FROM €50

Store Street, Dublin 1, Central Dublin; ☎ 01-813-4700; fax 01-836-5390; hotel@isaacs.ie; www.isaacs.ie

Location Central Dublin, near O'Connell Street and Connolly Street train station. **Buses** 27A, 27B, 53A; DART: Connolly Station. **Amenities and services** 90 units; air-conditioning in some rooms, bar, e-mail facilities, garden, hair dryers, in-room safes, in-room tea and coffee facilities, irons and ironing boards, nonsmoking rooms, restaurant, trouser press. **Elevator** Yes. **Parking** In nearby car parks, about €20 per day. **Price** Many special rates available, some including breakfast; otherwise, breakfast available from about €10 (best to find a bite in the neighborhood). **Credit cards** MC, V.

The most important thing to know about this outlet of an Irish chain is that you should book far, far in advance, because it's no secret that these are some of the best-value lodgings in town. (You might also keep in mind that it's the hotel you want and not the adjacent hostel of the same name.) The grandiose lobby suggests the place is a bit fancier than it really is, but the guest rooms are surprisingly attractive, in a generic hotel/motel sort of way, plus they are immaculate and equipped with shiny tile bathrooms. Rooms facing the street can be noisy, and the pleasant staff always seems a bit overworked, but there are more pluses here than minuses. A leafy courtyard is a nice oasis in this hectic neighborhood; a restaurant, bar, and Internet cafe supply the essentials; and the O'Connell Street shops, as well as the airport bus and other transportation links, are just a few blocks away.

Jurys Inn Christchurch   ★ ★ ★

QUALITY ★ ★ ★	VALUE ★ ★ ★ ★	€98–€140

**Christ Church Place, Dublin 8, Dublin Castle and the Cathedrals;
☎ 01-454-0000; fax 01-454-0012; info@jurys-dublin-hotels.com;
www.jurys-dublin-hotels.com**

Location Near Temple Bar, across from Christ Church Cathedral. **Buses** 21A, 50, 50A, 78, 78A, 78B. **Amenities and services** 182 units; bar, coffee bar, hair dryers, in-room tea and coffee facilities, laundry, nonsmoking rooms, restaurant. **Elevator** Yes. **Parking** In nearby car park, about €11.50 a day. **Price** Breakfast about €5. **Credit cards** AE, MC, V.

This chain hotel gives guests a lot for their money. The location, across from Christ Church Cathedral, provides a convenient base for exploring all of central Dublin; you can walk just about anywhere or hop on one of the many buses that pass just outside the door. While the guest rooms are a bit bland in their standard-issue faux-traditional furnishings, they are spacious and bright, and many have scenic views over the cathedral and other historic buildings. All rooms are equipped with two beds, or a bed and a pullout couch, and can accommodate three adults or two adults and two children. Rates are per room rather than per person, so Jurys is quite economical—you'll have a hard time finding lodging of this quality at this price elsewhere in Dublin, with the exceptions of several other Jurys around town. Other convenient locations in central Dublin are Jurys Inn Custom House (Custom House Quay, Dublin 1; ☎ 01-607-5000) and Jurys Inn Parnell Street (Moore Street Plaza, Parnell Street, Dublin 1; ☎ 01-878-4900). Whichever one you choose, book early, because Jurys is justifiably popular.

Longfield's Hotel   ★ ★ ★

QUALITY ★ ★ ½	VALUE ★ ★ ★	€99–€165

**10 Lower Fitzwilliam Street, Dublin 2, Georgian Dublin; ☎ 01-676-1367;
fax 01-676-1542; info@longfields.ie; www.longfields.ie**

Location Between Fitzwilliam and Merrion squares. **Buses** 11, 11A, 11B, 13B. **Amenities and services** 23 units; bar service, in-room tea and coffee facilities, Internet access, restaurant. **Elevator** Yes. **Parking** In nearby car parks, about €20 a day. **Price** Includes full Irish breakfast. **Credit cards** AE, DC, MC, V.

An old-world ambience prevails in these two interconnected houses in the heart of Georgian Dublin. Traditional furnishings, high ceilings, and old-fashioned wallpaper lend an air of nonfussy comfort to the lounges and bedrooms and do justice to the surroundings. A little more fussiness might be in order, though: plumbing does not always operate at top form, and soiled bedspreads and worn carpets aren't acceptable, especially given the prices charged. Some general refurbishment and the addition of a few more amenities—maybe minibars and on-premises e-mail facilities—would make a stay here more comfortable. One recent addition is Longchamps, an excellent restaurant on the ground floor of the hotel. Keep in mind when booking that bedrooms vary considerably in size (some are large enough to accommodate four-poster beds, while those on the top floor are quite small), and most bathrooms are equipped with showers only.

Merrion Hotel   ★ ★ ★ ★ ½

| QUALITY | ★ ★ ★ ★ ½ | VALUE | ★ ★ ★ | €370–€470 |

Upper Merrion Street, Dublin 2, Georgian Dublin; ☎ 01-603-0600; fax 01-603-0700; info@merrionhotel.com; www.merrionhotel.com

Location In Georgian Dublin, near government buildings. **Buses** 5, 7A, 13A. **Amenities and services** 142 units; babysitting, bar, broadband Internet access, CD players, concierge, gym, hair dryers, in-room fax machines, in-room safes, laundry service, minibars, 2 restaurants, satellite and cable TV, spa, steam room, swimming pool, 3 telephones in each room, trouser press, 24-hour room service. **Elevator** Yes. **Parking** Free valet. **Price** Continental breakfast, €22; Irish breakfast, €27; many special offers available. **Credit cards** AE, DC, MC, V.

Dublin's most luxurious hotel consists of four Georgian townhouses and, beyond large formal gardens, a stylish contemporary wing. One of the country's most extensive private collections of 19th- and 20th-century Irish art hangs in the public lounges, where fires burn beneath original ornate plasterwork, and the efficient staff seems to appear out of thin air to provide superb service. Large and gracious guest rooms are traditionally yet stylishly furnished. Swathed in yards of luxurious Irish fabrics, they cater to comforts that guests weren't aware of desiring (three telephones?), and many, such as huge walk-in showers, to which it is quite easy to become accustomed. A beautiful swimming pool and excellent spa lend a resortlike air to the urbane surroundings. The Merrion manages to pull off all this pampering without pretense, creating a truly great hotel. Should you be lucky enough to stay here, have a meal in the hotel dining room, Restaurant Patrick Guilbaud (page 159), which—not surprisingly, given where it is—is the best in town.

The Morrison Hotel   ★ ★ ★ ★

| QUALITY | ★ ★ ★ ★ ½ | VALUE | ★ ★ ★ | FROM | €285 |

Ormond Quay, Dublin 1, Central Dublin; ☎ 01-887-2400; fax 01-874-4039; sales@morrisonhotel.ie; www.morrisonhotel.ie

Location On the north side of the River Liffey. **Buses** 70, 80; DART: Tara Street. **Amenities and services** 148 units; bar, cafe, CD players, in-room safes, Internet access, minibars, restaurant, room service, spa. **Elevator** Yes. **Parking** In nearby car park, about €20 a day. **Price** À la carte breakfast from about €7; many special offers available. **Credit cards** AE, DC, MC, V.

The "cool" quotient is not necessarily the best criterion for a good hotel, but this creation of Irish designer John Rocha proves that a hotel can be stylish, edgy, and extremely comfortable all at the same time. Rocha had the good sense to expend his theatrics in the glamorous and colorful public rooms (including the excellent Halo restaurant; see page 155) and to use a spare hand in the guest quarters, many of which have river views. There, minimalist surroundings of modern furniture, natural fabrics, and warm tones of cream and brown create environments that are both soothing and exciting—it's a pleasure to kick off your shoes and bask in the ambience (or soak in one of the deep tubs). When you're ready to hit the streets, you'll discover the advantages of this location north of the Liffey: O'Connell Street shops are a short stroll away, as are many of the museums and other attractions south of the river, yet you are comfortably removed from the noisy antics of Temple Bar, just across the river.

Number 31 ★ ★ ★ ★

QUALITY ★ ★ ★ ★	VALUE ★ ★ ★ ★ ½	€110–€150

31 Leeson Close, Dublin 2, Georgian Dublin; ☎ 01-676-5011; fax 01-676-2929; number31@iol.ie; www.number31.ie

Location South of St. Stephen's Green. **Buses** 11, 11A, 11B, 13, 13A. **Amenities and services** 20 rooms; garden, in-room tea and coffee facilities, lounge. **Elevator** No. **Parking** Free private car park. **Price** Includes full Irish breakfast. **Credit cards** AE, MC, V.

For those willing to forgo the services of a full-scale hotel, Noel and Deirdre Comer's distinctive and extremely appealing guest house (composed of a coach house and a Georgian terrace house, separated by a lush garden) should be among the top choices for a place to stay in central Dublin. The coach house bears the mark of a previous owner, Sam Stephenson, one of Ireland's leading 20th-century architects. The stunning interior is pleasantly contemporary, with a sunken conversation pit surrounding a fireplace where aromatic peat is usually burning. Brick walls are painted in soothing tones of white and cream, tile floors are covered with kilims, windows are tall, and a conservatory breakfast room opens to a roof garden. The five rooms in this wing have an informal feel to them, with low wooden ceilings and, in several, small sitting areas that open to private patios. The large, high-ceilinged rooms in the Georgian house, reached through the rear garden or a separate entrance on Fitzwilliam Street, are decorated in an uncluttered traditional style with contemporary touches; those facing the garden are blessedly quiet. Breakfast, which includes treats such as homemade potato cakes and cranberry bread, is as memorable as the other ingredients of a stay in this wonderful place.

The Townhouse ★ ★

QUALITY ★ ★ ★	VALUE ★ ★ ★ ★	€60–€102

47–48 Lower Gardiner Street, Dublin 1, Central Dublin; ☎ 01-878-8808; fax 01-878-8787; info@townhouseofdublin.com; www.townhouseofdublin.com

Location Central Dublin, near train and bus stations. **Buses** 27A, 27B, 53A; DART: Connolly Station. **Amenities and services** 30 units; garden, hair dryers, in-room tea and coffee facilities, lounge. **Elevator** Yes. **Parking** In nearby car parks, about €20 a day. **Price** Includes full Irish breakfast. **Credit cards** MC, V.

A convenient location near the bus and train stations and the very reasonable rates account for the appeal of this popular bed-and-breakfast that sprawls through two Georgian houses (the former homes of two 19th-century playwrights, Lafcadio Hearn and Dion Boucicault) and a new extension. While the lounge and the rooms in the older wings bear the mark of this heritage with dark, traditional décor, the rooms in the new wing are surprisingly contemporary and chic—the wood floors, handsome furnishings, fluffy duvets, and well-appointed bathrooms would pass muster in a more expensive hotel. Keep in mind, though, that a few shortcomings do come with the low prices. The same management operates the adjoining hostel, so the public areas are always busy and the small staff is perpetually on the run (service is efficient but can be brusque). Rooms facing busy Gardiner Street as well as the garden (a popular gathering spot for guests at the hostel) can be noisy, and apart from the convenience of being near the airport link and other transportation, the busy, traffic-ridden neighborhood is not as appealing as others in Dublin.

The Westbury ★ ★ ★ ★

QUALITY ★★★★	VALUE ★★★	€340–€380

Grafton Street, Dublin 2, Grafton Street; ☎ 01-679-1122; fax 01-679-7078; westbury@jurysdoyle.com; www.jurysdoyle.com

Location In city center, off Grafton Street and near St. Stephen's Green. **Buses** 10, 11A, 11B, 13, 20B. **Amenities and services** 210 units; babysitting, bar, business services, concierge, gym, in-room entertainment, in-room safes, laundry, minibars, restaurant. **Elevator** Yes. **Parking** On property, free. **Price** Some packages include buffet breakfast; many special offers available. **Credit cards** AE, DC, MC, V.

This modern, rather nondescript building announces itself as one of Dublin's poshest hostelries by its privileged location, on a cul-de-sac just off Grafton Street. For many guests, the elegant lobby and well-appointed suites and guest rooms are the ultimate in graciousness. Bright, spacious, and beautifully furnished in traditional style with large desks and comfortable lounge chairs, they are sumptuous and appealing. The 25 so-called executive rooms are especially large, and depending on availability, you can upgrade to these for a relatively small extra charge. An attentive staff takes very good care of guests, ensuring that business execs and leisure travelers alike have everything they need. The only element lacking at the Westbury is pizzazz; a new crop of hotels, including the nearby Fitzgerald, provide similar levels of comfort with a little more dazzle.

EXPLORING DUBLIN

DUBLIN IS COMPACT—a pleasure to explore on foot and easy to navigate by public transportation. However you get around, the city will keep you entertained, enthralled even, but won't overwhelm you.

TOURS OF DUBLIN

THESE TOURS SHOW OFF THE BEST sides of Dublin and treat you to a uniquely Irish gift for gab. Many tours can fill up quickly during summer months, so book as far in advance as you can.

ᴛY SIGHTSEEING AND DUBLIN CITY TOURS Both outfits
ᵖp-on, hop-off schemes, with stops at 14 or so major attrac-
ɑnd the city and either canned or live commentary (the latter
ᵘunds as canned as the taped version). The convenience of
ᵗs, which are virtually identical, is that you can ride around
oying the view from an open-top bus, and get off whenever
like visiting a sight. Tickets are good for 24 hours. You
quite a bit of sightseeing into a full day or, better, an after-
ɑ the following morning (this gives you a chance to rest up
between bouts). The tours include stops outside the city center—at
Guinness Storehouse, Kilmainham Gaol, and Phoenix Park, among
other attractions—so concentrate on those to get the most bang for
your euro; you can reach the city-center sights on foot. Buy tickets
from Dublin Tourism, from vendors at some of the well-marked
stops, or on the buses. City Sightseeing Tours start at 14 Upper
O'Connell Street and cost €15 for adults, €6 for children ages 5 to 15,
free for children under age 5, €12.50 for seniors and students, €35 for
families; ☎ 01-872-9010 or **www.citysightseeing.com.** Dublin City
Tours start at 59 Upper O'Connell Street and cost €14 for adults,
€6 children under age 14, €12.50 for seniors and students; ☎ 01-873-
4222 or **www.dublinbus.ie.**

DUBLIN LITERARY PUB CRAWL Dublin produced three Nobel
Prize–winning authors—Samuel Beckett, George Bernard Shaw,
and William Butler Yeats—as well as many literary geniuses who
were not so rewarded (James Joyce and Brendan Behan come to mind).
At one time or another, most Dublin writers found inspiration at the
bottom of a pint glass in the hundreds of pubs around the city, and
you can follow in their footsteps to enjoy the *craic* and literary ambience of four famous writerly haunts. Visits are accompanied by
recitations and a bit of song. Tours start at the Duke Pub, 9 Duke
Street, Dublin 2, Temple Bar; April to November, 7:30 p.m. daily and
12:30 p.m. Sunday; December to March, 7:30 p.m. Thursday through
Sunday; €12 adults, €10 students; ☎ 01-670-5602 to reserve or go to
www.dublinpubcrawl.com.

HISTORICAL WALKING TOURS OF DUBLIN Walking through Dublin
with these locals who know their history inside and out is a pleasure,
and it's one of the best ways to get to know the city. Tours concentrate on some places you might otherwise rush by to get to leafier
precincts or more-appealing streets: the Old Parliament House, City
Hall, and the like. The guides are history buffs and graduates of Trinity College, and as they speak about the 1916 Easter Uprising and
other events with flare and ease, they put the complexities of Irish
and Dublin history into welcome perspective. The two-hour tours
meet at the front gate of Trinity College, College Green, Dublin 2;
May to September, 11 a.m. and 3 p.m. daily; April and October,

Walks and Drives around Dublin

From the capital, it's easy to get away from it all into seascape, mountain wilderness, and history-filled countryside.

GREAT WALKS

HOWTH HEAD

Only 15 minutes from central Dublin yet more like a seaside village than a suburb, Howth is justifiably popular with Dubliners in search of a breath of sea air or a splash in the chilly waters of the Irish Sea. Walkers can get even more of a sense of getting away from urban life on the paths that skirt the shorelines and climb the summits of the Howth Peninsula (see also page 171).

The DART station is at the edge of **Howth Harbour,** a busy port that shelters fishing fleets and pleasure craft. A cliff path begins near the **East Pier;** once you round the **Nose of Howth,** you will soon find yourself in a remote-seeming seascape that combines heather-covered moors and a rocky coast that is home to huge colonies of seabirds and seals. A walk of about half an hour will bring you to **Baily Lighthouse** on the southern side of the peninsula. If you want to extend the walk to a half-day's excursion, you can follow the sea as far as the **Martello Tower,** one of 27 such watchtowers the British built along the east coast of Ireland in the early 19th century to help thwart a possible French invasion. From there, make the climb to **Ben of Howth,** the peninsula's 170-meter (510-foot) summit from which views extend to the Wicklow Mountains to the south and the Mourne Mountains to the north, then descend the side of the summit back toward Howth.

BRAY HEAD

An especially beautiful and dramatic stretch of coastal scenery lies between **Bray** and **Greystones,** south of Dublin. Both towns are suburban, and both also have the flair of popular seaside retreats, with beaches and boardwalk-type amusements. Both towns are on the DART line from Dublin; for the best views, take the train to its terminus at Greystones, walk north to Bray, and catch a DART train back to Dublin there. Linking Greystones and Bray is a well-trodden ten-kilometer (six-mile) coastal path, full of views across Dublin

11 a.m. daily; November to March, 11 a.m. Friday through Sunday. You can purchase tickets at the meeting point: €10 adults, €8 seniors and students. For more information, call ☎ 01-878-0227 or go to **www.historicalinsights.ie.**

MUSIC PUB CRAWL Want to spend some time in Dublin pubs? Want to hear some good traditional music? Want to learn about those strange instruments you see folks playing? Know the stories behind some of the songs you hear around Ireland? Then sign on to one of these pleasant

Bay to **Howth Head, Bray Head,** and the twin summits of **Little Sugar Loaf** and **Great Sugar Loaf** to the west. Leave the coastal path for a short climb up the heather-covered hillsides of Bray Head to a viewpoint with a stunning outlook. You can reward yourself at the end of the walk with a dip in the sea at **Bray Beach** or with a tip of the elbow in any number of pubs in Bray.

ALONG THE WICKLOW WAY

The Wicklow Way, one of Ireland's finest walking paths, extends for 137 kilometers (85 miles), from **Marlay Park** on the south side of Dublin through the Wicklow Mountains to the village of **Clonegall** in County Carlow. Several companies and clubs in Dublin organize walks along the way, allowing you a chance to experience the moor-and-mountain scenery on a day's excursion (see page 178). If you want to get a taste of the way on your own, you can take the number 16 bus from O'Connell Street to Marlay Park and then follow the way into **Kilmashogue Wood** and up the flanks of **Kilmashogue Mountain;** enjoy the views over Dublin Bay from one of the viewpoints, and backtrack to Marlay Park. For a more rewarding walk, drive or take the bus to **Glendalough,** and from there follow the way as it passes the **Upper and Lower lakes,** the **Pollnass Waterfall,** and the beautiful monastic remains (see page 178). The **Wicklow Mountains National Park Visitor Centre** at Glendalough provides maps and information on walking the way and other trails.

GREAT DRIVES

THE BOYNE VALLEY

A relatively easy day's outing from Dublin exposes you to millennia of Irish history—from the fields where the Battle of the Boyne was fought in 1690 to the 5,000-year-old passage tombs at **Newgrange** to the seat of the medieval High Kings of Ireland at the **Hill of Tara.**

Leave Dublin to the north on M1 and follow this busy motorway about 32 kilometers (18 miles) to the turnoff for **Drogheda,** where you will pick up R132 east across the River Boyne to the Battle of the Boyne site. Here, in 1690, the

Continued on next page

expeditions departing from Oliver St. John Gogarty's (the upstairs bar) on Fleet Street. Two good-natured musicians take you to three pubs, play an assortment of instruments, sing a lot, and talk knowledgeably about the fine points of Irish music. Tours last about two and a half hours. All in all, a really good way to spend—or start—an evening. April to October, 7:30 p.m. daily; November to March, 7:30 p.m. Thursdays, Fridays, and Saturdays; €12 adults, €10 students; ☎ 01-478-0193 or reserve at the Dublin Tourism Office.

Walks and Drives around Dublin (continued)

GREAT DRIVES (CONTINUED)

THE BOYNE VALLEY (CONTINUED)

armies of the Protestant William of Orange defeated the forces of the Catholic James I. Excellent signage at the site will lead you to **King William's Glen,** where William's soldiers hid and launched their victorious surprise attack on James's armies, and to **Townley Hall Estate,** where walks through the forest lead you to overlooks of the valley where the battle was waged.

Some eight kilometers (five miles) west on N51 is **Slane,** a pretty village built around a castle and overlooked by the Hill of Slane, on which St. Patrick allegedly lit his paschal fire in AD 433, defying pagan King Laoghaire. Allegedly, the king allowed Patrick to preach Christianity after the saint brandished a shamrock to explain the mysteries of the Holy Trinity.

Newgrange (see page 176) is just three kilometers (two miles) south of Slane. This 5,000-year-old passage tomb is one of several prehistoric tombs and other archaeological sites collectively known as Brú na Bóinne, where the visitors center provides insight into the significance of some of the world's most impressive prehistoric structures.

Follow N51 12 kilometers (7.5 miles) west to Navan, and from there take R163 two kilometers (one mile) south to **Kells.** A round tower and the small, charming **St. Kevin's Church** are what remains of the great monastic complex that St. Colomba founded here in the sixth century AD. It is widely believed that Scottish monks brought the celebrated illuminated manuscript known as the **Book of Kells** to this monastic settlement, from which it was removed to Trinity College in Dublin and where it now resides in splendor (see page 131).

From Navan it's about ten kilometers (six miles) southeast on N3 to the **Hill of Tara** (see page 176), seat of the High Kings of Ireland through the pre-Christian centuries to as late as the 11th century. A climb up the grassy knoll towering over the site affords fine views of the surrounding plains.

A final stop on this history-filled itinerary is **Trim,** 15 kilometers (9 miles) west of the Hill of Tara on R154. Trim Castle is one of Ireland's finest medieval ruins, a huge Anglo-Norman complex that King Edward III fortified heavily in the 14th century. Oliver Cromwell attacked and destroyed the

VIKING SPLASH TOURS Driving around Dublin in a World War II–era amphibious vehicle is sort of silly. So is wearing a Viking helmet and roaring at passersby. Or splashing into a canal and floating past the apartments of rock stars. But the Viking folks pepper these antics with amusing and excellent commentary on city landmarks and history, and they deserve credit for proving that a tour can be informative without being stuffy. Tours last 75 minutes and run every half hour: February,

town and castle in 1649. Remnants include the keep, the turrets, portions of the outer wall, the nave and chancel of the cathedral, and, on the opposite banks of the River Boyne, the ruins of the Hospital of St. John the Baptist.

You can make a speedy return to Dublin from Trim on R154 and N3, a trip of about 50 kilometers (30 miles).

THROUGH THE WICKLOW MOUNTAINS

These mountains begin to rise in the southern suburbs of Dublin, providing city folks with a nearby retreat. In fact, the Wicklows encompass some of Ireland's most rugged scenery and also cradle monastic ruins and some charming villages.

Leave Dublin and head south on the M1, but you won't go far before you come to **Enniskerry,** a pretty village surrounding a square and a large 19th-century Gothic Revival church, but best known for **Powerscourt,** probably Ireland's most magnificent house and garden (see page 180).

From Enniskerry follow R755 through the forested mountains to **Round-wood,** notable not only for the mountain scenery that surrounds it but also for the fact that, at 250 meters (800 feet) above sea level, this small collection of houses surrounding a market square is the highest village in Ireland.

More spectacular scenery unfolds as you follow R759 and R115 deep into **Wicklow National Park** and through a pass in the mountain ridges known as **Sally Gap.** The road follows heather-covered hillsides through stands of pine and extensive bogs where peat is still cut for fuel. This stretch of road then passes high above **Glenmacnass,** a deep, impossibly green valley, at the end of which is the attractive village of **Laragh,** then **Glendalough** (see page 178). One of Ireland's most impressive medieval monastic communities, it is beautifully set in a valley beside a set of twin lakes.

You may want to return to Dublin by retracing your steps, so you can enjoy the scenery around Sally Gap again. Or head west on R756 and R758 for about 30 kilometers (18 miles), following the shores of **Blessington Lakes,** which is actually one large reservoir, **Poulaphouca,** which provides Dublin with its water. The village of **Blessington,** on the lakeshore, comprises an attractive assemblage of Georgian houses. From there you can return to Dublin on N81, a trip of about 50 kilometers (30 miles).

Wednesday through Sunday, 10 a.m. to 4 p.m.; March to October, daily, 9:30 a.m. to 5 p.m.; and November, Tuesday through Sunday, 10 a.m. to 4 p.m. €16 adults, €18 weekends in June and all of July and August; €8.95 children, €9.50 weekends in June and all of July and August; €52.50 for families of two adults and three children, €60 weekends in June and all of July and August; 64–65 Patrick Street, Dublin 8; ☎ 01-707-6000; **www.vikingsplashtours.com.**

walks and drives around dublin

REPUBLIC OF IRELAND

Dublin ★

N52
N2
R165
N33
Ardee R170
R166   Dunany
R170
R169   R170
N52
R168
R162
R163   N51
Ceanannus Mór   Slane
N3   Newgrange
N51
Navan   R150
R153   R152
Hill of Tara
R154   N2
Trim   R130
N3   R125
R160
R156   R121
N4
R403   R401

Drogheda

M1

Balbriggan

R127

Irish Sea

Swords Malahide
Malahide Castle

Howth

★ **DUBLIN**

M50

To Douglas →
To Liverpool & Mostyn →
To Holyhead →
To Holyhead →
To Cherbourg →

Ferry Route

0   10 mi
0   10 km

N7
R114   Brittas
Nass
R410
R759   R115
Blessington   Enniskerry
Powerscourt House
Kildare
N78
R415   N9
N81   Hollywood
R412
R756   Roundwood
Glendalough Abbey   Laragh
R418   R755   R752
Baltinglass

Dalkey
Loughlinstown
R117   **Bray**

N11

Wicklow

R418   R726
R727
N9   Tullow R725
R747   R747
R749   R748
R753
R747

Arklow

Great Walks
1. Howth Head
2. Bray Head
3. Along the Wicklow Way

Great Drives
4. The Boyne Valley
5. Through the Wicklow Mountains

DUBLIN WALKS

WALKING IS THE EASIEST WAY to get around Dublin and, given the number of fascinating places to see, a pleasure, even when holding an umbrella. Here's a look at the various neighborhoods and what to see on a walk through each of them. (For more on Dublin neighborhoods, see page 103.)

A Walk up O'Connell Street

To those who live here, known as Northsiders, this is the real Dublin, and O'Connell Street is the heart of the city. (Southsiders will make that claim about Grafton Street and St. Stephen's Green.) Begin your walk at the foot of O'Connell Street, on the River Liffey at **O'Connell Street Bridge.** A statue of Daniel O'Connell (1775–1847), a statesman and fighter for Catholic emancipation in Ireland, stands just a little ways up the street. He's overshadowed these days by the **Monument of Light,** a 120-meter (396-foot) steel pole that has inspired many rude names; one of the few that can be repeated in polite company is "stiletto in the ghetto." The **Abbey Theatre,** home of the Irish National Theatre, is just to the east, down Abbey Street (see page 160). Just north on O'Connell Street is the **General Post Office,** which became far more famous than its usual business warranted in 1916, when the building became the Republican command center of the Easter Uprising. Rebels stormed the building, issued the Proclamation of the Irish Republic, and held out against British troops for five days. Bullet holes still riddle the facade, and you can follow the events of the uprising (which led to the Anglo-Irish Treaty and independence for 26 counties of the Irish Free State in 1921) on the painting cycle in the lobby (open Monday through Saturday, 8 a.m. to 8 p.m.).

Henry Street, just beyond the post office, is one of many pedestrian-only thoroughfares in this part of town, leading to a European-looking outdoor market, on **Moore Street;** the stalls here (open Monday through Saturday, 8 a.m. to 6 p.m.) are far more colorful than their neighbors, the chain stores and shopping centers that line Henry Street. A few steps east off O'Connell on Cathedral Street is **St. Mary's Pro-Cathedral,** the principal Catholic church of Dublin but never designated as a cathedral (that honor goes to two Church of Ireland outposts across the river, St. Patrick's and Christ Church). St. Mary's is severely classical and temple-like in its design, a suitable setting for a Latin mass, which is sung by the famed Palestrina Choir every Sunday at 11 a.m. (the church is open daily, 8 a.m. to 6 p.m.).

Another place that is sacred to Dubliners is the **Gresham Hotel,** a bit faded these days but still the best address on O'Connell Street and famous as a spot to enjoy a cup of tea while watching the parade of strollers and shoppers on the avenue (see hotel profile on page 115). O'Connell Street ends at **Parnell Square,** named for Charles Stewart Parnell, a 19th-century champion of home rule who was brought down in scandal-ridden tatters when he was named in divorce proceedings against his mistress, Kitty O'Shea. This handsome square does the so-called Uncrowned King of Ireland justice as Dublin's cultural bastion. Fine old buildings on and around the square house the **Gate Theatre,** founded in 1929 and one of Europe's most respected stages (see page 161); the **Hugh Lane Gallery** (see page 139); and the **Dublin Writers Museum** (see page 137). On the north side of the square is the so-called **Garden of Remembrance,** a lovely and moving tribute to all those who have died fighting for Irish freedom.

Trinity College and Temple Bar

These two landmarks represent two sides of Dublin—or do they? **Temple Bar** is the haunt of inebriated youth and **Trinity College** is the haunt of ineb . . . well, youth at Trinity study hard, too, and do so in a famous and markedly lovely institution founded by Queen Elizabeth I in 1592. Oscar Wilde, J. M. Synge, Jonathan Swift, Bram Stoker, and Samuel Beckett are among the alumni, and behind the college's walls are 40 acres of greens, atmospheric structures, and one of the world's most famous volumes, the **Book of Kells** (see page 131).

Temple Bar lies just beyond the college gates, on the other side of the **Bank of Ireland.** This handsome building was the seat of the Irish Parliament until 1801, when that body voted itself out of existence with passage of the Act of Union, transferring government rule to London. You can still visit the chamber of the **House of Lords,** richly paneled, hung with tapestries depicting the Battle of the Boyne and the Siege of Derry, and illuminated with a splendid Waterford chandelier. (Open to the public Monday through Friday, 10 a.m. to 4 p.m.; free guided tours on Tuesday at 10:30 a.m., 11:30 a.m., and 1:45 p.m.). Busy, traffic-choked **Dame Street** leads west from College Green. From here you can catch a bus to just about anywhere in Dublin, hear music in the wonderfully Victorian **Olympia Theatre,** and easily escape the noise and the bustle by following any of the alleylike streets north into the neighborhood known as Temple Bar.

In recent years, young merrymakers from throughout Europe have been drawn to this old riverside quarter like bees to honey, with encouragement from restaurateurs and pub owners. Saving the neighborhood from complete debauchery are several cultural institutions on and around **Meeting House Square.** Most popular is the **Irish Film Centre,** where the cinemas, bar-cafe, and bookstore are always packed with film enthusiasts (see page 151). The center occasionally screens films outdoors in the square on summer evenings, providing some of Dublin's favorite free entertainment. Also free, and facing each other from opposite sides of the square, are the **Gallery of Photography,** which exhibits works by Irish and international photographers (Monday through Saturday, 11 a.m. to 6 p.m., Sunday, 2 to 6 p.m.; ☎ 01-671-4654) and the **National Photographic Archive,** which rotates its collection of historic Irish images (Monday through Friday, 10 a.m. to 5 p.m., Saturday, 10 a.m. to 2 p.m.; ☎ 01-603-0371).

From the north side of Temple Bar, pass through Merchant's Gate onto Wellington Quay, where **Ha'Penny Bridge** beckons you to cross the Liffey; this span has connected the two sides of the city since 1816 and those who used it once paid the eponymous toll.

Into Georgian Dublin

Grafton Street, just south of Trinity College, is first and foremost a statement about Ireland's newfound prosperity: this pedestrian way is a road well traveled by shoppers, who step in and out of expensive boutiques and pop into **Bewley's** for a cup of tea (see page 150). At the north end of the street is a reminder of a more humble Dublin: a statue of **Molly Malone,** the comely 17th-century fishmonger who also plied a nighttime trade and inspired the song "In Dublin's Fair City, Where the Girls Are So Pretty . . . ." (Dubliners refer to the statue of the unfortunate lass wheeling her load of mussels and cockles as "The Tart with the Cart.") About halfway up Grafton Street, a narrow lane leads west to the former townhouse of the Viscount Powerscourt, whose country seat was the magnificent **Powerscourt** in County Wicklow (see page 179). The viscount would no doubt be vexed by the fact that his 18th-century Palladian-style mansion, made of limestone quarried from his estate, is now the centerpiece of the **Powerscourt Townhouse Centre,** a posh shopping mall.

Grafton Street ends at **St. Stephen's Green,** 11 hectares (27 acres) of lawns and formal gardens surrounding a lake. Once used for hangings, the park is these days a lovely place for a stroll and a rest on a bench; you'll find yourself in the good company of James Joyce, W. B. Yeats, the Countess Markievicz, and other Irish luminaries, commemorated with busts and statures. The north side of the Green (which is how Dubliners refer to it) was known as Beaux Walk well into the 20th century, when it was still a row of gentlemen's clubs. One of these male bastions is now the pleasant **Brownes Hotel** (see page 114). A little ways down the street is the most popular hostelry and gathering spot on the Green, the **Shelbourne** (closed for a cellar-to-attic renovation), and down from that, the **Huguenot Cemetery,** a small burial ground that ensures its interred a good address for eternity.

Just to the east of the Green are Merrion Street and **Merrion Square,** elegant remnants of 18th-century Georgian Dublin. You can tour two of the fine houses that line these squares and streets, the **Oscar Wilde House,** at One Merrion Square (see page 144), and **Number 29,** east of Merrion Square on Fitzwilliam Street (see page 143). It's quite satisfying simply to admire the houses, with their large fanlights and brightly colored doors, from the pavement, as you can do repeatedly on the long stretch of **Fitzwilliam Street** known as the "Georgian Mile."

Between the west side of Merrion Square and Kildare Street is "official" Dublin, where government offices and museums (including the **National Gallery** and the **National Museum;** see pages 141 and 142, respectively) abut one another in all their limestone pomp. **Leinster House,** tucked between Merrion Square West and Kildare Street, inspired James Hoban's designs for the White House in Washington, D.C.; this formidable mansion, built for the Duke of Leinster in 1745, also serves a governmental function—it's the seat of the Oireachtas, the Irish legislature. Trinity College is at the north end of Kildare Street.

Dublin Castle and the Cathedrals

Dublin Castle, off Dame Street at the west end of Temple Bar, seems purposely built to separate that raucous quarter from some of Dublin's holiest ground, Christ Church and St. Patrick's Cathedral. You can get a taste for the might and glory of the castle (see page 130) just by looking at its formidable stone walls. But do take the time to step into nearby **City Hall,** built as the Royal Exchange and completed in 1779, and admire the domed rotunda surrounded by columns, the mosaic floor, and the frescoes depicting fact and fiction (legend and actual events) in Irish history (Dame Street, ☎ 01-672-2204; Monday through Friday, 10 a.m. to 5 p.m.; Saturday and Sunday, 2 to 5 p.m.; free admission).

Castle Street leads uphill to **Christ Church Cathedral** (page 133) and its neighbor, **Dublinia and the Viking World** (page 136). Between the old stones of the one and the ersatz re-creations of the other, you will learn a bit about medieval Dublin—more of which is in evidence in the delightful **St. Patrick's Cathedral** (page 146), just to the north up St. Nicholas Street.

Phoenix Park, the Liberties, and Kilmainham

To the west of St. Patrick's Cathedral lies a slice of Dublin life that many visitors see little of: a real neighborhood. **The Liberties,** settled by Huguenots in the 17th century, was appallingly poor through much of the 19th and 20th centuries, and the area is still less prosperous than other parts of Dublin. Oddly, the glossy **Guinness Storehouse** (see page 138), Dublin's most popular tourist attraction, is out here, just off Thomas Street. Should you feel up to the trek, the **Royal Hospital Kilmainham–Irish Museum of Modern Art** (see page 145) and **Kilmainham Gaol**

unofficial **TIP**
Seeing all these far-flung attractions in one outing is beyond the scope of even the most energetic walker. You may want to approach this part of Dublin in segments— visits to the **Guinness Storehouse, Royal Hospital Kilmainham– Irish Museum of Modern Art,** and **Kilmainham Gaol** can more than amply fill a day's sightseeing agenda, and **Collins Barracks, Phoenix Park,** and the **Old Jameson Distillery** another. Consider, too, the advantages of a hop-on, hop-off bus tour, which whisks you from one of these attractions to the next, allowing you to spend as much time as you want at each (see page 121).

(see page 140), which so eloquently pays tribute to Irish nationalism, are farther west, along James and Old Kilmainham streets. Across the River Liffey is **Collins Barracks,** housing the Museum of Decorative Arts (see page 136). **Phoenix Park,** with 1,750 acres that stretch five kilometers (three miles) along the banks of the river to compose Europe's largest public park, is just to the west of the Barracks, and the **Old Jameson Distillery** (see page 144) is just to the east.

ATTRACTIONS IN DUBLIN

 Book of Kells ★ ★ ★ ★

APPEAL BY AGE	PRESCHOOL ★	GRADE SCHOOL ★ ★ ★	TEENS ★ ★ ★
YOUNG ADULTS ★ ★ ★		OVER 30 ★ ★ ★ ★	SENIORS ★ ★ ★ ★

College Green, Trinity College, Dublin 2, Trinity College and Temple Bar;
☎ **01-608-1661; www.tcd.ie/library/heritage**

Type of attraction Illustrated manuscript. **Buses** 5, 7A, 8, 15A, 15B, 15C, 46, 55, 62, 63, 83, 84; DART: Tara Street. **Admission** €8 adults, €7 seniors and students, free for children under age 12, €16 for families of up to 2 adults and 4 children. **Hours** May–September: Monday–Saturday, 9:30 a.m.–5 p.m.; Sunday, 9:30 a.m.–4:30 p.m.; October–April: Monday–Saturday, 9:30 a.m.–5 p.m.; Sunday, noon–4:30 p.m. **When to go** Midweek and early in the day to avoid crowds. **Special comments** You can buy a combination ticket for admission to the Book of Kells and the Dublin Experience (see page 147), a sound-and-light show in Davis Theatre, also on the campus. **How much time to allow** 2 hours.

DESCRIPTION AND COMMENTS The Book of Kells is one of the world's most exquisite manuscripts. Scholars are still debating where the book was crafted, though many believe it is the work of ninth-century monks working in the great scriptorium at the monastic community of St. Colomba, on the island of Iona off Scotland. For most of the Middle Ages, the 680-page book, in which four gospels are illustrated with elaborate designs that show the influence of Eastern Christianity and Celtic cultures, was in the Colomban monastery at Kells, north of Dublin. The manuscript now occupies pride of place in the Long Library of Trinity College. Two sets of facing pages, one set displaying text and the other ornamental illumination, are shown at one time, and viewing them often requires standing in long lines; you catch only a brief glimpse of the treasures as the crowd presses forward. Nearby, fairly elaborate but nonetheless yawn-inducing displays chronicle the restoration and conservation of the text and reproduce some of the most elaborate pages, such as the one showing the symbol of Christ, the XPI monogram. The crush is less pressing around two other medieval manuscripts, the ninth-century Book of Armagh, a copy of the New Testament, and the seventh-century Book of Durrow; while these two less-noted volumes are mules to the show pony, they are exquisite and can be appreciated at your leisure.

How Attractions Compare in Dublin

ATTRACTION	DESCRIPTION	AUTHOR'S RATING
Chester Beatty Library and Gallery of Oriental Art	Library and art gallery	★★★★½
Hugh Lane Municipal Gallery of Modern Art	Museum of 19th- and 20th-century art	★★★★½
Kilmainham Gaol	Historic prison	★★★★½
National Gallery of Ireland	Ireland's premier collection of art	★★★★½
National Museum of Ireland	Treasure trove of Irish artifacts	★★★★½
Book of Kells	Illustrated manuscript	★★★★
Collins Barracks	Museum of decorative arts	★★★★
Dublin Writers Museum	Museum honoring writers who lived in Dublin	★★★★
Marsh's Library	Ireland's first public library	★★★★
Number 29	Historic home	★★★★
Oscar Wilde House	Home of famous author	★★★★
St. Patrick's Cathedral	Church	★★★★
Royal Hospital Kilmainham– Irish Museum of Modern Art	Historic building and art museum	★★★½
Shaw Birthplace	Home of famous author	★★★½
James Joyce Centre	Museum and learning center devoted to James Joyce	★★½
Christ Church Cathedral	Church	★★
Dublinia and the Viking World	Historical re-creation	★★
Guinness Storehouse	Brewery	★★
Old Jameson Distillery	Museum in a historic distillery	★★

TOURING TIPS   Take time to admire your surroundings. The library, also known as the Long Room, is an exquisite expanse of paneling and shelving beneath a barrel-vaulted ceiling. Glass cases running down the center of the room display the letters of Robert Emmet, expelled from Trinity for his anti-British convictions and executed in 1803 for acting on those sentiments. Marble busts of Jonathan Swift and other famous Trinity alumni oversee the comings and goings in the busy room.

Chester Beatty Library and Gallery of Oriental Art   ★ ★ ★ ★ ½

APPEAL BY AGE	PRESCHOOL ★	GRADE SCHOOL ★★	TEENS ★★★★
YOUNG ADULTS ★★★	OVER 30 ★★★★½	SENIORS ★★★★½	

Clock Tower Building, Dublin Castle, Dublin 2,
Dublin Castle and the Cathedrals; ☎ 01-407-0750; www.cbl.ie

Type of attraction Library and art gallery. **Buses** 50, 51B, 54A, 56A, 77, 77A, 78A, 123. **Admission** Free. **Hours** May–September: Tuesday–Friday, 10 a.m.–5 p.m.; Saturday, 11 a.m.–5 p.m.; Sunday, 1–5 p.m.; October–April: Tuesday–Friday, 10 a.m.– 5 p.m. **When to go** Anytime. **Special comments** The library cafe, the Silk Road, serves excellent Middle Eastern food. **How much time to allow** 2–3 hours.

DESCRIPTION AND COMMENTS Sir Alfred Chester Beatty (1875–1968) was an American who became a British subject (and later an honorary Irish citizen) after making his fortune as a mining entrepreneur. He spent much of his life collecting sacred texts, illuminated manuscripts, and miniature paintings from the great religions of the world. The library he established in Dublin in 1953 is one of those rare places where visitors pause in wonder in front of case after case of these rare artifacts, perhaps the greatest such collection in the world. Holdings include cuneiform clay tablets, ancient Biblical papyri, 270 copies of the Koran, paintings from India's Mughal era, and some of the earliest bound books, dating from the Renaissance. It's a comment on the greatness of this place that the prints of the old masters, including many by Albrecht Dürer, are overshadowed by the sheer magnitude of the rest of the collection.

TOURING TIPS The library is close enough to Trinity College and the Book of Kells that you can easily combine a visit to both on a mission to see old manuscripts.

Christ Church Cathedral ★★

APPEAL BY AGE	PRESCHOOL ★	GRADE SCHOOL ★★	TEENS ★★
YOUNG ADULTS ★★	OVER 30 ★★★		SENIORS ★★★

Christ Church Place, Dublin 8, Dublin Castle and the Cathedrals;
☎ 01-677-8099; www.cccdub.ie

Type of attraction Church. **Buses** 21A, 50, 50A, 78, 78A, 78B. **Admission** €5, free for children accompanied by adults; reduced rates for those who have paid admission to Dublinia. **Hours** June–August: Monday–Friday, 9 a.m.– 6 p.m.; Saturday, 10 a.m.–4:30 p.m.; Sunday, 12:45–2:45 p.m.; September–May: Monday–Friday, 9:45 a.m.–6 p.m.; Saturday, 10 a.m.–4:30 p.m.; Sunday, 12:45–2:45 p.m. **When to go** Try to visit during Evensong: Sunday at 3:30 p.m., Wednesday and Thursday at 6 p.m., and Saturday at 5 p.m. **Special comments** Save your time and money for a visit to St. Patrick's Cathedral next door. **How much time to allow** 1 hour.

DESCRIPTION AND COMMENTS A Victorian restoration, funded by whiskey magnate Henry Roe, took the life out of the 12th-century stone edifice that rose on the site of an 11th-century wooden Danish church—all but demolishing the medieval craftsmanship that graced this hilltop throughout much of Dublin's long history. Some stone work and quaint carvings in the nave, transepts, and choir, plus the wonderfully spooky old crypt, are about all that remain, hardly enough to warrant the steep entrance fee.

dublin attractions

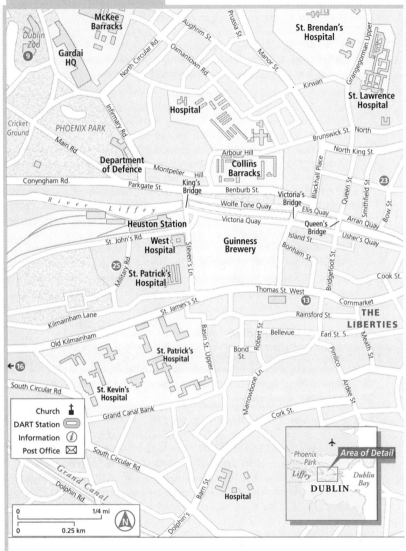

McKee
Barracks

Dublin
Zoo
9

Gardai
HQ

St. Brendan's
Hospital

Aughrim St.

Prussia St.

Oxmantown Rd.

Manor St.

North Circular Rd.

Grangegorman Upper

Kirwan

St. Lawrence
Hospital

Hospital

Cricket
Ground

PHOENIX PARK

Infirmary Rd.

Main Rd.

Brunswick St. North

North King St.

Department
of Defence

Montpelier Hill

Arbour Hill

Collins
Barracks

Blackhall Place

Queen St.

Smithfield

23

Conyngham Rd.

Parkgate St.

King's
Bridge

Benburb St.

Bow St.

River   Liffey

Wolfe Tone Quay

Victoria's
Bridge

Ellis Quay

Arran Quay

Heuston Station

Victoria Quay

Queen's
Bridge

Usher's Quay

St. John's Rd.

West
Hospital

Steven's Ln.

Guinness
Brewery

Island St.

Bonham St.

Bridgefoot St.

Cook St.

Military Rd.

25

St. Patrick's
Hospital

Thomas St. West

13

Cornmarket

St. James's St.

Rainsford St.

THE
LIBERTIES

Kilmainham Lane

Bellevue

Earl St. S.

Meath St.

Old Kilmainham

St. Patrick's
Hospital

Basin St. Upper

Robert St.

Bond
St.

Pimlico

Ardee St.

←16

St. Kevin's
Hospital

Marrowbone Ln.

Cork St.

South Circular Rd.

Grand Canal Bank

Church	✝
DART Station	⬭
Information	ⓘ
Post Office	✉

South Circular Rd.

Barn St.

Dolphin's

Grand Canal

Dolphin Rd.

Hospital

✈

Phoenix
Park

Area of Detail

Liffey

Dublin
Bay

DUBLIN

0		1/4 mi
0	0.25 km	

N

1. Abbey Theatre
2. The Ark
3. Bank of Ireland (Former
   Parliament House)
4. Book of Kells
5. Chester Beatty Library
6. Christ Church Cathedral
7. Dublin Experience
8. Dublin Writers Museum

9. Dublin Zoo
10. Dublinia and the Viking World
11. Gate Theatre
12. General Post Office
13. Guinness Storehouse
14. Hugh Lane Gallery
15. James Joyce Centre
16. Kilmainham Gaol
17. Marsh's Library

18. National Gallery of Ireland
19. National History
    Museum
20. National Museum of Ireland
21. Newman House
22. Number 29
23. Old Jameson Distillery
    and Chimney
24. Oscar Wilde House

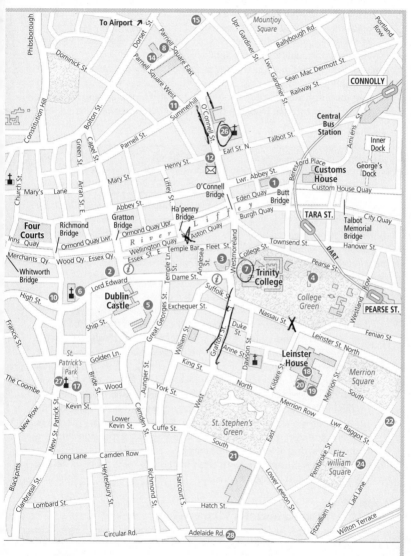

Should duty draw you in, a brief tour must include a stop at the tomb of Strongbow, the 12th-century Norman warrior who conquered Ireland for Henry II and who founded the cathedral; Strongbow's original resting place was destroyed and replaced in the 14th century. Adding to the allure of the dank crypt are the mummies of a cat and a rat, allegedly trapped in an organ pipe midchase in the 1860s.

TOURING TIPS   The far more interesting St. Patrick's Cathedral, another bastion of Irish Protestantism, is just to the north, so you can easily visit both on one round of churchgoing; you can also easily combine a visit to Christ Church with a stop at Dublinia, connected to the cathedral by a bridge.

Collins Barracks   ★ ★ ★ ★

APPEAL BY AGE	PRESCHOOL ★ ★	GRADE SCHOOL ★ ★	TEENS ★ ★ ★
YOUNG ADULTS ★ ★ ★		OVER 30 ★ ★ ★	SENIORS ★ ★ ★

Benburb Street, Dublin 8, Kilmainham; ☎ 01-677-7444; www.museum.ie

Type of attraction Museum of decorative arts. Buses 34, 70, 80. Admission Free. Hours Tuesday–Saturday, 10 a.m.–5 p.m.; Sunday, 2–5 p.m. When to go Anytime; the museum does not draw big crowds the way the city-center branch does. Special comments The staff leads highly informative tours, showing off the prizes of the collection that you might otherwise overlook; times vary, so check with the information desk. How much time to allow About 2 hours.

DESCRIPTION AND COMMENTS   The official name of this sprawling collection is National Museum of Ireland–Decorative Arts and History, at Collins Barracks, but that doesn't quite capture the nature of the eclectic collection, which includes stunning silver, fine furniture, and bizarre petrified bits from Captain Cook's voyages. The barracks is a handsome example of military architecture dating from the 18th century. The recently restored halls show such off treasures as 14th-century Chinese porcelain and furniture designed by Eileen Gray, an Irish designer who made her mark on the upper echelons of early-20th-century interior design (seeing her swanky rooms is worth the trip out here). The natural-history pieces are a recent addition, part of the museum's ongoing expansion into the realms of earth science and ethnography.

TOURING TIPS   The museum is quite close to the Guinness Storehouse and the Irish Museum of Modern Art.

Dublinia and the Viking World   ★ ★

APPEAL BY AGE	PRESCHOOL ★ ★ ★	GRADE SCHOOL ★ ★ ★ ★	TEENS ★ ★ ★
YOUNG ADULTS ★ ★ ★		OVER 30 ★ ★	SENIORS ★ ★

St. Michael's Hill, Dublin 8, Dublin Castle and the Cathedrals; ☎ 01-679-4611; www.dublinia.ie

Type of attraction Historical re-creation. Buses 50, 78A, 123. Admission €6 adults, €3.75 children, €5 seniors and students, €16 families of up to 2 adults and 3 children. Hours April–September, daily, 10 a.m.–5 p.m.; October–March, Monday–Friday, 11 a.m.–4 p.m., and Saturday–Sunday, 10 a.m.–4 p.m.

When to go Weekdays, if possible; the place swarms with kids on weekends. **Special comments** Children enjoy putting on medieval costumes and engaging in activities. **How much time to allow** At least 1 hour, longer if you will be explaining the exhibits to young companions.

DESCRIPTION AND COMMENTS Neither fish nor fowl, this place is not really a museum but not flashy enough to be first-rate entertainment. The prototype for this theme-park approach to history is the Jorvick Centre in York, England, where visitors travel through Viking times in vehicles similar to those in an amusement park. Here, in a 19th-century Gothic annex to Christ Church Cathedral, theatrical exhibits re-create everyday life in Viking and medieval Dublin with models and mannequins, accompanied by sounds and the occasional odor. Kids especially will enjoy the scenes, and even adults will leave the premises a little more enlightened about who did what when in historic Dublin (the name means "Black Pool," by the way). Even so, the experience could be a lot more engaging were the theatrics a bit more sophisticated and less reliant on text panels. Interestingly, the old-fashioned approach best succeeds here: some of the most intriguing items are the bona fide scientific finds on display in the museum section, such as the skeleton of a middle-aged woman buried in a shallow grave near the former city walls. Satisfying, too, is the view of Dublin from the adjoining tower.

TOURING TIPS A charming bridge links Dublinia to Christ Church Cathedral, which you can enter at a reduced price if you show your Dublinia receipt.

 Dublin Writers Museum ★ ★ ★ ★

APPEAL BY AGE	PRESCHOOL ★	GRADE SCHOOL ★ ★	TEENS ★ ★
YOUNG ADULTS ★ ★ ★	OVER 30 ★ ★ ★ ★		SENIORS ★ ★ ★ ★

18 Parnell Square, Dublin 1, Central Dublin; ☎ 01-872-2077; www.writersmuseum.com

Type of attraction Museum honoring writers who lived in Dublin. **Buses** 11, 13, 16, 16A, 22, 22A. **Admission** €11.50 adults, €7 children, €9.50 seniors and students, €32 families. **Hours** January–May: Monday–Saturday, 10 a.m.–5 p.m.; Sunday, 11 a.m.–5 p.m.; June–August: Monday–Friday, 10 a.m.–6 p.m.; Saturday, 10 a.m.–5 p.m.; Sunday, 11 a.m.–5 p.m.; September–December: Monday–Saturday, 10 a.m.–5 p.m.; Sunday, 11 a.m.–5 p.m. **When to go** The museum is a perfect place to spend a rainy afternoon. **Special comments** The cafe also serves an international school and is filled with European students sipping coffee (at the rear of the museum); a bookstore carries a small but admirable collection of works by Dublin writers. Chapter One, among Dublin's top restaurants, is on the ground floor. **How much time to allow** At least 2 hours.

DESCRIPTION AND COMMENTS The fairly steep price of admission buys hours of pleasurable browsing through extensive letters, manuscripts, photos, news clippings, audio recordings, and some other fascinating memorabilia—such as the lorgnette of Lady Augusta Gregory (patron of W. B. Yeats) and a postcard from Brendan Behan, then living in California ("great place for a piss-up"). A lively audio tour and the varied nature of the displays can accelerate whatever mild enthusiasm visitors might have for Oscar Wilde, James Joyce, Samuel Beckett, Jonathan Swift, and scores of other writers (most of whom appeared to have been both stifled and inspired by Dublin) into full-throttle fascination. While there have been many Dublin writers who left much behind, the museum's large collections are not overwhelming. They are tidily arranged in two salons of the Georgian mansion that was once home to a scion of the Jameson whiskey family—one room brings visitors up to the end of the 19th century, and the other is devoted to the 20th century.

TOURING TIPS You can continue a literary pilgrimage at the James Joyce Centre, a couple of blocks away on North Great George's Street.

 ## Guinness Storehouse ★ ★

| APPEAL BY AGE | PRESCHOOL ★ | GRADE SCHOOL ★★★ | TEENS ★★★ |
| YOUNG ADULTS ★★★★ | | OVER 30 ★★★★ | SENIORS ★★★★ |

St. James's Gate, Dublin 8, the Liberties; ☎ 01-408-4800; www.guinness-storehouse.com

Type of attraction Brewery. Buses 51B, 78A, 90, 123. Admission €14 adults, €9.50 seniors and students over age 18, €7.50 students under age 18, €5 children ages 6–12, free for children under age 6, €30 families of up to 2 adults and 4 children. Hours July–August, daily, 9:30 a.m.–8 p.m.; September–June, daily, 9:30 a.m.–5 p.m. When to go In the morning to beat the crowd; the Gravity Bar is especially pleasant on summer evenings. Special comments A very large shop sells T-shirts, key chains, and many other items emblazoned with the Guinness logo. How much time to allow 2 hours.

DESCRIPTION AND COMMENTS It's not surprising that Dublin's most famous tourist attraction is this shrine to Ireland's favorite beverage. What is surprising is that so many people are willing to pay so much to see what amounts to so little. Visitors do not see the actual brewery, but instead are treated to an unabashed display of self-promotion housed in a renovated fermentation plant. Arranged around a five-story glass atrium shaped like a pint are flashy high-tech exhibits showing how Guinness and the barrels that store it are made. The sophisticated displays, with lots of flashing lights, rushing water, and sound effects, are certainly impressive, but isn't it all a bit overdone? Guinness is, after all, a brewery—they're making beer here, not splitting the atom. The most engaging bits of paraphernalia are the advertising posters by John Gilroy, a spin master of the 1930s and 1940s who sold millions of pints of beer with charming illustrations of toucans and other animals, accompanied by such lines as "Guinness Is Good for You" and "It's a Lovely Day for a Guinness." In good weather, you will find it is indeed a lovely day for a Guinness when you step into the top-floor Gravity Bar, where you will be treated to a free pint and 360-degree views of Dublin. Enjoy it, because this is one of the most expensive pints you'll ever quaff.

TOURING TIPS You might want to combine a Guinness visit with stops at some of the other attractions in this part of town, including Collins

Barracks and Kilmainham Gaol; if you're primed to pay homage to other Irish spirits, the Old Jameson Distillery is also nearby.

Hugh Lane Municipal Gallery of Modern Art ★ ★ ★ ½

APPEAL BY AGE	PRESCHOOL ★★	GRADE SCHOOL ★★★	TEENS ★★★
YOUNG ADULTS ★★★★	OVER 30 ★★★★½		SENIORS ★★★★½

Parnell Square North, Dublin 1, Central Dublin; ☎ 01-222-5550; www.hughlane.ie

Type of attraction Museum of 19th- and 20th-century art. **Buses** 11, 13, 16, 16A, 22, 22A. **Admission** Permanent collection: free; Francis Bacon studio: €7 adults, €3.50 seniors and students, free for children age 18 and under; half price on Tuesday, 9:30 a.m.–noon. **Hours** Tuesday–Thursday, 9:30 a.m.–6 p.m.; Friday–Saturday, 9:30 a.m.–5 p.m.; Sunday, 11 a.m.–5 p.m. **When to go** Thursday morning, when you can see the Bacon studio for half the price and the galleries are not particularly crowded. **Special comments** Guided tours are conducted July–September, Tuesday, 11 a.m., and Sunday, 1:30 p.m. At noon on Sundays, the gallery hosts free concerts presenting classical works as well as pieces commissioned for the series. Postcards and a good selection of art books are for sale in the bookshop. **How much time to allow** About 2 hours.

DESCRIPTION AND COMMENTS The grandest dwelling on Parnell Square, built for the Earl of Charlemont in 1762, houses an exquisite collection of 19th- to early-20th-century art. It's only fitting that these handsome rooms still display fine art—the earl was a great collector, amassing Titians and other masterpieces. Much of the collection now hanging here is that of Hugh Lane, an aristocratic connoisseur who went down with the *Lusitania* after it was torpedoed by the Germans off the Irish coast in 1915. You can savor lovely works of the French Barbizon and Impressionist schools such as Renoir's *Les Parapluies* and Monet's *Waterloo Bridge.* Note that some of the dazzlers are moved back and forth to the National Gallery in London, but most of the paintings do remain here. The museum also exhibits many works by Irish artists, including canvases by the painter Jack Yeats, brother of the poet W. B. Yeats, and stained-glass panels by Irish artisans Harry Clark and Evie Hone. One of the museum's most stunning holdings is the studio of the 20th-century Irish painter Francis Bacon, moved here in its entirety from a London mews and painstakingly preserved, with the used paint tubes, rags, slashed canvases, and all the other clutter perfectly intact.

TOURING TIPS The Gallery is part of a cultural enclave in this part of Dublin; it can be included in an itinerary that would also include the Dublin Writers Museum and the James Joyce Centre.

James Joyce Centre ★ ★ ½

APPEAL BY AGE	PRESCHOOL ★	GRADE SCHOOL ★★	TEENS ★★
YOUNG ADULTS ★★	OVER 30 ★★½		SENIORS ★★½

35 North Great George's Street, Central Dublin; ☎ 01-878-8547; www.jamesjoyce.ie

Type of attraction Museum and learning center devoted to James Joyce. **Buses** 3, 10, 11, 13, 16, 19, 22, 123. **Admission** €5 adults, €4 students and seniors, free for children under age 12. **Hours** Monday–Friday, 9:30 a.m.–12:30 p.m. and 1:30–3:30 p.m. **When to go** Anytime; the center is rarely crowded. **Special comments** The center has a bookstore and a cafe. **How much time to allow** About 1 hour.

DESCRIPTION AND COMMENTS Reading *Ulysses* is pretty stringent prep for a museum visit, but knowing the ins and outs of the Dublin of Leopold Bloom will certainly help you make sense of many of the exhibits in this Georgian townhouse (which, incidentally, is one of the few places in Dublin where Joyce seems never to have lived). *Ulysses* aficionados can spend hours in front of the massive chart diagramming characters, events, and places in the novel, and pay homage at the door to 7 Eccles Street, home to the Blooms and one of the most famous addresses in literature. Those who appreciate Joyce's genius but don't live and breathe his work may be content with what's to be learned about the great man at the nearby Dublin Writers Museum. Quite interesting here, though, are the exhibits about tenement life in Dublin in the 19th and 20th centuries, when the neighborhood went into decline and dozens of families lived in once-grand houses such as this one. The center, devoted to Joyce scholarship, contains a large library of the writer's works, hosts lectures, and provides excellent walking tours through Joyce's Dublin.

TOURING TIPS Walking tours past the pubs, lanes, houses, and other venues of Joyce's works depart from the center from May to August on Tuesday, Thursday, and Saturday at 2 p.m.; fees are €10 adults, €9 seniors and students.

 Kilmainham Gaol ★ ★ ★ ★ ½

APPEAL BY AGE	PRESCHOOL ★ ★ ★	GRADE SCHOOL ★ ★ ★ ★	TEENS ★ ★ ★ ★
YOUNG ADULTS ★ ★ ★ ★	OVER 30 ★ ★ ★ ★ ½		SENIORS ★ ★ ★ ★ ½

Inchicore Road, Dublin 8, Kilmainham; ☎ 01-453-5984; www.heritageireland.ie

Type of attraction Historic prison. **Buses** 51B, 78A. **Admission** €5 adults, €3.50 seniors, €2 children and students, €11 families. **Hours** April–September, daily, 9:30 a.m.–6 p.m.; October–March, Monday–Saturday, 9:30 a.m.–5:30 p.m., and Sunday, 10 a.m.–6 p.m. **When to go** Try to arrive early in summer, as tours fill up quickly later in the day. **Special comments** The jail has a small tearoom. **How much time to allow** 2 hours.

DESCRIPTION AND COMMENTS This formidable prison opened in 1798 and closed in 1927; today it serves as a testimonial to Irish revolutionary history. A museum, an introductory slide presentation, and a highly informative guided tour provide excellent background on such 18th- and 19th-century revolutionary heroes as Robert Emmet, executed for his role in the Dublin riots of 1803, and Charles Stewart Parnell, the 19th-century nationalist leader and member of the Irish Parliament. Most gripping are the displays and commentaries recounting the 1916 Easter Uprising, when the Irish Republican Brotherhood mounted an armed revolt in Dublin, for which the British executed 15 of the leaders, many of them here at Kilmainham. On the guided tour, among the moving tales you'll hear about this event is that of young Joseph Plunkett, who married Grace Gifford in the prison chapel shortly before his execution. You will leave Kilmainham knowing a fair amount about Irish national history, and you will also see one of the most impressive rooms in all of Ireland—the elliptical central hall surrounded by tiers of cells.

TOURING TIPS   If you leave the museum and walk north a few blocks to the banks of the Liffey, you'll come to the War Memorial Gardens, laid out by the British architect Sir Edwin Lutyens. Ask for directions at the prison admission booth.

Marsh's Library   ★ ★ ★ ★

APPEAL BY AGE	PRESCHOOL ★	GRADE SCHOOL ★ ★ ★	TEENS ★ ★ ★
YOUNG ADULTS ★ ★ ★	OVER 30 ★ ★ ★ ★		SENIORS ★ ★ ★ ★

St. Patrick's Close, Dublin 8, Dublin Castle and the Cathedrals;
☎ **01-454-3511; www.marshlibrary.ie**

Type of attraction Ireland's first public library. **Buses** 50, 50A, 54, 54A, 65, 65B, 77. **Admission** €2.50 adults, €1.25 students and seniors. **Hours** Monday and Wednesday–Friday, 10 a.m.–1 p.m. and 2–5 p.m.; Saturday, 10:30 a.m.–1 p.m. **When to go** Anytime. **Special comments** Visitors are welcome to browse the library's catalogs and certain sections of the holdings. **How much time to allow** 1 hour.

DESCRIPTION AND COMMENTS   Ireland's oldest public library, founded in 1701, is an atmospheric repository of rare manuscripts and books from the 16th through 18th centuries. Many of these are so valuable that scholars must be locked into mesh cages to view them. Other visitors are free to peruse the fascinating exhibits, which are rotated frequently to display the collection's most precious holdings. The library, incidentally, is named for its founder, Archbishop of Dublin Narcissus Marsh (1638–1713), who is buried nearby on the grounds of St. Patrick's Cathedral.

TOURING TIPS   The library is set in a cottage garden at the edge of the grounds of St. Patrick's Cathedral, so you may want to combine a visit to both these landmarks of old Dublin.

National Gallery of Ireland   ★ ★ ★ ★ ½

APPEAL BY AGE	PRESCHOOL ★ ★	GRADE SCHOOL ★ ★ ★	TEENS ★ ★ ★
YOUNG ADULTS ★ ★ ★	OVER 30 ★ ★ ★ ★ ½		SENIORS ★ ★ ★ ★ ½

Merrion Square West, Dublin 2, Georgian Dublin; ☎ **01-661-5133;**
www.nationalgallery.ie

Type of attraction Ireland's premier collection of art. **Buses** 7, 7A, 8, 10, 10A, 44, 47. **Admission** Free. **Hours** Monday–Wednesday and Friday–Saturday, 9:30 a.m.– 5:30 p.m.; Thursday, 9:30 a.m.–8:30 p.m.; Sunday, noon–5:30 p.m. **When to go** Thursday evenings, when you'll have galleries to yourself and can spend as much time as you want in front of the canvases. **Special comments** The museum has a well-stocked bookshop where you can pick up postcards of the works that appeal to you, as well as an attractive cafe. **How much time to allow** At least 2 hours.

DESCRIPTION AND COMMENTS Ireland's national collection of European art is not overwhelming, but it does boast an impressive number of master-pieces. The top floor is especially satisfying: Caravaggio's *The Taking of Christ,* Andrea Mantegna's *Judith with the Head of Holofernes,* and Vermeer's *Lady Writing a Letter with Her Maid* hang among works by Degas, Tintoretto, Rembrandt, Poussin, and Verona in a string of pleasant and well-lit galleries. The Caravaggio is the museum's most newsworthy painting of the moment: presumed lost but recently discovered hanging inconspicuously in a rectory, covered with grime, it is the subject of a fascinating book, *The Lost Painting.* A ground-floor gallery houses works by Jack Yeats, Ireland's most famous 20th-century painter and brother of W. B. Yeats; the artist's impressionistic style and vivid palette capture many Irish scenes, including *The Liffey Swim,* still an annual Dublin event. Other Irish paintings make a decent showing too, as do British artists, but none more prominently than Reynolds, whose *First Earl of Bellamont* is an unintentionally mirthful portrayal of Georgian foppery.

TOURING TIPS The museum hosts an excellent lecture program and conducts guided tours; check with the information desk for times.

 ## National Museum of Ireland ★ ★ ★ ★ ½

APPEAL BY AGE	PRESCHOOL ★ ★ ★	GRADE SCHOOL ★ ★ ★	TEENS ★ ★ ★ ★
YOUNG ADULTS ★ ★ ★ ★	OVER 30 ★ ★ ★ ★ ½	SENIORS ★ ★ ★ ★ ½	

Kildare Street, Dublin 2, Georgian Dublin; ☎ 01-677-7444; www.museum.ie

Type of attraction Museum of national treasures. **Buses** 7, 7A, 10, 11, 13. **Admission** Free. **Hours** Tuesday–Saturday, 10 a.m.–5 p.m.; Sunday, 2–5 p.m. **When to go** Weekdays, when the museum is less crowded. **Special comments** Guided tours (45 minutes; €2 a person) leave regularly from the information desk and provide a rewarding overview of the collections. **How much time to allow** At least 2 hours.

DESCRIPTION AND COMMENTS Ireland's treasure trove of artifacts dating from 6,000 BC to the 20th century is housed in suitably grandiose quarters, behind an imposing 19th-century facade and beneath a soaring rotunda. Understandably, the crowd-pleaser is the stash of Irish gold: Celtic scepters, jewelry, crosses, a gold boat from the first century AD, a collar from about 700 BC, and other items fill one glittering case after another. Other priceless relics gathered from around Ireland include the Tara

Brooch and Ardagh Chalice, both from the eighth century, and the elaborately decorated Cross of Cong, from the 12th century. Remnants of the centuries of Viking occupation fill the upstairs galleries. This being the national museum, several galleries off the rotunda house an in-depth, evocative collection devoted to the Easter Uprising of 1916, paying due homage to the events that led to Irish independence in 1921, with uniforms, posters, and other artifacts. Collins Barracks, in west Dublin, houses the museum's collection of decorative arts (see page 136).

TOURING TIPS You may want to combine visits to the National Museum and the nearby National Gallery of Ireland (pages 141 and 142, respectively). The Museum Cafe at the National Museum is a good spot for lunch.

Number 29 ★ ★ ★ ★

APPEAL BY AGE	PRESCHOOL ★★	GRADE SCHOOL ★★★	TEENS ★★★
YOUNG ADULTS ★★★	OVER 30 ★★★½		SENIORS ★★★½

29 Fitzwilliam Street Lower, Dublin 2, Georgian Dublin; ☎ 01-702-6165

Type of attraction Historic home. Buses 7, 8, 10, 45; DART: Pearse. Admission €3.50 adults, €1.50 seniors and students, free for children under age 16. Hours Tuesday–Saturday, 10 a.m.–5 p.m.; Sunday, 2–5 p.m. When to go Anytime. Special comments A pleasant cafe on the ground floor serves tea and pastries, and a shop sells a small but good selection of books on history and architecture. The staff here is knowledgeable and most willing to answer questions about the house and other attractions. How much time to allow At least 1 hour.

DESCRIPTION AND COMMENTS The guided tour of these posh surroundings begins "below stairs," with a strong dose of egalitarian reality. A 15-minute video, narrated by the ghost of one of the residents of this comfortable 1797 residence, doesn't dwell long on domestic grandeur but instead spells out the appalling poverty, class distinctions, and miserable living conditions that prevailed when such elegant Georgian homes were built in Dublin. This puts a bit of perspective on the comforts upstairs, where the National Museum of Ireland has painstakingly restored sitting rooms and bedrooms with authentic detail. Especially notable are the various hidey-holes in which tea, food, jewels, and other valuables were stashed in case the starving servants succumbed to temptation. The fine bones of the old house itself are the standout, though: the huge fanlight and windows and the generous yet sensible proportions speak volumes about the beauties of Irish Georgian architecture.

TOURING TIPS Number 29 sheds light on the prevailing architecture in this section of Dublin. After the tour, with your newly acquired appreciation, walk up Fitzwilliam Street and around Merrion Square to admire the rows of Georgian homes. Also note the hideous concrete building just to the south of Number 29: this is the headquarters of the Electricity Supply Board, which in the 1960s tore down a row of Georgian houses to build the eyesore. Rumors are afoot that the building may be redone to better suit its surroundings.

Old Jameson Distillery ★ ★

APPEAL BY AGE	PRESCHOOL ★	GRADE SCHOOL ★	TEENS ★ ★
YOUNG ADULTS ★ ★ ★	OVER 30 ★ ★ ★		SENIORS ★ ★ ★

Bow Street, Dublin 7, the Liberties; ☎ 01-807-2355; www.pernod-ricard.com

Type of attraction Museum in a historic distillery. **Buses** 67, 67A, 68, 69, 79, 90. **Admission** €8 adults, €3.50 children, €6.25 seniors and students, €20 families of up to 2 adults and 2 children. **Hours** Daily, 9:30 a.m.–5:30 p.m. **When to go** If you're planning on going to the top of the Chimney as well, wait for good weather. **Special comments** The distillery pub serves meals and light snacks; the gift shop sells whiskey and a great deal of whiskey-oriented paraphernalia. **How much time to allow** 1½ hours.

unofficial **TIP**
As you travel around Ireland, you will have the chance to visit whiskey distilleries other than the Old Jameson—in Midleton, outside Cork, and in Bushmills (the only operation that provides a look at a working distillery). Save your hard-earned money and your yearnings to see how Irish whiskey (known locally as *uisce beatha,* or "water of life") is made for one of those facilities.

DESCRIPTION AND COMMENTS Homage is due this Dublin distillery, which dates from 1791, because it has contributed mightily to the local economy through many hard times; however, there are others that offer a more satisfying look at the whiskey-distilling process. Here, a dull video presentation and humdrum guided tour past an array of dusty exhibits, housed in an old warehouse, provide a pedantic lesson in the steps of the process, from growing grain to filling barrels. Your reward for sticking with the tour for the full hour is a free shot of whiskey in the tasting room, but for this price, you can enjoy two shots and some nice chatter at any pub.

TOURING TIPS For a bird's-eye view of Dublin, head next door to the old distillery chimney, where an elevator whisks you up to a viewing tower. The Chimney is open Monday through Saturday, 10 a.m. to 5:30 p.m., and Sunday, 11 a.m. to 5:30 p.m.; ☎ 01-817-3800 for information. Fees are a steep €5 for adults, €3.50 for children, and €15 for families.

Oscar Wilde House ★ ★ ★ ★

APPEAL BY AGE	PRESCHOOL ★	GRADE SCHOOL ★ ★	TEENS ★ ★ ★
YOUNG ADULTS ★ ★ ★	OVER 30 ★ ★ ★		SENIORS ★ ★ ★

1 Merrion Square, Dublin 2, Georgian Dublin; ☎ 01-676-8939; www.amcd.ie

Type of attraction Home of famous author. **Buses** 6, 8, 10, 45; DART: Pearse. **Admission** €5. **Hours** June–August, Monday and Wednesday, guided tours at 10:15 a.m. **When to go** Anytime you can; the house is rarely open. **Special comments** The extremely limited visiting hours may be expanded; call or check the Web site for updates. **How much time to allow** 1 hour.

DESCRIPTION AND COMMENTS Oscar Wilde was raised in this house, then as now one of the finest residences on one of the most elegant squares in Dublin. His eye-surgeon father, Sir William, and socialite-poet mother, Speranza, filled the salons with fine furnishings and a stream of privileged guests, who no doubt provided young Oscar with material for the comedies of manners he would later write. Owned and recently restored by the American College Dublin, the rooms are oddly devoid of personality, given the larger-than-life character the home honors. The reception hall, dining room, Speranza's salon, and Sir William's surgery room have been painstakingly furnished and painted in exacting detail to replicate the styles of the second part of the 19th century. Missing, though, are books and personal effects that might provide some clue to the enormous talent that took root here. Perhaps this patina will come with ongoing restoration efforts; in the meantime, the guides could fill in the gap with commentary that is more illuminating than it is currently.

TOURING TIPS For a more insightful look at domestic life in Dublin of yesterday, step around the corner to Number 29 (see page 143), a restored Georgian house on Lower Fitzwilliam Street.

Royal Hospital Kilmainham– Irish Museum of Modern Art ★ ★ ★ ½

APPEAL BY AGE	PRESCHOOL ★	GRADE SCHOOL ★ ★	TEENS ★ ★ ★
YOUNG ADULTS ★ ★ ★	OVER 30 ★ ★ ★ ½		SENIORS ★ ★ ★ ½

Military Road, Dublin 8, Kilmainham; ☎ 01-612-9900; www.modernart.ie

Type of attraction Historic building and art museum. Buses 79, 90. Admission Free. Hours Tuesday–Saturday, 10 a.m.–5:30 p.m.; Sunday, noon–5:30 p.m. When to go In good weather, if possible, so you can enjoy the gardens. Special comments The galleries often host temporary exhibitions of contemporary art; check the Web site. A small cafe serves light snacks. How much time to allow About 2 hours to see the historic rooms and the galleries.

DESCRIPTION AND COMMENTS This building, one of the finest in Ireland and completed in 1684, is a replica of Les Invalides in Paris. Like the more famous landmark, this structure once housed disabled and retired soldiers. A painstaking restoration has returned the great hall, chapel, staterooms, courtyards, and gardens to their former glory—a magnificent setting for a small but worthy collection of contemporary European art. You will get a heady dose of visual pleasure here as you admire the glories of the baroque chapel and paneled staterooms, then wander through galleries hung with works by Damien Hirst, Francesco Clemente, and other modern masters.

TOURING TIPS Guided tours show off the staterooms of the Royal Hospital; check with the information desk for times. Take time, too, to wander through the beautifully restored formal gardens.

St. Patrick's Cathedral ★ ★ ★ ★

| APPEAL BY AGE | PRESCHOOL ★★ | GRADE SCHOOL ★★★ | TEENS ★★★ |
| YOUNG ADULTS ★★★ | | OVER 30 ★★★★ | SENIORS ★★★★ |

St. Patrick's Close, Dublin 8, Dublin Castle and the Cathedrals;
☎ **01-453-9472; www.stpatrickscathedral.ie**

Type of attraction Church. **Buses** 50, 50A, 54, 54A, 65, 65B, 77. **Admission** €5 adults, €4 seniors and students, €12 families of up to 2 adults and 2 children. **Hours** March–October: Monday–Saturday, 9 a.m.–6 p.m.; Sunday, 9–11 a.m., 12:45–3 p.m., 4:15–6 p.m.; November–February: Monday–Friday, 9 a.m.–6 p.m.; Saturday, 9 a.m.–5 p.m.; Sunday, 10–11 a.m., 12:45–3 p.m. **When to go** Plan a visit to coincide with a lunchtime recital or evensong. **Special comments** The cathedral hosts lunchtime recitals throughout the year. The highly acclaimed cathedral choir sings twice on weekdays, during matins at 9:40 a.m. and evensong at 5:30 p.m. **How much time to allow** 1 hour.

DESCRIPTION AND COMMENTS These days, the centuries-long rivalry between Dublin's two neighboring cathedrals, Christ Church and St. Patrick's, seems to have swung in favor of the latter. Both edifices were built in the 12th century, and both were restored in the 19th century with profits gotten from spirits: St. Patrick's benefited from the Guinness brewing fortune, while whiskey magnate Henry Roe was the benefactor for Christ Church. However, while the restoration of Christ Church was heavy handed, that of St. Patrick's left much of the cathedral's medieval magnificence intact. St. Patrick's, built on the site where its namesake is said to have preached in the fifth century, is these days the largest church in Ireland as well as the flagship of the Church of Ireland. The grounds are littered with the tombs of some of Ireland's greatest sons and daughters. The most famous tomb here is that of the satirist Jonathan Swift, who wrote *Gulliver's Travels* and most of his other great work while he was the dean of St. Patrick's (1713–1745); his epitaph reads, "Swift has sailed into his rest; / Savage indignation there cannot lacerate his breast." Swift's lifelong companion, Stella (Mrs. Esther Johnson), lies nearby. Other memorials honor the Irish who died in the World Wars.

TOURING TIPS Marsh's Library (see page 141), at the southern edge of the cathedral grounds, is well worth a visit.

Shaw Birthplace ★ ★ ★ ½

| APPEAL BY AGE | PRESCHOOL ★★ | GRADE SCHOOL ★★★ | TEENS ★★★ |
| YOUNG ADULTS ★★★★★ | | OVER 30 ★★★½ | SENIORS ★★★½ |

33 Synge Street, Dublin 8, St. Stephen's Green; ☎ 01-475-0854

Type of attraction Home of famous author. **Buses** 16, 19, 22. **Admission** €6 adults, €3.50 children, €5 seniors and students, €17 families. **Hours** May–October: Monday–Tuesday and Thursday–Friday, 10 a.m.–1 p.m., 2–5 p.m.; Saturday–Sunday, 2–5 p.m. **When to go** Anytime. **Special comments** A shop sells postcards, gifts, and copies of the author's work. **How much time to allow** 1 hour.

DESCRIPTION AND COMMENTS Far more evocative than the sparsely furnished Oscar Wilde House, this modest terrace house says more about middle-class life in 19th-century Dublin than it does about young George Bernard Shaw. He would leave Ireland for London at the age of 23 and go on to be one of the greatest playwrights of the late 19th and early 20th centuries, winning the Nobel Prize for Literature. You can feel the claustrophobia of the confines of family life here as you peer into the cramped, over-furnished parlors, the primitive kitchen, and the wee bedroom on the landing where the playwright slept as a youth. The excellent recorded commentary is full of juicy tidbits about his unhappily married parents and his mother's infatuation with another man.

TOURING TIPS The house is just off the South Circular Road, about a ten-minute walk due south of St. Stephen's Green, so it can be added to a tour of that part of Dublin.

OTHER SIGHTS

kids **THE ARK: A CULTURAL CENTRE FOR CHILDREN** Eustace Street, Dublin 2, Temple Bar; ☎ 01-670-7788; about €7, depending on activity; open daily, 10 a.m. to 4 p.m., often closed to all but school groups during the week; buses 37, 39, 51, 51B; **www.ark.ie.** With the presence of this wonderful activity center, tourist folks really can honestly say the boozy Temple Bar district is family oriented. Kids sign up for programs to make stained glass, learn about Irish music, watch plays, and otherwise engage themselves in creative and mean-ingful activities.

DUBLIN CASTLE Dame Street, Dublin 2, Dublin Castle and the Cathe-drals; ☎ 01-677-7129; €4.50 adults, €3.50 seniors, €2 students; open Monday through Friday, 10 a.m. to 5 p.m., Saturday and Sunday, 2 to 5 p.m.; guided tours every 20 to 25 minutes; buses 50, 50A, 54, 56A, 77, 77A, 77B; **www.dublincastle.ie.** The former seat of British govern-ment in Ireland is appropriately somber and formidable, dating from the 13th century. Tours show off staterooms, the chapel, and parts of the royal apartments, but the place is better suited to the state func-tions it now hosts than to a fun tour. In other words, it's a bit of a bore, and you'll see more interesting interiors in castles and great houses elsewhere in Ireland.

DUBLIN EXPERIENCE Trinity College, Davis Theatre, Dublin 2, Trinity College and Temple Bar; ☎ 01-608-1688; €4.20 adults, €2.20 chil-dren, €3.50 seniors and students, €8.40 families; open late May to late September, daily, on the hours from 10 a.m. to 5 p.m.; buses 5, 7A, 8, 15A, 15B, 15C, 46, 55, 62, 63, 83, 84; DART: Tara Street. All you need to know about the history of Dublin, and then some, pre-sented in a snappy multimedia show.

kids **DUBLIN ZOO** Phoenix Park, Dublin 8, Phoenix Park; ☎ 01-677-1425; €13.50 adults, €9 children ages 3 to 16, free for children under age 3, €11 for seniors and students, €38 for families of two adults and two children, €43 for families of two adults and three children, and €47 for families of two adults and four children; open summer, Monday through Saturday, 9:30 a.m. to 6 p.m., and Sunday, 10:30 a.m. to 6 p.m., and winter, Monday through Saturday, 9:30 a.m. to dusk, and Sunday, 10:30 a.m. to dusk; buses 10, 25, 26; **www.dublin zoo.ie.** The third oldest zoo in the world opened in 1830, following the examples set by zoos in London and Paris. Others around the world have long since surpassed this one in size and sophistication, although recent expansion and restoration have made accommodations for the animals much more humane (many of the habitats are cageless). The Dublin zookeepers' big claim to fame is the ability to breed lions in captivity, and they have successfully bred and nurtured 700 lion cubs over the past 150 years; one of the progeny posed for the famed MGM trademark.

NATURAL HISTORY MUSEUM Merrion Street Upper, Dublin 2, Georgian Dublin; ☎ 01-677-7444; free; open Tuesday through Saturday, 10 a.m. to 5 p.m., and Sunday, 2 to 5 p.m.; buses 44, 48; DART: Pearse; **www.museum.ie.** Founded in 1857, this wonderfully old-fashioned collection of bones seems locked in the Victorian era. You'll find more-complete (and more-sophisticated) collections elsewhere, but few are as evocative of the great 19th-century age of discovery as Dublin's.

NEWMAN HOUSE 85–86 St. Stephen's Green, Dublin 2, St. Stephen's Green; ☎ 01-706-7422; €5 adults, €4 seniors and students; open by guided tour only, June to August, Tuesday through Friday, at noon, 2 p.m., 3 p.m., and 4 p.m.; buses 10, 11, 13, 14, 14A, 15A, 15B. Two sides of Dublin come together in this grand residence, which actually combines two houses: the rococo swirls of plasterwork, grand staircase, ornate Apollo Room (where the sun god is lavishly depicted), and baroque Saloon are the most extravagant examples of Georgian décor in the city. The premises were the original locale of the Catholic University of Ireland, founded by Cardinal John Henry Newman in 1850. The poet Gerard Manley Hopkins was a student here, and his quarters are included in the tour; you'll learn that the nude nymphs that are part of the décor were covered up to protect him and other young men from temptation.

WHITEFRIAR STREET CARMELITE CHURCH Whitefriar Street, Dublin 2, Dublin Castle and the Cathedrals; ☎ 01-475-8821; free; open daily, 8:30 a.m. to 6:30 p.m.; buses 16, 16A, 19, 19A, 22. Of Dublin's many places of worship, this one stands out as the repository of the relics of St. Valentine, making the church a popular venue for lovers, those disappointed in love, and those who are simply romantically inclined.

DINING *in* DUBLIN

DINING IN DUBLIN IS A DELIGHT. Even a decade ago, a statement like that would have elicited laughs. But with prosperity comes a taste for fine food, and Dubliners these days have a wide choice of excellent restaurants serving a variety of cuisines. While Dublin chefs are experimenting with international flavors, two factors remain fairly constant: service is, for the most part, excellent, and friendliness, courtesy, and other hallmarks of Irish hospitality are much in evidence. And even in the most formal restaurants, a meal remains a relaxed, comfortable affair; you'll rarely be rushed and, to the contrary, will be encouraged to linger.

How Restaurants Compare in Dublin

NAME	CUISINE	OVERALL	QUALITY	VALUE	PRICE
Jacob's Ladder	modern Irish	★★★★½	★★★★½	★★★★	mod/exp
L'Ecrivain	modern Irish	★★★★½	★★★★½	★★★★	very exp
The Tea Room	Continental	★★★★½	★★★★½	★★★★	exp
Chapter One	modern Irish	★★★★½	★★★★½	★★★½	very exp
Restaurant Patrick Guilbaud	French	★★★★½	★★★★½	★★★½	very exp
Enoteca della Langhe	wine bar	★★★★	★★★★	★★★★½	inexp
La Mère Zou	French	★★★★	★★★★	★★★½	exp
Les Frères Jacques	French/ Continental	★★★★	★★★★	★★★½	exp
Ely	modern Irish	★★★★	★★★½	★★★★	mod
101 Talbot	Irish/ vegetarian	★★★½	★★★★	★★★★	mod
Beshoffs	fish and chips	★★★½	★★★½	★★★★	inexp
Halo	French	★★★½	★★★½	★★★★	exp/ very exp
Pearl Brasserie	French	★★★½	★★★½	★★★½	mod/exp
Mermaid Cafe	seafood/ modern Irish	★★★	★★★½	★★★	exp
Eden	Continental	★★★	★★★	★★★	mod
Peploe's	wine bar	★★★	★★★	★★★	mod/exp

unofficial **TIP**

Tipping is not necessarily straightforward in Dublin; some restaurants add a service charge to the tab, but many don't. If the policy isn't stated clearly on the menu, don't be shy about asking. But don't bother to ask if you can light up over your coffee, because the answer will be no—smoking is prohibited in all public spaces in Ireland.

Here's a third factor you can count on—Dublin restaurants are expensive. You won't spend as much for a good meal here as you will in London or New York, but you will pay quite a bit. A tab of €60 to €80 for dinner for two is pretty common, and it's very easy to pay much more than that (see Part Three, Lodging, Dining, and Shopping). Lunch is usually less expensive than dinner, and many of the finest restaurants in Dublin dish up especially good value for the noon meal, usually on reasonably priced prix-fixe menus. Many restaurants also offer set menus at dinner, but these are often available only before 7 or 7:30 p.m.

TEN CHOICES FOR A CHEAP MEAL IN DUBLIN

BEWLEY'S CAFÉ 78–79 Grafton Street, Dublin 2, Grafton Street; ☎ 01-679-4085; all city-center buses. Dublin's favorite cafe closed a while back (amid much public protest) and reemerged in this new guise that retains several floors of nooks and crannies (though lingering is now only permitted in the ground-floor cafe; part of the premises houses a mediocre sit-down restaurant). Bewley's is still bathed in the mellow light of its tall Arts and Crafts windows, and while the food may be a bit lackluster, the cafe does make a handy stop for a sandwich or pastry and a cup of tea while making the Grafton Street rounds. And though much of the old Bewley's ambience has fallen by the wayside, its beloved 45-minute-long lunchtime theatrical productions have been revived. Monday through Saturday, 7:30 a.m. to 7 p.m.; Sunday, 8:30 a.m. to 6 p.m.

ELEPHANT AND CASTLE 18 Temple Bar, Dublin 2, Temple Bar; ☎ 01-679-3121; buses 51B, 51C, 68, 69, and 70. If you're homesick for a juicy burger or just looking for a quick bite along Temple Bar, you can't go wrong at this dinerlike purveyor of American-style grub. Food is served throughout the day. Monday through Friday, 8 a.m. to 11:30 p.m.; Saturday and Sunday, 10:30 a.m. to 11 p.m.

EPICUREAN FOOD HALL Middle Abbey and Lower Liffey streets, Dublin 1, Central Dublin; buses 70 and 80. Dublin's main food hall is a tempting collection of stalls, many with tables and counters where you can grab a quick bite; this is also the place to load up on cheeses, salamis, and other snacks to stuff into the minibar in your hotel room. **Caviston's,** an excellent all-around deli with a superb selection of Irish farmhouse cheeses, is here, as are outposts of world cuisine such as **Miss Sushi** and **Itsabagel.** Daily, 10 a.m. to 6 p.m. (open later on some Thursdays and Sundays).

GRUEL 68A Dame Street, Dublin 2, Temple Bar; ☎ 01-670-7119; buses 50, 50A, 54, 56, and 77. Jam-packed, noisy, and really not very comfortable, Gruel overcomes its shortcomings (and humble name) with a fine array of soups, salads, and sandwiches, dispensed all day long at very reasonable prices. Monday through Wednesday, 10 a.m. to 9:30 p.m.; Thursday through Saturday, 10 a.m. to 10:30 p.m.; Sunday, 10 a.m. to 9 p.m.

IRISH FILM CENTRE 6 Eustace Street, Dublin 2, Temple Bar; ☎ 01-677-8788; buses 21A, 78A, 78B. Dublin's wonderful screen for serious film (international, classic, documentary) is blessed with a lively cafe and bar that are popular even for those not lining up at show times. The creative, ever-changing menu includes many Mediterranean-inspired and vegetarian dishes, with price tags that hover comfortably around €8 a plate. Monday through Friday, 12:30 to 3 p.m. and 6 to 9 p.m.; Saturday and Sunday, 12:30 to 3 p.m. and 6 to 9 p.m.

LEO BURDOCK'S 2 Werburgh Street, Dublin 8, Dublin Castle and the Cathedrals; ☎ 01-454-0306; buses 21A, 50, 50A, 78, and 78A. You'll have to dine standing up, but you'll be in good company—Dubliners come from all over town to feast on what is considered to be the best fish and chips in town. Burdock's is almost as sacred as nearby Christchurch and St. Patrick's Cathedral, and a must-stop when visiting this end of town. Monday through Saturday, noon to midnight.

NATIONAL GALLERY OF IRELAND CAFÉ Merrion Square West, Dublin 2, Georgian Dublin; ☎ 01-677-7444; buses 7, 7A, 8, 10, 11, and 13. The cafeteria—a comfy room facing a cobbled court—is preferable to the pricier, more formal restaurant. The self-service counter is laden with salads, sandwiches, stews, quiches, and other plain fare made fresh daily, which can be enjoyed at leisure in pleasant, laid-back surroundings. Monday through Wednesday and Friday and Saturday, 9:30 a.m. to 5:30 p.m.; Thursday, 9:30 a.m. to 8:30 p.m.; Sunday, noon to 5 p.m.

PUBS It won't take you long to discover that it's not the food that draws Dubliners to their pubs. Even so, in many you can dine decently, if not fancily, on sandwiches and other light fare, and in some you can eat very well. Keep in mind that some of the busier, more tourist-oriented pubs draw visitors in with music and feed them mediocre but expensive meals. An exception is **Oliver St. John Gogarty** (58–59 Fleet Street, Dublin 2, Temple Bar; ☎ 01-671-1822), a busy multilevel place from which music fills the night air of Temple Bar; the top-floor restaurant here is a nice reminder of old Dublin, with formal service, starched linens, and heaping plates of fresh seafood and such classics as Irish stew (not to mention fairly steep prices). Some pubs have earned a solid reputation over the years for serving more-modest yet reliable and fairly priced meals. In James Joyce's *Ulysses,* Leopold Bloom stops into **David Byrne's** (21 Duke Street, Dublin 2, Grafton Street; ☎ 01-677-5271) for a sandwich and a glass of wine, and you can do the same, or you can dine on one of the daily specials. **O'Neill's** (2 Suffolk Street, Dublin 2, Grafton Street; ☎ 01-679-3671) has a carvery that packs in a big lunch crowd. Another busy lunch spot is the **Stag's Head** (1 Dame Court, Dublin 2, Temple Bar; ☎ 01-679-3701), where you can enjoy sandwiches and hot meals amid Victorian splendor and beneath the enormous, eponymous showpiece.

(Also see pub profiles on page 162.)

QUEEN OF TARTS 4 Cork Hill, Dublin 8, Dublin Castle and the Cathedrals; ☎ 01-670-7499; all city-center buses. Fresh baked goods and scones so light they float off your plate are the main temptations, but you shouldn't indulge in the sweets until you polish off one of the equally excellent sandwiches, salads, or tarts. The surroundings are cramped but aromatic and homey, and the prices most reasonable. Monday through Friday, 7:30 a.m. to 6 p.m.; Saturday, 9 a.m. to 6 p.m.; Sunday, 10 a.m. to 6 p.m.

WAGAMAMA South King Street, Dublin 2, St. Stephen's Green; ☎ 01-478-2152; all city-center buses. The ubiquitous London chain, a favorite for yummy and inexpensive noodles and other Asian dishes, has arrived in Dublin, bringing with it the communal tables, minimalist surroundings, and very reasonable prices that make it a megahit across the Irish Sea. Monday through Saturday, noon to 10:50 p.m.; Sunday, noon to 9:50 p.m.

RESTAURANTS IN DUBLIN

 Beshoffs ★ ★ ★ ½

FISH AND CHIPS	INEXPENSIVE	QUALITY ★ ★ ★ ½	VALUE ★ ★ ★ ★

6 Upper O'Connell Street, Dublin 1, Central Dublin; ☎ 01-872-4400
14 Westmoreland Street, Dublin 2, Trinity College and Temple Bar;
☎ 01-677-8026

Buses All city-center buses. **Reservations** No. **Entree range** €3–€7; full meals from €6.95. **Payment** Cash only. **Bar** Beer and wine only. **Disabled access** Yes. **Hours** Monday–Saturday, 10 a.m.–9 p.m.; Sunday, noon–9 p.m.

MENU RECOMMENDATIONS There's only one reason to eat here.

COMMENTS Dubliners have been stepping into this venerable "chipper" since the early 20th century, and no one can say standards have slipped. The freshest salmon, haddock, and sole are served alongside chips made from potatoes grown on the outfit's own farm. The O'Connell Street establishment, the flashier of the two, has recently been done up in a vaguely Edwardian style, but that barely disguises the fact that this is a no-nonsense self-service sort of place where the emphasis is on dispensing an excellent product.

dublin dining

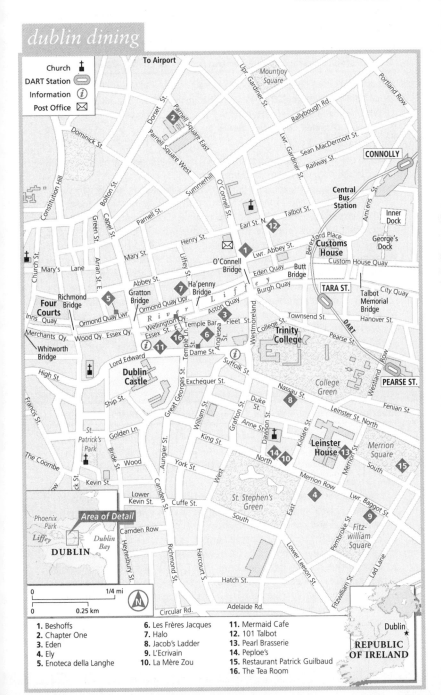

Church
DART Station
Information
Post Office

1. Beshoffs
2. Chapter One
3. Eden
4. Ely
5. Enoteca della Langhe
6. Les Frères Jacques
7. Halo
8. Jacob's Ladder
9. L'Ecrivain
10. La Mère Zou
11. Mermaid Cafe
12. 101 Talbot
13. Pearl Brasserie
14. Peploe's
15. Restaurant Patrick Guilbaud
16. The Tea Room

Dublin
REPUBLIC OF IRELAND

Chapter One ★ ★ ★ ★ ½

| MODERN IRISH | VERY EXPENSIVE | QUALITY ★ ★ ★ ★ ½ | VALUE ★ ★ ★ ½ |

18–19 Parnell Square, Dublin 1, Central Dublin; ☎ 01-873-2266

Buses 11, 13, 16, 16A, 22, and 22A; **DART:** Connolly Street. **Reservations** Required. **Entree range** €27–€45; 2-course lunch, €27.50; 3-course lunch, €31; pre-theatre menu, Tuesday–Saturday, 6–7 p.m., €32.50. **Payment** AE, MC, V. **Bar** Full service. **Disabled access** Yes. **Hours** Tuesday–Friday, 12:30–2:30 p.m., 6–11 p.m.; Saturday, 6–11 p.m.

MENU RECOMMENDATIONS Selections from the charcuterie trolley, chicken wrapped in pancetta, roasted scallops.

COMMENTS Depending on how you choose to look at it, the cellar of the Dublin Writers Museum is either an odd or an appropriate locale for this bastion of good taste and fine cuisine. Granted, few of the scribes you will encounter in the exhibits upstairs could ever have afforded to dine in a place like this (though the excellent €20 house wine might appeal), but the elegantly modern décor beneath brick arches, the flawless service, and the sublime preparations of Chef Ross Lewis will transport you to poetic realms. Many smart innovations make this lovely place all the more appealing: The charcuterie trolley, laden with Irish hams and salamis, provides a fine start to a meal; the lunch menus provide an affordable treat while exploring the sights north of the River Liffey; and a special pre-theatre menu makes an evening at the nearby Gate all the more memorable.

Eden ★ ★ ★

| CONTINENTAL | MODERATE | QUALITY ★ ★ ★ | VALUE ★ ★ ★ |

Meeting House Square, Dublin 2, Temple Bar; ☎ 01-670-5372

Buses 51B, 51C, 68, 69, 79. **Reservations** Recommended. **Entree range** €18–€28; 2-course lunch, €19.50; 3-course lunch, €24. **Payment** AE, DC, MC, V. **Bar** Full service. **Disabled access** Yes. **Hours** Daily, 12:30–3 p.m., 6–10:30 p.m.

MENU RECOMMENDATIONS Scallops, venison, duck confit, smokies (smoked haddock with crème fraîche and melted cheddar), vegetarian dishes.

COMMENTS This bright, airy room facing a lovely square is furnished in white vinyl and chrome, a throwback to the 1990s that looks so dated as to be stylishly retro. The overall effect, though, is soothing, especially when tables spill into the square in warm weather, and once the appetizers arrive it soon becomes clear that Eden is not just about trendy appearances. Instead, the emphasis is on creative and truly excellent cooking that brings together fresh seafood, game, and Irish produce; many specials are prepared daily, often including vegetable curries and other meatless dishes. Weekend brunches are popular and an especially good value.

Ely ★ ★ ★ ★

| MODERN IRISH | MODERATE | QUALITY ★ ★ ★ ½ | VALUE ★ ★ ★ ★ |

22 Ely Place, Dublin 2, St. Stephen's Green; ☎ 01-676-8986

Buses 7, 7A, 8, 10, 11, 13. **Reservations** Not necessary. **Entree range** €8.50–€24. **Payment** AE, MC, V. **Bar** Full service. **Disabled access** Limited. **Hours** Monday–Wednesday, noon–3 p.m., 6–9:30 p.m.; Thursday and Friday, noon–3 p.m., 6–11 p.m.; Saturday, 1–3 p.m., 6–11 p.m.

MENU RECOMMENDATIONS Bangers and mash, fresh oysters, burgers, carpaccio of beef.

COMMENTS Clearly, Dubliners welcome an alternative to the traditional pub, given the way they crowd into this two-level brick-walled wine bar and good-value eatery near St. Stephen's Green. No one will boot you out if you ask for a Guinness, but what a pity when dozens of excellent wines are available by the glass, accompanied by food that ranges from the light-snack variety to full meals.

Enoteca della Langhe ★ ★ ★ ★

| WINE BAR | INEXPENSIVE | QUALITY ★ ★ ★ ★ | VALUE ★ ★ ★ ★ ½ |

24 Ormond Quay, Dublin 1, Central Dublin; ☎ 01-888-0834

Buses 70, 80. **Reservations** Not necessary. **Entree range** €8–€12. **Payment** MC, V. **Bar** Wine only. **Disabled access** Yes. **Hours** Monday–Wednesday, 12:30 p.m.–midnight; Thursday–Saturday, 3:30 p.m.–1 a.m.; Sunday, 3:30 p.m.–midnight.

MENU RECOMMENDATIONS Bruschetta, cheese and salami plates, pastas.

COMMENTS Time was, the only reason to hang out here on the quiet, moody north banks of the River Liffey was to sip tea and browse through books at the recently closed, much-missed Winding Stair bookshop and cafe. With bright lights and lively chatter, this delightful and serious-minded purveyor of wine by the glass and Italian ambience does an admirable job of filling the gap. Many patrons stop by only to sip wine and watch soccer, but you can make a very satisfying meal out of the simple and delicious offerings.

Halo ★ ★ ★ ½

| FRENCH | EXPENSIVE/VERY EXPENSIVE | QUALITY ★ ★ ★ ½ | VALUE ★ ★ ★ ★ |

Morrison Hotel, Ormond Quay, Dublin 1, Central Dublin; ☎ 01-878-2999

Buses 70, 80. **Reservations** Required. **Entree range** €20–€45. **Payment** AE, MC, V. **Bar** Full service. **Disabled access** Yes. **Hours** Daily, noon–3 p.m., 6–10 p.m.; sandwiches and other light fare served 3–6 p.m.

MENU RECOMMENDATIONS Salmon with horseradish, lamb rump with lamb sausage, short ribs of Irish beef.

COMMENTS Stepping into the exotic dining room of the über-hip Morrison Hotel is a little like entering a circus tent: great swaths of purple fabric, angled mirrors, multiple levels, and a lively buzz create a theatrical environment. Trappings aside, though, dining well is serious business here, and if one Dublin restaurant epitomizes the city's bold new culinary frontier, this is it—the kitchen sends out French classics with a slight fusion twist. Inventive pricing makes the experience quite accessible—many of the tempting appetizers, such as fresh oysters with an anise glaze and salads laden with Irish produce, are also available as reasonably priced dinner plates.

 Jacob's Ladder ★★★★½

| MODERN IRISH | MODERATE/EXPENSIVE | QUALITY ★★★★½ | VALUE ★★★★ |

4 Nassau Street, Dublin 2, Trinity College; ☎ 01-670-3868

Buses 7, 8, 10, 11. **Reservations** Recommended. **Entree range** €15–€30. **Payment** AE, MC, V. **Bar** Full service. **Disabled access** Limited. **Hours** Tuesday–Friday, 12:30–2:30 p.m., 6–10 p.m.; Saturday, 12:30–2:30 p.m., 6–11 p.m.

MENU RECOMMENDATIONS Seafood stew, panfried filet of cod.

COMMENTS A ladderlike climb indeed is required to reach these upstairs rooms, but the effort is rewarded with lovely views through high windows over Trinity College. Simple furnishings and plain wood floors don't detract from this pleasant outlook, and the excellent service does nothing to dispel the myth that you're in a special place high above the city. Adrian Roche's careful preparations do homage to the freshest local ingredients, with an emphasis on seafood.

La Mère Zou ★★★★

| FRENCH | EXPENSIVE | QUALITY ★★★★ | VALUE ★★★½ |

22 St. Stephen's Green, Dublin 2, St. Stephen's Green; ☎ 01-661-6669

Buses 10, 11A, 11B, 13, 20B. **Reservations** Recommended. **Entree range** €20–€28; prix-fixe lunch, €25; early-bird dinner, Monday–Saturday, 6–7 p.m.; Sunday, all evening, €24. **Payment** AE, MC, V. **Bar** Full service. **Disabled access** Yes. **Hours** Monday–Thursday, 12:30–2:30 p.m., 6–10 p.m.; Friday, 12:30–2:30 p.m., 6–11 p.m.; Saturday, 6–11 p.m.; Sunday, 6–9:30 p.m.

MENU RECOMMENDATIONS Mussels (prepared any way).

COMMENTS Lacquered orange walls and orange-and-yellow-plaid fabrics brighten the basement quarters of this lovely little outpost of rural France facing St. Stephen's Green. The cuisine, as charmingly country French as the décor, includes reliable old standbys such as mussels (prepared in many different ways) and confit of duck. The set menus are of excellent value and are most welcome on Sunday, when a set menu is available throughout the evening, making La Mère Zou especially appealing for a homey dinner.

L'Ecrivain ★★★★½

| MODERN IRISH | VERY EXPENSIVE | QUALITY ★★★★½ | VALUE ★★★★ |

109a Lower Baggot Street, Dublin 2, Georgian Dublin; ☎ 01-661-1919

Bus 10. **Reservations** Required. **Entree range** €40–€45; 2-course lunch, €35; 3-course lunch, €45; prix-fixe dinner, €75. **Payment** AE. **Bar** Full service. **Disabled access** Yes. **Hours** Monday–Friday, 12:30–2 p.m., 7–10 p.m.; Saturday, 7–10 p.m.

MENU RECOMMENDATIONS Seared scallops, baked oysters, filet of Irish Angus beef.

COMMENTS One of Ireland's few restaurants to have earned a Michelin star continually lives up to its reputation as the second-finest dining room in town (after Patrick Guilbaud), and Chef Derry Clarke's traditional-yet-innovative approach to meat and seafood classics never fails. The food is sublime, and the two-course lunch special is a relative bargain enjoyed by what seems to be half the business crowd of Dublin. The soothingly toned, peak-ceilinged upstairs dining room is surprisingly casual and welcoming, filled with light during the day and complemented by service that manages to be both adept and casual.

Les Frères Jacques ★ ★ ★ ★

FRENCH/CONTINENTAL   EXPENSIVE   QUALITY ★ ★ ★ ★   VALUE ★ ★ ★ ½

74 Dame Street, Dublin 2, Temple Bar; ☎ 01-672-7258

Buses 50, 50A, 54, 56, 77. **Reservations** Recommended. **Entree range** €25–€35; prix-fixe menus: 2-course lunch, €17.50; 3-course lunch, €22.50; 4-course dinner, €36. **Payment** AE, MC, V. **Bar** Full service. **Disabled access** Yes. **Hours** Monday–Friday, 12:30–2:30 p.m., 7:30–10:30 p.m.; Saturday, 7–11 p.m.

MENU RECOMMENDATIONS Panfried foie gras and apple tarte Tatin; mixed grill of lamb, beef, and veal; crab-stuffed monkfish.

COMMENTS This small, plush room that opens right onto busy Dame Street is a welcome retreat and a bastion of old-world service, atmosphere, and cooking that doesn't shy away from decadent treats such as foie gras and rich sauces. One of the best French restaurants in Dublin, this is a top choice for a romantic dinner, but lunchtime prices, among the biggest culinary bargains in town, are the big draw.

Mermaid Cafe ★ ★ ★

SEAFOOD/MODERN IRISH   EXPENSIVE   QUALITY ★ ★ ★ ½   VALUE ★ ★ ★

69–70 Dame Street, Dublin 2, Temple Bar; ☎ 01-670-8236

Buses 50, 50A, 54, 56A, 77, 77A, 77B. **Reservations** Recommended. **Entree range** €20–€30; prix-fixe lunch, €23.95; prix-fixe dinner, €34.95. **Payment** MC, V. **Bar** Full service. **Disabled access** Yes. **Hours** Monday–Saturday, 12:30–2:30 p.m., 6–10:30 p.m.; Sunday, 12:30–3:30 p.m., 6–9 p.m.

MENU RECOMMENDATIONS Antipasto platter, crab cakes.

COMMENTS You know the food has to be good when diners are willing to pay a lot to crowd into cramped rooms that open unromantically to busy Dame Street through huge windows. Seafood is favored in the kitchen, and many fresh fish dishes, Maryland-style crab cakes (a concession to the fact that the cuisine is American inspired), and a creamy seafood casserole are standouts. Rib-eye steaks and several lamb dishes are served as well. Mermaid Cafe also serves the best Sunday brunch in Dublin, with pancakes, bagels, and other fare that will remind you of home; the restaurant also has a good traditional Irish fry.

101 Talbot ★ ★ ★ ½

| IRISH/VEGETARIAN | MODERATE | QUALITY ★★★★ | VALUE ★★★★ |

101 Talbot Street, Dublin 1, Central Dublin; ☎ 01-874-5011

Buses 27A, 31A, 31B, 32A, 32B, 42B, 43, 44A. **Reservations** Recommended. **Entree range** €11–€18; 2-course early-bird dinner, €21. **Payment** AE, MC, V. **Bar** Full service. **Disabled access** Limited. **Hours** Tuesday–Saturday, 5–11 p.m.

MENU RECOMMENDATIONS Pasta, fresh fish, daily vegetarian specials, organic Irish steak.

COMMENTS A big yellow upstairs room, floored in red linoleum, is completely devoid of pretension, rightly suggesting that the emphasis here is on warm service and good cooking. Vegetarians and the health conscious will delight in a menu that offers several inventive pasta dishes and choices such as couscous topped with vegetables, but the highest-grade Irish beef and pork, along with market-fresh fish, also appear on the daily-changing menu. This wonderful cuisine, excellent value, the location north of the River Liffey (where good restaurants are few and far between), and the proximity of the Gate and Abbey theaters draw a loyal crowd of Dubliners.

Pearl Brasserie ★ ★ ★ ½

| FRENCH | MODERATE/EXPENSIVE | QUALITY ★★★½ | VALUE ★★★½ |

20 Merrion Street Upper, Dublin 2, Georgian Dublin; ☎ 01-661-3627

Buses 10, 11A, 11B, 13, 20B. **Reservations** Recommended. **Entree range** €20–€28; prix-fixe menus: 1-course lunch, €16; 2-course lunch, €21.50; 3-course lunch, €26; dinner, €43 and €51. **Payment** AE, D, MC, V. **Bar** Full service. **Disabled access** Yes. **Hours** Tuesday–Friday, noon–2:30 p.m., 6–10:30 p.m.; Saturday and Sunday, 6–10:30 p.m.

MENU RECOMMENDATIONS Dublin Bay prawns wrapped in smoked duck, pan-fried sea bass, oysters.

COMMENTS A cellarlike downstairs room, warmed by fires and always lively, hits just the right note for a pleasant meal. This is a good place for a long and affordable lunch on a rainy day (lunchtime menus are an excellent value), and a bit of a scene on evenings, when a young, upwardly mobile crowd converges—then, the oyster bar is a perfect choice for light grazing and lively chatter.

Peploe's ★ ★ ★

| WINE BAR | MODERATE/EXPENSIVE | QUALITY ★★★ | VALUE ★★★ |

16 St. Stephen's Green, Dublin 2, St. Stephen's Green; ☎ 01-676-3144

Buses 10, 11A, 11B, 13, 20B. **Reservations** Not necessary. **Entree range** €10–€18. **Payment** AE, MC, V. **Bar** Full service. **Disabled access** Yes. **Hours** Daily, noon–midnight.

MENU RECOMMENDATIONS Braised rump of lamb, rabbit stew, smoked-fish cakes.

COMMENTS In theory, this suite of stylish rooms on the ground floor of a Georgian terrace seems like a welcome retreat, as it is for a crowd of regulars—an informal spot for lunch or a snack while shopping on nearby Grafton Street or visiting the nearby museums. But be warned: The place isn't really all that casual, and while the offerings are temptingly inventive, you can easily end up spending a lot on a full meal when all you wanted was a snack and a glass of wine.

Restaurant Patrick Guilbaud   ★ ★ ★ ★ ½

FRENCH	VERY EXPENSIVE	QUALITY ★ ★ ★ ★ ½	VALUE ★ ★ ★ ½

The Merrion Hotel, 21 Merrion Street, Dublin 2, Georgian Dublin;
☎ **01-676-4192**

Buses 10, 11A, 11B, 13, 20B. **Reservations** Required. **Entree range** €35–€50; 2-course lunch, €30; 3-course lunch, €45; evening tasting menu, €130. **Payment** AE, DC, MC, V. **Bar** Full service. **Disabled access** Yes. **Hours** Tuesday–Saturday, 12:30–2:15 p.m., 7:30–10:15 p.m.

MENU RECOMMENDATIONS Ravioli of lobster, honey-roasted quail.

COMMENTS It's easy to feel like a country mouse in Dublin's (and Ireland's) most celebrated restaurant, although the surroundings soon put you at ease. Lovely works by Irish painters enliven the simple and elegant décor, and large windows open onto a terrace and the lush and colorful gardens of the Merrion Hotel. The most economical way to sample the classic French cuisine is at lunch, when relatively economical set menus are served, but if you feel like a splurge, try the tasting menu at dinner—from Guinness and oysters to an Irish whiskey dessert, this is an Irish culinary feast that only a Frenchman could devise.

The Tea Room   ★ ★ ★ ★ ½

CONTINENTAL	EXPENSIVE	QUALITY ★ ★ ★ ★ ½	VALUE ★ ★ ★ ★

Clarence Hotel, 6–8 Wellington Quay, Dublin 2, Temple Bar;
☎ **01-407-0813**

Buses 51B, 51C, 68, 69, 79. **Reservations** Recommended. **Entree range** €22–€35; 2-course lunch, €26; 3-course lunch, €30; Sunday lunch, €34.50; 2-course dinner, €47.50, 3-course dinner, €55. **Payment** AE, DC, MC, V. **Bar** Full service. **Disabled access** Yes. **Hours** Monday–Saturday, 12:30–2:30 p.m., 7–10:30 p.m.; Sunday, 12:30–2:30 p.m., 7–9:30 p.m.

MENU RECOMMENDATIONS Daily fresh fish, pheasant and other Irish game.

COMMENTS The main dining room of the Clarence is as chic and cool as the rest of the hotel, awash in light oak and starched linens and bathed in mellow light. But as befits an operation owned by rock band U2, this excellent restaurant pulls off its trendiness without a lot of pretense. An obliging staff and the commodious surroundings (with widely spaced tables and acceptable noise levels) put diners at ease, ready to focus on the marvelous creations of chef Fred Cordonnier. Irish game, fish, and produce provide the basics, and you can sample the excellent preparations on the good-value lunch menus; Sunday lunch, especially, fills the bill if you feel like treating yourself to a luxurious afternoon without breaking the bank.

ENTERTAINMENT *and* NIGHTLIFE *in* DUBLIN

TO KEEP UP WITH WHAT'S HAPPENING in Dublin, check out **www.dublinevents.com** and **www.eventguide.com** for up-to-the-minute entertainment listings, and **www.ireland.com,** the online version of the *Irish Times.* Handy print resources include *In Dublin,* published every two weeks and available at newsstands (€3); the Thursday edition of the *Irish Times* (€0.50); and *Where: Dublin,* handed out free at better hotels. Another place to check out what's happening in Dublin is **www.ticketmaster.ie**—scan the listings, but avoid paying the high per-ticket service charge by purchasing directly from the box offices.

THEATER

DUBLIN, WHICH HAS A LONG TRADITION of staging good theater, can claim Richard Brinsley Sheridan (*The School for Scandal*), George Bernard Shaw (*Major Barbara* and many others), John Millington Synge (*The Playboy of the Western World*), Sean O'Casey (*The Plough and the Stars*), and Samuel Beckett (*Waiting for Godot*) as its own. While the theater scene in Dublin is, naturally, much smaller than those in New York and London, the Abbey and the Gate are among two of the world's great theaters, and Dublin has several excellent smaller stages as well.

ABBEY THEATRE 26 Abbey Street, Dublin 1; ☎ 01-878-7222; **www.abbeytheatre.ie;** buses 27B, 53A, most city-center buses to O'Connell Street stops; DART: Connolly. Tickets €15 to €30, €9 for seniors and students at some performances; box-office hours Monday through Saturday, 10:30 a.m. to 7 p.m. Ireland's national theater, founded in 1904 by W. B. Yeats, Lady Augusta Gregory (Yeats's patron), and playwright J. M. Synge, is famous for introducing many of the major Irish works of the 20th century. The Abbey continues to stage traditional Irish theater, while its smaller stage, the Peacock, strays into more experimental terrain.

BEWLEY'S CAFÉ 78–79 Grafton Street, Dublin 2; ☎ 086-878-4001; **www.bewleyscafetheatre.com;** all city-center buses. One of Dublin's most beloved institutions is this upstairs stage with its lunchtime presentations of short (less than 1 hour long), often innovative dramas. Performances, accompanied by soup and sandwiches, are Monday through Saturday at 1:10 p.m. and cost €12.

THE GATE Cavendish Row, Dublin 1; ☎ 01-874-4045; **www.gate-theatre .ie;** buses 3, 10, 11, 13, 16, 19. Tickets €20 to €25; box-office hours Monday through Saturday, 10 a.m. to 7 p.m. This lovely Georgian hall is the setting for Ireland's "second stage," where the repertoire includes the classics and contemporary works, usually by better-known European and American playwrights.

SAMUEL BECKETT CENTRE Trinity College, Dublin 2; ☎ 01-608-2266; **www.tcd.ie;** all city-center buses. Ticket prices and box-office hours vary. The theater is the stage for Trinity College drama students, whose work can be exceptional, and also hosts visiting theater and dance companies.

CLASSICAL MUSIC, OPERA, AND DANCE

DANCE THEATRE OF IRELAND Bloomfields Centre, Lower Georges Street, Dún Laoghaire; ☎ 01-280-3455; **www.dancetheatreireland.com;** DART: Dún Laoghaire. Ticket prices and box-office hours vary. Innovative choreography set against multimedia backdrops is the hallmark of this troupe.

HUGH LANE MUNICIPAL GALLERY OF MODERN ART Parnell Square North, Dublin 1; ☎ 01-222-5550; **www.hughlane.ie;** buses 11, 13, 16, 16A, 22, 22A. Dublin's exquisite museum of Impressionist and other 19th- and 20th-century art hosts popular Sunday-at-noon concerts, when jazz and classical musical are on tap. The free concerts last one hour. Admission is on a first-come, first-seated basis.

NATIONAL CONCERT HALL Earlsfort Terrace, Dublin 2; ☎ 01-417-0000; **www.nch.ie;** buses 10, 11, 13, 14, 14A, 15A, 15B. Box-office hours Monday through Friday, 10 a.m. to 3 p.m. and 6 p.m. to end of performance. The hall is home to the National Symphony Orchestra and the Concert Orchestra, both linked to RTE, the national broadcast network; also hosted are many visiting orchestras and artists. Tickets for the National Symphony Orchestra and the Concert Orchestra cost €10 to €32.

OPERA IRELAND Gaiety Theatre, King Street South, Dublin 2; ☎ 01-677-1717; **www.gaietytheatre.com;** buses 10, 11A, 11B, 13, 20B. Tickets from €10; box-office hours Monday through Saturday, 10 a.m. to 6 p.m. or to performance start times. Ireland's best-known and highly respected opera company does a varied repertoire from classics to new works in the fall and spring.

OTHER PERFORMING-ARTS VENUES

GAIETY King Street South, Dublin 2; ☎ 01-677-1717; **www.gaiety theatre.com;** buses 10, 11A, 11B, 13, 20B. Ticket prices vary; box-office hours Monday through Saturday, 11 a.m. to 7 p.m. Another remnant of Victorian Dublin, this theater is the home of Opera Ireland and also hosts concerts and drama.

OLYMPIA 72 Dame Street, Dublin 2; ☎ 01-679-3323; **www.mcd.ie/olympia;** all city-center buses. Ticket prices vary; box-office hours Monday through Saturday, 10 a.m. to 6 p.m. This Victorian music hall is an atmospheric place to see any kind of performance, which here could be anything from a rock concert to a ballet.

POINT DEPOT North Wall Quay, Dublin 1; ☎ 818-719391; **www.thepoint.ie;** bus 53; DART: Connolly. Ticket prices vary; box-office hours Monday through Saturday, 10 a.m. to 6 p.m. This is Ireland's premier venue for big-name concerts, from Bruce Springsteen and Elton John to touring musicals.

PROJECT ARTS CENTRE 39 Essex Street East, Dublin 2; ☎ 01-881-9613; **www.project.ie;** buses 21A, 50, 50A, 78, 78A, 78B. Tickets €10 to €20; box-office hours Monday through Saturday, 10 a.m. to 6 p.m. Dublin's venue for the cutting edge often features performance art, modern dance, and fringe-theater pieces.

ROYAL DUBLIN SOCIETY (RDS) Merrion Road, Ballsbridge, Dublin 2; ☎ 01-668-0866; **www.rds.ie** (go here for event information and ticket prices, and to book online); buses 7, 45, 84. Best known as the setting for the Dublin Horse Show, this huge arena occasionally hosts concerts by really big names.

TIVOLI 135–138 Francis Street, Dublin 8; ☎ 01-454-4472; buses 50, 78A. With a broad repertoire ranging from Shakespeare to musicals, the Tivoli is one of the venues for the Dublin Theatre Festival. For more information, go to **www.dublintheatrefestival.com.**

 PUBS

DUBLIN NIGHTLIFE, INDEED Dublin social life, still revolves around the pub—you'll find one around every corner. Many host sessions of traditional music, often nightly and almost always beginning at about 9:30 p.m. and lasting until 11 or so.

unofficial **TIP**
At many pubs, last call is 11:30 p.m., though the Temple Bar establishments frequently serve a bit later.

AULD DUBLINER 17 Anglesea Street, Dublin 2; ☎ 01-677-0527. Overlook the cutesy name and appreciate the merits of this typical Dublin pub, including first-rate nightly sessions of traditional music.

BRAZEN HEAD 20 Lower Bridge Street, Dublin 8; ☎ 01-677-9549. Claims to be the city's oldest may well be justified: the cozy, stone-walled establishment just off the River Liffey was first licensed in 1661 and operates on the site of a drinking establishment from 1198. Robert Emmet and other rebels once met here to discuss Irish freedom; these days crowds gather for nightly traditional-music sessions.

CAFÉ EN SEINE 40 Dawson Street, Dublin 2; ☎ 01-677-4567. A slightly decadent fin-de-siècle atmosphere of Art Deco furnishings seems almost Parisian, and it draws a crowd of upwardly mobile young professionals—as well as Dubliners of every other stripe.

THE CASTLE INN 5 Lord Edward Street, Dublin 2; ☎ 01-475-1122. Stone walls, stone fireplaces, stone floor—the place seems more like a castle than nearby Dublin Castle and is an appropriate setting for Irish music and dance sessions.

DAVY BYRNE'S 21 Duke Street, Dublin 2; ☎ 01-677-5217. In James Joyce's *Ulysses,* Leopold Bloom pops in for a sandwich, and that fictional repast has put the place on the map forever. Most pleasant for lunch or during the afternoon, and a quiet refuge from nearby Grafton Street.

DOHENY AND NESBITT 5 Lower Baggot Street, Dublin 2; ☎ 01-676-2945. Snug, Victorian, and wonderfully quiet on a rainy afternoon, this remnant of old Dublin accommodates a nighttime crush with the grace of an old-timer who's seen it all.

HARCOURT HOTEL 60–61 Harcourt Street, Dublin 2; ☎ 01-478-3677. Not so much a pub as a barroom, the emphasis here is on traditional Irish music, some of the best in the city and performed nightly.

THE LONG HALL 51 South Great George's Street, Dublin 2; ☎ 01-475-1590. This Dublin pub looks the most like a Dublin pub, slathered in polished wood. The place is frequented by habitués who seem to be permanently affixed to the bar, said to be the longest in town.

THE LORD EDWARD 23 Christchurch Place, Dublin 8; ☎ 01-454-2158. Almost as sacred to Dubliners as the medieval cathedral across the street, the two levels of pubdom here provide relaxed surroundings for a pint and a quiet chat.

NEARY'S 1 Chatham Street, Dublin 2; ☎ 01-677-7371. The hushed and upholstered refuge has been a retreat for performers and patrons at the nearby Gaiety Theatre since Victorian times.

O'DONOGHUE'S 15 Merrion Row, Dublin 2; ☎ 01-676-2807. Students, locals, and tourists jostle for elbow room here, but amid the crowds an impromptu traditional-music session is likely to break out.

OLIVER ST. JOHN GOGARTY 57–58 Fleet Street, Dublin 2; ☎ 01-671-1822. The most adult watering hole in Temple Bar—by chronological age, not by behavior—sprawls over several levels and hosts boisterous traditional-music sessions most evenings and on Saturday and Sunday afternoons.

THE STAG'S HEAD 1 Dame Court, Dublin 2; ☎ 01-679-3701. Smoky mirrors and Victorian stained glass provide atmospheric surroundings for a drink after a performance at the nearby Olympia Theatre.

BARS

A FEW WATERING HOLES in Dublin offer a cocktail-lounge atmosphere rather than a pub atmosphere—and there *is* a difference.

COCOON Royal Hibernian Way, Dublin 2; ☎ 01-679-6259. Fashionable young things find themselves wrapped in soothing tones of cream and beige, paying homage to owner and Formula 1 driver Eddie Irvine.

THE LIBRARY Central Hotel, 15 Exchequer Street, Dublin 2; ☎ 01-679-7302. A book-lined, fire-warmed room weathers its current spate of popularity to provide a quiet retreat.

THE MARKET BAR Fade Street, Dublin 2; ☎ 01-613-9094. Cool, cavernous, and adult, this is a fine spot for a quiet conversation and a light meal. No pub grub here for this crowd—first-rate tapas instead.

THE MINT Westin Hotel, College Green, Dublin 2; ☎ 01-645-1234. The Westin occupies a fine old bank, and what better place to escape for a quiet drink than the former vaults?

MORRISON HOTEL BAR Morrison Hotel, Ormond Quay Lower, Dublin 1; ☎ 01-887-2400. Beautiful, comfortable, and with water views—a lovely spot for a cocktail.

OCTAGON BAR Clarence Hotel, 6–8 Wellington Quay, Dublin 2; ☎ 01-407-0800. A little too cool for its own good, Dublin's sleekest, hippest watering hole is nonetheless a treat to experience, and the best place in town to spot a celeb (if you really want to).

GAY AND LESBIAN DUBLIN

THE WINDS OF CHANGE SWEEPING OVER Ireland in recent years have brought with them a little more tolerance for gays and lesbians, but this conservative Catholic country, Dublin included, is a lot less gay friendly than much of the rest of Europe.

THE GEORGE 89 South Great George's Street, Dublin 2; ☎ 01-478-2983. Dublin's largest, longest-established gay bar is part pub, part nightclub, always busy, and open until 2:30 a.m.

IRISH FILM INSTITUTE BAR Irish Film Institute, 6 Eustace Street, Dublin 2; ☎ 01-679-5744. Gay friendly, not gay, this is a delightful place to hang out regardless of your sexual leanings and whether or not you're catching one of the excellent films screened here.

OUT ON THE LIFFEY 27 Ormond Quay, Dublin 1; ☎ 01-872-2480. Second fiddle to The George and not nearly as lively, this watering hole welcomes both men and women in pleasant, laid-back surroundings.

CLUBS

DUBLIN'S CLUB SCENE IS FAIRLY NEW, and, though growing, still small. But, clubgoers here can exude just as much attitude as those in London and New York. When you're ready to switch from cozy pub to trendy club, check out these places.

Lillie's Bordello

TRENDY PLACE TO BE SEEN

**Adam Court, Dublin 2, St. Stephen's Green; ☎ 01-679-9204;
www.lilliesbordello.ie**

Cover €15. **Drink prices** Expensive. **Food available** None. **Hours** Monday–
Saturday, 11 a.m.–2:30 a.m.

COMMENTS The name, inspired by red walls and portraits of nudes, is
as slickly ersatz as the posturing among the well-dressed, 20- and 30-
something poseurs trying to appear cool. You want to shout over the
music (a mix of rock, 1970s and 1980s tunes, and disco): "Will everyone
just relax and be themselves!"

Ri-Ra

FRIENDLY PLACE TO DANCE

**Dame Court, 1 Exchequer Street, Dublin 2, Temple Bar;
☎ 01-677-4835; www.rira.ie**

Cover €5–€10. **Drink prices** Moderate. **Food available** Snacks. **Hours**

Monday–Friday, 11 p.m.–2:30 a.m.; Saturday and Sunday, 10:30 p.m.–2:30 a.m.

COMMENTS The name means "uproar" in Gaelic, but this place is a lot tamer
than that—just a friendly scene for a 20s, 30s, and even older crowd to
hang out and dance to soul, disco, and other hits.

Spirit

CLUB WITH A HOLISTIC APPROACH

**57 Abbey Street, Dublin 1, Central Dublin; ☎ 01-877-9999;
www.spiritdublin.com**

Cover Varies. **Drink prices** Expensive. **Food available** Snacks. **Hours**
Thursday–Sunday, 11 p.m.–5 a.m.

COMMENTS So many experiences under one roof: the Virtue Room provides
a serene atmosphere with incense, aromatherapy, and very mellow
music to help patrons—a mixed bag of youngsters from all walks of life—
chill out. Thus prepared, they can venture into a bar and relax the
old-fashioned way or shake their stress-free limbs on a big dance floor.
To top it off, Spirit also has a performance space where plays and shows
are staged.

Spy and Wax

TWO CLUBS IN ONE

**Powerscourt Townhouse Centre, Dublin 2, Grafton Street;
☎ 01-677-0014; www.pod.ie**

Cover Spy: free, €8 Saturday after midnight; Wax: €5–€8. **Drink prices** Expensive.
Food available None. **Hours** Monday–Saturday, 6 p.m.–3 a.m.

COMMENTS An upstairs-downstairs set of clubs on the swanky Powerscourt
Centre attracts an appropriately well-heeled crowd of young Dublin

professionals. Sometimes patrons are allowed to sashay back and forth between the two spaces, but most times you must pick the experience you want: upstairs Spy is a mellow cocktail lounge, while downstairs Wax centers on the dance floor, where R&B holds sway.

SHOPPING *in* DUBLIN

SHAMROCK MOTIFS STEAL THE SHOW in many Dublin shops, but these days the wares offered are far more alluring than the souvenirs and booze that were once the mainstays of the city's shopping scene. Shopping in Dublin can be an extremely satisfying experience, all the more so because shopkeepers maintain old-fashioned standards such as courtesy, knowledge of the stock, and helpfulness. In general, shops are open Monday through Saturday, 9 a.m. to 6 p.m., and Sunday, noon to 6 p.m. On Thursday evenings, many shops don't close until 8 or 9 p.m.

WHERE TO SHOP

TO MANY DUBLINERS, **O'Connell Street** is still the city's main shopping avenue, although the venerable and wonderful **Clery's** department store is one of the few old-time establishments to remain. Most Dubliners who find themselves in this part of town head west off of O'Connell onto **Henry Street,** a busy pedestrian zone lined with emporia of the large-chain-store ilk. The most fashionable shopping is south of the river these days, on **Grafton Street** and a cluster of other streets around St. Stephen's Green. **Temple Bar,** more famous for restaurants and bars than for shopping, caters to the neighborhood's brisk tourist trade with many small boutiques, while **Nassau Street,** near the national museums, also caters to tourists with souvenirs and excellent made-in-Ireland goods.

SHOPPING CENTERS

BRINGING NEW LEVELS OF SOPHISTICATION to the shopping-center experience is **Powerscourt Centre** (59 William Street, off Grafton Street, Dublin 2), which occupies the former 18th-century townhouse of the Viscount Powerscourt. The likewise upscale **Stephen's Green Centre** (Dublin 2) is on the west side of the Green. North of the River Liffey are **ILAC Shopping Centre** (Henry Street, Dublin 1) and the **Jervis Centre** (Jervis Street, off O'Connell Street, Dublin 1). One could argue that **St. George's Arcade** (Dublin 2), the city's oldest shopping center, is really a covered market, Dublin's grand bazaar, if you will. The attractive old place is filled with tony shops as well as stalls selling jewelry and bric-a-brac; all and all, it's a down-to-earth retreat from the glitter of nearby Powerscourt.

DEPARTMENT STORES

ARNOTTS 12 Henry Street, Dublin 1, Central Dublin; ☎ 01-872-1111; all city-center buses. Dublin's largest department store carries just about everything, as well as a smaller selection, focusing on designer fashion, in a Grafton Street branch.

BROWN THOMAS 88–95 Grafton Street, Dublin 2, Grafton Street; ☎ 01-605-6666; all city-center buses. Exclusive, expensive, and a showcase for top designers, among whom are many from Ireland.

CLERY'S O'Connell Street, Dublin 1, Central Dublin; ☎ 01-878-6000; all city-center buses. Old-fashioned and as comfortable as an old glove, Clery's is a bastion of traditional clothing and home furnishings.

DUNNES STORES Henry Street, Dublin 1, Central Dublin; ☎ 01-671-4629; all city-center buses. This is the flagship of a popular chain that dependably outfits Dubliners in cheap casual clothing.

MARKS AND SPENCER 15–20 Grafton Street, Dublin 2, Grafton Street; ☎ 01-679-7855; all city-center buses. The British chain is a hit in Dublin, too, stocking sensible and sensibly priced fashions and basics (from groceries to undies).

MARKETS

LIBERTY MARKET 71 Meath Street, near Christ Church Cathedral, Dublin 8; Friday and Saturday, 10 a.m. to 6 p.m.; Sunday, noon to 5 p.m.; buses 21A, 50, 50A, 78, 78A, 78B. Bric-a-brac, clothing, and crafts.

MEETING HOUSE SQUARE Temple Bar, Dublin 2; Saturday and Sunday, 10 a.m. to 5 p.m.; buses 50, 50A, 54, 56, 77. Produce, fruits, cheeses, and other goods fresh off the farm.

MOORE STREET MARKET West of O'Connell Street, Dublin 1; daily, 10 a.m. to 4 p.m.; buses 25, 34, 37, 38A, 66A, 67A. Local color is abundant in the city's main market, along with fruits, vegetables, flowers, and inexpensive clothing.

TEMPLE BAR SQUARE Temple Bar, Dublin 2; Saturday and Sunday, 11 a.m. to 4 p.m.; buses 50, 50A, 54, 56, 77. Used and rare books, magazines, and prints are lodestones for browsers.

WHERE TO FIND . . .
Antiques

There are two Dublin stops for any hunter. **Francis Street** (near Christ Church Cathedral) is one long row of antiques shops; buses 21A, 50, 50A, 78, 78A, 78B. **O'Sullivan** (43–44 Francis Street, ☎ 01-454-1143) is internationally known for its fine furniture, and many shops on this street sell similarly exquisite pieces. A large and much-attended **Antiques and Collectibles Fair** draws vendors from throughout Ireland to Newman House (85–86 St. Stephen's Green) every second Sunday; buses 10, 11, 13, 14, 14A, 15A, 15B.

Books

Dubliners are still lamenting the closure of **The Winding Stair,** a wonderful old shop overlooking the River Liffey. Some good substitutes are **Cathach Books** (10 Duke Street, Dublin 2; ☎ 01-671-8676), which is oriented toward rare books and first editions, and **Secret Book and Record Shop** (15A Wicklow Street, Dublin 2; ☎ 01-679-7272), good hunting grounds for less-expensive secondhand editions. **Books Upstairs** (36 College Green, Dublin 2; ☎ 01-679-6687) is a large general-interest shop that caters to students at nearby Trinity College, as does **Hodges Figgis** (56 Dawson Street, Dublin 2; ☎ 01-677-4754). **Eason's** (40 O'Connell Street, Dublin 1; ☎ 01-858-3800) is a big, brightly lit chain with a fairly unliterary stock of books, but it's a great spot for stationery needs and European magazines. For all, city-center buses.

Crystal and China

Brown Thomas department store (see page 167), on Grafton Street, Dublin 2, carries a large line of Irish china and crystal. You'll find another huge selection at the **China Showrooms** (32–33 Abbey Street, Dublin 1; ☎ 01-878-6211; buses 27B, 53A), where Waterford, Belleek, and all the other big Irish names are available.

Heritage

Nassau Street provides one-stop shopping for souvenir hounds, and two shops even send visitors home with an Irish pedigree. **House of Names** (26 Nassau Street, Dublin 2; ☎ 01-679-7287) and **Heraldic Artists** (3 Nassau Street, Dublin 2; ☎ 01-679-7020) affix your family name and crest to everything from coasters to sweaters to shields; buses 5, 7A, 15A, 15B, 46, 55, 62, 63, 83, 84. If you're not sure if you do indeed have a heraldic Irish name, not to worry—Heraldic Artists will help you investigate your Irish heritage.

Irish Crafts

The **Kilkenny Design Centre** (6–10 Nassau Street, Dublin 2; ☎ 01-677-7066) and **Blarney Woollen Mills** (21–23 Nassau Street, Dublin 2; ☎ 01-671-0068) are both in Georgian Dublin; buses 5, 7A, 15A, 15B, 46, 55, 62, 63, 83, 84; DART: Pearse. Conveniently located just down the street from one another, these shops provide easy shopping for superb handwoven sweaters and other knitwear (especially at Blarney, an outlet of the Cork-based mills), as well as distinctive Irish ceramics and pottery (especially at Kilkenny). Other high-quality woolens and housewares are available just around the corner at **Avoca Handweavers** (11–13 Suffolk Street, Dublin 2; ☎ 01-677-4215; same buses). Another popular neighborhood spot of the same ilk is **House of Ireland** (37–38 Nassau Street, Dublin 2; ☎ 01-671-1111), carrying tweeds, crystal, and all things Irish.

Whichcraft (5 Castlegate, Lord Edward Street, Dublin 2; ☎ 01-670-9371; buses 50, 54A, 56A, 65, 65A, 77, 77A, 123, 150) features the work of artisans from throughout Ireland, creating a showcase for the latest and finest in pottery, weaving, glass, and more. **Craft Centre of Ireland** (atop the Stephen's Green Centre, Dublin 2; ☎ 01-475-4526; all cross-city buses) also showcases the work of Irish artisans. **Tower Craft Design Centre** (Grand Canal Quay, Dublin 2; ☎ 01-677-5655; bus 2 or 3; DART: Pearse) is an enclave of artisans who work in an old sugar-refining plant, creating everything from cards to carpets. **Louis Mulcahy** (46 Dawson Street, Dublin 2; ☎ 01-670-9311; **www.louismulcahy.com;** buses 10, 11A, 11B, 13, 20B) is an Irish institution, creating ceramics from his studio on the Dingle peninsula, of which this shop is an outlet.

Irish Music

Most Dublin music shops—even the megastores such as **HMV** (Grafton Street, Dublin 2; ☎ 01-679-5334; all cross-city buses) and **Tower Records** (around the corner at 6–8 Wicklow Street, Dublin 2; ☎ 01-671-3250)—sell traditional Irish music, and employees usually know quite a bit about it. **Claddagh Records** (2 Cecilia Street, Dublin 2; ☎ 01-677-0262; all cross-city buses) stocks the city's largest selection and also posts notices of who's performing where in Dublin and elsewhere in Ireland. At the **Celtic Note** (12 Nassau Street, Dublin 2; ☎ 01-670-4157; buses 5, 7A, 15A, 15B, 46, 55, 62, 63, 83, 84), you might even hear live music as you browse the extensive stock.

EXERCISE *and* RECREATION *in* DUBLIN

WHO KNEW? Dublin is paradise for the recreation enthusiast.

BEACHES

A DOZEN OR SO ARE WITHIN EASY REACH from the city, many via public transportation. **North Bull Island, Malahide,** and **Howth,** all to the north of the city center, have clean sands and good swimming; bus: 130 from Abbey Street to Bull Island; DART to Howth and Malahide. **Killiney** and **Sandymount,** to the south, also have nice long beaches, although tides at Sandymount can be extremely strong; DART to both.

FISHING

A FISHING TRIP IS JUST A DART RIDE AWAY to the shores of **Dublin Bay,** to **Howth** or **Malahide** north of the city center, or south to **Dún Laoghaire;**

unofficial **TIP**
A good source of information on sea angling and freshwater fishing around Dublin is the **Irish Tourist Board**'s Web site, **www .angling.travel.ie,** which provides info on guides, where to fish, and other resources.

all locations offer fishing from rocks and/or piers. For more information on these places, see "Day Trips from Dublin," on facing page.

GOLF

YOU DON'T HAVE TO STRAY FAR from the Dublin city center to experience the links for which Ireland is famous. The course closest to the city center is **Elm Park Golf and Sports Club** (Nutley Lane, Dublin 4, Ballsbridge; ☎ 01-269-3438; **www.elmparkgolfclub.ie**), located in a southern residential neighborhood near the Ballsbridge hotels. Greens fees are about €80 weekdays, €100 on weekends. One of the world's leading courses is at **Portmarnock Golf Club,** about 16 kilometers (10 miles) north of the city center and seaside in Portmarnock (☎ 01-846-2968; **www.portmarnockgolfclub.ie**); greens fees of €165 weekdays and €190 weekends. Similarly well known is the **Royal Dublin Golf Club** (☎ 01-833-6346; **www.theroyaldublingolfclub.ie**), located on Bull Island in Dublin Bay; greens fees are about €120.

HORSEBACK RIDING

BY THE WAY, TO THE IRISH this activity is known as "horse riding." Horse trails lace Phoenix Park, where you can rent a horse from **Ashtown Riding Stables** (Ashtown, Dublin 15; ☎ 01-838-3807; buses 37, 38, 39, 40). The stables are open daily, 9:30 a.m. to 5 p.m.; guided trail rides and instruction are available, as is independent riding; rates begin at about €30.

JOGGING

YOU'LL SEE JOGGERS RUNNING through the center of town, but you will be wise not to follow their example—heavy vehicular and pedestrian traffic make city streets less than ideal for exercise. A far better option is **Phoenix Park,** with its acres of greenery and many paths; from the city center, the quickest routes are on buses 10, 25, and 26.

SWIMMING

ONE OF THE BEST PUBLIC POOLS in Dublin is right in the city center, at the **Markievicz Leisure Centre,** Townsend Street, Dublin 2; ☎ 01-672-9121; all cross-city buses; DART: Tara Street. Open Monday through Friday, 7 a.m. to 10 p.m.; Saturday, 9 a.m. to 6 p.m.; Sunday, 10 a.m. to 4 p.m.; €4.70, €8.50 families. The center also has an excellent gym.

WATER SPORTS

Surfdock (Grand Canal Dockyard, Dublin 4; ☎ 01-668-3945; **www.surfdock.ie;** bus 2 or 3; DART: Grand Canal) is the in-town center for sailing, kayaking, and windsurfing, with 17 hectares (42 acres) of enclosed waterway around the Grand Canal. Equipment rental and instruction are available. **Fingal Sailing School,** north of the city in Malahide (☎ 01-845-1979; **www.fingalsailingschool.com;** DART: Malahide), rents sailboats and other craft for excursions in Dublin Bay.

SPECTATOR SPORTS

FOR SCHEDULES AND OTHER INFORMATION, check out the city's many entertainment resources (see page 160).

Football

The game Americans know as soccer is as popular in Ireland as it is elsewhere in Europe. Big international matches are played at **Lansdowne Road Stadium** (62 Lansdowne Road, Dublin 4, Ballsbridge; ☎ 01-668-4601; DART: Lansdowne Road), while matches of the **Eircom League** usually take place at **Dalymount Park** (Phibsborough, Dublin 7; ☎ 01-868-0923; buses 10, 19, 19A, 121, 122), home turf of the locally popular **Bohemians Football Club.**

Gaelic Football and Hurling

These two games are uniquely Irish, and wildly popular. Gaelic football is a blend of soccer, rugby, and football (the American version), while hurling might be compared to lacrosse. Both games involve getting the ball into a net or through goalposts; in Gaelic football the ball can be played with hands or feet, and in hurling it's propelled down the field with hurley sticks. Both games provide plenty of fast action and engender a great deal of enthusiasm at citywide matches organized by the Gaelic Athletic Association; competition comes to a head during the All-Ireland Championship in summer. For information, call the Gaelic Athletic Association at ☎ 01-836-3222 or visit **www.gaa.ie.**

Horse Racing

The main Dublin course, and the closest to the city center, is **Leopardstown** (Foxrock, Dublin 18; ☎ 01-289-2888). Steeplechases are the main events here, including the **Hennessy Gold Cup** in February, although flats are also run throughout the year as well. You can reach the track on bus 46A from the city center; for schedules and other information, go to **www.leopardstown.com.**

DAY TRIPS *from* DUBLIN

HOWTH

A SUBURB SOME 13 KILOMETERS (8 miles) north of Dublin, Howth seems more like a seaside village. Pretty old houses surround a lively fishing pier that's usually thronged with Dubliners buying some of the city's freshest seafood, and the fringes of the town meander toward **Howth Head.** An 8.5-kilometer (5-mile) path skirts the flanks of the rugged headland, providing sensational views of the sea, mountains, and the **Eye of Ireland,** a rocky islet just offshore. DART zips out to Howth from Connolly and other Dublin stations, with service about every 15 to 20 minutes; the trip takes about 20 minutes.

Howth's primary appeal is the chance to catch some sea air on a walk around the busy harbor and along the piers past bobbing fishing boats, then, for some real exercise, around Howth Head. In spring and early summer, you may also want to step into **Howth Castle Rhododendron Gardens,** where some 12 hectares (30 acres) of colorful blossoms create a carpet of color beneath the castle walls. The castle is the ancestral home of the St. Lawrence family and closed to the public, but the rhododendron gardens are open April to June, daily, 8 a.m. to sunset; admission is free; ☎ 01-832-2624.

Attraction in Howth

 National Transport Museum of Ireland ★ ★ ★ ★

APPEAL BY AGE	PRESCHOOL ★★★★	GRADE SCHOOL ★★★★	TEENS ★★★
YOUNG ADULTS ★★★		OVER 30 ★★★	SENIORS ★★★

Grounds of Howth Castle, Dublin 13; ☎ 01-832-0427; www.nationaltransportmuseum.org

Type of attraction Museum of commercial and military vehicles. Admission €3 adults, €1.25 seniors and children, €8 families. Hours June–August, Monday–Saturday, 10 a.m.–5 p.m.; September–May, Saturday, Sunday, and public holidays, 2–5 p.m. When to go In good weather, because many of the exhibits are outdoors. Special comments Kids love this place. How much time to allow About 2 hours.

DESCRIPTION AND COMMENTS An earnest collection tended by transportation buffs is dedicated to preventing buses, trucks, and trams from rusting into oblivion on the junk heap. The 60 vintage vehicles will evoke nostalgia in some, and perhaps a sense of wonderment in visitors accustomed to the comparatively mundane-looking vehicles that clog the road today. Especially appealing is the Pig, an all-purpose truck with a pointed snout that once plied the streets of Dublin and other Irish cities. Even vehicles that look surprisingly like their modern-day descendants, such as the generations of double-decker buses and trams, delight young visitors and may transport their adult companions back to days of yore.

TOURING TIPS If you don't have kids in tow and aren't fascinated by vintage vehicles, spend your time instead walking around Howth Headland.

MALAHIDE

MALAHIDE WOULD BE A PLEASANT TOWN even without its stunning castle and botanical gardens. Attractive lanes run from a green down to the sea, where marinas are cluttered with colorful pleasure craft. Just north of the town center is the vast parkland that surrounds the castle and lends the impression that Malahide is a country town rather than a suburb. DART zips out to Malahide from Connolly and other Dublin stations, with service about every 15 to 20 minutes; the trip takes about 20 minutes.

The 100 hectares (250 acres) of parkland surrounding Malahide Castle are laced with walking paths, and within the park is the 8-hectare (20-acre) **Talbot Botanic Garden,** where more than 5,000 species, many from New Zealand and Australia, thrive in well-tended beds, a walled garden, and a conservatory. The garden is open May to September, daily, 2 to 5 p.m.; €3.50, free for students and seniors. Also on the grounds is the **Fry Model Railway Museum,** where dozens of model trains chug through gorgeous, minutely fabricated Irish landscapes. The price of admission also includes **Tara's Dollhouse,** a collection of antique dolls and toys. The museum is open April to September, Saturday through Thursday, 10 a.m. to 1 p.m. and 2 to 5 p.m.; €6.70 adults, €4.20 children, €5.70 seniors and students, €19 families.

Attraction in Malahide

Malahide Castle ★ ★ ★ ★

APPEAL BY AGE	PRESCHOOL ★★	GRADE SCHOOL ★★	TEENS ★★★
YOUNG ADULTS ★★★	OVER 30 ★★★		SENIORS ★★★

Malahide; ☎ 01-846-2184; www.malahidecastle.com

Type of attraction Medieval castle. **Admission** €6.70 adults, €4.30 children under age 12, €5.70 seniors and students, €19 families. **Hours** January–March, Monday–Saturday, 10 a.m.–5 p.m.; April–September, Monday–Saturday, 10 a.m.–5 p.m., and Sunday, 10 a.m.–6 p.m.; October–December, Monday–Saturday, 10 a.m.–5 p.m. **When to go** In good weather, so you can spend time in the gardens and other parts of the grounds; you'll also want to explore the town and waterfront. **Special comments** For an additional fee of about €5, you can buy a ticket for combined admission to the castle and one of the following: Fry Model Railway Museum (on the grounds), Dublin Writers Museum (see page 137), James Joyce Tower in Sandymount (see page 177), and the Shaw Birthplace (see page 146). **How much time to allow** The better part of a day if you want to visit the gardens, park, and other attractions on the grounds, plus explore the town.

DESCRIPTION AND COMMENTS   The Talbots lived at Malahide Castle for close to 800 years, until the last of the clan sold the place in the 1970s to pay estate taxes and then moved to Tasmania. While the turrets and towers bear the mark of medieval builders, first and foremost Malahide stands out as a place to view the domestic manners of the aristocracy. Accompanied by a taped commentary clumsily broadcast over loudspeakers, visitors step in and out of the salons and bedrooms, brought up to mid-20th-century tastes and conveniences, and where the family once socialized and spent rainy afternoons writing letters. The castle's masterpiece is a Van Wyck portrait of the clan eating breakfast on a morning in 1690—that happened to be the day of the Battle of the Boyne, from which none of the breakfasters returned.

TOURING TIPS   Try to combine a tour of the castle with a visit to the Talbot Botanic Gardens, but note that hours are spotty. Young visitors who deserve a reward for their patience will be delighted with the Fry Model

dublin day trips

Balbriggan

R127

Skerries

St. Patrick's Island

Bernagearagh Bay

Shenick's Island

N1

R127

R128

R108

R126

Donabate

Lambay Island

*Irish
Sea*

Swords

R106

Malahide

4

R106

R122

N1

Dublin
Airport

M1

Portmarnock

Ireland's Eye

R107

R104

Sutton

Howth

N2

R103

2

▲ Ben of
Howth

5

R105

N3

Clontarf

North Bull
Island

N4

DUBLIN

Dublin Bay

Liffey

N7

Royal Canal

R119

N11

R117

R112

Dún
Laoghaire

3

Sandycove

Dalkey

Dalkey Island

R113

Dalkey Hill ▲

Killiney Hill ▲

To Shankill

8

Killiney

7

0 | 2 1/2 mi
0 | 2.5 km

Area
of Detail

Dublin
REPUBLIC
OF IRELAND

1. Hill of Tara
2. Howth Castle
   Rhododendron
   Gardens
3. James Joyce Tower
4. Malahide Castle
5. National Transport
   Museum of Ireland
6. Newgrange
7. Powerscourt House and
   Gardens
8. Glendalough Abbey

ilway Museum and Tara's Dollhouse. A cafe on the castle's ground
por is quite gloomy but will take off the chill with hot meals and deli-
ous pastries.

HILL OF TARA AND NEWGRANGE

TWO OF IRELAND'S MOST IMPORTANT historic sights, both
of them associated with the pre-Christian era, are just to the
h of Dublin.

he **Hill of Tara,** meeting place of pagan princes and Druid priests, is
ilometers (20 miles) northwest of Dublin via the N3; **Newgrange,**
of the world's most extensive prehistoric tombs, is 60 kilometers
(36 miles) north on the N2. Public transportation to both is via bus, to
Navin for the Hill of Tara and to Slane for Newgrange; for schedules
and tour information, check with **Dublin Tourism** (see page 106).

Hill of Tara ★ ★ ★ ½

APPEAL BY AGE	PRESCHOOL ★★	GRADE SCHOOL ★★★	TEENS ★★★
YOUNG ADULTS ★★★		OVER 30 ★★★½	SENIORS ★★★½

North of Dublin, outside Navan; ☎ 046-902-5903

Type of attraction Center of pre-Christian Ireland. **Admission** €2 adults, €1
children and students, €1.25 seniors, €5.50 for families. **Hours** Mid-May–
mid-September, daily, 10 a.m.–6 p.m. **When to go** In good weather, because you'll
be outdoors. **Special comments** A tearoom on the grounds serves snacks and
light meals. **How much time to allow** At least 1 hour, to walk on the hill and visit
the Interpretive Center.

DESCRIPTION AND COMMENTS The seat of the High Kings of Ireland, was,
through the pre-Christian centuries to as late as the 11th century, home
to rulers and an assembly point for tribal and religious leaders from
throughout Ireland. It's significant that when St. Patrick defied Druid
leaders in the fifth century and lit his famous bonfire on Easter Eve, he
did so within sight of the Hill of Tara—making it known to the powerful
elite that Christianity had arrived in Ireland and would challenge pagan
rites. Wooden assembly halls and any other structures of note have long
vanished; what remains is a 90-meter (300-foot) knoll that commands
a view of much of central Ireland. The sight is impressive, but to fully
comprehend the significance of the site, spend time in the well-done
Interpretive Center, where re-creations, timelines, and other exhibits
bring pre-Christian Ireland to life.

TOURING TIPS If you're traveling by car, it's easy to continue on from the Hill
of Tara to Newgrange; the two are about ten kilometers (six miles) apart.

Newgrange ★ ★ ★ ★ ★

APPEAL BY AGE	PRESCHOOL ★★★★	GRADE SCHOOL ★★★★	TEENS ★★★★
YOUNG ADULTS ★★★★		OVER 30 ★★★★½	SENIORS ★★★★★

Outside Slane; ☎ 041-988-0300; www.knowth.com/newgrange

Type of attraction Prehistoric tomb complex. **Admission** €4.25 adults, €1.50 children over age 6 and students, free for children under age 6, €2.75 seniors, €10 families. **Hours** May and mid- through late September, daily, 9 a.m.–6:30 p.m.; June–mid-September, daily, 9 a.m.–7 p.m.; November–February, daily, 9:30 a.m.–5 p.m.; March–April and October, daily, 9:30 a.m.–5:30 p.m. **When to go** Early in spring through summer, to avoid crowds. **Special comments** Admission is by guided tour only, on a first-come, first-served basis; you may have to wait for admission or be turned away. **How much time to allow** At least 1 hour.

DESCRIPTION AND COMMENTS   One of the world's most impressive prehistoric sites predates Stonehenge by 1,000 years. Although lacking the drama the tall monoliths impart to that place, Newgrange is just as transporting. It is estimated that a workforce of hundreds labored for at least two decades to construct the passage tombs, covered by a mound 100 meters (330 feet) across and constructed from some 250,000 tons of stones most likely transported overland from the Wicklow Mountains, 80 kilometers (50 miles) south. Newgrange appears to have done double duty as a burial place and an observatory. On each of five days on and around the winter solstice, the main chamber is brilliantly illuminated by sunlight for 20 minutes—thousands apply to witness the illumination, of whom less than 100 are selected by lottery.

TOURING TIPS   Tours begin at the Brú na Bóinne Visitors Centre, where you will see exhibits introducing the site. Visitors are taken to the mound by coach from there. The center is also the departure point for tours of nearby Knowth, another passage tomb, at which there is no access to the passage and chambers.

DÚN LAOGHAIRE AND SANDYCOVE

A BUSY SEASIDE TOWN at the southern edge of Dublin, **Dún Laoghaire** is known to many travelers as the ferry port for the trip across the Irish Sea to and from Holyhead, in Wales. Those who linger here a bit can walk out to the end of **East Pier,** one of a twin set, each extending for 2.5 kilometers (1.5 miles). Another option is to stay closer to shore and follow the harbor south along **Marine Parade** about one kilometer (less than a mile) to the little seaside settlement of **Sandycove.** Dubliners come here to brace the cold waters of **Forty Foot Bathing Pool,** once reserved for men only, few of whom wore suits—until a decade or so ago, when women stormed the waters and staked a claim. Suit or no suit, the pool can be mighty chilly in winter, but that doesn't seem to deter the hardy. Rising above the waters is **James Joyce Tower,** a rounded, stone tower built in 1804 to help thwart a Napoleonic invasion of Ireland and now famous for its tenuous, though effective, association with James Joyce.

unofficial **TIP**
Dún Laoghaire and Sandycove are both on the DART line, with service from Connolly and other Dublin stations about every 20 minutes.

Attraction in Sandycove

James Joyce Tower ★ ★ ★ ★

| APPEAL BY AGE | PRESCHOOL 1 | GRADE SCHOOL ★ ★ ★ | TEENS ★ ★ ★ |
| YOUNG ADULTS ★ ★ ★ | | OVER 30 ★ ★ ★ | SENIORS ★ ★ ★ |

Sandycove, Dublin; ☎ 01-280-9265;
www.dun-laoghaire.com/dir/jjtower.html

Type of attraction Museum in historic tower. **Admission** €6.50 adults, €4 children, €5.50 seniors and students, €18 families. **Hours** March–October, Monday–Saturday, 10 a.m.–1 p.m. and 2–5 p.m.; Sunday and holidays, 2–5 p.m. **When to go** Anytime. **Special comments** The museum occasionally hosts readings and other Joyce-related events. **How much time to allow** About 1 hour.

DESCRIPTION AND COMMENTS James Joyce stayed here for a week in August 1904, and that sojourn both inspired the opening scene of *Ulysses* and put this distinctive round martello tower from 1804 on the map as a must-see stop on a James Joyce itinerary. The story behind the visit is the most interesting aspect of the place—that and the spectacular views of Dublin Bay from the tower's weapon platform, installed as defense against a potential invasion by Napoleon. Joyce's host was Oliver St. John Gogarty, another literary figure who appears in his guest's great novel (not flatteringly) as Buck Mulligan. The collection of letters, photographs, and first editions is commendable, but you'll learn and see more about the writer at the Dublin Writers Museum and the James Joyce Centre (see pages 137 and 139, respectively).

TOURING TIPS Don't even think of coming here without taking a walk along the sea, either to and from Dún Laoghaire or both; you might want to take DART to Sandycove, visit the museum, then walk back to the DART station in Dún Laoghaire.

THE WICKLOW MOUNTAINS

MANY DUBLINERS CONSIDER THESE gentle, lovely mountains—rising 3,000 meters (10,000 feet) just 30 kilometers (18 miles) to the south—to be one of their city's greatest assets. As well they should: dense forests cover the slopes, and rushing streams sprint through valleys into clear mountain lakes. The mountains are all the more appealing because they cradle one of Ireland's grandest estates, **Powerscourt,** and one of the country's most romantic monastic ruins, **Glendalough Abbey.**

The **Wicklow Way** walking path crosses the mountains, passing through rugged country as well as villages. For information on hiking on the way, and the many other outdoor activities in the park, stop in at the Visitor Centre of **Wicklow National Park,** Glendalough, ☎ 0404-45425; open May to August, daily, 10 a.m. to 6 p.m., and April and September, weekends only, 10 a.m. to 6 p.m.

Tours of the Wicklows

If you're without a car, the only practical way to see the mountains is on a tour. For a strenuous excursion, set off with **Dirty Boots Treks.** You'll be picked up in front of Trinity College and driven high into the mountains for four- to five-hour hikes through gorgeous scenery. Resting and conversation are allowed, and among the rewards is a pint in a country pub before heading back to Dublin. One-day treks are €50; longer treks are also on the calendar. For more information, call ☎ 01-623-6785 or go to **www.dirtybootstreks.com.**

Wild Wicklow Tours pack a lot into a day's outing and embellish the Wicklow scenery with smart and witty commentary. Trips include a brief tour of Dublin, a stop at Sandycove, a shopping break at Avoca Handweavers, a guided tour of Glendalough Abbey and hike through the valley, a pub lunch (not included in the price), a drive over Sally Gap (a scenic mountain pass), and a return through Dún Laoghaire. Chances are you'll have a better time on this tour, and see more, than you would on your own in a car. Tours run daily, with pickup in central Dublin beginning at 8:50 a.m., and returning at 5 or 5:30 p.m.; €28 adults, €25 children and students. For more information, call ☎ 01-280-1899 or go to **www.wildwicklow.ie.**

Attractions in the Wicklows

 ## Glendalough Abbey ★ ★ ★ ★ ½

APPEAL BY AGE	PRESCHOOL ★★★	GRADE SCHOOL ★★★★	TEENS ★★★★
YOUNG ADULTS ★★★★		OVER 30 ★★★★½	SENIORS ★★★★½

About 50 kilometers (30 miles) south of Dublin; ☎ **0404-45325**

Type of attraction Ruins of monastery. **Admission** Free. **Hours** March–mid-October, daily, 9 a.m.–6 p.m.; mid-October–mid-March, daily, 9:30 a.m.–5 p.m. **When to go** Out of high season or early in the day to appreciate the setting with a semblance of peace and solitude. **Special comments** The only drawbacks to this remarkable place are the entrance, where vendors sell wares such as souvenirs and postcards, and a modern hotel that intrudes upon the scenery. **How much time to allow** At least 2 hours, to allow time for a walk around the lakes.

DESCRIPTION AND COMMENTS Glendalough pleases on so many levels. These stone buildings on the floor of a peaceful valley once composed one of Europe's great centers of learning. Remains of the churches, tower, and other buildings (rendered to ruin by 14th-century British plunderers) present a satisfying look at what Ireland's monastic communities were like. Nestled beneath forested mountain slopes alongside a set of interlocking lakes, the place is incredibly romantic. The founder was St. Kevin, one of Ireland's favorite saints and the son of early Irish royalty, who came here in the sixth century to live like a hermit in a dank, creepy cave

no   s St. Kevin's Bed. Kevin probably oversaw the building of
th   hurch of the Oratory; a later church, named for the saint,
sti   its remarkable barrel vaulting. The best-preserved struc-
tu   th-century round tower, and from its 100-foot height a
lar   guided the faithful and those hungry for sustenance and
lea   e monastery.

TOURI   ow the shores of the lakes to the Visitors Centre of
W   onal Park, where you can stock up on information about
th

Powerscourt House and Gardens ★ ★ ★ ★ ½

| APPEAL BY AGE | PRESCHOOL ★ ★ ★ | GRADE SCHOOL ★ ★ ★ ★ | TEENS ★ ★ ★ ★ |
| YOUNG ADULTS ★ ★ ★ ★ | | OVER 30 ★ ★ ★ ★ ½ | SENIORS ★ ★ ★ ★ ½ |

25 kilometers (15 miles) south of Dublin on R117; ☎ 01-204-6000; www.powerscourt.ie

Type of attraction Historic home and magnificent gardens. **Admission** House and garden: €9 adults, €5 children ages 5–16, free for children under age 5, €7.50 seniors and students; waterfall: €4.50 adults, €3 children under age 16, €4 seniors and students. **Hours** House and garden: daily, 9:30 a.m.–5:30 p.m.; waterfall: daily, 10:30 a.m.–7 p.m.; closes at dusk in winter. **When to go** Spring to see the best blooms, or any summer morning to avoid crowds. **Special comments** A shop and a cafe, both run by Avoca Handweavers, feature excellent woolen goods and good food. **How much time to allow** At least half a day to appreciate the gardens and make the trek to the waterfall.

DESCRIPTION AND COMMENTS The first viscount of Powerscourt, a favorite of King James I of England, commissioned this Palladian-style house in 1731, hiring the architect Richard Castle. The handsome facades and ballroom are all that remain of what was one of Ireland's finest houses, which was gutted by a fire in 1974. The gardens, a Victorian addition, have fared better. They are the creation of the gout-afflicted, sherry-swizzling Daniel Robertson, who allegedly had to be pushed around the grounds in a wheelbarrow as he brought his vision to magnificent fruition. His lawns, dells, ponds, statuary, and even a pet cemetery create a showcase of European garden design; they're a delight to explore at random, treating you to one vista after another. Untamed nature lends a hand in the magic of the place, too: Powerscourt Waterfall, on the grounds but a hefty 6 kilometers (3.5 miles) from the house, is Ireland's tallest cascade, plummeting 120 meters (400 feet) into the Dargle River.

TOURING TIPS Wear walking shoes, because you'll be covering quite a bit of ground to see the gardens and the waterfall. You might want to forgo the busy and glitzy cafe and bring a picnic to enjoy in a dell.

unofficial **TIP**
To reach Powerscourt by public transportation, take DART to Bray and bus 185 from there; Dublin Bus and other companies offer tours to the estate. For more information, contact **Dublin Bus** (☎ 01-703-2574) or **Dublin Tourism** (☎ 01-605-7700, www.visitdublin.com).

PART FIVE

THE SOUTH
of IRELAND

IF YOU THINK YOU'LL HEAD SOUTH from Dublin into the boon-docks, you're in for a bit of surprise. While the landscape does roll across the greenest farmland you'll ever see, southern Ireland is an amazingly sophisticated part of the world. You'll enjoy lively towns and cities such as **Cork** and **Kilkenny,** remarkable medieval monuments (none more haunting than the **Rock of Cashel**), and, in places like **Cobh** and **Kinsale,** a good dose of Irish history served up in seaside surroundings.

KILKENNY

KILKENNY OFTEN IS DESCRIBED as Ireland's loveliest medieval city, and in fact it might be fairly said that it's Ireland's loveliest city, period. A castle of mellow stone looms, benevolently these days, above the banks of the River Nore, while medieval houses and churches line charming lanes.

The city's greatest fame came in the Middle Ages, when the Irish Parliament met in **Kilkenny Castle.** But if you've heard of Kilkenny, you're more likely to associate it with cats. Legend has it that Oliver Cromwell's soldiers, occupying the city in 1650, tied the tails of two cats together. They fought each other to the end, and the term "Kilkenny cats" has come to connote those who fight relentlessly, whatever the cost. The apocryphal incident also inspired a verse that many an Irish schoolchild can recite: "There wanst was two cats of

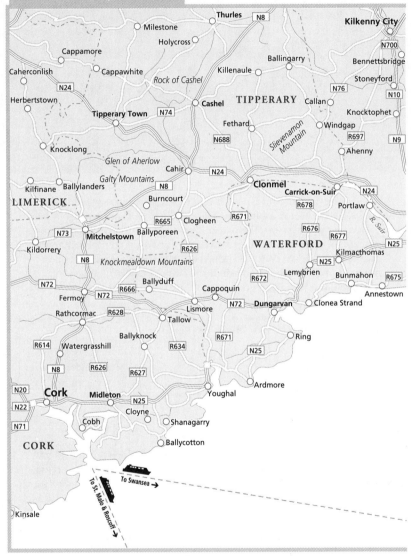

the south of ireland

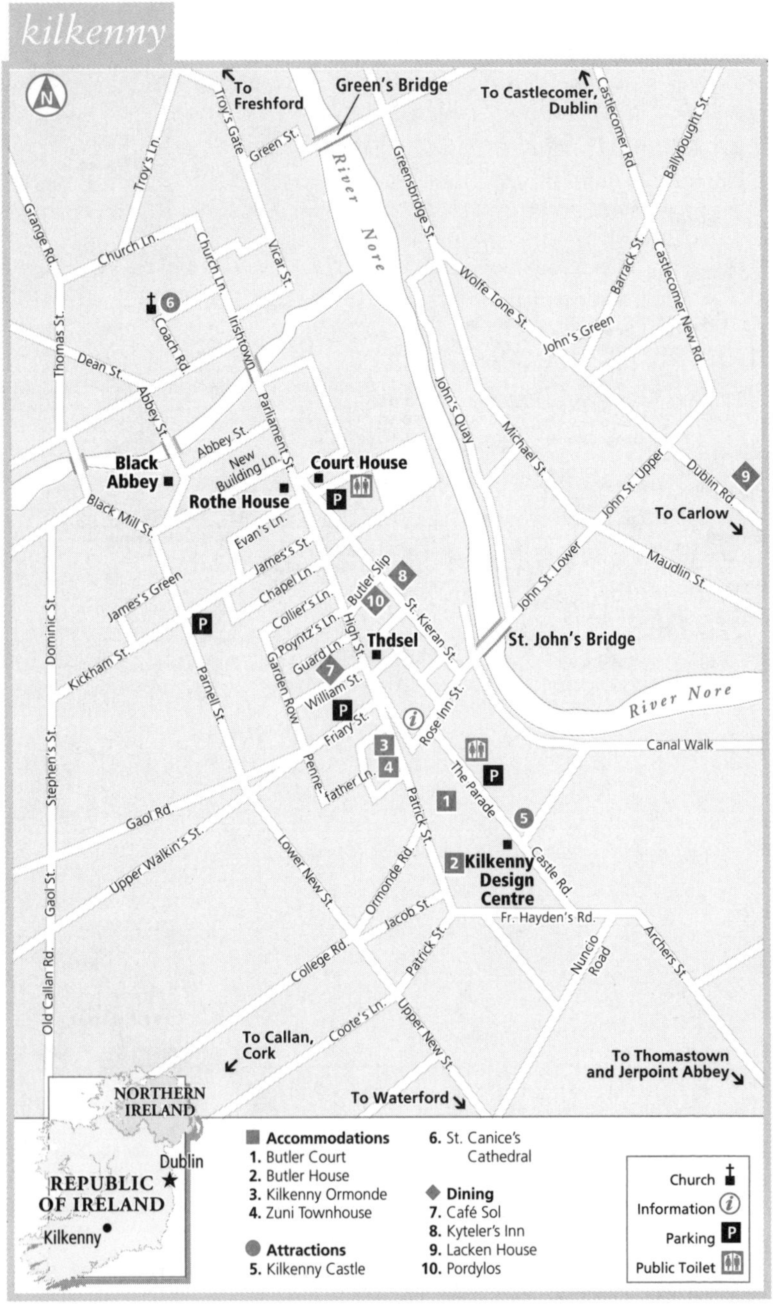

kilkenny
N
To Freshford
Green's Bridge
To Castlecomer, Dublin
Troy's Gate
Green St.
River Nore
Greensbridge St.
Castlecomer Rd.
Ballybought St.
Troy's Ln.
Grange Rd.
Church Ln.
Church Ln.
Vicar St.
Barrack St.
Castlecomer New Rd.
Wolfe Tone St.
John's Green
Coach Rd.
Irishtown
Thomas St.
Dean St.
John's Quay
Michael St.
Abbey St.
Parliament St.
Abbey St.
New Building Ln.
Black Abbey
Court House
Rothe House
Dublin Rd.
John St. Upper
To Carlow
Black Mill St.
Evan's Ln.
James's St.
Maudlin St.
Chapel Ln.
Butler Slip
John St. Lower
James's Green
Collier's Ln.
St. Kieran St.
Poyntz's Ln.
High St.
Thdsel
St. John's Bridge
Dominic St.
Kickham St.
Guard Ln.
Garden Row
William St.
Parnell St.
Rose Inn St.
River Nore
Friary St.
Canal Walk
Stephen's St.
Penne-father Ln.
The Parade
Patrick St.
Gaol Rd.
Upper Walkin's St.
Lower New St.
Ormonde Rd.
Kilkenny Design Centre
Castle Rd.
Gaol St.
Jacob St.
Fr. Hayden's Rd.
College Rd.
Patrick St.
Nuncio Road
Archers St.
Old Callan Rd.
Coote's Ln.
Upper New St.
To Callan, Cork
To Thomastown and Jerpoint Abbey
To Waterford
NORTHERN IRELAND
Dublin
REPUBLIC OF IRELAND
Kilkenny
Accommodations
1. Butler Court
2. Butler House
3. Kilkenny Ormonde
4. Zuni Townhouse
Attractions
5. Kilkenny Castle
6. St. Canice's Cathedral
Dining
7. Café Sol
8. Kyteler's Inn
9. Lacken House
10. Pordylos
Church
Information
Parking
Public Toilet

Kilkenny / Each thought there was one cat too many / So they fought and they fit / And they scratched and they bit / 'Til instead of two cats there weren't any." And now you'll understand why cats appear on so many signs around Kilkenny.

PLANNING YOUR VISIT TO KILKENNY

NICELY HOUSED in a 16th-century almshouse on Rose Inn Street (the lower part of Ormonde Street), the **Kilkenny Tourist Office** provides information on places to stay, what to see and do, and where to dine in Kilkenny and the surrounding region. The staff also will check train and bus schedules for you, and they are really helpful in planning excursions to outlying sights. For information, call ☎ 056-775-1500 or visit **www.southeastireland.travel.ie.** The center is open April to October, Monday through Saturday, 10 a.m. to 6 p.m.; November to March, Monday through Saturday, 9 a.m. to 1 p.m. and 2 to 5 p.m.

Special Events in Kilkenny

Kilkenny's full roster of events includes the **Carlsberg Kilkenny Rhythm & Roots Festival** in late April, a celebration of what can only be described as an Irish version of country music; call ☎ 056-779-0057 or visit **www.kilkennyroots.com.** The **Cat Laughs Comedy Festival,** in June, is one of Europe's leading comedy events; call ☎ 056-776-3416 or visit **www.thecatlaughs.com.** The **Kilkenny Arts Festival** brings music, dance, and theater to town for ten days in August; call ☎ 056-776-3663 or visit **www.kilkennyarts.ie.**

ARRIVING AND GETTING ORIENTED IN KILKENNY

KILKENNY IS APPROXIMATELY 120 KILOMETERS (75 miles) south of Dublin. Trains arrive from Dublin and other Irish cities at McDonagh Station, on the east bank of the River Nore. About four trains per day run between Dublin and Kilkenny; the trip takes a little less than two hours, and the fare is about €20 each way. For information, call toll free ☎ 1850-366-222 or 01-836-6222, or visit **www.irishrail.ie.**

unofficial **TIP**
Parking is severely limited in Kilkenny; the best bet is to park immediately in the large car park in the center of town on Ormonde Street for about €1 per hour or €8 per day. Most hotels in town offer free parking for guests.

By car, Kilkenny is easy to reach on Ireland's national road network; allow about two hours for the trip down the N9 and N78 from Dublin.

Bus Éireann coaches arrive at the train station from throughout Ireland; regional service also operates to and from stops along the Parade in the city center. Buses leave from Dublin for Kilkenny about every three hours, and the trip takes three and a half hours; the fare is about €10 one way and €15 for a round trip. For information, call ☎ 056-776-4933 or visit **www.buseireann.ie.**

How Hotels Compare in the South of Ireland

HOTEL	OVERALL	QUALITY	VALUE	PRICE
KILKENNY				
Zuni Townhouse	★★★★	★★★★½	★★★	€90–€120
Butler House	★★★★	★★★★	★★★	€80–€120
Kilkenny Ormonde	★★★	★★★★	★★★	€110–€160
Butler Court	★★★	★★★	★★★	€60–€120
CORK				
Lancaster Lodge	★★★★	★★★★	★★★★	€74–€100
Hotel Isaacs Cork	★★★★	★★★½	★★★	€75–€100
Lotamore House	★★★½	★★★★	★★★½	€75–€130
Hayfield Manor	★★★½	★★★★	★★½	€200–€240
MIDLETON AND EAST CORK				
Glenview House	★★★★★	★★★★	★★★★	€65–€140
Ballymaloe House	★★★½	★★★★	★★½	€135–€240
Barnabrow Country House	★★★	★★★½	★★★	€80–€120
KINSALE				
Old Presbytery	★★★★	★★★★½	★★★★	€95–€150
Chart House	★★★★	★★★★	★★★	€50–€120
Old Bank	★★★½	★★★	★★½	€170–€245
Friar's Lodge	★★★	★★★	★★★★½	€60–€120
Trident	★★★	★★★	★★½	€110–€140

HOTELS IN KILKENNY

Butler Court ★★★

QUALITY ★★★	VALUE ★★★	€60–€120

Patrick Street, Kilkenny; ☎ 056-776-1178; fax 056-779-0767; info@butlercourt.com; www.butlercourt.com

Location City center. **Amenities and services** 10 rooms; hair dryers, Internet connections. **Elevator** No. **Parking** On property, free. **Price** Includes Continental breakfast; off-season rates are available. **Credit cards** AE, MC, V.

Just around the corner from the castle, John and Yvonne Dalton's ten pleasant contemporary-style units are tucked into an attractive courtyard. The arrangement is a little like that of a motel, in that all rooms open to the outdoors, whether to a patio-like lower court or to an upstairs balcony. The off-the-street location ensures plenty of quiet, despite the central location, and the courtyard is especially welcome in good weather for a relaxing break from sightseeing. Guest rooms are furnished in a comfortable but fairly standard hotel style, with a few touches to add a bit of character (such as cherry hardwood floors) and modern conveniences (such as power showers, which use pumps to create stronger water flow).

Butler House   ★ ★ ★ ★

QUALITY	★ ★ ★ ★	VALUE	★ ★ ★	€80–€120

16 Patrick Street, Kilkenny; ☎ 056-772-2828; fax 056-776-5626; res@butlerhouse.ie; www.butler.ie

Location City center, near castle. **Amenities and services** 13 rooms; hair dryers, satellite TV, in-room tea and coffee facilities, trouser press. **Elevator** No. **Parking** Nearby, free. **Price** Includes full Irish breakfast; off-season rates and Internet specials are sometimes offered. **Credit cards** AE, MC, V.

In the 1970s, the Irish State Design Agency renovated this lovely Georgian mansion that was once part of the Kilkenny Castle estate, blending historic details and a restrained contemporary design that is now a bit out of date but classic enough not to be jarring. Marble mantelpieces, tall windows, and sweeping staircases are accented with soft natural fabrics and soothing earth tones for a distinctive, relaxing atmosphere. Many of the guest rooms are enormous, overlooking well-maintained gardens through huge bow windows; lounge chairs, kilims, contemporary art, and soft lighting add comfort to these remarkable surroundings. Not as stunning are the large but rather spartan bathrooms, although ongoing renovations include improvements such as tub-and-shower combinations. Fresh baked goods and hot breakfasts are served in the Design Centre Café at the end of the garden.

Kilkenny Ormonde Hotel   ★ ★ ★

QUALITY	★ ★ ★ ★	VALUE	★ ★ ★	€110–€160

Ormonde Street, Kilkenny; ☎ 056-772-3900; fax 056-772-3977; info@kilkennyormonde.com; www.kilkennyormonde.com

Location City center. **Amenities and services** 118 rooms; 2 bars, child care, gym, hair dryers, indoor swimming pool, in-room tea and coffee facilities, Internet connections, irons, minibars, nonsmoking rooms, 3 restaurants, room service, satellite TV, sauna, steam room, trouser press. **Elevator** Yes. **Parking** On property, free. **Price** Includes full Irish breakfast. **Credit cards** AE, D, MC, V.

This sprawling modern hotel, handily situated in the center of town, does a large convention and meeting business during the week and caters to family getaways on weekends. The striking contemporary design nicely accommodates the crowds, which always seem to be passing in and out of the hotel, with flowing public spaces, lively bars and restaurants, and a large leisure center. (If you want lodgings that reflect Kilkenny's medieval atmosphere, this is not the place for you.) Guest rooms are decorated in unexciting business-hotel style and loaded with conveniences such as large writing desks; many are set up to accommodate families and, in addition to having a double and single bed, are linked to an adjacent room through an interconnecting door. Some of the rooms and all of the suites have sweeping views over the castle and the old town.

Zuni Townhouse ★ ★ ★ ★

QUALITY	★ ★ ★ ★ ½	VALUE	★ ★ ★	€90–€120

26 Patrick Street, Kilkenny; ☎ 056-772-3999; fax 056-775-6400; info@zuni.ie; www.zuni.ie

Location City center. **Amenities and services** 13 rooms; hair dryers, Internet connections, restaurant, satellite TV. **Elevator** Yes. **Parking** Nearby, free. **Price** Includes full Irish breakfast. **Credit cards** AE, MC, V.

The ground-floor restaurant is the main business here, and a great deal of care goes into providing memorable meals in stylish, edgy surroundings. Unlike many establishments that tack on guest rooms as a second thought, Zuni also minds the hotel end of the business, providing some of Kilkenny's nicest accommodations. Smart and hip, the guest quarters are an oasis of sleek contemporary furniture, brightly painted walls, glamorous fabrics, and high-tech lighting. Sensibly, the décor doesn't take precedence over comfort, and the large, high-ceilinged rooms are soothing and relaxing, plus they're equipped with such welcome amenities as large bathrooms with power showers.

EXPLORING KILKENNY

KILKENNY CASTLE DOMINATES ONE END of the medieval city, **St. Canice's Cathedral** the other. Beginning at the castle, a walk down High Street leads past the **Tholsel,** built in 1761 as the commodities exchange. The handsome arcaded building, topped with a clock tower, later became the assembly rooms, where dances, meetings, and Kilkenny's other social and civic events transpired. Now it houses the municipal archives. Just beyond is **Butter Slip,** the most appealing of the medieval lanes that lead off High Street. The commerce that once transpired here is remembered in a famous Kilkenny verse: "If you ever go to Kilkenny, look for the hole in the wall, where you get 24 eggs for a penny, and butter for nothing at all."

Slip down the alley to Kieran Street, turn left, and you will come to **Kyteler's Inn,** now a pub and the onetime home of Alice Kyteler, who entered the annals of history in 1323 as the subject of Ireland's first witchcraft trial. More likely Alice was simply a crafty poisoner—after doing away with four wealthy husbands, she disappeared during the trial; her lady-in-waiting wasn't so fortunate and was burned at the stake. Kieran Street soon comes to Parliament Street and the **Courthouse,** where the ground floor houses dank prison cells. Just across the street is the exquisite **Rothe House,** a merchant's home from 1594 with three wings facing two courtyards. The house, with period furnishings and beautiful wood ceilings, is open January to March and November to December, Monday through Saturday, 1 to 5 p.m.; April to June and September to October, Monday through Saturday, 10:30 a.m. to 5 p.m.; Sunday, 3 to 5 p.m.; and July to August, Monday through Saturday, 10 a.m. to 6 p.m.; Sunday, 3 to 5 p.m. Admission is €3 adults, €1 children, €2 seniors and students; for more information, call ☎ 056-772-2893.

Black Abbey, just beyond the house at the end of Abbey Street, was founded in 1225 by the Dominican order of monks. Oliver Cromwell more or less destroyed the nave when he occupied Kilkenny in 1650. Although the stone structure has been overrestored, it once again functions as an abbey; the church is open daily, 8 a.m. to 6 p.m. The name is derived from the black capes the Dominicans once wore or, more darkly, from the fact that so many of them died in the Black Death of 1348. St. Canice's Cathedral is a little farther north, at the end of the medieval city.

unofficial **TIP**
Tynan's Walking Tours provide an excellent way to survey the city as you walk through the medieval streets with a local historian. Walks depart from the Kilkenny Tourist Office on Rose Inn Street, March–October, Monday–Saturday, 9:15 a.m., 10:30 a.m., 12:15 p.m., 1:30 p.m., 3 p.m., and 4:30 p.m.; November–February, Tuesday–Saturday, 10:30 a.m., 12:15 p.m., and 3 p.m.

ATTRACTIONS IN AND AROUND KILKENNY

Jerpoint Abbey ★ ★ ★ ★

APPEAL BY AGE	PRESCHOOL ★★	GRADE SCHOOL ★★	TEENS ★★★
YOUNG ADULTS ★★	OVER 30 ★★★★		SENIORS ★★★★

Thomastown, 14 kilometers (9 miles) south of Kilkenny on R700;
☎ **056-772-4623**

Type of attraction Evocative ruins of a medieval abbey. **Admission** €2.75 adults, €1.25 children, €2 seniors, €7 families of up to 2 adults and 3 children. **Hours** March–May, daily, 9:30 a.m.–5 p.m.; June–mid-September, daily, 9:30 a.m.–6 p.m.; mid-September–mid-November, daily, 9:30 a.m.–5 p.m.; mid-November–December 1, daily, 10 a.m.–4 p.m. **When to go** In good weather because the abbey is in ruin and you will be exposed to the elements. **Special comments** Reaching Jerpoint Abbey by public transportation is difficult; a taxi costs about €30 round trip. The Kilkenny Tourist Office can provide bus schedules, but if you don't have a day to spare spend your time exploring Kilkenny instead. **How much time to allow** At least 1 hour.

DESCRIPTION AND COMMENTS These remains of a 12th-century monastery, built for the Benedictines but handed over to the Cistercians a century later, are evocative and utterly charming, lost in time in a bucolic setting. The compound's stellar attractions are the Romanesque carvings in the side chapels and on the tombs littering the roofless nave. The rough works are tenderly human in their aspect—clergymen grin while legions of long-forgotten souls look forlorn and vulnerable. Just as impressive, though, is the serenity that surrounds the place. Visit any time other

How Attractions Compare in the South of Ireland

ATTRACTION	DESCRIPTION	AUTHOR'S RATING
KILKENNY		
Jerpoint Abbey	Evocative ruins of a medieval abbey	★★★★
St. Canice's Cathedral	Second-largest medieval cathedral in Ireland	★★★★
Kilkenny Castle	Castle, family home of the Butler clan	★★★½
CASHEL		
Rock of Cashel	Majestic ruins of an early fortress and medieval church complex atop a massive rock	★★★★★
WATERFORD		
Waterford Crystal Factory	World-famous manufacturer of glass	★★★
CORK		
English Market	A covered food market	★★★★
Church of St. Anne Shandon	A historic and beloved church	★★★½
Crawford Municipal Art Gallery	An excellent small art gallery	★★★½
Cork City Gaol	Former prison, now a museum	★★★
Blarney Castle	One of Ireland's most famous castles	★★
MIDLETON AND EAST CORK		
Fota House	Historic home and grounds	★★★★
Fota Wildlife Park	Zoo	★★★
Old Midleton Distillery	Historic whiskey distillery	★★½
COBH		
Cobh, the Queenstown Story	Exhibit tracing Cobh's dramatic maritime history	★★★½
KINSALE		
Charles Fort	Historic fort overlooking Kinsale Harbour	★★★★

than the height of summer, and you may have the well-preserved cloisters and peaceful grounds to yourself. At these times, as you look over the surrounding countryside, it's easy to imagine this as an isolated community of about 100 monks and brothers who worked the gardens, ground their own grain in the now-ruined water mill, worshipped in the still-impressive church, and were buried beneath the stones in the cemetery. A small interpretive center adjoining the ruins is well worth a quick visit to learn about the carvings and monastic life; should Sheila Walsh or one of the other guardians be on duty and offer to lead a tour, by all means take advantage of the opportunity.

TOURING TIPS The setting is lovely, and the grounds are a nice place to stretch out and relax; bring a bag lunch to enjoy in the picnic area.

Kilkenny Castle ★ ★ ★ ½

APPEAL BY AGE	PRESCHOOL ★★	GRADE SCHOOL ★★	TEENS ★★
YOUNG ADULTS ★★★	OVER 30 ★★★★		SENIORS ★★★★

Center of Kilkenny, ☎ 056-772-1450

Type of attraction Castle, family home of the Butler clan. Admission €5 adults, €2 children and students, €3.50 seniors, €11 families of up to 2 adults and 2 children. Hours April–May, daily, 10:30 a.m.–5:30 p.m.; June–August, daily, 9:30 a.m.–7 p.m.; September, daily, 10 a.m.–6:30 p.m.; October–March, daily, 10:30 a.m.–12:45 p.m. When to go Anytime. Special comments Access by guided tour only; includes a 15-minute audiovisual presentation that may make young visitors restless. How much time to allow 2 hours (including 1 hour to walk on the grounds).

DESCRIPTION AND COMMENTS Strongbow, an Anglo-Norman warrior and settler, built a wooden fortress here in 1172, and a castle has commanded the bend of the Kilkenny River ever since. As you'll learn on the guided tour (the only way to see the castle), the present structure dates to the Middle Ages; from 1391 well into the 20th century, it was the home of the Butler family, who were given the title Earls of Ormond. The Butlers were such a force in Irish politics that the Irish Parliament often met at the castle, and clearly the family did well. Improvements went on well into the 19th century, including extensive gardens, a massive stable block (now housing the Kilkenny Design Centre), and elaborate interiors. The drawing room, library, and other family rooms are Victorian, providing a glimpse of the splendor in which 19th-century landholders lived. The tour ends with a bang in the Long Gallery, where portraits of generations of Butlers hang beneath a hammer-beam ceiling. A humorous endnote in this family legacy is the story of how one of the last of the Butlers, a member of the American branch of the family, came to Kilkenny to hand over the keys to the castle and the last claims to ownership; a member of the rock group U2 happened to wander into the ceremonies and stole the show.

TOURING TIPS Cross the street to the former stable block, now housing the Kilkenny Design Centre. Filled with the work of craftspeople from throughout Ireland, the center provides one of Ireland's best shopping experiences, and the Design Centre Café is an excellent spot for lunch.

Walks and Drives in the South

The varied landscapes of the South can best be enjoyed on foot and on drives through backwaters and along unspoiled coastlines.

GREAT WALKS

THE BLACKWATER WAY

If you cross the Vee in the **Knockmealdown Mountains** and descend toward Cashel, you'll encounter the Blackwater Way a couple of times. This 188-kilometer (113-mile) route begins in the village of **Clogheen** on the River Tar and crosses the Knockmealdowns into the Blackwater Valley to the town of **Fermoy.** You can get a taste for the walk and enjoy some nice riverside scenery on a short amble out from the village of Clogheen (see the Blackwater Valley drive, opposite). For a more strenuous mountain walk, join the way as it passes through the top of the Knockmealdowns. You'll find the way well marked off a parking area in the part of the mountain pass known as the **Gap.** From there, you can climb the way across mountainside moors toward the summit, for stunning views over what seems to be all of central Ireland.

THE SCILLY WALK

One of the pleasures of a visit to **Kinsale** (see page 224) is a seaside stroll along Scilly Walk, a path that begins at the end of **Long Quay** on the east side of the port and follows the harbor for about three kilometers (two miles) to **Charles Fort.** The path passes through several attractive harborside communities and comes temptingly close to two atmospheric pubs, the **Spaniard** and the **Bulman.** Tour the fort on one of the excellent guided tours, and if you are up for more walking, you can continue another five kilometers (three miles) out the peninsula to **Frower Point,** for excellent harbor views.

CORK CITY RIVER WALKS

In addition to the many city walks to be enjoyed in Cork, you can also easily get away from the bustle of the city center. One such walk is along the **Maradyke,** a tree-shaded pedestrian avenue that follows the River Lee west for about 2 kilometers (1.2 miles) from the city center, skirting **Fitzgerald Park.** Near the end of the park, you can cross the **Daly Bridge** and ascend the hill to **Cork City Gaol** (see page 210). Another walk follows the south bank of the River Lee for about five kilometers (three miles) east, along a shaded walkway, toward the the village of **Blackrock** near **Cork Harbour.** There's plenty of activity to observe on the wharves along the river, and Blackrock is a pleasant place that retains the air of a fishing port.

GREAT DRIVES

**THROUGH THE BLACKWATER VALLEY AND THE KNOCKMEALDOWNS
TO CASHEL**

The **Rock of Cashel** provides all the sightseeing thrills you might need for
a day, but if you visit this medieval monument from Cork City or eastern
County Cork, you can add a scenery-filled drive up the Blackwater Valley and
through the Knockmealdown Mountains. The route begins at the old port
and resort of **Youghal,** on busy N25, 48 kilometers (30 miles) east of Cork
City and 74 kilometers (45 miles) south of Waterford.

Youghal, at the mouth of the Blackwater River, once belonged to Sir Walter
Raleigh, a gift from Queen Elizabeth I. Allegedly, Raleigh introduced the
potato to Ireland in his farmlands here. (Beware: Many other places in Ireland
make the same claim.) A long stretch of walls still surrounds part of the old
city, built on a natural harbor with a miles of sandy beaches.

From Youghal, follow the Blackwater River north, but note that finding the
riverside route takes a bit of alert navigating. Follow N25 north from Youghal
about 2 kilometers (1.5 miles), and you'll see a turnoff for the **River Blackwater;** a series of minor roads designated as Scenic Route follows the rushing
river north and in about 30 kilometers (20 miles) comes to Lismore.

Lismore Castle, looming high on a cliff above the river, is the Irish seat of
the Duke and Duchess of Devonshire. Past residents include the chemist
Robert Boyle, who was born in the castle in 1627 and is still known for his
Boyle's Law. Adele Astaire, sister of Fred and his onetime dancing partner,
gave up Hollywood to marry a Devonshire duke in the 1930s and lived in
the castle for many years; her brother was a frequent visitor. You can visit the
extensive gardens from May through October, daily, 1:45 to 4:45 p.m.; admission is €4 adults and €2 children under age 16.

From Lismore, R668 climbs through woods and moors as it crosses the
Knockmealdown Mountains, passing the summit through a wide natural
pass known the **Vee;** the narrow valley leading into the Vee is known as the
Gap. Pull into one of the turnouts on the north side of the pass for stunning
views over the fields that dot the plain below. As you descend into the valley, cross the River Tar at **Clogheen** and follow the river east to **Clonmel,**
passing through the pretty villages of **Newcastle** and **Kilmanahan.**

Clonmel, about 35 kilometers (21 miles) from Lismore, is still partially walled
and gated. The seat of County Tipperary, it has some serious literary associations: **Laurence Sterne** (1713–1768), author of *Tristram Shandy,* was born here;
another novelist, **Anthony Trollope** (1815–1882), was a town postmaster.

Continued on next page

Walks and Drives in the South (continued)

GREAT DRIVES (CONTINUED)

THROUGH THE BLACKWATER VALLEY AND THE KNOCKMEALDOWNS TO CASHEL (CONTINUED)

Cashel, where a giant outcropping of rock is topped with the spectacular remains of a medieval church complex (see page 200), is 25 kilometers (15 miles) northwest on R688. You can make a quick return to Cork City and its surroundings on N8.

ALONG THE COAST OF WEST CORK

The coastline of County Cork is attractive and relatively unspoiled, etched with bays and headlands.

From **Kinsale** (see page 224), follow R600 west for 20 kilometers (12 miles) to **Timoleague,** a pleasant seaside village built around the ruins of a 13th-century Franciscan abbey. Among the stone window-frames and foundations of the chapel and refectory is a most unusual feature: the remains of a wine cellar. **Timoleague's Castle** is long gone, but the palm-shaded gardens remain and are open to the public June through August, daily, noon to 6 p.m.; admission is €2.

Follow R601 from Timoleague around **Courtmacsherry Bay** through the fishing village of the same name to **Butlerstown,** and then around the headlands to the shores of **Clonakilty Bay.** The peninsula that separates these two bays is known as the **Seven Heads,** for its seven headlands; the large peninsula to the east of Courtmacsherry Bay is the **Old Head of Kinsale,** off of which the *Lusitania* was torpedoed by the Germans in 1915, killing 1,198 people. The peninsula is now the grounds of an exclusive golf club (see page 231).

Clonakilty, about ten kilometers (six miles) from Timoleague, is an extremely attractive village with several sandy beaches nearby. About five kilometers (three miles) west of town off N71 is the birthplace of **Michael Collins** (1890–1922), the resistance fighter who was killed in an ambush outside nearby **Macroom.** The house burned to the ground in 1921, and little remains but the foundation.

Beyond **Rosscarbery,** another five kilometers (three miles) down N71, join the coast again on R597; after about three kilometers (two miles), come to **Drombeg Stone Circle,** a ring of 17 standing stones thought to be 2,000 years old. Adjacent to the site is a stone cooking-trough from the fourth through seventh centuries, in which it is believed hot stones were placed to heat water.

Retrace the route back to Kinsale, or if you are returning to Cork, follow N71 northeast.

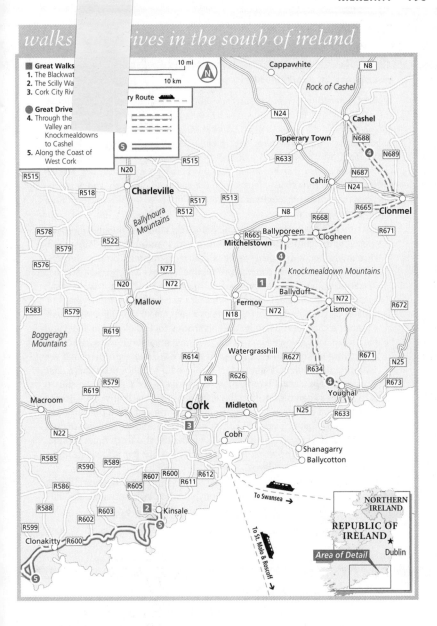

walks [and dr]ives in the south of ireland

■ **Great Walks**
1. The Blackwat[er]
2. The Scilly Wa[lk]
3. Cork City Riv[er]

● **Great Drive[s]**
4. Through the [Blackwater]
   Valley an[d the]
   Knockmealdowns
   to Cashel
5. Along the Coast of
   West Cork

10 mi
10 km

[Ferr]y Route

Cappawhite

Rock of Cashel

N8

N24

Cashel

Tipperary Town

N688

N689

R633

R515

Cahir

N687

N24

R515

N20

R517

R513

R512

Charleville

N8

R668

R665

Clonmel

R518

Ballyhoura Mountains

R665 **Ballyporeen**

Clogheen

R671

R578

R522

Mitchelstown

R579

N73

Knockmealdown Mountains

R576

N20

N72

Ballyduff

N72

R672

Mallow

Fermoy

N18

N72

Lismore

R583

R579

Boggeragh Mountains

R619

R614

Watergrasshill

R627

R671

N25

R619

R579

N8

R626

R634

R673

Macroom

CORK

Midleton

Youghal

R633

N22

N25

R585

Cobh

R590

R589

○ **Shanagarry**
○ **Ballycotton**

R586

R607 R600 R612

R605 R611

To Swansea →

NORTHERN IRELAND

R588

R603

Kinsale

REPUBLIC OF IRELAND ★

R599

R602

To St. Malo & Roscoff

Clonakitty R600

Area of Detail

Dublin

St. Canice's Cathedral ★ ★ ★ ★

APPEAL BY AGE	PRESCHOOL ★ ★	GRADE SCHOOL ★ ★ ★ ★	TEENS ★ ★
YOUNG ADULTS ★ ★ ★	OVER 30 ★ ★ ★ ★		SENIORS ★ ★ ★ ★

Dean Street, ☎ 056-776-4971

Type of attraction Second-largest medieval cathedral in Ireland. **Admission** €3 adults, €1.50 children under age 12; separate admission to round tower: €2 adults, €1 children under age 12. **Hours** May, daily, 10:30 a.m.–5 p.m.; June–August, daily, 9:30 a.m.–7 p.m.; September, daily, 10 a.m.–6:30 p.m.; October–March, daily, 10:30 a.m.–12:45 p.m. and 2–5 p.m. **When to go** Anytime, but try to find a slot of fair weather if you plan on climbing the round tower. **Special comments** Take time to wander through the cathedral randomly and enjoy the medieval monuments throughout. **How much time to allow** 30 minutes, 1 hour if you climb the round tower.

DESCRIPTION AND COMMENTS   This is one of Ireland's most impressive medieval monuments, completed in the 13th century and, after St. Patrick's in Dublin, the second-largest medieval church in Ireland. Commanding the north end of Kilkenny, the massive Gothic hulk has weathered a number of catastrophes. Part of the roof collapsed in 1332, and it was rebuilt as penance by William Outlaw, who was accused of relations with the alleged witch Alice Kyteler (see Kyteler's Inn, page 198). Oliver Cromwell seized the cathedral when he and his troops took Kilkenny in 1650 and did the usual Cromwellian damage, leaving the church walls intact but destroying the monuments. Most of them have been retrieved and are rather haphazardly but charmingly displayed throughout the chilly, dark interior, clad in black Kilkenny marble. The appeal of a visit to the church is to wander the aisles noting the effigies of knights in armor, elaborate carvings, and other medieval artifacts. For centuries before the cathedral was built, St. Canice's was the center of a large monastic settlement, and the round tower, once a beacon guiding the faithful from miles around, still stands, a little the worse for wear; a climb to the top affords stunning views over County Kilkenny.

TOURING TIPS   Combine a visit to St. Canice's with a look at several other nearby remnants of medieval Kilkenny, such as Black Abbey, Butter Slip, and Rothe House (see "Exploring Kilkenny," page 188).

RESTAURANTS IN KILKENNY

Café Sol ★ ★ ★ ★

MEDITERRANEAN	MODERATE	QUALITY ★ ★ ★ ★	VALUE ★ ★ ★ ★ ★

6 William Street, Kilkenny; ☎ 056-776-4987

Reservations Recommended for dinner. **Entree range** Lunch, €5–€10; dinner, €10–€20. **Payment** AE, MC, V. **Bar** Full service. **Disabled access** Yes. **Hours** Monday–Friday, 10 a.m.–9 p.m.; Saturday, 10 a.m.–5 p.m.

MENU RECOMMENDATIONS   Scones, soups, grilled sausages, pastas.

COMMENTS   This terra-cotta–colored, light-filled room brightens even the grayest Irish weather, and a welcome air prevails as the wooden tables

How Restaurants Compare in the South of Ireland

NAME	CUISINE	OVERALL	QUALITY	VALUE	PRICE
KILKENNY					
Café Sol	Mediterranean	★★★★	★★★★	★★★★★	mod
Lacken House	Irish	★★★★	★★★★	★★★★★	mod
Kyteler's Inn	pub food	★★★★	★★★	★★★★½	mod
Pordylos	Irish	★★★★	★★★	★★★	mod
CORK					
Jacobs on the Mall	Continental	★★★★½	★★★★	★★★★	mod/exp
Farmgate Café	Irish	★★★★	★★★★	★★★★½	inexp/mod
Fenns Quay	Continental	★★★★	★★★★	★★★★	mod/exp
Jacques	modern Irish	★★★★	★★★★	★★★½	mod/exp
Les Gourmandises	French/ modern Irish	★★★★	★★★★	★★★	exp
Nash 19	modern Irish	★★★★	★★★★	★★★★½	inexp/mod
MIDLETON AND EAST CORK					
Farmgate Restaurant and Country Store	Irish	★★★★	★★★★	★★★★★	mod
O'Donovan's	modern Irish	★★★★	★★★★	★★★★	mod
Ballymaloe House	modern Irish	★★★★	★★★★	★★★½	exp
KINSALE					
Fishy Fishy Café	seafood	★★★★	★★★★	★★★★★	mod
The Vintage	Irish	★★★★	★★★★	★★★	mod
Little Skillet	Irish	★★★½	★★★★	★★★★	mod
Blue Haven	pub/Irish	★★★	★★★	★★★★/ ★★★ (pub)	mod/exp

fill throughout the day for delicious breakfast pastries in the morning, good-value lunches, and light but delicious evening meals. The simple surroundings belie the sophistication of the kitchen, which turns out flavorful variations on salmon, lamb, and other local staples.

Kyteler's Inn ★ ★ ★ ★

| PUB FOOD | MODERATE | QUALITY ★ ★ ★ | VALUE ★ ★ ★ ★ ½ |

St. Kieran's Street, Kilkenny; ☎ 056-772-1064

Reservations None. **Entree range** €8–€15. **Payment** AE, MC, V. **Bar** Full service. **Disabled access** Yes. **Hours** Meals: daily, noon–3 p.m., 6:30–9 p.m.; pub: 11:30 a.m.–1 a.m.

MENU RECOMMENDATIONS Witches brew (vegetable soup), fish and chips (not always available).

COMMENTS In lieu of haute cuisine, this medieval inn serves up nightly music and plenty of atmosphere along the lines of stone walls, heavy beams, a dark cellar, and even a resident witch, Alice, infamous for allegedly poisoning four husbands. Alice's evil aura doesn't seem to deter legions of diners, who tend to wash down the plain offerings of sandwiches, the occasional curry, and simply grilled salmon and steak with pints of Smithwick's, brewed in Kilkenny for almost 250 years.

Lacken House ★ ★ ★ ★

| IRISH | MODERATE | QUALITY ★ ★ ★ ★ | VALUE ★ ★ ★ ★ ★ |

Dublin Road, Kilkenny; ☎ 056-776-1085

Reservations Recommended for dinner. **Entree range** €24.50–€28.50; 5-course dinner, €49.50. **Payment** AE, MC, V. **Bar** Full service. **Disabled access** Yes. **Hours** Tuesday–Saturday, 7–10:30 p.m.

MENU RECOMMENDATIONS Foie gras, Lacken House filet of beef, rack of lamb, roast duckling.

COMMENTS The restaurant that helped make Kilkenny famous for its cuisine continues to lead the way and takes pride in using Kilkenny products. The menu pays homage to the local suppliers and shops who keep the kitchen stocked with lamb, beef, fish, and other fresh ingredients. You can experience the mastery with which chef Barry Foley assembles these components on the excellent-value prix-fixe menu, although the à la carte menu, full of such surprises here in the interior as fresh oysters and pan-fried wild turbot, is a pleasure to explore. A great deal of effort has also gone into bringing the 11 guest rooms up to the same high standards of the restaurant, so you now can enjoy an excellent meal and immediately retire in comfort. Lacken House offers bed, breakfast, and dinner packages that make this notion especially appealing.

Pordylos ★ ★ ★ ★

| IRISH | MODERATE | QUALITY ★ ★ ★ | VALUE ★ ★ ★ |

Butter Slip, Kilkenny; ☎ 056-777-0660

Reservations Recommended for dinner. **Entree range** €17–€25. **Payment** AE, MC, V. **Bar** Full service. **Disabled access** No. **Hours** Tuesday–Saturday, 12:30–3 p.m., 6–10:30 p.m.

MENU RECOMMENDATIONS Lamb, fresh fish.

COMMENTS The upper floor of a medieval building on the atmospheric alley known as Butter Slip is a justifiably popular spot for a decent meal; be sure to book early, because the small room fills up fast. Cuisine here doesn't soar to quite the same levels as those of some of the neighbors, but neither do the prices, and the overall experience may be the most pleasant in town. The beamed, candlelit room is amiable, the service is adept, and the less elaborate offerings—such as stews or simply prepared chops, lobster (chosen from a tank near the door), or filets of fresh fish—are quite good.

ENTERTAINMENT AND NIGHTLIFE IN KILKENNY

KILKENNY'S OWN **Smithwick's Brewery** keeps the city's lively pubs well supplied. You can taste a Smithwick's (pronounced without the *w*) while enjoying traditional music at **Kyteler's Inn** (St. Kieran's Street, ☎ 056-772-1064) and **Caislean Ui Cuain** (The Castle Inn; on the Parade, ☎ 056-776-5406. Everyone's favorite Kilkenny pub is the amiable and cozy **Eamon Langton's** (69 John Street, ☎ 056-776-5133). If you want to expand beyond the pub scene, check out the **Westgate Theatre** (Parliament Street, ☎ 056-776-1674), which often hosts visiting performers for plays and concerts. **John Cleere's Theatre** (Parliament Street, ☎ 056-776-2573) highlights local bands.

SHOPPING IN KILKENNY

THE FORMER STABLE BLOCK OF KILKENNY CASTLE is now one of Ireland's leading showcases for crafts, the **Kilkenny Design Centre** (Castle Yard, ☎ 056-772-2118). Artisans from all over Ireland assemble here to show a stunning array of ceramics, glassware, pottery, jewelry, and knitwear. Prices are not low, but the quality is about as high as you're going to find. A light-filled cafe serves an excellent selection of salads, sandwiches, and hot dishes; a bit of shopping and lunch is a pleasant way to top off a visit to the castle across the road. The Design Centre is open year-round, Monday through Saturday, 9 a.m. to 6 p.m.; June to September, Sunday, 11 a.m. to 5 p.m.

AROUND KILKENNY

CASHEL

RISING ABOVE THE PLAIN OF TIPPERARY some 60 kilometers (38 miles) southeast of Kilkenny, the **Rock of Cashel** may well be Ireland's most imposing sight. Cashel is an easy day trip from Kilkenny, or it's a handy place to stop for a few hours if you're driving west from Kilkenny toward Limerick.

Attraction in Cashel

 Rock of Cashel ★ ★ ★ ★ ★

APPEAL BY AGE	PRESCHOOL ★★★★	GRADE SCHOOL ★★★★	TEENS ★★★★
YOUNG ADULTS ★★★★	OVER 30 ★★★★½	SENIORS ★★★★½	

Cashel, ☎ 062-61437

Type of attraction Majestic ruins of an early fortress and medieval church complex atop a massive rock. **Admission** €5 adults, €2 children and students, €3.50 seniors, €11 families of up to 2 adults and 2 children. **Hours** Mid-March–early June, daily, 9 a.m.–5:30 p.m.; early June–mid-September, daily, 9 a.m.–7 p.m.; mid-September–mid-October, daily, 9 a.m.–5:30 p.m.; mid-October–mid-March, daily, 9 a.m.–4:30 p.m. **When to go** In good weather, if possible, because the rock is exposed to the elements; with clear skies, the views over the Plain of Tipperary are extensive. **Special comments** You may or may not choose to step into the theater and watch the slick 15-minute audiovisual presentation; the informative commentary does a good job of summarizing the Rock's complex history, but this modern incursion detracts from the location's romance and sanctity. By all means see it before touring, because the perspective will come in handy; plus, you'll have time to regain a sense of the mood while you tour the ruins. **How much time to allow** 2 hours.

DESCRIPTION AND COMMENTS One of Ireland's most visited attractions is alluring in spite of the crowds it attracts. The giant rock topped with medieval remains is a spectacular sight, even when swept with clouds and rains, and the ruins are richly evocative and telling of the church's onetime power. Early kings settled the Rock as early as the fourth century; virtually impregnable and commanding the countryside for miles around, it's easy to understand the Rock's strategic importance. The Catholic Church took over in the 12th century and remained until the late 18th century; it didn't take long for the harsh elements to render the complex the ruin you'll see today. As befits a gloomy ruin, the Rock of Cashel is well endowed with lore. One of the most popular legends surrounds the 12th-century cross (a replica of the original) that stands near the entrance to the complex. The cross not only commemorates the church's acquisition of the Rock, but also the spot where, in AD 432, St. Patrick baptized King Aengus, Ireland's first Christian ruler. (Allegedly, Patrick became so caught up in the importance of the event that he failed to notice he had driven his staff through the king's foot. Aengus didn't complain, thinking the pain was part of the ritual.) On the same day, Patrick allegedly held up a shamrock to explain the mystery of the Holy Trinity, and the symbol took hold in the hearts of the Irish people.

Begin a tour in the newest building, the restored 15th-century Hall of the Vicars Choral. This appealing timbered hall, warmed by an enormous hearth, served as quarters for vicars who were chosen to sing during services. The largest building on the Rock is St. Patrick's Cathedral, now a roofless ruin marred by the events of 1647, when Cromwell's troops attacked Cashel and set fire to the cathedral where hundre_____ _____people had taken refuge. Weatherworn sculptures and ca_____ _____transept depict the lives of the saints and other biblical s_____ _____argoyles still surround the window frames. The best-prese_____ _____g is Cormac's Chapel, built in 1127 by king and bishop Corm_____ _____y. One of Ireland's finest Romanesque structures—note the _____ _____hes and twisted columns typical of that style—retains som_____ _____oes (a rarity in the moist climate of Ireland). The oldest buil_____ _____ound tower, 92 feet high and built as a beacon and lookout_____ _____e stone structure has been beckoning travelers to the Rock ev_____ _____. still does. A few souls remain forever, in the gloomy graveyaru _____ _____he cathedral walls.

TOURING TIPS   In summer, try to avoid visiting the Rock between 11 a.m. and 3 p.m., when visitors arrive by the busload.

WATERFORD

THIS BUSY AND SOMETIMES SHABBY PORT, 50 kilometers (30 miles) south of Kilkenny, was founded by the Vikings 1,200 years ago. Among the industries the town has supported over the years, none is more famous than the **Waterford Crystal Factory,** and a visit to the factory and shop is what draws most visitors here.

Attraction in Waterford

 Waterford Crystal Factory ★ ★ ★

APPEAL BY AGE	PRESCHOOL N/A	GRADE SCHOOL N/A	TEENS ★ ★
YOUNG ADULTS ★ ★ ★	OVER 30 ★ ★ ★		SENIORS ★ ★ ★

Cork Road; ☎ 051-373311; www.waterfordvisitorcentre.com

Type of attraction World-famous manufacturer of glass. **Admission** Free for audiovisual presentation, gallery, and showrooms; tour: €8 adults, free for children under age 12, €6.50 seniors, €4 students. **Hours** Tours: March–October, daily, 8:30 a.m.–4:15 p.m.; November–February, Monday–Friday, 9 a.m.–3:15 p.m.; Gallery and showrooms: March–October, daily, 8:30 a.m.–6 p.m.; November–March, Monday–Friday, 9 a.m.–5 p.m. **When to go** Avoid busy weekends if possible. **Special comments** Children under age 10 are not allowed on factory tour. **How much time to allow** 1 hour for audiovisual presentation and tour; as long as you want for shopping.

DESCRIPTION AND COMMENTS   One of Ireland's most popular attractions (right up there with tours of the Guinness Brewery and the Jameson and Old Bushmills distilleries) is also the largest crystal factory in the world and modern Waterford's most important industry. That explains the no-nonsense approach to this well-run factory tour and shopping experience. A superb audiovisual presentation explains such chapters in the company's history as the bleak times when the Famine forced it to close; Waterford didn't begin producing again until 1947, and the prestige the company has regained since then says much about the quality of the product. A brief but fascinating factory tour shows off the glass-blowing and cooling processes, and then visitors are left on their own to roam through the shop and a gallery showing off historic pieces. Alas, no discounts are to be had in the shop (although the selection is first rate), and unlike purveyors of beer and whiskey, Waterford does not hand out free samples at the end of the visit.

TOURING TIPS Call ahead to reserve a place on the tours, which fill up quickly.

CORK

IRELAND'S SECOND-LARGEST CITY is also one of its oldest, dating to the seventh century, when St. Finbarr founded a monastery in marshy land along the River Lee (*Carcaigh*, the city's Gaelic name, means "marsh"). Today, Finbarr is remembered in a massive Gothic Revival cathedral that looms over an appealing city encircled by two arms of the River Lee, where docks once sent goods all over the world. Alleys and pedestrian streets, many of which were once waterways, bustle with students at **Cork University** and businesspeople working in new buildings going up alongside the river. A noted free-spiritedness made the city a major center of rebellion in the 1919–1921 War of Independence; these days the Rebel City turns its attention to jazz festivals, a lively pub scene, and some of the finest cuisine in Ireland.

PLANNING YOUR VISIT TO CORK

FOR INFORMATION ON PLACES TO STAY, what to see and do, and where to dine in Cork and the surrounding region, contact the **Cork Tourist Office** (Tourist House, 42 Grand Parade; ☎ 021-425-5100, **www.corkkerry.ie**). The center is open Monday through Saturday, 9:15 a.m. to 5:30 p.m.

Special Events in Cork

Cork celebrates Ireland's patron saint with a lively **St. Patrick's Festival** March 17 to 19, when poetry readings, traditional-music concerts, and other events take place around the city; for information and tickets, call ☎ 021-480-2596 or visit **www.corkstpatricksfestival.ie.** The **Cork International Choral Festival,** April 26 to 30, is one of Europe's top choral competitions and draws singers from around the world for concerts in Cork City Hall; for information, call ☎ 021-422-3535 or visit **www.corkchoral.ie.** The other big musical event is the late-October **Guinness Cork Jazz Festival,** one of the world's most acclaimed jazz fests, attracting more than 1,000 performers to stages around the city; for information, call ☎ 021-427-8979 or visit **www.corkjazzfestival.com.** The **Cork Film Festival** screens features, documentaries, and shorts for one week in late October; for information, call ☎ 021-427-1711 or visit **www.corkfilmfest.org.**

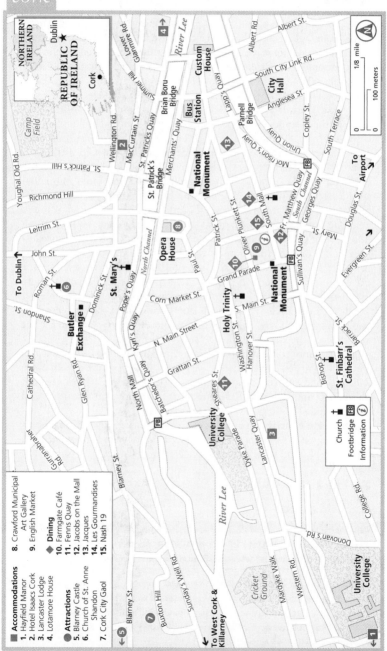

cork

REPUBLIC
OF IRELAND

NORTHERN
IRELAND

Dublin ★

Cork ●

Accommodations
1. Hayfield Manor
2. Hotel Isaacs Cork
3. Lancaster Lodge
4. Lotamore House

Attractions
5. Blarney Castle
6. Church of St. Anne
   Shandon
7. Cork City Gaol

8. Crawford Municipal
   Art Gallery
9. English Market

◆ **Dining**
10. Farmgate Café
11. Fenns Quay
12. Jacobs on the Mall
13. Jacques
14. Les Gourmandises
15. Nash 19

Church +■
Footbridge FB
Information i

0   1/8 mile
0   100 meters

To Dublin ←

To West Cork &
Killarney ↓

To Airport →

University
College

Custom
House

Bus
Station

City Hall

Opera
House

St. Mary's

Butler
Exchange ■

National
Monument

Holy Trinity

National
Monument

St. Finbarr's
Cathedral

University
College

ARRIVING AND GETTING ORIENTED IN CORK

CORK IS 260 KILOMETERS (160 miles) southwest of Dublin. Trains arrive from Dublin and other Irish cities at Kent Station, off MacCurtain Street in the northeast corner of the city. Trains run between Dublin and Cork about ten times a day, and the trip takes about 2 hours and 45 minutes; fare is about €52 each way. For more information, call toll free ☎ 1850-366222 or ☎ 01-8366222 or visit **www.irishrail.ie.**

By car, Cork is easy to reach on Ireland's national road network; allow about four hours for the trip down the N8 from Dublin. If you're traveling from Shannon Airport or elsewhere in the West, take N20 from Limerick and allow about three hours for the trip. Parking is severely limited in Cork, and it is much to the city's discredit that more effort has not been made to restrict city traffic and build municipal garages on the outskirts. You'll find a handy garage near the tourist office on Grand Parade and several others on the eastern end of town, near the bus station and Lapp's Quay. Expect to pay about €1.50 an hour. Street parking is limited, and in most spots you are required to purchase a disc, available at newsstands; these usually are good for only three hours maximum at a cost of about €1.80 an hour. (Scratch off your arrival time, and display the disc on the dashboard.) There are also park-and-ride lots on major approaches to the city; fees of about €3 a day include transportation to and from the city center. If you're staying in Cork, take our advice and don't drive—stash the car and explore the city on foot.

Bus Éireann coaches arrive from throughout Ireland at the bus station on Parnell Place. Buses leave from Dublin for Cork about every 2 hours, and the trip takes 4 hours and 30 minutes; fares are low, about €10 one way and €15 round trip. For more information, call ☎ 021-450-8188 or visit **www.buseireann.ie.**

Once you've arrived, you can get around Cork easily via local buses operated by Bus Éireann; the fare is €1.10, and service is frequent from 7 a.m. to 11 p.m., with limited service after that.

HOTELS IN CORK

Hayfield Manor ★ ★ ★ ½

QUALITY	★★★★	VALUE	★★½	€200–€240

Perrott Avenue, Cork City; ☎ 021-484-5900; fax 021-431-5940; sales@hayfieldmanor.ie; www.hayfieldmanor.ie

Location West of city center. **Amenities and services** 88 rooms; bar, beauty salon, business center, cafe, hair dryers, Internet access, minibars, restaurant, room service, satellite TV, sauna, spa, swimming pool, trouser press. **Elevator** Yes. **Parking** Free, on property. **Price** Includes lavish breakfast; special packages available. **Credit cards** AE, MC, V.

Built in 1996 in the style of a grand Georgian country house, Hayfield Manor makes no concession to contemporary design. In fact, it dishes up more old-world ambience than many of the genuine country-house hotels it imitates, but not always to the best effect—the opulent surroundings can seem a bit stuffy and over-the-top. The drawing room is filled with antiques, heavy paneling lines the hushed library, and a grand staircase sweeps up to the exceptionally large and finely furnished bedrooms. You might feel a bit self-conscious plopping down with a good mystery in any of these public spaces. The traditionally furnished guest rooms are genuinely comfortable, with cushy wing chairs, thoughtful lighting, and fine bedding. The modern world intrudes in the form of in-room sound systems, flat-screen TVs, and stunning bathrooms with long, deep tubs, separate power showers, and marble vanities. An attractive leisure complex includes an indoor swimming pool, a sauna, a small gym, and spa facilities. A formal restaurant overlooks a small garden; casual meals are served in a woody bar and an airy conservatory cafe—these amenities are especially welcome, because Hayfield Manor is tucked away in a residential neighborhood about a mile away from shops and restaurants.

Hotel Isaacs Cork ★ ★ ★

QUALITY ★ ★ ★ ½	VALUE ★ ★ ★	€75–€100

48 MacCurtain Street, Cork; ☎ 021-450-0011; fax 021-450-6355; cork@isaacs.ie; www.isaacs.ie

Location City center. **Amenities and services** 50 rooms, 11 apartments; air-conditioning in some rooms, Internet access, minibars in some rooms, nonsmoking rooms, room service, safes in some rooms. **Elevator** Yes. **Parking** On property, free. **Price** Includes full Irish breakfast. **Credit cards** AE, MC, V.

Much about this member of a small Irish chain is appealing and distinctive, not least of which is the location on an up-and-coming commercial street on the north bank of the river. It's convenient to all the sights but just enough off the beaten track to give you the feel of a real Cork neighborhood. Shops and restaurants surround the hotel, and in the same 18th-century warehouse are two popular eateries, Greene's and the eponymous Isaacs. Both are a good value, serving solid modern-Irish cuisine in relaxed surroundings. Beyond a cobbled court and garden (enlivened with a waterfall) are busy and welcoming lounges; in the comfortable guest rooms upstairs, wood floors and attractive pine furnishings lend a lot more character than you'd expect to find in a chain hotel at this price. Windows are double-glazed to minimize traffic noise from busy MacCurtain Street, and the shiny bathrooms have tubs with power showers. Apartments sleeping four to six guests are also available.

Lancaster Lodge ★ ★ ★ ★

QUALITY ★ ★ ★ ★	VALUE ★ ★ ★ ★	€74–€100

Lancaster Quay, Cork; ☎ 021-425-1125; fax 021-425-1126; info@lancasterlodge.com; www.lancasterlodge.com

Location City center. **Amenities and services** 39 rooms; hair dryers, in-room tea and coffee facilities, Internet access, nonsmoking rooms, safes, satellite TV, 24-hour desk/concierge, trouser press. **Elevator** Yes. **Parking** On property, free. **Price** Includes full Irish breakfast; 10% discount for seniors; special offers available on Internet. **Credit cards** AE, MC, V.

At first sight, this guest house on the banks of a branch of the River Lee, at the southern edge of the city center, seems a bit forlorn, surrounded by car parks, new offices, and apartment blocks. The entryway doesn't do much to dispel the austere feel of the modern building, but just beyond are a handsome lounge and breakfast room with light-colored wood floors and striking contemporary furnishings. Guest rooms are likewise appealing: large and relaxing; decorated with care in soothing tones; and fitted out with sleek chairs and sofas, thoughtful lighting, amenities such as wireless broadband access and satellite TV, and spacious bathrooms with counter space and tub/shower combinations (two with Jacuzzis). The best rooms are those at the front of the hotel facing the river and overlooking the city. Modern as the surroundings are, breakfast is traditionally Irish, with a nice array of cereals and fruits on the buffet, plus eggs and other hot dishes cooked to order. St. Patrick's Street and other places in the city center are within a five-minute walk, and some of Cork's best restaurants, including Fenns Quay (see page 212), are just outside the door. You can stash the car in the ample car park and explore Cork on foot.

Lotamore House ★ ★ ★ ½

QUALITY ★★★★	VALUE ★★★½	€75–€130

Tivoli, Cork; ☎ 021-482-2344; fax 021-482-2219; lotamore@iol.ie; www.lotamorehouse.com

Location East of city center. **Amenities and services** 20 rooms; complimentary tea and coffee, hair dryers, honor bar, nonsmoking rooms, satellite TV, trouser press. **Elevator** No. **Parking** On property, free. **Price** Includes full Irish breakfast. **Credit cards** AE, MC, V.

Generations of Cork burghers lived in this Georgian mansion atop a grassy knoll on the banks of the River Lee. Although Cork's busy wharves and a busy highway now lie at the end of the long drive, Lotamore still has the air of a country house. The gracious interior, remarkably unspoiled, recently has been refurbished with a careful eye to style. In the lounges and guest rooms, deep-red hues and earth tones cover the walls, cushy old chairs are covered in handsome fabrics, and tables and sideboards are antique. Over-stuffed couches surround the hearth in the drawing room, and guests help themselves to coffee, tea, or a drink from the honor bar. A grand staircase leads to large and rather posh bedrooms filled with handsome old armoires, deep reading chairs, and good beds dressed with fine linens. Most rooms have nice views down the river to the Cork hills beyond, and several ground-floor rooms overlook the lawns and rhododendron gardens. Bath-rooms are modern and have tub-and-shower units. A few lapses are in evidence: reading lamps are in short supply, making it difficult to hunker down in the guest rooms, and breakfast is a bit meager. Keep in mind, too, that although Lotamore is just ten minutes away from the city center, it is not near shops or restaurants, and it can only be reached conveniently by car or taxi.

EXPLORING CORK

SURROUNDED BY TWO ARMS OF THE RIVER LEE, Cork sometimes is called an Irish Venice. That is a bit of an exaggeration, but the quays and alleys leading to the river's arms do give Cork a maritime feel. It's a pleasure to walk through the small center of Cork at random, allowing yourself to get lost—which you inevitably will do, because streets are poorly marked. If you wish to follow any sort of logical route, arm yourself with a map from the tourist office and keep your sights set on the steeple of the **Church of St. Anne Shandon,** a conspicuous landmark and handy navigation guide on the north side of the river.

A good place to begin is on the river at **St. Patrick's Bridge,** the city's most famous span. The enormous statue just along Patrick Street honors **Father Matthew,** a 19th-century leader of the Temperance Movement who's due some respect, as the fellow must have had a pretty hard time of things in a hard-drinking town like Cork. **Patrick Street** is Cork's busiest shopping street; rather than letting that take you inland, stick to the river and the quays where the city's commerce bustled until the early 20th century. A walk along **Lavitt's Quay** brings you to the **Opera House** and the **Crawford Municipal Art Gallery** (see page 210). A turn south onto Paul Street takes you into the **French Quarter,** settled by Huguenot refugees from France, and from there to the **Grand Parade.** This wide avenue, once a canal, is graced with two of the city's most revered landmarks: off the Grand Parade is an entrance to the **English Market** (see page 211), Cork's historic food emporium, and the lacy, spirelike **National Monument** at the south end honoring Irish patriots. If you cross the river at the monument and continue south, soon you'll find yourself beneath the hulk of **St. Finbarr's Cathedral,** dedicated to Cork's founding saint and appropriately elaborate, with piles of Gothic Revival stonework and a colorfully painted interior. The cathedral is open daily, 9 a.m. to 6 p.m.; admission is free.

A walk north across St. Patrick's Bridge takes you into the hilly **Shandon Quarter,** where **St. Mary's Dominican Church** faces the river from behind an imposing portico of thick Ionic columns. Just beyond the church, on John Redmond Street, is the **Butter Exchange,** a late-18th-century building that did a lively business grading butter in the days when that was the city's principal commodity, shipped from the Cork wharves to Australia and South America. A fitting end to a walk through Cork is a climb up the tower of the **Church of St. Anne Shandon** (see page 209) for an aerial survey of the city.

Tours of Cork

You'll get a nice look into the history and architecture of Cork on the **guided walking tours** that start at 8 p.m., June to August, Monday through Friday, from the tourist office in Grand Parade. The cost is €7 and ends with a pint at a local pub. For more information, check with the tourist office or call ☎ 021-488-5404. An easy way to get around Cork and see the sights is on **Cork Panoramic** buses. The open-top hop-on, hop-off vehicles circuit the major sights, allowing you to get on and off as you wish; this is an especially handy way to outlying attractions such as **Cork City Gaol.** Buses operate April to October, daily; €12 adults, €4 children, €10 seniors and students; for information, call ☎ 021-430-9090. **Bus Éireann** offers a narrated Cork City tour in July and August for about €9; call ☎ 021-450-8188 for information.

ATTRACTIONS IN CORK

 Blarney Castle ★ ★

APPEAL BY AGE	PRESCHOOL ★★	GRADE SCHOOL ★★★★	TEENS ★★★★
YOUNG ADULTS ★★★		OVER 30 ★★★	SENIORS ★★★

Route R617, Blarney, about 8 kilometers (5 miles) northwest of Cork City center; ☎ 021-438-5252; www.blarneycastle.ie

Type of attraction One of Ireland's most famous castles. **Admission** €7 adults, €2.50 children ages 8–14, €5 seniors, €16 families of up to 2 adults and 2 children. **Hours** May, Monday–Friday, 9 a.m.–6:30 p.m.; Sunday, 9:30 a.m.–5:30 p.m.; June–August, Monday–Friday, 9 a.m.–7 p.m.; Sunday, 9:30 a.m.–5:30 p.m.; September, Monday–Friday, 9 a.m.–6:30 p.m.; Sunday, 9:30 a.m.–5:30 p.m.; October–April, Monday–Friday, 9 a.m.–sundown; Sunday, 9:30 a.m.–sundown. **When to go** Avoid midday in summer, when busloads of visitors arrive. **Special comments** Kissing the stone requires a climb and some uncomfortable positioning; not suitable for visitors with limited mobility. **How much time to allow** 2 hours for the stone and grounds.

DESCRIPTION AND COMMENTS *Blarney* means, basically, nonsense, and you'll encounter a lot of it in this ruin of the onetime stronghold of the McCarthy clan. When 16th-century owner Cormac McCarthy hesitated to turn the castle over to Elizabeth I, the English queen referred to his tactics as "blarney." Today a well-worn path leads past crumbling rooms and dark passageways and up a watchtower, where a blasé attendant will hold your legs as you dangle backward to kiss the most famous of Irish emblems, the Blarney Stone. The stone, formally known as the Stone of Eloquence, is allegedly half of an orb presented to McCarthy as a medal of honor for his valor in the Battle of Bannockburn in 1314; kissing it is said to impart the "gift of the gab," something Ireland doesn't need more of.

Essentially, this experience involves waiting (up to half an hour at busy times) to get into an uncomfortable and unflattering position and kiss a slobber-covered chunk of rock. A photographer catches you in the act and offers to sell you a print for €10. These shenanigans are fun for kids, but if you don't have any youngsters with you, skip the blarney and spend your time enjoying the rest of the castle and grounds. If you insist on engaging in another ritual of superstition, step into the Rock Close, an eerie grotto said to be haunted by ancient spirits and in which several rock outcrops resemble the face and hat of a witch and other such beings. Here, you make a wish, back down the steep and slippery Wishing Stairs to a little pool, and then retrace your steps backward—with your eyes closed the whole time, without stepping into the pool, and without breaking your neck on the steps. Do so successfully and your wish will come true. You also can engage in tamer pursuits such as strolling through the colorful gardens, a beautiful spot to which the ruined castle towers in the background add romantic flair.

TOURING TIPS Be sure to spend some time on the grounds.

Church of St. Anne Shandon ★ ★ ★ ½

APPEAL BY AGE	PRESCHOOL ★★★★	GRADE SCHOOL ★★★★	TEENS ★★★★
YOUNG ADULTS ★★★★		OVER 30 ★★★	SENIORS ★★½

Church Street; ☎ 021-450-5906; www.shandonbells.org

Type of attraction A historic and beloved church. **Admission** €3 adults, €2 seniors and students, €8 families of up to 2 adults and 2 children. **Hours** Monday–Saturday, 8:30 a.m.–6 p.m. **When to go** On a clear day to enjoy the view from the tower. **Special comments** With the tower climb, view, and bell ringing, St. Anne's is a big hit with kids. **How much time to allow** 1 hour.

DESCRIPTION AND COMMENTS Cork's most famous landmark stands on a hill on the north side of the River Lee. The pepper-pot steeple, topped with a salmon-shaped weather vane rising above a neighborhood across the river from the city center, is a handy point of reference as you navigate the alleys and twisting lanes of downtown Cork. This 18th-century structure is so integral to life in Cork that the local football and hurdling teams take their colors from the limestone that covers two of the tower's four sides and the red sandstone that covers the other two. St. Anne's is also known as Shandon Church, and its famous bells are commemorated in "The Bells of Shandon," a piece of sentimental fluff by early 19th-century bard Francis Mahony: "With deep affection and recollection, I often think of those Shandon Bells, whose sound so wild would, in the days of childhood, fling round my cradle their magic spells." The bells will sound wildly throughout your visit to Cork, as visitors are invited to become bell ringers and take a turn at playing a tune on the six-ton monsters. Once you've tried your hand, continue up the steep stairs to the top of the tower for a stunning view of Cork and the hills that surround the city—this aerial view is a handy way to get the lay of the land. St. Anne's has yet another name, too. It is blasphemously but affectionately known as the four-faced liar, because until 1986 each of the clock faces on the church tower told a different time.

TOURING TIPS A fair amount of climbing is required to ring the bells and enjoy the view, so St. Anne's is not a good choice for visitors with limited mobility.

Cork City Gaol ★ ★ ★

APPEAL BY AGE	PRESCHOOL ★★	GRADE SCHOOL ★★★★	TEENS ★★★★
YOUNG ADULTS ★★★	OVER 30 ★★★		SENIORS ★★★

Convent Avenue, about 2 kilometers (1 mile) west of the city center; ☎ 021-430-5022; www.corkcitygaol.com

Type of attraction Former prison, now a museum. Admission €5 adults, €3 children, €4 seniors and students, €14 families of up to 2 adults and 3 children. Hours March–October, daily, 9:30 a.m.–5 p.m.; November–February, daily, 10 a.m.–4 p.m. When to go Anytime. Special comments Architecture buffs who otherwise may not be interested in this aspect of Irish history should note that the jail is an important example of early-19th-century public architecture. How much time to allow 2 hours.

DESCRIPTION AND COMMENTS Opened in 1824 as a model prison, this assemblage of towers and high walls is remarkably intact, and, despite the grim history of place and the icy chill that still prevails within the stone walls, it is a remarkable piece of architecture. In fact, it's so easy to get carried away with the Victorian beauty of the jail that you might forget the human misery once endured in the tiny cells—that is, if it weren't for the excellent audio tour (included in the admission price). A riveting narration tells the stories of half a dozen inmates incarcerated here over the years. As you stand in the multistory elliptical compounds and peer into cells containing realistic dummies, you learn that most of the inmates were poor and on the brink of starvation, reduced to crimes such as stealing pieces of cloth, for which they received long terms of hard labor. Even the prison's skimpy gruel and flea-ridden mattresses were an improvement on life in the tenements of Cork. After closing in 1928, the prison stood empty for many years. In the 1950s, part of the compound became headquarters for Radio Éireann (there's good transmission from the hills above Cork). A small museum traces the history of radio and displays a remarkable selection of the devices—with due mention of the fact that Guglielmo Marconi, inventor of the radio, was part Irish.

TOURING TIPS The tour ends on a false note, with an over-the-top film that summarizes the prison's history, complete with trial scenes—the film doesn't add much to the experience, and you'll be more moved if you make an escape before it starts.

Crawford Municipal Art Gallery ★ ★ ★ ½

APPEAL BY AGE	PRESCHOOL ★	GRADE SCHOOL ★	TEENS ★★
YOUNG ADULTS ★★	OVER 30 ★★		SENIORS ★★★

Emmet Place, off Lavitt's Quay; ☎ 021-490-7855; www.crawfordartgallery.com

Type of attraction An excellent small art gallery. **Admission** Free. **Hours** Monday–Saturday, 10 a.m.–5 p.m. **When to go** Anytime. **Special comments** The museum's cafe is a destination in itself; operated by the Allen family of Bally-maloe, it serves an excellent selection of fresh Irish fare. **How much time to allow** At least 1 hour.

DESCRIPTION AND COMMENTS One of Ireland's best collections of art fills the 18th-century brick customs house plus a modern extension, and it is all the more enjoyable to view because it is small enough not to overwhelm. A ground-floor gallery is filled with one of the museum's prizes, a collection of casts of Greek and Roman sculptures. This area usually is thronged with art students leaning over their drawing pads. A stroll through the galleries beyond, though, reveals the heart of the collection, a couple dozen or so canvases by 19th- and 20th-century Irish artists. Jack Yeats, brother of the poet W. B. Yeats, is well represented by works such as *Off the Donegal Coast* (1922); Sean Keating's *Men of the South* (1921) is a moving depiction in browns and grays of nationalists during Ireland's War of Independence. Earlier works include canvases by Cork's own James Barry (1741–1806). The museum regularly hosts special exhibitions and displays work by contemporary Cork artists.

TOURING TIPS Occasionally, much of the permanent collection is taken down to make room for special exhibitions; the Greek and Roman casts are almost always on view, as is a small selection of works by Yeats and other artists.

 English Market ★ ★ ★ ★

APPEAL BY AGE	PRESCHOOL ★ ★	GRADE SCHOOL ★ ★	TEENS ★ ★
YOUNG ADULTS ★ ★	OVER 30 ★ ★ ★ ★	SENIORS ★ ★ ★ ★	

Off the Grand Parade

Type of attraction A covered food market. **Admission** Free. **Hours** Monday–Saturday, 9 a.m.–6 p.m. **When to go** Morning, when the market is at its liveliest. **Special comments** This is an excellent place to forage for breakfast, especially the pastries from Cork Bakery Company and a cup of coffee from Iago. **How much time to allow** At least 1 hour.

DESCRIPTION AND COMMENTS Every city should have a market like this at its center. You haven't experienced real Cork life until you've taken a leisurely stroll through this vast covered hall dating back to 1881 (rebuilt after a fire in 1980). More than 140 stalls brim with Irish produce, fish, and meat, making it easy to see why Cork is one of Ireland's culinary capitals. Who sells the best of what is a matter of ongoing debate in Cork, but Iago consistently gets nods for Irish cheeses, and O'Reilly's is the place to stop for tripe (cow stomach) and *drisheen* (blood sausage). The liveliest spectacle is the ongoing show in the fish aisles, where restaurateurs and nattily attired office workers alike pick over mussels, eels, and other denizens of the deep. Many of the stalls offer free samples, so come prepared to snack, and if you can't resist the hunger pangs, head upstairs to the Farmgate Café, where the kitchen is supplied by the market stalls and a table provides a bird's-eye view of the proceedings below.

TOURING TIPS Because the market is in the city center near the shops and city-center attractions of Patrick Street, consider nipping in more than once during your rounds.

RESTAURANTS IN CORK

Farmgate Café ★ ★ ★ ★

IRISH	INEXPENSIVE/MODERATE	QUALITY ★ ★ ★ ★	VALUE ★ ★ ★ ★ ½

English Market, Cork City; ☎ 021-427-8134

Reservations None. **Entree range** €8.50–€16. **Payment** MC, V. **Bar** Wine and beer. **Disabled access** Yes. **Hours** Monday–Saturday, 8:30 a.m.–4 p.m.

MENU RECOMMENDATIONS Lamb stew, fish chowder.

COMMENTS Fresh Irish fare gets no fresher than this: the wooden tables and chairs line a gallery overlooking the English Market, the stalls of which keep the kitchen in steady supply of produce, meat, fish, and cheese. These ingredients appear in some typical, elsewhere-hard-to-find Cork dishes, such as tripe and *drisheen* (sausage made with pig's blood), as well as savory tarts and hearty soups. Berry crumbles and other desserts are memorable, too, as is the experience of savoring the buzz of the market from this welcoming perch.

Fenns Quay ★ ★ ★ ★

CONTINENTAL	MODERATE/EXPENSIVE	QUALITY ★ ★ ★ ★	VALUE ★ ★ ★ ★

5 Sheares Street, Cork City; ☎ 021-427-9527

Reservations Recommended. **Entree range** €16–€25; €20 2-course dinner; €25 3-course dinner. **Payment** AE, MC, V. **Bar** Full service. **Disabled access** Dining room, yes; restrooms, no. **Hours** Monday–Saturday, 10 a.m.–10 p.m.

MENU RECOMMENDATIONS Black pudding with potato pancake, seafood chowder, Irish lamb burger.

COMMENTS In this bright, welcoming space, white-brick walls are covered with splashes of contemporary art, and the kitchen sends out delicious food to keep patrons happy throughout the day. Freshly baked muffins appear at breakfast time; soup and sandwiches are available for quick lunches; and, most notably, innovative twists on Irish beef and lamb, freshly caught fish, hearty salads with farm cheeses, and pasta dishes made with fresh vegetables appear on the evening menu. Plan to arrive before 7:30 p.m. so you can sample the offerings on the small but excellent early-dinner menu.

Jacobs on the Mall ★ ★ ★ ★ ½

CONTINENTAL	MODERATE/EXPENSIVE	QUALITY ★ ★ ★ ★	VALUE ★ ★ ★ ★

30A South Mall, Cork City; ☎ 021-425-1530

Reservations Recommended; required on weekends. **Entree range** €17–€25. **Payment** AE, D, MC, V. **Bar** Full service. **Disabled access** Yes. **Hours** Monday–Saturday, 12:30–2:30 p.m. and 6:30–10 p.m.

MENU RECOMMENDATIONS Seared scallops with pancetta salad, breast of free-range duck, any daily preparation of fresh local fish.

COMMENTS Cork's most distinctive dining room, a vaulted contemporary space that occupies a former Turkish bath, is also arguably the city's best restaurant, serving deceptively simple preparations of local produce, fish, and meat. Asparagus is from nearby Kinsale, the fish from local waters, breads fresh from the kitchen ovens; even the simplest offerings, such as farmhouse cheeses with homemade biscuits, can be sublime. Service is relaxed but adept, and while the airy, light-filled space is quite appealing at lunch, you may want to return for a long evening in these soothing, sophisticated surroundings.

Jacques ★ ★ ★ ★

MODERN IRISH	MODERATE/EXPENSIVE	QUALITY ★ ★ ★ ★	VALUE ★ ★ ★ ½

Phoenix Street, Cork City; ☎ 021-427-7387

Reservations Recommended. **Entree range** €19.90–€25.90; €15.90 2-course lunch; €19.90 2-course early dinner (6–7 p.m.). **Payment** D, MC, V. **Bar** Full service. **Disabled access** Yes. **Hours** Monday–Saturday, noon–3 p.m. and 6–10 p.m.; Sunday, 5–9 p.m.

MENU RECOMMENDATIONS Warm salad of crispy chicken and watercress, free-range chicken stuffed with Parma ham.

COMMENTS Now serving food for a quarter of a century, sisters Jacqueline and Eithne Barry helped put Cork on the culinary map. They pride themselves on the close relationships established with local suppliers over the years. In the kitchen, these fresh ingredients are transformed into preparations that the Barrys refer to as "simple fresh Cork food," served with care but without fuss in subtly modern surroundings.

Les Gourmandises ★ ★ ★ ★

FRENCH/MODERN IRISH	EXPENSIVE	QUALITY ★ ★ ★ ★	VALUE ★ ★ ★

17 Cook Street, Cork City; ☎ 021-425-1959

Reservations Recommended. **Entree range** €23.50–€28; €39.50 dinner, Tuesday–Thursday all evening, Friday–Saturday 6–7 p.m.; €55 tasting menu. **Payment** D, MC, V. **Bar** Full service. **Disabled access** Yes. **Hours** Tuesday–Saturday, 6–10 p.m.; Friday, noon–2 p.m.

MENU RECOMMENDATIONS Les Gourmandises tasting plate, hot and cold foie gras, roasted sea scallops.

COMMENTS Chefs-owners Pat and Soizic Kiely trained at top Michelin-starred restaurants in England and Dublin (including the latter city's acclaimed Patrick Guilbald) before bringing their skills to Pat's native Cork in 2002. Their handsome cream-colored room, warmed by an open fire, is as comfy as a French bistro, as are such bistro classics as beef bourguignonne and roast-duck-leg confit. The friendly, low-key service is in perfect keeping with the atmosphere. Any meal here is memorable, but the tasting menu puts a real shine on an evening.

Nash 19 ★ ★ ★ ★

MODERN IRISH   INEXPENSIVE/MODERATE   QUALITY ★★★★   VALUE ★★★★½

19 Princes Street, Cork City; ☎ 021-427-0880

Reservations Not necessary. **Entree range** €8.50–€11.50. **Payment** AE, MC, V. **Bar** Beer and wine. **Disabled access** Yes. **Hours** Monday–Friday, 7:30 a.m.– 4:30 p.m.; Saturday, 7:30 a.m.–4 p.m.

MENU RECOMMENDATIONS   Scones, soups, warm salads, berry crumbles.

COMMENTS   The only complaint you're likely to have about this amiable, bustling city-center gathering spot is that it is not open into the evening hours. Instead, you'll have to settle for a breakfast of hot scones and free-range eggs or one of the casseroles or other sumptuous lunch dishes, all of which Claire Nash prepares with fresh ingredients from local suppliers. Daily choices are seen in an open-style pantry near the door; place your order, take a seat in the series of attractive small rooms, and the accommodating servers will bring your meal to you. Lunchtime lines can be long, but the food is well worth the short wait.

ENTERTAINMENT AND NIGHTLIFE IN CORK

OFF LAVITT'S QUAY IN THE CITY CENTER, the **Cork Opera House** is Cork's major venue for live entertainment, with a lively year-round schedule of opera, drama, and concerts; for information and tickets, call ☎ 021-427-0022 or visit **www.corkoperahouse.ie.** The domed **Firkin Crane Cultural Center,** part of the historic Cork Butter Exchange, takes its name from a Danish term for a unit of measure. The center, which is dedicated to promoting contemporary Irish dance, often hosts troupes from around Ireland and throughout the world; call ☎ 021-450-7487. **Everyman Palace** is a beautifully restored Victorian entertainment hall on MacCurtain Street that stages plays and other performances; call ☎ 021-450-1673.

The heart of Cork nightlife is the city's lively pub scene. At the **Franciscan Well Brew Pub** (North Mall, ☎ 021-421-0130) you can enjoy the house's own brews (including Blarney Blonde and Rebel Red) and soak in the history of the surroundings—the brewery occupies the site of a 12th-century Franciscan monastery. **An Spailpin Fanac** (The Migrant Worker; Main Street, ☎ 021-427-7949) and **An Bodhrán** (42 Oliver Plunkett Street, ☎ 021-427-4544) are Cork's choice spots for live traditional music (a *bodhrán* is a Celtic drum). An Spailpin Fanac dates from 1779, which makes it Cork's oldest pub; the second oldest is the **Mutton Lane Inn** (3 Mutton Lane, off Patrick Street; ☎ 021-427-3471), where an old-world, dark-wood, heavy-beam aura prevails.

SHOPPING IN CORK

CORK'S MAIN SHOPPING VENUE IS PATRICK STREET, and setting the gold standard for the avenue's many shops is **Brown Thomas,** a venerable old Dublin-based department store at Number 18; ☎ 021-480-5555. Paul's Lane, which cuts a swath through the French Quarter between Patrick Street and the quays, houses a number of antiques shops, including **O'Regan's** (Number 4, ☎ 021-427-2902) and **Mills** (Number 3, ☎ 021-427-3528). The **Living Tradition** (40 MacCurtain Street, ☎ 021-450-2564) stocks a large selection of traditional music and instruments, and the place for books of Irish interest is **Mercier** (5 French Church Street, ☎ 021-427-5040); the shop is run by Mercier Press, Ireland's oldest independent publisher. Irish crafts are on offer at **Crafts of Ireland** (11 Winthrop Street, ☎ 021-427-5864), while the **Shandon Craft Centre** is a co-op where potters, weavers, and other artisans offer distinctive wares (in the Cork Butter Exchange; John Redmond Street, ☎ 021-430-0600). **Blarney Knitting Mills** (☎ 021-438-5280) takes advantage of the Blarney Stone–kissing crowds with a huge shop on the castle grounds, offering one-stop shopping for everything from hand-knit sweaters to fine crystal to key rings.

EXERCISE AND RECREATION IN CORK CITY

CORK IS SURROUNDED BY GOLF COURSES. Among the top links are the **Cork Golf Club** (on Little Island, eight kilometers [five miles] east of town, ☎ 021-435-3451) and **Douglas Golf Club** (five kilometers [three miles] east in Douglas, ☎ 021-489-5297).

MIDLETON *and* EAST CORK

JAMESON'S OLD MIDLETON DISTILLERY, where the fine Irish whiskey is produced, has put the busy market town of **Midleton** on the tourist track. **Midleton** a good base from which to explore the countryside, coast, and even Cork City, and the town is surrounded by a number of excellent country-house hotels where you can enjoy rural Irish life in comfort.

PLANNING YOUR VISIT TO MIDLETON AND EAST CORK

HOUSED IN THE JAMESON DISTILLERY in the center of town, the **Midleton Tourist Office** provides information on where to stay, what to see and do, and where to dine in the surrounding region. For information, call ☎ 021-461-3702 or visit **www.corkkerry.ie.** The center is open May to September, daily, 9:30 a.m. to 5 p.m.

ARRIVING AND GETTING ORIENTED IN MIDLETON AND EAST CORK

IT'S DIFFICULT TO EXPLORE EAST CORK WITHOUT A CAR. Midleton is within easy reach of Cork City, about 20 kilometers (12 miles) east via N25; the trip takes about 20 minutes. If you opt for public transportation, you're better off using Cork City as a base and traveling by bus or train to Midleton and other places in East Cork from there. **Bus Éireann** coaches travel between Cork City and Midleton about every half hour. One-way fare is about €3; for information, call ☎ 021-450-8188 or visit **www.buseireann.ie**.

HOTELS IN MIDLETON AND EAST CORK

 Ballymaloe House ★ ★ ★ ½

QUALITY ★★★★	VALUE ★★½	€135–€240

Shanagarry, Midleton, County Cork; ☎ 021-465-2531; fax 021-465-2021; res@ballymaloe.ie; www.ballymaloe.ie

Location 23 kilometers (14 miles) southeast of Cork. **Amenities and services** 33 rooms; croquet, gardens, 9-hole golf course, hair dryers, lounges, playground, swimming pool, tennis court, TV room (no in-room TVs). **Elevator** Yes. **Parking** On property, free. **Price** Includes full Irish breakfast; special offers available on the Internet. **Credit cards** AE, D, MC.

The 160-hectare (400-acre) estate of the Allen family may be the most famous country-house hotel in Ireland. Since the dining room opened in 1964, three generations of Allens have become world renowned as restaurateurs, instructors (at the nearby Ballymaloe Cooking School), and authors of books on cooking and entertaining (for sale in the hotel shop). The patina of fame washes over the premises, and not necessarily to the advantage of the place—you get the feeling that the old house is the center of an empire rather than a relaxing retreat. In fact, many guests are not here to relax or enjoy the grounds but to dine or attend classes at the school, which operates out of a house about a mile down the road. Even so, the Allens remain very hospitable, and they have done a smart job with the guest rooms. Distinctively decorated yet comfortably simple, these occupy the original house, tastefully and seamlessly attached newer wings, and the old farmyard. Accommodations vary considerably in size, and not all are accessible by elevator, so discuss your needs when booking. Some of the nicest rooms are on the ground level, with small patios adjoining the lawns. Rooms in the farmyard are small but cozy, and a few of these are suites with conservatory-like sitting rooms. Ballymaloe offers special midweek breaks and other cost-saving plans, usually including a meal or two in the acclaimed dining room, so call or visit the Web site to see what's available when you plan to stay.

Barnabrow Country House ★ ★ ★

QUALITY ★★★½	VALUE ★★	€80–€120

Cloyne, Midleton, County Cork; ☎ 021-465-2534; fax 021-465-2534; barnabrow@eircom.net; www.barnabrowhouse.ie

Location Countryside, between Cloyne and Ballycotton. **Amenities and services** 21 rooms; babysitting, gardens, hair dryers, restaurant. **Elevator** No. **Parking** On property, free. **Price** Includes full Irish breakfast. **Credit cards** AE, MC, V.

Lambs, ponies, and chickens roam the grounds surrounding the imposing 17th-century farmhouse at the heart of this estate, where guests find quiet corners in the extensive gardens to relax and soak in the rural atmosphere. Five of the rooms are in the main house. The best in the place, these rooms are large and light, painted in soothing hues, floored with African teak, and furnished with a pleasing mix of traditional, contemporary, and African pieces; several of the large bathrooms are equipped with claw-footed soaking tubs. Other accommodations are in outbuildings grouped around the farmyard, and while smaller than those in the main house, these can accommodate families and are nicely appointed with casual, handsome furniture. Most rooms open directly to the outdoors, making them ideal for kids to come and go and wander the grounds. Guests enjoy a large breakfast served at a communal table in the main house, as well as excellent lunches and dinners made with local game, fish, and produce grown on the farm, in a beamed dining room. Unfortunately, Barnabrow is increasingly popular with large wedding parties, so sometimes it is unavailable to other guests.

Glenview House ★ ★ ★ ★ ★

QUALITY ★ ★ ★ ★	VALUE ★ ★ ★ ★	€65–€140

Midleton, County Cork; ☎ 021-463-4680; fax 021-463-4680; info@glenviewmidleton.com; www.glenviewmidleton.com

Location 3 miles west of Midleton, off Fermoy Road. **Amenities and services** 4 rooms; dinner sometimes available upon request; gardens, honor bar, hair dryers, in-room tea and coffee facilities, lounge. **Elevator** No. **Parking** On property, free. **Price** Includes full Irish breakfast. **Credit cards** AE, MC, V.

Ken and Beth Sherrard set the gold standard for a stay in an Irish country house. This hospitable, well-traveled couple are unobtrusively on hand to share advice on exploring the region, and they graciously ensure comfort during your stay in the house and grounds they have lovingly restored over the past 40 years. In 1965, Ken ingeniously salvaged the contents of a row of Georgian townhouses on Fitzpatrick Street in Dublin that were slated for demolition, and many of the mantelpieces, floors, cornices, and other architectural details now grace Glenview. Guests relax in the handsome drawing room, where a fire blazes in colder months, and upstairs are three commodious and thoughtfully appointed guest rooms overlooking the rolling countryside. One room on the ground floor is equipped for travelers with disabilities. The coach house has been converted to two comfortable apartments, one with two bedrooms and another with one bedroom; both have pleasant sitting rooms and full kitchens, one of which is designed to be used by guests in wheelchairs. An Irish breakfast is served at the huge family table and includes eggs from Beth's hens as well as fresh fruit and home-baked breads. Beth also prepares exquisite dinners on request.

EXPLORING EAST CORK

TO THE EAST OF CORK, rich farmlands roll down to the sea. The coast is lined with sandy beaches and still-thriving fishing ports such as **Ballycotton, Shanagarry,** and **Youghal. Midleton** and the surrounding countryside are also convenient to **Fota Island** and **Cobh.** You may want to spend a full day exploring the region east of Midleton, and another in Fota and Cobh. From Midleton, Route R629 leads south across farmlands to **Shanagarry** and **Ballycotton,** and from there you can follow the coast north and east on R633 to **Youghal,** a busy port town of which Sir Walter Raleigh was once mayor. To reach Fota and Cobh, simply follow N25 back toward Cork for about ten kilometers (six miles) and take the well-marked exit that leads you first to Fota Island then around the northern shores of Cork Harbor to Cobh.

ATTRACTIONS IN MIDLETON AND EAST CORK

Fota House ★ ★ ★ ★

APPEAL BY AGE	PRESCHOOL ★ ★	GRADE SCHOOL ★ ★	TEENS ★ ★ ★
YOUNG ADULTS ★ ★	OVER 30 ★ ★ ★ ★		SENIORS ★ ★ ★ ★

Fota Island, about 5 kilometers (3 miles) west of Midleton; follow N25 west toward Cork City and take the well-marked exit to Fota Island; if you are driving from Cork, follow N25 east and take the same exit; trains run from Cork to Fota Island and on to Cobh; contact Irish Rail, ☎ 1850-366-222 or 01-836-6222, or visit www.irishrail.ie; Fota House: ☎ 021-481-5543; www.fotahouse.com

Type of attraction Historic home and grounds. **Admission** €5.50 adults, €2.20 children, €4.50 seniors and students, €12.50 families of up to 2 adults and 3 children. **Hours** April–September, Monday–Saturday, 10 a.m.–5 p.m.; Sunday, 11 a.m.–5 p.m.; October–March, Monday–Saturday, 10 a.m.–4 p.m.; Sunday, 11 a.m.–5 p.m. **When to go** In good weather, if possible, to enjoy the grounds. **Special comments** The house is sparsely furnished, which may disappoint some visitors. **How much time to allow** 2 hours to see the house, garden, and arboretum.

DESCRIPTION AND COMMENTS The Smith-Barry clan traces its roots to the 12th-century Anglo-Saxon invasion of Ireland, so they had 900 years in which to amass their vast lands, which at one time encompassed much of the eastern part of County Cork. At the center of these holdings was Fota Island, where the family built a house and planted gardens and an arboretum. The house and grounds had fallen into disrepair by the end of the 20th century, but ongoing restorations have made Fota a showcase that you should go out of your way to visit.

The present house was built in the Regency style in the 1820s, and the 70 rooms (only those on the ground floor can be visited) are an impressive assemblage of columns, friezes, and plasterwork. After touring castles and ornate manor houses, you'll appreciate Fota's clean lines and classical proportions. Some visitors may be disappointed in the sparse furnishings, as much of the family collection was sold off over the years to settle debts. Then again, you may find the absence of furniture an asset because it allows the architectural detailing to take center stage. The servants' wing shows off life on the other side of the house. An octagonal larder is equipped with a massive carousel for hanging game and fowl; rows of bells summoned staff to different rooms of the house; a massive charcoal stove and shelves stocked with copper pots were essential parts of everyday life in a great house.

The walled garden is beautiful, but the arboretum is the standout here. The family commissioned plant-collecting expeditions to the far corners of the world, and trees and plants from China, Japan, and South America continue to thrive at Fota. One tall specimen may look familiar to visitors from the western United States—it's a sequoia, one of the first to be planted in Europe, brought back from California in the early 19th century.

TOURING TIPS Videos in each room of the house tell the stories of residents and servants and provide a wealth of information on architecture and period tastes; take the time to view these sophisticated viewing aids. A pleasant cafe serves light meals and snacks.

Fota Wildlife Park ★ ★ ★

APPEAL BY AGE	PRESCHOOL ★★★★	GRADE SCHOOL ★★★★	TEENS ★★★★
YOUNG ADULTS ★★★★		OVER 30 ★★★	SENIORS ★★★

Fota Island, about 5 kilometers (3 miles) west of Midleton; follow N25 toward Cork City and take the well-marked exit to Fota Island; if you are driving from Cork, follow N25 east and take the same exit; trains run from Cork to Fota Island and on to Cobh; contact Irish Rail, ☎ 1850-366-222 or 01-836-6222, or visit www.irishrail.ie; park: ☎ 021-481-2744; www.fotawildlife.ie

Type of attraction Zoo. **Admission** €11.50 adults; €7 seniors, students, children under age 16; free for children under age 2; €45 families of up to 2 adults and 4 children. **Hours** April–December, Monday–Saturday, 10 a.m.–6 p.m.; Sunday, 11 a.m.–6 p.m.; January–March, Monday–Saturday, 10 a.m.–4:30 p.m.; Sunday, 11 a.m.–4:30 p.m. **When to go** In good weather. **Special comments** A visit involves a walk of about 2 kilometers (1.2 miles) along a well-marked route; wheelchairs are available. An open-air tour train is €1 to ride from the entrance to the park's far end, or €2 round trip. **How much time to allow** About 2 hours.

DESCRIPTION AND COMMENTS The deer and the antelope really do roam free on these 70 acres, along with flamingos, giraffes, and 90 other species of creatures exotic to Ireland. Human admirers watch their antics from a path that for the most part is separated from the grazing grounds only by low electronic fences. Fota is not as spectacular as world-renowned zoos in San Diego and some other North American cities, but it does an admirable job of showing off its inhabitants in natural surroundings. In the past 20 years, the park also has done a much-lauded job of breeding endangered species. The cheetahs (the only denizens confined to an enclosure) now number in the hundreds, and most were born here; Fota also has helped rescue an Irish native, the white-tailed sea eagle, from the brink of extinction.

TOURING TIPS   If you want to extend a day in the fresh air, combine a trip to the wildlife park with a visit to the Fota House gardens and arboretum.

 ## Old Midleton Distillery   ★ ★ ½

APPEAL BY AGE	PRESCHOOL ★★	GRADE SCHOOL ★★	TEENS ★★
YOUNG ADULTS ★★	OVER 30 ★★		SENIORS ★★

Off Main Street, Midleton; ☎ **021-461-3594; www.whiskeytours.ie**

Type of attraction Historic whiskey distillery. **Admission** €7.95 adults, €3.50 children under age 16, €6.25 seniors and students, €20 families of up to 2 adults and 2 children. **Hours** March–October, daily, 10 a.m.–6 p.m.; November–February, daily, 10 a.m.–6 p.m. with tours at 11:30 a.m., 2:30 p.m., and 4 p.m. **When to go** Anytime. **Special comments** Much of this tour is conducted outdoors, so dress warmly and bring rain gear as needed. **How much time to allow** Tour and tasting take about 1½ hours.

DESCRIPTION AND COMMENTS   Irish distillers not only make good whiskey but also run a slick business in whisking visitors through its three distilleries: the one here, the Jameson Distillery in Dublin, and the Bushmills Distillery to the north in County Antrim are among Ireland's most popular attractions. The Midleton operation traces its roots to 1825, when James Murphy converted a woolen mill on the banks of the Dungourney River into a distillery that operated until 1975; a new plant adjoins the site. A self-congratulatory introductory video gives visitors the lowdown on the distillery's history as well as the process of making Irish whiskey, and it also reveals tidbits such as how Paddy and Powers, other mainstays of an Irish pub, joined the Jameson family. Another bit of knowledge that will be drilled into you is that *uisce beatha*, Irish for whiskey, means "river of life." A guided tour of the historic premises shows off the world's largest pot still and convinces you that Jameson is smooth as silk because it's distilled three times, whereas Scotch whisky (spelled without the *e*) is distilled only twice. You don't see the actual distilling process, which transpires in the modern plant. You do, however, dip into the river of life at a free tasting at the end of the tour, when you can also stock up on premium whiskeys or key chains shaped like whiskey bottles. In the meantime, for the price of admission you can get a couple of drops of the dew at any pub, and that might be the best way to appreciate this excellent beverage.

TOURING TIPS   If you're traveling to Northern Ireland, you might want to save your distillery tour until you get to Old Bushmills on the Antrim Coast (see page 404), where you can see distilling and bottling in process—far more interesting than looking at old vats.

RESTAURANTS IN MIDLETON AND EAST CORK

Ballymaloe House   ★ ★ ★ ★

| MODERN IRISH | EXPENSIVE | QUALITY ★ ★ ★ ★ | VALUE ★ ★ ★ ½ |

Shanagarry, Midleton, County Cork; ☎ 021-427-7387

Reservations Recommended. **Entree range** €30–€35 lunch; €60 dinner. **Payment** D, MC, V. **Bar** Full service. **Disabled access** Yes. **Hours** Seating times are Monday–Saturday, 1–1:30 p.m., 7–9 p.m.; Sunday, 1–1:30 p.m.; buffet dinner, 7:30–8:30 p.m.

MENU RECOMMENDATIONS   Any fish or seafood from nearby Ballycotton, fresh vegetables and greens from the farm gardens, free-range pork and lamb, farmhouse cheeses.

COMMENTS   Ballymaloe, in the capable hands of the Allen family of culinary stars, has a well-deserved reputation for turning the freshest ingredients into masterpieces of modern Irish cuisine and serving them in perfect country-house surroundings. Just about everything on the exquisite menu is from the farm and local suppliers, and these ingredients emerge from the kitchen of chef Rory O'Connell in deftly prepared, simple dishes. Even the potatoes accompanying the roasts are memorable. Service is flawless but not fussy, and the intimate dining rooms are enlivened with reproductions of the Allen family's collection of paintings by Jack Yeats (many of the originals are in the National Gallery in Dublin). Meals can begin and end with drinks in one of the lounges or the conservatory, or maybe a walk in the well-tended gardens.

Farmgate Restaurant and Country Store   ★ ★ ★ ★

| IRISH | MODERATE | QUALITY ★ ★ ★ ★ | VALUE ★ ★ ★ ★ ★ |

Coolbawn, Midleton, County Cork; ☎ 021-463-1878

Reservations Recommended for dinner. **Entree range** €10–€20. **Payment** AE, MC, V. **Bar** Full service. **Disabled access** Yes. **Hours** Monday–Saturday, noon–4 p.m.; Thursday–Saturday, 7–9:30 p.m.

MENU RECOMMENDATIONS   Cheeses, baked goods, Irish stew.

COMMENTS   The displays of fresh produce, cheeses, and baked goods in the shop at the front of this popular spot are a good omen of what to expect. Like the outlet in the English Market in Cork City, Farmgate has put Midleton on the culinary map for its fresh-as-can-be, simple-yet-superb renditions of soups and salads, as well as stews and other Irish classics—with the occasional fancy surprise, such as stuffed duckling. In fact, you may want to make the effort to come to Farmgate on one of the three evenings dinner is served, because the menu then expands impressively and often includes memorably fresh fish.

O'Donovan's   ★ ★ ★ ★

| MODERN IRISH | MODERATE | QUALITY ★ ★ ★ ★ | VALUE ★ ★ ★ ★ |

58 Main Street, Midleton, across from Old Midleton Distillery; ☎ 021-463-1255

Reservations Recommended. **Entree range** €16–€23; €19 2-course early dinner (6–7 p.m.). **Payment** AE, MC, V. **Bar** Full service. **Disabled access** Yes. **Hours** Monday–Saturday, 12:30–2:30 p.m. and 6–9 p.m.

MENU RECOMMENDATIONS Warm salad of lamb kidneys and Ballycotton crab salad.

COMMENTS This former pub–turned–restaurant remains one of Midleton's most popular gathering spots, with Pat O'Donovan keeping a close eye on the low-key dining room to make sure his guests are content. The menu relies heavily on fresh seafood just off the boats in nearby Ballycotton, as well as produce and meats from Pat's suppliers throughout East Cork. You may want to plan a late-morning visit to the Old Midleton Distillery across the road so that you can lunch here—in fact, a meal at O'Donovan's may be the highlight of the day.

AROUND MIDLETON *and* EAST CORK

COBH

WHAT NOW SEEMS LIKE a pleasant seaside town of Georgian and Regency terrace-style houses was once Ireland's busiest port. With an excellent position at the end of Great Island in Cork Harbor, Cobh (pronounced "cove," and known as Queenstown for a while under British rule) was a naval base in the Napoleonic Wars. It also served as the point of embarkation for convicts transported to Australia and emigrants sailing for America, as well as the last port of call for the *Sirius* (the first ship to steam across the Atlantic) in 1838 and for the *Titanic* on her first and only voyage in 1912. Survivors from the *Lusitania*, which was torpedoed by a German boat off nearby Kinsale Head in 1915, were brought to Kinsale.

Cobh wears this mantle of history well and shows it off in its excellent **Heritage Centre.** The waterfront is littered with a few touching monuments and memorials, including those to the victims of the *Lusitania* and *Titanic*. Most moving, though, is the statue of Annie Moore and her siblings, who sailed from Cobh in 1891; on January 1, 1892, Annie became the first immigrant to pass through New York's Ellis Island. On a hill behind the waterfront looms massive **St. Colman's Cathedral,** completed in

unofficial **T I P**
A good way to see Cobh is on Michael Martin's **Titanic Trail tours**. These lively and informative 60- to 70-minute-long walk takes in former steamship offices, popular gathering spots for passengers, the quays, and other landmarks. Tours begin at the Commodore Hotel: April–May and September, daily, 11 a.m.; June–August, daily, 11 a.m. and 2 p.m.; October–March, varying times. Cost is €8.50 for adults, €4.25 for children under 12. For more information, call ☎ 021-481-5211 or visit **www.titanic-trail.com.**

1915 and topped with a graceful spire. The church is open daily from 8 a.m. to 6 p.m., but the best reward of a walk to the entrance is the fine view over the harbor.

Arriving and Getting Oriented in Cobh

Cobh is about 20 kilometers (12 miles) west of Midleton and the same distance east of Cork, and easily visited on a day trip from either. If you are driving from Midleton or Cork, follow the well-marked exit off N25 for Cobh–Great Island. An easy way to reach Cobh from Cork is by rail; the trip takes 25 minutes, affording excellent views of the coast, and ends next to the *Queenstown Story* exhibit. Trains run about every half hour to hour throughout the day, and the round-trip fare is about €6. For more information, call Irish Rail, ☎ 1850-366-222 or 01 836-6222, or visit **www.irishrail.ie.**

Attraction in Cobh

 Cobh, the Queenstown Story ★ ★ ★ ½

| APPEAL BY AGE | PRESCHOOL ★ ★ | GRADE SCHOOL ★ ★ ★ | TEENS ★ ★ |
| YOUNG ADULTS ★ ★ | OVER 30 ★ ★ ★ ½ | SENIORS ★ ★ ★ ½ |

Cobh Heritage Centre, on waterfront in old train station;
☎ **021-481-3591; www.cobhheritage.com**

Type of attraction Exhibit tracing Cobh's dramatic maritime history. **Admission** €6 adults, €3 children, €5 seniors and students, €16.50 families of up to 2 adults and 4 children. **Hours** May–October, daily, 10 a.m.–6 p.m.; November–April, daily, 10 a.m.–5 p.m. **When to go** Weekdays, if possible; the exhibit can be crowded on weekends. **Special comments** The exhibits are informative, but a walk around the town gives more of a sense of place; try to join one of the Titanic Trail tours (see Unofficial Tip on facing page), and don't miss the *Titanic* and *Lusitania* memorials or the emigrants' statue on the waterfront. **How much time to allow** 2 hours.

DESCRIPTION AND COMMENTS Cobh's maritime past is remembered in an extensive exhibit that is quite engaging, not only because it's well done, but also because Cobh's history is so colorful. The town once was Ireland's major emigration port; millions embarked from here between 1750 and the mid–20th century. Not all went willingly, as Cobh Harbor was filled with "coffin ships" used to transport prisoners to Australia, so called because of the hideous death rates during the long crossing. The Famine of 1844–48 brought millions of eager emigrants desperate to flee starvation and start a new life in the New World. Extensive exhibits, most with lavish audiovisual components, trace conditions in Ireland and life aboard the outgoing ships. Cobh was also the first and last European port of call for transatlantic liners, and other exhibits explore two momentous events in this history. The *Titanic* called here in 1912, just days before hitting an iceberg and sinking. Also, the *Lusitania* was torpedoed off nearby Kinsale Head by the Germans in 1915, with a loss of

1,198 lives; the attack catapulted the United States into World War I. Survivors were brought to Cobh, and many of the dead are buried in the town cemetery. After exposure to the misery Cobh has witnessed, it's refreshing to see the exhibits filled with advertising posters and other memorabilia recalling the glory days of ocean liners.

TOURING TIPS If you're of Irish heritage, chances are your ancestors shipped out of Cobh. You can trace your roots at the adjacent genealogy search center, where the staff will lend a hand; the fee for a genealogical profile is €30. The Cobh Heritage Centre also has a gift shop and a good cafe.

KINSALE

SMALL AND UNDENIABLY CHARMING, Kinsale comes complete with a fascinating history, a beautiful harbor, and excellent restaurants and hotels. The harbor has drawn everyone from Stone Age tribes to British troops seeking an Irish stronghold against invaders to modern-day yachting enthusiasts. Kinsale will easily entertain you for two or more days, and it is also a handy base from which to visit Cork, Cobh, Fota Island, and other places in County Cork.

PLANNING YOUR VISIT TO KINSALE

FOR INFORMATION ON WHERE TO STAY, what to see and do, and where to dine in Kinsale and the surrounding region, contact the Kinsale Tourist Office (Pier Road, ☎ 021-477-2234, www.corkkerry.ie, or www.kinsale.ie). The center is open March to June, Monday through Saturday, 9:30 a.m. to 5:30 p.m.; July to August, Monday through Saturday, 9 a.m. to 7 p.m.; Sunday, 10 a.m. to 7 p.m.; March to June, Monday through Saturday, 9:30 a.m. to 5:30 p.m.; December to January, limited hours, often weekends only.

unofficial **TIP**
As soon as you arrive, stash your car in the large lot near the harbor next to the tourist-information office (about €1.80 per hour, €10 per day, or €17 overnight), or find a spot on the street (about €0.50 per hour, sometimes with a two-hour minimum; pay at one of the self-service pay stations and display the ticket in the car window). Fortunately, many of Kinsale's accommodations provide free parking.

Special Events in Kinsale

Kinsale's first big event of the year is a **St. Patrick's Day Parade** on March 17. In late April, the town hosts the **Heineken Kinsale Sevens by the Sea,** one of Europe's largest rugby meets, drawing 80 teams from ten countries; for information and tickets, call ☎ 021-477-2783 or visit www.kinsalesevens.com. In early October, the **Kinsale International Festival of Fine Food** offers tastings, special meals, demonstrations, and other events that promote Kinsale as the "Gourmet Capital of Ireland"; for information, call ☎ 021-477-9900. Kinsale's **Jazz and Blues Festival** in late October coincides with the Guinness Cork Jazz Festival; for information, call ☎ 1-477-2135.

ARRIVING AND GETTING ORIENTED IN KINSALE

KINSALE IS 30 KILOMETERS (18 miles) south of Cork; the most direct route by car is on R611. Driving in the town's narrow lanes can be difficult during the busy summer season. If you're traveling between Kinsale and Cobh, the most scenic route takes you via R600, R613, and R610, with a trip across an inlet of Cork Harbor on a small ferry; the fare is €3.50 per car.

Bus Éireann coaches from Cork run about every hour and arrive at the Esso Station on Pier Road near the tourist office. The fare is about €5 one way or €7 round trip. For more information, call ☎ 021-450-8188 or visit **www.buseireann.ie**.

Kinsale has no public transportation, but most sights, with the exception of **Charles Fort** (see page 228), are within easy walking distance in the town center; for a taxi, call **Kinsale Cabs, ☎** 021-477-2642.

HOTELS IN KINSALE

Chart House ★ ★ ★ ★

QUALITY ★ ★ ★ ★	VALUE ★ ★ ★	€50–€120

Denis Quay, Kinsale, County Cork; ☎ 021-477-4586; fax 021-477-7907; charthouse@eircom.net; www.charthouse-kinsale.com

Location City center. **Amenities and services** 4 rooms; hair dryers, Internet connections, irons, satellite TV, sauna, tea and coffee, trouser press. **Elevator** No. **Parking** On street, free. **Price** Includes full Irish breakfast. **Credit cards** AE, MC, V.

Mary and Billy O'Connor have turned their 200-year-old house, the former home of a sea captain and just steps from the harbor, into Kinsale's most comfortable and luxurious bed-and-breakfast establishment. The four bedrooms, filled with majestic old bedsteads and other fine antiques, are well appointed with modern amenities such as deep whirlpool soaking tubs and power showers. Two of the upstairs rooms are especially spacious and have sitting areas. A snug little single on the ground floor is a great value given that occupants can easily spread out to the charming living room, where a fire glows in colder months and Billy and Mary serve tea and coffee. The couple also serve an excellent breakfast at a highly polished antique table in an elegant dining room.

Friar's Lodge ★ ★ ★

QUALITY ★ ★ ★	VALUE ★ ★ ★ ★ ½	€60–€120

Friar Street, Kinsale, County Cork; ☎ 021-477-7384; fax 021-477-4363; mtierney@indigo.ie; www.friars-lodge.com

Location City center. **Amenities and services** 18 rooms; 3 self-catering apartments also available; DVD players, hair dryers, in-room tea and coffee facilities, Internet connections, irons, laundry service, pillow menus, satellite TV, turndown service. **Elevator** Yes. **Parking** On property, free. **Price** Includes full Irish breakfast; off-season rates and Internet specials sometimes available. **Credit cards** AE, MC, V.

When Maureen Tierney, a longtime veteran of the hospitality industry and a traveler herself, built her guest house a few years ago, she had strong ideas about the sorts of amenities she preferred. Her rooms may not be as atmospheric as those at some of the neighboring inns, but they are extremely large; well furnished in traditional, comfortable style that is more functional than luxurious; and loaded with little extras. Complimentary sherry is on hand in the cozy lounge in the evenings. A long list of surprising in-room extras includes DVD players (films are available at the front desk and at a shop around the corner), turndown service, and even a choice of down or synthetic pillows (for allergy sufferers). A full Irish breakfast is served in an attractive dining room, and most of Kinsale's well-reputed restaurants are just a short walk away.

Old Bank ★ ★ ★ ½

QUALITY	★ ★ ★	VALUE	★ ★ ½	€170–€245

Friar Street, Kinsale, County Cork; ☎ 021-477-4075; fax 021-477-4296; oldbank@indigo.ie; www.oldbankhousekinsale.com

Location City center. **Amenities and services** 17 rooms; golfer friendly (information on courses, tee times, and more); limited room service, no smoking. **Elevator** Yes. **Parking** On property, free. **Price** Includes full Irish breakfast; off-season rates sometimes available. **Credit cards** AE, MC, V.

Michael and Marie Riese have created a stylish little inn that commands the best spot in Kinsale: facing the harbor at the end of the charming main street. A mix of antiques and fine fabrics adds a touch of luxury to the high-ceilinged guest rooms; beds can be configured as singles or zipped together as kings, and the well-designed bathrooms have tub-and-shower combinations. Nice touches, such as window seats from which to watch the boats and a well-appointed drawing room with an open fire, encourage you to settle in and relax. To get the most out of a stay, request a room at the front of the house (for the best views). If you're up for a splurge, ask for the postmaster's suite—a capacious room with a sitting area and fireplace. Michael is a master chef and prides himself on his elaborate breakfasts, which are served in a stylish dining room.

Old Presbytery ★ ★ ★ ★

QUALITY	★ ★ ★ ★ ½	VALUE	★ ★ ★ ★	€95–€150

43 Cork Street, Kinsale, County Cork (closed December 1–February 14); ☎ 021-477-2027; fax 021-477-2166; info@oldpres.com; www.oldpres.com

Location City center. **Amenities and services** 6 rooms; 3 self-catering apartments also available; hair dryers, in-room tea and coffee facilities. **Elevator** No. **Parking** On property, free. **Price** Includes full Irish breakfast. **Credit cards** AE, MC, V.

Kinsale's most atmospheric accommodations are at the top of the old town in this fine old house, where an alluring warren of alcoves and staircases leads to six attractive and comfortable guest rooms. Phillip and Noreen McEvoy have decorated each tasteful room differently, with a penchant for plain pine Irish antiques (they opt for a more ornate look in the Victorian lounge). Several rooms have balconies, and number six is especially appealing with its glassed-in sitting room and terrace; a penthouse suite is on two levels, with a rooftop bedroom reached via a winding staircase. Phillip is a chef, and his breakfast feasts of smoked and fresh fish, crepes, and fresh pastries provide a memorable start to a day. None of the rooms in the main house are suitable for guests who can't manage stairs, and all guests would be well advised to leave heavy luggage in the car. Easier to reach are the three self-catering apartments in an adjoining house, reached from the rear car park. All of these have two bedrooms and two bathrooms, as well as large sitting rooms with gas fires and well-equipped kitchenettes; they are available for several days or longer periods.

Trident   ★ ★ ★

QUALITY ★ ★ ★	VALUE ★ ★ ½	€ 110–€ 140

World's End, Kinsale, County Cork; ☎ 021-477-9300; fax 021-477-4173; info@tridenthotel.com; www.tridenthotel.com

Location City center. **Amenities and services** 75 rooms; bar, gym, hair dryers, in-room tea and coffee facilities, Internet connections, restaurant, satellite TV, sauna, steam room, whirlpool. **Elevator** Yes. **Parking** On property, free. **Price** Includes full Irish breakfast; off-season rates and package specials sometimes available. **Credit cards** AE, MC, V.

Kinsale has so many small, cozy inns that it seems odd to settle for a large and rather anonymous hotel such as this. That may be the point, though—the large, sleekly appointed rooms are like those in an upscale business hotel and offer solid comfort and few surprises, with the exception of the best water views to be had from any Kinsale hotel. When booking, request a room in the newer wing closest to the harbor, particularly one of the suites hanging directly over the water—two of these have large terraces. While the long hallways are a bit dispiriting, the Savannah Restaurant is airy, provides refreshing water views, and serves excellent local seafood. The Wharf Tavern, all dark wood and stone, serves excellent pub grub.

EXPLORING KINSALE

KINSALE'S MEDIEVAL LANES CLIMB FROM THE HARBOR toward Compass Hill, and the well-preserved streets are endowed with remnants of the town's long past. The tallest structure in Kinsale is the steeple of **St. Multose Church.** The Dutch-style **Old Courthouse,** at the far end of Church Place, was built in the 17th century. It enjoyed the spotlight in 1915, when officials from around the world gathered in the courtroom for the inquest into the sinking of the *Lusitania* by a German torpedo boat off Kinsale Head. That tragedy and other episodes in Kinsale's past are evoked in the small **Regional Museum,** open Wednesday through Saturday, 10:30 a.m. to 5:30 p.m.; €2.50; for more information, call ☎ 021-477-7930. **Desmond Castle,** around the corner on Cork Street, houses the **International Museum of Wine**—not as much of a stretch as it may seem in vineyard-deprived Ireland. As you'll learn, Irish emigrants helped establish the wine trade around the world. More interesting are the modest exhibits honoring other events in the building's past: The Spanish quartered here during the thwarted Spanish-Irish attempt to oust the British in the Battle of Kinsale in 1601; the British imprisoned American sailors here during the American Revolution and French soldiers during the Napoleonic Wars; and starving farmers took refuge here during the Famine, when the building served as a workhouse. The castle is open mid-April to mid-June, Tuesday through Sunday, 10 a.m. to 6 p.m.; mid-June to October, daily, 10 a.m. to 6 p.m.; €2.75 adults, €1.25 children, €2 seniors and students, €7 families.

ATTRACTION IN KINSALE

Charles Fort ★ ★ ★ ★

APPEAL BY AGE	PRESCHOOL ★★★	GRADE SCHOOL ★★★★	TEENS ★★★★
YOUNG ADULTS ★★★★	OVER 30 ★★★★		SENIORS ★★★★

Summercove; on the harbor, about 2 miles south of Kinsale;
☎ **021-477-2263**

Type of attraction Historic fort overlooking Kinsale Harbour. **Admission** €3.50 adults, €1.25 children under age 12, €2.50 seniors, €8.25 families of 2 adults and 2 children. **Hours** Mid-March–October, daily, 10 a.m.–6 p.m.; November–mid-March, daily, 10 a.m.–5 p.m. **When to go** In good weather. **Special comments** Even if you're not a military-history buff, this place is fascinating, and the views over the harbor and headlands from the ramparts are worth the price of admission alone. **How much time to allow** 2 hours (1 hour for guided tour, 1 hour to wander on your own).

DESCRIPTION AND COMMENTS The British began work on this mighty star-shaped bastion overlooking Kinsale Harbour in 1677, still feeling vulnerable after British forces had successfully thwarted a joint invasion of Irish and Spanish forces in the Battle of Kinsale in 1601. Consider the fort's strategic position at the entrance to the harbor to understand its military importance—the extent and thickness of the walls seem to make it impregnable. Ironically, it was attacked only once, and despite its mighty defenses, the fort failed the test and was taken. You can walk the ramparts and wander through the fort on your own, but be sure to take one of the frequent tours included with the admission price. The resident historians are gold mines of information, and you'll get an hour-long earful, all of it illuminating and most of it true. (You be the judge of the veracity of the tale about the officer's bride whose ghost can still be seen taking an evening stroll on the ramparts.) Several buildings within the massive complex have been renovated, and one of them houses an excellent exhibition that chronicles the long history of the fort and includes a brief film reenacting the life of an Irish soldier.

TOURING TIPS If the weather cooperates, venture out to the fort on the Scilly Walk, which follows the harbor through little hamlets and park-like groves; a stop for a pint at the Bulman, just below the fort in the village of Scilly, is mandatory.

RESTAURANTS IN KINSALE

FIRST CHOICE FOR A CASUAL MEAL IS **Mother Hubbard's** (Market Street, ☎ 021-477-2440), a popular breakfast spot that bakes memorable pastries and serves soup and sandwiches into the afternoon hours.

Blue Haven   ★ ★ ★

PUB/IRISH   MODERATE/EXPENSIVE   QUALITY ★ ★ ★   VALUE ★ ★ ★ ★ (pub),
★ ★ ★ (restaurant)

3 Pearse Street, Kinsale, County Cork; ☎ 021-477-7858

Reservations Recommended for restaurant. **Entree range** €10–€18 pub; €20–€37 restaurant; €35 3-course early dinner. **Payment** AE, MC, V. **Bar** Full service. **Disabled access** Yes. **Hours** Pub: daily, 12:15–3 p.m. and 6:30–10 p.m.; restaurant: daily, 7–10 p.m.

MENU RECOMMENDATIONS *Pub:* Fresh oysters, beer-battered haddock and fries, banana banoffi pie; *restaurant:* crab linguine, caramelized scallops, grilled filet of sea bass.

COMMENTS This friendly old hotel in the center of Kinsale serves food to suit any mood and appetite, in a woody pub, an airy daytime cafe, or an elegant conservatory-style restaurant. You'll find good food and service in all, but the pub is especially appealing in that it offers that hard-to-find, good-but-light evening meal. The more-elaborate restaurant menu is appealing, too, laden with excellent preparations of seafood and game. You may want to settle in next to the fire or on the patio with a pint and take a look at the different menus to see what suits your fancy.

Fishy Fishy Café   ★ ★ ★ ★

SEAFOOD   MODERATE   QUALITY ★ ★ ★ ★   VALUE ★ ★ ★ ★ ★

Guardwell, Kinsale, County Cork; ☎ 021-477-4453

Reservations None. **Entree range** €10–€15. **Payment** AE, MC, V. **Bar** Wine and beer. **Disabled access** Yes. **Hours** Daily, noon–3:45 p.m.

MENU RECOMMENDATIONS Grilled prawns, seafood chowder, smoked salmon on brown bread.

COMMENTS Seafood doesn't come any fresher than it does at this fish market with a scattering of indoor and outdoor tables. The menu is small and hinges on what's fresh off the boats—crab and scallops are often available, as are John Dory and other local fish. You should see no need to stray from the listed offerings, but if you do the kitchen will prepare any fish in the cases as you like it. Little wonder Fishy Fishy has a devoted lunchtime following, so arrive early or late.

Little Skillet   ★ ★ ★ ½

IRISH   MODERATE   QUALITY ★ ★ ★ ★   VALUE ★ ★ ★ ★

Main Street, Kinsale, County Cork; ☎ 021-477-4202

Reservations Recommended for dinner. **Entree range** €16–€20. **Payment** MC, V. **Bar** Full service. **Disabled access** Yes. **Hours** Daily, 12:30–2:30 p.m. and 6–10:30 p.m.

MENU RECOMMENDATIONS Seafood chowder, Irish stew.

COMMENTS The stone-walled room with open hearth and simple furnishings has the feel of a country kitchen, and the offerings do nothing to dispel the feeling that you're enjoying a knowledgeably prepared home-cooked meal. Seafood offerings are made from the freshest fish, and the vegetables are chosen carefully from local suppliers. The charms of the place are well known, so plan on enjoying a pint in the little bar across the street while you wait for a table—not an unpleasant proposition. Anne and Richard Ennos offer likewise-engaging accommodations upstairs.

The Vintage ★ ★ ★ ★

| IRISH | MODERATE | QUALITY ★ ★ ★ ★ | VALUE ★ ★ ★ |

50 Main Street, Kinsale, County Cork; ☎ 021-477-2502

Reservations Recommended for dinner. **Entree range** €10–€20. **Payment** AE, MC, V. **Bar** Full service. **Disabled access** Yes. **Hours** Mid-February–mid-April and mid-October–December, Tuesday–Saturday, 6:30–10 p.m.; May–mid-October, daily, 6:30–10:30 p.m.

MENU RECOMMENDATIONS Dublin lawyer (a flaming lobster), oven-roasted duck, fresh fish prepared any way.

COMMENTS An oak-beamed, stone-walled room is the setting for an excellent meal based on ingredients that change with the seasons. The cozy surroundings are especially well suited to the fowl and game dishes that prevail in the colder months, but an evening here in any season is an occasion that is well orchestrated by proprietors Diana and Frank Ferguson (like the kitchen team, they are of relatively new vintage in this long-established institution). An excellent selection of wines is available, and the service is highly polished yet friendly.

ENTERTAINMENT AND NIGHTLIFE IN KINSALE

TWO OF KINSALE'S MOST POPULAR AND ATMOSPHERIC PUBS are on the harbor outside of town. The **Bulman** (just below Charles Fort in Summercove, ☎ 021-477-2131) has cozy rooms warmed by fires and a seawall-cum-terrace across the road from which to watch the sun set; an upstairs restaurant serves good seafood. The **Spaniard** (Scilly, ☎ 021-477-2436), on a hillside above the harbor closer to town, sports a maritime-themed interior beneath a thatched roof and packs in an evening crowd with live music. In town, the **Shanakee** (*Seanachai,* or "storyteller" in Gaelic; Market Street, ☎ 021-477-7077) is the best of the pubs that offer live music.

EXERCISE AND RECREATION IN KINSALE

WATER-SPORTS ENTHUSIASTS SHOULD MAKE A BEELINE for **Oysterhaven Holiday and Activity Centre,** which rents sailboards, kayaks, wet suits, and more; the center also has tennis courts. Oysterhaven is eight kilometers (five miles) outside of town; call ☎ 021-477-0738. Sailboats can be chartered from **Sail Ireland Charters** at the Trident Hotel;

call ☎ 021-477-2927 or visit **www.sailireland.com.** Bicycles are available for rent at the **Hire Shop** (18 Main Street, ☎ 021-477-4884), providing an excellent way to explore the paths around Kinsale Harbour; the shop also rents rods and other fishing equipment. The most famous golf course in the area is the **Old Head Golf Links on Kinsale Head,** with a fine reputation and greens fees to match; for information call ☎ 021-477-8444 or visit **www.oldheadgolflinks.com. Kinsale Golf Club,** five kilometers (three miles) to the north, is also well regarded and much less expensive; call ☎ 021-477-4722. Walkers can set out on the maintained paths following the shores of Kinsale Harbour. The much-trod **Scilly Walk** provides a scenic route from the town center to Charles Fort.

PART SIX

THE SOUTHWEST *of* IRELAND

EASYGOING, DEEPLY RURAL, RUGGED, BEAUTIFUL, friendly, fun loving—it's pretty easy to see why this corner of Ireland is, for many visitors, what Ireland is all about. You won't find much here to grouse about, except maybe the weather, and even then the locals will tell you to wait five minutes and that will change. Settle into **Kenmare** or **Dingle Town,** hike across the magnificent mountain-and-lake scenery of **Killarney National Park,** inch along on cliff-hugging coastal roads, and you'll see why the people who live here are in no rush to see things change in these parts. Of course, things do change, and you'll run into some hard-core tourism in places such as **Killarney Town** and some spots along the **Ring of Kerry.** When you do, take a cue from the locals—just take a turn off the beaten path.

KENMARE

ONE OF THE MOST LOVELY TOWNS in Ireland is tucked neatly into the hills at the head of the Kenmare River. The river, as you'll soon notice, is actually a bay, dividing the Beara and Iveragh peninsulas. British settlers, including the 17th-century Sir William Petty, surveyor general for Oliver Cromwell, found it more convenient to call the bay

the southwest of ireland

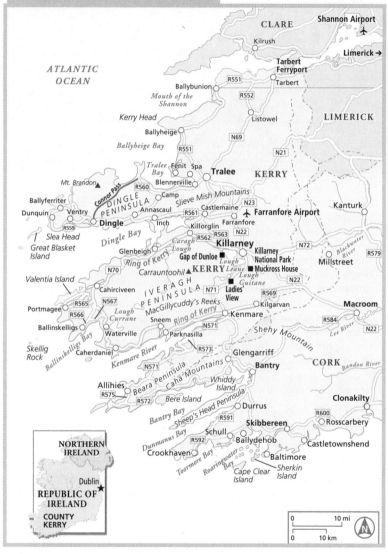

a river because by law fish farming was allowed only in rivers and not in open waters. The name lives on, to the confusion of visitors, who are nevertheless much taken with the sight of the purple mountains of the peninsulas rising across the gleaming waters.

Kenmare is a cheerful place of brightly colored houses and store-fronts, a remnant of a 19th-century overhaul when the town was tidied up as part of the sprawling Lansdowne Estates. Another aspect of Kenmare's heritage is also much in evidence—lace. In the wake of the Famine, the nuns of the order of the Poor Clares taught young women lace making, and Kenmare lace soon became the rage of Victorian English society. A member of the order, Sister Mary Francis Clare Cusack, known as the "Nun of Kenmare," is famous for her stance against the indifference of British during the Famine.

Today Kenmare, with a number of fine hotels and restaurants, is an excellent base for exploring much of County Kerry, and even County Cork just to the north. From here, you easily can make excursions northwest to the Ring of Kerry, Killarney National Park, and the Dingle Peninsula, or northeast to Cork City and its environs.

PLANNING YOUR VISIT TO KENMARE

THE KENMARE TOURIST OFFICE IS HANDILY located in the town square; the bad news is that it's open only from May to October, Monday through Saturday, 9 a.m. to 6 p.m.; Sunday, 10 a.m. to 5 p.m. If you're visiting outside of those dates, try to stock up on info at other Cork/Kerry tourist offices, such as those in Cork City or Dingle Town. When you're in the Kenmare office, be sure to pop into the free **Kenmare Heritage Centre** in the back room; small but earnest displays do an excellent job of explaining the town's history. Also on the premises is the **Kenmare Lace and Design Centre,** where you can see demonstrations of Kenmare lace making, which follows a technique similar to the craft practiced in Venice. Unfortunately, both these attractions are, like the tourist office, closed in the winter and early spring. For more information, call ☎ 064-41233 or visit **www.corkkerry.ie.**

unofficial **TIP**
If you're in town in late May, you can enjoy some pleasant treks into the surrounding countryside organized by the **Kenmare Walking Festival;** ☎ 064-42639. In mid-August, Kenmare celebrates an old-fashioned Irish Fair, with livestock and crafts exhibits; for information call ☎ 064-42653 or go to **www.kenmare.com.**

ARRIVING AND GETTING ORIENTED IN KENMARE

KENMARE IS ABOUT 65 KILOMETERS (40 miles) southwest of Cork, an easy trip by car along N22, with a turn west on R569. **Bus Éireann** coaches arrive from Dublin, Cork, Killarney, and other points in Ireland, with about three buses per day to and from Dublin; for the eight-hour trip the fare is about €15 one way and €20 round trip. For more information, call ☎ 064-34777 or visit **www.buseireann.ie.**

HOTELS IN KENMARE
Foley's ★ ★ ½

QUALITY ★★★	VALUE ★★★★	€50–€80

Henry Street, Kenmare, County Kerry; ☎ 064-42162; fax 064-41799; info@foleyskenmare.com; www.foleyskenmare.com

Location Center of town. **Amenities and services** 9 rooms; pub downstairs. **Elevator** No. **Parking** On street. **Price** Includes breakfast. **Credit cards** MC, V.

Foley's is a bar-and-restaurant operation that keeps busy serving drinks and meals throughout the day and evening, and the pleasant accommodations upstairs are a cut above the norm for "rooms above a pub." While there are no public rooms, except for the bar, you won't mind spending time in the guest rooms, which are decent in size and rather snappy, with bright colors and handsome traditional furnishings. All have adjoining bathrooms, and all have multiple beds in traveler-friendly configurations such as a double and a single, two queens, or, in the family room, a double and two singles. The big draw is the in-town location, right on the main street with easy access to restaurants and shops; Foley's is a good choice for a night or two when you don't have the time to settle into the more-relaxing guest-house routine.

Sallyport House ★ ★ ★ ½

QUALITY ★★★★	VALUE ★★★	€100–€170

Sound Road, Kenmare, County Kerry (closed mid-November–March 1); ☎ 064-42066; fax 064-42067; port@iol.ie; www.sallyporthouse.com

Location The edge of town near the mouth of the Kenmare River. **Amenities and services** 5 rooms; gardens, in-room tea and coffee facilities. **Elevator** No. **Parking** Free, on grounds. **Price** Includes full Irish breakfast. **Credit cards** MC, V. *Note:* Not suitable for children under age 13.

Jane and John Arthur, a brother-and-sister team, have converted their family home into an extremely comfortable guest house. Built at the head of the Kenmare River in the 1930s, it has just five rooms overlooking the gardens and estuary waters that surround the house on three sides. Much about this house suggests you are in a private home: you can watch sailboats from a telescope on the upstairs landing or relax in a quiet corner of the garden. The handsome downstairs lounges are filled with old family furniture, and one chimney contains stone salvaged from a workhouse that once stood on the site. Extremely large bedrooms are individually decorated with antiques and extras such as sofas and window seats, and one of the rear rooms has a separate sitting room; all have queen- and king-size beds (with orthopedic mattresses and fine linens) as well as lavish bathrooms. The center of town is an easy ten-minute stroll away through parkland.

Sea Shore Farm ★ ★ ★ ½

QUALITY ★★★★	VALUE ★★★½	€70–€120

Tubrid, Kenmare, County Kerry (closed November 15–March 1); ☎ 064-41270; fax 064-41270; seashore@eircom.net; www.seashorefarm.com

How Hotels Compare in the Southwest of Ireland

HOTEL	OVERALL	QUALITY	VALUE	PRICE
KENMARE				
Shelburne Lodge	★★★★½	★★★★	★★★★	€80–€160
Sea Shore Farm	★★★½	★★★★	★★★½	€70–€120
Sallyport House	★★★½	★★★★	★★★	€100–€170
Foley's	★★½	★★★	★★★★	€50–€80
DINGLE				
Castlewood House	★★★★	★★★★½	★★★	€100–€180
Greenmount House	★★★★	★★★★	★★★★	€50–€150
Milltown House	★★★★	★★★★	★★★	€60–€150
Captains House	★★★★	★★★	★★★★	€60–€100
Doyle's Townhouse	★★★	★★★½	★★★	€120–€145
Old Pier	★★★	★★★	★★★★	€40–€80
Heaton's Guesthouse	★★★	★★★	★★★	€60–€150

Location On the bay, about 1.5 kilometers (1 mile) outside of town. **Amenities and services** 6 rooms; beach, gardens, hair dryers, in-room tea and coffee facilities. **Elevator** No. **Parking** Free, on grounds. **Price** Includes full Irish breakfast. **Credit cards** MC, V.

The aptly named home of the O'Sullivans is on the shores of the Kenmare River amid the rich farmlands that co-owner Patricia O'Sullivan's grandfather settled almost a century ago. Such beautiful surroundings are the greatest appeal of this well-run guest house. In good weather, chairs and tables are set out on the patio and lawns overlooking the sea; you can fish from the pier or, if you don't mind the frigid seawater, swim from a small beach on the property. In colder months, a fire burns in the pleasant lounge, but the emphasis here is really on privacy. Guest rooms are comfortable, bright, and extremely large; all have views of the sea and fields, and all have new baths with power showers. Furnishings are eclectic, and rooms are sprinkled with 19th-century armoires, Art Deco tables, and other pieces that Patricia picks up at flea markets—the house is geared to guests who want homey surroundings, not to those who prefer generic hotel rooms. Two ground-floor rooms open to patios, while the upstairs rooms have large floor-to-ceiling windows that slide open. One of the downstairs rooms is unusually large and, with three exposures, exceptionally bright, and one of the upstairs units is well suited for guests with children because it has a small adjoining bedroom. A refrigerator and microwave in the upstairs hallway are among the thoughtful touches that make a stay here all the more comfortable. A nice walk of about 20 minutes along a little-traveled country lane brings you to town.

Shelburne Lodge ★ ★ ★ ★ ½

QUALITY ★ ★ ★ ★	VALUE ★ ★ ★ ★	€80–€160

Cork Road, Kenmare, County Kerry (closed December 1–March 1);
☎ **064-41013; fax 064-42135; shelburnekenmare@eircom.net;**
www.shelburnelodge.com

Location About 0.5 kilometers (a fifth of a mile) outside the city center on the Cork Road (R569). **Amenities and services** 9 rooms; gardens; tea, coffee, wine, and other drinks available; tennis **Elevator** No. **Parking** Free, on grounds. **Price** Includes full Irish breakfast. **Credit cards** MC, V.

Maura Foley has long been in the hospitality business (she was once the chef at Packie's restaurant in town), and now she extends her amazing talents to make guests feel welcome in her 18th-century stone farmhouse at the edge of town. The grounds are stunning, with gardens, lawns, a grass tennis court, and fine old trees. And Shelburne may have the most stylish lodgings of any Irish guest house. Fine kilims and carpets are scattered on highly polished floors throughout, bold but soothing colors and artwork cover the walls, and a drawing room and smaller sitting room are stocked with books and furnished with comfortable couches and chairs. Welcoming, attractive guest rooms are a good size and contain a mix of antique and classic furnishings, excellent beds and fine linens, and large bathrooms that are as tastefully done as the rest of the house; a large unit in the rear of the house is well suited to families. Maura shows off her culinary skills with a breakfast in which breads, preserves, cheeses, and hot choices are all fresh and delicious. It's worth a stop in Kenmare just to stay in this guest house, and you might want to consider settling into Shelburne Lodge for several days as a base for exploring the Southwest.

EXPLORING KENMARE

YOU CAN TOUR THE TOWN ON A FAIRLY SHORT STROLL, because most shops and restaurants are concentrated in a small triangle between Henry, Main, and Shelbourne streets. Just to the north is the leafy town square, including the tourist office, the **Kenmare Heritage Centre,** and **Kenmare Lace and Design Centre.** Be sure to take a walk out to the **Druid Stone Circle**, conveniently located just to the south of the town center off Market Street and much more accessible than these monuments usually are (more than 100 such stone circles dot the remote landscapes of Counties Cork and Kerry). The 15 stones here surround a center dolmen (perhaps used for rituals). The site is at least 3,000 years old and is thought to have been used to plot solstices.

RESTAURANTS IN KENMARE

An Leath Phingin ★ ★ ★ ½

ITALIAN	MODERATE	QUALITY ★ ★ ★ ½	VALUE ★ ★ ★

35 Main Street, Kenmare; ☎ 064-41559

Reservations Recommended. **Entree range** €14–€23. **Payment** AE, MC, V. **Bar**

How Restaurants Compare in the Southwest of Ireland

NAME	CUISINE	OVERALL	QUALITY	VALUE	PRICE
KENMARE					
The Purple Heather	café	★★★★	★★★★	★★★★½	inexp
Packie's	bistro	★★★★	★★★★	★★★★	mod
Lime Tree	seafood/ modern Irish	★★★★	★★★★	★★★	exp
An Leath Phingin	Italian	★★★½	★★★½	★★★	mod
DINGLE					
Global Village	modern Irish	★★★★	★★★★	★★★★½	mod
Chart House	modern Irish/ seafood	★★★★	★★★★	★★★★	exp
Goat Street Café	modern Irish	★★★½	★★★★	★★★★	inexp
Doyle's	seafood	★★★½	★★★½	★★★	exp
Out of the Blue	seafood	★★★	★★★★½	★★★½	exp
Lord Baker's	Irish	★★★	★★★	★★★★	mod/inexp
Fenton's	modern Irish	★★★	★★★	★★★	mod

Full service. **Disabled access** Ground-floor room only. **Hours** Thursday–Monday, 6–10 p.m.; closed mid-November–mid-January.

MENU RECOMMENDATIONS Prawn risotto, pizzas, homemade pastas.

COMMENTS The name is Gaelic (meaning "half penny"), but the menu is Italian. Both the cozy stone-walled downstairs room and the jauntier, more formal room decorated with Italian advertising art at the top of the narrow stairs are well suited to the homemade focaccia bread and excellent pizzas and pastas. More-elaborate dishes, such as local salmon and strip loin of Irish beef grilled over an open fire, are prepared simply.

Lime Tree ★ ★ ★ ★

SEAFOOD/MODERN IRISH   EXPENSIVE   QUALITY ★★★★   VALUE ★★★

Shelburne Street, Kenmare; ☎ 064-41225

Reservations Recommended. **Entree range** €16.95–€24.50. **Payment** AE, MC, V. **Bar** Full service. **Disabled access** Yes. **Hours** Daily, 6:30–10 p.m.

MENU RECOMMENDATIONS Blue-cheese tartlet, smoked-salmon-and-fennel risotto, roast Kerry lamb.

COMMENTS A 19th-century stone schoolhouse that also did duty for officials doling out passage to famine-stricken farmers now serves up some of

Kenmare's best fare and its most atmospheric dining experience. Stone floors and handsome country furnishings set a rustic tone, and French doors open to the flowery terraces that surround the building; an upstairs art gallery sells works by local artists. This place isn't all show, though—the cooking is down-to-earth, with an emphasis on the freshest local ingredients. Kerry lamb is oven-roasted to perfection, and wild salmon done on an oak plank elevates this Irish staple to new heights.

Packie's ★ ★ ★ ★

BISTRO	MODERATE	QUALITY ★ ★ ★ ★	VALUE ★ ★ ★ ★

Henry Street, Kenmare; ☎ 064-41508

Reservations Recommended. **Entree range** €14–€28. **Payment** AE, MC, V. **Bar** Full service. **Disabled access** Yes. **Hours** Tuesday–Sunday, 6–10 p.m.; closed January–mid-March.

MENU RECOMMENDATIONS Sole stuffed with prawns, roast duck, Irish lamb stew.

COMMENTS If you're staying in Kenmare for more than a few days, return to this cozy, candlelit, center-of-town bistro a couple of times to dine your way through the tempting menu. Seafood plays a large part in the preparations, but not exclusively so, and you may want to sample the diverse and creative offerings to make a meal of starters, many of which you won't see on a lot of menus: seafood sausages, a salad of warm duck livers, smoked cod cakes. Main courses, too, are innovative, and sole and other fish caught just hours earlier are accompanied by vegetables from the restaurant's own kitchen garden.

The Purple Heather ★ ★ ★ ★

CAFE	INEXPENSIVE	QUALITY ★ ★ ★ ★	VALUE ★ ★ ★ ★ ½

Henry Street, Kenmare; ☎ 064-41016

Reservations Not necessary. **Entree range** €5–€15. **Payment** Cash only. **Bar** Full service. **Disabled access** Yes. **Hours** Monday–Saturday, 11:30 a.m.–6:30 p.m.

MENU RECOMMENDATIONS Salads, toasted open-faced sandwiches.

COMMENTS It's hard not to consider this bar and cafe the center of Kenmare social life. Drop into the appealing room of dark wood and deep hues any time during the day for informal fare that's actually rather exciting—heavenly omelets, salads full of local produce and farmhouse cheeses, excellent pâtés and hearty soups, all of it accompanied by homemade dark bread.

ENTERTAINMENT AND NIGHTLIFE IN KENMARE

SEVERAL KENMARE PUBS WOO CUSTOMERS with traditional music, nightly in summer, in the off season less frequently, usually one or two nights a week at most. **Foley's** and **Davitt's,** both on Henry Street, are the most likely to have music year-round; in summer, just stroll along Henry and Main streets, and let your ears lead you into the pub with the music that appeals most to you.

How Attractions Compare in the Southwest of Ireland

ATTRACTION	DESCRIPTION	AUTHOR'S RATING
KENMARE		
Bantry House	Historic home in a magnificent setting	★★★½
KILLARNEY NATIONAL PARK		
Muckross House and Traditional Farms	Victorian home and grounds	★★★★
Ross Castle	Medieval stronghold	★★★
IVERAGH PENINSULA		
Skellig Experience	Museum of life on the Skellig Islands	★★★★
Derrynane House	Historic home of Daniel O'Connell	★★★
DINGLE		
The Blasket Centre	Museum of life on the Blasket Islands	★★★★

AROUND KENMARE

THE BEARA PENINSULA

SOUTHWESTERN IRELAND STRETCHES into the Atlantic in a string of craggy peninsulas. The Iveragh Peninsula (christened the "Ring of Kerry" by tourist authorities) and the Dingle Peninsula are well known and well traveled, but the Beara Peninsula remains remote, at least relatively so. You needn't travel far out of Kenmare (west on R571) before you find yourself with the Kenmare River on your right and the purple spine of the heather-covered Caha Mountains on your left. At the far western tip of Beara, a creaky cable car with room for "three passengers and one cow" swings across the sea to **Dursey Island,** where colonies of seabirds nest amid the ruins of a medieval castle. At **Castletownbere,** the main town on the peninsula, fleets of foreign fishing trawlers anchor in a harbor that once sheltered the ships of smugglers who traded Irish fish for French brandy.

It isn't necessary to venture all the way out to the end of the peninsula to enjoy spectacular scenery. At the village of **Lauragh,** about 16 kilometers (10 miles) from Kenmare, R574 heads south into the mountains and across one of the most thrilling routes in all of Ireland, **Healy Pass.** This narrow road traverses the mountainous border between Cork and Kerry, where the backdrop of desolate moors and purple peaks looks more like a stage set than a real place. Just to the

walks and drives in the southwest

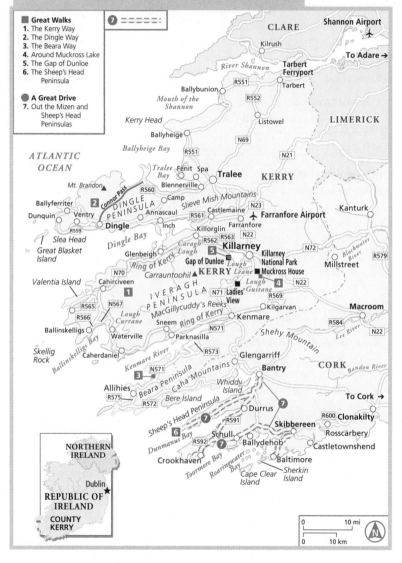

Great Walks
1. The Kerry Way
2. The Dingle Way
3. The Beara Way
4. Around Muckross Lake
5. The Gap of Dunloe
6. The Sheep's Head Peninsula

A Great Drive
7. Out the Mizen and Sheep's Head Peninsulas

CLARE

Shannon Airport

Kilrush

To Adare →

River Shannon

Tarbert Ferryport

Ballybunion   R551   Tarbert
              R552

LIMERICK

Mouth of the Shannon

Kerry Head

Listowel

Ballyheige

N69

Ballyheige Bay   R551

N21

ATLANTIC OCEAN

Tralee Bay   Fenit   Spa

Mt. Brandon   R560   Blennerville   **Tralee**

KERRY

Ballyferriter   Connor Pass   Camp   Slieve Mish Mountains

DINGLE PENINSULA   Annascaul   Castlemaine   N23

Dunquin   Ventry   **Dingle**   R561   Killorglin

Farranfore

Kanturk

✈ **Farranfore Airport**

R559   Inch   Farranfore

Slea Head   Dingle Bay   R562   R563   N22

Great Blasket Island   Glenbeigh   Caragh Lough   **Killarney**   N72

Ring of Kerry   Gap of Dunloe   Lough   Killarney   Millstreet   Blackwater River   R579

N70   Carrauntoohil ▲ **KERRY**   Leane   National Park

Valentia Island   Cahirciveen   IVERAGH   Lough   ■ Muckross House

PENINSULA   N71   Ladies'   Guitane   N22

R565   N567   MacGillycuddy's Reeks   View   Kilgarvan

R566   Lough   Ring of Kerry   R569   **Macroom**

Ballinskelligs   Currane   Sneem   **Kenmare**   R584   Lee River   N22

Waterville   Parknasilla   N571   Shehy Mountain

Skellig Rock   Caherdaniel   Kenmare River   R573   Glengarriff   CORK   Bandon River

Beara Peninsula   **Bantry**

N571

Allihies   Caha Mountains   Whiddy Island   To Cork →

R575   R572   Bere Island   Sheep's Head Peninsula   Durrus   R600 **Clonakilty**

Dunmanus Bay   R591   **Skibbereen**   Rosscarbery

Schull   R592   Ballydehob   Castletownshend

Crookhaven   Toormore Bay   Baltimore   Sherkin Island

Roaringwater Bay   Cape Clear Island

NORTHERN IRELAND

Dublin ★

REPUBLIC OF IRELAND

COUNTY KERRY

0   10 mi
0   10 km

south of the peninsula, facing the windswept expanses of Bantry Bay, is one of the greatest of Irish great houses, **Bantry House** (see below).

Attraction around the Beara Peninsula

Bantry House ★ ★ ★ ½

APPEAL BY AGE	PRESCHOOL ★ ★	GRADE SCHOOL ★ ★ ★	TEENS ★ ★ ★
YOUNG ADULTS ★ ★		OVER 30 ★ ★ ★	SENIORS ★ ★ ★

Outside Bantry on N71, County Cork; ☎ 027-50047; www.bantryhouse.ie

Type of attraction Historic home in a magnificent setting. **Admission** Houses, gardens, and French Armada Centre: €10; gardens and French Armada Centre: €5. **Hours** March–October, daily, 10 a.m.–6 p.m. **When to go** Try to find a break in the rain showers so that you can spend time in the gardens. **Special comments** Bantry House provides a good break in the journey if you're traveling between Cork and Kenmare, and the tearoom is a decent spot for a sandwich or other refreshments. **How much time to allow** About 2 hours for the house, gardens, and French Armada Centre.

DESCRIPTION AND COMMENTS   The White family came to Bantry Bay in the 17th century and ingratiated themselves with the British a century later. In 1795, Richard White raised the alarm when an armada of French ships, in an alliance with Irish nationalist Wolfe Tone, attempted an invasion of Ireland. Tone's plan was to land 50 ships laden with 15,000 troops at Bantry Bay; White heard rumor of the fleet's arrival and posted lookouts. Irish weather proved more effective than British bravado and forced the ships to turn back to France, but White was made the First Earl of Bantry for his loyalty. Set amid terraced gardens overlooking Bantry Bay, the house has been richly embellished through the years, most lavishly by Richard White, the second earl. He scoured Europe for treasures, bringing back furnishings that include Gobelin and Aubusson tapestries (those in the Rose Room are said to have been commissioned by Louis XV for Marie Antoinette) and portraits of George III and Queen Charlotte by Allan Ramsay, the celebrated 18th-century Scottish portraitist. The small French Armada Centre next to the house details the events of 1795 with excellent exhibits accompanied by sound effects. Most interesting are a model of the frigate *Surveillante*—which the French were forced to scuttle off the coast—and the artifacts found on board when it was recovered in 1982.

TOURING TIPS   Leave at least one hour to explore the gardens, which are spread across seven terraces above the bay. Formal plantings include the first earl's Rose Garden and the second earl's Italian Garden, but most exhilarating are the views over the mountains and bay from the top terrace, reached by stone stairs known as the "Staircase to the Sky."

⚐ KILLARNEY NATIONAL PARK

ONE OF THE MOST BEAUTIFUL CORNERS OF IRELAND, this wilderness of heather-covered mountains, lush forests, and shimmering

Walks and Drives in the Southwest

While it wouldn't be quite fair to other regions to say the Southwest is Ireland's most scenic region, let's just say that in the Southwest an amazing amount of beautiful scenery is compressed into a relatively small area. It's no accident that many of Ireland's most traveled walking paths and favorite drives criss-cross the Southwest.

GREAT WALKS

THE KERRY WAY

Some of Ireland's finest scenery unfolds along this 214-kilometer (128-mile) route that passes through **Killarney National Park** and circles the **Iveragh Peninsula** (aka the Kerry Way). You can pick up the way at any number of spots as you explore the park (for instance, it skirts the shores of Muckross Lake) and drive around the peninsula. A very nice and relatively easy way to enjoy some of the Kerry Way's best coastal scenery is around **Derrynane,** on the southern side of the Iveragh Peninsula. In addition to views of the sea, mountains, and Skellig Islands, this segment of the way also provides a bit of historical insight—it begins in **Derrynane National Historic Park** (see page 251), which preserves the birthplace of Daniel O'Connell, known as the Liberator for his efforts on behalf of independence and against the oppression of Catholics. The route first follows the trails of the **Derrynane Dunes Nature Trail** to the Coomnahorna River estuary, where you're likely to see many shorebirds. From the estuary you can follow a lovely stretch of beach for one kilometer (half a mile) east to the beginning of a mass path, one of the rough tracks common in the countryside that were once used for funeral processions and other religious rites. The path follows a rugged coastal hillside, affording views of headlands and offshore islands, and comes to another small beach. By the time you've retraced your steps to Derrynane from here, you will have covered about seven kilometers (four miles).

lakes has been popular with tourists since the middle of the 19th century. The huge expanse of natural beauty is now protected as a 10,000-hectare (25,000-acre) national park, much of which can only be explored on foot and by boat. You'll see enough from the roads that skirt the park to whet your appetite to get out of the car and explore the park further.

Approaching from Kenmare, N71 passes through a cleft in the mountains known as **Moll's Gap,** affording the first views over the park's lake-filled valleys and sheltering mountain ranges. Continue on a few miles to the even-better spectacle from **Ladies' View,** so named for

THE DINGLE WAY

This 153-kilometer-long (92-mile-long) walking route circumnavigates one of Ireland's most scenic peninsulas and is one of the country's most popular long-distance routes. Casual walkers can pick up the well-marked way anywhere along the peninsula for a short trek. In fact, the most scenic stretch, around **Slea Head,** is easily accessible and only about seven kilometers (five miles) west of **Dingle Town** (see page 254). If you're traveling by public transportation, you can take the bus from Dingle to **Ventry** and begin the walk from there; if you're traveling by car, follow the coast road west and pick up the way where it crosses the road about three kilometers (two miles) east of Slea Head. As you walk west, you'll pass some of the Dingle Peninsula's many early ruins, including 2,500-year-old **Dunbeg Fort** (see page 263), with thick earthenwork ramparts rising precariously above the sea, as well as groupings of *clocháns,* beehive-shaped huts built without mortar by early-Christian hermits. As you approach Slea Head, the views over the sea, adjoining **Dunmore Head** (the westernmost point in Ireland), and the **Blasket Islands** are stunning.

THE BEARA WAY

Another of County Kerry's walking circuits circles the **Beara Peninsula,** covering 196 kilometers (118 miles). One stretch, from the village of **Castletown Bearhaven** on the southern side of the peninsula, introduces you not only to spectacular scenery but also to some fascinating archaeological remains. From the village, follow the signs for **Derreena Taggart Stone Circle,** about 2 kilometers (1.2 miles) west; this ring of 12 standing stones is about 2,000 years old. From here the path continues across bogs where peat was once cut and over beautiful moors for about three kilometers (two miles) to another remnant of early life on the peninsula, the **Teernahilane Ring Fort.**

Continued on next page

Queen Victoria's ladies-in-waiting, who enjoyed the outlook when the Queen was a guest at **Muckross House** (see page 248). The **Torc Waterfall** cascades down a nearby mountainside, but any sense of wilderness comes abruptly to an end as N71 enters Killarney, a town that long ago sold its soul to the god of tourism and should by all means be bypassed. On the other side of town, though, the romantic ruins of the seventh-century monastery that once flourished on Innisfallen Island rise out of the lake, and beyond lies the **Gap of Dunloe,** accessible only on foot, horseback, or bike. Here is some of the park's most enchanting scenery, where enormous boulders litter a pass that cuts

Walks and Drives in the Southwest (continued)

GREAT WALKS (CONTINUED)

THE BEARA WAY (CONTINUED)

Another good walk follows the Beara Way as it skirts **Coulagh Bay** from the village of **Eyeies,** on the north side of the peninsula. Leaving this colorful village to the east, follow the Way as it winds along the rugged coast of Coulagh Bay for about 4 kilometers (2.5 miles). Tides permitting, you can walk part of this route on nearly deserted beaches. Near the headland at the northern end of the bay, follow a well-marked path inland to the **Ballycrovane Ogham Stone,** one of some 300 such stones in Ireland, most of them in Counties Cork and Kerry, that are inscribed with a pre-Christian Celtic script known as Ogham. This stone and many others like it are thought to mark burial grounds.

AROUND MUCKROSS LAKE

A half-day walk, about 11 kilometers (8 miles) around this lake in the heart of **Killarney National Park** (see page 243) exposes you to the varied and delightful scenery of one of Ireland's six national parks: waterfalls, rugged mountains, bubbling streams, and, of course, the lake itself. As you follow the well-marked **Lake Shore Path** south from **Muckross House,** you pass through lovely woodland to a short path into **Torc Waterfall,** where flights of rough stone steps lead to viewpoints over the 20-meter (60-foot) cascade and, to the north, the peaks of **MacGillycuddy's Reeks,** Ireland's tallest mountains. The path then skirts the southern shores of the lake and comes to a beautiful spot called **Meeting of the Waters,** where the waters of Muckross Lake, Lough Leane, and a small river flow together beneath the **Old Weir Bridge,** then to **Dins Cottage** (no public access), set amid lovely gardens of azaleas, magnolias, and eucalyptus. As you proceed north, then east, the path skirts the shores of Lough Leane as well as Muckross Lake. You'll come to small **Doo Lough,** a relatively secluded spot surrounded by woodlands, then **Reenadinna Wood,** Europe's largest yew forest, before

through MacGillycuddy's Reeks, Ireland's highest mountains, and ends at one of the park's most remote expanses of water, Upper Lake.

Exploring Killarney National Park

Hiking trails crisscross the park, and many of the trailheads are on or around the grounds of Muckross House. Even a quick hike up the Old Boathouse Nature Trail along a peninsula in Muckross Lake or up the Blue Pool Trail to the pretty eponymous lake will introduce you to the park's beauty. For more information on the park and its attractions, visit the **Killarney National Park Visitor Centre,** on the grounds of Muckross House.

the path crosses beneath a stand of magnificent oaks and returns to the grounds of Muckross House. You may well want to take time at the end of the walk to join a tour of one of Ireland's finest homes (see page 248).

THE GAP OF DUNLOE

No signage is necessary to guide yourself through this gorgeous boulder- and lake-laced gorge—simply follow the crowds who partake in one of Ireland's most popular outings. The 6.5-kilometer (4-mile) trek between **MacGillycuddy's Reeks** and **Purple Mountain** is all the more appealing because of the noticeable absence of motorized traffic. If you're coming from Killarney and other points in the Southwest, it's most convenient to begin the walk at the north end of the gap, at **Kate Kearney's Cottage,** once the home of a maiden who sold *poteen* (moonshine) and now a lively pub. Should you be worried about having the stamina to walk the length of the gap, you can rent a jaunting car to take you halfway in. The walk, however, is quite comfortable and relatively easy, combining so many views of mountains and lakes that you won't mind the summertime crowds. If you want to get away from the crowds and add quite a bit more exertion to the walk, you can climb out of the Gap about halfway through and make the climb to the summit of **Purple Mountain,** 830 meters (2,700 feet) high. Another pub, **Lord Bandon's Cottage,** is at the south end of the gap, the so-called **Head of the Gap.** From there you can retrace your steps back to Kate Kearney's Cottage or board a boat for a cruise across the Upper Lake and Lough Leane to **Ross Castle** (see page 250), near Killarney Town.

THE SHEEP'S HEAD PENINSULA

One of the least visited peninsulas on the Southwest Coast stretches west from **Bantry.** The 88-kilometer (53-mile) **Sheep's Head Way** takes full

Continued on next page

Tours of Killarney National Park

One of the easiest ways to see the park is in a horse-drawn jaunting car, an open carriage that accommodates up to four passengers; about €20 per person, per hour; tours are available at Muckross House and other points within the park. **Adventure Tours** offers a scenery-filled excursion in a jaunting car through the Gap of Dunloe, followed by a boat trip across three of the park's lakes; for more information, call ☎ 064-30200 or visit **www.gapofdunloetours.com.** For a rougher trek, horses can be rented at **Muckross Riding Stables,** Mangerton Road, Muckross; call ☎ 064-32238. The scenery is especially beautiful when viewed from one of the lakes. Board the *Lily of Killarney* or *Pride of the Lakes* on

Walks and Drives in the Southwest *(continued)*

GREAT WALKS (CONTINUED)

THE SHEEP'S HEAD PENINSULA (CONTINUED)

advantage of the rural settings of the peninsula's interior and the rugged coast-lines. You can a nice taste of the way at its most dramatic point, a 4-kilometer (2.5-mile) loop around **Sheep's Head.** Begin in the parking area at the end of the road along the south side of the peninsula. From there, a well-marked path leads across rocky headlands to the **Sheep's Head Lighthouse** and then follows the tops of sea cliffs high above Bantry Bay on the return loop.

GREAT DRIVES

The peninsulas of the Southwest are ringed by some of Ireland's most popular driving routes. The **Iveragh Peninsula** (see page 251), christened the Ring of Kerry by the tourism powers, is the most traveled, though more-rewarding drives can be enjoyed on the **Dingle Peninsula** (see page 263), the **Beara Peninsula** (see page 241), and on the relatively unknown **Mizen** and **Sheep's Head peninsulas.**

OUT TO THE MIZEN HEAD AND SHEEP'S HEAD PENINSULAS

A trip out to Mizen Head begins in **Skibbereen,** about 85 kilometers (53 miles) west of Kinsale on N71. This lively town hosts two markets, one of cattle on Wednesdays and one for farm-fresh vegetables, local seafood, cheeses, and other local produce on Fridays. **Lough Hyne,** about six kilometers (four miles) southwest of town, is a saltwater lake and much warmer than the sea, providing a habitat for sea anemones and a wide variety of other marine species. Skibbereen is also graced with the lovely lakeside gardens of the **Liss Ard**

the pier at Ross Castle. Hour-long cruises operate April to October: every hour and a half or so beginning at 10:30 a.m.; €8 for adults, €4 for children; for reservations on the *Lily of Killarney* call ☎ 064-31068, and for *Pride of the Lakes* call ☎ 064-32638.

Attractions around Killarney National Park

Muckross House and Traditional Farms ★ ★ ★ ★

APPEAL BY AGE	PRESCHOOL ★★★	GRADE SCHOOL ★★★★	TEENS ★★★★
YOUNG ADULTS ★★★★		OVER 30 ★★★★	SENIORS ★★★★

In Killarney National Park, about 5 kilometers (3 miles) south of the town of Killarney, County Kerry; ☎ 064-31440; www.muckross-house.ie

Type of attraction Victorian home and grounds. **Admission** Muckross House: €5.50 adults, €2.25 children and students, €4.25 seniors, €13.75 families of up

Foundation, which you can visit from May through October, daily, 10 a.m. to dusk; admission is €5.

A detour of 12 kilometers (8 miles) southwest from Skibbereen on R595 brings you down to **Baltimore,** a beautiful fishing village and pleasure port; ferries connect the town with **Sherkin Island,** where only 90 residents live among the ruins of medieval **Dún na Long Castle** and **Sherkin Abbey,** and with **Cape Clear Island,** the southernmost point in Ireland and well positioned for excellent bird-watching and sightings of whales and dolphins.

From Skibbereen, follow N71 west along the River Ilen and the shores of Roaringwater Bay to the attractive village of **Ballydehob;** then follow R592 out to the port of **Schull.** From there, continue around Toormore Bay to **Goleen,** then past sandy beaches and spectacular seascapes where waves crash into the high cliffs of **Mizen Head.**

After returning to Toormore, follow R591 along the north side of the Mizen Peninsula to **Durrus,** at the head of Dunmanus Bay and the Sheep's Head Peninsula. A narrow road leads west out to the village of **Kilcrohane** and beyond that to **Sheep's Head** (see the Sheep's Head Peninsula walk, page 247). The drive out to the head is adventurous enough, but you should also head north from Kilcrohane on the steep, narrow road aptly named the **Goat Path** over Seefin Mountain. At the summit, get out and make the easy walk to the viewpoint on the mountaintop to see the remarkable views over Bantry Bay and the Beara Peninsula to the north and Dunmanus Bay and the Mizen Peninsula to the south.

Follow the Goat Path down to the shores of Bantry Bay, and then drive east to **Bantry,** from which you can continue north on N71 toward **Kenmare** (see page 233) or east toward **Kinsale** (see page 224).

to 2 adults and 3 children; Traditional Farms: €5.50 adults, €2.25 children and students, €4.25 seniors, €13.75 families of up to 2 adults and 3 children; joint ticket: €8.25 adults, €3.75 children and students, €6.25 seniors, €21 families of up to 2 adults and 3 children. **Hours** Muckross House: July 1–August 31, daily, 9 a.m.–6 p.m.; September 1–June 30, daily, 9 a.m.–5:30 p.m.; Traditional Farms: March–April, Saturday–Sunday, 1–6 p.m.; May, daily, 1–6 p.m.; June–September, daily, 10 a.m.–6 p.m.; October, Saturday–Sunday, 1–6 p.m. **When to go** The house tour is a good refuge when the skies open up, but try to find a break in the weather so you can explore the grounds; the Traditional Farms are not enjoyable in the rain, especially if you are accompanied by children. **Special comments** The Muckross Walled Garden Centre is a glass-fronted complex facing the walled Victorian gardens and housing a self-service restaurant and shops selling local crafts. **How much time to allow** At least 1 hour if you're visiting only the house, 3 hours to include the grounds and Traditional Farms.

DESCRIPTION AND COMMENTS Much of the lands that now compose Killarney National Park were part of the Welsh-Irish Herbert family estate, a fortune made through copper mining on the Muckross Peninsula. Henry Arthur Herbert and his wife, the watercolorist Mary Balfour, built this Victorian mansion at the heart of the estate on the shores of Lough Leane, completing it in 1843 and furnishing the 20 rooms much as they appear today. Queen Victoria spent a few days at Muckross in 1861, and the expense of bringing the house up to snuff for the royal visit is said to have contributed to the family's financial woes. They lost the house in 1898; a member of the Guinness family bought it in 1899; and William Bowers Bourn, an American who made his millions in California gold mines, presented the house as a wedding gift to his daughter, Maud, and Arthur Rose Vincent, in 1910. Muckross is filled with heavy furniture, antlers, portraits, and elaborate silver services, but it has the feel of a family home. Even Queen Victoria's suite, specially fitted out for the visit, is not particularly grandiose. Note its ground-floor location—the queen was terrified of fire and never slept in an upstairs room. Downstairs is a warren of pantries and kitchens that show how the other half spent their days at Muckross House.

So, too, do the Traditional Farms, where authentic-seeming replicas of three working farms from the 1930s and 1940s depict rural life in those not-so-long-ago days in Ireland when machinery was still horse drawn and cottages were lit by kerosene lamps.

TOURING TIPS Take one of the free house tours if available; guides are a font of gossipy background.

Ross Castle ★ ★ ★

APPEAL BY AGE PRESCHOOL ★★★★★ GRADE SCHOOL ★★★★★ TEENS ★★★★★
YOUNG ADULTS ★★★★★   OVER 30 ★★★★½   SENIORS ★★½

On Lough Leane, 2 kilometers (about 1 mile) south of Killarney off N17, County Kerry; ☎ 064-35851; www.heritageireland.ie

Type of attraction Medieval stronghold. **Admission** €5 adults, €2 children and students, €3.50 seniors, €11 families of up to 2 adults and 2 children. **Hours** April and October, daily, 10 a.m.–5 p.m.; May and September, daily, 10 a.m–6 p.m.; June–August, daily, 9 a.m.–6:30 p.m. **When to go** Anytime, but it's best in spring or fall when the crowds thin out and you can get a better sense of the place. **Special comments** In the busy summer months, you may have to wait to enter. **How much time to allow** About 1 hour.

DESCRIPTION AND COMMENTS The O'Donoghue Ross clan of Irish chieftains built this castle on the shores of Lough Leane in the 15th century. Substantial portions of the fortification walls and two of the round towers remain intact. Though today the castle makes an incredibly romantic appearance, with its tall walls and towers rising from the misty waters of the lake, this positioning, with most of the castle protected by the water from land attack, was purely defensive—and ineffective. In 1652, inhabitants held off an invasion by more than 2,000 Cromwellian troops for days, until the British floated batteries onto the lake and bombarded the beleaguered castle from two sides. Somewhat ironically, this defensive stronghold is rather charmingly, even cozily, fitted out with some splendid 16th- and 17th-century furniture.

TOURING TIPS After touring the castle, take a walk along one of the paths that follow the lakeshore, or board one of the boats that depart from the castle pier (see page 247).

THE IVERAGH PENINSULA (RING OF KERRY)

NATURE BESTOWED THIS LONG PENINSULA with more than its fair share of shadowy mountains and rugged coastlines, and where nature slacked off, advertising flacks picked up the slack. The so-called Ring of Kerry is Ireland's most publicized national attraction, and fleets of tourist buses heed the call in summer. The scenery is captivating, but no more so than in many other parts of Ireland (the adjoining Beara and Dingle peninsulas are more appealing), and if you've already visited Killarney National Park, you won't find scenery to top those glorious mountains and lakes.

If you approach from the south, the first stop is the pretty and much-visited village of **Sneem,** full of gaily painted cottages. Set on a forlorn hillside beyond Sneem is **Staigue Fort,** a well-preserved, circular Iron Age stone enclosure that probably functioned as a fortified homestead some 2,500 years ago, providing protection to farmers and their cattle. The fort is open Easter to September daily, 10 a.m. to 9 p.m.; free (although you'll pay a €1 fee to cross private land to reach the fort); €3 for for the small museum, where drawings and artifacts will enlighten you on the fort's function.

The next village along the coast is **Caherdaniel,** where **Derrynane House** was the home of Daniel O'Connell, the "Liberator," who won equal rights for Irish Catholics in 1828. The house is now a fascinating museum (see profile, page 252), and the grounds compose the 128-hectare (320-acre) **Derrynane National Historic Park,** a nice place to stroll on the beach. Just beyond is one of the most scenery-filled stretches of the Ring, the **Coomakista Pass,** where pulling off the road affords stunning views up and down the coast.

Just beyond Waterville you have the option to make the 32-kilometer (20-mile) loop around **Skellig Ring** at the tip of the peninsula; do so, because

unofficial **TIP**

If you can't resist doing the Ring, keep in mind that a complete circuit covers a slow 180 kilometers (112 miles) on route N70, more if you want to make the dramatic **Skellig Loop** at the western tip of the peninsula, and will take the better part of a day.

unofficial **TIP**

The northern flank of the Ring is not as dramatic as the southern side. If you don't mind twists and turns and a little fancy clutch work, you might want to consider returning east on one of the inland roads, which follow isolated valleys and rugged mountainous terrain, showing off the Ring's remote beauty. If you do follow the northern coastal road, stop at **Glenbeigh,** a pleasant resort generously endowed with palm trees and a nice beach.

the views of crashing surf and the conical **Skellig Islands** (see below) are fantastic, the best part of the Ring of Kerry circuit. The largest island, **Skellig Michael,** rises more than 230 meters (700 feet) out of the Atlantic surf; for six centuries it sheltered a colony of early-Christian monks. You can learn more about this settlement and the islands' wildlife at the **Skellig Experience** (see page 254).

Attraction on the Iveragh Peninsula

 Derrynane House ★ ★ ★

| APPEAL BY AGE | PRESCHOOL ★ | GRADE SCHOOL ★ ★ ★ | TEENS ★ ★ ★ |
| YOUNG ADULTS ★ ★ | OVER 30 ★ ★ ★ | | SENIORS ★ ★ ★ |

Off N70 outside Caherdaniel, County Kerry; ☎ 066-947-5113; www.heritageireland.ie

Type of attraction Historic home of Daniel O'Connell. **Admission** €2.75 adults, €1.25 children and students, €2 seniors, €7 families of up to 2 adults and 2 children. **Hours** May–September, Monday–Saturday, 9 a.m.–6 p.m., Sunday, 11 a.m.–5 p.m.; April and October, Tuesday–Sunday, daily, 1–5 p.m.; November–March, Saturday–Sunday, 1–5 p.m. **When to go** Anytime, but wait for coach tours to leave before entering the house. **Special comments** A small tearoom serves sandwiches and pastries. **How much time to allow** About 45 minutes.

DESCRIPTION AND COMMENTS   In this old house, once the center of a small estate, you'll learn about the man known as the Liberator and a fascinating period in Irish history. O'Connell was educated in France because Catholics were not entitled to schooling in Protestant-governed Ireland, but he returned home and ran for Parliament in 1828, becoming the first Irish Catholic to be sent to Westminster. He won Catholics full rights of citizenship in 1829, and he founded the grassroots Catholic Association to promote education and representation. O'Connell is very much a presence in the old rooms, many of which he remodeled with his own hands and filled with family portraits and artifacts such as the pistol with which he won a duel.

TOURING TIPS   Take one of the guided tours if available; if not, ask for one of the handouts that explain the contents of each room.

THE SKELLIGS

YOU'LL SEE THESE THREE CONICAL-SHAPED ISLANDS as you round the Iveragh Peninsula. Learn about the early-Christian monastic community that flourished on one of them, **Skellig Michael,** at the **Skellig Experience** on Valentia Island (see page 254). A visit to that excellent exhibit also includes a two-hour sea cruise around the islands. Even so, it's well worth the time and energy to visit the islands, about 14 kilometers (8 miles) offshore, where the beehive cells that housed monks for many dark centuries still remain and colonies of seabirds roost on the rock faces. A community lived on Skellig Michael (the largest of the islands, and the only one that can be visited) from about AD 600 to 1100. Life must have been austere even by monkly standards, given that the monks' diet consisted almost entirely of fish, birds, and eggs, save for grains or other foodstuffs they might have obtained from passing ships. Viking raiders and other passersby were not always friendly, though one Viking, Olav Trygvasson, lingered in friendly fashion long enough to be baptized on the island in AD 956; this future king of Norway later introduced Christianity to his country. Just east of Skellig Michael is **Little Skellig,** noted not for monks but for huge colonies of an estimated 45,000 gannets and other seabirds, as well as gray seals, which laze around the base of the island on huge rocks. A third Skellig, slightly removed from the others, is known for its shape as **Washerwoman's Rock.**

Planning Your Visit to the Skelligs

The first stop for anyone planning to visit the Skelligs is the **Skellig Experience** on Valentia Island (see page 254). The next step is to contact one of the outfits that run excursions to **Skellig Michael,** usually for about €40 a person. From Valentia Island, these include **Des Lavelle** (☎ 066-947-6124) and from Portmagee, **O'Keefe's** (☎ 066-947-7103), **Murphy's Sea Cruise** (☎ 066-947-7156), and **Joe Roddy** (☎ 066-947-4628); you'll see plenty of signs for Skellig cruises at this far end of the Iveragh Peninsula, but make sure that the outfit you deal with actually goes ashore—some just circumnavigate the islands. You'll also need to wait for good weather, because boats can land at the narrow, concrete pier on Skellig Michael only when seas are relatively calm. Weather permitting, boats leave at about 10:30 a.m. for the hour-long crossing to Skellig Michael and give passengers about two hours to explore the before the return trip, which usually includes a spin around the base of Little Skellig to see the birds and other sea life. Government guides often meet the boats on Skellig Michael and give an informative talk before letting visitors wander on their own. Bring your lunch for a picnic in a memorable setting, as food is not available on the island.

Exploring the Skelligs

A visit to Skellig Michael begins at the foot of the steep and slippery steps that ascend the flank of the rock 180 meters (600 feet) to the monastic colony. Six beehive-shaped huts and two cavelike oratories and a church seem barely habitable, but they are little different now than they were through the six centuries when they housed a devout community, members of which spent their days in prayer and hunting and fishing for their meager sustenance. Pilgrims have been coming to the island for centuries, too, many of whom used to crawl out to a cross (no longer there) on a precipitous outcropping near the summit of the peak as an act of death-defying penitence.

Attraction around the Skelligs

Skellig Experience ★ ★ ★ ★

| APPEAL BY AGE | PRESCHOOL ★ ★ ★ | GRADE SCHOOL ★ ★ ★ ★ | TEENS ★ ★ ★ ★ |
| YOUNG ADULTS ★ ★ ★ ★ | | OVER 30 ★ ★ ★ ★ | SENIORS ★ ★ ★ ★ |

Valentia Island, off causeway from the mainland; ☎ 066-947-6306; www.skelligexperience.com

Type of attraction Museum of life on the Skellig Islands. **Admission** Exhibit: €4.40 adults, €2.20 children, €3.80 seniors and students, €10 families of up to 2 adults and 2 children; exhibit and cruise: €21.50 adults, €10.70 children, €19.40 seniors and students, €57 families of up to 2 adults and 2 children. **Hours** April–May, daily, 10 a.m.–6 p.m.; June–August, daily, 10 a.m.–7 p.m.; September–November, daily, 10 a.m.–6 p.m. **When to go** Visit the exhibit any time, but the experience is much more rewarding when the cruises are operating. **Special comments** Sea cruises do not operate in rough weather; call ahead. **How much time to allow** 3 hours with sea cruise, 1 hour without.

DESCRIPTION AND COMMENTS These innovative exhibits re-create life on the Skellig Islands, the rocky outcroppings in the Atlantic just southwest of the Ring of Kerry, with models and audiovisual effects. Replicas of the stone oratories and cells of the early-Christian monastic community that flourished on Skellig Michael, light effects demonstrating the Skellig Lighthouse, and models of storm petrels and other seabirds pay due homage to the islands and their rare habitats. More thrilling, though, is the two-hour sea cruise around the base of the islands, where you'll see seabirds, gray seals, the Skellig Lighthouse, and the rocky remains of the monastic settlement.

TOURING TIPS If you take the sea cruise, you won't have time to dally elsewhere on the Ring of Kerry.

DINGLE TOWN

unofficial **TIP**
Dingle Harbour is busy in August with several events: the **Dingle Races** on the second weekend, the **Dingle Regatta** on the third weekend, and the **Blessing of the Fishing Fleet** at the end of the month. For information on these and other events, go to **www.dingle-peninsula.ie.**

AT HEART A FISHING PORT but also a popular seaside getaway for ordinary Irish folks and foreign visitors alike, Dingle is an agreeable place to settle in for a few days. A number of really good guest houses and many excellent restaurants make it all the more appealing. Don't expect to find yourself completely off the beaten path, though. The town is still small, at about 1,500 year-round residents, but holiday bungalows march across the green hillsides and smart shop windows line the cobbled streets—signs that Dingle is no longer the quaint, out-of-the-way village it was even as recently as 30 years ago.

PLANNING YOUR VISIT TO DINGLE

ON THE WATERFRONT NEAR THE CENTER OF TOWN, the **Dingle Tourist Office** is open mid-April to October, Monday through Sunday, 9 a.m. to 5 p.m.; November to March, Tuesday through Saturday, 9 a.m. to 5 p.m. The office is actually a souvenir shop, but the staff can be helpful regarding accommodations and local sights. For more information, call ☎ 066-915-1188 or visit **www.corkkerry.ie.**

ARRIVING AND GETTING ORIENTED IN DINGLE

DINGLE IS ABOUT 70 KILOMETERS (42 miles) west of Killarney, and by car the most direct route is via N22 and R561. **Bus Éireann** coaches link Dingle with Dublin, Cork, Galway, and other points in Ireland, but a trip just about anywhere involves a transfer in Tralee to the north or Killarney to the south. The trip to Dublin takes almost eight hours; about €20 one way, €35 round trip; for information, call ☎ 066-712-3566 or visit **www.buseireann.ie.** Buses arrive and depart from the Quay, in front of the supermarket.

HOTELS IN DINGLE

Captains House ★ ★ ★ ★

QUALITY ★ ★ ★	VALUE ★ ★ ★ ★	€60–€100

The Mall, Dingle, County Kerry (closed December 1–March 15); ☎ 066-915-1531; fax 066-915-1079; captigh@eircom.net; homepage.eircom.net/~captigh

Location Center of town. **Amenities and services** 8 rooms; in-room tea and coffee facilities, satellite TV. **Elevator** No. **Parking** On street, free. **Price** Includes full Irish breakfast. **Credit cards** AE, CB, D, DC, JCB, MC, V.

Snug is the word for this old house (actually, two narrow townhouses joined together) in the center of town, where Jim Milhench, a retired sea captain, and his wife, Mary, run a tight ship. Downstairs is a cozy parlor filled with mementos of Jim's travels and warmed by a turf fire in colder months, as well as a conservatory, where a large breakfast is served. A long garden at the rear of the house runs down to the River Mall; it's a delightful place to relax after a day of sightseeing. Guest rooms, reached via steep stairs and twisting hallways full of nooks and crannies, vary considerably in size. Although most rooms are quite small and not unlike cabins on a ship, they are extremely comfortable, with good beds and tidy little bathrooms, and the best are in the rear of the house overlooking the garden. This is not a good choice for anyone who has a hard time with stairs, and all guests would be well advised to leave heavy bags and, given the tight quarters, superfluous belongings in the car.

Castlewood House ★ ★ ★ ★

QUALITY ★ ★ ★ ★ ½	VALUE ★ ★ ★	€100–€180

The Wood, Dingle, County Kerry; ☎ 066-915-2788; fax 066-915-2788; castlewoodhouse@eircom.net; www.castlewooddingle.com

Location West edge of town. **Amenities and services** 12 units; hair dryers, in-room tea and coffee facilities, Internet access, minibars. **Elevator** Yes. **Parking** Free, on property. **Price** Includes full Irish breakfast. **Credit cards** AE, MC, V.

Little wonder that this beautifully appointed house at the edge of Dingle Bay has the feel of a luxury hotel: owners-managers Brian Heaton and Helen Woods Heaton trained at some of Ireland's finest hotels before returning to Dingle to open their own guest house next to Heaton's, the well-known inn run by Brian's parents. In fact, the two houses look like a matching set of McMansions; Castlewood is the more luxurious property, although both live up to the family's reputation for hospitality. The 12 individually decorated and tasteful rooms at Castlewood are all oversize; the largest are set up like suites and have welcoming sitting areas overlooking the bay and king-size beds covered in fine linens. The individually decorated bathrooms are large, with expanses of marble, long vanities, deep whirlpool tubs (in many), and separate power showers. Overstuffed couches surround a hearth in the handsome lounge, and a large breakfast is served in a sunny room overlooking the bay. Treats include porridge with Bailey's Irish Mist and made-to-order omelets.

Doyle's Townhouse ★ ★ ★

QUALITY	★ ★ ★ ½	VALUE	★ ★ ★	€120–€145

John Street, Dingle, County Kerry; ☎ 066-915-1174; fax 066-915-1816; cdoyles@iol.ie; www.doylesofdingle.com

Location City center. **Amenities and services** 8 rooms; in-room tea and coffee facilities, irons, satellite TV, trouser press. **Elevator** No. **Parking** On street. **Price** Includes full Irish breakfast. **Credit cards** AE, DC, MC, V.

A Victorian-style parlor, visible from the street, sets a warm and welcoming note for this stylish guest house, where the rooms are large and well furnished, sometimes overly so, with antiques and country-style pieces, richly upholstered chairs and sofas, and beds outfitted with fine linens. The rooms do not have sea views, but the trade-off is the in-town location amid Dingle's many pubs and restaurants—in fact, the famous, long-established, in-the-same-family Doyle's is right next door (see page 260). The best accommodations are the rooms at the rear of the house; two on the ground floor open to small patios, and those upstairs have small terraces that overlook a garden.

Greenmount House ★ ★ ★ ★

QUALITY	★ ★ ★ ★	VALUE	★ ★ ★ ★	€50–€150

Gortonara, Dingle, County Kerry; ☎ 066-915-1414; fax 066-915-1974; info@greenmount-house.com; www.greenmount-house.com

Location East edge of town. **Amenities and services** 12 units, including 6 suites; garden, in-room tea and coffee facilities, turndown service. **Elevator** No. **Parking** Free, on property. **Price** Includes full Irish breakfast. **Credit cards** MC, V.

A hillside perch overlooking the town and bay is only part of the appeal of John and Mary Curran's legendary B&B; for many visitors it's the highlight of a tour around Ireland. The Currans have been welcoming guests for almost 30 years in their expanded family bungalow, and they never seem to tire of improving the property (some ground-floor rooms were expanded this past winter). Most rooms are really suites, with comfortable sitting areas, large windows filled with views, and many with terraces or patios. Furnishings in the guest rooms and the lounges are tasteful, colors and fabrics throughout are soothing, and bathrooms are continually being refurbished. The day begins with breakfast in the conservatory, and the buffet table is so laden with homemade cakes, breads, and farmhouse cheeses—augmented with a large selection of cooked dishes—that few guests manage to leave Greenmount without gaining a pound or two. The center of town is an easy walk down the hill.

Heaton's Guesthouse ★ ★ ★

QUALITY ★ ★ ★	VALUE ★ ★ ★	€60–€150

The Wood, Dingle, County Kerry (closed late November–early February);
☎ **066-915-2288; fax 066-915-2324; heatons@iol.ie;**
www.heatonsdingle.com

Location West edge of town. **Amenities and services** 16 rooms; garden, in-room tea and coffee facilities. **Elevator** No. **Parking** Free, on property. **Price** Includes full Irish breakfast. **Credit cards** AE, MC, V.

This pleasant house across the road from Dingle Bay is comfortable and low-key, with rooms overlooking the water and lawns. Many include lounge chairs and sofas, and most are furnished in an unobtrusive contemporary style that may be a welcome break from the woody, chintzy clutter of many B&Bs. Note, though, that styles vary throughout the house, and rooms are continually being refurbished; if you don't like the décor of your room, ask to see another. Owners Cameron and Nuala Heaton are on hand to see to the needs of their guests and provide advice on what to see and where to eat. A large, delicious breakfast is served in a sunny front room that, like the comfy lounge, overlooks the bay. Heaton's is next door to the slightly more upscale Castlewood (see page 55), run by the Heatons' son Brian and his wife, Helen Woods Heaton; the properties are at the edge of town, about a ten-minute walk away.

Milltown House ★ ★ ★ ★

QUALITY ★ ★ ★ ★	VALUE ★ ★ ★	€60–€150

Dingle, County Kerry (closed November 15–March 15);
☎ **066-915-1372; fax 066-915-1095; info@ milltownhousedingle.com;**
www.milltownhousedingle.com

Location On the bay, just west of town. **Amenities and services** 10 rooms; garden, hair dryers, in-room movies, in-room tea and coffee facilities, trouser press. **Elevator** No. **Parking** Free, on property. **Price** Includes full Irish breakfast. **Credit cards** AE, MC, V.

This fine old house, set amid lawns on the shores of Dingle Bay, is a country-like getaway only about 1 kilometer (0.5 miles) from the center of town. This is the sort of place that guests return to often and think of fondly. Robert Mitchum stayed here when he was filming *Ryan's Daughter,* and his room, number ten, is one of several oversize doubles that have large bay windows furnished with easy chairs facing the bay and town. Geared for relaxing, all of the rooms have sitting areas, and while the furnishings are old-fashioned, they include firm beds and modern amenities such as flat-screen TVs. *Ryan's Daughter* and *Far and Away,* also set on the Dingle Peninsula and starring Tom Cruise and Nicole Kidman, are aired on the in-house movie system. While many hotels try to create as many revenue-producing rooms as possible, the Kerry family takes the opposite approach, continually enlarging rooms to make them more comfortable. Two of the ground-floor rooms open to private patios, and another, number eight, has its own entrance to the gardens that surround the house. A lavish breakfast, which always includes fresh fish, is served in a delightful conservatory; other public rooms include a large lounge, and tables and chairs are set out in the lawn next to the bay in good weather.

Old Pier ★ ★ ★

QUALITY ★ ★ ★	VALUE ★ ★ ★ ★	€40–€80

Feothanach, Ballydavid, County Kerry; ☎ 066-915-5242; info@oldpier.com; www.oldpier.com

Location On the north side of Dingle Peninsula, about 15 kilometers (9 miles) outside of Dingle Town. **Amenities and services** 5 rooms; hair dryers, in-room tea and coffee facilities. **Elevator** No. **Parking** On property. **Price** Includes full Irish breakfast. **Credit cards** MC, V.

The surf crashes into the rocks just steps from the front door of this five-room guest house in a tiny fishing village on the north side of the Dingle Peninsula, setting the stage for a scenery-filled seaside getaway. Rooms are large and snug, with wood floors, nice pine furniture, and tasteful fabrics. Most have wonderful views of the sea. A family room is equipped with extra beds for children, who will enjoy the expansive grounds and nearby beaches. The best part of staying at the Old Pier is the proximity of the dining room downstairs, which serves some of the freshest and best-prepared seafood in the region. This is where locals come for a good seafood meal, and guests can arrange very attractive dinner and bed-and-breakfast deals.

EXPLORING DINGLE

DINGLE IS COMPACT, WEDGED BETWEEN THE BAY and the mountains, and the town's few sights are within easy walking distance. The **Chapel of St. Joseph's Convent,** off Green Street, is lit with the heavenly light from 12 stained-glass windows by Harry Clark, one of Ireland's leading 20th-century artisans. Completed in 1922, the windows charmingly depict scenes from the life of Christ and are nicely documented in a free audio-guide tour; Monday through Friday,

9:30 a.m. to 1 p.m. and 2 to 5 p.m. Dingle's flashiest attraction is the rather modest **Ocean-world Aquarium,** on the harbor, call ☎ 066-915-2111 or visit **www.dingle-oceanworld.ie.** Skip this unless it's raining and the kids are restless. The effort to show native fish is sincere, and there are plenty of chances to pet starfish and other creatures, but the experience pales if you've visited more-ambitious aquariums elsewhere. Open daily, 10 a.m. to 6 p.m.; €10 adults; €6 children; €7.50 seniors and students; €27 families of up to

unofficial **TIP**
Besides the boat tours, another way to see Fungie is to walk out along the east side of the harbor, following the seashore path beyond the Coast Guard Station to the lighthouse; Fungie often frolics just offshore.

two adults and four children. Dingle's most famous attraction can be hard to pin down, is often out of sight, and is prone to getting you wet—this, of course, is **Fungie,** a bottlenose dolphin who swam into the harbor in 1983 and, much to the delight of local entrepreneurs, decided to stay. Boat operators charge €12 for adults and €6 for children for the cruise out to see Fungie, who appears with such regularity that the trip comes with a money-back guarantee if the star is a no-show. Boats leave from the pier near the tourist office every half hour in the summer, less frequently off season.

RESTAURANTS IN DINGLE

A COUPLE OF CHARMING CAFES ARE TUCKED AWAY on Dingle's cobbled streets; most are open only during the day. **An Café Liteartha,** behind the bookstore of the same name on Dykegate Street, serves soup, sandwiches, and freshly baked scones; open Monday through Saturday, 9 a.m. to 6 p.m., this is a delightful place to sit for a spell and read.

Chart House   ★ ★ ★ ★

MODERN IRISH/SEAFOOD	EXPENSIVE	QUALITY ★ ★ ★ ★	VALUE ★ ★ ★ ★

The Mall, Dingle; ☎ 066-915-2255

Reservations Recommended. **Entree range** €17–€24. **Payment** MC, V. **Bar** Full service. **Disabled access** Yes. **Hours** Wednesday–Monday, 6–10 p.m.; limited hours November–February.

MENU RECOMMENDATIONS Roasted cod, peppered filet of pork.

COMMENTS This handsome stone building near the bay provides the most pleasant dining experience in town, with sophisticated yet informal surroundings in a wood-floored, rose-hued room overlooking the water. Friendly but polished service pairs with superb preparations of seafood from the local waters and meats from Kerry farms. Sauces are perfectly flavored, while interesting risottos and vegetable concoctions accompany the main courses. Several vegetarian dishes are served every evening as well—a warm polenta tartlet, perhaps, or simple homemade ravioli stuffed with spinach and brie. Desserts include homemade ice creams and a wonderful selection of Irish cheeses.

Doyle's ★ ★ ★ ½

SEAFOOD	EXPENSIVE	QUALITY ★ ★ ★ ½	VALUE ★ ★ ★

John Street, Dingle; ☎ **066-915-1174**

Reservations Recommended. **Entree range** €21–€32; early-bird dinner, 6–7:15 p.m., €35. **Payment** AE, MC, V. **Bar** Full service. **Disabled access** Yes. **Hours** Monday–Saturday, 6–10 p.m.

MENU RECOMMENDATIONS Fresh oysters, mussels, fish pie.

COMMENTS Doyle's, which comprises several stone-floored, stone-walled dining rooms in an old house, has been a popular dining destination since 1974, long before Dingle was a stop on the tourist trail. The restaurant sticks to a time-honored formula: serve the freshest seafood right off the boats and prepare it simply, as often as possible according to old local recipes. Lobster is a house specialty, chosen from a tank near the entrance. Meat dishes are served, too, but they aren't just afterthoughts for carnivores who might stumble in—the juicy Kerry lamb pie is just as memorable as the creamy fish pie.

Fenton's ★ ★ ★

MODERN IRISH	MODERATE	QUALITY ★ ★ ★	VALUE ★ ★ ★

Green Street, Dingle; ☎ **066-915-2172**

Reservations Recommended. **Entree range** €18–€24; value meal, €22 for 2 courses. **Payment** MC, V. **Bar** Full service. **Disabled access** Yes. **Hours** Tuesday–Sunday, 6–9:30 p.m.; closed November–March.

MENU RECOMMENDATIONS Hot buttered lobster, black sole à la meunière, roast rack of lamb with rosemary and thyme, apple and berry crumble.

COMMENTS When locals want a relaxed evening out, they often come to this cozy old house in the center of town, where Patricia Fenton makes her guests feel at home in a cheerful wood-floored room warmed by a fire in an old stone hearth. A small menu sticks to local produce—lamb reared on the family farm, lobster and other seafood from Dingle Bay, and homegrown vegetables, all deftly prepared.

Global Village ★ ★ ★ ★

MODERN IRISH	MODERATE	QUALITY ★ ★ ★ ★	VALUE ★ ★ ★ ★ ½

Main Street, Dingle; ☎ **066-915-2325**

Reservations Recommended. **Entree range** €17–€24; early-bird menu, 5–7 p.m., €19 for two courses, €24 for three courses. **Payment** MC, V. **Bar** Full service. **Disabled access** Yes. **Hours** Daily, 5–9:30 p.m.; closed mid-November–February.

MENU RECOMMENDATIONS Thai curry, duck, fresh fish of the day.

COMMENTS Chef Martin Bealin claims to have been inspired by his world travels—hence some interesting spices and the appearance of a curry dish or two on the menu—but he has not forgotten his Irish roots. His cooking is honest and down-to-earth, with an emphasis on the freshest fish from

Dingle waters as well as prime Irish beef and lamb. His excellent presentations are served with great warmth and attention to guests; the pleasant, relaxed tile-floored room features works by local artists.

Goat Street Café   ★ ★ ★ ½

MODERN IRISH   INEXPENSIVE   QUALITY   ★ ★ ★ ★   VALUE ★ ★ ★ ★

Goat Street, Dingle; ☎ 066-915-2770

Reservations None taken. **Entree range** €9–€10. **Payment** Cash only. **Bar** Wine and beer. **Disabled access** Yes. **Hours** Monday–Saturday, 10 a.m.–5 p.m.; some weekend evenings, especially in July and August.

MENU RECOMMENDATIONS Lamb tagine, pasta with smoked salmon.

COMMENTS This modest little place has just a few tables and makes no attempt at décor, but the kitchen is much more ambitious than the surroundings suggest. The menu, available at lunch and occasionally in the evening, changes daily and usually includes such simple fare as homemade soups and farm-fresh salads. But the more sophisticated fare, including a salad of warm duck confit, is such a surprising treat that it would be a shame to miss.

Lord Baker's   ★ ★ ★

IRISH   MODERATE/INEXPENSIVE   QUALITY ★ ★ ★   VALUE ★ ★ ★ ★

Main Street, Dingle; ☎ 066-915-1277

Reservations Recommended. **Entree range** €15–€25; early-bird dinner, €16.50; prix-fixe menu, €24.95; lunches and light evening meals, about €9–€14. **Payment** AE, MC, V. **Bar** Full service. **Disabled access** Yes. **Hours** Friday–Wednesday, 12:30–2 p.m. and 6:30–10 p.m.

MENU RECOMMENDATIONS Seafood chowder, rack of lamb, lobster.

COMMENTS More Dingle restaurants—which tend to serve full meals only at dinnertime—should take their cue from the oldest pub in town, where you can choose from a bar menu and enjoy a lighter, less expensive evening meal or opt for a full dinner. Certainly, the lighter option—maybe a bowl of seafood chowder or lobster bisque followed by crab claws or a crab sandwich—is a satisfying meal in itself. The best place to enjoy your meal is the handsome old stone-walled barroom warmed by a turf fire; a more formal dining room and walled garden are just beyond.

Out of the Blue   ★ ★ ★

SEAFOOD   EXPENSIVE   QUALITY ★ ★ ★ ½   VALUE   ★ ★ ★ ½

Waterside, Dingle; ☎ 066-915-0811

Reservations Required. **Entree range** €18–€32. **Payment** MC, V. **Bar** Beer and wine only. **Disabled access** Yes. **Hours** Thursday–Tuesday, 12:30–3 p.m. and 6–9:30 p.m.

MENU RECOMMENDATIONS Fresh catch of the day.

COMMENTS This simple, brightly covered shack is the talk of Dingle these days, and the basic room has far fewer seats than can accommodate diners eager to eat here. The menu depends entirely upon what's available from the boats that dock just outside the door, and chef Eric Maillard prepares the catch simply but interestingly, with a dash of spices and skillful sauces, accompanied by delicious soups and chowders, fresh vegetables, and homemade breads. The only flaws: the premises are far too small for the crowds of appreciative patrons, and long waits, cramped seating, and rushed service are common.

ENTERTAINMENT AND NIGHTLIFE IN DINGLE

THINK PUBS, WITH WHICH DINGLE IS WELL ENDOWED. Many offer live traditional music a couple of evenings a week, some more often, and the musicians are usually in tune and ready to begin by 9:30 p.m., winding down around 11:30 p.m. This means that if you want to enjoy some pub grub, you'd better order by 8:30, because most pubs stop serving at 9 p.m. to accommodate the heavy-drinking music crowd. Two of the best pubs for music are **An Driochead Beag** (The Small Bridge) and **O'Flaherty's,** both on Bridge Street. In the old days, pubs doubled as shops, and this tradition lives on in Dingle. **Dick Mack's,** on Green Street, is still part leather- and shoe-repair shop, and the smell of leather mingles nicely with that of beer. **Foxy John's,** on Main Street, is also a hardware store, and **O'Currain's,** across the street, does double duty as a clothing shop. Dingle's other nighttime entertainment is the **cinema** on the Mall, where a first-run film, often British, usually is showing.

SHOPPING IN DINGLE

SHOPPERS WITH AN EYE FOR GOOD CRAFTSMANSHIP will be pleased to find some high-quality work in Dingle's shops. **Gaileari Beag** (18 Main Street, ☎ 066-915-2976) is a showplace for local artisans, with excellent pottery and other works on display, including fused-glass jewelry and lamps by Fiona and Jazz Wood. **Greenlane Gallery** (Green Street, ☎ 066-915-2018) shows works by local painters and sculptors. The **Weaver's Shop** (also on Green Street, ☎ 066-915-1688) features scarves, shawls, tablecloths, and distinctive decorative pieces by Lisbeth Mulcahy, one of Ireland's most noted weavers.

EXERCISE AND RECREATION IN DINGLE

DINGLE IS A GOOD BASE FOR ACTIVE VISITORS. The peninsula is skirted by some excellent beaches, the best being the five-kilometer-long (three-mile-long) strand at Inch, backed by dunes; much of David Lean's film *Ryan's Daughter* was shot on the beach. Inch is about ten kilometers (six miles) east of Dingle on R561. **Mountain Man** (Strand Street, ☎ 066-915-2400) rents bikes and equipment and dispenses a lot of advice on where to ride. Most cyclists head out to Slea Head at the eastern tip of the peninsula. You can golf at the **Dingle Golf Club,** about

16 kilometers (10 miles) north of Dingle Town in Ballyferriter; ☎ 066-915-6255; about €60 for 18 holes. If you want to explore the mountains or trot along a beach on horseback, rent a mount at **Dingle Horse Riding** (Ballinaboula House, ☎ 066-915-2199). Walkers can choose a stretch of the **Dingle Way,** which circles the peninsula for 150 kilometers (90 miles); the tourist office in Dingle sells guides to walking the path.

AROUND DINGLE

 **THE DINGLE PENINSULA**

THE WESTERNMOST TIP OF IRELAND stretches some 50 kilometers (30 miles) from the mainland into the Atlantic surf—a spine of rugged mountains, rocky cliffs, and soft sands. Remnants of prehistoric and early Christian cultures litter the hilly countryside, where farmers still speak Irish, and fishing boats set out from tidy harbors along the coast. None of these charms are lost on visitors, who crowd the peninsula in summer, but the empty landscapes accommodate them well. Besides, the Dingle Peninsula is far enough off the beaten track that for much of the year the towns and villages settle back into their quiet ways, and the sense of otherworldliness is enhanced by thick mists, good stout, and the ever-present traditional Irish tunes.

Exploring the Dingle Peninsula

The most dramatic scenery on the peninsula lies to the west of Dingle Town, and you can enjoy the sights on a well-marked 50-kilometer (30-mile) loop from the west end of town. Be prepared to drive slowly (roads are twisting, often one lane, and shared more often than not with sheep) and to stop frequently, as there's much to see, from Iron Age forts to early Christian settlements to spectacular scenery.

About 13 kilometers (8 miles) beyond Dingle Town the road comes to 2,500-year-old **Dunbeg Fort,** with thick, earthen ramparts rising precariously above the sea. In fact, much of the enclosure has already crashed into the waves, but enough remains to show the defensive strength of the enclosure and its strategic position on a wave-washed promontory; entrance is free, but you'll pay €2 to cross private land to reach the fort. About 1 kilometer (0.5 miles) or so down the road is a colony of stone beehive huts said to have been built by early Christians; you'll pay another €2 to get to them. After you ford a stream, the road comes to **Slea Head,** where you should pull over next to the stone crucifixion scene to enjoy views of the wild surf racing ashore and the Blasket Islands looming in the near distance. Just beyond is another scenic spot, **Dunmore Head,** the westernmost point in Europe, and the village of **Dunquin,** where the ruins of stone cottages abandoned during the Famine years litter the hillside around a small harbor and boats depart for the Blasket Islands. Life in this bleak outpost is chronicled in the nearby **Blasket Centre** (see below). **Bally-ferriter,** about eight kilometers (five miles) down the road, is the largest village at this end of the peninsula. It's dominated by the glossy operations of the Louis Mulcahy Pottery studios; sophisticated pottery and dinnerware made from local clay is displayed in a large shop daily, from 10 a.m. to 6 p.m.; ☎ 066-915-6229.

Several more early Christian settlements are clustered on this part of the northern coast. At **Reasc,** a 6th- to 12th-century monastery enclosure includes remnants of an early church and an intricate cross carved into a Celtic stone pillar from 500 BC. More intact, though, is the nearby **Gallus Oratory,** a beautiful, remarkably well-preserved 1,300-year-old church resembling the keel of a boat, constructed with dry-stone corbeling developed by prehistoric tomb builders; daily, 10 a.m. to 5 p.m. (hours vary in off season); €3 includes a film introduction to Ireland's prehistoric and early Christian cultures. Running into a cove just down the coast is **Brandon's Creek,** a landing stage for fishing boats. St. Brendan the Voyager is said to have set out from here sometime in the middle of the sixth century and sailed across the Atlantic to the New World in a *currach,* a fragile little vessel of hide stretched over a wood frame. In 1976, an adventurous scholar who embarked on the same voyage from this spot in a similar boat made it all the way to Newfoundland.

Return to Dingle Town over the **Connor Pass,** a view-a-minute ride (in good weather, that is) through a breach in the spine of mountains that runs the length of the peninsula.

Tours of the Dingle Peninsula

Tim and Michael Collins, a father-and-son team, introduce visitors to the peninsula's prehistory and early-Christian cultures on their fact-filled **Sciuird Archaeology Tours,** which depart from Dingle Town. These guys know all the back roads, and they will show you tombs and forts you'd never find on your own, while giving you an earful about life in these parts. Tours last about 2.5 hours; May to September, 10:30 a.m. and 2 p.m.; call for times in the off season; ☎ 066-915-1606; €20.

Attraction on the Dingle Peninsula

 The Blasket Centre ★ ★ ★ ★

APPEAL BY AGE	PRESCHOOL ★ ★	GRADE SCHOOL ★ ★ ★	TEENS ★ ★ ★
YOUNG ADULTS ★ ★	OVER 30 ★ ★ ★ ★		SENIORS ★ ★ ★ ★

Dunquin, tip of Dingle Peninsula, about 16 kilometers (10 miles) west of Dingle Town on R559; ☎ 066-915-6444; www.heritageireland.ie

Type of attraction Museum of life on the Blasket Islands. **Admission** €3.50 adults, €2 seniors and children. **Hours** Easter–June, September–October; daily,

10 a.m. –6 p.m.; July–August; daily, 10 a.m. –7 p.m. **When to go** Anytime. **Special comments** A stop here is mandatory before visiting the islands. **How much time to allow** About 1 hour.

DESCRIPTION AND COMMENTS   The remote Blasket Islands were home to several hundred inhabitants until the early 1950s, when the last of the islanders went to the mainland. For centuries the only contact an islander had with the rest of the world was to row across 12 miles of open ocean in a *currach* (a boat made of animal hide) to this end of the Dingle Peninsula. It's not surprising that the islanders developed their own ways—their own dialect, musical variations, and a small body of literature (referred to as the Blasket Library). This well-designed museum preserves the Blasket culture with fascinating photographs, manuscripts, and models of island houses; a 20-minute video contains rare footage of the last days of life on the islands, as well as some lyrical readings of poetry. Large windows at the front of the museum overlook the islands.

TOURING TIPS   If you're inspired to see the islands, board the Blasket ferry in nearby Dunquin Harbour. Boats run hourly in the summer, but not at all from mid-October to March, and not in bad weather, when rough seas make it foolhardy to dock at the tiny landing stage on Great Blasket; €20 round trip.

PART SEVEN

THE LOWER SHANNON

THE SHANNON, THE LONGEST RIVER in the British Isles, flows into the Atlantic Ocean through a wide estuary in County Limerick. While many travelers, who know the region only as a gateway to Ireland through Shannon Airport, rush through on their way to other places, the green landscapes that roll away from the estuary merit a visit of several days or more. The countryside is littered with castles, pretty towns and villages, and some of Ireland's grandest hotels. One of Ireland's largest cities, **Limerick,** is here, too. You might want to settle down for a spell upon first arriving in Ireland, or perhaps enjoy the region as a last taste of the country before taking off.

unofficial **TIP**
The Lower Shannon region is tucked conveniently between Kerry and Galway, so it makes a nice stopover when traveling between places in those two counties.

NOT TO BE MISSED IN THE LOWER SHANNON

Adare (see below)   Bunratty Castle and Folk Park (page 288)

Ennis Friary (page 290)   The Hunt Museum, Limerick (page 282)

The Loop Head Drive near Kilrush (page 294)

ADARE

ADARE IS A PICTURE-BOOK PLACE that's the self-proclaimed "prettiest village in Ireland." Who's to say if that is really true in this country with so many pretty villages, but Adare is certainly attractive. The thatched-roof cottages lining its main street look as if they were built solely for the pleasure of photographers. Actually, the Earls of Dunraven built the rose-covered village cottages and houses in the middle of the 19th century for tenants on their estate, which straddles the banks of the River Maigue at the edge of town. The estate's parklands

the lower shannon

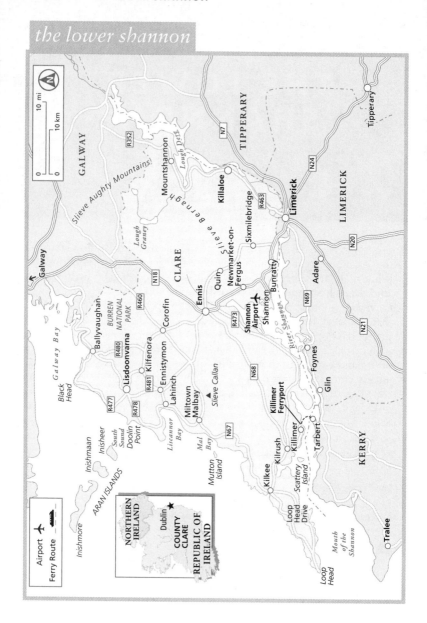

are a delight for walkers, and the Dunravens' Gothic Revival manor house is one of Ireland's most luxurious hotels.

Just 40 kilometers (25 miles) south of Shannon Airport, Adare is a good choice for a first or last stop in the old country. Comfortable hotels plus good restaurants, activities, and attractions add to the appeal.

PLANNING YOUR VISIT TO ADARE

YOU'LL FIND INFORMATION ON ADARE and the surrounding region at the **Adare Heritage Centre** on Main Street; it's open May to September, Monday through Saturday, 9 a.m. to 7 p.m., Sunday 9 a.m. to 6 p.m.; and October to April, Monday through Saturday, 9:30 a.m. to 5:30 p.m.; call ☎ 061-396666 or visit **www.shannonregiontourism.ie.** The information desk is not always staffed, especially around lunchtime; if this is the case, ask someone in the shop or elsewhere in the center when the info folks are coming back or if they can tell you what you need to know. The Heritage Centre galleries present displays, a model of the town, and an audiovisual presentation highlighting Adare's history.

unofficial **TIP**
Admission to the **Adare Heritage Centre** is steep for what you'll see: €5 adults, €3.50 children, €15 families. You can learn just about all you really need to know about Adare on the historical placards in front of the building or from one of the free handouts from the information desk.

ARRIVING AND GETTING ORIENTED IN ADARE

ADARE IS JUST 20 KILOMETERS (12 miles) southwest of Limerick City; the trip is a quick 15 minutes by car on N20. If you're coming from **Shannon Airport,** follow N18 to Limerick and continue from there on N20 to Adare. If you're coming from County Kerry, follow N21 north, which will bring you right to Adare, as will N20 north from Cork; from Dublin, take N7 through Limerick and N20 from there. **Bus Éireann** buses run frequently throughout the day between Limerick and Adare, and the fare is about €3.10 each way; from Shannon Airport, take the coach to Limerick (€5.20; service about every hour throughout the day, more frequently during morning and evening rush hours), and continue from there to Adare. Limerick will also be the transfer point if you're traveling to Adare by train or coach from most other parts of Ireland. For more information on Bus Éireann service, call ☎ 061-313333 or go to **www.buseireann.ie.**

HOTELS IN ADARE

Adare Country House ★ ★ ★

QUALITY	★ ★ ★ ½	VALUE	★ ★ ★ ★ ½	€50–€70

Adare Village, County Limerick; ☎ **061-395986; adarecountryhouse@eircom.net; www.adarecountryhouse.com**

How Hotels Compare in Lower Shannon

HOTEL	OVERALL	QUALITY	VALUE	PRICE
ADARE				
Adare Manor	★★★★	★★★½–★★★★★	★★★	€250–€540
Dunraven Arms	★★★★	★★★★	★★★★	€125–€190
Adare Country House	★★★	★★★½	★★★★½	€50–€70
ENNIS				
Dromoland Castle	★★★★½	★★★★–★★★★½	★★★½	€150–$500
The Old Ground	★★★★	★★★	★★★★½	€80–€120
KILRUSH				
Hillcrest View Bed and Breakfast	★★★½	★★★½	★★★★	€40–€70
LIMERICK				
Jurys Inn Limerick	★★★	★★★	★★★★	€59–€79

Location At the edge of Adare. **Amenities and services** 12 units; garden, hair dryers, in-room tea and coffee facilities. **Elevator** No. **Parking** Free, on property. **Price** Includes full Irish breakfast. **Credit cards** MC, V.

A courtyard entry sets a welcoming note at Denis and Eileen Moroney's appealing bed-and-breakfast at the edge of Adare. Pubs and shops are just a five-minute walk away, but the house is set on a country lane amid fields and gardens; these surroundings, along with wide-planked floors and handsome pine furnishings, lend a country-house feel. Most of the rooms are on the ground floor, making access easy; they are quite large, and the oversize modern bathrooms are equipped with deep bathtubs. The Moroneys serve a good breakfast in a handsome dining room, and they have set aside a small lounge for guests to use. The only amenity inconveniently missing is a telephone—even a public phone on the premises would be a welcome addition.

 Adare Manor ★ ★ ★ ★

QUALITY	★★★½–★★★★★	VALUE	★★★	€250–€540

Adare Village, County Limerick; ☎ **061-396566; fax 061-396124; reservations@adaremanor.com; www.adaremanor.com**

Location At the edge of Adare. **Amenities and services** 63 units; bar, beauty salon, bicycling, business center, fireplaces in some rooms, fishing, gardens, golf, gym, hair dryers, horseback riding, in-room tea and coffee facilities, Internet connections, restaurant, room service, safes, shop, spa, swimming pool, tennis, turndown service, walking. **Elevator** Yes. **Parking** On property, free. **Price** Full Irish breakfast, €23; many special offers available. **Credit cards** AE, DC, MC, V.

The Earls of Dunraven built their neo-Gothic manor house on the banks of the River Maigue, fitting it out with intricately carved woodworking, acres of leaded glass, dozens of chimneys, and fine furnishings. The house has been a hotel since the 1980s, one of Ireland's finest. Connoisseurs of architecturally distinctive lodging will be heartened by the assemblage of stone walls, winding stairs, glowing hearths, and even a gallery lined with elaborate choir stalls (ask to see the risqué carvings). With two staff members for every guest, service is exceptionally attentive and professional, enhancing the feeling that guests are in a private home. The best accommodations are the so-called staterooms in the old house; these enormous and generously furnished suites—some even have fireplaces in the cavernous marble bathrooms—have hosted many heads of state and celebrities. A new wing holds less sumptuous, but nonetheless luxurious, accommodations. Disappointingly, though, these rooms are reached off long, dispiriting hallways. Stuffy and rather unexceptional furnishings make for less character than found in the older wing; these rooms could benefit from a tasteful makeover that better captures the spirit of the old house. Most rooms throughout the hotel have nice views over the river, boxwood gardens, and the fairways of a Robert Trent Jones golf course. The grounds also include the romantic ruins of a castle and monastery.

Dunraven Arms ★ ★ ★ ★

QUALITY ★ ★ ★ ★	VALUE ★ ★ ★ ★	€125–€190

Adare Village, Country Limerick; ☎ 061-396633; fax 061-396541; reservations@dunravenhotel.com; www.dunravenhotel.com

Location In the village center. **Amenities and services** 88 units; bar, beauty salon, bicycling, fireplaces in some rooms, fishing, garden, gym, hair dryers, horseback riding, hunting, in-room tea and coffee facilities, Internet connections, 2 restaurants, room service, safes, swimming pool, walking. **Parking** On property, free. **Price** Includes full Irish breakfast; many special offers available. **Credit cards** AE, MC, V.

This handsome mustard-colored inn not only retains a friendly small-town-hotel atmosphere, it also offers a great deal of luxury. The paneled bar is the most popular gathering spot in town, and several snug, fire-warmed guest lounges are to the rear of the reception area. The high-ceilinged guest rooms at the front of the hotel retain a solid, old-fashioned air, but Dunraven Arms breaks the older-is-better rule—a new wing that extends through gardens at the rear of the hotel is, despite the long hallways, just as attractive. The rooms in this new wing are large, handsomely furnished with traditional pieces (including four-poster beds in many), and outfitted with spacious bathrooms and separate dressing rooms; several rooms have fireplaces. Aside from offering a beautiful indoor pool and well-equipped gym, the hotel arranges fishing, golf, horseback riding, shootings, and other recreational activities.

EXPLORING ADARE

ADARE IS WELL SUITED TO WALKING, and your route should begin on Main Street, a postcard vision of brightly colored thatched-roof cottages with roses climbing around the doorways. A more somber presence is that of the **Trinitarian Abbey,** built in the 13th century by a French order of monks whose raison d'être was to raise ransom money for Christians taken captive by the Moors during the Crusades. The stone compound was enlarged after English troops under King Henry VIII severely damaged such monasteries throughout Ireland in a campaign to wipe out Catholicism; it now serves as a Catholic church. The placid **Wishing Pool** across the street, backed by a double-arched stone bridge, once did double duty as a communal laundry and watering hole for horses.

Main Street ends at the ornate gates that mark the entrance to the vast, beautiful, and emerald-green parklands surrounding **Adare Manor,** the ancestral home of the Earls of Dunraven. The manor is now a hotel (see profile on page 270), and the links of its golf course wind through the grounds, but visitors are welcome to stroll the paths and lanes shaded by majestic old trees. The ruins of **Desmond Castle,** begun in the early 13th century within an ancient ring fort, rise from the banks of the River Maigue near the manor; the towers and Great Hall are discernible among the terribly romantic piles of stone rubble. Nearby, a 25-meter (75-foot) tower looms over the ruins of a **Franciscan monastery** founded in the 15th century by the Friars of the Strict Observance. Another monastery, this one in good repair, is the **Augustinian Priory** just to the north; a fascinating example of medieval architecture, it now serves as a Protestant church. A good vantage point from which to enjoy the River Maigue is the nearby **village bridge,** built of stone in the 14th century and, although widened over the centuries, still medieval in appearance.

RESTAURANTS IN ADARE

Inn Between   ★ ★ ★

MODERN IRISH	MODERATE	QUALITY ★ ★ ★	VALUE ★ ★ ★ ★

Rose Cottage, Main Street, Adare; ☎ 061-399-6633

Reservations Recommended. **Entree range** €13–€22. **Payment** AE, MC, V. **Bar** Full service. **Disabled access** Yes. **Hours** Tuesday–Sunday, 6–10 p.m.; lunches available in summer.

MENU RECOMMENDATIONS Salmon and smoked-haddock cakes, linguine with prawns, lamb's liver.

COMMENTS One of two restaurants at Dunraven Arms, this airy bistro with warm-hued, skylighted rooms and a pleasant patio occupies a thatched-

How Restaurants Compare in Lower Shannon

NAME	CUISINE	OVERALL	QUALITY	VALUE	PRICE
ADARE					
Wild Geese	modern Irish	★★★★	★★★★	★★★½	exp
Inn Between	modern Irish	★★★	★★★	★★★★	mod
LIMERICK					
Green Onion	modern Irish	★★★★	★★★½	★★★	mod
ENNIS					
The Cloister	modern Irish/ seafood	★★★½	★★★½	★★★½	mod
Durty Nellie's	pub fare	★★½	★★½	★★★	mod/inexp
KILRUSH					
Kelly's	pub food	★★★★	★★★½	★★★★	inexp

roof cottage across the road from the hotel (the Maigue Restaurant, in the hotel, is more formal). You can dine lightly if you wish (the home-made soups and juicy burgers are excellent) or a little more elaborately, choosing from a range of meat dishes and locally caught fish. The Dunravens' woody bar, a good choice for even lighter fare, serves sandwiches and snacks.

Wild Geese   ★★★★

MODERN IRISH	EXPENSIVE	QUALITY ★★★★	VALUE ★★★½

Rose Cottage, Main Street, Adare; ☎ 061-396451

Reservations Recommended. **Entree range** €22–€27; €30 for two courses, €36 for 3 courses. **Payment** AE, MC, V. **Bar** Full service. **Disabled access** Yes. **Hours** Tuesday–Sunday, 6–10 p.m.; also lunch on Sunday, May–September.

MENU RECOMMENDATIONS   Roasted Adare lamb, wild pheasant stuffed with rosemary, any fresh fish.

COMMENTS   Diners come to Adare just to enjoy a meal in these country-style dining rooms arranged throughout one of the village's famously pretty cottages. Chef David Foley is a local man—well, almost. He trained at Tralee, over the border in County Kerry, and worked at several restaurants in Southwest Ireland before moving on to London and Dublin, returning to the region in 1999 to open his own restaurant. Foley uses the freshest local game, seafood, and produce in preparations that are creative but sensible—fresh crab appears in soufflés; Adare lamb is enhanced only with fresh herbs; monkfish is enlivened with tempura vegetables. The service, like the food, is down-to-earth but polished.

EXERCISE AND RECREATION IN ADARE

HEADQUARTERED NEAR ADARE IN BALLINGARRY, **Celtic Angling** offers fly-fishing excursions (with equipment and instruction) to local streams and lakes as well as salmon-fishing outings on the River Shannon; call ☎ 069-68202 or go to **www.celticangling.com.** The 18-hole **golf course at Adare Manor,** designed by Robert Trent Jones, meanders through woodlands, around the shores of three lakes, and along the banks of the River Maigue; for greens fees and other information, call ☎ 061-395044 or go to **www.adaremanor.com.** Horseback riding is available at **Clonshire Polo and Equestrian Centre** (☎ 061-396770; **www.clonshire.com**).

AROUND ADARE

ALONG N69

A SHORT DRIVE NORTH FROM ADARE brings you to the **Forest of Curragchase,** which is laced with trails, and then to Route N69, which follows the wide estuary of the River Shannon west through old river towns such as **Foynes** (see below). At **Tarbert,** you can board a ferry to cross the river to **Killimer** and **Kilrush** (see page 292). N69 continues south from Tarbert into County Kerry to **Tralee,** the county capital, and from there you can continue on to the nearby **Dingle Peninsula** (see page 263).

Attractions along N69

Foynes Flying Boat Museum ★ ★ ★

| APPEAL BY AGE | PRESCHOOL ★★ | GRADE SCHOOL ★★ | TEENS ★★ |
| YOUNG ADULTS ★★ | | OVER 30 ★★★ | SENIORS ★★★ |

Foynes, County Limerick; ☎ **069-65416; www.flyingboatmuseum.com**

Type of attraction Aviation museum. **Admission** €5 adults, €3.50 seniors and students, €2.50 children under age 14, free for children under age 5, €12 families of up to 2 adults and 4 children. **Hours** April–October, daily, 10 a.m.–6 p.m. **When to go** Anytime; the museum is indoors. **Special comments** Children may find the film and exhibits a bit dull, and visitors with limited vision may find it difficult to view the print-heavy exhibits. **How much time to allow** About 1 hour.

DESCRIPTION AND COMMENTS In the late 1930s, the little harbor town of Foynes on the Shannon Estuary became the port for the first transatlantic air-passenger service, Pan American's "flying boats." Foynes's fame was short-lived, as longer-distance aircraft introduced during World War II made the flying boats obsolete, but the town's prominence in the history of aviation is remembered in this earnest little museum in what was once

How Attractions Compare in Lower Shannon

ATTRACTION	DESCRIPTION	AUTHOR'S RATING
ADARE		
Glin Castle	Ancestral home of the FitzGerald family on the banks of the River Shannon	★★★★
Foynes Flying Boat Museum	Aviation museum	★★★
TRALEE		
Kerry County Museum	Exhibits highlighting the history and scenic beauty of County Kerry	★★½
LIMERICK		
Hunt Museum	Museum of art and antiquities	★★★★
King John's Castle	Restored medieval castle	★★★½
ENNIS		
Bunratty Castle and Folk Park	Restored medieval castle and re-creation of Irish rural life	★★★★½
Ennis Friary	Ruins of monastic complex	★★★
Craggaunowen	A re-creation of prehistoric Ireland	★★
KILRUSH AND THE WEST CLARE PENINSULA		
Dolphinwatch Carrigaholt	Boat trip in the Shannon Estuary	★★★★
Vandeleur Walled Garden	Garden	★★★

the terminal building. Conspicuously absent is one of the luxurious crafts that set down here. Instead, an excellent film, as well as photographs, news clippings, and radio equipment, musters some exciting nostalgia for the era. You'll learn that the Foynes–New York journey took 25 hours, passage came with a bed and seven-course meals, and there was a 50–50 chance the plane would have to turn back at the point of no return when it became clear there wasn't enough fuel to get to the next stop. While you can't step aboard a flying boat, you can take a seat in the terminal canteen and order an Irish coffee, invented here on a wet winter's night in 1942.

TOURING TIPS Foynes is a handy rest stop if you're following the Lower Shannon between the Dingle Peninsula and other places in County Kerry, and places in County Limerick and County Clare.

Walks and Drives in the Lower Shannon

River and ocean scenery dominate the lush land surrounding the estuary of Ireland's longest river.

GREAT WALKS

SEASIDE RAMBLES

You can walk the entire **Loop Head Drive** (see page 294), east of **Kilrush,** in a couple of days, and almost any segment offers a thrilling shorter walk. Especially scenic is the section just south of **Kilkee,** where the narrow road hugs the tops of high cliffs battered relentlessly by enormous waves. **Ballybunion** is also a prime walking spot, with vista-filled cliff-top walks along the sea.

COUNTRY AMBLES

You'll find especially pleasant, path-laced parklands at **Adare Manor** in Adare (see page 270), the former estate of the Earls of Dunraven, where the scenery includes the ruins of a castle and monastery and the rushing waters of the River Maigue. The **Forest of Curraghchase,** just north of Adare off N69, shelters beautiful formal gardens as well as a vast arboretum planted with fine specimens of native Irish trees.

A GREAT DRIVE

ALONG THE BANKS OF THE SHANNON

A good place to begin this drive along the shores of the **Shannon** to the coast of the Atlantic is the pretty village of **Adare.** If you're staying in or around **Ennis** or elsewhere north of Limerick, you can easily reach Adare via the N20.

Adare (see page 267) is a pleasure to explore on foot, with a pleasing number of thatched-roof cottages, the ruins of a castle, and several monasteries and abbeys. Especially inviting are the tree-shaded lanes that crisscross the parklands of **Adare Manor.**

From Adare, follow N20 west for about eight kilometers (five miles) to **Rathkeale,** where Sir Walter Raleigh and the poet Sir Edmund Spenser stayed at **Castle Matrix** in 1589. Legend has it that Sir Walter planted Ireland's first potatoes, imported from the Carolinas, at Rathkeale, but the "first potato" claim is one you'll encounter frequently throughout Ireland. The headquarters of the Irish Heraldry Society, the castle houses some fine period

Glin Castle ★ ★ ★ ★

APPEAL BY AGE	PRESCHOOL ★★	GRADE SCHOOL ★★	TEENS ★★★
YOUNG ADULTS ★★	OVER 30 ★★★★		SENIORS ★★★★

Glin, off N69; ☎ 068-34173; www.glincastle.com

furnishings and a famous set of documents pertaining to the Wild Geese, Irish mercenaries who served in Continental armies in the 17th and 18th centuries. It's open mid-May through mid-September, Saturday through Thursday, 11 a.m. to 5 p.m.; admission is €5.

Leaving Rathkeale, follow R518 north for ten kilometers (six miles) to **Askeaton.** Ruins dominate this appealing town on the River Deel. **Desmond Castle,** a stronghold that the Desmond clan built on an island in the river in the 15th century, fell to the British in 1580, though the banqueting hall and chapel remain in ruined splendor. A 15th-century Franciscan abbey, of which only the cloisters remains, is on the nearby shore of the Deel.

A drive of another ten kilometers (six miles) west on N69 brings you to the banks of the Shannon at **Foynes.** The views of the river are sweeping, and the **Foynes Flying Boat Museum** (see page 274) pays homage to the town's service as the European terminus for transatlantic Flying Boat service.

Glin, 13 kilometers (8 miles) west on N69, is the riverside domain of the Knights of Glin, whose current castle, dating from 1785 and open to the public, is filled with fine furnishings (see below).

Tarbert, six kilometers (four miles) farther west, is the port for ferry service across the Shannon to **Killimer** in County Clare. Before embarking, time permitting, make a jaunt west for 25 kilometers (15 miles) to the mouth of the river at **Ballybunion.** This attractive little resort offers some fine beaches and bracing cliff-top walks above the Atlantic.

From Tarbert, ferries run year-round, daily, with departures every hour. (The fare is €15 one way, €25 round trip, for one car and passengers). Board a boat for the 20-minute crossing, and, once in Killmer, make the short drive east to **Kilrush** (see page 292).

After exploring Kilrush, follow the **Loop Head Drive** (see page 294) through the seaside resort of **Kilkee.** From there, follow the well-marked route along the high cliffs of the Atlantic coast southwest to **Loop Head Lighthouse,** then along the **mouth of the Shannon.** The entire loop covers about 50 kilometers (30 miles).

If you're staying in or around Ennis, the quickest return is on N68; Ennis is only about 40 kilometers (24 miles) from Killrush on this route. If you're staying in Adare or somewhere else south of Limerick, you'll save considerable time by taking the ferry back across the Shannon to Tarbert and traveling east from there on N69.

Type of attraction Ancestral home of the FitzGerald family on the banks of the River Shannon. **Admission** €7 adults, €3.50 children. **Hours** Summer, 11 a.m.– 2 p.m. or by appointment (castle is often closed to the public). **When to go** Anytime, but especially in summer when the gardens are blooming. **Special comments** Glin Castle also operates as a country-house hotel and is sometimes rented in its

walks and drives in the lower shannon

Great Walks
1. Seaside Rambles
2. Country Ambles

A Great Drive
3. Along the Banks of the Shannon

entirety, so the premises are often closed to the general public. Young visitors may be disappointed by the absence of such medieval-castle trappings as ramparts and dungeons. **How much time to allow** About 1 hour.

DESCRIPTION AND COMMENTS The FitzGeralds have been the Knights of Glin since the 14th century. Their current castle dates only from 1785 and, in a dash of retrofitting, was adorned with crenellations and other medieval-looking adornments in the 19th century. The current knight is the noted art historian Desmond FitzGerald, who has filled the castle with a stunning collection of 18th-century Irish furniture. Neoclassical columns and elaborate plasterwork provide a suitable setting for these wonderful pieces, and the centerpiece of the castle is a flying staircase, with a double set of stairs that rises to a central flight for the final ascent. The magnificent gardens are a sea of color in spring and summer.

TOURING TIPS Should you be swept away by Glin Castle, inquire about overnight stays in one of the beautifully appointed guest rooms; rates begin at about €250.

TRALEE

THE CAPITAL OF COUNTY KERRY, about 80 kilometers (50 miles) south of Adare, is an attractive yet unassuming workaday place where inhabitants are much more in evidence than tourists. During the last week of August, though, Tralee becomes frivolous as it stages the **Rose of Tralee International Festival,** with events that include a beauty contest to nominate the "Rose of Tralee" (a namesake of the popular Irish song), live music, and a horse race. Tralee is also home to **Siamsa Tíre,** the National Folk Theatre of Ireland, with a permanent home next door to the Kerry County Museum (see below) in the Town Park. Performances bring folk tales and traditional rural ways to life through music, dance, and mime. Shows are seasonal, from May to October, with the most performances in July and August. For more information, call ☎ 066-712-3055 or visit **www.siamsatire.com.**

Exploring Tralee

A popular excursion from Tralee is aboard the **Tralee–Blennerville Steam Train,** a mere three kilometers (two miles) along narrow-gauge track to Blennerville, where the largest working windmill in Ireland, 20 meters (60 feet) tall and built in 1800, is once again in operation after standing idle for decades. The train leaves from Ballyard Station in Tralee, with departures every 30 minutes from May to October, 10:30 a.m. to 5 p.m.; round-trip fare is €5 adults, €2.50 children, €3.50 seniors and students, and €12 families; for more information and to check on schedules, which can vary, call ☎ 066-712-1064. Guided tours of the **Blennerville Windmill** explain the flour-making process, and a small exhibit covers the bases from windmill operations to the fate of Kerry farmers during the Famine years; also on the grounds are a restaurant and a crafts shop. The Windmill complex is open from April to October, daily, 10 a.m. to 6 p.m.; €5 adults, €3 children over age 5, €4 seniors and students, €13 families. For more information, call ☎ 066-712-1064. To learn more about local attractions and events, visit the **Tralee Tourist Office,** which also houses the Kerry County Museum (Ashe Memorial Hall on Denny Street, ☎ 066-712-1288). The office is open Monday through Friday, 9 a.m. to 1 p.m. and 2 to 5 p.m., and on some weekends in the summer.

Attraction in Tralee

Kerry County Museum ★ ★ ½

APPEAL BY AGE	PRESCHOOL ★ ★ ★	GRADE SCHOOL ★ ★ ★ ★ ★	TEENS ★ ★ ★ ★
YOUNG ADULTS ★ ★ ★ ★		OVER 30 ★ ★ ½	SENIORS ★ ★ ½

Ashe Memorial Hall, Denny Street; ☎ 066-712-7777; www.holidaytralee.com

Type of attraction Exhibits highlighting the history and scenic beauty of County Kerry. **Admission** €8 adults, €6.50 seniors and students, €2.50 children, €12 families. **Hours** January–March, Tuesday–Friday, 10 a.m.–4:30 p.m.; April–May and September–December, Tuesday–Saturday, 9:30 a.m.–5:30 p.m.; June–August, daily, 9:30 a.m.–5:30 p.m. **When to go** Anytime; the museum is a good rainy-day excursion with kids. **Special comments** This is one museum that kids are likely to enjoy more than their parents—the video presentations and medieval re-creations are especially popular with young visitors. **How much time to allow** About 2 hours.

DESCRIPTION AND COMMENTS Three exhibits present an overview of County Kerry. The least imaginative of these is "Kerry in Colour," a humdrum slide presentation in which scenic images are projected onto a large screen to the accompaniment of traditional Irish music. The museum's treasure trove of Celtic crosses, Norman pottery, and other artifacts is displayed in "The Story of Kerry," but here, too, overly ambitious audiovisual technicians have added such distractions as faux newsreels tracing the history of the county in modern times. The museum's big extravaganza is "Geraldine Tralee," a reconstruction of the medieval town complete with sounds and smells; an audio guide explains what's transpiring in the various tableaux. (The Geraldines are the Anglo-Norman family that more or less ruled Counties Kerry and Limerick for centuries.) All the showmanship here is a bit amateurish, and while you'll come away from the museum knowing more about local history than you did when you entered, a few rooms full of old-fashioned display cases could have achieved the same goal in less time—and a smaller outlay of cash.

TOURING TIPS The tourist office is the same building, so stock up on touring info while you're here; a cafe serves a tasty lunch selection of soups, other hot meals, and sandwiches.

LIMERICK

THIS INDUSTRIAL PORT CITY at the mouth of Shannon Estuary has thrived on its terrible portrayal in Frank McCourt's international bestseller, the Pulitzer Prize–winning *Angela's Ashes*. Fans of the memoir flock to Limerick to see for themselves the scenes of the author's grim, impoverished childhood, though the "gray place with a river that kills" is fairly natty these days. Rows of elegant Georgian houses are clustered around the city center, and even the once-grimy quays have been spruced up a bit.

You won't want to allot too much of your valuable travel time to Limerick, and you'll probably want to stay in more-appealing places such as Adare or Ennis, but a half day here is well spent.

PLANNING YOUR VISIT TO LIMERICK

ON ARTHUR'S QUAY, the **Limerick Tourism Centre** provides information on attractions in the city and throughout the Shannon region and also helps arrange accommodations. Call ☎ 061-317522 or visit **www.shannonregiontourism.ie.**

ARRIVING AND GETTING ORIENTED IN LIMERICK

LIMERICK IS JUST 25 KILOMETERS (15 miles) southeast of Shannon Airport, one of the two major international gateways to Ireland (see page 60). If traveling by car, follow route N18, one of the few four-lane highways in Ireland, which connects the city with the airport. From County Kerry, N21 leads north into Limerick; from County Cork, N20 leads to Limerick; and from Dublin, N7 crosses the center of the country to Limerick. **Bus Éireann** buses run frequently throughout the day between Limerick and Shannon Airport; the fare is about €5.20, and service runs about every hour, more frequently during morning and evening rush hours. Bus Éireann also provides service between Limerick and all other parts of Ireland. For more on Bus Éireann service, call ☎ 061-313333 or go to **www.buseireann.ie.** Limerick is on a rail line, and **Irish Rail** provides service from Dublin, Cork, Killarney, and other cities; the trip from Dublin's Heuston Station takes about two and a half hours, and the fare is about €41. For more information, call ☎ 061-315555 or visit **www.irishrail.ie.**

HOTEL IN LIMERICK

Jurys Inn Limerick ★ ★ ★

QUALITY ★ ★ ★	VALUE ★ ★ ★ ★	€59–€79

Lower Mallow Street, Limerick; ☎ 061-207000; fax 061-400966;
www.jurysdoyle.com

Location Center of Limerick. **Amenities and services** 151 units; bar, hair dryers, in-room tea and coffee facilities, laundry. **Elevator** Yes. **Parking** In nearby car park, €7.50 a day. **Price** Breakfast available from à la carte menu. **Credit cards** AE, MC, V.

DESCRIPTION AND COMMENTS   This outlet of a well-known Irish chain provides some of Limerick's most comfortable lodgings, right in the city center and very well priced, too. No-nonsense business hotel–style rooms, some with views of the River Shannon, are large and comfortable, and unlike rooms in most Irish hotels, rent for a flat rate regardless of the number of guests. Most rooms sleep three adults or two adults and two children, making Jurys a good value for families. What the hotel lacks in character it makes up for with location—Arthur's Quay shopping, the Hunt Museum, and the castle are all an easy walk away.

EXPLORING LIMERICK

O'CONNELL STREET, a row of unimposing but serviceable shops, runs through the center of Limerick. The city's flashier shopping quarter is now **Arthur's Quay,** at the northern end of O'Connell, and just north of that is the **Hunt Museum** (see below), an excellent collection of art and antiquities housed in the city's old Custom's House that no visitor to Limerick should miss. Just north, on **King's Island,** rise the city's two most famous landmarks, **King John's Castle** (see page 284) and **St. Mary's Cathedral.** The cathedral dates to 1172, but only an exquisite Romanesque doorway and parts of the nave survive intact from that time. The church is open from June to September, Monday through Saturday, 9 a.m. to 5 p.m.; October to May, Monday through Saturday, 9 a.m. to 1 p.m.; €1.30 donation.

Tours in Limerick

A COMMUNITY-BOOSTING ORGANIZATION, **St. Mary's Integrated Development Programme** leads excellent walking tours that introduce visitors to historic sights in Limerick as well as points of interest from Frank McCourt's *Angela's Ashes*. All tours cost €4, €7.50 families, and depart from St. Mary's Action Centre (44 Nicholas Street on King's Island). The 90-minute historic tours depart Monday through Friday, 11 a.m. and 4 p.m.; *Angela's Ashes* tours depart daily at 2:30 p.m.

ATTRACTIONS IN LIMERICK

Hunt Museum ★ ★ ★ ★

APPEAL BY AGE	PRESCHOOL ★ ★	GRADE SCHOOL ★ ★ ★	TEENS ★ ★ ★ ★
YOUNG ADULTS ★ ★ ★		OVER 30 ★ ★ ★ ★	SENIORS ★ ★ ★ ★

Rutland Street, Limerick; 061-312833; www.huntmuseum.com

Type of attraction Museum of art and antiquities. **Admission** €7.20 adults, €5.80 seniors and students, €3.50 children, €16.50 families of up to 2 adults and 2 children. **Hours** Monday–Saturday, 10 a.m.–5 p.m.; Sunday, 2p.m.–5 p.m. **When**

limerick

NORTHERN IRELAND

Dublin

Limerick City

REPUBLIC OF IRELAND

■ **Accommodations**
1. Jurys Inn Limerick

● **Attractions**
2. Hunt Museum
3. King Johns's Castle

◆ **Dining**
4. Green Onion

Nicholas St.

■ St.Mary's Cathedral

Merchants Quay

Mary St.

Georges Quay

Charlotte Quay

Michael St.

Clancy Strand

Arthur's Quay

Francis St.

Patrick St.

Sarsfield Bridge

Denmark St.

Mungret St.

William St.

■ Milk Market

River Shannon

Henry St.

O'Connell St.

Cecil St.

Roches St.

Catherine St.

Glentworth St.

To Foynes and Glin

Mallow St.

Parnell St.

Hartstonge St.

Pery Square

Bus & Rail ■ Station

People's Park

To Adare

0   1/8 mile
0   100 meters

N

Information ⓘ
Post Office ✉

to go Anytime. **Special comments** The museum hosts Sunday-evening concerts and frequent lectures; the ground-floor Du Cartes Café is an appealing spot for lunch or, if you want an early dinner after a museum visit, try the Green Onion, across the street (see page 285). **How much time to allow** About 2 hours.

DESCRIPTION AND COMMENTS Barely a decade old, this handsome museum occupies Limerick's elegant 18th-century Customs House. On display are the amazing collections of the late John and Gertrude Hunt, avid collectors themselves and advisers to noted collectors such as William Randolph Hearst and the Aga Khan. The Hunts' wide-ranging tastes and vast knowledge are what make the excellent displays in this museum so fascinating. The couple amassed a trove of Celtic and medieval artifacts second only to those on display at the National Museum in Dublin, along with 18th-century ceramics, 19th- and 20th-century paintings by Renoir and Picasso, and other decorative arts spanning the centuries. Three of the most stunning artifacts are a shield from the eighth century BC, a ninth-century-AD cross from County Antrim in Northern Ireland, and a bronze horse believed to have been crafted by Leonardo da Vinci. But the pleasure of visiting this eclectic and charming collection—small enough not to overwhelm— is just to wander and come upon the many unexpected treasures that most attract your notice.

TOURING TIPS Take advantage of one of the free guided tours often available; these show off the highlights or focus on one period, such as medieval artifacts, or one topic, such as jewelry.

King John's Castle ★ ★ ★ ½

APPEAL BY AGE	PRESCHOOL ★★★	GRADE SCHOOL ★★★★	TEENS ★★★★
YOUNG ADULTS ★★★★		OVER 30 ★★★★	SENIORS ★★★★

King's Island, Limerick; ☎ 061-360788; www.shannonheritage.com

Type of attraction Restored medieval castle. **Admission** €7.50 adults, €5.95 seniors and students, €4.50 children, €18 families. **Hours** January–February and November–December, daily, 10 a.m.–4:30 p.m.; March–April, daily, 9:30 a.m.– 5 p.m.; May–October, daily, 9:30 a.m.–5:30 p.m. **When to go** In good weather, if possible, to enjoy the ramparts and courtyard. **Special comments** Try to be in Limerick at some point after dark to see the castle illuminated by floodlights. **How much time to allow** About 2 hours.

DESCRIPTION AND COMMENTS This imposing 13th-century fortress, built by order of King John of England on an island in the heart of the city, is especially impressive when viewed from across the rivers that surround it, with the long, high walls and round towers rising above the water. The castle is one of Ireland's most intact medieval monuments, and massive restorations and ongoing archaeological excavations ensure a rich and informative visit that includes a heady mix of Viking houses, a reconstructed medieval courtyard where costumed craftspeople and merchants ply their trades, and rampart walks. An excellent audiovisual presentation brings to life events such as the siege of 1642, which all but destroyed the castle and the rest of Limerick. Much of what we know about the siege was brought to light by a soldier's diary that is among a thousand-some artifacts unearthed in the castle to date. The city and castle repelled another siege, this one by William of Orange, when Irish troops retreated to the castle after the Battle of the Boyne in 1690.

TOURING TIPS Kids probably will get bored with some of the archaeological displays, in which case you might want to let them enjoy the medieval courtyard while you tour the galleries. Combine a visit to the castle with a look at St. Mary's Cathedral, also on the island.

RESTAURANTS IN LIMERICK

MANY OF LIMERICK'S HISTORIC PUBS SERVE DECENT MEALS as well as pour a fine pint. Especially atmospheric is the 300-year-old **Locke** (2A-3 George's, ☎ 061-413733), where you'll find fresh seafood along with traditional Irish music on Sundays and Tuesdays. **Du Cartes Café** in the Hunt Museum (see page 282) is a good spot for lunch.

Green Onion ★★★★

MODERN IRISH	MODERATE	QUALITY ★★★½	VALUE ★★★

Old Town Hall Building, Rutland Street, Limerick; ☎ 061-400710

Reservations Recommended for dinner. **Entree range** €13–€22. **Payment** AE, MC, V. **Bar** Full service. **Disabled access** Yes. **Hours** Monday–Saturday, noon–10 p.m.

MENU RECOMMENDATIONS Daily salad specials, wild-mushroom-and-garlic soup, steak and Guinness stew.

COMMENTS Limerick's most talked-about restaurant hasn't changed with the justifiable fame it's earned over the years—the softly lit two-level dining room still has an informal air to it, augmented with jazz in the background. This is the sort of place where you'll want to linger awhile. The cafe is crowded most evenings, about as close to a scene as Limerick stages, but it is especially mellow in the afternoon and early evening.

SHOPPING IN LIMERICK

THE CITY'S SMART NEW SHOPPING COMPLEXES are **Arthur's Quay** and **Cruises Street Shopping Centre,** both in the city center. These malls have done much to revitalize downtown Limerick, although travelers looking for a slice of old Ireland may be disappointed to discover that, with some exceptions, they provide a fairly generic blend of find-them-anywhere shops. More authentic are the locally crafted sweaters and other garments at 100-year-old **Irish Handicrafts** (26 Patrick Street, ☎ 061-415504). **Milk Market,** east of the city center at Ellen and Wickham streets, houses a decent Saturday-morning food market, when wonderful produce and cheeses from throughout central Ireland fill the stalls; on Fridays, arts and crafts take over the premises.

ENNIS

MANY TRAVELERS SPEED RIGHT PAST Ennis en route to County Kerry, Galway, and other better-known places to the north and south, but don't do the same. The seat of County Clare boasts only one great monument, **Ennis Friary,** but it's an appealing place of medieval appearance, with narrow lanes and attractive old houses along the banks of the River Fergus.

PLANNING YOUR VISIT TO ENNIS

THE ENNIS TOURIST OFFICE is on Arthur's Row, O'Connell Square; ☎ 065-682-8366; it is

unofficial **TIP**
Ennis is a good place in which to alight after arriving at Shannon Airport or to enjoy a last night before flying home (**Dromoland Castle** is well geared to a splurge).

open from May to September, Monday through Saturday, 9:30 a.m. to 5:30 p.m.; Sunday, 9:30 a.m. to 1 p.m. and 2 p.m. to 5:30 p.m.

Special Events in Ennis

Ennis is known for its traditional music, performed at pubs around the town and at the **Glór Irish Music Centre** on Friar's Walk. For a week in late May, the **Fleadh Nua** brings together musicians and dancers for one of Ireland's largest festivals of traditional music; ☎ 065-686-7777. The **Ennis Trad Festival** in early November also showcases traditional music as well as jazz and bluegrass; ☎ 065-684-4522.

ARRIVING AND GETTING ORIENTED IN ENNIS

ENNIS IS 25 KILOMETERS (15 miles) north of Shannon Airport and 37 kilometers (20 miles) north of Limerick, connected to both by N18. **Bus Éireann** buses connect Ennis with many cities in Ireland, although many connections are through Limerick. The same is true of train service. For more on Bus Éireann service, call ☎ 061-313333 or go to **www.buseireann.ie.** For more information on **Irish Rail** service, call ☎ 061-315555 or visit **www.irishrail.ie.** Bus Éireann also provides service throughout the day between Shannon Airport and Ennis; the fare is about €5 and buses run about every hour, more frequently during morning and evening rush hours.

HOTELS IN AND AROUND ENNIS

 Dromoland Castle ★ ★ ★ ★ ½

QUALITY	★ ★ ★ ★ – ★ ★ ★ ★ ½	VALUE	★ ★ ★ ½	€150–€500

Newmarket-on-Fergus, County Clare; ☎ **061-368144; fax 061-363355; sales@dromoland.ie; www.dromoland.ie**

Location Outside the village of Newmarket, at Dromoland exchange off N18, about 16 kilometers (10 miles) north of Shannon Airport. **Amenities and services** 100 units; 2 bars, beauty salon, bicycling, business center, fishing, gardens, golf, gym, hair dryers, horseback riding, in-room tea and coffee facilities, Internet connections, nonsmoking rooms, 2 restaurants, room service, safes, shop, spa, swimming pool, tennis, walking. **Elevator** Yes. **Parking** Free valet. **Price** Includes full Irish breakfast; many special offers available. **Credit cards** AE, DC, MC, V.

One of Ireland's best-known castle hotels is a delightful warren of finely paneled galleries and twisting stone passageways that manages to be both grandly impressive and comfortably welcoming. The staff works very hard to make guests feel at ease, and the relatively few public rooms are nicely outfitted with cushy chairs and sofas custom-tailored for long hours of reading in front of a fire. (Public areas tend to be crowded, though, and the castle is in need of at least one more lounge in which guests can relax.) Many of the guest rooms, especially those in the older part of the hotel, are luxuriously large and supremely appointed with firm king-size beds, cozy arrangements of couches and armchairs, and double sinks and separate tubs and showers in the commodious bathrooms. Rooms in a relatively unobtrusive new addition across the entrance court match the hotel's high standards, but even their grand size and such amenities as luxurious marble baths can't conceal the smack of cookie-cutter newness. Ask about the various styles of accommodations when booking, and if you want genuine character, request a room in an older part of the hotel. Dromoland is just minutes from Shannon Airport, so the hotel is ideally situated for a grand introduction to Ireland or a treat-yourself last-night splurge. With a world-famous golf course, an indoor pool overlooking a walled garden, and miles of walking paths crisscrossing the grounds, the castle offers plenty of diversions, so don't overbook on sightseeing excursions. Instead, take time to relax and get the most out of these extraordinary surroundings.

The Old Ground ★ ★ ★ ★

QUALITY	★ ★ ★	VALUE	★ ★ ★ ★ ½	€80–€120

O'Connell Street, Ennis, County Clare; ☎ 065-682-8127; fax 065-682-8112; reservations@oldgroundhotel.com; www.flynnhotels.com

Location Center of Ennis. **Amenities and services** 114 units; bar, cafe, hair dryers, in-room tea and coffee facilities, restaurant, room service, trouser press, turndown service. **Elevator** Yes. **Parking** Free, on grounds. **Price** Includes full Irish breakfast; many special offers available. **Credit cards** AE, DC, MC, V.

This ivy-covered house in the center of Ennis, dating from the 18th century, has served as a town hall and jail at various times in its long history. The house yields few surprises within its thick old walls. Furnishings in the guest rooms are by-the-book traditional, with canopied beds, wing chairs, and heavy chests. These rooms are well done and well appointed, and all have up-to-date bathrooms, but they're a bit characterless; even a whole floor of new rooms is infused with a predictable patina of tradition. A little more quirkiness would be most welcome, although you'll find plenty of charm and character in the delightful staff. The lounge, library, and other public rooms are more atmospheric than the guest quarters, with genuine antiques, open fires, and charming bow windows. A cozy bar, the Poets Corner, hosts live music sessions in the evenings, and the delightfully airy Town Hall Café is a nice place for a cup of coffee or light meal.

EXPLORING ENNIS

THE RIVER FERGUS SURROUNDS THE OLD CENTER of Ennis, giving the town its name—*inis* means "island" in Irish—and riverside walks follow the torrent. From the riverbanks, narrow streets, connected by arches known as bow-ways, twist and wind through the town's medieval layout, although many of the handsome, brightly colored houses are from the 19th century. The finest remnant of medieval Ennis is the Friary, founded in 1240 by Donnchadh Cairbreach O'Brien, King of Thomond, and now in ruin (later generations of Thomonds built nearby Bunratty Castle; see profile below). Two of the town's great-est heroes are commemorated with statues. Daniel O'Connell (1775–1847), whose Derrynane House can be visited in County Kerry (see page 252), was known as "The Liberator" for his efforts on behalf of Catholic emancipation, and he represented County Clare in Parliament from 1828 to 1831. Eamon De Valera (1882–1975) was born in the United States but returned to his ancestral County Clare and served as prime minister of Ireland from 1937 to 1959 before becoming president.

ATTRACTIONS IN AND AROUND ENNIS

IN ADDITION TO THE FAMOUS DROMOLAND and Bunratty castles, among the many other castles that surround Ennis is **Dysert O'Dea,** nine kilometers (six miles) north in Corofin. Built in 1480, this impos-ing tower house is now filled with Bronze Age to medieval artifacts from 25 nearby monuments, all of which can be reached on foot from the castle. It's open daily, May 1 to September 30; admission is €4 adults, €3.50 students and seniors, €10 families, free for children under age 5; ☎ 065-683-7401.

kids Bunratty Castle and Folk Park ★ ★ ★ ★ ½

APPEAL BY AGE   PRESCHOOL ★★★★½   GRADE SCHOOL ★★★★★   TEENS ★★★★★
YOUNG ADULTS. ★★★★★   OVER 30 ★★★★½   SENIORS ★★★★½

Off N18, Bunratty, County Clare; ☎ 061-360788; www.shannonheritage.com

Type of attraction Restored medieval castle and re-creation of Irish rural life. **Admission** €11 adults, €8.50 students and seniors, €5.95 children, €26 families. **Hours** January–March and November–December, daily, 9:30 a.m.–5:30 p.m.; April–May and September–October, daily, 9 a.m.–5:30 p.m.; June–August, daily, 9 a.m.–6 p.m. **When to go** Try to avoid weekends, when the castle and park can be especially crowded. **Special comments** Bunratty is not to be missed for families with younger children; the park staff makes young visitors feel especially welcome, and craft demonstrations, grazing animals, and cottage visits will keep them amused for hours. **How much time to allow** At least half a day.

DESCRIPTION AND COMMENTS Ireland's most intact medieval castle is also one of the country's most visited tourist attractions, known to busloads of visitors as the scene of nightly banquets. Home to the O'Briens, Earls of Thomond, from around 1500, the tall fortress has been beautifully restored down to its last medieval timber and is filled with stunning 15th- to 17th-century furnishings. Despite the crowds and the commercial buzz, the castle is a pleasure to visit (forgo the banquet, though, unless you think you might enjoy eating mediocre food with hundreds of strangers as wenches sing "When Irish Eyes Are Smiling"). Even when the castle is jammed with visitors, rooms such as the Great Hall and the paneled guest apartments manage to evoke life in a medieval castle.

The adjoining Folk Park is a serious undertaking that manages to be a heck of a lot of fun and educational at the same time. A complete village is pleasant but the least successful re-creation in the park—many authentic villages await you on your Irish travels. Far more interesting are the laborers', farmers', and fishing families' cottages, some moved intact from other locales and all authentically furnished. Some, such as the Byre dwelling, are extremely humble cottages in which families and livestock shared one earthen-floored room. Golden Vale is the well-furnished home of a prosperous farmer, and the Victorian-era, stuffily comfortable Hazelbrook House was the home of a manufacturer of a popular brand of Irish ice cream. A walled garden flourishes, yielding a healthy amount of fresh produce, and water mills continue to function. During the summer the grounds are abuzz with blacksmiths, millers, and other costumed craftspeople demonstrating the old ways, but even without them the Park does an admirable job of portraying a way of life that endured in Ireland until not too many decades ago.

TOURING TIPS Mac's Pub, in the re-created village, serves light meals and a good pint of Guinness.

Craggaunowen ★ ★

APPEAL BY AGE	PRESCHOOL ★ ★	GRADE SCHOOL ★ ★ ★ ★ ★	TEENS ★ ★ ★ ★
YOUNG ADULTS ★ ★ ★ ★		OVER 30 ★ ★	SENIORS ★ ★

Near Quin, County Clare, about 30 kilometers (18 miles) north of Bunratty; ☎ 061-360788; www.shannonheritage.com

Type of attraction A re-creation of prehistoric Ireland. Admission €7 adults, €4.20 for children ages 6–18, free for children under age 6, €17.50 families of up to 2 adults and 4 children. Hours April–mid-October, daily, 10 a.m.–6 p.m. When to go In good weather, if possible, because many attractions are outdoors. Special comments Kids will probably enjoy this place more than their parents will; for an outing the whole family will enjoy, Bunratty Castle and Folk Park is a much better choice. How much time to allow About 2 hours.

DESCRIPTION AND COMMENTS What will they think of next? Craggaunowen is a prehistoric theme park, with re-creations of ring forts, dolmen, and other fragments of Ireland's long past. Before you fork over the admission fee, you may well want to consider visiting the real prehistoric monuments that are so thick on the ground in Ireland. Kids may fall for the neat-looking *crannog,* a fortified island dwelling, and the costumed Celts and Iron Age farmers, but their parents might be reminded of Fred Flintstone and Barney Rubble. One of the most interesting artifacts here is the leather-hulled boat in which Tim Severin sailed across the Atlantic to re-create St. Brendan's alleged sixth-century voyage to the New World.

TOURING TIPS Adjoining Craggaunowen Castle, the real McCoy and built in 1550, towers over the park. Also nearby is Kannpogue Castle, in Quinn; here you should enjoy the view from the outside (especially dramatic when the castle is floodlit at night) and spare yourself the €11 entrance fee.

Ennis Friary ★★★

Abbey Street, town center; ☎ 065-682-9100; www.heritageireland.ie

Type of attraction Ruins of monastic complex. **Admission** €1.50 adults, €1 seniors, €0.75 children and students, €4.25 families. **Hours** April–May and mid-September–October, 10 a.m.–5 p.m.; June–mid-September, daily, 10 a.m.–6 p.m. **When to go** Anytime. **Special comments** When the friary is closed, you can get a decent view of the ruins through the gates. **How much time to allow** About 30 minutes–1 hour.

DESCRIPTION AND COMMENTS Founded in 1240 and one of Ireland's great medieval centers of learning, this large, now ruined monastic complex once housed 350 monks and as many as 600 students. The old moss-covered stones still evoke the friary's great wealth and importance. Among the many carvings that litter the ruins are an endearingly primitive statue of St. Francis and the alabaster MacMahon tomb. An elegant stone window frame still graces the chancel, and the 15th-century tower rises above the ruins.

TOURING TIPS After touring the friary, step into Cruise's Pub, in a 17th-century house next door, for a drink or a light meal; the low ceilings, beams, and open hearths seem much in keeping with the medieval atmosphere of the friary, and the patio overlooks the ruins.

RESTAURANTS IN AND AROUND ENNIS

MEDIEVAL CASTLES ARE POPULAR DINING SPOTS in these parts. The experience doesn't have a lot to offer aside from the thrill of feasting in a genuine banqueting hall: food and entertainment are generally bland, and your entertainment budget will go a lot further if you opt for a more authentic experience, such as enjoying a pint and some traditional music in a pub. Banquets are staged year-round at 5:30 p.m. and 8:45 p.m. at **Bunratty Castle and Folk Park,** €48.50; and April to October at 7 p.m. at **Knappogue Castle,** €47.50. Call ☎ 061-360788 for more information and to make reservations.

The Cloister ★★★½

Club Bridge, Abbey Street, County Clare; ☎ 065-682-9262

Reservations Recommended. **Entree range** €14–€23. **Payment** AE, DC, MC, V. **Bar** Full service. **Disabled access** Yes. **Hours** Daily, 12:30–3 p.m. and 6–9:30 p.m.

MENU RECOMMENDATIONS Fresh mussels, oysters, and other seafood.

COMMENTS The scent of turf fires permeates these beamed rooms built into the remains of a 13th-century church, overlooking the monastery gardens. Part of the premises are given over to a publike room where excellent lunches are served and traditional music is often played, but evening dining is a serious business, too, with an emphasis on local seafood and game.

Durty Nellie's   ★ ★ ½

| PUB FARE | MODERATE/INEXPENSIVE | QUALITY ★★½ | VALUE ★★★ |

Next to Bunratty Castle, Bunratty, County Clare; ☎ 061-364861

Reservations Not accepted. **Entree range** €8–€20. **Payment** AE, MC, V. **Bar** Full service. **Disabled access** Yes. **Hours** Daily, 11:30 a.m.–10 p.m.

MENU RECOMMENDATIONS Sandwiches and other light meals.

COMMENTS Given the hordes of visitors who pass through the doors, this character-filled 400-year-old pub—once a drinking spot for the guards at the adjacent Bunratty Castle—does a commendable job of preserving some atmosphere, serving passable food, and even offering live music on occasion. Keep your menu choices simple, and don't even think of darkening the doorway if you're looking for an authentic Irish-pub experience—this is an unabashed tourist trap.

ENTERTAINMENT AND NIGHTLIFE IN ENNIS

AT THE EDGE OF THE OLD CITY on Causeway Link, the **Glór Irish Music Centre** is a strikingly designed theater that stages traditional music and dance concerts as well as drama and other events. Check the schedule to see what's on tap when you're in Ennis: call ☎ 065-684-3103 or visit **www.glor.ie.** Ennis keeps more than 60 pubs in business, many of which host traditional-music sessions. Some of the most atmospheric are **Ciaran's** (1 Francis Street, ☎ 065-684-0180), **Paddy Quinn's** (7 Market Street, ☎ 065-682-8148), and **Cruise's** (Abbey Street, ☎ 065-684-0180).

SHOPPING IN AND AROUND ENNIS

THE BELLEEK SHOP (36 Abbey Street, ☎ 065-682-9607) stocks an impressive array of Irish china and crystal, including a line by the eponymous china house, as well as selections from other big-name European producers. **Custy's** (2 Francis Street, ☎ 065-682-1727) does the town's musical heritage proud with a good selection of music by traditional artists, as well as instruments. Bunratty Castle, not surprisingly, adds shopping to its tourist-oriented activities. **Bunratty Village Mills** (on the castle grounds, ☎ 061-364321) is a collection of shops housed in quaint cottages that sell crystal, tweeds, and other Irish products, some tacky but many of high quality.

EXERCISE AND RECREATION
IN AND AROUND ENNIS

ONE OF MANY 18-HOLE GOLF COURSES IN THE REGION, the **Ennis Golf Club** (Drumbridge Road, ☎ 065-682-4074), charges a modest €25 to €35 for a round; **Dromoland Golf Club,** on the grounds of the castle hotel (see page 286) and one of the most famous courses in Ireland, charges €100. Walkers have a choice of several well-marked routes through the County Clare countryside, including the **Mid-Clare Way,** which leads to the **East Clare Way,** providing almost 300 kilometers (180 miles) of walks along paths and country lanes through spectacular scenery; ask for maps and information at the tourist-information office in Ennis.

KILRUSH

THIS ATTRACTIVE TOWN ON THE WEST CLARE PENINSULA is deceptively grand at first appearance. The wide streets and large central square, which give the impression that Kilrush is more prominent than it really is, are part of an improvement scheme by 18th-century landlords, the Vandeleurs, who attempted to put Kilrush on the map as a model estate town. For most travelers the real appeal of Kilrush is its off-the-beaten-track location and proximity to rugged, little-visited coastal scenery. Kilrush is a good place to stop for a day or two as you travel north to County Galway or south to County Kerry; you'll get a nice glimpse of an Irish country town that's relatively unconcerned with tourism.

PLANNING YOUR VISIT TO KILRUSH

The **Kilrush Tourist Information Centre** (in the center of town on Moore Street) is open June to September, daily, 9 a.m. to 6 p.m.; ☎ 065-905-1577. Outside of these hours, you can consult information boards in the town square for listings of hotels, restaurants, and services.

ARRIVING AND GETTING ORIENTED IN KILRUSH

KILRUSH IS ABOUT 45 KILOMETERS (27 miles) west of Ennis on N68, about a 45-minute trip by car. **Bus Éireann** buses connect Kilrush with Ennis, where you can make connections to Galway, Dublin, Cork, and other parts of Ireland; buses run about every three hours (more frequently during the summer), and the trip takes a little less than an hour; the fare is about €10. For more information, call ☎ 061-313333 or go to **www.buseireann.ie.**

If you're approaching County Clare from the south, you might want to cross the Shannon Estuary on the car ferry that runs between Tarbert, in County Limerick on the south side of the estuary, and Killimer, on the north side near Kilrush. If you're traveling, say, from the Dingle Peninsula, and want to see the sights of West Clare, the 20-minute ferry crossing saves you the 130-kilometer (80-mile) loop around the Shannon Estuary through Limerick. Ferries run year-round, daily, with departures every hour. The fare is €15 one way, €25 round trip, for one car plus passengers. For more information, call ☎ 065-905-3124 or visit **www.shannonferries.com.**

HOTEL IN KILRUSH

Hillcrest View Bed and Breakfast   ★ ★ ★ ½

| QUALITY   ★ ★ ★ ½ | VALUE   ★ ★ ★ ★ | €40–€70 |

Doonbeg Road, Kilrush, County Clare; ☎ 065-905-1986;
fax 065-905-1900; ethnahynes@eircom.net; www.hillcrestview.com

Location At the edge of Kilrush. **Amenities and services** 6 units; garden, hair dryers, in-room tea and coffee facilities, lounge. **Elevator** No. **Parking** Free, on grounds. **Price** Includes full Irish breakfast. **Credit cards** MC, V.

Ethna and Austin Hynes show great prowess as innkeepers at their stylish and comfortable bed-and-breakfast, the nicest lodging in Kilrush. The couple began by hosting guests in two tidy bedrooms in the front of the family home. In the late 1990s, they built a thoughtful addition with four new rooms designed to their specifications, two upstairs and two on the ground floor. These new rooms are especially comfortable, large, and sunny, with polished-pine floors, firm beds, attractive yet unobtrusive furnishings, thoughtful lighting, and windowed bathrooms equipped with excellent showers. Austin cooks a delicious breakfast (including homemade porridge) that Ethna serves in a conservatory overlooking a walled garden. It's a wonderful place to relax after a day of sightseeing.

EXPLORING KILRUSH AND THE WEST CLARE PENINSULA

TWO EXHIBITIONS IN KILRUSH PLOT THE REGION'S HISTORY. The **Kilrush Heritage Centre,** in the Town Hall on Market Square, concentrates on the local landlords, the Vandeleurs, and how they developed Kilrush as an estate town. The exhibit tells you a little more than you ever thought you wanted to know about Kilrush, but the detailed explanation of estate towns, common throughout Ireland, is revealing, as are the sad details of the plight of the tenants during the Famine. The center is open June to August, daily, 10 a.m to 6 p.m.; admission costs €4 adults, €1.50 children, €7 families; ☎ 065-905-1047. The **Scattery Island Centre,** on Merchants Quay, tells the story of the monastic community founded by St. Senan in the sixth century on an island just offshore from Kilrush; it is open from June to mid-September, daily, 10 a.m. to 6 p.m.; admission is free; ☎ 065-905-2139. From the harbor you can see the stark and spooky ruins of the round tower and several churches. In the summer, fishermen make extra cash ferrying the curious who want a close-up look at the island (beware, though, as one of St. Senan's accomplishments was slaying an enormous sea monster out there); boats run irregularly, depending on demand, and the fare is about €15 round trip.

Kilrush is at the edge of the West Clare Peninsula, a finger of land that juts into the mouth of the Shannon and the Atlantic. The peninsula is far off the well-beaten tourist track, so you'll feel as if you have the rugged coastal scenery to yourself. The well-marked

Loop Head Drive begins in the seaside town of Kilkee, follows the high cliffs of the Atlantic coast southwest to Loop Head lighthouse, and then heads back to Kilkee on the south side of the peninsula, along the mouth of the Shannon.

Kilkee, 12 kilometers (8 miles) west of Kilrush, might seem alien to Americans who have a preference for long, deserted beaches and easygoing seaside towns. The Victorian-era bathing resort is a tidy and densely packed collection of brightly colored row houses that have been the summer quarters of generations of Irish families. An air of gentility hangs over the town, and a long seaside promenade follows a sheltered, sandy strand on a bay that provides safe swimming. Pools in the rocks at the edge of the bay, known as the Pollock Holes, teem with fish and plant life and are especially popular with snorkelers.

Kilkee is the starting point of the **Loop Head Drive,** a thrilling route along the rugged and unspoiled coast. The loop is much less traveled than more famous scenic coastal drives on the Ring of Kerry and Dingle Peninsula, imparting a sense that you've found a corner of wild Ireland. The scenery just south of Kilkee along the Atlantic is especially dramatic. Here, a narrow road hugs the tops of high cliffs, surf crashes through blowholes, and enormous waves charge relentlessly against rocky headlands. At the **Bridges of Ross,** a natural arch spans two rocky outcroppings, providing a dizzying look at the sea crashing beneath your feet; the sense of adventure may be heightened by the fact that a second bridge crashed into the sea not too long ago. The lighthouse at the tip of the peninsula is not open to the public, but a path leads to land's end, one of many such headlands in the west of Ireland where the green landscape drops into the Atlantic surf. Just inland, along the southern coast of the peninsula, is the little village of **Kilbaha.** The modern village church shelters the **Little Ark of Kilbaha,** a relic of mid-19th-century Catholic persecution. The British, and therefore Protestant, local landlords refused to allow their Catholic tenants to build a church. When the village priests held mass in workers' cottages, the landlords had the cottages torn down. One enterprising priest, or so the story goes, went to Kilkee and saw the portable bathing boxes that were pulled, with costumed swimmers inside, to the water's edge, allowing bathers to immerse themselves without exposing themselves immodestly. The priest built a chapel in the same style, had it wheeled to the beach on Sundays, and there preached to his faithful, who knelt in the sand. At **Carrigaholt,** farther east along the peninsula, forbidding MacMahon Castle overlooks the Shannon. A "murder hole" over the entrance reveals a lot about the no-nonsense purpose of the tall fortress, the inhabitants of which once dropped burning oil and heavy objects through the hole onto the heads of would-be invaders.

ATTRACTIONS IN KILRUSH AND THE WEST CLARE PENINSULA

Dolphinwatch Carrigaholt ★ ★ ★ ★

APPEAL BY AGE	PRESCHOOL ★★★	GRADE SCHOOL ★★★★	TEENS ★★★★
YOUNG ADULTS ★★★★		OVER 30 ★★★★	SENIORS ★★★★

Carrigaholt, on the Loop Head Peninsula outside Kilrush; ☎ 065-905-8156; www.dolphinwatch.ie

Type of attraction Boat trip in the Shannon Estuary. **Hours** April 1–October 31, daily, call for schedule. **Admission** €18 adults, €9 for children ages 4–16, free for children under age 4. **When to go** Anytime. **Special comments** The M/V *Discovery*, another dolphin-watching vessel, operates out of the Kilrush Marina, with as many as 3–4 excursions per day from April to October; call ☎ 065-905-1327 or visit **www.discoverdolphins.ie. How much time to allow** 2 hours.

DESCRIPTION AND COMMENTS The mouth of the River Shannon is home to a school of bottlenose dolphins, and they are well accustomed to daily visits from the Dolphinwatch boat. But the antics of the playful creatures are just part of the show. It's a pleasure to be out in the brine-scented air of the wide Shannon Estuary where it meets the Atlantic, and the water-level views of rugged cliffs and green pasturelands are stunning. Sightings of grey seals are also common, and many species of seabirds populate the waters and surrounding shores. Commentary is intelligent, amusing, and salty at times, although it's hard to top the sound of the dolphins communicating with one another, heard through underwater microphones.

TOURING TIPS Don't rush away from Carrigaholt once the boat docks; allow some time to take a look at the 15th-century castle that once protected the port and, weather permitting, to enjoy a pint on the patio of one of the village pubs overlooking the Shannon.

Vandeleur Walled Garden ★ ★ ★

APPEAL BY AGE	PRESCHOOL ★★	GRADE SCHOOL ★★★	TEENS ★★★
YOUNG ADULTS ★★		OVER 30 ★★★	SENIORS ★★★

Killimer Road, Kilrush; ☎ 065-905-1760; www.westclare.com

Type of attraction Garden. **Admission** €5 adults, €3 seniors and students, €2 children ages 6–18, €10 families of up to 2 adults and 3 children. **Hours** Summer, 10 a.m.–6 p.m.; winter, 10 a.m.–4 p.m. **When to go** Best in spring and summer. **Special comments** A stone building at the entrance to the garden houses a pleasant coffee shop. **How much time to allow** 30 minutes–1 hour.

DESCRIPTION AND COMMENTS The Vandeleur clan came to Kilrush in 1687 and built a 400-acre estate that is still surrounded by the formidable walls you pass as you head south out of town. The house long ago fell into ruin, but a walled garden built nearby to nurture rare plantings has been beautifully restored. You might not think so when a gale blows in off the Atlantic, but Kilrush enjoys a fairly mild climate, which is enhanced by the tall walls surrounding this two-acre garden. Banana trees, hydrangeas, ferns, and roses grow in profusion, and the colorful beds are laid out along well-tended paths. Vandeleur is not the grandest garden in Ireland, but it's a delightful spot and a surprising oasis in the fairly rugged terrain of West Clare.

TOURING TIPS Much of the rest of the Vandeleur Estate is set aside as a forest park, and from the garden you can follow paths through lush woods.

RESTAURANT IN KILRUSH

Kelly's ★ ★ ★ ★

PUB FOOD	INEXPENSIVE	QUALITY ★ ★ ★ ½	VALUE ★ ★ ★ ★

Henry Street, Kilrush; ☎ 065-905-1811

Reservations Not necessary. **Entree range** €7–€15. **Payment** MC, V. **Bar** Full service. **Disabled access** Yes. **Hours** Monday–Saturday, 11 a.m.–9:30 p.m.; Sunday, 12:30–9:30 p.m.

MENU RECOMMENDATIONS Fresh seafood.

COMMENTS This friendly place looks like old Ireland, with a handsome oak bar and small tables grouped around a fire up front, and snug booths in the tile-floored dining room. Half the clientele comes in for a pint and gossip, the other half for the best food in town. Delicious open-faced prawn sandwiches on homemade brown bread are served throughout the day, and evening specials often include grilled fish fresh from the sea that day.

EXERCISE AND RECREATION IN KILRUSH

THE WATERSIDE GOLF LINKS AT THE **Kilrush Golf Club** on Ennis Road afford views over the Shannon Estuary; a round costs €30 weekdays, €35 weekends; ☎ 065-905-1138. The **Doonbeg Golf Club,** designed by Greg Norman, is a somewhat controversial course in the village of Doonbeg, north of Kilkee—the links carpet beautiful coastal dunes and hills that many locals thought should have been preserved as parkland. Greens fees are about €185; ☎ 065-905-5600.

PART EIGHT

THE WEST *of* IRELAND

IT DOESN'T MATTER IF YOU'RE TRAVELING from Kerry and Dingle to the south or Sligo and Donegal to the north. Just when you think the scenery couldn't get any better, you discover the rugged sea, mountain, bog, and moorland landscapes of the real West of Ireland. These lands west and north of the River Shannon, parts of the province once known as Connaught, are so wild—and until recently unknown—that Oliver Cromwell would condemn those who would not conform to his hard rule "to Hell or Connaught." Little wonder that the independent and uncivilized West resisted outside influences for centuries, and is still *Gaeltacht* (Irish speaking) in many parts. Do not be put off by the foreignness of this part of Ireland. The West is amazingly hospitable, relatively unspoiled, and home to a city that all Irish love, **Galway.**

CLIFFS *of* MOHER

THE CLIFFS OF MOHER, 40 kilometers (25 miles) west of Ennis on N85 and R478, rise some 230 meters (700 feet) out of the sea in an eight-kilometer (five-mile) swath of spectacular scenery. Puffins and other seabirds nest and roost on shelves of black shale and sandstone, the **Aran Islands** float in a cloud of mist in the distance, and the surf rushes ceaselessly ashore. A path follows the top of cliffs to vantage points such as **O'Brien's Tower,** a viewing platform built during the Victorian tourist days, and **Hag's Head,** a rock formation about an hour's walk south that resembles a woman looking out to

unofficial TIP
The best way to see the Cliffs of Moher is on a boat trip—you will avoid the crowds, and the perspective from the bottom of the towering rock faces is far more dramatic than it is from the top. Hour-long Cliffs of Moher cruises depart April–October, daily, from the pier in Liscannor at 9 a.m. and from the pier in Doolin at 1:30 p.m. and 5:30 p.m.; €20, with discounts for families and students. For more information and to book (strongly recommended), call ☎ 065-707-5949 or go to www.moher cruises.com.

the west of ireland

ATLANTIC
OCEAN

Newport Bay   ○ **Newport**
Clew Bay   ● **Castlebar**   [N5]
Westport   [N17]
Louisburgh ○   [N60]
[R395]   *Sheffrey Hills*   **MAYO** Claremorris ○   **Ballyhaunis** ○
[N59]   *Lough Cara*
Inishbofin   *Killary Harbour*   *Lough Mask*   ○ Ballinrobe   **Dunmore**
Inishark   Renvyle ○   *Lough Fee*   ○ Leenane   **Cong**
Cleggan ○   *Maamturk Mountains*   **Tuam** ○
Letterfrack   CONNEMARA NATIONAL PARK   *Lough Corrib*
Omey Island   ○ **Clifden**   **Maam** **Headford** ○
Ballyconneely   **Recess**   [N59]   **Cross**   **Oughterard** ○   [N17]
[R342]   ○ Screeb   **GALWAY**
Roundstone   ○ Lettermore
[R340]   **Athenry** ○
Carna ○   Lettermore ○   **Costelloe**   **GALWAY**
○ Rossaveel   **Bearna**
[R336] ○   ○   ● **Salthill**   [N6]
Inverin   **Spiddal**
Galway
Inishmore   *Black Head Bay*   [N18]
Inishmaan   **Kinvarra**
ARAN ISLANDS   *Inisheer*   **Gort** ○
Doolin ○
Cliffs of Moher   **CLARE**

NORTHERN
IRELAND

Dublin ★

REPUBLIC OF
IRELAND

0   10 mi
0   10 km   Ferry Route ◄━━━►

sea. Be advised that human visitors far outnumber seabirds at the cliffs, and the former pay €4 to park at the visitors center, a tacky shop-and-cafeteria combo. Scheduled to open sometime in 2007 is a controversial new complex buried within the cliff face, providing a James Bond–like stage set from which visitors will be able to view the sea and length of the cliffs without going outdoors.

DOOLIN

THIS SMALL VILLAGE ON THE RUGGED COAST of north Clare, six kilometers (four miles) north of the Cliffs of Moher on coastal road R479, is famous throughout the world for traditional Irish music, drawing droves of enthusiasts. The irony is, the crowds who come to enjoy a small Irish coastal town all but obliterate the small-village ambience. However, the music—although increasingly performed by musicians from throughout Europe—is generally first rate. For a bit of authentic village atmosphere, head out to **Doolin Pier,** where fishermen bring in a bounty of lobster, salmon, and other fresh catches; for a bit of exercise and some stunning scenery, walk south along the Cliffs of Moher.

HOTEL IN DOOLIN
Atlantic Coast ★ ★ ★

QUALITY ★ ★ ★	VALUE ★ ★ ★	€60–€70

The Pier, Doolin, County Clare; ☎ 065-707-4189; atlanview@eircom.net; www.bedandbreakfastireland.net/clare_atlanticview

Location On coast, near Doolin Pier. **Amenities and services** 12 rooms; garden, in-room tea and coffee facilities, lounge. **Elevator** No. **Parking** Free, on property. **Price** Includes full Irish breakfast. **Credit cards** MC, V.

Doolin is really just one long string of bed-and-breakfasts. This one manages to stand out because of its overall quality and its edge-of-the-sea location. Nearly all the rooms in the rambling two-story gabled house have views over Galway Bay to the Aran Islands and down the coast to the Cliffs of Moher; a couple of rooms on the ground floor open to a seaside lawn. The large rooms contain unobtrusive pine furniture, and the bathrooms, most with showers only, are spacious; many rooms have multiple beds for families. The upstairs hallway opens to two pleasant alcoves that are well equipped with couches and books, providing cozy places for guests to relax outside their rooms. Plus, you can walk to the pier, which makes this B&B a handy base for a trip to the Aran Islands or a cruise past the base of the Cliffs of Moher. Doolin's famous music pubs are also within walking distance.

RESTAURANT IN DOOLIN
McGann's ★ ★ ★ ★

PUB FARE	INEXPENSIVE	QUALITY ★ ★ ★ ½	VALUE ★ ★ ★ ★

Main road, near the bridge, Doolin; ☎ 065-707-4133

Reservations Not necessary. **Entree range** €10.50–€12.50. **Payment** MC, V. **Bar** Full service. **Disabled access** Yes. **Hours** Daily, food served noon–9 p.m.

How Hotels Compare in the West of Ireland

HOTEL	OVERALL	QUALITY	VALUE	PRICE
DOOLIN				
Atlantic Coast	★★★	★★★	★★★	€60–€70
GALWAY				
Killeen House	★★★★½	★★★★½	★★★★½	€100–€180
Great Southern Hotel	★★★★	★★★★	★★★½	€100–€250
Glenlo Abbey	★★★★	★★★	★★★	€155–€275
Park House Hotel	★★★	★★★★	★★★	€100–€185
Jurys Inn Galway	★★★	★★★	★★★★½	€64–€86
CLIFDEN				
Ballynahinch Castle	★★★★★	★★★★½	★★★★	€120–€240
Foyles Hotel	★★★½	★★★½	★★★★½	€50–€80
Abbeyglen Castle Hotel	★★★	★★★	★★★	€90–€170
CONG				
Ashford Castle	★★★★	★★★½	★★★	€225–€450
WESTPORT				
Delphi Mountain Resort and Spa	★★★★	★★★★	★★★	€150–€240
Atlantic Coast	★★★	★★★½	★★★	€140–€220

MENU RECOMMENDATIONS Seafood chowder, mussels with garlic.

COMMENTS Doolin's other music pubs serve food, too, but this small, cozy room hits just the right note. A turf fire takes off the chill in the cooler months, service is always friendly, the seafood is fresh from the pier, and the place is full of local chatter. Plan to arrive around 7 or 7:30 p.m. for dinner so you'll have a table when the music starts at 9:30.

ENTERTAINMENT AND NIGHTLIFE IN DOOLIN

DOOLIN'S CULTURAL LIFE—AND FAME—centers on three pubs. All offer nightly music (but not every evening in the winter; schedules vary), and the entertainment is generally first rate, best if the music is traditional. The largest and most famous of the pubs is **O'Connor's** (☎ 065-707-4133); the music is usually pretty good and decent meals are served, but the place is geared toward tourists. **McDermott's** (☎ 065-707-4328) and **McGann's** (☎ 065-707-4133), across the road from each other near the bridge on the main road, are local hangouts

How Restaurants Compare in the West of Ireland

NAME	CUISINE	OVERALL	QUALITY	VALUE	PRICE
DOOLIN					
McGann's	pub fare	★★★★	★★★½	★★★★	inexp
GALWAY					
Nimmo's	Continental	★★★★½	★★★★	★★★★	mod
McDonagh's	seafood	★★★★	★★★★	★★★★	inexp/mod
Malt House	modern Irish	★★★★	★★★★	★★★	exp
K C Blakes	modern Irish	★★★★	★★★½	★★★½	mod
The Quays	pub fare	★★★★	★★½	★★★	inexp/mod
CLIFDEN					
Owenmore Restaurant	modern Irish	★★★★	★★★★	★★★	exp
Marconi Restaurant	modern Irish	★★★½	★★★½	★★★★	mod
WESTPORT					
Quay Cottage	seafood	★★★★	★★★★	★★★½	mod

with a feel of authenticity that's lacking at O'Connor's. Pop into all three during an evening to see what sort of music is on tap. Music usually begins at 9:30 p.m. and continues until midnight.

THE BURREN

THE BURREN (DERIVED FROM *boireann,* Gaelic for "rocky land") is a plain of limestone that covers some 1,600 hectares (4,000 acres) of western County Clare, a portion of which is protected as **Burren National Park.** The land is not conducive to farming, to say the least; as one of the surveyors for Oliver Cromwell put it, this is "a savage land, yielding neither water enough to drown a man, nor tree to hang him, nor soil enough to bury." While the Burren is not hospitable to human habitation, it's a natural wonderland, home to rare butterflies, puffins and other seabirds, and goats and hares. For most of the summer, the Burren becomes a sea of color as plants flower in profusion from cracks in the limestone. The Burren was more welcoming, even forested, when prehistoric and early Christian settlers built forts and tombs here, hundreds of which still dot the stark landscape.

unofficial **TIP**

You won't miss much if you skip **Aliwee Caves,** the Burren's outpost of grossly commercialized tourism: cheese shops, a "potato bar," and other such enterprises surround the entrance to a warren of rather dull caverns. If you must visit, expect to pay a hefty €9 (€22 for families) to enter; the caves are open daily, 10 a.m.–6:30 p.m., but intermittently in December and January.

EXPLORING THE BURREN

IF YOU'RE COMING FROM THE SOUTH, you would do well to make the village of **Kilfenora** your first stop, because the **Burren Centre** (see below) does a good job of introducing the region's geology, botany, and history. From there, head east on R476, and at **Leamaneh Castle** turn north into the barren landscape. Leamaneh Castle, not open to the public, is a 15th-century fortified manor house, not much of which remains but the tall walls. At **Caherconnel,** a stone enclosure is one of the Burren's many ring forts; just north along the road is the well-marked path to the **Poulnabrone Dolmen,** a slablike tomb that dates from 2500 to 2000 BC. Another tomb, a wedge-shaped slab, is at nearby **Gleninsheen;** a neck collar found near the tomb dates to around 700 BC and is in the National Museum in Dublin. **Cahermore Stone Fort,** continuing north, was probably inhabited well into medieval times. **Ballyvaughn,** the largest town in the region, is a pleasant little crossroads and fishing village on the shores of Galway Bay. The **Burren Exposure** (see lower right) is another exhibit that captures the uniqueness of the region.

ATTRACTIONS IN AND AROUND THE BURREN

The Burren Centre ★ ★ ★

APPEAL BY AGE	PRESCHOOL ★ ★	GRADE SCHOOL ★ ★	TEENS ★ ★
YOUNG ADULTS ★ ★	OVER 30 ★ ★ ★		SENIORS ★ ★ ★

Kilfenora; ☎ 065-708-8030; www.theburrencentre.ie

Type of attraction Exhibits with multimedia displays. **Admission** €5.50 adults, €4.50 seniors and students, €3.50 children, €15 families. **Hours** March–May and October, daily, 10 a.m.–5 p.m.; June–September, daily, 9:30 a.m.–6 p.m. **When to go** Anytime. **Special comments** The center has a good tearoom, and its shop sells crafts that are a cut above the wares found in most tourist spots, including beautiful handmade Aran sweaters and eerily lifelike porcelain dolls made in the region. **How much time to allow** About 1 hour.

DESCRIPTION AND COMMENTS   The snazziest exhibit in this modest museum is a three-dimensional map of the region, a high-tech and sophisticated piece of gadgetry that allows visitors to trigger video and audio shows with a touch of a button and learn whatever they want to know about flora, fauna, or geology. Meanwhile, a 25-minute film tells the fascinating story of how this limestone wasteland came to be some 300 million years ago and why so many unique plants, many of Mediterranean origin, flourish in cracks in the rocks. Other exhibits focus on the history of human habitation in the region, explaining the significance of the many

How Attractions Compare in the West of Ireland

ATTRACTION	DESCRIPTION	AUTHOR'S RATING
THE BURREN		
Kilmacduagh	Ruins of monastic complex	★★★½
The Burren Centre	Exhibits with multimedia displays	★★★
The Burren Exposure	Exhibits with multimedia displays	★★★
GALWAY		
Galway Irish Crystal Heritage Centre	Crystal factory with a history museum	★★
CONNEMARA		
Kylemore Abbey and Garden	Manor house	★★★★
WESTPORT		
Westport House	Historic home and amusement park set in gardens	★★½

ring forts and tombs. If you are interested in knowing about this unique region, you'll find these earnest, well-done displays to be highly informative; some young travelers and those eager to hurry on to Galway and other places may be bored stiff.

TOURING TIPS Step next door to the 12th-century Kilfenora Cathedral, a fairly humble place that's partly in ruin. By an ecclesiastical fluke, the Pope is the absentee bishop of the cathedral and its diocese. Five high crosses grace the graveyard.

The Burren Exposure ★★★

APPEAL BY AGE	PRESCHOOL ★★	GRADE SCHOOL ★★★	TEENS ★★★
YOUNG ADULTS ★★★		OVER 30 ★★★	SENIORS ★★★

4 kilometers (2.5 miles) north of Ballyvaughan; ☎ 065-707-7277

Type of attraction Exhibits with multimedia displays. **Admission** €6 adults, €3.50 seniors and students, €14 families. **Hours** One week before Easter–October, daily, 10 a.m.–6 p.m. **When to go** Anytime. **Special comments** Kids probably will find the slide shows at the Burren Exposure to be more of a thrill than the rather staid exhibits at the Burren Centre. **How much time to allow** About 90 minutes.

DESCRIPTION AND COMMENTS Like the Burren Centre (see above), the Burren Exposure tells the story of this unique region with the help of sophisticated technology. Here, the exhibits are a lot slicker than those at the Burren Centre, and three slide shows cover the region's flora, geology, and human history. You'll come away from either exhibit with more or

Walks and Drives in the West

Some of Ireland's most spectacular scenery is in the West, where the landscapes encompass the soaring **Cliffs of Moher,** the stony expanses of the **Burren,** and the craggy mountains and moors and bogs of **Connemara.**

GREAT WALKS

THE BURREN

The 3.5-kilometer-long (2-mile-long) **Green Road** traverses **Burren National Park,** providing an easy way for walkers to get a close-up view of the limestone plateaus and other geological features unique to this region. The Burren Way begins in **Ballyvaughan,** on Galway Bay, and makes a 35-kilometer (22-mile) trek through the region; the southern terminus is the coastal village of **Doolin** (see page 299). The way follows some remote country tracks into the heart of the limestone plateau, where in spring and summer you'll be surrounded by exotic wildflowers growing from fissures in the limestone. Burren National Park does not have a visitors center, but you can find information on walks in this region at the **Burren Centre** and the **Burren Exposure** (see pages 302–303).

CONNEMARA NATIONAL PARK

Nature trails within the park (see page 324) are short and easy; the longest, **Sruffaunboy,** is only 1.5 kilometers (1 mile) long but shows off a section of bog and comes to an observation point over the moors where Connemara ponies graze. You may also spot some of the red-tailed deer that have been reintroduced to the park, and you can observe the lichens, moss, and orchids that flourish in the region. The most popular walk in Connemara is up the flanks of **Diamond Hill,** rising some 450 meters (1,500 feet) from the northeastern corner of the park and affording wonderful views over moors, bogs, and the **Twelve Bens Mountains.** A path to the top (not always open; check with the park's visitors center) crosses boardwalks and climbs wooded steps in many parts to prevent erosion and protect the fragile bogland environment.

less the same knowledge. It's important, though, to make a stop at one or the other before touring the area, because your appreciation of the landscape will be much greater with such an introduction. If you're coming from the south or west (Doolin, Cliffs of Moher, or Ennis), stop at the Burren Centre; if you're coming from the north (Galway), stop at the Burren Exposure.

TOURING TIPS The Whitehorn Café, next to the center, is worth a stop in itself and offers good lunches and stunning sea views.

UP CROAGH PATRICK

One of the most popular walks in Ireland follows the well-worn **Pilgrims' Path** up the flanks of this 760-meter-tall (2,500-foot-tall) mountain rising above **Clew Bay.** You see this conical-shaped peak from miles away as you make the drive between **Leenane** and **Westport.** Legend has it that St. Patrick retreated to the mountaintop for 40 days during Lent in AD 441, and while there lured all the serpents in Ireland to the side of a precipice and commanded them to slither off—and that's why you never see a snake in Ireland. As many as 25,000 pilgrims make the climb to a chapel at the summit every year; in fact, some of them crawl to the top, rendered all the more uncomfortable by all the stones and boulders that strew the steep path. The official date for the pilgrimage is the last Sunday in July, though the faithful and those who simply want to enjoy the views of Clew Bay and the mountains of Connemara make the climb year-round. The path begins in the small village of **Murrisk,** eight kilometers (five miles) south of Westport on R335, and the walk to the top and back takes a little more than two hours.

GREAT DRIVES

FROM THE CLIFFS OF MOHER INTO THE BURREN

The Cliffs of Moher provide a dramatic starting point for a drive through one of Ireland's most striking landscapes, the Burren.

The **Cliffs of Moher** (see page 297) are a spectacular eight-kilometer (five-mile) swath of sea cliffs that rise some 230 meters (700 feet) out of the surf. You can view from many different angles on a cliff-top walk (see above).

From the cliffs, follow R478 inland through a bleak, stony landscape for about ten kilometers (six miles) to **Lisdoonvarna,** a rather faded-looking spa town once famous for its sulfurous springs. You can still plunge into a sulfur bath at the **Lisdoonvarna Spa and Bath House.** If you roll into town in late September, you can also partake in the **Matchmaking Festival,** a holdover

Continued on next page

Kilmacduagh ★ ★ ★ ½

APPEAL BY AGE	PRESCHOOL ★★	GRADE SCHOOL ★★★	TEENS ★★★
YOUNG ADULTS ★★★		OVER 30 ★★★	SENIORS ★★★

About 5 kilometers (3 miles) outside Gort on the road to Corrofin; no phone; www.irelandmidwest.com

Type of attraction Ruins of monastic complex. **Admission** Free. **Hours** Sunrise to sunset. **When to go** In good weather; you'll spend much of your time here

Walks and Drives in the West (continued)

GREAT DRIVES (CONTINUED)

FROM THE CLIFFS OF MOHER INTO THE BURREN (CONTINUED)

from the days when farmers would come to town around harvest time look-ing for wives; marriages may still develop from the festivities, which include a great deal of lively music and dancing.

A trip of about ten kilometers (six miles) up to **Ballyvaughan** on coast road R477 provides sweeping views over **Galway Bay,** as well as a chance to visit the **Burren Exposure** (see page 303), an exhibit that celebrates the unique flora, geology, and human history of this region in high-tech displays.

The **Burren** (from *boireann,* Gaelic for "rocky land"), a plain of limestone that covers some 1,600 hectares (4,000 acres), unfolds as you travel south from Ballyvaughan on R480 and R476. If you're making the trip in summer, the Burren will be a sea of color as plants flower in profusion from cracks in the limestone. Many rare flowers, including Mediterranean and Arctic species, take root in fissures in the Burren's limestone.

Just outside Ballyvaughan you can visit **Aliwee Caves,** but the region's above-ground topography and prehistoric and early-Christian remains are far more interesting.

You will encounter both as you travel south, coming to such well-posted sights as **Gleninsheen** and **Poulnabrone Dolmen** stone tombs, and **Caher-more** and **Caherconnel,** two of the Burren's many ring forts (see page 302).

At **Corofin,** 23 kilometers (15 miles) south of Ballyvaughan, the **Dysert O'Dea Castle Archaeology Centre** does a good job of putting the Burren's archaeological heritage into perspective with excellent displays. The castle itself is a fascinating relic, built in the 15th century on a forlorn outcropping and surrounded by no fewer than 25 historical monuments, all within a three-kilometer (two-mile) radius via a well-marked walking route. These points of interest include an eighth-century church and a tenth-century round tower. The castle (☎ 065-683-7401) is open May through mid-October, daily,

walking through fields and crouching over stones to interpret carvings. **Special comments** If you're driving from the Burren to Galway, it's easy to reach Gort and Kilmacduagh on a short detour; at Kinvara, head south off N67 to the monastery. **How much time to allow** About 1 hour.

DESCRIPTION AND COMMENTS Of Ireland's many ruined monasteries, Kilmac-duagh stands out because of its eerie isolation on a plain at the edge of the Burren. Enough remains of the stone complex to impart a sense of the importance of Kilmacduagh, which, founded in AD 610, flourished for almost a thousand years—give or take, that is, a couple of centuries

10 a.m. to 6 p.m.; admission is €4 adults, €3 seniors and students, €2 children, and €9 families.

You will see more of the stark Burren landscape as you travel the 16 kilometers (10 miles) west to **Kilfenora** on R476. The **Burren Centre** (see page 302) is another well-done exhibit of the Burren's geology and human history.

From Kilfenora you can make the ten-kilometer (six-mile) trip back to the Cliffs of Moher on R476 and R478.

INTO CONNEMARA

A scenery-filled circuit of **Lough Corrib** provides a taste of medieval abbeys and castles, as well as the bog-and-mountain scenery of Connemara. For a longer circuit of Connemara, see page 324.

From **Galway City,** N84 follows the western shores of **Lough Corrib** to **Cong.** The lake, the second largest in Ireland, is one of the country's best spots for freshwater angling, a beautiful expanse of water that is especially appealing when it reflects a blue sky. About 15 kilometers (9 miles) north of Galway you'll come to **Annaghdown Priory,** founded by St. Brendan the Navigator in the sixth century.

Another religious ruin, that of **Ross Errilly Abbey,** stands next to the Black River about eight kilometers (five miles) up the road, near the town of **Headford.** This Franciscan community dates from the 14th century.

Cong (see page 330), another 12 kilometers (7.5 miles) north, is tucked between Lough Corrib and **Lough Mask,** just to the north. It's famous as the setting for the 1952 film *The Quiet Man,* starring John Wayne and Maureen O'Hara, and for its ruined Augustine monastery in the village center, on Abbey Street (free, always open). The monastery's famous relic, the **Cross of Cong,** is now in the National Museum in Dublin, though some structures embellished with wonderful Romanesque carvings and archways remain.

Continued on next page

of Viking raids between AD 900 and 1100. Signage is scarce, and visitors are left to pick their way across pastures littered with old stones and clusters of graves. Much of what remains dates from the peaceable centuries that followed the Norman occupation of Ireland. A round tower from the 11th century leans a bit but is remarkably intact, as are the walls of the now-roofless cathedral.

TOURING TIPS Kilmacduagh is a nice spot for a picnic; you can get supplies in Gort or other towns in the Burren.

Walks and Drives in the West (continued)

GREAT DRIVES (CONTINUED)

INTO CONNEMARA (CONTINUED)

From Cong you can begin a circuit of Lough Mask on R345. Not only will you be treated to lovely lake views, but in the village of **Ballinrobe,** 9 kilometers (5.5 miles) north of Cong, you can admire stained-glass windows by Harry Clarke, the 20th-century artisan who also fashioned the windows of the Chapel of St. Joseph's Convent in Dingle Town (see page 258).

A circuit of Lough Mask on R330 and R345 brings you, in about 40 kilometers (25 miles), back to the northern shores of Lough Corrib around the villages of **Maam** and **Maam Cross.** You're now in a typical Connemara landscape, where brown moors and bogs extend to craggy mountains. If you arrive in Maam Cross during one of the town's frequent cattle fairs, you encounter a real slice of rural Ireland. A detour of 16 kilometers (10 miles) west on N59 to brings you to **Recess** and, just beyond, **Ballynahinch Castle** (see page 328), a delightful hotel where you can have a sandwich and a pint in front of the fire in the handsome pub or take a stroll along the banks of the Ballynahinch River.

About 15 kilometers (9 miles) south of Maam Cross on N59 is the attractive village of **Oughterard,** a low-key resort on the shores of Lough Corrib. Galway City is 27 kilometers (17 miles) southeast on N59.

ALONG THE GALWAY COAST INTO CONNEMARA

You can enter Connemara the traditional way, north along N59 past the shores of Lough Corrib, or by the back door, but what a back door it is—the relatively unspoiled coast west of Galway City.

From **Galway City,** follow R336 west and north through a string of appealing seaside villages: **Spiddle, Rossaveel, Scrib,** and **Roundstone.** In

GALWAY

ONE OF IRELAND'S MOST CHERISHED cities is an agreeable place that fans out from a cluster of medieval lanes running down to the River Corrib and Galway Bay. Anglo-Normans settled the city as a trading post, and their medieval descendants—the Tribes, as the original 14 merchant families were called—established a lively commerce with far-flung ports in Spain and elsewhere around the globe that continued well into the 19th century. Given its geographic isolation in the West, Galway long remained a land apart from the rest of Ireland, allowing Irish cul-

all of these villages you'll find a smattering of thatch-roofed cottages, as well as a large contingent of Irish speakers.

After about 40 kilometers (25 miles) you'll come to **Clifden** (see page 327), an appealing town that seems especially well endowed by nature, surrounded as it is by the sea, a rocky coastline, and such typical Connemara features as bogs and mountains.

Leave Clifden to the north on the **Sky Road,** a thrill-a-minute, 14-kilometer (9-mile), cliff-hugging coast road that drops you in **Letterfrack,** about 15 kilometers (9 miles) north of Clifden. The town houses the headquarters of **Connemara National Park** (see page 324), where trails cross bogs and moors in the shadows of the Twelve Bens Mountains.

Just seven kilometers (four miles) beyond Letterfrack, N59 enters the **Kylemore Valley,** between the Twelve Bens to the south and the Dorruagh Mountains to the north and the beautiful setting of **Kylemore Abbey** (see page 325).

About 15 kilometers (9 miles) west of Kylemore Abbey, N59 comes to **Leenane,** famous for playwright Martin McDonagh's *Leenane Trilogy* but notable too for its setting on the shores of fjordlike **Killary Harbour.** This inlet carved by a glacier, extends inland for 16 kilometers (10 miles). **Mweelrea** and other Connemara peaks rise from the shores of the harbor, in which waters plunge to depths of 150 meters (495 feet). A visit to the **Leenane Sheep and Wool Museum** will give you more information that you ever realized you might want on shearing, weaving, and dyeing, as well as about the breeds that graze just outside the door. The museum is open April through October, daily, 9:30 a.m. to 7 p.m., and admission is €4; ☎ 095-42231.

The return to Galway City is direct but scenery filled. Follow R336 south to Maam Cross, and from there take N59 to Galway, passing through the lake, bog, and moor scenery that is typical of Connemara.

ture to take a strong hold here. You'll still hear Irish in the streets and cafes, and many of the Irish speakers are young students at the university. The sense of ease you're likely to feel in Galway may be bolstered by the fact that there's not a lot to see. Attractiveness is the city's main attraction, and you can spend a pleasant day simply following the many pedestrian lanes and riverside and bayside walks.

PLANNING YOUR VISIT TO GALWAY

REALLY JUST A BIG TOURIST SHOP, the **Galway Tourist Office** is handily located off Eyre Square, near the train and bus stations on *walks and drives in the west*

Forster Street; it is open from May to June and September, daily, 9 a.m. to 5:45 p.m.; July to August, daily, 9 a.m. to 7:45 p.m.; October to April, Monday through Friday, 9 a.m. to 5:45 p.m., Saturday, 9 a.m.–12:45 p.m. You'll have to stand in line to speak to someone, but the staff tends to be very helpful. If you don't want to wait, look for a copy of the *Galway Tourist Guide* or one of the other free handouts available. For more information, call ☎ 091-537700 or visit **www.westireland.travel.ie.**

Special Events in Galway

Galway's full roster of events includes the **Galway International Rally** in early February, one of Ireland's major car races; **www.galwayinter national.com.** The **Early Music Festival** in mid-May presents a week of medieval, Renaissance, and baroque dance and music concerts in theaters and churches; for more information, call ☎ 087-930-5506 or visit **www.galwayearlymusic.com.** More than 150 musicians fill Galway pubs for **Galway Sessions,** a week of traditional music and jazz concerts in June; ☎ 087-243-2644 or **www.galwaysessions.com.** The **Galway Film Fleadh Festival** screens Irish and international films, showing more than 70 features, in July; ☎ 091-751655 or **www.galwayfilmfleadh.com.** **Galway Cathedral Recitals** presents more than a month of concerts from mid-July to mid-August, **www.galwaycathedral.org/recitals.** The **Galway Races** attracts thousands of horse-racing enthusiasts the first week of August, with other meets in the fall; ☎ 091-753870 or **www.galway races.com.** The **Galway International Oyster Festival,** held in the outlying seaside villages of Clarenbridge and Kilcolgan, is a five-day party in late September with music, dancing, oyster-shucking contests, and other festivities; ☎ 091-587992 or **www.galwayoysterfest.com.** A season of classical music, **Music for Galway** presents concerts from September through April; ☎ 091-705962 or **www.musicforgalway.ie.**

ARRIVING AND GETTING ORIENTED IN GALWAY

GALWAY IS ABOUT 90 KILOMETERS (54 miles) north of Shannon Airport, an easy trip by car along N18. If you're coming from Doolin or the Burren, the quickest route takes you along N67 to its junction with N18 south and east of Galway. You'll enter the city through a series of busy but well-marked roundabouts; simply follow the signs to "City Centre." Good train service runs six times a day between Dublin and Galway. The trip takes about three hours; one-way fares begin at €29. For more information, call toll free ☎ 1850-366222 or ☎ 01-836-6222, or visit **www.irishrail.ie. Bus Éireann** coaches arrive from Dublin, Limerick, and other points in Ireland, with about 15 buses a day to and from Dublin; the trip takes about 3.5 hours and the fare is about €15 one way. For more information, call ☎ 064-34777 or visit **www.buseireann.ie.** The train and bus stations are near Eyre Square and the tourist-information office on Forster Street. You can also reach Galway by plane, on one of the two daily flights that **Aer Lingus** operates from Dublin. The airport is 16 kilometers (10 miles) east of the city center off N6.

HOTELS IN AND AROUND GALWAY

Glenlo Abbey ★ ★ ★ ★

QUALITY	★ ★ ★	VALUE	★ ★ ★	€155–€275

**Bushypark, Galway; ☎ 091-526666; fax 091-527800;
info@glenloabbey.ie; www.glenlo.com**

Location 5 kilometers (3 miles) north of Galway on N59. **Amenities and services** 46 units; bar, garden, golf course, hair dryers, in-room safes, room service, shoe shine, trouser press, 2 restaurants. **Elevator** Yes. **Parking** Free, on property. **Price** Includes full Irish breakfast; many special offers available. **Credit cards** AE, DC, MC, V.

Galway's famous country-house hotel is a 58-hectare (138-acre) estate on the shores of Lough Corrib, where an abbey, a manor house, and a tasteful new wing provide the feeling of an exclusive retreat. Glenlo, though, is not necessarily about getting away from it all: the abbey now serves as a small conference center, and two old rail cars on the property house the distinctive Pullman restaurant—these facilities are frequently booked for seminars, weddings, and other events. The most atmosphere on the property can be found in the lounges at the old house, where fine old furniture surrounds the large fireplaces. Guest rooms, most of which are in the new wing, have a bit less character. These are extremely large and very well appointed with luxurious, ultratraditional furnishings that often include four-poster beds; however, while exceedingly comfortable, the décor does not break new ground in design. Rooms vary considerably in size, view, and configuration, so if the hotel is not full, ask to see what other accommodations are available.

Great Southern Hotel ★ ★ ★ ★

QUALITY	★ ★ ★ ★	VALUE	★ ★ ★ ½	€100–€250

**Eyre Square, Galway; ☎ 091-564041; fax 091-566704;
res@galway-gsh.com; www.gshotels.com**

Location City center, on Eyre Square. **Amenities and services** 99 units; bar, hair dryers, in-house movies, in-room tea and coffee facilities, Internet access, irons, laundry and dry cleaning, nonsmoking rooms, restaurant, room service, shoe shine. **Elevator** Yes. **Parking** In nearby car park, about €10 a day. **Price** Some rates include full Irish breakfast; many special offers available. **Credit cards** AE, DC, MC, V.

Galway's grandest city-center hotel, part of an Irish chain, faces Eyre Square and, like that space, has recently undergone extensive renovations to emphasize the structure's Victorian opulence. The marble-floored entry and sunny, hearth-warmed lounges are especially appealing—grand enough to let all those who enter know that the Great Southern is still the best address in town. Many of the oversize guest rooms have been redone to capture the hotel's 1870s affluence, while others reflect a crisp yet soothing contemporary style. The top floor houses suites with their own exclusive lounge and a state-of-the-art spa facility. Tariffs vary wildly and can be quite high on weekends, when the hotel is booked by Irish visitors enjoying a couple of days in Galway, but room rates often come down considerably midweek.

Jurys Inn Galway ★ ★ ★

| QUALITY | ★ ★ ★ | VALUE | ★ ★ ★ ★ ½ | €64–€86 |

Quay Street, Galway; ☎ 091-566444; fax 091-568415; jurysinngalway@jurysdoyle.com; www.jurysinn.com

Location City center. **Amenities and services** 128 rooms; bar, cafe, hair dryers, in-room tea and coffee facilities. **Parking** In nearby car park, about €10. **Price** Breakfast not included. **Credit cards** AE, MC, V.

Location is the greatest appeal of this link in one of the U.K.'s most respected budget chains. Rooms look upon the rushing River Corrib or out to Galway Bay; the pedestrian streets of the city's charming city center, with their many pubs and restaurants, are just outside the door. The hotel's airy public areas include a contemporary bar and cafe, and the guest rooms are large, immaculate, and uniformly but pleasantly furnished in an unobtrusive standard business style. Jurys is especially well suited to families or those traveling in pairs or groups, because the hotel has a "one room, one price" policy, by which a flat rate applies to rooms no matter how many guests use them. Most rooms sleep three, either with a double and a single bed, or with a double bed and a pullout sofa. Rates vary with the demands of the season and days of the week, but always represent a good value for the standard of comfort.

Killeen House ★ ★ ★ ★ ½

| QUALITY | ★ ★ ★ ★ ½ | VALUE | ★ ★ ★ ★ ½ | €100–€180 |

Bushy Park, Galway; ☎ 091-524179; fax 091-528065; killeenhouse@ireland.com; www.killeenhousegalway.com

Location On N59, about 5 kilometers (3 miles) north of Galway. **Amenities and services** 7 units; complimentary tea, gardens, hair dryers, in-room tea and coffee facilities, nonsmoking rooms, turndown service. **Elevator** Yes. **Parking** Free, on property. **Price** Includes full Irish breakfast. **Credit cards** MC, V.

Catherine Doyle has exquisite taste and a great knack for hospitality. These qualities are on display throughout her gracious guest house just outside Galway. Public rooms include an attractive and comfortable lounge, but it's in the guest rooms that you'll most appreciate the many comforts you won't find in even the most expensive hotels: freshly cut flowers, flat-screen TVs, fine linens, crystal drinking glasses, and fluffy towels on heated racks. All of the accommodations are extremely spacious and overlook the grounds through large windows; most are suites, with attached sitting areas or small bedrooms and/or dressing rooms. Each is tastefully decorated in a different style, although the décor is not overdone. The rooms are elegant and uncluttered, with fine period chests, armoires, bedsteads, and armchairs with nearby reading lamps. The Georgian Suite is especially large, with a snug bedroom attached and an exquisite, handsomely tiled bathroom. Throughout the house, bathrooms are equipped with large basins, deep bathtubs, and, in many, separate showers. The bright, airy Garden Suite opens directly to the gardens that cover much of the 25-acre property and run down to the shores of Lough Corrib. Breakfast, served in a sun-filled dining room, includes homemade breads, preserves, and muesli, as well as farm-fresh eggs cooked to order.

Park House Hotel   ★ ★ ★

QUALITY	★ ★ ★ ★	VALUE	★ ★ ★	€100–€185

Forster Street, Eyre Square, Galway; ☎ 091-564924; fax 091-569219; parkhousehotel@eircom.net; www.parkhousehotel.ie

Location City center, off Eyre Square. **Amenities and services** 57 units; hair dryers, in-room safes, in-room tea and coffee facilities, Internet access, laundry service, nonsmoking rooms, satellite TV, trouser press, turndown service. **Elevator** Yes. **Parking** Free valet. **Price** Includes full Irish breakfast. **Credit cards** AE, MC, V.

Just steps from Eyre Square, this large hotel seems to be perpetually busy, and the lively lobby and adjacent bar are some of the town's most popular meeting spots. The Park House couples this prime location with unusually spacious accommodations that are much more sedate and relaxing than the bustling public areas. Deluxe rooms are the size of suites, with separate sitting areas, and the junior suites comfortably sleep four with plenty of extra room for lounging and working. Even the standard rooms are large; while these face an interior courtyard and don't have city views, they are extremely comfortable, and many provide a combination of queen-size and single beds to suit families. Rates vary considerably, and special offers (check the hotel Web site) provide especially good value.

EXPLORING GALWAY

YOU'LL PROBABLY FEEL IMMEDIATELY AT HOME in Galway on account of the soft gray stone; narrow, twisting streets on which the only traffic is two legged; and homely sensations that combine the tang of salt air from Galway Bay with the sound of rushing water from the River Corrib. Galway is compact, wedged as it is between the river and bay, and invites a leisurely stroll. In fact, a walk through the town is an attraction in itself: while Galway does not have major museums and other such sights—not yet, anyway—you'll find plenty to do just soaking in the local color.

The center of town is **Eyre Square,** a pretty patch of cobblestones and trees from which radiate any number of pedestrian-only lanes. The main thoroughfare, which begins on the north side of Eyre Square and runs to the River Corrib, changes its name from William Street to Shop Street to High Street to Quay Street.

You could probably find all the sustenance and goods you might ever need for your stay in Galway without ever straying from this series of streets, but the alleyways and lanes that twist away in various directions tempt you into the depths of the **Latin Quarter.** The medieval

heart of the old city gets its name from the brisk trade that once transpired from here with Spain. On the corner of Abbeygate Street is
Lynch's Castle, a sturdy 16th-century fortified house made necessary by
raids from other Irish tribes. The gloominess of this structure, home to
the prominent Lynch family, foretells the fate of one of its residents.
Judge Lynch FitzStephen was forced to hang his own son after the lad
was found guilty of murdering a Spanish sailor who had stolen his girl-
friend. The so-called Lynch Memorial Window, an elaborate carved
frame embedded in a medieval stone wall around the corner from the
castle and next to the **Collegiate Church of St. Nicholas,** marks the spot
where the deed transpired. St. Nicholas, which dates to the 14th century,
does honor to its ranking as one of Ireland's best-preserved medieval
churches with many fine carvings and gargoyles.

A more recent episode in Galway's history comes to light just around
the corner, opposite the church clock tower, in the **Nora Barnacle House.**
On June 16, 1904, James Joyce had his first date with Nora, the daughter of a Galway baker. The two married, and Joyce set his epic novel
Ulysses on this date, which he calls Bloomsday. The modest dwelling
is filled with a touching collection of the couple's photos, letters, and
other memorabilia. It is open mid-May to mid-September, Monday
through Saturday, 10 a.m. to 5 p.m.; €1.50; ☎ 091-564743.

The banks of the River Corrib are just a block away, and you can
follow the rushing torrent on the **Corrib River Walkway.** From spring
into early summer, a spectacle unfolds in the waters beneath the
Salmon Weir Bridge, when salmon climb upstream to their spawning
grounds in Lough Corrib. On an island at the western end of the
bridge rises the imposing **Cathedral of Our Lady Assumed into Heaven
and St. Nicholas,** completed in 1965 and said to be the last major stone
structure to be completed in Ireland.

Now a pub, **Tigh Neachtain,** near the intersection of High and Cross
streets, was the 18th-century home of Richard "Humanity Dick" Martin,
a local politician who promoted animal-rights legislation and patrolled
the streets looking for mistreated beasts. He was also known as "Hair
Trigger Dick" because of his dueling acuity. Quay Street ends near the
Spanish Arch and the old docks at the juncture of the River Corrib and
Galway Bay, where Spanish ships once unloaded their goods of wine
and brandy. The waterfront neighborhood just to the west of the arch is
Claddagh, a collection of thatch-roofed fishing cottages until the middle
of the 20th century, when more-conventional housing and worldly ways
replaced the close-knit, independent community.

One tradition that persists is the **Claddagh ring,** in which a pair
of hands encloses a heart topped with a crown to symbolize
love, friendship, and loyalty. If you buy a Claddagh ring in one
of Galway's many souvenir shops, be careful how you wear it. When
worn with the heart facing inward, the ring indicates the wearer is
spoken for; with the heart facing outward, the ring tells the world
that the wearer is available.

Tours in Galway

Kay Davis, a local woman who knows Galway like the back of her hand, leads two-hour walking tours through the old city from late June to September, Monday, Wednesday, and Friday, 11:30 a.m.; €8. Tours depart from the tourist-information office. For more information or for a private tour throughout the year, call ☎ 091-792431. **Lally Tours** is one of several outfits that offer bus tours of Galway. (Actually, Galway is so compact and easy to navigate on foot that only visitors with limited mobility might require a bus tour.) Fare is €10; for schedules and other information, visit the offices at 19–20 Shop Street, call ☎ 091-562-2905, or go to **www.lallytours.com.**

Corrib Princess cruises take 90-minute trips from Galway Bay up the River Corrib into Lough Corrib, providing a nice look at the city and the pastoral shoreline beyond; May to June and September, daily, 2:30 p.m. and 4:30 p.m.; July to August, daily, 12:30 p.m., 2:30 p.m., and 4:30 p.m.; €10 adults, €5 children, €9 seniors and students, and €25 families. You won't see a lot of enormous interest on the cruise, but the trip up the river is pleasant and provides a nice way to get off your feet and relax while enjoying a pint and a snack from the onboard bar.

ATTRACTION IN GALWAY

Galway Irish Crystal Heritage Centre   ★ ★

APPEAL BY AGE	PRESCHOOL ★ ★	GRADE SCHOOL ★ ★ ★	TEENS ★ ★ ★
YOUNG ADULTS ★ ★	OVER 30 ★ ★ ★		SENIORS ★ ★ ★

Dublin Road, Galway; ☎ 091-757311; www.galwaycrystal.ie

Type of attraction Crystal factory with a history museum. **Admission** €4 adults, €3 seniors and students, €2 children, €10 families. **Hours** Monday–Friday, 9 a.m.–5:30 p.m.; Saturday, 10 a.m.–5 p.m.; Sunday, 11 a.m.–5 p.m. **When to go** Anytime. **Special comments** The center has a cafeteria and, of course, an excellent shop. **How much time to allow** 1 hour.

DESCRIPTION AND COMMENTS Galway's only real pack-'em-in tourist trap is this factory, shop, and history museum. It seems as if every bus tour in the land makes a potty stop here, so expect big crowds. If you can, turn your back on the general bustle and immerse yourself in the exhibits, most of which are quite well done. Especially engaging are the displays that highlight the old way of life in Claddagh, the Irish-speaking fishing enclave on the bay at the edge of the old town (see page 315). Beware, though, that the photos of thatched-roof cottages and fisher folk mending nets will instill in you a sad nostalgia for life the way it was until the middle of the 20th century. Other displays will help you make sense of the confusing hierarchy of 14 Irish tribal families that held a grip on Galway for many centuries. *Fiona,* a nifty hooker (as the broad-hulled, thick-masted boats that sail Galway Bay are known), is preserved in all her glory. The main business at hand, though, is making and selling

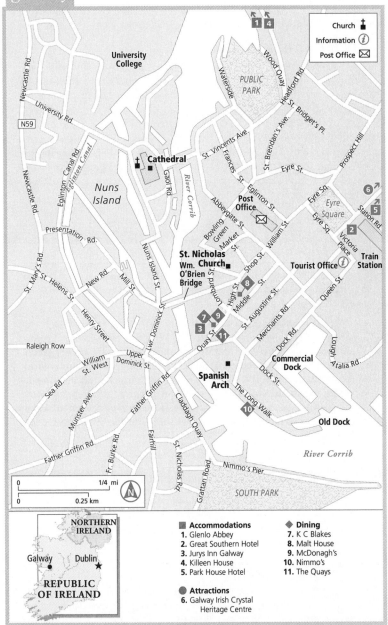

galway

Church †
Information ⓘ
Post Office ✉

University College

PUBLIC PARK

Wood Quay

Newcastle Rd.

University Rd.

N59

Eglinton Canal Rd.
Eglinton Canal

Nuns Island

Newcastle Rd.

Presentation Rd.

St. Mary's Rd.

St. Helens St.

New Rd.

Mill St.

Nuns Island St.

Henry Street

Raleigh Row

William St. West

Upper Dominick St.

Lwr. Dominick St.

Sea Rd.

Munster Ave.

Father Griffin Rd.

Fr. Burke Rd.

Fairhill

Claddagh Quay

St. Nicholas Rd.

Grattan Road

Father Griffin Rd.

Waterside

Headford Rd.

St. Bridget's Pl.

Prospect Hill

St. Vincents Ave.

St. Frances St.

St. Brendan's Ave.

Eglinton St.

Eyre St.

Cathedral †

Gaol Rd.

River Corrib

Abbeygate St.

Bowling Green

Market St.

Post Office ✉

Eyre Sq.

Eyre Square

Eyre Sq.

Station Rd.

Victoria Place

St. Nicholas Church ■
Wm. O'Brien Bridge

Lombard St.

High St.

Shop St.

William St.

Middle St.

St. Augustine St.

Merchants Rd.

Tourist Office ⓘ

Train Station

Queen St.

Lough Atalia Rd.

Quay St.

Dock Rd.

Dock St.

Commercial Dock

Spanish Arch ■

The Long Walk

Old Dock

River Corrib

Nimmo's Pier

SOUTH PARK

7 9
3
11
8
6
5
2
10
1 4

0 — 1/4 mi
0 — 0.25 km
N

NORTHERN IRELAND

Galway • • Dublin ★

REPUBLIC OF IRELAND

■ Accommodations
1. Glenlo Abbey
2. Great Southern Hotel
3. Jurys Inn Galway
4. Killeen House
5. Park House Hotel

● Attractions
6. Galway Irish Crystal Heritage Centre

◆ Dining
7. K C Blakes
8. Malt House
9. McDonagh's
10. Nimmo's
11. The Quays

crystal, and guided tours will steer you through the work areas to the fancy shop.

TOURING TIPS Paid admission is for a guided tour; you can see the history exhibits and visit the shop on your own at no charge.

RESTAURANTS IN GALWAY

YOU'LL PROBABLY NOTICE THE **Goya** name as you dine your way through Galway, as this wonderful bakery supplies bread and desserts to many restaurants. To experience the baked goods at the source, step into the delightful bakery and cafe on Kirwan's Lane (☎ 091-567010). **Sheridans** (☎ 091-564829), also on Kirwan's Lane, is well stocked with a tempting array of Irish cheeses, plus olives, sausages, and other treats for a hotel-room snack. **G.C.B.,** or **Galway City Bakery** (7 Williamsgate Street, ☎ 091-563087), is a handy stop for baked goods or a sandwich, and the upstairs restaurant serves salads and other light fare.

K C Blakes ★ ★ ★ ★

MODERN IRISH	MODERATE	QUALITY ★ ★ ★ ½	VALUE ★ ★ ★ ½

10 Quay Street, Galway; ☎ 091-561826

Reservations Recommended. **Entree range** €12–€23. **Payment** AE, MC, V. **Bar** Full service. **Disabled access** Limited. **Hours** Wednesday–Saturday, 12:30–2 p.m.; daily, 5–10:30 p.m.

MENU RECOMMENDATIONS Beef-and-Guinness stew, pasta, seafood.

COMMENTS This stone tower house is a remnant of medieval Galway, although the two dining rooms, one on each floor, are strikingly contemporary lairs with dark polished floors, soothing lighting, and colorful art. In the kitchen, the emphasis is on the freshest local ingredients, which appear at the table in deft and creative preparations, some of which are quite casual, such as open-faced sandwiches, often pairing unusual spices with standard offerings such as the freshest possible sole and salmon.

Malt House ★ ★ ★ ★

MODERN IRISH	EXPENSIVE	QUALITY ★ ★ ★ ★	VALUE ★ ★ ★

High Street, Galway; ☎ 091-567866

Reservations Recommended. **Entree range** €14–€25; €20 for two courses, 6–7:30 p.m. **Payment** AE, MC, V. **Bar** Full service. **Disabled access** Yes. **Hours** Monday–Saturday, 12:30–3 p.m. and 6:30–10:30 p.m.

MENU RECOMMENDATIONS Honey-glazed duckling, rack of lamb with parsley crust, panfried scallops.

COMMENTS A quiet courtyard off busy High Street sets the welcoming tone for this cozy hideaway, where hearty traditional fare is served in a beamed dining room. In a nod to the old-fashioned surf-and-turf concept, the menu offers steak and other meat from the land (in this case, often from the farms around Galway) and fresh-that-day seafood from local markets. Service is gracious and unhurried, and you can polish off an evening here with an after-dinner drink in the attractive bar.

McDonagh's ★ ★ ★ ★

| SEAFOOD | INEXPENSIVE/MODERATE | QUALITY ★★★★ | VALUE ★★★★ |

22 Quay Street, Galway; ☎ **091-565001**

Reservations Not necessary. **Entree range** €8–€30. **Payment** AE, MC, V. **Bar** Full service. **Disabled access** Yes. **Hours** Daily, noon–10 p.m.

MENU RECOMMENDATIONS Fish and chips, fresh oysters.

COMMENTS Galway's one-stop shop for the freshest seafood is part old-fashioned fish-and-chips restaurant, part restaurant, and part fish market. Fish and chips—fried to perfection—are made with mackerel and other fish caught that day. In the more formal restaurant you can eat simply but divinely on a heaping plate of mussels, fresh oysters on the half shell, or crab claws, washed down with a selection from the excellent wine list.

Nimmo's ★ ★ ★ ★ ½

| CONTINENTAL | MODERATE | QUALITY ★★★★ | VALUE ★★★★ |

Long Walk, Spanish Arch, Galway; ☎ **091-561114**

Reservations Recommended. **Entree range** €12–€24. **Payment** MC, V. **Bar** Full service. **Disabled access** Limited. **Hours** Tuesday–Sunday, 12:30–3 p.m. and 7–10 p.m.

MENU RECOMMENDATIONS Fish soup, beef bourguignonne.

COMMENTS One of the most romantic restaurants anywhere occupies an old stone house on a quay beside the River Corrib. The torrent rushes right beneath the windows of the rustic, heavily timbered wine bar on the ground floor and the charming candlelit restaurant upstairs. Dinner is served in both sections; a menu of daily specials often includes a hearty fish soup and succulent roast lamb. Even the desserts, "imported" from Galway's best bakery, Goya, add to the feeling that an evening here is a special night out.

The Quays ★ ★ ★ ★

| PUB FARE | INEXPENSIVE/MODERATE | QUALITY ★★½ | VALUE ★★★ |

11 Quay Street, Galway; ☎ **091-568347**

Reservations Not necessary. **Entree range** €8–€16. **Payment** MC, V. **Bar** Full service. **Disabled access** Limited. **Hours** Daily, 12:30–9 p.m.

MENU RECOMMENDATIONS Poached salmon, burgers.

COMMENTS One of Galway's most popular and atmospheric pubs incorporates carvings, pews, and arches from a medieval French church. The several levels of dining rooms are lively spots for lunch or an early dinner, when it seems that much of the working population of Galway packs in for salads, sandwiches, and hot meals that often include a nice selection of seafood. In late evenings, The Quays stages live music.

ENTERTAINMENT AND NIGHTLIFE IN GALWAY

THE WOODY, CARVED INTERIOR OF **The Quays** (11 Quay Street, ☎ 091-568347) was salvaged from a medieval French church, making this multilevel space an especially atmospheric place to hear music; not all of it, unfortunately, is traditional Irish—or particularly good. **Tigh Neachtain,** or **Naughton's** (17 Cross Street, ☎ 091-568820), is the favorite hangout of many locals and visitors, partly because the old interior has not changed in more than a hundred years and also because the nightly sessions of traditional music are reliably first rate. The Rabbitts have run their family pub, appropriately named **Rabbitt's** (23–25 Forster Street, ☎ 091-566490), since the 1870s, and the old place has changed little during their tenure. **Au Pucan** (11 Forster Street, ☎ 091-561528), just down the street from Rabbitt's, is hard to miss with its thatched roof, beneath which a loyal cadre of locals gathers for good traditional-music sessions.

Galway supports a lively theater scene. **Siamsa,** the Galway Folk Theatre, stages a summer-only show of dance, music, and folk drama that calls to mind the step-dancing format of *Riverdance*. The theater is in **Claddagh Hall,** Nimmos Pier, and operates June to August, Monday through Friday, 8:45 p.m.; €20; ☎ 091-755479 or **homepage.tinet.ie/~siamsa. Taibhdhearc Theatre** focuses on Irish-language plays, and summer brings an excellent program of song, dance, and folk drama in a handsome theater on Middle Street; performances run July to August, Monday through Friday, 8:45 p.m.; €10–€12; ☎ 091-563600. **Druid Theatre** presents Irish drama as well as Anglo-Irish and other works from the international repertoire; year-round, 8 p.m.; €11 to €20; ☎ 091-568617 or **www.druidtheatre.com.**

In summer, if you have a car, consider an evening drive south along Galway Bay to the village of **Kinvarra.** There, **Dunguaire Castle,** a fortified medieval tower house is an imposing presence above the rocky shore. The old vaulted banquet hall is the scene of nightly feasts that are a cut above the tourist pageants staged at several other castles. Seating is limited to 55, sparing participants the bus-tour crush; the food is quite good, and entertainment includes spirited readings of works by Yeats and other Irish poets. Banquets are staged April to October, nightly, at 5:30 p.m. and 8:30 p.m. For information and reservations, call ☎ 061-360788 or visit **www.shannonheritage.com.** Kinvarra is about 25 kilometers (15 miles) south of Galway via N18 and N67.

SHOPPING IN GALWAY

CLADDAGH AND CELTIC JEWELLERY COMPANY (next to Jurys Inn at 1 Quay Lane, ☎ 091-534494; **www.claddaghandceltic.com**) carries a huge selection of Claddagh rings in silver and gold. **Mulligan's** (5 Middle Street, ☎ 091-564961) stocks a large selection of traditional Irish music, while **McCambridges** (38–39 Shop Street, ☎ 091-562259) is a good place to stock up on Irish cheeses and chocolates, as well as delicatessen-type fare for a picnic. **O'Maille** (16 High Street, ☎ 091-562696) carries a fine selection of Irish knits and tweeds, and **Treasure Chest** (William Street at Castle Street, ☎ 091-563862; **www.treasure chest.ie**) is well stocked with lines of high-quality Irish china and crystal. The **Galway Crystal Heritage Centre** (Dublin Road, ☎ 091-757311) is a strange combination—glass-blowing studio, shop, and heritage center with decent exhibits on Galway's history. The fine crystal produced on the premises is beautiful, and Belleek china and other high-line Irish crafts are also sold; note, though, that prices here are about the same as they are in any other shop.

EXERCISE AND RECREATION IN GALWAY

GOLF COURSES SURROUND GALWAY. Especially scenic links can be enjoyed at the **Galway Bay Golf and Country Club** (in Renville, ☎ 091-790503) and the **Galway Golf Club** (in Blackrock, ☎ 091-522033); greens fees at both are about €50 weekdays, €60 weekends. To explore the town and countryside by bicycle, stop in at **Celtic Cycles** (Queen Street, ☎ 091-566606), where you'll pay about €20 per day for a rental. Anglers should step into the offices of the **Western Regional Fisheries Board** (Weir Lodge, Earl's Island, ☎ 091-563118) for info on where to fish, what flies to use when, and other advice.

THE ARAN ISLANDS

THESE THREE ISLANDS—**Inishmore, Inishmaan, and Inisheer**—some 48 kilometers (30 miles) out to sea off the West Coast—retain their rugged beauty, if no longer their rugged way of life. For more than 1,000 years, fishermen and farmers on the once-remote outposts eked a meager livelihood from the rough sea and stony soil; you may have seen the hard way of life here depicted in Robert Flaherty's classic documentary, *Man of Aran* (1934). Among the illustrious visitors who have sought solitude on the islands in the past is the Irish playwright J. M. Synge (1871–1909), who set his *Riders to the Sea* here. These days, some 1,500 islanders subsist mainly on the proceeds of some 200,000 annual tourists, but they maintain their independence from mainlanders, a distinctly simple way of life, and the Irish language, spoken unless otherwise necessary. The islands have managed to escape the worst incursions of modern life and retain their beautiful landscapes, in which emerald-green fields sweep down to the sea and such fabled mainland sights such as the **Twelve Bens in Connemara** and the **Cliffs of Moher** at the edge of the Burren are within view on a clear day.

PLANNING YOUR VISIT TO THE ARAN ISLANDS

BY BOAT, YOU CAN REACH THE ISLANDS from Doolin (see page 299) on service from **Doolin Ferry Company;** several boats sail daily from the Doolin pier from mid-April through September; round-trip fare is €27 to and from Inishmore and €25 to and from Inishmaan; for more information, call ☎ 065-707-4455 or visit **www.doolinferries.com.**

Aran Island Ferries sail from Rossaveel, 37 kilometers (23 miles) west of Galway City, and from Galway during high season. You can count on three a day from April through October, at 10:30 a.m., 1 p.m., and 6 p.m., and two a day the rest of the year, at 10:30 a.m. and 6 p.m.; shuttle buses run from Victoria Place (near Eyre Square) in Galway to the Rossaveel dock. Sailings take about 45 minutes, but count on two hours for a trip that includes connections on the shuttle bus. Round-trip fares are €19 adults, €15 seniors and students, and €10 children. The shuttle bus costs €6 extra round trip. In summer, you can travel directly from Galway Dock, for an extra €6.50 per ticket. You can purchase tickets at the **Galway Tourist Office** (see page 309) and at the Aran Island Ferries Office on Victoria Place. There is also a ticket office on the dock in Rossaveel. For more information, call ☎ 091-568903 or visit **www.aranislandferries.com.**

You can reach the islands by air on **Aer Arann Islands,** with ten-minute flights from Connemara Airport, 32 kilometers (20 miles) west of Galway City, to the three islands. Service departs almost hourly from April through September and three times a day out of season, at 9 a.m., 10:30 a.m., and 3 p.m. A shuttle service connects the airport and Victoria Place in Galway. Round-trip fares are €45, €25 for children; the bus is an additional €6. For more information, call ☎ 091-593034 or visit **www.aerarannislands.ie.**

ARRIVING AND GETTING ORIENTED IN THE ARAN ISLANDS

A SMALL TOURIST-INFORMATION OFFICE near the docks on Inishmore distributes a useful map of the islands and other information. The office is open June through August, daily, 10 a.m. to 5 p.m., and less frequently in the off season. Accommodations on the islands are provided by B&Bs. Arrange reservations in advance at the **Galway Tourist Office** (see page 309); the office in Inishmore can also help.

You will probably be met in Kilronan on Inishmore by a fleet of minibuses with drivers offering tours of the island. For about €10, you get a nice intro to the lay of the land in about two and a half hours. Other modes of transportation are your own feet, jaunting car (a horse-drawn carriage; an island tour for two costs about €40); and bicycle. Bikes are available from any number of outfits near the docks, including **Aran Bicycle Hire** (☎ 099-61132). The only easy way to see the other islands, which are considerably smaller, is on foot.

EXPLORING THE ARAN ISLANDS

THE BUSIEST AND LARGEST OF THE ISLANDS is **Inishmore,** eight kilometers (five miles) long and three kilometers (two miles) wide; most of its 800 or so residents live in the little settlement of **Kilronan.**

While the island has some attractions to draw your interest, the greatest pleasure of being on any of the Arans is to get away from it all and walk or bike through meadows and the small, stone wall–enclosed fields and along the coasts.

The **Island Heritage Centre** in Kilronan introduces you to the island's traditional ways, as well as its unique limestone geology and accompanying flora—the Arans are in many ways an extension of the Burren, and many of the same Mediterranean flowers that blossom there in spring and summer also sprout in the Arans. Take a seat in the Centre's theatre for one of the frequent daily showings of the hour-long *Man of Aran* for a good look at how harsh life here was not so very long ago. The Centre is open April through June, daily, 10 a.m. to 5 p.m.; July and August, daily, 10 a.m. to 7 p.m.; and September through October, daily, 10 a.m. to 5 p.m. Admission is €3.50 for the museum only, €2 extra for the film.

Inishmore's big attraction is **Dún Aenghus,** one of Europe's best-preserved prehistoric monuments, dating to about 2,000 BC. The fort, surrounded by walls that are 4 meters (13 feet) thick and 3 meters (10 feet) high, was built by Celts. This mighty enclosure now sits precariously at the edge of a 100-meter (330-foot) cliff that drops to the crashing surf, which occasionally claims sections of the ramparts. The fort is open April through October, daily, 10 a.m. to 6 p.m.; and November through March, daily, 10 a.m. to 4 p.m. Admission is €2. In high season, guides occasionally give excellent tours.

Inishmaan, with a population of about 300, is the most remote-seeming of the islands and a pleasure to explore on foot. Trails and country tracks will lead you to a smattering of sights, including the stony ruins of early Christian churches and Conor Fort, an earthen fortress that is a smaller-scale Dún Aenghus.

Inisheer, the smallest of the islands, is relatively flat and especially well suited for walking. You can hike around the island in an afternoon, taking in the flower-filled meadows and sights such as the early-Christian Church of St. Kevin. This sturdy little structure is buried in sand every winter and dug out in time to celebrate St. Kevin's Day on June 14.

CONNEMARA

JUST NORTH OF GALWAY BEGINS THE VAST and empty landscape known as Connemara. From Galway, the main road into Connemara is N59, a scenic route around the shores of Lough Corrib to the town of **Clifden,** and from there into **Connemara National Park.**

Connemara is mountainous in parts, covered with prairielike moors in others, and dotted with forests of pine and fir that surround rushing streams and glittering lakes. The largest of the lakes—in fact, the second largest lake in Ireland—is 175-square-kilometer (65-square-mile) **Lough Corrib,** one of the country's best spots for freshwater angling. You might be tempted to compare this rugged terrain to that of the American West, but Connemara is really like no place else. Its dark, brooding mountains and brown bogs create a uniquely Irish landscape that is quite desolate. Even in summer, you're likely to have parts of this wild region to yourself.

Twelve craggy mountains—the **Twelve Bens,** also known as the **Twelve Pins**—rise from the center of the region. The tallest, **Benbaun,** reaches 730 meters (2,400 feet). Bogs cover a third of the landscape, and you'll see the long, dark trenches left by turf cutters who dig turf, or peat, from the bogs, dry it, and sell it for fuel. All over Ireland you'll smell the sweet scent of turf fires dug from landscapes like this, but the supply is quickly dwindling.

Some 2,000 hectares (4,942 acres) of the region is preserved as **Connemara National Park,** which spreads across bogs and moors up the flanks of the Twelve Bens. The park's visitors center is in the village of **Letterfrack,** about 95 kilometers (57 miles) north of Galway on N59. Earnest, fairly engaging displays point out the area's geology and ecology. You'll learn about peat and how it is harvested; meadowlarks, merlins (small falcons), and other birds that inhabit the park; and the famous Connemara ponies, said to have descended from stock grounded when the Spanish Armada was wrecked offshore. Enthusiastic staffers dispense maps of hiking trails and copious advice on what to see and how best to enjoy this beautiful place. In summer, rangers guide hikes and conduct nature programs for kids. The park is open year-round, but the visitors center is open seasonally, April to May and September to mid-October, 10 a.m. to 5:30 p.m.; June, 10 a.m. to 6:30 p.m.; July to August, 9:30 a.m. to 6:30 p.m.; €2.75 adults, €2 seniors, €1.25 children and students, €7 families.

Major towns that surround the Connemara wilderness are **Clifden,** on the coast in the west; **Cong,** on the shores of Lough Corrib to the east; and **Leenane,** on the shores of Killary Harbor to the north. **Westport,** on the other side of fabled Crough Patrick from Leenane, is an appealing town on the shores of Crew Bay.

EXPLORING CONNEMARA

YOU CAN GET A NICE TASTE OF CONNEMARA in a day's outing from Galway. A good loop tour would take you out of Galway on N59, with your first stop in **Oughterard,** about 25 kilometers (15 miles) west. In this fishing village and resort you can get a good look at Lough Corrib, take advantage of some of Ireland's best freshwater angling, or embark on a lake cruise. A string of lakes lies to either side of N59 as you continue north into scenery that becomes starker and more dramatic as the peaks of the Twelve Bens begin to rise above moors and bogs. At **Maam Cross** you have the option to head north toward

Leenane and Cong, but unless you are in a hurry to get to Cong, continue west. At Recess you might want to make a slight detour to **Ballynahinch Castle** (see page 328), a delightful hotel where you can have a sandwich and a pint in front of the fire in the handsome pub or take a stroll along the banks of the Ballynahinch River. The road then passes through some of the region's most beautiful landscapes as you skirt the Twelve Bens and drop into **Clifden** (see page 327). After stretching your legs around the jaunty town square, get a taste of Connemara's seascapes on the **Sky Road.** At the end of that scenic route, N59 heads east to Letterfrack and the visitors center at Connemara National Park. Just down the road is spectacular **Kylemore Abbey** (see below), and in the village of Leenane you'll pick up route R336 and drop south to **Cong** (see page 330). From Cong, it's 35 kilometers (21 miles) back to Galway on R334 and N84. If you're continuing to Westport, head north from Leenane on N59 or R335.

Tours in Connemara

The easiest way to visit Connemara is by car, but if you're not driving, consider one of several tours that operate out of Galway. These include summer tours from **Bus Éireann,** the national bus network (☎ 091-562000 or **www.buseireann.ie**), and from **Lally Tours** (☎ 091-562905 or **www.lallytours.com**). Both provide a full day of sightseeing with stops at Clifden, Kylemore Abbey, and other sights. Fares are €22 adults; €16 for seniors, students, and children; and €55 families of up to two adults and three children. At the village of Oughterard, you can board a **Corrib Cruise** from May to September, daily, for sailings in Lough Corrib that last 90 minutes or half a day and include a stop at the village of Cong; the longer cruise also includes a quick stop to see the ruined monastic complex on Inchagoil Island. You can also board the boats in Cong. Short cruises from Oughterard: 11 a.m. and 2:45 p.m.; €12 adults, €6 children, €25 families. Long cruise: 11 a.m.; €16 adults, €7 children, €32 families. For more information, call ☎ 092-460029 or visit **www.corribcruises.com**.

ATTRACTION AROUND CONNEMARA

Kylemore Abbey and Garden ★ ★ ★ ★

APPEAL BY AGE	PRESCHOOL ★★★	GRADE SCHOOL ★★★★	TEENS ★★★★
YOUNG ADULTS ★★★★	OVER 30 ★★★★		SENIORS ★★★★

Outside Letterfrack, off N59; ☎ 095-41146; www.kylemoreabbey.com

Type of attraction Manor house. **Admission** €10 adults, €6.50 seniors and students. **Hours** Abbey and grounds: daily, 9 a.m.–5:30 p.m.; walled garden: Easter–September, daily, 10:30 a.m.–4:30 p.m. **When to go** In good weather to enjoy the grounds. **Special comments** A pottery workshop, a shop selling high-line crafts and clothing, and a cafeteria are on the grounds. **How much time to allow** About 2 hours.

DESCRIPTION AND COMMENTS Kylemore is the home of the order of Irish Benedictine nuns and an exclusive boarding school for girls, but the allure of the faux-Gothic castle and its lavish grounds is primarily secular: Kylemore was for many decades a pleasure dome for wealthy and entitled residents. From 1867 to 1871, Mitchell Henry, heir to a Manchester, England, cotton fortune, built the house and landscaped the 5,500-hectare (13,000-acre) estate at the base of the Twelve Bens for his wife, Margaret. She had admired the spot, with its lake and glens, on a carriage ride during their honeymoon. Margaret died in 1874, but Mitchell remained on the estate for 30 years, representing Galway in the House of Commons; in 1903, he sold Kylemore to the Duke and Duchess of Manchester. The noble couple's elaborate lifestyle came to an end when the duchess's wealthy American father, who bankrolled the enterprise, died in 1914. The nuns, bombed out of their convent in Ypres, Belgium, during World War I, took over the estate in 1920, and ever since have paid the bills by educating the daughters of Ireland's elite. In the abbey you'll see a few opulent reception rooms that are furnished in a fairly humdrum style (most of the original furnishings have been removed, so you really don't get a sense of the house as a wealthy residence). More impressive are the lovely grounds, a small chapel that's built like a cathedral in miniature, and an elaborate stream-laced garden in which exotic fruits and flowers flourish behind thick limestone walls.

TOURING TIPS A shuttle bus runs between the abbey and the walled garden, in a sheltered vale about 1.6 kilometers (1 mile) from the house, but walk at least one way.

EXERCISE AND RECREATION IN CONNEMARA

A ONE-STOP SHOP FOR LAND- AND WATER-BASED activities is **Delphi Adventure Holidays,** located next to the Delphi Mountain Resort north of Leenane. The center makes use of the surrounding mountains for hill walking, mountain biking, and mountaineering, and Killary Harbor is well suited to waterskiing, kayaking, and many other water sports. For more information, call ☎ 095-42307 or go to **www.delphiadventureholidays.ie. Connemara Walking Centre** caters to walkers with half- and full-day hikes throughout the spring and summer in many different parts of Connemara. Walks are March to October, costs begin at about €20, and groups assemble at Island House on Market Street in Clifden for bus transportation to the different starting points; ☎ 095-21379 or **www.walkingireland.com.** Lough Corrib is known as some of Ireland's best angling waters; an excellent source for information on renting boats and tackle, advice on flies to use, and more, is **Angling West,** Rushveala Lodge, Oughterard; ☎ 091-557933 or **www.anglingwest.com. Irish Cycling Tours** in Leenane rents bicycles and other equipment and leads tours; ☎ 095-42276 or **www.irishcyclingtours.ie.** Golf courses include the **Connemara Golf Club,** outside Clifden in Ballyconneely, ☎ 095-23502, and the **Oughterard Golf Club,** outside Oughterard, ☎ 091-552131.

CLIFDEN

BACKED BY THE PEAKS OF THE TWELVE BENS, Clifden seems almost like an Alpine village, but the bogs and the rocky coastline that surround the town remind you that you are indeed in Connemara. The year-round population barely tops 1,000, but Clifden is by far the largest town in Connemara as well as the region's self-proclaimed capital. Clifden is also the start of the Sky Road, a scenic drive along Clifden Bay.

unofficial **TIP**
With lively pubs and shops in the compact town center, Clifden is a good place to stop for a break from touring or for an overnight stay.

Arriving and Getting Oriented in Clifden

CLIFDEN IS 80 KILOMETERS (48 miles) northwest of Galway on N59. A drive here from Galway takes you through some stunning Connemara scenery that includes the shores of Lough Corrib and the craggy, heather-covered Twelve Bens. A tourist-information office, on the Galway Road (N59) at the entrance to the town center, is open May to September, daily, 9 a.m. to 6 p.m. If you're heading into Connemara in other seasons, you can stock up on the same info at the Connemara National Park Headquarters or at the Galway Tourist Office.

Special Events in Clifden

From June through August, Clifden stages a show of traditional dancing and music in the town hall on Tuesday and Thursday evenings. In late July, you can see Connemara ponies at the **Claddaghduff Pony Show;** these handsome beasts make a reappearance during the **Festival of the Connemara Pony** in mid-August.

Hotels in and around Clifden

Abbeyglen Castle Hotel ★ ★ ★

QUALITY	★ ★ ★	VALUE	★ ★ ★	€90–€170

Sky Road, Clifden; ☎ 095-21201; fax 095-21797; info@abbeyglen.ie; www.abbeyglen.ie

Location Just outside Clifden's city center. **Amenities and services** 38 rooms; bar, garden, hair dryers, helipad, in-room tea and coffee facilities, irons, pitch-and-putt golf, restaurant, swimming pool. **Elevator** Yes. **Parking** Free, on property. **Price** Many special offers available, including low-season packages that include dinner, bed, and breakfast at very reasonable rates. **Credit cards** AE, DC, MC, V.

This 175-year-old castlelike manor house, complete with turrets and crenellations, is set in a sheltered glen laced with streams and lovely gardens. Abbeyglen has all the trappings of a romantic getaway and is beloved by many repeat visitors. A comfortable, informal atmosphere permeates a series of lounges and a game room, while a parrot jabbers at the reception desk. You can enjoy a drink or complimentary afternoon tea in front of a peat fire or relax for hours in one of the armchairs in the lounge. The lawns and pleasant swimming pool are inviting without being fussy. A recent refurbishment scheme has ensured that the rooms and large bathrooms, most with big tubs, are comfortable; the furnishings, however, are a bit drab and uninspired. In the rooms and in the dull hallways and worn public areas you get the feeling that the property is not yet quite up to snuff—too institutional to be casually chic yet several marks shy of being luxurious.

Ballynahinch Castle ★ ★ ★ ★ ★

QUALITY	★ ★ ★ ½	VALUE	★ ★ ★ ★	€120–€240

Recess, County Galway; ☎ 095-31006; fax 095-31085; bhinch@iol.ie; www.ballynahinch-castle.com

Location About 15 kilometers (9 miles) east of Clifden off N59. **Amenities and services** 40 rooms; cycling, fishing, gardens, nonsmoking rooms, room service, tennis, walking; closed at Christmas and part of February. **Elevator** No. **Parking** On property, free. **Price** Includes full Irish breakfast; many special offers available. **Credit cards** AE, DC, MC, V.

One of Ireland's most noted country-house hotels occupies an 18th-century manor on the banks of the Ballynahinch River, surrounded by 450 acres of woodlands and mountain pastures. Former residents of the estate include Grace O'Malley, the "Pirate Queen" of Connemara; "Humanity Dick" Martin, founder of the Royal Society for the Prevention of Cruelty to Animals; and HRH the Maharajah Ranjitsinji, also known as "Ranji, Prince of Cricketeers." Even without this colorful provenance, Ballynahinch is an utterly delightful place that doesn't miss a beat in providing a memorable retreat. Open fires and Persian carpets grace the welcoming public rooms, where guests seem to spend many contented hours sitting quietly and reading; when the urge strikes, fishing, walking, and many other activities await just outside the front door. The woody pub is a popular gathering spot for guests and locals alike, and the Owenmore Restaurant is the best dining room in Connemara. Forest trails, riverside walks, and gardens grace the grounds. Delightful guest rooms are situated in the old house and in thoughtful, light-filled new extensions strung out above the river, which can be viewed through floor-to-ceiling windows. The furnishings are airily Georgian; excellent beds are covered with fine linens; and bathrooms are new, large, nicely outfitted, and often reached through dressing rooms. The attentive service caps off the feeling that guests are enjoying a casually elegant country house—which they are.

Foyles Hotel ★ ★ ★ ½

QUALITY	★ ★ ★ ½	VALUE	★ ★ ★ ★ ½	€50–€80

Main Street, Clifden; ☎ 095-21801; fax 095-21458; foyles@anu.ie; www.foyleshotel.com

Location Town center. **Amenities and services** 30 rooms; hair dryers, in-room tea and coffee facilities. **Elevator** No. **Parking** On street. **Price** Includes full Irish breakfast. **Credit cards** MC, V.

The in-town location, just steps away from Clifden's shops and pubs, is one of the many appeals of this nicely old-fashioned hotel. A sunny lounge filled with oversize armchairs faces the town square, and a small patio surrounded by a flowery garden is at the rear of the reception area. Upstairs, the high-ceilinged guest rooms are well done, with solid, beautifully maintained old furniture, including handsome chests and armoires and firm beds. Color schemes are restful, and the décor is appealingly traditional without being overbearingly so; bathrooms have been updated with large basins, deep bathtubs, and good showers. Rooms in the front of the hotel afford entertaining views of the town's comings and goings, but those on the side and at the rear of the hotel are completely free of traffic noise.

Restaurants in and around Clifden

Marconi Restaurant   ★ ★ ★ ½

MODERN IRISH	MODERATE	QUALITY ★★★½	VALUE ★★★★

In Foyle's Hotel, Main Street, Clifden; ☎ 095-21801

Reservations Recommended in summer. **Entree range** €14.95–€18.95. **Payment** MC, V. **Bar** Full service. **Disabled access** Yes. **Hours** Daily, 6:30–9:30 p.m.

MENU RECOMMENDATIONS Fresh Connemara oysters, Connemara lamb, fresh Atlantic salmon.

COMMENTS The dining room of Foyle's Hotel is, like the rest of the establishment, slightly formal and old-fashioned; these surroundings impart the feeling that a meal is a special occasion. The service can be rushed when staff is short, but the kitchen reliably prepares fish and seafood fresh off the boats. A good light meal for seafood lovers might begin with oysters, washed down with a glass of white from the decent wine list and followed by one of the other excellent seafood appetizers, such as calamari, crab cakes, or mussels steamed in white wine. (Incidentally, Guglielmo Marconi, Italian inventor of the radio and the restaurant's namesake, was part Irish.)

Owenmore Restaurant   ★ ★ ★ ★

MODERN IRISH	EXPENSIVE	QUALITY ★★★★	VALUE ★★★

Ballynahinch Castle, Recess; ☎ 095-31006

Reservations Recommended, as is smart attire. **Entree range** €45, prix-fixe dinner. **Payment** AE, DC, MC, V. **Bar** Full service. **Disabled access** Yes. **Hours** Daily, 7–10 p.m

MENU RECOMMENDATIONS Poached wild Atlantic salmon, rack of roasted Connemara lamb.

COMMENTS This elegant dining room in Ballynahinch Castle hotel is the finest restaurant in Connemara. Chef Robert Webster takes inspiration from the surrounding landscapes as he artfully prepares local lamb, seafood, and produce. The room does much to enhance the pleasure of a meal here:

*un*official **TIP**
For lunch or a snack, drop into the daytime-only **Two Dog Café** (Church Street, ☎ 095-22186), where the baked goods are delicious.

huge windows overlook the Ballynahinch River, and the lovely atmosphere is augmented by smooth, attentive service that makes guests feel welcome and pampered.

Shopping in Clifden

CLIFDEN CATERS TO ITS MANY VISITORS WITH SHOPS selling goods of unusually high quality. These stores include an outlet of the noted Irish chain **Avoca Handweavers,** which showcases its excellent tweeds, along with carvings and other Connemara souvenirs, in a bright shop set next to the sea about ten kilometers (six miles) outside town on the Clifden–Leenane Road; ☎ 095-41058. Right in town is **Millars Connemara Tweed Ltd.** (Main Street, ☎ 095-21038), justifiably famous for its wool from local sheep; you can buy it by the yard or woven into hats, blankets, and other attractive apparel and household items.

CONG

THIS LITTLE VILLAGE, TUCKED BETWEEN Lough Corrib to the south and Lough Mask to the north, would be noteworthy in its own right, but Cong is still resting on the fame it garnered as the setting for the 1952 film *The Quiet Man.* John Wayne and Maureen O'Hara got star billing, but the green countryside and pretty cottages—still much in evidence—steal the show.

Arriving and Getting Oriented in Cong

CONG IS ABOUT 35 KILOMETERS (21 miles) north of Galway on N84 and R334. A longer but slightly more scenic route takes you out of Galway on N59, with a turn north on R336 at Maam Cross, from which it's about another 20 kilometers (12 miles) to Cong. The busy **Cong Tourist Office** (town center near abbey, ☎ 094-954-6542) is open March to June and September to November, daily, 10 a.m. to 6 p.m. and July to August, daily, 10 a.m. to 7 p.m.

Hotel in Cong

Ashford Castle ★ ★ ★ ★

QUALITY	★ ★ ★ ½	VALUE	★ ★ ★	€225–€450

Cong, County Mayo; ☎ 094-954-6003; fax 094-954-6260; ashford@ashford.ie; www.ashford.ie

Location At edge of village. **Amenities and services** 83 rooms; bicycles, boating, fishing, 9-hole golf course, health club, horseback riding, nonsmoking rooms, shooting, tennis. **Elevator** Yes. **Parking** Free, on property. **Price** Includes full Irish breakfast; many special offers available. **Credit cards** AE, DC, MC, V.

One of Ireland's most acclaimed hotels gives credence to the old real-estate maxim that location—and, in this case, a breathtaking one—is everything. The 19th-century castle, built with its many turrets and towers around a

13th-century manor, is nestled stunningly between Lough Corrib and the River Cong. Inside, oil paintings glimmer on paneled and stone walls, and suits of armor stand sentry beneath grand staircases. Despite the grandeur, though, there's a certain lack of authenticity to the place. Ashford can seem more like an American resort hotel than an Irish castle; service can be brusque (so atypical of Ireland); and some of the public areas seem to have had their last bit of life polished out of them. The guest rooms are furnished to a very high level of traditional comfort and offer every amenity, but some, especially those in the newer wing, are actually a bit dull. Most rooms, however, have wonderful outlooks, and because the castle is surrounded by water, there is no need to pay extra for a lake view. Many guests, who include a long roster of celebrities, would not think of staying elsewhere and extol virtues such as the hotel's two excellent restaurants, the Connaught Room and the George V; two atmospheric bars; a state-of-the-art spa; and a wealth of activities. But if you're looking for a relaxed retreat where you'll feel like a guest in an Irish country house, set your sights instead on nearby Ballynahinch Castle (see page 328).

Exploring Cong

CONG'S MOST AUGUST MONUMENT IS THE RUINED **Augustine monastery** in the village center, on Abbey Street (free, always open). The monastery's famous relic, the **Cross of Cong,** a processional object emblazoned with gems and enamel, is now in the National Museum in Dublin. What remains here are some wonderful Romanesque carvings and archways, a chapter house, and a charming and ingenious fishing hut, raised above the river on stone pilings. The crafty monks would lower a basket on a rope with a bell attached; when a fish swam into the basket, the bell would ring.

Many visitors still come to Cong in search of the region's Technicolor beauty made famous by *The Quiet Man*. The village caters to these film buffs with the **Quiet Man Cottage,** a replica of the dwelling used in the film. It's hard to imagine anyone actually plunking down hard-earned cash to see the grainy production photos and dusty costumes, but if you can't resist this bit of Hollywood memorabilia, you'll pay €4 to indulge yourself; open mid-March to October, daily, 10 a.m. to 5 p.m.; ☎ 094-954-6089. If you are such an ardent fan of the Duke that you need to see more, **Paddy Rock** leads tours of the locations used in the film; contact him at ☎ 094-954-6155.

Shopping in Cong

STEP INTO **Kate Luskin's shop** at the edge of town near the entrance to Ashford Castle for a wonderful selection of handmade Aran knitwear, made from the wool of local sheep and colored with natural dyes. You can select a sweater from the shelf, or Kate will make one to order. Prices are extremely reasonable for the quality of the materials and craftsmanship, beginning at €125. If Kate's not there, ring the bell and she'll pop over from her house nearby; ☎ 094-954-6757.

WESTPORT

THIS ATTRACTIVE TOWN OF WIDE STREETS and gracious squares, designed by architect James Wyatt in the 1770s, is to the north of Connemara, on the other side of the Doolough Valley and Croagh Patrick, a conical-shaped peak close to the hearts of the devout. In the fifth century, St. Patrick spent the 40 days of Lent atop the mountain, fasting, praying, and ringing a bell to expel all snakes from Ireland; a small white oratory marks the site of his hermitage. Thousands of pilgrims, some of them barefoot, still make their way up a wide path to the summit, as do hikers devoted more to exercise than to Ireland's patron saint.

Westport is one of Ireland's most appealing towns, though its current prosperity is fairly recent—the town fell into a 200-year-long stretch of hard times when British mills supplanted the local linen industry around the turn of the 19th century.

unofficial **TIP**
Walking tours of Westport depart from the clock tower on nearby Bridge Street at 8 p.m. in July and August; cost is €5.

PLANNING YOUR VISIT TO WESTPORT

THE WESTPORT TOURIST OFFICE (James Street, ☎ 098-25711) is open May to October, Monday through Saturday, 9 a.m. to 6 p.m.; November to January, Monday through Friday, 9 a.m. to 6 p.m. and Saturday, 9 a.m. to 1 p.m.

At the **Heritage Centre,** downstairs, you can learn all you need to know about Westport House, the Pirate Queen, Crough Patrick, and other people, places, and episodes in local history; €3.

ARRIVING AND GETTING ORIENTED IN WESTPORT

WESTPORT IS ABOUT 20 KILOMETERS (12 miles) north of Leenane on N59. A slightly longer and much more scenic route takes you out of Leenane on N335 through the **Doolough Valley** and along the southern shores of **Clew Bay.** This route first takes you just outside Leenane around **Killary Harbor,** a fjordlike body of water carved by a glacier. Near the entrance to the Doolough Valley, **Aasleagh Falls,** reached by a short trail from the road, cascades down a hillside where ferns and wild rhododendron flourish. The valley is beautiful, though the remote landscapes were the setting for the Famine Walk, one of many gruesome episodes during the Great Potato Famine of the 1840s. Some 600 tenants walked through the valley to ask their landlord at Delphi Lodge, south of the village of Louisburgh, for food and were turned back; most died of starvation on the side of the road. Archbishop Desmond Tutu is one of many pilgrims who have retraced their steps on an annual commemorative walk.

HOTELS IN AND AROUND WESTPORT

 Atlantic Coast ★ ★ ★

QUALITY	★ ★ ★ ½	VALUE	★ ★ ★	€140–€220

**The Quay, Westport, County Mayo; ☎ 098-29000; fax 098-29111;
info@atlanticcoasthotel.com; www.atlanticcoasthotel.com**

Location Facing Westport harbor, about 1 mile from town center. **Amenities and services** 85 rooms; bar, cafe, hair dryers, in-room tea and coffee facilities, non-smoking rooms, restaurant, satellite TV, swimming pool, spa. **Elevator** Yes. **Parking** Free, on property. **Price** Includes full Irish breakfast; many special offers and family rates available. **Credit cards** AE, DC, MC, V.

Behind the facade of an 18th-century mill on the old Quay facing West-port's harbor, the Atlantic Coast is strictly contemporary, with light and airy public spaces and large guest rooms facing the sea through big windows. While the atmosphere throughout is more functional than cozy, any feeling of anonymity is offset by the friendly service and the presence of many families who come here for short getaways, especially on weekends. Many of the rooms have a double bed and a single bed; folding beds can be wheeled in for no extra charge; babysitting is available; and the hotel is equipped with an indoor swimming pool—all attractions for travelers with children. Adults are catered to with a spa and an excellent top-floor restaurant, while the ground-floor bistro serves casual meals well suited to young guests. Westport House (see page 334), with its many kid-friendly attractions, is nearby, a pleasant walk along the Quay and through the estate parklands.

Delphi Mountain Resort and Spa ★ ★ ★ ★

QUALITY	★ ★ ★ ★	VALUE	★ ★ ★	€150–€240

**Leenane, County Galway; ☎ 095-42987; fax 095-42303; delphigy@iol.ie;
www.delphiescape.com**

Location Above Killary Harbor, south of Westport. **Amenities and services** 22 units; bar, bicycles, fishing, hair dryers, horseback riding, in-room tea and coffee facilities, nonsmoking rooms, restaurant, spa, walking. **Elevator** Yes. **Parking** Free, on property. **Price** Includes full Irish breakfast; many special offers and spa-treatment packages available. **Credit cards** AE, MC, V.

You will fall under the spell of this lovely retreat, which promises to offer an escape from the stresses of modern life, the moment you step inside—or perhaps as you approach, because the stone-and-timber building blends so unobtrusively with the mountain landscape that surrounds it. Inside, a turf fire burns in a stone hearth in the lobby, color schemes are soothingly neutral, and walls of glass bring the outdoors inside. Guest rooms are simply but comfortably decorated with natural fabrics, hardwood floors, and appealing contemporary furnishings; many are suites with loft bedrooms, and all have large tiled bathrooms and either patios or small balconies. The spa is especially restful, and guests have access to a large Jacuzzi overlooking the mountains, a sauna and other facilities, and a full range of pay-as-you-go treatments. Even the dining room, which specializes in Irish seafood but also serves meat and vegetarian dishes, is extremely relaxing. The cocktail bar caters to the broad tastes of guests, serving smoothies and fruit juices as well as beer and cocktails. Delphi offers a range of multiday spa and outdoor-activity packages but is open to overnight guests as well.

EXPLORING WESTPORT

WESTPORT WARRANTS A LEISURELY STROLL to take in the harmony and elegance of the 18th-century town plan. All streets converge on the Octagon, architect James Wyatt's innovative take on a town square. A gurgling river rushes past one side of the appealing space, and a riverside walk is shaded by lime trees. Westport's harbor is about 1 kilometer (0.5 miles) west of the town center on Clew Bay. The 17th-century mills lining the Quay now house shops, apartments, and a hotel (see Atlantic Coast, page 333), though there's still a salty tang to the place. **Westport House** (see below) elegantly commands a green hillside just above the bay.

ATTRACTION IN WESTPORT

 Westport House ★ ★ ½

APPEAL BY AGE	PRESCHOOL ★★★★	GRADE SCHOOL ★★★★★	TEENS ★★★★
YOUNG ADULTS	★★★★	OVER 30 ★★½	SENIORS ★★½

Outside Westport; ☎ 098-27766; www.westporthouse.ie

Type of attraction Historic home and amusement park set in gardens. **Admission** House and gardens only: €9.50 adults, €6 children, €7.50 seniors and students; house, gardens, and attractions: €18 adults, €11 children, €10 seniors, €14 students, €59 families of up to 2 adults and 4 children. **Hours** House and gardens: March and October, Sunday–Friday, 11:30 a.m.–4 p.m.; April–June and September, 11:30 a.m.–5 p.m.; July–August, Sunday–Friday, 11:30 a.m.– 6 p.m.; attractions: April 9–13 and 30, 11:30 a.m.–5 p.m.; May, Sundays, and bank holidays, 11:30 a.m.–5 p.m.; June, Sunday–Wednesday, 11:30 a.m.–5 p.m.; July– August, Sunday–Friday, 11:30 a.m.–6 p.m. **When to go** Avoid Sundays, when every child in the West of Ireland descends upon the place. Oddly, Westport House is closed on Saturdays. **Special comments** If you've been dragging your young companions through museums and historic homes, the rides, zoos, and other commercial attractions of Westport House will be a welcome treat for them. **How much time to allow** About 1 hour for the house, and as long as the kids want for the rides and other attractions.

DESCRIPTION AND COMMENTS This stately home on the shores of Clew Bay is the work of two of Ireland's leading architects, Richard Cassels (Powerscourt, see page 179, is his masterpiece), and James Wyatt, who laid out the handsome streets and squares of Westport. Cassels began the house in 1730 on the site of an earlier castle, of which some dungeons remain, and Wyatt completed the job in 1788. Stately touches such as the grand staircase and elegant dining room are Wyatt's. The collections of paintings, Waterford crystal, and fine silver are the family treasures of the Browne family, owners of Westport House and descendants of Grace O'Malley, the infamous 16th-century "Pirate Queen" who made her fortune raiding ships off the coast of western Ireland. Parts of the grounds, including some formal gardens, are indeed lovely, but, sadly, the estate has become a money-generating theme park with intrusive and unstately amusements that include swan-boat rides, a log flume, and a mock farmyard.

TOURING TIPS   If you want to enjoy a slice of Irish history without commercial intrusions, limit your tour to the house.

RESTAURANTS IN WESTPORT

THE TOP CHOICE FOR A CASUAL MEAL IN Westport is **McCormack's** (Bridge Street, ☎ 098-25619), a casual cafe that shares its premises with an art gallery and a deli–butcher shop. Chowders, stews, and baked goods are sublime; cheese and other foods are available for takeout in the shop downstairs. A mandatory evening stop is **Matt Malloy's** (Bridge Street, ☎ 098-26655), a down-to-earth pub owned by Matt Malloy of the Chieftains; traditional music is on tap many evenings.

Quay Cottage   ★ ★ ★ ★

SEAFOOD	MODERATE	QUALITY	★ ★ ★ ★	VALUE	★ ★ ★ ½

The Harbour, Westport; ☎ 098-26412

Reservations Recommended. **Entree range** €18–€25; prix-fixe dinners, €25 and €35. **Payment** AE, MC, V. **Bar** Full service. **Disabled access** Yes. **Hours** May–October, daily, 6–10 p.m.; November–April, Tuesday–Saturday, 6–10 p.m.

MENU RECOMMENDATIONS   Fish chowder, garlic grilled oysters.

COMMENTS   A stone cottage at one end of Westport's historic quay reflects the gentrification that has turned what was once a working port into a leisure district, but there's nothing casual about the approach to food here. Many of the dishes that arrive at the pine tables in the nautically themed room are based on seafood from Clew Bay just outside the front door, though duckling and other land-based choices are available, too. Service is adept, and a view of the bay gleaming in the moonlight awaits when you emerge at the end of a meal.

NORTH *of* WESTPORT

NORTHERN COUNTY MAYO IS WILD AND WINDSWEPT, a landscape of moors, isolated farms, and a rugged coastline. Among the reasons to linger here—and to simply enjoy rural Ireland is a big one—is the opportunity to visit **Achill Island** and **Céide Fields,** a 5,000-year-old Stone Age site.

ACHILL ISLAND

THE LARGEST IRISH ISLAND COMPRISES 147 square kilometers (57 square miles) of bogs, moors, and wild coasts and is only 6 meters (20 feet) off the coast, about 60 kilometers (36 miles) north of Westport via the N59 and R319, which crosses a causeway to the island. In good weather, Achill Island is incredibly beautiful, remote, and wild, with wonderful walks along sea cliffs, some of which rival those at Slieve League (see page 360) in height. Conversely, when mist and fog set in for days on end, as they often do, the island can seem like the bleakest place on earth.

You can drive around the island on well-marked **Atlantic Drive,** coming to beautiful beaches, small villages, and ascending, on the north coast, around the bases of **Croaghaun,** 688 meters (2,270 feet) tall, and **Slievemore,** topping off at 671 meters (2,214 feet). One of the most haunting spots on the island is **Slievemore Village,** where more than a hundred ruined, overgrown cottages are reminders of the Famine, when villagers left in search of food, and of evictions by landlords seeking higher rents. **Heinrich Boll,** the Nobel Prize–winning German novelist and essayist, lived in the village of Doogort during the 1950s and based his *Irish Diary* on his experiences. Doogort isn't much more than a small collection of houses backed by the flanks of Slievemore, next to a beautiful beach.

CÉIDE FIELDS

THIS MODEST-LOOKING SITE SOME 80 kilometers (50 miles) north of Westport seems like an outpost at the end of the world, which indeed it was when a Stone Age settlement flourished here 5,000 years ago. Boglands covered the houses and farm plots millennia ago, beautifully preserving the stone foundations of houses and the fences that parceled off fields. It takes a little imagination, and some time in the excellent visitors center, to appreciate the significance of the place, which is also enhanced on one of the guided walks. The site is on coast road R314, near Ballycastle; ☎ 096-43325. Open mid-March through May and October, daily, 10 a.m. to 5 p.m.; June through September, daily, 10 a.m. to 6 p.m.; and November, daily, 10 a.m. to 4:30 p.m. Admission is €3.50 adults, €2.50 seniors, €1.25 students and children, and €8.25 for families.

The drive to Céide Fields from Westport is especially scenic if you follow the coast north through **Castlebar** and **Ballina** to the pleasant seaside village of **Killala** and around **Downpatrick Head,** where the sea erupts in plumes through a string of blowholes.

PART NINE

THE NORTHWEST
of IRELAND

NORTHWEST IRELAND IS LIKELY TO HIT YOU like a big gust of salty sea breeze: the rugged landscapes are never far from the wild North Atlantic, and they're as wild as the sea. A string of maritime peninsulas jut in and out of the sea; inland, brown and purple heaths and moors climb the sides of craggy mountains. The British settled so-called Plantation Towns throughout the region and still control the lands just across the border in Northern Ireland; however, much of the rural, desolate Northwest is Irish speaking, and even the signs are in Gaelic. The major towns of the Northwest, **Sligo** and **Letterkenny,** are boomtowns these days, but even so their populations barely top 25,000 each. Most of your travels here will be on country roads where the only traffic you might encounter for miles is four legged.

SLIGO TOWN

AN OLD-FASHIONED CHARM still prevails in this sturdy commercial town spanning the banks of the River Garavogue near Sligo Bay, but there's quite a buzz in the air, too. New shops, a new riverside walk along the Garavogue, and new prosperity might bring to mind the often quoted line by William Butler Yeats, "All changed, changed utterly." Yeats, incidentally, is Sligo's most famous son. Though born

the northwest of ireland

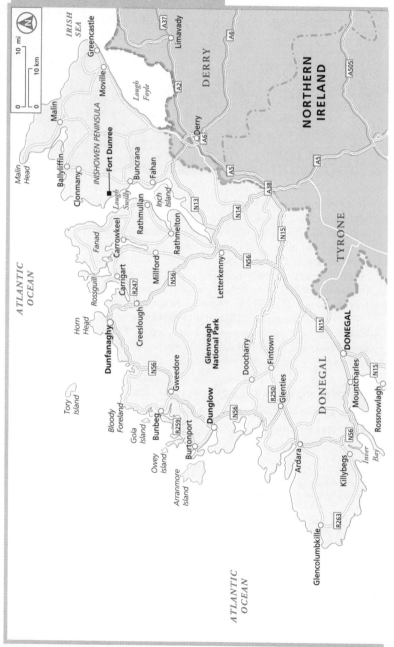

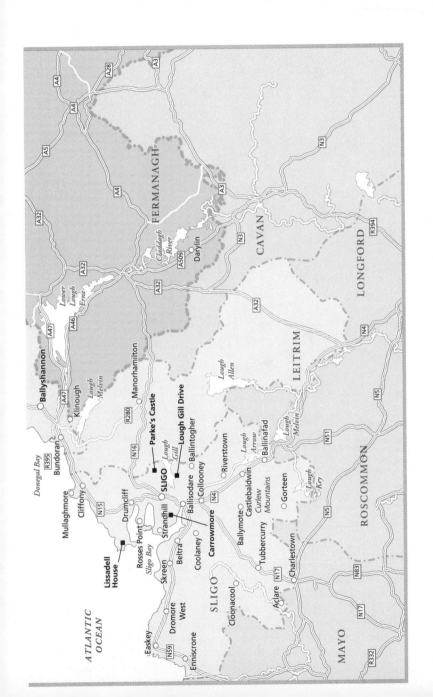

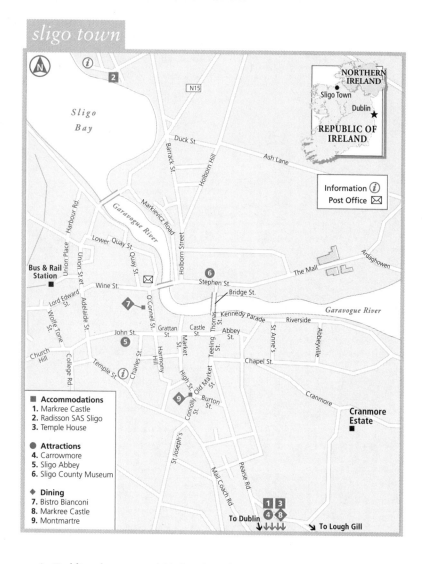

sligo town

NORTHERN IRELAND

Sligo Town

Dublin ★

REPUBLIC OF IRELAND

Information ⓘ
Post Office ✉

Sligo Bay

N15

Duck St.

Ash Lane

Barrack St.

Holborn Hill

Markievicz Road

Garavogue River

Harbour Rd.

Lower Quay St.

Holborn Street

Ardaghowen

Union Place

Union St.

Quay St.

The Mall

Bus & Rail Station ■

Wine St.

✉

Stephen St.

6

Bridge St.

Garavogue River

Lord Edward St.

Adelaide St.

7

O'Connell St.

Kennedy Parade

Riverside

Abbeyville

Wolfe Tone St.

John St.

5

Grattan St.

Castle St.

Thomas St.

Teeling St.

Abbey St.

St. Anne's

Church Hill

College Rd.

Temple St. ⓘ

Charles St.

Harmony Hill

Market St.

Chapel St.

9

High St.

Old Market St.

Connolly St.

Burton St.

Cranmore

Cranmore Estate ■

St. Joseph's

Mall Coach Rd.

Pearse Rd.

To Dublin

1 3
4 8

To Lough Gill

■ **Accommodations**
1. Markree Castle
2. Radisson SAS Sligo
3. Temple House

● **Attractions**
4. Carrowmore
5. Sligo Abbey
6. Sligo County Museum

◆ **Dining**
7. Bistro Bianconi
8. Markree Castle
9. Montmartre

in Dublin, the poet and his brother, the painter Jack Yeats, had their roots in Sligo and spent much of their lives here. Those for whom the name Yeats recalls the poet's famous line "I will arise and go now, and go to Innisfree" will be inspired by Yeats Country, to be explored on a lovely route that skirts Lough Gill, affording views of the Lake Isle of Innisfree. Sligo Abbey, in ruin, is the sole reminder of the town's prominence as a trading center in the Middle Ages—and of a savage attack on the town by the British, under Sir Frederick Hamilton in 1642, in which the abbey and most of the rest of Sligo were destroyed.

Most of the handsome town center dates from the 19th century, when in the pre-Famine days the docks and warehouses along the Garavogue and Sligo Bay brought wealth and prominence to Sligo.

PLANNING YOUR VISIT TO SLIGO TOWN

SERVING THE NORTHWEST REGION, the **Sligo Tourist Office** provides information on the town as well as the rest of Counties Sligo and Donegal. Located at the edge of the city center (Temple Street, ☎ 071-916-1201), the office is open daily year-round, 9 a.m.–5 p.m.; **www.ireland northwest.ie.**

Special Events in Sligo Town

Sligo's most famous annual event is the **Yeats International Summer School,** for two weeks in July and/or August, when lectures, readings, and other events honor the town's famous poet; for information, call ☎ 071-69802 or visit **www.yeats-sligo.com.** The **Scriobh Literary Festival** in September attracts writers from throughout Ireland, as well as international literary figures, for readings and workshops; for more information, contact the Model Arts and Niland Gallery, ☎ 071-914-3694. Several musical festivals include the **Yeats Country Music Festival** in June, with country-music performers from throughout Ireland and the United States; ☎ 01-605-7707, **www.showtours.ie;** and the **Sligo Feis Ceoil,** also in June, with choral singing, sessions of traditional music, and more; ☎ 087-960-2866, **www.sligofeisceoil.com.** In October, the **Sligo Festival of Baroque Music** focuses on music from the 16th to 18th centuries; ☎ 071-914-1405, **www.modelart.ie.** November's **Sligo International Choral Festival** brings together choristers from around the world; ☎ 086-259-2290, **www.sligochoralfest.org.**

ARRIVING AND GETTING ORIENTED IN SLIGO TOWN

SLIGO IS ABOUT 138 KILOMETERS (85 miles) northeast of Galway and 217 kilometers (135 miles) northwest of Dublin. By car, follow N3 across Ireland from Dublin to Sligo; from Galway, take N59 north. **Irish Rail** runs five trains per day between Dublin and Sligo, and the trip takes about three hours. Standard one-way fare is €25. The Sligo train station is on Lord Edward Street; for more information, call ☎ 071-916-9888 or go to **www.irishrail.ie.** About six **Bus Éireann** buses travel between Dublin and Sligo daily; the trip take about four hours and costs €9. The Sligo bus station is near the train station on Prince Edward Street.

HOTELS IN AND AROUND SLIGO TOWN

Markree Castle ★ ★ ★ ★

QUALITY ★ ★ ★	VALUE ★ ★ ★	€83–€165

Collooney, County Sligo; ☎ 071-916-7800; fax 071-916-7840; markree@iol.ie; www.markreecastle.ie

How Hotels Compare in the Northwest of Ireland

HOTEL	OVERALL	QUALITY	VALUE	PRICE
SLIGO TOWN				
Temple House	★★★★½	★★★★	★★★★	€105–€170
Markree Castle	★★★★	★★★	★★★	€83–€165
Radisson SAS Hotel Sligo	★★★	★★★★	★★★	€120–€160
DONEGAL TOWN				
St. Ernan's House	★★★★	★★★★	★★★	from €230
NORTH DONEGAL				
Frewin	★★★★½	★★★★	★★★★	€70–€140
Rathmullan House	★★★★	★★★★	★★★	€130–€220
Castle Grove Country House Hotel	★★★★	★★★½	★★★	€80–€160

Location 13 kilometers (8 miles) south of Sligo Town, outside the village of Collooney. **Amenities and services** 30 rooms; bar, fishing, gardens, horseback riding, nonsmoking rooms, restaurant. **Elevator** Yes. **Parking** Free, on property. **Price** Includes full Irish breakfast. **Credit cards** AE, MC, V.

Built in 1640, this rather ominous, fortresslike castle is the ancestral home of Charles Cooper, who operates the 400-hectare (1,000-acre) estate as a hotel providing some of the most charmingly idiosyncratic lodgings in all of Ireland. You'll know the place isn't run-of-the-mill from the moment you enter the front doors and climb the stone staircase to the paneled and galleried Great Hall. Markree has ample comforts—roaring fires burn in hearths (including an elegant matched pair in the drawing room), central heating keeps drafts at bay, and the plumbing is up-to-date. In the guest rooms, tucked into corners and towers and reached by a labyrinth of stairways and passages, furnishings are sometimes mismatched and a bit worn; however, ongoing improvements are raising the level of accommodation. Each room is different, and some are easier to reach than others without climbing stairs—the elevator serves only some levels, so be sure to mention any accessibility needs you may have when booking. Public rooms include the sunny double-length drawing room, a cozy bar, and an elegant rococo dining room where an excellent prix-fixe dinner is served with delightful old-world formality. The River Unsin sprints past the front door, while paths crisscross the wooded grounds to the estate's own lake. If you want a break from the ordinary, this is the place.

Radisson SAS Hotel Sligo ★ ★ ★

| QUALITY ★ ★ ★ ★ | VALUE ★ ★ ★ | €120–€160 |

Ballincar, Rosses Point Road, County Sligo; ☎ 071-914-0008; fax 071-914-0006; info.sligo@radisssonsas.com; www.radissonsas.com

Location About 3 kilometers (2 miles) north of Sligo Town in direction of Rosses Point. **Amenities and services** 132 units; bar, in-room safes, in-room tea and coffee facilities, Internet, irons, minibars, nonsmoking rooms, restaurant, room service. **Parking** Free, on property. **Price** Includes full Irish breakfast; special Internet rates available. **Credit cards** AE, MC, V.

Sleek outlets of this chain have opened in towns around Ireland, and in places such as Sligo, which have a dearth of inner-city hotels, they provide a high standard of comfort not readily available. The only drawback to this business-oriented hotel is the fact that it doesn't reflect the character of this colorful town and region. That said, service is friendly and professional; the swimming pool, gym, and spa are delightful; and the clean lines, contemporary décor, and warm hues are soothing—as are all the standard hotel comforts and an added perk, views over Sligo Bay. Be sure to request a room with this view, and for extra space and comfort, upgrade yourself to a business-class room or a junior suite.

Temple House ★ ★ ★ ★ ½

| QUALITY ★ ★ ★ ★ | VALUE ★ ★ ★ ★ | €105–€170 |

Ballymote, County Sligo (closed December–March); ☎ 071-918-3329; fax 071-918-3808; enquiry@templehouse.ie; www.templehouse.ie

Location Outside the village of Ballymote, about 20 kilometers (12 miles) south of Sligo Town, off N17. **Amenities and services** 6 rooms; bird-watching, boating, dinner available on request (€40), fishing, gardens, high tea for children, nonsmoking rooms, shooting, walking. **Elevator** No. **Parking** Free, on property. **Price** Includes full Irish breakfast. **Credit cards** AE, MC, V.

The Perceval family has lived in this grand Georgian mansion, one of Ireland's largest homes still in private hands, since 1665; the estate rolls across more than 400 hectares (1,000 acres). Perceval predecessors at Temple House built the Knights Templar castle, now in ruin on the grounds. Today, Roderick and Helena Perceval oversee the guest-house operation Roderick's parents undertook almost 40 years ago. Sensible changes, such as updating bathrooms and heating, have been made, while leaving all the wonderful qualities of Temple House intact. Guests make themselves at home in country-house surroundings that are delightfully lived-in—Temple House is a real home, not a polished hotel. The marble-floored hall features cases displaying stuffed game birds and fish landed on the estate; a grand staircase is lined with Perceval family portraits; a handsome sitting room, warmed by a fire in winter, opens to a terrace overlooking the lough; and Wellingtons wait by the door for those who want to wander through the wooded grounds or down to the dock for a row. Guest rooms—huge and filled with old family armoires, canopied beds, and writing desks—remain outfitted much as they were a century ago, with the exception of stylish new bathrooms with power showers. A wonderful breakfast and evening meals (the latter on request and featuring local produce) are served in a beautiful dining room. Children are most welcome at Temple House, and all guests enjoy the warm attention of Roderick and Helena, who are gracious and gifted hosts.

EXPLORING SLIGO TOWN AND ITS ENVIRONS

SLIGO'S CITY CENTER STRADDLES THE RIVER GARAVOGUE, but most commerce transpires south of the river. The main shopping district is on and off **O'Connell Street,** a lively thoroughfare that climbs away from the river toward the ruins of Sligo Abbey (see lower right). At the foot of O'Connell Street, alongside Hyde Bridge, is the **Yeats Memorial Building,** home to the Yeats Society and the venue for the popular annual Yeats International Summer School. Despite the academic-sounding name, the "school" is actually a festival celebrating the poet's work. Readings, musical performances, and other events round out the workshops and other scholarly undertakings. Yeats is remembered on the north side of the bridge with an impressionistic and beloved statue; just beyond, up Stephen Street, the **Sligo County Museum** (see page 348) houses a small selection of letters and other Yeats memorabilia.

Copious remnants of the neolithic peoples who inhabited the region some 7,500 years ago litter the hills that surround the center of Sligo. The most striking remains are those at **Carrowmore** (see below).

ATTRACTIONS IN SLIGO TOWN

Carrowmore ★ ★ ★ ★

APPEAL BY AGE	PRESCHOOL ★ ★	GRADE SCHOOL ★ ★ ★	TEENS ★ ★ ★
YOUNG ADULTS ★ ★ ★		OVER 30 ★ ★ ★ ★	SENIORS ★ ★ ★ ★

Southern edge of Sligo Town, marked off N4; ☎ 071-916-1534

Type of attraction Megalithic cemetery. **Admission** €2.10 adults, €1.10 children and students, €1.50 seniors, €5.50 families of up to 2 adults and 2 children. **Hours** May–September, daily, 10 a.m.–6 p.m. **When to go** Try to visit in good weather, because you'll spend most of your time outdoors. **Special comments** Rising above Carrowmore is Knocknarea, a mountain that crowns a promontory in Sligo Bay. You can walk to the summit, a moderately difficult 45-minute climb, to enjoy the views. A huge stone mound, known as a cairn, is said to be the tomb of Maeve, the first-century-BC Celtic queen; more likely, archaeologists say, the stones cover another large passage tomb. **How much time to allow** At least 1 hour.

DESCRIPTION AND COMMENTS These passage tombs (burial chambers dug into the hillside, with entrances constructed of stone) span several prehistoric centuries. Most date from around 5,000 BC, making them even older than Stonehenge in England. One of the tombs, from about 5,500 BC, is believed to be the oldest piece of freestanding stone architecture in the

How Attractions Compare in the Northwest of Ireland

ATTRACTION	DESCRIPTION	AUTHOR'S RATING
SLIGO TOWN		
Carrowmore	Megalithic cemetery	★★★★
Lissadell House	Historic home	★★★½
Parke's Castle	Historic home	★★★½
Sligo County Museum	Museum of local history	★★★½
Sligo Abbey	Medieval abbey and friary	★★½
DONEGAL TOWN		
Old Abbey	Monastic ruins	★★★½
Donegal Castle	Castle and fortified house	★★½
NORTH DONEGAL		
Glebe House	Historic home and art gallery	★★★★
Glenveagh Castle	Historic home	★★★★

world. Quarrying in the not-so-distant past destroyed many of the tombs, which once numbered in the hundreds, although the 40 or so that remain still comprise the largest collection of prehistoric tombs in the British Isles. Most importantly, standing on this windy hillside—one of the world's great ancient sites—and staring into the tombs so carefully constructed millennia ago is a haunting experience. Exhibits in a small stone cottage help illuminate the significance of Carrowmore.

TOURING TIPS   Another prehistoric grave site, Carrowkeel, lies to the east of Carrowmore, high above the shores of Lough Arrow outside the town of Castlebaldwin. Carrowkeel is much more remote than Carrowmore, and much less visited and developed, so you may find yourself alone on the hillside exploring the 14 tombs. To reach Carrowkeel, follow the well-marked single-lane road up the hill from Castlebaldwin.

 ## Sligo Abbey ★★½

APPEAL BY AGE	PRESCHOOL ★★	GRADE SCHOOL ★★	TEENS ★★
YOUNG ADULTS ★★	OVER 30 ★★½		SENIORS ★★½

Abbey Street, Sligo Town; ☎ 071-914-6406; www.heritageireland.ie

Type of attraction Medieval abbey and friary. **Admission** €2 adults, €1 children and students, €1.25 seniors, €5 families of up to 2 adults and 2 children. **Hours** April–October, daily, 10 a.m.–6:30 p.m. **When to go** Anytime; the ruins are especially evocative in the rain. **Special comments** If you are traveling north to Donegal and are pressed for time, you may want to give Sligo Abbey a quick

Walks and Drives in the Northwest

Rugged and often desolate, Northwest Ireland is graced with wild moors, rocky coasts, and stark mountains that are among some of the most beautiful landscapes in Ireland.

GREAT WALKS

SLIEVE LEAGUE

Hands down, the most dramatic walk in Ireland is along these soaring sea cliffs (see page 360) about 50 kilometers (30 miles) west of **Donegal Town.** A short but unforgettable walk begins in the small village of **Bunglass** and follows the tops of the cliffs for three kilometers (two miles), traversing Eagle's Nest and other heights before reaching the **Slieve League** summit via **One Man's Pass,** an aptly named narrow ridge with dizzying drops on either side.

ERRIGAL MOUNTAIN

A scramble up this distinctively shaped mountain, 752 meters (2,476 feet) tall and the highest peak in Donegal, is one of Ireland's most scenic hikes. The most popular, and least demanding, ascent covers about eight kilometers (five miles) and begins at a well-marked turnoff on R251 three kilometers (two miles) east of the village of **Dunlewey.** Soon after you cross the grassy lower slopes of the peak, you will be rewarded with views across the surrounding mountains, moors, and glens and from the summit, extending all the way to the Inishowen Peninsula to the north and Slieve League to the south and east.

THE NORTHERN HEADLANDS

Malin Head, at the tip of the **Inishowen Peninsula,** is officially the northernmost tip of Ireland. A view-filled walk begins at **Malin Well Beach,** about one kilometer (half a mile) east of the town of Malin Head and follows cliff tops east along the peninsula to **Black Hill.** The round-trip trek is 12 kilometers (7.5 miles), but even a short walk affords wonderful views of the **Antrim Coast** in Northern Ireland (see page 400) and the **Kintyre Peninsula** in Scotland.

glance and tour the more dramatic abbey ruins in Donegal Town. **How much time to allow** About half an hour.

DESCRIPTION AND COMMENTS Modern-day Sligo bustles just outside the walls, but the significant remains of a once-important religious community are a reminder of the role this medieval settlement played. Maurice Fitzgerald, a Norman baron and one of the founders of Sligo, brought the Dominicans to Ireland and built this elaborate complex for the friars. They taught, studied, and worshipped here, and the friary also served as a place for public worship. The remains include much elaborate stonework,

ARDS

Ards Forest Park, about 30 kilometers (18 miles) northwest of **Ramelton** on Sheephaven Bay, encompasses more than 600 hectares (1,000 acres) of woodlands and beaches, as well as lakes, bogs, and even a few prehistoric stone circles. A network of trails follows the shores of **Lough Lilly** and the bay, crossing terrain that seems barely touched. An especially scenic walk (three kilometers or two miles round trip) leads from the main parking area (where a sign shows trails within the park) to **Black Strand** on Clonmass Bay. Follow the dune-backed beach to a path that leads east through woodlands to **Binnagorm Point,** for stunning views of the bay and surrounding hills.

GREAT DRIVES

AROUND THE NORTHERN HEADLANDS

Northwest Ireland meets the sea in a string of mountainous peninsulas, most of which can be circumnavigated on scenery-filled drives.

Carrigart, some 14 kilometers (9 miles) north of Ramelton on R245, is the start of **Atlantic Drive** around the Rosguill Peninsula. You might want to linger a little while on **Rosapenna Beach,** just to the north of town, before following the signs onto the 15-kilometer (9-mile) circuit.

Atlantic Drive passes bays on one side and mountains on the other, coming to beaches at **Downings** and **Tranarossan Strand.** As you round the tip of the peninsula, you'll have spectacular views of the coast, with **Horn Head** to the west, **Fanad Head** to the east, and **Errigal Mountain** to the south.

At the southern end of the peninsula, pass through Carrigart again, and then continue 11 kilometers (7 miles) south on R245 to the town of **Creslough,** on Sheephaven Bay. Just outside of town, on a promontory at the southern end of the bay, is **Doe Castle,** not much more than a stone tower surrounded by thick walls. In the 15th century, the castle was the residence of MacSweeney Doe, a *gallowglass* (foreign mercenary) hired by the O'Donnell

Continued on next page

including the framework for 13th-century lancet windows, one of the few sculpted altars to remain from a medieval Irish church, an elaborate rood screen, and lovely cloisters. Tombstones rather gloomily litter the ruins, as the abbey was destroyed during the British sacking of Sligo in 1642 and became the town burial ground. Among the tombs are medieval markers above the graves of princes and princesses of Sligo, and their presence among the ruins is a comment on the fleeting nature of earthly might.

TOURING TIPS You can learn more about Sligo's long history at the Sligo County Museum (page 348).

Walks and Drives in the Northwest (continued)

GREAT DRIVES (CONTINUED)

AROUND THE NORTHERN HEADLANDS (CONTINUED)

clan; the site is not attended but is usually open, and you can visit the stark, damp rooms daily, 10 a.m. to 5 p.m.; admission is free.

Also near Creslough is **Ards Forest Park,** where the wonderfully varied landscapes include slat marshes, wooded valleys, and long, sandy beaches and are crisscrossed with excellent hiking trails (see page 363); ☎ 074-53271; open daily, 8 a.m. to dusk; free admission, parking fees.

From Creslough, follow N56 north 11 kilometers (7 miles) to **Dunfanaghy,** on the western shore of Sheephaven Bay. The tides here are extreme, so the town's **Killyhoey Beach** becomes a vast tidal flat at some times and is completely submerged at others. A small road to the north of town rounds **Horn Head,** which drops to the sea in steep cliffs where gulls, puffins, and other seabirds roost.

Once back in Dunfanaghy, you can retrace your steps east to Carrigart or continue west into more-rugged scenery. If you opt for the latter, follow N56 west for 11 kilometers (7 miles) through stony, barren terrain to **Falcarragh,** then another 13 kilometers (8 miles) to **Meenlaragh.** Weather permitting—and it's often not—boats sail from this scrappy little village to desolate, treeless **Tory Island,** inhabited by a few hearty fishermen.

The mainland is not much more hospitable, and as you head west on R257 you won't see much but stone-studded moors and stark mountains. This is the **Gweedore Headland,** where Irish is the first language in the tiny villages and lonely farms. The singer Enya comes from Gweedore, and it's easy to see a connection between the barren landscapes and her soulful music. The western edge of the headland, about 30 kilometers (18 miles) south of Meenlaragh, is **Bloody Foreland,** named for the color of the rocky seaside cliffs as they catch the rays of the setting sun.

AROUND ERRIGAL MOUNTAIN

A short drive west from **Letterkenny** brings you into some of Ireland's wildest

Sligo County Museum ★ ★ ★ ½

APPEAL BY AGE	PRESCHOOL ★ ★		GRADE SCHOOL ★ ★	TEENS ★ ★
YOUNG ADULTS ★ ★		OVER 30 ★ ★ ★ ½		SENIORS ★ ★ ★ ½

Stephen Street, Sligo Town; ☎ 071-42212

Type of attraction Museum of local history. **Admission** Free. **Hours** June–September, Tuesday–Saturday, 10 a.m.–noon and 2–4:50 p.m.; October–mid-December and mid-March–May, Tuesday–Saturday, 2–4 p.m. **When to go**

and most spectacular mountain scenery. Here, the slopes of the **Derry-veagh Mountains** are covered with moors, bogs, stands of birch, and carpets of ferns.

From Letterkenny, follow R250 and R251 for 16 kilometers (11 miles) to **Gratan Lough,** a large lake surrounded by forested slopes. The lakeside village of **Church Hill** is said to have been the birthplace of St. Colomba in the sixth century. **Glebe House,** on the northwest shores of the lake, is an oasis of civilization—the 19th-cenutry manor is filled with a fine collection of 19th- and 20th-century art and surrounded by beautiful gardens (see page 364).

Gratan Lough is at the edge of **Glenveagh National Park.** These 10,000 hectares (24,000 acres) of moors, mountains, and lakes compose what may just be the most beautiful and wild scenery in Ireland, and the park is an enchanting place to spend as much time as you can manage. Within the park the summits of the Derryveagh Mountains rise; the lush valleys of the River Owenbeagh are filled with stands of oak; and Lough Veagh cuts a shimmering blue swath through the northeast corner. The **Derrylahan Nature Trail** is one of many paths that traverse the wilderness. You can get information on walks and other activities in the park at the visitors center, just outside Church Hill; open mid-April through October, daily, 10 a.m. to 6 p.m.; ☎ 074-913-7090. Not all of the charm of Glenveagh is natural: **Glenveagh Castle** (see page 365) is a lavish home reflecting 20th-century tastes and comforts, surrounded by well-tended gardens.

For close-up views of **Errigal Mountain** or a trek to its 752-meter (2,476-foot) summit (see above), follow R251 around the northern fringes of the park to the little village of **Dunlewey,** beautifully perched between the shores of Dunlewey Lough and the flanks of the mountain. A trail to the summit begins from a roadside trailhead three kilometers (two miles) east of the village on R251. The **Lakeside Centre** in Dunlewey, occupying a 19th-century weaver's home, aptly features demonstrations of old weaving techniques and also provides short boat trips on the waters of Dunlewey Lough; ☎ 075-31699; open April through May, Saturday and Sunday, noon to 6 p.m., and June through September, daily, noon to 6 p.m.; admission is €5.

Anytime. **Special comments** For fans of William Butler Yeats, the manuscripts and other memorabilia are fascinating; all visitors will be entranced by the paintings of Jack Yeats. **How much time to allow** At least 1 hour.

DESCRIPTION AND COMMENTS This small museum houses two collections. One shows earnest but humdrum exhibits of artifacts that pertain to local history; however, it comes to life with regard to the works of William Butler Yeats, who is lovingly remembered with first editions, letters, and other memorabilia—a gold mine for Yeats fans. The adjoining

walks and drives in the northwest

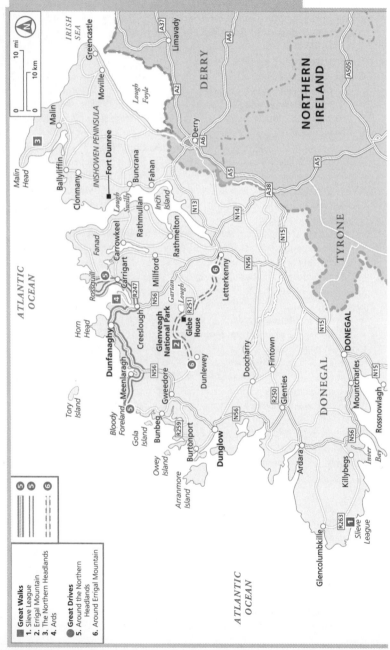

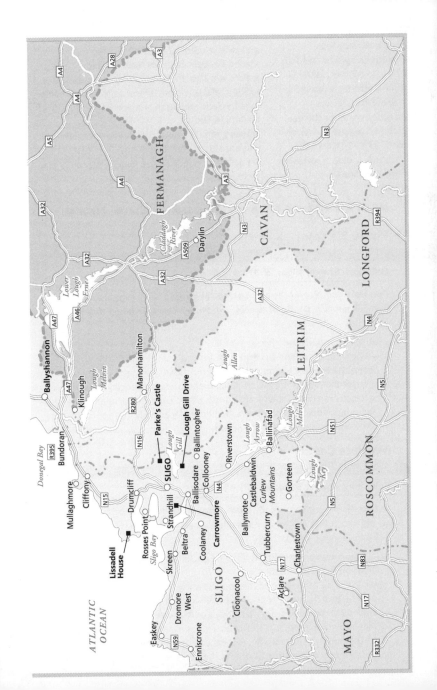

unofficial TIP
For a picnic, step into aromatic **Cosgrove and Son** (32 Market Street, ☎ 071-42809), offering a tempting array of Irish cheeses and soda breads, or **Kates Kitchen/Hopper** (24 Market Street, ☎ 071-914-3022), which sells a wide assortment of deli selections.

Niland Gallery is devoted to the works of the poet's brother, Jack Yeats, who was one of the most important painters of 20th-century Ireland and whose colorful canvases evoke many local scenes. Portraits by John Yeats, the father of both artists, are also on view. The family had its roots in Sligo, and this is the largest collection of paintings by Jack and John outside of the National Gallery in Dublin.

TOURING TIPS If you are continuing north, you will encounter more works by Jack Yeats at the art gallery of Glebe House near Letterkenny (see page 364).

RESTAURANTS IN AND AROUND SLIGO TOWN

Bistro Bianconi ★ ★ ★

ITALIAN	MODERATE	QUALITY ★ ★ ★ ★	VALUE ★ ★ ★

O'Connell Street, Sligo; ☎ 071-914-7000

Reservations Not necessary. **Entree range** €13–€28. **Payment** AE, MC, V. **Bar** Full service. **Disabled access** Yes. **Hours** Daily, 12:30–2:30 p.m., 5:30–midnight.

MENU RECOMMENDATIONS Pizza.

COMMENTS Some of the best pizza in Ireland comes out of the wood-fired ovens here, and carryout is available for those wishing to indulge in summertime pizza on the beach. A full menu of Italian specialties is served in a handsome room of white tile and light-colored wood, as are some delicious appetizers (including a baguette decadently topped with many different cheeses) and hefty salads.

Markree Castle ★ ★ ★ ★

CONTINENTAL	EXPENSIVE	QUALITY ★ ★ ★ ★	VALUE ★ ★ ★

Collooney, County Sligo; ☎ 071-916-7800

Reservations Recommended. **Entree range** Prix-fixe dinner, €40. **Payment** AE, DC, MC, V. **Bar** Full service. **Disabled access** Yes. **Hours** Monday–Saturday, 7–9 p.m.; Sunday, 1–3 p.m., 7–9 p.m.

MENU RECOMMENDATIONS Roast lamb or duckling, salmon and other fish and seafood from Sligo Bay.

COMMENTS This atmospheric castle is the ancestral home of Charles Cooper, and he and his wife, Mary, were well-known restaurateurs before they took over the day-to-day operations of Markree. Accordingly, a group of elegantly plastered and mirrored dining rooms is the setting for some of the region's best cuisine. A meal can be followed by coffee or a drink in front of a roaring fire in one of the lounges.

How Restaurants Compare in the Northwest of Ireland

NAME	CUISINE	OVERALL	QUALITY	VALUE	PRICE
SLIGO TOWN					
Montmartre	French	★★★★½	★★★★	★★★★½	mod
Markree Castle	Continental	★★★★	★★★★	★★★	exp
Bistro Bianconi	Italian	★★★	★★★★	★★★	mod
DONEGAL TOWN					
The Weaver's Loft	Irish	★★★	★★★½	★★★★	inexp
KILLYBEGS					
Kitty Kelly's	seafood/Irish	★★★★	★★★★	★★★★	mod
NORTH DONEGAL					
Weeping Elm	modern Irish	★★★★½	★★★★½	★★★½	exp
Green Room	Continental	★★★★	★★★★	★★★★	exp
Bridge Café	seafood	★★★½	★★★	★★★★	mod

Montmartre   ★ ★ ★ ★ ½

FRENCH	MODERATE	QUALITY ★★★★	VALUE ★★★★½

Market Yard, Sligo; ☎ 071-916-9901

Reservations Recommended. **Entree range** €14–€23; early dinner, €15; prix-fixe dinner, €35. **Payment** AE, DC, MC, V. **Bar** Full service. **Disabled access** Yes. **Hours** Tuesday–Sunday, 5–11 p.m.

MENU RECOMMENDATIONS   Fish soup, roast rabbit.

COMMENTS   Chef Stéphane Magaud does credit to the airy and charming bistro-like surroundings in an old building at the top of the city center. Excellent preparations of French classics are made modern with many imaginative twists. Service has a twist, too, as the French wait staff are as friendly and accommodating as their Irish counterparts. The wine list is exceptional, with many exciting choices available by the glass and half bottle.

ENTERTAINMENT AND NIGHTLIFE IN SLIGO TOWN

SLIGO'S MOST ATMOSPHERIC PUB IS **Hargadon Brothers** (4 O'Connell Street, ☎ 071-917-0933), a dark and welcoming place of paneled walls, stone floors, cozy little alcoves, and crackling fires. **Hawk's Well Theatre** (Johnston Court, ☎ 071-916-1526) is Northwest Ireland's leading theater, hosting top companies from throughout the country.

EXERCISE AND RECREATION IN AND AROUND SLIGO TOWN

EXCELLENT BEACHES RING THE SHORES of Sligo Bay (beware, though, as the water is cold), the most popular being those at **Rosses Point** and **Strandhill.** If you tire of the beach and fancy a round of golf, head inland to the **Strandhill Golf Club** (Strandhill, ☎ 071-916-8188, **www.strandhillgc.com**) or the **County Sligo Golf Club** (Rosses Point, ☎ 071-917-7134, **www.countysligogolfclub.ie**).

AROUND SLIGO TOWN

ENGAGING SCENERY SURROUNDS SLIGO TOWN, from rugged maritime landscapes to green glens and mist-shrouded mountains littered with prehistoric remains.

LOUGH GILL

THIS SERENE BODY OF WATER (the name aptly means "Lake Beauty"), shimmering beneath green hills, is endowed with a great deal of romance. The lake lies at the center of what the tourist industry has termed "Yeats Country," referring to the prominence of this region in the poetry of William Butler Yeats. Although the poet and playwright was born in Dublin and raised in London, he held these landscapes close to his heart and wrote of them often. Another romantic notion associated with the lake is the legend of the bell of Sligo Abbey. The story goes that when Sir Frederick Hamilton sacked Sligo in 1642 and demolished the abbey, his soldiers sank the silver bell in the lake. Unlikely as the tale is (the plunder would no doubt have been carted off), it's said still today that the pure of heart and deed can hear the bell tolling.

An extremely popular route, and a must-do for Yeats fans, is the **Lough Gill Drive.** This well-marked circuit follows R287, R288, and R286 around the lake, affording wonderful views. From the south end of the route, a lane leads to a landing stage where a boatman may or may not be waiting to ferry visitors to the **Isle of Innisfree.** For Yeats fans, the island may recall such lines as "I hear lake water lapping with low sounds by the shore." Others may experience slight disappointment upon seeing the nondescript little islet. Even so, this island, the subject of Yeats's "The Lake Isle of Innisfree," summoned for the poet all the nostalgia he felt for Sligo. On the lake's eastern shore stands formidable **Parke's Castle** (see below). The suburbs of Sligo appear a bit farther along R286 and dispel the romantic aura of Lough Gill.

Attraction along Lough Gill

Parke's Castle ★ ★ ★ ½

APPEAL BY AGE	PRESCHOOL ★ ★ ★	GRADE SCHOOL ★ ★ ★ ★	TEENS ★ ★ ★
YOUNG ADULTS ★ ★ ★ ★		OVER 30 ★ ★ ★ ½	SENIORS ★ ★ ★ ½

Eastern shore of Lough Gill, ☎ 071-916-4149

Type of attraction Historic home. **Admission** €2.75 adults, €1.25 children and students, €2 seniors, €7 families. **Hours** April–May, Tuesday–Sunday, 10 a.m.–5 p.m.; June–September, daily, 9:30 a.m.–6:30 p.m.; October, daily, 10 a.m.–5 p.m. **When to go** Anytime. **Special comments** From the castle, you can make an easy walk to the remains of Creevelea Abbey, founded by the Franciscans in 1508; the remains include a charming cloister and carvings depicting the life of St. Francis of Assisi. **How much time to allow** 1 hour, 2 hours to also explore the lakeshore and nearby Creevelea Abbey.

DESCRIPTION AND COMMENTS   The O'Rourkes, a clan of local rulers, built a fortress on the shores of Lough Gill in the Middle Ages, but the present structure dates from the 17th century. That's when Captain Robert Parke, a British planter, arrived, confiscated the surrounding lands from Irish Catholics, and used materials from the original structure to build a fortified castle that would offer him protection from the hostile populace. Despite this tumultuous history and the injustices of the Plantation system, by which King James I of England meant to supplant the native Irish and subject them to British rule, Parke's Castle is a beautiful place, a tall, handsome house of light stone and sturdy timbers. Beyond the enclosed courtyard is a massive great hall and several other drafty rooms that overlook the lake through tall windows.

TOURING TIPS   In good weather, board one of the boats that depart from the dock below the castle for a tour of Lough Gill.

ROSSES POINT AND DRUMCLIFF

A DRAMATIC HEADLAND at the entrance to Sligo Harbour, **Rosses Point,** about eight kilometers (five miles) northwest of Sligo, is ringed with long, golden beaches that are especially attractive in the low light of the sun setting over the Atlantic Ocean. William Butler Yeats and his brother, painter Jack Yeats, spent their boyhood summers at Rosses Point. The former Yeats and his wife, Georgina, are buried nearby in the churchyard at **Drumcliff.** The poet's simple tombstone is engraved with words he penned himself: "Cast a cold eye / On life, on death. / Horseman, pass by!" Behind the graves rises the dramatic, flat-topped summit of **Ben Bulben.** From Sligo, R291 leads out to Rosses Point, and N4 leads seven kilometers (four miles) north from Sligo to Drumcliff.

Attraction around Drumcliff

Lissadell House ★ ★ ★ ½

APPEAL BY AGE	PRESCHOOL ★★	GRADE SCHOOL ★★	TEENS ★★
YOUNG ADULTS ★★	OVER 30 ★★★½		SENIORS ★★★½

On Drumcliff Bay, 3 kilometers (2 miles) west of Drumcliff on N15; ☎ 071-916-3150; www.lissadell.com

Type of attraction Historic home. **Admission** €6 adults, €3 children; garden tours: €6, 1 hour, €10, 2½ hours. **Hours** Mid-March–late-September, 11 a.m.–6 p.m.

When to go Try to find a patch of good weather so you can enjoy the grounds.
Special comments Tours are unusually enlightening, as they provide fascinating
details of the house's history and its past inhabitants, as well as ongoing restoration efforts such as refurbishing the original wall coverings and gas fixtures. **How
much time to allow** 1 hour for the house, half a day to tour the gardens and
grounds as well.

DESCRIPTION AND COMMENTS This neoclassical Georgian mansion of local
limestone is not only lovely, but it also has witnessed some remarkably
colorful history. For most of its history, the house has been home to the
Gore-Booth family, the most famous member of which is best known as
the Countess Markievicz (the title Constance Gore-Booth acquired
when she married a Polish count). Constance was a prominent figure in
the 1916 Irish Rising, for which she was imprisoned and sentenced to
death (the sentence was reversed), and she became the first female
member of the British House of Commons and the Dáil Éireann, or Irish
Parliament. The count's family portraits grace pilasters in the dining room.
Constance's forebear Sir Robert Gore-Booth distinguished himself as an
enlightened landlord when he mortgaged Lissadell House to raise funds
to save his tenants from starvation during the Famine; Constance's
brother, Josslyn, carried on this tradition, selling more than 28,000 acres
to his tenants at affordable rates and instituting vast agrarian reforms.
William Butler Yeats, a frequent visitor to the house, became close friends
with Constance and her sister, Eva; he wrote, "The light of evening, Lissadell, / Great windows open to the south, / Two girls in silk kimonos."
Edwin Walsh and his wife, Constance Cassidy, have recently purchased
Lissadell House, where they are raising their seven children. Several rooms
are open to the public on guided tours, as are the gardens.

TOURING TIPS The woods surrounding Lissadell House are home to Ireland's
largest colony of barnacle geese, as well as many other wildfowl and birds.

▌ DONEGAL TOWN

DONEGAL TOWN IS A FRIENDLY PLACE, nestled into a valley of the
River Eske near its mouth in Donegal Bay. Even the proud 15th-century
castle that dominates the town center is a benign presence these days,
and a convivial atmosphere prevails in the Diamond, the triangular
marketplace upon which major streets converge. The name Donegal
derives from *Dún na nGall*, or "Fort of the Foreigners"—a reference to
the Vikings, who sailed in and out of Donegal Bay and in the ninth century set up a garrison here as a handy base for raiding and pillaging the
north. The O'Donnell clan drove out the Vikings and built the fortified
house that has become **Donegal Castle** (page 358), and soon a colony
of scholarly monks flourished at Donegal's now-ruined abbey. A monument in the Diamond commemorates the Franciscan friars who painstakingly preserved the history of Gaelic Ireland in their *Annals of the Four
Masters*, which traces the history of Ireland up to 1618. It is easy to

understand why the monks found it necessary to preserved Gaelic culture: the British took over the town in the 17th century, drove out Catholic land-holders, and gave their properties to Protestant colonists from England.

ARRIVING AND GETTING ORIENTED IN DONEGAL TOWN

DONEGAL IS APPROXIMATELY 66 KILOMETERS (40 miles) northeast of Sligo Town; the direct route by car is on N4 and N15. At least six **Bus Éireann** buses travel between Donegal and Sligo daily; the trip takes about 1 hour and costs €3.50. Buses stop on the Diamond, the Donegal mar-ketplace. For information about the town and surrounding region, step into the **Donegal Tourist Office** on Quay Street; ☎ 074-972-1148; Easter to September, Monday through Friday, 9 a.m. to 5 p.m.; Saturday, 10 a.m. to 6 p.m.; Sunday, noon to 4 p.m.; October to Easter, Monday through Friday, 9 a.m. to 5 p.m.

unofficial **TIP**
Donegal Bay Waterbus tours provide lovely views of the town and the ruined abbey while cruising down the river into Donegal Bay. In the bay, the rugged shoreline, seabirds, and seals at Seal Island nicely fill 90 minutes of sightseeing. Tours run May–September, but times vary widely depending on the weather and the tide. Tickets are available at the small office on the Pier (Donegal Town, ☎ 074-972-3666) for €8 adults, €4.50 children and seniors.

EXPLORING DONEGAL TOWN

YOU'LL FIND IT A PLEASURE to spend an hour or two walking through Donegal, strolling on and off the Diamond, visiting the town's two sights of note (see below), and eyeing the many woolen goods that fill the shop windows.

HOTEL IN DONEGAL TOWN

St. Ernan's House ★ ★ ★ ★

QUALITY ★★★★	VALUE ★★★	FROM €230

Donegal, County Donegal; ☎ 074-972-1065; fax 074-972-2098; www.sainternans.com

Location In Donegal Bay. **Amenities and services** 12 units; boating, dining room, garden, lounges, swimming. **Elevator** No. **Parking** On property, free. **Price** Includes full Irish breakfast. **Credit cards** AE, MC, V.

DESCRIPTION AND COMMENTS This remarkable retreat occupies its own island in Donegal Bay, providing magnificent water views along with a great deal of luxury and a real sense of escape from the world. Guests make themselves at home in a series of handsome, fire-warmed lounges and retreat upstairs to room that vary considerably in size but attain the same level of taste and comfort. Donegal Town is only 2 kilometers (1.25 miles) away from the end of the causeway that connects the island to the mainland, but it would be easy to hole up here for a couple of days—especially since superb prix-fixe dinners (from €55) are served in a dining room as tasteful as the rest of the house.

ATTRACTIONS IN DONEGAL TOWN

 Donegal Castle ★ ★ ½

APPEAL BY AGE	PRESCHOOL ★ ★	GRADE SCHOOL ★ ★	TEENS ★ ★
YOUNG ADULTS ★ ★		OVER 30 ★ ★ ½	SENIORS ★ ★ ½

Castle Street, Donegal Town; ☎ 074-972-2405

Type of attraction Castle and fortified house. **Admission** €3.50 adults, €1.25 children and students, €2.50 seniors, €8.50 families. **Hours** Mid-March–October, daily, 10 a.m.–5:15 p.m. **When to go** Anytime. **Special comments** After visiting the castle, take a good look at the Diamond, the marketplace that Sir Basil Brooke also designed as part of his efforts to make Donegal a model British Plantation Town. **How much time to allow** About 45 minutes for castle and grounds.

DESCRIPTION AND COMMENTS Standing mightily in the center of town, Donegal Castle is partly in ruin, but it incorporates the splendid and beautifully restored 15th-century fortified house that was once the residence of the O'Donnells, a ruling clan ousted by the British in 1607. The O'Donnells did not leave without a fight—Hugh Roe O'Donnell managed to fend off at least one onslaught of British troops and died not in battle but of fever in Spain, where he had gone to muster a force to fight a British invasion. When Englishman Sir Basil Brooke finally took possession in 1610, he added the turrets and gables that lend the castle its distinctive appearance. You can wander the pleasant grounds, enclosed behind high walls, and visit the Great Hall and a few other rooms on informative and blessedly short (25 minutes) guided tours. All in all, though, as far as Irish castles go, this one is fairly dull.

TOURING TIPS From the castle, walk across the Diamond, the center of Donegal, and from there follow Quay Street south to the Old Abbey. This route will give you a nice sense of the town.

Old Abbey ★ ★ ★ ½

APPEAL BY AGE	PRESCHOOL ★ ★ ★	GRADE SCHOOL ★ ★ ★	TEENS ★ ★ ★
YOUNG ADULTS ★ ★ ★		OVER 30 ★ ★ ★ ½	SENIORS ★ ★ ★ ½

The Quay, Donegal Town

Type of attraction Monastic ruins. **Admission** Free. **Hours** Always accessible. **When to go** In good weather, if possible. **Special comments** If you're traveling on to Dublin, be sure to seek out the facsimile of *Annals of the Four Masters,* compiled here and on view at the National Library. **How much time to allow** 45 minutes.

DESCRIPTION AND COMMENTS The O'Donnells, the ruling clan of this region, established a monastery for the Franciscan Order in 1474, at about the same time that they constructed their castle. The two centuries that followed were unusually tumultuous for what had been intended to be a quiet religious community on the banks of the River Eske. The abbey was important enough to attract a gathering of clergy, scholars, and political leaders in 1539, but it soon was torn asunder by the fierce fighting that ensued as the British stepped up their attempts to dominate this part of Ireland. Attacks in 1593, 1601, and 1607 all but destroyed the complex, though the friars remained. From 1632 to 1636, four resident scholars endeavored to preserve the Celtic culture in *Annals of the Four Masters,* a compilation of old Gaelic manuscripts that trace Irish history and mythology from the earliest times; a facsimile of this precious work is on view at the National Library in Dublin. What remains today are the choir and other portions of the church, as well as two walls of the cloisters, all romantically perched above the river near its mouth at Donegal Bay.

TOURING TIPS The abbey ruins are particularly impressive from the water; look for them as you enter Donegal Bay on a Waterbus tour (see page 357).

RESTAURANT IN DONEGAL TOWN

The Weaver's Loft ★ ★ ★

IRISH	INEXPENSIVE	QUALITY ★ ★ ★ ½	VALUE ★ ★ ★ ★

Above Magee's, the Diamond; ☎ 074-972-2660

Reservations Not necessary. **Entree range** €6–€10. **Payment** AE, MC, V. **Bar** Beer and wine only. **Disabled access** No. **Hours** Monday–Saturday, 10 a.m.–5 p.m.

MENU RECOMMENDATIONS Fresh seafood from Donegal Bay.

COMMENTS This pleasant cafeteria above Magee's, Donegal's famous woolen-goods shop, is a handy place for a meal before or after sightseeing and shopping. Hot meals change daily but often include Irish stew and fish chowder, both made with care. Hefty salads, sandwiches, and pastries are always available.

SHOPPING IN DONEGAL TOWN

ANYONE LOOKING FOR HANDWOVEN Donegal tweeds need look no farther than **Magee of Donegal,** famous throughout the land for its handsome jackets and coats, as well as a fine array of woolen goods and fabrics. Magee's, in fact, is one of Donegal's main attractions, and it commands pride of place on the Diamond; ☎ 071-972-1526.

AROUND DONEGAL TOWN

KILLYBEGS

BUSY AND FAR MORE BUILT-UP than other places on this relatively remote stretch of North Donegal coast, Killybegs is made picturesque by its harbor full of vessels from around the world. The town is one of the major fishing ports in Ireland, and huge trawlers from as far afield as Eastern Europe unload their catches at sundown, when the town is especially lively. Killybegs is 28 kilometers (17 miles) west of Donegal Town on R293.

Restaurant in Killybegs

Kitty Kelly's ★ ★ ★ ★

SEAFOOD/IRISH	MODERATE	QUALITY ★ ★ ★ ★	VALUE ★ ★ ★ ★

Largy, Killybegs; ☎ 074-973-1925

Reservations Recommended. **Entree range** €8–€10. **Payment** MC, V. **Bar** Full bar. **Disabled access** Yes. **Hours** Daily, 7–9:30 p.m.

MENU RECOMMENDATIONS Fresh fish and seafood.

COMMENTS This pink-toned cottage on the coast road five kilometers (three miles) west of Killybegs is hard to miss, and not just because of its distinctive paint job—it seems that most of Killybegs heads here for dinner. The cozy, old-fashioned interior can be a Tower of Babel as crews from the many foreign ships that dock in town settle in for a meal of mussels from Bruckless and other delicious homemade fare.

SLIEVE LEAGUE

PERHAPS THE MOST DRAMATIC VIEW in all of Ireland—and that is saying quite a lot—is the prospect of these multihued ocean cliffs rising some 600 meters (2,000 feet) out of the raging surf. The tallest sea cliffs in Europe, they are much more thrilling to behold than even the Cliffs of Moher (see page 297) near Galway. The remote location is no small part of the appeal, and you may find yourself alone standing on a precipitous ledge regarding the spectacle of the majestic cliff face, framed by sea and mountains.

From the the village of Carrick, follow the signs to Bunglas and Slieve League. At the tiny village of Teelin, signs will direct you to the road that precipitously climbs the slopes of Slieve League, passing stunning (if hair-raising) views of the sea far below and the cliffs ahead. After about three kilometers (two miles), the road comes to a ledge that affords dead-on views of jagged cliffs. From here you can walk to the summit on One Man's Pass, not recommended for those who suffer from vertigo or for anyone when the path is slippery. The apt name derives from the fact that at one point the path is wide enough for only one walker to pass through the sheer drop-offs on both sides of the narrow track.

NORTH DONEGAL

THE MOST NORTHERLY REACHES of Ireland meet the sea in a series of rugged headlands. The interior is a rugged landscape of mountains, lakes, and forests, where many of the villages of whitewashed cottages are *Gaeltacht,* or Irish speaking.

The major town in the far north is **Letterkenny,** which is said to be the fastest-growing place in Ireland. Unfortunately, it may soon also be the least attractive: town planners are taking their cues from the worst sort of development, and Letterkenny these days is an un-appealing collection of parking lots, shopping malls, and megastores. Don't linger here—**Ramelton** and **Rathmullan,** just a bit farther north on the shores of Lough Swilly, are much more pleasant places to spend your time and to use as a base.

ARRIVING AND GETTING ORIENTED IN NORTH DONEGAL

LETTERKENNY, ABOUT 115 KILOMETERS (70 miles) northeast of Sligo Town, is the main hub of the North Donegal region. If you are traveling by car, follow N15 from Sligo through Donegal Town and north to Stranoriar, where the road continues north as N56. **Bus Éireann** buses travel between Letterkenny and Dublin four times a day; the trip takes about four hours and costs €10. The bus station is at the end of a shopping-center parking lot at the north end of town. Keep in mind, though, that the only easy way to explore the often lonely countryside is by car. Letterkenny is also the place to stock up on information. The **Tourist Information Office** occupies a flashy new building rather inconveniently located outside the town center, on a roundabout on the Derry Road; ☎ 074-21160, **www.irelandnorth west.ie.** The office is open September to May, Monday through Friday, 9 a.m. to 5 p.m.; June, Monday through Saturday, 9 a.m. to 6 p.m.; and July to August, Monday through Saturday, 9 a.m. to 8 p.m., and Sunday, 10 a.m. to 2 p.m.

HOTELS IN NORTH DONEGAL

Castle Grove Country House Hotel ★ ★ ★ ★

QUALITY ★ ★ ★ ½	VALUE ★ ★ ★	€80–€160

Letterkenny, County Donegal; ☎ 074-915118; fax 074-915118; reservation@castlegrove.com; www.castlegrove.com

Location Off R245, about 3 kilometers (2 miles) north of Letterkenny. **Amenities and services** 14 rooms; bar, boats, disabled access, hair dryers, nonsmoking rooms, restaurant, walking. **Elevator** No. **Parking** Free, on property. **Price** Includes full Irish breakfast. **Credit cards** AE, MC, V.

Though the sprawl of Letterkenny encroaches, this delightful estate remains intact, tucked away on the shores of Lough Swilly on grounds laid out by the great British landscape designer Capability Brown in the 18th century. Sheep graze beneath magnificent old oaks as the sea glimmers in the distance, and the house merges old-world elegance with thoughtful attention to comfort and amenities. A series of drawing rooms, a library, and a conservatory are welcoming and much used. Guest rooms are located upstairs and in an adjoining carriage house; all are large and furnished with comfy old pieces (including the occasional four-poster bed), and come with some nice touches—some rooms on the ground floor open to the beautifully maintained gardens, and those at the front of the house have wonderful views of the grounds and sea. The hotel's restaurant, the Green Room, offers the best dining in the region (see page 366).

Frewin ★ ★ ★ ★ ½

| QUALITY ★★★★ | VALUE ★★★★ | €70–€140 |

Ramelton, County Donegal; ☎ 074-915-1246; fax 074-915-1246; flaxmill@indigo.ie; www.frewinhouse.com

Location Outside Ramelton, 11 kilometers (7 miles) north of Letterkenny off R245. **Amenities and services** 4 units plus a housekeeping cottage; garden, lounges, nonsmoking rooms. **Elevator** No. **Parking** Free, on property. **Price** Includes full Irish breakfast. **Credit cards** MC, V.

Thomas and Regina Coyle restored a Victorian rectory and filled it with their collection of antiques, memorabilia, books, Persian carpets, and old prints—all handsomely displayed in the warm, uncluttered lounges and private rooms of this wonderful guest house. The Coyles' fine taste and the good bones of the old house are a winning combination, and guests soon feel at home in an airy sitting room as well as a small library where a fire burns in colder months. A shady garden on a bluff above the River Swilly is a perfect summer retreat. Guest accommodations have sitting areas with snug armchairs and cushy couches, while firm beds in the sleeping alcoves are dressed in fine linens. Rich cream-colored tones and soft lighting are notably relaxing, and three of these suitelike rooms have large soaking tubs in their well-equipped bathrooms. Regina's full Irish breakfast is accompanied by home-baked breads and delicious preserves; dinners can be arranged for €40. A lovely cottage on the grounds is available for €500 per week.

Rathmullan House ★ ★ ★ ★

| QUALITY ★★★★ | VALUE ★★★ | €130–€220 |

Rathmullan, County Donegal; ☎ 074-915-8188; fax 074-915-8200; info@rathmullanhouse.com; www.rathmullanhouse.com

Location On Lough Swilly at the village's edge. **Amenities and services** 30 units; bar, beach, disabled access, gardens, nonsmoking rooms, restaurant, swimming pool, tennis court. **Elevator** Yes. **Parking** Free, on property. **Price** Includes full Irish breakfast; good-value "last-minute deals" available at Web site. **Credit cards** AE, MC, V.

This fine 19th-century mansion, built for a Belfast banker, faces a two-mile-long beach that's perfect for long strolls. The Wheeler family has owned and operated Rathmullan House for four decades now, and they supply their guests, many of whom return year after year, with a great deal of easygoing comfort. The hotel is quietly luxurious but relaxed, and social life centers on the inviting drawing room, library, lounge and bar, and restaurant, as well as an indoor swimming pool and leisure center. Accommodations vary considerably in size and price, but all are comfortable and full of character. Unlike many owners of vintage hotels who have tacked on characterless modern extensions, the Wheelers have expanded with great taste, adding a wing of enormous, bright, and appealing rooms that open directly to the gardens.

Glamorous bathrooms are equipped with deep soaking tubs and freestanding showers. The old-fashioned bedrooms at the front of the house, which face the sea with huge bay windows, have all the modern amenities, including updated bathrooms. Four family-friendly rooms tucked under the eaves can accommodate up to six.

EXPLORING NORTH DONEGAL

AN ATTRACTIVE SETTLEMENT on the River Lennon, about 12 kilometers (7.5 miles) north of Letterkenny on R245, **Ramelton** is a so-called Plantation Town, settled by British Protestant colonists brought to Ireland to displace Catholic landowners and to establish a British presence. Many of the fine houses date from the early 17th century, and near the town center is the oldest Presbyterian church in Ireland. Francis Makemie (1658–1708) emigrated from Ramelton to the United States, where he founded the American Presbyterian church.

Rathmullan, today a pleasant beach town 11 kilometers (7 miles) north of Ramelton on R247, was the scene of the Flight of the Earls in 1607, when the last of the noble Irish chieftains fled by ship, ensuring British dominance of Ireland. This momentous event is very well chronicled in the **Flight of the Earls Heritage Centre,** which overlooks the harbor; ☎ 074-915-8131, **www.flightoftheearls.com.** Open June to September, Monday through Saturday, 10 a.m. to 6 p.m., and Sunday, 12:30 p.m. to 6 p.m.

A drive north of Rathmullan on R247 and R246 takes you out to **Fanad Head,** one of the many dramatic headlands that jut into the Atlantic from the northernmost reaches of Ireland. On these peninsulas, spines of rugged mountains drop down to the rocky coast and often violent surf. An excellent place to explore these coastal landscapes is **Ards Forest Park,** about 30 kilometers (18 miles) northwest of Ramelton via a circuitous route through valleys and over mountain passes (a more direct route takes you north from Letterkenny on N56). Crisscrossed with hiking paths, the park encompasses more than 600 hectares (1,000 acres) of woodlands and beaches, as well as lakes, bogs, and even a few prehistoric stone circles.

The largest of the northern peninsulas is **Inishowen,** the tip of which, **Malin Head,** is officially the northernmost tip of Ireland and affords stunning views of the sea. Views are also spectacular from the **Gap of Mamore,** a mountain pass on the western coast that climbs to 250 meters (820 feet) and is crowned with a strategically placed viewpoint. Some of the peninsula's attractions are man-made rather than natural. **Grianan Ailigh,** at the southwestern tip of the base of the peninsula 30 kilometers (18 miles) northeast of Letterkenny on N13, is a 3,500-year-old ring fort that until the 12th century served as the fortress of the region's ruling clan, the O'Neill chieftains. Unfortunately, the aura of the historic place was diminished severely by an aggressive 19th-century restoration. Another fort, about 20 kilometers (12 miles) up the western edge of the peninsula at **Dunree Head,**

unofficial **TIP**
You can circumnavigate the **Inishowen Peninsula** on a well-marked 160-kilometer (100-mile) driving route, but to see the peninsula in its entirety requires a lot of driving to enjoy scenery that's not as pleasing as that of more-accessible headlands such as **Fanad Head.** If you've had your fill of coastal scenery elsewhere in North Donegal, limit your visit to a stop at **Grianan Ailigh.**

was built in 1798 to repel a possible invasion by Napoleon's forces. The fort now houses a museum of military history, in which the most interesting exhibits trace the use of bases and ports in Northern Ireland during World War I. The museum is open June to September, Tuesday through Saturday, 10:30 a.m. to 6 p.m.; Sunday, 12:30 to 8 p.m.; October to May, Tuesday through Saturday, 10:30 a.m. to 4:30 p.m. Admission is €4 adults, €2 seniors and students.

The heaths and woodlands of **Glenveagh National Park,** 27 kilometers (17 miles) northwest of Letterkenny on R251, climb the slopes of the Derryveagh Mountains, presenting some of the most beautiful and dramatic landscapes in Ireland. Most of the 10,000 hectares (24,000 acres) were amassed by an unusually notorious landlord, John George Adair, who evicted hundreds of tenants and destroyed their cottages in order to create the estate. Glenveagh passed through the hands of several owners before becoming a national park in 1984. Deep in the heart of the estate is the charming **Glenveagh Castle** (see facing page). The most popular landmark in and around the park, though, is **Errigal Mountain,** with a pyramid-shaped peak that is covered with snow for much of the year.

ATTRACTIONS IN NORTH DONEGAL

Glebe House ★ ★ ★ ★

APPEAL BY AGE	PRESCHOOL ★ ★	GRADE SCHOOL ★ ★ ★	TEENS ★ ★ ★
YOUNG ADULTS ★ ★ ★		OVER 30 ★ ★ ★ ★	SENIORS ★ ★ ★ ★

Church Hill, 18 kilometers (11 miles) northwest of Letterkenny on R251; ☎ 074-37071

Type of attraction Historic home and art gallery. **Admission** €2.50 adults, €1.20 children and students, €1.90 seniors, €6.30 families. **Hours** Mid-May–September, Saturday–Thursday, 11 a.m.–6:30 p.m. **When to go** Anytime. **Special comments** If you are pressed for time, skip the house tour and see the gallery only; however, try to see both, as the house is extraordinary. **How much time to allow** About 2 hours.

DESCRIPTION AND COMMENTS An 1820s rectory surrounded by gardens was the home of the 20th-century English landscape painter and portraitist Derek Hill, who donated the house and his remarkable collection of art to the Irish nation in 1981. The house, visited by guided tour only, is a delight, filled with Islamic and Japanese art, William Morris wallpapers, Regency chairs, and other eclectic furnishings. A converted stable now houses a light-filled gallery hung with works by Oskar Kokoschka, Pierre Bonnard, Jack Yeats, and others; each piece is a gem, and browsing this lovely assemblage is a treat you would not expect to find in the remote reaches of North Donegal.

TOURING TIPS Glebe House is at the edge of Glenveagh National Park, so it can easily be included as part of a visit.

 Glenveagh Castle ★ ★ ★ ★

APPEAL BY AGE   PRESCHOOL ★ ★ ★ ★ ★   GRADE SCHOOL ★ ★ ★ ★ ★   TEENS ★ ★ ★ ★ ★
YOUNG ADULTS ★ ★ ★ ★ ★   OVER 30 ★ ★ ★ ★ ½   SENIORS   ★ ★ ½

Glenveagh National Park; ☎ 074-913-7090; www.heritageireland.ie

Type of attraction Historic home. **Admission** €2.75 adults, €1.25 children and students, €2 seniors. **Hours** Mid-March–early November, 10 a.m.–6:30 p.m. **When to go** Early enough in the day to allow time for a hike in the park before or after touring the castle. **Special comments** A minibus runs from the parking lot to the castle; the fare is about €1, and tickets can be purchased at the park's visitors center. You might want to make one leg of the 3-kilometer (2-mile) trip on foot, as the walk along the lakeshore is delightful. A tearoom in the former stable block serves excellent salads and hot meals, which you can enjoy on the terrace in good weather. **How much time to allow** At least 2 hours to see the house and gardens.

DESCRIPTION AND COMMENTS One of the most delightful historic homes in Ireland is perched on the shores of Lough Beagh in the midst of Glenveagh National Park. Woodlands, moors, and heath-covered mountainsides surround the castle, creating a sense of remoteness. The rugged landscapes are welcoming, with their shades of purple and russet reflected in the lake waters, and the Italian and English gardens surrounding the house add a note of civility. This is the sort of wilderness where you can imagine happily getting away from it all, which is what a succession of wealthy residents and their visitors have done here. The castle was the creation of John George Adair, a notorious landlord who ruthlessly evicted his tenants in 1861 to create the 14,000-hectare (35,000-acre) estate that now comprises Glenveagh National Park. His widow, Cornelia, planted the elaborate gardens. The pleasing, refined rooms, swimming pool, and terraces are largely the work of an American, Henry P. McIlhenny, heir to the Tabasco sauce fortune and president of the Philadelphia Museum of Art. McIlhenny spent part of every year at Glenveagh from 1937 to 1983, entertaining such guests as Greta Garbo. You can visit the house only on a 45-minute guided tour that's filled with anecdotes and shows off the delightful and extremely livable rooms; it's easy to fall under the spell of Glenveagh.

TOURING TIPS You can spend a very pleasant full day at Glenveagh. Stroll through the castle gardens, and then turn your attention to the rest of the enormous park. Follow the maps available at the visitors center to explore the park on one of the many trails.

RESTAURANTS IN NORTH DONEGAL

Bridge Café ★ ★ ★ ½

SEAFOOD	MODERATE	QUALITY ★ ★ ★	VALUE ★ ★ ★ ★

End of bridge, Ramelton; ☎ 074-51119

Reservations Recommended. **Entree range** €14–€25. **Payment** MC, V. **Bar** Full service. **Disabled access** No. **Hours** Monday–Saturday, 7:30–10 p.m.

MENU RECOMMENDATIONS Oysters, wild salmon.

COMMENTS The Bridge Café is Ramelton's most popular pub, perched romantically beside the River Swilly and often bathed in fog. The downstairs barroom is warmed by a roaring fire and local chatter; dinner is served upstairs in several nicely lit, low-ceilinged rooms with wood floors. Sit by the fire downstairs and have a pint or a cocktail while regarding the menu; then place your order and wait to be called to your table upstairs. The pub often hosts sessions by local musicians, a pleasant way to end an evening here.

Green Room ★ ★ ★ ★

CONTINENTAL	EXPENSIVE	QUALITY ★ ★ ★ ★	VALUE ★ ★ ★ ★

Castle Grove Country House Hotel, Letterkenny; ☎ 074-915-1118

Reservations Recommended. **Entree range** €18–€30; prix-fixe lunch, €15 and €22; prix-fixe dinner, €30 and €48. **Payment** AE, MC, V. **Bar** Full service. **Disabled access** Yes. **Hours** Monday–Saturday, 12:30–2 p.m., 6:30–9 p.m.; Sunday, 6:30–9 p.m.

MENU RECOMMENDATIONS Fried fillet of beef, fresh fish and seafood.

COMMENTS A handsome, light-filled extension to this old country house is quite stunning—suitably fancy surroundings for the accomplished cuisine of Chef Pascal Desnet. Meals are served with polish and flair, making even a light lunch a memorable occasion. To take full advantage of a meal here, stroll through the well-maintained gardens and enjoy coffee and an after-dinner drink in one of the welcoming lounges.

Weeping Elm ★ ★ ★ ★ ½

MODERN IRISH	EXPENSIVE	QUALITY ★ ★ ★ ★ ½	VALUE ★ ★ ★ ½

Rathmullan House, Rathmullan; ☎ 074-915-8188

Reservations Recommended. **Entree range** €18–€35. **Payment** AE, DC, MC, V. **Bar** Full service. **Disabled access** Yes. **Hours** Daily, 7:30–8:45 p.m.

MENU RECOMMENDATIONS Crab and other local seafood, Rathmullan lamb.

COMMENTS The dining room of Rathmullan House is as inviting as the rest of the hotel. Innovative preparations of mostly local ingredients are served in an exciting dining room beneath sweeping tentlike ceilings. The floor-to-ceiling windows, which open to a stunning garden, lend the impression that you are eating outdoors, whatever the weather. Lunches and light early dinners are served in the hotel's Cellar Bar in summer.

PART TEN

NORTHERN IRELAND

THE VERY NAME OF THIS REGION connotes political unrest and violence, but with peace has come a discovery for 21st-century visitors—this is one of the most beautiful and rewarding corners of Ireland.

British and Scottish settlers began flooding into the North in the 17th century, as the British sought to establish a strong footing here and keep the lands out of Catholic (Irish) hands. The six counties of Northern Ireland, often called **Ulster,** remain under British rule, as established in the Anglo-Irish Treaty of 1921, under which the remaining 26 counties of Ireland became independent. Many of our present-day impressions of Northern Ireland were formed in the 1970s and 1980s, when violence erupted in Belfast and Derry as a groundswell gathered behind the Irish Republican Army (IRA) and demanded independence and, with it, better conditions for the often oppressed Catholic population in the North. A cease-fire inaugurated in 1994 and confirmed by the Good Friday Peace Agreement of 1998 has held, and Northern Ireland is a relatively peaceable kingdom these days. Its complex politics and turbulent past are not to be ignored, but to be accepted along with the many other attributes of the North—natural beauty, architectural treasures, and a great deal of warmth. The North is still off the well-beaten tourist path, and the sense of discovery adds considerably to the pleasure of a visit.

NOT TO BE MISSED IN NORTHERN IRELAND

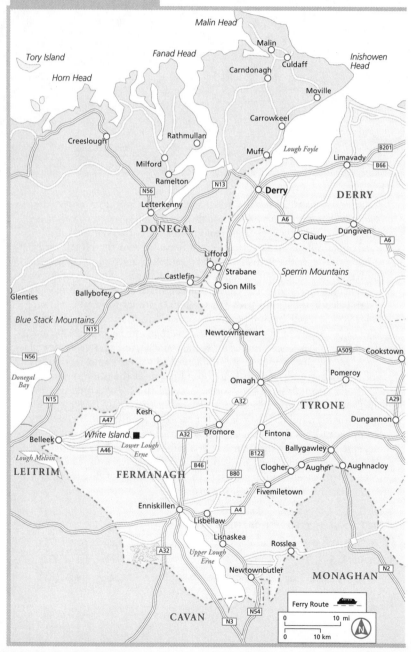

northern ireland

Malin Head

Tory Island

Fanad Head

Malin

Horn Head

Carndonagh

Culdaff

Inishowen
Head

Moville

Carrowkeel

Creeslough

Rathmullan

Muff

Lough Foyle

B201

Milford

Limavady

B66

Ramelton

N13

Derry

DERRY

N56

Letterkenny

A6

Dungiven

DONEGAL

Claudy

A6

Lifford

Strabane

Sperrin Mountains

Castlefin

Sion Mills

Glenties

Ballybofey

Newtownstewart

Blue Stack Mountains

N15

A505

Cookstown

N56

Pomeroy

*Donegal
Bay*

Omagh

TYRONE

A29

N15

A32

Dungannon

Kesh

A47

White Island ■

Dromore

Fintona

A32

Ballygawley

Belleek

B122

Aughnacloy

*Lower Lough
Erne*

A46

Clogher

Augher

Lough Melvin

B46

B80

LEITRIM

FERMANAGH

Fivemiletown

Enniskillen

A4

Lisbellaw

Lisnaskea

Rosslea

*Upper Lough
Erne*

A32

Newtownbutler

MONAGHAN

N2

Ferry Route

0   10 mi

CAVAN

N54

0   10 km

N3

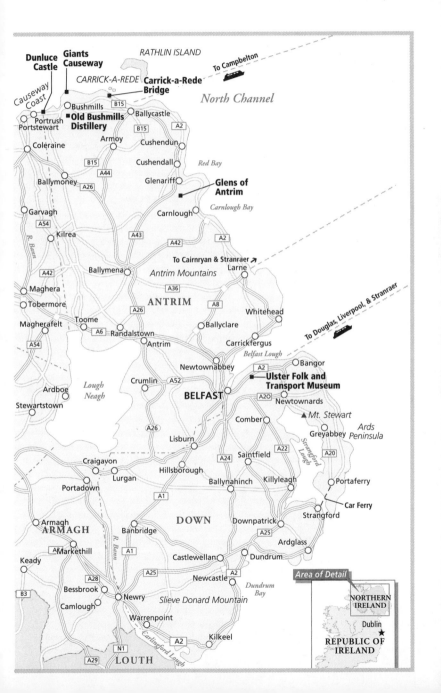

Dunluce Castle
Giants Causeway
Causeway Coast
RATHLIN ISLAND
To Campbelton
CARRICK-A-REDE
Carrick-a-Rede Bridge
North Channel
Bushmills   B15   Ballycastle
Portrush
Portstewart
Old Bushmills Distillery
Armoy   B15   A2   Cushendun
Coleraine
Ballymoney   B15   A44   Cushendall   Red Bay
A26   Glenariff   Glens of Antrim
Garvagh   Carnlough   Carnlough Bay
A54
Kilrea   R. Bann   A43   A42   A2
A42   Ballymena   Antrim Mountains   To Cairnryan & Stranraer   Larne
Maghera   A36
Tobermore   ANTRIM   A8   Whitehead
Magherafelt   A26   To Douglas, Liverpool, & Stranraer
A54   Toome   A6   Ballyclare
Ardboe   Randalstown   Carrickfergus
Stewartstown   Antrim   Belfast Lough   Bangor
Lough Neagh   Newtownabbey   A2   Ulster Folk and Transport Museum
Crumlin   A52   BELFAST   A20   Newtownards
A26   Comber   ▲ Mt. Stewart   Ards Peninsula
Lisburn   Greyabbey
Craigavon   A24   Saintfield   Strangford Lough   A22   A20
Lurgan   Hillsborough   Ballynahinch   Killyleagh   Portaferry
Portadown   A1   Car Ferry
Armagh   DOWN   Downpatrick   Strangford
ARMAGH   Banbridge   A25
Markethill   A1   Ardglass
Keady   Castlewellan   Dundrum
A28   A25   A2
Bessbrook   Newcastle   Dundrum Bay
Camlough   Newry   Slieve Donard Mountain
B3   Warrenpoint
Carlingford Lough   A2   Kilkeel
N1
A29   LOUTH

Area of Detail

NORTHERN IRELAND

Dublin ★

REPUBLIC OF IRELAND

belfast

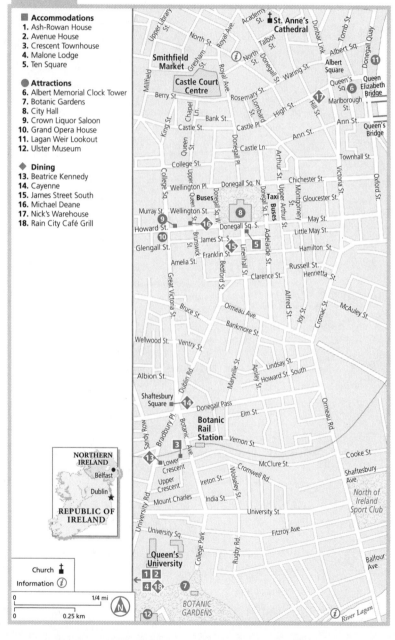

Accommodations
1. Ash-Rowan House
2. Avenue House
3. Crescent Townhouse
4. Malone Lodge
5. Ten Square

Attractions
6. Albert Memorial Clock Tower
7. Botanic Gardens
8. City Hall
9. Crown Liquor Saloon
10. Grand Opera House
11. Lagan Weir Lookout
12. Ulster Museum

Dining
13. Beatrice Kennedy
14. Cayenne
15. James Street South
16. Michael Deane
17. Nick's Warehouse
18. Rain City Café Grill

Church ✝

Information ⓘ

0 _____ 1/4 mi

0 _____ 0.25 km

NORTHERN IRELAND
Belfast
Dublin ★
REPUBLIC OF IRELAND

BELFAST

BELFAST HAS HAD A LOT OF BAD PRESS TO OVERCOME—after all, no other city in Western Europe, with the possible exception of Derry, has been as war torn in recent decades. The talk in Belfast these days is about rebirth, and peace has brought with it the pleasure of discovering a beautiful, fascinating, and often overlooked city of fine avenues, ornate architecture, pleasant neighborhoods, and, surprisingly, perhaps, a crop of outstanding restaurants. The whole city seems to be caught up in rebirth, with new hotels and shops opening all the time and streets taking on a gentrified air. Step into the pubs (some of the friendliest in the land), and you'll feel a sense of pride, a notion that Belfast has always been a fine place to be—it's just that now we visitors can feel comfortable learning this firsthand.

Belfast is a busy metropolis, as it has been since the late 18th century, when French Huguenots imported linen weaving, British settlers established shipyards and factories, and immigrants came from throughout Ireland to find work. The city is home to some 300,000 souls, about a third of the population of Northern Ireland.

PLANNING YOUR VISIT TO BELFAST

STAFFERS AT THE **Belfast Welcome Centre** work hard to ensure that visitors get the most out of a visit to Belfast and other places throughout Northern Ireland. You will receive maps and a wealth of helpful information about accommodations, attractions, walking, and other activities. You'll want to make a beeline for the office when you get to town; 47 Donegall Place, ☎ 028-9024-6609; **www.gotobelfast.com.** June to September: Monday through Saturday, 9 a.m. to 7 p.m.; Sunday, noon to 5 p.m.; October to May: Monday through Saturday, 9 a.m. to 5:30 p.m.

Special Events in Belfast

November's **Belfast Festival** at Queen's University is the city's big cultural bash of the year, staging plays, concerts, dance performances, film screenings, and many other events; for more information, contact the festival office at ☎ 028-9066-6321.

ARRIVING AND GETTING ORIENTED IN BELFAST

BELFAST IS ABOUT 170 KILOMETERS (105 miles) north of Dublin, an easy trip by car along N1 and A1. You'll take the A6, M22, and M2 from Derry; connect to these routes at Derry if you're traveling from Donegal and Letterkenny. If you're traveling into the North from Sligo, you'll take the A4. Good train service runs eight times a day between Dublin and Belfast Monday through Saturday, with five trains on Sunday. The trip takes about two and a half hours; one-way fares begin at £29. For information, call **Irish Rail** toll free at ☎ 1850-366222 or ☎ 01-836-6222 or visit **www.irishrail.ie**; you can also

unofficial **TIP**
Note: There are no longer border crossings from the Republic into Northern Ireland.

contact **Northern Irish Railways** at ☎ 888-BRIT-RAIL or 028-9024-6485. Trains arrive and depart from Belfast's Central Station. **Ulsterbus** coaches arrive from Dublin and many other points in the Republic, with about seven buses a day to and from Dublin Monday through Saturday and three trains on Sunday; the trip takes about three hours and the fare is about £15 one way. For more information, call ☎ 028-9033-3000 or visit **www.translink.co.uk.**

Belfast is also served by air, with many flights from the U.K., other parts of Europe, and via connection from North America. Ferries also connect Belfast and the North with the U.K. For more information on air and boat service to Northern Ireland, see Part Two, Arriving.

HOTELS IN BELFAST

Ash-Rowan House ★ ★ ★ ★

QUALITY ★ ★ ★ ★	VALUE ★ ★ ★	£54–£79

12 Windsor Avenue, Belfast, County Antrim, BT9 6EE;
☎ **028-9066-1758; fax 028-9066-3227; ashrowan@hotmail.com**

Location In University area, south of city center. **Amenities and services** 5 rooms; complimentary snacks, in-room tea and coffee facilities, lounge, library. **Elevator** No. **Parking** Free, on property. **Price** Includes full Irish breakfast. **Credit cards** AE, CB, D, DC, JCB, MC, V.

Sam and Evelyn Hazlett's guest house is a Belfast institution, and these life-long veterans of the hospitality industry welcome many return guests at their charming, antique-filled townhouse. The Hazletts have good taste and appreciate luxury, so they pamper guests with linen sheets, complimentary robes, fresh flowers, and tea and snacks served on good china. They outdo themselves in the morning, serving a choice of eight traditional breakfasts, including a hearty Ulster fry. The best rooms are the two on the top floor, where king-size beds are fitted into bright alcoves, but any of these delightful accommodations will make you feel that you've found a home in Belfast.

Avenue House ★ ★ ★

QUALITY ★ ★ ★	VALUE ★ ★ ★ ★	£40–£50

23 Eglantine Avenue, Belfast, County Antrim BT9 6DW;
☎ **028-9066-5904; fax 028-9029-1810; info@avenueguesthouse.com;**
www.avenueguesthouse.com

Location University area, south of city center. **Amenities and services** 4 units; hair dryers, in-room tea and coffee facilities, Internet access, nonsmoking rooms. **Elevator** No. **Parking** Free, on street. **Price** Includes full Irish breakfast. **Credit cards** MC, V.

The top choice among the many bed-and-breakfasts in the Eglantine Avenue area occupies a nicely refurbished terrace house and provides a wonderfully

How Hotels Compare in Northern Ireland

HOTEL	OVERALL	QUALITY	VALUE	PRICE
BELFAST				
Ten Square	★★★★★	★★★★★	★★★★	£80–£180
Ash-Rowan House	★★★★	★★★★	★★★	£54–£79
Crescent Townhouse	★★★½	★★★½	★★½	£85–£105
Malone Lodge	★★★	★★★★	★★★	£95–£109
Avenue House	★★★	★★★	★★★★	£40–£50
DERRY				
Merchants House	★★★★	★★★	★★★	£40–£50
Tower Hotel Derry	★★★	★★★	★★★★	£60–£70
ANTRIM COAST				
Bushmills Inn	★★★★½	★★★★½	★★★	£100–£160
Maddybenny Farmhouse	★★★★	★★★★	★★★★	£40–£50

convenient base—the lively Malone shops and cafes, Queen's University, the Botanic Gardens, and the Ulster Museum are all within a five-minute walk, and the city center is easily reached just ten minutes away on foot. Stephen and Mary Kelly will tell you how to go about enjoying the local attractions and will engage you in delightful and topical conversation as well. Rooms are large and more comfy than chic—beds are firm, reading chairs are adjacent to large bay windows, and there is plenty of room to spread out. Bathrooms are small but new and nicely equipped. The Avenue is a good base for families because three of the rooms are triples; the top-floor triple is especially large and homey.

Crescent Townhouse   ★ ★ ★ ½

QUALITY ★★★½	VALUE ★★½	£85–£105

13 Lower Crescent, Belfast, County Antrim BT7 1NR;
☎ **028-9032-3349; fax 028-9032-0646; info@crescenttownhouse.com;**
www.crescenttownhouse.com

Location Off Botanic Avenue, just south of city center. **Amenities and services** 17 rooms; bar, business services, Internet access, nonsmoking rooms, restaurant, trouser press. **Elevator** Yes. **Parking** Free, on street. **Price** Weekend rates available. **Credit cards** AE, MC, V.

Many Belfast residents know this handsome old building mainly for its Metro Brasserie (especially popular for lunch, with a good-value early-dinner menu) and Bar 12, a rather posh hangout that hosts cabaret shows and other live entertainment. (Given late-night comings and goings from this popular club, ask for a room far from the entrance.) Upstairs are large and handsome guest rooms, nicely done in varying styles, some traditional and others soothingly contemporary; baths are new, with state-of-the-art fixtures that include, in many rooms, large power showers. Photocopying and other business services, as well as meeting rooms and the proximity of the city center, make the Crescent popular with business travelers, but the hotel is also gracious and laid-back, a nice base for a leisure visit to Belfast, too. The surrounding neighborhood, near the Botanic Gardens and Queen's University, is one of the most pleasant in Belfast.

Malone Lodge ★ ★ ★

| QUALITY ★ ★ ★ ★ | VALUE ★ ★ ★ | £95–£109 |

60 Eglantine Avenue, Belfast, Country Antrim BT9 6DY;
☎ **028-9038-8000; fax 028-9038-8088; info@malonelodgehotel.com;**
www.malonelodgehotelbelfast.com

Location University area, south of city center. **Amenities and services** 80 rooms; bar, gym, hair dryers, in-room tea and coffee facilities, Internet access, restaurant, sauna, 2 telephones in each room. **Elevator** Yes. **Parking** Free, on property and on street. **Price** Includes full Irish breakfast; weekend rates and special offers available. **Credit cards** AE, MC, V.

Unexpectedly tucked away amid the terrace houses and B&Bs along Eglantine Avenue, this smart, well-run business hotel is spacious and comfortable, a wonderful retreat from the city streets. Public spaces include Macklins Bar, extremely popular for its lunchtime carvery, and seem to be perennially busy. Guest rooms, though, are unusually restful; most are enormous, twice the size of most modern hotel rooms, and face the avenue through bay windows fitted out with handy arrangements of tables and chairs. Earth tones and unobtrusive furnishings are soothing, while bathrooms are large and updated, many with corner tubs and separate showers. The Malone Lodge is a far better choice than the better-known Wellington Park around the corner.

Ten Square ★ ★ ★ ★ ★

| QUALITY ★ ★ ★ ★ ★ | VALUE ★ ★ ★ ★ | £80–£180 |

10 Donegall Square South, Belfast, County Antrim BT1 5JD;
☎ **028-9024-1001; fax 028-9024-3210; reservations@tensquare.co.uk;**
www.tensquare.co.uk

Location City center. **Amenities and services** 22 rooms; bar, DVDs, in-room tea and coffee facilities, Internet access, minibars, nonsmoking rooms, room service, safe, trouser press, 2 restaurants. **Elevator** Yes. **Parking** Nearby car park, £8 overnight. **Price** Includes full Irish breakfast; many specials available. **Credit cards** AE, MC, V.

Belfast boasts a new crop of small, stylish hotels (the nearby Malmaison, **www.malmaison.com,** and Merchant, **www.themerchanthotel.co.uk,** also fall into this category), but Ten Square holds its own as the first and best. While it might be easy to be put off by the self-conscious trendiness of the place, you're likely to soon see past this attitude—Ten Square is lovely, luxurious, and comfortable, and hospitality is taken very seriously. One of the most delightful spots is the handsome alcove off the reception area, where a fire is always burning. The ground-floor Grill Room is a relaxed place for a good-value meal or snack; Porcelain, upstairs, is a dark, uphol-stered, modern hideaway in which to enjoy a fine meal. Guest rooms manage to be both showy and peaceful—tall windows graced with shutters of milky glass bring to light creamy whites and neutrals, and the modern furnishings are unobtrusive and comfortable amid excellent lighting and appealing art. Bathrooms are outfitted with deep tubs, oversize sinks, power showers, and other amenities. These rooms pass the ultimate test—they are so relaxing and enjoyable that you will want to stay put.

EXPLORING BELFAST

DECADES OF INDUSTRIAL WEALTH in compact central Belfast have bestowed the city with broad avenues and many grand public build-ings. **Donegall Square** is the city's central hub; the main avenues con-verge at the square, and the domed **City Hall** dominates one side. The square is a good departure point for a walk around the city center; a longer trek or short bus ride takes you south to such sights as **Queen's University,** the **Ulster Museum,** and the **Botanic Gardens.** The best way to see **Falls and Shankill roads**—respectively, the main streets of the Catholic and Protestant neighborhoods that were for years the epicenters of the Troubles—is on a guided tour (see page 379).

Monuments in **Donegall Square** provide a quick overview of great moments in the city's past; especially worth seeking out are those commemorating the *Titanic* (the doomed luxury liner was built in the city's vast shipyards) and honoring the U.S. Army forces that made first landfall in Europe here in early 1942. You can step inside the main hall of **City Hall,** completed in 1906 and modeled on St. Paul's Cathedral in London; crane your neck to look up the heights of the ornately decorated dome, and take the time to join one of the free guided tours that show off the receptions halls and council chambers, all wonderfully grandiose; the foyer is open Monday through Satur-day, 9 a.m. to 5 p.m.; guided tours take place Monday through Friday at 2:30 p.m., more frequently June to September. The other monu-mental structure on the square is **Linen Hall Library,** founded in 1788 and these days the world's largest repository of materials relating to the Troubles; political posters and other fascinating materials relating to the city's turbulent past hang in one of the galleries; ☎ 028-9032-1707; open Monday through Friday, 9:30 a.m. to 7:30 p.m. and Sat-urday, 9:30 a.m. to 4 p.m.

Two other remnants of Belfast's Victorian heyday are just to the west of Donegall Square. Follow Howard Street to Great Victoria Street and the **Grand Opera House,** an elaborate 1895 structure that,

Walks and Drives in Northern Ireland

Spectacular coastal scenery, some of Europe's best cruising waters, and wind-swept mountains are among the diverse, and little explored, landscapes of Northern Ireland.

GREAT WALKS

GLENARIFF FOREST PARK

In the most beautiful of the Glens of Antrim, you can follow the Inver and Glenariff rivers as they cascade through forests and mossy valleys. The visitors center (open daily, 9 a.m. to 4:30 p.m.) provides maps of the many trails in the park. The most popular walk, on the **Waterfall Trail** (4.5 kilometers/ 3 miles), follows a series of cascades on the Glenariff River, and the **Nature Trail** (2.5 kilometers/1.5 miles) follows the Inver River.

THE CAUSEWAY COAST WAY

A well-maintained and well-used walking path follows the Causeway Coast for 52 kilometers (31 miles), from **Portstewart** in the east to **Ballycastle** in the west. The most scenic part is the section around the **Giants Causeway** (see page 403), although the route passes rocky sea cliffs, green mountains and lush inland valleys along its entire length.

THE MOUNTAINS OF MOURNE

This moor-covered seaside range of 600-meter (2,000-foot) summits, just 50 kilometers (30 miles) south of Belfast, is little traveled and makes for beautiful walking country. An easy place to get a taste of the mountain scenery is **Tollymore Forest Park,** 6 kilometers (3.5 miles) west of the town of **Newcastle.** Four well-marked trails crisscross forests and follow the valley of the River Shimna; the longest trail, the **Long Haul,** covers 13 kilometers (8 miles); trail maps are available at the park entrance, and the park is open daily, 10 a.m. to dusk.

like most other buildings in Belfast, was bombed (as recently as 1991) and then rebuilt in all its extravagance. These days the hall is the venue for some rather mediocre entertainment, such as traveling road shows of big musicals, that doesn't always do justice to the surroundings. The Grand Opera House never fails to steal the show; the box office is open Monday through Friday, 8:30 a.m. to 9 p.m., and Saturday, 8:30 a.m. to 6 p.m. The **Crown Liquor Saloon,** just down the street at Number 46, is an august assemblage of carved wood, colorful tiles, and gilded mirrors that is now owned by the National Trust; business

ALONG THE CAUSEWAY COAST

Travelers who make it to the North discover that some of Ireland's most spectacular scenery, and one of its most scenic drives, is on the **Causeway Coast,** between the resort of Portush and the Glens of Antrim.

The route follows narrow, winding A2 west from **Portrush,** a faded Victorian resort town. Almost as soon as you leave town, though, you find yourself among green hills and a rocky seacoast that stretches for miles. Just eight kilometers (five miles) outside Portrush is **Dunluce Castle** (see page 402), a ruined 13th-century fortress perched on the edge of a cliff high above the sea.

After another eight kilometers (five miles) comes an even more spectacular sight: **Giants Causeway** (see page 403), where some 35,000 basalt columns extend into the sea, dramatic evidence of volcanic activity 60 million years ago.

Just two kilometers (one mile) south of Giants Causeway is **Bushmills,** an attractive village put on the map by the fame of its local industry, the **Old Bushmills Distillery** (see page 404), the oldest licensed distillery in the world.

Carrick-a-Rede Bridge, 13 kilometers (8 miles) east of Giants Causeway, is another memorable sight, albeit man-made (see page 402). Here, a rope bridge connects the mainland and an island of the same name, swaying in daredevil fashion above the turbulent surf far below.

Ballycastle, eight kilometers (five miles) east, is a delightful seaside town with fine old pubs and shops, a long beach, and docks that bustle with the hubbub of the local fishing fleet. The town is the gateway to the **Glens of Antrim,** nine wooded valleys that etch the mountains along the coast from here for 66 kilometers (40 miles) to **Glenariff.**

From Ballycastle, continue east along the coast on the narrow road around Murlough Bay to **Fair Head,** a barren headland that affords sweeping views up and down the coast.

Continued on next page

goes on as usual, so sit down in a snug and enjoy a pint. Just across the street is a Belfast landmark of more recent vintage: the nondescript **Europa Hotel,** which has the dubious distinction of being Europe's most bombed hotel, having survived 11 IRA blasts, but has quickly gotten back to business as usual after every one.

St. Anne's Cathedral, a somber, forbidding edifice, is north of the square, on Donegall Street; the cavernous interior is brightened somewhat by the presence of delightful mosaics. A far more appealing piece of architecture is the **Albert Memorial Clock Tower,** at the end of High

Walks and Drives in Northern Ireland (continued)

GREET DRIVES (CONTINUED)

ALONG THE CAUSEWAY COAST (CONTINUED)

Cushenden, 26 kilometers (16 miles) east and south of Ballycastle, is an orderly arrangement of squares and terraces that came into being two centuries ago when the local nobility, Lord Cushenden, married a Cornish woman and commissioned the architect Clough Williams-Ellis to create a village that would remind his bride of her native Cornwall.

Cushendall, ten kilometers (six miles) south, is notable for **Turnley's Tower**, built in 1820 as a jail for "idlers and rioters"; you can't miss the red-stone structure, sitting in the middle of a crossroads at the center of the village.

Glenariff, another 11 kilometers (7 miles) farther south, faces Red Bay and lies at the entrance to some of the most magnificent scenery in the Glens, which you can enjoy as you explore the woods and valleys of **Glenariff Forest Park,** open daily, 8 a.m. to dusk; £1 admission fee per car.

AROUND LOUGH ERNE

Just south of **Derry** lies Northern Ireland's so-called **Lakelands,** comprising the waters, shores, and islands of Lough Erne.

From Derry, it's a fairly quick drive through pretty countryside down the River Foyle along B48 to **Omagh,** 50 kilometers (30 miles) south. This ordinary market town in the stark Sperrin Mountains would be unremarkable if it weren't for an IRA bombing in 1998 that killed 29 people.

Omagh's main attraction is about five kilometers (three miles) north, the **Ulster-American Folk Park.** Exhibits here trace the contributions that Irish from the north have made to American culture. The ancestral home of industrialist **Andrew Mellon** (1855–1937) is a simple whitewashed cottage, all the more poignant given the millions that Mellon made in the steel business. Re-creations include a log settlement like those where emigrants settled in the New World two centuries ago and a ship that took them there. Castletown, Camphill, Omagh, County Tyrone; ☎ 028-8224-3292. Easter through September: Monday through Saturday, 10:30 a.m. to 6 p.m.; Sunday, 11 a.m. to 6:30 p.m. October through Easter: Monday through Friday, 10:30 a.m. to 5 p.m.

Street on Victoria Square; the elaborate tower, a tribute to Queen Victoria's husband, Prince Albert, is made all the more interesting by a distinct tilt and the background presence of huge cranes in the shipyards along the River Lagan. You can take in the scene from the **Lagan Weir Lookout,** on Donegall Quay just beyond the square; if you think you might enjoy displays documenting the control of tides in Belfast harbor, you can fork over £1.50 to step inside the **Lagan Lookout Visitors Centre;** Monday through Friday, 11 a.m. to 5 p.m.; Saturday, noon

Admission: £4 adults, £2.50 seniors and children ages 5 to 16, £10 families of up to two adults and two children.

A drive of 40 kilometers (24 miles) southwest of **Omagh** on A32, B4, and A47 brings you around the northern shores of Lower Lough Erne, surrounded by green hills, to **Belleek.**

Lough Erne, divided into lower and upper lakes (the "lower" lake is the northern section) is considered one of Europe's finest cruising locales, with miles of open water and many inlets and islands.

About halfway between Omagh and Belleek, visible from the lakeshore, is **Boa Island,** connected to the mainland by two bridges. In the island's Caldragh cemetery you'll encounter two pagan stone idols, one double faced.

Belleek is a factory town famous for its handmade china, often created in a distinctive basket weave. You can tour **Belleek Pottery Ltd.** (on weekdays, tours every half hour; ☎ 028-6865-8501) and shop in the showroom, where you'll find a lot of quality and few discounts. Belleek, by the way, is a border town, so you can easily slip west from here to the Republic and zip down or up the N15 to Sligo or Donegal.

From Belleek, follow the shores of Lough Erne on A46 about 35 kilometers (21 miles) to **Devenish,** a ruined monastic community. About three kilometers (two miles) before reaching Devenish, though, make a short, well-marked detour off the highway to **Monea,** a ruined 17th-century castle built by Planters, as colonists from Britain who settled in Ireland were called.

Devenish is on a island just off the mainland and reached by ferry (see page 398). St. Molaise founded a monastery on the island in the sixth century, and medieval remains, including a 12th-century round tower visible for miles around, now litter the marshy terrain.

Enniskillen, six kilometers (four miles) south, is a pleasant resort town that's wedged on a spit between the lower and upper lakes (see page 397). Local attractions include **Castle Coole,** one of the grandest homes in Ireland (see page 398).

From Enniskillen, follow the east side of the lake north for 12 kilometers (7.5 miles) to **Castle Archdale,** a busy resort with several marinas. From there take B4 30 kilometers (18 miles) to Omagh, and then return to Derry.

to 5 p.m.; Sunday, 2 to 5 p.m. Far more enjoyable is a walk through the old riverside warehouse neighborhood between the cathedral and the clock tower, laced with narrow alleyways known as entries.

Tours in Belfast

The most compelling reason to take a tour in Belfast is to see **Falls Road** and **Shankill Road,** epicenters of the Troubles. Whether you tour by cab

Continued on page 382

walks and drives in northern ireland

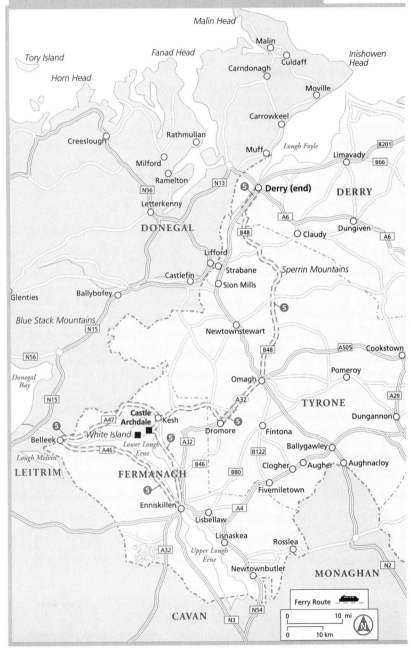

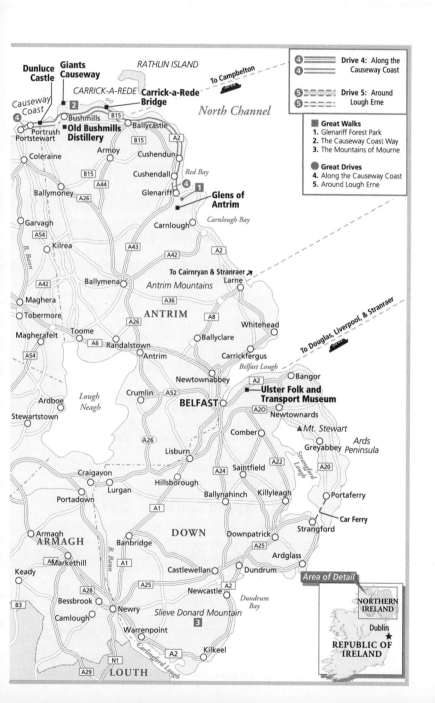

RATHLIN ISLAND

To Campbelton

Dunluce Castle
Giants Causeway

CARRICK-A-REDE

Carrick-a-Rede Bridge

Causeway Coast

4

2

Bushmills
Old Bushmills Distillery

B15

Ballycastle

North Channel

Portrush
Portstewart

Coleraine

Armoy

Cushendun

B15

A2

Ballymoney
A26

B15
A44

Cushendall

Glenariff

Red Bay

4 **1**

Glens of Antrim

Garvagh
A54

Kilrea

Carnlough

Carnlough Bay

A43

A42

Ballymena

Antrim Mountains

To Cairnryan & Stranraer ↗

Larne

Maghera

Tobermore

A36

ANTRIM

A8

Magherafelt

A54

A26

Toome

A6

Randalstown

Antrim

Ballyclare

Whitehead

To Douglas, Liverpool, & Stranraer

Carrickfergus

Belfast Lough

Ardboe

Lough Neagh

Crumlin

A52

Newtownabbey

BELFAST

Bangor

A2

Ulster Folk and Transport Museum

Stewartstown

A26

Comber

A20

Newtownards

▲*Mt. Stewart*

Greyabbey

Ards Peninsula

Lisburn

Craigavon

Portadown

Lurgan

Hillsborough

A24

Saintfield

A22

Strangford Lough

A20

A1

Ballynahinch

Killyleagh

Portaferry

Car Ferry

Armagh

ARMAGH

Banbridge

DOWN

Downpatrick

Strangford

Markethill

A1

A25

Keady

A28

Castlewellan

A2

Dundrum

Ardglass

Area of Detail

B3

Bessbrook

A25

Newcastle

Dundrum Bay

Camlough

Newry

Slieve Donard Mountain

3

Warrenpoint

N1

A29

A2

Kilkeel

LOUTH

Carlingford Lough

NORTHERN IRELAND

Dublin ★

REPUBLIC OF IRELAND

Drive 4: Along the Causeway Coast

Drive 5: Around Lough Erne

Great Walks
1. Glenariff Forest Park
2. The Causeway Coast Way
3. The Mountains of Mourne

Great Drives
4. Along the Causeway Coast
5. Around Lough Erne

or bus, you can count on two things: commentary will be highly informative (and despite the gravity of recent events here, entertaining), and you'll most likely begin with a drive through the Catholic neighborhood around Falls Road, close to the city center. You'll pass the **Sinn Féin** offices and endless murals, then go through the so-called peace wall to **Milltown Cemetery,** where hunger striker Bobby Sands and other IRA members are buried, then into the Protestant Shankill Road neighborhood, where murals include Union Jack motifs and even elaborate portrayals of the victory of the Protestant William of Orange over the Catholic King James II in the Battle of the Boyne in 1690.

Black taxis run by several companies ply this route regularly, charging about £22 for one to three passengers, £25 for four to six passengers. You can also arrange with the drivers to travel farther afield to see sights such as the **Wolf Shipyard,** where the *Titanic* was built and which is now slated for development as a huge commercial district aptly named the Titanic Quarter (although the nomenclature is bound to launch endless jokes about sinking fortunes and businesses that can't stay afloat). Among the taxi companies are **Belfast Black Taxi** (☎ 08081-271125), **Belfast City Black Taxi Tours** (☎ 028-9030-1832), and **Black Taxi Tours** (☎ 028-9064-2264). You can also see Falls and Shankill roads, along with sights in the city center and outlying neighborhoods, on a **Belfast City Sightseeing** tour bus. Departing from Castle Place, these 90-minute tours, accompanied by intelligent commentary, operate daily from May to September, 9:30 a.m. to 4:30 p.m., and October to April, 10 a.m. to 4 p.m.; £9.50 adults, £6 children, £7.50 seniors and students; ☎ 028-9062-6888; **www.belfastcitysightseeing.com.**

Belfast Safaris provides a look at the city through the eyes of residents, who lead guided walks—either along established routes (£8) that explore different neighborhoods and historic sights or on a route you design (£21); ☎ 028-9022-2925; **www.belfastsafaris.com. Belfast Pub Tours** depart from the Crown Liquor Saloon and take in historic pubs around the city center; May to October, Thursday, 7 p.m.; Saturday, 4 p.m.; £6; ☎ 028-9268-3665; **www.belfastpubtours.com.**

ATTRACTIONS IN AND AROUND BELFAST

Botanic Gardens   ★ ★ ★ ★

| APPEAL BY AGE | PRESCHOOL ★ ★ ★ ★ | GRADE SCHOOL ★ ★ ★ ★ | TEENS ★ ★ ★ ★ |
| YOUNG ADULTS ★ ★ ★ ★ | | OVER 30 ★ ★ ★ | SENIORS ★ ★ ★ |

Stranmillis Road, ☎ 028-9032-4902

Type of attraction Victorian gardens. **Admission** Free. **Hours** Daily, dawn to dusk; Palm House and Tropical Ravine House: Monday–Friday, 10 a.m.–5 p.m.; Saturday–Sunday, 1–5 p.m. **When to go** When the Palm House and Tropical Ravine House are open. **Special comments** One of the advantages of staying in the Stranmillis neighborhood is the opportunity to pay frequent visits to these delightful gardens, a pleasure even in bad weather, when the glass houses provide

How Attractions Compare in Northern Ireland

ATTRACTION	DESCRIPTION	AUTHOR'S RATING
BELFAST		
Botanic Gardens	Victorian gardens	★★★★
Ulster Folk and Transport Museum	Museum of social history	★★★★
Ulster Museum	Museum and art gallery	★★★½
DERRY		
Tower Museum Derry	Museum of local history	★★★★
Workhouse Museum	Museum that chronicles the Famine and Derry's role in World War II	★★★★
ENNISKILLEN		
Castle Coole	One of Ireland's finest country estates	★★★★
ANTRIM COAST		
Giants Causeway	One of Europe's most unusual natural phenomena	★★★★★
Carrick-a-Rede Bridge	Hair-raising rope bridge	★★★★
Dunluce Castle	Castle ruins	★★★★
Old Bushmills Distillery	Whiskey-making factory	★★★★

tropical refuge; kids will welcome the chance to be outdoors. **How much time to allow** At least 1 hour.

DESCRIPTION AND COMMENTS Dating from 1827, these gardens sloping down to the banks of the River Lagan are as much a part of Victorian Belfast as the ornate buildings in the city center. Plantings throughout the gardens come from every corner of the globe; the most exotic are the trees and blossoms in the enormous Palm House, a glass-and-wrought-iron greenhouse completed by Belfast architect Charles Lanyon in 1839, and the junglelike foliage of the Tropical Ravine House. Many of the beds surrounding these glass houses are beautifully planted with roses and other flowering plants that thrive in Ireland, enlivening the garden from early spring through fall.

TOURING TIPS If you're up for a walk, follow the gardens to the River Lagan and take the towpath back to the city center. Or you can continue south through the outer reaches of the city. After about five kilometers (three miles), the path comes to the Giant's Ring, a 2,000-year-old stone circle that's 200 meters (600 feet) wide and was used in part for burials; you can also reach the Ring on bus 13 from the city center.

kids Ulster Folk and Transport Museum ★ ★ ★ ★

| APPEAL BY AGE | PRESCHOOL ★ ★ ★ ★ | GRADE SCHOOL ★ ★ ★ ★ | TEENS ★ ★ ★ ★ ★ |
| YOUNG ADULTS ★ ★ ★ ★ | | OVER 30 ★ ★ ★ ★ | SENIORS ★ ★ ★ ★ |

Cultra, 11 kilometers (7 miles) northeast of Belfast on the A2;
☎ **028-9042-8428; www.uftm.org.uk**

Type of attraction Museum of social history. **Admission** Folk Museum: £5 adults, £3 seniors, students, and children ages 5–16, free for children under age 5, £14 for families of up to 2 adults and 3 children; Transport Museum: £5 adults, £3 seniors, students, and children ages 5–16, free for children under age 5, £14 for families of up to 2 adults and 3 children. Combined museum visits: £6.50 adults, £3.50 seniors, students, and children ages 5–16, free for children under age 5, £18 for families of up to 2 adults and 3 children. **Hours** March–June: Monday–Friday, 10 a.m.–5 p.m.; Saturday, 10 a.m.–6 p.m.; Sunday, 11 a.m.–6 p.m.; July–September: Monday–Saturday, 10 a.m.–6 p.m.; Sunday, 11 a.m.–6 p.m.; October–February: Monday–Friday, 10 a.m.–4 p.m.; Saturday, 10 a.m.–5 p.m.; Sunday, 11 a.m.–5 p.m. **When to go** Much of the folk park is outdoors, so try to find a day when showers are at least infrequent. **Special comments** The museum is a wonderland for kids, who will delight in the cottages, the demonstrations of spinning and other crafts, the trains, and the attractive grounds. **How much time to allow** A full day to do both the folk and the transport museums, half a day for each.

DESCRIPTION AND COMMENTS The two sections of this vast 70-hectare (176-acre) museum compound, one a collection of old structures and the other showcasing cars, planes, and other modes of transportation, all built in Ireland, are seemingly disparate, but together they provide a fascinating and touching look at Irish social history. The folk park is an ambitious assemblage of about 20 structures, ranging in size and grandeur from humble farm cottages to Cultura Manor, an early-20th-century estate house on whose grounds the park is built. The earthen floors and crude furnishings in many of the dwellings speak volumes about the hardships that led so many Irish to emigrate. Even so, the simple farmhouses, workers' cottages, and rudimentary public buildings such as the school are more satisfying to visit than the more refined manor house and lavish reconstruction of a town. Superb exhibits in the Folk Galleries show off artifacts from the rural past and explain social norms and customs that prevailed in many parts of Ireland until only a few decades ago. Locomotives, horse-drawn carts, and some genuine surprises—such as the car that General Motors maverick John DeLorean had built in a Belfast factory—fill the airy galleries of the Transport Museum. The *Titanic* was also built in Ireland, in Belfast shipyards, and a fine exhibit provides an in-depth look at the liner's design, manufacture, and doomed maiden voyage.

TOURING TIPS Plan on breaking up a visit with a meal or tea; the main tearoom is in Cultura Manor, where a lavish Sunday lunch is also served.

Refreshments are available at kiosks around the grounds, and many picnic sites are on the grounds.

Ulster Museum ★ ★ ★ ½

APPEAL BY AGE	PRESCHOOL ★★	GRADE SCHOOL ★★★	TEENS ★★★
YOUNG ADULTS ★★★		OVER 30 ★★★½	SENIORS ★★★½

Botanic Gardens, Stranmillis Road; ☎ 028-9038-3000; www.ulstermuseum.org.uk

Type of attraction Museum and art gallery. **Admission** Free. **Hours** Monday–Friday, 10 a.m.–5 p.m.; Saturday, 1–5 p.m.; Sunday, 2–5 p.m. **When to go** Anytime. **Special comments** The museum publishes an excellent guidebook, available free at the information desk, which is most helpful given the wide-ranging nature of the exhibits. The museum has a small cafe, but Stranmillis Road, just outside the doors, boasts a nice row of cafes and shops. **How much time to allow** About 2 hours.

DESCRIPTION AND COMMENTS The most comprehensive museum in Northern Ireland is devoted to history, the natural sciences, and art. While it might be easy to assume that a collection this far-flung is not going to excel in any arena, the 19th-century neoclassical building in a corner of the Botanic Gardens is filled with a remarkably worthy mix of treasures, displayed in well-designed galleries. It is a pleasure simply to wander and come upon a mummy, mask, or painting that catches your eye. A collection of African arts and crafts from the 19th and 20th centuries is unmatched. Several galleries thoughtfully explain the history of Ireland with an unflinching look at the Troubles and the developments that led to the formation of the North as a separate entity; the painting galleries are hung with masterpieces by Gainsborough, Reynolds, and the late-20th-century American abstract painter Morris Louis. Some of the most exquisite treasures are Spanish gold, salvaged when the Spanish galleon *Girona* sunk off the northern coast in 1588.

TOURING TIPS Take advantage of a visit to the museum to see the Botanic Gardens and the rest of this appealing neighborhood, which lies about two kilometers (one mile) south of the city center and includes the handsome campus of Queen's University, modeled on Oxford's Magdalen College.

RESTAURANTS IN BELFAST

Beatrice Kennedy ★ ★ ★ ★

MODERN IRISH	MODERATE/EXPENSIVE	QUALITY ★★★★	VALUE ★★★½

44 University Road, Belfast; ☎ 028-9020-2290

Reservations Recommended. **Entree range** £12.95–£15.95; 2-course express menu, 5–7 p.m., £12. **Payment** AE, MC, V. **Bar** Full service. **Disabled access** Yes. **Hours** Tuesday–Saturday, 5–10:15 p.m.; Sunday, 12:30–2:30 p.m., 5–8 p.m.

MENU RECOMMENDATIONS Seared salmon with cabbage and bacon, Peking duck breast.

COMMENTS The onetime residence of the eponymous genteel lady provides relaxed and refined surroundings, warmed by fires and accented with a few pieces of Victoriana. Meals here never fail to surprise—for their unfailing quality, outstanding presentation, and, more to the point, unexpected touches such as hints of Thai curry and other exotic ingredients that add a great deal of zest to the deft cooking. Even the homemade dessert chocolates are memorable.

Cayenne ★ ★ ★ ½

| FUSION | MODERATE/EXPENSIVE | QUALITY ★ ★ ★ ★ | VALUE ★ ★ ★ ½ |

7 Ascot House, Shaftesbury Square, Belfast; ☎ 028-9033-1532

Reservations Recommended. **Entree range** £11–£18. **Payment** AE, DC, MC, V. **Bar** Full service. **Disabled access** Yes. **Hours** Monday–Friday, noon–2:15 p.m.; Monday–Thursday, 6–10 p.m.; Friday and Saturday, 6–11 p.m., Sunday, 5–8:45 p.m.

MENU RECOMMENDATIONS Crispy duck salad, chargrilled calamari with chorizo, fresh fish.

COMMENTS Chef-owner Paul Rankin is one of Ireland's most beloved food celebs and has several Belfast restaurants. None disappoint, although some are better than others: Cayenne earns high marks for creative use of the freshest ingredients in innovative preparations with a spicy Asian twist. Many who've been dining on standard Irish fare think they've died and gone to heaven when they walk into these sleek, restful surroundings of rich wood, contemporary art, and subdued lighting to enjoy one of Rankin's innovative creations. The superb service is both polished and welcoming. At another nearby Rankin restaurant, Roscoff Brasserie (7–11 Linehall Street, ☎ 028-9031-1150), classic dishes are served in a restrained, contemporary room.

James Street South ★ ★ ★ ★

| MODERN IRISH | MODERATE/EXPENSIVE | QUALITY ★ ★ ★ ★ | VALUE ★ ★ ★ ★ |

21 James Street, Belfast; ☎ 028-9043-4310

Reservations Required. **Entree range** £12–£20; pre-theatre menu, £15.50 for 2 courses, £17.50 for 3 courses. **Payment** AE, MC, V. **Bar** Full service. **Disabled access** Yes. **Hours** Monday–Friday, noon–2:45 p.m.; Monday–Saturday, 5:45–10:45 p.m.

MENU RECOMMENDATIONS Roast loin of rabbit with artichoke and pear, roast loin of venison.

COMMENTS A few pieces of colorful art, polished wood floors, crisp linens, and dramatic but warm lighting create just the right contemporary atmosphere in this refined room facing narrow James Street through arched windows. The minimalist environs strike just the right note in suggesting that the emphasis here is on the expertly served exquisite preparations of Chef Niall McKenna—lunch or dinner in this accomplished place is always a special occasion.

Michael Deane ★ ★ ★ ★

| MODERN IRISH/FUSION | VERY EXPENSIVE | QUALITY ★ ★ ★ ★ | VALUE ★ ★ ★ |

38–40 Howard Street, Belfast; ☎ 028-9033-1134

Reservations Required. **Entree range** Prix-fixe dinner, £33–£59. **Payment** AE, MC, V. **Bar** Full service. **Disabled access** Yes. **Hours** Wednesday–Saturday, 7–9:30 p.m.; Friday, 12:15 p.m.–2 p.m.

MENU RECOMMENDATIONS Ravioli of lobster, roasted scallops, and filet of Irish beef.

COMMENTS One of Ireland's finest restaurants—and the only dining room in Northern Ireland ever to have earned a Michelin star—never fails to deliver a memorable dining experience. Michael Deane trained in Bangkok, and subtle spices work their way into simple local ingredients such as squab, fresh fish, and seafood. The result is stunning. There is nothing outlandish about dishes such as the mashed potatoes infused with lemongrass or carpaccio of salmon with sticky rice—dish after dish, you wonder why no one has thought of doing this before. The dining room is located above the less formal and rather disappointing Deanes Brasserie; don't settle for a meal downstairs when culinary heaven is just above your head.

Nick's Warehouse ★ ★ ★ ★

MODERN IRISH	MODERATE/EXPENSIVE	QUALITY ★ ★ ★	VALUE ★ ★ ★ ★ ½

35–39 Hill Street, Belfast; ☎ 028-9043-9690

Reservations Recommended. **Entree range** £8.50–£17.50. **Payment** AE, MC, V. **Bar** Full service. **Disabled access** Yes. **Hours** Monday–Friday, noon–3 p.m.; Tuesday–Saturday, 6–9:30 p.m.

MENU RECOMMENDATIONS Shepherd's pie, roast chump of lamb (the portion between the leg and loin), grilled filet of salmon.

COMMENTS Chef Nick Price was a pioneer when he opened his warm and welcoming eatery in a warehouse district on an alley near St. Anne's Cathedral. The neighborhood is booming these days, but Nick remains the local star, serving in a lively ground-floor wine bar and an upstairs dining room—a meal downstairs tends to be more fun, with a lot of animated chatter among the regulars, especially at lunch. Nick's serves a stellar selection of wines by the glass.

Rain City Café Grill ★ ★ ★ ½

MODERN IRISH	MODERATE	QUALITY ★ ★ ★ ½	VALUE ★ ★ ★ ★

33–35 Malone Road, Belfast; ☎ 028-9068-2929

Reservations Recommended. **Entree range** £7.95–£14.50. **Payment** AE, DC, MC, V. **Bar** Full service. **Disabled access** Yes. **Hours** Daily, 9 a.m.–10 p.m.

MENU RECOMMENDATIONS Rain City burger, fish and chips, grilled Irish steak.
COMMENTS In this informal bistrolike outlet of the Paul Rankin empire near Queen's University, the emphasis is on casual fare and good value. Cream-colored brick walls and pine tables set just the right mood for an easy meal of a burger or a plate of sausages, while more-substantial fare—including some excellent fish preparations—is also available. The service is friendly and attentive, and kids are most welcome.

ENTERTAINMENT AND NIGHTLIFE IN BELFAST

NOT SURPRISINGLY, PUB LIFE is no less active here in the North than it is in the Republic. Belfast's most celebrated watering hole is the **Crown Liquor Saloon** (Great Victoria Street, ☎ 028-9027-9001), a wonderfully atmospheric Victorian showcase of mirrors and carved wood; the Crown is protected as part of the U.K.'s National Trust, but this museum-like status and the place's popularity on the tourist trail do not detract from the pleasure of enjoying a pint and a plate of oysters or other light fare in these ornate surroundings. Atmosphere is also on tap at the pubs on the narrow lanes of the **Cathedral Quarter.** At **White's Tavern** (2–4 Winecellar Entry, ☎ 028-9033-0988), business goes on beneath brick arches pretty much as it has since 1630, with great conversation and traditional music some nights. **The Spaniard** (3 Skipper Street, ☎ 028-9023-2448) is a snug little place that serves soups and tapas into the early evening, and then pints of excellent Guinness are poured for a crowd of regulars who crowd around the long bar and cozy tables. For a taste of Belfast student life, head out to the "Bot" (the **Botanic Inn**) or the "Egg" (the **Eglantine**)—across Malone Road from one another and attracting throngs of thirsty scholars who pass many an evening in one or the other (Botanic Inn, 23–27 Malone Road, ☎ 028-9066-0460; Eglantine, 32–40 Malone Road, ☎ 028-9038-1994).

For traditional music, settle into the **Fountain Bar** (16–20 Fountain Street, ☎ 028-9032-4769) on Friday evenings; **Maddens** (74 Berry Street, ☎ 028-9024-4114) on Monday, Friday, and Saturday evenings; **McHughs** (29–31 Queens Square, ☎ 028-9050-9990) on Thursday and Friday evenings; and **Fibber Magee's,** behind the Crown Liquor Saloon, every evening. For disco, R&B, and other (often live) entertainment, check out **La Lea** (43 Franklin Street, ☎ 028-9023-0200) and **Milk** (10–14 Tomb Street, ☎ 028-9027-8876).

The two major performing arts venues in Belfast are the **Grand Opera House** and **Waterfront Hall.** The former, located on Great Victoria Street, is a beautifully restored Victorian music hall that these days hosts road shows and other visiting companies, with a penchant toward smash musicals from London and New York; for tickets and information, call ☎ 028-9024-1919 or visit **www.goh.co.uk.** Waterfront Hall, the city's main stage, hosts symphonic concerts, dance, traditional Irish music performances, rock concerts, and other big events; to check out what's scheduled during your stay in Belfast, call ☎ 028-9033-4400 or visit **www.waterfront.co.uk. Kings Hall Exhibition and Conference Centre** (☎ 028-9066-5225; **www.kingshall.co.uk**), in Balmoral, also hosts concerts, along with trade shows and other events. **Ulster Hall** (Bedford Street, ☎ 028-9032-3900; **www.ulsterhall .co.uk**) is home to the Ulster Orchestra and the Northern Ireland Symphony Orchestra. Belfast's leading stage for plays is the **Lyric Theatre** (Ridgeway Street, ☎ 028-9038-1081; **www.lyrictheatre.co.uk**).

Odyssey, on Queen's Quay, is a one-stop spot for sports and entertainment. The huge arena is home to the **Belfast Giants,** an ice-hockey team, and is yet another venue for major concerts. The complex also has a bowling alley, IMAX theatre, and 12-screen cinema complex, the best place in town to catch a major new release; for general information, call ☎ 028-9045-1055 or visit **www.theodyssey.co.uk.**

SHOPPING IN BELFAST

DONEGALL PLACE, ROYAL AVENUE, AND HIGH STREET are the main shopping venues in the city center. Belfast is at best a serendipitous place for the shopper, though, with many outlets of the typical British chains, including a **Marks and Spencer** on Donegall Place. Two places worth seeking out are **Smyth's Irish Linens** (65 Royal Avenue, ☎ 028-9024-2232) and **St. George's Market** (May Street and Oxford Street, ☎ 028-9043-5704), a colorful piece of 19th-century Belfast that hosts food and craft vendors every Tuesday and Friday morning, starting at 8 a.m.

DERRY

IN KEEPING WITH ITS COMPLEX NATURE, this appealing and underrated city has two names—those in favor of British rule still call the city Londonderry, an understandably controversial appellation that Catholics have over the years rejected in favor of simply Derry. The city is still officially labeled Londonderry, though the city council and other political bodies within the city often use Derry. What the city is called, one can truly say in this case, depends on whom you are talking to.

Derry commands a lovely and strategic position on the banks of the River Foyle, and given the possibilities for shipping, British and Scottish Protestants settled the city in the early 17th century and surrounded their stronghold with thick walls that still stand—some of the most intact medieval walls in Europe. The city repelled a siege by the forces of the Catholic King James II in 1688–89, and for its impregnability has earned yet a third name, the Maiden City. The strong Protestant presence and large Catholic population made Derry rife with conflict during the Troubles: beginning in the late 1960s the city saw considerable violence, with daily bombings and horrible bloodshed, including the murder of 14 innocent civilians during the Bloody Sunday protests of January 30, 1972. You'll never be far from the palpable presence of the Troubles in Derry, though these days they make themselves known by colorful, politically charged murals rather than violence.

PLANNING YOUR VISIT TO DERRY

HOUSED IN A HANDSOME PAVILION near the banks of the River Foyle, the **Derry Visitor and Convention Bureau and Tourist Information Centre** (44 Foyle Street, ☎ 028-7126-7284; **www.derryvisitor.com**) is at the south end of town across from the Foyleside Shopping Centre. The extremely helpful staff is full of advice on what to see and do in

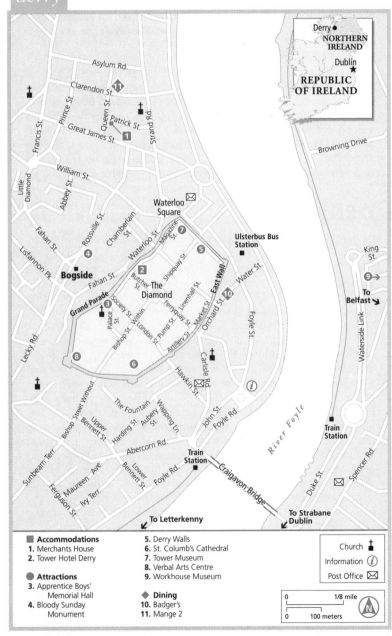

derry

Derry ●
NORTHERN
IRELAND
Dublin ★
REPUBLIC
OF IRELAND

Asylum Rd.
Clarendon St.
Prince St.
Queen St.
Patrick St.
Strand Rd.
Great James St.
Francis St.
Little Diamond
William St.
Abbey St.
Rossville St.
Fahan St.
Chamberlain St.
Waterloo St.
Magazine St.
Waterloo Square
Ulsterbus Bus Station
Listannon Pk.
Fahan St.
Bogside
Grand Parade
Butcher St.
Shipquay St.
The Diamond
Society St. Within
Palace St.
Bishop St. Within
London St.
Ferryquay St.
Linenhall St.
Market St.
Pump St.
Artillery St.
East Wall
Orchard St.
Water St.
Foyle St.
King St.
To Belfast
Waterside Link
Lecky Rd.
Hawkin St.
Carlisle Rd.
The Fountain
Bishop Street Without
Upper Bennett St.
Harding St.
Aubery St.
Wapping Ln.
John St.
Foyle Rd.
River Foyle
Browning Drive
Train Station
Sunbeam Terr.
Maureen Ave.
Ivy Terr.
Lower Bennett St.
Abercorn Rd.
Train Station
Foyle Rd.
Craigavon Bridge
Ferguson St.
Duke St.
Spencer Rd.
To Letterkenny
To Strabane Dublin

■ **Accommodations**	5. Derry Walls	Church ✝
1. Merchants House	6. St. Columb's Cathedral	
2. Tower Hotel Derry	7. Tower Museum	Information ⓘ
	8. Verbal Arts Centre	
● **Attractions**	9. Workhouse Museum	Post Office ✉
3. Apprentice Boys' Memorial Hall		
4. Bloody Sunday Monument	◆ **Dining**	0 1/8 mile
	10. Badger's	0 100 meters
	11. Mange 2	N

Derry and the surrounding region (stock up on info about the Antrim Coast here, too), arranges accommodations, and leads excellent walking tours. Mid-March to June and October: Monday through Friday, 9 a.m. to 5 p.m.; Saturday, 10 a.m. to 5 p.m.; July to September: Monday through Friday, 9 a.m. to 7 p.m.; Saturday, 10 a.m. to 6 p.m.; Sunday, 10 a.m. to 5 p.m.

Special Events in Derry

Derry stages several major cultural events throughout the year. The **City of Derry Drama Festival** in early March is Ireland's most acclaimed showcase for amateur drama; ☎ 028-7126-4455. Irish music is celebrated at the **Feis Doire Cholmcille** during March and April, while the **Celtronic Festival** in late June and early July is a festival of Irish dance; ☎ 028-7126-4455. The **City of Derry Jazz Festival** in early March to late April brings together an international roster of jazz and big-band enthusiasts; ☎ 028-7137-6545, **www.cityofderryjazzfestival.com.** Derry's most famous—and notorious—event is the **Relief of Derry Celebration** (held on the Saturday that falls closest to August 12), which commemorates the 1688–89 siege during which Protestants loyal to William of Orange kept the forces of the Catholic King James II at bay for 100 days. In a ceremony that has stirred up violence over the years, members of the Protestant all-male Apprentice Boys organization walk the walls in remembrance of those who lost their lives during the siege.

ARRIVING AND GETTING ORIENTED IN DERRY

DERRY IS ABOUT 110 KILOMETERS (70 miles) north of Belfast and 230 kilometers (145 miles) northwest of Dublin. By car, follow the A6 motorway across Northern Ireland from Belfast to Derry, which takes a little more than an hour. **Northern Ireland Railways** runs eight trains per day between Belfast and Derry, and the trip takes about two hours. Standard one-way fare is £5. Derry's Northern Ireland Railways station is on the east side of the River Foyle on Duke Street. Bus service is faster and much more frequent, with about 16 buses a day making the trip in one and a half hours. The bus station is conveniently located next to the tourist information office on Foyle Road. For information on both train and bus service, go to **www.nirailways.co.uk.**

unofficial **TIP**
The only easy way to see Derry is on foot. If you're driving, stash the car as soon as you get to town. The most convenient car park is at **Foyleside Shopping Centre,** across from the tourist office. The massive parking area is open daily, from 8 a.m. into the evening hours; expect to pay about £2.50 to park for most of the day. From here it's an easy walk to sights, shops, and restaurants.

HOTELS IN DERRY

Merchants House ★ ★ ★ ★

QUALITY	★ ★ ★	VALUE	★ ★ ★	£40–£50

16 Queen Street, Derry, County Londonderry BT48 7EQ;
☎ **028-7126-4223; fax 028-7126-6913; saddlershouse@btinternet.com;**
www.thesaddlershouse.com

Location 5-minute walk from city center. **Amenities and services** 5 units, 1 with private bath; in-room tea and coffee facilities, sitting room. **Elevator** No. **Parking** Free, on street. **Credit cards** None.

If ever a hotel was so appealing that you'd be willing to forgo a private bath, this lovely old house—a rare Georgian gem—might be the place. The atmosphere of a private home really does prevail here: The sitting room will tempt you to linger for hours and read, guest rooms are commodious and charming with their eccentric but comfortable furnishings, and breakfasts are memorable; shared baths are plentiful, spotless, and just steps from the rooms. Joan and Peter Pyne, who run this delightful guest house, also operate the Saddler's House a few blocks away. That too is a historic home lovingly restored, featuring seven rooms, three with private bathrooms. Both establishments provide character-filled accommodations in one of Ireland's most distinctive cities.

Tower Hotel Derry ★ ★ ★

QUALITY	★ ★ ★	VALUE	★ ★ ★ ★	£60–£70

Butcher Street, Derry BT48 6HL; ☎ **028-7137-1000; reservations@thd.ie;**
www.towerhotelgroup.com

Location City center. **Amenities and services** 93 rooms; bar, gym, hair dryers, restaurant, room service, wireless Internet access. **Elevator** Yes. **Parking** £5, on property. **Price** Includes full Irish breakfast; special weekend rates available. **Credit cards** AE, MC, V.

The only hotel within the city walls of Derry can just barely make that claim—the walls soar past one end of the hotel, creating a dramatic view from the ground-floor bistro and some of the guest rooms. Other than this location, the Tower makes few claims to distinction, instead focusing on providing standard hotel amenities at a good price. The busy public areas include the pleasant Lime Tree Bar, where sandwiches and other light fare are available throughout the day, and the Bistro, an airy restaurant serving Mediterranean-influenced cuisine (including many pasta dishes). Guest rooms are amply sized and warmly decorated in a safe, traditional style; those at the rear of the hotel offer views over the River Foyle and sections of the city walls.

EXPLORING DERRY

TAKE IN A NICE OVERVIEW OF DERRY and its history, past and recent, on a fairly easy walk along the medieval walls that still surround the central city, and then into the once-strife-torn **Bogside** neighborhood. You will get a lot more out of a visit to Derry if you make this walk in the company of a knowledgeable guide; see "Tours in Derry,"page 394.

The completely intact **Derry Walls,** built by British settlers between 1614 and 1618, are the only such set in Ireland and one of the few in Europe. A walkway of a little more than 2 kilometers (1.25 miles) follows the tops of the walls, affording wonderful views over the historic city within the enclosure, as well as the metropolis that has sprung up over the centuries outside the walls. Frequent stairways lead off the walls, providing access to the places you will want to visit in the city center. If you mount the walls near the **Tourist Information Centre** at Bridge Street and walk in a clockwise direction, you will soon come to **St. Columb's Cathedral,** built in 1633 and a powerful symbol of Protestant Derry. Among the many relics from the 1688–89 siege is a 270-pound mortar ball that the Catholic forces of King James II of England lobbed over the walls with conditions of surrender attached. Legend has it that the citizenry of the besieged and starving city rushed to the walls and shouted "No Surrender!"—a popular chant during the Troubles. Find the Stars and Stripes in the forest of flags and banners that hang in the church; this was the flag brought to Northern Ireland by the American troops who used Derry as their first entry point into the European theater of World War II.

A little farther along is another edifice that's almost as sacred to the Protestant hearts of Derry, the **Apprentice Boys' Memorial Hall.** Built in 1867 in a faux-Gothic manor, this imposing bastion serves as headquarters of the all-male, all-Protestant Apprentice Boys Society, which was formed in 1715 to honor the 13 young apprentices who in 1688 closed the city gates on the advancing troops of King James II, setting in motion Derry's great siege. Members of the organization still meet within the bar and lounges of this ornate structure, where some 20,000 members have been sworn in over the years in the initiation chamber. The Society sometimes opens its doors to nonmembers (check with the Tourist Information Centre), and members make a great showing every year on the Saturday closest to August 12 when they march on the city walls. Violence frequently flared up when thousands of Protestant marchers allegedly flaunted their might to Catholics in the Bogside neighborhood beneath the walls; since the Good Friday Peace Accords of 1998, in a gesture of peace, only a small contingent of the Society is allowed to march past the Catholic precincts.

From this section of the walls you can look down into **Bogside,** so called for the marshy, less-desirable ground upon which the neighborhood took shape around the 1840s famine, when starving peasants from Donegal came to Derry looking for work. The violence that erupted in this neighborhood during the Troubles accounts for the presence of the British military lookout tower on this section of the walls; much of the installation has been dismantled, and next to the tower is the **Verbal Arts Centre,** a peace-promoting concern that encourages the development of local literary efforts. From the walls you can pick out some of the murals depicting the heated political climate of the past decades (walk into the neighborhood later for a closer look; see below). You can also see the **Bloody Sunday Monument,** which honors the 14 civilians shot by British soldiers during a march on Sunday, January 30, 1972, because they were protesting laws allowing imprisonment without trial.

Just outside the north end of the walls is the **Guildhall,** an 1890 mock-Gothic fortress and the seat of city government; a bomb blast ripped through the building in 1972, a time when bombings were a daily occurrence in Derry. Like most other damaged structures, the Guildhall was rebuilt, and the magnificent stained-glass windows were remade to the original designs still on file at the glassmaker's studios in Belfast. One of the convicted bombers, Gerry Doherty, took a seat in the council chamber when he was elected to the City Council in the 1980s. The excellent city museum, **Tower Museum Derry,** is just inside the walls here.

Bogside

The Catholic neighborhood beneath the walls has been largely rebuilt since the violence of the past decades, but political murals are stunning reminders. While those promoting the British cause have appeared in Protestant neighborhoods since the division of Ireland in the 1920s, they were outlawed in pro-independence Catholic neighborhoods but began to reappear during the Troubles of the 1970s. The murals one sees today are recent—from the 1990s—and vivid statements of the ideologies that emerged from the strife. If you leave the walled city through Butcher's Gate and turn west (left) toward Rossville Road, you'll soon encounter the murals, usually painted along the gable ends of buildings. Most commemorate significant events in clashes between the IRA and the police and military: *Death of Innocence* portrays Annette McGavigan, a 14-year-old killed in crossfire between police forces and the IRA in 1971; *Rioter* shows a youth armed only with a stone facing a British military vehicle; *Operation Motorman* depicts a British soldier attempting to demolish the neighborhood barricades with which Bogside residents once surrounded themselves. One of the most poignant reminders of the neighborhood's past is the huge sign painted on the end of a building: "You Are Now Entering Free Derry," capturing the quest for independence that ignited the Troubles.

Tours in Derry

The **Derry Visitor and Convention Bureau** conducts an excellent walking tour that more or less circumnavigates the walls, with stops at St. Columb's Cathedral and other landmarks along the way; you look down on the Bogside neighborhood from overlooks on the walls while your guide explains the murals and monuments, but for a close-up look you'll need to head down there on your own. Tours, which last an hour and a half, depart from the **Tourist Information Centre;** July to August, Monday through Friday, 11:15 a.m. and 3:15 p.m.; September to June, Monday through Friday, 2:30 p.m.; £5 adults, £3 seniors and students. For an in-depth look at the murals, consider joining one of the hour-long walks offered by **Bogside Artists;** for times and fees, call ☎ 028-7129-0371 or visit **www.bogsideartists.com.**

ATTRACTIONS IN DERRY

Tower Museum Derry ★ ★ ★ ★

| APPEAL BY AGE | PRESCHOOL ★ ★ | GRADE SCHOOL ★ ★ ★ | TEENS ★ ★ ★ |
| YOUNG ADULTS ★ ★ ★ | | OVER 30 ★ ★ ★ | SENIORS ★ ★ ★ |

Union Hall Place, Derry; ☎ **028-7137-2411;**
www.derrycity.gov.uk/heritage.htm

Type of attraction Museum of local history. **Admission** £5 adults; £3 seniors, students, and children; £10 families. **Hours** July–August: Monday–Saturday, 10 a.m.–5 p.m.; Sunday, 2–5 p.m.; September–June: Tuesday–Saturday, 10 a.m.–5 p.m. **When to go** Weekdays, if possible, because the museum can be quite crowded on weekends, making it harder to enjoy the exhibits. **Special comments** The museum is an essential stop on a trip to Northern Ireland, in that it is probably the visitor's best source of information on the Troubles and the complex conditions that fostered the conflict. **How much time to allow** At least 2 hours.

DESCRIPTION AND COMMENTS Derry's civic museum, which occupies a reconstructed tower house from the 17th century, is a fascinating place, not simply because Derry is such an interesting city, but also because the exhibits are superb. If you've come to Derry thinking the city is simply a blighted war zone, this museum will go a long way toward convincing you otherwise and leaving you with a much greater appreciation for the town's architecture, strategic importance, and colorful forebears. The latter include—as you'll learn in the galleries—characters such as Frederick Augustus Hervey, the high-living late-18th-century bishop, and aviator Amelia Earhart, who once landed in a field outside Derry. Multimedia exhibits dramatically reenact the siege of 1688–89 and sensitively explain the historic roots and many tragedies of the Troubles. A new wing shows off one of Northern Ireland's greatest treasures: loot found in the wrecks of Spanish galleons that sank off the coast in 1588.
TOURING TIPS Budget at least half your time to explore the exhibits dealing with the Troubles, as these deserve time and concentration.

Workhouse Museum ★ ★ ★ ★

| APPEAL BY AGE | PRESCHOOL ★ | GRADE SCHOOL ★ | TEENS ★ ★ ★ |
| YOUNG ADULTS ★ | | OVER 30 ★ ★ ★ ½ | SENIORS ★ ★ ★ ★ |

23 Glendermott Road; ☎ **028-7131-8328;**
www.derrycity.gov.uk/heritage.htm

Type of attraction Museum that chronicles the Famine and Derry's role in World War II. **Admission** Free. **Hours** Monday–Thursday, 10 a.m.–4:30 p.m. **When to go** Anytime. **Special comments** The grim nature of the workhouse and the fate of children here can make a visit unsuitable for young visitors. On the other hand, the section devoted to Derry's role in World War II is of enormous interest to veterans of that conflict and others interested in the war. **How much time to allow** About 1 hour.

DESCRIPTION AND COMMENTS   The sense of misery is almost palpable here, and a floor of exhibits movingly depicts the fate of many impoverished victims of the Famine of the 1840s, who had no choice but to throw themselves at the mercy of institutions such as these. The workhouse was essentially a forced labor camp in which families were separated forever. Untold numbers died of hunger and disease. Derry was the North's major port of emigration; many of the inhabitants of the Derry workhouse walked to the city from rural counties hoping to find passage on ships bound for America. Sadly, many could never scrape together the fare and essentially had no choice but to die in the grim dormitories here. Part of the museum chronicles the Battle of the Atlantic, especially the role of the U.S. troops who arrived in 1942 and, three years later, oversaw the surrender of the German U-boat fleet in Derry Harbor.

TOURING TIPS   The museum is across the Foyle from the city center, about a ten-minute walk; if you're traveling by car, consider stopping on your way into or out of the city.

RESTAURANTS IN DERRY

Badger's ★ ★ ★

PUB FARE	INEXPENSIVE	QUALITY ★ ★ ★	VALUE ★ ★ ★ ★

16–18 Orchard Street, Derry; ☎ 028-7136-0763

Reservations Not necessary. **Entree range** £5–£10. **Payment** MC, V. **Bar** Full service. **Disabled access** Yes. **Hours** Monday, noon–3 p.m.; Tuesday–Thursday, noon–7 p.m.; Friday–Saturday, noon–9:30 p.m.

MENU RECOMMENDATIONS   Beef-and-Guinness stew, sandwiches.

COMMENTS   What may well be the most popular pub in Derry attracts neighborhood locals as well as a highly talkative crowd of journalists and artists (let them do the talking—you don't want to voice an unpopular political opinion in these parts). The Guinness is excellent, and a satisfying meal is easy to come by; check the board for daily specials.

Mange 2 ★ ★ ★ ★

IRISH/INTERNATIONAL	MODERATE	QUALITY ★ ★ ★ ★	VALUE ★ ★ ★ ★

2B Clarendon Street, Derry; ☎ 028-7136-1222

Reservations Recommended. **Entree range** £8–£10. **Payment** MC, V. **Bar** Full service. **Disabled access** Yes. **Hours** Monday–Saturday, 11:30 a.m.–3 p.m., 5:30–11 p.m.; Sunday, 10:30 a.m.–3 p.m.

MENU RECOMMENDATIONS Fresh fish.

COMMENTS Simple, straightforward preparations here are almost always satisfying, and meals are served with care in an unpretentious but pleasing cafelike setting of pine tables and uncluttered walls. Don't let the lack of pretense fool you, though—this is one of Derry's most respected kitchens and most pleasant dining experiences.

SOUTH *of* DERRY

THE SPERRIN MOUNTAINS RISE JUST SOUTHEAST of Derry, reaching their peak at **Sawel,** 661 meters (2,204 feet) tall. For the most part these are gentle mountains, covered with moors and woodlands above valleys parceled into small farms.

South of the Sperrins, green hills run down to the shores of **Lough Erne.** The Ernes are actually two lakes, Upper and Lower Lough Erne, and they compose one of Ireland's most popular spots for boating. Monasteries flourished on the lakeshores in the Middle Ages. Some of Ireland's greatest estates were built in the region in the 18th century, while a pleasant, low-key resort atmosphere prevails today.

ENNISKILLEN

ABOUT 100 KILOMETERS (60 MILES) SOUTH OF DERRY, Enniskillen is beautifully lodged between Lower Lough Erne to the north and Upper Lough Erne to the south; the River Erne runs through town, connecting the two. Enniskillen, the capital of County Fermanagh, has the look of a prosperous county seat, with rows of redbrick Georgian houses running down to the river and the lakeshore.

Arriving and Getting Oriented in Enniskillen

Ulsterbus runs daily coach service to and from Enniskillen, with several trips a day; one bus departs from Derry at 9 a.m. and returns at 5:30 p.m., allowing plenty of time for a day's outing. The two-plus-hour trip requires a change in Omagh and costs about £7. The trip is all the more pleasant if you travel by car, allowing yourself time to meander south through Belleek on A47 and from there around the lakeshore (see page 379) to Enniskillen and the attractions that surround the town.

Exploring Enniskillen and the Region

Enniskillen's charms are greatly enhanced by the green hills and blue waters that surround the attractive town, as well as by the hulking presence of **Enniskillen Castle.** This mighty fortress began to take shape in the early 15th century, when the Maguire clan established a foothold in the region to protect the passes that led into the rest of the North. The castle's most prominent feature is the Watergate, a tall, turreted, fortified structure that rises on the banks of the River Erne. Watergate, oddly, contains no gate but is near a breach in the castle's thick walls.

Much the appearance of the present-day castle is the work of Sir William Cole (1576–1653), a Londoner by birth who was responsible for overseeing boat traffic on Lough Erne and who was eventually given the lease to the castle and the land on which the town took shape. The castle houses a fairly dull collection of local history and wildlife, as well as weapons and uniforms of the Royal Inniskilling Fusiliers. Open year-round Monday, 2 to 5 p.m.; Tuesday through Friday, 10 a.m. to 5 p.m.; also open Saturday, May through September, 2 to 5 p.m., and Sunday, July and August, 2 to 5 p.m. Admission is £2.75 adults, £2.20 students and seniors, and £1.65 children. For more information, call ☎ 028-6632-5000 or visit **www.enniskillencastle.co.uk.**

Enniskillen's **Portora Royal School,** established by King James I in 1608, educated Samuel Beckett, Oscar Wilde, and several other noted alumni. The town's other attractions include two of Ireland's finest houses, **Castle Coole** (see below) and **Florence Court,** 13 kilometers (8 miles) southeast off A32. The latter, an appealing manor set on extensive grounds in the Cullcagh Mountains, was built in the 18th century and is richly embellished with elaborate rococo plasterwork. The grounds, laced with hiking trails, are open year-round, daily, dawn to dusk. The house is open in summer only: June, Monday and Wednesday through Sunday, 1 to 6 p.m.; July and August, daily, noon to 6 p.m.; and September, Saturday and Sunday, 1 to 6 p.m. Admission to the house and grounds is £4.25 adults, £2 children, and £10.50 for families of up to two adults and two children; admission to the grounds is £3 per car. For more information, call ☎ 028-6634-8249 or visit **www.nationaltrust.org.uk.**

Devenish Island, in the lake just southeast of Enniskillen, is graced with the best-preserved round tower in Ireland, built in the 12th century as protection against Viking raids. St. Molaise founded a monastery on the island in the sixth century, and the Augustine order of monks built the Abbey of St. Mary here in the 12th century. Chapels and convents lie in picturesque ruins, with the tower rising above them and the lake glimmering in the background. Ferries sail to the island from Trory Point, 6.5 kilometers (4 miles) south of Enniskillen, April through September, £2.25 round trip. Call ☎ 028-6862-1588 for schedules and information.

Attraction around Enniskillen

Castle Coole ★ ★ ★ ★

APPEAL BY AGE	PRESCHOOL ★★	GRADE SCHOOL ★★★	TEENS ★★★
YOUNG ADULTS ★★★	OVER 30 ★★★★		SENIORS ★★★★

2.5 kilometers (1.5 miles) southeast of Enniskillen off the A4;
☎ **028-6632-5665; www.nationaltrust.org.uk**

Type of attraction One of Ireland's finest country estates. **Admission** £4.50 adults, £2 for children under 12, £11 for families of up to 2 adults and 2 children.

Hours June, Friday–Wednesday, 1–6 p.m.; July and August, daily, noon–6 p.m.; September, Saturday and Sunday, 1–6 p.m.; grounds are open year-round, daily, dawn to dusk. **When to go** Midweek and early in the day, when you are likely to have the grounds to yourself. **Special comments** The house is often used for weddings and other functions, so check to make sure your visit does not coincide with an event that takes over parts of the estate; the house hosts concerts throughout the year (on the grounds on some summer evenings). **How much time to allow** 3 hours for house and grounds.

DESCRIPTION AND COMMENTS The starkly elegant neoclassical facade of this manor, built for the Earl of Belmore at the end of the 18th century, is one of the most stunning architectural sights in all of Ireland. The earl served in the Irish Houses of Parliament and was one of the wealthiest landowners in Ireland; accordingly, he hired the finest architect of the day, James Wyatt, to build his estate here in the remote wilds of County Fermanagh. The earl more or less retired here when the Act of Union dissolved the Irish Parliament in 1800, and the family remained in residence until the seventh earl of Belmore sold Castle Coole to the National Trust in 1951. The staterooms include several salons furnished in Regency style, a great hall, and a bedroom prepared for a royal visit from King George IV in 1821 (the king never showed up). Just as intriguing are the servants' quarters and a tunnel that connected them to the house, the only entrance help and tradesmen were allowed to use—eliminating the unsightly blemish of a service door on any of the house's four facades.

TOURING TIPS Plan on spending time walking in the beautiful grounds.

Restaurant in Enniskillen

Blake's of the Hollow ★ ★ ★ ★

PUB FARE/MODERN IRISH   INEXPENSIVE/MODERATE   QUALITY ★ ★ ★ ★   VALUE ★ ★ ★ ★

6 Church Street, Enniskillen; ☎ 028-6632-0918

Reservations Not required. **Entree range** £6–£14; early-dinner menu in Café Merlot daily, 5:30–7:30 p.m., 2 courses £11.95. **Payment** AE, MC, V. **Bar** Full service. **Disabled access** Yes. **Hours** Daily, 12:30–2:30 p.m. and 5–9:30 p.m.; pub, daily, 11 a.m.–midnight.

MENU RECOMMENDATIONS Aged filet of beef, any fresh-fish preparation.

COMMENTS Enniskillen's most venerable pub retains all the Victorian grandeur that was in vogue when it opened in 1887. The operation has expanded and now offers, aside from pub grub in the woody old bar, a formal dining room, Number Six, and the informal Café Merlot. The latter is a good place for a casual meal, but if you don't mind settling for a sandwich, the old bar is still the most atmospheric place in town to drink and dine.

Exercise and Recreation in Enniskillen

Understandably, many visitors come to Enniskillen with the single-minded intention of getting out onto the waters of Lough Erne. **Lakeland Canoe Centre,** on Castle Island just west of town (☎ 028-

6632-4250), rents canoes, sailboats, and windsurfers, as well as bikes for a land-based excursion. Should you wish to enjoy the lake without physical exertion, you can cruise the lake, with a stop at Devenish Island, on scheduled two-hour sailings from May through September with **Erne Tours Ltd.** (Brook Park, near town center; call ☎ 028-6632-2882 for schedules and fares).

THE ANTRIM COAST

TO THE NORTH AND EAST OF DERRY lies some of the most spectacular scenery in all of Ireland, along the Antrim Coast. You can explore this coastline on a scenic road, A2, that hugs the green hills dropping down to the sea. Any reluctance you might feel toward leaving this beautiful coastline behind is offset by the pleasures of exploring the **Glens of Antrim,** nine densely wooded river valleys etched out of the mountain terrain along the sea.

ARRIVING AND GETTING ORIENTED ON THE ANTRIM COAST

THE ANTRIM COAST BEGINS OUTSIDE the resort town of **Portrush,** about 60 kilometers (36 miles) northeast of Derry. Not surprisingly, the easiest and most satisfying way to tour the region is by car, although in summer open-top buses run along the coast from Portrush to the Old Bushmills Distillery and the Giants Causeway; for more information, contact **Translink,** ☎ 028-9066-6630; **www.translink.co.uk.** You'll find an excellent **tourist-information center** at Giants Causeway, ☎ 028-2073-1855; open year-round, Monday through Friday, 9:30 a.m. to 5 p.m., Saturday, 10 a.m. to 4 p.m., and Sunday, 2 to 4 p.m. You will also find reams of information on the Antrim Coast and the Glens at the tourist-information office in Derry.

HOTELS ON THE ANTRIM COAST

Bushmills Inn ★ ★ ★ ★ ½

QUALITY ★ ★ ★ ★ ½	VALUE ★ ★ ★	£100–£160

9 Dunluce Road, Bushmills, County Antrim BT57 8QG; ☎ 028-2073-3000; fax 028-2073-2048; mail@bushmillsinn.com; www.bushmillsinn.com

Location In the village of Bushmills, near the historic distillery and Giants Causeway. **Amenities and services** 22 rooms; bar, hair dryers, nonsmoking rooms, restaurant. **Elevator** Yes. **Parking** Free, on property. **Price** Includes full Irish breakfast. **Credit cards** AE, MC, V.

One of Ireland's most beloved inns maintains its character and high level of comfort year after year. Guests are greeted by turf fires and old beams, setting the stage for the traditional style admirably and tastefully maintained throughout the hotel. Lounges and a circular library, reached through a secret panel, along with a woody pub and attractive restaurant, are among the appealing public spaces. Guest rooms are continually being upgraded to a very high standard; these are attractive in a country-house style and, like the rest of the premises, not overdone—with fine old beds and armchairs, plus nicely equipped baths, they provide solid comfort. All the attractions of the Antrim Coast are within easy reach; some, such as the Giants Causeway (see page 403), can be reached via an exhilarating hike.

Maddybenny Farmhouse ★ ★ ★ ★

QUALITY ★ ★ ★ ★	VALUE ★ ★ ★ ★	£40–£50

Loguestown Road, Portrush, Country Antrim T52 2PT; ☎ 028-7082-3394; accommodation@maddybenny22.freeserve.co.uk; www.maddybenny.com

Location Outside Portrush. **Amenities and services** 5 units; garden, hair dryers, in-room tea and coffee facilities, lounges. **Elevator** No. **Parking** Free, on property. **Credit cards** MC, V.

The late Rosemary White, one of Northern Ireland's most celebrated inn-keepers, extended her 17th-century farmhouse many times over the years, but always with the comfort of her guests in mind. The front of the house, overlooking gardens and lawns, is now a series of delightful and sunny lounges, behind them a snug parlor warmed by a fire in colder months. Upstairs, the guest rooms are likewise comfortable; all but one small single are suitelike arrangements, extending into cozy sitting areas that also double as extra sleeping accommodation for families. Rooms are furnished with quaint old family pieces and equipped with thoughtful touches such as alarm clocks and, in the hall, a refrigerator for guests to use. The enormous breakfasts are part of Rosemary's legacy.

EXPLORING THE ANTRIM COAST

YOUR FIRST IMPRESSION OF THE COAST—the faded resort town of **Portrush**—may be a bit disappointing. A few terraces of Victorian houses and a busy harbor are pleasant enough, but continue east on A2 for just five kilometers (three miles) to the first of many spectacular sights, this one man-made: the ruins of **Dunluce Castle** perched on a rocky headland (see page 402). Just down the road is another man-made attraction well worth a stop, the **Old Bushmills Distillery,** a venerable institution that is the oldest licensed distillery in the world. If you do enough elbow bending in the tasting room, you will fall for the local blarney that the sea of rocks down the road—the marvelously strange natural phenomenon known as **Giants Causeway**—is the work of a likeable giant named Finn MacCool. Whatever the lore that surrounds the causeway, the sweep of cylindrical basalt outcroppings extending far out to sea toward Scotland is remarkable, all the more enticing because of the many hiking trails that lace the green hillsides around it.

The **Glens of Antrim** begin to grace the landscape around the small port and resort town of Ballycastle. **Glenariff,** the most beautiful of the glens with its dense woodlands and cascading cataracts, is also the most accessible, on the road and trails lacing **Glenariff Forest Park;** open daily, 8 a.m. to dusk; £1 per car.

ATTRACTIONS ON THE ANTRIM COAST

 Carrick-a-Rede Bridge ★ ★ ★ ★

APPEAL BY AGE	PRESCHOOL ★ ★	GRADE SCHOOL ★ ★ ★ ★	TEENS ★ ★ ★ ★
YOUNG ADULTS ★ ★ ★ ★		OVER 30 ★ ★ ★	SENIORS ★ ★ ★

8 kilometers (5 miles) west of Ballycastle; ☎ 028-2073-1582; www.nationaltrust.org.uk

Type of attraction Hair-raising rope bridge. **Admission** £2. **Hours** April–June and early September, daily, 10 a.m.–6 p.m.; July and August, 10 a.m.–8 p.m. **When to go** Only in good weather, because the bridge is closed when conditions are windy and wet. **Special comments** Do not even think of stopping if you're afraid of heights; kids have a ball crossing the bridge. **How much time to allow** ½ hour.

DESCRIPTION AND COMMENTS For some 200 summers, fishermen have been putting up a rope bridge to make the short crossing to Carrick-a-Rede Island, where they set out nets to snare salmon that swim toward the rivers to spawn. In recent years, the savvy fisherfolk have figured out that they can net more than some big fish—tourists by the busloads are willing to fork over £2 to timorously cross the rope-and-plank concoction swaying a dizzying height above the sea. So what if you're falling prey to gimcrack tourism? Crossing the bridge is a heck of a lot of fun, provided you don't suffer from vertigo, and the view of the surf and seabirds is exhilarating; this is one of those experiences you'll be telling the folks back home about.

TOURING TIPS If you see tour buses in the parking lot, try to come back another time—the experiences loses its appeal when the bridge is mobbed.

Dunluce Castle ★ ★ ★ ★

APPEAL BY AGE	PRESCHOOL ★ ★ ★	GRADE SCHOOL ★ ★ ★	TEENS ★ ★ ★
YOUNG ADULTS ★ ★ ★		OVER 30 ★ ★ ★	SENIORS ★ ★ ★

On a headland on the coast; ☎ 028-2073-1938; www.northantrim.com/dunlucecastle.htm

Type of attraction Castle ruins. **Admission** £2 adults, £1 seniors and children under age 16. **Hours** April–May and September: Monday–Saturday, 10 a.m.–6 p.m.; Sunday, 2–6 p.m.; June–August: Monday–Saturday, 10 a.m.–6 p.m.; Sunday, noon–6 p.m.; October–March: Monday–Saturday, 10 a.m.–4 p.m.; Sunday, 2–4 p.m. **When to go** Try to avoid a visit during a rain shower; the site can be muddy. **Special comments** Although it's easy to pass by the castle for more-noted attractions such as Giants Causeway and Bushmills Distillery, take the time to stop—a visit to these evocative and poetically perched ruins is a memorable experience. **How much time to allow** About ½ hour.

DESCRIPTION AND COMMENTS The elaborate castle complex, incorporating two 14th-century Norman towers, was the stronghold of the powerful MacDonnell clan, the Counts of Antrim. It wasn't rival clans that did them in, but the forces of nature—the sea churned relentlessly away at the precipitous cliffs on which the castle sits, and on a dark and stormy night in 1639 half the kitchen wing, and part of the staff, plunged into the surf. Over the ensuing centuries, surf and storms completed the job, leaving the castle basically a shell; even so, the ruins romantically evoke life in a medieval castle at the edge of the sea. An engaging staff gives short tours, during which they fill in the architectural gaps with colorful stories of the MacDonnells, life in the castle, and ongoing restoration efforts.

TOURING TIPS Tours do not follow a set schedule, so ask at the entry gate whether someone is available to show you around—a guide adds a lot to the experience.

 Giants Causeway ★ ★ ★ ★ ★

Near Bushmills; ☎ 028-2073-1582; www.giantscausewayofficialguide.com

Type of attraction One of Europe's most unusual natural phenomena. **Admission** Free; parking, £5. **Hours** April–September, daily, 10 a.m.–6 p.m.; October–March, daily, 10 a.m.–4:30 p.m. **When to go** In good weather. **Special comments** Take time to watch the 12-minute film in the visitors center for a good roundup of the legends surrounding the Causeway and a concise explanation of the equally compelling geologic forces that formed it; exhibits in the small museum are also well done. **How much time to allow** Several hours, more if you want to spend time hiking along the coast.

DESCRIPTION AND COMMENTS Legends concerning the formation of these pillars of basalt that litter the coast and sea for about six kilometers (four miles) of the coast are as plentiful as the stones themselves. Most concern a giant named Finn MacCool, who allegedly laid down the stepping stones to reach his beloved across the sea in Scotland. The only reason we mortals can't also use the stones to get to Scotland is that a rival giant, the lady giant's boyfriend, came to Ireland to settle the score. The story goes that he was terrified when he heard how big and fierce Finn was, and he tore up the stepping stones while beating a quick retreat. Just as awesome, actually, is the science-based theory that the stones were formed when lava erupted from underground fissures some 60 million years ago and crystallized in the cooler seawater. Begin a tour of this fascinating natural phenomenon, administered by the National Trust, at the visitors center. From there you can take a shuttle bus down to the causeway or walk the 2 kilometers (1.5 miles) along a delightful path that sticks to high ground for some wonderful views before descending past bizarre rock formations to the sea via stairways.

TOURING TIPS Unless you really want the exercise, consider walking down the Causeway to enjoy the views as you approach, and then take the minibus back. You can walk the length of the Antrim Coast on the Ulster Way hiking path, so you might consider walking to the Giants Causeway from Bushmills or from the Giants Causeway to the Carrick-a-Rede Bridge.

 ## Old Bushmills Distillery ★ ★ ★ ★

APPEAL BY AGE	PRESCHOOL ★	GRADE SCHOOL ★	TEENS ★★
YOUNG ADULTS ★★★	OVER 30 ★★★½		SENIORS ★★★½

Main Street, Bushmills; ☎ 028-2073-1521; www.bushmills.com

Type of attraction Whiskey-making factory. **Admission** £4 adults, £2 children, £3.50 seniors and students, £11 families. **Hours** April–October: Monday–Saturday, 9:30 a.m.–5:30 p.m.; Sunday, noon–5:30 p.m. (frequent tours to meet demand); November–March: Monday–Saturday, tours at 10:30 a.m., 11:30 a.m., 1:30 p.m., 2:30 p.m., and 3:30 p.m.; Sunday, tours at 1:30 p.m., 2:30 p.m., and 3:30 p.m. **When to go** During the week when the plant is in operation; it's actually quite interesting to see bottles being filled and set into boxes. **Special comments** If you've visited the Old Midleton Distillery (page 220), consider bypassing the tour here and settling for a visit to the shop; aside from actually seeing the operation at work, you won't learn anything new; the coffee shop–pub is a good stop for lunch while touring the coast. **How much time to allow** About 1 hour for the tour and tasting and a visit to the gift shop.

DESCRIPTION AND COMMENTS When King James I granted a whiskey-making license to Bushmills in 1608, the locals were already old hands at distilling—allegedly, a distillery has stood on this site since the 13th century. By the time you reach Bushmills, you too may be an old hand at touring distilleries if you've already paid visits to the Jameson operations in Dublin and Midleton. What sets Bushmills apart is the quality of the product, generally regarded as the best Irish whiskey, and the fact that this is a working plant—you actually see workers mashing and bottling, which adds a bit of veracity to the guides' lectures on how whiskey is made. As at other distilleries, the tour ends with a bang, in the tasting room, and you exit the premises through an enormous gift shop.

TOURING TIPS During the busy summer months, call in advance to reserve a place on one of the tours, which fill up fast.

RESTAURANT ON THE ANTRIM COAST

Ramore Wine Bar ★ ★ ★

PUB FARE	INEXPENSIVE	QUALITY ★★★	VALUE ★★★

The Harbour, Portrush; ☎ 028-7082-4313

Reservations Not necessary. **Entree range** £6.50–£8. **Payment** AE, MC, V. **Bar** Full service. **Disabled access** Yes. **Hours** Monday–Friday, 12:15–2:15 p.m., 5–10 p.m.; Saturday, 4:45–10:30 p.m.; Sunday, 12:30–3 p.m., 5–9 p.m.

MENU RECOMMENDATIONS Burgers, lamb steaks, grilled fish.

DESCRIPTION AND COMMENTS Previous visitors will remember Ramore's as an elegant and excellent restaurant. While that no longer exists, Ramore's is still a big presence on the harbor in Portrush these days. The informal and lively Wine Bar, really more of a family-oriented bistro, serves decent, wide-ranging casual fare in relaxed surroundings with sweeping harbor views. Coast, a pizza parlor, is just down the street, and the nicest part of the operation is the adjacent Harbour Bar, a cozy pub that retains its century-old character.

ACCOMMODATIONS INDEX

Note: Page numbers of accommodation profiles are in **boldface** type.

RESTAURANT INDEX

Note: Page numbers of restaurant profiles are in **boldface** type.

SUBJECT INDEX

Unofficial Guide Reader Survey

If you would like to express your opinion in writing about Ireland or this guidebook, complete the following survey and mail it to:

> *Unofficial Guide* Reader Survey
> P.O. Box 43673
> Birmingham, AL 35243

Inclusive dates of your visit:_____

Members of your party:

	Person 1	Person 2	Person 3	Person 4	Person 5
Gender:	M F	M F	M F	M F	M F
Age:					

How many times have you been to Ireland? _____

On your most recent trip, where did you stay? _____

Concerning your accommodations, on a scale of 100 as best and 0 as worst, how would you rate:

The quality of your room?   The value of your room?
The quietness of your room?   Check-in/check-out efficiency?
Shuttle service to the airport?   Swimming pool facilities?

Did you rent a car?_____   From whom?_____

Concerning your rental car, on a scale of 100 as best and 0 as worst, how would you rate:

Pick-up processing efficiency?_____   Return processing efficiency?___
Condition of the car?_____   Cleanliness of the car?_____
Airport shuttle efficiency?_____

Concerning your dining experiences:

Estimate your meals in restaurants per day? _____

Approximately how much did your party spend on meals per day? ____

_____

Favorite restaurants in Ireland: _____

_____

Did you buy this guide before leaving? _____ While on your trip?_____

How did you hear about this guide? (Check all that apply.)

Loaned or recommended by a friend □   Radio or TV □
Newspaper or magazine □   Bookstore salesperson □
Just picked it out on my own □   Library □
Internet □

What other guidebooks did you use on this trip? _____
_____
_____
_____

On a scale of 100 as best and 0 as worst, how would you rate them?
_____
_____
_____

Using the same scale, how would you rate the *Unofficial Guide*(s)?

_____

Are *Unofficial Guides* readily available at bookstores in your area? _____

Have you used other *Unofficial Guides*? _____

Which one(s)? _____
_____
_____

Comments about your Ireland trip or the *Unofficial Guide*(s):
_____
_____
_____
_____
_____
_____
_____
_____
_____
_____
_____
_____
_____
_____
_____
_____
_____
_____
_____
_____
_____

Praise for

WARREN BEATTY and DESERT EYES

"A thoughtful, analytical and juicily detailed account of Beatty's rise to his present, somewhat problematical Hollywood eminence." —*Washington Post*

"This doesn't really qualify as a beach book; it's too smart. But Thomson, one of our most gifted film critics, writes so compellingly that this is the kind of book you could take just about anywhere....It's quite a read."
—*Atlanta Journal and Constitution*

"David Thomson is by far the most imaginative film critic working in this country.... [His] essay on Warren Beatty's life, full of thoughtful speculation as well as hard fact, alternates chapters with...a witty, often brutal Hollywood story that resolves quite charmingly....Anyone who likes fine writing will appreciate this book." —*Austin American-Statesman*

"At the age of 50, the most elusive Hollywood legend since Garbo has at last been captured and defined....Like Beatty himself, Thomson's book is a maverick. It brings a cinematic and literary sensibility to the much-abused genre of 'celebiography,' and it leaves us with a new way of looking at both the nature of Warren Beatty and the style of the 'creative biography' that brings him to life." —*Stockton Record*

"It almost takes fiction to explain Beatty fully, and between the two aspects of this remarkable book, Thomson has produced an imaginative, unfailingly exciting total biography." —*Anniston Star*

"A madcap gamble of a book...an insightful meditation on movie stardom, and it is Thomson's skill as a critic and observer that gives it coherence. The book's aphoristic wit...confounds conventions and expectations just as surely and delightfully as its manner and form do. An audacious success." —*Kirkus*

WARREN BEATTY

and DESERT EYES

WARREN BEATTY

and

DESERT EYES

A Life and a Story

David Thomson

VINTAGE BOOKS

A Division of Random House

New York

First Vintage Books Edition, June 1988

Library of Congress Cataloging-in-Publication Data

Thomson, David, 1941–
Warren Beatty and Desert Eyes.

Reprint. Originally published: London: Secker & Warburg,
1987.
Bibliography: p.
1. Beatty, Warren, 1937–   . 2. Motion picture actors and
actresses—United States—Biography.   3. Motion picture
producers and directors—United States —Biography.   I. Title.
PN2287.B394T5 1988   791.43′028′0924 [B] 87-45934
ISBN 0-394-75756-4 (pbk.)

Display typography by Marysarah Quinn

Manufactured in the United States of America

10 9 8 7 6 5 4 3 2 1

for Jim, Robert and David

Author's Note

There are two strands to this book, one biography and one that is fiction. The biography treats a real movie star, Warren Beatty, his life and work and the ways in which he has inspired a part of the romantic imagination of this century. The fiction concerns an imagined star, with the absurd but perhaps prophetic name of Eyes. His story is set vaguely in the future and entirely in legend. But the purpose of his fable is to shed light on a world inhabited by both Warren Beatty and his unknown spectators. For it is in the nature of stardom, movies and our times that bright, photographed faces do coexist with dark wonderings.

A Life and a Story

"His enemies may say that it is the only thing he has; but to me to have charm is fundamental. That accusation is like saying this fellow is only a genius, or that fellow is only an angel."
– Jorge Luis Borges on Oscar Wilde, *Twenty-Four Conversations with Borges*

"I bet you think this song is about you."
– Carly Simon

WARREN BEATTY

and DESERT EYES

THERE HE IS

There he is, on what is called the facing page, watching you before you begin, looking to see what you will think, ready to smile as soon as you like him, but quite prepared to be above it all if you're left in doubt. Don't think he's not going to be there looking over your shoulder, or coming up behind you very softly. Don't count on him wearing some obtrusive Jockey Club cologne you'll always pick up. He'll just be *there*, intrigued, suspicious and downright hooked that you're thinking about him. For while Warren is certainly the center of this book, and of his own view of things, there's nothing so attractive in him as his own avid attention – his watching and listening, his being so alert that he takes control of the passing moment. He likes to telephone women in the night and ask, "What are you wearing? Let me guess." And so later they wonder if it is them he likes or simply the phone's authority.

Can you attempt the "life" of anyone still alive? Does responsible biography need as a first condition the death of its subject and the stillness of his life? Does an aspiring biographer have to dispose of his target before he can write with a clear conscience?

I began with an essay on Warren Beatty, published in the January 1982 *California* magazine, to coincide with the opening of *Reds*. The article described the making of that film; it had the benefit of telephone talks with Richard Sylbert, the film's production designer, and Jerzy Kosinski, the novelist enlisted by Beatty to play Zinoviev. It drew upon a meeting and several amiable conversations with David MacLeod, Warren's cousin and the associate producer on *Reds*. It had even a telephone contact with Beatty himself, or with an actor claiming to be Beatty. This immediately intimate voice called me, without secretarial

1

threshold, to say that while he appreciated what I was doing he wasn't talking to anyone.

Only high perversity takes the trouble to say that; and only a shell-shocked showman declines to promote the biggest picture he has ever made. He said, "Well . . . If you're going to write this article, I won't stop you. After all, I couldn't." But Paramount, the distributor of *Reds*, may have been begging for it. Movie distributors want us to know their picture is there. And for a movie starring Beatty, as well as produced and directed by him, they might have had cover stories in *Time* or *Newsweek*, as well as a dozen other magazines, not to mention appearances on television, perhaps a privileged hour with Barbara Walters as Warren said what the film really meant to him, giving Barbara that coax-me grin when she urged him, "Warren, you can tell *me*."

Paramount gathered none of these boosts. Yet Warren could tell me, gracefully, that he appreciated but had decided against aiding my effort. *Reds* was not a success. It was well received critically; it was a prestigious film, liked by many. But it did not recover its costs on initial release. It was the first failure of Warren Beatty the producer.

The industry estimated that if he had given more of himself then *Reds* might have stood a better chance of success. For Warren, perhaps, this had to be believed. Otherwise, the picture's failure was incomprehensible. After all, he is famous for his charm and seductiveness, yet he had been turned down by America. A few months later, when he accepted an Oscar for directing *Reds*, he gave an earnest speech about wanting to reclaim a lost chapter of America's history. That same sentiment offered earlier, to Barbara Walters and Walter Cronkite (the three of them in armchairs in the Library of Congress?), might have put several million on the film's rentals. Who can doubt Warren's ability to make Communists tasty for middle America? In the film itself, the Reeds had been made adorable, sexy puppies.

But that campaign could not have saved the film. And if nine-tenths of Beatty was opposed to failure, still perhaps the last tenth was fascinated by it and saw it as the way of doing less in the future. For there is no such creature now as an aging or middle-aged movie star. There is not much left between being Warren Beatty at 47 and Cary Grant at 81. Nothing but the time to fill.

It is Beatty's ambivalence about himself that makes me most interested in examining him. He has a way of catching sight of us looking at him and asking, "You want to be here? If I move over?" Who else has been so shyly conscientious about being the larger-than-life figure stardom requires, yet so irked by its excesses and so determined to withhold himself? These warring impulses make a perplexing result – Warren is simultaneously legendary, yet barely existing. Everyone "knows" him, but wonders what is there. His superiority is what a ghost might command.

If you do not appreciate this phantomness, try a game: imagine Jack Nicholson and Warren. Now imagine each one on his own, in the sancta of their homes (not unalike, not far apart – there is a stretch of Mulholland Drive where the gods live, tended by the same caterers, art dealers and security experts). No one is with them; the homes are ticking over efficiently; time and deals are passing. Just Jack. Just Warren.

Nicholson is all cracks, ledges and handholds for the imagination. I can hear his stomach rumbling: he farts and chuckles at the sweet afterburn of last night's gingered lobster. I can hear him breathing, enjoying the peace of the day, inhaling now and then on a fine smoke he has made for himself. He is a kind of Caliban, a jolly bad boy, scratching on his too-large belly, seething gently with his own good time, crawling over to the bookcase, sniffing at it, and then going pie-eyed over a page of Thomas McGuane or the I Ching, and beginning to suspect he'll be horny in an hour.

But Warren sits in shadow, perched on the edge of a Bauhaus chair, still, tense, poised, not sure he isn't being sapped or sucked on by secret recording devices, even the imagination of the world. He is so paranoid, so intelligent, he *knows* we are there. And so he schools his body to be quiet and reserved. He is a Prospero who has kept the look of an Ariel. But he has too many dreads to be a virtuoso self when alone. He may be as tempting as ice cream; but don't taste, and if you don't, he won't melt. So he finds a young woman (the numbers are all in his head), takes her to a restaurant, and then frets and trembles that his privacy is being jeopardised by the bold stares of other diners saying "Isn't that him?" And he smiles at her, as if to say, "Imagine when we are alone."

I am entering Warren Beatty's life, pen at the ready, to puzzle out his dismay. He has not welcomed me, or sat down with me. And though I asked for that once, I am glad he refused. For I see now how he could hardly listen and hesitate without applying control. And how can you warn someone you like if he insists on keeping power?

He should think of me as a rescuer, not a threat. I may have some understanding of him and his anxiety, and I am drawn to stardom. Hollow as that condition may be in any sensible consideration, I wouldn't mind being there. This ardor drew me once into the romantic assertion that Howard Hughes had arranged to die in the air, the "there" he loved most. Friends who heard this yearning laughed at it. But I think Warren, another Hughes fan, would have understood the principle involved. Of course, Warren is not laughed at much; the lack colours his loneliness a little. He does not let his crazy romanticism show, but keeps it sheathed in grim elegance and holds himself taut and cool. 47, 48, 49 – he begins to look like someone afraid his back could go out at any minute. It is a time of life where grace meets surgical support.

This is not a biography that inches across the knowable facts like a vacuum cleaning the carpet. Such bodies of page-time fall into place after death; and only then because, without presence in the life, a writer proceeds by way of research. The richest biographies concern those who kept diaries, sent many letters and had the wisdom to cultivate survivors. Research bestows order and temporal progress on a life. But it makes muddlers and neurotics seem more purposeful, and it forgets how life can feel empty, untidy and beset by indecision. For it keeps putting facts in order – as if the chief task of the subject had been to put his affairs in order before dying, instead of raising a good mystery. And if Warren wants to be mysterious, then a life written while he lives has the best chance of responding to the puzzle. He may come clearer afterwards. But he may look dull and minor.

"Being Warren Beatty" may be what his autobiography or some posthumous biography settles on – especially if he finds himself caught in some political backwater. "Being Charles Dickens", we may say now, is best rendered by the biography by Edgar Johnson – best, that is, if you insist on not reading the novels. But for Dickens, the part was a ferment of possibility that helped exhaust him. The writing of his novels included everything he omitted as well as what is now the settled text. The life is left standing, but its living was all the effort and hope that sought to prop it up. And the momentary electricity of this desperate being is especially important in a film star's enigma. For great stars change before our eyes; it is their disguise of growing old. Being Warren Beatty is sharing those flickering transitions with millions, sighing to them in the rapture of a close-up, "Imagine me", until the unknown answer, "O Warren, baby, come to *me*."

The image remains for history, but not its intensity. To appreciate an actor you must have seen their work. To know a movie actor, you must have been moved when their films were new. It is impossible now to feel all that Lillian Gish meant before 1920, or Garbo in 1930. The excitement turns camp nearly as quickly as ripe cheese becomes inedible. It is enough to make a picture actor wonder whether it is worth working.

There are two lives here. The one is Warren's, or as close as I could get to it in reading, talking to his friends and associates, seeing his films and in simply thinking about him. The other life comes out of all that thinking: it is a fiction, a life one might offer to him, a part fit for him to play. The story helps me explore the Hollywood Warren inhabits – and this is a book about the atmosphere of that place – but it also contributes to the portrait of a man who is always looking at stories, judging whether to give them life, and who may sometimes be uncertain where the facts of his life end and the possible pictures take over.

Beatty sent a message to me once, through a mutual friend, that he couldn't understand anyone writing about someone else without having met them. I sent a message back – that he should think of Clyde Barrow and John Reed. For Warren knew in 1967, in the first film he produced, *Bonnie and Clyde*, that lives, lies and insights abound before an outlaw is shot to pieces, especially if he is capable of that ecstatic, knowing glance – for death and immortality – exchanged between Warren and Faye, Bonnie and Clyde, just before their firing squad. Clyde did not look like Warren; the outlaw's passion on the brink of death is invented. But Warren aspires to art and transcendence, and he has carried Barrow into history with him.

And the potency of movie stars depends on their remarkable bond with strangers. They have established a peculiarly modern "knowledge", that of familiarity without contact, intimacy without experience. Beginning in movies, it has already reached out into most forms of public discourse. The stars may think it crazy for millions of the unknown, people in the dark, to invest so much in imagining them. But there is a matching folly in the stars being so available for the kindness, or the demon, of strangers.

It is a measure of the great stars that they seem to speak privately to the individual stranger: that is their shyness and our sensitivity. For it is essential to the great public show of stardom that it whispers to every pair of eyes in the dark, "Here, here is my secret. For *you*." The secret shines like a gift; the same offer of knowledge and privilege is made in love or seduction. The viewer's enormous desire has been recognised, but the trick is to let him or her believe that no one else has noticed their need. The great show is as furtive, and as bound by loneliness, as every voyeur's pleasure must be.

It is all desire at the movies – wanting to get on the screen. Suppose Warren had been drawn to movies once for no better reason than to get into that fame, and to meet women? When the public thinks of him now they feel the undertow of his seductiveness, his longing to be secret. He gazes at desire in the certainty that it can never quite be satisfied, not if the secret is to last. The public may not fathom this, but they see Warren has a design upon them evident in his guarded mind as well as his rationed appearances. So they are wary with him.

There is no welling up of imminent merriment and affection, as there is for Nicholson. There is not the amused respect accorded to Clint Eastwood, the securely unimaginative Clint, safe in his timidity. When Beatty's films are thought of it is in scenes of sexual allure – the orgasm in death in *Bonnie and Clyde* (so stroked by photography and cutting), Julie Christie going under the table in *Shampoo*, or even a poster picture, the angel of death and sex in *Heaven Can Wait*. The public has not quite kept up with his halting career. But they hear the legend of his prodigiousness in love; he is proverbial. They suppose it accounts for the gaps between pictures. He says he has been busy with serious things, like politics; and the public smiles. They know politics have become foolish. They wonder if he is trying to seduce them with his earnest smile. He is so sultry to the public mind he is nearly feminine. Which other actors seem so challenged to make us think of desire?

Give him some credit for the idea's currency. Say you have a list of 792 known women with whom he has had sexual congress; or 1,316; or realise that he is old enough for 10,000. Then look at this abiding youth and feel the mystery. Tell the stories of the several notable and prolonged affairs in his life. And find some decent way of letting the reader feel the heat and theater in Hollywood sex, as well as the sex in most acting. It is a place made out of looking and longing, fearful of physical decay and wear. Still, there *is* the real thing, rising every night like an old story.

There is also a legend to which others ascribe, willingly, helplessly or with envy. It is enough for Warren to keep a demure silence over that, sure that in the end he will be as good as they say he is. For instance, Orson Welles told his biographer, "The only way I can hold Warren's attention is to cease to be a gentleman and trade off marks on the gun, you know. It's the only way an old man could keep him interested. He'll listen for hours to *anything*." And so Welles told Warren about an actress with whom he had had an affair, until the woman's affections were stolen away by Billie Holiday.

Warren "was so fascinated with it," said Welles, "that he stopped for a week until he got to know the girl and asked her if it was so. He's that obsessed by the subject. It struck him as so exotic and unlikely and probably a lie. And he found out it was true. *That's* all he thinks of, day and night. Oh yes, he's a real satyrite . . . calling different people all morning long to be sure that in the evening there's going to be somebody new. You know, that's the *real* Casanova."

Welles comes off as the Falstaff in the story, or as the fond old fool who has been outstripped. That may only mean there are always roles in Hollywood, and a certain sense of the crown being passed on. His story aids the warm myth that performing genius fucks them all, and has a pistol feathery with notches. Beatty learned long ago not to own up, but to tease and deflect such leading questions. A rumor lurks in Warren's bedroom eyes – don't you wonder if it's all true?

It's an intellectual mystery that beguiles as much as the sensual promise. For it seems to say not just, here is the fuck of your life, but what do you suppose it is, finally, to fuck? If you were sufficiently seduced, or that much in love with love, could you measure the quality, could you tell a Don from your husband? Warren Beatty's eyes allude to the chance that sex is imaginary, whatever its physical antics, and that in carnal knowledge only the knowledge lasts – and sometimes that goes the way of forgetting. He has seldom taken off his clothes on screen. But he has a head and face for dreamers – poised, recessive, lyric and secret. And like any Narcissus, he will keep his looks so long as desire moves him. If that ever goes, if it becomes a mere idea, then youth will be replaced by something like Dracula's haggard smile.

You may have come to this book for some fresh-cut slice of Hollywood revelation in which this or that flagrant young woman is tripling with Warren at her conventional bower and Jack at the back door, axing his way in with "Here's Johnny!" You are left to your own imaginative devices, the most solid sharing you will have with Warren, Jack or any of the blatant dames.

There are some films made, but many more declined or lost in delay. It makes you wonder at the other things Warren *hasn't* done. Aren't real lives just as consumed with thoughts of things not done as with the glee or misery that recalls things checked off and done with? Isn't it sometimes – because regret may be so much more lasting than glee – more challenging to contemplate things not done? One might think for many years about a lover never bedded, not even asked. But once the act is managed, doesn't the hope fill a smaller part of the dreamed day?

It's all very well to say that, on the balance of the evidence, it seems probable that Beatty had sexual relations with Joan C. and Natalie W., and so on. But he never "knew" Grace Kelly – did he? Further, I think we can safely eliminate Vanna White, Margaret Thatcher, Marlene Dietrich, Marilyn Monroe, Louise Bryant, Emma Bovary, Miss America, the usherette in Edward Hopper's painting *New York Movie* and Miss Piggy. I can find no jot of evidence that he has had any of those beauties. Believe me.

But suppose you don't. And suppose you have ears still for some whisper of gossip which says, well, with one of them, yes, he has, we'd have to call if f-cking. Whom would you guess? Can't you see how it might have been any of them?

It makes you wonder about other available pursuits. Do we think he has read Gibbon's *Decline and Fall of the Roman Empire*? Has he seen Goya's sketches in the basement of the Prado? Has he drunk calvados in the evenings in small Normandy towns? Did he ever see Carl Yastrzemski go hitless at Fenway? Has he read every book in his house? Has his car broken down on Mulholland Drive? Has he thought of going to a monastery, or some rather less severe retreat, for the rest of his life? Has he listened to Charlie Parker for days on end, been seasick, overslept or spent Christmas Day alone? Will he read this book? Will he think it's about him?

D goes home

D hurried home through gruesome streets, his new script under one arm, its copy under the other. He had had to take one of the rubber'nlead sheets to protect himself. The kopyshops gave them out now because of the radiation in copies. It was a stiff, soiled square with ragged edges. It left his side clammy and hot: his shirt was already soaked and stained from it. Would the cotton disintegrate? Shirts were essential for meetings. So he moved the drab protector and used it to guard the script against a collision on the street.

He could feel the cool pack of pages now against his body. D smiled to think of the rays seeping into his bones with the rubber sweat. He needed his work. What if it did destroy him? He had no age insurance, anyway. Something would happen before he turned old.

Though it was a little out of his way, D did not resist the routing of his legs towards the Eyes Building. He loved its shine, and the idea of it. It was eleven stories, an arrangement of selenium panels, in all of which there was a hinge with a dozen or more panels that could slip forward to help compose the facade. Thus the building had the appearance of a shower of tears. Its firmness as a structure was made poignant by the shimmering mutability in the facade. After all, it was only a building, a front; nothing happened inside.

And what the front pulsed with was the face of that great star Eyes – or the face as last seen in a movie made . . . how many years ago was it now? There were over a thousand panels and every one was a piece of Eyes' face. Since every panel-space had a dozen variants that could slip forward (at eleven different speeds) according to the programing of the computer, Eyes' face was always alive. The building breathed and shifted with the sensual possibilities of his smile or his frown. Even his stillness fluctuated. There were always people watching the building, their attention making a pilgrimage from his brow to his lip. As D looked up, the tongue swept across the mouth – a tongue like Moby Dick – and for a

9

few seconds a dew of readiness glistened on his lips. Another building might have dragged out its foundations and lurched across the plaza to kiss it – the Tuesday Weld Memorial Hall, maybe, from the other side of the street.

It was remarkable what they could do now. D was sure it was not mere partisanship, but truly the color quality in the Eyes Building was the most refined in the city. He felt so proud of his daughter, V, who worked on the process. For the past four months she had had responsibility for Eyes' upper right cheek, where a pink as delicate as Albertine rose had been appearing. D joked that she was the apple in Eyes' smile.

The problem at the intersection was no easier. Years ago, as people complained of boredom waiting for the lights to change, the authorities had mounted videos on the traffic light posts. They had changed behavior. People now thronged to the corners to watch; there were scuffles over the best positions. And so, gradually, the vehicles had noticed that people did not cross when they were entitled. Inevitably, some drivers grew impatient and began to go against the red. In a few months, there was traffic anarchy and several pedestrians who had seen an episode already, or who were blind perhaps (one heard only the stories), seeing the green or hearing its meek tone, stepped out and were killed. One had to take one's chance. Reports said that an average citizen was later home by fifteen minutes. "Intersections" did $7.2 billion in the first year. New lights were being pretexted all the time. Fresh, narrow streets were stuck into hitherto solid blocks. Between 52nd and 53rd there was now A as far as F.

D passed the Personal Appearance Arcade. There was not much of a crowd, but several camera crews at the entrance were recording the night's couple. D recognised them. They were actors who had met on a commercial and gone on to several series. She wore a boysenberry-colored fur coat, with the fall of her amber hair piled on the collar. Her lean face and lovelorn eyes turned from one camera to another. Her husband had distinguished gray hair, rimless dark glasses and strands of silver chain round his brandy-hued neck. He wore loafers and a cowboy suit, and held two Dobermans on lurex leashes. These hard brindle animals, pop-eyed in the Kliegs, surged against the wife so that she swayed and sighed. On the video, this tossing and her breathing were clear, but the dogs were out of the frame.

Interviewers were asking them the secret to their lustrous, enviable marriage, and she was giving the same answer, take after take, for different crews:

"Well, we do it one day at a time, we respect each other, and we have fun. We do."

Another sigh. And the gray head of the husband nodded while the dogs arched against their mistress's fur. D saw the hot-pins of the dogs' penises, and when he looked at their yellow eyes he thought of a scene in which the dogs might rape the lady – and she could dream it was her unaccustomedly ardent husband. You could have her in a sun-mask, so that she did not actually see her lovers. And then pups a little later . . .? D could not decide whether it was a comedy or a grisly.

D peeled back the flimsy door to the apartment ready for the assault of cooking, noise and family. There was always too much crammed in there. The warmth, the density of things, the impossibility of being alone. What magic D felt in emptiness. How steadily people of their poverty dreamed of airiness, space and time, of solitude, that lovely suspension that beckoned from films and videos whenever a star was alone with the camera.

The children, their evening occupations, the hungry pets, the cracks and flaws in the apartment ran out to meet him like sour water from a burst pipe. He would embrace them all, letting the stain sink further into him, laughing and chattering, welcoming it all. He could not bear to see how worn he must be, or the shame of tiredness in movie's light. People in the tenements did not often look at one another; they moved like bats, bowed and humble, bumping and apologising, ready to kill, moving away, edging into corners, dreading bare mirrors.

The family fed in a hunched group every evening, like card players worrying over their hands. The meal was consumed in a few minutes to the hiss of soda cans and the discord of three videos left playing. The licence had been halved a year ago if the set was always left on: it played gentle sleeping sounds at night along with shots of colored scarves falling, sinking, on a marble floor in slow, voluptuous motion. D sat up many nights, waiting for this infinite cascade to turn sinister, daydreaming of sleep and new clothes and bumping awake with steel in the morning sky and computer fractions hopping across the screen with tremors of the Market.

The poster for *Heaven Can Wait*

Weegee, *Palace Theater, New York*, 1945

While he washed up in the kitchen, he studied the video set in the sink. It was easy, looking down, and there was something whimsical in having the picture swirled by waves of greasy water. The picture was a patio and a lounge, in daylight, up in Bel Air. It was an actress a lot of people were talking about, Arlene Loomis; she had an aching quality, D could tell. In this moviette she was alone in her home, alone with a saluki, trying on kaftans. Each one was lovelier than the last – she went from perfect to plus-perfect. But Arlene became vexed by choice. And so at last she lay on a bird's egg blue sofa made like a moccasin and stroked her sex until she fell asleep with her hand still folded, nostalgically, between her legs, and the saluki's sad head resting on her calf. She was hot – D could feel it. She would be cast soon. He wondered if she was right for the female lead in his script. She was too old, of course – they were all, always, too old – but you got a vivid extra panic if you cast an actress younger than her age.

D walked around the apartment. His dear V, nineteen, had fallen asleep over a half-finished jigsaw of Eyes. Her face rested in the hole in the center of the puzzle and her dribble was flowing onto Eyes' face. D soaked it up with his shirt tail and shut his daughter's mouth. She worked so hard. Little T was asleep at the end of his cot, the Jagger doll on the rubber band above his head. P, seven, was playing a game show with a video, and G, twelve, the studious one, was writing his paper on Wink Martindale.

And so D turned to the cleared table, to play hearts with his wife, C. He did not look at how exhausted she was – she irons transfer faces on T-shirts all day. He knows it is kindness not to let her see disappointment.

She deals the cards from the pack so old that the image of Loretta Young on the backs is scarred and worn in so many ways they can, both of them, identify several of the cards. But they do not mention this, and sometimes play from habit alone, not keeping score or noticing gross errors, but freed from the day and able to talk fondly in the placid rhythm of cards as heavy as skins.

"Did you decide on a title for the script?" asked C, sorting her hand, still believing in shape.'

"Well," said D. He had not made up his mind. He still favored *Imagine Me*. But he suggested, "*The Center of Attention?*"

C pursed her lips and inclined her head, as if trying to name a scent. "I think I like that very much," she decided.

Her pleasure was so brave, D looked into her battered, gratified eyes.

14

D goes home

If it had been a movie, he might have wept. C went on, "I know, my dear, this one will be a success. It's the finest thing you have done."

"Have you the two?" D asked politely, ready to scream if their little game didn't start. He wasn't sure if she meant these things, or was an acute parody of his dreams. Did he hear C any longer, or only her lines and her role?

"You work so hard to be famous, we all love you for it. You are our hero. Why, V keeps a photograph of you in her —"

"The three?" he asked.

This might have gone on much longer: they were both void in clubs. But then the apartment door opened and Scrug looked in. "Phone," he sneered, looking at D. "I'll play your hand." He was the building supervisor, a lout they feared so much they lived with unreported breakdowns.

"Oh no," C began.

"Why argue?" said Scrug. "Phone."

So D reassured his C and went out into the dimly lit hallway. *Streets of Fire* was playing on one wall, and the usual corridor porn on another. The phone was dangling; a three-legged kitten was beating at it with its head. As D reached down, the cat clawed him. He looked at the pink raking on his knuckles.

"Well, now," said the phone. "Is that D?"

"Yes," he cried, naked with hope. He could never quell his amazement with the phone, of finding that someone was thinking of him. He was weeping. His tears stang the scratch marks. "D," murmured the phone, privately. "This is Clear. With Eyes. I was wondering if we might meet." D knew he would go anywhere to meet this understanding voice and its easy reference to magnificent authority.

"I believe this may be your break, D," said the phone with a modesty not comfortable with such stale promises, but duty-bound to say it just this once. "Are you there still? Surprise hasn't stunned you, I hope? Not dropped dead?"

LITTLE HENRY

Beatty lacks those handicaps of birth or upbringing so often used to justify ruthlessness in stars, or desperation. He does not come from the wild side; and he never persuades us he might lose control. He cannot turn on some executive in a dispute over terms, or confess to a woman on the beach at Malibu at twilight, "What you have to know about me is I come from nothing. So I have nothing to lose." Indeed, he has more the pinched air of a man who fears some intense, inner theft.

His line will have to be more mysterious, one without much screen tradition – "I don't have to do this, you know" – as if, one day, he might not if the woman or the studio heads don't lay restraining hands and deals on him now. He is going to hint, "You could lose me." And because he lets it be felt that he is in movies out of some private, incommunicable decision, he carries a patina of mysterious intelligence. This is a suspicious commodity in Hollywood. Who else there would bother to have his mind on anything except the place and its contest? And a game becomes philosophy if the players are amused by their intensity.

But in an unreflective setting, he who treasures his intelligence may end up a fool. Next to the raw thrust of Eastwood or Sylvester Stallone, Beatty seems to lack the confidence required in his medium. Beside the younger generation, he looks fussy and distracted. And while Beatty prefers to draw our attention to his loftier purposes, we might ask whether any thoroughly intelligent person could exist, let alone work, in Hollywood?

He is a child of teachers, born in 1937, when the education establishment is inclined to regard Hollywood as a dangerous place, where lies are concocted for the American imagination, and specious dreams divert the people from knowledge, reason and hard times. In 1937, despite Depression and Fascism, Hollywood makes *History is Made at Night*, *Wee Willy Winkie*, *The Awful Truth*, *Lost Horizon* and *A Star is Born*. In 1938, from the Garden of Allah Hotel, Scott

Fitzgerald, seeing himself as a cracked-up literary figure, writes to Max Perkins, his New York editor:

> ". . . this amazing business has a way of whizzing you along at a tremendous speed and then letting you wait in a dispirited, half-cocked mood when you don't feel like understanding anything else, while it makes up its mind. It is a strange conglomeration of a few excellent overtired men making the pictures, and as dismal a crowd of hacks and fakes at the bottom as you can imagine. The consequence is that every other man is a charlatan, nobody trusts anybody else, and an infinite amount of time is wasted from lack of confidence."

Henry Warren Beaty is born a year and twenty-four days before that letter is written. Yet he will go on to illustrate its several points, and there are times when he will share Fitzgerald's wounded tone. As if Warren Henry's parents have not filled the house with warnings.

He is born in Richmond, Virginia, on March 30, 1937; in the South, the capital of the old Confederacy, the city where, in the summer of 1932, there has been held one of the last great parades of Civil War veterans. There is then a home for old soldiers in Richmond, where white-haired men run up the Confederate flag and bitterly contest the possibility that a statue of Robert E. Lee can be assigned to a sculptor from Ohio, or that a monument at Appomattox – fifty miles to the west – may bear the healing inscription, "North-South: Peace-Unity".

Richmond then is the headquarters of the cigarette industry and of Civil War nostalgia – a place of smoke and statues, neither of which will impress the boy any more than the considerable conservatism and untroubled racism. Ira Owens Beaty is a respected figure in the town, a teacher who will go on to be superintendent of Richmond High School. He is a southerner, married to another teacher, Kathlyn Maclean, from Nova Scotia originally, not just of the North but Canadian. She is a thin woman, very quiet in the marriage; he is large, authoritarian and domineering.

The father has been a promising young violinist in his home, Front Royal, Virginia. A teacher has heard him playing with the amateur symphony orchestra and recommends special tuition, Europe and a career as a soloist. But Ira Beaty turns the prospect down and, years later, gives this explanation to his daughter:

> "The competition was too rough, Monkey. And that would have been no way to make a living. It wouldn't have been dependable. Sure, I would have seen Europe, maybe been wined and dined by royalty, but if I had done it, I

probably wouldn't have met and married your mother and we wouldn't have had you and Warren. So I think I did the right thing."

The daughter is never sure her father believes this. In his drinking and in his provocative way of raising arguments which sometimes get to the exposed souls of his family, he seems frustrated and disappointed. His children learn the lesson not to compromise with possible talent, and the son may see in himself the same turbulent mixture of search for glory and the need for security.

Ira Beaty reads philosophy at Johns Hopkins, and he is a professor of psychology and education at Maryland College, in Baltimore, when Kathlyn Maclean comes there to teach drama. They have a kind of sacrifice in common, for she has wanted to be an actress. They fall in love and they marry, despite Kathlyn's sense that Ira has been hurt by an upbringing in which he was dominated by his mother.

At the birth of Henry Warren, Ira and Kathlyn already have a daughter, Shirley, who will be as outspoken as Warren is reserved. Shirley MacLaine will give a portrait of her parents in 1970 like scenes from a family drama about repression and escape. It might be by Ibsen or O'Neill. It is nowhere near as painful or drastic as *Long Day's Journey into Night*; it is lit up with hope and freedom. But it is a play in which the daughter understands and rids herself of emotional shadow by becoming an actress. She leaves a brother behind who, when his turn comes, will also act; but this troubles the brother, for he is never to be a happy actor, sure of having found himself. Warren is part-participant, part-onlooker in Shirley's battle. We cannot tell from her story whether he noticed the same threat, or felt her need to survive it. But just as she presents her father as an obstacle she has to overcome, so it is possible that the strongest force in Warren's early life was his older sister. There is still a look of wistful patience on his face sometimes that has had to wait out the tirades of her quicker spirit, its glorying in earnestness and its certainty that she is a soul who has been many other people in earlier lives. She too is loved by America.

Shirley says she has "loving parents", but then she adds that there are things left wanting – "feelings". The children are caught in "a cliché-loving, middle-class Virginia family", in a house of objects, furniture and possessions too precious to be touched, yet fake sometimes, like the "Chippendale" mirror. She grows up with a sense of fineness in the family, and its aspirations; yet, in hindsight, she sees just "a plain, modest, middle-class, red-brick house – mortgaged and everything". The failure that haunts her adult account is that of honesty and sentiment, and the warping that springs from it which she was too strong or determined to endure:

"My father was the autocratic head of the family, well educated, with a portly build moving toward rotundity whenever there were peanuts around. He was a stern man with light blue eyes full of suspicion, the censor of all he surveyed, and the guardian of our safety. He was sometimes terrifying, because he always acted as though he knew not only about the 'bad' things we *had* done, but also those 'bad' things we were *going* to do. Then there were times when he was so moved with pride for us that his chest puffed out even further than his stomach. His sensitivity was bottomless, but the fear of his own feelings was sometimes too painful to witness.

"Mother was a tall, thin, almost ethereal creature with a romantic nature, who found even the most insignificant unpleasantness difficult to accept. In fact, it didn't exist – nothing unpleasant existed; it was a mistake or misinterpretation."

In all of this, Warren is a child follower, what Shirley calls her "companion in adjustment and rebellion". She recalls being handed her baby brother wrapped in a blanket – "He spent most of his time yelling, and with growing finesse and sometimes astounding precision, he has been doing so ever since." That is an odd change of tone and time focus in a childhood recollection, a belated recognition of control in the young ally, as if she has needed time to appreciate his mastery.

She says their parents were perfectionists, but that the father was defeated, a man of great ambition who had abandoned his own hopes and become bitter or depressed. It is clear how often father and daughter challenge one another, how steadily the mother observes the fights until she has to say, "All right Ira, that's enough." And that seems to do it; in the end, the Beaty males do not have authority. There is a crucial confrontation. Warren is not there – Shirley remembers this. As an actor, he will not court fights. His eyes can seem stunned or baffled by the pain of others, at a loss to help and so a little more drawn to coldness and distance.

This incident occurs when she is sixteen, and Warren thirteen. It "still blazes in my memory". She is studying to dance, in addition to her regular schooling at Washington-Lee High School in Arlington. She goes into Washington for dancing classes. But she loses the part of Cinderella in a Christmas production, and comes home in tears. Her father witnesses her return and the spectacle of her failure releases his loathing of any type of success (it does require an O'Neill):

"He stopped, and with finger wagging told me that that should teach me to stop trying to do things I wasn't capable of."

They are on the staircase, like people in a crisis in a Hitchcock film: "wasn't this episode proof enough for me that, if I attempted to go beyond my range, I would only be crushed? Hadn't he told me many times during my life? When would I believe him, when would I understand that if I tried I would only get hurt?"

Shirley remembers a few years before when his scorn at her performance as Ado Annie in a production of *Oklahoma!* ("I'm just a girl who can't say no") had stopped her singing completely. She says she fell on the stairs, with her father above her berating her. She cries so hard she vomits, but he never stops telling her off. The mother says that is enough, Ira. It's the one line Shirley gives her, and it's as haunting as something from *Long Day's Journey*. And Shirley sees the whole thing in one of those flashes that can be blinding to the enlightened, but never noticed by faraway brothers. It is victory and defeat, a curtain moment:

"He could see, even though I had dissolved into a little pile of protoplasm, that I would never stop dancing. And he seemed to understand that ironically he, in effect, was teaching me to dare because I saw that he was such a spectacular disappointment to himself for having never tried it. A strange clear look of understanding came into his eyes [this is the passion of movies and movie-going] as he realised I didn't want to be like him. He stepped over the vomit and went to fix himself a drink."

A couple of years after that, Shirley leaves home, with her mother's support, to become an actress. But in the book that includes these family scenes, *Don't Fall Off the Mountain*, she goes back home years later, in 1968, on a visit. She has come from Mississippi, the deep South, where she has been watching voter registration and school desegregation. In 1968, Shirley will be a delegate at the Democratic Convention. At home, her father hears she has been in the company of blacks and – he is a southerner – jokes: "Don't you want to have a nice, long hot shower before you tell us – we just had the upholstery cleaned."

Instead, she tells him, a teacher and school superintendent, about a black girl whose chair in class is spat on by her fellow-students.

"Dad listened to my story about Thelma with clenched teeth and when it was over I could see tears streaming down his face. He slumped deeper into his favorite chair like an old man and said, 'God, I want to change, but it's so hard I think I'll die first.'"

Shirley tries to open the windows in the room, but her father tells her they are fixed shut. It is really Ibsen now – the windows have *always* been closed. The mother comes in carrying meatloaf for dinner.

"'Why aren't these windows open?' I asked. 'It's hot this afternoon and there's a breeze outside that would help.'

"Her eyes stopped dancing and she quickly darted a look toward my father. 'I don't know,' she said. 'Daddy says they've never been opened.'"

The curtain comes down again, on the frozen scene of father and daughter staring at one another in horror and an airless room.

The set for *A Loss of Roses*, designed by Boris Aronson

Clear's appointment

The next day D set out to see Clear. That night, on the phone, like an idiot (how easily one hated oneself), he had blurted out, "I could come now." He took it for granted that this Clear never rested. But Clear had paused, chuckled amiably and said, well, he was in the bath. There was a sound of water stirring, and then a more significant gathering of waves, as if someone close to Clear, in the same tub, had stood up and water had tumbled from their body, rills sliding off their shoulders, scoops abandoned by their flattened belly. It was like darkness broken and pushed aside by the bright face in a close-up.

D strained to picture this person before he or she vanished into towelling. It seemed an impressive figure, if immaterial; substantial, yet only a slip of a thing. It could have been a boss, or a hooker hired for the night. But D could tell that Clear was watching, too: his voice when it returned was upturned and expectant, waiting to see if this other person smiled.

"Come any old time," said Clear. He was so intent, he might have been watching his heart have an attack on a measuring machine.

"*Any* time?" D could not endure such vagueness.

"Call when you're coming." Clear sounded sleepy now.

"I could come tomorrow."

"You could?" Was Clear taking advice? Or watching a toy drift in the tub?

"Easily."

"Why not then? I suppose so."

The click that told D the call was over was preceded – his eager ear was attuned now – by a rising in the tiny lapping of water, as if the phone floated beside ducks, drinks or waterproof volumes of poetry. He could imagine the perfumed steaminess. D felt a little dirty. He remembered that his pants were soiled and no shirt had all its buttons. Could he manage a casual look? For an instant, he wished he lived in the desert and

22

never saw another human being. He was shaking with strain after the call.

"Don't bleed on my floor," growled Scrug, looking at his hand. Of course, the floor was rancid. Just thinking about it made D fear his wound was infected.

"I have an engagement tomorrow," said D, but Scrug muttered, "Swine", out of habit. No one believed D was going to be famous. Even D thought sometimes that his best chance was to kill Scrug and seven or eight others in the building. "Crazed Author Runs Amok!" he could see the headline, and a Weegeepic of himself scathed by flashlight, his face hanging like a rag, his eyes struggling to get out of his head.

Not very cheering stuff, thought D in the fishy morning light. The place that Clear had told him to go was a four-hour walk away, above Sunset. D planned his journey to arrive in the early afternoon. There was no transportation that went there, but D knew the city well enough to avoid the worst climbs and keep to the shaded sides of the street. He would probably arrived soaked in his own sweat anyway.

He wrapped the script in a towel to protect it. Obviously he had to take it. Clear hadn't mentioned it, but why else would Clear call? He hardly wanted to see D for social reasons. D knew he was an embarrassment; he had made up his mind to let it be that way. An agent once had told him he had no charm, not enough to get any invitations. "You would have to write *soooo* well," the agent said to himself, and he had declined to take D. "Go on, viper," he'd said as a joke. "Keep all the loot yourself!" And so D had been without proper representation. "It's a life for strong spirits," the agent had said on parting, the last lash on a flayed soul.

The building at the end of D's journey was made of azure glass: from a distance it was only lines etched in the surrounding sky, a fancy, a diagram. But coming closer, up the last inescapable hill so steep he had to use his free hand to hold on to the ground, he realised it had block, depth and a parking lot. There was a space inside the glass that flung back the world's sated look at itself. He was exhausted, and the last mile was filled with an irrational dread that the script might fall from his sopping grasp, the pages skipping in the fractious breeze. D could never subdue these fears, or shut out of his mind the dazzling, despairing liberty of hurling away this and every other script, all that neurotically numbered paper, with CONTINUED on top of the pages, from the highest hills of the city. Suppose LA smog was really only the waste of all its abandoned stories, all unmade, poisoning the air.

There were colors up there. In D's part of town, you forgot color in the smog; it erased it. But in the lobby of the building there was a pink carpet that hurt his eyes; or rather, not exactly the retinae, but their old association with feelings. Wherever he looked, up here, D saw the surface of desirable emotion. He wanted it all for himself, as well as the girl at the walnut console, a lone lean creature, fiercely tanned, in a black halter top, with fresh black grapes in her hair. She wore moist ivory lipstick, and when she spoke to him a tremor of expectation ran through her body. She was excitement. There was a way people here embodied mood and need. Everyone was a degree of desire. It was the way he remembered old movies, where apples and automobiles, blondes or killers, were all sexy because they were being seen.

"Hi," said the girl. "Like a grape?"

D reached out a wavering hand. As it touched the grape, the firm soft fruit dropped into his palm, and he heard the girl say, sigh rather (the lips did not move), "Oh, you're gentle." Was it an answering machine?

"You must be the appointment for Mr Clear?"

This was marvelous! In a twelve-storey building, to be known and expected. "That's right," smiled D.

"Why don't you take a video? I'll tell his office you're here."

D examined the row of watermelon velvet chairs, each with video in its arm, like a nail on a finger. He sat down and realised that the picture was Miss Grapehead herself. How witty! And when he smiled, her picture looked up and gave a sly wink back to him. The soundtrack had her breathing and the slight flexings of her clothes. He could feel the self-satisfied interplay of her good health and her Frederick's lingerie. He was a fly resting on her lustrous skin, and he noticed his seat was not quite still. It breathed in time with the receptionist! This was like being between her breasts. He felt so rested. The face on the screen looked up at him, and said, "It's D, isn't it? Sure, that's right. Our old fiddle-dee-D. So good to have you," and then, "So sweet," as if treasuring a lost civilization.

A moment later he heard her voice again, but now it was petulant in the flocked air of the lobby. He strolled over to the console, quite impishly for a wreck, saying it was a droll device. But she was altered, unfiltered. She had become a receptionist at the tag-end of a humiliating day. Her mascara had run with her confidence.

"What?" she said, out of patience.

D sailed on, too full of rapture. "To have the seat over there adjusted to your breathing . . ."

She looked at him as if he was mad, as well as ugly. "Mr D, that's quite absurd. This is only a lobby. Do you think people are made of money? God! Go on up, will you." She said it as if he was an assassin. He had ventured out of his shell, and made a fool of himself. From the console, those palpitating seats looked crude and inert, like seats at a bus station. It was late afternoon. The building had turned itself into a place everyone longed to quit.

"The eleventh floor?" said D in a daze.

"That's right," from the snappy bitch. "And don't repeat everything up there. They'll throw you out of the window – if they can get the window open, that is." This seemed to amuse her, but she laughed in a panic-stricken way. D hurried past, before she came to tears.

The elevator was the size of D's living room. He marvelled to think of such a space, empty as often as not, rising and falling through the heart of the building like a pump. How many such rooms were there, all over the city, each with its signed inspection certificate and the chiselled warning that no more than sixteen persons were to be there at one time? D admired the braille dots to show the floor numbers. Suppose there were seventeen blind men in the elevator? Even at the end of the day, bedraggled and daunted, he was a story man. That was the kind of bucking up C would have given him. C, his wife, so far away, in the ironing room, trying to tell the sky from the lead tone in the sweatshop skylight. Poor dear C, with wizened eyes and gaunt limbs. He loved her, he told himself, as the elevator whispered to the passing walls. It groaned and bumped at 11.

He realised as he got out, there had been no video in the elevator. It made him sure that he had been watched. He looked back at the panelled interior. There was no hint of a lens. But who was there to fear these days if they couldn't fashion a spy-hole invisible to the naked eye?

He had to withdraw his searching head as the doors began to close automatically. Wedges of polished steel met in front of him. He saw the frosted outline of a man behind him in the sheen. Before he could turn, hands fell on his shoulders and a close, muted voice said, "It must be D, isn't it? Don't disappoint me." Anxiety is so catching, thought D, as he closed his eyes and made to turn his battered body round.

FEMALE INFLUENCES

When Shirley makes a family drama of the childhood she shares with Warren, then he is cast in the role of her best audience. Their mother is as committed to duty and endurance as the grim scenery; Warren is the attention Shirley looks for, to make sure that her rightness has got across. When Shirley finally leaves Virginia, she says to herself about her brother, "He'll do something. And it will be his way, just as I am going off to do something my way. But I knew that, whatever it was, somehow it would continue to be a joint plan against the established way of doing things.'"

But suppose Warren does not feel all of that jointness, and is not as hurt by the defeated force in the house that drives Shirley away? Suppose he is more attuned to the necessary forlornness of energy and selfhood. Thirty years or more later, Shirley MacLaine is convinced of the reach of reincarnation – apparently so eccentric, so dotty – whereas it is hard to think that Warren believes in anything except what really happens and the decent doubt one retains about even that.

Yet he does follow his sister; he goes off to be in show business. That can only boost her hope that he is her ally. But it might haunt his wish to be his own man. It might make him tactically cold to her, as and when they do meet in their other world, show business. Does he need to say to her, Don't always think you understand me, Don't think loyalty covers everything? He is someone who wants to keep an indefatigable puzzle at his center, even an emptiness that others must try to fill. But if she lectures him when they are children, if she tells him her problems with their parents, so often and with such narrative bravura, then he may be afflicted by the condition of audience and the sibling resentment that feels we were always talking about *her*. No wonder she is baffled at his silent rebukes later: she was brought up as the center of things. She is the story-teller, so Warren cannot escape the meekness of a listener, with the imprisoned needs of someone who imagines more than he can ever

26

describe and who sometimes asks himself why the power and the glory can't come to *me*.

Warren Beatty will make his name in a profession where a very few do and are, and the many watch them doing and being. This is one of the equations of our times, a neon equals sign surrounded by fear and superstitions. It allows that the few have more vivid identity and more public worth than the many. But they are also regarded as vain, unreal and vaguely corrupt. Those human failings actually count as ingredients of exemplary public value. For such figures are loved and despised. A great trouble with actors, you hear it said, is that they are always "on", always performing, with only "off" as an alternative. It is as if they are versions of electricity; and like electricity they are used, taken for granted and then scorned because their light is not natural.

Shirley MacLaine is an example of such brilliant, "electric" presence, a star worthy of the lights that emblazon her name, or some such. She is famous for an energy beyond her years. At fifty, she has an exuberant, "unbelievable" one-woman show. She comes off soaked in sweat, crystalline, as if it was the residue of electricity. Her screen work is broad, explosive, larger than life; she has red hair; she is called outspoken; she struts, she laughs out loud, she bumps and grinds; she pours out her heart. The public is fond of her and sees her "inner life" – the thing about reincarnation – as part of her exalted condition. She could end up another Ethel Merman – superhuman, an immortal, the spirit of show business and America.

These two warm winds become more alike during Warren Beatty's childhood and the pride of stars in uniform. He is seven when Franklin Roosevelt is re-elected in 1944; it will be the first presidential election he notices, and it seems to say that the leadership of America is the focal point in international crisis. That is why this one man goes on being elected, why a man so ill and physically depleted that he has become a photographed figure, a movie man, all shots and close-ups, has defined a crisis that needs him. America knows FDR is a cripple but it is shown what it wants to believe – the pictures of power. There is no sharper time in which to learn about the presidency's modern drama.

Another actor, the young genius of his time, is very prominent in the Roosevelt campaign. We have encountered him already: Orson Welles. He speaks for FDR, on the radio and at public meetings, and he writes in *Free World*. The actor and the president are on friendly terms, exchanging notes. Not yet thirty, Welles has made and acted in a film about a man who sets himself at the highest power in America, *Citizen*

Kane, a film that directly compares politics and theater and shows the same imaginative drive going from one to the other. When Roosevelt wins again in 1944, he writes to Welles:

"I may be a prejudiced spectator who had a special interest in the action, but I want to thank you for the splendid role you played in the recent campaign. I cannot recall any campaign in which actors and artists were so effective in the unrehearsed realities of the drama of the American future. It was a great show in which you played a great part."

Warren does not know this, of course; or, he does not read the letter. But he is a seven-year-old boy, looking out at the drama and its movies, bathed in their light, and he would know already as part of the great show that a president might talk to an actor, waving to him above the dark throng, winking even, like kin. Long before the voting in of Ronald Reagan, there is a pressure building in America: the natural consequences of its idealism, its dreaming and its media.

Millions partake vicariously in stars' blithe risk-taking, their high kicks, and their willingness to be invented people. Some find it easier to live with Ronald Reagan as president, because he is so good at being president. This is not the same as being a good president; it is to take the role as one laid down in that messy genre made up of the news, documentary and political announcement. The detail of his administration may seem comically inept. But he has made that reality transparent beside the humdrum radiance of his show. He is a star for anxious unknowns or humble tyrants, a model for salesmen, the more removed from criticism because he is so expertly wry and amateur. His administration is the best celebration of ordinariness yet managed by stardom. Like Will Rogers or Johnny Carson, he identifies the power possible in being likeable.

Such a presidency functions like the movies. It takes our minds off our own awkwardness and failure and our fear that perhaps nothing now is likeable. We so identify with him that we can vote for him while ignoring his wretched, irrational policies. This "we" has given up several birthrights – observation, evidence and judgement, at least. For we are believing in the unbelievable. The only compensation is that we have in so doing affirmed imagination. From our own dank place in the dark we can feel for, be with, these electric stars. They do not know us, cannot see us; but we know them as if they were us. Somehow, this presumption of ours fills the empty space they worry over in their hearts. For they let us lead entirely other, phantom lives: thousands of them, as many as a satyr could mate with. And if we elect one star as a lover supreme, it is because we are fucking crazy.

Many people felt better on seeing *Bonnie and Clyde* – more relaxed, more energized, clearer. All American movies are restoratives of a kind: they are ointment and lubrication to the reckless process of imagining that the medium encourages. Stardom gives us fantasy, which is so much more up-to-date than the afterlife: we can have it now. As we sit in the corners of gloom and chaos (remember D), we can pretend we are Eyes (or Mouth). Far from the reckless or irresponsible escapism, this is proof that we have inner potential; it is a fineness that corresponds and communes with the empty, impossibly electric quality of those we watch. This is not really so far from the apparently crazy scheme of reincarnation – close enough to see that a brother might still be fascinated by what a sister believes.

If Warren Beatty is the most intelligent actor in Hollywood, then he must think on these things. No wonder he dines sometimes with Orson Welles and tells him, yes, he is serious about being president. And Beatty will have looked at *Citizen Kane*, taken its love of mystery to heart; he may even have read around enough to find that, reviewing the film, Jorge Luis Borges said "it is a labyrinth without a center". Which could help explain why he acts so seldom, and so absentmindedly, as if the work never convinced him. He has a shyness that suggests he would rather be watching, and that he is not sure why or how he became an actor, unless it was the helpless response to his beauty, his inspiring sister and the way his America is so ready to look at pictures.

The boy Henry Warren Beaty was a watcher not given to opinions. He tiptoed away from what he saw so as not to be questioned about it. Did he really howl as a child, as Shirley remembers, or did he just exist? It is so hard to hear his raised voice or forceful enunciation. His grown-up authority is deferential. Shirley looked at him and knew he was prettier than she could ever be, beautiful in ways that are contingent on silence. Too much talking can tire a face and eat away its calm.

The few things Warren has said about his childhood omit the stresses felt by Shirley – because they are hers alone, because they are too intimate to be revealed, or because he hates being known. He has remarked on his parents' interest in the arts. His mother directed plays, his father played the violin. He felt their wish to have creative children, just as Shirley says they resisted it.

"I never thought I would be an actor. I watched my mother direct, my father play the violin, and Shirley dance. I played the piano; maybe I just waited to spring. But no thought of getting up to perform. I was interested in the theater as a place to control, to manipulate."

Shirley was the best boy he knew. She was called "powerhouse" as a mighty hitter of home runs in softball games. When bigger boys picked on him, Shirley would rush in "like Rocky Graziano". And then "Warren would look grateful but bewildered, because he really wanted to take the risk himself".

He *was* her companion in escapades she designed, emptying garbage on neighborhood doorsteps, ringing doorbells and running away, pretending to drop dead in the middle of busy streets. At home, they were well behaved, hard-working and dutiful, so Shirley says. Yet Warren may have been lazier and more reclusive. His room had a spacious, walk-in closet, with a window of its own. It was a place to hide out in, a place to live away from others. Shirley envied it, and did not seem able to penetrate it. She only learned years later – when he must have told her – how in the empty house, in the basement, when no one else was home, he would be "acting out his soul to every Al Jolson record ever made, and memorizing in detail every play that Eugene O'Neill ever wrote."

There was a Jolson revival when Warren was nine, ten, eleven and twelve. Columbia made *The Jolson Story* and *Jolson Sings Again*, with Larry Parks as the singer. But O'Neill was an odder taste for a boy, unless he too was drawn to some of the unspeakable stories in reputable, creative families with fathers who had been actors and mothers who had to go upstairs to lie down; or unless he was making his devoted attempt to hear and be in the kinds of drama his sister insisted was their lot.

Warren has a forceful father, yet the father's example is one he may decline to follow, more a set of mistakes than a model. And Warren will have a way, later in life, of searching out men's weaknesses. Is he more comfortable with women, and more wholeheartedly admiring of them? He has at least three strong female influences in his early life – not just mother and sister, but his maternal grandmother. She had been Dean of Women at Acadia University, in Wolfville, Nova Scotia. Warren's mother will remember that Warren had a special rapport with this grandmother:

"I remember he used to get all dressed up to come to the dinner table because he knew Mother would be dressed. She never came to the table without having dressed, with a new hairstyle and perfume. And she wouldn't use a paper napkin. She insisted on a real linen napkin. Anyway, as soon as Warren and Mother sat down, Warren would snuggle up to her and say, 'Oh, Grandmother, you smell so good.' He never left her side. There was something very profound between the two of them."

Drew

"*N'est-ce pas?*" Clear asked again at the elevator. His life seemed to depend on the answer, until he saw his reflection swimming in the steel doors. He put up one arm to be sure it was him there. D suspected he had too much to do, and could no longer concentrate. It was a condition that came from lifelong readiness without action.

Clear was tall, yet curved, in an attentive forward droop, like a stick of celery. He wore rimless spectacles and his hair was a fine, brindle cover poised on his lean head. There was no doubting his quickness of thought. But his reactions came a shade slowly and his pale blue eyes had gazed on a prairie where only patience survived.

"It's D?" he hoped. D surged with the great responsibility of not wanting to disappoint Clear. He liked him on the spot, and he was intrigued by the way efficiency and dreaminess met in him but did not fit exactly, like a face cut in half and the halves restored a millimeter out of true.

"D," said D, in as hearty a way as possible.

"Terrific," said Clear. He stuck out a splay of long, narrow fingers. It was a hand to span a dinner plate, with a dry palm that might have given one last caress to a finished statue, as if the sculptor wanted to say, "Well, there you are, that's the best I can do." And now this hand fell on D's shoulder like an epaulette.

"My word. You're damp," said Clear. "Shower? We have everything here."

"Well," said D. He regarded his soiled state as a measure of integrity.

"Why not?" asked Clear. "I have to run out, anyway. My number just came up on television as a winner, if I can get there in five minutes." He shifted from one foot to another to show the boyish hurry behind his tranquil smile. "Of course, it's nonsense," he added. "But I've never won and I'm curious to see what people do win. The procedure?"

"You should go," urged D.

"It's not foolish?" The eyes had gone otter gray. The skin near them ran with deep lines. Clear was so willing to be laughed at.

"You'll be blue later if you don't go," said D, out of unexpected wisdom. It didn't seem like him.

Clear's face rose. "That's exactly it. This is the start of a proper friendship, I can tell." And he contrived in maybe thirty seconds to show D the suite, tell him how the shower worked and take a silver tray of canapés from the refrigerator, without seeming rushed or putting his five-minute deadline in jeopardy. D wanted to ask, "Well, why am I here, then?" But it would be unsporting when Clear was so valiant.

"Good luck," called D.

Clear's face had time to reappear at the doorpost, a milky sun of good will. "Thanks so much, old fellow," he said, and vanished.

D stood for a moment, alone in the suite. There was a large reception area with many other rooms leading off it, some doors flung back, others only ajar, but nothing closed. Degrees of daylight from these rooms seeped into the reception area and mingled with the frosted lilac and vanilla of the overhead. All the machines were working. The carpet felt like spring grass. D walked here and there through the reception area, past artwork and copying machines, admiring throw cushions and the telex. Something like pride filled and refreshed him. It was arousing to be alone in such a spanking place. D had the feeling that anything he touched or needed would be new, exact and ready.

He breathed deep the dry gin air of power and command. But the conditioning tickled his throat. He had a panic of choking. How ghastly to splutter in this groomed silence.

As if the place divined his horror, there came the sound of a piano being played in one of the rooms. Apparently in a far corner of that room. The notes were distant, tender and speculative. It sounded like a blind man tip-tapping a way into the tune, not sure if he was composing or remembering. D thought the melody might be "I Don't Want to Play in Your Yard", but he had a hopeless ear.

He wondered if he should go into that room, greet the pianist, interrupt his revery. Whoever it was had heard his frantic coughing. The tentative notes were a message on the wall to the latest newcomer in a prison. It was a way of saying welcome, but warning don't come in here, I'm here, let me stay here, but don't fret, be of good heart.

D realised there might be several people in the suite, quietly engaged in their tasks or stunned by the ebbing of the day, waiting for night. D looked up, towards the room with the piano. The light coming from there faltered or flinched, not naturally, as if a breeze had blown mist across the failing sun, but methodically. It was as if the aperture in the building had been closed half an f stop. D felt dirty.

He went to the bathroom outlined by Clear. It was a compact chamber of self-improvement, hard to determine in size because all its surfaces were black. When D shut the door, it did not smack or boom closed, but met with the sound of bare feet landing on the ground. Light came on, a suffusion of mooniness where the walls met the ceiling. The room was made of black tile. The towels were black, the soap and the toilet paper. There was even a book on the stool beside the black lavatory bowl, an album of Ad Reinhardt pictures. Did the ebony faucets disgorge black water? It would not be much more trouble, or any less fanciful. How might it feel to be cleansed in a sooty cascade? D imagined black lather on his chest, like curls growing beneath his eyes.

As his timid hand touched his own sad buttons and fasteners, he saw a black bowl of black cherries on the table. They were young and cold, but of a perfect softness that perhaps lasted only an hour. He took one and ate it: authentic juice filled his mouth and worked his jaws until only the pit remained. D dropped it in the dish. This small black room had a mastermind undaunted by the pallor of his body.

D turned his back on the mirror where he had been a fearful, scruffy intruder in the room. He let his hateful clothes drop where they would and he turned on the faucets. The water roared, then preened and sighed as he made adjustments. He stepped into the shower, slid the black doors shut and felt the heat on his back like a lover's support. The small of his back swelled with well-being. If he had had any doubts, his hand immediately found the dry egg of new soap in its recess.

He noticed out of the back of his mind – he was too superstitious or polite actually to observe it – that the water changed as soon as he wished. Both the temperature and the force leaped to meet his desire. He played with this facility. He imagined himself for a moment a slave after a day's labor in torrid Macao: the water began to chill, and soon it was a stream of invigorating cold. Then it was Christmas Eve, and he had been out in the snow chopping down a tree. "Into the shower with you" his family urged, snapping icicles from his nose, before he could have so much as a slice of spiced ginger cake. Then the water steamed and he felt restored by its brave warmth. He let his desires roam. He called for the water to stroke him and the filigree of spray made him giggle. Then he willed its fierceness and his skin tingled with the force of so many stinging droplets. He was laughing out loud with the fun when the water stopped and a recorded voice sounded in the shower, "Thank you". Then there was just D and the piles of silent steam in the black room.

Stepping out of the shower, he saw black towels and a black bathrobe, but his clothes had gone. D was concerned lest some system in the floor tiles had vaporised or consumed them. His key had been in his pants pocket. And there was the key, placed on the corner of the black marble table, beside the bowl of black cherries, replenished. The one pit had gone and a new cherry was in its place. The scene was ready to be replayed – taken again.

"Thank *you*," said D, under his breath, slipping into the bathrobe; it was heavy, embroidered towelling, but soft as mother's love. This phrase came into his head as fully formed and unplanned as the changes in the water. His hand explored the pockets. There was a black case filled with unnamed, unfiltered cigarettes and a lighter in one pocket, and a handy revolver in the other.

He left the bathroom, his feet enjoying the lawn-like texture of the carpet. In the reception area there was a young woman, a quite suddenly gorgeous youthful female creature – he was in love – sitting on the floor doing exercises in time with those offered on television. Her body, D did see, was very white. She wore nothing but the black wool leggings that dancers had in aerobics advertisements. They gave the odd impression of her body having been omitted between her capable white feet and all the white rest above her thighs. The black splash of pubic hair was like a hand holding her black and not-quite-there legs together.

She grinned at him, but did not stop her exercises until the television called for a break.

Then, "Hi," she said, "I'm Drew." She picked up a hand towel and dabbed her armpits. Then she stepped into a black leotard, a wisp of cotton that filled with her. She was a dancer, D assumed, with just the stark white bone of her feet, her hands, her neck and the heartbreak face that came up to D and kissed him. At the same time, her hand (so frail) pushed through the folds of his robe and found his thing. Her hands were cool and mastering. There was no complaining.

Drew squatted. D heard the sinews crackle. Her mouth closed on his thing and worked at it. He was on top of his mountain looking down. He saw her hairs on top of her head. The piano-player tested one note. D was just a loyal prop to this ardent action, being drawn out of himself. He thought of hospital. Her taut throat gulped; she took it all in. He wavered and thought he would fall. So weak, so helpless.

Then there was sound and arrival – Clear. D sought to free himself, but Drew was too determined. Clear did not refer to D's predicament. He was interested in the soft toy he held.

"Look!" he cried. "A teddy bear – isn't it? I don't think I've ever had one."

There was a small noise, as of a vacuum being released. A moist mouthed Drew, still crouched, looked up and said, "You had one once, when you were a little boy."

"I did?" Clear was pierced by lost memory.

Drew was already making herself scarce. "I remember from typing your profile. Bye," she whispered to D. He sniffed the breath of his own life. So salt. And wanted to keep her there.

Clear nodded as if it must be so. He was too delighted to worry. It was an orange bear in a green suit. "D," he sighed. "You've brought me luck. And how are you, old fellow?"

It took a moment for D to see Clear was not addressing the bear.

VIRGINIA KID

He is a boy in war, and a youth in cold war. After the family moves in 1946, he lives on the edge of Washington, in Arlington, where the National Cemetery is located. When he is seven, eight, nine, that cemetery has a steady supply of those who have won special honor dying for their country. In 1944 or 5, such a boy cannot know that there are Americans who do not attend to the running of the country as part of their natural responsibility. He will be politically minded in the way a film fan is Hollywood-minded. He will sometimes seem humorless about this, and he may explain that to himself as a measure of his extra seriousness. If there ever comes a moment when he notices that neither Hollywood nor Washington quite merits intelligence or dedication, then he will have to put himself above it all, too solitary to be taken, too cool to back a loser.

He might be president – if he could make it without first committing to the contest. Could he go from that bedroom closet philosopher, with his private window, his books and the stewing envy of his sister, to being the nation's studio chief? Is there a way all the intervening, democratic fuss could be avoided? Could it be managed so that the humorlessness never comes apart in its owner's hands or lap, so that he never has to see that his integrity has been spoiled?

In later years, people writing about him will fall upon his wry remembrance that, "My earliest childhood ambition was to be President of the United States. That was until I was six years old. At seven I decided to be Governor of Georgia. At eight I decided to become an actor. People become actors because of a need within themselves."

That thought is published in 1962, when Beatty is twenty-five, just arrived on the movie screen. At that time he works hard to imagine what reporters want to hear, and so he may try to give himself a Beaver-like American charm. Today, the remark has become prescient, for the years since have provided a president who was Governor of Georgia first. But in 1962 and 1944 (when Beatty is seven), that ambition testifies to the place of the South and civic duty in his mind. Of course, no one interviews kids when they are seven except the kids themselves, lying on the floor in their closed rooms, filling the light of the window with their future, chatting away in their heads or out loud to the only properly respectful world, the one they can invent.

Perhaps the kid has such thoughts, and then thinks of being a bum, a nobody, by the time he is ten or eleven – not a true nobody, but one like Vag, the emblematic vagrant, in Dos Passos's *U.S.A.*, or Montgomery Clift in the movie *A Place in the Sun*, a dark stripling hitch-hiking, backing towards and then turning to face the camera. And the camera says, that's someone. *A Place in the Sun* opens in 1951, when Warren is fourteen.

The new actor in Hollywood in 1962 is organising the way people think of him. But to be famous one day, he may have begun early, talking to himself with the patience of a Washington reporter, schooling his mind in the solitude of his closet on the humble jokes that become celebrities. A kid imagines himself famous already. Most go on to failure and dismay. Yet Warren Beatty has not failed, or has not let failure register. The most intriguing possibility of the 1962 story is that the teller still had some sense of being a destined child. The very ordinariness the story seems to pose and polish could be a role founded in the child's inexperience of being thwarted. The purest power in America is having your fantasy realised. Such hopes can still exist in men far more affected by age, grind and disappointment than Warren Beatty. If Ronald Reagan can survive his errors and unfitness, it may be because the shortcomings never adhere to his dream. In any manipulation of the media, the most vital mind to sway is the first one that will entertain the impossible dream. For if *you* can believe, you can make anyone follow you.

The Beatys are Baptists; they are taught to be truthful, clean and meticulous; they are children in awe of their parents. There is even a year, 1945–6, when the father works as principal at an elementary school in Arlington. Warren is taught to read at four, by his father, so he is able to follow newspaper accounts of Pearl Harbor and keep up with the course of the war, as well as the Little Henry cartoon in the comics section. He is called Little Henry by the family. He is a pretty little boy with a gentle, brilliant smile; his dark hair is parted on the right and much curlier than it will be. He has a large collection of toy cars, and he will grow up knowing all the details of 1950s automobiles. He does his homework, he listens to his parents and his sister; he talks to himself and he absorbs his parents' love of the arts.

His school record is not outstanding. Between them, the daughter and son of two teachers will amass one year of college after which Warren backs off because the educational system is not serious enough. In later years he will be called an omnivorous reader, an extraordinary memory, a tenacious arguer and negotiator. But those who observe these traits remark on the way he imposes his own terms on discussion and dealing. Like the self-educated, with equal amounts of pride and insecurity, Beatty is not always emotionally capable of being defeated. His intelligence has worked towards what we might call self-improvement, not the fostering of general discourse and debate. And for the self to stay improved, it cannot be wrong. This timidity trusts no one else with its education. Years later, on the set of *Reds*, when some people marvel that there is no script, Diane Keaton will observe that Warren is keeping it all in his head. That speaks for the capacity and power of the head, and for its need for advantage and privacy. It also shows an ignorance of how the ordinary educated man may use a library, and know that knowledge is there outside his head – safe, unstealable.

Self-improvement, after all, can be absolute and abstract; or it can be driven by competition. It can be a very American pursuit, idealistic yet paranoid. It can lead to those sad testaments of self-nagging like Jay Gatz's *Schedule* in which the Mid-West nobody who would one day be the supreme but unrecognised host at his own great parties set himself to do dumbbell exercises, to "practice elocution, poise and how to attain it", to study needed inventions, give up smoking and chewing, "read one improving book or magazine per week" and "be better to parents." Little Henry has a grandmother who teaches elocution, and he will be an actor who takes pride in never speaking clearly.

He goes to Washington-Lee High School in Arlington, and when he is thirteen he is challenged by a teacher and a system because he spends all his time with books when he is plainly the best athlete in the school. He switches. He takes up every sport and becomes an exceptional football player. Yet he is not a wide receiver, not a running back or a quarter-back (the position he gives his character in *Heaven Can Wait*). He is a center: at the nub of battering contact, without much chance of touch-downs, visible glory or space in the game reports. But he is over six feet, and his weight is close to 200 pounds. He is a big boy and, briefly, a team player. He makes president of his high school class. Football has become very important to him: it earns him offers of ten scholarships to college, in the era before face-masks. Singer John Phillips, from a rival school, remembers, that, on the gridiron, he was called "Mad Dog Beaty".

It is easier now to think of him as a coach or a field general. If football is ever his game, it must be because of its scope for planning. Yet all a center has to do is urge himself forward across a foot or so of overshadowed ground into the collision with his blocker. The center is a large body the general wants, and can replace. Within a few years, Beatty will scorn football. He does not follow it much now; he does not take an interest in sport. He explains his earlier involvement as "Maybe it has to do with at a certain age in high school you want to prove you're a man."

In 1985, *People* magazine runs a story on misfit kids who grew up to be showbiz stars. It has comments from Cher, Woody Allen, Barbra Streisand, and so on; and it includes Warren. *People* does not get him to speak, but it quotes *the mother of a friend*: "Warren would come to my house, sweep in and give me a big theatrical kiss. He gave the impression of being self-confident; actually, he was essentially a loner, never wanting to be committed and tied down."

People prints a picture of Warren at seventeen, his large, rather jowly jaw, his fat grin and his sultry teen eyes all pressed down by a savage cropped haircut. He looks like a brash stud athlete who could so flirt with friends' mothers that they'd recall a kiss thirty years later and the impossibility of tying him down. In five years' time, on Broadway, Warren will be playing a provincial kid who goes to bed with a friend of his mother. And in 1985, in *People*, the cocky 50s grin is saying, "Is that right, Mrs . . . . I actually kissed you? I did?" When he is famous he will look back on his school years as those of "a cheerful hypocrite".

"I think he graduated in . . .," the biographer stumbles. He is not above feigning dullness, for sometimes rescuers volunteer the most.

"55," says the woman's voice. "He graduated the same year as me."

"Oh, really . . ." Oh, really. This woman is a Mrs L-----, secretary now, in 1985, to the principal of the Washington-Lee High School. The biographer has come upon her by chance in an effort to ascertain that Warren's father, Ira, never taught at Washington-Lee. (He didn't; he had given up teaching for real estate.)

"Did you know him well?" he asks his newfound treasure, wondering what "well" will mean to her.

"Well . . . I didn't know him 'well'. He was class president and all those good things."

The biographer sighs. He might call back, of course, might make friends with Mrs L-----, ask for her home phone, or urge her to call him collect when she is out of the office. And so perhaps at home at night she fidgets round her phone until Mr L asks, "What *are* you doing?", and she explains, and he says, "He'll just want dirt," and Mrs L has to decide whether to betray or whether to admit she was always outside the charmed circle that might have had the dirt. She does not call, and the biographer does not call again.

But he notes the way in which a class president, center of so many "good things", is lost to the school while someone never quite in the swim now works there every day, nine to five, an hour for lunch. Speculate: do not call. This is an imaginative biography. And, anyway, as Mrs L tells the biographer, Washington-Lee has no alumni organization where one might round up the good things gang. No alumni organization? Is that Warren covering his tracks?

In 1954, the summer before his senior year in high school, he hangs around the National Theater in Washington D.C. He is hired as the kid who will stay out in the alley every evening to scare off the rats. The theatre has been invaded by rats; an actor has been bitten. And so Warren Beaty waits in the alley, with sticks and stones maybe, a big boy with a Baptist dread of rats, while Helen Hayes works inside on a production of Thornton Wilder's *The Skin of Our Teeth*. The play is a parable about how easily the world might end, and brave families with it, and this is 1954 with Eisenhower president, the H-bomb shared by Russia and America, in the lull between Dien Bien Phu and "Vietnam". It is just before rock and roll and James Dean.

Piano player

D was far from home, even if this splendid suite was only a city's breadth from the apartment where he lived. He might have felt as homesick as an African slave dressed in silks as a lady's toy in a Nash house. Amid such ease and grace – when the flicker of need in his numb head was leaped at by supple bodies – he could not forget the harder lot of those at home. Then again, he had never been serviced so comprehensively as he had been by Drew. He remained puzzled whether he had been technically unfaithful. After all, it had been her idea, her power, with D simply a baby, made all the more absurd because he was giving her suck. But he had been pleased. It perplexed D that he could measure technical ethics where something like desire seemed to have been involved. Nor was he accustomed to lounging in a designer robe with a gun in its pocket, his toes delighting in the carpet and the cool azulejo tiles.

But if ever D feared fainting from embarrassment, there was Clear with some small question – the date of Magna Carta? the credits of Clifton Webb? – to set D on his feet again. And talking of those feet, when Drew reappeared with a silver tray of drinks – she was dressed for company now, in a pink sheath – she looked at the floor in amazement. D thought he must have dropped something. But Drew's voice was somber with wonder.

"Oh, those feet. I don't think I have ever . . . ." The ice in the drinks shivered. "Clear, have you . . .? They are the most amazing, I only just noticed them. Who, I have to know, you have a podiatrist? Clear, have you seen D's feet?"

Clear was smiling with contentment. "Among the first things I appreciated in D." He had the gentlest way of saying this. It seemed to tell the air why, yes, D's feet were majestic; but likely D shrank to hear this mentioned so much; not that Drew should feel brash for speaking; she had only declared her heart, and wasn't that the stuff of life, recommended in Humanities 101 and TV Inspirationals?

"Those feet are Praxiteles," said Drew. "Tell me they aren't."

"I won't," whispered Clear. "But the ears are nobler. If you can pick some murderers by their ears, D must be a saint." Drew's gaze came up, like a Grand Canyon telescope, unlocked by a coin, and Clear slipped D away to meet others, leaving Drew in a pose of resolute awe.

Clear seemed to give all his thought to putting others at ease, yet this left no trace of weariness or resentment in him. He was *for* others, a sort of service. D had never met such benevolence.

"Eyes is fortunate to have you," he said.

"Well . . . his sort are lonely, you know – masters of the world, but so shy."

"It's the reticence that is most magical," said D. "In this age of pressing and boosting."

Clear's arm rose and settled on D's shoulder: it was a garland of team spirit. "Just look at that," said Clear, for they were at a vast window, confronting the city.

The last flare of amber fell across the view to their right as the sun dropped into the sea. The buildings were gray and mauve, except when their windows held a final coppery facet of the sun. The streetlights were on and along the highways every vehicle was pushing and dragging its small jewels through clots of smoke and cloud. A fabulous threat fluttered in the view. It was the passion of evanescence, like seeing a face make up its mind. It was in the harmony of twilight and man's lighting schemes, and in the contrast of their vantage and the muddied infinity of the hot, hectic city, a fever of business on the ground and a dust that seemed in danger of being wiped away.

"Now, D," asked Clear, "where are you?"

D reached out for an area of the dying fire beyond the bright light of the smarter zone. "There," he said, as if he was touching C and the children.

Clear peered forward. His nose quietly bumped the glass, and he murmured in amused surprise. The place was a measurable distance away, yet it was another level of location, a part of the far indigo grime from which Clear could now say he had met someone.

"I should be going back, I think," said D. The nearness haunted him.

"Not yet," Clear whispered. "It's too soon."

D looked wistfully at the spot he had picked. How could he admit it all looked alike from here? He had insisted he knew where home was; it had such desirability when he was away. He felt warm tears of separation sliding down his face.

"D," said Clear, full of soothing discretion. "Please don't fret. We'll have you there very soon. It's touching that you miss them. Why, the last fellow we had in, he looked me straight in the eye, and do you know what he said?"

D shook his head: it made his teeth ache.

"He had a family or some-such out there, and he said, 'Mr Clear, call me callous, but do away with them. Please. You want, I'll go there and do it myself. But I can't take this failure much longer.' He was garish. Not a bad writer, though."

"What did you do?"

"Oh, we hired him as a bodyguard. I told him it was nothing to be ashamed of. But we do keep an eye on him. I'm not confident he wouldn't go out there on his day off and slaughter them all. For attention. There is often a suppressed killer in a good bodyguard."

"I guessed the same." D nearly said it to himself.

"Why, of course you did," Clear remembered with pleasure. "It's one of the scenes we most enjoyed."

"You've read the script already?"

"Oh, yes. We get instant print-outs. You can't wait for final submissions these days. I was reading it as it was typed. Typists have their little side-lines. May I say, here and now, without prejudice to any future negotiation – a work of genius, D." Clear licked his lips. "And as you know me better, you will find I do not use that word lightly."

"Has Eyes read it?" asked D, sticking to the straight line.

"Not yet. No so far. Or, I don't believe so."

"He must be so busy." D was furious with himself for having presumed.

"In a way," Clear agreed.

"Is he here? This evening?" D ventured.

Whereupon Clear lightly struck his brow. "Good Lord, I never thought to say. D, what have you been thinking? I haven't even introduced you. I tell you – and please don't tell another soul – I have too much to do. You find me at a vulnerable moment."

"I wouldn't say a word."

"That's your quality, your rareness. Others, of course, would expose me."

"Loyalty is the ticket," said D.

"You must meet Eyes," Clear had made up his mind. This was the best reward he could imagine. "Did you hear him earlier?"

D had been on the track all along. "The piano player?"

44

Clear chuckled. "You're too sharp. He's there now, I think. Come along, won't you?"

Like a messenger from some outer part of the empire, D followed Clear into the most private lounge. There was a white grand piano on the far side of the room, and someone sitting at it, but hidden by the raised lid. Drew was squatting on the floor, easing away hard dry skin from the player's feet with pumice stone. There was a worldly tilt to her lovely head, as if she dreamed of greater feet. The piano player's right hand was drifting idly in her hair, as the left picked over the pieces of a melody.

"Here we are," Clear announced, and then, "No, don't go," as Drew made to disappear from the big meeting.

She settled again and the legs above the bare feet she had been grooming straightened. A blinding image of a man stood up. He wore white slacks and a cream shirt. He was the right sort of height and build; with the same aura, more or less. His head seemed to have been dipped in aroused, headstrong hair. He had a tip-top air of retiring grandeur. He was emphatically *there*, yet receding, sentimentally drawn to vanishing. It looked like Eyes – as far as anyone can look like a picture. The spectacle had all the poignance of the real thing at last revealed, like Angkor Wat still there in the jungle, secure and mysterious.

But . . . wasn't the context more persuasive than the image itself? Was this Eyes or just the mask of beauty, incapable of his authentic, devouring look?

FRESHMAN

Why does he go to college in September 1955, and why is he no longer there a year later? Is this part of a plan already, the traces of solitariness or reluctance to work with others? Does he calculate in advance that he can spare one year of "waste" so that, in years to come, anyone may look back and hear Warren Beatty muttering to himself (at a School of Speech) that the system is not good enough? Is a part of him already living in reverse, arranging biography as a mystery, with the wishfulness-waiting-for-genius of a kid piano-player taking apart tunes?

Some young people go so automatically to college, they do not have to absorb its philosophy. They go because it is there, and has been expected of them, and because the going averts some tougher choices waiting in the dark. College can be a safe way of leaving home; in the mid 1950s it has the promise of smoking, booze and sex, accretions of illicit worldliness. Some American colleges are the slackest way imaginable of carrying the young forward into the national dream of success. Whatever else they teach, they instill an hysterical approach to learning that crams and forgets, and an air of casualness that could go on forever. It is a moment at which absurdity can enter American life, and middle-class repression explode in indulgence, all in the name of making good minds.

It is not easy in an American college to explore intelligence without feeling opposed to the system. That is one more of its crippling conditions, something contributed to by any student's share of flat, passable classes and back-slapping alumni organisations hitting him for donations as soon as he graduates. You learn those economics, whatever your major. You see that higher education can be a transaction in which a degree is purchased by so much accumulated tuition and residence, with courses and grades to suggest you got this or that percentage of the product. It is a process not designed to make you think, but to prepare you for process. And we are talking of the middle 1950s, of the Eisenhower era, before alternative curricula, student government and a world panorama to make America doubt itself.

This is a general description few feel driven to make in the 1950s. And if the American college was then, and is still now, indicative of the business ethic, a kind of societal and work preparation program, then we may consider the possible virtue in one kid, raised to it, the son of an educator, breaking away after his freshman year.

Warren Beaty enters the School of Speech at Northwestern University, at Evanston, Illinois, a northern suburb of Chicago, to be a drama major. An attraction of the school is the drama teacher, Alvina Krause. But Northwestern is not an acting school or a place that offers professional training. It is a university that requires a liberal arts major to meet basic standards in English, mathematics, a foreign language and to have had some experience with science and social science. Charlton Heston has been there, and in 1955 he is playing Moses in *The Ten Commandments*. No student can spend all of his or her time in the theater, and no would-be actor can escape the assumption by the institution that he or she will be a better artist knowing about the world.

It is reasonable to propose that an actor should read novels and history, listen to music and watch dance; that he may understand the ways of rendering character better if he is acquainted with biology and biochemistry – what is happening in Iago's brain and Hamlet's body chemistry?; that he will be more alert in Strindberg if he knows Swedish history and geography; that he can bring more to Restoration Comedy if he knows what was being restored and why; that he can be a surer Moses if he believes in the Law; that he can hardly be serious in experimenting with the psychology of characters if he does not read Freud; and, finally, how will he play Shylock if he does not grasp the principles of interest?

An actor could know all there is to know . . . or does he only need to sense the range of everything in which he can create his particular person on the stage or screen? It is a problem like that of the biographer, torn between research and writing. But people anxious to know as much as possible about everything, and people dedicated to stringent application of the laws of evidence, do not seem to go into acting. It has a better record with liars and dreamers. The stage does beckon those with a special, heightened mixture of insecurity and arrogance, knowing nothing but the lines, their part and the cues. They want the stage, they want to take it over, so their pain, their indecision, their pause, can reign there.

Actors want to get on stage and do it; they want the lights, a scene, the dark, an audience, applause and a pay check. They will tolerate a script, a character, a director, other actors and quite extensive theories if they can get on stage and act. But they soon learn the need to know agents, producers and contacts as well as Aristotle and the texts of Antonin Artaud.

The actors who do make it will range from those who regard thinking about what they do as like walking under ladders to those who can talk-show for a year and a day on stage stories. But in 1955–6 there is in America a passionate fusion of practice and theory, a way of justifying self-absorption. If we think of one college student facing it, in 1955, it is not hard to see the Method as harbinger of all the intensity of self-determination that distracts American campus life ten years later. And to the extent that Lee Strasberg's Method acting is a celebration of movie presence, there are Method politics, in which our votes may fall, with our sympathy, into those wry presidential shrugs, shucks and pauses that fill television. Here is the apotheosis of not knowing but winning. Ronald Reagan has no superior at offering problems a cheery, polite "God bless". Much Method acting has been more agonized. It is still the case that the Method and the close-up have made the act of thinking hallowed, and given it a potency that goes far beyond the reach of thinking itself. We are talking about the desire to know, as romantic as knowledge is realistic. And we are trying to explain the look on Warren's waiting, intelligent face.

There are always reasons for dropping out of college: you can easily suppose you are wasting your time if you accept the college-based theory of the measurability of things; you may be irritated at the humorless way in which the Introduction to Drama always starts at 10.10 a.m.; because you are a freshman you may get no parts in any production, or because you are afraid of being rejected you may not try-out for parts; you may realise that you are part of a community in which most members are trying to become like one another; you may notice that, whatever their claims and hopes, teachers never have enough time to teach enough; you may worry that you are not out in the world, but enclosed in a place for which the term "intramural" was invented; you may want a way of rebuking your parents' expectations; you may be a lazy no-good bum more interested in laying a wider range of females than coeds constitute; you may have been struck rigid that a few days after you began your college career, on September 30, 1955, James Dean was killed, aged twenty-four.

At Northwestern, Beaty dates some, especially a girl named Ellie Wood. He knows athletes, but he doesn't do sports himself. He sings a song in a show. He lives in a dorm, he takes classes, and then he gets out. In the years since, he gives two oblique commentaries on his departure. He says that the Northwestern approach to acting was "slovenly, lackadaisical". And in 1967, he tells Rex Reed about one encounter with a jock:

> "A guy actually became an all-American. He was big and he was tough. He was from Ohio. I rather liked him. One night I came home late to a freshman dorm and they said, 'So-and-so is really sick, got drunk tonight, and he's asking for you. He vomited in the mens' room.' 'How sick was he?' I asked. 'Go in and see.' I saw, for one second, a whole cabbage, a carrot, an unchewed lamb chop – I said, 'Man, I'm too sensitive for *this*!' And I quit."

So he has very little of what is called a higher education – which may mean he knows he must learn on his own. He flinches from packed male company – he does confess to being more at ease with women. That he is, for a time, a drop-out, may account for dismay in his parents. That he becomes, so soon, a success could obscure the fact that he may have been ready to stay a drop-out. The sequence helps him believe in himself, and in no external entities. There may be no alternative for him to being a king or an outcast, best of all a role that partakes of both. To be alone, to stay private, becomes more appealing as the crowd presses in, more dense, more likely to vomit. But what a pressure on this loner if he also wants to be famous. He may smile as he hears of Dean's death, seeing past our loss, knowing now Dean is famous forever and free from the vomit. He may imagine himself as Dean, enjoying the nihilistic liberty, hurrying away from the bogus camaraderie of college.

Years later, the biographer calls Northwestern University. He is put through to the Evanston campus, and then to the office of the Registrar, which listens to his query and says, "You need Verification." It is clearly a capital V, no matter that that department or resort turns out to be a smart, amused kid, someone on work study and maybe going through *Madame Bovary* with a yellow underlining pen as he mans the phone. He has, perhaps, just remarked on "Emma was like all his mistresses; and the charm of novelty, gradually falling away like a garment, laid bare the eternal monotony of passion," with a note to himself that this is

49

more than just French, when he gets this guy on the phone asking about Warren Beatty at Northwestern.

The biographer has to stay on hold for several minutes before the student comes back, sauntering, cockily, let's goose this guy, with, "Sir, I have an H. Warren Beaty, one t. Did you know that?"

"Aha," the biographer sighs. And, yes, a year, fall 55 to spring 56, in the School of Speech. "What courses?" the biographer wonders, a little shocked to hear himself prompting garrulousness.

"Oh, I couldn't tell you that, sir."

The biographer has expected confidentiality, and has no wish to trick it. But the kid at Evanston is quite a character; one can hear his grin. It's the voice that goes with that highschool picture of crew-cut Warren. And so the biographer murmurs something about whether H. was in good standing – and would be still, presumably, could go back and pick up where he left off? The kid might like that: "Hey, Warren, split a brew?" The quality of those freshman grades is what the biographer is wondering about – not so much the specifics as their tone.

"Well," the Evanston Flaubert hesitates, surveying the old grade card and grinning again to see courses that are still torture, "he didn't do so great, but he didn't fail anything." There is a pause, as two innocents wait to see how worldly they can be. "All right?"

And the biographer does not even have a name to add to the Acknowledgements, even if for an instant it has *been* Warren, or at least H. Warren Beaty.

Wheel of Fortune

D never knew it, but Clear stayed outside, peering through the door's crack to see if D would pick up the trick.

There was a video camera aimed at the piano player at his white piano and at Drew, attending to his feet. Its pictures played on a large television screen set just inside the door and in the pianist's easy line of sight. D perceived the triangular arrangement, the hallowed "there" being repeated on the screen, like a nose pursuing itself across a cubist face. He moved aside so as not to impede the star's view and stepped round the prow of the grand. Looking to make sure the screen was visible, he saw his furtive self slip into the picture.

"There you are, kiddo," the man sighed. He was happier talking to the image of D. The frame was pleasing, with most of the piano, the man at its controls, swivel-faced D and Drew's delectable head at the bottom of the frame like the silver ball in a puzzle that one must coax into some shallow hole without disturbing the other elements.

"Well then, D," said the man. "Old Didi," he crooned. "Dee-dee-I-oh. Diddle di-dee fiddle di-dee. Dee-dipity-dee. Dee-di-daddy-o." And then a lengthy amount of yodelling on the dee-dily-deadly scheme, rising to a climax with "Yes indeedee!" D was horrified; there must be a mistake. This wasn't Eyes.

"That's neat," murmured Drew. She was bowed over, moving so slightly, as patient and painless with his horny feet as water depleting rock in the Dordogne caves. D could see the tranquility in being slave to a god on Earth. He noticed, not for the first time, the appeal of inventive forms of imprisonment. Liberty had had its historical rage. Most slavery could be adjusted to if it was not rushed. Only suddenness alarmed.

D wondered if the actor was contemplating the role of Gershwin, Liszt or Liberace in a biopic, judging how he might look in a keyboard shot. Key-bored, D decided. This man was stagnant or stupefied. As the scales were eased from his feet so they seemed to have formed on his soul.

There was none of the liveliness of the real Eyes, only glossy, stale resemblance.

With a lunge and a snarl, the man's hand came up from the keys to a channel-selector. He cut from the lulling self-enshrinement to a game show. The tense noise of a studio audience filled the room.

"Wheel of Fortune," the man announced. It was like telling the time.

Drew looked at the host in his plaid soup jacket quivering in the electric storm. Then she smiled at D. He was struck that she had more focus than the piano man. She was attentive; she had interest and warmth; she saw feelings pass. Was she a better actress than the star? D looked at this alleged Eyes: the head was transfixed by the game show, but so slow, so coarse. D had to face his disappointment. Then he looked at Drew again. Did she read his reading? She was inspecting the piano-player in a sly and mocking way, her brow furrowed with the labor of his thought. And then she winked at D, as if to say, what a stiff, this "Eyes", and what fools they were to go along with him.

"It's a phrase," said the piano-player, nodding with the explosive discoveries of the game show.

Wearily, Drew gave another glance to the screen. D looked, too: it seemed polite to join in. Surely, soon, this dreadful, unlikely Eyes would want to discuss plans. He would probably dismiss Drew then, D thought gloomily. There was something necessary about her. She might be sewing down there on the floor, stitching up this unresolved scene.

The game was hanging on a four-word phrase:

T-- ---T-- -- -TT--T---

"Shit," said the piano player. "This is hard." Drew smiled in an absent-minded way.

Then a contestant, a flight attendant from Buena Vista, called for an N and Vanna White swished forward in her cherry-colored slant-cut dress, and Ns rattled into frame against a crackle of applause:

T-- --NT-- -- -TT-NT--N

"That last word's giving me a headache," the man cried.

"I think it's ATTENTION, baby," said Drew, studying his feet. Did she have the image screened for her in his big toenail?

"It is? Yeah? It could be."

"So," said Drew. "What's the first word gonna be. Gonna be an article, don't you think?"

Another contestant, a black schoolteacher from Palms, asked for an H, and the first word could only be THE.

"Only one H, though," the pianist grumbled, and he urged the players to buy a vowel. But they pushed on, sportsmen all, until the third of them, a body-builder and encyclopedia salesman from Lancaster, hit on C:

TH- C-NT-- --- -TT-NT--N

"I know!" he yelled. "The Country of Attention."

"I don't think so, honey," said Drew. "It doesn't fit. I think they want an R."

"Yeah?" he struggled with this clue. His face crinkled, like the land mass in a time-lapse movie about continental cooling. Then he bounced on the piano stool and shouted out "The Central is Attention!"

Drew laughed, as if a ghost had tickled her. "That's not a phrase," she told him.

"The Center of Attention," said D, quietly. He had not meant to speak but the coincidence would not stay modest.

"I bet you're right," said Drew. She was looking straight at him, not smiling, but entirely concerned to see what was happening to him. He faced her, but her gaze was too strong for him. D blinked. His head dropped. He was such a sissy. And the piano player was bellowing, for he and the flight attendant from Buena Vista had solved the puzzle. His noise precluded the risk that another had been there first. He stood up and moved forward to look at the prizes. His feet gone, Drew looked at the window and the night, an estimating smile on her face. Was she seeing all the way to the desert where the night was an hour older?

The flight attendant was claiming her bounty: kitchen machinery, a year in Hawaii and a jigsaw puzzle of the home of Wayne Newton on which his face was superimposed. It looked like a puzzle testing enough for all that year in Hawaii while the kitchen steel festered.

"Pussy time," announced the man. He had to have some prize.

"Not now," said Drew, but she was warning D. He heard her fear of the star's brutal whim.

With one quick movement, the man brought down the lid of the piano. The room vibrated with crushed notes. "Up you go," he said, and Drew was dragged onto the smooth white surface.

"D shouldn't –" Drew began.

"He stays." The man's blunt finger prodded D's papery chest.

D could only watch. The man's hands tore away the pink of Drew's clothing; she was left as pale as the white lid. He dropped his head into her profuse dark bush. His head was lost in it. No wonder he sounded afraid.

He was eating, lapping, snorting over her. Drew's face was only a foot from D's hand. Her eyes were blank; he wanted to tilt his face to see if there was any expression. But soon her face could not resist the tremors coming from his animal intrusion. Her light body was bubbling on the piano. When the player looked up for air, drool was hanging from his gunmetal fillings. Then he plunged down again and Drew groaned. It could have been the piano's broken chords rising to protect her. But the cry that came next was hers.

She was sliding helplessly towards a climax when her gaze caught D's and looked at the channel selector. D understood. But how did the tool work? He struck at it until he found the answer. On the set, across the room, the game show was wiped away by a diagonal spectrum and replaced by the old standard, the piano, and Drew's turmoil. Sounds of feeding and surrender came from the set. Drew's head turned to watch herself. The scene went on, all its action and terror. Her face was contorted, but her eyes rose in sympathy: she had become the show.

D could not stay there. He staggered away from the piano – the man was too intoxicated to notice – and he went out into the larger room. There were several more people there now. But D did not look at any of them. He was walking, he did not know where, when Clear's arm stopped him.

"What ever –?"

"Horrible! That man . . ."

"Yes?"

"It cannot be Eyes. I may be a fool. But this is a creature without tenderness or spirit or . . ."

"Humor?" suggested Clear. "Of course it isn't him. This is his idiot stand-in. And you knew it, you champ." He embraced the trembling D. The two men swayed together, and D thought he must faint. But over Clear's shoulder, D saw the naked scrap of Drew in the doorway, so weak she clutched the door, but eager to see what D thought and felt.

HEALTH

He goes to New York. In 1956, in all of America, where else can a Northwestern drop-out go and expect to retain the least reputation for seriousness? And wanting to be taken seriously is already palpable – it may be a little like fear in combat or the guarded edge that makes women believe he is interesting. He wants to be taken seriously; he wants to be respected. And so he makes himself aloof, as if to say, look, he doesn't care about those very things.

No matter that he gives every indication in the next few New York years of wanting to be an actor, still at the time and years later he says he is not/was not ever sure. Maybe it was a director he was going to be. Don't mark him down. Don't be sure you ever know what Warren's intending. It is so much harder to fail if your own needs stay masked. Other people do not see your depression or disappointment. You may even keep your own simple limits for yourself if you can believe you are so clever a fellow you have ambitions intricate enough and necessarily veiled so that no one knows them. The country and the leader secure against espionage is the one who has no plan. If there is, finally, nothing final to be found out, why, possibility goes on forever. You can get a reputation for being dreamy, floating somewhere between the sublime and the downright humorless.

"You know, I think there is no such thing as reality," Shirley MacLaine says in her one-woman stage show. It's all a matter of perspective. That very same principle could be the motto for a handsome, formidable, very intelligent ghost. In 1956, we are on the edge of an age where being thought of will come to rival being. Acting, for that sort of philosopher or adventurer, could be less a profession than a kind of yoga of the soul, and a way towards flexibility and emptiness. Sometimes the very great personalities feel most conscious of their own nothingness.

"I don't think either of us ever seriously considered that we *wouldn't* be able to make something of ourselves. We *had* to; it was the only way

55

we'd have any respect for ourselves. We *wanted* to live up to whatever our potentials might be. The frustrating spectacle of people who hadn't, who had been afraid to, and were bitterly disappointed in themselves as a result, had been crippling to us in many ways as we grew up; but, on the other hand, their failures and frustrations had been so clear that Warren and I had a precise blueprint of how *not* to be."

That is Shirley, years later, thinking about her parents, herself and her brother. She had gone to New York in 1952. She had an apartment at 116th Street and Broadway, a succession of roommates, crackers and honey and auditions. She was broke by the time she got an audition for the Servel Ice-Box Trade Show which was going on the road. She got noticed.

" 'You mean me, sir?' I asked timidly.

" 'Yeah. What's your name?'

" 'Shirley Beaty, sir.'

" 'Shirley Batty? That's a funny name.'

" 'Not Batty. Beaty.'

" 'Yeah, that's what I said: Beauty.'

" 'Not Beauty, Bay-tee.'

" 'OK, so it's BAY-TEE. Don't you have a middle name or something?'

" 'Yes, sir – MacLaine.'

" 'OK, Shirley MacLaine, you're hired.' "

So those long legs go on the road to arouse gatherings of travelling salesmen to the virtues of refrigerators. With such nightmarish confusion of being hot and cold, it may be as well to reassure yourself you are nothing but a figure in the light going through those motions. No, it's not me; it's just the part.

By 1954, Shirley had got the task of being understudy to Carol Haney, one of the leads in what would be a hit show, *The Pajama Game*. It opened when Warren was 17, and then Carol Haney broke her ankle. In going to New York, in the family, Warren was showing his foolishness. One child had gone into show business – against advice and tradition – and she had been a success. But she had striven for it throughout her childhood; she was so outgoing; and she was a girl, pretty and vivacious. Warren had always seemed so much more serious and reticent. There had been talk of him becoming a lawyer. Did he now expect that the mad future that makes a success in show business – not to mention stars – would hit on one small family twice? Shirley must have been asked to dissuade him. He must have been warned that he was making a fool of himself; he must have wondered if he was so immature, so under-developed, that he could only see the path that his sister had pioneered. And could aloofness work where she had needed all of her drive and all her great appetite for change?

But he went to New York and, like a cool guy who didn't dance, he took acting lessons at the Stella Adler Studio. This is the short hard time of Warren Beatty – the second "t" comes in in these years – in which he has as the center of his life something that doesn't pay. In a few years' time, by the time he is twenty-five, he will be considering and refusing offers that would look magical to the peanut-butter-sandwich brigade who want to be actors. And by that stage, he will no longer have interest in being a theater actor. For this kid "makes it" not in a hit show where the star has a mishap and youth is thrown "on", with the audience's applause ready to mingle with the cheers of history and posterity, already attending to the larger show. No, Warren Beatty is in one Broadway play, a flop, in a company that goes away convinced of his intractability, and he has never yet tried another play. He is not quite the trouper, not exactly like the sister who, at fifty, is doing eight performances a week of her one-woman show in the course of which she tells the audience that you're cheering or you're not, you call a glass half-empty or half-full, and that you have to love yourself before you can love others, whereupon a female voice in the audience shouts out "Don't tell Warren," and Shirley says, "You have great taste," and the audience laughs so warmly that maybe even Shirley thinks it was a warm remark.

So Warren lives in a room on West 68th Street, a furnished room for $24 a month. "It was a junk heap," he said. "I mean a real junk heap because a junkie had lived there before. And the smell was still there." Did the kid who flinched at a football player's vomit lie awake warm summer nights inhaling and reeling in that sinister smell? Did he know what it was? Do junkies smell more than or different from other deadbeats? How do out-of-work actors smell? Or is it a line from a picture about a kid who has really lived, had it tough? Is it a line dropped in a reporter's notebook with a wry grin?

He works at this and that, apparently: he washes dishes, helps a brick-layer, he is a sand hog in the Lincoln Tunnel, one of the crew carving out its third tube – or so it is said – this is back-flap territory, the early life of the later great that lists so many unlikely jobs and which might be God's truth or the bitterness of fame that has known anonymity and says how much nonsense will these idiots take. It is the

Catherine Deneuve in *The Hunger*

Andrew Dasburg in *Reds*

short life in which I once saw that William Faulkner had been a factory caretaker and wrote *As I Lay Dying* between midnight and two a.m. Just one two-hour slog? I thought. It is a short book, and I knew what I was meant to expect of genius.

But Warren has to have money for the rent, the acting classes and the peanut-butter sandwiches. So he does this and that, and maybe there is some money coming from home or even from Shirley. By 1956, she has made *The Trouble with Harry*, *Artists and Models* and *Around the World in Eighty Days*.

It seems a little more interesting that occasionally – it may be no more than once or twice, and even unpaid – he plays cocktail bar lounge piano at Clavins on East 58th Street. He does play; he enjoys jazz. And in all his later work, the aroma or aura of these shabby days in New York City is captured only once, in *Mickey One*, one of his stranger, least known pictures, in which he plays a nerve-racked nightclub entertainer, a comic and a piano player. *Mickey One* is a low life picture about a kid who goes undercover in some unnamed city (a city out of Kafka by Orson Welles) because he thinks the mob, or even the Mob, is after him.

Is it? Who knows. Reality is wondering. In *Mickey One*, Warren is unshaven and dirty. It is a black-and-white film, with a feeling for exotic poverty and human wreckage. But it ends with the camera craning up above a penthouse where Mickey - rehabilitated, cocky again – is hammering out chic jazz, like Erroll Garner in a Concert by the Night. More of the film anon, but it is a window on Beatty's sense of the lustre in performing.

And he contracts hepatitis at this time, and is so sick he has to go home to Arlington to be looked after.

The question of health arises. The young man has made his attempt on fame and been compelled to come home with a serious illness, one that can leave lasting weakness in the organism, and one supposed to accompany reckless and unhygienic living. "You've not taken care of yourself," he is told, and he has to work out a reply about the risk if he is to protect his dangerous ambitions.

He has worked in tunnels and lived in rooms sour from junkies. What happens to a face deprived of sunlight and washed over by junkie atmosphere? What happens to any face that grows old, exposed to the elements of unhappiness and failure in which the face is known only to those who meet you and see you in life? This is the kind of face a mother looks at every day to judge whether the yellow is receding from the eyeballs. It is a face that must look up at the inspection of the mother, whose face "no one" would recognise. Real life, ordinary life, is truly the secret territory for those whose faces are famous.

Suppose he takes a safer line with his life, in real estate or business? Suppose he becomes an unhappy drunk? It would make his face sag or turn scarlet; it would strain the blood vessels, the eyes and the hopes behind the eyes. "I was born tired," Warren's father says, "and every morning I have a relapse." By forty, the hair might recede, the face flabby and the eyes ringed with the stains of depression. Or it would be collapsed from the worry of taxes, children and holding its strained substance and security together. It could be a face like yours or mine, and by forty we are content to have it not much known.

At forty, Warren Beatty will be making *Heaven Can Wait*. When that film opens, it is said how beautiful he is, how well preserved. He plays a Superbowl quarterback and a sweet absent-minded millionaire. This man wins the love of Julie Christie, eats health foods and has his own accidental death corrected by Heaven's bureaucracy. He looks as good as any man of forty can look – ideal or exquisite – while playing out the fantasies of someone only thirty.

By 1977, it will be clearer in how many obvious and subtle ways Warren Beatty has taken care of himself. He has not smoked, drunk or taken drugs. It is not that he has never done these things. But in the context of actors, obsessives and Hollywood people, it is notable how little of them he has done.

His weight does not fluctuate. He has resisted anything like his father's weakness for peanuts. He has not rivalled the Brando, huge with dismay and idleness, likely to be "taken" against his will by scandal-sheet photographers at airports. He has disdained being a Jack Nicholson, prophet of commonness at $4-6 million a movie, prepared to let his lovely gut hang out in view of the camera. It is hard to imagine Warren doing what Robert De Niro did for *Raging Bull*, stuffing himself for the character. Warren would have known that even if that new weight was shed again, the face would never be the same. De Niro may be nearly as thin as he was, but the face cannot recover from the excess and the tiny shifts in bone structure to hold it. Nor can it erase the indignity and the repression in the diet that stays with you and makes you look like a fugitive from the law. What is most special about Beatty's face is still that it is not haunted. It is the face of someone who thinks well of himself, without being a fool.

61

So Warren takes care, and knows he merits the care. Yet few see the strain of such effort. He does not run like Bruce Dern, or jump up and down at basketball games like Jack; he does not ski Redford's slopes, or swim and play tennis like Robert Towne. And on those very few movie occasions when he has to run or fight, he looks like someone embarrassed by the actions, who would prefer not to be seen exerting himself.

He has private ways and tricks. ". . . it's something I got from Warren," says Nicholson, "a trick he learned in English theater. If you're going to be lit for a photograph, you put dark powder here [points to hairline] because it keeps the light from making the hair you do have disappear. There are certain things Warren is just not ashamed about, but I am." Warren is loyal to a movie code from the 30s and 40s, in which the parts were subservient to an actor's glamor.

There are several aspects to this process. The most obvious is to play roles younger than oneself, and have no one remark on the gap. When John Reed died, he was thirty-two; when Warren plays Reed, he is forty-two. Movie lends itself to this by the bold lies of casting, the soft deceits of make-up and lenses, and the simple phenomenon whereby an actor can look back at his films and see himself younger, cheating death.

The next is to be good-looking. This is where physical well-being and thinking well of oneself come together. For in movies, beauty is inseparable from moral worth. It is a form of idealism; we know it is irrational and contrary to life's evidence, but we adhere to it helplessly. We think beauties reach the greatest heights of passion and compassion. We think Garbo's elevated face was the imprint of her fineness. And so Garbo did not play Mother Courage or Baby Jane, and she retired from pictures when this idealism put its greatest test on photography, when she was thirty-six. It tends to happen ten years earlier for women than for men.

Today's movies do not pursue perfection as devotedly as once the medium did. Film has lost primacy and confidence; it is in advertising now we see the richest display of "good-looking". But screen actors still prefer to play "good" characters, those liked by an audience; for they want to be seen in an agreeable light. They cling to the notion that the look is substance – it becomes part of their diet or regime.

Photographs and film have taught us a kind of beauty and goodness that are only photographic. I mean a tone and texture to the skin, a shine in the eyes and mouth, not observed in life. They have to do with light, emulsion and the quality in prints called "glossy". These measures do massage age, but that is a minor effect. The larger achievement is a look that enshrines health, and adds this to the definition of "good-looking" – that it feels good to be seen. Because all photographs are still, this aura lasts. There is a vague hope of averting decay in wanting to look like photos. Glossy prints have a radiance beyond fingerprints or aging, fatigue or infection. Was it into a version of photography that Howard Hughes hoped to escape?

There is a climate and a place in photography we aspire to; it is our mythic kingdom. For the photographed are at a different level of existence, poised, friction-free, alive and unaging. They are seen and imagined but not lived with or in. They are proof against time, preserved in a situation and a pose emblematic of their whole being. Star photos are the stars' hope for themselves. They are the uplifted moment that transcends ordinariness, just as any still has won an edge on death. If you regard death as natural and proper to life, then they represent a peak of health verging on insanity. But they are the most subversive cultural influence in a society far from sure now that death is necessary.

The smallest family snapshot begins to make the life-like more impressive than life. The close-up in a movie drama projected to the height of two or three storeys is so potent it is hard to grasp the discrepancy. Those images have been made by the best film-making skills. None has been passed unless it is free from error . . . or illness. Movies want to get everything right. That means saying the lines correctly, with the intonation that is revelatory. But long before the actor acts, the camera has been cleaned, fresh film has been loaded, the lights have been set and the camera has been put in what must seem the only position. The result is a record of appearance and a piece of the story. But it is also perfection vindicated. Even villains seem resplendent with health; they are right on. The lack of doubt is monstrous.

Most people, given the option, would rather not be photographed. How remarkable then if someone believes his nature deserves this gigantic, broadcast photography. It is not enough to call the confidence "vanity", though there is vanity to the point of delusion in some movie stars. One of the most intriguing implications in Warren Beatty's career is that he persists in being a star, but worries at it, and would therefore often rather not work, not be seen. He is like a man who makes a great quest for treasure, but who has an urge to back away at the threshold – as if he knew the quest was more precious than the jewels and the gold. He seems drawn to find out how long the very famous person can remain invisible. He has a sense – far more profound than his evident talent as a director – that the ultimate force of movies rests in the things unseen.

Of course, in his real life, he does show signs of actual decay or neurosis, the ordinary failures in fineness. One lover who meets him again after several years notices:

"Alas, his college boy looks were becoming slightly crumpled. The eyelids were heavy, the cheekbones mottled. Much of the charm was still there, but the old magic was missing. It looked like Warren had made himself too available: it seemed to me that practically anyone could have him."

That could be spite: Britt Ekland is not what she was herself. But she is not just talking about the audience having Warren come to them, like a dream. And Beatty has not posed for formal still photographs since 1978 and *Heaven Can Wait*. He has rationed his film appearances. No one thinks he is anything but very healthy, yet he handles his reputation with something like the first fear of invalidism. Is this coming closer to Howard Hughes? Is it being so intuitive a magician of well-being that he resembles a witch doctor?

There is an old story about Warren. It has him crossing wires and overhearing a telephone conversation between strangers. He listens as one man tells the other about his symptoms, and what the doctors reckon they amount to.

"No," says Warren. He interrupts; he emerges from the silence. "It's not that, it's — ." And he names another rare illness that his private research has studied. He proves correct. It is magic.

He deserves this story, even if it has no basis in fact. And that is one reason why we can believe nearly anything about the great suggestive faces.

Stand-in

Coming out of the music room and falling into the arms of Clear, D realised the turn his life was taking. He had a huge wish to say, "Let me go home, now." But it would seem craven to burst into tears. Spoiled children cannot run this world. It did occur to D that he might not see home again. How easily one could fall off the carpet. He had been sucked into this sinister party where death was sipped from canapés and wounded sexual eyes.

But Clear was not inconsiderate. He had the remote compassion of an overworked psychiatrist. He sat D down on a sofa so charcoal it was scarcely visible in the twilight.

"D, a wicked game has been played on you. Well, not quite wicked – "

"Oh, it was, it was!"

"My dear, good fellow, do shut up." Clear said it in such an easy way.

D did as he was told and he heard stealthy chuckles in the rest of the party. Was he on show?

"Eyes," said Clear, "is not here. Eyes is often not here. He is there, you see." And he nodded with his head towards some other level of being.

"He is ill?" asked D.

"No, very fit," replied Clear. "He jogs an hour every day and, for a man of his age, well. . . ." He waved a hand in the air, as if reputation was enough. "No, it is the danger. Stars are inviting targets. I daresay you've felt the itch to stone some lustrous vapid face."

"I see the prudence," agreed D: there is a policeman in anyone who lives in fear.

"Moreover, he is an artist."

"I was going to say –"

"And he needs peace. Therefore, we employ Chuck – you met Chuck – as a look-alike, a live-in."

"So if there is an attempt on Eyes' life," D hoped, "this Chuck will get it?"

"No one wishes Chuck less than the best. He takes the risk."

"He is *like* Eyes," D admitted.

"Well," Clear searched for the word, "only like him."

"It's merely a resemblance."

"You felt the difference," Clear reminded him. "Between ourselves, D, he is a bore. It is good for the rest of us; it makes us more appreciative of the real thing."

D could not conceal his further questions.

"You're wondering how much Chuck does? Appearances – he opens malls and charity benefits. He takes young actresses to restaurants and has apparent liaisons at discreet hotels. After months of work we have got him to do a fairly respectable absent-minded routine in this or that lobby with some model on his arm. We do not let him say much, and this restraint meshes intriguingly with Eyes' own. . . . You will like Eyes."

And then, as if to say too much talk was morbid, Clear stood up and did five fast knee-bends. There was no effect of exertion: it was like a tic. "I've not had my squash today," Clear remarked. "I feel the loss immediately. When the body is finely honed, it can notice an ounce of fat on an angel's wing. Who said that? Was it Julia Child or Victoria Principal?"

With that question, Clear whirled and headed for the party. Yet he stopped and held out a white hand at D. "Come, let's mingle. These are your new friends."

The place was becoming crowded, shadows moving to the shuffle of a samba and the aroma of snacks. A spiffy young restaurateur, Stephen, was presiding over the eats, and the three gaunt waiters he employed. Stephen, Clear said, was the group's chef and picnic-man. Whenever there was a gathering he would bring in his latest nouvelle outrages. Tonight he was offering a lamb pâté cut with ginger and served in a vinaigrette of white tomatoes; there was a salad of eleven different leaves in walnut oil with crumbled pieces of old Turkish delight; and a bloody swamp of sun-dried tomatoes – "Tenderised, slightly chillied ears from El Salvador, try them yourself," quipped Stephen.

Stephen had a lacquered head like a barber's mannequin advertising hair-dressing. His baby face moved in and out with snide jokes, and he left the impression of being a cocky eleven-year-old close to ruin. He was bold, undaunted by a discard's future. So he did whatever came into his head and dressed it with crackling devil's patter.

Then there was Doc, a gangling gray-haired figure, who strolled around forbiddingly, a learned amateur in matters of health who, it was said, had polished up or reworked key scenes in just about every interesting movie of the last fifteen years. He had a windswept look and a philosophical gaze: aging swiftly, he might have played the Astrologer in an adventure set in Tibet or Nepal.

And so on . . . writers for the magazines, fashion consultants, agents, lawyers, accountants, automobile repair experts, gunsmiths, tennis professionals, masters of the hunt, gallery owners, dealers, crooks, whores and lyricists, all in the soft gray light where business was done and promises shared over quiche.

D was assaulted by names and brief lives, as Clear led him around, always saying "And this is D, who is going to be very important." At last the circuit ended. Clear had business to attend to. "But I want you to tell us the story of your script. Pitch it for us. It's the nicest way for everyone to know you. Do it after *Network Superstars*." He nodded at another room where the TV's light flared.

And so D withdrew from the rush and smartness. He backed away until he felt the softness of a body at his side. It was Drew. She seemed fully recovered. D would notice here that women had the capacity to restore themselves to a pre-sexual state, groomed and ready, as if nothing had happened and anything could happen like new, for the first time.

"Same shit," said Drew quietly.

"Isn't it?" D agreed. "Are you feeling better?"

"Oh sure."

"How can you be?"

"I'm not, but I say I am. It's what they expect."

"Why do you do this?"

"I want to be in a picture with Eyes." She took the last dead embryo in cilantro aspic on her plate and put it in her mouth. "We're alike, lovebunch. Wouldn't you kill for a break?"

FIRST PARTS

A would-be actor is desperate to have the small opportunities to be other people for money. He inhabits a folk-lore that says if you have real talent you will make it, or that talent is never enough – you need perseverance, the absolute readiness to humiliate yourself, and blind luck. It is out of your control, or it is something that only you can change. You must regard yourself as a helpless leaf or as the wind.

If you have been brought up in an educating household, and if you have dallied with thoughts of a career in law, it is like going over the edge into voodoo and darkness. Rationalism and intelligence do not sit well on actors; in the eyes of casting directors, agents and other actors, they may be taken as marks of coldness, lack of insight, reservation about commitment. Actors live with legendary tales and rumors – that, say, one in a hundred young people who seek the stage will make it; that one in ten thousand hopeful movie-players will ever have their pictures sold to the public; or that it should be one in ten thousand and one in five hundred thousand. You are gambling without any accurate sense of the odds: the mythology says merely that it is impossible. There are drunks, derelicts and the dead to point to, people who had one great review, who seemed poised on the edge of eternity, but who could not go all the way; there are ex-actors selling insurance in Des Moines, working as a mental nurse in North Carolina, or just gone, vanished. If you fail as an actor, you may at least have learned the tricks or picked up the illness that keeps you from being a fixed, findable you. So you dissolve in and out of many different lives and personae and you go missing and roaming, a person without identity but vivid to all who see you pass by and who offer you the chance of a passing performance. People may tell you, "You should have been an actor" as if *you* betrayed the trust, the talent and the arrangement of destiny.

You could drift between bottomless cynicism and demented faith; you might be alienated and superstitious, at a loss as the fierce member of small, intense religious cults. You could be killed, or a killer. You begin to resemble a coin.

If you fall ill, with hepatitis or acute depression, you do not so much blame bacteria or chemical imbalances in the brain; you try to feel out the pressure in the occult scenario that brought you these burdens. So intent on getting into stories, you cannot help but see yourself moving in a stream where fiction is the best version of current. Actors take acting lessons, they may have their noses and their teeth corrected, they may go into analysis. But they read horoscopes, they have their fortunes told, they live for coincidence – and, if it occurs, they wonder whether it is lovely or horrific. They may watch religious shows on television: there is work there, and the message of such shows, the strange pattern of anonymity and celebrity, speaks to the loneliness of their lives. Actors believe in gods, seldom one, but many of them; actors collect horoscopes, like line readings, sure that truth is in the collage. And if you know all your possible star charts, then you may imagine that you can control their real course. "If I know everything this character might do now, then I can decide what he must do." Or, "Knowing all the possibilities, I am helpless in the face of decision." In movie acting there can be an intense hiatus, a depth of being that will not speak, move or decide, where the actor's presence opposes itself to the machinery's need to move forward and says. "Wait. I can suck you in." It is observable in the young Warren Beatty.

Your world cannot make up its mind what it thinks about actors, which in itself supports the dread that the life is dangerous and daft. It has an age-old faith that actors are what they are because they have no real person to be – and the 1950s is a time strong on "real" people. It thinks what actors are paid is ridiculous, a travesty of sensible careers and proper work ethics. It believes that show business is a mess of falsehood and corruption; it assumes that actresses sleep with the system before they sell themselves to the larger public; so in popular fiction, "actor" or "entertainer" are synonyms for whore. Acting and pretending are symptoms of madness; the stable, sleeping world cannot forget that the performance is a lie, no matter that it lives it every night for its dreams. Liars are scoundrels, aren't they?

Yet in the 1950s, for the first time, acting has broken out of the bounds of its business. It is everywhere. There are fewer films being made, but television is devouring American attention and it will provide far more work for actors not just in *its* films and series, but in commercials and in all those interweaving moments and situations when people have to go on the small screen and project. In a few years' time, the American presidency will be won by a man hooked on movie stars and successful (so they say) because he was better on camera. Where do they say it? On television. At last, "good-looking" is taking on a natural, metaphysical depth at a national level. The president will very soon be the person who is photographed to denote certain formal state occasions. The televised press conference will become the central governmental process. A public that once saw a couple of movies a week is well on its way to witnessing, or accepting, a couple of movies' worth of screen time and imagery a night.

Warren Beatty looks for work, for parts, for jobs. He must recognise the likelihood of failure, of being turned down and sent away. Very early on, he elects for himself the posture of one who will not abuse himself, who will not be comically ingratiating, who will not take too much shit. He says to himself that *they* will be lucky to have him. It may be the only way to maintain dignity – or to overcome the terror – in the situation of going for auditions. He will say of his studies with Stella Adler, "She equipped me with a certain amount of arrogance – arrogant self-confidence, I should say – which enabled me to bluff my way through a few sidescrapers." In the next few years, he will earn the reputation as someone likely to walk out on auditions if he dislikes the atmosphere. When one director criticises him for mumbling, Beatty hands back the script and the role without a word. It is a great gamble – if it is all trick; but the situations are so testing that a young actor must believe in the way he is playing. The pride, the difficulty, the aloofness, are heartfelt. They are dignity coming to life.

He gets small parts in television and in local stock. He works on an early morning religious show; he has parts in Studio One and Playhouse 90 for CBS; he plays the lead in *The Curly-Headed Kid* for Kraft Theater and NBC. And there are two New York-area theaters where he plays in repertory: the North Jersey Playhouse in Fort Lee, New Jersey, and the Gateway Theater on Long Island. He has parts in plays of the time – *A Hatful of Rain*, *The Happiest Millionaire*, *Visit to a Small Planet*, *The Boy Friend* and *Compulsion*.

He is acting hard; the work will never be as intense again, if we think simply of the number of roles. This is also the effective end of whatever formal training Warren Beatty has as an actor – which is to say, part of a year at Northwestern and some classes in New York. It is not much, not if one compares what young actors must submit to with the training of musicians, dancers, painters, or even writers. But, of course, in Warren's time there is a way of believing that actors in America function rather less through craft and steady work than by touching their own deepest and most neurotic inspiration. It is in their nature and their liberty that they should not have to submit. This can lead to the modern appraisal that Marlon Brando is a great actor who stays away from the corruption of work.

We do not have to accept that trust in magic, or conclude that Beatty is anything but an able and professional actor like all the others. Still, the thing that he does is something he does rather seldom. By the age of fifty, Warren Beatty will have appeared in some ten plays and in just seventeen films. At the same age, quite apart from many roles in school, in training and in repertory before he was twenty, Laurence Olivier has played in over sixty stage productions and starred in twenty-eight films, three of which he has directed. Cary Grant has made fifty-seven pictures.

Elevator

D detached himself from the party – he was a professional story man, if he ever earned anything, no one people wanted to meet. He felt hideous among the smooth beauties. All he wanted was an empty room, somewhere he might wait until the socialising died down. Solitude was the only answer to mortification. But he could think of nowhere free except the elevator. He was not sure he dared occupy it, with all the risk of being found there, so evidently hiding. Unless he could suggest that elevators were a hobby or a fad, a perversion these people would understand. He decided to work there; wouldn't that be honored? So he took his script and a pen and slipped away towards the elevator.

Barefoot still, he approached so silently he did not disturb Drew who was sitting in the corner of the elevator reading a paperback – *The Eye of the Beholder*, by Marc Behm. He paused to examine her, holding his breath. It was delicious, she did not know she was being watched. Her diligent, sexpot face flickered with the developments in her book. He could see every sentence wriggle, like a snake across a pond.

"Hi," she grunted, never looking up.

"I didn't mean to disturb you," said D.

"Looking for a hideout?"

"Well," he didn't want to offend, "this isn't quite my sort of thing."

"You'll fall in that well," said Drew, gloomily.

"What?" He saw a figure falling down an empty elevator shaft.

"Don't worry. I don't mind it. I kind of like it."

"What are you talking about?"

"Saying 'well' before you say something. It's like a doorway, something you're behind."

"It's just that I don't know what I should say."

"You'd rather say nothing."

"Sometimes." He couldn't tell if this dialogue was gaining momentum, or she was teasing him.

72

"Rather be writing scenes."

He shrugged, he did smile, he was blushing, "Well –"

Drew laughed and D felt the warmth.

"You look very beautiful here, on your own," he whispered. "I spoiled it for you."

"Certainly did not. Who knows I look good if you don't come by?" she asked him. "That's the problem," she added.

"What problem?"

"Being alone but being seen. That's the trick. That's what Eyes is so damn good at." She assumed it was all clear to him, and he didn't want to seem stupid. "Won't you come in?" Her small hand patted the floor beside her.

D felt he was getting into much more than an innocent elevator – not that he trusted that one's simplicity. But he went in, and Drew pressed the doors shut.

"You want to ride?" she asked.

He grinned in agreement; it all seemed so playful. They sat in opposite corners, their toes close but not touching. He saw that hers were bent and smudged.

"You see, writers," she told him, "they're always thinking pictures and story and construction and character motivation and dialogue that fits together. The whole dramatic thing. Right? I'm not saying that's not important. You have to have it. But it's not all. You know what actors like? They like scenes like 'She is alone with the camera'. Now if the writer writes that he feels like a jerk. Right? What does that mean? So he writes a whole lot of extra stuff about what she's thinking. But the actress really gets off if the script just says, 'Alone with the camera.' She loves it. So she just prowls around her room, lazy but loose, lights a cigarette maybe, straightens an ornament. She's doing nothing whatsoever for the story. She's like the music and the light. No lines, no interaction. Yummy! It's immense, total. And audiences love it. They just float on it, watching the beast up there on the screen. It's the most erotic thing. I wouldn't even have to do any flesh. I just let the camera see me, and I don't know it's there. You know, D, if I had one good scene like that, a minute, thirty seconds, I could make the world fall in love with me." The shine on her eyes left no doubt about her capacity for so much admiration.

"Oh, yes," D breathed. He could see it, better than he usually saw anything, as if he had been given new glasses that made him younger and more hopeful. She was captivating. He was already envisaging a whole

73

film about her, a meditative epic in which she met not another soul, had no need of any, with her own sleek surface to buff, an egg or an orange to eat and a book to be stirred by. She could sing beneath her breath, and audience hearts would fly up to the illusion of her skin, like sparrows going after bread. Well, D gave in, it looks like I'm in love.

"Of course," Drew laughed, "there's maybe ten million girls in the US who could do it, too. And you'd fall for all of them."

"Oh, no," said D, "not nearly so many."

"You in love with me?" she asked, and then before he could begin, "Don't say 'well'."

So he said nothing. However astute her analysis, this strategy had not occurred to him before. It gave him a strange sensation, as of shedding gravity or his body. But it seemed to work.

"Bet you are," she probed. "I just bet you are. I can tell. Oh, you're wicked." She was grinning; she had seen what he was up to. "You really not going to talk?" It irked her and made her move for him. She was no longer poised in her corner, confident about letting his gaze wander over her. She looked at him, and looked away, trying to hook and scramble his concentration. Her knees came up, and then slipped sideways as she shifted her position. It was a test of wills, and she had become a plucky girl, ready to cry with frustration or peal with laughter at the heady game.

"Tell you what," she said, "I'll do something I've never done before. I mean it. I'll tell you a story about my life. And it's a great story. I just need someone to write it, to *see* it properly, and put it down on paper. Then I could play it. All right? I'll tell you." Her voice dropped and her eyes swung away to the corner of the elevator – bright and empty. "You'll be the only one who knows."

The elevator stopped. "Why, there, you see," she was not surprised. "It heard me."

"Where are we?" said D. His alarm always let him down.

"Oh, you spoke!" Drew was petulant, but she was pleased not to be thwarted any more. She came across the floor on her knees and put herself between D's legs. She fitted so easily, like a letter put in a book. "There," she said, looking at him. "Oh, and there," she remembered, seeing something within the fold of his black robe. "You are awful," she warned him, as if he was invading her. Or telling dreadful things about her.

"Your life story," he said, trying to distract her.

"Oh, yeah. Some other time."

74

"You said —"

"So." She was insolence. "That was to get you talking. Now you're talking. Love me?"

"When did you meet Eyes?"

Her hand had been penetrating the robe, but it stopped. She considered his question and all the ways of answering it. "I don't usually talk about him," she said. She was disappointed.

"But he must be an important part of your story," D told her.

"Oh, you think so?".

"I daresay he made you lovable," D suggested.

It went home. He saw her appreciate that he was more than she had reckoned on, a stooge maybe, but someone who could see. "That's real smart," she said. "And it's right. Know how he saw me? I was kidnaped up in New Hampshire. Yes, I was. That's where I came from. This creep up there he went crazy one winter and took me off to his cabin. He was a packer at the IGA."

"Against your will?" D asked.

"In a way. Yeah, it was really."

"But not quite?" He was trying to be adult about it.

She looked at him and rolled her eyes. She seemed to say, guess, sucker, to suggest that maybe she and this madman had had some bizarre thing together and what a fox D was to work it out. But D wasn't sure she had not been carried off, raped, whatever, but only now made the incident more vague, more suggestive, for his benefit and her own sense of story.

"Well," she decided, "I was rescued after a while. And there were police and everything up at his cabin, and there was TV – not that I saw it then – what are you looking at?"

"At nothing." He kept his face straight.

"Oh, you cheat, you slut," she murmured. "Anyway, there was coverage. I was national. And Eyes saw it. There was this shot of me being pulled both ways, by the guy and by a cop. That cop was hot for me, I'll tell you. And Eyes said the look on my face stopped what he was doing." She grinned. "I don't know *what* he was doing."

"You never saw this shot?"

"Yeah, I saw it. Later."

"And?"

"I don't know. It was OK." She thought about him. "You want me here, D? Now?"

"What did Eyes do?" D did not answer her question, but he got up and

75

while she started to answer, he merely urged Drew onto her back on the floor. She never altered what she had to say.

"He called me and said I should come and see him. If I wanted. Because he'd been so impressed, you know."

D put his hand inside her clothes. She had changed again, but it hardly mattered what she was wearing. The clothes were just clues or signs to follow. He found his way between her legs, and she was moist already, sure all along that he would get there.

"So I went down to New York city on the bus," she was telling him, but her eyes were already reacting to where his hand was. "He wouldn't send me a plane ticket. Get that. I went to his hotel. Oh yeah, and you know what, on the telephone I had talked to him and we'd made a date and I was so nervous I said, 'How will I know you?'" She laughed out loud; the floor hummed with her mirth. "And he loved that. He said he thought it was the wittiest thing he'd ever heard. You listening?"

D was looking directly into her face. But he had his whole hand in, the fingers moving as if she were a ball in there that he was deciding how to throw. And the back of his hand rode against her so that she breathed quicker and was becoming slowly thrilled and shuddery as if the torture could not be escaped.

"And he, he said I had a skin so white. It shone. From the winters."

"Your skin is still very white," D told her.

"Yeah?" She was anxious for it all to be true. "And I became his lover and he made me feel so good about myself. I never had. For all of February."

"But he never put you in the picture."

Furious, she shook her desperate head. "Not yet. Get in me. I want you. Don't you want to?" He saw her mind accelerate. "You can tell yourself it's somewhere Eyes has been before you. Don't you want to be there?"

And D knew he did, and would be, and though the elevator suddenly resumed its progress, he knew not even that would deter him.

"Can you really write?" she hissed in his ear.

But he chose again to answer her without talking, and he rocked her to the timing of her gentle, stricken cries there in the stuffy space of the lightly rising elevator.

DISCOVERED

Discovery is a vital moment in the self-sustaining ritual of show business. It enables everyone involved to believe that they are involved with magic and excitement. If the world is seething with those ready to be discovered, then boredom is staved off. And if all those participating can believe in the fact of talent, its mystery and its fateful manifestation, then it becomes rather easier to live with and overlook the mass of hard work, sacrifice, corruption and mere chance that also goes into the making of stars. After all, if you are a member of a religion, you want to believe in our ability to recognise the god. One of the benefits of divinity is that the gods carry the responsibility: if we don't notice them, then that is part of their design. We don't have to realise that we are stupid. Show business would be harder than it is to endure if you believed that quantities of talent missed the net, smashed up on the rocks and just went unnoticed. Stars have to believe they deserve their stardom, and the business clings to the divine right of true stars. Otherwise the shit is also a bagatelle, and perhaps unforgivable. Whatever happens then, is divine and designed: if fools and monsters thrive, and fine young people kill themselves . . . that's show business.

You may do nothing, or you can try to manipulate every last taxi ride and telepone call – it does not matter, profoundly, because discovery depends upon some higher, deeper purpose. You may be resigned, or you may be the most fearsomely ambitious creature anyone can remember – still, discovery absolves you from your own way towards the light. You may be infinitely ruthless and calculating, and still think you did nothing. In the end it is easier to think you are blessed than talented. For talent is a matter of skill, sensibility and unending pursuit. It is a good that might be lost. If you trusted talent, you might end up hopelessly anxious and neurotic. But if you think you are blessed, then "it" does not go, and does not involve your unceasing effort. You have only to be saved. Anxiety may be replaced by madness: it is the difference between being Marilyn Monroe and Norma Desmond. And whereas a Monroe must have known how easily she might have been missed, and lived with the daily fear of being dumped, a Norma Desmond knows no luck or gratitude.

Warren Beatty is discovered twice at once. Two people see him in the same small part in *Compulsion* at Fort Lee and are moved to action. For it is just as moving to discover as it is to be discovered. It is another heartfelt part of show business mythology to know when your robe has been touched, to look into mid-West beauty contests, chorus lines, summer stock or casting photographs and say "that one". It is another way of wanting to be magical to aspire to magical insight. And the business is thrilled by stories of discovery, not just for the unknown, but for the director or producer whose vision crystallises in the nick of time. God needs to be identified, too.

We know Josef von Sternberg as the man who found Marlene Dietrich for *The Blue Angel*. We remember the story how in the early days of shooting *Gone With the Wind*, David Selznick turns away from the lurid lights of his burning Atlanta and is introduced to Vivien Leigh. In the Cukor *A Star is Born*, James Mason goes in search of a singer who rescued him at the premiere and finds her after hours in a club, singing "The Man That Got Away". He knows, and his life is going to be saved for love and purpose. It is the moment in thousands of movies and perfume ads when he or she stops and notices he or she and the cutting and the music sigh with rapture or "I want to fuck you". The movies, more than all the rest of show business, believe in magic noticing. And he who notices is given bliss, power and a kind of parenthood in picking out the new wonder. It is a very erotic siezure, even if the two people on either side of fate's margins do not couple.

Joshua Logan notices Warren Beatty. He is a director and a producer, a man of fifty-one in 1959, who started in pictures in the 1930s, then moved to Broadway and directed the original productions of *Annie Get Your Gun*, *Mister Roberts*, *South Pacific* and *Picnic*. Then in the mid-1950s he had gone back to movies and directed *Picnic*, *Bus Stop*, *Sayonara* and *South Pacific*. It is notable that in the movie of *Picnic*, he has "discovered" Susan Strasberg and given Kim Novak an opportunity denied her in her earlier work; and in *Bus Stop*, he has so earned Monroe's confidence and recognised her strength that the picture will survive as one of her best. Logan is a writer and a master of big shows, but his work shines with affection for players.

In Fort Lee, he wonders if Beatty could be right for a new project he is supposed to make for Warners, a picture called *Parrish*. "I sent for him. He was all a director could hope for: tall, humorous, extremely male. He even sat down at the piano and played and sang. His name was Warren Beatty, and I decided to use him though he had never been on the screen before."

Logan had Beatty fly to Los Angeles where he screen-tested him with another newcomer whom he had thought of using in *Parrish*, Jane Fonda. It is impossible now to think of those two, both graced by family connections, on the wrong side of success, caught in the same waiting room. We can only imagine them as stars pretending to be ingenues. The story is that they kissed in their screen test and could not be stopped, or awakened, by repeated calls of "Cut!". Why not? They wanted to be remembered, noticed. You may not do just as you are told if you are desperate to be remembered. You may change your lines, pause until the camera comes back to wait for you. The two of you may say to one another, "let's show them", or one of you may plan to surprise and ravish the other. Perhaps they both surprised each other, and went off afterwards in laughter and in love. There is eroticism left over in filming, not least in tests, for it to change the real lives of actors. But people talked – the crew perhaps, crusty, unsentimental types who know it is their duty to propagate that very sentimental mode of rumor, legend.

But *Parrish* doesn't happen. Warren Beatty's first movie is one he will not make. When the script of the film arrives, Logan does not like it. He asks Warners to reassign it. It is made by Delmer Daves who casts his hot discovery Troy (*A Summer Place*) Donahue in it. That picture opens in 1961, and it begins to suggest that Donahue's discovery has been an error. For the business believes that it can disappear people as easily as it can discover them: if they will let that happen, if their magic is not strong enough.

Instead, Logan agrees to make a movie of *Tall Story*, about a college basketball star and a cheer leader. He sees Jane Fonda as the female lead and he thinks of using Warren Beatty opposite her. But Logan's short-term personal contract with the actor had lapsed, and he was persuaded to cast Anthony Perkins in the role instead. This does not work out perfectly, for Perkins persuades Logan to let him and Fonda rehearse the love scene alone.

"They worked very hard," Logan writes later, "devotedly in fact, on their intimate scenes. When they showed them to me they were strangely slow and full of pregnant pauses, but apart from that quite attractive, so I filmed them as rehearsed. Unfortunately, when cut into the picture they were endless and, I think, hurt the picture almost more than the charm of the two people in those scenes helped it."

Tall Story is at least the second picture Beatty does not make. "At least" because he spends a few weeks in Hollywood, long enough to inspire a five-year contract offer from MGM starting at $400 a week, and long enough, no doubt, for him to be surefire casting for this movie over dinner, or that movie over the weekend. "Discovering" does not wait for divinity. There are just as many matchmakers as there are suitors. Beatty will discover that there may be twenty projects talked about and believed in for any one made. The amazing possibilities of sweet deals are always circulating. To be in the city is to be a piece that might be fitted into any of them. To this day, Beatty's aura and reputation are just as much those of a piece as they are those of a maker of films.

MGM has a first picture to go with their contract offer – *Strike Heaven in the Face* it's called, the last great 30s title of the 1950s. He turned it down and got out of the enclosing contract. He went back to New York, too smart to see his "big break" or already a better reader of real opportunity than most people in the city. For someone else had noticed him in *Compulsion*, the playwright William Inge.

Ham and cheese

Chuck was sitting on the floor in front of the television, eating cream of wheat. He turned to look at them as Drew led D into the room. The party was listless and broken, here and there around the suite. The night was complete now, a black-brown cloth like Guinness with a sparkling head of traffic and night trade. D traced the lines of the streets until they vanished. He imagined C putting together the humble evening meal, wondering where he was. He wanted to wave and say, "Don't worry, I'm here." And he imagined her amazed, foreboding "There!"

"Hey, buddy, don't jump," said Chuck.

"Oh, I had no intention –"

"Plate glass. You'd just bounce off." Chuck snorted to think of the wasted energy. "Not ordinary glass. New stuff. They tested it. Got a kamikaze plane to hit the window. Wham!" His hand described a rebounding arc. "Just caromed off, like a little bee. It was on *Real People* when they built this building."

"Did you keep bees?" D asked.

Chuck's face fell half an inch, or rather the clench of eagerness slipped from perplexity. He seemed shorter.

D tried to be conciliatory: "I wondered if as a boy perhaps you had a hive."

Drew was crouched by the television, in a lotus position, "He's just asking if you kept bees, you jerk, back in De-troit City."

"Shit, no," said Chuck, aghast at where small talk could go. "They sting. What do I want with 'em?"

"Honey is super virile," suggested Drew. "And that Queen Bee jelly, oooh," she shivered thinking of it.

"Yeah?" said Chuck, and he turned to D, "You a diet doctor?"

"D is a writer, Chuck," Drew enjoyed explaining. "He has done a new script, which I hear Eyes is crazy for."

"Isn't he always? That guy uses scripts like toilet rolls."

81

"This is a special script" She was guiding him along, like a mother making sure he finished his dinner. "Doc has been looking at it already."

Chuck grunted. He was impressed. It was an early mark of trust in a project if it had sicknesses enough for Doc's attention.

D was just as surprised, and more alarmed, but Drew had a quick private smile for him, "Don't worry. It's a good sign," she said.

"Wouldn't it be something to be working again?" sighed Chuck.

"Everyone's excited," said Drew.

"Training all the time's brutal for the body." Chuck had his problems.

"Oh sure," said Drew. "All foreplay and no coming gets you muscle-bound."

"Kid!" scoffed Chuck, and he threw a playful hook at her jaw. D winced for her, but it was an old routine and she knew how to ride the haymaker. "You're all right," he told her.

"Thanks Chuck." It was a sweet answer, without irony. As D would learn, remarks there drifted into the air like chlorine in a pool without the cultural guarantee of being heard.

"Listen, D," said Chuck a moment later. "You want to watch some TV with me?" It was something he had been planning, a way of getting to know an important writer better. D was nervous enough from the strain of this new world to swim in the lines a little. Chuck gathered arms of cushions and the two men stretched out in the light of the screen.

There were two shows Chuck was watching, and he went from one to the other with a proven instinct, seldom missing big moments and managing a rhythm, like that of a large yacht in a heavy swell, that was invigorating without being frightening. The shows were *Family Feud* and *Network Superstars*.

In the one, a Mexican family from San Diego was competing with a Swedish family from Solvang, and the crisp-haired Richard Dawson was giving them just three seconds to say what things a husband and wife do simultaneously. A hot pepper seventeen-year-old daughter had X'd out on a giggly "Kiss?" and Lars, the cousin from the old country, whose sandpaper face was tuned pale cherry on the Sylvania, got all the money with "They sleep, I tink, Richard."

And in the other, at a sun-drenched college track, there was a steeplechase in progress in which men raced with women on their backs. D noticed Doc Severinsen, hardly able to toot beneath the soft statue, Loni Anderson; Jim Palmer and Mary Lou Retton; William Shatner, puffing a mite but dignified in conversation beneath Dr Joyce Brothers, her thighs gripping his jowls in approved Eastern-taught riding style;

82

and Carl Lewis, with Brooke Shields up. Al Michaels (on a ride-along camera car) was interviewing the contestants as they plunged through the water jump.

"Make one of these shows," said Chuck. "Boy, that's it!"

"The rewards?" D surmised.

"Unbe-fucking-lievable. You've got a prize for this meet, has to be two mill. Then there's the play-offs, and the endorsements. And the winning couple get a series." Chuck whistled at the way a few sportsmen had it soft.

"So, anyway, D," Chuck began, "this scripteroo . . .? The real thing, huh?"

"Well. . . ."

"All the signs are good, I hear."

"You hear that, too?"

"What she, what Drew just said."

"Ah," D was feeling his way. "And if it's done, that will be good for you?"

It was obvious to Chuck. "Gets me visibility. The stunts, the stand-in stuff. Eyes doesn't take no risks, now."

"Of course not," said D. Just the bits alone with the camera, so peaceful and so insurable.

"I have told them all – Clear and the high command – we should take some of the action pictures. Those offers don't go on forever. Eyes takes his time, that's OK, that's his thing, but we get offers it's dumb to turn down. It's spitting at money. A lot of action pictures, they could send me out and who knows?"

"The audience would think it was Eyes?"

"Right. Adventure pix, they're heavy into long shots, anyway. What is so hard for Eyes' integrity we pick up some cash and give people a good time?"

"Those films are popular," D admitted.

"It would broaden Eyes' appeal. And the exercise would be good for him."

"But," said D, "you would be doing it."

Chuck wasn't deterred. "Oh, right. Anyway, why not? I'm off four weeks, no more. No sweat. Eyes has to take some of his ass out to eat at Michael's, Spago, wherever, himself."

"You often do that for him?"

"Do I? It's freaking my body."

"Too much rich food," D could imagine.

"And all at once. Secret is, little and often. You have to break your slavery to the meal. I dip. I keep a bag of nuts and dried tomatoes with me. And sitting down when you eat is worst. You ever think what is occurring in the lower intestine and the colon when you sit down?"

Whereupon, Chuck stood up and started running on the spot. One of Stephen's young fauns had just entered with a tray of canapés. Since this was not a full meal – and was plainly little things coming around often – Chuck took a miniature kiwi quiche with a slice of foie gras on it, a pasta horn filled with red caviar and a piece of marinated raw goat flesh.

"Don't you want something?" Drew asked D. She gave the impression of being anxious about his strength. "What would you like?"

"Well . . . do you think a ham and cheese sandwich?" D hadn't had one for years.

"You have to be kidding," drawled Flex, their waiter.

"You don't have it?" D was unhappy to make trouble.

"They can make one," said Drew, defiant.

"Would you like that with a, with a pickle?" asked Flex, not bothering to hide his amusement.

"Could I?" D wondered, and Drew kissed him on the cheek.

Flex went away, churlish and subservient, and then Clear came into the room with all the pleasure of reunion after many a long year. He embraced them all, but kept his best hugs for D, who saw Drew's smile as he was held tight against Clear's fine cold-stone ear.

"It's nearly time for your story," said Clear.

"Have many read the script already?"

"Very few," Clear promised. "Think of us all as virgins. It's more lively that way. Just take charge of us. Put us in the palm of your hand."

Flex reappeared, carrying a silver tray. On the tray was a folded white napkin, on the napkin a plate, on the plate a sandwich, and on the bread, still damp, a pickle.

"Ham and cheese," said Flex in a sultry way, "on rye. I held the mayo. Until it wept."

D thanked him and took the plate. He picked up the sandwich and brought it to his mouth. Then he caught the old wolfen scent of Drew's sex, like rich land where water must lie, or was it bodies buried in the woods? The smell was so close to life and death.

"What's the matter, old chap?" Clear saw any hesitation.

"Oh, déjà vu," said D. And he bit into the several textures, tearing at the ham, his eyes watering from the Dijon mustard, his nose in ecstasy at the hard, dry decadent tang of the Swiss. It was the best sandwich he'd ever had.

What a whirl! The picture business! Here was D, hours only away from dingy home, eating a rare sandwich and remembering the stealthy musk of his lover's cum, about to pitch his own story to a round table of Hollywood excellence. He let the mustard excuse his tears, and saw the fluctuating Drew coming up to him and kissing him. She couldn't get enough.

"There," she said soothingly. "There, there."

It did seem as if he was there at last. Now all he had to handle was the being here, too.

LOSS OF ROSES

KENNY: I want *you*, Lila. I can *talk* with you and feel at home with you.

LILA: Kenny, you don't mean those things you're saying. You shouldn't talk like that to a woman if you don't mean it. Things like that excite a woman, so much more'n you know. They raise her hopes, and then, when you don't mean them, those hopes have to fall again. That's happened to me, Kenny. It's happened to me several times. And each time, I think I'm gonna die. I even *pray* to die. Don't tease me, Kenny.

KENNY (*Believing himself completely*.): Lila, I never talked this way to anyone in my life.

— William Inge, *A Loss of Roses*, Act 2, Scene 1.

William Inge is forty-six in 1959. He is from Independence, Kansas, where he has acted in college plays and summer stock. This settled, provincial world, and the effect of loving, smothering families, is the material of plays that change his life after the end of the Second World War. He goes from being a teacher at Iowa State College to arts critic on the *St Louis Star-Times* to successful Broadway playwright. He differs from Tennessee Williams and Arthur Miller in being closer to the American heartland and to that point where small-town romanticism takes fire with Freudian insight into the parent-child relationship and the perennial struggle between stability and adventure.

He writes *Farther Off from Heaven* in 1947 (which is filmed in 1960 as *The Dark at the Top of the Stairs*); *Come Back, Little Sheba* in 1950; *Picnic* in 1953; and *Bus Stop* in 1955. Their terrain is Kansas, Oklahoma, and the period is often set back a little from the present, out of nostalgia and the need to explain how a middle-aged man feels now. An abiding theme is the longing to get away, to fall in love, to take a risk and escape the sober, sedate mid-West upbringing. The plays are poignant studies of happiness missed because of ordinary failures and everyday insecurities. The Beaty household in Virginia in the 1940s would have been ideal Inge material. This is not said casually: Beatty moves and inspires Inge, and Inge more than anyone helps launch the young man on a transforming career. And even if Warren will become a cosmopolitan hotel-dweller, he never shakes off the wholesomeness or the bourgeois politeness that speaks of the influence of Home. No Inge play quite realises it, but when his characters do break away they begin to remake the kind of life that was so recently suffocating. In revolution, they lose their edge. The John Reed of *Reds*, twenty years ahead, is an Inge character. Beatty, after all, grew up in the 1950s, and we never escape the dramatic atmosphere of our own initiation.

At the end of that decade, Inge is hot as a writer. It is an odd state of glamor which moves the rather depressive, kindly Kansan more than he can say or show in his life. He has a Pulitzer for playwriting; his plays have made successful movies – *Picnic*, *Bus Stop* and *Come Back, Little Sheba*. In early 1959, Inge is writing a movie original (his first), which will become *Splendor in the Grass*. Beatty is one of several young actors talked about for its male lead.

Splendor is being developed by Inge and Elia Kazan, who in 1957 has directed *The Dark at the Top of the Stairs* on the New York stage. The two men become friendly and want to work together again. Inge tells Kazan a number of possible stories and Kazan picks one that comes from Inge's own life. But the picture is postponed because Kazan is busy with the Broadway production of *Sweet Bird of Youth* and another movie, *Wild River*.

But Inge has seen and been impressed by Beatty, and when the actor returns to New York after his first period in Hollywood, the playwright backs him for the role of Kenny Baird in his new play, *A Loss of Roses*. It is set in a small town outside Kansas City in 1933. Kenny, aged twenty-one, lives with his mother Helen in a modest but cosy bungalow. Kenny is written to be "a nice-looking boy who wears a mysterious look of misgiving on his face, as though he bears some secret resentment that he has never divulged, that he has perhaps never admitted to his consciousness." The father has been dead for years: Kenneth Sr drowned, saving Kenny in a swollen river.

The Bairds are comfortable together – Kenny is willing to be mothered for ever. He is turning into a lazy, dishonest lout, ready to live at home and be spoiled. Helen has no other life, except for the Church. But the play seeks to touch on a buried level of love – Helen has gone cold after her husband's death, and she and Kenny are living in peaceful ignorance of how far they have become unadmitted sexual figures for each other.

Then Lila comes to the house. She is in her early thirties, "a small-time tent-show actress," who was once so friendly with the Bairds that Kenny called her "Aunt". Helen decides to take her in until she can get a job again. In fact, Lila is a failure, someone who is never going to be discovered, who has had breakdowns and who is close to making the shift from show business to prostitution. She is the catalyst in the action: she sleeps with Kenny, even dreams of marrying him. Then she moves on, fatalistically, to a sex show. But the action has been enough to make Kenny leave home, too.

The play proves to be Inge's first great flop; and it is a production marred by disputes in which Beatty exercises a power quite unexpected in someone making his Broadway debut. The play no longer reads well. It seems both over-obvious and too discreet, as if stagecraft was covering up the depths possible in the mother-son relationship. Indeed, there is another, avoided, play close at hand, in which Kenny might sleep with Helen. But a pall of decency hangs over the dangerous prospects. Even so, when the play is published, in 1960, Inge says in the Foreword, "I have never gone into a production with a play in which I had such complete confidence."

The director is Daniel Mann, who has directed both the stage and the screen versions of *Come Back, Little Sheba* and *The Rose Tattoo*. To play Helen, Shirley Booth is cast, the star of *Sheba* and of another film directed by Mann, *About Mrs Leslie*. In addition, Mann has directed the movies of *I'll Cry Tomorrow*, *Teahouse of the August Moon* and *Hot Spell*, the cast of which includes Shirley MacLaine. The part of Lila is given to Carol Haney, who has become famous with the "Steam Heat" number in *The Pajama Game*, and whose broken ankle has afforded a big chance to MacLaine. *A Loss of Roses* is Haney's opportunity to play a big dramatic part, though no one could call her "an extraordinarily beautiful woman of thirty-two, blond and voluptuous" as described in the play. She is not the last actress who may feel daunted by the looks of her romantic partner when playing with Beatty.

A Loss of Roses has textual difficulties. Inge, as he admits, is prevailed upon to do a lot of rewriting, even to the point of making the play's climax Kenny's decision to leave home, rather than Lila's crestfallen but brave acceptance of a career in polite pornography. "I can't remember why all the changes were thought necessary," Inge writes in 1960, "but working under the pressure that exists in the theater today, people become excited and mistrust their best instincts."

The great crisis occurs after a week's try-out in Washington D.C. – at the very theater where Beatty has been hired to watch for rats – when Shirley Booth quits the production. This may be because she is unhappy with her part and with the play as a whole, but she is also troubled by the influence exerted by Warren Beatty.

Beatty and Mann are not getting on, which does not mean a lack of communication so much as persistent attempts by Beatty to stop to discuss every detail. There are stories, too, that he is coming to rehearsal late and then questioning everything possible about the play and its direction. This could be wilful sabotage; it could be the decision to impose himself at all costs, or to impress Joan Collins, often a visitor at rehearsals; and it could be chronic indecision in need of more support and conference than anyone else is disposed to provide. Mann is taken aback by his arrogance and vanity: "I have to say that Warren was one of the few problems I've had in a forty-year career, and I've directed actors like Anna Magnani, Marlon Brando, Vanessa Redgrave, Susan Hayward and Elizabeth Taylor."

Mann keeps Beatty's understudy, Dennis Cooney, in rehearsal too, and entertains the thought of firing Warren. But Beatty has Inge as his warmest defender, and Inge is not only the author. He has put $100,000 of his own money in the production. When Booth walks out, she is replaced with Betty Field, and Inge undertakes rewriting that builds up the role of Lila and plays down that of Helen. Mann says, "Warren won't listen to me, he's going to do nothing until opening night and then he'll play on the sex appeal and charm and all the crap and do something on-stage we don't even *know* about."

Apparently, Beatty will not settle into a way of playing the part that other actors can depend on. He is improvising, or – without the inspiration – shifting, hesitating, brooding, letting his doubts take over the production, like Dean drawing a scene into himself in *East of Eden*, treating a theater as if it were a camera.

A few months later, Inge tries to defend Beatty:

"Warren is really kind of like a young colt who's out in a new green pasture. He's nervous about making a picture and it brings out a most self-protective quality. As a result, he's very reluctant to trust people in charge. He has the feeling he has to design the set, the costumes, the make-up, and sometimes you want to say, 'Oh, shut up and do your part.' But he's basically a very fine kid who will eventually learn a way of working with people."

Inge does go on to publish a "restored" version of *A Loss of Roses*. But if he ever feels unduly influenced by Beatty, he never turns on him. There are two more collaborations ahead, and two roles that are undoubtedly enriched by Inge's chance to observe the actor. Still, a few days before Broadway opening – at the Eugene O'Neill Theater on November 28, 1959 – Inge knows *A Loss of Roses* "was not happening on stage".

It closes after twenty-five performances and an opening night on which, according to another actor in the production, "Warren changed lines, business, blocking, and completely screwed up Carol Haney so badly that she ran into her dressing-room in tears".

There's no reason to think Beatty knows this will be his final stage appearance, late in 1959. (Even now, in 1986, we cannot rule out a return to theater – though we may bet against it.) *A Loss of Roses* is a tumultuous experience, but he may not notice that or regard it as a cause for regret. If he does not trust, he may not sympathise. At the same time, it is a career failure, despite his own good notices, and a failure that owes something to the shortcomings of the play. And it is a play about lost hopes and social fear. When a movie is made from the play a few years later – *The Stripper*, with Richard Beymer and Joanne Woodward, the first film directed by Franklin Schaffner – it is not a good film, but it is about sex. It is possible that, on the stage, Beatty feels himself labouring with Inge's evasions, with the plodding uncovering of unsurprising things and with an actress he is not attracted to. Perhaps he is not excited, and cannot pretend arousal, no matter that Kenneth Tynan, writing in the *New Yorker*, can see that he is "sensual around the lips and pensive around the brow".

Does that face think the world must come closer and doubt be made a part of the material? He is an actor who prefers to be invaded by the perplexity of a moment, and this is something the camera delights in. It fosters the skin's worry about what to say, the eyes' uncertainty; and it is close enough to hear sighs and breathing, not just the script you have to learn – as if anyone in life, Warren says, *knows* the lines. Yet such a doubting actor is a tyrant too, not just determined to have his way, but incapable of bending to the necessity of collaboration, performance and giving to order that constitutes theater. For on the stage, the actor is servant to the play and the public – it is not him on show but his pretending. But in the movies, it is all him.

Tusk & Zale

D would never have guessed the ritual with which these major motion picture people regarded his script. For him it was a recent labor in which he hoped the regular pages, the carefully checked typing and the complex lay-out were compelling without being distastefully anal. There are so many things that can be wrong in a script – the numbering of the scenes, the use of capitals for every character, the consistent indentation of dialogue, not to mention the proper use of technical terms and the leanness whereby 120 pages can be scanned in thirty minutes without loss.

A writer is intent on correctness, on eliminating errors, typos and blemishes in his paper. The bound block of pages must be without guilt. It is mortification to have someone show you a "freind" on page fifty-six, or a "MICHA@L" at the point of climax.

But here, at the apogee of the movie pyramid, D was expected to tell the story to some faces he recognised from the celebrity press, and others full of sultry spite or lavish innocence current in fashion and fitness imagery. He had kept to himself his bewilderment at how Clear had cognisance of the script. D concluded that the Eyes' organization had access to the computer xerography he had employed to make copies of his script. But with the load of scripts being prepared in the city – D had heard as high as 77,000 a day – no human reader could have picked his out. No, Clear's computer must have seen his script's absolute correctness, been triggered by its title and passed that on for eyes which noticed the desirable male lead factor. Of course, D had used the approved system of color coding – red for violence, blue for talk, silver for motion and white for nakedness. Clear might have seen an intricate print-out – an emotional map, or a wave involvement profile – but he had probably not read it.

Such thoughts were soon confirmed. For Clear took D aside into a smaller and noise-reduced room that had no windows. There was a

John Gutmann, *Cynics, Hollywood*, 1944

severe and exquisite white table in the middle of the room at which two men sat in sharkskin suits, vests and ties. Clear introduced them as Zale and Tusk, lawyers to Eyes Enterprises. They greeted D slavishly, and had him sit facing them. There were no papers, no cases, no folders, no phones on the table. Business here was as ideological as torture.

"D," said Clear, "a *petit* formality."

"A dull preliminary," added Tusk, while Zale studied the corners of the ceiling. As his partner's attention slowly sank, Tusk teased, "You're not going to be difficult?"

"Certainly not," D assured them.

"Because you have a lot to gain here," Zale said.

"Exactly," Tusk noted, "and we only need you to sign an agreement that we and all members of Eyes Enterprises have not seen your script . . . what's it called? My head is jello, today."

"*The Center of Attention*," supplied Clear. "Such a good title."

"You think so?" asked Zale.

"Don't you?" Clear asked.

Zale considered. "Seems cold to me. Of course, my wife's the title man. She knows as soon as she hears them. She writes titles, you know. Likes to have something to do in the day."

"It's the only way," said Tusk, "otherwise the bitches start fucking the gardener, the plumber, the chimney-sweep —"

"You have chimneys still in Brentwood?" Clear wanted to know.

"Just for decor," Tusk told him. "But if you've got 'em, clean 'em, is what I say."

"You want I should call my wife?" Zale asked. "She was the one who did *A Virtuoso Personality* and *Everything That Goes With a Kiss*."

"I don't know those," said wide-eyed D.

"Never made," said Zale. "But they got heavy development. They were very big for a time."

"So," said Tusk to D, "we just want your John Hancock."

"However," D began, and the room went quieter. Nothing else in the world could be heard, and D's bold point of view dropped to a whisper. "You *have* seen it."

"Well," Clear simpered, indulgent of technicalities.

"We are *discussing*," D explained.

"He's trouble," sighed Tusk.

"You have expressed *interest*."

"Not a warm enough word," Clear smiled.

"We have talked of *seeing Eyes*."

"Very soon." Clear stood up and strolled around the room. Zale and Tusk never took their eyes off D. "You are a breath of fresh air, if that doesn't sound patronising."

This remark didn't trouble D at all; he had always thought well of fresh air, but as seldom as he thought of living in the South Seas.

"I believe we are going to make this picture," said Clear.

"It's 80:20," said Zale.

"85:15," was Tusk's estimate.

"Let me add," Clear went on, "that I have never known these two so bullish at this stage of a project."

"That's true," the partners confessed, and D saw that, if the optimism was rare, the two hardnoses were not ashamed of it.

"Still," said Clear, "experience has taught us it is injudicious –"

"Very dangerous," said Tusk.

"A no-no," was Zale's rule.

"– to be seen to have seen a script," Clear finished.

"Ah," said D. It was all he had to do to give a rhythm to the explanation.

"Open a package," Clear speculated, "slip off a rubber band, return a script with thanks but no thanks and we are open to the charge of having read it. Then years later perhaps, if a name, a line, a situation crops up in some other film – and nothing is ever utterly original – we may be liable to a hole-in-the-wall verminous lying whine that we stole it. I abhor the cunts!"

"Clear has suffered for this," said Zale.

"It gets him wild," said Tusk.

"Fellows," Clear was his old self again, "you are salt of the earth. But still, D, I hope you see the problem. We have been hit for a great deal in the past."

"Mucho cash," said Zale.

"Not to mention professional respect," was Tusk's unhealed wound.

"As a result," Clear picked up the ball, "it is our policy when entertaining a project to first get the writer's signed statement that we have not seen the script. Then, if by any chance, we do not make the picture, we are not shitface down the road."

"We have the papers here," Tusk added, sliding three copies of the one sheet from a card-thin drawer in the white table.

"Now, D," said Clear, "I am your friend, and I should tell you that you might seek advice at this point."

"Oh, Cleary," groaned Zale.

"I don't care," said Clear. "D is special, and I value his trust."

"Fiddle-de-dee," said Zale, looking the other way.

"Of course," Clear admitted, "delay can spoil a mood. And this is a moody art. Hesitation could also mar what promises to be an exciting night."

"I don't want to hesitate," said D.

"This is an intelligent man," Tusk noticed.

"Though I should see my family."

"Oh yes," Clear dismissed the delay, and then to the lawyers, "Isn't he a brick?"

"I suppose I should sign," said D. "But –"

"You want an option?" Zale knew it.

"Well –"

"It's not unreasonable," Tusk agreed.

"D *is* coming to meet us," said Clear, "and I daresay a little short of funds?"

"No funds," said D.

"You could buy some things for the little ones," said Clear.

"My wife has a gift boutique on Camden," said Tusk. "If you'd like to look. Here's her card."

"So the feeling is for some modest passing of . . ." said Zale.

"Money?" Clear filled in the blank.

"Done and done," said Zale. "Give us your signature, kid," and he rolled a pen across the table to D, who signed the three pages with the best writing he could muster. Not that D is a rich name calligraphically.

Tusk returned the three sheets to their drawer. He then stood up and, as it appeared, broke a corner off the very table!

"Hurrah!" cried Clear.

But D saw that Tusk had not a broken, ragged corner of the table in his hands, but a clean oblong. The corner was a separate piece waiting to be detached. It was a slender briefcase, which Tusk now pushed across the table towards D.

"Enjoy yourself," he told him.

One white catch secured the case. D pressed it and the lid bounced up. He felt a cool air come up from inside the case. He wondered if he was gazing at salad, lettuce, cucumber and so on, there was such an impression of green and white. But it was money. Six packs of bills, all with Benjamin Franklin on them, his wise face unflustered.

"Fifteen thou," said Zale.

"For starters," Tusk reminded.

D heard a click in his rapture, then a rattle. By the time he looked up, Clear was able to present him with a photograph of an amazed face. His. He looked like someone in a comedy.

"Your first souvenir," said Clear.

JEWEL IN THE NAVEL

Joan Collins is close to twenty-six when she first sees him. She is English, married once to another actor Maxwell Reed, divorced and upheld by the judge as not having to pay him support. She has made pictures since 1951, and her late teens. But in 1954, she has her big break, playing a vicious wanton in Howard Hawks' enchantingly silly *Land of the Pharaohs*. Not the least point of note about this film is that in her abbreviated costume, Joan has to wear a ruby in her navel to satisfy the censors. She has a very taut stomach, and admirable muscle control, but still a little glue has to be employed to hold the jewel in place.

She plays with Errol Flynn and Bette Davis in *The Virgin Queen*; she is Evelyn Nesbit in *The Girl in the Red Velvet Swing*; she is under contract to Twentieth Century Fox and they put her in *Island in the Sun*, *The Bravados* and *Rally Round the Flag, Boys*. She is attractive; she can be "sexy" in that rather deliberate English way that can never quite take it seriously; she has a sense of fun, and she enjoys herself in Hollywood. Her money comes and goes; she has several boy friends. Fox are not likely to renew her contract. She has had her moments.

In a restaurant, La Scala, with friends, she realises she is being studied by a young man at another table. "That boy who's looking at you," says the friend, "is Shirley MacLaine's brother, Warren something or other."

This is the spring of 1959, during Beatty's first visit to Hollywood. He is an actor without any movie credits, a pretty face most easily placed in a possible scheme of nepotism. Living cheaply at the Chateau Marmont Hotel on Sunset Boulevard, he had seen photographs of Collins, been interested, and gone to see her in *The Bravados*, a Gregory Peck Western. That disappointed him: it is a man's picture, and Joan has little chance to look glamorous in the glaring sunlight. But then he sees her at La Scala. He is with Jane Fonda – they may have just done their screen test, or perhaps they are on their way to it, plotting that impacted kiss.

Joan notices that she is being noticed. This may not be her chief reason for eating out, but she is like any movie personality in that she can eat and chat with a friend while registering everyone who comes and goes in the dining room and what attention they pay to her. If you are not of the business, you may think such a personality is neglecting you. But they can tell you everything you have said; they can break away and still pick up the old conversation a moment later. You may feel slow, dogged or limited, but they will not admit shame or ambition. It is their life to be seen, and they see themselves as if they were on a screen. Technical details so preoccupy them that vanity seems eclipsed. They are not always quite there. Their loveliness is there, their presence. But their inner being may be removed, watching how the show goes. Their presence is hugely sensitive, as the body and the image must be when they are detached from the soul. It is like a child's first adventure without parents.

Joan looks at the other table and sees: "He was about twenty-one or twenty-two. Blondish slightly curly hair, worn rather longer than was fashionable, a square-cut Clark Kent type of jaw with a Kirk Douglas dimple in the chin – rather small greenish eyes, but a cute turned-up nose and a sensual mouth. From where I sat it looked as though he suffered from a problem I had once had – *spots*! He wore a blue Brooks Brothers shirt and a tweed jacket. All in all, he looked rather appealing and vulnerable, and my interest was somewhat piqued."

He is talking all the while to Jane Fonda, and she is listening to him intently. Perhaps he looks away sometimes, into empty space, as he schemes the kiss of their futures, the better to see whether Joan is noticing being noticed. There is a moment where he raises his glass to her in an unspoken toast, a movie gesture in which the code of seeing and being seen has been formulated and broadcast for forty years already.

Some days later, Joan is invited to a Beverly Hills party at the house of Debbie Power, the widow of Tyrone. It is crowded when she gets there – "The usual mob doing the usual things – drinking, gossiping, talking box-office grosses, whiling away another forgettable evening," – but she realises that someone is playing the piano rather well. It was Warren something-or-other, doing imitations of Oscar Peterson, George Shearing and Erroll Garner. She drew nearer – Warren at the piano, intent on the keys, but looking up at the dark-haired beauty (who happened to be wearing Bermuda shorts, a shirt, a ponytail and no makeup – "A cross between Jackie Cooper and Betty Coed."). He looks up, notices her and smiles, "but he appeared totally absorbed in his music."

With Joan Collins

The next day, Sunday, Joan goes to the beach and returns to her Shorelawn Drive apartment to get ready for a cocktail party. She checks her answering service and discovers that a Warren Beatty has called six times from the Chateau Marmont. She wonders how he discovered her number. The calls are better than roses. She puts down her phone, and, like magic, it rings again.

"Hi, did you get my messages?" says the voice, without identifying itself.

It takes movie people, ardent for magic, to cling on to the transcendent intuitive power of the telephone. They do not take it for granted. They realise that two people talking on the telephone are like two close-ups, two streams of film, that could be cut and blended together in the flow of a love scene. The phone is better still for movie lovers for the close-ups stay intact. When at last, in film, two faces kiss, they so easily squash and obscure one another. It may be most romantic for a picture to pause on the edge of the kiss, the two beautiful faces still alone in narcissistic splendor. Let the audience go home and kiss.

This may sound fanciful, yet the dynamics of the phone conversation are very close to the grammar of movie sequences. Infinite use of the telephone is a measure of wealth, and of feeling ignoring budget. And the phone call that finds you unexpectedly may be as sudden and erotic as a hand coming to rest on a thigh in the dark. The love affair that follows between Joan and Warren is an experience of two would-be stars, of sex appeal, of fondness, of a fellow-feeling for publicity. It is all of these, surely, but it is the phone speaking, too. For the telephone is, among all other things, the instrument of intimacy for those who may not want actually to be with one another. The service, and now the answering machine, are further manifestations of the power it offers.

Joan is near the end of an affair at this moment with George Englund, a producer, who has talked about but never quite managed to leave his wife Cloris Leachman. Joan and Warren have a Mexican dinner that Sunday night at Casa Escobar, and he follows her back to her place in their separate cars. He goes up for coffee.

"We became inseparable." She thinks they have everything in common. They talk all night and make love and when she goes to work on her current picture, *Seven Thieves*, she looks the worse for wear. Friends tell her he's too young, too blatantly ambitious, probably using her to get ahead. But she likes him, his attentiveness, his talk, his quiet mind and the way he understands her. She's sure he will be a success without her. She goes to meet Englund at the Cock and Bull, to end that affair, but she kisses George in the parking lot and when she gets back to the apartment Warren is not there. He comes in in a moment, throwing off his jacket and his glasses. She remembers he tipped over a stool without those glasses. He had followed her to the rendezvous, driven around the Cock and Bull for two hours, seen the kiss. They have to make up. If they could either of them admit it, they do not want a settled life, for it would seem to negate ambition. If they fight a good deal, it may be vital to all their loving.

They are committed to each other before he has to go east to rehearse *A Loss of Roses*. "He plunged into rehearsals with enthusiasm and optimism," she remembers. When *Seven Thieves* is completed, she joins him in Washington DC for the try-outs. They stay at the Willard Hotel, but she meets and likes his parents. No matter the problems with the Inge play, Warren has time to advise her. Jerry Wald has just offered her the part of the older woman in his forthcoming picture of *Sons and Lovers*. It is the most demanding part she has ever had a chance at – it will win Mary Ure an Oscar nomination – but Warren tells her she shouldn't do it. He doesn't like the script and he doesn't want her leaving now for England. "Don't go, Butterfly," he begs. "Don't leave your Bee."

They go on to the Blackstone Hotel in New York for the opening of *A Loss of Roses*. When the play fails they stay on over the holiday period, after eating at the Harwyn Club, which gives them free meals for the publicity.

Then early in 1960 they return to Los Angeles. It is an election year, and John Kennedy is running. They live in an apartment at the Chateau Marmont. Warren works with her on scripts, they get into a health food diet and they prowl drugstores looking for pictures of themselves together in the magazines.

A film is being talked about for Warren – *Splendor in the Grass*, written by William Inge, directed by Elia Kazan. She says he was on the phone all day, to his agent and to Inge, who was pressing for him to be cast. "He was never happier than when he was on the phone, and he didn't need a phone book to remember the important numbers he constantly called." So he telephoned, she read scripts, and they made love – four or five times a day. He would take calls when they were in bed, when he was in her, rolling aside a little to make them both a little more comfortable and so that he could look away at the wall to concentrate and imagine. On the other end of the line, people noticed his pauses, the sound of his breathing, as if he was doing something else. The legend of his prowess was being bugged, at his own instigation. As

Joan remembers him, working with her on a script, "He was an excellent director and a patient teacher, with an intense and intellectual approach to exploring the depths and details of a characterization."

The pitch

A whimsical equilibrium had overtaken D. He smiled when he noticed it. He had these tidy white blocks under either arm: the script and the case of money. And since the two looked so abstract, D thought of himself as a jockey carrying weights in his saddle for a handicap. So far, his story seemed worth its weight in money.

D recognised that the bulk of the $15,000 could have been avoided. A check might have come in an envelope, no thicker than a Valentine. But the system had a sentimental side; it appreciated measure for measure. And D realised that, just as they did not want to look at his script, so it would be vulgar in him to open the case and peep. It was enough to know what was there, a solidity of cash. He might slide it into a vault and never touch it. He would die a pauper, a pauper with a happy dream, knowing the dry, green paper waited in its darkness. Money! D whispered, under his arm like a new girl.

And so D followed Clear, Zale and Tusk into the large room. The people there were deployed as if to indicate trepidation that their entertainment had depended on the legal negotiations. There was a smattering of applause as D emerged in which he heard well-bred restraint and sheer lust for sensation. To have money and be wanted, he thought; it was enough to make one beautiful. And D noticed now that not one of the handsome men or women skipped over him. They looked at him, their eyes brimming and fascinated.

"Take it away, D, baby," a soft voice called out of the twilight, and D noticed an elan coming over him, a vibrance he had always wanted. Perhaps he *was* made for show business. Still, he wished he could absent himself quickly for a wee-wee. He hardly wanted to spout his story standing cross-legged.

Zale and Tusk were supervising the setting up of a video camera in the corner. A younger man was in charge of the equipment, but the two lawyers were fussing to be sure its lens swallowed the whole assembly. D guessed his talk was to be taped, and perhaps sent on to Eyes, who must be too busy to be there himself. How inventively the new technology let the busy become busier.

The people in the room turned towards the camera, and in a low but clear voice – not stale from habit, but reverent, like nuns saying grace – they chanted, "I swear that, despite any information or anecdotes being shared in what follows, I have not seen the screenplay of *The Center of Attention*. Furthermore, I attest that I will in no way seek to sell, offer or report on the story of the script. So help me, God. Now this."

Like any good grace, it was appetite-whetting, a proof of readiness and spirits open for wonder. D had not been prepared for the simple disclaimer – he could hardly join in it himself, though (like a good Jew in a Catholic Church) he was sufficiently moved by the sense of the congregation that he might have joined in to be sporting.

"D," said Clear, "I think at long last we are ready for you."

"Well," said D, stepping forward with a will.

"Go on," said Clear.

"What was that?" asked D. Something in the fundament, he thought, had shifted.

"Did the earth move, D, honey?" a droll female wondering came up from the cushions.

"It's your excitement," Clear ventured to explain.

But D was not convinced. He had felt a bump, as when reels change, even reels on a fresh print, and his inner eyes had seen the two blobs in the top corner of the screen, sunspots in the brightness. Had anything altered? As if he owned the place and the entourage, D strode to the window and looked down on the city. His Drew came to his side. The buildings were as they should be, erect in their places, poised and unmoving like the advancing gang in grandmother's footsteps. The traffic was burning out the dark core of the highways.

"Tell us your story, D," said Drew, a child disturbed by talk of trouble.

D was not scared, no matter his certainty that something had happened. He looked out towards the horizon, the twinkle of lights going so valiantly into the tawny black of the sky, and there above, the crinkled edge of ground, a few stars. He felt Drew's tentative hand on his arm, and it did not stop his imagination soaring out there to the desert, to the supposedly devastated lands which somehow seemed more tranquil and possible than this jittery city.

He walked forward to the shack where the equipment was kept. It was cold and the wind tugged at his fine cotton slacks. He should have put shoes on.

"What was it?" he couldn't walk all the way, not in the dark, with scorpions about.

George's studious voice came back from the shack, "Four seven."

"I knew it," said Eyes. "I can feel 'em."

There was an anxious hush in the room when D turned round. Not one of them, maybe, had noticed anything, but they could not dismiss the force of his intuition. The storyteller always knows. Clear came up to D so filled with scrutiny that D felt like a large, late Rothko, or a two-way mirror.

He could see Clear was too much in awe to speak.

"There is the look of an adventurer on your face. Like a deep, prosperous tan," said Clear. D smiled and looked away at Drew who appeared as struck by his unwitting grandeur.

"By the way, what time is it?" D asked.

"Just past eight," said Clear.

"Nine in the desert," murmured D.

He was about to reclaim the center of the room, but he paused very near Clear so that no one else could hear them. "You understand, this thing, the entire enterprise – chaff in the wind."

"Oh, absolutely," smiled Clear, and D realised that this master of poise had a touch of desperado in him. Or desperation.

"Let's start, then," D decided.

He stood for an instant, considering how to tell the story. Then the story came up behind him like a wave and it told him:

There is a young man, an orphan, brought up by an uncle and aunt. He has not found a persuasive course in his life, one to match his uncle's success in business or his aunt's glory in charity.

So the young man spends his time at one of his family's homes, a modernist mansion in the West.

It is a house in the high desert, still, hot and dry, and the young man does little except shoot pool, confront the view, talk to the black man who looks after him and watch television in the basement.

This black, who is fond of the young man, is beginning to think the young man's mind is disturbed by the solitude and the emptiness of his days.

The young man has taken to recording the appearances of a beautiful young woman weathercaster. He has a three-hour assembly of her forecasts.

He writes to this woman at the network that employs her. But the letters are not answered.

He tries to telephone her, but the calls are not taken.

"Why do you like her so?" the black man asks.

The young man points to the screen. The woman is saying, "torrid winds tomorrow".

He learns that the President of the country is in the habit of riding in a nearby valley in the mornings.

He goes there at dawn and sees a figure riding, probably the President, guarded by an entourage. Up and down the valley.

Then he writes again to the weathercaster saying how much he wants to be with her, and how he knows where the President rides. But this letter is not answered.

There is a day in the mansion when the kindness of the black man, peppery enchiladas and trick shots at pool cannot lift the young man from his depression.

The next day the young man goes to the nearby valley at dawn and fires at the President with a rifle, wounding him.

The young man is instantly apprehended by the President's guards.

There is a national frenzy at this latest violence, the threat to the presidency and the sinister influence of television on a deranged personality.

The officers of the network that has the woman's weather are savaged in the press. The woman is cast in a movie.

"I never knew him," announces this new actress.

"We are mortified," say the aunt and uncle.

The booming of editorials is heard in the land.

The black man says, "This is a sad kid with a great hurt."

The President says, "He only winged me."

The actress's secretaries discover letters from the young man in the rooms of unanswered mail.

The pitch

"I admire her," says the young man, "and I wanted to get her attention."

The actress visits the President in hospital.

The young man is examined by psychiatrists, who decide he manifests an inability to recognise obstacles to desire.

The young man is tried for attempted murder and found guilty but insane.

Restored to work, the President reaffirms policies of eliminating the deficit by growth, says he feels niftier for the rest and reckons that America is getting happier than ever.

The actress's film does poorly. Entertainment pundits believe it is because of public reaction to the "example" she set the young man.

The uncle says his nephew should be shot, while the aunt wonders if he had adequate love or understanding.

The aunt calls on the President and they are photographed.

She visits the actress and they go on *Donahue* together.

An article is written by a film professor on how the affair is a consequence of stardom and imagery's generation of a supra-human identity for the weathercaster.

The actress's agent and personal manager devise a plan whereby – with full coverage – the actress will visit the young man in the hospital, proving to him that she is an ordinary young woman.

The aunt asks for the young man to be restored to her custody so that she can re-initiate the process of love and maturation left lacking.

The uncle says justice has been travestied.

The President admits he doesn't understand the fuss.

The actress does visit the hospital and she is allowed to meet the young man, but neither can recognise the other as dull or ordinary. Instead they fall in love.

Enlisting the aid of her personal bodyguard and saying he can come along to make sure she is not in danger, the actress engineers the young man's escape from the hospital.

The three of them go away to the parks of the West pursued by the authorities, the security forces, doctors and lawyers, the uncle, the aunt, the President and sundry movie deal-makers.

"Mad Lovers in Desert" say the headlines.

And D paused there. He knew the resolution to the story. But in the telling, he had seen the desirability in movie stories of having no ending, the plot left in suspense, so that the story can go on forever. Movies, being a medium that shows things – which sometimes threaten to show everything, or to arrive at a reality in which nothing exists if it cannot be seen – secretly aspire to enigma and the unseen. There is no moment so precious in a film as that in which terror is promised but not yet disclosed. And so D learned from this opportunity to tell his story the special potency of the answer withheld.

So D waited and looked at the begging faces of his listeners. There was a faraway rumbling of thunder as if the dream he was telling snored or groaned in the slight ruffling of its sleep.

In his retreat in the halfway high desert, Eyes pondered the prospects of the erstwhile weather woman and her young man blown across the landscape by love and flight. And he wondered if he could be young again.

NATALIE

A moment in the TV night: a segment from *60 Minutes*, on the famine in Ethiopia, with Mike Wallace at a relief settlement center in Bati, being shown around by a white Catholic priest, assessing the drought, the failure of harvests and the many hundreds of thousands who make their way across the barren veldt hearing the rumors of food, a baby born in front of the camera, somehow no larger than a hydrocephalic embryo, and then wrapped in rags, the children's eyes on sticks, the folds of unfilled skin, the heads like cellophane stretched around the ovoid skulls and always the eyes, not like parts of their devastated bodies, but creatures unto themselves, the body eating itself and the certainty of permanent brain damage in the babies from the malnutrition, the possibility of a generation of idiots if they survive, the home of the dead where the bodies are brought every day, the one doctor and the four nurses, and the children as thin as spiders staggering across the grassless plain, and the priest saying to Mike Wallace, "Do you know the President, the President of America?" – this is greater than CBS – and Mike says yes and the priest says tell *him*.

Into the announcer's voice and the flourish of music: "Tonight, Charlton Heston, George Kennedy, Ava Gardner, Lorne Greene and Geneviève Bujold face the natural disaster we all fear the most. It could happen anytime. Tonight on Channel 2, *Earthquake*. Portions of this movie may not be suitable for young children."

In the early part of 1960, Joan Collins realises she is pregnant. She and Beatty talk of marrying, or of having the child and then putting it out for adoption. But they settle on an abortion, and Beatty calls friends in New York to discover the best operative. There are moments when Joan changes her mind and wants the child, but he dissuades her. She says he

109

tells her, "Butterfly, we *can't*, we can't do it. Having a baby now will wreck both of our careers – you know it will."

So they fly to New York together, where he will soon start filming *Splendor in the Grass*, and one day he drives her to a high-rise in Newark. When they get there, she notices that he is sweating with anxiety. They comfort one another that nothing will go wrong. She has the operation and they spend a night in a cheap hotel as she recovers. In the course of the next few days, she discovers that her diamond necklace is missing. In her book, *Past Imperfect*, Joan Collins surmises that it was probably stolen by a hotel maid.

The couple take an apartment on Fifth Avenue and Warren begins filming *Splendor in the Grass*, with Elia Kazan and co-star Natalie Wood. A little younger than Warren, Wood is already a veteran star. She has begun in movies as a child, playing in *Tomorrow is Forever*, *Miracle on 34th Street* and *No Sad Songs for Me*. Her own teenage years coincide with the explosion of interest in adolescents in films, and she has had success and a kind of immortality by playing opposite James Dean in Nicholas Ray's *Rebel Without a Cause*, the essential Dean movie in that its setting and its melodrama of teenage frustration are contemporary.

Thereafter, for Warners, she has appeared in John Ford's *The Searchers*, she has won the part of *Marjorie Morningstar* and been borrowed by Frank Sinatra for *Kings Go Forth*. But nothing has had the raw emotional impact of *Rebel*, and nothing has yet established Wood as a mature, disciplined actress rather than a desperate risk-taker who responded to the mood of *Rebel* and the authority of Dean. Her career is at a turning point, and in *Splendor in the Grass* she has by far the most complex role of her career.

Though set in Inge's Kansas again, locations for *Splendor* are found on Staten Island and Long Island, and interiors are filmed at New York's Filmways studio. Joan Collins sees a few scenes being filmed and envies Warren having such a celebrated director, probably the best living director of young actors, for his first film. But she has to give most of her time to taking Italian lessons, for she is due to depart for Rome, where her career has worked its way around to *Esther and the King*, a biblical epic.

Before she goes, she and Warren become engaged. As she describes the proposal it is as charming as a scene from a 1930s romantic comedy. In the middle of the afternoon, as she is reading the *Esther* script, he says he fancies some chopped liver. There is some in the refrigerator. Joan gets up to find it, he waits and calls out, "Does it fit?" He has put a gold ring with diamonds and pearls in the chopped liver.

"'It's your engagement ring, dummy,' he said, grinning like a Cheshire cat. 'I figured, since you're going away soon and we'll be separated we should um, well, um, you know . . .' He shuffled embarrassedly. Took the glasses off. Put them on again. Grabbed a couple of Vitamin C tablets and crunched them. 'Get – well, engaged. What do you think?' He looked anxious.

"'I think it's a great idea – just terrific,' I squeaked happily. 'Are you sure you really want to – I mean you're not just doing this to make me feel secure, are you?'

"'No, Butterfly, I'm not – you know I don't do anything unless I want to . . . and . . . um . . . well . . . um . . . I guess I want to. We . . . er, could get married at the end of the year.' He took his glasses off again and we burst out laughing."

If it *is* a movie, anyone saying "you know I don't do anything unless I want to" is testifying to his own insecurity. For a young actor, like any actor, is hoping to be liked, hoping to be hired and then told what to do and say, which way to look, when to smile and pause, and hoping in all of this performance that he will be good and that he will be liked . . . It is a natural part of that insecurity for a young, decently attractive and reasonably sexed young actor to fall in love with his leading lady, not simply out of proximity and kissing scenes, or because their roles are those of people forever thwarted in coming together, but because they are both in the same dilemma – hoping to be liked – and in a predicament where they are the most likely reassurance for one another. Elia Kazan may have a hunch, and a hope, for the good of his picture, that Beatty and Natalie Wood will have an affair. There's no reason for him to think it need outlast the filming; he does not care for them as much after that, and it is not callous to be so devoted to his project. It is important for him that the kids look loved, and in love. Movie acting sucks on the real personality of the actor; the emptied areas are sometimes filled up with vanity and insecurity. For in acting, and American acting especially, there can be a nearly complete confusion of the character's aspirations and the actor's professional desire.

Kazan can explain this, in terms of theory: "There's a basic element in the Stanislavsky system that has always helped me a lot in directing actors in the movies. The key word, if I had to pick one, is 'to want'. We used to say in the theatre: 'What are you on stage *for*? What do you walk on stage to get? What do you want?'"

Actors fall in love with actresses for so many reasons – they may have to kiss each other over and over again, and the practice can make perfect;

their success in the fiction depends upon the expression of yearning in their faces; and desire is the engine of movies, the energy they cling to. There is another reason, nearly occult: actors are worthy of each other, they have the same rating in the currency of fame, and it endangers stardom to seem happy with unknown people. No one knows of a lengthy relationship in Warren's privacy-seeking life that is not with a famous woman. There is a caste system, and Natalie Wood is at his level and moment.

She has played the child who didn't believe in Santa Claus in *Miracle on 34th Street*. But in her own life, she has never realised that one has a choice about being a movie star. Her mother has done everything possible to foster her career – she is photographed wherever she goes, and she is encouraged to look on Dennis Hopper, Tab Hunter, Elvis Presley and others as possible boyfriends. When she graduates from Van Nuys High School, there are movie studio photographers there ready to transmit the event to the fan magazines. She is internationally famous, yet she is the princess of a small principality – greater Los Angeles, the very backdrop for the drama of *Rebel Without a Cause* – a bride for its courtiers and its lights.

When she is nineteen, she is married to Robert Wagner, a perennial Prince Charming of Beverly Hills who will never manage to get character into his acting or the little boy out of his face. Wagner is in his mid-fifties today. He was eight years older than Wood, but a less forceful screen presence. When Wood is shooting *Marjorie Morningstar* in the Adirondacks, living at a hotel with her mother and her sister, Lana, Wagner joins her and sleeps with Natalie in one suite, with her mother and Lana next door. According to Lana, their mother quells any doubts and serves the young lovers breakfast in bed. When he proposes, Wagner calls on Natalie with a bottle of champagne and two glasses. The engagement ring is waiting at the bottom of her glass. Everything sparkles.

They go by train to Florida for their honeymoon. But Wagner has allowed one photographer to ride with them and, though he tells Natalie the pictures are private, for their use alone, still they get into all the papers. There is no reason to doubt that Wagner and Wood are in love, but just as little to deny that in the principality such a union is a dynastic offering to the media. It is one thing to surmise that professional show people, that actors, do not have any sense of privacy. It is another to wonder whether we are already the self-righteous advocates of privacy because we know we will never achieve fame. It is the culture of movies that has led us to respect intimacy being posted up on a screen twenty-feet high.

How does one describe such marriages as that of Wood and Wagner except to say that its mythic appeal for the lovers themselves was so great that they would need to do it twice? Natalie spends time and money decorating their Beverly Hills home in white and gold, and becomes a talk of the principality because her taste is less than exquisite. The bride is terrified of all the pressures in her life. She takes sleeping pills, because it is important that the camera sees her untired, but also because at her level of the principality you do not have a problem without seeking recourse in purchase and action. She goes into analysis, against Wagner's wishes. It is possible that a famous actress is close to being a human wreck, and that her desirability on screen is the consequence of her vulnerability. Perhaps the analyst has thought of telling her to give up acting. But if being has not yet been worked out, what else is there? And analysts are like Los Angeles High Schools, they are eager to keep famous names on their rolls.

No one has ever thought to look upon Warren Beatty as a human wreck. It is the measure of his distinction, his dark understanding of Hollywood and his superior intelligence that he has taken care of himself. But he will be, and he certainly wants to be, the closest thing Natalie Wood has encountered, since his death, to James Dean. A princess only knows it is her duty to find a prince; analysis may also tell her it is her freedom and her nature to be royally joined.

Elia Kazan is known for his work with actors – Brando, Steiger, Dean, Clift – but he believes he is most sympathetic to actresses:

> "I'm better with actresses. And I think your remark about the tenderness is true because for me it's part of sex. I like womanliness, I like character in a woman."

Directors do not always sleep with actresses, and actresses do not fall in love with every director – at least, not every actress. But I doubt that good, vital films – I am trying to edge around the unerring erotic part in the life of films, which has as much to do with their invocation of voyeurism as with working affairs – are made without the possibility. The actress needs to trust the director, to believe that she is better understood, more seen into, more naked, more honestly presented, than she has ever been before. The director needs to see the actress as potentially veiled or obscured and to believe that at this moment he can decently undress her. It is not unlike analysis, and if either party is ever disconcerted by the closeness of an affair or of the way seeing is standing in for fucking, then they can use the process as a version of therapy, a step towards inner cleanliness.

Something intriguing happens during the filming of *Splendor in the Grass*. The film has a scene in which Natalie Wood has to cry. She tells Kazan she doesn't think she can do it. Whereupon, Kazan asks Barbara Loden to join them. She is an actress playing a smaller but striking part in the film, that of Warren Beatty's sister. She is blonde, not quite beautiful, but with a bitter, wolfish, intelligent face. Kazan asks her to cry for Natalie, on the spot.

Loden lowers her head and puts her hands over her eyes. In less than a minute, she looks up and tears are pouring from her eyes. Kazan asks Wood what she thinks of that. Natalie is very impressed, and jealous. "But did you feel anything?" Kazan asks. "No," says Natalie, "I was in awe of her being able to do that. But I wasn't moved."

"Exactly," says Kazan. "Barbara can do it in an instant. She has a special ability. But she was just doing it, just showing you. There was no emotion involved. As long as you are honest with yourself, as long as you show genuine emotion, it won't matter if there are tears or not. The scene calls for you to show pain, not necessarily tears. Show pain, Natalie, and if it is real it will be all that is needed."

When Natalie plays the scene, the crew gives her an ovation. She will be nominated for Best Actress Oscar; I think *Splendor in the Grass* is the best thing she ever did, and I am sure that owes something to the affection and trust shared by her and Kazan, as well as the stimulus of Warren Beatty. But the story also helps show the movies' manipulation of feelings, as well as their sometimes desperate insistence that they deal in the real thing. Barbara Loden never made it as a movie actress; that face was too sharp, too hard in its refusal to try to be lovely. But she directed one very fine film, *Wanda*, before she died, a low-budget, 16 mm, independent picture, not very well known. By then she was married to Elia Kazan, for his first wife had died in 1963 after a long illness.

Word of mouth

The premises of Eyes Enterprises were now beset with word of mouth. Even deaf, you would have recognised the fever people breathed in one another's ears. Wherever you looked, in corners or corridors, in camera or in conclave, heads were turned, face to face, like flowers gossiping over some panic their roots had felt in the ground. Mouths moved, heads dipped and swayed, and as eyebrows arched so hands came up, lifting the weight of amazement. There were already discreet lines at the phones as word was passed out, around the town, to brokers, agents, career-makers, hairdressers and astrologers.

D wondered about the communal oath taken not so long ago, and now tossed to the wind, like confetti. He was stirred by the tribute to his story. But it impressed him that the ceremony of the vow had all along fostered loose talk. It had initiated the low, superstitious murmur. In Hollywood, censorship has been among the greatest stimuli of the creative process. And while there is an intimacy thrilled by "just between you and I", "strictly off the record" and "don't let this go any further" – like the caressing of a private part – still, it is a world in which the urge to be seen must broadcast its privacy. It is a precious gift to these people to be told a secret, and ordered not to divulge it. Word of mouth is bearing witness, and so secrecy is a convention or a genre, like sincerity or the Western, archaic but admired.

A cynic or an outsider might be scornful of such deviousness. But that misses the idealism in word of mouth, and what it reveals of the religious instinct in the community. For they long to believe; and nothing fires the longing better than the prospect of a great film.

D saw faces transformed by his story. They were younger; they were in love. Eyes shone in the dead, handsome faces. People were approaching him all the time with their touching attempts to convey the effect he had had on them. He felt like an evangelist. He wanted to bless them and assure them that everything would be all right soon. Was there ever a people so anxious to have their lives and their exhausted bodies massaged by the wind of fiction?

"D, it gave me hope."

"It did?"

"I see a colossal first weekend, and I know it has legs."

"We are all very eager to make sure of the legs."

"There are Oscars here. This is the one that makes Eyes untouch-able."

"He does deserve it."

"D, you're a genius. No, don't blush. You are, you really are. And you're cute – I saw it before the others, I said so. Why don't you come to my aerobics class Tuesday, and maybe my lime sorbet after?"

"I'm not entirely clear about Tuesday."

"So, name your day, D. Who's proud if Jesus is in Town?"

Chuckling helplessly, and backing away with his hands raised – like someone in a dream who finds himself before a firing squad – D realised the need to urinate. He recalled the black bathroom; it seemed an age ago that he had showered in there, and come out to find Drew ready with her last rite. Still carrying his two white packets, he stumbled towards the bathroom, praying it would not be busy. He was beginning to feel the close horror of having to pee in a sink or even, hissing and steaming, on the carpet itself, his performance slowly stilling even word of mouth. If only he had the nerve. He should have done it as he told the story, without pausing. It would have been a sign of confidence to those people. He would have had their hearts forever. "I was there when D pissed," old ladies would treasure it in the rest homes thirty years from now.

The black bathroom was empty. D looked in all its dark corners for some chat about *The Center of Attention*. Nothing. No one. The bliss of an empty bathroom. D knew he could live in a bathroom the rest of his life, saying "just a moment" to every knocking, knowing he would never emerge. He talked silently to himself in bathrooms, about how he would guide the Lakers, master the stockmarket, run wars on the tiled floor or steer his family's way to safety despite the collapse of world order and the cracking apart of Earth.

D had just unzipped, and the first fall of his golden piss was on its way to the sloping wall of black porcelain above the oval of flat water – D did not want a noisy splash-down – when the door to the bathroom opened and Doc came in. He sat on the vanity, blinking, and started to talk.

"Young man, I have been in this business so long I tell myself I must love it."

116

"Oh," said D.

"And I do, don't misunderstand me. I'm saying this because I want you to know this isn't some old lady telling you that was a great story."

D tried to turn to show Doc his grateful smile.

"And I have worked on most of the best scripts since – "

"I know, I know," said D.

"God, it's a wonderful thing," said Doc. "I'm honored to think I'm going to be working on it."

"You are?" said D, surprise making his cascade waver.

"Clear says Eyes wants me on the rewrites."

"Rewrites?"

"Only the good scripts get rewritten. The bad ones, they make 'em straight away."

It was difficult to hear these unexpected developments while emptying a bladder that he had trained over the years to be commodious in case of emergency.

"How do you feel about Joan Collins for the aunt?" asked Doc.

"Well . . . " said D. "I hadn't thought about that." In truth, he had, and his heart was set on Mercedes McCambridge.

"I got these flashes of Joan in black underwear and the young guy weeping in her lap. I think the aunt wants to fuck him, don't you?"

D thought as quickly as he could. "I did want to suggest that the aunt and uncle have not given him a full measure of affection."

"Sure, sure," said Doc. "Jesus, kid, what have you got there, the Colorado River?"

"I beg your pardon."

"You piss for ever. Never seen anything like it. You get to be my age and it comes in dribs and drabs, like the dialogue in an Eastwood picture. You piss like Orson Welles selling sherry."

D laughed nervously, "It just keeps coming."

"Thing of beauty. I have to tell the others."

"Oh no, please," D cried, but Doc was unhearing; and though he tried mightily, pushing on his river to end it, D's fine arc was still there when several others crowded into his bathroom.

"What did I tell you?" Doc asked them.

One lady moved to get a side-on view. "Oh, I've only seen anything as fine from a Navajo guide I knew in Monument Valley. When he tinkled it was D. H. Lawrence."

"You better join the Fire Department, D," joked Chuck.

"And it's a pretty dick too." This was Drew, squatting down so close she could have trailed her hand in the spray. D was so startled by her coming up on his blind side he could not stop himself turning towards her, a movement that would have drenched her if her sure hand had not reached out to stay the swing of his admired part. "It's warm," she said, sentimentally.

At last, D felt an easing in the flow. The curve began to droop. He had to lean towards the bowl. Like a ship docking after a voyage, the slowing went on a very long time. Then there were tardy passengers, until the last ashore, one pinging drop that fell into the inch-deep amber froth. There was a clatter of applause in the black room, and Chuck whistled in approval. When the noise subsided, Doc said:

"How about this for a scene? Our hero has to take a leak. He goes into the men's room and he's got his dick out. He's got a bag with him with something special in it. Secret stuff. And he's put it down beside him, and just when he's in full flood a thief comes by and snatches it. The guy wants to chase but he can't stop pissing."

"Oh, wow," said someone.

"That *is* neat," said another.

"Now, I don't know if it would fit," Doc admitted.

"In *The Center of Attention*?" D asked.

"It's a good scene. We're going to need a few of those."

"What would be in the bag?" D was aghast.

"Who knows?" said Doc. "I'm just making pictures."

"It *is* intriguing." This was Clear's voice. D was horrified that *he* should be taken with it. He choked.

"D, what is it?" asked the solicitous Clear.

"Nothing," yelped D bravely. "A minor mishap securing my zip."

"Oh no!" cried Doc. "Don't hook that fish." There was laughter, and many pats on D's patient back. "Hey, remember?" Doc asked of Clear.

"What's that?" Clear wanted to know.

"Don't sell that cow," said Doc wistfully, and the black bathroom filled with the good cheer of former triumphs.

SPLENDOR

The tragedy in *Splendor in the Grass* is of a desire which cannot find fulfilment. Deanie Loomis and Bud Stamper are high-school seniors in south-east Kansas in 1928. The kids are in love, still on the virginal shore of sex. But they are compromised by the screen presence of Natalie Wood and Warren Beatty, twenty-two and twenty-three when the film is made, lush, carnal and very likely their own lovers by the time the shooting is complete. Yet their characters are fearful of going all the way with anyone they love. There lies abortion, divorce and disgrace. Boys can use whores, and girls must tame their needs by telling themselves that sex is a nasty tithe they pay for marriage, children and respectability.

But the anxiety about this beast sex seems all the more dementing because the leading actors cannot – no matter how well they act – lose their sexual assurance. There's an irony of more potential than Hollywood could handle that, as Wood and Beatty beat their heads on the sets with pretend sexual frustration, so they get hornier over the real bodies they might get to feast on, once relinquished by the roles.

So *Splendor in the Grass* is period distress brought to hysteria by conscientious acting and Kazan's feeding of its fires. It is also a touching picture, never as solemn as its makers might hope, but never simply ridiculous as some critics have claimed. Whether or not it is plausible for such lovers to refrain from sex, the clash of desire and what is allowed has its roots in cinema. That these lovers come so close to madness – Deanie spends two and a half years in a mental hospital when all she seems to need are the lays that Natalie Wood's false eyelashes know – is part of the awkward but heartfelt attempt to trace such repression to the stupidity of parents and the Crash of 1929. *Splendor in the Grass* thinks bad sex, or the lack of sex, may be what cripples society. For Warren Beatty, the thematic righteousness of his first film is an emotional pointer in the direction of *Bonnie and Clyde*.

More accurately, it is a film about acting: so often with Kazan, the story and its issues are pretexts for performance. His great talent is in making actors work. Wood was the more experienced of the two, and the picture is set up to be about her. She has the several virtuoso scenes (she was nominated for an Oscar), and the Wordsworthian title runs in her head. We remember the film for her in a red dress seemingly walking through a waterfall, nearly swooning with dreams of orgasm and guilt in the steam of her hot bath, and suddenly discovered up to her neck in a cool lake, letting the water subdue her heat. She is the water nymph who will not swim and who therefore thinks of drowning herself.

She is very good, even if she is a young actress seeking to regain what was raw instinct a few years before. She is at her best when alone, a face thinking of what she wants but cannot have, an icon beset by the imagery of water and agonising that Kazan pumps in. She seldom shows us the kind of sudden, shocking "mistake" in performance, such as illuminates *Rebel*. She is too accomplished now to give way to nervous breakdown, except that the script calls for it and Kazan has conjured up the set-pieces of would-be drowning for her. We never quite believe Deanie has thought of them.

Beatty seems to be her support. The credits say "and introducing Warren Beatty"; the posters add, "in his very first picture – a very special star!". He is paid only $15,000 for the picture. On the other hand, the story is based in William Inge's own life, and may be intended from Bud's point of view. There are signs of Inge's interest in the young Beatty: Bud is a high-school athlete with an older sister urging him to break away from parental control. But most important, in its subtlest moments, *Splendor in the Grass* is a film about Bud in which Beatty's acting is the more intriguing because it is less spectacular.

The debut is not always comfortable. There are moments when Beatty cannot handle long lines, because of an attempt at regional accent, or even a small lisp of his own not quite smoothed away. A mix of narrowed eyes and open mouth conveys meanness, excessive suspicion and sheer monotony. There are scenes where he is too busy – dropping his gaze, turning his head away, groaning, fluttering his eyes, putting a hand to his head. If movie acting is allowing the camera to inspect your thoughts, Beatty seems untrusting and eager to escape. There are times when his cheeks bulge and his face shines in a disconcerting way. Is he forcing himself to look frustrated? Is there a humor native to him that wants to deflate the portentousness of Bud's situation, a grumbling that cannot quite credit the forbidden fuck?

Still, Bud determines the action. He is the son of a vulgar oil man, carrying the burden of his father's search for more success because his older sister Ginny (Barbara Loden) is a rebellious outcast. Bud wants to marry Deanie, but his father tells him to go to Yale. That is why he drops Deanie, the perfect love who won't put out, and instead dates the famously "loose" girl in class. As a result, Deanie goes to pieces.

Beatty's Bud is a miscast hero, angelic-looking, but unable to meet everyone's expectations. Early on, he mouths silently as his father talks to him. He cannot always finish or grasp what he wants to say. He turns away physically from situations that baffle him. He tends to violence because of the confusion, and he has a habit of shutting off – when his schoolmates discuss girls in the locker room, Bud closes his eyes and lets the shower water flood his face.

He is browbeaten by his father; he is mocked and effectively castrated by a more sexually knowing sister ("If you weren't my brother you wouldn't come near me," she tells him. "I know what you nice boys are like. You just want to talk to me in the dark."). And Bud is overawed by Deanie and the force of her loving refusals. The film does not state this explicitly, but perhaps their frustrated need has bred the fatal, maddening love between them. Deanie is a romantic, and Bud a down-to-earth fellow who cannot fly at her wild heights.

Everyone "remembers" *Splendor in the Grass* as a Wood–Beatty love story, the plot so compelling the actors were carried away. Yet, in truth, they are uneasy together. It is hard for such ambitious actors to play people so much more naive than they are; and so in the love scenes they seem to condescend and watch themselves. Kazan crowds them together, kissing, petting, flustered by touch. He does not let the lone faces watch – and that is the movies' height of love. Natalie is outgoing, and Warren reticent. But Bud needs to be seduced, while Deanie wants protection. So there is a stand-off between them, as when he has to look up, archly, so she can only kiss his neck, and he taunts her, "You're nuts about me." In one of the fullest love scenes, he pushes her to her knees and she says "I'd do anything for you," as if to hint at fellatio.

As soon as Bud moves out of Deanie's aura, Beatty becomes more penetrating. His dismal time at Yale is beautifully captured in a scene where he comes back to his room, contemplates his desk, then calmly sweeps its contents onto the floor and begins to play solitaire. It is the first quintessential Beatty moment in which an unlaughing but amused fatalism refuses to accept the world's clutter. He is more grown up, alone with the camera, than ever he has been with company. He laughs like

With Barbara Loden in *Splendor in the Grass*

someone not just touched but discovered when the dean at Yale says of his father, "He isn't a very good listener, is he?" For Beatty in this first film establishes his skills in that very area. He listens, he watches: he takes it all in.

This reaches its height in his scenes with Zohra Lampert, the pizza waitress Bud meets in New Haven and marries. He is sitting alone in the restaurant when she talks to him. There is no tension or anxiety, just an immediate conversation. She asks him what Kansas is like, and he says, as if just realising it, "It's very friendly. That's what it's like." This is Beatty's best moment; at last a real Bud emerges from the flux of others' influence and the melodramatic set-up of the piece.

In the film's conclusion, Bud is married to the waitress, a farmer, with one child and another on the way. He has become quieter and stronger. He is dirty from his work and tanned by the sun. Deanie, out of the hospital, comes back to see him. It is the one passage of the story that deals with adults, and it comes as welcome relief to see compromise working. The marriage is ordinary. The ex-waitress feels what Deanie meant to Bud, and Zohra Lampert registers the helpless concern more effectively than Natalie Wood does anything in the picture. The Wordsworth runs over Wood's face as she drives away – about growing up and growing sad.

The fine ending exposes early limits and strains. *Splendor in the Grass* is too narrowly about sex to be as erotic as it hopes; and too ready to settle for half-baked equations of sexuality and politics. But it is in Beatty's troubled, cautious display of a mind working at its problem that we glimpse what Kazan said about his own movie:

"As for Bud, you want to know the truth? I think he is sort of scared of her (Deanie), after she comes out of the institution. She is too complicated for him. I think he felt, 'I've got a nice wife, she doesn't make any demands on me, we help each other, we have some aspirations, I'm comfortable here, what the hell do I need more trouble for? What do I need romance for? It's bullshit!' He's happy that way. I think he realises: this is what I want. The American notion, that love is the solution of all life's problems, is only true for an inhibited society. Even if you get the right woman you still have the same problems: you have to solve them within yourself."

Death of air conditioning

No matter the soothing onset of money and success, or the tingling unsteadiness whenever Drew's lissome, casual body pierced his vicinity (she *was* the shiver in his cold), D was anxious to make some contact with his family. As well he might be. After all, this city – as C, his wife, saw it, from their abode – was a cyclorama of peril.

"But you're perfectly all right here," Clear began again. "I would have thought things were more uncertain . . . over there." His hand waved in what he recollected of the direction.

"Exactly!" D was quivering. But it was Drew's fingertips xylophoning his vertebrae.

"Anyway," Clear sighed, "there's a party for the famine tonight. We're all invited to at the Lighthiser house on Mulholland. Cy will slay me if I don't bring you."

He did not expand on the prospect; he was having to shepherd guests out of the building and into a necklace of jet limousines for the trip up to Mulholland Drive. D was again struck by the limitless patience and tact in Clear which never let him appear as a hack or a crawler. Who would want to manhandle a score of piquant personalities, many of whom had calls to make, bathrooms to visit and petty delays if their feelings were not to be crushed? Yet Clear made them all sure that his destiny was to cater to them. He was not unlike the black bathroom, for he met everyone's desires. It crossed D's mind that he might be a warm machine, a very subtle, fleshed-out robot. But no chance: Clear had humor; he saw how silly he was – that was his redemption.

Doc rode down with D in the elevator, as D tried to recall just how Drew had presided over its floor.

"Been thinking about the script," said Doc.

Doc thought as he spoke. It was like jazz, assertive but vulnerable, and an essential defense against interruption. "Let me say, it's a hell of a script. Hell of a basis, anyway."

"It needs more work?" D asked.

"I don't know about work. Concept, perhaps. We have this guy who shoots the President?"

D nodded vigorously.

"We're imagining Eyes there?"

"Well – "

"Ah, you see. You hesitate. I like that, it's a mark of quality. This is not exactly Eyes, is it?"

"The part is somewhat younger," D conceded.

"I don't mean that. We could age this guy up, and you'll be amazed what Eyes can do when he goes into training. But shooting at the President."

"He's mentally unbalanced," D tried to explain. "Obsessed with being famous."

"I get that. And the actress is going to save him. That I like, and Eyes'll be crazy for it. But does he have to shoot at the President?"

"He doesn't kill him."

"That's something," Doc supposed, not convinced. "But it could throw off a lot of public sympathy. I wonder if Eyes – our character – could simply *oppose* the President on some more politically appealing thing."

"Like what?"

"Save the whales, do you think? Or defending a hospital for poor black kids. Orphans?"

"Shooting is much more filmic."

"Well, theoretically, I have to agree. But you see my worry? I don't know if Eyes sees himself as someone who'd shoot at the President."

"So much of my subject here," said D with a zeal that did seem strident in an elevator, "is the matter of fame and death, desire and immortality."

Doc was sheepish: "Well, sure, in the Aristotelian sense you're on the money." He reflected more. "Just suppose Eyes played the Pres, and we built *that* part up, and the girl rescues the President? A youngish President."

The talk went on, repeating itself, and D and Doc rode up and down in the elevator. There they were, amiably argumentative craftsmen, until they realised that the office suite was empty. Whereupon they went down again and out onto the street, where Clear was checking off names on a list.

There was a dense, disconcerting air in the street. It was turgid and static, as if an ominous dung hovered only a few feet above human heads. Two dogs were fighting, and D saw flecks of red in their jaws. Some curse in the stagnant air had destroyed their urge to run away yelping for a better day. They were killing themselves.

It was like the death of air conditioning, but etched with some greater loss, as if oxygen had been made into char. When you moved, you felt the urge to push aside curtains of dust. Your movement set up a rolling wake so that the waves of congealed air fell dead and silent against the buildings. It was like a dream in which you are dying and, when you wake, you believe the dream's plan is carrying over. D shuddered, and heard Clear say something about the Santa Ana imprisoning air up in the canyons until it frets and stirs. He wanted to reach up and rip the sky apart, letting breeze or change in. He felt they were in a picture, a painting, *Evening in L.A.*, being poisoned by the oils.

"May be fresher in the hills," said Doc, looking for a limousine.

D was following, when Clear called out, "You're over here, D. Drew wants you to ride with her." Clear winked at him; it made his face seem mechanical. The wink could not match the rare sensitivity, the delicacy, between him and Drew. And then D thought again, recalled his distant C, and wondered if there was an understanding that could be delicate.

A limousine door was opened, and a long, bare arm beckoned. "Hurry, D," her voice called. "We're going to a party."

Closing his eyes, for who could see in its smoked dark?, D ducked into the aroma of new leather until he pressed against Drew's pliant delectability. His coming released sighs of jasmine perfume from her.

"There you are," she crooned, and her arms reached across him to the door, to shut him in. It closed with no more sound than a safety catch makes in a long shot, and Drew's arm came back to rest on his thigh. Thank God, he still had his script and the money, thought D, as the limousine crept forward and those inside it raised a low, camp cheer like hunger sniffing food. Drew's hand moved up his thigh, and in, and D calculated the distance to Mulholland Drive.

MOMENTS

Biography is supposed to gain in pace and detail as a life comes into its own – as if the famous really did more, or had more minutes in their hours than the unknowns. In the summer of 1960, Warren Beatty makes his first movie; it will prove a considerable success, and it is talked about a good deal in the year that elapses between principal photography and actual release. He knows famous people: he is caught in love affairs with two actresses better known than he is. It is in the nature of things that he acquires an agent, a publicity representative, would-be managers and advisors, as well as lawyers, accountants and people who will be pleased to be known as his tailor, his barber, his mechanic, his tennis coach or his man for all those little things he cannot entirely manage himself.

His life is led day by day. It is as well to remind ourselves of this, for the legend and the dynamics of a movie star's medium let us believe in the power of cutting – instantaneous transports and alterations in which desire or a whim are accomplished in a twenty-fourth of a second. It is the wondrous or magical nature of a movie star that he has the potential to be everywhere – in 2,000 theaters across the nation, opening this Friday, on the upper East side of Manhattan and in Midwestern malls, his fiction unwinding 2,000 times at once; or he is "seen" by gossip columns simultaneously in London, Madrid and Los Angeles – for, after all, a busy man might sit down in all these cities in one twenty-four-hour space, if he was peculiarly driven by being busy or by ample credit card aimlessness; and anyway, in a movie he is everywhere – he is sitting sad in a New Haven pizza joint, in the end alcove, and he is the picture being studied by his old amour as she lies on a couch and talks to her analyst. A movie star is someone whose vital parts we can take home with us after the movie, in the Midwest or in the suburbs of European cities. Which leaves him, the other him, with a day-to-day existence that may seem faintly, comically absent or immaterial. How boring it may seem – how unnecessary? – for these great figures to live minute by minute when

127

they have seen the force they can convey in a five- or six-second take or cut, recorded in the summer of 1960, held in the dark and in the cutting room for a year and then released in darks all over the world as a kind of recurring eternity. To be wonderful, could you have the patience, the stamina or the spiritual persistence to tie your shoes every day? Or won't you opt for slip-ons, and leave broken-backed shoes in the hotels and boudoirs of the smart world so that sometimes, in amazement, you notice your own barefootedness and wonder about a movie that begins with a beautiful, and beautifully dressed amnesiac, wandering into the Pierre Hotel in New York, or the White House, with some intense message, meaning or plot the size of which is mysteriously promised by his having no shoes on? If you are dreamed about, here and there, how long is it before the pressure of these fictions enters your own sleep?

Yet stars must observe the verities of time and place. If you slept last night with —— at her beach-house, you have to drive back to the Beverly Wilshire (if your car starts, or when the cab comes), shower and change into fresh clothes that will please the other lady you are lunching at 12.30 at . . . where was it, Michael's or Spago? And you have to know how long it takes to get the car out of the Wilshire garage, how long it takes to go down from your floor to El Camino Real where the car will arrive. You have to judge how many of the accumulated calls you can answer; you have to shave – you must do it yourself, you cannot rely on the mirror and the presence of so-and-so for Men simply dissolving that monotonous rash of bristle away. And can you find the clean shirts, or has the laundry screwed up again? When can you find the time to sit down and really assess the pluses and minuses of laundering your shirts or simply and only ever wearing new shirts? You are late. You are always late. You had better develop and cultivate the reputation of being late, ambitious, unreliable, impulsive. And who is this woman you're having lunch with? Didn't you fuck her in Rio five or six months ago – wasn't it her? – and didn't she become a slightly more conventional and clinging goddess after you'd made love? So why not call the restaurant – no, you can't do that – better send five dozen orchids to her, at her table, with a note, a note from . . . Valparaiso (the florist can do it) saying gosh, darn it. It will be the greatest moment of her life, the poor bitch. She may get a part because of it, some producer seeing her, levitating in all those orchids, knowing that even in Chile – it is Chile? – you did not forget her.

And you can get a club sandwich or room service and watch game shows, and sleep, and when you wake at last the laundry will have come,

and you can sink your head in the fresh white shirts and feel restored. There is a screening at five; another at seven; dinner dates, two at nine and one that is rather more supper at ten, and there is a call from Jack which you know is an invitation to see a Lakers game. It is nearly his best part, you know, Lakers fan – active, urgent, crazed, merry, a man of the people. Jack is ready and happy to let himself be watched watching. And so you may stay at home, watching the minutes creep away, feeling the pathos in a movie star who is bored and empty. So much later, in revery, you turn up somewhere, anywhere, and you find three women whose names you don't know. The reality is sustained because they know who you are. One never tells a soul, hoping you will value discretion and call her again. One does tell, but she is notorious in LA as a liar, and another makes mocking allusions to the occasion for the rest of her life, so no one ever knows. There will come a day when neither you nor she will ever quite know if you did it, minute by minute, or as in a movie, momentarily and forever. Do you come instantaneously, like the light, or never, as in a powerful promise?

What this means to say is that biography is a literary form in which dates, times, references, source notes, quotations and verifiable sources conspire in an illusion – that, yes, life was lived day-by-day, moment-by-moment, and this is how it was. The strong line of narrative gives the writer and the reader confidence: it keeps them both going. But it is as well to remember that the life they are insisting on reading had no such decisions to make. It was helpless: it was there, in a jacuzzi where time was the water.

A movie star leaves more records than most people. He leaves parts of his life on film and tape. Beatty, before *Ishtar*, has acted in sixteen films, the accumulated running time of which is 1,809 minutes, or 30.15 hours. Now, of course, he is not on screen for every one of these minutes (I would need a special research grant to give you *that* figure). But we may overlook that discrepancy in view of a much larger and vaguer figure: the total time in minutes that Beatty has had recorded on film. For in respectable film production, the scene chosen to be on screen is the best of all the times that scene was filmed or taken. There is a term, the shooting ratio, which is the amount of film exposed on a production in relation to the length of the film as released. A 10:1 ratio is uncommonly low in Hollywood. The production companies would have records of all the film shot somewhere. But it would need more research grants still to discover them, and I am not sure that it would be using our time well.

I prefer to consider that somewhere, probably, the discarded footage of these sixteen films still exists, in cases, in vaults, in dubious safety and preservation, perhaps. But exists. If we suppose an average ratio in Beatty's films of 15:1 (high for some, maybe, but very low for others, like *Reds*) then we can propose a round figure of 27,000 minutes of Mr. Beatty's life preserved in silver acetate – nearly nineteen days of second-by-second imprint of smiles, scowls and the hoverings between the two.

An eternity of presence, of which a fifteenth (by a formula which, I repeat, is modest) constitutes his screen career, his Work, his oeuvre, that which may yet win lifetime achievement awards (with perhaps another three or four days to be added to the eventual total).

There are so many other ways of tracing Warren Beatty. How many still photographs have been taken of him, how many times 1/100 or 1/50 of a second, decently enough exposed for there to be no question of who it is? Of course, not many of those pictures have a calendar in them so that we can ascertain his exact whereabouts for those moments. Still, the world in which he moves is more generous to the latterday researcher than you might suppose. There is a photograph of Beatty and Joan Collins together at a dining table. There is an ashtray in front of them with a crown motif on it, and a name, "The Harwyn". This was a club that allowed the young couple to eat free, says Joan Collins. So we might suppose that a manager of or agent for the Harwyn pushed the ashtray into the picture, checked that it was in focus and in frame, and maybe then went so far as to give the couple cigarettes, so that the ashtray should seem reasonable and familiar. But the legend says Warren Beatty does not smoke, despite the cigarette in his hand. Is this why he is smoking with such superiority. Did he know we would be coming, and had he seen that early that there is not a photograph taken that is not designed and directed?

There may be a reservations book for the Harwyn with "Beatty 2, 9.30" here and there, and some appointments crossed out. The data bank of the world's airlines would have his flights – he must have frequent flier bonuses akin to the GNP of small states by now. There will be credit card records, hotel bills, telephone bills – which university press will publish those six or seven volumes, properly annotated, I trust? There will be other records – more or less unquestionable – of where and when he was: a matter-of-fact litany of commotion.

There may be records a little more uncertain and without a doubt illegitimate. Who knows how many friends have recorded Warren at parties – this is a community so adept at recording machines, small tape geniuses that could fit in the pocket, video cameras in the corners as if the house was a bank. Imagine all the telephone answering machines – wiped, or held in perpetuity – that have something like "Hi kiddo, I'm thinking of you, but I'm off to Helsinki," which might be Warren, as well as decent boyfriends having a little fun with their lovers. Think of all-night parties where the coming and going was preserved on videotapes that no one yet has had the time to examine. Consider that some ladies may have had the foresight to flip on some hidden tape recorder just before they felt their last self-control slipping away (and yes, some, later, find that, in the dark, they had had Warren on fast forward by mistake). Moreover, how many agencies, agents and whatever may have attempted to tap Warren's calls? Presidential offices? He was an active campaigner on behalf of Richard Nixon's opponent in 1972. Movie business rivals, jealous husbands, eager biographers, or Warren himself, quietly aware of a duty to posterity?

The bank of all those records might go on forever, taking far more than one normal life to type or read, and it would simply say how minute-by-minute Warren Beatty did this or that. And it would give no adequate hint of how much he was at a loss, of how far his experience was always hanging between doing everything and nothing.

Like a movie

It was like a movie. Wasn't it? That's what Doc had been saying all along, get it like a movie and then it goes of its own accord.

Imagine you're D, Doc had said.

Imagine I'm me? D started to giggle.

And Doc said right, make that separation, see yourself in the car going north on Beverly Glen, climbing and twisting. You're there, inside, like a vine growing on Drew. But you're outside, too, sucked along in the slipstream, catching the scene.

And D got the odd hang of it, being in two places at once, protagonist and voyeur.

What do you want? Doc asked – the car, the night, this amber-bodied, kiss-me, love-me girl? You want music on the radio, a ball game in the dark? Blossom Dearie, Dodgers and the Mets? You can play with the arrangement, have D say this, do that, polish the lines till they shine like the green clock on the dash.

Getting used to it, D looked at himself in the limo, saw himself locked in that rush of immediacy, the now-ness, and felt himself the spectator. It was uncanny – the dark and the cabin of light hurtling along, side-by-side, the show and its secret watcher.

Anything? he asked Doc.

Sure, there's nothing you can imagine that it could not become. That's what It is, said Doc.

It?

Sure, said Doc, what Hollywood used to say was sex, Clara Bow on a tiger rug. But there's a bigger it than little Clara, or even Drew now. It's watching, don't you see? It's being there and watching at the same time.

Oh yes, sighed D, I see. And he laughed out loud.

"Share the joke, D," said Drew. The line was tipped with her mock lust. But that was how D heard it, how he reckoned she had played it. That sweet Drew might never quite greet you with spontaneity again.

133

You wondered who set her up to this, who cast and wrote her? You never shook that paranoia.

"What?" asked D, just a small peak of worry on the optical track.

"What are you on, D?" Chuck leered from the black-bead gloom beyond Drew.

"Doing stuff?" Drew asked. And you look at whatever packet they have of this drug or that, and you laugh because what I'm on is I'm not here, I'm out there.

The car goes through curves like liquid taking the line of flow – we'll do it Steadicam at 32 f.p.s., says Doc. There is no shock or jolt from the steel rectangle fighting the arcs of highway. The limo is a motile S, and so the space inside seems to flex at its joints, the walls closing in and oozing out.

Arrange it however you like. Have total dark in the car, a swaying uncertainty and just the wriggle of Drew's fingers opening you up, freeing the cavalier, the feather in her hand. You could wonder whether her other hand, the left, is not another scurrying monkey for Chuck. You could speculate about Drew's handedness, and which one is closer to her soul.

The soul is tough in movie, says Doc. It doesn't photograph.

But she has one, you say, and Doc looks at you with what could be pity or envy.

Or there could be deadpan chit-chat between you and old Chuck, not such a bad guy, men of some world together, as the so supple (you can hear her sinews stretching) Drew bends to your two horsemen. And the two stupefied fellows could look to heaven or the satin roof of the limo without disclosing the intensity of the sensation. To be a you there, you must meet triumph and nirvana with Apache impassivity. You know you are being watched, so give nothing away. Don't look at the camera.

There are other sights to glimpse along the way – the topaz light from pools wavering on adobe walls, the blooms and blossoms like flesh in the streetlights, and the shimmering shapes of people seen through the half-shut Venetian blinds. You could have a three-legged dog lurch across the road, its tail drawn between its legs in terror, and the driver could surmise in walk-on Latino, "I tink I see it onze b'fore, in Monterrey before the – ", but you do not catch the last word in the cha-cha-cha on the radio, and when you look at Drew her nostril is crystalline with too much right stuff. You wish it could be only you and her, curled up under a rug, like lovers riding in Central Park, clip-clop, kiss-kiss, on an endless summer night of personal learning experience.

You cheat! You are an actor, watching what you're doing. Why should anyone ever trust you?

"The car's dying," said Drew, and so it was, drifting into the incline just short of Mulholland's crest, its strength ebbing. The car stopped. They felt the handbrake save it from further indignity. Then they heard the wind searching along the ridge of the hills. You could imagine wolves, or worse, loping along, looking for you.

Couldn't you?

LOVING EVERY MINUTE

The family of Natalie Wood lives at this time in a house in Sherman Oaks. One day – it must be 1960 or early in 1961 – Natalie rushes in, in tears, an emotional escapee from the house she has lived in with Robert Wagner. Natalie's sister, Lana, eight years younger, remembers her sister's hand is bleeding "because she had squeezed and broken one of her cherished crystal wineglasses". Wagner has left their home; the marriage is at an end.

When the shooting of *Splendor in the Grass* is beginning, observers reckon that Natalie is in love with Elia Kazan. Why not? This is a movie about desperate love and its thwarted consummation. The actress must be brought, time and again, to a peak that never breaks, never gives her release. Kazan is older, wiser, cunningly skilled in drawing an actor's personality into that of the character they are playing. He is attractive, ugly, physical, dynamic; he has magic, and he makes actors believe he can urge it upon them with his pushy, zealous eyes and his strong brown hands. Any actress needs to think that she has some hitherto hidden power that this director can set free. But then, it may come to pass that she sees how far the director is already a little bored with her and the tricks he can make her play, and that he was always there to escort her towards the young actor whom she kisses in the picture. If the director is very clever, the camera will see the instant at which these two recognize each other properly for the first time.

It may not always work out so tidily, or so well for the picture; and whether or not it does depends on the kind of romanticism in the minds of the actor and the actress. Something like infatuation develops on the set of *Splendor in the Grass*. Falling is so natural a response if you feel raised up by adventure and art, if you are exhausted and insecure, and if you have been brought up in the codes of the Method. Kazan may tell his young players they are doing well, he may bolster them with reassurance; or he may choose the opposite ploy, exposing them, goading them with a disappointment he cannot conceal – which director is a poor actor? But nothing will convince Natalie or Warren more than if they, the real selves, as well as Bud and Deanie, fall in love. And in this, Warren Beatty is the less experienced. Bud will not have Deanie in the film, but suppose the actor can lure the actress away from her husband? This is not cold-blooded, it is passionate. But it is also something that an unusually intelligent man, or one as much drawn to retreat and skepticism as to magic, will one day see as ridiculous.

And life is not straightforward, even if it passes hour by hour. The telephone is always at hand, offering whispered exchanges across 8,000 miles, transformation and betrayal, the sound of static and the little coughs when the medium clears its throat.

Joan Collins is in Rome, on *Esther and the King*. Along with all the other Biblical costumes, she wears the engagement ring that Warren has given her. He has asked her not to live in a hotel, but in the apartment of a friend – there she is less open to temptation, closer to a known phone, and so much less surrounded by anonymity and discretion. He sends her many letters and telegrams, though I would suspect that the letters (needing seven or eight days) are quickly made archaic by cables and phone calls. It may be that a letter arrives with sentiments, beautifully expressed and carefully thought out, but made redundant by a breathless phone confession of five nights ago.

Joan is moved by how much he misses her – "he sounded so forlorn and depressed." She surprises him by flying to New York for the week-end. They spend the time in their apartment, and she watches him filming before she flies back to Rome. When she gets back there, Warren writes with amusing comments on "How to make a Biblical film," for they have agreed that her project is junk. The points are discerning and sarcastic; they show someone already scornful of the way most pictures are made:

"1. It is always best to try to show as much emotion in all scenes as possible. It is generally best if the actor cries in each scene, taking special pains not to be out of control or realistic to the extent that members of the crew or other actors will be made to feel embarrassed. All gestures and facial expressions should be worked out in front of a large mirror. These should not be deviated from. Remember that the audience is not involved until the actor cries. Be very careful not to let the mascara run.

2. In doing Biblical pictures it is best to try to imagine how Jesus Christ would have said the necessary lines and done the prescribed movements and then to emulate his work.

3. Never change the words in a movie script. These have been written by great creative forces.

4. Do not challenge the director, or especially the producer. These are dedicated men.

5. Do not tire yourself out with thinking about the script between takes or at night away from the set. This destroys spontaneity."

We are cross-cutting as we advance, as in any Hollywood story about a fellow with two girls: in 1960, in Hollywood, it could be Tony Curtis in the lead, with Janet Leigh and . . . Joan Collins as his two loves. In the summer of 1960, Beatty and Natalie Wood are being seen about together. When reporters catch up with them they say they are just friends. At times, Warren blushes and laughs, just like any other shy fellow in love, and spied upon by journalists.

There are sequences of these times available to us like passages of film, and who knows exactly their proper order? Montage – that rapid, giddy, exhilarating editing style to cover a passage of time – is but one of the ways in which Hollywood asserts that atmosphere, energy and momentum are more important than history.

Joan Collins has suspicions in Rome. The telephone is as available to malicious friends, gossips and provoking reporters as it is to lovers. She wonders about Warren and Natalie, and she recollects the opinion of her astrologer, Ben Gary, that Warren is "stubborn and aggressive, but he is unyielding in his ambition and because of his tremendous drive and energy will have an early and immense success." And, after all, says Gary, he's an Aries, "Ruled by their cock. How delightful for you, my dear."

Warren hears that Joan is being seen with an Italian actor, Gabriele Tinti, and when he calls her she is on the phone for hours at a time. He begs her to go to New York again, and she goes. Years later, when she writes her book, *Past Imperfect*, she recollects sadly that Warren never went to Rome.

After *Esther and the King*, she returns to America and she and Warren live together again on Sunset Plaza Drive. Perhaps, now they are reunited, they think nostalgically of when they were forever quarrelling and making up on the phone, when they knew the local Alitalia numbers by heart. The wedding dress, designed and purchased, lies carefully wrapped in the closet.

There is a brief intrusion from the mundane world: military service. Beaty, Henry Warren (or 44.9.37.130, as the Selective Service regards him), has been classified 1-A since June 1958. But in February 1960, when he takes his physical, he is classified as "Accepted", one level below "Qualified", indicating some imperfection. We cannot say what it is, for the relevant remarks in his record are destroyed under the authority of the National Archives and Records. And so, in March 1960, Beaty is classified 1-D (member of a reserve component).

This takes him to George Air Force Base in Victorville, between Los Angeles and Barstow, on a three-week tour of duty. As soon as he is there, he frets and hates the waste of time. He starts to send cables again and to monopolise Joan's phone, "expressing his misery, loneliness and undying love. So why did he fight with me and harass me all the time when we were together?"

Joan Collins says she was too independent and aggressive. And since he was insecure and determined to have his own way, they make a volatile couple. She has the added difficulty of being dropped by Fox and having to look for work. That is no problem for Warren. He is in great demand, and he reads the scripts offered her as well as those sent to him. He tells her hers are rubbish, and he throws them in the wastepaper bin. He can hardly fail to notice a career that is slipping.

It is February 1961, and in the London Clinic Elizabeth Taylor may be dying – in which case, Twentieth Century-Fox want Joan as her replacement on *Cleopatra*. For a few days they live by the phone. Warren has to go out and find another phone for his calls. Then the word comes that Elizabeth is getting better. There are situations in real life too, where some training in talking (and thinking) like Jesus Christ proves its use. "It's showbiz, baby," says Warren, "as in there's no biz like it."

Warren has a second film, *The Roman Spring of Mrs Stone*, and it will be shot in London. With nothing to do for herself except see her family, Joan goes with him. They rent a home belonging to the director, Peter Glenville, just behind Harrods. She visits the set at Elstree and sits in the dark watching Warren's character, Paolo, in the brightness, making love to Mrs Stone, played by Vivien Leigh. Joan is well aware now that women are finding Warren attractive. When the three of them take lunch in the studio restaurant, Leigh deplores Joan's dress sense and advises her to invest in jewellery. She says Joan looks a little like a man.

"What do you think, Warren darling?" she asks her co-star.

Joan looks at that gentleman as he considers how to answer: "His hair had been darkened for the part of the Italian gigolo. He had a deep tan, which, although it was out of a bottle, looked as if it came straight from

139

Portofino. He wore a beautifully cut beige silk suit from Brioni, a cream crêpe-de-chine shirt from Battaglia, and a brown-and-beige St Laurent tie. No wonder half the females in the restaurant were tripping over themselves to get a glimpse of him. The Warren Beatty sex-symbol was beginning to emerge. Women adored him. He was loving every minute of it."

Limo death

The limousine swayed off the road and was stilled in the incline of red earth and shale. It had stopped thirty yards from a telephone – just a pole, a perspex hood over the instrument and a light above it. It seemed a recent installation, a fresh, clean phone, put there that morning perhaps. Drew poked with her toes at the arrowed heart and initials put in the cement by a laborer's quick finger. But the crusts stayed hard. She was carrying her sandals, flimsy silver platforms, walking on the warm pavement.

Stretch, the driver, got the hood up. The light from the phone shone into the bed of glossy, succulent machinery. There was a scent of newness under the hood, as sweet as the leather inside. D was backing up the hill to study the view. Chuck threw rocks out at the darkness.

This was not far short of Mulholland, not that late in the evening. When they looked down at the city they could still see movement and intelligence there. How could a stranded car be forgotten up there in the desolate canyon where the air felt thick around them? A phone call would do the trick, wouldn't it?

Drew was jittery at the lack of motion after the serene journey: it was like finding herself in a crack in the desert after panning the spider-trailed floor from a cruising 747. It was like having the movie stop. Drew had had a fit once when the projector blew out during a movie. She had had to be sedated. She had played on it afterwards and said the doctors told her she was subject to fits if the 24-a-second rhythm was interrupted. It was a lie, but one she liked. And now, she did feel rattled, ready to sit down and rant at the sky.

"Call, won't you?" she nagged Stretch.

"I can handle this," the driver's voice said, under the hood. She saw his white cuffs in the car's black stomach.

"No, you can't," snarled Drew. She sounded hideous, and in one bold swing the heel of her palm knocked the wing mirror from its mounting.

141

Stretch looked up at the jolt and ping in the heavy car. He giggled stupidly.

Drew crossed the road, the angry mirror of her face like a baby she was carrying. She found a space of hard, clear ground in the light from the phone, and set the mirror down.

From higher up the hill, alone in the dark, but seeing all of them, children playing in the light, D saw Drew take a packet from her bag. She tipped white powder on the mirror: there was no breeze. Her hand worked over the powder. She must be holding some edge too fine for him to see. The mirror was white. Then Drew made brisk movements that left white ridges on the glass.

She saw the stripes across her watching face, bent down her head and sniffed the three lines up into the mirror and into her face. The glass was clean, and she could see the first smile falling down from the brain and the bone, into the lowered look of Drew. What a sweet smile. The pain dropping too. This girl could be something. Her face in the mirror was liquidising with hope and the hit. Cocaine made you long for your own next minute; it let you feel your heat.

Without bothering with his consent, Drew spoke quietly and firmly to D, never looking away from the mirror, "Come along, come and get it."

D edged forward, to see if he was in the mirror yet. But there was only black around her brilliant face. Did the silvering etch her features with glamor, or do all instruments of seeing polish what they see? D had never seen Drew so desirable, doting on her own intoxication, gossiping with her reflection.

Stretch was sneering at his passengers. "This won't take a moment," he warned Drew.

"You're going to have to call," she sang back.

Chuck had picked up the mirror. Holding it like a pizza to go, he shook cocaine on it. The powder spilled. He groaned and swept some away. It fell to the ground in a shimmer. Then he put his nostrils to the mound, snorted crudely and blew away as much as rushed into his black nose.

"Pig," Drew noted calmly. And then, looking up, pretty please, "D, you have to try. At least, you should try."

Chuck laughed. "If he's never done it, don't let him try this stuff."

"I'm gonna make D a special line," crooned Drew, "just a very thin line, a very short nice line." She was as diligent as a mother picking a baby's first oyster – not too startling, large or odd, an oyster that might be a jelly baby, one that would release its meaning beyond the child's nervous throat, so deep within the system that he felt safe.

"D's going to be very fixed up here," she was murmuring – it was wicked and irresistible, the model of the age. "D is going to be in heaven," she was saying as the razor blocked off a line as thin and crisp as thread. If only more personal, less chemical pledges could be made, D thought. He would take it if he must, if it was a way to win this girl's nervy interest.

He held the tube. He was nervous of botching it. But as he moved it down towards the line, he saw the end grains lift and dither towards it. They were so eager to please, they rose and hurried like white balls in an educational movie about busy atomic particles. He was whole and handsome in the second it took. The line filled in his nerves, a Pac-Man gobbling up doubt. He floated back on the ground and looked up at the stars, cold and amaretto in his mouth. And he heard the thrilled company of Drew's body like surf bursting on his own. The two of them, side by side, and Chuck and Stretch at the phone, beggars at their feast, looking stupid and ill-fed.

He heard Stretch on the line asking for rescue. Chuck was doing wind sprints into the peak of the hill. And Drew was romancing him, her trusty tongue inside the mansion of his mouth. D closed his eyes and the slumbering roll in the ground seemed part of his being with Drew. But when he opened his happy face, Chuck was sitting on the ground up the hill, holding onto the pavement as if it had billowed and tried to escape, and Stretch was clinging to the phone, a man overboard.

"The ground moved," said Drew, bleary in her several worlds, but certain and unsurprised.

ROMAN SPRING

Not every movie contrives so grim an overlap between its story and the lives of those making it as *The Roman Spring of Mrs Stone*. But hardly a picture is entirely free from that peculiar haunting.

Joan Collins, when she is in London, watches Warren acting with Vivien Leigh, and wonders whether her fiancé is actually involved with the forty-eight-year-old actress whose marriage to Laurence Olivier has just ended, at his request, with Olivier planning to marry the much younger actress, Joan Plowright. It has been a tormented marriage for many years: she is unstable, depressive, drawn to many affairs, disappointed in her career. Perhaps she is mad – acting is a profession and a life in which that illness is hard to detect or prove. Vivien Leigh believes by 1960 that several irredeemable forms of ruin have overtaken her, not the least of which is age and its effect on her looks.

The Roman Spring of Mrs Stone, from a novel by Tennessee Williams, concerns an actress, Karen Stone, aged about fifty. She has a disaster, trying to play Rosalind in *As You Like It* – the production comes to a grinding, out-of-town halt at the Washington Theater! She decides to retire. Her husband, an older, wealthy man, takes her to Rome for a holiday. But on the flight there he suffers a fatal heart attack. Mrs Stone settles in Rome, an angel of death in attendance in the form of an impoverished but beautiful young man who watches her apartment and follows her.

Karen Stone is "drifting," not really aimlessly, but like a leaf on a river feeling the quickening in the water as the weir approaches. She is fixed upon by the Contessa, a pimp who provides Italian gigolos for older women, generally Americans. One of the Contessa's boys is Paolo. She trails him before Mrs Stone until the ex-actress is helplessly in love. Paolo is a cunning, narcissistic opportunist, played by Warren Beatty. It is to the credit of those making the film that his character is never softened. Not for an instant do we think that the male prostitute has been compromised, or deepened, by feeling love for this forlorn woman. Instead, there is a sense of ritual. He is the man who will destroy Mrs Stone's spirit, so that she is ready for the other young man – who appears before Paolo – and who will fulfil or execute the role of killer that Paolo casually describes to her one afternoon.

The film is all the more acute and troubling in that it is not simply the story of a romantic woman's tragedy in which Paolo is the cruel instrument. It is also a story about acting and ambition, for Paolo will not remain a Roman gigolo, one of the Contessa's hirelings. He wants to get into the business of acting which Mrs Stone has quit. His final betrayal of her is presented as the rite of passage of a shameless, beautiful young man into movie-making.

As Karen Stone becomes infatuated with Paolo, she gives him clothes, jewellery and a movie camera. He plays with it. Then the Contessa – out of sheer malice and the destined urge to destroy Mrs Stone – tells Paolo that their affair is getting him the right sort of attention. He is on magazine covers with her; he is being talked about by film people. There is a young Hollywood actress in Rome at the moment, Barbara Bingham (Jill St John), and she has set her eyes on Paolo, if only to vex and thwart the older, stage actress.

A small but exquisitely dreadful party is arranged at Mrs Stone's apartment – for her, Paolo, Miss Bingham, the Contessa and a couple of the rich ghouls from this cut of *la dolce vita*. It is a party to view the home movies Paolo has shot with his camera. The group is more interested in seeing the shots of Paolo than those of Karen: it is clear which one the camera loves. There is a shot of the statue of an Egyptian god. Across the hot, active projector, Barbara Bingham asks Paolo:

"What's he holding?"

"er . . . That's a cornu-copia. Horn of plenty. There's a lot of . . . Karen before we get to me. Why don't you come outside – I show you the seven hills of Rome."

They move out to the balcony – the facet of Mrs Stone's apartment that Paolo most envied on his first visit – and Karen can no longer deny her love or Paolo's heartlessness. The young couple leave together, and Mrs Stone tosses the key to her apartment, wrapped in a loose handkerchief, to the killer waiting patiently outside. The humiliation complete, she is ready to play out her death scene, as foreshadowed in an earlier scene with Paolo, one of the best in this very dark movie:

PAOLO (seeing the younger vagrant in the street below): Who is this boy that follows you?

KAREN: What?

PAOLO: You must have noticed him. He's everywhere we go. Come here.

KAREN: I never saw him before in my life.

PAOLO: The trouble is, you make a spectacle of yourself.

KAREN: What do you mean?

PAOLO: Spectacle? That's something that's conspicuous. You. Your photograph in the magazine pointed out on the street.

KAREN: And you adore it. It's you they look at, Paolo. Not at me.

PAOLO: Ah! You don't hear the comments.

KAREN: Oh, yes, I do. *Che bello uomo* – what a beautiful man. That's what they say on the café sidewalks. And you bask in it like a sunflower. If I'm conspicuous, it's because you've made me so.

PAOLO: It's no use contradicting you. An American woman's never going to admit she's wrong about anything. But you don't hear all the comments. Last week I was compelled to challenge a man to a duel on account of a remark he made.

KAREN: You fought a duel?

PAOLO: I sent a challenge and the man left Rome.

KAREN: And what was this remark?

PAOLO: Too disgusting. I can't repeat it. Hasn't it ever occurred to you, Karen, that women of your kind are very often found assassinated in bed?

KAREN: What?

PAOLO: It's true. Only last week on the French Riviera a middle-aged woman was found in bed with her throat cut from ear to ear. There was no broken lock, no forced entrance. Just stains of hair oil on the pillow. Obviously, the lady had asked the assassin to come in.

KAREN: Does this mean you're going to kill me?

PAOLO: Ay-eie. That's right. Make a joke. Show your sense of humor. And in three or four years I pick up a paper and read about your death.

KAREN: Three or four years is all I need. After that, a cut throat will be a convenience.

Vivien Leigh dies in the summer of 1967, aged fifty-three, about a month before *Bonnie and Clyde* opens. She has made only one other film after *Roman Spring* – *Ship of Fools*.

If *The Roman Spring of Mrs Stone* is not quite a vehicle for Vivien Leigh, still it is the work of three men who admire her very much – Tennessee Williams, in whose *Streetcar Named Desire* Leigh has won an Oscar; screenwriter Gavin Lambert, and director José Quintero, who has lately directed Leigh on the London stage, in Giraudoux's *Duel of Angels*.

Beatty is the interloper. The first plan for *The Roman Spring of Mrs Stone* is that it be shot in Italy with a young Italian playing Paolo. But Warner Brothers are anxious to put a starrier figure opposite Vivien

146

Leigh. Beatty has seen the script. *Splendor in the Grass* is a Warners picture, and its director, Elia Kazan, may have spoken on Beatty's behalf.

But Beatty decides that he must convince Tennessee Williams. He may be encouraged in this by the story of how Brando won the lead in *Streetcar Named Desire* by meeting and impresssing Williams. And so he puts on an Italian suit and olive make-up and goes in search of the playwright in Puerto Rico. As Beatty describes his conquest: "I walked up to him in a gambling casino and began to talk to him in an Italian accent. In fact, I brought him a glass of milk on a tray, because I had been told that he had ulcers from his reviews of *Sweet Bird of Youth*."

He proposes himself for the part, and he reads for the writer, with accent and without. Williams is charmed; he says sure, why not? There is a coda to this story, told by Dotson Rader, who only meets Williams years later. He says that Tennessee tells him how, later that night, Warren comes to his hotel room wearing a bathrobe. Williams sighs and he says, "Go home to bed, Warren. I said you had the part."

Then Beatty has to win the favor of Vivien Leigh, who has casting approval. She is charmed by him, too. José Quintero is over-ruled. It will be speculated subsequently that Beatty may have given himself in sex to Leigh: his Paolo does have an icy humor that regards everyone as waiting to be used. But nothing is established; the casting is forever tinged by rumor and Williams' instinct that the Puerto Rican gesture showed Beatty's suitability. Perhaps Tennessee sees a grin of danger beneath the make-up and feels that heat of reckless ambition.

The Roman Spring of Mrs Stone does not fare well at the box office but Williams regards it as the most faithful screen adaptation of his work. The picture is not helped by the late decision of producer Louis de Rochemont to shoot it in London, instead of Rome. Screenwriter Gavin Lambert, barred from the set by de Rochemont after three weeks, remembers "the difficulty of creating a Roman spring in the deadly foggy English winter, with a producer as sullen as the weather". This hurts Beatty especially, he thinks, for it prevents the actor from absorbing the life of Rome, seeing real Paolos and hearing Italians speak English.

Lambert thinks that Beatty's Paolo sounds more Mexican than Roman. The voice does fluctuate, but most of all it sounds like an actor experimenting. No transcription can convey the sound Beatty makes before saying, "That's right. Make a joke," in the scene quoted. It is credibly Italian. But it stays in the mind because it seems like narcissistic cunning caught playing with itself. This is not merely an actor at work, but a man who knows everything is always an act. The sound itself lets us know that this Paolo – too cowardly for a real duel – has himself thought of murdering Mrs Stone.

Roman Spring has poor camerawork and studio sets that never seem a part of the sweaty, sexy Rome that would make Paolo more credible. The film is stagy: Quintero is a fine theater director. But it is Vivien Leigh who presents most problems, I think. She *is* the role, painfully so. But she has a tendency to posture whenever her character is most hurt or moved. She is excellent when quiet, watchful or thoughtful, but vague and melodramatic when put to the greatest ordeal.

There is a story told about Lotte Lenya (the Contessa), amused and gloating over her chance to steal the picture because Vivien Leigh was so smitten with Beatty. I think that is ill-founded. Lenya is excellent in what is a rather easy part, but there are really no moments where the three of them are playing together and a scene can be stolen. The true theft is more a matter of Beatty's own lust for the nastiness of Paolo overwhelming Leigh's uncertainty.

He is very good in the part. The inconsistency with the accent actually substantiates our feeling that Paolo is a fake, and draws attention to those moments when he is lying or making an appealing spectacle of himself. In effect, Leigh's voice is like a classical statue, while Beatty's is somewhere between a worm and a serpent, slithering over and around her, letting us feel a constant awareness of Paolo's Machiavellian traits. This gigolo acts with the heart, but never stops thinking and planning. And Beatty was apparently ready to be such a character, never flinching, never clutching at a moment that will let the audience like Paolo.

The movie might be better if its narrative fixed on the way two actors cross paths. If there was one good scene in which Mrs Stone coaches Paolo as an actor, this theme would be stronger, and for a moment at least Paolo might love a true teacher. As it is, the cold-blooded detail is superb. He is sleek, if a little too fleshy for a Roman who might starve if he can't sell himself. His mouth parts like a polyp, and the serene inaccessibility of his face becomes bogus whenever it smiles or frowns. For both are shows for the world: Paolo is really as deadpan as poker. When Mrs Stone gives herself to him sexually, he comes into her bedroom, in a black shirt and black pants. He drops his white jacket on a chair, he closes the drapes, he surveys her and then as he approaches the bed he goes into silhouette. It is a cultivated performance, without warmth or spontaneity, by a man always thinking how he is looking.

One cannot say, of course, if it is the actor's skill, the director's grace, or the simple nakedness of the man pretending to be Paolo. More than the stage, films study that balance of nature and artifice, and in playing an intelligent man, for the first time, Beatty touches on the impossibility of real feeling.

There is one breathtaking scene in which that question exactly coincides with the drama. Paolo is on the phone to the Contessa: she is hinting that he may have a chance at a movie career. The camera is in his lap nearly, as he leans back in an armchair. He is listening to her, thinking, stroking his tie absent-mindedly, his hand cocked, the phone curved around his face like a caress. His eyes dart back and forth, as if watching a fly. It is all brilliant and incisive; it is selfish, rapid thinking made manifest. And if it is acting – if the gesture with the tie was calculated, not thoughtless – then it is just a deeper, darker lie that it can seem so natural. But does this young hustler know when he is on, and when he is not? Or has he taken an imaginary camera into his solitude for company?

When the shooting of *Roman Spring* is concluded, he takes a vacation – in Rome. He is in a café there with the actress Inger Stevens when he meets Susan Strasberg, the daughter of teacher Lee Strasberg and another actress. (Does he let them pass him on? Or are there chambermaids and housewives who also catch his eye?)

He is still wearing Paolo's costume from the picture and Strasberg asks if he can sit down in such tight pants. They go out to dinner, and hit it off so well he moves in to her Rome apartment. "I found him charming and intelligent," she says, "with a tremendous need to please women as well as conquer them."

They go everywhere in Rome together, including the salon of Luchino Visconti, the film director. Visconti is "surrounded by priceless antiques and a handful of beautiful young men, while advocating Communism for the masses". A little more scarlet than red, perhaps, the connoisseur Visconti is attracted to Warren. After a little of this directorial scrutiny, Warren elects to visit the bathroom. He whispers to Susan on his way that she is to linger a moment and follow him.

Soon, they are in the small interior. You could safely imagine marble, rare lotions and elegant luxury, if it helped. She asks what they are doing there, *there*, in the john, and he says he'll show her. There is a breathless, cramped and necessarily ingenious twenty minutes before the two Americans stroll back to the salon and all the ardent, waiting gazes. Those eyes have their reward, for Susan has not noticed, she says, that her blouse is still unbuttoned. Or has Warren written the scene and schooled her in the proper display of carelessness? "I wasn't quite sure how to act," says Susan, "but Warren beamed, at one and all, an enchanting, ingenuous smile."

In 1962

Truth and other tales

A wind had sprung up, searching through the canyons. It was not a prevailing wind, but a brief panic in the air, the stir of some pressure in the ground, like the gasp after an explosion or a sunspot's belated gale. D shivered in the wind. It was such a mourning sigh of the faraway, it left him wistful. He was, he admitted it, a failure, a chump who grew sad listening to the wind. Such a pitiful romantic. But what could he do to stop fate dropping him in love with this unexpected and disarming Drew? Was he to blame? Wasn't it absurd to posit moral order or responsibility when this city could be wrecked in a commercial break? And wasn't D there just because he had striven to improve himself – never giving up? He had to learn to regard himself as the ball on the roulette wheel, falling where it might, ready for another play, free from regret or triumph.

"It's stopped," said Drew. She sounded disappointed.

"I suppose the earthquake must come one day," said D, trying to be fair with such hazards.

"I want it," Drew whispered. She was looking for fresh chasms or dust in the air from landslides. Far away the city twinkled on. The surface of Stone Canyon Reservoir was a sleepy sweat in the moonlight. The noise of the city was the familiar tiny booming, the old beat. It all went on, one minute after another, the cars slipping from third to top, the pins being reset after a strike.

"I want it all gone," she insisted.

"How can you?" It was the disbelief he felt someone ought to voice.

He saw her hair shift, like breathing. "I want to see the hills splitting and the reservoir spilling into the city. If this whole city got shaken up," she was straining with the thought, "anything could happen." She laughed as it struck her. "I could get my chance then." She turned on him; there were suspicions in her eyes. "Don't you want it?" She knew his answer. "I don't care! It deserves it." That was her clincher.

152

"It?" asked D. Perhaps she was religiously inclined? So many actors believed in long-shots bets.

"The city, the business." For Drew there was an "it" in there – the power by which the house rigged a game D accepted as open. "It" was the demon of her paranoia, and she wanted it revealed. "When it starts to shake," she tried again, "something in me says, 'Go on. Don't stop.' I want to be the cave woman in the new world." She smiled with relief, for she had got it clear as a role: the ruined city, and Drew in tousled hair and scorch marks, a marauder.

She was so much more molten than he was. D saw how, in life, the manner of actors could seem loose and distasteful, a little demeaning. He led her to a flat piece of ground and urged her to lie down.

"Won't there be snakes?" Her eyes were darting into the darkness, past the clumps of bush and weed.

"Surely not." D hoped the odd rabbit might hop past to live up to her fever. He told Drew to rest. He watched over her stern face, younger once her eyes closed, trying to sleep but growing tense again.

"Know what I did once?" Her eyes opened, grinning already, eager to see how he would take it. It made D think a story was coming, or at least a treatment.

"In Miami, I got in with some guys. They liked to have me lie down on the floor so they could putt golf balls at my pussy. On the carpet in a hotel. For gambling."

He waited. He never knew what traps she had. "That's horrible," he said. The line had been shaky the way she said it, but he wasn't sure whether this was the line's lurid flatness or her shortcomings as an actress. Yet she did not mock his upset. She tried to explain a certain ordinariness in the Miami scene.

"They weren't so bad. I like golfers. They've never let me down, you know." D could see the men, in shirtsleeves, with beer, studying their lie and tossing bills on the table.

"These weren't professional golfers?"

She hooted. "No, you bunny. They were just people in the business. You know who Truth is? A wrestler. He had handmaidens, two of us, dressed like slave girls and he came into the ring carrying us, one in each arm."

"You didn't wrestle?"

"That's death to a career. I wore a veil." Drew smiled at him, remembering the camouflage. "I even wore it to the gym for rehearsal."

"Where this Truth trained?"

"He didn't train. He walked his wife's dachshund. Truth was fifty, easy, and he wrestled three, four times a week. He used to specialise in beating Spanish kids. The Mexicans hated him. Their women called us whores – Cherry and I." He could see those old days jazzing past her romantic eyes.

"One night one of these young Mexican wrestlers took it to him. See, you can hurt someone if you want to, and if you're smart you can make it look like a mistake. This kid broke Truth's leg. Crowd went mad. Truth was weeping, sitting on the canvas. And you know what the Mexican kid did? He smacked Truth in the face, sitting there, so the blood poured out of his nose. It was like the kid thought the crowd wanted blood. But they didn't. They went absolutely silent and I hit the Mexican in the face with a bucket. They loved it. They roared. I just knew it was the time to take off my veil. You wouldn't believe it – the cheering, they threw flowers and the women blessed me. Anything like that happen to you?"

She could see the answer in his face, and so she hurried on. "I was on the Carson Show one night. One of the girls they have who bring out the new products? I wore a white bikini and I had a cake mix."

"And Carson flirted with you?"

"He's a frost."

"Still, the *Tonight* show."

"Yeah, but the white bikini didn't help me. My thighs had built at the gym. I should have had a black one-piece. I could have made it then."

"But Eyes saw you?" D presumed.

"He'd seen the pictures I did."

"Pictures?"

A gleeful idea surged across her face. "You think they were porno."

D blushed, "I didn't know."

"You kinky little D."

"I meant no such thing."

"You thought it. You thought private blue movies for Eyes alone. These were stills in travel brochures. Mexico, South America. Beaches and hotel pools. I was in a lot of those. And Eyes collects brochures. He found me through the agency. Just called me one day. Know what he said?"

"I'd never guess."

"He said, 'Hi'" her voice dropped down to her knees, "'this is Eyes. I just wanted to say I think you have terrific skin.'" Drew laughed, not sure whether to be proud or play the story for absurdity.

"Well, so you do," D told her.

"Yeah? I'll tell you about skin some day. Here's the car."

Another limousine was coming up the hill, slowly, looking for them. D brushed the dirt off his clothes, "We didn't have wolves."

"Oh we will," said Drew, "don't you worry."

"I'm puzzled." D had to say it – there is a stickler in him. "There was the New Hampshire story?"

"What?" Alarm loomed up in her guessing face.

"How Eyes saw you on TV, torn between that man who abducted you and the cop."

"Oh. That." It was an old story. She looked like a girl reminded of having to see grandmother when Randy Red Raider has just called.

She was so pretty a thing, such a scrap of dark foreboding. And when she stood, her body arched like a bow his love was pulling back. But D had lost track of how to humor or reassure her. She wanted very hard to be appealing, to have sway, but D could see that she was too desperate. It was her protection against a life of having to be liked. He knew she was more dangerous to his wish to be reasonable than snakes or wolves. Because he had the sense to shun those creatures.

As they gathered to transfer to this new car, D thought of travel brochures and all the young women you saw in them, sophisticated at the casino or sunning by the pool. He had regarded them as a Kodak army, alike, bronze, slender and blank in their wish-you-were-here. He thought of the determination in Drew that had lifted her out of that army.

"I'm glad for you that you are with Eyes."

"Oh sure," he heard her hurt. "Lucky me."

Another kind of slavery? He considered the allure of being a cave woman in this city, rendered back to chaos and primal struggle. D had the first unequivocal sense that he might see the end of the world. As if she guessed it, Drew took his hand and said, "Hang on, dearie. We're going to the party."

JOAN AT THE STAKE

Warren Beatty's attractiveness is being talked about as if it is a great talent, or a phenomenon apart from his character. People encounter it long before they meet him. A movie star never meets anyone to whom he is a stranger or a newcomer. His picture has been seen and appraised in magazines; if he has given interviews, they have been read and allowed to grow in the readers' minds; and in his movies, by giving several seconds at a time of his presence, his watching, listening, waiting self, he has allowed absolute strangers to develop a peculiar sense of familiarity with him. It will be particularly charming or offensive to anyone who is uncertain of himself to find that people he meets believe they have met him before, that they know him, and that when he smiles or jokes they knew he was going to do that. It may leave him suspicious of being, and in certain moods he may make a lavish, exaggerated, self-mocking imitation of this version of himself known in advance. And sometimes that act will go undetected. There may even come a moment in which he can perhaps be "Warren Beatty" in public – it satisfies so many, all the strangers checking in with the freak – and explore himself quietly, secretly, behind the closed doors of his smile. It is something all celebrated actors are likely to encounter, and it has the appeal of seeming to give the person control of a mad, frivolous world. But it is a kind of madness, too, for it initiates a split in the self that can become so constant it will not be noticed. And so you may some day read this or that about yourself, and chuckle, and say, "Look what 'Warren Beatty' is doing today. That rogue, that actor."

While they are in London and he is filming *The Roman Spring of Mrs Stone*, Joan Collins lives with Beatty. They may tell one another that they are in the greatest intimacy either of them has ever known in life. And he is learning lines for the next day, watching himself in the mirrors in the apartment or in the warmth of her responses. The role he is hoping to perfect for the film is that of a young man who exploits women. There are scenes in the movie where he is affectionate to and considerate towards women, where he makes love to them, with words or with his body. Then there are scenes where he is alone, or with men, with whom a quite different scale of candor is in order. He goes to the barber, and there he discusses his looks, his women and their gifts to him with a gloating, "professional" manner. He is the character and the actor in control of the character in *The Roman Spring*.

There is a moment in the barber shop when a waif-like young woman supposedly sauntering past on the Roman street sees this gorgeous young man through the window and stops to look at him. The actress playing this part has no lines. She and Beatty's Paolo are only cut together, each of them looking at the other. But the woman has a lean, wide-eyed face, and long hair that she tosses to him like a fisherman's line going out on the water. It is Sarah Miles, aged twenty, before she is known, before *Term of Trial*, or *The Servant*. For her it is only a day's work, but perhaps she talks to the star of the film between shots, perhaps he says to her, "What do you do?" and she says, "Oh, I just look at you." Perhaps there is no meeting. Joan Collins will wonder every day, and he can tell her, "You know what movies are like. Don't you trust me?" All actors are learning the facility that can make responsibility as slippery as soap in the shower.

Joan and Warren go to Paris for a few days, and they spend some time there with Joanne Woodward and Paul Newman, who is making *Paris Blues*. One night the four of them go to the Carousel, a gay night club in Montmartre. The acts at the club involve young men dressed as women – female impersonators, trans-sexuals perhaps. In their performance, the look-alikes for Marilyn Monroe, Ava Gardner, and so on, flirt with Newman and Beatty. One of them sings "Diamonds Are a Girl's Best Friend" and draws her boa across Warren's shoulders. The men blush, the women feel upstaged.

Then, at the end of the show, the performers invite the movie people backstage. Warren is a little nervous, but Joan says she urges him to go. And in the dressing room, attention shifts. The men are in various stages of bold undress, and they dote upon Joan and Joanne, professionally alert to *their* clothes, *their* hairstyles, and their interesting example of famous, beautiful women. How long is the career of female impersonators? Long enough, perhaps, for someone in Montmartre to be doing an outrageous "Alexis Carrington" still based on memory.

Joan and Warren live together again in Los Angeles after *The Roman Spring of Mrs Stone*. But it is not going well between them. It is her home, but he is irritated when her mother and young brother arrive from London on a visit. She tells him to stop being such a rat, and perhaps he blinks at that word and its failure to mesh with his vision of what is happening.

"It was obvious I had to be the one to end it with Warren. He seemed content to let it drift sloppily along. What happened to the glorious romantic fun we used to have? Why did all of my relationships with men turn sour? Was it my fault? Was I too strong? Or was I too weak? Or was it – and this I knew deep down to be the truth – that I really *wanted* only the neurotic ones, the men unable truly to love, truly to support and truly to give. Only by gaining the love of one of these impossible men could I prove to myself that I was a worthy person."

Joan is offered the female lead in *The Road to Hong Kong*, a reunion of Hope and Crosby. It is fifteen years since the last Road film, and this one will be filmed in England. "It's crap," says Warren, tossing the script aside. "Why do you need to do it?"

"Two reasons: for the money – and to get away from you." He had become a man and almost a star, says Joan, and I had marked time.

But her career is not quickly saved. Indeed, she will never make another good or significant movie again. She works all over the world in quick adventure films, empty comedies and in soft-core pornography – *The Stud*, *The Bitch*, *Nutcracker*. For theaters or television, she lists twenty-six films starting with *The Road to Hong Kong*. Beatty, in the same period, will make fourteen pictures. She exemplifies the kind of career he dreads – forever slipping, but never giving up, taking anything to keep in work.

There may be times in later years when she would go out of her way to avoid a meeting, and to hear his polite questions about what she's doing, knowing she's still doing what he regards as crap. Of course, she marries twice in those years, and she has three children, one of whom suffers but survives a serious road accident.

And then she becomes utterly famous again. In 1981, producer Aaron Spelling offers her a role in the soap opera, *Dynasty*. She says she'll think about it, and she accepts. In the next few years, she becomes one of the best known women in the world. The show is a hit, still running high in the ratings in 1986. Her character catches the popular imagination and "Joan Collins" becomes the epitome of a wicked, scarlet woman. At Christmas 1983, she is on the cover of *Playboy*, and inside, revealing not quite all, but far more than most fifty-year-olds would feel comfortable about. Her cheerful, disarming autobiography, *Past Imperfect*, published in England in 1978 but withheld in America—she is paid $100,000 for this discretion—appears in America in 1984.

In February 1982, already a hit as Alexis, Joan appears at Radio City Music Hall in the "Night of 100 Stars". There are actually over 200 stars, and Warren Beatty is another of them. They are on the same crowded stage for a few moments, and the camera does catch a suave grin thrown in his direction. He looks tired still from *Reds*.

There is no simple rivalry in such careers. *Reds* is not *Dynasty*. But there are no actors so sophisticated that they do not feel the raw power of celebrity. And *Reds* is not really so unlike *Dynasty*. They work according to similar rules of storytelling and casting. Of course, more people see *Dynasty*. And if it is crap, then it may be that a cheerful, middle-aged actress would ask isn't most of show business crap? No other woman in Warren Beatty's life seems to have survived his quiet judgment so well or so merrily. An inspired producer would try them together now, in comedy. It would be for Warren to have to consider such an offer.

Lighthiser house

The Lighthiser property was on the southern side of the ridge, and not what you'd expect at the end of a dirt track that straggled away from the smart curves of Mulholland. It looked like a spur that must narrow and choke in weeds, just beyond the blind bend that was all anyone could see from the road. D supposed that it was contrived to look as shabby as possible, with the undergrowth raised to be daunting. He remembered that Cy Lighthiser had made his first fortune in LA as a florist and landscape gardener. This was just a little touch of wilderness in the theater of the Santa Monica Mountains.

For as the limousine wallowed in the dune-like sand, it soon bit on a deeper layer of gravel, and D could see in the car lights ahead a wider swathe of cultivated drive. Through the back window, beneath the clouds left by the car, he saw its deep tire tracks in the act of vanishing. Subtle vents at ground level, hidden in the chaparral, were blowing away all traces of their entry. In a moment, it would look like a dead-end again. D wondered if there was a sound system in the undergrowth that played those small, indistinct hisses that might be animals only a step away. After all, the movies were an art and a technology in which reality had been commandeered for atmosphere. One never knew in Los Angeles which street scenes were spontaneous, and which the sport of story-telling.

The drive now was broad enough to accommodate flanks of parked vehicles and two lanes of traffic in between. There were Mexicans in white, moving in and out of the headlights, to supervise parking. Some of them had rifles strapped across their backs, bandido style. D wondered if brigands were ever hired for the night to come across the hillsides in threatening forays so that guests could be thrilled by the crackle of firing.

They parked the car and stepped out into the warm dust, fragrant with jasmine and mesquite. There were eucalyptus trees farther down the track and D could smell their pungent, mentholating resin. He felt how

easy to float down to the party, or to negotiate the distance on a cut. But Drew wanted to walk, barefoot, and D did as she asked. He took off his shoes and socks and left them in the car. Even dowdy D had an inkling of how this abdication enhanced his "look". On impulse, he borrowed a wide-bladed knife from one of the Mexicans and slashed at the ends of his pants to still their forlorn straightness. Drew studied her new pirate.

"You need a bloodstain," she reckoned, and as he was saying, "Do you think so?", he felt a slip of blade scathe his cheek and then stood patiently as Drew arranged a few drops of blood on what had been, at best, D's gesture towards a fresh white shirt – ironed, how long ago, by C, with typewriter white-out to cover its threadbare edges?

"Perfect," said Drew.

He felt the damp drying on his face.

"Act as if you hadn't noticed it," she told him. She was, in her way, as caring as C. Yet she had been armed with that tiny sharpness. D could not recall any pointedness in C; she had been his soft cushion. What a pity she couldn't be there to enjoy the eucalyptus and the trepidation.

"I think this is near the Bugsy Siegel house," said Drew, as they sauntered along, beckoned by the sounds of music – the bass of dance – glasses kissing and the torn strips of laughter.

"Is that so?" D liked to have historic sites identified. "When was that?"

"Oh," she moved away from him, "I don't know the dates."

D had intimidated her. In truth, he believed the Siegel home had been farther over, nearer Silverlake. But he did not want to deter Drew from stories that might be quite as revealing as the facts. So he said, "You could easily hide out in these canyons."

"I know it," she asserted. "I was up here one summer with Eyes. In a world of our own." It was like a caption.

"Near here?"

"Near here," she allowed. "Bugsy Siegel," she decided to say, "he used to dress up and go out, and no one ever recognised him. And then he'd answer the door at his house as the butler, and he'd say, 'Oh no, regrettably Mr Siegel's gone away, out of town – he's in Africa, or he's in jail.'"

"He had an amusing name," said D.

"He was Benjamin really," Drew volunteered.

"I didn't know that."

"Oh sure," Drew paused. "He was only forty-one when he died."

"As young as that?"

"Know what Bugsy said?" The little girl was pleased as punch now. "He said, 'I never thought I'd live to be forty.'"

"Ah," said D. "Forty is a serious step."

"Eyes and I used to picnic around here," Drew was saying. "We'd sleep out nights and make love under the stars."

Was he meant to ask for more, or show some flickers of jealousy? She stooped to examine him. Her old child's face noticed his muddle.

"You could go home, you know. Whenever you want."

"I don't think so, not now," he admitted.

"Don't think of me," she warned him.

"What does that mean?" He was haughty, he knew, trying not to break.

"Don't believe in me, that's all."

D knew there was blunt, inescapable advice in this, amply evidenced by the veering of this slick kid. But her miserable way of saying it made him feel protective of her. The prettiness was so shadowed by fatigue in its act – it looked like illness sometimes.

Then a Mexican came up behind them, polite but not to be refused. "Senor, senora," he said, "you hurry on party. These hills scary at night."

"Of course," said D, and he winked at Drew. "You never know who's sleeping in the undergrowth."

The gallantry touched her. One eye became a tear that slid onto her face. "It really happened, D. Eyes was so bright then. He could have saved the world."

"I know," said D. "I had an idea once for a story for him – he would have been a derelict who discovers a power of healing, and he becomes a famous evangelist. Yet he never knows whether his power is real."

"Oh yes," said Drew – she could see it. "That's a great seventies picture."

SUITCASE LIFE

Maybe Joan Collins throws him out, or is it just that she's left with the impression that she threw him out, while he believes that she was going to England so he didn't see any point in hanging around? This is not a community or a business where very many people break down and tell you, "I was the fool." And it is not that they are necessarily lying to you or themselves. They have got into the habit of seeing how they are on top. They are like Clint in Clint Eastwood movies, always thinking out those cutting one-liners that have an air of being in charge. But Clint uses those lines on other people. Most people talk to themselves with them. Of course, it is not exactly a community or a business. It is more of a séance.

And he is disinclined to unpack. Whether they are living in places she has taken and is paying most of the rents on, in borrowed apartments in London or in hotels, he tends to live out of a couple of suitcases, flat and often open on the floor. The clothes go from the cases to his body to the laundry, and they come back pressed and folded like new shirts so they can go back in the cases again. He knows were everything is – that's why no one else is allowed to touch, because that will disturb the order or further the disorder.

So when the time comes it is going to be a little easier for her to know she kicked him out because she can say to herself, "Just zip your bags, buster, and on your way." It's not that he's picked out magnolia trees for the garden and fed them a little mulch every day. There aren't any evident emotional investments. And if he is thrown out, he can always remind himself that he wasn't ever really, or thoroughly, *there* – not a resident, but someone who was staying there, waiting. It's no humiliation; he was going anyway. Couldn't she see he was his own man? Couldn't he see she knew he was scared?

Not living anywhere, or not having a home, is a strange condition in the extensively middle-class world from which Warren Beatty makes movies. Most of the audience has a home; it is the place they leave to go out to the movies. It is the firm site of security in the lives they expose to fantasy at the movies. If the picture lags, they may get to wondering whether the babysitter is molesting the children, or whether they are being robbed, or how they are going to finance the new room for when the kids get to be of an age when they've gotta do those things – like laying one another, or smoking grass – and you'd rather they did it in the safety of the home, but somehow out of sight.

Most movie stars have homes, eventually; they all die, too, of the same withering and merciless failures. And there have always been magazines that take you inside the homes of the stars, just as there are bus-tours that will lead you past their barred and walled properties. But it is sad to see exactly how a star lives – even if it is Edward G. Robinson with a Gauguin, or Debra Winger with Christmas stockings hanging all year over the hearth. Because it ties them down, it confines them. It is wonderful for a moment to have the detail, but then you realise you have lost the infinite possibility.

So, finally, living out of suitcases, living everywhere for no matter how long as if the place were a hotel, is a form of imaginative complicity with the audience. It is the self-denial of a pilgrim, the rootlessness of an actor who is happiest in the dressing-room, living like a slut, but emotionally secure in the eternal readiness for change. There is a frontier of not having which has a unique appeal to those millions who will be mulling over what they have left at home, worrying so much that a part of them would feel lightened if the message was flashed up in the middle of the movie – "Mr —— come home, your house has burned down."

So Warren moves in with Natalie Wood. Which complicates relations between Natalie and her sister Lana, eight years younger. Lana is not happy at home, and when Natalie leaves Robert Wagner, to live first in Bel Air and then in Benedict Canyon, Lana is around enough to have a room of her own. On Lana's sixteenth birthday, Natalie gives her a Jaguar XKE convertible. "All gold," says Lana.

Sometimes the girls play together, dressing up, exchanging confidences. But then, suddenly, Natalie is a sophisticated young woman with an affair and a kid sister – and an attractive kid sister who in a couple of years will outrage Natalie by posing for *Playboy*. When Natalie makes *Gypsy* – at the same time – she never takes *her* clothes off.

Lana says Warren moves into Natalie's home – the one in Benedict Canyon in which a waterfall outside is made into a stream that runs through the house, complete with mosquitoes – because their love is so intense. "Together in public," says Lana, "they were something to behold: beautiful, exciting, sophisticated." But at home, they fight and live on different tracks. Lana says Warren would talk about his dreams of producing and directing. But then there is a night when the sisters are together, and Natalie is becoming tense. She and Warren are expected at a party, but he has not come home. (They are an evident couple. Norman Mailer will report them at a party at Peter Lawford's Malibu home, which Marilyn Monroe leaves hours before her death.) By the time he returns it is too late, and Natalie is too overwrought for anything but a fight. So he storms out again, and Lana is there to sympathise, to blame him – though she has noticed that he sometimes looks at her – and to save it all up. One night Lana says that Warren is "only chronologically" older than she is when Natalie orders her to apologize to him.

"They occasionally had friends to dinner," Lana will say in her book. "But more often than not it was Natalie and Warren and, on weekends, just the three of us. It seemed to me that whenever Warren was in one room, Natalie was in another. Natalie would lie by the pool in the sun for an hour and then when Warren would appear in his trunks, his usual book tucked under his arm, she would get up and go into the house. It wasn't hostility, it certainly wasn't disinterest, and I have since come to think of it as two lives coming together briefly, but always at cross-purposes. There was always a distance between them."

There are incidents not likely to improve trust, such as the story of Warren and Natalie dining together at a restaurant. Warren's eye is captured by a hat-check girl. Not that Warren comes with a hat. It might be a waitress or a hostess; it might be another diner. But in the version that casts the hat-check girl, Warren excuses himself in the middle of the meal, finds the girl and persuades her to give up her job. They go off then and there, leaving Natalie alone at the table, with a hat-check costume tossed on the dressing-room floor.

Who knows now exactly how or whether it happened? It may have been only a meeting at the restaurant that developed into something later. It may be that Natalie did not know where Warren had vanished to for seven days, without his usual book. The story may be correct, or nothing more than a fabrication Natalie heard being spread around town. Whatever, she knows she is with a man who is the quicksilver center of more stories than she has dresses; and it plays upon her insecurity. Stories are torment to the imaginative. And if she asks him to explain, she can expect a shy denial – as if he is too proud to act it out well

165

With Natalie Wood

for her. "Well, of course," he can say finally, "if you don't trust me . . ." This is how the wanderer gets left.

It lasts about a year, with many storming outs as well as plans to make a picture of the Neil Simon play *Barefoot in the Park*, about newly-weds in New York. (Several years later, Jane Fonda will make this film with Robert Redford as her husband.)

Near the end of the year, Natalie has to go to New York for publicity. She invites Lana on that trip, to be a fellow-shopper. One night they are to have dinner with the journalist Tommy Thompson: Natalie is having a "brief affair" with him. Then Warren invites all three to dine with him.

It is an awkward meal, with arguments and silences between Warren and Natalie. At last, she and Thompson leave to go to their suite. Lana remains at the table with Warren. She knows he is a philanderer, but she says she is astonished when Warren suggests they adjourn to her room.

> "He told me I was always provoking him running around Natalie's house in a bathing suit, that even though I pretended not to know what was happening I knew exactly what the score was. I smiled sweetly – and insincerely – and said it couldn't be so because I was never interested in him and, in fact, considered him the cause of much of my sister's unhappiness."

But she has him take her back to her hotel. She asks him to get her room key from the desk, and while he's away she telephones Natalie for sisterly advice. She asks to be taken in for the night, but Natalie can't manage that. Warren reappears with the key and Lana tells him no, she can't do it. The hotel room is a convenience, but it is an institution. It is somewhere where, whatever happens, it need not be regarded as a defeat on one's home turf, an action embodying commitment. It is a well-appointed stage, with room service and fresh linen, in which the desperation can seem like freedom.

Same old party

The closer D and Drew came to the sounds of the party, the more likely it seemed that the house was not quite there. For they felt themselves close to the brink of a cliff or some drastic collapse in the land. They could feel that coolness which promises there is no ground to warm the air a few yards ahead. There was a point of utmost illusion at which they were hesitant to step forward while hearing phrases from conversations ahead as well as boredom and curiosity in the languid voices.

Then suddenly the house and its garden were beneath them on a last shelf in the hillside. It was a white-walled hacienda with a red-tile roof. Music and amber light were spilling from it onto the first of two terraces where people were dancing on a swimming pool. Yet it was a dancefloor made like a pool, the couples turning to and fro, partners offering and withholding on a surface of rippled turquoise, lit from below so that they did appear to be stepping on water. The Latin dance band was deployed on the three levels of diving board.

But on the second terrace there was a true pool. Guests were swimming there. There was a tang of chlorine and the noise of splashing lifted up by the canyon draft. For beyond the second terrace there was nothing but the vague forms of trees on the valley slope beyond, their top leaves gilded by moonlight. The estate was on the edge of inhabited land. The drop may have been only several hundred feet, but at night it seemed more complete.

There was a large video screen at the entrance to the house, set up near the statue of Aphrodite that Cy Lighthiser had brought back from Florida and surrounded with a bed of roses. The floodlighting made it difficult to distinguish the colours of the roses – they all resembled flesh – but the scents were so astonishing that no one went too near them. The video showed Lighthiser and his wife, the actress, Claudia Cannon. He wore white evening dress, without a tie, his swarthiness protruding at the cuffs and throat. And she wore a jungle green dress from which her

168

shoulders rose like volcanic peaks. Standing between Cy and Claudia was an African couple, in rags, the woman holding a hydrocephalic child. These natives were smaller than Cy and Claudia – like matted-in figures from another movie, taken on a different lens. The hosts ignored the couple: still, they were there, a point of tacit reference in the video.

CY: Hi. Welcome to our home.

CLAUDIA: We thought that as the crowd grew we might have trouble meeting every one of you personally.

CY: So we've chosen this unusual hallo. There's no reason for the party.

CLAUDIA: Except to say that somewhere else others are less well off.

CY: So, eat and drink.

CLAUDIA: And dance and play.

CY: And if you see anyone around who looks like us.

CLAUDIA: Don't be afraid to talk, or touch.

CY: Just don't forget we live in a large world. And don't pick the roses.

Whereupon, his lime-colored consort shivered with laughter. Then they both smiled during an undue delay, like a newsreader waiting to go to pictures, before the image went blank and was replaced with clips from Cy's latest movies.

"What a chic occasion," drawled Clear, coming up to D and Drew. "The Ethiopian pledges, I hear, are enough to have made a mini-series." He had the same wry smile, patient enough to do without obvious irony.

"What about our earthquake?" asked Drew.

"Did you have one? I don't think we felt anything here."

"Our car died," D explained, and Clear smiled again as if he understood all the reasons to stop along the way. "And there was a quake?" he asked politely.

"How's this party?" demanded Drew, disdaining detail.

"Same old party, if you know what I mean. Pasta salads and shoptalk. Some bright young things. A few deals closing before morning. All the old folks cracking the same jokes. The party that moves around town."

"Why do they come if it's not so special?" asked D. To him, it looked as perilous as a zoo where the visitors were expected to stroll in the same paddock as the animals.

"It would be rash to miss it," Clear explained. "You see, giving and going to parties here is like charity in other empires – gifts to the gods. Our starving Africans are the ultimate celebrities. That's why you won't be introduced."

Clear was so alert to the folly that D had to ask, "Eyes will not be here?"

"I doubt he will. It wouldn't be the first time I'd been wrong. He'd be more likely to drop in if he knew I was handing out his regrets. But with parties, in general, Eyes has slowly detached himself. Though, I remember when he was partial to intimate dinners – six or eight people, good talk, that sort of thing."

"Well," said D, not wanting to think badly of this pomp, especially if he was a guest, "it must be better than the Black Death."

"Oh, that's good," said Clear. "We should tell Cy that. I think he'd like it. Look, I have to take a call. Drew, circulate D. Show him the sights. There's anything you'd want." He spread his hands in an air of amiable defeat. Then he moved on, brushing cheeks as he went, and backhanding sly fives.

"Always working," said Drew, bitterly.

"He is agreeable, though."

"Do you think so?" she wondered. "He only carries the messages."

"He has been very kind to me," D assured her.

She considered what this opinion revealed. "You shouldn't be here," she told him. "These people could feed you to the fish."

"I don't think so." D laughed boldly. He wanted to be up to it all.

"Or make you fall in love with them," she murmured. "Would you bathe naked?" This question came so quickly after the barbed remark, D could not deal with both.

"In the pool," Drew nodded her head, leaning that way with a body that wanted the cool in her armpits, between her legs, in the spaces between her toes.

"No bathing suits?" he asked her.

"I told you about skin. Come and watch. There'll be other old gentlemen."

"Is that what I am?"

"I'm fond of old gentlemen," she said. She made him think they were always the most knowing.

"I might watch."

"That's riskier than swimming."

"Don't you want me to watch you?" Was it the tenderest question he had asked her?

"Why not?" said Drew. She looked at him as sad as if he had come along too late, but wondering if there might yet be a best to be made of it. "I'm a slut," she added.

"This is a splendid evening," said D. He wanted her to know how eager he was.

"Until you're sick to your stomach," she threw in.

ALL FALL DOWN

Sometimes an alchemy appears in the early careers of stars. From one picture to the next, a mood hangs in their air as if to say these movies are not really separate, individual dramas in which a Warren Beatty happens to have been cast, but stages in a conspiracy or a cult that *is* the actor. Sometimes this is the shared wisdom at rival studios that he is especially well cut out for some moment or stance that fits easily into many dramas – a way of seeming to arrest the action, looking up at the other characters and at the entire process of the film, saying, "What did you say?" or "You mean me? You think that's me?" Sometimes it is the actor and the actor's agent besieging a project with pleas for a scene they know he looks good in – a star has to realise how he should be photographed, he easily acquires the code for his own looks, and he is likely to chat casually, on a man-to-man basis, with directors of photography ("Lionel, how are we today?" – when he means by "we" the photosensitive pact in which the two are furnishing a kind of religion). Or it may be chance, an unavoidable, rising nature seen and used by different people, without prodding or prompting, just as – it is alleged – some great natural discoveries are made simultaneously all over the world.

Early on in *All Fall Down* there is a scene in a bar in Florida. Clinton, in his late teens, has come south from the family home in Cleveland, looking for his older brother, Berry-Berry. Clinton has brought $200 that was meant to help his brother get set up in business; but is has to be spent to get him out of jail. Berry-Berry is a loner, a drifter, a wastrel, a womaniser. "If he was my brother, I wouldn't brag," someone warns Clinton. But the kid is too much in awe of his brother: they are Brandon de Wilde and Warren Beatty, wide-eyed love and wonder and the narrowed face that hates itself.

So the brothers go to a bar – fond, related, but with nothing in common and no evident thing to do except for Berry-Berry to disillusion the kid. A rich young woman comes in, Mrs Mandel. She is played by

Constance Towers – tall, blonde, a little bitter and repressed – it is one of those many fine performances that seem stimulated by Beatty's presence. She talks to the barman first:

"Good evening, Mrs Mandel."

"Good evening, Tony."

"Are you leaving tonight?"

"Yes, we're going on a little cruise to the Bahamas. My husband's had a terrible time finding a crew today. They all want such enormous wages. Shocking."

The cutting and the framing of the film have already alerted Mrs Mandel and Berry-Berry to one another: it is a medium hooked on attractions. Faces look and the leap of editing gives their ardor an object of desire. It has to, otherwise the film falls apart. Berry-Berry moves over to be nearer, but this is as much an effect of breathing as of real motion. The medium lets him come closer, and Beatty is already an actor in whose sagging mouth breath is the most intense physical activity. His voice comes from his nose – it is crucial to his sexiness.

"Lady, if I had a yacht, I wouldn't complain."

"Do you resent people with yachts?"

"No . . . Just that I got an old man at home who talks about a share of the wealth, and all that."

"Oh, I'm perfectly willing to share any of my possessions," says Mrs Mandel, and she opens her white cardigan on that line. This is the kind of effect – so "right," so slick – that we must begin to feel that people are already helplessly in the debt of movies they have seen, and of their codes. And yet, something in the actress, a certain innocence, still makes the director's touch poignant. We are seeing a frightened woman pretending to be brazen, a woman claiming to be an actress. It is sexy because of this insight into pretense.

She goes on: "Perhaps you'd like to join us? You might enjoy the Bahamas." (There is something wonderful and surreal in movies before the end of sexual censorship – that this cool white sweater holds semi-tropic isles, with the word "Bahamas" on the sound track, passing into radio's eroticism.)

Berry-Berry considers and then says something utterly out of keeping with the compelling naturalism of this scene, but something so right if it is really a scene about actors: "How do you know I'm not some dangerous maniac that goes around killing beautiful women like you?"

She relaxes; the threat is balm because he has noticed her greatest worry, he has called her beautiful. She is stupid for him, and he is in control. *All Fall Down* does not much like women: "Well, in that case, I won't have to take a sleeping pill tonight." This is why the picture is in black-and-white, and is years ahead of anything that could be made now, more than two decades later. It has a lucid pessimism, not flaunted and not evaded, a quiet terror at the way people are and at their destructiveness.

"Well. These are the only clothes I got," says Berry-Berry.

"I think I can find a pair of trunks that will fit you."

"Well, I've got another problem here," – power in pictures always humiliates others – "my kid brother, I gotta take care of him. Need about fifty bucks to get him home."

Mrs Mandel hands over the money: it is her body printed in neat, flat, oblong forms – Grant's tomb.

"Be down on the pier in half an hour. If you don't come I'm going to have to have you shanghaied."

Berry-Berry is a gambler, and a self-destructive. Even the "golden" offer is one to take risks with: "Didn't I hear you say you had a husband?"

And the film leaps with danger, as Mrs Mandel has her moment: "Oh, I do, but I don't think he'd appeal to you at all."

All Fall Down is two films that never mesh. It is the story of the Cleveland home, of parents who insist that their sons call them by their first names as if to ignore their constant need for infants. Ralph and Annabel (Karl Malden and Angela Lansbury) are failures: he drinks, she nags; they are craziness kept decent by domestic habit. And Clinton, their son, has been driven to spying on them and recording their conversations on his way to being a writer: *All Fall Down* was first of all a novel, by James Leo Herlihy. Clinton is a sweet hero, who loves life. Will he survive this family?

Berry-Berry is another film, that of a sexual roadie whose dark hair has golden ends from the Florida sunshine. He lives off fools and women. He beats them, because he hates life and himself. He could be a good deal more depraved if the film were bold enough – he might sleep with Mr and Mrs Mandel, he might be an adventurer a little less burdened by self-pity and a little more capable of true intelligence.

But Berry-Berry is there to teach Clinton about life in the kindly, conventional and circumscribed scheme of William Inge, John Frankenheimer and James Leo Herlihy. And so he must behave so badly that Clinton sees the light. Berry-Berry comes home. You mustn't ask why. The family's house guest, Echo (Eva Marie Saint), falls in love with him.

She is a thirty-one-year-old virgin of the kind that Hollywood keeps in the trunk next to the one for drifters, wastrels and womanisers – just so long as the two breeds can sniff each other's begging blood. Echo gets pregnant. Berry-Berry wants his freedom. She drives off into the night and the rain and crashes. The studious film has already established her as a good driver.

It may be the craziest measure of *All Fall Down*'s "family virtues" that this young mother's suicide is utterly condoned. Like most of Inge's work, this movie wants to tear the family limb from limb, but it can only sit there in its awful shadow, suffering. Annabel loves Berry-Berry but the emotion is repressed. It is a far better film if Berry-Berry offers sex to his mother. Beatty seems just as interested in Angela Lansbury as he does in Eva Marie Saint. Their love is a plot device in which love-making is dissolved with shots of swans and emotional embraces so much less acrid and pointed than the talk with Mrs Mandel.

Beatty is on screen for rather less than half the film. He cannot handle the implausibility in his actions. He never makes us believe that he loves Clinton or Echo. Nor is Beatty remotely successful in either a final tearful breakdown or a devilish, laughing display of nihilism. It is clear here how far – in a certain professional sense – he cannot act: these are types of scenes in which his effort is merely perfunctory. When he has to cry, Frankenheimer despairs of the actor moving us and employs a series of cuts moving in on ever closer shots to register an intensity Beatty cannot give the lens.

It is the "sincerity" dearest to this concept in which Beatty fails. It is as if the real man in the actor is too guarded to play such revelatory scenes. Warren Beatty has extraordinary screen presence, but it is confined to situations of thought, guile and artifice. He has to play an actor. He does not believe in the generosity that gives of the self. Given that in Beatty, Berry-Berry should only come to the Cleveland home like a terrorist, bent on ripping away all its veils of disguise.

The film is an interesting failure, then. But in its first half, it has two of Beatty's best scenes. The first is with Mrs Mandel, where the game and the act are everything: indeed, they are the best sex Mrs Mandel is going to get, however many garments she is ready to open up for him. The second scene comes when Berry-Berry has moved on to work at a gas station. It is just before Christmas when a woman comes in for a fill-up. The actress is Barbara Baxley, and it is the best thing she will ever do on the screen.

"You new here?" she asks. Her voice is shifting from the tired, thin

Southern scream of a teacher who no longer believes in talking, to the deeper, more careful delivery of someone who knows she may be on the verge of a "great scene." Now she is becoming the teacher who always wanted to be an actress.

"I'm just helping out for a while." He hasn't noticed her yet.

"I wondered. I drive here regularly, and I knew I hadn't seen you before. I think I would have remembered you if I'd seen you before. I mean, you're not the kind of young man one expects to see in a job like this." She is already essaying the Blanche DuBois no one will ever ask her to attempt.

"Why's that?" There's the line, sighed to the car as much as to her, but coaxing the picture to address him.

"Well, if I were a young man, and I were as good-looking as you, I think I'd go to Hollywood. Try and get in the movies." In Beatty's career, no subject will ever loom larger than the career itself, and we are left as cultural explorers wondering whether such a scene is conscious or natural.

"That where you're headed?" He is saying so little, working on the car, while she is talking. She is like an actress auditioning for him, and he is too busy and callous to give her all his attention.

"No, I'm going to Louisville for my Christmas vacation. I'm a teacher. I have three weeks' vacation. I'm going to Louisville. I have a sister there. I hate to drive all the way to Louisville by myself. I don't suppose you know any young man who'd drive me, do you? Somebody reliable? Who'd be a kind of companion, too."

"I don't suppose you'd like to change your mind by any chance and go to Cleveland?"

"Cleveland! I don't have any relatives in Cleveland." There's a tremor in the air, disturbing her small hopes, saying just how much would you give up for the part? Order? Sanity?

"Well, what if this young man didn't have any bread. He couldn't afford a room?"

"Bread?"

"Didn't have any money."

"Oh, well, teachers aren't ever rich, but I'm sure I could afford a room for him some place. As long as my vacation lasted. And provided he'd drive me back. And if he'd take me a few places in Louisville. My sister and her husband don't go out very much, and sometimes I get very lonely." The would-be actress wants the play to be about her; it may be her miracle play.

"You got yourself a driver." She will never catch this blunt pace. He will come and come again while she is getting in the mood.

"You mean you can go?" (The actress is exquisitely good: we know exactly how far desire's dream is destroying her philosophy.) "You mean you can just pack up and leave? My goodness. You can't just go, right now. And leave the station without anyone to take care of the customers."

"You want me or not?" This is Attila at the gates of her vagina.

"Well, I'd be delighted if you took the job, but I don't want to inconvenience other people."

This is the peak of *All Fall Down*. There is a short scene to come, in Louisville, where the teacher knows she has been humiliated and where Berry-Berry hits her because, "You made me do it. I didn't have any choice." But it is unnecessary after the dark comedy of the pick-up which lets us imagine all the damage to come while never losing the acidic mirth of the spider keeping the fly in the corner of its wicked mind.

It is telling that Beatty so wanted to play Berry-Berry and to emphasise his waywardness. When people saw (or see) *All Fall Down* they cannot like Berry-Berry at the level of the movie's conservative consciousness. But they cannot forget Beatty because while he is poor, abject or nearly non-existent in several scenes, still he is the heart of the movie's best scenes, those in which it has the power available to the medium.

It might be a kinder world if movies awakened us to human depths that let us behave better. But they are more concerned with power, glamor and seductiveness, and that is why they can make danger and darkness so attractive. Movies always say do you want me or not?, and now, not just when you're ready. Movies race on at *their* pace and energy and they say leave your belongings and your attachments. On a cut, let us go from Florida to Louisville, or from propriety to desire's nakedness. Berry-Berry knows the energy of the medium: its fuel is his air and nothing is as frightening or as exciting as this readiness to go now, leaving the dull, real world for what it is.

The medium celebrates such drifters, however much the script scolds them. Perhaps William Inge knew why Beatty's own family experience equipped him for *All Fall Down*. Maybe he wrote scenes for the young actor he liked, and feared a little. But we must remember that Inge's world wants home and family to work, and it could be that Inge himself would have gone crazy if he had ever had to live out of a suitcase or literally give up the ship that placed him in the world. *All Fall Down* is the worried lament of middle America, too nervous to really use the animal it half-wants as its nemesis. The movie is still disturbing just because of that conflict of wish and energy. It is the kind of failure that can enhance a career.

Drew dives

Drew was in her dive, a twist and somersaults, the whorl of pubic hair the screw fastening her to the scene. D would have watched her all the way down. But the tall woman in black went on talking to him. "Mr D, I'm telling you about my art event," dragging his head away from the leggy spin his naked Drew made in the floodlight before the streak of body cut the water and an uncomplaining lifeguard went in after her. She was a spectacular diver, but she could not swim, and had to keep a certificated man around.

D could not take it all in, along with the silver trays of canapés, the ever-fresh tulips of champagne, or the smoldering joints. He was not accustomed to parties: he was like the Ethiopians, and he wondered if his eyes were as terrified as theirs. His head was swivelling. Yet he was aware of all he was missing.

The party was one space, not with precise distances between the magnolia tree and the parrot on its perch, but an inner montage in which these images were superimposed. For he was always in one place, with his attention in another, shutting down talk at his ear to pick up whispers over there. And he could alter his tuning, just as he could believe that everything was happening at once, that the party was not a night or several hours, but a bulging instant.

At the pool, Drew met several children putting a kitten on the water on a square of white styrofoam; and the kitten was clawing at its small raft, destroying it. So Drew chided them and lifted the cat to safety. But its hair-thin claws raked her arm, and the children oohed to see blood. It was like chocolate in the floodlighting.

Then it was teenagers, hard with muscle, impervious to the fudge sundaes they were eating. They ganged up on Drew, and tossed her in and out of the water. She was their ball, nearly sick with laughter. Then at last she was left hanging on the rail in the water until one of the boys swam back to her, stood behind her and drove her flat against the wall. D

178

was left to wonder if he was penetrating her. She tried to beat at him and he knifed away through the water like an indolent shark. Drew sagged from the rail, her eyes shut. He saw her mouth muttering. D had done nothing but watch.

He attached himself to a ring of savagely attractive faces and their conversation:

"So I will have this affair with Teddy," said a woman in orange hair. She had the air of being dead, examining her old life.

"Not Teddy! I hoped he was gay," said the man with her.

"Of course he is. But he wants to humiliate Maxene."

"I know I'm going to kill Maxene," another woman promised them all.

And another man, "Have you forgotten? I did kill her a year and a half ago, but then a few months later she just came back from a trip, re-cast and no one bothered."

A butler brought D a white telephone: "For you, sir."

"How can it be?"

But the fellow only smiled and put the phone to D's head.

"Having fun?" said the voice on the phone.

"Well," D tried to explain. "It's extraordinary." He had just noticed that another group was exploring the floor of the valley below with a laser beam. The small lemon of light pierced through woods, patios and houses. It found a couple asleep. The light stopped. The woman stirred. The light had focused as a pinpoint in her open armpit. She tried to get away. D felt her agitation. She never woke, but the intrusion reached into her sleep.

"I've been talking to Eyes," said the voice.

"Who is this?" asked D.

"Look up towards the house," the voice told him.

D did as he was told, and he saw a man by the terrace balustrade, looking down, smiling at him. The man was on the telephone. The man was Clear.

"No, stay there," said Clear on the telephone, as D looked for the steps so that he might be with his colleague. "It's easier like this. Anyway, I talked to Eyes about the script."

"Is he here?"

"The telephone. He loves it – I told you that – but he puts his finger on something that troubled me."

"What's that?"

"Well, it does rather dwell, in terms of time and space."

179

"I see," said D. He could not decide whether this was a mortal problem or akin to an unpleasing color in the paper.

"We weren't sure," said Clear. "So we called your wife, and she concurred."

It was a shivery knife in his back. He looked up and Clear was still amiable – thank God now for the distance of the phone. Clear must have foreseen this.

"You could reach her?" D felt sick.

"By good luck. We called and some rather grim man answered. He got her to the phone."

"Scrug," said D. The man was menacing at night, when he might have been taken from some favorite show.

"He seemed very nasty," Clear recalled.

"And she agreed?"

"You don't mind us asking?" Clear's voice wormed into his ear.

"She does know the script," D reasoned.

"And your pluses and minuses. Anyway, think about it. Let's talk soon."

"Soon?" D asked. In ten minutes or later in the year?

"I have to run." When D looked up, Clear was gone.

He returned the phone to the rest, and noticed a silence crowding in on him except for the voice of a woman, who, apart from being rather overdone, looked like Barbara Howar. She was saying, "But even at a party like this, entertainment business goes on and the hopefuls may find out whether this is the place for them or whether they should get the next Greyhound back to Omaha."

There was a camera pointing at him, as well as lights. D read "Entertainment Tonight" on the camera. He looked again and it *was* Barbara Howar, not exactly overdone but in the swing of her indefatigable desire to catch the system at work. D felt mortified. He was sure people were laughing at him, yet he tried to find out from the crew what night this segment might be shown.

SOUR APPLE

It *feels* orchestrated, even if there has been no master plan. "Warren Beatty" bursts upon the world like a campaign. His first three films open in the period from October 10, 1961 to April 11, 1962. Initially this is because of the unusual interval between the shooting of *Splendor in the Grass* and its release. But it is also because other pictures feel they may be harboring a phenomenon to be exploited immediately. And so, *The Roman Spring of Mrs Stone* opens three days after Christmas 1961, in time to secure Oscar possibilities for that year and to catch the wake of interest left by *Splendor*. *All Fall Down* is pushed out early, in part because MGM have a disaster in *Four Horsemen of the Apocalypse*, but also because in early 1962 people are talking about Warren Beatty. There are the films, and there are the love affairs; and if it may sometimes trouble an earnest young romantic to see how the two are confused, still the careerist has a complete understanding of how seductiveness works. But if he *is* a romantic, he will dislike himself for his cool calculation. And if he is Warren Beatty, too, he will see how far his own sensual presence, his uncanny need to be alluring, and his own wish to be in control of it all, leaves many people disliking him. There are moments when it could put a kid off romantic life for good.

All Fall Down is a severe failure; *The Roman Spring of Mrs Stone* does not do well; and, while it is well reviewed and is clearly an event, not even *Splendor in the Grass* excels at the box office. These are all despondent views of life, grim, sad or resigned. They are the natural material of novels or plays trying to find outlet on the screen, but never convincing the American audience. For, all too plainly, they deal with reality, and both the entertainment force and the artistic achievement of American films have always and will always depend upon turning reality into energised metaphors – they are called genres – that take the crowd for a ride and let the moral sink in peacefully.

In the early 60s, the picture business in America is going out of control: nothing else may irk Warren more. The studio system has broken down, just as the mass audience has given its imagination to the small screens. Hollywood is making hugely expensive throwbacks – like *Cleopatra* – or small, old-fashioned, literary studies of harsh reality, like *All Fall Down*. Neither works. We are still a few years away from the reclaiming of movies by the young as a vital American form and from the new forging of American genres, something that prevails from, say, *Bonnie and Clyde* to *Taxi Driver*, a period in which Warren Beatty is a clear leader and a figure of unquestioned charisma.

There is no reason to think Warren foresees all this: the story goes dead if he does. But he knows things are wrong in the business he is entering, and if he and that business do not get on well in many ways it may be because his skepticism keeps nagging at its failure to understand and change. He does not trust the business to run his career, and he does not see the sense in the inane round of empty interviews entailed in promoting a film. So he angers the studios and the press – all of which makes him more desirable, and surely schools him in an insight which may never have been far from his nature: that it can be seductive to stay silent, to be difficult, to treat your admirers badly. The seducer despises his conquests, for they have failed to see that the charm was just a trick, the play of an intelligence that does not much like life or the world.

When *All Fall Down* opens it gets reviews that manifest the nation's urge to confuse the star and the characters he is playing. When we are sensible and pious we always deny this; but it is central to the nature of celebrity as it attaches itself to movie actors. In *The New York Times*, Bosley Crowther says: "Everybody in the story is madly in love with a disgusting young man who is virtually a cretin. At least, Warren Beatty plays him so he seems like one. This persistent assumption that everybody should be so blindly devoted to this obnoxious young brute provokes a reasonable spectator to give up finally in disgust. Surly, sloppy, slow-witted, given to scratching himself, picking his nose and being rude beyond reason to women and muttering about how much he hates the world – this creature that Mr Beatty gives us is a sad approximation of modern youth."

Film criticism is doing just as badly as the business in the early 60s. Yet Mr Crowther inadvertently touches on a mysterious appeal in pictures – a puzzle that fascinates, which is, who picks his nose? Is it Berry-Berry, or Warren Beatty? There is no answer; it is the question that is most relevant and illuminating. For the audience and actor alike there is a freedom in letting it be both at the same time, and it is a liberty that works best in the deserted intimacy of the movies, where "he" is "here", "now" and never here, never now, never knowing us, his watchers. You can show the spy outrageous things about yourself if you are certain the spy cannot warn you he is there.

The press grumbles about Warren Beatty in the way Bosley Crowther preaches against the character he plays. Even those who work with Beatty despair of him and sometimes turn on him with the kind of rejection that the Willart family realise is all their Berry-Berry deserves.

In 1962, the Hollywood press give Beatty their Sour Apple award for being uncooperative. That covers everything from rudeness, silences, evasions when he is being interviewed, to doing all he can to avoid and deny the press. The particular section of the press that covers "entertainment" is not known for its intelligence or its restraint. And Beatty will not have to wait long to discover how far he is wasting his time and his thought on them, especially if they keep asking about his plans to marry or his special intentions towards a few specific ladies – questions he cannot solve when the ladies themselves ask. So he has reason to be aloof or uncooperative.

But John Houseman, the producer of *All Fall Down*, sees someone who is also intensely ready to sell himself. It is Houseman who has asked MGM to let him turn the James Leo Herlihy novel into a film. "Almost against my will", says Houseman, the cause of Beatty for Berry-Berry is promoted. William Inge is the actor's chief spokesman, a writer in whom at the time Houseman sees a depression that sometimes becomes suicidal. Houseman allows that Beatty himself has done the rest: "In an astonishing campaign of self-promotion this young man . . . had managed to get pictures of himself, together with feature articles, into every major magazine in the country. Using charm, sex and unmitigated gall, he kept the country's female columnists in a tizzy".

Houseman remarks on the fact that Beatty has made himself a name and a personality that quite outdims more experienced professionals like Karl Malden, Angela Lansbury and Eva Marie Saint. And he attests to something not easily believed today – that Beatty at the start of his career is interviewed all over the media. That he is sometimes morose and difficult in those interviews does not contradict the zeal with which he and his agents go after them. His reticence toward the press in later years might be explained as the rueful lesson of those early years. But that has to suppose that Warren is not in charge. If he seeks interviews and then plays difficult – as if that was his role – then it is in character that, after a time, he decides to withhold himself from the press. The control is *not* complete: there is a pathology beneath control, the one area it prefers not to notice. But there is always an experimenter at work in Beatty, watching and refining the alchemy of being liked and hated, known or forgotten.

He may have to put up with more lovers than friends. "From the start," John Houseman says of the making of *All Fall Down*, "our most serious problem was young Mr Beatty. With his angelic arrogance, his determination to emulate Marlon Brando and Jimmy Dean, and his half-baked, overzealous notions of 'Method' acting, he succeeded in perplexing and antagonising not only his fellow actors but our entire crew."

Houseman repeats that the cameraman Lionel Lindon – the one I imagined Beatty attempting to charm with, "Hi Lionel, how are we today?" – grew so enraged that "he flew a camera-bearing helicopter within a few inches of his head". But Houseman knows Lindon as "Curly". Perhaps Beatty is too shy, too hip, to know how to talk to a veteran. Maybe he is seeking friendliness when he calls the gaffer "kid", only to alienate that grizzled stalwart. It is hard to be easy with the crew, to pretend there are no gaps, when they are dowdy technicians to the glossy dream.

At the end of location shooting in Florida, the crew and the local police plot together, and Beatty is left to spend a night in a Key West jail cell. This is exactly where *All Fall Down* discovers Berry-Berry – the ironies outlive the laughter.

The reviews are not all bad. In the *New Republic*, Stanley Kauffmann admires Beatty's Berry-Berry: "Physically, Beatty has the requisite magnetism; emotionally, he has the coiled-snake tension of black lower-middle-class frustration. What he needs now, as an actor, is to develop a more reliable voice, with a wider range."

At this point, a certain kind of movie star biography would launch out on that widening range to see the actor growing. But it has never happened. Warren Beatty acts less now than he did in the early 60s. But when he does and when he is good he is exactly like his Berry-Berry, watching himself, dark, fatalistic, as fascinating as a cobra, and in charge.

The young man does not accede to all the best hopes around him for how he will grow up. And he stays young: approaching fifty, Beatty is still a Kid. His greatest denial or refusal is towards the leavening of experience, or even towards its risk.

In January 1962, an interview appears in *Cosmopolitan*, conducted by Jon Whitcomb. It is far from the toughest or coldest Beatty gives. When the tape recorder is turned off, Whitcomb recalls, Beatty expands, relaxes, grins and talks like a kid. But while it is on, he is grudging, suspicious and difficult, like a kid paying James Dean lines:

"To break another silence, I asked him how he happened to meet Mr. Inge.

"'I met him for *Splendor in the Grass* in a most conventional way. My agent introduced me to him.'

"'Had he seen you?'

"'Who, my agent?'

"'No, Inge.'

"'No. He was trying to cast this picture, and I was introduced to him by my agent.'

"'What sort of play was it?'

"'What play?'

"'*A Loss of Roses.*'

"'Well, I met him for *Splendor in the Grass.* Then the picture was canceled, and he had this play, so then I did the play.'

"'What was your role like?'

"'You're trying to get me to say something I don't wanna say?'"

Later in the same piece, Whitcomb describes a talk with William Inge. It is full of insight: Inge anticipates that Beatty may give up acting; he speaks of his instincts and his conscience. The remarks reveal Inge as a sad, hopeful, kind man, a man moved by Beatty, knowing him well in some respects, seeing but perhaps too afraid to look all the way to the end of the tunnel:

"This young man is still high, still exhilarated at the turn his life has taken. His birthday comes early in the summer, I think, and he's just turned twenty-four. I think he may start closing the doors on the press pretty soon. I doubt if he will give interviews at all much longer. When I first met him he seemed marked for success. He was the kind of boy everyone looked at, knowing he was going to make it big . . .

"I don't think he knows how he acts. He's hard-working and instinctive. He's got a healthy ego. And a good ego, a really sound ego, has its negative side, too. There's an awful lot of negativism in Warren, but he has real intelligence. And he has a basic self-confidence that's made of iron. Indestructible! . . .

"He's been so intent on his career that he's devoted his entire self to it. He's just sitting around now, waiting for the rest of his life to come back to him."

Thinking of running

D was worn down by the gaiety on the terraces. He was like an electrician who ruined every shot by being caught on camera, endeavoring to conceal a cable or scrim a brute while the beautiful action went on. And so he wandered, to avoid attention. He had time to appreciate how every scooped surface on the property was filled with humus so that some velvet bloom could be reared there. No one but D examined the flowers, he was solitary enough to be a connoisseur. He grew dizzy dipping his head into all the startling scents, and even a little sick.

These "grounds" were not as substantial or as organic as that word suggested. There was an odd sensation in having the ground beneath one's feet, of coming upon rock gardens, streams and trees, yet feeling exposed and thrust out into the canyon. At the very edge, by peering over, he discovered that the Lighthiser property was all on a platform. There might be twelve feet of earth or fill on top of a base which jutted out from the hillside and was supported by steel struts. There were large birds swooping between the stanchions. D guessed owls, or carrion crows, waiting for chicken thighs to slip from the careless fête.

He looked farther down and heard a breeze grazing on the invisible canyon floor. Or was it a more full-bodied roar? Was there a river below, or a factory busy in the night? D had never known what happened in the folds of these hills. Being there only heightened the mystery. How rare for such uncertainty to prevail – no wonder the area was so desirable.

Looking into the prickling darkness D was ready for monsters to rear up or for sprites to beckon him down. What a spot for suicides – it was so tempting to step up onto the balustrade and walk into the solid, balmy night. Stunt men, D decided, were mystics as well as droll mechanicals perplexed to have so many women around. They had their affair with impossible ventures. They dived off cliffs, time and again, so brave but such insiders with death.

There was a rumbling in the valley, several ridges away. Then, quite distinctly, he heard a cry rise up from the canyon, full of despair. Half a mile away, D knew the person would never heal the wound that had sent up the cry. He had heard anguish tearing. It was as if the person had accidentally found the complete betrayal of their life. He waited, but there were no further cries. He knew he would have to forget the cry.

He wandered into the house, in and out of different lounges, and found Doc alone in front of a television set that was following some late election results.

"You got the whole damned thing laid out tonight," said Doc, in the spirit of a soothsayer ignored by his age.

D looked at the picture: the numbers changing, the disarray of campaign headquarters, exhausted kids who had forgotten their foolish, sloganising clothes, and studio pundits talking it all to sleep. It was vaguely political, D supposed, with brash art and color.

"I didn't know there were results tonight," said D.

"Every week now there are some run-offs or other," said Doc. "Contests, prizes. Where democracy meets the lottery."

"It's not popular where I live," said D.

"It's sleepwalking, that's what it is."

"That too," D agreed.

"Anyway, he won."

"He was cheerful?"

"He was hunky-dory. He's an amiable guy."

"I find myself liking him," D admitted.

"Don't you, though?"

"It makes you nostalgic."

"This city has perfected it," said Doc. "It's the swansong of the easygoing pal. There used to be a kind of pal in adventure pictures – it was just casting. No writing or direction. The guy had to watch the hero, grin and talk to him, say 'OK, Jeff', back him up in shootouts, agree with him. Just a soldier ready to do anything because he wanted to be liked."

"And cast?" said D.

"Exactly! The same urge to please on the silly face. And now it's a dry old-timer who doesn't know much and makes knowing look stuffy. And he just darned well refuses to see that it's difficult or impossible. He just says 'Have a good day' to whatever it is and takes you to the zoo instead, and you feel like you're four and he's grand-dad with a warm brown hand for you to hold on to."

"Yes," D knew that satisfaction. He could feel the comfort, and he remembered the ease in going out with his own grandfather, and of riding serenely in a tobacco haze, confident about where he was being taken. It was puzzling, for D had not known his grandparent.

"There was a moment tonight," Doc wanted to talk. "He was up in his hotel suite, and she was down at the headquarters addressing the people and there was this great screen on the wall behind her. It was like her insignia. And some of the time while you were watching they put the faces of people listening to her on the screen. And sometimes there were vistas of America – the cornfields, the Mississippi, the steel mills, the Rockies, the malls. But then, when she finished, there was cheering, the screen cut away to him in his room, on the sofa, and there was a camera crew there with him and after about five seconds the old fart got it that he was *on, there*. And he waved, and she waved back. He was so tickled, and the noise got louder and he and she were grinning away at each other. 'Hey, look! We're on TV!' Straight to the heart."

D was excited by Doc's treatise: "If only the people could hear you say that."

"I'd sound crazy. You start analysing TV and you look fatuous, a spoilsport. You sound like thought – you'll pardon the expression – it's poison. That's why Eyes doesn't have a chance."

"He is thinking of running?"

"The whole time he's thinking."

"Ah."

"Eyes is always going over the arguments. And that shows." Doc was gloomy and clear about the dead-end.

"Aha."

"No one will trust him. The intelligent look wicked on TV. As if they're plotting against us."

"That's it!"

"Anyway, he'd never stand to be on TV, just grinning there, walking from the helicopter, riding his horse. No, you got him, D."

"I did?"

"Absolutely. He's someone who might try to shoot the President – just to see if he was real. I have to admit it, Eyes could be our assassin."

"As a matter of fact," said D, "I understand he's having some doubts now himself."

"You bet he is. Did you ever meet anyone that thoughtful who didn't have a lot of doubts?"

"I suppose not."

"What did he say?"

"It was rather vague – too much dwelling on space and time."

Doc reflected. "He read that somewhere. Or he dreamed it. He could have woken up with that line in his head."

"What do you suppose it means?"

"He expects you to tell him."

"How can I?"

"He's like a Pharaoh who wants his dream given footnotes."

"This could hold up the deal?"

Doc was smiling. "Something has to. Eyes and I have a project – seven years old – but I can't crack his worry."

"What is it?"

Doc grinned, admiring the trap he was in. "He says, 'You don't think I'm too old for it?' How do you like that?"

D nodded ruefully. It was good to have this professional fellowship with a veteran like Doc. "What a strange business," he admitted.

"It's a madhouse. And we're lucky."

"Yes?"

"Eyes is head and shoulders the thinking guy in town. He'll headgame you till you're as stuck as he is. But he'll pay you while you're figuring the answer. So long as you don't ask."

DOING...NOTHING

It is something like the privilege of being at your own funeral: being a movie star, but doing nothing. Consider this parable – there are two young men who meet in acting school, or in summer stock. They tell each other how much they want to be actors; they both impress their various audiences, on and off the stage. The one is truly addicted to acting; he is not comfortable off the stage; he pursues work, sometimes in defiance of poor pay and billing. It is said of him, as he says himself, that he loves the theater. He comes in time to be regarded universally as a master actor. Late in life, when he has married again and had children, and when he has had several illnesses, he does television commercials and what he admits are bad pictures because he needs the money. But it is a great deal of money that comes in, and yet he goes on working. If he is a great actor, perhaps it is this insecurity that drives him. He would rather act than be, and so he happily adopts disguises and character parts. He is never, quite, a star: he never takes the risk of saying "Here I am, let *me* be famous."

The other does not work as hard at acting. He turns down interesting low-money offers; he is determined on the best billing. He never lets his looks change on the screen. He does not much enjoy acting; he does not really have a rich technique. But he is a star. And being a star was always so much his only ambition that he wants to see if he can be only a star – not a star kept alight by regular work and appearance, but a star who exists according to the self-perpetuating mechanics of stardom. There is a power in going on stage, commanding the silence and attention of strangers, and bringing them to tears. There is another power in being known, in being known to be *there* by millions of people. Where is there? It is stardom, and it is located on the edge of some Los Angeles pool. It is a place to be for ever, or for as long as you can manage – well, at least for twenty minutes. One of the most beautiful, heartfelt pictures of Hollywood I have ever seen is of Faye Dunaway, the morning after the

1977 Oscars, when she won for *Network*. It is a sunny dawn and she is sitting besides a pool with her Oscar on a table. Maybe they have to get up very early to get the picture. Maybe there is a throng of friends, servants, gigolos, pool-cleaners, renters, process servers and shy assassins they have to clear out of the sight-line to get the right, splendid aloneness. But it is a picture the actress needs. It shows her on the edge of a mythology she believes in as much as anyone. "I was there," she can say when she is old and ruined. It is a small trinket against death, her most precious jewel.

Hollywood is a very hard-working community – if waiting, talking, dealing, planning are work. But there is no peace, no leisure, not if a career is as desperate and ruthless as it must be. There are pools as little used as Gatsby's, except that they constitute the "there" that journalists, producers and the family can see when they visit from the East.

Warren Beatty does nothing – so to speak – from late 1961 to the middle of 1963. By which I mean to say, he does not shoot a film, his apparent line of business. Of course, his days and nights are full enough to account for some of his bad temper. He reads many scripts, and some of them he reads several times. He travels, he sees women, he discusses projects. He is in and out of grand hotels, he is giving interviews, he is going to parties, there are days when he gets to sit beside some of the several hundred thousand pools there are in Los Angeles, and maybe dozes with a book folded on his dry trunks. There is possibly a moment in this time – it could even be in October 1962, as the TV gets ready for a war, the big one, for Cuba – that he realises how, in a way, he is doing nothing, just to see whether it can be done. He laughs to himself, for he has proven how absurd this world he has conquered is. But then he realises he must take a firmer grip on himself, for a man could easily go crazy so angelically poised between such heavy things and nothing.

He is not under contract to a studio – such pieces of paper still exist, even if they are no longer identification cards for an industry. Beatty does not commit. He has one agreement, with Elia Kazan, a personal service contract of a kind common with big directors who reckon that they are the ones making the new stars. It talks about other projects, but none ever comes along and nothing significantly disturbs Beatty's line (over the years) that Kazan is a great director, or the best.

As yet, he has been paid only $105,000 for his three pictures – $15,000 for *Splendor in the Grass*; $30,000 for *The Roman Spring of Mrs Stone*; and $60,000 for *All Fall Down*. And he does not get all of that, of course: there is an agent and a secretary sometimes, and he has to consider whether it is worth hiring a lawyer to save him money with the IRS. But, despite the generally poor box office of the three pictures, he is asking $150,000 for his next movie. His expenses are going up, after all. And his reputation is going up, despite the reviews and the bad press. A true star does not have to make good or successful films. Hollywood has always told itself that was not so: failures vanished, three strikes and you're out, as good as your last picture. But Hollywood is changing. Different perceptions of how to place works are becoming possible. One crucial law in the famous breakdown of old Hollywood is the notion that it was a business run on hard facts and common sense. This was never the case, but now it is becoming easier to see that Hollywood was always an inane business, just as dependent on superstition and magic as on the numbers. Even the numbers are not firm. The numbers are like songs, a way of keeping cheerful.

And if you are asking $150,000 a picture in 1962, and turning down scripts, you can charge anything you want in LA. People sometimes stay there a year in the grand hotels, the bills waiting on the deals that are known to be coming. That is why the deals are so important: they determine whether you can live day-by-day. Warren Beatty will die with a record in which deals out-number finished films four or five to one. That is how one kind of inflation works; the overhead has to eat all the incomplete development deals. So he rents a pink stucco house – not large – above the Sunset Strip, and moves his suitcases in. One day as he lifts one of those cases, thirty-five uncashed checks fall out, along with some unpaid bills. He may not need a bank account or a credit rating; word-of-mouth will be enough. Alexander Korda, the Hungarian producer, once gave this advice for handling LA – move into the best hotel, be seen with the most beautiful women, charge everything and harbor any cash for lavish tipping. Wait for offers.

The scripts flow in to Beatty. Sometimes, not scripts, but ideas. He and Natalie Wood are talking about *Barefoot in the Park*. There is word that he is offered a lead in *The War Lover*, John Hersey's novel about American pilots in Britain during the Second World War – Steve McQueen and Robert Wagner end up playing its two leads. Which is Beatty offered? Which do you want, Warren? He could have had the part taken by Alain Delon on Luchino Visconti's film of *The Leopard*, shooting in Italy, being dubbed, working for a prestigious foreign director, spending more time in his bathroom.

In the middle 60s, the American director based in Europe, Joseph Losey, develops an espionage script set on the Russia-Finland border –

The Most Dangerous Game, written by John Paxton. Beatty is to play the lead, but the script is never quite right and the location presents serious weather problems. The snow and the ice will have to wait for Warren. At another time, Losey will think of doing William Faulkner's *The Wild Palms* (a novel of parallel stories), with Warren, Julie Christie and Elizabeth Taylor.

Moss Hart's autobiography, *Act One*, is to be filmed by the one-time MGM boss Doré Schary. It is a best-selling book about a showbiz hero. Beatty is interested, but in the end the role has to make do with George Hamilton and the picture is a flop. It is a mistake to deduce that Beatty could have rescued the film, or that it would have been made with him. Casting is the Hollywood stock exchange. Everyone is considered for everything. Someone would have been ready to make *The Godfather* as *The Godmother*, if Barbra Streisand had said yes, and the songs were right. We only see the pictures that are made. Bad as many seem, they have fought through the jungles of those only thought about. Beatty does a few projects that are simply demonstrations of his power, films that would not exist but for him. Some say he turns down 75 scripts a year. Casting is more vital than actor-director rehearsal; that is one reason why rehearsal is dying away. It is a vagueness that lets a Beatty believe he might have been in 80 per cent of the pictures of his time.

So his agent, Charles Feldman, is on the phone to him a lot. He gets used to having Warren answer, "What's new, pussycat?", a line he has used for the many women. And when Feldman becomes a producer, he adopts the line and its life-style and sets up a picture about a fashion editor with more lovers than he can remember. But Peter O'Toole plays the part in a movie that is Woody Allen's first script credit.

The next famous refusal concerns *PT 109*, a movie about John F. Kennedy's alleged wartime exploits as the commander of a PT boat. The Kennedys are movie mad. They have made pictures and had actresses as mistresses for a couple of generations. No matter that he knows how generously exaggerated the original book was, John Kennedy is not averse to the picture being made. (After all, it will open in 1963, just before re-election year.) Warner Brothers persuade themselves that it is a hot property. They put veteran Bryan Foy in charge of the picture. And Foy was irked to find that Kennedy's quiet choice to play himself when younger and glorious was Warren Beatty. Pierre Salinger, the presidential press secretary, acted as envoy. But Beatty doubts the chance of war pictures, especially this script, and may flinch from playing so well-known and so apparently real a personage. Cliff Robertson gets the part, and the movie fails. But before then, a part of the press have treated Beatty's refusal as arrogance and even lack of patriotism. Bryan Foy says, "Actors today will drive you crazy if you pay any attention to them."

Beatty extends his circle. He goes to meet Jean Renoir, the French film director who lives in Beverly Hills, and he probably sees a few Renoir films. The French New Wave – Truffaut, Godard and so on – are having an unexpected commercial impact in America, and they all vow the greatness of Renoir and his influence. A friend of Renoir's is the playwright Clifford Odets. Beatty collaborates with him for a time on a screenplay, and probably listens to the older man's stories about the Group Theater, about true work and selling out, about being married to actresses and loving them, about Luise Rainer and Frances Farmer.

The press portrait of a sulking Adonis builds up. The story goes around that when Beatty made *All Fall Down* at MGM he got a star dressing-room and then posted the name Gregor Krocp on it, so that he could sleep undisturbed. Is this star behavior or is it satire? In England, the press are similarly agitated when the Beatles simply refuse to be interviewed "properly". It's what comes of having a president who cracks jokes at a state banquet; it's a new, cool style; it begins to look suspiciously like the 60s.

In July 1962, the *Saturday Evening Post* carries a profile on Beatty, "Brash and Rumpled Star" they call it. The writer is Joseph Laitin, and early on in the piece he has Beatty turning on him, "I've given you too much of my time, much too much. All you're interested in is the neurotic side of me. You don't want to write about my work. You haven't asked me a single question about my ideas on acting, about the theater or anything I consider important. My childish ego is excited by the prospect of your writing a story about me, but all you're interested in is trivia."

Laitin is chastened. He does his best to give Beatty's point of view, and he tells the story how in New York a few months earlier Beatty had spent days at the bedside of an old friend from the theater until the man died.

Then he says that, in the middle of a conversation, Beatty vanishes and comes back in his swim trunks. Then he goes out to the pink pool, brushes away some of the leaves that have accumulated there and discovers a dead lizard. The young actor pokes at the reptile's corpse, sighs and maybe takes a grip on himself. He has a great line to deliver: "If Natalie knew a lizard died in this pool, she'd never swim here again. . . . Let's go over and use Natalie's pool."

Pool life, from *Sunset Boulevard*

Cy

Some people had quit in an hour of goodbyes, fur wraps unwinding from closets, and dust in the headlights down the drive. But this evacuation passed, and there were still fifty or so who showed no sign of leaving. A game of pun charades occupied the terrace. D kept away. Its howls signalled a ruthless cult.

"Can't you smell the hostility in the air?" said the man in the kitchen, lopping flowers off broccoli. "I take a few crudités around this time of night. Flushes out the system."

D knew it would be easy to sentimentalise raw vegetables in this luxurious setting. He thought it wisest to be casual, so he nibbled at the rugged greenery.

"You don't know me?" It pleased the man.

"I don't know anyone here," D confessed.

The man chuckled. "I know you. I been looking for you, D."

There was only a worktop light on in the kitchen. The man's smile was in half-shadow. "Cy Lighthiser," he explained, but it sounded equivocal, as if the pun charades had come inside to eat away all assurance. "Would I lie?" This was a slim, wiry man, hair receding, in slacks and a sports shirt, cutting up raw vegetables. He was so much more commonplace than the man on the screen who had welcomed guests to the party.

"Disappointed?" asked Cy, his head tilted to study the grain in a root of fennel. Then he attacked it and came up with a white moon hanging from his knife. "Try it," said Cy. "Today, from Frieda's Finest. I like it quick roasted in a walnut oil with fresh pepper. But I don't know how this range works." He indicated the gunmetal chambers where cooking could be done.

"This is not your home?" asked D.

"We're not here a lot. Claudia gets spooked if she's up here on her own. So, if in doubt, don't eat cooked things. And what's the oil going to do but coke your arteries?"

"The oil is not good?"

"We eat like decadents," said Cy. "The red meat, marbled with fat." He pinched the items between his fingers. "The butter, the sauces. Night before my heart attack I had three servings of a creamed scallop bisque you could have built on."

Cy crunched a carrot, reflecting. "Life's too precious. I'm not going, you know." His voice dropped, "And I don't believe we have to."

It took D a second to see the destination Cy was ducking.

"My heart. It didn't work. New parts. They can do it. They don't boast they can do it, they're going to be mobbed. Listen, D, this is as hard a business as it gets. It's not the Sistine Chapel. But for worry and heartbreak it has no match. So . . . exercise, diet, relaxation, only let pure things into your home, and your body is your best home. Be tranquil when you can. Then do your work, screw the slimes when you have to. No desserts. A little grain, fibre, a lot of salad, toffuti. I'm still here. I'm better than ever. And I tell you – this is not just my opinion, read the trades – I'm making better pictures. These guys fuck with cigars, cocaine and red meat, they're making crap. Nouvelle cuisine, nouvelle movies. Claudia, now – she has our new kid – she is breastfeeding. Her, taking that risk with her gilt-edged. You can hear that mother's milk flowing, and she is sexier than ever. She stinks with it. The camera never really gets all of her. There's magic left. That's the kick in knowing her. She and Eyes, they gotta work together. And Eyes, he is all yeast-shakes and nice light meals with roughage. What ruined Monroe was not her pussy, it was the calories: ice cream, Danish and lamb chops. I've known sweet kids – I won't name 'em – dolls, Miss Cutesville, and I've seen them eat steak dinners with éclairs to follow. Your liver can take only so much. And it makes a pit of the skin. Your stars that last have skin like photo paper, and they never eat all they'd like. It's will power. You end so hungry you want to kill. Anger!" Cy Lighthiser's eyes shone. "It's the best diet."

"It has always intrigued me, the dilemma of staying a star," said D.

"It's a duel with death."

"As much as that?"

"That's what movies are. The defiance of death. Think about it. It's a magnificent thing."

"A legendary quest," mused D.

"That's very true. So, how is our old Eyes, the monkey?"

"Oh," said D, indicating how hard it was to be sure.

"I hear he's hot for your script. That it?"

Cy

Cy's eyes went in as fast as Duran to the body to the script still tucked under D's arm. "I know you shouldn't ought to let me see it."

"I shouldn't," D agreed.

"So why not maybe put it on the counter. I'll hit the fan, and the pages riffle by. While we're talking. I can sometimes get the taste of a script that fast."

"You are interested in it for your wife?"

"I don't see it, I don't get to touch her, know what I mean? Otherwise I have to go out get a hooker." He stopped chopping. "Unless we have some here. Did you notice any?" He was deadpan, as if the talk concerned the first swallows of summer.

"I'm not sure I would know them."

"John Public," said Cy, pointing the knife at him.

"Me?"

"Sure. The wonderful thing about the picture business is the audience never recognise the whores. Put it down." Cy smacked his hand flat on the counter top.

"I shouldn't," said D. "I couldn't."

"If I was you I'd want my work seen. There are scripts Eyes has bought and paid for, he makes paper airplanes out of them."

"But sometimes – "

"An unmade Eyes beats a Lighthiser?"

"Well – "

"I know. He's a pathfinder. But the pathfinder – "

"Can get too far ahead?"

"Out of sight is what he can get. Is he coming tonight? I got flim-flam from Clear."

D could not resist the momentum of all this sliced and curving chatter: "Clear's a lot of air – but I like him."

Cy caught the shift, and made a little swastika of celery sticks. "We all had aides like Clear, we'd be collecting Nobel prizes. He's a saint. He is also an empty space when he has to be. What I'd like to know is how he'd turn out if there was nothing he had to be."

"Burn off by eleven?" D wondered. How quickly his allegiances could switch on cross-talk. He was a slut. He remembered Drew saying it of herself.

"We asked him tonight, of course," said Cy. "He said he'd call back."

"He doesn't go out much."

"He likes to refuse. 'I'd rather not.'" Cy said it in mockery of the loftiness. "He has this thing for refinement. It does credit to us all."

"A man ahead of his time."

"This business is garbage, and you should never lose the feel for dirt. Maybe he stays out in the desert or wherever, balling young girls and thinks he's a prince of darkness. That's not. That's just horny. There are bankers in this city married to schoolgirls, still paying for their braces. You get outa touch – know what I mean?"

"Living with reptiles – " D began.

And Cy was with him, " – is just a matter of practice." He was already scooping untouched crudités into the waste disposer. It ground down on the stalks – "This house pees V8," said Cy – when they heard the scream from outside and realised what a hush had befallen the pun charades.

LILITH

Lilith is the best film Warren Beatty has made at that point in his career; you could make a case that it is the best he will ever make. A failure in its day, the picture grows more profound and beautiful as the years pass by. It is a lake that resists every effort to plumb its depths. It is not easily explained, critically or intellectually; it is a rapture, just like the madness of its central character. And this sense of belatedly revealed tragedy is surely enhanced by our knowing what became of its actress, Jean Seberg, and by the realization that this was her best work and that she was wasted and rebuffed when at her best. But Beatty does not like the film. After it opens, he calls it a disaster, something he could have made better himself. To this day, I believe, it is one of the movies he does not like to hear mentioned.

Lilith is a movie about sex, about nymphomania, about a rapture so intense it must be a matter of judgement whether it is termed madness or nature. Perhaps no other American movie has addressed this subject so thoroughly, or been so convinced that woman is the ultimate source of sexual power.

The film is taken from a novel by J. R. Salamanca, published in 1961. It will be the last film of writer-director Robert Rossen, the maker of *All the King's Men*, a victim of McCarthyism, lately returned to America to direct *The Hustler*. Rossen is struck by an idea in the book – "that of comparing the person whom people call 'adjusted' to the one called 'maladjusted' in our society. Society considers the person who is outside its norms as sick. Now, my own feeling is that society, itself sick, is only refusing a certain form of unreason."

There speaks a Hollywood radical, possessed of a simple notion of social malaise and looking for a movie vehicle to embody it. McCarthyism feared such intentions, and never saw that the film industry always translated such "ideology" into a personal melodrama. Thus the film *Lilith* is about sex, not madmen; ecstasy, not malfunction.

201

It may not be exactly the picture Rossen believed he was making – but the elements of myth in the material cannot be prevented from marrying with the medium's urge toward legend. If a beautiful woman plays Lilith, if she is starry, then any view of her society pales in her brightness.

The film does change the novel's ending. In both, the protagonist is a young man, Vincent Bruce, who takes up work as a nurse in an asylum for the wealthy. He is a troubled figure, trying to seek out his nature and do good by the world. The asylum where he works has Lilith as a patient, and Vincent is seduced by her. In the novel, Vincent manages finally to break away from her power. He gives up the job. Lilith's parents remove her from the asylum and she is sent to Europe. While there, she drowns, apparently, though the lake in question is too deep for her body to be recovered. Her possibility is eternal. Vincent survives. He restores the relationship with his grandfather and he writes the book, like someone coming back from an encounter with a demon.

This would be a diffuse conclusion for the film, and so Rossen's script has Vincent being increasingly led away from sanity by Lilith's influence. The picture ends with Vincent walking towards the people who have employed him and towards the camera and saying "Help me." It is fearsome, but tidy: the nurse becomes an inmate, but the moment is given life by the terror and intensity with which Beatty delivers the line. For whatever it says, and whatever the character must do, somehow the actor refuses to ask for help.

If only because of their shared water imagery, it is reasonable to think that *Splendor in the Grass* influences Rossen in preparing *Lilith*. The first actor he engages is Beatty to play Vincent, persuaded by the Kazan picture that Beatty can convey a normal young man driven crazy by desire. At this stage, the actor and the director are very close. *Lilith*, after all, is the film that will bring Beatty out of his "nothingness"; and Rossen is an anti-establishment figure, surely recommended by Odets. It is in this mood of friendly collaboration that Beatty suggests Jean Seberg for Lilith.

Several other actresses have been in line for the part – Yvette Mimieux, Samantha Eggar, Diane Cilento, Sarah Miles, and even Natalie Wood, who had gone crazy for *Splendor in the Grass*. Beatty has seen Seberg not just in her first films for Otto Preminger (*Saint Joan* and *Bonjour Tristesse*), but in Jean-Luc Godard's *A Bout de Souffle* and perhaps even in a charming romantic comedy, *L'Amant de Cinq Jours*, in which her hair was long, as opposed to the close-cropped look that had made her famous. Rossen casts Seberg, despite her seeming to have "gone over" to low-budget, French movies. When he makes the announcement to the press, he says "She's got that flawed American-girl quality – sort of like a cheerleader who's cracked up."

Beatty goes with Rossen on the trip to Paris to decide on Seberg: he is being paid three times her fee, even if the woman is bound to be the object of the film's worship. When pre-production begins in April 1963, in New York and in Maryland, where the chief locations are sited, Beatty and Rossen have what Seberg sees as a "fraternal, very intimate" relationship. The three of them visit several mental hospitals, they talk to patients. They work on the script. As they rehearse, and come to the scene where Lilith must say, "You know what is wrong with Lilith? I want to possess all the men in the world," it is Beatty who guesses that that line will work better if she says it in the third person.

The shooting is an agony. Seberg sees the bond between Rossen and Beatty deteriorate from the day filming begins. Rossen is not well. He is suffering from a mysterious illness in which dark spots appear on his skin. He may sense that this is his last film, he may fall under the sway of Lilith and Seberg as shooting starts. I do not mean he sleeps with his actress. But he ravishes her with his camera. No other Rossen picture has anything like *Lilith*'s erotic intensity – and if Rossen smells his own death then this turning of desire into art may be like a way of clinging on to life, a panic that leads to very little coverage of Beatty in the love scenes.

Or perhaps the persistent impression from the film of Beatty scowling, his head lowered or his back to the camera, is because he is so unmanageable, and so reluctant to act. He delays the shooting with doubts and anxieties. There is a famous argument as to whether, early in the film, Vincent should say "I've read *Crime and Punishment* and *The Brothers Karamazov*." Beatty thinks the character never finished *Karamazov*, and should say so. It does sound better that way, but such arguments cloud every scene. Is the actor really more in touch with the material than the director? Can an actor ever have that advantage if a film is to be shot? Or is Beatty aware that it is not "his" picture, and trying – in a mix of cunning and unconscious maneuvering – to drain the picture into his own hunched disquiet?

Has Seberg made it clear that she does not want Beatty as more than a professional colleague? One of Rossen's assistants says, "Warren is a brilliant, charismatic person, and he made sure he got his share of the spotlight. He has the charm of the stalking cat, and he preyed on Jean with all his power as a seducer. But nothing was ever what it seemed to be on the surface. He was busy playing games, manipulating people and situations. For Jean, it was a terrible handful."

There is a fight scene between the two of them in which Lilith has to slap Vincent. Time and again as they try to shoot it, Beatty puts up his arms to ward off the blow – is the character flinching, or is there something in the action that the actor cannot allow? Seberg's arm is battered and bruised. Peter Fonda, in a supporting role, threatens to beat the shit out of Beatty. There are fears of real violence between the two actors. There are stories that Beatty's trailer is vandalised, and that he is asked not to appear at the wrap party. The shooting goes on through the summer of 1963 amid growing arguments and a decline in Rossen's health. When he dies, in 1966, it will be said that he names Beatty as one of his death blows.

It is all the sadder that Beatty, the only one of the three major participants in *Lilith* still alive, seems not to like the film. His performance cannot be separated from the achieved tragedy, no matter how much he was an outcast or a problem to those making the picture. And it takes only a moment to see how fully *Lilith* fits in with the slowly emerging screen persona of Beatty. In *All Fall Down*, there is a conversation between Clinton and Berry-Berry in which the older brother proclaims his hatred of life. Still in awe, Clinton tries to agree, and he asks Berry-Berry, "What do we live for?"

"You mean what's the point of everything?" says Berry-Berry, and he looks away at one of his women: "Well, maybe *that's* the answer. It's the only thing I could ever figure out."

Lilith, the movie, is an exploration of that possibility, the picture that most clearly engages Beatty in something like his own appetite for sexual encounters without the codifying legitimacy of marriage. Yet *Lilith* is an American movie made before the real relaxation of censorship and the work of a director who chooses to romanticise sex with poetic dissolves. The animality of Lilith's desires is not shown; in 1963, I don't think it could be. There was a silly press thrill when it was thought that a semi-nude scene was to be filmed.

But the movies are more erotic if the thing, the ultimate *there*, is not shown, but evoked or gilded in rapture. *Lilith* is a very rare movie in that it understands the force and primacy of sensuality and portrays it thematically as Lilith's urge to have everyone, without condemning her. Vincent is the chief enemy to her desire: he is a therapist, supposed to guide her into normalcy, and a lover who wants her all for himself. He

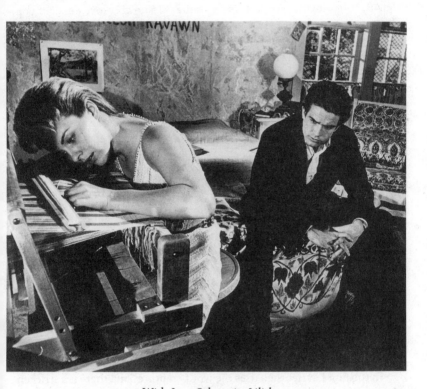

With Jean Seberg in *Lilith*

cannot endure the ease with which she turns to other men and women. Beatty's rather grim, tight face – sometimes reminiscent here of Elvis Presley, but tight-assed and disapproving – is the embodiment of outraged decency and propriety.

"You dirty bitch," hisses Vincent, finding Lilith with another woman, and Seberg's lovely face flowers in a smile: "I show my love for all of you and you despise me." How many times in life has some such dialogue been played, in reverse, between Beatty and a woman who has had to discover his helpless need for others? Of course, he need not be mad for Vincent to be an irrationally disconcerting part for him to play. The seducer never feels he has been seduced: it is the most complete usurpation of his power. The thought might destroy him.

Perhaps this is reading too much into movies. Perhaps movies are just a job. Perhaps. See *Lilith* and decide. And notice how imprisoned Beatty looks and feels; see what a good job he does for this remarkable film. In particular, there is a scene in which the new therapist talks to Dr Lavrier, the head of the asylum. Vincent is talking about how the work is going. He is hunched. There seems to be a great tension in his body as he struggles to give answers. He is half turned away from Lavrier as they talk about Lilith's charm.

"It's almost like she wants to share this magic little world of hers," he says.

And quietly and gently, Lavrier asks "Do you ever feel like accepting?"

"Yes!" says Vincent. It bursts out, his body nearly falls over across the frame, his face opens, the wall cracks, and he is like a child confessing to a terrible wish. It is one of the best things Warren Beatty will ever do. Perhaps it is great acting; perhaps the final giving of self.

In the film Lavrier then uses the word "rapture" and there is a stricken but uplifted close-up of Vincent repeating the word. In the novel it is Vincent who comes up with the term – "She has a kind of . . . rapture about her which is very compelling. Do you know what I mean? A kind of rapture that perhaps I'm jealous of."

It is a bad time for Warren after *Lilith*. The picture does poorly, and the ailing Robert Rossen does not hesitate to tell others the young actor is a trial. We should remember that there are other careers of the early 60s which do not last at the star's level – Fabian, Dean Stockwell, Richard

Beymer, George Hamilton, Terence Stamp, Troy Donahue. There is a chance that Warren too may be a three-year wonder.

He is in a restaurant one day, the story goes, when a letter is delivered to him from the office of Darryl F. Zanuck, the head of Twentieth Century-Fox. The two have never met, but the letter from Zanuck says, in effect, be of good cheer, you are *the* actor of your generation, I can see your career reaching ahead, anything you want to do, or anything you hear of, just bring it to Fox. Something like that, a letter for his dreams.

He is hugely cheered up: here is valuable evidence that he was once a young man. He tells his world about this unexpected endorsement; he looks for projects to take to Fox. The mishap of *Lilith* falls into place.

A few days later he encounters an old friend who remarks on how much more cheerful Warren is. Warren tells the friend about the letter. Oh, you liked that? Did I ever! You wouldn't believe the trouble I had getting the letterhead stationery, admits the friend. (Is this really friendship? remains a question for Plato or Miss Manners.)

This is the story I heard. I don't have the letter. I'm not sure of the friend. But in the story, Warren is aghast. He wonders, what can I do? I've told so many people. Must I explain to everyone that I was fooled, had? He considers; he waits a day or so; and he decides – what the hell, let the story run . . . .

And now here is his biographer, years later, wondering whether or not to believe the legend. I think the story plays, and in Hollywood that is always the ultimate transcending of history.

Body in the pool

Cy Lighthiser moved to the bookcase in the walnut lounge and pressed a switch where Elmore Leonard met Lermontov. There was no thrill of strings, but a section of fiction turned into a smoked window in which it was still possible, from the secret angle, to see the spines of the books. They were engraved in the glass, or a picture printed there. The switch simply rearranged the dots and molecules to provide a way of looking out at the terrace and the pool. D assumed from Cy's openness that nothing of this subterfuge was visible from outside.

The people on the terrace were gathered at the pool: the water cast a blue glow on the women's legs and the men's slacks. D was struck by the chromakey frieze at the pool's lip.

"Is there someone in the water?" said Cy.

D shared the anticipatory stillness of those by the pool. "Should we go out?" he said.

Cy did not move. He was so entertained staying there, waiting to find out.

D could not expunge the loneliness of watching. He wanted to be out there, a part of the wonder or amusement. Then, quite plainly, but from farther away than the pool, Cy and D heard a rumbling, as if something had been irrevocably disturbed. Then one woman at the pool turned. It was Drew, and her face was blind and agonised, staring towards them and crying, but knowing nothing.

"Look at that one," Cy asked.

Drew's distress isolated her. Some pitch of feeling had made her a membrane, helplessly bearing witness.

"Who is that?" Cy wanted to know.

D did not pause to recommend her to the producer. He went out through the kitchen to the terrace. He heard water lapping and the muttering of the people. Doc bumped into him, still looking back over his shoulder but trying to get to the house.

"Where's a phone?" he said.

"What happened?" asked D.

"Someone drowned."

"Was he drunk?" D imagined the man slipping into the water without a sound, opening himself to it.

"I heard he made a dumb guess in the game."

"And for that he drowned himself?"

Doc was flustered, still thinking of how to phone in a crisis. "No one knows," he said.

"It was only a game?" D remonstrated. "Was there money at stake?"

"Probably. But he made a fool of himself."

"Everyone here is already foolish," D burst out.

"You think so?" Doc had given up on the phone now. "Everybody says it's a madhouse here." He hated the cliché. "That's no help. You loathe it, but you're here, aren't you?"

There was nothing D could say. He wished a sweeping force could reach across the hillsides, obliterating the party and his own failure to grasp its sickness.

"Try to see it," said Doc. "Let's say this man was ambitious. He was a designer, I think. He may have been close to making it, and then one slip –"

"What slip?"

"What does it matter? Perhaps he got a title wrong."

"And so he killed himself?"

"Maybe he knows he's lost it. Feels he's sliding down the snake all the way to the bottom."

"A game!" D's smothered fear escaped with the cry.

"There's always some game," said Doc. He made it sound past blame or dispute.

The body was in the pool, face down, scrutinizing the water – a man in pink shirt and yellow pants. Of course, someone was taking photographs. Cy presided. A windowless white limousine came for the corpse; it had a stretcher that reached out, like a tongue. Statements were taken, with the tone of press interviews. There were arguments over the man's name: some said Richard Burger, others Rick Berg. A few claimed Ricky Burr or Rich Blur. People discussed his credits – a horror film and several music videos. There were those who felt he had had brilliance, but others began to see a derivativeness that should not be overvalued.

D searched for Drew. Since leaving the house – expressly to comfort her – he had lost her. More people were leaving, in talk of imminent storms. Some said they had seen lighting in the gaps between the hills. D guessed it was past two in the morning. He felt he could go on forever. A contempt for time and order was dawning in him, and he was not afraid. He saw that this Berg blur might have glanced at the empty pool and seen the electricity of his colors there, knowing he wouldn't be forgotten, going out on a hot shot.

D called cautiously to the pale averted figure on a stone seat by a fig tree. A face on the figure turned, and he hurried down the steps towards Drew. She was not crying now.

"Know what happened?" D asked.

Her mind moved back up to the terrace, to an hour ago. "Oh, that," she recollected, touched by the far incident.

"Doc says the fellow was ruined by some minor mistake in the game."

"It's not a game of minor mistakes." She gazed away, addicted to private knowledge.

He guessed she had taken some other drug. She was so cut off now from help or his presence.

"Go away," said Drew, without interest.

Her heavy head swung round: it looked like death challenging him. "You don't do the game. You think it's enough to say ha-ha, isn't it senseless?"

"Why were you crying then?" This should hold her in his faith.

She couldn't remember.

"At the pool. You turned away. I saw it."

It was as remote as her childhood, out of her reach. "I just did that." She was weary, and doing could be trivial.

"Did it?"

"Everyone was eyeballing the water." She made the face of stupid staring. Then it was her again. "I wanted to fix the memory," she wavered, like someone telling Merv a confidence, "so I made it into a scene." She laughed out loud to see his glum face. "I like acting! It's what I do."

"Well, Cy Lighthiser saw it and seemed impressed."

"He did?" Drew was aroused by this news, but D could not tell whether because of its promise or because it was a cherry on absurd cream. "Cy'll put it in Claudia's next picture, you wait. Claudia and Chuck were very twosome earlier. What do you think of that?"

"What is there to think?"

"Wouldn't you say that in seven or eight shots out of ten Claudia and Chuck could pass for Claudia and Eyes?"

"He has none of Eyes' flair."

"Oh, Eyes," said Drew, as if the name was a curse and flair the cheapest trick.

MICKEY ONE

Mickey One is flash when we first see him, when he goes by a name we will never learn. That name is like an apartment he knows will be staked out, so he never risks going back to it. But if you had to guess at the name, it could be Tony Lombardi or Tommy Terrific. He's a night club comic, and he says he's Polish. But that's an act already, a Polish joke. He's New Jersey Italian, or maybe he's just a smart Harvard kid trying to hide his shyness in this awful act. He *is* a lousy comic. That's the funniest thing in the picture. He could be Rupert Pupkin's father. Arthur Pupkin – got it. Not so much flash as hair oil, sewn-on sequins and silver shining through the mirror. But a pretty kid who might be nice-looking if he wasn't so dumb or if he wore glasses and a masseur could get rid of that little knot of loose flesh above the nose where he holds everything together and tries to pretend he is a cool mother who is never going to be taken.

He is a comedian working in Detroit, at a place called Lapland, owned by Ruby Lapp, a guy with a destroyed face and a capacity for grand speeches that can echo all the way from a chance remark to the tomb's shade.

Something happens one night at Lapland, something so important that we have to know it was the dream of Arthur Pupkin's life, the bit that would make him Terrific so he could tip twenties and sit there with the girl reflected in his dark glasses. In Detroit.

At the start of the movie we get a series of fragments. There is "Mickey" sitting in a steam room, concentrating on wearing his overcoat and a black derby while smoking a cigar: he is all routines. And the four fat old guys in towels are laughing at him – not at the act or the material, but at his sweet thought of being a comedian. One guy gets up and smacks him on the back – like he's an idiot, but a decent idiot – and the actor playing "Mickey" lets his head drop so that the derby rolls down his arm and onto his hand. You have the feeling that the actor probably worked four weeks on the trick and could get it to work cleanly three times out of ten.

Then you see a sports car come out of a highway tunnel with the sign (to downtown Detroit). It's daylight. It stops and the driver, Mickey, looks back at another sports car with a girl in it who might have been second or third in a Miss Breck competition. If it was held in Detroit. He seems to have noticed her in his rear-view mirror. She is played by an actress named Donne Michelle, and the name is the best part about her. But Mickey thinks the girl is sensational, and he waves to her and signals a direction they should both take.

You think he wants her. But in the next fragment it's night and the girl is climbing up on the hood of his car and trying to kiss him through the windscreen. So he turns on the wipers, because he's cool.

You see the girl on a bed from up above, from the ceiling mirror; or maybe the shot is looking up at the mirror. Mickey comes to her. Then they're both in front of his dressing-room mirror, and he has white cream and make-up on his face. But he starts to kiss her, which gets the cream on her face too.

Then Mickey is looking into a dark alley where two men are beating up another, and the girl comes up behind him – she's maybe just been to the bathroom – slips off his jacket and starts to kiss him. He shoots craps in a club. The girl dances. Men are watching: large, ugly faces, thrilled by what they see and what it means. You see the girl on her own, off in some ecstatic, unwinding dance. And then it is later and Mickey comes looking for her and there is nothing but her dress or her wrap on the deserted drum kit.

You might think that this Arthur has been the victim of a montage in the silly yet wonderful American artiness of *Mickey One*. But he *is* a Harvard kid, versed in Kafka and the literature of alienation, and perhaps an assassination buff on the side (who thought "Ruby Lapp – Jack Ruby" when he arrived at Lapland). So he reckons that he messed with a gangster's moll the night before, took her from the gangster, maybe lost her money at the crap table and asked her to put the dice in her panties and to get them *hot*. And now she's gone, and he's in trouble.

He talks to Ruby Lapp – what's that ruined face and its sepulchral eloquence for?

MICKEY: Ruby, what did I do? What do they want? All right, so tell me how they set me up at least. Shooting craps drunk? That's the only thing they could have. How much did they fix I should lose? You can tell me that. Five grand? Ten. Twenty? Tell me! Why? Was it the girl? I've been playing around this time somebody's private stock?

She ain't private anymore. Who owns me? Ruby? You know, I really was nuts about that girl. I can't three times a night go out and make jokes on my own grave. I can't! Maybe I can raise the money and pay 'em up. You help me – 20,000 – it ain't the end. Why not?

RUBY: How do you know it's 20,000– I didn't say it? How do you know it's only money?

MICKEY: Why? – shooting craps? It's –

RUBY: You say. How do you know it's not all the other crap games they tore up on you? And the bookie slips? How do you know it's not the car they gave you you smashed up? And the liquor, and the good times and the apartment and the clothes, and Christmas and birthdays and the rehearsal hall?

MICKEY: They were favors!

RUBY: Favors as long as they want them to be favors. How do you know it isn't all the trips they paid for? Or the special material, and the arrangements in music? The dentist. The law suits. The parties. The expenses. 20,000? 20,000's just a fraction. How do you know it's not your whole life you're living?

Mickey One is a Hollywood Kafka job, in black-and-white, handled by a French photographer, made for under $1 million, with Stan Getz's wistful tenor saxophone improvisation drifting across its squalid scene like the last smoke of hopefulness. It is filmed largely in Chicago (the place to which the comic flees after his Detroit disaster), on wasteground, in wretched tenements and on the shabby streets. Like an allegory, it is made with a few very beautiful players (Beatty, Alexandra Stewart as the good girl who helps him, and Hurd Hatfield as Ed Castle, the jittery, organic food aesthete who owns the Xanadu, the big club where Mickey might play) and a surrounding world of the picturesquely ugly, ranging from Franchot Tone's Ruby Lapp through a dwarf, giant ladies and a bum with an S-shaped nose who studies his features in an arcade mirror, standing beside the muddied and messed up Mickey, who is still only a disguise for the magnificent Warren.

It is difficult not to chide *Mickey One*. No matter that it is the collaboration of an actor bristling to show his intelligence and his scorn for Hollywood conventions and of a director, Arthur Penn, who embodies the hope that cultivated New York theater traditions can take over the movies, still it is the kind of pretentious picture that exposes the huge gap in depth between literature and film. In time to come, Beatty will say, "It's not a bad film. It's not a waste of time." But he finds it unduly obscure: "It reaches further than it needs to." This is Hollywood's fear of difficulty or evident strain. "I didn't know what the hell Arthur was trying to do," he says. "I'm not sure that he knew himself."

Mickey One is solemn, spectacular and flashy in its pessimism, and downright juvenile in an optimism it never flinches from spelling out. For Mickey is not just an actor going crazy, he is an Everyman who has the wise and tender reassurance of his girl and the recurring example of a speechless but enthusiastic Oriental who gathers together scrap metal and turns it into Tinguely-like art works entitled "Yes". His work and vivacity have a message, spelled out by the girl – "Courage is Freedom": come on, Mickey, you can go, you can go back to the business. That is the slogan set up as a polar opposite to the moment at which Arthur Pupkin is re-named, at the Rent-a-Man Agency, and assigned to his job in a cafeteria: "Mickey One – Garbage".

His girl, Jenny, tries to coax him back to reason and work, but her therapist talk is always tangled up in his spirals of fear and loathing. The actress, Alexandra Stewart, has the forlorn task of being gentle to Beatty's snarls. Just in the sound of their voices, and in the pattern of "be nice" – "I'm bad", there is a power not really noticed by the film's schematic parable.

> MICKEY: 4½ years I travelled up and down the back end of the South – an animal. Tried, two, three times to get in touch with Ruby Lapp, Detroit. Nothin'. Now today they have pressure on me.
> JENNY: They know?
> MICKEY: I don't know for sure they know who I am or not. Yet. But I haven't got the kind of guts to stick around and find out.
> JENNY: Can't you talk to them?
> MICKEY: I talk to you. 'Cause you don't talk. Nobody's gonna talk to you.
> JENNY: I don't understand. Anything. I mean, hiding from you don't know who. For a crime you're not even sure you committed.
> MICKEY: The only thing I know – I'm guilty.
> JENNY: Of what?
> MICKEY: Sure you don't want a drink?
> JENNY: Of what are you guilty?
> MICKEY: Not being innocent. What the hell am I – a lawyer?

The stories from the set in Chicago say that Beatty is as surly and unapproachable as Mickey. Actors say they can't hear what he's saying when he talks in scenes; years later it is impossible to know exactly what Mickey says from repeated study of tapes of the sound track. It is said he orders tailor-made "old clothes" for Mickey's underground life, and then loses his temper when they don't fit. That he spends all his time combing his hair to get the right tousled look for a Mickey who sleeps in alleys. That when he tries to pick up female extras they are turned off by his arrogance. He has a stand-in, John Gibson, who says: "I spent about ten weeks with Beatty, and we exchanged about twenty words. The rest of the time he tried to give me orders – 'Get my water!' 'Get my yogurt!' 'Get my orange juice!' After a few days of that, I told ol' buddy Warren to 'Get lost!' " Which is the kind of cocky story Mickey might have told. Is it chance or design, or does Beatty have the power to turn real people into the kind of support his characters need? Or has this always been the way movies would take over the world?

Mickey One is a failure when it opens, as nearly everyone anticipates. If there is an exception, someone who reckons on good reviews, festival garlands and a modest profit, it is Beatty, for this is his first step towards being a producer, someone who says "let us make this," rather than "yes, I will appear in that." *Mickey One* is still, in many respects, half-baked, fatuous and full of that unconscious humor which takes it for granted that a comedian is the ideal figure for a universal story about alienation and madness. Nevertheless, it was made – in defiance as much as creative absorption – and it endures as an attempt at a statement in which underground forces struggle against the deliberate but adolescent concept.

Suppose for a moment that *Mickey One* is a curiously penetrating and oblique portrait of acting. Then, it has no more daring or interesting aspect than that Mickey is a bad comic. But was that the intent or the inadvertent residue of such arty ambitions? The framing of the story seems to turn on a great talent whose paranoia takes him out of circulation. His agent, his girl and Ed Castle all want Mickey to risk the crucial audition at the Xanadu. He is presented as a kind of natural, someone whose great fears cannot quite overcome his urge to get up on stage, take the mike and start talking.

But his act is hackneyed, cynical and mean-spirited. Mickey can never fully give of himself. He snarls at the audience, at the idea of jokes and at the situations and the spotlights he craves. He has a problem about being a performer for which the possible Mob vengeance is only a pretext. The film does not notice, let alone explore this, but it is there in the hunched bearing and delivery of Beatty and in his convoluted sense of his own glamor. For this is a contradiction, a movie about reclusiveness, in which Mickey One, taken up by a kind but not especially alert girl, turns on her, bitter, cruel and liberated, and says, "I'm the king of the silent pictures – I'm hiding out till talkies blow over. Will you let me alone?" And says it as if even the generosity of words hurt his soft, pulpy, ego-blown mouth. There is an anger in Beatty far greater than that in Brando or Dean, for it is closer to the core, and it turns upon a loathing of himself as spectacle, his own visible glory and his role of speaking the big speeches. He is a star wanting to become a black hole.

Reviewers in 1965 say that Beatty plays the role badly. In *The New York Post*, Archer Winston writes: "Beatty gives it the fast-clatter routine which he seems to have learned for the occasion, but it doesn't come out of him with authority. For instance, he's not up to the style of the minor burlesque hall comic who has a bit. He's not in total control of the rest of his character either because that's not his kind of character. It can't fool anyone who believed him in his good ones likes *All Fall Down* and *Splendor in the Grass*. This is all a surface act, surface sweat. It's not inside him because he doesn't understand it."

But suppose the situation is really that of someone not very skilled as an actor, highly ungiving as a presence, chronically averse to becoming a part but addicted to observing his own attempt. *Mickey One* comes into focus if we reappraise it as a picture about self-denying narcissism. Of course, no one has that plan for the film. This is the biographer wanting, wishing the picture had dropped its black-and-white harshness, its Chicago and its stage-like message of courage. If only *Mickey One* had been in color and in L.A. with a performer who was searching for an excuse not to perform, and who had to find a girl and a Mob and woo or bribe them into pretending to be cross with him. For Mickey truly is someone who wants to shape the world to fit his fears. And what is paranoia but the self-willed melodrama of the shy?

There are moments in which its confusions suddenly lift – a slow dissolve in which one image of Mickey/Beatty seems to be watching another walk towards him; or when he closes out one act by playing the piano, grinning like a kid and singing "I'm coming, Virginia"; or that fragment of his act, in shades, tuxedo and cigar smoke (the teenager playing Lucky Luciano), and he chats up the mike: "How do you do, gentlemen, welcome to the Pickle Club. You all remember me, the human tranquiliser. I'm the management's answer to the cold shower," and then adds this line, as if trying it out, "A tidal wave just wiped out all sex in Chicago," tempted by the thought that there could be someone there, but really believing in his own isolation. And then there is the end of the film – at night, on the roof of some building, open to the air and the city skyscrapers, with Mickey sitting at a piano, alone in the spotlight, and the camera craning upwards, swept away by the majesty of this bashfulness that has finally become legendary and no longer needs the daily grind of telling jokes three times a night on its grave, not even at the Xanadu.

Claudia Cannon

Those left at the Lighthiser house had been inspired by witnessing death. The show had had such force – tragedy can be as bracing as three hard sets. Those left felt freed, the story-tellers and not its victim. Cy Lighthiser was exhilarated. He talked of putting a statue by the pool or a gold plaque in its tile floor. He encouraged rumors that the deceased was melancholy, that he had been fatally ill, that the incident was a mishap, inexplicable and marvellous because of that, that it was murder (hadn't everyone wondered?), or that it was the young man's gift to the assembly, a mystery they could always ponder.

"Rick and his splash," said a slender, tanned youth – sixteen or so – said to be a son of Cy by another marriage. His name was Beau, and he was just back from somewhere: his bare feet were stained and scarred. He might have walked across a burning desert. But everything else about him had a high finish, like the radiance of a sword that guarantees its danger and the sword's indifference.

"By the way," Beau whispered to D, "my stepmother wants you." D could tell that Beau liked to exploit whatever lurked in another's shadows.

"I beg your pardon." D was trembling.

The stark face was insolent with wonder. "Do you say that sort of thing all the time? The 'I beg your pardon' and 'What did you say?' Cy will kidnap you from Eyes. It's all talk with Cy – routines, sketches, lines. You'd be his dreamboat. Oh," this over his shoulder, as his example bade D follow him, "and I like the crestfallen look, too." Beau's laugh was like water scuttling from a bath.

D hurried down a corridor in the perfumed slipstream left by the youth.

"Seen her?" asked Beau.

"Only on screen," D was struggling to distinguish 'knowing' and 'seeing' with famous people. "Of course, I know who she is."

"Not even the lady knows that," Beau sighed. "If she ever thought she was catching up with herself she'd take a sleep cure. She has to guard that uneasiness." Then he added, "It's feeding time. You'll see her mummies, you wolf. Don't attack her. And one thing." He suddenly stopped, so D could not avoid bumping him.

"Don't laugh."

"No?"

"Not at her. *With* her is fine. But never at, over, under or about. She'll throw a blue fit."

"I'm glad you told me," said D, though he couldn't recall the last time he had laughed.

"You'll love her."

"I expect to."

"Oh, you're perfect," Beau pinched his cheek. "Tip-toes now, we mustn't alarm the little usurper."

There was a powder-blue ante-room, like an air-lock, and then a door and its jamb both edged in white felt and velcro so that the door would not mar a babe's sleep. The air was warm and it smelled of Johnson & Johnson, milk and shit.

"Highness," whispered Beau, and Claudia Cannon looked up from her Queen Anne nursing chair. Her ivory robe was in folds at her waist, crystalline slime from which the goddess was emerging. The child was attached to one of her prime white bosoms, the left, its small leaf of a hand on the bowl of her right breast. Claudia was looking down at it with brave wariness.

"Have you got it?" she demanded of Beau.

"Of course I've got it, step-mama."

"Fuck you," she murmured, her expression toward the baby never altering. She had not seemed to see D.

"Ma petite soeur," drawled Beau. He stroked the baby's brow with a finger, and emptied a sachet onto a saucer on the side table where Claudia had put baby's gripe water. A rough white cone stood up in the lamplight.

"Voilà."

"You're hateful," she told him.

"I'd only do it for you, Claudia."

"Until you tell it to the *Enquirer*," she replied.

"Never!" cried Beau. "I want enough for a book. I want it to be in libraries and book clubs. You deserve hard covers, an index and pictures." And then Beau, on his knees at the side table, looked across at D. "I'll show you my pictures if you're good, D. Claudia likes me taking

219

her. She says it's massage. No one knows how young she looks. Her ass is still as high as a back pack." And then to Claudia: "You know you shouldn't be sitting."

"Nursing mothers sit," she told him.

"What's that got to do with it? You're just getting off on the brat's soft gums. Admit it. I'll bet you're wet."

"Claudia Cannon is always wet, mousehole." It was proverbial.

"That's a chapter in my book," Beau promised D.

D could not tell how often they had run this conversation. It sounded spiteful and natural, but that could be Ms Cannon's genteel reluctance to get into further unpleasantness in front of strangers. D was still inclined to think she cherished this baby, its small grumpy face being led into affection by her bodily sustenance. D liked to believe mothers were brought closer to abiding calm in nursing. He had loved to watch C feeding their children. He could remember lying in the dark, listening to the lapping, the tiny belches and the sense of being on the edge of a sea of benevolence. The smell of shit came from a diaper, tossed on the carpet. It did not go away.

"Look at her," said Beau. He was sitting on the floor, watching his half-sister like a chess player who sees an intricate check coming.

"I enjoy your envy," said Claudia, slipping a transparent tube from the baby's gown. It was a foot long, bringing the cocaine closer. The glass slanted past the baby's head. D was fascinated by the different beats involved – inhalations by the mother and the placid swallowing of the child's system. The baby's hand reached up for the tube. D saw white grains settling in it when Claudia paused.

"Isn't that good stuff?" Beau asked.

She could not answer. She was gasping. The baby's eyes widened. The mother regained control and peace came back to the baby.

Claudia turned to D. She was revealed, that was the effect, intruded on before she had got the decent mask on her face and screwed it down. "You don't see me at my best," she said to D. It was an apology, but a seduction, too, letting him know she was ready for him to survey greater disarray. Then she looked at her stepson and said, "Out, Beau."

"Ma mère!" he pouted.

"And take that shitty rag with you."

Beau crawled across the floor like a drowsy dog (you could see him amusing his little sister), and sniffed at the diaper. Then he picked up the towelling in his teeth, and went away, dragging it with him.

"Come closer, D," said Claudia Cannon. "I want to whisper."

PROMISE HER

If a handsome man wants to be esteemed for his intelligence, he will become contemptuous of a world whose stories only concern his looks, his attractiveness and his romantic aura. He may then endeavor to insist upon the power of his mind by treating his relationships with women with some extra detachment or humor – just to stress that he is in control of, and superior to, them. He says to himself that if the world sees only a Don Juan, just a lover, then he will play that part with dark glee. He will have them all. Then perhaps some of the women will go away with the story that he was thinking all the time, that however many times his body climaxed and came, the hard on behind the eyes never lost its grip, never diminished.

Of course, it could drive him crazy, this attempt to smother himself with intelligence. There are not many more tortuous or gradual ways of going mad than being supremely intelligent about everything. And it will be especially warping if this man has amounts of kindness or affection that he would like to offer people, but which he learns to guard against because so many of his relationships have a twisted way, sooner or later, of becoming public, and because after a time he notices that there are women coming to him with the frank opportunism of tourists who want a story and a picture to prove they were there. He makes his real there more inaccessible, and provides a false front, the popular veneer of himself, for most of them. And when he fucks them, the popular image is doing the work, and the real one, the true one, is sitting in the dark watching. The man known for his love of women may be a ghost who loathes them by the age of forty and whose fucking does not hide the edge of disdain. Will no-one have the courage to cast him as Bluebeard?

And if he gives interviews, he is badgered with questions, "Will you marry *her*, or her?" or even "Will you ever marry?" He learns how to smile and say, "You know . . . I really don't know," and it is years before he appeciates how true that is, and how the easy satisfaction of every

221

sexual desire is a cover for not knowing. Then intelligence begins to worry, for it cannot convince itself that it is still in control. Suppose this man is in the movies, he takes his dismay to see films and he comes slowly upon this last comfort: that there is an attractiveness, an eroticism and a desire – maybe even a love – in seeing but not being seen. He sees the new movies, and he sees the new hot actresses, and he gets to meet most of them, and his chance with them. But he realises that maybe he felt most about them before he met them. And he has seen some lovers become as bored with him as ever he has been with them. The distance becomes alluring. And if he remembers all he has fucked, he may say to himself it wasn't really always him who did it. It was the other one, it was Beatty. After all, how could *he* have had so many, and not remembered them all? But intelligence begins to see a dilemma in all of this, a riddle: does this almost obligatory infidelity mean that the mind's control is necessarily dark and pessimistic? And compelled by its nature to permit no roots, no family attachments, no children? Must it be a martyr to itself, only at home in a kind of resentful loneliness?

Whatever he says about the films when they are made, Beatty is making pictures in the early 60s that seem to be experiments with self-hatred: a gigolo; a cold, nihilistic exploiter of women; a nurse who sleeps with an insane patient; and a neurotic comic who seems to have wallowed in garbage before appearing on the set. Such parts are a corollary to the way aggrieved journalists squeak at his surliness and his uncooperativeness. But the world, which entails chiefly those journalists, continues to say that he is gorgeous, sexy, beautiful etc. Some of them add, as if to establish that they were there, that he has a charisma, or a glamor, in person that exceeds even the best that the studios can do for him.

He meets Leslie Caron early in 1963 at a Hollywood party at the Bistro given by her agent, Freddie Fields, to boost her recent Oscar nomination for her performance in *The L-Shaped Room*. Caron is six years older than Beatty, and she is in her second marriage, to Peter Hall, the director of the Royal Shakespeare Company in England. She and Hall have two children; she is thirty-two, the star of such Hollywood films as *An American in Paris*, *Lili* and *Gigi*. On stage, she has been directed by Jean Renoir in his own play, *Orvet*, and by Peter Hall in a version of *Gigi*. Of course, she is French, and originally a dancer. She falls for the American actor. "It was quite strong wooing," she says later. "We practically didn't leave each other after that party for the next couple of years."

Peter Hall contents himself with Chicago, Jamaica and Beverly Hills as instances of togetherness established by a private detective when he names Beatty as co-respondent. This is some eighteen months later, in the summer of 1964, as Hall files for divorce, charging his wife's adultery as the grounds. Chicago represents *Mickey One*; Jamaica is for when Caron films *Father Goose* with Cary Grant; Beverly Hills is where they go to when not working, the place to which Caron wants to bring her two children.

The relationship with Caron has some reason to be judged the most serious of Beatty's life: it leads the perfectionist into making two pictures, *Promise Her Anything* and *Kaleidoscope*, that are not just bad, but trivial, foolish and unnecessary beyond the fact that they give him some income while he is in London. That is forced upon him because a London court accedes to Hall's request that the two children should not leave England.

The court hearing to decide the divorce is in February 1965. Beatty is ordered to pay the costs. Shortly thereafter, shooting starts on *Promise Her Anything*. The picture is made in London, but it claims to be set in New York. Caron plays a young widow with a baby son who moves into Greenwich Village. Beatty's character, Harley Rummel, lives upstairs. He wants to make serious films but is for the moment sidetracked into tasteful pornography. It is a romantic comedy, or so its advertisements say. Mr Rummel goes so far as to use the baby in one of his dirty movies, but then the hound redeems himself, saves the infant's life and wins the heart of his mother.

It is the film of an actor with something much more important on his mind, a disaster so great that it can only be explained as not being noticed. Beatty is in love, ready, perhaps eager to have his life changed. He and Caron live together in her house in Montpelier Square, in the most fashionable part of a London going through all the motions of what the media will soon identify as "swinging." This is the first great age of the Beatles. English movies have come to life. London is the center of the world for exciting, cut-price fashions.

One does not have to take the notion of "Swinging London" at face value. Still, it is a more stimulating environment than Beverly Hills. Moreover, the show business circle in London to which Beatty is attached is likely to include writers, painters, musicians, designers and even politicians and restless members of the royal family. The sojourn in London allows Beatty to live more steadily with a woman than he has ever dared since leaving home. He meets and talks to children, as a shy prospective step-father. And he lives in the time and mood of films like

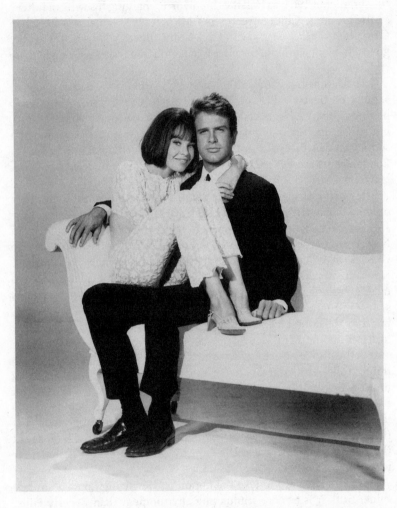

With Leslie Caron, a publicity pose for *Promise Her Anything*

Losey's *The Servant*, the Beatles films, directed by Dick Lester, Kubrick's *Dr Strangelove*, Jack Clayton's *The Pumpkin Eater*, *What's New, Pussycat?*, Polanski's *Repulsion*, John Schlesinger's *Darling* (with Julie Christie) and Antonioni's *Blow Up*. The films Beatty makes in London are not nearly as interesting, but it is out of the London experience that he comes more fully into his own as both an actor and a producer with a new kind of American film.

The influence of Leslie Caron may be even more important than that of London. She is never just a sexual partner. In the summer of 1965, the usually taciturn Beatty is ready to tell columnist Sheilah Graham that he will marry Caron "whenever she wants . . . when she says 'Now!'." That might be a lie, or part of the subtle gaslighting that says to the woman, you haven't ever asked me, dear . . . oh, you were waiting for me to ask . . . well, I've been asking, haven't you heard? . . . no, of course, I'm not being difficult . . . well, if you say so, let's think about it. But that habitual masquerade doesn't need to woo by way of the press. Everything suggests that in Caron, Beatty finds a woman wise in the ways of show business, intelligent, forthright and creative. Someone he can talk to.

Earlier on, in Jamaica, when Beatty is on the island with her, as incognito as he can manage, he lives quietly in her house and waits for her to come home from the shooting. Night after night they talk, and the chief topic is his career and its troubles. He tries to place himself in the tradition of Brando and Clift. They are taken seriously, he complains. "He was considered just a playboy," Caron says years later. "He had spent too much time wooing women in the public eye. Of course it bothered him that he wasn't taken seriously. We used to talk about it. He was in despair about it."

Beatty has reason to be upset with his status. But if he looks hard at Clift and Brando, he must see larger difficulties in being a movie star. Clift will be dead in 1966; he is nervewracked, dependent on drugs and drink, terrified at the loss of his looks. Brando is increasingly disenchanted with his career. The picture he directed, *One-Eyed Jacks*, has been a failure. He finds little pleasure left in acting. *Last Tango in Paris* and *The Godfather* lie ahead, but he is near the end of his patience as a regularly working actor and utterly perplexed at how to secure more power in the business.

Kaleidoscope is not quite as bad as *Promise Her Anything*, largely because it casts Beatty as a rogue, Barney Lincoln, a playboy who eases his boredom by planning a gambling coup that requires breaking into a playing card factory and marking cards soon to be used in a big casino. This "caper" is couched as another romantic comedy, with Susannah York as his partner. Beatty is no more at ease in comedy than he was before. He does not deliver jokes properly: he seems to feel the silliness in serving up laughs. He even looks humorless, cute or heavy. Here is a real paradox in his nature as an actor: ask him to play comedy and he is forlorn; put him in certain near-tragic situations, and he can deliver an exquisite humor. It is as if he cannot deal with his own image at the speed of slapstick or in a ridiculous light.

But when Lincoln has to be the casual mastermind, when he sits at the gambling table, a little like a Yankee James Bond, then he seems excited by himself and the context. You can believe he often falls asleep thinking of himself in fantasies of power and command, the lone gambler who walks off with a fortune, favoring those who guess he cheated but cannot prove it with a slanting grin in which you see the shark has a diamond set in one of his teeth.

One more film in this line and Beatty might have died of boredom – if he was noticing the films. We have to think he was in love with Leslie Caron, happy to be with her, and to go with her to Paris.

Dive into darkness

Being alone with Claudia Cannon! – except, of course, for her new babe, whose world and library were its mother's warm teat. D was persuaded that the child was not yet spoiled by the pipeline of cocaine that slanted across its feeding like an hypotenuse. And he preferred to let the baby's meek adoration fill his mind. But being alone with Claudia Cannon was like confronting a famous painting. There was a powerful urge to have all the serenity for himself, or deface it irretrievably. But the most poignant feeling was of being with an entity culturally apart. As she turned her grave and lovely head this way and that, without any bidding or eye contact, D appreciated that he was like history for her. She did not look at him when she spoke, but alluded to his possibility.

"So, dear Eyes stood us up, the prick." The words were sharp with animosity, but the light of Claudia Cannon's gaze stroked her baby's brow. D wondered at that brow and its waiting mind being impressed by the mother's saintly glance. It was a pose that might have found its way into Claudia's emotional filing system on some trip to an art museum. She was in her prime now to play the Virgin Mary. Cy was probably planning the Christmas card, and haggling with Helmut Newton on which serpents there might have been close to the manger.

"I'm sure he's upset not to be here." D tried to be diplomatic. How often strangers found themselves excusing or conjecturing a hopeful best in Eyes.

"He didn't call," she carped, but her face steered straight on for baby's bliss. "Mr Hold-the-Phone didn't have the grace to touch-tone us, did he?"

"I believe he is in a retreat." D struggled to be plausible. "Away from a phone."

"He has one implanted in his body." Claudia was smiling now, in a wicked dream. "He's just doing it to show us how small we are, Cy and I, Cy and Me." She had winced at the echo. Claudia had a taste for melody.

She had learned over the years which lines worked for her, and now her mind spun them out as effortlessly as the DNA, or whatever, generated her beauty. With both looks and dialogue, thought had been circumvented. There was just effortless nature being endlessly consistent, a passionate persistence. "I'd like to cut off his royal dick," she said, "and feed it to baby – suitably moulinexed, of course. Let her eat it early, before she has to swallow humiliation with it."

A shudder coursed through D's body at what Claudia had said. She was not looking at him, but she detected the spasm. She was so tuned to alterations in atmosphere or vibration, a nerve to her vicinity. Wasn't there often a scene where the Virgin felt a hand touch her in the crowd? D could not control his seeing of Claudia in the eternity of scenarios.

"Ah, D," she said softly. "You are moved by children."

"I may have eaten something a little off." He wanted to make a joke of it.

"We all have," she promised. "We have all of us here sucked such poison," she was looking away into the depths of ignominy, "and kissed their cancerous asses."

"Please!" yelped D. He had the first heaves of nausea, and this was no time to vomit, not alone with Claudia Cannon.

"Dear D, I meant only that I felt the true parent in you." So saying, her unencumbered right hand reached out into his groin. His rod of parenting had shrunk – exhaustion, the occasion and sheer bewilderment – but Claudia had a discovering touch. And very soon, she had a respectable part of him in her hand. "You're very handsome, very fine," she told him. She knew; she never looked. D did wonder if his dimensions or even a living video image were put up for her, off in the dark, like the lines in a soap opera, when work is too intense for dialogue to be learned. But her eyes did not focus narrowly, as in reading. They communed with the faraway, with absence, her truest lover.

"Wouldn't you like to touch me, D?" she asked. "I'm nearly ready again. What you might call a restored virgin." She simpered; it must be her silly hope to be intact again, always love's fresh fruit. "You would have to be very gentle, slipping in and out. Could you be like a mouse?" She did not wait for his opinion of this. "I think you could. I do think so. Not that I want you to be *un*obtrusive. No, I do want to notice. Astonished even. What say you?" The lilt of regality had carried her close to Quentin Durward or the Round Table. But what chance had D of impinging when Washington had Cary Grant and Eva Marie Saint on his face and never flinched?

"Will you tell me stories, D, if I lie in your arms? I am so fearful of the dark, and so restless a sleeper."

D was crushed, "I can seldom think of stories."

"You must have told them to your children," said Claudia. "I can see their rapt faces, imploring you not to stop or go away."

"Ah," sighed D, for he saw the same picture, and it stirred him with guilt and fondness.

"You and I are parents, D. We know. Not like the Eyes of the world, so promiscuous and unestablished. We have children here and there, and we know those tuggings of duty that we can never quite fulfil. We are grown up, that's the difference." D was always staggered at where her speeches carried her.

Her hand had to come away from her loyal swain. The baby was full. Claudia placed the child on her shoulder, and eased a stupefied belch from its little balloon of a body. She sighed with gratification at the effect, and then took the infant to its cradle, plying it with crocheted blankets like lace handkerchiefs.

"There, baby," she said to the powdered air. "Go to sleep, wake up strong and true – and watch the bedbugs don't bite." She tiptoed away from the cradle – it took a couple of minutes – so as to be certain the child was sleeping. Then, as if with her last strength, she drifted to a day bed and sank upon it.

"I'm so drained when I have fed my baby. I feel I have given it my life." There was a sense of true loss.

"Should you rest?" D wondered.

"With you here, foolish? What kind of hostess do you think I am? Come sit beside me." And her hand flapped on the few inches of the day bed not filled by her and that liquid ivory robe, just another version of flesh. Such a hand. D could not take his eyes from its gloss of marble. It was the hand she had held him with.

"You do desire me, don't you?" Her eyes were closed now, in tribute to sleep.

"Well," D began.

"Tell me truly," she ordered. "Is it me you want, or just the star? I cannot bear to be used."

"I'm sure it must be you," said D. He did not add that, while her stardom was unquestioned, he was not himself among her greatest fans. Indeed, he groaned at announcements of her new pictures.

"You would have to be so very careful. I am not fully healed."

D imagined the inner Claudia Cannon beneath the loose robe, with

229

flaps of unknit wound, like sails in the doldrums, and the funk of blood. There might be scars still, white and blue in their new state, skin ready to tear again, so that if he entered her there might be the look of invadedness in her suddenly opened eyes.

"Do it anyway," she said. "You only live once, and when it's done we can trash that rascal Eyes together. Come along, darling, pop it in," and in a trice she had rolled up the yards of silk and swung her legs apart, like a dockyard whore.

"Well," said D, and dived in the darkness.

IN BED

What is Warren Beatty like in bed then? He must wonder himself. We are not supposing from this book someone so monotonously secure or self-adoring that he does not scrutinise the tremblings and the commotions in his ladies (and in himself) like a seismologist on the San Andrea Fault. And it is very much to the book's point that he will have seen himself named – on bathroom walls or in the gossip columns – like a Kilroy or a Casanova, so earnestly imagined, so zealously trumpeted, that he must have recognised how far he stands for the *idea* of sexual splendor. No doubt he has his moments in bed, but can any of them match the thinking in advance or the neo-poetic descriptions? In the end – no matter which end or which way – there is a purely factual, physical aspect to what goes on in bed, so ecstatic in its nature, so brief, so high, that it is bound to move in legend in one of two directions – it will be lied about, or forgotten. There is no surer function in art than its ability to pin down the imagined sexual peak. Movie stars are as sexy as their pictures, and there must come a day when they know the drudgery and thankless labor of actually being in bed with anyone. It testifies to our Warren's sense of ordinariness if he has persevered.

Britt Ekland has this to say, in a book in which she never gives a mealy-mouthed impression of herself in bed:

> "Warren was the most divine lover of all. His libido was as lethal as high octane gas. I had never known such pleasure and passion in my life.
>
> "Warren could handle women as smoothly as operating an elevator. He knew exactly where to locate the top button. One flick and we were on the way."

Where is the man who couldn't stand to have this printed about him? Who can tell the revelation of intimacy from the enhancement of legend? And it is in the nature of this sort of legend that intimacy has been transcended, with the star exploding to fill space.

Ekland's account surpasses the racy gentility of Joan Collins' "four or five times a day". Here is a metaphor that might allude to a history of visiting Warren at the Beverly Wilshire, going up and down for him. Is it a fond tease, saying, remember when we nearly did it in the elevator itself, jammed in a corner, all awkwardness forgotten, romantic effort racing the ponderous rattling climb of the walnut cabinet?

Warren and Britt could not have done it in the Beverly Wilshire elevator: it is only a ten-story building, and the elevator has an operator. But I can never enter the elevator without the thought occurring. When mortals dream about stars, or when one person wonders about another, it is the thought that counts. Which lovers alone in an elevator have not calculated the chances, or considered what would happen if the box halted between floors?

The Ekland metaphor does offer the woman's body as the elevator, with man the dextrous operator, existing in and out of that body as need arises, like an engineer at a power plant. It is a description of the woman's body that seems passive and submissive at first. But it is so extensive, so elemental, as to be more powerful than the man's. (No one finds the little engineer if the power plant melts.) The elevator could have other kids to press its buttons. But what would those boys do if they had no elevator to play with? Warren in Britt's scenario is a master, but a potentially homeless expert, the servant to her existence, merely skilled (and humbled) in the face of authentic power.

In this context of biography – admittedly discursive, playful and speculative – isn't the nature of metaphor the best hope for insight? It is not enough to depict Warren as a womaniser. He is used too. It is likely that from time to time Warren Beatty has received carefully handwritten letters from young women in Arkansas or Zagreb, with snapshots of the writers enclosed, nude pictures even with the girls grinning patiently at the camera, their legs spread to show targets and prizes, or that the letters have said, "Dear Warren, what I would like is for you . . . (all put so bluntly that a romantic skims across the alarming words) . . . And I will be your slave and do anything you ask, and I can go all night, Warren, can you?" Or daunting words to that effect, so that the reader feels exhausted already.

Now imagine, if you will, that I had found ladies ready to describe such scenes with Warren and stand by them. I cannot believe that my publisher would dare to put such words in print. For it is in the true and noble nature of sexual or romantic intimacy that the act occurs in such a way that even the parties wonder what happens. There is no sex without the imagination, and no way of rendering it that does not reach out for fiction.

It may not be necessary always for Warren to do it. He may become more culturally potent with abstinence. The French director Roger Vadim recalls a Malibu party in 1965 when Warren, "surrounded by young actresses, explained that he had become suddenly impotent and would be leaving for India the next day". In those 60s, India is supposed to hold so many answers and rescues. Vadim sees that it is a ruse – "sometimes Warren loves to mystify people". He knows already that an idea can be more magical than its thing. And teasing can merge with the mind's heavenly India or philosophy.

Let us say he thinks such things on the flight to Paris, while dozing through the movie, holding hands with Leslie Caron. I buy the hand-holding; so many women speak of Warren's kindness. And if he's dreamy with sex and flying as their palms grow moist, isn't he growing into Howard Hughes?

Why Paris? Because it is where Caron grew up, ballet-crazy amid Occupation, Resistance and Relief. There is even a chance now that she and Beatty will act together in the movie of *Is Paris Burning?* And because, once before, Caron was the guide to an American in Paris, and now sees a need to broaden the young actor's mind and awareness. There are things she knows he has not heard of, and he probably listens to them quietly until he has learned them.

One has to do with the history of the movies. It goes as follows. The movies were invented simultaneously in France and America, but the word the world uses is American because in the first two decades of the form American commercial power took such charge of the medium and its business. The French made small films for themselves and for those parts of the world prepared to deal with "foreign" films. In France, it was possible for leading writers, painters and musicians to be interested in film and occasionally involved with it. The pictures made there won a reputation for being "adult". The greatest film director in the world, Jean Renoir, was French. Many years later, while he is discussing a venture with Martin Scorsese, Beatty will see a picture of Renoir's *La Règle du Jeu* on Scorsese's wall, and he will say, "That's *Shampoo*."

Meanwhile, America makes movies for the world, so many of them that in the next four decades film alters the way people regard reality. For we look at things and consider how they compare with the photographs, and when we think of how life's own drama and narrative work, we remember and are influenced by the plot structure and the romantic imagery of movies. The movies made in America are intended as versions of real life, albeit versions made for fiction and entertainment. But as time goes by, so the Hollywood story structures – the genres – become at least as familiar as, and rather more reliable than, the ways of life.

By the late 1950s, the task of broadcasting those genres and their extensive, implicit ideology has been passed on to television. American theatrical movies are therefore stranded, far from life and losing their audience. There are a few pictures which, consciously or not, respond with a wicked, desperate creative energy, as if to make films about this movie ideology. They are absurdist, camp, and the best American films of their time – *Rio Bravo, Psycho, Some Like it Hot, Written on the Wind, Men in War, Touch of Evil* – extraordinary works, full of dark humor, in which the various genres are going cubist and crazy.

This is not much noticed in America at the time. But in France there is a resurgence in adventurous, small films, made now by men younger than movie-makers have ever been. The movement is called the New Wave; its directors are Truffaut, Godard, Chabrol, Rivette, Rohmer, and so on. They love the natural photographed look of life and new, casual actors. Some say their films are very real. But they are, in truth, films about film made by young people who think of themselves as artists and who have grown up in the notion that the cinema is a guiding part of reality.

Why Paris? Because this new attitude has been discovered there and vindicated. Films are about films. It is a more appealing insight than a self-absorbed actor could ever have imagined. And if he loves Leslie Caron very much, as much as he can, it may be because he is deriving from her not just her body, her lessons, her love and herself, but glimpses of a way ahead for himself. Yet this is not a simple discovery, with eyes suddenly widening in delight. No, there is something in Beatty that does not like to be seen discovering; it does suggest he was not as intelligent as he wants to be if there is so vast a novelty, one that requires discovery. So if revelation comes his way, he is cool about it, and learns to grin through clenched teeth and say, "Uh-huh, I see," giving away as little as possible.

How is he in bed, if he is so reluctant to be surprised?

This is a story about a party at Marianne Hill's house, some time in the middle 1970s. And Warren Beatty arrives with Michelle Phillips; and an observer sees his act.

First Michelle vanishes into the kitchen and Warren stands there surveying the room. He picks on this woman – not an especially beautiful woman, but sharply dressed. She has come with a man, but Warren comes on over and he just positions himself between them with his back to the man, and after a while the man just goes away.

Warren says, "Don't I know you?" to the woman.

She says no.

Then he starts his whole shy thing. The head down, muttering, not very articulate. He even kicks at the floor with his toe, trying to get it out. And he offers the woman a cigarette.

She says, "No, thank you. I don't smoke."

"Neither do I," says Warren.

So she points out, "You're smoking now."

And he says, "That's only because I'm nervous." And he says, "I'd really like to get to know you better."

She says to him, "Didn't you come with someone?"

"Yeah, Michelle," says Beatty. "Have you seen her?"

"I don't think so," says the woman.

And at that Warren gives up, and he retrieves Michelle Phillips from the kitchen and they leave.

Torn room

"Let me tell you," announced Claudia Cannon, a swan's neck of an arm thrust back for emphasis, and knocking the backboard. "And you may quote me – look at my hand, I'll be bruised."

"Heavens," D called from a more southerly spot on the day bed.

"Anyway," Claudia was looking for the pain to peep through. "Eyes has nothing on you. Rien!"

This news did not swell D's head. It supported his caution with most popular myths. Every cat is gray in the dark was his opinion, plus the likelihood that all wangs waned. There is a law of gravity in such things, like aging and the fading of swish tricks.

"Now let's see what we have on Eyes," Claudia cajoled.

"What do you mean?" asked D in the tented shade of the sheet she had drawn over them.

"All those distant, lordly ways," complained Claudia, "pretending he's different from the rest of us. Ducking my party. Being so stingy with himself. What are our strings if not to be plucked?"

"Indeed," said D, whose own fingers were still tingling from ostinato attention to Claudia's viola.

"He has a debt to the public. Eyes does get a touch solemn. It's a kind of sadness. I have never once seen him at the Lakers, he disdains Superstars and I know for a fact, the producer is an old pal, that Eyes will not do *Donahue*."

"And he would be good with Phil," D surmised. "Two genuine worriers addressing a broad range of issues. And no suckers."

"So right," said Claudia. "And if he is serious about politics, the poor dear, it's the only way to get yourself about."

A little time went by in silence – it can be cut.

"Kiss me, sweetie," she asked, and D dipped his head again into the vanilla blancmange. He felt his renewal stirring, the spent & thinking again of being a ! for her *.

Torn room

"And tell me the story, I wish you would. I can be quite unrestrained next time, you know. I really am a wicked thing. Just tell me what's on your mind. So long as we don't wake baby."

D reminded her of her very recent fluttering, rising and falling like an anesthetist's bladder, her face gorged on excitement, but without so much as a sound.

"Every mother has to learn the muted orgasm," Claudia told him. "And, after all, the great actresses needed no sound. Anyway, you were driving me wild. What else could I do?"

"I guessed as much," he said demurely.

"Weren't you going to tell me the story? Unless you want to come in my face first?"

This target astonished him.

"It is more beneficial than any oils or creams on the market." She liked to sound practical.

The dilemma for D was that he could only be loyal to Eyes and Clear by making love to Claudia. It did distract her from the script. He was still in a blithe state of mindless desire for her, but simple prudence said neither that supply nor his! could last for ever. Moreover, D's view was complicated by his chronic problem: he was already in love with la Cannon. When she sighed and shut her eyes with pleasure it convinced him that she liked him and gave him open house, this very celebrated star. But love needs sleep.

"This script," said Claudia, "I know you shouldn't tell me," she put a tangy finger on his lips. "And you mustn't. But it's daring, isn't it?"

"I think it is." He saw the fate of the future turning in her heady eyes.

"Good work must be," she knew. She smiled shyly and caressed his !; her touch was so cool still.

"Oh my!" D moaned.

"Yes, yours," she allowed, and in a moment she had him like a corkscrew, so anxious to obey her request for hush, but so impelled to give voice, until the sweet relief and he was pouring into her cupped hand. From which she next sipped and then lathered the rest into her breasts until they shone.

"We should be in a film." He was besotted with her. "Our love-making should be shown."

"Oh, really?" she said.

"Without censorship."

"I had a slightly different idea," she confessed.

"Yes?" She was the expert, after all.

"I believe you should direct your script. Only you can understand it. Now, of course, directing is a chore –"

"Oh no," said D, a writer who had no doubt where authorship rested.

"You would have to watch some Eyes or other doing his feeble best to make love to me."

At this moment, D could see worse fates.

"But you would know I was thinking of you."

He tried to imagine exactly how that would be knowable.

"And you could spite him by making sure the camera saw me."

"Just the back of his head, burrowing away," D could picture that unruly mop doing its best.

"I think the true exaltation is female, don't you?"

"How could you guess I wanted to direct?" he asked her.

"We have had . . . knowledge of one another. Secrets travel with that cargo. I felt it. I do feel things." It is the knowledge, isn't it? Not the body, that cocky meringue. So saying, she took his hand and led it to the mouth of her *. The flood was so great, D worried there might be blood there.

"Put your hand in, your whole hand," she urged. There was room for him to feel around the swimming softness, testing the elastic walls of the chamber.

"Mmmmm," she said to him, so simple and quiet, he was smitten to the quick. They both sighed at being there. "Tell me the story," she said.

"Well," began D. But he had to roll to get a firm base on his elbow if he was to keep his whole hand in the honey and tell the story. The manoeuver must have turned his wrist for he saw a tremor of bliss hurry through her eyes, not conventional, not movie-like, but scary and untidy, as if she thought her insides would rip.

"What was that?" she asked. There was fear in her voice. She was asking not D, but the story.

"I had to move a little, my arm was going to sleep."

"Not that." She dismissed the details. She waited but there was nothing. Then, when she had subsided again, the room cracked apart and a rift of earth, air, night, cold and a smoking, wrenching noise came between them and the baby. There was a sucking sound and D's damp hand came free as the naked Claudia scrambled from the bed to the brink of the chasm, looking out across it at the rest of the room and the baby's cradle floating away.

Her scream began, and D saw his script, a white tablet, tumbling into the pit. Now he had only the money.

PARIS

In Paris, with Leslie Caron, Beatty encounters François Truffaut at a party. They have lunch together. This is not their first meeting, for Truffaut has been in Chicago during the shooting of *Mickey One*, visiting his girl friend, Alexandra Stewart. At lunch, Caron and Beatty talk movies and parts. They would like to do something together more worthwhile than *Promise Her Anything*. Truffaut says there is this script that has been offered to me which would be more suitable for you. After all, it is an American story, and Truffaut hardly speaks English.

The script is the work of two young American writers who met at *Esquire*, David Newman and Robert Benton. They do not have a movie credit between them, and their story concerns a pair of outlaws who had a brief fame in Texas and Oklahoma in the early 1930s. Their names are Bonnie Parker and Clyde Barrow. They are both killed by Texas Rangers and assorted deputies on May 23, 1934. Neither of them has reached the age of twenty-five. They have robbed small banks and killed people who got in their way. They are the sort of brutes we go in dread of meeting; unless we meet them in imagination, in which case they are raw energy, recklessness and a kind of exemplary panache – part theirs, part the savagery of gleeful, demented newsprint – ready to assist our fantasies. Their lives seem to have been lived in the American instinct and desperation that fame would be enough, and that it would change all else.

Newman and Benton have sent the script to Truffaut because they have been inspired by his films (especially by *Jules et Jim*), and because they do not think the American business is capable of making, or even understanding, their picture. They have liked the quality of a ménage in *Jules et Jim*, two men and a woman, and the unexpected juxtaposition of laughter and tears in Truffaut's films. They regard this as a lifelike spontaneity not evident in American films, not quite seeing that it is in the influence of montage and scene-making on his scenario, that it is film making the new conditions for the medium.

239

In America, in 1964, Truffaut has met Benton and Newman, and startled them by showing them a French translation he has had made of the script, the better to deal with it. The three men talk about the project, and Truffaut suggests an improvement: "Bonnie writes 'The Poem of Bonnie and Clyde' in a car, then cut to a Texas ranger reading the poem in a newspaper, then cut to Bonnie and Clyde lying on a blanket in the meadow with Clyde reading the poem in the paper." This sequence will be intact in the finished picture, the climax in its notion of star identity as a liberating aphrodisiac.

But Truffaut says he cannot take the script as he is trying to make *Fahrenheit 451* in England. His generosity has been for its own sake. And now, over lunch, he sketches in the story for Beatty, with Caron translating when Truffaut's English lets him down. It is an awesome moment for those sentimentally inclined to believe in luck and drama. For it is the chance of a great American movie in which American ways have been bypassed. And for the lovers looking for material to secure their unofficial marriage, it looks like a blessed fantasy. The press has made Beatty and Caron outlaws already – which they resent and regard as wrongful reports. Let them make their own ballad then and be a team, peppering the hostile world and its media with bullets and grins. Sooner or later, if an American movie is going to work, its stars must believe it tells *their* story. For if the picture frees their desires, then it has a chance of capturing the large audience, too. All sensational American pictures delight in outlawry, whether the shooting up of banks or the soaring above everyday dullness.

Leslie Caron must see herself as Bonnie. She may be leaping ahead of her winning translation with plans for Bonnie Parker's French mother, a woman from New Orleans. Who ever really knows the reliable truth, ze 'ole truth, about such desperadoes? These are lost loves, *n'est-ce pas?* More than that, Caron has been urging Beatty to be his own master, not to play according to the system, but to be another kind of outlaw. Here is a project he can tell himself he found. Of course, its actual authors are in New York, but Beatty can go back to them, woo them with offers, and then let them realise, slowly, how in France he saw the picture afresh, and his seeing made it his so that now, in a way, they, the writers, have the chance to serve *his* version. Let Warren seduce you – if you want your script made.

Someone who knows Beatty at this time says, "He likes and can get on with every woman, any woman. But every man is a competitor." Moreover, Beatty has been taking on a psychological stance towards older men in which he wants to give them respect, awe, reverence and service. He wants a hero and a leader, but his inner nature is so competitive and so mistrustful of these men that he begins to battle with them until he finds and fixes on a flaw, some small way in which they fail or let him down. And then he judges them, and says, "Oh, yeah, so-and-so . . ." and smiles with superiority.

This has happened with William Inge and Elia Kazan. It is what accounts for the awful breakdown in the relationship with Robert Rossen. When Beatty first knows Clifford Odets in Hollywood, he approaches the worn-out, compromised, alcoholic and neurotic writer, only a few years from death, and wants to talk books and art with him. All Odets wants to do is play gin rummy, and Beatty goes along with this and then remembers with a cool mixture of sorrow and triumph that he's a better player than Odets.

When Beatty meets Arthur Penn in *Mickey One* they are in love with their own closeness and the feeling of having discovered a comrade. Before the shooting, Penn says Beatty must live with him and his family in New York so they can talk all the time. And in the six weeks that follow Beatty finds Penn's faults, his limitations – let us say his human nature – and again feels victory and that old detachment. There are those who will hail *Bonnie and Clyde* as Penn's triumph, his self-expression. So it is in part, but Arthur Penn always knows who is in charge, and he may realise that he is the first leader who has become a follower. It is part of Beatty's gradual realisation that he must take control that he sees the need to hire instead of be hired. He will not say this, but inwardly he thinks he has control of the vital, dynamic, brilliant Penn. He would not hire a true rival.

To be so judgemental, to go so zealously and ruthlessly in search of flaw in order to feel secure seems like immaturity. It is not necessarily conscious behavior, and it does not block out the class or the intelligence of Warren Beatty, or his very good instincts about those who need to be loyal to him. There is a way in which he is using people, but the manner is ambiguous and the goals are often very worthwhile. Moreover, Beatty is always in search of some other figure he can believe in – his eyes have the hopeful smile of a disciple. It is just as real a need as the mechanism that begins to undermine the hero. Occasionally, it finds a perfect model.

A few years later, in 1971, Beatty pursues a young actress after a party. They walk together through the streets of Beverly Hills and he points out houses to her where stars live and he tells her how ten years before, as a newcomer, he had walked the same streets at night and wondered whether he could ever take over one of these houses. The young woman realises he did the tour – not in company, on a bus – but privately, secretly. He is a movie buff, in love with all the old Hollywood history. As if to dramatise what she is thinking, a darkened limousine drives by and enters the grounds of one of the larger houses.

"Do you know what that is?" Beatty asks her. "That's the hearse with Mike Romanoff's body." The death has just occurred, at the age of eighty plus, of the man who said he was related to the Tsar, who had become a restaurateur and a pillar of Hollywood society. As far as such things are ever known for sure it was known he was a fraud. But Hollywood is crazy over frauds, if they get away with it – that's what acting is – and maybe this Romanoff, real name possibly Harry Gerguson, did have a French mother. Romanoff was a young romancer: he seduced women, he advised on movies about old Europe, he told stories, and he became one of the city's first magical hosts. You knew Mike was a bullshitter, but you listened because the city is so superstitious.

And Warren has timed this nocturnal stroll to pay homage to the hearse. What a part Romanoff would be for him, and what a hero, for Romanoff is dead. The flaws are wiped away by his going. You could maybe love yourself as a killer, too, if the killer died in time. To be up there on the screen is to partake of life and death simultaneously, it is to be the most vivid thing in life and absolutely out of touch, the only secure hero. As Warren Beatty finds himself, he is working out the nature and the necessity of being a certain kind of magical ghost, of being more imagined than real.

Doolywohl

It was now only a flap on the edge of wilderness, but the door to what had been Claudia's room before the new ravine struck through it, opened and the weathered face of Doc appeared. He was windswept in the gale left by disruption. There was a look of long-suffering on his face, as if he doubted that any story could proceed without his watching over it. He had the manner of a plumber at a domestic flood.

"You had to do it, didn't you?" he said.

"Do what?" asked D, sheepish but defiant.

"Have your precious earthquake!"

"Well –" D felt caught in the act.

"Not enough to hint at it, keep the reader guessing. You could have had all your metaphors without bringing the damned thing down on us. Everyone gets the point!"

"I know, but –"

"Do you have any idea what it entails?"

D was too mortified to speak. He had been crass.

"This'll need months of effects work. You get those guys in, it's all bureaucracy and things you never see properly until you preview in Seattle, and then you're in the can. You have a decent thing going with actors, you're working up a nice idea, and then it's blown. Your actors are left making faces at blue screens. They go bananas. They lose the picture. And those effects people, they talk a language no one understands. It's giving the picture away for some stupid gotcha. To say nothing of the damage and the lives. I'm disappointed. I thought you could keep it cool."

The gloomy Doc prowled into what was left of the room, stood by the naked Claudia frozen in a scream on the brink, and looked out at the other half of the room, receding, and at all the wasteland in between. It was like a back projection.

"Right here, you've got another million, million two. What else do you have in mind? Jesus," he groaned, "this could be as bad as that thing with Heston and Geneviève Bujold."

"Oh no," D was worried now. "This is simply to get the action out of the city and into the desert."

Doc considered the options. "How about a modest local disaster up on Mulholland? Enough to get your characters driving. But not so we have to show Westwood or downtown coming apart."

"Well," D began.

"You'll thank me."

"I did have a scene coming where they pause in their flight, look back at the city and see the HOLLYWOOD sign start to hop and jump."

"It does?" Doc was interested in spite of himself.

"DOOLYWOHL," D offered. "OLDWHOLYO."

"Well, I can see the charm of that," Doc admitted. "The big shake comes after they've got away?"

"That's what I thought."

"I suppose one good model shot of the sign would get you a lot of mileage."

"Exactly," said D. "And then later we can have radio reports –"

"Cut off in mid-sentence," guessed Doc.

"That's not too much?"

"It never fails. Just silence and the faces of Angelenos wondering. But no effects shit."

"As little as possible."

"It's like having a SWAT team in."

D shuddered sympathetically.

"How many dead?" asked Doc.

D looked at the texture of the goose bumps on Claudia's unwavering shoulder. "Millions, I suppose," he said tentatively.

"Has to be," said Doc.

"I don't know what to say," said D. "The writing gets a momentum of its own."

"Still," said Doc, drawing his fingers through the strands of Claudia's hair, as if he was sorting fossilised time. "There isn't one of them living here doesn't expect it to happen." He looked into the abyss – it stank now of sewage and summer waste. "Or want it."

D said nothing; what could professionals say? It was more important that silence prevailed between them, so that the howling and the din in nature washed up against their resilience. Two tough writers - hardboiled, some said? Or just two wordy fellows, hopelessly susceptible to destruction, hoping their terse dialogue might mask the fear. Talking well is an honorable courage, when the earth's plates are grinding in opposite directions, and a baby is being swept away on the rush of lost ground with the mother at your feet, as fixed and wounded as a Weegee face. But Doc and D did have their saving port at the aghast edge: they could putter about there; time passed through their shifting images, like light through blinds; and they could chat.

"So what do you reckon?" asked Doc.

"I was going to have a panic – nothing fancy – and Clear getting the escape together."

"Yeah, Clear's the one. Who goes?"

"Claudia and Cy," D began to make a list.

"And his scumbag son," added Doc.

"Certainly. And Chuck, and all the entourage that's here."

"They're here still," Doc knew. "They're always last to leave."

"Tusk and Zale?" D asked.

"I saw them running old Perry Mason tapes," said Doc.

"And Drew, of course," D was contrite at not having named her sooner.

"You have a problem there," said Doc.

"Really? I thought just a bitter moment when Drew realises what must have happened with D and Claudia. One piercing close-up and perhaps an acrid remark."

"Oh, it's easy to *show*," said Doc – what a task it was to be a teacher, what a test of faith and dismay. "But then you've got a sweet kid pissed off at you. I mean, that is a good young woman, and she's going to be hurt. That doesn't wear off with one nice close-up. Added to which," Doc nodded down at Claudia, "you've got this bimbo who's going to be Gish-ho on 'Where is my poor babe?'"

"I do see that," said D, ruefully. There was so much to look after.

Doc smiled crookedly, "You know, you have turned into a major ladies' man."

"It just seemed to happen," D protested.

"Oh, it did?" Doc's eyebrows went up like hawks. "That *is* tough."

"Well," D struggled, "let's hope the crisis can cover it all up."

"Where we going?"

D took fresh heart in the plans that had to be made, "I thought a motley caravan of limos and trucks."

"With Clear as traffic cop."

"Making our way out of the city."

"The roads?" Doc had done this sort of thing before.

"Just as you said, this was an early tremor. They – we – make it to safety before the big quake."

Doc nodded, "So you get your local mayhem *and* the grand panorama, the sign doing anagrams?"

"What do you think?"

"I've heard worse." And he had. This was a city used to slapdash disasters. "Do we have enough vehicles?"

"I'm sure."

"You're sure," Doc was nagging now. "You've done a body count? You have to line-produce as well as spin the yarn."

"Well, no –"

"Too busy counting the freckles on Claudia's ass, I suppose? Come on, D, you have obligations. Fuck the star on your own time. So, then, where we going?"

"To the desert, of course."

"Out to see Eyes?" Doc could imagine this for himself.

"Isn't it neat?" D was proud.

"Well, it's about time. But just remember, because you wanted to get D and Eyes together, you razed the greater Los Angeles area." Doc was a pillar of civic integrity.

D fudged. "You said yourself it would come as no surprise."

"No surprise! Philosophically it's right. But don't kid yourself that there isn't going to be a lot of ground-level distress."

"I understand," said D, biting his lip.

"No, you don't," Doc added. "The tenements, over on the other side, where your wife and kiddies live. Where *you* live." Doc's finger struck him in the chest. "That's all coming down like a house of cards. Gas explosions. And no one to fight the fires or go through the rubble listening for cries. That's how bad it is, and you'll be wrapping up this coked-out mother in her mink, calming her down and reminding her of the story so you can juice her again."

"I –" D was loud and brief with protest.

"You would."

"I would. It's true." These creatures were so available, and no one could be in movies without discovering the appeal of power.

A silence resumed between them. But Doc was not sanctimonious, and he knew the rigors of writing. He'd had a heroine once he'd taken to bed and then let the cops shoot her eyes out. A writer was so full of desire but so sure of disappointment.

"So where in the desert?"

"Well," D had the map in his hand. "I was going out by way of Lancaster and Mojave."

"That's good," said Doc. "You could have planes in the air over Edwards. Planes that can't land because the runways are ruined."

"Oh, I like that," cried D.

"Use it," said Doc.

"And then by way of China Lake and Death Valley and into Nevada." He loved the name, its sound of emptiness with burnt mauves at dusk, the ghost towns and the big breaks.

"Where would you cross the line?" Doc wanted to know – clearly another desert buff.

"At Beatty?" D hazarded.

"Seems reasonable," said Doc. "And then a life in the desert for this weird crew?"

D paused in time. "I don't want to spoil it for you." He knew he had the master hooked.

"OK, OK," grumbled Doc, looking around the room, and getting ready to go. "Just one thing."

"What's that?"

"What about me?" This question was muttered. Doc was too bashful, too squeamish, to make it a plea.

"Why," D laughed out loud. "You come with us."

"Oh, I do?" Doc was asking. "You're sure about that?"

"I can't do it without you." This was said so naturally that D knew it must be true.

Doc was fidgeting at the door. "If you're certain."

"I am!"

Doc nodded, thought to speak, abandoned the project, and then told himself, hell, no, it has to be said.

"Don't say it," said D.

"No?"

"No need."

"OK. It was just that the earthquake bit was . . ."

"Vulgar?"

"Kind of. Promise me something."

"What's that?"

"You don't have a nuclear holocaust lined up for us, do you?"

"Never entered my head."

"That's good. I can't stand that shit. A new life in the desert."

"A new life," repeated D, hoping it could be so, and turning to attend to Claudia. She was beginning to move again and coming back to reclaim her scream.

PARIS–TEXAS

Warren Beatty comes back to New York from Paris. He calls Robert Benton and says he would like to read the script of *Bonnie and Clyde*. This is not a conversation between agents. Half an hour after the call, the movie star himself turns up on Benton's Lexington Avenue doorstep to collect the script. Of course, Benton hands it over, along with his doubts. He and Newman have set out to write a French film; they cannot quite see a movie star as a film-maker; and their script has an important homosexual relationship between Clyde and his gang-member, C.W. Moss. *Can you be gay, Warren?* I'd really like to read the script. *I don't think you're going to like it.* I just want to read it.

Later that day Beatty calls Benton and says he wants to do it. *How much have you read, Warren?* I'm at page thirty-eight. *Wait until you get to sixty-four. That'll curl your hair.* I want to do it.

There is another call a few hours later, and the actor's mind is still made up. Benton cannot talk him out of it – that is the story that will be told years later, as part of the legend of *Bonnie and Clyde*. As if Benton had somehow been put in the negotiating position of trying to deter his only buyer, and as if no one remembered that Beatty got the script for $10,000. So let's suppose that there were also moments like *Well, Warren, that's wonderful that you want to do it. We've always liked your work.* Yeah, it's an interesting script. Not a flawless script. *Well, what is?* Exactly. *Truffaut loved it.* But he's not American. *Well, what exactly is wrong with it?* It needs a lot of work yet, don't you think? *Maybe, but what kind of work?* You mentioned the homosexual thing yourself. *But that's very important to us, and we did warn you.* So maybe we need another writer to look at that afresh. *Where does that leave us, Warren?* Well, you fellows have to see that I'm going to need to put a lot more work and money into this project. There's no way of knowing if it's ever going to get made. *So, $10,000?* I'm taking a hell of a chance.

249

He is, though on terms by which he can afford to lose. In business, he is like an actor watching his own performance, an actor who is master of the show – just like the pick-up scene in *All Fall Down*. From the outset, Beatty has been drawn to *Bonnie and Clyde* not simply as an actor, but as an impresario and a manager. Morever, just as when acting he has insuperable problems in revealing himself, as a businessman he is at his most naked and least compromised.

When it comes to a director for the picture, Beatty defines the ground by saying he could do it himself. *That's an awful lot for one person to do, Warren.* I know. But Orson Welles did it. *True, but Citizen Kane, you will recall, was not a hit.* Maybe it is asking too much of myself. *It is, you'll feel easier with a director.* Exactly. *Who do you think would be good?* Well, I think I'd like to hear your suggestions. *There's ——.* Oh, I don't think so, he's ——. *True, what about ——?* I heard bad things about him. *Oh. Well, there's Penn, of course. You boys like Arthur? He's damned good at psychological action, and I know he'd kill to do it.* Yeah, he has that feeling for danger. *So you'd like Penn, Warren?* If he's the one you fellows want. If you really think it's him then I'm not going to stand in the way.

In fact, Penn is not certain about doing it straightaway. Other directors are in the running. One of them is Brian G. Hutton, but he is typical of Hollywood sentiment in his reactions. He is looking at the Benton-Newton script one day with a young writer Beatty knows, Robert Towne. Hutton asks, "What do you see in this?" Towne tells him, at length; he loves the original screenplay. But Hutton looks at him as if he is crazy. "Well," he sighs, "I just don't see it. I'm going off to do *Where Eagles Dare*." Hindsight is not kind to this choice, but it shows industry wisdom at that moment.

And so it is Arthur Penn who has the central task of persuading Benton and Newton (and Warren to some degree) that the homosexuality is not right for the film. He tells them it confuses the story, that they don't know enough about it. *I mean, you boys aren't gay, are you?*

The re-writing of the script begins, and as Benton and Newman are offered more and more suggestions, so they are given help. It comes in the form of Robert Towne, then in his early thirties, a man who has written a couple of horror movies for Roger Corman, and some television work as well as a Western, *The Long Ride Home*, from which he removes his name. This is the start of a way of working that Towne will make famous – of having helped out on scripts without official credit. It is called script doctoring, and it is a measure of secret insiderism and unspoken pacts in a city of cliques that rattle like castanets in flamenco. Beatty sees and likes the script of *The Long Ride Home*, and Towne becomes one of his first most abiding disciples. In time, people will say Towne is maybe Beatty's closest friend. Twenty years later, they are just as close.

Towne will be credited on *Bonnie and Clyde*, in the head credits, as "Special Consultant". It is a unique credit, and perhaps the best public rumor anyone in Hollywood has ever had. Benton and Newman get the screenplay credit. But it is Towne who writes some scenes fifty times for Penn, and for Warren. It is Towne who is on location and who sometimes even corrects a line reading. On a good and successful movie there is enough credit for everyone, but there is a battle for it, too. The idea was Benton and Newman's. Much of the detailed craft is Towne's. All three prosper from the film in terms of work, if not money. But it is Beatty who brings them together, and who keeps them all a little uneasy. And it is Beatty who would blame himself if there was one word, glance or frame that he didn't like. And this man with some self-hatred is on the edge of an opportunity to rise above all his own doubts. He is flying, as anyone will when picking and goading talent is his greatest skill.

And now skill must cut through fondness. Leslie Caron says that even as Beatty was reading the script he called her for advice. He wonders if it isn't too much like a Western, a dead genre? No, Caron tells him, it's a new kind of movie. Maybe she even says it's a movie about fame, and about movies – she may be the most intelligent woman Beatty has ever lived with. So, she urges him, buy it for us. And he buys it.

But when she comes back to America, he tells her she's not quite right for Bonnie Parker. "The way he discarded me after I got him to buy *Bonnie and Clyde* was rather ruthless. Anyone who has come close to Warren has shed quite a few feathers. He tends to maul you." Not that Warren can even tell Leslie straightaway who will play the part. It's just that it won't be her.

He has Natalie Wood in mind: she was the kid on the run with James Dean in *Rebel Without a Cause*. But Wood is reluctant to go to Texas for two months with Warren without her psychiatrist. According to her sister Lana, Natalie has tried to kill herself some time in 1966 after a visit from Warren. He is far from her only problem, but he is someone who reminds her of how easily she can be manipulated.

Carol Lynley and Tuesday Weld come close to getting the role of Bonnie. It may only be Weld's pregnancy that keeps her from it. They are not the only names considered. Beatty is one of those Hollywood

people for whom casting is a way of life: he does not just cast and recast pictures in his head; he looks at real situations in terms of "casting". Casting is a power in which the imagination plays with the future, and even puts an ad in the trades saying that any beautiful and interested young woman should be at the door at 8 a.m. and still ready to show her best at 6 p.m.

In thinking about which actress should be the one to bring his Clyde to sexual fulfilment, Beatty thinks of everyone he knows or could dream of knowing. Afterwards, Shirley MacLaine says, yes, he talked to her once or twice: "You know how he is, sitting in the corner of the Beverly Wilshire coffee shop and acting mysterious while he's on the phone. Then he never called again. All that stuff in the cornfields. I guess he couldn't do it with his sister. But come to think of it – maybe he could!"

Casting is wondering who you could do it with. And in time it will become a deliberation that slows the actual making of movies. Faye Dunaway gets the part. So obvious now, so uncertain then.

And casting goes all the way down the line: it picks on Gene Hackman, so good in *Lilith*; on Michael J. Pollard, who played with Beatty in *A Loss of Roses*; it chooses Estelle Parsons and Gene Wilder (for a one-scene part), sure that they have something. It can go from a veteran cameraman, Burnett Guffey, known for mastery of black-and-white, to a young production designer, Dean Tavoularis. It awards costuming to Theadora Van Runkle, a brilliant newcomer, and make-up to Robert Jiras, a good friend from *Mickey One*. It must think about all these areas, for there is to be a new look in this film that springs up at parties within months – it involves clothes, long skirts and hats, as well as make-up. Indeed, when Clyde first meets Bonnie he tells her to make a small alteration in her hair, dropping a cutesy curl for free fall. It does improve her, and it shows us Clyde as a producer of history. Maybe the scene comes from Towne seeing Beatty stroll among actresses adjusting hairstyles here and there, like a sultan becoming a genius. A film is full of details, and Beatty has learned in his movies so far that sometimes people are too tired or too casual or too bad to chase down all the details. He collects them, to prove himself.

Bonnie and Clyde goes on location to Dallas, with a base at the modest North Park Motor Inn. It is never set up as a big picture. This is only three years after the John Kennedy assassination, and people on the crew are impressed by the local aftershock. And so the history of American violence seeps into the picture, where it will become a shocking new beauty. Very quickly, relatives and buddies of the real Bonnie and Clyde come by, with stories of the "hard times" and the understandable outlawry. Robert Towne spends time with Clyde's nephew, who was eleven when the gangster died, and picks up anecdotes about Clyde's skill with cars and the way "he could cut a corner square when he drove".

They are filming here and there, thirty miles to the north of Dallas, at Pilot Point and Ponder, having no difficulty in finding desolate fields that feel like the 30s and drawing very few spectators to their shoot-outs. A routine sets in of filming, with Towne in the Motor Inn re-writing pages for the following day. When the crew comes back in the evening, he has dinner with Arthur Penn, and sometimes Warren, to discuss the work, and then they all go to a theater in downtown Dallas to look at the dailies.

A lot of the time, these are printed in black-and-white to save money. Warners are cutting back on the picture as it proceeds, shaving the budget so that Beatty personally has to make up the difference. As a result, by the end of production, he owns a more substantial share of it than was ever envisaged – let the kid carry the risk, says the studio.

"Warren was truly a great producer," says Towne. "I remember a scene we had, it's just before the final deaths, and Bonnie is supposed to get some fruit and be eating it with Clyde in the car as they drive towards the ambush. Well, we wanted a peach that would squirt and squish on the big screen.

"The day before shooting, Warren asked the property master if it was going to be all right with the peach.

" 'I don't have them,' the guy said, and Warren's face went white.

" 'They're not in season,' the guy said. 'I got apples.'

" 'Somewhere in the world they're in season,' said Warren. 'In South America or North Pakistan. I want peaches tomorrow.'

"Well, in the end, we couldn't wait for peaches. We got a pear and we injected it with water with a syringe. But I never forgot Warren's response and the feeling that it was a detail that was going to be on the screen a long time. And Bonnie and Clyde *were* peaches, not apples. Warren said, 'It's hard to argue, but you've got to keep doing it.' "

He does his best to keep everyone content. Faye Dunaway is not the least eccentric of actresses, and she has to worry that her co-star – not quite thirty – is running the show. But Warren gets on with her as well as anyone in Texas does. Estelle Parsons will later praise his care and consideration. You have to be the producer every person needs – confidant, confessor, fan, bully, tease, buddy, and amateur juice-maker for stand-in pears. There is a moment when Towne has to go back to Los Angeles for a few days, and Beatty – grinning – goes down on his knees to beg him not to, because he knows that Towne is going anyway, but will treasure the grace of the act. And Towne comes back to Texas early.

He is having to argue his case all the time. Warners regard Warren as a famous young actor whose films lose money. There have been seven before *Bonnie and Clyde*, and no one says that any except *Splendor in the Grass* made money. And since Warners distributed that, and three others, they're ready to dispute even that claim. *Kid, the people don't like you. You're very bright, but sometimes that frightens the public.* The pictures have been bad. *You chose them.* Yeah, but I was working for others. Now I'm working for me. I will never make a failure when I'm working for me. *Until you start to second-guess yourself, baby!*

The stories all have Beatty on his knees to Jack Warner saying let me do it, let me cut it my way. Joe Hyams, a long-time Warners man, says he was *there*: he saw Warren *kiss* Jack's feet, begging to have the picture in better theaters than the marketing people had booked. Those lips? Those shining shoes? Perhaps. There is not an office on show at Warners, with grooves in the carpet where this supplication occurs. You can imagine Beatty on his knees, with Warner grinning, *Whatever next?*, and Warren grinning back – it's all camp in such offices, actors trying to upstage one another. You can picture the kid on his knees, asking. You really think I should do it, Jack? Little me? The shy thing, head down, hair tousled. Not all the stories add that Beatty's deal and his buying in on Warners' fear and bewilderment have got him up to forty per cent of the profits.

Getaway

It was a scene of mythic significance: the escape from a civilization in cataclysm for a wilderness as empty and hypothetical as a billiard table. They had all anticipated it, uncertain whether dread or energy would carry them through. They had bags packed, lists of things they could not do without. And when they foresaw the terror of the metropolis, they were as sure of passing through it as Crusoes, taking dry flints, bean seeds and Rock and Roll's Greatest Hits to their private shore. For heartfelt frontier people had thought ahead and picked out a little desert refuge, somewhere off the map.

Cy Lighthiser had typed inventories of the things to go and a truck in his garage with camping materials, sterile water, cases of dried tomatoes, board games and worry beads. Clear, whose practice it often was to go out to the desert to consult, had a company camper and a stock of safari clothing, guns, Fontella Bass tapes and iron rations. So many show people, having been so long homeless, or unattached, are constitutionally suited to such a departure.

So Cy was sweeping up his collection of bound screenplays while kicking his best Persian cushions into a basket with the aplomb of Pele or Puskas. Even D had the wisdom to rake the surface of Claudia Cannon's vanity into a wastepaper bin, while imprisoning the lady in yards of Indonesian silk. (He found no mink.) Sooner or later she would want her make-up, but for now it was all "My baby! Oh Lord, the child", as grating as Blanche in *Bonnie and Clyde*, until D hit her once, speculatively, in the jaw, the golden scallop, and was touched to see her sag in silence.

"Guessing her weight?" asked Drew, coming upon D, his arms full of the vermilion-wrapped Claudia. Only her dainty feet and head protruded from the silk, with a smudge of blue on her chin.

"I am rescuing her," D answered his former amour. He had meant to be firm about the strife in his feeling. But when he saw Drew's woeful look, his heart lurched again. He was ready to toss the dire Claudia after the babe. That girl had been hurt by his wandering eye. How she must care for him. Hadn't she warned him to have nothing to do with any of them? Was there a surer sign of virtue?

"Where's Claudia's kid?" she asked.

"She was carried off by the landslide."

"We'll look for her on the way down," said Drew.

"She may be lost forever," D pointed out. He was anxious to get on. You had to keep the line going forward.

"Don't say that!" Drew's eyes fell on the absent, set face of the mother. "She doesn't get off that easy." D thought he saw a flicker in Claudia's eyelids. He was shocked by Drew's severity, until he saw the strength of necessity in her face. She had never been more beautiful. She made Claudia look effete. He was so thrilled he wanted her there, on the dangerous spot. She felt it, too. For she smiled and told him he was still her D. "Do you think we're going to die?" she asked.

"Perhaps," he agreed.

"Then we may have to kill," she told him, and he nodded.

The crisis was enough to make D act and change his mind without regret. He was ready for death or murder; it was like being in a fire without burning. All ordinariness had fallen away. He felt like someone in a story, not simply willing to kill, but pledged to the implacable destiny of plot.

The strange convoy made off into the night. But one car, a Mercedes, would not start. It blocked the way, so Chuck, driving a Lincoln, rammed it repeatedly, the celadon metal becoming as crumpled as a dress tossed on the floor. They all roared encouragement, and at last he barged the soft sedan off the road. Those whose car it had been looked back with loathing. "Shoot it!" someone cried to the night. It was Beau. There was a pause and then shots, and in an instant the wreck exploded in a gasp of orange heat, putrid with gasoline. The assembly bathed in the heat, their bared faces amber and delirious.

D was in the camper with Drew and Clear. Chuck was driving and Claudia was still stretched out where D had put her along a bench seat. Her body bounced helplessly as Chuck surged into every bend, braking to save them. The vehicle groaned and bucked from his driving, and Chuck laughed out loud, fighting the bastard of a road and shouting at those ahead to go faster. D wanted to go up to him and poleaxe the idiot. But the camper was riding such a stormy drive, and who but Chuck could handle it? So D held on and felt the jarring in his head.

This jagged immediacy broke in on Claudia's rest. D was crouched at her side, ready to apologise.

"Miss Cannon," he began.

"I dreamed of you," she held his wrist.

"I had to strike you."

"Is that what you did?" Her eyes widened.

"We beat a very hasty retreat."

"Did we?" said Claudia. She sat up, and her silk sheath could not hide her nakedness. "Oh my," she murmured. "Gentlemen, forgive me. I appear to have come out au naturel."

Drew spoke to her from the other side of the jolting camper: "Claudia," she said, "we've lost your daughter."

"Claudia?" she echoed, wan and fitful. "Who is she?"

"That's you, mama," said Drew. "Your baby went sliding down the hillside in the earthquake."

"I really don't remember," said Claudia. "I had a child?"

"Oh Jesus," Drew realised, "the amnesia bit."

"Was she pretty?" Claudia had to know.

"We'll find her, of course," D told her.

"Oh no," she wearied. "I don't expect so. These hills are so wild and so many. And there are such fearsome people around. We will have to wait for the ransom demands." Her voice was piteous but firm, a victim with a hold on her pathos.

"Why did you hit me?" she asked D.

"Well, I –"

"I know." She put a hand on his. "It was to protect me from the loss. You are my knight. And what a puncher, too, that I should lose all recollection."

And so on, down the twisty hillside, into a city more asleep than dreaming. Drew and D sat side by side. Claudia drew closer to Clear and began to think aloud with him.

"Do you know," she said, "that I have a lost child? A poor babe taken by the sudden violence of the land. Of course, I shall search for her, no matter how long it takes. It will become like a legend. People will ask one another whether they have ever seen the mother whose child was lost. And the woman will go on and on, roaming everywhere, hardly aging, her spirit is so taut and ardent in this quest. Do you like it?"

ESQUIRE PIECE

Just before *Bonnie and Clyde* opens, in its August 1967 issue, *Esquire* publishes a profile on Beatty, written by Rex Reed. It is somewhere between a report of the actor's life and an attempt on it. But it qualifies for its chapter here because it is also an event in the life, a moment which helps the subject discover his own *mysterioso*.

The article is still entertaining and expressive. More than just good reportage, it helps define a new relationship between "adventurous," "creative," "gonzo" journalism and the few remaining giants of the movie business, increasingly cut adrift from the studio protection and the pre-prepared publicity kit. Reed's article may not be the first "new" movie profile, but it does become a model for others. Which means that it influences the movie people getting ready to be interviewed, as well as the writers sent out to capture them.

There is a history to this development worth sketching in. In the past, American movies have been promoted by studio publicity departments. Stars have made tours of personal appearance, photo occasions and the passing on of homilies, lies and good cheer to every shorthand reporter in the room. In the great age of stardom, an engaging but quite false glare is broadcast on the human nature of these stars. There is a general tendency in the media in the 60s to look deeper and to discover the crass and dishonest roots of heroism and glamor.

In film writing, its first great example is the series of articles Lillian Ross writes for the *New Yorker* on the making of *The Red Badge of Courage*, published as a book in 1952, called *Picture*. The innovation in these pieces is that if a writer simply sits in on the meetings that make up the process of American film-making then the recall will be hilarious, startling and fascinating because picture people only reveal their stupidity, vulgarity and duplicity when they open their mouths. And they cannot help but open their mouths, because they are all of them actors at heart.

259

The business is appalled by *Picture*, but it can temper neither its way of talking nor its occasional weakness for letting itself be overheard. In 1968, Twentieth Century-Fox will let John Gregory Dunne's retentive ears onto the premises and the devastating result is *The Studio*. Of course, ears are not enough. Nobody on *The Red Badge of Courage* noticed Lillian Ross writing it all down – perhaps she just learned the timing and the rhythm and then recreated it later. By the 1960s, small tape recorders are giving us every grunt and delay. Hollywood narcissism finds a fresh form – the sentence that goes on for ever without achieving form or period.

As the power of the studios declines, so their promotional machinery falters. The big actors, and especially those determined to be masters of their fate, take on publicity agents or agencies. When a film opens, the studio has to deal with these agents, who may put out the word, "Warren's not doing press," or some such. Partly out of fear of their own inarticulacy, and partly because the new power gives them something to control, actors begin to flinch from promotion. It leads to a bizarre anomaly, that of people striving to become movie actors and then refusing any further prostitution of themselves in selling their pictures. Warren Beatty is a patron saint to this reticence, and the Rex Reed interview will stand as a warning test case to all those beauties afraid of getting trashed.

Still, such profiles as Reed's do not happen by accident. A magazine editor, and its writers, are eager for good material. They assume that the public is most (or only) concerned with a star as one of their films opens. But it is often the publicity agent who initiates such pieces and arranges the key meeting with the star. Beatty has as his agent Pat Newcomb, who came of age in the business by being one of Marilyn Monroe's closer confidantes. These agents can be very powerful figures, prevailing upon their clients and even instructing them how to behave. In other cases, they are not much more than the star's answering service. For it is a part of Beatty's developing nature and influence in the business that public image is too important to be trusted to others. It may be more central than the film. It may be more vital than the person.

Reed's article is entitled "Will the Real Warren Beatty Please Shut Up." This may or may not be Reed's choice – but for the star, and his peers, it is testament to the attitude of the press, begging their time and talk and then slapping them publicly in the face.

The article is in some ways a meditation on such pieces with an undertone of disdain in the writing and an ambivalence in the subject.

We are left to decide whether that is instinctive or calculated, or whether it is Beatty's own shyness and vanity being professionalised and brought almost to the point of myth by his own realisation that the process can be teased.

Why should a man, much less a star, not adopt elusiveness as his own style when the article opens with U.C.L.A. students not knowing who Beatty is, confusing him with Tab Hunter and generally contributing towards a New York writer's sense of how silly California is, and how flimsy its products must be? After that, Reed does a round-up of rumors (in the new way of outflanking libel lawyers) as a build-up for the article's high concept:

"Back in New York, I had skipped the public and asked Those Who Know, and from them I learned that Warren was a draft dodger, a Communist, that he had two illegitimate children living in London, that he had been arrested three times by the Los Angeles vice squad, that he was a sadist who loved to invite ten girls to his hotel room at one time and not show up, that he wore black leather pants and carried a whip when he was not working, and that 'at least fifty women were seduced by him' as one man swore. Above all I learned that Those Who Know knew everything but the truth.

"The Truth – as I came to find out – is that nobody knows very much at all about Warren Beatty, including Warren himself."

Now, Truth or even truth may be a little heavy a label for this insight. But I am not averse to it: there is something essentially Warren in his screen depths of perplexity, of language spilling into a hole of stricken silence. But it is more interesting still to see this dumbfoundedness as one more actor's trick, as a caption for closing off the question of who he is – so that even he need not puzzle any longer.

The interview complains about Beatty being hard to pin down. We get a feeling of the bored Reed trapped in his hotel in Los Angeles waiting for the call. And then Warners press agent, Guy McElwaine, gives Reed his shtick, drives him in circles, says Warren's hard to get and why doesn't he do Nancy Sinatra instead?

At last Beatty is discovered in his office, "a tiny pink room at the end of an empty corridor in a tiny pink stucco building that looked like a temporary wartime army hut for training-center personnel." Reed is still in the mindset that finds it hard to believe in pink. Reed describes Beatty's staring look, his "rather slow and cumbersome" way of speaking. He fixes on "the desperation to be liked, approved of, the fear (the greatest terror of his life, to be exact) of being considered

261

unintelligent. At least four or five times during our talks, he would turn to me defiantly and say, as if in self-assurance, 'I *am* intelligent; I *know* I am intelligent.' "

My own research and wonderings would not dispute the gist of Reed's point. But his accusation, his superiority, is misplaced: wanting to be intelligent is not inconsistent with the thing itself. It is only Hollywood that defies intelligence. And Reed gives not nearly enough credit to what his recorder has Beatty saying: a stunning litany of accuracy that should have terminated the project there and then in *Esquire*'s mind and offered the life and work of Beatty up to some rather more adventurous writing:

> "There is, as far as I can see, no reason to do a story on me. Most of what I have to say you couldn't print anyway. [Such magazines do nag their writers to get scandalous revelations that their lawyers then forbid them to use.] Most movie stars are not interesting, so to sell papers and magazines in the fading publications field a writer has to end up writing his ass off to make somebody look more interesting than he really is, right? What this all boils down to is publicity because somebody's got some movie to sell, right? What do I need with publicity? You want to see me driving up and down the Sunset Strip in my car picking up girls, right? Well, you don't think I'd be stupid enough to let you see *that* side of me, do you?"

This may not qualify as intelligence in those circles where intelligence is adjudicated. But it's smart. It rattles off like a big speech. And it manages to blind even the sour Reed to the fact that no one – not even Jack Warner – was keener to promote the pants off *Bonnie and Clyde* than Warren Beatty.

A few years later, while travelling for George McGovern, Beatty is interviewed by two young reporters for The *Daily Cardinal*, the newspaper of the University of Wisconsin at Madison. They ask him about Rex Reed and the *Esquire* interview:

> "I don't know what to say about a person like that. You would have to address yourself to the symptoms of American journalism and what allows that kind of sickness to sustain itself.
>
> "This was a guy who said he thought I was the best actor of my generation and that he'd seen these films of mine over and over again. He tried to get me to pose for a picture with thirty girls. I thought that was insane. Why would I do a thing like that? I only spent an hour talking to him – certainly an hour of a mistake. He made up the article largely out of things out of columns. He had me involved with women I'd never met in all sorts of incidents that never took place. I would say the whole thing may come out of some homosexual anxiety.

"As I remember Rex Reed sat there for that hour . . . the only word I can think of is 'dewy-eyed'. I remember having a feeling of sympathy for him and trying very hard to answer seriously the questions he asked.

"I think the man is contemptible, dishonest, and a very hostile creature."

The *Cardinal* boys may be hopping in their chairs with excitement at getting such candor. "Do you mind if we print that?" they ask.

And there in Madison, in 1971, Warren Beatty has one of his great moments when life allows him to utter a movie line:

"What do you think I said it for?" he asks.

Night man

Driving through the great city at night, with as much circumspection as a glittery caravanserai could muster, none of them missed the destruction poised in the air. They looked on every glass tower as a shower of splinters still held in place by the need for dignity. They saw the loops and strands of freeway ramps like curls about to fall on a barber's floor. And if they saw night people in doorways, wrapped in *The Times* or plastic bags, they felt the soft centers waiting for the collapse of rubble.

"Can't we warn any of them?" Drew whispered. "Not even D's wife and children?"

"No cigar," said Clear.

So they drove on, with the hiss of wheels and Claudia's developing story. She was muttering to herself and feeding from a giant jar of peanuts, the small dry pellets churning with her scenario: "I'm the most wretched woman alive. I had a child, a newborn child . . ."

It needed work on the dialogue, a montage of changing scenery, some soaring score to reach to the edge of eternity, and Claudia could lose a few pounds – but such things were easy enough to manage. D had to admit he was touched by the concept. He could see it working. Nothing so constituted the nature of an actress as her readiness to serve us all in metaphor. Claudia had no steady reality. Even being with her, locked in some of the sweatier Sutra holds, D felt she came and went. Her nature was always ready to slip "out there" into story, to pose on the horizon of imagination, to belong to everyone.

They had reached the eastern edge of the city when they pulled into the forecourt of a filling station. They must have every drop of gas for the desert trek. Clear was having spare cans filled and taking a collection of credit cards to pay for it all when it was appreciated that the station was untended.

"No one here?" Clear asked of a man filling up his car, a pale black in a faded orange suit.

"We're here, man. I know we're here."

"I meant the operatives, the officials."

"Night man's in there," the black man nodded towards the office.

"He's not working?" Clear asked.

"He's not breathing." The black took the nozzle from his tank, careful not to spill a drop. "This a freebie night."

D moved towards the office. The door could not close because the body of another black was there, lying in its own blood. The man's hand had sought to write something in the blood before he died. There was a scrawl, or a shape: it might have been a name, or the outline of a face, all the man could do to express rage or his disappearing self.

"See that market over there," Chuck was saying. "There's a pick-up backed in a window and guys loading it." Chuck edged closer to Clear. "What you say we freshen up on supplies?"

"You don't think we should escape now?" asked Clear.

"We're nearly out of the city. The fault doesn't reach this far. This is almost the edge of your desert."

"Who knows who's over there?" said Clear doubtfully.

"We can take guns," Chuck answered him. "It's wide open. Whatta you say, Cy?"

Lighthiser had joined them; he was brisk and cheery, like one enjoying the outing. "Let's take them," he said. "Six, seven of us go over there with Uzis, who's gonna get in our way?"

"It's against the law." Drew's warning came from inside the camper.

"It's the early hours in east LA," said Chuck, "and there's an act of God coming."

"Who says?" Drew challenged him.

"Everyone says," Chuck told her. He was talking to a kid. "You too stoned to see the hole in the ground on Mulholland?"

"I've seen holes there before."

"On what you do, you've seen Aladdin's caves."

"Well," said Drew, "if you're going, get me a box of Tampax for the desert."

"In the desert!" Chuck was shouting and shaking. There was an excitement in him too great to fit into words. "In the desert, you bleed." It was as if Chuck knew he would be vindicated there. All around him, D felt the mood for the crisis. People wanted their babies lost, the gas stations open so that you had to drive in over bodies as well as the rubber lines that rang a bell in the office. And all of them wanted to go shopping in the market with the limits off. D could imagine himself grabbing up

265

armfuls of oranges, laughing with glee. All those dayglo fruits, and all of them dry as cobwebs in the desert in a week. The supplies would only scratch the desert's surface. What they would always need there would be the liberty to take anything and shoot any face that got in their way.

"Let's go," said D, picking up a rifle, the first he had ever touched. It leaped up to meet him, and the oiled black metal told him, "I'm your lover, fellow."

BONNIE AND CLYDE

When you think about *Bonnie and Clyde* now, you see their last car on the country road, stopped to help a friend, then peppered by bullets that come back at the gorgeous creatures like an explosion put in reverse. It is a shooting picture, from the target practice with the hanging tire that rebukes the Depression, through the motor court ambushes to the last stake-out. Too many bullets to count, but enough to inaugurate the new movie lyricism of bodies ripped, pecked, chafed and urged into abandon by lead.

This is the crucial American movie about love and death, lit up by fresh-air faces that have been burning underground for years, too much in the dark to admit, yes, we're in love with death, let's fuck death. But *Bonnie and Clyde* surpasses its early, easy claim that violence is aphrodisiac (Bonnie stroking Clyde's casually offered, groin-crossing gun) and reaches the far more dangerous idea that death brings glory and identity. If you want to know what the film is about, think how thoroughly Bonnie and Clyde have given up the ghost for sex-crazed American immortality.

There are enough bullets to constitute the film's musical score. What can be counted are the references to identity and fame and the instances of naming. When Bonnie and Clyde meet, and his hard-on limp threatens to steal into her airless West Dallas stew of heat, boredom and unused skin, they stroll down the art director's street of 1931, falling into a ritual of spot-on small talk in which she vamps and drawls and he tells her just exactly who she is – the sexiest insight.

She asks him what armed robbery is like and puts her hand on his bashful barrel. He lurches into the store and comes out clutching cash, like weeds he has pulled up Then it's off and away in her car – one of the great lovers' meetings in movie history, and proof that this picture must be watched as closely as the fine points in a movie deal contract. And as they tear off, happy at knowing they've found a way to die, they introduce themselves, just as smartass droll as actors who foresee the fun of fucking each other in the roles they are playing.

After that, the picture never stops the naming process. There are over thirty blatant namings. I do not mean the natural occasions in conversation; I mean a heightened, boastful stream of namings – enough to suggest that America has a greater dread of anonymity than of poverty.

The characters are introduced flamboyantly. Thereafter, they chew over one another's full names, as if they suspected they were bogus – "Well, Mister C. W. Moss" and so on, full of leers and goosings. When the dispossessed farmer and his black come upon the target practice, and get a shot at their own old windows, Clyde is like Jack Benny in the lush, delayed timing that introduces Bonnie and himself and adds, "We rob banks", trying to get the ex-farmer's vote. He has a self-destructive glamor that wants to give death and the cops a chance.

It's not long before Beatty's shy, muttered "This is a stick up" (which he has to repeat, shouting, before he gets respect) has turned into a smooth, matinée act in which the gang strolls onto a bank set, and Clyde allows himself to drawl, "Good afternoon, this is the Barrow gang," half expecting a round of applause. Bonnie and Clyde want to be known; they are sublimely committed to this openness, so misguided in real outlaws. But they are not as crass as brother Buck, who pushes his ugly mug in front of a policeman so he won't forget Buck Barrow. Bonnie and Clyde do not want to be vulgar; they want the billing and streamlining of stars.

The plot of this very skillful movie turns on identity. The Texas Ranger who pursues Bonnie and Clyde is not just their nemesis, but their servant, lured into dealing out death by the cunning that has compromised his reputation. When Frank Hamer comes upon them, off the road, the gang consider killing him. But Bonnie's poetic genius elects to have Hamer photographed with them so the gang can send the pictures to the papers making a stooge of the Ranger. The ploy is carried filmically by the avidity of Faye Dunaway's face and by Bonnie's urge to French-kiss Hamer's frosty mustache. The real guile in the photo session enlists Hamer's implacable need to get them. Of course, this is not spelled out directly. You can believe, some of the time, that Bonnie and Clyde do have a notion to grow old and plain and settle down.

Hamer's posse kills Buck and captures his distraught widow. Blanche is so intriguing – the gang member whose polite living-death style is something the gang are desperate to escape. Blanche is blind, in a cell, when Hamer creeps in to question her. "Blanche Barrow" he roars in her ear – the naming never stops, and is always more than is necessary. He coaxes a whole name out of her, the one gang name he didn't know, "C. W. Moss", and the lip-smacking bravura of the film has Blanche's whining coming out of Hamer's sullied mouth.

The Ranger finds Moss's family home – where the wounded Bonnie and Clyde are hiding out. He draws C. W.'s father into a death plot on the grounds that C. W. can be spared – not officially named yet as a gangster, he can get off lightly in return for the father's act of betrayal. And so the summer afternoon roadside is arranged, and our lovers drive towards it with all the aplomb of movie stars who have so given themselves away they've brought the slowest and most stupid of posses down on them. They want it, and they are ready.

"Everyone" now knows how *Bonnie and Clyde* met death: in their passing they became fixed forever, like Lincoln, John Kennedy, James Dean, Billy the Kid and the man in the Weegee photograph, poised in mid-air, saved from hitting the certain sidewalk. But the real Bonnie and Clyde died . . . how? The answer is lost along with their blunt, rural faces and the strained clutter of their teeth. But in the picture they are the best-looking couple in the world, actors togged up with rare enterprise, yarning away in smart Texas accents, and shameless about their bright teeth and the strange cult of being movie stars. Thus, to the parable of fame, *Bonnie and Clyde* adds the metaphor of performance.

The first day in West Dallas, Clyde is like a kid with a snappy impersonation of a Hollywood producer. So it's lucky Bonnie is at her upstairs window naked with a window steamed up enough to let Clyde *know*, without getting the scissors out. And Bonnie *knows* opportunity has knocked. She has gone to the window and called out, "Hey, boy! What you doing with my Mommie's car?" And Clyde has looked up with a grin so savage she yells, "Wait there!", so she can throw on a flimsy dress and leap down the stairs after him. She comes in a lovely rush, the camera looking up her flying skirts, so quickly done you do not *know* if you saw it or not. But you know why she's hurrying. This early Bonnie is untapped orgasm in need of a showman.

They walk. She puts on a brittle act which Mr Producer cracks by asking her, "What do you do – a movie star? A lady mechanic? A maid?" before letting her have the answer he's known all along, "A waitress?", uttered with Beatty's most intimate, withering disapproval. As if to say, if you think I could trouble with a waitress, think again. It's like not doing television interviews.

As they drive away from Clyde's demo hold-up, Bonnie just wants to get fucked. She can't wait for him to stop the car. This is the ingénue naivety that thinks Hollywood is just getting laid. The producer has to educate his new actress. She begins to think he doesn't like sex, or that he can't even do it: "Your advertising is just dandy. Folks would never guess you don't have a thing to sell." At which Warren grins — it's maybe more of a sucking smile — and goes into a heartfelt scene in which the famed lover asks the world to look past mere sex to its drive for something more ineffable:

CLYDE: All right, all right, if all you want's a stud service, you get on back to West Dallas and you stay there the rest of your life. You're worth more than that, a lot more than that, and you know it, and that's why you came along with me. You could find a lover boy on every damn corner of town, and it don't matter a damn to him whether you're waiting on table or picking cotton. But it does make a damn to me.

BONNIE: Why?

CLYDE: Why? What do you mean why? Because you're different, that's why. You know why you're like me? You want different things. You want something better than being a waitress. You and me travelling together, we could cut a path clear across this state, and Kansas! and Missouri! and Oklahoma! And everybody'd know about it. You listen to me, Miss Bonnie Parker, how would you like to go walking into the dining room of the Dolphin Hotel in Dallas, wearing a nice silk dress? And have everybody wait on you? Do you like that? Does that seem like a lot to you? That seem enough to you? You've got a right to that!

BONNIE: Hey! When did you figure all that out?

CLYDE: Minute I saw you.

BONNIE: Why?

CLYDE: Well, you may be the best damn girl in Texas.

This seduction is audacious because it has been launched on Clyde's sexual failure. That may be traumatic impotence, if one wants to live with the idea that the gun brings sexual liberation to Clyde. It is much more interesting to see how far fame is his key aphrodisiac. For Bonnie will "free" Clyde from his reluctance by writing a poem about him and sending it to the newspapers. What makes the movie so lastingly fascinating is the glimpse we get of a great seducer setting himself the hardest task, of withholding his most celebrated force and asking us to see that reputation, the mystery of being known, is what most compels him. It is the producer's film, the imprint of his views about the world and himself.

The scheme could be arid and merely clever without its filmic embodiment. The credit for this can be shared among many. But, amid all the death and violence, see the beauty in the movie. Beatty had never been so giving on the screen, so ready to laugh and smile, so little addicted to hiding. You can hear what he says, because Clyde enjoys talk. Further, despite the very active intelligence in a smart actor who is also producing, Beatty does begin to reveal his potential for being less bright than he might like. Clyde is a kind of wizard: C.W. says no one can catch him. But he has limits in awareness, and Beatty lets the movie see them.

He shows fear sometimes, a dumb swagger and a slowness on the uptake. He even fidgets when driving because he needs to take a leak. He has no larger design than having a good time for the moment. Asked how he might live his life afresh he has nothing more than a new strategy for taking banks. He is Buck's brother, caught in the same stupor of easy-going perplexity when the question arises, well, apart from having a good time, what shall we do next? There is a country-boy stoicism and sweetness in the way he says he chopped off two toes to get off work detail in prison and then got paroled a week later, free but limping. "Ain't life grand?" he chuckles in a sudden ravishing close-up.

But Clyde is less perceptive than Bonnie. He does discover her, he does have the vision that alters her life and the eye to know she should get rid of her cute kiss curl. Clyde runs the gang and overrules Bonnie on new members and cutting Blanche in on the take. But it is Bonnie who sees the future, tells Clyde's story and gracefully conducts her man towards death.

It is Bonnie who feels fatality in their beauty. She turns to ice on hearing that the man they have picked up in the reverse car chase is an undertaker. She sees that all their going is getting nowhere, with no way they can come to rest, close to their kin. There is no ordinary life. The future is all Dolphin Hotel, self-announcement and taking the risk (a kind of Hollywood).

The poem Bonnie sends to the newspapers is as slick and shallow as film. But it is what the characters want. "You told my story," Clyde exults – this is his rapture, and Beatty's too, the acting is so open. "You told my whole story, right there. One time I told you I'd make you somebody. That's what you done for me." They make love on the picnic grass, with the pages of the poem blowing in the wind.

It is a transforming passion, but more discreet than the earlier scene in which Bonnie was ready to fellate Clyde and he rolled away in despair. But there is an afterglow in which she tells him, "You did just perfect," and the self-reflexive layering of the movie is laid bare as Warren says, "I did, didn't I? I really did."

But love isn't perfect or memorable enough. The real love scene is the finale when bodies separated in space twist, roll and sigh from the fire of ardor. The death scene is the climax, and it is graced and consented in by the rapid exchange of knowing close-ups as they look and see what is coming. Naming is no longer necessary. Death is greeted as something as rare as ecstasy because of the great outlawry. Being famous has been shown as the most certain way to beauty. The only way.

24-hour market

It was a 24-hour supermarket, but someone had backed a small truck through the plate-glass front. There were nuggets of glass strewn underfoot and squashed shopping carts beneath the wheels of the truck. This outrage excited the gang moving liquor, frozen chickens and quivers of baguettes into the truck. But other shoppers were still going in and out of the regular doors, determined not to notice. D saw no bodies around, nor any other damage. The lights were on, and muzak was falling on the merchandise like snow. Robbery went on smoothly, beside the calm, digestive measure of shopping. People picked over porterhouse steaks and waited patiently to get at the special offers on swordfish and sunchokes.

"What's the plan?" Chuck wanted to know.

Clear shook his head. "I was always a hopeless shopper."

"Shopping's a great way to meet women," Doc suggested. "You run your cart accidentally into theirs. It gets a conversation going. The market's like an old matinée."

Chuck was tapping the barrel of his gun on Doc's shopping cart. "You're right," said Doc, sheepishly. "It's just that I look at a market and I picture chance meetings at the coffee grinder."

"It's charming," said Clear.

"And it sucks," said Chuck.

"Then it's a good thing we have you here, too," said the diplomatic Clear.

Meanwhile, Claudia had accosted a large black woman pushing a cart full of groceries and small children to the car park.

"Have *you* seen my baby?" Claudia asked the woman.

"Ain't seen no baby."

"Mama," said one of her kids.

"I lost my child, my only child."

"Where you do that?"

"Oh," said Claudia, "up in the hills."

"Why you lookin' here, then?"

"Gravity, my good woman, the cradle was moving downhill in the landslide."

"No slide here, lady," said the black woman. "We got a toxic cloud last year."

Chuck was assigning the men. D was to get meats. Doc was told to collect liquor and beer. Clear was sent after pasta, rice, grains and pulses. Then, unwilling to yield to his weakness for potato chips, Chuck wandered towards fresh produce, sentimental about desert scurvy.

He came to a range of melons, green with rough hides. Chuck felt one, and it was soft – wouldn't last as far as Nevada. He slammed the fruit on the floor. It burst. Juice and seeds ran out on the polished floor.

"Hey man, easy," called out a black, who was packing a crate with oranges. "Folks can slip on that, break their legs."

"That's right," said his friend, who was juggling mint-colored apples from a bin to his cart.

Chuck looked at the two blacks, sensing threat.

"What's it to you?" he asked.

"We don't want our grandmother breaking her hips. Old folks get a bad hip it's misery for the family."

The elan of these blacks curdled Chuck. They were doing a song and dance with the robbery. They weren't true low-lifes, but trained dudes, maybe some FBI blacks ready to arrest him. He looked up and saw the video camera eating them all, stirring slowly from side to side. That was the plan. Get the evidence, make the snatch. Fucking spooks. He took his rifle and splattered the camera with fire.

"What you doing?" reasoned one of the blacks. "We can't be on no TV now."

"Real gun, man?" the juggler wanted to know. The camera was still dripping its splinters on the ground.

"You didn't see?" Chuck was sulky.

"I saw." The smile had gone now. "What you going to do? Going to shoot us, too? Want us to be the baddies? We hide behind the dried fruit, ambush you, you come on like Chuck Norris? We throw up our arms, jump in the air, shout, 'Wow, I's dead'? You like that?"

"I'll take your oranges," said Chuck.

"Plenty more, man."

"I like yours," said Chuck. "I like that asshole way you packed them."

"They're for my granny. She got a C deficiency."

"Get yourself some more."

"I don't think so."

So Chuck took them out. One waft of fire wrapped them in falling blood. They were weeping on the floor, their blue-brown hands trying to stop the wounds. The muzak did not pause, but the aisle emptied of people. Chuck took one of the crates of oranges and sauntered on, adding Idaho potatoes, heads of broccoli and bundles of carrots to his cart.

In another part of the market, D heard the chattering noise. He thought it was a cash register gone berserk with figures. He had seen that before. There was a girl near him, in the market's pink uniform, restocking the cold meats. She was lovely in her sharp-eyed way. He thought of Rosanna Arquette.

"What was *that*?" the girl said, eager to gossip.

"Firing?" D speculated.

"You think?"

"The market seems to have been abandoned by the staff," D added in an off-hand way, letting her draw her own conclusions.

"Rats!" she was stranded, dumped on.

This girl was so piquant, with a nose like a pickle and a mouth as emblematic as the heart on a Valentine. Her eyes slipped around her face when she looked at anything. It gave an erotic sense of surface instability. How one stumbled on untrained beauties in the most unlikely neighborhoods. California! She had noticed his admiration.

"You want to make it?" she asked him. Being watched aroused her.

"Here?"

"Uh-huh." She was acting the hoodlum, daring him with a dead-eyed leer.

"You do that with customers?"

"Well, you look like you're going somewhere," she was examining his cart. "With two hundred cans of beef stew. You can tell the guys with plans." She was a little dry comic, on her honor not to laugh at the jokes.

"Actually," said D, "we have a trip ahead."

"I love trips." The girl took off her pink cap and shook free brown hair that had streaks of green and red under the lights.

"What's your name?" asked D.

She put on an innocent face, as if she hadn't heard of names.

"You look like Rosanna Arquette?" But she did not respond; she let her eyes roll. *"Baby, It's You?"* he added.

"I know," she pouted. "And it's you, and it's all it is. So why don't we?"

276

"Well," said good old D, resigned to his sway as a sex object. The girl was already down, shivering on the floor – the uniform had a free, skating slipperiness – and he could see the glint of her sex. He could not shut out the label picture on all the stewed beef cans.

"Oh," the girl shook, and "Oh, I love you, I love you," in time to the drive of his body with hers. Her breasts spilled like Dutch cheeses on the ground, smelling of custard, walnuts and ripe strawberry.

"I'm not going to ever let *you* go," she said. "We'll make it in all the wild places – in photo-booths, in banks. If they have banks still."

D might have slept. But there was no time. His head on the floor watched the wheels of shopping carts pass by. They churned and squealed. He started to get up and perhaps peril hardened him anew, for as he stood she came with him, impaled and as cheery as a kid on a ride.

"Wow!" she cried, and he saw the soaring face of his child mate.

"You can come too," promised D. "Wherever we're going."

"My name's Look," she told him. When he watched the slide in her vivid face it seemed he had always known this.

LIFE OF DRAGONFLIES

It is never enough to make a picture. You must secure the image and the reputation of the picture, too. You are exhausted, physically and emotionally, when you deliver your final cut to the studio. And you will have had to protect that final cut and speak out against all worries on a cut, a transition, a scene, a shot over which you may yourself have had enough doubt to occupy nine nights in a row. So you are tired from the exercise of fine judgment and by testing and re-testing your own response to inner rhythms. It may be the trimming and the fretting over the transcendence in the close-up and the "ain't life grand". Your tiredness may have reached the point of craziness that *knows* if that flicker of all the feelings thirty years have gathered is you, then the film will be all right. You may be so tired you are impotent and lucky to have a woman who lets you alone and hopes for you. It could be as close as you ever come to marrying.

Why not? You will never be more tender, going deeper and deeper in the folds of your film. You may discover that you love the form, that you could work in it like this forever. Except that you know you would die of the tiredness. Indeed, you are shocked at how much you have extended yourself, afraid of the passion you have seen and maybe a touch too fond of yourself, of your own looks and health, to risk it. But you are at your best, and you know it is good, just as you vowed that no one else would ever be blamed by you for this film. That is not hard, if you do not naturally trust others. But paranoia, too, yields to fatigue, and you may never have felt so warmly for others before, or seen the silliness in mistrust more clearly.

But this best does not equip you for what is to come, immediately. Prints will be made from the cut, and someone has to check the quality of those prints before they reach theaters. The laboratory does it; the studio does it. It would be so sweet when so tired to trust them. You learn you cannot. The decision is taken at the studio on when and where to open your film. The advertising campaign is designed. Posters and trailers are made. You have been in the business seven years and these are matters that you left to others, that you never understood and never much believed in. You told yourself a picture took care of itself: if it worked, the audience bought it; if not, well . . . Tiredness would so like to hang on to that principle. Then you see a terrible ad, and you know you must not trust the studio publicity people. Then you discover that they will open your picture on the 13th of August. You knew they meant to destroy you.

Beatty has fought for the power to make *Bonnie and Clyde* his way, even fending off Jack Warner's exasperation on seeing the rushes. But there is a debt incurred in such a victory. It is that Jack now calls it "Warren's picture" and smiles a little sadly when the subject comes up. Those forty-five years' seniority have to find their moment and their advantage, and they come in the chance to be patronizing. The studio machine feels that and knows, even if Jack does not quite know it, that the studio head will bear up nobly if *Bonnie and Clyde* is a failure. A kid has to learn, after all. So we'll open it in the middle of August, at the end of the summer, but before the important fall pictures. And we'll open it in New York City, in the summer of 1967, let's see how those people back east like this weird shoot-'em-up. It may never make its way into words, but there is an attitude about – this picture will be limited.

Bonnie and Clyde opens in New York City in two theaters, the Forum and the Murray Hill, and nowhere else. The reviews are, at best, mixed. Judith Crist in *Vogue* and Hollis Alpert in the *Saturday Review* are impressed. But *Variety* sees only inconsistency and incongruity. In *The New York Times*, Bosley Crowther calls it "a cheap piece of baldfaced slapstick comedy that treats the hideous depredation of that sleazy, moronic pair as though they were as full of fun and frolic as the jazz-age cut-ups in *Thoroughly Modern Millie*" (another film of the moment, and a hit). In *Newsweek*, Joseph Morgenstern is equally offended by the clash of "the most gruesome carnage since Verdun . . . accompanied by some of the most gleeful offscreen fiddling since Grand Ole Opry . . . For those who find killing less than hilarious, the effect is also stomach-turning." He calls the picture "a squalid shoot-'em for the moron trade."

And in *Time* magazine, in an issue with a cover story "Inside the Viet Cong", there is the same horror at such jaunty violence: "Both Producer Beatty and Director Arthur Penn have elected to tell their tale of bullets and blood in a strange and purposeless mingling of fact and claptrap that teeters uncannily on the brink of burlesque. Like Bonnie and Clyde themselves, the film rides off in all directions and ends up full of holes."

There is one review of the picture that is both favorable and discerning, and it comes from Penelope Gilliatt in *The New Yorker*. She alone grasps how far the picture is concerned with fame and with reflecting on the process of film itself. She says it "is about two real thieves of the early thirties who behaved as if they thought of themselves as film stars in a movie . . . The film shows them holding up grocery stores and banks as if the two of them were box office draws who were bound to survive because of their audience pull . . . *Bonnie and Clyde* could look like a celebration of gangster glamor only to a man with a head full of wood shavings. These two visibly have the life expectancy of dragonflies: their sense of power and of unending gang fun is delusion, and to see them duping themselves is as harrowing as the spectacle of most other hoaxes. Their motive isn't gain but an urge to be theatrically remembered . . . The picture often makes you think of Lee Harvey Oswald."

Something happens in theaters that seems to bear out Ms. Gilliatt's insight. *Bonnie and Clyde* does $59,000 in its first week at two theaters. And then, in the second week, the gross goes up to $70,000. There is no way of knowing why or how – no matter how hard you work at carrying your film to the public, or how much experience you have of the business, there is a mysterious chemistry. Very quickly, a controversy arises over the violence, fuelled by repeated attacks from Bosley Crowther, never a Beatty admirer and now seemingly furious.

Of course, the violence is very real and very fake – at the same time. Some critics and moral guardsmen are outraged that attractive people are being violent and that the film rushes them away from hold-ups and murders on merry banjo music. But audiences may see how boldly the film is exploring the absurdity of violence, and the absurdist potential of film in which "reality" and fantasy work off one another. This is but a few years after the death of John Kennedy and Lee Harvey Oswald, and in a time increasingly faced by newsreel coverage of Vietnam. There are many appalled at violence, and there are some who see how far it has become a show, a reality that cannot be regained for the larger public. Real people are becoming mythic – that is what Beatty has done to those allegedly real, dog-faced desperadoes, Mr Barrow and Miss Parker. There is already an unvoiced urging – awful but compelling – in which fame is overpowering ethics and decency. And *Bonnie and Clyde* has this very enduring sub-text to the later 60s, it hates and fears authority and system.

There is also an uncommon reversal by *Newsweek* and Joseph Morgenstern. A week after his first review, he speaks again, calling his original notice "grossly unfair and regrettably inaccurate". He has seen the film a second time, with a large audience, "enjoying itself almost to the point of rapture". He may also have had a call from the producer: the telephone is not to be wasted, and if no critic will respond to bullying, still few critics are averse to flattery or to some such hesitant prattle as "I respect what you say . . . and I really value you saying the film was 'interesting', and I wish if you had the time you'd look at it again".

Morgenstern's second thoughts are not really much more intelligent that his first, but he has made a great effort, and done something that critics usually avoid: he has looked again, and he has risked the company of a large audience of "innocent" moviegoers. Now he realises that the film "knows perfectly well what to make of its violence, and makes a cogent statement with it – that violence is not necessarily perpetuated by shambling cavemen or quivering psychopaths but may also be the casual, easy experience of only slightly aberrated citizens, of jes' folks."

In its third week in Manhattan, the take is up to $74,000. By that time, the film has played two weeks at a single theater in Los Angeles, the Vogue, and takes $28,000 and $29,000. In week four, it does $69,000 in New York (the first decline) and $22,000 in Los Angeles. The following week, these declines continue, but the movie adds Cleveland to its market and picks up $30,000 there. Detroit and Chicago are added in the sixth week, and in Chicago it gets good reviews and $42,000. By its seventh week, it is the third most successful film in the country, running behind *To Sir, With Love* and *Thoroughly Modern Millie*. By week eight it is in major cities across the country, still taking $39,000 in New York, doing $40,000 in Kansas City and $18,000 at the Charles in Boston, despite local interest in the World Series.

Beatty studies the figures and uses them in his assaults on Warner Brothers. He travels widely, angling himself into local promotions. He notices the early rage for the picture in London and uses the lessons there to challenge American cities where the film is doing less well. He knows that it is doing less well than was possible. He makes himself a pest to Warners, who are taken aback by its good opening. When he should be pleased, he's asking for more. He earns dislike as well as respect for his persistence. He is told, what a pity, if only we'd known earlier, because you can never get over the first release of a movie. He starts agitating for

281

re-release, and in the moment of fiercest bargaining he trades back a part of his ownership so that Warners will re-open, with a new campaign. This comes early in 1968, after *Bonnie and Clyde* is nominated for ten Oscars.

By then, it is an unmistakable phenomenon, and in this second, wider distribution it secures its full success, amounting to net rentals in its first year of at least $30 million. For that second release, the general audience comes out, the country kids most like the real Bonnie and Clyde, older people initially alarmed at the talk of violence but now wooed by prestige. In short, a working version of everyone, at last aware that *Bonnie and Clyde* is as much of its time as the Beatles – hard and soft, a kind of charming rape that we all like and deserve.

For its December 8, 1967, issue, *Time* has thoroughly rewritten its past. It has a cover story, "The New Cinema: Violence . . . Sex . . . Art . . .", with a silkscreen collage by Robert Rauschenberg devoted to *Bonnie and Clyde*. It reassesses its earlier review for comparing the real and the fictitious Bonnie and Clyde – "a totally irrelevant exercise". And it claims, in Stefan Kanfer's story, that America is now ready to handle complex movies and deal with them as it would with . . . art! The New Wave has reached Hollywood and Warren Beatty is its boss. The Earl Scruggs record of *Foggy Mountain Breakdown* is a hit. Chic young women look like Faye Dunaway's Bonnie.

A Californian film critic comes to New York, fired from *McCall's* and unhappy at the *New Republic*. It is Pauline Kael, who writes a 9,000-word essay on the film for the *New Yorker* in October. It is a stimulating piece of work, and it helps get Ms Kael on the staff of the *New Yorker* even if it does not match the briefer insights in Penelope Gilliatt's first review. But it is an event, a little like Bonnie's poem in the papers, and it surely tells Beatty's story in a way he likes.

Among other things, Kael remarks that Beatty is for the first time less burdened by his limits as an actor. She goes to the heart of American film-making in seeing how power and success are the greatest stimulants:

". . . in a number of roles Beatty, probably because he doesn't have the technique to make the most of his lines in the least possible time, has depended too much on intuitive non-acting – holding the screen for too long as he acted out self-preoccupied characters in a lifelike, boringly self-conscious way. He has a gift for slyness, though, as he showed in *The Roman Spring of Mrs Stone*, and in most of his films he could hold the screen – maybe because there seemed to be something going on in his mind, some

282

kind of calculation. There was something smart about him – something shrewdly private in those squeezed-up non-actor's eyes – that didn't fit the clean-cut juvenile roles. Beatty was the producer of *Bonnie and Clyde*, responsible for keeping the company on schedule, and he has been quoted as saying, 'There's not a scene that we have done that we couldn't do better by taking another day.' This is the hell of the expensive way of making movies, but it probably helps explain why Beatty is more intense than he has been before and why he has picked up his pace. His business sense may have improved his timing."

He also learns how extensive the business is, how many things there are to worry over. Time and again, people are touched and impressed by the dogged way this star comes off the screen with persistent questions about why his image there is not quite clear or his voice not loud enough. It is a way of learning humor.

He goes with *Bonnie and Clyde* to London for its opening there, and he attends the critics' screening at the Warner Theatre in Leicester Square. It is a large place, and he is struck by how modest the sound is, especially that of gunfire. In making the picture, he has drawn upon years of viewing and remembering, and he has always liked the emotional force of the gunfire in George Stevens' Western, *Shane*, made in 1953. He has talked to Stevens about the innovative techniques used on that film, and with his own sound man, Francis Stahl, he has played with different ways of recording shots so that they "jump out at you", moving the viewer with a mixture of fear and arousal.

But in London, the shots sound tame. "So I ran up to the projectionist, and I walked into the booth, and he was a little surprised to see me, because I was in the movie. He didn't know I'd produced it. And he said, 'You're the producer of this picture?' And I said, 'Yeah.' And he said, 'Well, I've really helped you out in the sound here. I've made a chart, and I turn it up here and down here, and so on. It's the worst mixed picture . . . I haven't had a picture so badly mixed since *Shane*.'"

Check-out

"What's happening?" asked Cy Lighthiser, over his shoulder. He was at the check-out, reading an *Enquirer* story on how Lee Majors had lost 21 pounds in seven days and was about to make astonishing career headway.

"Hey," said Cy. He looked twice at D's companion. "Take-away Rosanna Arquette?"

D put his arm around the young woman – her identity could so easily get out of his control.

"Looks like Rosanna," said Cy. He was examining her, as if she were an antique of controversial provenance, holding back his bid.

"That's right?" said Look. She let her head loll to one side, as if it was so boring it was a scream, and she showed Cy the ball of gum in her mouth.

"You could go on shows," he reckoned.

"This is Look," D explained. "Can't you see it?"

"Sensational!" cried Cy. And Look grinned so Cy added, "Right!" with feeling, and the shelf-filler about to be hoisted from humble circumstances writhed up to Cy in bashful twitter so that he picked her gum as cinnamon. "You're a quiet riot," he told her, Lee Majors' redemption forgotten.

"Yeah?" she asked. It was a movie moment.

"What was that racket back there?" Cy nodded towards the far reaches of the market.

"Backfire?" D surmised.

"Backfire, back story – what's the diff?" Cy was studying the shelves and their divisions, brooding on the sugar and cake mix aisle. "Kids, I have just had a hell of an idea. You can tell your grandchildren you were here when I had it."

"Fantastic," giggled Look.

"Can't tell you now," said Cy. "Wait till we're on our way." Then a doubt crossed his mind and he looked at D. "She's coming?"

Look said, "I guess so," her olive oval eyes swinging from one man to the other, trying to assess the originating force in the going. Then she winked at Cy, "D swept me off my feet, you know."

"Do I?" said Cy. "He's a musketeer."

There should be some musical flourish as this crew of adventurers and frauds put their all together in limousines and campers to make it away to the desert. Chuck comes backing into the camper, his leveled Uzi holding off the several blacks whose pals he had wasted. The bounty was brought in and loaded, with Clear at his best in the arrangements. They were at the point of being off, when a gaunt black woman came up to Claudia, led by Beau, carrying a bundle of rags.

"Oh, sweetheart," called Beau. "A moment."

"What is it?" cried Claudia to the air. She was not quite focusing, but speaking to the fates and the darkness outside her gathered light.

"You the one los' the chile?" asked the woman.

"I am, I am —"

"Got one here," said the woman.

"It's at least a possible," whispered Beau.

"How could this woman find my child?" wailed the mother.

"Claudia, you never know. What you have lost, someone else must find." Beau pulled back the shabby wrappings to disclose a baby.

"It's white," said the black woman.

"I don't know," Claudia complained. "How can I know?"

Cy came up to offer his opinion. He tried to remember – babies do look alike. Then he shrugged and told his wife in a bargaining way, "What you got to lose?"

"Claudia dear," said Beau. "You could be a universal mother, like Ingrid in that Chinese orphan picture." D saw him slip a twenty into the old blanket in which the black woman had wrapped the baby. The child had already been inserted in a more suitable shawl.

"You all be well in Christ," said the black woman and hobbled away.

"What a fine soul," sighed Beau.

"It's not your step sister." D was ready to be indignant.

"How should I know?" protested Beau. "It surely wasn't the old crone's, was it? You want Claudia doing her woeful Crawford bit forever?"

"And this gives your lawyers a better chance at the inheritance."

"You're cynical, baby," said Beau, with the utmost fastidiousness.

As they bundled themselves and their provisions into the vehicles, Drew came up beside D, as silent and mournful as an assassin.

"Picking up more women?"

"I bumped into her."

"You're a disgrace."

"If I am —"

"If?" She was proud of him, no matter the hurt.

"Look will be useful to us," said D, on the spot. "She has experience storing foodstuffs."

"Look?" Drew glanced swiftly at her rival. "Looks like Debra Winger. That's what she looks."

"Others think Rosanna Arquette," said D.

Drew scowled. "No way. No comparison." She was bitter a moment. "Rosanna could have played me. You know, if they'd done me."

"You should play yourself," said D.

"Too late. They're used to me. 'Old Drew' they say. They like me. They understand my position. But I'm gone. Best chance I had was for some hot-shot writer," she glared at him, "to write a script about me. Then Arquette would have been made for it."

"I do see it," D admitted, hoping to make her see that he had eyes for her *and* the Arquette look.

"You horny goof," she was smiling at him. "Why don't you get out?"

"Not again."

"We could get out together. You can do what you want with me. You know that, don't you?

"Well, yes, I —"

"But it bores you? Let me tell you, you'll wish you'd settled for being bored." She looked at him again, struck by something new.

"What is it?" The worry came so quick.

"You're getting better looking," said Drew. "I swear you are."

AS GOOD AS IT GETS

It is as good as it gets. It may be all he can imagine ever wanting, without straining or altering himself. He is so high, he sees other people around using drugs and he laughs like a happy kid wondering why they need them, when you can do success. But it may never be better for him, and he is young enough to have ample time for discovering. He has been famous before, and no one has had difficulty thinking the worst or the best of him romantically. He did stand for a breathtaking limit – call it cool or callous. But the face was that of a tight-minded, spoiled kid. Now everyone has to admit a different kind of emergence, a Beatty they had not seen or understood. It is heaven if you think you have been misunderstood, but it is the first moment in which the intelligence, the watchfulness, or just the smarts he prizes, may falter, and may even be seduced by what people think of him.

He has a hit that runs counter to one of Hollywood's great warnings – that a picture never transforms itself commercially once it has opened. So he can wear the magical exception lightly, and know that everyone in the business knows it was his extraordinary persistence and accuracy – his being right – that lifted *Bonnie and Clyde* into new life. There will be a great deal of money coming to him over the years. And he feels so good about it all that he may even look forward to keeping such an eye on the numbers that he is never cheated. Once upon a time at a party, Beatty knows, Jack Warner had cornered John Wayne, who had been avoiding the studio head. What is it, Duke? Warner asked. And the Duke shuffled and reddened, too angry but too proud to say out loud that he thinks Warners were cheating him. But the Duke spat it out, and Jack Warner grinned and said, "Duke, I know, but that would have happened anyway, and we're your friends!" Warren could always ask Warner to stop embarrassing him if he thinks the studio is cooking the books.

Beatty has accountants and lawyers who actually urge him to spend more or invest more. This book is not going to get access to Warren's

David Hockney, *Chair and Shirt*, 1972

Swimming pool, as seen from the old wing of the Beverly Wilshire Hotel; now the site of the new wing (Beverly Wilshire Hotel)

financial records. We have to guess. And I'd guess that over the years he has paid rather more tax than he might have done, because he never takes quickly to advice or investments (no matter he pays for the advice) and never realises that their is sense in spending money that will otherwise go in taxes. Not that he's being stupid. It's just that he may not trust anyone to be as clever as possible, and just that he is not naturally daring, generous or free with money. And when he signs the IRS check, he tells himself it is being responsible and public-spirited; it is a hint to himself that he takes the good of the country seriously.

Of course, he spends money, but never at a rate that will put his reserves at risk. He stays at the best hotels, he wears good clothes, he eats at expensive restaurants, and he travels a lot. He has whatever he wants – cars, places to live, clothes sometimes. But the business is himself. He never seems to think of owning the things that appeal to so many young successes in the business – boats, planes, palaces, islands, studios and even the business. He has never yet sought to make or distribute a picture with his own money. In 1967, he looks like the new man in Hollywood, and he can be cold and insolent to the stalwarts of the old system, scorning their stupidity, but he is not averse to the system, he will never go near partnership with any of the other young geniuses who come into film after *Bonnie and Clyde*.

He does not buy a house; he prefers what is always a modest arrangement at the Beverly Wilshire. Indeed, success may make him feel vindicated in *leaving* home, in enjoying his detachment. He relaxes a little: everyone says he is more open, and more amusing. And he has Julie Christie as his new princess, as if to prove he is moving on and attuned to now.

It is in 1968 – which is easily recollected as a terrible time, because of assassinations, Vietnam and Chicago. But it is a moment in which people feel as internally alive as they do close to death, and *Bonnie and Clyde* is often cited as an instance of this. One of the appealing undertones of the 60s – and a source of the age's subsequent betrayal – is the sense of thrill. For that exquisite, dangerous momentariness will pass, and there will be more disappointment left after it than true change.

But in 1968, Warren Beatty can feel he has risen above the silly system of pictures, that he is closer to the heartbeat of the country than movie people have been before. And it will still be a while before other people in the business think of him as part of the bullshit, and a while longer still before he realises that.

He is so happy that he may not notice how far the tiredness has reduced him to doing very little. But his body and his soul will pick up on this rhythm of doing everything and then nothing. And the most intriguing and mysterious part of that habit, and the part that beckons undying reticence and shyness, is nothing. What now proves his success is, for days on end, for a year if he wills it, he can do nothing. It does make all the contorted, fussy and aggrandising forms of something seem foolish. He has always been an actor of pauses, of hesitation. And if *Bonnie and Clyde* made him quicker, then the peace that comes when it is over may make the attraction of a much larger pause all the greater. It is like being dead, yet still alert to your own funeral: watching the show and imagining you are its director.

Julie Christie is the perfect mate for happiness, she is so fully given to experience and lack of cant. He has encountered her while he was with Leslie Caron in London: he may explain to Leslie, wide-eyed, that it's very difficult being in London in their particular circle, and *not* meeting glorious young women. Caron will only see how ready he is to be met, however strenuously he is campaigning for the wisdom of marriage to her. And Christie is not just physically gorgeous: she is the promise of a new kind of wild, uninhibited actress who sees the sham of movie-making and will not be deterred from addressing the issue of how to be a decent person.

Christie has had a small, striking part in John Schlesinger's *Billy Liar* in 1963. Two years later, she has won the Oscar for the same director in *Darling*, about a young woman who proves her own moral ruin as a success in pictures. Immediately, she is winning some of the best female roles around: Lara in *Dr Zhivago* and the two women in Truffaut's *Fahrenheit 451*. She lives in London with an art teacher: they are devoted, she tells the press he is the only man for her, as if she wanted this to be so, wanted to convince him and her, and felt the pressure of her fame. In 1967, she opens in *Far from the Madding Crowd*.

It is not really Beatty who takes her away from the art teacher – her destiny cannot escape moving out. Caron says it is simply Warren's weakness for Oscar nominees. We might see the relationship as part of his continuing attraction to women who are not American, and who may help him see the narrowness and naivety of his country. But Christie is appealing because her need for liberty is more demanding than Warren's, because she surprised him by volunteering for freedom he is shy to spell out. And he must guess, quickly, that he is never going to find a better screen partner. The event is buried in the future still, but in hindsight, in 1975, he may realise that there never was another actress as likely, as happy, to risk her prestige, her respectability, by saying out loud, "I'd like to suck his cock", the line from *Shampoo* that flusters Beatty a good deal more than it does Christie.

In 1967, when she is making *Petulia* in San Francisco, Warren is up and down the Pacific coast to see her. He does follow her, and arrange his busy schedule to see her as much as possible. Christie comes to Los Angeles for the 1968 Academy Awards. Warren does not win anything personally. *In the Heat of the Night* is reckoned to be the best picture, Rod Steiger is best actor in the same picture and Katharine Hepburn best actress for *Guess Who's Coming to Dinner?* Hollywood is still at the stage of being impressed by its own ponderous racial liberalism. *Bonnie and Clyde* wins for photography, and Estelle Parsons as best supporting actress. Which is as much as to say Hollywood is still perplexed by the picture. But at Oscar time, the movie is riding very high and Warren smiles away the loss – he must feel his best chances are ahead, and cannot foresee the hard night he has to come at the Oscars.

Christie stays on with him at the Beverly Wilshire: there will be a similar gap in productivity in both their careers. They must be very much in love for Julie Christie to be content to live so long in Warren's suite, the Escondido, at the Wilshire, a very good hotel wedged between a Boulevard that is really a highway and blocks of composed suburbia. There is nowhere to walk to – no parks, no lanes, no secret places – and nothing to do once one knows the several bars, restaurants and the bookstore at the hotel. Every time you come or go you have to let your car be parked by the valet. It is not easy to storm out after a row if the car is not waiting, but must be retrieved by the polite Mexican kids.

The suite at the Wilshire is modest – Elvis Presley had used it as a rehearsal room when he stayed at the hotel – two rooms and a bathroom, with a balcony, many mirrors and the untidiness of someone who says he knows where everything is – books, scripts, magazines, contracts, correspondence. There is another room in the hotel where his secretary works, but he keeps the things he wants to read or refer to in the suite. And after *Bonnie and Clyde* he is being sent everything – not just scripts, but the galleys of any novel anyone hopes could be filmed. He does his best to look at them, even if he starts to employ readers. It is a strange dilemma, so duty-bound to literature and so conscientious about hard work, suspecting a masterpiece in the pile if he can find it, but knowing he could probably pick up any book, say "This?", and get it done. Every month or so, someone throws out the old and the stale. He is a publisher's clearing house, not a man with a library.

There are room service trays buried in paper in the suite. There is a large bed, the telephones and the mirrors, and the weights he works out with. Over the two and a half decades of his career, no one has seen Beatty out of condition or overweight. Yet he does not jog on Rodeo, Wilshire and Charleville; and he is not seen on courts or at the gym. He does his exercises upstairs, on the carpet and in the mirror or on the balcony. It is as if his perfection had to seem casual, or as if the ex-jock was reluctant to show strain in public. He may even wonder whether he should murmur to one or another of the would-be interviewers that he gets his best exercise in bed, or trust them to deduce it? This is a joke Warren's father sometimes tells – a man of no greater fame than having two top stars for children. Proud and overwhelmed at the same time: "I did my greatest work in bed." What sort of man would be content with that?

Because of Julie Christie he is often in London, and he becomes closer friends with Roman Polanski, who is also there. They have had an acquaintance since the Pole's first feature film, *Knife in the Water*, caused such a stir in Europe and America. Fox had an idea to remake the story, in 1964, with Burton and Taylor as the couple and Beatty as the interloper who separates them. In London, Beatty meets Polanski at parties given by Victor Lownes, an executive with the Playboy organisation. Polanski asks Beatty if he would play the husband, the devil's agent, in his forthcoming picture, *Rosemary's Baby*. But, "He procrastinated, as usual, and finally rejected the role as not important enough. Warren's parting shot was, 'Hey, can I play Rosemary?'" John Cassavetes will get the husband's part.

And again, Beatty is in London, in August 1969, when Polanski's wife, Sharon Tate, and others, are murdered at the director's house on Cielo Drive in the canyons beneath Mulholland. Beatty, Lownes, Richard Sylbert and others do what they can to look after Polanski. Beatty is one of the close group that flies with him, back from London to Los Angeles, to confront the horror. He is one of those who takes turns to keep the Pole company, maintaining "a stream of improbable stories, mostly relating to his hyperactive sex life" which Polanski supposes are meant to make him laugh.

Beatty and Polanski have tastes in common: beautiful women, movies in which violence plays a part, and the roving life of show business celebrities. But put the two side-by-side, and one must see how circumspect and middle-class Beatty is in comparison. Yet this is not the only time he will be fascinated by those who live much closer than he to danger. Why should he not be curious about what disaster does, as well as friendly with Polanski?

When Polanski thinks of working again, he sees Beatty as his natural actor. He wants to make a film of the book *Papillon*, about escape from Devil's Island. He approaches Warren – "Like Papillon, he could con anyone into anything" – and Beatty is enthusiastic. Polanski goes to Paris to raise money for the venture, and a few days later Warren follows. They are supposed to discuss the script. But several nights pass with nothing but "parties, discos, and girls."

Recognising Beatty's characteristic delay, Polanski tells him it is time to work. "You're absolutely right," grins Warren, "we've had our fun." But perhaps he is still set on therapy for Roman. There is another night of partying and in his hang-over Polanski is frustrated.

He goes to London for a break and gets a call there from Warren, who seems now to have read the script. He refers to one scene that it calls for: "I'm not going to appear bare-ass. It's a hang-up I have. What did you say the budget was?" Polanski reads this as refusal. They part and the project drifts on, to another director and to Steve McQueen in the lead.

There are other parts to be turned down, of course; that is steady employment now. He does not do *Laughter in the Dark*, from Nabokov's novel, and he will not play Michael Corleone in *The Godfather*. The first has a tinge of gayness to it, he thinks, and as for the second, he has had his shot at being Italian. Suppose he and Christie laugh together at the foolishness of contrasting accents and foreigners for all those absurd scripts. This is the late 1960s, when acting can seem like an escape from the richness of life's responsibilities. It is in a state of laughter and happiness, of a power that could do anything or nothing, that he agrees to act in *The Only Game in Town*.

This picture comes from a play by Frank Gilroy that failed on Broadway: it is about an aging showgirl and a gambler who meet in Las Vegas and fall in love. Tammy Grimes and Barry Nelson play the leads on stage. When it is all done with, and the $7 million loss is clear, no one can recall why this film was made, except in the search for success. It is a vehicle for Elizabeth Taylor that will reunite her with George Stevens, who directed her in *A Place in The Sun* and *Giant*; and it is a property full of the worldly sadness stars think becomes them. It also promises to be an easy film to make, for it is essentially a play for two characters.

Yet it turns out a kind of monster. Originally, Frank Sinatra is cast as the gambler, Joe Grady, but he withdraws when the start is held up by Ms Taylor's hysterectomy. And so Beatty takes the part at the eleventh hour: some say for $750,000 , some for $1.2 million. The movie is to be made in Paris, despite location research in Las Vegas, because Taylor wants to be close to Richard Burton, who is making *Staircase* in the same city. And so much of the aura of Nevada is brought in to the Paris studio – craps tables and gambling apparatus have to be flown in and a vast Vegas perspective is built, of hotel towers and mountains beyond, to be seen through the windows of the story.

The shooting begins in October 1968, and it will last over 100 days, with time in Los Angeles at Fox and even a few days on location in Las Vegas. Despite two stars so potent and prominent, the film is not released until March 1970, which is a sign that some people have been asking, "What are we going to do with it?" It does not work; it takes maybe $3 million towards its cost of $10 million.

There is a story about its making that may help explain this. The first day on the set in Paris, Warren strolls over to where Elizabeth is sitting. What follows is like a parody of his seductive routine to those who have observed it. He studies the actress, never losing a polite but slightly bewildered smile. She knows she is being looked at, and she rises to the scrutiny and its challenge. She has heard of him. She's only seven years older than he is, and she has noticed his taste for brunettes and English origins. But she is engaged in one of the world's most celebrated romances, with Richard Burton. They may recall the earlier prospect of Polanski's *Knife in the Water*, and its hint of Warren's power. Will Warren test her out himself, will he make her decide whether she has to turn him down and have his failure show? Does he work out in public view?

So he prowls around her and then he laughs out loud, but to himself. "What is it?" she asks. He has aroused her curiosity. He has started by making her ask – to show what he might do. "Oh, nothing," he says. "It's nothing." And he walks away.

The following day there is still no explanation. So Taylor goes to him, and asks again, "Why did you laugh, Warren?" He has the timing to wait here, long enough for both of them to see the world press howling with another coup for Liz, to see the lunacy and the indignity. Then he says, "I laughed because nobody can be that beautiful." It is a sweet and voluminous line, and it tells her from the start that she is not quite real, not even possible, not simply or definitely there. She is her image, and he is just a mortal.

The film they make preserves this odd, close-company distance. *The Only Game in Town* is not a movie about people. In the script, they are

With Elizabeth Taylor in *The Only Game in Town*

both failures, downcast and flaky; but in the casting they have become inexplicably disconsolate gods. The picture is about two actors considering what they are doing. That puts it more in Beatty's vein than in Taylor's. When the script says they are in bed and in love, he looks wary – of her emotional power, or of her recovery from illness. He wants to edge away. For he has elected to play his role as a fake watching impossibility, mocking the lines, the character and the gigolo-stooge way he gets to play the piano for her. "Give me a kiss," he asks her. "Why should I?" she says. And he answers, "Because I'm a winner, and winners are irresistible." But there is something in his stance and distance that knows he cannot risk himself, and it feels camp or contrived when he has to be a helpless gambler. Self-control is the cool, dark place where he is hiding. Years later, Beatty will note he has played gamblers three times (here, in *Kaleidoscope* and in *McCabe and Mrs Miller*), but never actually gambled himself. This is a curious omission when it would be so easy for so wealthy a researcher to play seriously one night, or one week-end, or . . . Is it a thrill he fears? Or does he say everything is a gamble, every word, meeting or kiss?

As for Taylor, her great emotional need is warned off. Perhaps she wants a more reckless lover. The picture is a failure and a curiosity, often touching and funny, and filled with Warren's elegant, charming promise of himself that finds he is making the picture, absent-mindedly, when he thought he had refused it. "It was like telling a joke underwater," he remarks afterwards, dismissing failure.

The writer, Frank Gilroy, meets briefly with Beatty in Paris, after he has written the script. But when Warren is cast, George Stevens asks Gilroy to go to Beatty's Paris hotel for an evening and read the entire script to him. Read it into his record.

Much later, Gilroy sits down to look at a rough cut with Stevens. "It became very apparent the movie was a disaster. I had been ready to make notes. It was beyond that. Warren was the best thing in it. He was working hard and well. But other things had gone hopelessly wrong. And it proved to be Stevens' last film, and the last film of producer Fred Kohlmar too. I think it was sunk when they went to Paris. Maybe if they could have gone to Vegas and made it very real for $1.98. And yet it had meant a lot to Stevens. Something in the story moved him very much."

And George Stevens will be one of the few directors Beatty refers to when he thinks of the best – an instinctive and emotional man, but a controlled, careful director, sometimes a little academic. He has a way of arriving at very strong scenes and then filming them studiously from every camera angle he can think of. George Stevens makes several very successful films; he is a respected liberal and a heartfelt American; he likes order and decency, and he believes in the outsider getting his chance in the system. But he never quite proves himself as a film artist. And he is not far from Beatty's model for directing, a very significant influence on *Reds*.

Terrific note

"I feel strong on how we stand," announced Cy Lighthiser as the camper made its way through gray-dawning suburbs. "Not solid, but positive." None of the traffic lights was working now, and Clear – who had head position in the convoy – edged across intersections, looking for movement in the dingy streets. "Of course," Cy conceded, "things could be better."

"Right," snapped Drew. "I could have a part and someone to trust. You could have your baby, and we might be hopeful about next week."

"I never have five cents for next week," said Cy. "I take 'em day by day."

Drew regarded him as if it was that attitude that had let things get out of hand. "What about you?" she turned on D. He had known there would come this lunge in her attention. He would have to suffer for his Look.

"It might be worse?" he suggested carefully. "We're getting out of the city."

"And you like to have the story moved on, get some momentum going, the smell of wild flowers and gunpowder on the hot air – kind of thing?"

"Well, I've not been out of the city before. I'm curious to see a desert."

Drew was shut out by this innocence. It sounded docile but mad. She looked at him askance, in case he had been teasing. But all she saw were his eyes set on whatever he imagined desert to be.

"I've seen films about the desert," he added. "*Zabriskie Point* –"

"That's very desert," said Drew.

"And a lot of Peckinpah," said D.

"Oh well," she breathed, waving her hand, dismissing more talk with benediction. "I was the only woman I know went with him he didn't turn on."

"He was very rough with Claudia," Cy commented.

Drew was grinning as she remembered: "He put you in the position of defending him, and he had that wicked look because he knew you wanted to say how terrible he was."

"I wrote a picture for him once," said Doc. "He was going to do it. We just couldn't get the right actress."

"What was that?" Cy wanted to know.

"About a woman with a false eye and a wooden leg. And she was bald. Only, she's also very sexy and attractive. But most men don't see it at first. So she becomes a contract killer. Sam was high on it."

"I would have done that," said Drew.

"There was this great ending when she finally gets the guy she's wanted. And he decides he's in love with her. He realises she's sensational looking –"

"I can see it," Drew was carried away.

"And they're in bed, and he screws her all he can. And then it's a while later, and he's still in her, and she says, 'You stay here. I'm going to cook us some eggs.' And she gets up and goes to the kitchen. And he's lying there, half-asleep, but very slowly he realises she's left the part of her he's in in the bed."

Drew was laughing out loud at the end of the story. And Look was laughing too, but that didn't deter Drew. The two women were guessing they might get along.

"How would Sam have done that?" asked Cy.

"Done it?" Doc never smiled.

"The bit of her he was still in."

"Well," said Doc, "I told you. We couldn't get the actress."

"Sam said actresses weren't worth patience," said Drew proudly.

"I like his deserts," said D, after a pause.

And then Cy, a while later, put it to Doc, "You made that up?"

"The story? Sure. I'm a writer."

"I mean you made it up that Sam was going to do it? You couldn't *do* that."

"He could have done it, Cy."

"A woman who comes apart?" Cy was outraged. Claudia had bred in him an ideal of feminine completeness.

"Just a woman who's lived hard," said Doc. "One day, we'll all be parts."

"One bright day I'll have Eyes' dick," snorted Cy. "What'll he do then?"

"Oh, he'll go back to the magic wand," said Clear from the driver's seat.

The camper shook with laughter; the unevenness of the unmaintained streets was lost in merriment. It is natural in any company in awe of someone or some thing, or travelling toward it from afar in a spirit of reverence, that there should be a momentary need to laugh at the person or the object. For there must be a humor in greatness if it is not to soar into absurdity or tyranny. Gods should have the wit to reckon on this and deal tenderly with prayers that cannot be met, responding with a courteous rejection slip. A paranoid in Eyes – if such a creature existed – could have felt threatened by the laughter and sent a drunken truck to smash them. But our Eyes would have known the laughter was normal.

D realised they were going to pass close to his home. Here were trashy corners and foul alleys he knew, desolate sites where he walked the children on hot afternoons. Without drawing attention to it, at the proper turning he stared down the long gray chute towards his building. It was there still, not stirring. Perhaps all his children were asleep, their small snores freshening the damp on their pillows. What bliss to look at the surrender of their sprawled heads, to be so tired that rest came in like a tide.

The wheels screeched: D imagined a streak of cat squeezed beneath them, a bloody fur skid on the blacktop.

But Clear called out cheerfully, "D, we could easily look in on your family. Aren't they hereabouts?"

"Well –" he struggled to dissemble.

"Oh, treats," cried Beau. "Let's see D's place."

D felt hot shame pouring from his face. "There's really no need," he said.

But Drew wouldn't have it. "No need to tell your wife you're going?" He wished she wouldn't say it, but there was an unfailing kindness in her saying it for his sake. It was only in persistent ties that ethics had any chance, stretching to encompass dilemmas that the solitary could always regard as fate's ill-will.

"Down there," D admitted. Clear worked at the steering wheel and brought the unwieldy caravan around behind him, as cumbersome as a python turning a corner while it swallowed a donkey.

"Maybe your wife could lay on breakfast?" said Cy. "Pancakes perhaps?"

"We couldn't impose on her," said Clear. "And there's a breakfast stop planned in the desert."

"We shouldn't be late then," urged Cy.

"A quick call," said Clear. "I won't even turn off the engine." D caught his reassuring smile in the mirror (the sweet pacts people put together), but he wondered if Clear was fearful of never starting again.

"Here, I think," said Clear, coming to a halt outside the mottled charcoal front of a block. Amid blocks so similar, there was nothing to make this building stand out. Of course, Clear knew it; he probably had specifications.

"I'll hurry in, then," muttered D.

"I'm coming," said Drew. And Look would not let him go either. So D, it seemed, had to say hallo-and-goodbye to his official loved ones with two new goodies, both a little the glossier for recent loving. How many times in one day would D have to do it? He did stagger as he stepped down from the vehicle, but Drew and Look were there with hands in his armpits, like angels lifting an amazed soul into heaven.

They went up the echoing stone staircases, stepping over the garbage, and came to D's floor, wintry and fishy.

"This is so like my building," said Look.

Drew was ready to talk about her Westwood duplex and parents in the Valley. But how could she touch this pitiless, unpromising world? It made her more impressed by D's politeness – he might have turned out a killer.

The door to the unit was open.

"They're up?" asked Drew. No doubt the poor had to be.

But D was surprised. Had C been up all night, trying to find some authorities? Had she had to deal with the odious Scrug? He shuddered. What had he left them to?

He went in, and his girlfriends surged in behind him, hushed but blatantly curious, like kids examining a party spread.

There was no one in the unit. All the beds were made.

"Gone back to mother, maybe," said Drew.

"There is no mother," D explained. "Nothing like that." He saw that his scripts were gone, too, along with his dictionaries and favorite reference books. As far as he could tell, very few clothes had been taken in the departure, but all his vital papers were missing.

"They could be at an all-night entertainment center," Look offered.

The suggestion horrified D. Could his influence die so quickly?

The plainness of the unit was sinking in on Drew, leaving a sadness she could not express. Yet Look was discovering a blackened stove on a broken floor like those in her home. Drew felt her distance from it all, and she half-supposed that D and this Look were made for each other – if the world must always stay as it was. Then she rallied. "Well, sweetheart," she said to D. "We know they'll be all right. And we should be moving on."

D wanted to get away, but he felt the urge to stay, too, to wait for their return, to be here as if nothing had happened or ever would.

"You've started to go, D," said Drew. "I expect your wife knows."

That would explain their unaccountable absence. It was the sign he was looking for, the bleak response to his own desperate measure.

"I'll leave a note," said D.

"Oh yeah, a note would be terrific," Look agreed.

And so D wrote this – "I got back early in the morning. Found you all out. I am off to the desert, to see Eyes. Hope the earthquake has not troubled you. Such tumultuous times. Take care of yourselves. Who knows what will happen to us all? My love, D" – and left the page on the table with an empty milk bottle on top of it. Then he reconsidered and replaced the milk bottle with the white case of money he had been carrying. He was pleased to be rid of it, and he felt freer now for whatever was to come.

With Julie Christie in *McCabe and Mrs Miller*

McCABE AND MISS CHRISTIE

Warren loves Julie – are there enough conifers in the British Columbian forests for them to carve out their feelings? But if you're filming there you don't want every tree in sight branded with their heart-and-arrows. No, if you're making a movie with an actor and an actress who are in love, better to have their days spent somewhat apart and their screen roles not always, all the time, in kissing scenes and bedroom sprawls. They have enough of that in their honey evenings together; imaginative creatures that actors are, they may even be close to having enough of it altogether, with Warren discovering the problem of dialling directly in the north-west wilderness. It is perfection for the picture, and the lovers, if the script thwarts them, if it makes them partners beset by misunderstanding and mettlesomeness. That way, they look at one another as they might have done when they first met – and it is the looking that film wants, no more. The medium is so callous to those whose looks it sucks on – it is a lesson in modern coldness.

McCabe and Mrs Miller thrives. It is a Robert Altman picture, made a couple of years after the career-making hit of his *M.A.S.H.* And let us note that that picture – and then its influence on modern television – might not have been possible without the example of *Bonnie and Clyde*. For *M.A.S.H.* works on the same stew of apparent opposites: a field hospital in the Korean war where the blood and ruin of the operating table exists a foot and a half beneath banter from a 1930s comedy. It works, and the sleepy public learns another lesson – that in the pits of horror and death it is possible to make jokes. Indeed, the survivors may be distinguished by the intriguing harmony of their poker faces and their jazzy lines. Early in *M.A.S.H.*, at least, there are moments of life that have somehow crept on to the screen, so adult, so startling, the medium may be changing: it is probably nearing its end. Altman is one of the best directors America will ever have, and it is Beatty's good fortune that – in love with Christie – he waltzes into the director's demanding arms.

As if someone has felt the true meaning of *Bonnie and Clyde*, or something in the air is climatically leaned upon by it, *McCabe and Mrs Miller* is a gentle mockery of identity and reputation. It is as if, in four years (the space of a college education, after all), wisdom has settled in so that it can see, whereas the blaze of meaning in one film is valid and fun, a decent man a few years later has to move on, has to be subject to more doubt and to the altogether larger feeling for things that knows in art (as opposed to sensation) identity is always mistaken.

And so we have John Q. McCabe (the Q is never filled out by the picture, allowing us to play with thoughts of Quentin, Query or even Quilty – or is McCabe a true modernist, and is the Q just Q, not Q., standing for something, but like the O in David O Selznick, a beat for rhythm, meaning nothing?). He comes plodding into Presbyterian Church some time around 1900, looking as good as Warren Beatty ever will. He wears a fur coat, black shirts, a bushy beard and flowing dark hair, mysteriously shampooed all the time, the whole set off by a crisp black derby, just as hard, curly and detachable as the frosty little sayings that McCabe pops out to ward off conversation or investigation of himself.

They are, "You know how to square a circle? You shove a four by four up a mule's ass" or "If a frog had wings he wouldn't bump his ass so much, you follow me?" McCabe does look like a dandy on this woebegone frontier; he is taken for a very lethal and distinguished gunslinger; and he begins to deport himself like a business genius, a gambler, an impresario and the manager of the few whores who do not have access to his shampoo. But he is worried about his ass, and quite properly so, for he is one of the great idiots of fiction. Let us be clear: Q is the best role Warren Beatty has yet taken.

There then arrives in Presbyterian Church Mrs Miller, an English (I would guess south London) madam who has a team of girls that includes Shelley Duvall. She moves in on the town and on the truly frail brain of John McCabe. He watches her eat a zesty meal (his own stomach settles for raw eggs in whiskey), and while she scoffs that and sniffs his "cheap Jockey Club cologne", she devours him in a snatched glance and tells him, "You think small, because you're afraid to think big."

So she gives him a deal: his money, her girls and know-how. She'll pay back the investment, and then they'll go 50–50. But they are partners only, and if, say, John Q comes knocking on Mrs Miller's door for solace, why he has to drop his grubby dollars in her pink, heart-shaped box, along with all the others. When the caution and the timidity and the business pride of McCabe watches the brisk dexterity with which he is taken over, the pain and wonder in Warren's eyes – the sheer perplexity of guardedness taken out of itself – is a thing of beauty. His watching, listening face, and its efforts to mask amazement, will never be finer. You notice, within the beard, those big soft lips, like tenderness hoping to be mistaken for a tough cat. Whereas Julie Christie's mouth is made to wolf oysters as big and soft as men.

The business flourishes. In its gloomy days and mole-like mining spirit, Presbyterian Church grows a little happier. McCabe is cock of the walk, and only Mrs Miller yearns for something else, and looks for it in opium. Then bigger business comes to find them, to swallow them. Mrs Miller knows, of course: we realise that, eater as she is, she has been chewed over in her time. She knows the name of the larger company, Harrison & Shaughnessy, and she knows they are not to be temporised with. But McCabe has never heard of them. Where has he been? Maybe in his room alone, working up his cryptic jokes ("You boys know about the frog that got ate up by the eagle?")?

He makes jokes about the messengers' names and their offers. They are decent enough men, troubled that this innocent does not understand the offer is one he cannot refuse. They do not wish him dead; they no doubt have a case in their set minds that big business getting bigger is good for the world, and they regard outsiders and losers as unhappy, unwholesome creatures who should be pleased to be asked in out of the cold.

But McCabe struts as well as a gimpy man can – he does not quite seem to have all his toes either – and says, not nearly enough, even if he was inclined to sell. Mrs Miller despairs of his stupidity. She sees death settling on him, ignoring the fur coat. And he is not quite so unaware that he doesn't respect her instincts. But when he looks for those agents again, to renegotiate, they are gone. There isn't a second chance. And when McCabe seeks out a magnificently inane lawyer (out of Mark Twain) the client is baffled by the fulsome picture of the example that is to be made of the case. McCabe sees slowly that he may end up a martyr for liberty.

His idiocy would not be as dramatically fine if it was merely dumb. In her otherwise exciting writing on the picture, Pauline Kael makes the mistake of saying McCabe is "too simple" for Mrs Miller. Whereas, I think he is a very complex character, as rich in interest as anyone anxious to be deemed smart and whose shyness does not have the muscle that knows how to ask or apologise, and who is not cunning enough to get out of a fix because he is afflicted with a quite disastrous sense of nobility and honor. McCabe is a beautiful man in much more than looks or ironic contrast – he can act bold and tough, he deals in whores and so forth, and he does not say he *hasn't* killed people. His shyness is a part of his kindness and his helplessness; but it gets him into trouble because it is mistaken for swagger. He is chronically beset by virtue and integrity, this would-be operator. That is the stubborn impediment to his intelligence. He is so romantic, his snarls are a bluff waiting to be called. His caution dreads this exposure, and makes him more hidden, more laconic . . . until fatalism descends on him as a final, cold peace. As with all great movie roles, the credit belongs to many: to Edmund Naughton for the novel, *McCabe*; to Altman and Brian McKay for the script; and to the actor for providing such a living example and some of his own lines. For being there.

And he has timed his getting there exactly. The picture has not been easy to set up. The screenwriter, Brian McKay, recalls long, deteriorating struggles with nervous backers. Whereupon, Warren arrives from Europe with Julie Christie. He asks what's wrong, and McKay says the picture could be dead. At which, Warren flashes a grin and says, "No problem" – it is a grin that already has McCabe's silver-plugged tooth. Warren has been getting in character, and it makes him cocky. He admits it:

> "I like to play schmucks. Cocky schmucks. Guys who think they know it all but don't. It's been the story of my life to think I knew what I was talking about and later find that I didn't . . . McCabe made me laugh all during the movie."

A similar pattern of comeuppance affects McCabe in his relationship with Mrs Miller. She does not try to save him from his mess; she is too Tooting to think of rosy rescues. And she knows he can never change, anyway – that much insight is possible for characters, and sometimes Julie Christie looks hurt, as if she had caught sight of his lovely limits and a solitariness too great to be talked about in the evenings. McCabe is so tested by Mrs Miller that, when he is alone, he talks to himself about her. He is the only person he can ever come close to trusting, and it is part of his honor that he is inarticulate at this moment. It may be the best speech Beatty will ever have in a film, energy and jazzy talk beating up against the things that are beyond him:

> "Making me feel like I'm making a fool out of myself. Now we'll see who the fool is. Sons of bitches! Never did it in this goddam town. God! I hate it when

those bastards put their hands on you. I'll tell you, sometimes . . . sometimes when I'm taking a look at you, I just keep looking and alooking, and if I don't feel your little body up against me so much, I think I'm gonna bust. I keep trying to tell you, a lot of different ways – just one time if you can be sweet without so many around, I think I could . . . Well, I'll tell you something, I've got poetry in me. I *do*, I got poetry in me, but I ain't going to put it down on paper. I ain't no educated man. I've got sense enough not to try. Can't never say nothing to you. If you just *one time* let me run the show, I'd . . . Just freezing my soul, that's what you're doing. Freezing my soul. Well, shit, enjoy yourself, girl, just go ahead and have a time with it. It's just my luck, going with the one woman who's ever been something to me ain't nothing but a whore. But what the hell – I never was a percentage man. I suppose a whore's the only kind of woman I'd know."

Beatty and Christie live with a few friends in a cottage at Horseshoe Bay on Howe Sound in Vancouver during the shooting. It is a kind of wintry idyll in which she says he eats like a baboon, they stick pictures on the windows to deter gulls from flying at the glass headlong and killing themselves, and – when Christie has an eye ailment – Warren calls not the eye specialist of the world, but the ex-ophthalmologist of the picture business, Jules Stein of MCA. If it is cold at night they have McCabe's fur coat and their love. But on screen, love is so much more moving if the lovers' feelings remain as yearning, like the wish to be intelligent. But such hopes are vulnerable to life's ordinary failures and the realisation that there is a poetry which cannot be sent to the newspapers, which will never come out – because it is a man's death getting ready to spring at him.

The movie is well received, when it opens in June 1971, but too odd, too dark, too druggy for wide enjoyment. But it is the best thing Beatty has done; perhaps the best he will ever do. It is all the more intriguing because of the way he has understood McCabe, and perhaps himself. The film is made because of Warren (he has ten per cent of the gross instead of salary), because he is "interested" in Altman and inclined to give the film life with his name and presence. He therefore imagines he is in charge, and Altman has sometimes to tease this attitude along. Beatty does make suggestions, and surely some of them are blessed with his private pact with McCabe. Altman grabs good first takes from the impulsive Christie, and lets Beatty's performance build more slowly. Warren likes to keep going for takes; this is doubt and caution being creative, waiting and unwinding as he works. It is when Beatty acts well that you can see how fearful he is of himself; you can wonder how far inertia and delay are just guards against the fear. So intent on what is happening to him, the actor may not see that it is someone else's film, and that he is just a part of the greatness. He may not notice that the greatness has eaten him, like an eagle swallowing a frog.

Some years later, Gore Vidal remarks on how he meets Beatty at a party. Vidal says how much he has liked *McCabe and Mrs Miller*. Beatty asks Vidal to write him a picture. Did Altman write *McCabe?* Vidal asks. "Well, actually," says Warren, "but I did most of it." Whereupon Vidal replies, "If you can write that well you don't need me." And Warren sighs, "Oh, well . . ."

Why not? "Well —" or even "Well" are decent responses to the world's fury and cleverness, as D's progress makes plain. And don't imagine that an honest, outsmarted well-sayer isn't capable when the time comes of going out in the snow, or some other desert, and dispatching his three killers, wrapped in the silence of the muffled ground and a morning that has forgotten him.

Breakfast place

They drove into the desert and the rising sun; they were laughing because they could see nothing ahead in the rosy glare. The road was a silver line vanishing in the blood and the roar of the sun that effaced the faint edge of the pewter hills. By the time they got into the hills – to that "there" where the sun was tipping out its bucket of light – it would be higher and they might pass beneath it. So they drove on into the primitive condition, and if the road curved, or if there were obstacles in the light, no one would be to blame. Even Clear found himself driving at 110 miles per hour, and hardly moving on the steady plain of sun-washed gravel and mescal-clear plants. So he had time to count ants and dewdrops on the diamond-white stalks.

D took it all in – the mountains, with stains of white and mauve in the dung color, mineral bitters in the rock; he thought he saw jack-rabbits, dawn foxes and the slither of a snake by the roadside, but he knew maybe none of them had been there, except in his eager eyes; he might see the dead, too, those who had perished walking across the crinkled desert, maddened by thirst; or the Paiute, who knew which cactus flesh to score and how to suck its cold juice. He revelled in the distance and the deadpan availability of space. It was a world abandoned, but waiting for new life. He could imagine himself riding across the parched ground on a sure horse, with water, a gun, beef jerky and his favorite books, a survivor ready to make a start again with history and civilisation. In the desert, every man can believe he is the first and the last, and be unafraid.

". . . like a screen," Drew was saying. "Makes your head race."

"Oh yes," he agreed, in love with it, and with her for being his companion. He could believe that he and Drew in the desert might start a new family, even if the disaster had taken away everyone else. They would live in an abandoned stone house with the only well in the area. They would have an orange tree and a walnut tree. And they would study the colors and have children. It would be a castaway life, and they would give the world its new chance. D would cherish the insects and the

312

lizards, and learn to live with snakes so they were at peace with him and the rattlers were attentive at twilight when he read Dickens to his family. Or made up more CD if the books were lost.

"People go quite mad in the desert," Drew said, out of the blue.

"Will that happen to us?" D asked.

She didn't answer. She was more fearful than he had realised.

"Eyes will be there," he sought to encourage her.

"Or he's disappeared," she said.

"Why would he? He lives here now."

"In the desert? Big movie star just goes away to the desert?"

D felt like the spokesman for this man he had not met. "He is personally reticent, a little withdrawn. He likes to hide, prefers to peep out. He attains a unique status which he wants to preserve. So he moves away from the picture city. He goes off into wilderness. It is quite practical, yet very romantic."

"And insane," said Drew.

"Well," said D, "a little. It's hard without a little."

"The Eyes I know," Drew told him, "he liked room service and limousines, and lots of telephones. I bet he's been in the city all the time, at the heart of things."

"But Clear arranged this, and −"

"Clear doesn't always know. And Clear's on payroll."

"I imagine so."

"But Eyes doesn't pay regularly. He doesn't like to be taken for granted. So sometimes Clear is short. What would he do then?"

"Talk to Eyes." It seemed natural.

"But Clear knows Eyes wouldn't like that. He'd be embarrassed. Richies get so edgy. So Clear calls his laywer, and his lawyer talks to Eyes' lawyer, and then a messenger brings a check. And Clear and Eyes, they never have to mention it."

D thought about this eccentric discretion. "Well," he decided, "that kind of man could be holed up in the back end of a desert somewhere."

They were still on the western rim of the desert when they stopped at a small diner for the breakfast Clear had been recommending. It was getting on for eight, and they were the only customers, but the old-timer and his Indian helper had them sit at the counter and served them eggs, hot cakes, muffins, bacon, hash browns, coffee and orange juice. It was as if everything was provided for, this extensive fresh breakfast, this trading post, all set down and waiting for them.

"Much business here?" asked Cy.

The old-timer scratched his head to consider. "No sir, not exactly," he decided.

"Rocket-fuel OJ," said Look. You could see the C shining on her eyes.

"Thank you, miss. It's the fresh-squeezed does it."

Look grinned some more – it was as if she was being squeezed.

"How many breakfasts would you do in a week?" Cy wanted to know.

"In a week?" the old man took his time.

"Yeah," said Cy, wiping up wet yolk with a wedge of pancake.

"That'd be hard to say."

"In a month, maybe," said Doc, trying to help.

"Ah," the old face moved ahead, figuring. "Well, we do a breakfast most months."

Cy looked at the length of polished mahogany counter, every red-topped stool taken, with not one spare or one of them required to stand. "You stay in business for that?"

"We're a breakfast place," said the old-timer.

And the new desert pioneers murmured in consent as their knives and forks worked away over the thick plain plates gray with use.

"What a character!" said Cy to D and Drew later, as they were walking outside in the morning warmth, waiting for the one restroom the post possessed. There was a blush of violet and amber where the wild flowers grew in the desert.

"You really swallow this heavenly breakfast place," asked Drew, "and your grizzled old-timer cracking eggs and jokes?"

"Well –"

"Pretty convenient," she said in her off-hand, nagging way. "And pretty damn good-looking."

"We were in there," Cy begged her to consider.

"Like a set, wouldn't you say?" Drew would not be caught.

Cy shrugged. "It was what I'd hoped for."

"And there it was – in the desert – just what you wanted."

"Did she have grass in her hot cakes?" Cy asked D.

"Shit," said Drew. "Don't you think it's a pretty wonderful mirage?"

"Mirage?"

"We are in the desert!" Drew shouted at him. "On location!"

She walked away. It was her turn with the bathroom; she was already musing on whether it would be there or she would have to be inventive with the bare ground.

"Wasn't there a *Star Trek* like that?" Cy said to D. "Some planet they reached and it was anything they wanted it to be?"

Breakfast place

"People go crazy in the desert." D passed on the wisdom.

"If you can find the people," said Cy. "You know the trouble with deserts?"

D didn't answer. You never had to, and the serenity of the desert was seeping into him.

"No water," said Cy. "No rivers. No status quo."

"Right," said D. And the people talk like signposts, which is disconcerting if you don't believe you're lost.

THE MOST IMPORTANT MORAL FORCE IN...

He has been thinking about his country, and its management; and he is not sure that he might not have to become involved, for he has a taste for running things and he can feel the beguiling solitude there might be in being in charge of everything. "The American presidency is the most important moral force in the world," he says in 1972. There it is, the true transcendent voice of the screen – stirring, quotable piffle. It is a line, from the book of lines that can make thought archaic and unnecessary, just as existence may one day be subsumed in photo-opportunity.

In modern America, actors and politicians are rivals for the high, clear, intoxicating air. They watch one another with the same sort of bleak humor and respect we might imagine in opposed nuclear missiles. Few top politicians can do without acting now; and few stars do not feel the urge to run, or the chance to advise America in their pictures. Only a few back off:

> "I don't do those things," says one, in 1972. "I don't believe anyone cares what I have to say. Something funny happens to actors. As soon as people know you, you have some kind of power. As soon as people want to see you, you begin to think you really have something to say.
>
> "I think actors are suckers for politics. You've just begun to see what's going to happen. Ronald Reagan is only the beginning."

That is Robert Redford, in 1972.

But Warren is presidential timber, and a tree that feels the wind blowing that way. He has the equipment. He has such a memory, and he thinks so thoroughly ahead that he has nearly escaped the present. As Tommy Thompson says of him, in 1968, referring to his physical mobility, but foreseeing ubiquity: "He is seldom here or there in a definite place, as most of us are – he is simply 'somewhere.'"

This is a condition of modern leadership, an ability to be in the air. You can be motivated to seek the presidency by so many things –

ambition and martyrdom, calculation or altruism – but not least by the worry that no one else can be trusted with the job, so that your pervasiveness must count. "Do I have to do everything myself?" says one voice inside the head; and its friend answers, philosophically, "If you want something done, get a busy man to do it."

This chapter spans chronology. There are urges in a life that are always going on, driving the person forward, even if nothing appears to happen pertaining to these goals in a day, a week, or a year. Being president is vital; doing the job, a bonus. And Warren is an image in the mind – just like a modern leader – even if unseen. In the spring of 1986, anyone would recognise Warren Beatty as an actor, yet he has not acted for five years – in a film. But he has mastered acting without films, or parts. More than any of his contemporaries, he has set up an extreme imbalance between the wanting, wondering and thinking about doing a thing, and the thing itself. It is what makes him unequalled as a desiring spirit: film after film has the essential Beatty shot, of his face straining toward something, of beauteous desire kept alive. Women are overwhelmed by this look; it is what makes Warren unique for them, and tender despite the way he may eventually dislodge or ignore them. Indeed, the expression does not disappear, because so often he arranges events so that he is left, alone and still embalmed in desire's oil. It is the wishing in the eyes, and not everyone realises that the point of focus is beyond the level of immediate companions. He is looking out there.

And the presidency is not just out there, but the thereness of there. And as he comes to the time of life when people are presidents he has to decide whether the object of ambition or the steady state of desire matters most.

Moreover, he lives in a country and a time when intensity of desire in politics is honored and searched for because it is cleaner than the hash and muddle of the system. Of course, if any leader thrives on just that charisma, he will be chided for it and for the shallowness it is presumed to conceal. This is a nod to the old, lost order, like blaming stars for being fabrications when we feast upon their imaginative appeal. It is an American way of seeing that prefers to overlook the solid detail of party program and the onerous, depleting routine of political life, and see instead the supreme force and direction of the country in one man.

The language of American politics has required charm, amiability and mystery in leaders – to such an extent that it has become possible to see the system depending on nothing else. That is a fallacy: Washington is a city of detail, intricacy, meetings and monstrous labor in which passions are brutalised in winning half an inch there and revised wording here. But the nation's view of itself is that leadership must be finer than the dense, killing battle among clerks, lawyers and lobbyists. And so presidents have to shame the detail: we dread a tired leader, and we rejected early traces of it in Mondale. Nothing so establishes Ronald Reagan in this mood as much as the well-furnished legend that he does not over-work, or let the tangle in issues betray his clarity; that he may sometimes catnap in cabinet meetings. This is taken as a measure of his resilience, his nearness to us, his freedom from political compromise, his imaginative energy and his still active desire – for only those hoping to dream would sleep. And Reagan may have learned the value of a few zzzs in his movie days, when actors strove to keep moral force shining until the day's last close-up.

And we are not astonished if, on waking, this leader talks to microphones (they will always have more of him and his husky intimacy than other people get) about the Budget Committee that may be getting ready to propose a tax increase. His steadfast refusal on such cuts is already a glowing instance of desire overcoming reality or mathematics. And as he chuckles and ponders over what the Budget Committee may do (with lowered head and inward gaze), he tells the mikes, well, let them just try it – "Make my day!" He is like a seer who has quoted one of the holy lines, a second-rate actor still paying homage to stars as lofty and Whitney-like as Clint Eastwood. Some groan at the vulgarisation of political discourse, but the public has voted for this instinct for immediate identification. They can face not understanding all the problems, all the minutiae, if they know how the chief's fancy works. And the line refers not simply to Eastwood's refusal to be bought or used (God save it!), but to the ardor in all movie star eyes, the believing in being believed.

So, if the time comes, it can be recalled in Beatty's "literature" that his first childhood wish was to be President, until at seven he wanted to be Governor of Georgia, and only at eight an actor. This was before Jimmy Carter had used that governorship as a stepping-stone. It can be said that Warren is president of his high-school class, that he is a child of teachers, a young man who makes himself a millionaire. He can point to liberal sentiments, none so pronounced that it would detract from his practical ability. Above all, he is known. Every statistical survey reports that Americans vote for those they have heard of the most, and the best. Any decision on Beatty's part, to run or not, would turn on how he feels that word "best" is measured in the public mind.

He has already worked hard, if cautiously, in the machinery of the Democratic Party. Since 1968, he has participated seriously in every election but that of 1980, which coincides with the making of *Reds*. In 1968, he campaigns for Robert Kennedy. So did many show business figures: it is not hard for them to make easy gestures – to sign a petition, to buy a couple of plates at a fund-raising dinner, to let their names be used and to appear at a few events. This is routine endorsement, unlikely to impress real politicians any more than it does the electorate. Getting Hollywood celebrities lined up is a way of convincing yourself you are doing the basics if you are a candidate. There is a risk, though, in being associated too closely with such figures just because the public takes for granted their self-interest and their irrepressible urge for attention.

What marks Beatty's political campaigning is its developing personal reticence, the movement away from being a public speaker or a photographed presence. What impresses Pierre Salinger in 1968 is that "Warren was a 'guts' worker, not a movie star. He read every speech Bob had ever made in the Senate, and when he talked to hostile kids on college campuses, he won them over as skilfully as Bob himself did." The second Kennedy assassination only adds to Beatty's feelings about violence. He works on John Glenn's Emergency Gun Controls Committee, and in *The Parallax View* his character has a line, "Every time you turned around someone was killing off one of the best men in the country," that is plaintive and arresting. As he says it, the face is full of the longing for something better. For desire always focuses dramatically on its obstacles. And election day, 1968, is the day on which the action of *Shampoo* takes place. Not that that film is overtly political. Still, there is a pressing uneasiness in the possibility of some affinity between George Roundy's destiny and America's. It suggests that Beatty was an early sceptic of many of the libertarian dreams of the 1960s.

But it is in 1972 that he commits himself to political work, for a candidate defeated in one of the most famous of landslides. That man, George McGovern, says, "He took a year out of his life to do it. He traveled around the country making speeches, debating issues, interpreting me to the public, and he personally was responsible for raising more than a million dollars."

The core of Beatty's work in 1972 is to organise a series of star concerts. Gary Hart, McGovern's campaign manager, says that Beatty "invented the political concert" at which major performers would give their time and their act to boost the campaign funds. The concerts take place in Los Angeles, Cleveland, San Francisco, Lincoln, Nebraska, and

At Candlestick Park, San Francisco, July 6 1968

Madison Square Garden, New York. At Los Angeles, Carole King comes out of a temporary retirement to appear with James Taylor and Barbra Streisand. 18,700 attend and $320,000 is raised. At Cleveland, the audience is 14,000 for Joni Mitchell, Paul Simon and James Taylor.

Beatty prevails upon these stars to perform and directs the stage shows as well as the political themes they embody. It is the first time he has directed. At Madison Square Garden, he uses the slogan "McGovern Can Bring Us Together Again" for a concert that reunites famous teams: Simon and Garfunkel, Mike Nichols and Elaine May, Peter, Paul and Mary. Dionne Warwick shows up, but her former partner, Burt Bacharach, cannot make it. There are always some stars who let him down. At the Garden, there is a plan to have stars work as ushers. Some do, Goldie Hawn for one, but Beatty has to employ some of the arena's regular workers. The New York concert brings in 19,500 people and estimates of $450,000.

Warren Beatty is seen at these concerts, but not too much. He has learned to be wary of having himself seen. On July 6, 1968, weeks after the shooting of Robert Kennedy, he goes with Julie Christie to Candlestick Park and before the game between the San Francisco Giants and the St Louis Cardinals he stands at home plate and speaks to the crowd. "A sound and reasonable gun control law will only help curb violence in our society," he says. "Now is the time to act, and Americans should wire or write their Congressmen to approve a law that will impose reason and good sense on possession of firearms."

He is booed; he can hardly be heard. The 28,233 crowd wants Juan Marichal and Bob Gibson. Do they recall how recently Faye Dunaway stroked Warren's pistol and spent a movie teaching him it was flesh? That evening, Warren and Julie hit the Cow Palace with a similar speech before the Sonny Liston-Henry Clark fight. Beatty is asked about his attitude to real and movie violence: "I see no conflict. The movie simply tried to show a historical situation as it was . . . To my mind, the movies that are most dangerous are those that show violence but show it as not being dangerous – the type where all the shooting goes on but nobody gets hurt."

He is badly received again in 1971 at the University of Wisconsin. Such experiences prompt him into devising a role for himself as organiser, no matter that he enjoys talking about politics. Why is he booed? Is it just a few drunks or rowdies setting off an easily swayed crowd? Beatty has learned how to command and direct waves of cheering at McGovern rallies. (He may not know it yet, but this is a training undergone by John Reed at political pageants more than fifty years earlier.)

Would any star be booed at home plate, if he delayed the game? Henry Fonda? Paul Newman? Gregory Peck? Marlon Brando? Clint Eastwood? Is there an American crowd brave enough to taunt Clint? Or is there something in Beatty's reputation, even in 1968, that has stored up resentment or mistrust in the public? Do the people detect his innate guardedness, the veiled watching that is weighing his effect? Does he think it's sultry to keep his shades on? Is that why the crowd turns on him? Great lovers do not easily possess the vast, vague affection of the people. They don't seem to need it. They smell of private satisfactions, the privileged fruits of beauty.

Beatty supports his candidate. He says McGovern "has a greater degree of foresight than anyone I know. He is eight to ten years ahead of everyone else in what he perceives the truth to be, and if we can't deal with the truth then what the hell are we doing?" There is a whiff here of the political novice who wants to run by throwing out all the old, stale ways of the game. And in the campaign of 1972, he often sounds like an evangelist: "Before Florida and Wisconsin, people would ask 'Does he [McGovern] have a chance?' I'd say, 'What difference does it make? Do you want to be for someone who has a chance, or someone you think is right?' "

But when foresight fails to persuade voters, he blames McGovern for losing, and even for extracting such effort and dedication from himself in a losing cause. "The most desperate feeling in the world," he says, "is to hope people will vote for you." Yet, in a campaign how can a genuine candidate keep himself from some moments when he looks weary, ignorant, spiteful, petty, inadequate and wrong to those closest to him? The supporters must understand the ordinariness and live with it; this is how lovers negotiate marriage. The uncompromisingly idealistic may have to ignore or shun day-to-day politics because of its spectacle of drabness. And what self-control would it take in a candidate to go through that schedule and ordeal and never look petty or mistaken? People in show business have remarked on Beatty's frustrated search for heroes, and on his remorseless need to prove himself superior to those who might be models. McGovern too falls short, and shows how anyone "right" can still fail. There is very little about politics that is artistic.

Still on the edge of politics, Warren can sound easily hurt and child-like as he runs from one tough "line" to another: he is Butch Cassidy in, "I even tried to rope in Marlon, but he's so far out politically, he thinks the elections are a lot of bullshit"; he is Michael Corleone in, "You need organisation in politics, and I'm a good organiser. McGovern needed visibility, and he needed money, and we supplied him with both." But he is himself, spot on, in:

> "You drop everything to work for a guy who was *zero* a year ago and immediately you're doing it for publicity. These Washington writers feel guilty because they want to make it with Raquel Welch, so they take it out on us. I could have made $1.5 million this year, but I felt it was important to spend the time working for McGovern."

Beatty works as hard in 1984 for Gary Hart. It is not that he gives up or shelves movie considerations this time. He can never do that entirely. Film associates get used to him being interrupted by political phone calls. They wonder if anyone can control so many diverse things, or whether Beatty can be as earnest as he says he is about their picture project when he is apparently promising the time not just to a candidate but to the president that candidate wishes to become. Does Beatty know he has another loser in Hart? Does he count on it, or is he organising his life so that time is filled and nothing is ever done?

He does not appear in public for Gary Hart. The political concert has largely died away by 1984. But he is closer to the center of the campaign. For in 1972 there are times when Beatty may out-argue Hart, the manager, on how McGovern should be presented. Hart is never as much of a hero. He is the man who has Beatty's advice, and it is sometimes fiercer, quicker and more ruthless than Hart's nature. People who see them together in private situations say that Hart is in awe of Beatty, ready to be directed by him. They say Beatty is not always willing to be impressed by Hart. Beatty helps shape the campaign, the speeches and the issues. As late as the party convention, in San Francisco, he is in attendance as an official delegate, and he has written the drafts of speeches for Hart if he wins or loses. No one else in San Francisco believes Hart can win, but Beatty works on two speeches. He has come close to making a winner out of Hart. For Mondale's defeat by Reagan is always more likely than Hart's. In person, and by phone, Beatty is never out of Hart's decision-making process, and never as exhausted as Hart. He is defining a role for himself as power-broker, and he works decently for Mondale when he has the nomination, to ensure that the Party is not offended.

He would be 51 in 1988, 63 in the year 2000 and still only 71 (the age at which Reagan had his first year as president) in 2008. What will the country want then, and what will government entail? Suppose that by

The icon and the candidate: Clint Eastwood in *Pale Rider*, and in Carmel, California, running for mayor

1990, Beatty has made two more substantial movies – in the sense that they make him a great deal of money, and bring him prestige. Suppose he could somehow find a role that earned him our love? Suppose then that he ran for office in California – the Senate, the governorship? Then by 2000 he might be at least as plausible a candidate as Ronald Reagan ever was.

But there are liabilities. Crowds boo him, and the public regards him at best with coolness and an amused envy. His life has already accumulated love affairs that any opponent could present in a scandalous light. He would have to defend himself in public, be open to bitter, unfair, unreasonable questioning, whereas he has always preferred not to explain or justify, not even to speak much or appear. Any political campaign exposes the candidate to tedium, fatigue and triviality in a way he might not be able to stomach. He has always made use of secrecy in his life, whereas a major political figure must go in terror of being discovered and must master or own that generosity, a sheer openness of spirit and disposition that can let itself be seen and pictured and smile through the years with warmth and vitality. It is a look that too much intelligence can kill.

He may be too thoughtful, too restless, too private a sensibility to run for office, and too easily bored to ensure administration. Buck Henry has said, " 'Easygoing' is not a quality he has. You know how presidents age in office? If Beatty was president, either he would be dead after the first year or the country would be dead, because his attention to detail is maniacal."

And, of course, we hope that presidents are constitutionally opposed to death, whether theirs or America's.

Is it the closeness to politics, or just the irresistible force of flirtation that makes him say it?

This is 1974, and he is being interviewed by Joan Dew for *Redbook*. It has to be near the end of their time together, the thing she has been wondering whether to ask.

"What do you have anxieties about?" It may be the quietest thing on her recorder.

He pauses; she believes he is groping for a reply.

"I don't usually like to reveal those," he tells her.

Nothing can stop her now: the lines are carrying her into her dream movie. *She* is talking to *him*. "Why not?" It's loud now. "It would make you more human." Maybe *she* is the rescue she imagines.

This is when he says it. It has to be straight to the camera, as clearly the end as Tuesday Weld saying "Why not?" in *Play It As It Lays*. It is the line of a self-observing campaigner perhaps, breathtakingly dreadful.

"But I have no need to seem more human."

It is a line like handing someone a rattlesnake, until you see the harm the snake must have done while the person waited to hand it away. Waited years, perhaps.

Desert stop

"Perhaps here," said Clear. He spoke calmly, preferring to leave no eyelash of query in the seared sheen of the late afternoon. He was lost, but he knew the need for assurance in uneasy times, and his kindness wanted them to regard it as a group decision.

"Couple of hours to sunset still," complained Chuck.

"Why not stop and enjoy this light?" said Beau.

Look settled it. She lounged out of the camper and discovered that her hums, her giggles and any snatch of song came back at her, small and clear, from the ruffled wall of mountain nearby, its umber holding up in the blue smokiness of time of day.

This mountain was not deniable, yet it looked like creased silk dropped down from the sky. In the desert, the density of reality flattens into theory. And the clarity of light and the belated reach of every scratching sound is hallucinatory. D did feel he could walk up to the mountain and stroke its surface, yet he understood it was miles away. He could imagine he was the figure in a diagram in a physics book. He could see them being an exemplary society here. He noticed he had a hard on – an unaccountable rising, like something you find when waking from a dream – and so he promenaded for a spell into the emptiness until it woke and diminished.

"Taking a leak?" he heard Chuck's call. There was impatience in it, a first rip of panic. "Got to get that organised. Define our foul territory."

"Oh, really?" D sang back at him, noticing that he might not be suited to such rules. "Where should I go then?"

"Back of those mesquite trees?" guessed Chuck after lengthy deliberation. "You see a sidewinder, piss in its eye." D heard Chuck snort with mirth. "Don't miss, now, or it'll freshen up your pecker."

D examined every poised dead twig, every twist of gray leaf, every agonised stem, for glistening scales that might move if he unzipped. But his cock felt happy in the sun: it had always been the one tanned part of his body, the colour of Lena Horne, he thought. He let his gentle arc

328

reach out to the desert and the sunset; it sparkled above its tracer shadow on the dune. What could it matter? He saw a Kodak packet in the mesquite, blanched but recognisable.

They were somewhere in the northern end of Death Valley, where it comes up to the Nevada border. Their tinny noise of camp-making seemed fake and craven in the bed of silence. It was easy to believe they were not fully there, that the "there" was a vast fossil spectacle and they were people at a museum observing it. Though supplied with atmospheric heat, their "there" was a sheltered dome in the immensity. The stillness had already impressed D, as if a kind of nothingness that had always waited inside him was growing in the fantastic sun. The heat was beyond sweat or discomfort, he was already thinking of himself as mere air in it, his body discarded and dry as a snake's skin.

"A particularly desolate area," murmured Doc. "Known for its absence."

"Apparently," said D. He heard it.

"I was out here several years ago on a Foreign Legion pic," Doc was telling him. "Scotty's Castle must be somewhere out there. Then, beyond that, it's the Last Chance range. Fifty miles or so and not one soul or construction."

"Could we go there?" D felt the urge.

Doc weighed it: "With enough water we might."

"The empty quarter," said D.

"Eureka Valley, Slate Ridge, Deep Spring Lake. Nothing else. A hole on the map the size of an apple."

"And Eyes might have a place up there, a stronghold?"

"It's what he'd like us to think," said Doc. "But what kind of stronghold could you muster up there? How are you going to bring the strength in? Without it being noticed?"

"He might reside in a simple hut."

"Or a ghost town. Might have been mining hereabouts once. Or people who tried some prospecting."

The dusk drew in rapidly and the temperature fell away with a silent scream in which they heard the wind at the bottom of a saucepan. The vehicles made a circle. There was a scrappy mesquite fire, bitter in the air and burning too quickly in the night breeze. They tossed cardboard boxes on the fire; their panels floated on the hot air before sinking and melting.

Chuck was gloomy. "We can't go on like this."

"What do we do, great scout?" said Drew.

Chuck stared into the disappearing fire. "I hope that damn Eyes shows up."

"Don't doubt it," said Clear. "We should try to sleep."

"Anyone care to cuddle with me?" they heard Look's voice in the dark. "Just for practicality purposes."

"Sure," said someone in the dark, a voice no one quite recognised. But they were too enclosed in worry and too cold to wonder at it.

And Chuck helped them all to sleep with, "Don't we have to stretch something round the camp to keep off snakes?" They hesitated in the doubt. "I thought we did," he added wistfully.

"That's the moat," said Doc. "I did it."

"Right," said D. "We took a dip in it."

"Sure," said Doc. "Being in the desert is a holiday."

In the morning, no one had slept better than Look. "I had terrific dreams," she told them, "like fresh French fries." There was a honeymoon glow to her that surprised their faded faces.

"What a kid!" Cy laughed. "I'm in love with her."

And after their uncooked breakfast, and the decision to stay where they were for the day, Cy Lighthiser asked D and Doc to accompany him on a walk – to explore, he said, a direction that looked promising. They walked for a mile during which no landmark came closer, but the broken surface of the ground exhausted them.

"Let's sit," said Cy, pointing to a group of boulders. And so the three of them had a conference out there in Death Valley.

"What I have been thinking," said Cy, "is that our Eyes seems less and less likely to make a picture, and even less likely to say, no, he won't make a picture."

"At his age, a false move could be fatal," said Doc.

"Hysterical," said Cy, without warmth. "How are you guys on Chuck?"

"Low," they said together. They had always hoped someone would ask.

"Strictly visually," said Cy.

"He is like Eyes," said D. "I have a shock whenever I look at him."

"Correction," said Cy. "A lot like Eyes was. Which is better. Because who knows how he looks now?"

"You do wonder," D offered.

"When flesh goes, it rushes," Cy assured them. "Jayne Mansfield went in one summer." He still regretted that.

"So?" Doc could see it coming.

Cy looked from D to Doc, and back again. "Suppose Chuck makes the picture."

"What picture?"

"D's script," said Cy, amazed it took so long to get a breakthrough concept across. "It needs a polish – we've got Doc. We go with Chuck as the guy who shoots the president – Chuck is stranger than Eyes, anyway. And I like this Look for the actress."

"You'd bill Chuck as Eyes?" asked Doc.

"Why not? We can make it work. The guy shouldn't talk too much, right," Cy looked at D. "I like a silent assassin. We photograph Chuck OK, we can get a brooding quality. It'll be in the desert a lot of it, narrow eyes, heavy tan, wild hair, funky. I get excited talking about it."

"And Eyes?" asked Doc.

"We make a good enough box office, my guess is he doesn't say a word. He goes with it – sees the joke, Or," Cy had just thought of this, "he lies low, waiting to see if it's a conspiracy."

"What about Claudia?" Doc remembered. "She isn't going to be the actress?"

"I know, I know. I get to be the traitor. But I tell you, and it's heartache saying it, Claudia is bouncing her marbles on a hard floor. In which case she isn't going to look good."

"Maybe old D could write in another part," Doc was grinning in his foxy way. "I'd polish it, of course."

"Well," said D, cautiously.

"You could?" asked Cy. "The Eyes part could have a very sexy let's-say-forty therapist? A lot of ways that could be better for Claudia. She's still good at the rueful wisdom thing. Jeanne Moreauish. Our best chance with Chuck, I'd say, is steamy scenes." He looked at D directly, as one asks a mechanic what time this afternoon it'll be ready. "Can he fuck the aunt?"

"Tell me, Cy," said Doc. "Does this constitute an offer, this little chat?"

"Listen," said Cy, "we're a long way from where we can do reliable business. I haven't got a secretary out here, not even a copying machine. I just wanted to pitch the idea. You two don't like it – I'm an idiot. Tell me. I'll think again."

"I did take money," said D, "and sign a contract."

"Kid," said Cy, "this is the desert, and for all we know it's the end of the world. New rules. The survivor adapts the quickest."

"That's what Chuck says," said Doc.

"But he seems depressed," D pointed out.

"He's not swimming in the moat," said Doc, and D nodded.

"What is this moat?" asked Cy, scratching at a bite on his arm.

"Moat's at the castle," said D. "Where else?"

The sun cranked higher and their new life in the desert wilted in its gaze. Drew and Look lay beneath the camper in its oily shade, listening to the vehicle stretch in the sun.

"Anything happen to you last night?" asked Look.

"Not a thing."

"I thought you and D were an item?"

"He's a married man." Creak, crack. "What about you?"

Look sounded dreamy. "I thought I got off on the most sensational fuck last night."

"You thought?"

"I must have had a fever."

Some distance away, Clear was consulting with Zale and Tusk.

"Nothing on the radio," said Zale.

"What does that mean?" Clear wanted to know.

"That civilisation as we grasp it is kaput?" suggested Tusk. "That the quake took out LA and everything else?"

"It could be temporary," said Clear.

"You want the radio to put out a bulletin saying no, this is really the end?"

"That would help," admitted Clear.

"He has a point," said Zale to Tusk. "If we knew for sure that the Constitution was in suspension, so to speak, then there are powers we could assume."

"Like what?" asked Tusk.

"Like we could pick a leader and write out rules. Define sexual liberties and shoot enemies."

"What would Eyes do?" Clear wondered aloud.

"Where is he?" asked Tusk. "I have documents waiting for his signature."

"Documents, my friend," Clear lamented.

"Don't knock documents," Tusk told him.

And in the afternoon, when they had been there nearly a day, Doc said to D, "Maybe we should go look for Scotty's Castle."

"Do you know which way?"

Doc nodded up the valley.

"How far?"

332

"Probably too far, but I'm getting blue here."

"Listening to Cy's ideas?"

"That was a good story he had."

"You think we should do it?"

"No, not that. But I've been thinking about it as a story about a guy who takes over some star or tycoon who is not immediately present."

"Like Hughes and Clifford Irving?"

"Perhaps," said Doc; he was searching still. "Could make a nice role for Eyes."

"A fake who might be real?" D saw it in an instant.

"Right," said Doc. "Someone who gets hired to impersonate a lost millionaire because he looks like him —"

"And then wonders if he might not be him," D was excited again.

"You could have a scene," said Doc, "where he discovers that the guy's old shoes fit him."

"Or his spectacles," said D.

"Oh," groaned Doc. "That's lovely."

And the two of them, at twilight, slipped out of the camp with only a plastic bottle of spring water, a box of wheat thins and this new idea.

PARALLAX VIEW

The Parallax View aches with a loneliness and mistrust that the film cannot release or escape. It is, on the surface, a paranoid thriller about American politics in which a vagrant reporter discovers and then opposes a mysterious corporate force that assassinates promising presidential candidates. The film is not "about" Lee Harvey Oswald and the Kennedy killing, as those who make it are at pains to protest. Yet it would not have been imagined or made without that event or the ferment of unease that follows the hurry of the Warren Commission to explain what it is that happens in Dallas on November 22, 1963. The picture opens only six weeks before the resignation of Richard Nixon, yet it does poorly at the box office, no matter that it is frightening, well-acted and "spooky" in the way of greater successes and similar pictures made by its director, Alan J. Pakula, *Klute* and *All the President's Men*.

In Seattle, at a reception high up on the Space Needle, a Senator Carroll is shot and killed. The movie's flurry of murder shows us two men with guns, one of whom falls from the Needle moments after the assassination. The investigative commission says this man was the killer, and that he acted alone. A few years later, Lee Carter (Paula Prentiss), a television reporter present at the killing seeks out Joe Frady, a newspaper reporter of far lower status. Indeed, just prior to the killing, we have seen Frady attempt to gain entry to the reception by saying he is "with" Lee Carter. But she pauses, looks him in the eye, and denies it. We guess that some time before they have had an affair, and that she feels he let her down. And now, when she comes looking for him, Frady is with a much younger girl; her visit seems to have interrupted their love-making. Frady grins to himself at the bad luck of the world. The sullen girl trails away.

Lee tells Frady that witnesses to the Carroll killing have themselves been murdered. He says only a few have died, and they just died; there's no conspiracy. But she brings news of a death he hasn't heard of; and then a little later she dies herself. Frady is not in good standing with his

334

own editor, Edgar Rintels (Hume Cronyn) – he has had a drinking problem, apparently dealt with, but he has still to "curb your talent for creative irresponsibility". He is a loner and a reckless journalist who employs stunts to find his material.

Frady begins to investigate on his own, and as he finds more deaths and the existence of the Parallax Corporation, which seems to be hiring misfits and preparing them as assassins, so Rintels backs his campaign. Frady is nearly killed himself in the death of Austin Tucker, Senator Carroll's campaign manager, and when he returns from that mission he tells Rintels, "Print my obituary – I'm dead." He goes undercover, takes on a new identity and poses as an outcast to penetrate Parallax. He lives in a room in a rooming house, cooking ineptly on a hot plate. He is accepted by Parallax. But only because the Corporation is on to him. They kill Rintels. And then in a second major shooting, that of a Senator Hammond, they manage to frame Frady as the killer. The film ends on a freeze frame, as Frady runs from the area where the killing occurred, into a blast of gunfire. Another tribunal intones the verdict that Frady killed Hammond, that he was a lone agent.

Warren Beatty is Joe Frady. *The Parallax View* is not his production and yet it is known that he involves himself a good deal in the rewriting of the script, and that he has serious if constructive arguments with Alan Pakula over the film. It is also the first picture he makes after his experience on the McGovern campaign of 1972. Which makes it more significant that the movie has a dread of politics, power and the vulnerability of its America being manipulated. And while this fault can only be located in the film, it is plain that Beatty's presence as an actor is serving to pull the film in opposite directions, first to raise and then to deny a fascinating potential which leaves *The Parallax View* the most substantial failure in which he has yet been involved.

This is still in his time of supreme beauty. There is a close-up in the scene where Lee Carter discovers Frady with the sulky teenager, his face washed in morning light, with just a spoiled puff in his cheeks and a tired smile on his face, of confession turning into pride, that is among the most ravishing he will ever allow the camera. But the picture gives him no relationships, and after the death of Lee Carter there is not another grown woman in sight. The loveliness is stranded by the story, but it cannot quite sustain the proposition of Frady's dark solitude, his lack of success, and the picture is goaded into doing something about this anomaly. It has to admit to the angel's aura.

Thus, on one of his early investigations, Frady goes into a bar in a country town in the north-west. The sheriff and his deputy are sitting there telling stories. Two waitresses are with them, and both of them are instantly attracted by Frady. One of them, Gail, goes up to him at the bar.

"What can I fix you?" she asks him.

"I –"

"How about a martini?" she jumps in on a Beatty hesitation, eager to occupy his inner spaces. "You know what they say about martinis? They say that martini is like a woman's breast." She curls up inside, to draw him into the punch line. "One ain't enough and three is too many."

She chuckles and he tells her, dryly, that it is an amazing joke and he settles for a glass of milk.

At this point, the deputy comes up to the bar, looking to dispose of this glorious male stranger.

"Can I buy you a drink, miss?"

Frady sighs: he, too, has seen this movie scene too many times before. The bar is nothing but folklore, the place where anecdote occurs.

A big young guy, the deputy plugs on: "You know, for a moment I thought you were a man. But you aren't, are you?"

"No, I'm a, I'm a girl," Frady answers quietly.

"Why don't you go right over there and tell those people that, real loud?"

The deputy puts his hand on Frady's arm, and Beatty says, "Don't touch me unless you love me."

There is then a complicated, fancy fight: it is, really, the only extended physical struggle Beatty has ever had in his films, and he is not easy in it, no matter that he wins. Nor, later, does he seem convinced, fluent or eloquent when he has to run to jump on a truck to make an escape. His clothes seem tight, his spirit tighter. As an actor, he would always rather sit still, listen and talk a little, using his bland milk to mask a daring sexual speculation. No one can doubt he is fit; he was a footballer in college. But he appears reluctant to show strain, and he has none of the natural joy in prowess that marks Wayne, Gable, Cagney or so many other male stars. Sometimes he seems too shy even to move; as still as a watcher, his power is in his recessiveness.

The fight is one of several scenes in *The Parallax View* meant to provide action, but going nowhere and only serving to build up Frady as a conventional hero when the actor cast in the part has urges to take it elsewhere. There is this ponderous fist-fight, a battle to survive in a river, a car chase, and so on. There is, later, an elaborate sequence on a

In *The Parallax View*

plane where Frady realises there is a bomb aboard and wonders how to alert the crew without drawing attention to himself. Only there is the action properly addressed to Beatty's fastidious character as an actor: for he is trapped; he has to be casual and unobtrusive. There is even a moment in which he writes a soaped message on the restroom mirror, opens the door to find another customer waiting outside, goes in again and wipes away all trace of the message, that shivers with the weird neurosis that does not want to be seen or caught in a bathroom. It is a glimpse of a Frady we do not get enough of, as playful and paranoid as the lovely, visionary line: "Don't touch me unless you love me".

It is not that we are seeing a homosexual here, but a chameleon, someone who has grasped the encyclopedic range in acting and is therefore within touching distance of playing a person who is disintegrating. *The Parallax View* sets Frady up as a failure, and then has him masquerade as a psychopathic outsider. But it never challenges us, or Beatty, with that prospect. Quite simply, the film says he is pretending to get into Parallax; that he is by then so provably robust that we trust him and are "with" him. But the picture is cold, grim and distant, in awe of its own series of plots. We do not feel for Frady. Beatty's own inability to give of himself, to come out with the energy to win our love, has defeated the simple purpose of suspense or melodrama. We neither care about his loss, nor believe that the world of the film can be saved. *The Parallax View* is a totalitarian theorem that serenely proves itself, killing people and shutting out hope, amiability or untidiness. It is high on its own cool, sinister air. It is surely made by decent, liberal people, but it has the dead calm and elegance of fascist design.

The picture cries out for less of its irrelevant, unfelt action, and more of Frady's neglected intricacy. We need to examine his recklessness: there should be a threat of craziness in it. And we need more than the hint Lee Carter throws off in "As long as you were there", when Frady chides her suspiciousness, "You were always scared a guy might come up and attack you in bed." And it forsakes the richest ambiguity to have Frady seek advice on how to answer Parallax questions in order to qualify. There might have been a different film, a film always circling around Frady's inner life, his alienation from others and his absorption in a sheltering, reassuring imagination in which he *knows* already how to respond to the remarks we see on the Parallax personality inventory, because the shy eyes, looking out, discover themselves there:

"I am often frightened when I wake up in the middle of the night.

I am at my best in large groups.
Sometimes strange men follow me.
I have never vomited blood.
I would like to be an actor.
I can't understand why I have been so irritable and touchy.
Someone is out to get me.
My father would hate me if I got into trouble with the law.
I like to win when I play games.
I never liked school.
I want people to remember me when I'm gone.
I have never cried.
My friends always end up double-crossing me."

If we feel that person there is no need for the questionnaire or for the academic explanation that it is meant to draw out anger, repression, frustration and violence. Suppose, instead, that we have a fired reporter working on his own, living alone, masquerading as a personality type he is so close to being that he may pick up the rifle, unaware.

That would be like *Taxi Driver*, in that it would be a movie about a man of a certain kind of warped goodness driven to kill, for love and to be remembered when he is gone. It would be claustrophobic, dangerous, disturbing; it would endanger Warren Beatty's image, and it would be a commercial failure. But *The Parallax View* did not do well, anyway.

And if we saw, from within, the subterranean life of this Frady, then the movie would not need its very provocative but absolutely digressive sequence in which Frady has to watch a short film of potent images during which his responses are measured. It is the questionnaire made more vivid: key words like ME, LOVE, HOME, FATHER, MOTHER, COUNTRY, GOD, ENEMY, HAPPINESS in a montage of familiar pictures – a happy couple, children, old age, babies, mother and child, fatherhood, a still from *Shane*, baseball player, idyllic home, apple pie, cornfields, Thanksgiving, Statue of Liberty, Mount Rushmore, Lincoln, a church, Hitler, Mao Tse-tung, Castro, whiskey, red meat, and so on.

These are the clichés of Americana, a storyboard for Lee Harvey Oswald – and for Kennedy, too – and the variable ingredients of political advertising. Again, Beatty did not make the picture, or compose this sequence. But he lent himself to it, and to the overall Hollywood vision of politics as a popular spectacle directed by malign, faceless men whose desire it is to have control and to manipulate a gullible public.

We are not told what Parallax is for, though the suggestion is that it is of the Right. It could be the Left, or it could be a movement interested in power for power's sake. The picture of America arrived at by the movie is of a country propelled by imagery, largely unaware of small but crucial criminal sections that actually determine events. As such, it is so devoid of hope that it cannot find people who live or show any sign of optimism, independence or departure from this set pattern. It is politically despairing, but actually drawn to the mechanics of control that may be bringing America closer to totalitarianism. The two senators who are killed are resplendent but hollow creatures – TV figments (one is Jim Davis, soon to be in *Dallas*) who repeat homilies or are cut down in the rehearsal for their "spontaneous" triumph. It is bad enough that they are assassinated; but it is worse perhaps that they have not deserved to be elected. There is a way in which they are dead already. And that slackness gives silent support to the sinister effectiveness of Parallax. If these stooge candidates do not merit office, it makes them more deserving of the bullet.

Melodrama is so paranoid: suspense movies have plots into which every detail should fit. There is no life outside the dread, and no rationalism brave enough to overcome its power. And there is a polarity in the spiral of paranoia in which to be heroic you must be either President or the killer. Nothing else works. If America has had all its ordinariness stifled by cliché, then it is less a country and a people eager to be guided than communicative controls that wait to be possessed.

If *The Parallax View* disappoints, it is worth touching on some problems in its making. Director-producer Alan J. Pakula knows that he has to start shooting without a "ready" script. More work needs to be done. But Beatty has and insists on a pay-or-play deal, so shooting has to commence. As it goes along, the actor contributes many good ideas to the picture. But there is a control, a shape, never possible if it is not there early enough. Pakula has to impose some of the shape in the editing room, and so the mysteriousness of the film is compounded by the pressures of production.

Pakula is exasperated with Warren. When the film opens modestly, the star calls the producer, nagging him about its numbers. Eventually, Pakula has to tell Beatty that if he's concerned he should get out and do publicity for the picture. If not, then Pakula would rather not have his relentless calls.

But charm does not accept defeat. A few years later, Pakula has a sure hit, *All the President's Men*, and there is a party for its opening. When the director arrives, Warren is there, lounging in the doorway, shy and grinning, aloof but appealing. "So who do you like the most," he asks, "Redford, Hoffman or me?" And, as Pakula acknowledges, hard feelings dissolve with that smile.

But if *Parallax* had more of this mixture?

Scotty's Castle

They had kept up a steady pace through the night in the kind of unspoken agreement they treasured. And whose mind does not sometimes sway to treasure in the desert?

They did not walk at one another's side, but took turns in single file, leading and following. Five steps apart, the one behind could see the silver puffs of dust at the other's feet, disappearing in the moonlight. Their feet crunched on the cold shale and grit of the desert floor. If D closed his eyes he could imagine they were polar journeyers packing down the snow. He assumed they had fallen into a rhythm of walking, unaware, in one another's footprints, indifferent to the cold compress of their sweat. One night like this can be the perpetual bond for a significant friendship. Whatever minor professional rivalries there may have been before between D and Doc, whatever irritation in the latter at the former's rawness, they were by dawn like the last brothers on Earth.

They sat down in the first twinges of light as the sun loomed up again, the Valley's old dragon. This was the moment to be breakfasting, in air like an English Spring. They could smell the renewal amid all the mustiness of the desert. Miles away, like a parenthesis, a hawk cruised in the air, planning a quadratic equation. They saw their first snake, a fluid fucking diagonal, a muscle of Ss, making it's speedy way across the ground to hiding. It came close to them. Its oval eye went past like a non-stop train, a blind eye. And the two men felt suddenly sure that snakes did not think about men.

"We should find the Castle today," said D.

"If I'm not a buffoon," Doc reminded him.

"I have every confidence."

"I appreciate that," said Doc, snapping a wheat thin in two to prolong breakfast's glow.

They rested twenty minutes; it was already warm and pink when they started again. D was sure that if they went another full day in such heat and found nothing they would die. But he was not concerned about it.

The water slopped against the sides of the plastic bottle. It was a third down already. Neither of them said anything about estimates or limits. It was taken for granted they were going on. Realising that self-destruction was in prospect, D wondered about Drew's warnings of madness. But when he looked at Doc's face he saw only the calm eyes of one without worry. He hoped to hell he would not have to be so stupid as to ruin this bond by remarking on it.

Then Doc said, "This is the life," looking at the bland distance; it was nothing to do with them; they were like men admiring the fine brushwork in an Old Master. The desert was a classic, a fundament of their culture, a climate that would wear away their tragedies as it smoothed stones and snakes.

"You tell the first story," said D. It was so apparent that they would keep talk going as they made their way.

"I like Scotty's story," Doc told him.

"The man who built the Castle?" said D.

"Didn't build it," Doc explained. "There's the beauty of it. Walter Scott, that was his name; he was born in the 1870s in Kentucky."

"He was not a Westerner?"

"Only by inclination," Doc was smiling as he paced along, seeing the shape of the story. It was like watching a young creature take its first steps. "He worked for a time with Buffalo Bill's Wild West Show."

"He was a cowboy?" D wondered.

"I doubt it. The advertising and promotion part of the business."

"Which is what that business is," D added.

"Exactly. Which is fine. Anyway, some time early in this century, Scotty comes out to Death Valley and goes in for prospecting. I don't believe he ever found so much as a lost ring. But, because promotion was his calling, his character, he was good at having it thought that he had found gold."

D chuckled. So fearfully honest himself – dull, nearly, some say – he was warmed by the thought of an inventive fraud.

"He said he had a mine here in the Valley," Doc continued. "He said it was one hell of a mine, and he got some people to put up a little money. He told 'em he required it for equipment – which was encouraging."

"Then what did he do?"

"I'm telling you. Then he'd go to some town and spend that money, spend it in a showy way. So what did people think?"

"That he's rich. He must have struck gold!"

"And then they were lining up to give him more money!"

Road scene, Death Valley

D clapped his hands. "And there was nothing at the heart of it all!"

"Nothing but Scotty's native inventiveness," said Doc. "And then there was this rich man, Albert Johnson. He came West to convalesce after some serious illness. But what made him better was Scotty's company."

"Scotty told him tall tales," D surmised.

"He couldn't look at his breakfast without building it into a romance. And Albert, I suspect, was a dry stick. But he constructed this house in the Valley. The Castle. Where we're going, I hope."

"Scotty's Castle?"

"Except that Albert paid for it. But Scotty —"

"Said it was his," guessed D.

"Yes, sir," said Doc. "And they were grand friends. I don't mind telling you now," he added, "that I have always reckoned Scotty as a role for Eyes — whimsical, a charmer, a yarner, a tease, a will of the wisp, but an American. It was after I mentioned the project to Eyes himself that he got this hankering to live in the desert. He's a deadly researcher, you see."

"Know what you could do?" D was looking ahead. "You could have Eyes play Albert, too."

344

Doc went on another five steps before he stopped and turned. "In the same picture?"

D had to come to a halt. Doc's gaze was so demanding. "Right. Two roles."

Doc looked up at the blue sky, battered and beaten, without a cloud. "Jesus," he said. "That's it. That's singin' in the rain."

"The rogue and the recluse," said D.

Doc was grinning all over his face, "The story-teller and the sickly rich man."

"Don't you like it?" asked D.

"I'm having an orgasm over it. And no split-screen nonsense."

"Certainly not," D assured him.

"Just the two men watching one another in the cutting."

"So Eyes could do it comfortably."

"He'd be in his element. Always able to consider himself in another role."

"It's a fine plan."

"Well, it's yours," Doc told him.

"But I couldn't do it without you."

Doc considered this. "Have to do it together, then."

And each smiled at his portion of the far sandy distance, pretending to wince in the glare. The desert has these facilities. Though it may be a barbaric environment, still it can polish old souls.

Towards noon, without premonition or indication, they came round an outcrop and found before them a dell, a glade in the desert valley, a tidy flourish of trees surrounding a castle – there was no question in D's mind – so flagrantly designed that it had parts in diverse styles, the medieval fortress and the Spanish hacienda, the courtyard and the battlements. It looked an ingenious gathering of castellated sets where adventure serials might be shot. D looked to see if there was even the eagle of the old Republic perched on a turret.

"Not quite how I recall it," said Doc.

"Is there a choice of castles in Death Valley?" D asked him.

Doc was judging. "No, there's the wishing well."

He pointed at a low stone wall in the courtyard with a wooden arch. The timid fountain was dribbling out a little water. As they came closer they saw coins in the pool, shimmering, a little larger and cleaner than life.

The castle was abandoned. The café and the ticket office were closed, but the notice saying the Castle was open to visitors every day had not begun to fade. Looking through the windows of the gift shop, between the credit card decals, D could see souvenirs lined up on the shelves with the packets of film, the dark glasses and the candy.

"Door to the house is open," he heard Doc's call across the courtyard. There was excitement in his voice. The mood and its echo made it easy to appreciate the beguiling vacation place the castle might have been once. D went up to the door and saw a Packard saloon, 30s vintage, silent and dusty in the covered shade. He entered the house, on red tiles, with beams above and heavy Spanish furniture, in leather and brocade, where ranchers could rest up with the blinds down. There were leather curtains and small waterfalls to cool the air. Death Valley was 125 degrees in summer. The castle would not have been worth a nickel without its siesta mercy, a place where buddies could doze, with lemonade and an unread book on their laps.

The two men made their way about the house, marvelling here and there – at the pipe organ upstairs, at the thick yellow and green chinaware in the dining room and the plates with curled lips (for serving, said Johnson; from the heat, Scotty answered). They could hear the slow measure of such old repartee, lugubrious jokes and the amazed laugh of a rich man who had eluded death. They saw the white shirts, the sombreros and the row of red ties in the wardrobe in Scotty's room.

"What a country," murmured Doc, "when a man can wear red ties and be set up for life."

There was fresh food in the kitchen, with wine in the refrigerator. All the power was working. Whatever stroke had afflicted the land, Scotty's Castle had its own generator – there was an engine within the fake part of the castle – and it was still in touch with whatever source it had, the snow in the Sierras, the heat in the ground, or the spirit of two friends braving out the furnace days.

D and Doc fed a little and then they found a bedroom each and succumbed to the great force of the afternoon. They rested. They promised to meet again at dinner: they had no plans beyond that and a pink salmon in the icebox waiting for them, as firm and piquant as an untold story. And there were lemons they had found to squeeze on it as it broiled.

The room that D took himself to had a canopy bed. He was cautious, letting himself down on the coverlet; he thought it might be a museum bed, with only chips of styrofoam beneath the embroidered cover. But he felt a different kind of substance, and when he drew back the heavy drape material he found an unmade bed – tousled sheets, one sock and a pair of women's panties, pale chocolate in colour. The pillows were crushed from recent heads and there was a smear of lipstick on one of them. Moreover, D could feel a good-natured wildness in the bed that bespoke a college co-ed's room rather than this antique place of companionship. There was a sneaky whiff of sex, and when D lay down, he saw, close to his face, a coarse black hair in the shape of a comma.

He studied the beams in the ceiling, and the stucco walls. He let his gaze slip from one portrait to another, framed black-and-white photographs of women early in the century, in white, buttoned up at the neck, their hair bound in on itself like turbans. These must be beloveds of Johnson and Scotty, women still tense at having their pictures taken, or warding off Scotty's relentless comedies.

D's tired head lolled for a moment so that he saw, on the table beside the bed, a pair of spectacles with fine steel rims. They were not folded, but put down as taken from the head. He could see the lower moons of bi-focals, and then he was slowly impressed that in the upper, inner quarters of the lenses, there were still the fine, pinhead bubbles of perspiration, as if these glasses had been very lately worn, out in the sun, and only just set down by someone who had come in for a merited snooze. The glasses were as fresh (and every bit as up-to-date) as the salmon in the kitchen.

At which unnerving realisation, D heard steps in the corridor outside, the light flicker of a barefoot child – at most a slender young woman – making her way in familiar premises. The person was singing, "I Can't Give You Anything But Love"; the voice could have been a girl's or a woman's. D sat up. The breezy intrusion was coming his way. The door's ajar widened and a rippling young thing came in. She stopped in mid-stride, on the brink of singing "Baby", seeing a stranger in the bed.

"V!" cried D, a little less the finder than found.

"It's Virginia, now, Dad," she said, as if somehow the bed he was struggling on explained the enrichment.

347

SHAMPOO

In the early 1970s, he has been entertaining more and more ventures. As well as *McCabe and Mrs Miller* and *The Parallax View*, he has made a picture called simply *$*, written and directed by Richard Brooks, with Goldie Hawn as his co-star. It is another "caper" film, opening at Christmas 1971, in which he plays Joe Collins, a supposed security expert who becomes the thief of safe deposit boxes in Hamburg. Hawn plays Dawn Divine, a hooker who was once a showgirl in Las Vegas. There is a suspenseful scene in a bank vault, and a prolonged chase across ice. It is light and forgettable, a picture remarkable in this composed and brooding career for having been made at all. Gary Arnold, in the *Washington Post*, calls it sour, disorganised and dismally facetious. Beatty, he says, remains cute, "but is wasting his and our time (when he read the screenplay, didn't it occur to him that it was *Kaleidoscope* all over again, only worse?)."

He ponders many other proposals – to be in *Ryan's Daughter*, for David Lean, but in which part? – the Christopher Jones role, the young officer and lover, or Robert Mitchum's, the sad husband? He is at that in-between age. He does not make *The Adventurers*; a Yugoslav actor, Bekim Fehmiu, takes the part that Beatty probably never considers seriously. He declines to play the man Marlon Brando will be in *Last Tango in Paris* – and here we cannot fail to notice, hypothetically, the more dangerous commitment of which Brando is capable on screen, the depth and pain of his voice and the nakedness of self-revelation. Beatty in *Last Tango* could hardly sustain the defenselessness of its bare, empty apartment affair without names. He could not live up to its desperation. He is never a man that Francis Bacon would paint – David Hockney perhaps?

And he thinks about and rejects four roles that will become the body of Robert Redford's screen career – *Butch Cassidy and the Sundance Kid*, *The Sting*, *The Way We Were* and *The Great Gatsby*. On *The Sundance Kid*, he says he "didn't feel much like getting on a horse and riding around". But he has been interested earlier, when Polanski is in sight as a director and Elvis Presley is to be Sundance to his Butch. It is Presley, apparently, who rejects this opportunity. *The Sting* never impresses Beatty; the man in *The Way We Were* strikes him as apathetic; as for *Gatsby*, he delays, he asks to renegotiate, and the project lumbers on, leaving Beatty with this communiqué: "As an artist it wasn't something I felt I needed to do at this time." But, in fact, at another time, he has thought of producing *Gatsby* and having the producer, Robert Evans, as his Jay. Beatty may be the one actor in town who feels the charm of that role, but sees what a handsome nothing it is.

One can see Beatty in all these Redford roles: he could be the wary eyes in Sundance, watching the jazzy smoke rings of Paul Newman's talk; he could be the con man in *The Sting* who might be about to double cross the picture; he would inhabit the brittle Hollywood success in *The Way We Were* and the disappointment of promise that lacks stamina or the strength to face difficulty; as for Gatsby, he is a character who anticipates the narcissistic hollowness of just about every young Hollywood sensation.

He is entering other ideas and situations, just as enticing, but more immediate. In 1970, in London, at a dinner for Polanski, "Warren's gaze descended on" Britt Ekland. She has need of a new affair to detach herself from Patrick, Lord Lichfield; and she falls in love with Warren. They make love in her bed-sitter, and fall asleep exhausted.

She has to travel to Los Angeles: she has been invited to appear on Dean Martin's television show. He follows her: that is to say, Warren follows her, not Dean, follows her to Los Angeles. "I missed you a hell of a lot, Britt," it is said he says. They live in his suite at the Beverly Wilshire, sunbathing naked on the terrace, with Warren going inside occasionally to make a call. He worries that Julie Christie will find out; he tells Britt he is worrying about this. "But I guess that's one of the gambles we're gonna have to take."

They go to see a pornographic movie; they sit in its dark unnoticed. Afterwards, Britt says she was bored by it: "I will never make a porno film unless it's for real and only with you," she tells him. He laughs and says maybe they should bring in a camera crew to film their activities in the penthouse.

There are other names mentioned – Maya Plisetskaya, once a ballerina with the Bolshoi and twelve years older than Warren; Brooke Hayward, the daughter of Margaret Sullavan and briefly the wife of Dennis Hopper; Joni Mitchell, Liv Ullmann, Carly Simon – does she write

"You're So Vain" about him? It is the point of the song, its great rejoinder, that he is left wondering. And Lana Wood, Natalie's sister, becomes briefly his lover when he lets her live at his Wilshire suite when she is broke and down on her luck. "Warren is a passionate and inventive lover," she writes, "a curator of women. . . . Whatever his motives were, Warren helped to restore me, gave me shelter and some of my self-esteem back and for that I remain grateful."

His romancing has become not just a topic in the press, but a climatic constant for America that can be alluded to at any time without explanation. It is proverbial, which must make the real thing that much more elusive. It is like wondering what "they" think in Peoria, or when the first snows will fall in New England. Outlandish names and prospects are put next to Beatty's name – Princess Margaret, Jacqueline Onassis. One would not be caught off guard by a picture of Warren with Mother Teresa and a nudging caption that says, "Yes, she's human too!" For this legendary Warren could melt ice and eroticise all women just by looking at them, even if he was without his glasses at that moment. His seductiveness is helpless; it is a force of public need and faith that requires so little action from him, and which so lends itself to his caution and his indolence, that just a sigh could seem to suggest a touching. He has become a wind on open fantasies – there may be women sure he secretly ravished them when all he did was look at them once across a table or brush their cheek with a goodbye kiss in a crowded salon. "And he never even said hallo."

And he entertains a movie about this infinite capacity, a talent and a suggestiveness that are almost indistinguishable from the nature of film itself. For hasn't Warren Beatty's looking at women from the screen (without ever seeing them) become almost the same as contemplating them at a party, the image a little blurred perhaps because it is all in passing and he *is* short-sighted? One promise in his love is that he wants you to come very close so that he can really see you; he manages to make seeing seem a function of the whole skin, not just the eyes.

This film begins very soon after *Bonnie and Clyde*. Beatty rents a London house on South Audley Street, and Robert Towne is his guest there. They talk of a script that Towne might write for Warren, instead of one to re-write. A few years earlier, Towne has written an episode for the television show *Breaking Point*, "So Many Pretty Girls, So Little Time", which is about the dilemma of a womaniser. At the Chichester Festival Theatre in England, Towne and Beatty see a revival of the Wycherly play, *The Country Wife*, starring Maggie Smith as a woman seduced by a rake named Horner who deflects her husband's suspicions by pretending to be homosexual. These influences gather in a script Towne writes about a Beverly Hills hairdresser who has many women in his life. Its first working title is *Hair*, but between 1967 and 1975 that is taken by another venture.

The first script is 220 pages: it has two large female parts, but Beatty says he wants only one. According to Towne: "He was very angry about it, and I was very angry about his being angry about it, because I thought the script was really pretty terrific. For a period of about six months we hardly spoke, and the project was put aside for several years. It was like two brothers quarreling. I don't know anybody who's a bigger prick, but there's no one I love or admire more."

The project languishes, and then suddenly comes to life again, in 1974. Towne moves into the Beverly Wilshire with director Hal Ashby for an eight-day blitz. He discovers that, in the meantime, Beatty has himself written another draft of the script. Eventually, the two men share the writing credit and the stand in a trial when a woman says that the picture has plagiarised her 29-page treatment, *Women Plus*, which she has sent to Columbia in 1971. Moreover, the jury finds for her, until the judge throws out the verdict and is sustained by the California Supreme Court. The picture is *Shampoo*: it is Beatty's second production and, when it is released by Columbia, it will be a huge hit, with $22 million in rentals on its first release.

Shampoo covers a little more than a day in the life of George Roundy, the star of a hairdressing salon, who is trying to open his own business. He lives with Jill (Goldie Hawn), but in the time the movie covers he betrays her with a client Felicia (Lee Grant), with Felicia's daughter (Carrie Fisher) and with Felicia's husband's mistress, Jackie (Julie Christie). There is a moment when George seeks to reassure Jackie's lover, Lester (Jack Warden), by acting fey that is the single reference to *The Country Wife*. It comes when George has just done Jackie's hair for an Election Day party (this is November 4, 1968), and so transformed her that they make love, only to be interrupted by Lester. And Lester is straightforward enough to believe that women are not drawn to gays, and that strong men like himself need not feel threatened by them.

The film might more boldly have made George bisexual, or at least erotically appealing to everyone. That aside, its great insight is to see how far the Beverly Hills hairdresser is a servant who may have more power, knowledge and intimacy than lovers or tycoons. For he conjures appearance: when George softens and enhances Jackie for the party,

351

when he lifts her out of weary, common attractiveness into beauty, it is the greatest gift that movies or LA know. It is the generosity that could seduce anyone there – the accurate understanding of how they might be beautiful. There is a story told that one day Natalie Wood sees Leslie Caron at a party at the time of the Caron–Beatty affair. Isn't Leslie looking unusually lovely? people say. Warren, Wood replies, as if Caron has made herself look better for him, or as if he has willed and summoned it, been the mirror in which she reappraises herself. And surely Natalie has felt the same light lift her face, and seen her own radiance in the mirror. This is not just cosmetics; it is only grace that makes people feel better about themselves.

Body servants in Los Angeles are a priesthood: they know the stars and the star-lorn yearning in others, and they may have the power to make the person anew as well as the opportunity to hear their confessions. Such intimate attention to the flesh may easily prompt sotto voce revelations; the artist is only a few inches away from the ear and the mouth. There is a scene in *The Roman Spring of Mrs Stone* where Beatty's Paolo reveals himself to his barber. It is a clue that the best insight into Beatty might come, not from his women, but from Robert Jiras, his valued make-up man on several pictures.

Shampoo is a lucid moral disaster, with resemblances to comedy of confusion: it is funny, and it is bathed in the painless light of southern California and the downy glow of bodies better cared for than any in human history. But it is always on the edge of melancholy, as if it knew the horror of aging and decay. Its ambiguity grows out of the very level way in which so many characters are seen. No one is rejected, or seen as without faults. Lester is foolish and vulgar, but he is kindly and open-minded. Felicia is rapacious and selfish, but she believes in lust. Jill is superficial and Jackie opportunistic, yet the film steers away from condemning them. It regards such frailties as everyday things. Like a Jean Renoir picture, it never loses sight of the sound reasons we all have for what we do. But the picture does finally sink into George's pity. For while it is a comedy, still its central character has no humor about what he does. He is a philanderer – yet somehow he is hiding from his own promiscuity, saying it is only liberty. He wants to think well of himself; he longs for some Roundy of his own who will make him morally lovely and unimpeachable.

The election night party is a fiasco. George's betrayals all come to the surface when, at the dinner table, the tipsy but discerning Jackie tells the world she would like to suck George's cock. (Yet isn't even that what *he* would like, no matter that he has the performing instinct to look embarrassed by the confession?) Late at night, George is seen fucking Jackie – Beatty's bare ass on top of Julie Christie in the gloom. He loses everyone, and he rushes here and there, having to run and look stupid again, in the strobe light of a very Bel Air 60s party, Don Juan out of breath.

Next morning, he has his last scene with Jill. She has gone off at the party with another man who offers her a new life. She comes back to the apartment she has been sharing with George. It is a scene that, in script and preparation, Beatty must know is not just his big moment in the picture, but *his* scene. In rendering it for the page, a book must admit failure. It is not just that we are without the droop of Beatty's head and his chronic physical efforts to withdraw from the scene and its place, to fade out, as it were. It is that, as well as speaking he makes sounds. They are the moans and primal creakings of misery, of inarticulateness, of having to be honest when he is a poseur, of the knowledge that in words he will start lying again, not speaking but wooing, so eager to be liked he does not know what he thinks. The sounds are the edges of his voice; they come from behind his nose. They are very moving. They are the sounds that must have seduced a mother once, let alone adult lovers. They are beyond words, they are the naked creature. They amount to extraordinary performance, and yet they are a nakedness that cringes from being seen. They are the scream of someone too shy or proud to ask for help. They are called "noises" here.

JILL: I don't want to fight, George.
GEORGE: I don't want to fight, either. Look, er, I'm sorry. (This is said with boyish vigor, the shallow wish to be simple and direct, to look everyone in the eye, and to get the scene over with quickly.)
JILL: Bullshit.
GEORGE: *noise* Why didn't he come in?
JILL: Because I didn't want him to.
GEORGE: Well, I hope he doesn't mind me being here. (Be sorry for him.) Did you get a job out of it, at least? (And if you're not sorry, he'll jab you.)
JILL: I'd like you to leave now. And take this with you. (*She throws a small piece of female jewelry on the floor. He picks it up.*)
GEORGE: Where'd that come from?
JILL: Who knows? I'm sure you don't. But if it'll help any, I found it in your bed. Obviously there were others. Weren't there?
GEORGE: Obviously.
JILL: How many?
GEORGE: What do you want to know for? (A fending off that is also seductive: don't you want to know?)

353

In *Shampoo*

JILL: Because I want to know. (*She has to leave him: She will always think the way his mind works.*)

GEORGE: What difference does it make?

JILL: Because . . . I don't want girls looking at me and knowing, and me not knowing. No, it'll help me, really. It'll help me if you tell me. (*Yet the film is not essentially concerned for Jill.*)

GEORGE: How?

JILL: Because I'll know that you've lied to me all along, and I'll know that you're incapable of love.

GEORGE: *sighs* If it'll do any good. I, I just, you know, like, I, I . . . You really want to know?

JILL: Yes.

GEORGE: *sighs* There were a couple . . . I mean there *noises, sighs* Let's face it, I mean, that's what I do. *noises* That's why I went to beauty school. I mean, they were always there and I keep, I just, I – I – I *noise* You know, I, I, I don't know what I'm apologising for. *sighs* I go into that shop and they're so great looking, you know. And I, I'm doing their hair, and they feel great, and they smell great. Or I could be out on the street, you know, and I could just stop at a stop light, or go into an elevator, or, I . . . there's a beautiful girl. I, I, I don't know . . . I mean, that's it. I, it makes my day. Makes me feel like I'm gonna live forever. And, as far as I'm concerned, with what I'd like to have done at this point in my life, I know I should have accomplished more. But I've got no regrets. I mean, gee, because . . . I mean. *noises* Aaagh! *sighs* Maybe that means I don't love 'em. Maybe it means I don't love you. I don't know. Nobody's going to tell me I don't like 'em very much.

It is a riveting scene, but one better for a biography than for the film. For, in truth, it says what we have already gathered about George, and it takes away from *Shampoo* being about a group of liars, connivers and appealing fakes. It takes away from the place, the light and the froth of the title to have one character on the analyst's table, and so available for pity. There seems to me in the speech and its uncanny playing to be the instinct that the fault is not the speaker's, but a condition that has made him the victim. He is drawing the dilemma into himself, making it private, after we have seen his shortcomings clearly in a social sense. But if he can inhale it – there, behind the nose – it becomes his burden, not his failure.

Shampoo is a very good film, and very rare from Hollywood in that it is more about Los Angeles than it is a reworking of habitual movie genres. It is the second film to exhibit a brilliant, bold, self-obsessed producer; and it shows how in American film the producer can be the artist. Yet *Shampoo* might end more challengingly if it had a vision other than the producer's, or one that could be colder in looking at him. It might end more challengingly if the forlorn George was cheered up by the film's most frightening character, the Carrie Fisher part, in a blunt, unadorned, unalleviated scene of sexual excess, a home movie of them getting it on, with her sucking George's ankle and Warren's faraway face watching, nearly deserted.

V

His daughter's coming in so casually and happily had altered the room; it had shifted from being a composed monument, normally open to the public's hushed, "don't touch" inspection, to a motel cabin. V, Virginia, inched open the top drawer in a chest D had taken for solidity – time cast as walnut – and retrieved a packet of gum.

"Well," she said, perching her small self on the end of the bed and slipping an oblong wafer in her mouth.

"Virginia?" he wanted to be sure.

"I know," she groaned. "Eyes says it makes him think of England."

"He . . . he christened you?"

It was the first time his daughter had assessed the process. "He said he couldn't keep track of me in his head as V."

"I didn't know you were friends."

"Oh, yeah. You see, Dad, he thought that might upset you."

"How long have you, er, known him?"

"Don't *do* that," she grinned. "Since you were doing that script. He thought you'd feel uncomfortable if you were possibly writing it for Eyes and I."

"Eyes and me," D told her, and a flush of thunder swept across Virginia's face.

"Right, right," she dismissed it. "Anyway." Her eyes rolled at voices ranting in her head over dads' silliness.

"And you were telling him about the script? Reading scenes?"

She shrugged, "I thought you'd be pleased. Think how many scriptwriters wouldn't mind having their kid in the sack with Eyes."

"You are intimate with him?"

"He's not a pervert, you know."

"And you are – "

"Nineteen," she piped in, "in case you've forgotten."

"I've not forgotten," said D. How swiftly relatives could put one askew. "I remember quite clearly."

357

"Oh," she pondered. "I thought, you know, you'd been busy."

D smiled modestly at this understatement. "I have been through a lot," he admitted. "I am lucky even to be here." He wanted to say she was fortunate to have him still.

"You were with *them*, though," said Virginia.

"With them?"

"Clear and the gang." Then Virginia grinned, and D could see the ball of gum, rosy and salacious in her mouth. "And that Drew et cetera . . ." And as he made to speak, she dropped in one more "et cetera" and let the gum expand in front of her mouth, like a kiss in a nuclear blast. It popped and the tension faded.

"Anyway, Dad," she was conciliatory. "I think that's nice for you. My old Dad."

D didn't know how to respond. He could see a long line of lies ahead of him that might end in tyranny or running a movie company.

"I was stupid," he said.

"Listen," she told him.

"Yes?"

"What?"

"I was to listen?"

"Yeah? Oh, yeah. Well . . ." The chewing seemed to be what was interrupting thought in his daughter's head. But D saw that it was really the old thing, the difficulty of thoughts. Virginia gave it up. "Just be nice," she said.

"Is that your motto?"

"It sure is." Virginia nodded soberly, as if hand-on-heart issues were involved here. "I mean, you have to be loving."

"That's what Eyes says?"

"I'll tell you, Dad," she wriggled further forward, giving up her lotus position, levering on the cheeks of her bottom so that the old bed squeaked. "He is a very tender guy."

"I'm glad to hear that."

"Actors, you know," she explained. "They really see into people."

Especially those in the mirror, he was inclined to say, but he was learning to wait out the homilies of the young. She might surprise him. Sooner or later, everyone did. He had not dreamed she could be so calm or stoical, so far ahead of any possibility he had thought of for her. No, it was always D being caught unsuspecting. He was the idiot of the piece.

"You don't have any knicks there, do you?" she nodded at the bed.

"Chocolate colored?"

"Right. Eyes got 'em at Victoria's Secret." Her voice fluttered at the memory and D waited for insights into the fitting. But none came, so he fished behind him for the scrap of rumpled silk. How close he had come to sniffing their worn odor when he was alone.

Virginia took them, jumped off the bed and shimmied into them, drawing them up under her Navajo skirt.

"You gotta wear them," she passed it on. "Because of the snakes."

"Ah," said the father, relieved that he had made his peace with those reptiles. "Are there many in the desert?"

Virginia thought about it. "How many would many be?"

He shrugged. "Enough for you to take precautions."

"Oh, yeah. Enough for that. You see, Dad, what you have to face is there's no back-up now."

"No?"

"You get a snake bite there's no hospital, no flying doctor with the serum. It's curtains. Eyes says this is year zero."

"Aha," said D, recognising the political potential of a good caption. "Yes, that does clarify one's thinking."

"Does it ever. And you really have to carry a gun, whatever your feelings on the subject."

"To shoot a snake?" That tiny eye and the head not much larger. Slithering past. It would take genius.

"Uhn-uhn," she told him. "Survivalists."

"What are they?"

"People who live in the desert in new communities. They've been here since long ago, long before the disaster."

"Survivalists," he repeated the name.

"They're killers," she told him. "Shoot first. Don't ever get talking to them. They are so crazy you can't reason with them."

"You have a gun?" D asked her.

"Sure. It's outside in the basket on my cycle."

"You don't live here then?"

"No, this is Eyes' weekend place. He has the real base north. I rode over. It's great biking in the desert, and what it does for your body."

"I can see," D conceded with pride and true enjoyment for her innocent firmness.

"You gotta try it."

"It's a long time since I've cycled."

"In the desert it's a cinch."

"So," said D. "Eyes is to the north."

"Toxic Flat. The seat of government."

"He must be very busy?"

"Well," she considered, "no, there's not a lot to do. I thought he might even be here."

"These spectacles," D pointed to the table.

"Yep, that's him. He's gone off. Maybe he heard you and it frightened him away."

"I don't think I would frighten anyone."

"Oh, he's very timid." Her gum was losing its flavour, and she was looking for somewhere polite to dump it. "He broods. It's a load, you know."

"The seat of government?" D supposed.

His daughter looked at him. "Yeah, that too, I suppose." Then she made up her mind. "Listen, can you keep a secret?"

"Did I ever say anything about my time in espionage?"

Virginia's jaw stopped. Her eyes widened. "Fuck, no! That's aces."

"You begin to comprehend the nature of my secrecy."

"I'll say! What did you do?"

"How can I say more?"

"Oh," she was dashed, but respectful. "That's all gone now, I suppose, in the disaster. No structure."

"It'll be back."

"You think so?"

"Don't you imagine we are prepared for things like disaster?"

"You'd have to be, I suppose. God." It was sinking in, like evening watering in a bed of roses. Then she whispered, "How truly thrilling." D wished it could be true as well, but he took his small pleasures when he could.

"What secret?" he reminded her.

"Well," it was lovely for D to see his child having to organise a story: he knew no higher measure of civilisation. Was it really disaster if the instinct grew back to describe it?

"Well," she tried again. "You know Eyes has a reputation."

"He is a celebrated movie star."

"I know, but a rep, too."

"Romantically?"

"As a lover supremo. Well, some time ago he got a letter from the Smithsonian asking if they could have his . . ."

"Yes?"

His daughter blushed. He wished he had a picture of her, or could freeze her embarrassed heat and all the room and have it forever. "His splendid member," she said. "The scepter of his authority."

"They wanted that?" D had imagined the nose, but Virginia's eyes were looking sharply down and sideways, like a man in a skit about urinals.

"Look, they've got Archie Bunker's chair and Kareem's goggles. Julia Child's apple pie dish. Trademarks. Americana."

"Still," said D.

"He felt honored. He said it would be the first part of him established in Washington."

"They wanted it now?"

"Of course not, stupid." Virginia sighed that fathers could be so crass. "When the time comes – if it does. But they wanted to do the measurements and so on, so they'd have a nice satin case for it. Well, he had a deal going at that time and he couldn't go. If you leave LA they think you're bored."

"So?"

"So he FedEx'd it."

"It comes off?"

"You would be amazed what it does."

"So must the ladies be."

"You bet!"

D thought about the most delicate phrasing of his next question. "He's everything he's said to be?"

"It's like TV, I tell you."

"Ah," D's imagination raced. "And it comes off?"

"He's so far ahead of his time," said Virginia. "It's another entire level of consciousness. You see, Dad, most of you guys are just over-attached to your things."

"I know I am," D said, to be agreeable.

"Right. So he sent it."

"Don't say it got lost." D tried to remember the insurable limits on Federal Express.

"Worse."

"Damaged!"

She spoke very slowly and clearly: it was the punch line. "He thinks they sent back the wrong one."

"It doesn't fit?" D couldn't help but wonder whose Eyes might have acquired.

"As far as I'm concerned," said Virginia, "it's as pretty as ever, and no one I've talked to can detect a difference you could put your finger on."

"There's a group? A club?"

"Yeah, it's nice. Like a society. We talk on the phone."

"And does it perform . . . in the way it did?"

"Wondrous," said Virginia, full of honest admiration for older people.

"Still," D could see it, "he's suspicious."

"He is and he isn't. Sometimes he's sure it's his, but then other days he starts to wonder if it's a practical joke. It's occurred to him it could be bugged."

"He must need a great deal of reassurance."

"Well, men do, you know. No offense, Dad."

"Of course not. I feel proud that you can . . . cope with such rare problems."

"We all of us have to grow up fast now. That's the thing."

"True," D thought, "yet there's still a slower process that should be allowed to persevere."

"Yeah?" Virginia took the gum from her mouth and stuck it on her left elbow. "Seen Mom?"

"Not since – when was it? She wasn't at home when I called by."

"She's here. Up north. She's doing real well."

"That's wonderful. How did she get here?"

"Eyes arranged it."

"I am even further in his debt."

"Oh," she dismissed it awkwardly, for the young are so fearful of having done well. "What do you think is going to happen?"

"I really don't know. I expect we'll all be together again soon."

"I mean with the world." She made him feel dull and commonplace.

"Ah yes, the world. Well," he hoped to be broad in his view. "I daresay we can make a life in the desert."

"I suppose so," said Virginia. "But can we make movies? You gotta have the population base for real pictures. Otherwise they end up private art things."

D was saved from having to contemplate the future of the media by questioning calls from the courtyard. He left the room and bumped into a drowsy Doc in the hall.

"My daughter Virginia," he said.

"No kidding? How are you, Virginia?"

"I'm great, thanks."

And so into the sunlight where they found Drew and Look counting the coins in the wishing well.

V

"Hi," said Drew. "Know what we did? We followed your tracks. It works. You have any water?"

"We were going to drink this pool," said Look.

"How about a salmon dinner?" Doc suggested.

"Here?" Drew was amazed.

"With all the trimmings," D added.

"That's Eyes's salmon, you know," Virginia pointed out.

"This is my daughter," D explained.

"I'd have known," said Drew. "Same foxy look." And D was so happy to feel Virginia's slender arm slip into his. "Eyes would want us to have the salmon," she had made up her mind.

"Oh, that Eyes," said slypuss Drew, reading the whole picture there in the dazzle. Who says we need crowds or the dark for the picture show?

A PATTERN EVOLVING

As he grows older, he begins to seem youthful. But he has no children to play with. And as he puts more of his time and energy into money, business and calculation, so he explores a screen image that is impulsive and open, a man of good, rather innocent intentions, an inept idealist with never the time, or coolness, to get everything in order. His face stretches, to accommodate widening eyes; it is as if he is talking a lot to the young, and inhaling their naivety.

There is a flutter after *Shampoo*, the wake of his sexual prestige in which, the media assume, millions of women bob like corks. It is the start of an automatic reference to him that the press can make. But it comes from a picture of Beatty's own doing, in which he tempts the belief that the character on screen *is* the actor. At the same time, he cannot endure or dispense with this legend of Don Juan.

Not long after the film opens, he agrees to appear at a forum at a high school in New York where the subject is to be the treatment of women in films. Molly Haskell, the critic, is leading the forum. She is the author of a book on the treatment of women in film, *From Reverence to Rape*; she is also a native of Richmond, Virginia. She recalls that, as she is introducing the panelists, he leans over and polishes his spectacles on the tail of her jacket. This is done so everyone can see.

It irritates the audience, already prepared to be critical of Beatty. Yet he charms them by a policy of direct attack – yes, he says, he knows their view that Hollywood does bad scripts, but he sees the scripts that ordinary people submit and they are worse by far. He beguiles the audience, and at the end of the forum women flock round him. Next day, he telephones Haskell to apologise, in case his gesture with his glasses was misunderstood. She says she thinks she got the message.

"There does seem to be a pattern evolving," he says in March 1975, in

Boston to promote *Shampoo* and receive the Harvard Hasty Pudding Award. "It's very hard for me to play a guy who is a Superman. It just embarrasses me. I think it's funny. I guess I prefer to play men who are very stuffed-up, like a blowfish. I don't do it consciously but, it's funny, because, if I looked back on things that I've done, especially things that I've written, they are similar people. The guy in *McCabe*, for example was so full of b.s. and puffed-up that, when he gets into a situation where the heavy starts negotiating him down, he goes down, down, down. The guy is very timid. I mean, it would be very hard for me to play *High Noon*."

He has another film that opens in May 1975, *The Fortune*, to date the last picture in which he has simply acted. No one will understand why it is a failure, for it has two of the most attractive stars of the 1970s, Beatty and Jack Nicholson, playing inefficient confidence tricksters who do all they can to dispose of a young heiress. The partnership seems natural and fitting, for the two are friends and admirers, and there is the same streak of fatalistic, sardonic intelligence in the two of them as they partake of the same limelight. It is part of their modern hipness that they can suggest the attention is faintly ridiculous. This is the sort of wry kinship dictators must feel as they regard one another across oceans and purges.

Jack and Warren have been introduced by Jules Feiffer, somewhere in the area of Vancouver, when *Carnal Knowledge* is on location only a few miles away from *McCabe and Mrs Miller*. As the two actors approach one another, Nicholson, grinning and acting up, looks up at a Beatty who is five or six inches taller than he is, whistles, and says, "Now, *that's* what a movie star's supposed to look like." Feiffer witnesses instant mutual infatuation: Beatty is not averse to being teased, and Nicholson likes a tall straight man. A Chief to prowl around. Of course, the infatuation is etched with rivalry, as if each man knows and is saying to himself, "Well now, look here, this is the other good guy, and it's a damn good thing I think I'm going to like him, because otherwise I might have to kill him, and that could be a situation inclined to lead to my own death." They are both very keen to be natural fellows; but they cannot help but talk to one another in a script that their heads have been working out in advance. They are two bums who will try to be a little shabbier than the other; and they are skyscrapers hobnobbing as best they can.

The Fortune is written for them by Adrien Joyce. They are Nicky and Oscar – Nicky an aging dude with such combed back, greased down hair, and such a tidy, stuck-on mustache that, for the first time, Beatty looks

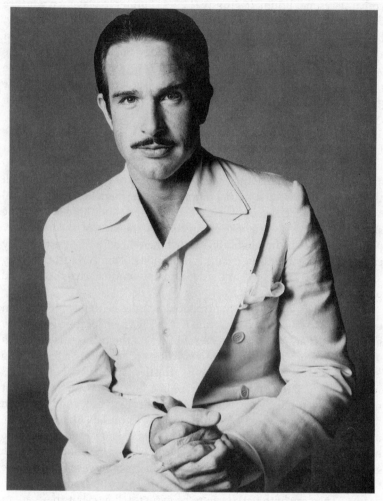

In *The Fortune*

Howard Hughes in 1947

like Howard Hughes; and Oscar, an untidy little scruffbag of a man, with a bald dome and wings of electric hair. Nicky has married the heiress (Stockard Channing) to get her money, and Oscar is suspicious. As the story develops, they become a ménage à trois, the men regularly confounded in their efforts to kill the woman and inherit from her.

The film is directed by Mike Nichols; it has a pleasing, cute air of the 1920s. The dialogue is pointed, and Beatty has been encouraged to rattle out such lines as "This is purely a love proposition between her and I, kiddo." Stockard Channing gives an engaging, funny performance, but a first fault may lie in her casting. For we do not feel that she has a sexual power over either man, or that she is capable of a craziness that overawes them. Until shortly before production, Beatty has been seeing and reading a young improvisational comedienne, Robin Menken. There might have been a restless queen bee center of sensuality and imperious unpredictability with her in the picture, a kind of danger.

As it is, Beatty allows Nicholson to steal our attention, or has to watch it happening, helplessly. Next to Jack, he looks suspicious, tense and almost constipated. The one rogue is loveable, and the other is outside our attention. In labelled comedy, Nicholson is so much surer of himself than Beatty, and the script or the actor does not seem quite ready enough to let Nicky be a properly vain idiot. Beatty does not have a free part of himself loose enough to put beside Nicholson's lazy, randy mercury. So he becomes clumsy fingers trying to pick it up. He often looks like a stooge, and the film allows him none of those pauses or those occasions for hurt noises in which he can become a center for pathos.

Jack and Warren also have Michelle Phillips in common. After her divorce from John Phillips and the break-up of the singing group the Mamas and the Papas, and after a short marriage to Dennis Hopper, Phillips lives with Nicholson for a time in the early 70s. She moves on from that to a relationship with Beatty sufficient to persuade him to inhabit the Mulholland Drive house he has owned for a few years but never really owned up to or taken possession of. He lives there with Michelle and her young daughter, China, and there is again talk that he may marry. He sometimes drives China to school. But he keeps his suite at the Beverly Wilshire, and if he sometimes confesses his awareness of growing older and feeling more sedate, no one close to him ever knows what other contacts have been cut off, or which flower in the dark. He will build himself a house on Mulholland Drive, but if a girl supposes this is an urge to settle he can murmur that he must, because the Beverly Wilshire addition has given other guests a view of his balcony.

In the audience, with Michelle Phillips, at the 1975 Hasty Pudding Man of the Year Award

How do such uneasy associations end? Warren is not in the habit of sitting women down and telling them that he is bored or depressed with them, that their laughs or their bodies have run their course for him, that stagnation is taking away his larger optimism with life and making him disagreeable, that he is seeing someone else so this is over. He is too kind for that, or too afraid, for it is not simply kindness to let the tedious party notice the fresh excitement that some novel party has aroused in endless Warren.

"The truth is," he says, "that whenever a relationship has ended, the decision has never been mine; it's always been the other person's." We could deduce from that that Julie Christie has come to her own wilful decision that it is time for her to move on, that she has found someone else – that Warren is left, just as George, in a purely technical sense, is "left" at the end of *Shampoo*. But suppose that Christie was driven to that end out of self-protection, from so many hints of other affairs and out of eventual fury at the delicate manipulativeness that wants always to see itself in the right, and not unkind?

The fury may not always last. Many of the associations never quite end, so much as drift. When old girl friends pass through town, then old habits pass through Warren: it flatters them and helps him sustain the thought that he was not brutal. Friendship is a fine and extensive thing, but it can be a veil to the ugly shifts in life that leave us older and wounded. Friendship can be another word for unchallenged promiscuity, a synonym even for disloyalty.

There are some hurt. A few years after the relationship with Michelle Phillips ends, she speaks out: "He feels that marriage isn't a happy, productive way of life. He prefers not to be involved. He prefers shallow, meaningless relationships – he thinks they're healthier, or at least the only kind he can have."

He would hardly accept that portrait in quite such cold lucidity. Yet he is aware of the rootlessness, fascinated by it and horrified: he sees George Roundy's sickness but he cannot spoil the guy's glamor. He has to argue this out in his own head – can a woman fuck him and still feel decent? Can he be Warren and survive the mirror?

He decides he is not suited to marriage and its ties. But he has such high, vague ambitions to be significant in America – and how can a president, say, seem, rootless? The manipulative mind sorts through the problem and begins to conceive of a notion of "maturity" that is free but committed to reason, liberalism and purpose. He spells it out sometimes, and it is as close as he comes to sounding stupid or crazy:

"One way to describe maturity is to say it could be the capacity to postpone gratification. And when someone with my particular history has not been asked to postpone certain gratification – and I'm not speaking just of sexual gratification – it's impossible not to sense that you might be cheated out of maturity. And I try not to get cheated out of that."

Women hover in the air, like projects; and like projects, they can be given wings with the telephone. Beatty is especially occupied with the thought that he might act in *Hardcore*. This is a screenplay by Paul Schrader, the author of *Taxi Driver*, about a Michigan businessman, a strict Calvinist, whose teenage daughter goes missing on a Church trip to California and who becomes an actress in pornographic movies.

Some time later in 1975, Beatty announces his interest in playing this role. He talks of directing the picture himself, or of hiring Arthur Penn. Schrader has himself been set to direct originally, but he defers to the wishes of so big a star in what is regarded as a difficult picture. He rewrites the script for Warren. According to Schrader, Beatty

"wanted the daughter to be a wife because he didn't feel he was the appropriate age to be a father – which is a very typical actor's fantasy. I went on one of those Warren Beatty shifts – it was two hours a day every day for a month. He was living in the Beverly Wilshire. I did not find it a very rewarding experience, though it was a very educational one. He set in motion a series of changes which, ultimately, to my mind, destroyed the script. A softening."

What Schrader discovers in Beatty is the prolonged, gradual, diffident, unyielding assertion of power:

"He will always win. If you have a particular disagreement with him, let's say on an artistic issue, you can sit and convince him for two hours and he will walk away from it and then one week later he will bring up the issue and you will convince him again. And this can go on for years. You get worn down. In the end you never really convince him. You help him to find what he has already decided. And he apparently derives great energy from this. Other people walk out of the room exhausted, and he walks out energised."

The softening of the script is not without benefits. Beatty, finally, will back off (in order to make his film about Howard Hughes, he says at the time), and Schrader resumes as director with George C. Scott playing the central role and with the woman being made a daughter again. But

Schrader keeps at least one scene from his days with Warren, a scene he allows that Beatty wrote and which mirrors his subtle ways of getting what he wants. It involves Jake Van Dorn talking to his designer about a display:

JAKE: Hmm. This all the display space you could get?
MARY: I tried to get more, but this is the limit. The De Vries line has the same area.
JAKE: What do you think of that shade of blue, Mary?
MARY: I like it, Mr Van Dorn.
JAKE: Don't you think it's a little . . . bright?
MARY: Not really. But if you want me to tone it down?
JAKE: I wouldn't hire a display designer if I didn't trust her taste. Maybe we could bring more of that shade in. Perhaps a panel?
MARY: No, that would be much too overpowering.
JAKE: Overpowering – that's the word I was looking for.
MARY: Mr Van Dorn, I've worked on this color scheme for weeks. I think it's just right.
JAKE: What do you call that shade?
MARY: Pavonine. It's the same shade as the fabric.
JAKE: Hmm-hmm. You still going with that fellow, that teacher over in Grand Valley?
MARY: Sam?
JAKE: Yeah. Nice guy. You don't want to lose him. Maybe we could take it *down* a little bit, it's such a –
MARY: Overpowering?
JAKE: Yeah.
MARY: OK, Mr Van Dorn, I think we could knock that pattern in blue a bit.
JAKE: Are you sure it's all right?
MARY: Yes, I think it'll look better.
JAKE: If you say so.

At least six months after Beatty has dropped out of *Hardcore*, Paul Schrader is at a party, talking to an actress. She says she is being considered for a part in a picture he has written; it is called *Hardcore*. Just a few days before, she has run into Beatty in the lobby of the Beverly Hills Hotel and he has asked her to read for the role of the woman – daughter, wife, whatever. "And apparently he read her," says Schrader, "whatever that entails. He discussed the role with her at length. To some degree you say it's just the machinations of Don Juan, but on another level it's a man who is a compulsive caster. And, if she had been totally right, maybe Warren would have picked up the phone and come back on *Hardcore*!"

Some years later, Beatty will be talking to another director with a project Beatty considers producing – when he is ready. The director says he risks losing actors and crew because of delays, but Beatty tells him, "I know what everybody's doing, and you're not going to lose anyone you wouldn't mind losing." This is a mind so full of reports, information and gossip, so much in control, so disposed to casting and arranging, that it may think it *is* the picture business. But there is a risk – that the game of casting takes over, and lets speculation dispel action.

He says, in 1976, that he will begin to make a movie about Howard Hughes. "I've been working on it for years," he discloses. "It seemed that the urgency of the project made the Schrader picture a more secondary priority." At the same time, he says it would be premature to suppose he is also about to re-make the 1941 picture, *Here Comes Mr Jordan*, about a boxer sent too soon to Heaven and allowed to return to life. "If you make that part of your story," he tells the *Los Angeles Times*, "you could be vastly incorrect." And he says he is thinking a lot about Hughes, about where he is and what a man of that stature is like, reclusive, in the desert somewhere or on the top floor of a luxury hotel, having a hand in the great affairs of the world, or simply existing, as an imagination.

Then, on April 5, 1976, Howard Hughes is reported dead, in the air, an hour out of Acapulco on the way to a hospital in Houston, a ninety-three-pound legend. One of his aides says that in the complex and scarcely plausible state of Hughes' business empire perhaps the mogul has had to die to establish that he was ever once legally alive.

Night desert

Not to disparage the salmon dinner they composed at Scotty's Castle, much less the deadpan amiability of Doc, or the entertaining conclave of whispering, spirit and conspiracy among Drew, Virginia and Look, still D had a hankering to be off, away for a while, in the capacious desert. He was moved by the prospect of its solitude and unobserved rites of mastery.

"Don't worry. We can be alone soon," Drew drawled as she passed his carved teak chair with salad. He must have been staring into his thoughts, gloomy with concentration.

Then Look asked him if he'd show her the house, at which Virginia recommended the organ, upstairs, and all of them fell about laughing. But they were soon dozing off the assault of their rich meal. There had been chocolate decadence waiting at the back of the ice-box, so heavy the wire shelf sagged beneath it.

When D awoke, there was no one to be seen. It was night yet it was warm with the day's heat gathered in the timbers and a scent of eucalyptus through the house. He went back to the bedroom where he had had his first rest, not sure why, until he found the note that Virginia had left him:

"I had to get back. I've taken Eyes' glasses. Look out for yourself with all these hot babes, Dad. Joking. Seeyasoon. V. I mean, Virginia."

The last stroke of the V soared like a tick. D was reminded of the note he had left in the city apartment, and he pictured it there still, unseen, paling as the crisis set in, relic of an earlier life and discarded cares.

In another bedroom, he found Doc and Look naked and sleeping on a bed, their arms tangled, their bodies turned to face each other. Doc was a stringy old athlete, and Look was like a ripe persimmon beside him. D did not breathe in the doorway, and he heard the tranquil creaking of their two minds in sleep. Doc made a sound and moved one leg: Look responded with a soporific moan, an opening in the air to accept his noise,

374

and her hip rolled in time with his, as if the two bodies were oiled by the sounds. It was like finding gorillas asleep in the jungle and realising that every snuffle was true to their existence. The sleeping brains were steaming fecund earth. The tiny amendments to silence soaked into the ground so that the two people might wake, not needing to speak, but amazed and refreshed by the complicity. D was happy for Doc and Look, and he saw nobility in his erection between them, standing like a guard dog.

D ventured out of the house into the courtyard. It was as hot as day-for-night; there were shadows on the ground, and none of the chill of other nights. It was like a night that Doc and Look might be dreaming, pumping it alive with their long, slow snores. He looked up and he saw Drew standing on top of a rocky outcrop. She waved to him; slivers of light ran down the tautness of her body.

"Climb up," she said. There was no need to shout.

He found a way, feeling the warmth baked into the stones and the smoothness of the surfaces. Drew was sitting on a broad slab, a table rock; and though it was night, she was sunbathing, her head tipped back to let her neck turn golden. She moved to kiss him and he smelled the lemon juice and herbs at her mouth, tarragon and thyme, as well as the nutty convection from the rock and her nakedness. She moved like a dolphin across the rock. He was driftwood beside her, a plaything in the waves, but he shut his eyes and found that she was water now and that he could ride along in her swell. Pressed against him, her fragrance spurted: there was chocolate on her breath, and a virulent fish in her armpits, the confidence she was a siren. She moved on him expertly and she was smiling above his pleasure – the smile was their moonlight – coaxing and timing it, like a mother powdering a child with affection after its bath. If only he could take such moments for what they were. But wherever he was, he looked further ahead, with dread or desire, and now he saw past Drew's bouncing immediacy and the artful love in what she did here, now, to a time of being bored, to guilt, horror and death, and to needing someone else, anyone, just to move on and stay alive.

"Frightened?" she asked. He could not stand the way she saw into his plans for thought.

"I'm the singer," said D. "Not much good at the song." It sounded like a quotation, but he didn't know where it had come from, or even what it meant.

She was just as perplexed, but more daunted. She backed away and sat up. "Do you think I'm beautiful?" she asked him suspiciously.

"Of course." He didn't see how she could worry over that.

She sounded bitter, or resentful. "We all want the beauty for ourselves." She had a stance; he had noticed it and loved it many times – of being erect and lonely, set in an empty space. It was desire filling the view of a single full shot. There were times when it filled his mind, like a picture on the wall. But the poise escaped her now, and Drew was left behind, shakier, like someone nearly struck in an accident.

"Movie people," she despaired. "Two or three parts every year for twenty years, maybe. Looking the same, but slipping along. Such a lot of lovely pretending, and never being tied to any dull you. But those rovers get scared too, sooner or later, and in the end they beg, 'Don't leave me.' Such leavers!"

"They sing to stop the quiet," said D.

She pulled on the large T-shirt she had brought with her. It was her nightshirt, the souvenir of some picture she had been on, a tube of white cotton emblazoned with a title, dripping in dead flames, some forgotten sensation.

They followed the ridge that circled Scotty's Castle and took a spur sloping down to the plain. Moonlight had brushed it clear of debris or coiled serpents. They were walking on a crushed velour, and they could see their footprints appearing soundlessly, with the raindrop circles of their toes.

"You think the air here is poisoned?" Drew asked him.

"The best I've known," he told her.

"That's not suspicious?"

"It's the lack of contamination," he said, but he wondered where the lemony hints and the salmon pink in her sex went in the night. Had they been the first womanly smells in this stretch of the dry desert?

"Or poison from the tests," Drew imagined. "In Nevada there are pieces of land sixty miles by sixty where you can't go."

D thought of Virginia cycling across them, leaving one closed zip of track to perplex the snakes.

She had a story: "Howard Hughes was in Nevada once, and very fearful for his well-being. He had given up sandwiches because where the bread met the mayo seemed a certain place for infection. Every item of his food came separately: the bread, the ham, the Swiss and his mustard."

"He liked mustard?"

"Adored it. All in airtight cellophane packets. And he had stopped seeing his business associates. He regarded friends as a source of tainting. He spoke to his people endlessly but on a phone that did not touch his skin. And he wore only new clothes that had been fumigated and kept in a vacuum. As far as he could, he existed in neutral – in air so clean it was barely air, in a life so sparse it was nearly coma."

"Yes?" D held his breath, trying not to blow away the gossamer Hughes.

"And then one day his chief physician called him and said, 'Oh, by the way, Howard, did you ever consider that sex and money are major contagion carriers?' There was a stricken silence. The doctor wondered if Howard was mortified, or might have passed out in panic. But then Howard coughed and said, 'Well, we all die – send in the next one.'"

They kept walking. D did not remark on the story, or question its likelihood. But Drew knew he was revolving in its spin. He could no more resist stories than some people can leave a last dry-roasted peanut in the jar. And if some stories were tall, D only felt more upright because of them.

"Going to write for Eyes?" she asked.

"It would mean security," he answered.

Drew laughed. "Whatever it brings you, it won't be that."

There must have been a look of innocence on D's face. It never goes – stupidity locks it in long after youth's shine wears off.

She was elaborating: "There was a writer once Eyes hired, a good enough writer. This was when I was in favor. There was such a time. But this writer and I had a little thing going, you see. Maybe it wasn't for any more reason than so Eyes could feel betrayed. And one night we were at the writer's cottage in Malibu. It was warm, and the beach doors were open. You could hear the waves. We were making love, very quietly and peacefully, when I saw the look on his face. The worst look I ever saw. He was staring over my shoulder. Know what? Eyes was screwing me from behind at the same time, so soft, so slinky, I hadn't noticed. And Eyes looked over my shoulder at the writer – they had a rhythm going, and I was just the space in the middle – and he said, 'Hi kid, how are my pages coming?'"

"You never felt Eyes entering you?"

She shook her head. "Try that on a girl's sensitivity."

They may have been a mile from the Castle. It is hard to be sure how far you are going when you talk. But they heard three shots, heavy as doors slamming, and then a woman's scream from the same direction. There was horror in the scream, a hopelessness that made them sure a mile was too far away to be of any avail or mercy. Then a second scream, years sadder than the first, full of woe and revulsion, as if some pain had eaten into the worm's rot of the scream itself. There was only one cure to that scream, and it was deafness.

"We have to go back," said Drew, and he answered yes, he knew, he had known that all along.

HEAVEN CAN WAIT

He is forty when he makes *Heaven Can Wait*, too young yet for the grim but ravaged face of Hughes. And this is a picture that one might use to pass the time while waiting for others that are weightier and which will test stamina to the limit. Of the films Beatty has made for himself, it is the least necessary and the most easily forgotten. Yet it will be his greatest financial hit and it is so slight and so frivolous on the one hand, and so momentous on the other, that it may mark a moment at which he wonders if he can get away with anything.

But suppose he can never be simply cocksure or cold-blooded. Suppose that in the misty, cloud-cuckoo muddle of *Heaven Can Wait* there is or was something that intrigues and moves Warren Beatty. Well, it is a picture about being dead and alive at the same time; about being forty but pretending to be the Los Angeles Rams' quarterback in the Superbowl, while also looking back on life from the sterile but perfect vantage of a white Heaven; and, not least, it is the first movie in which strenuous, nearly depleting efforts seem to have been made by Warren to deny, evade or transcend his real age. It has the kind of tender soft focus that in the 30s and 40s was used to reassure still lovely but cracking actresses.

Joe Pendleton, a health freak football player, is killed in a traffic accident just before the big game. On his way to Heaven, he establishes with his Escort (Buck Henry) and the Archangel Mr Jordan (James Mason) that he has been rounded up too early. It is an error in Heaven's book-keeping. They hurry Joe's soul back to LA, but his old body has already gone up in smoke. So they let him be Leo Farnsworth, instead, a millionaire lately murdered by his wife and secretary. It is akin to acting, which is the enclosure of an imagined spirit in an old body.

The story is framed as farce, and clumsy farce at that, but is that plot simply as contrived and absurd as farce is presumed to be? Or should we consider whether Warren Beatty is not unusually tickled by the notion of a spirit and a mind that can escape its own body and then find itself

379

stranded? The film does not grasp or develop the possibility, but there could be an extraordinary comedy here about a man who has managed to escape materiality, who talks to God (Beatty had wanted Cary Grant for that role, the locus classicus of his lounge suit acting) and has only occasional nostalgic twinges about doing something real and having a body for others to touch and . . . Suppose it was about a man able to watch and wander unseen through the life he had just left, pleased to find everyone waiting. I am guessing – but one has to do something with the disarray of *Heaven Can Wait*; and I am so fond of Warren I would rather think the best of his ventures. Let us just say there is a prospect worthy of *our* Warren here – a sublime film which, three or four times, peeps through all the busy untidiness of the picture that made a medium-sized fortune.

He has bought the movie rights to the original play from old Jed Harris. The play is *Here Comes Mr Jordan*, by Harry Segall. It has been filmed in 1941, with Robert Montgomery in the lead. The rights have come into the possession of Harris, seventy-five in 1975, sick, bitter, dying, once the greatest stage director in New York and one of the most feared and disliked men in the world. By the 1970s, Harris is forgotten, living in Los Angeles, a peculiar torture to the once famous, smoking himself to death. Beatty pays him $25,000 for the rights to *Here Comes Mr Jordan*, money for cigarettes and a hotel while Harris is "wasting time waiting to die".

Beatty hires Elaine May to write the script, and then becomes her collaborator. The script never seems to bear May's caustic charge, the instinct for danger and giving public affront evident in *Such Good Friends*, *A New Leaf*, *The Heartbreak Kid* and *Mikey and Nicky*. Elaine May is a regular in Beatty's telephone fold, an obsessively private woman whom he likes to hire and encourage, despite her reputation for dark and difficult films. One other associate says she is the sort of "smart, funny, cynical urban person he likes to have around".

Beatty talks to Peter Bogdanovich about directing *Heaven Can Wait*: after all, it is meant as a recreation of classic Hollywood, such as Bogdanovich has managed in *What's Up, Doc?* and *Paper Moon*. Bogdanovich is willing. But as they talk, Warren says, of course, he could direct it himself. The debate goes on many months, at the end of which Bogdanovich announces, "Warren, I'd like to dance with you, but I'm going to have to leave."

It has turned out so that he *has* to direct himself; the other person has walked out. But he is wary of being over-extended and he enlists Buck

Henry as a co-director. What does this mean? Henry never quite knows. He says of Warren, "He likes to work under pressure, and if it's not there he'll create it. He's a demonic producer . . . he fills every minute. Nothing deters him, nothing stops him. He barely sleeps and he likes to do as much as possible himself." Perhaps a co-director does lay off some of the pressure. He is also another opinion on the set, and another entertaining companion.

This is the first time Beatty has lodged one of his productions at Paramount. He likes it there. He gets on well with Charles Bluhdorn, the chairman of Gulf & Western, and with Barry Diller, the chairman of Paramount. He also gets the best deal he has ever had there, and secures exceptional power in the promotion of his film. I do not know the figures on the deal, but its outline shows the power Beatty has: first, Paramount pays for the production – Beatty does not use his own money; he gets a significant fee for his work – say, $3–4 million; and he gets a portion of the profits. Beatty is not alone in enjoying such a deal. Half a dozen other stars command similar terms. But he is unique in being a producer who does not let anyone outside his circle interfere in the film, in its conception or production, and now as little as possible in the marketing too. Yet he abides by the old Hollywood scheme of studios taking the risk. He is notably not like George Lucas and Francis Coppola, who seek to rid themselves of the old system and who put their own money in their projects, thus ensuring much more of the gain, and the loss. For Coppola it brings ruin, but for Lucas it is the means to wealth and power such as Beatty cannot approach. His business instincts stay conservative, faithful to Hollywood.

Heaven Can Wait opens in June 1978. It has a famous poster of Warren, legs crossed, head bowed, wearing a track suit and angel's wings. Indeed, it may be the wings that are keeping him upright. In the summer of *Grease* (a far bigger hit), *Heaven Can Wait* is material for a rather older audience in search of romance. There are laughs in the picture (mostly from Dyan Cannon and Charles Grodin), a great deal of undisciplined good nature, and much wishful thinking about true love surpassing death and other ecological threats. At the end of the picture, there are poignant looks between Warren and Julie Christie – as if they were both gazing at advertisements – which makes the public sentimental for a relationship that no longer functions in life. And in Beatty's millionaire masquerade there is a puppy-like naivety in which anyone can imagine they would handle being rich too without ever having to become more or less than decent and kind. (It has a sophomoric bounce, an unawareness of difficulty's existence, that is like the elixir than keeps Reagan young.)

In Beatty's own performance there is a blur of wide-eyed hurry and self-consious eccentricity that seems like the wish to be charming. But the picture never pricks the bubble. It obviously works in 1978, but it is such a departure from his earlier watchfulness, and it is the chief reason why he seems to be becoming younger on the screen. Something is asking us to see, and trying to make himself believe in, an earnest, idealistic, likeable Mr Beatty. He has seen a possible public image, and he strains after it. But short sight has left him in a fuzz. He is desperately trying to come out into the open. But the more he appears, the more lightweight he seems.

The picture earns $47.5 million in rentals in its first release. It is his third production in a row to be a big hit. He has never been richer, or attached himself to so minor a project. *Heaven* has several Oscar nominations, but no significant awards. Oscar night in 1979, in the company of Diane Keaton, brings him not much more than the test of his sister's wide-eyed jokes from the stage.

Warren and Shirley have at least two things in common – a place in the highest rank of American show business, and parents who are neither young nor especially well. They have something else to share, of course: a sibling they do not fully understand, who vexes and provokes them as naturally as he (or she) commands their love. This is not too uncommon. Few siblings close to the age of fifty still dream of absolute harmony. They get along as best they can, pleased (if they reflect) that their tiffs and silences do not get on television.

Warren has reason to regret that Shirley goes on about him so much. Over the years, she has talked about him to reporters, weighing the mischief and the fun, while he has said very little in public except that he doesn't talk about his sister. She has referred to him during her stage show and wondered at the number of women who have had him. On Oscar night, 1979, her jokes might not have been offered, except that he is sitting there in the audience and on camera. His smile that night says a good deal about family life, his ability to put on humor, and how long he has known her.

There may have been anger after that night, and no one could say she has not earned it. In her most recent book, *Dancing in the Light*, she says she respects his wish that she should not discuss his life. After all, he does not analyse her views on reincarnation in print; he appears to act as if it was natural and proper that she has her life and career, apart from him.

He is so reticent that you begin to appreciate how far her jokes, her jabs, have shown her need to win his interest and approval. He was her first audience, and maybe her toughest.

That said, she has been doing not much more than tease a tease. For anyone very fond of Warren and as experienced as Shirley in keeping up with him, there must be a great urge to puncture that immaculate, superior male grin and to let the world realise that Mr Wonderful has his common, shabby, inglorious moments, too – that it is all a grand act. There is a way in which Shirley serves as the wife Warren has not risked – adoring, enduring, but reckless with wondering whether his gravity has to be taken *so* seriously.

In both of them, there is an urge to surprise the other. On the occasion of the 1984 Academy Awards, Warren prepares a very complex gift for Shirley. It is something he has devised and fashioned personally, in several parts that reflect on his sister's life. He has it delivered to her just as she gets in the car to be driven to the ceremony where she will win an Oscar for *Terms of Endearment*.

In *The New Yorker*, in 1978, Pauline Kael says of *Heaven Can Wait*:

> "There isn't a whisper of personal obsession in the moviemaking. The film has no desire but to please, and that's its only compulsiveness; it's so timed and pleated and smoothed that it's sliding right off the screen. This little smudge of a movie makes one laugh a few times, but it doesn't represent moviemaking – it's pifflemaking. Warren Beatty moves through it looking fleecy and dazed, murmuring his lines in a dissociated, muffled manner. The film has to be soft-focused and elided – a series of light double takes – because if Beatty raised his voice or expressed anything more than a pacific nature, the genteel, wafer-thin whimsy would crumble."

So he hires her – as if to prove he is more than she fears. She has been the most noted and eloquent film critic in America for ten years. Ever since *Bonnie and Clyde*, she has followed and been impressed by his work – until this. But she is close to sixty and as worried over money as she is still ambitious for some complete, wild glory in film-making. And so she goes to Los Angeles, to an office on the Paramount lot, to work for Beatty, developing projects and ideas and perhaps, one day, coming to be a producer. One day, at nearly sixty? There are obvious reasons why this deal is dangerous: she is old for the change, she does not drive and she is likely to be flayed by the world of writing and criticism that she is now compromising and deserting. He may never really listen to her, or share her lust for danger. There may be a part of him that seeks to prove her wrong – or ordinary. But there is a headstrong romantic in Kael: it is what makes her sense of movies so eager and sensual. And he cannot lose his respect for intelligence.

There is an immediate project for Ms Kael. In 1977, James Toback directs his first film, *Fingers*. He has previously written *The Gambler*. *Fingers* is a commercial failure, yet it cost only $1 million. It is one of the most startling American debuts, expressing Toback's overwrought feelings for art and crime, for sensitivity and violence. The picture gets a few good reviews, one of them from Kael, who has known Toback a little in New York.

For his next film, Toback has written *Love and Money*, about a man who falls for the wife of a South American silver baron, and takes her away from him. Toback wants Beatty to play the hero. The script is bought by Columbia, but when the top management there changes after the David Begelman scandal, the picture goes into turnaround. Toback telephones Warren Beatty, who asks him to send the script to the Beverly Wilshire.

But Toback knows the suite there is crammed with old scripts, many of which are not read. He tells Beatty, "I've got to read it to you."

"I know how to read," says Beatty. "Besides, I wouldn't let Sergei Eisenstein read me a script.

Toback has a long history as a gambler. "Oh well," he says. "We can't do it."

The next day Beatty calls back and asks to see *Fingers*. It is screened for him and Ali McGraw. It is a very frightening film, visceral and passionate in its disregard of caution. After seeing it, Beatty walks around the screening room in agitation. "How did you get him to *do* that?" he asks Toback about the actor in *Fingers*, Harvey Keitel. Does he think that Toback might unlock his own final security? From the start, something in Toback intrigues and perplexes Beatty and maybe leaves him a little ashamed of his safety.

He meets Toback for dinner at the Four Oaks restaurant on Beverly Glen. Toback reads the script while Beatty feeds. It is in the primitive nature of survival that you cannot eat with someone else not eating without feeling his inferior. Beatty buys the script, and says he will produce it. He may act in it, too.

Then Beatty puts Toback with Kael to refine and develop the screenplay. They work together for a couple of months: she wants substantial changes in the script, but he will accept only a few. In the end, Beatty sides with the man and the film-maker in these disputes. But they are settled by the advance of *Reds*, by the termination of the arrangement with Kael and by Lorimar coming in to take over *Love and Money*.

Kael returns eventually to New York and the *New Yorker* where she works again as the film critic, more secure perhaps but less important in her authority and less potent as a writer. Soon she is cruelly attacked by Renata Adler in the *New York Review of Books*. *Love and Money* is made, with Ray Sharkey in the role meant for Beatty, and Klaus Kinski as the tycoon – the part that would have suited Warren better. The film is hugely inferior to *Fingers* and gets only a three-week run in New York. Warren is making *Reds*.

It all feels like a short story, about vanity, false hopes and hustling in Hollywood. And so it is. But it also concerns three fascinating people, full of creative energy and the urge to manipulate others. Perhaps Beatty has hopes of being not just a producer, but a patron, and hope for the future, a leader in the industry. Perhaps he puts two alarming people in a room together to see if they will destroy themselves. At the least, don't write the incident off as a whim or a wrong turning. Warren doesn't make mistakes. This play is as full of thwarted potential as *Heaven Can Wait*, a man harboring a strange, young hope.

There is another possibility that comes his way. In 1979, at the urging of his friend Henry Jaglom, Orson Welles writes an original script, *The Big Brass Ring*. It is about a senator in his forties, a Vietnam veteran, who runs for president, and a much older man, once an adviser to Franklin Roosevelt. The senator takes on this older man as his chief council and adviser in the presidential bid. And the old man falls in love with the senator, without ever disclosing what he feels.

Welles has known Beatty a little; they dine occasionally. And Welles thinks that perhaps he and Warren might play the two parts in *The Big Brass Ring*. It could be a significant return to American movies for Welles as a director. The script is offered to Beatty and he says he will do it if he can be the producer and if he has the power of final cut. If you think that Welles is the greatest film director America has had, this is a humbling proposal, even a humiliation. Welles refuses. Who knows how valuable a picture is lost here, or how tender and stirring a screen meeting?

Dog

Wavering with drink, but with his deadly suave act unimpaired, the man Dog was taking D on a tour of the Castle. Despite the heat, Dog wore a coat as heavy as carpet, with a fur collar. Wherever he ambled, he carried a ponderous rifle – D thought it might be a buffalo gun, its spear-long, tasseled gravity accounting for the absence of that creature. But Dog did not hold the gun with shooting in his mind. He cradled it, so that it resembled a rod of office.

"Now, of course," Dog explained, "I am in charge, and I believe I am safe in regarding myself as a gentleman."

"Yes?" said D.

"But . . . I do drink immoderately, as the day wears on. Immoderately," he repeated, for the word was his test of sobriety. "And the others are beasts, you see?"

D had guessed it from the wolfish jaw and the pink pit-bull eyes.

"It's just that I wouldn't want to instill any false confidence. I don't want you coming whining to me later."

Dog retrieved a pint flask of spirits from a poacher's pocket in his coat and took an extensive swallow. The hot air became more pressured. "We should bury that slut," he supposed, his wild head stretching in her direction, but impeded by the fur collar and an old crick in his neck.

"Look," said D.

"Be a horrid stink if we don't."

It must have been eleven in the morning, and there were three dead already in the steadfast courtyard of Scotty's Castle, where even the killers, weighed on by perils, looked wistfully at the wishing well.

Look was on her way to dying when D and Drew returned to the castle at dawn. Dog then had been sitting on the stone wall to the well, keeping a serene sideways cover on the weeping Doc, while Breed (an associate of Dog's) was beating up Look. It was like beating a lace handkerchief for dust.

Dog and Breed in *McCabe and Mrs Miller*

"I say, easy on," Dog was murmuring, and then, "Good Lord", to see such absurd violence in his associate. "She's a nice-looking girl," Dog remonstrated. "Not the sort of thing we're likely to find every day in the desert."

"Too pleased with herself," said Breed, and Dog sighed at Doc to indicate that benevolence could only go so far.

"Stop him!" howled Doc.

Breed did falter. When he had no strength left to hit Look, he scratched and gouged at her. And so she fell in the courtyard, and had been left there. She was bloody and broken, but in the space of two hours, without anyone noticing, she had moved a few feet, her body snailing its way on the ground.

"She wants the shade," Drew realised.

"What could I do?" Doc implored them. "I was asleep, and she tried to protect me."

They had stood by and watched the beating, directed by Dog's archaic gun and the lean hatefulness of Breed, a gaunt man in a poncho. "He's unpredictability itself," Dog had warned them, "a lost soul." Dog was sentimental about those born of two races, and he admired the way Breed had adapted to being unloved.

The morning passed: boredom and the enormous terror of expecting to be murdered co-existing like the heat and Dog's fur coat. There was something, D knew now, that permitted ugly power – it was a readiness in the humble to be ordered. It was like sitting beneath an amazingly frightening film in which no torture was spared, hoping it will end but obedient in the dark. There had always been a slavery implicit in watching movies.

"Is there anything we can do?" Drew whispered.

"You think so? What is there? I really don't see a thing we can do," D rattled off answers.

"Don't look so serious," she told him.

"Oh stop," begged D. He was crying, he noticed. Her hand went to his face to lift away the tears.

"I'd suggest," said Dog, "you didn't do that, little lady. Breed here is touchy."

"I'll do what I choose," Drew told Dog.

"Ah well," chuckled Dog, and left it there for the moment, not at all surprised to see D flinching from his lover's courage.

After noon, a troop of prisoners came into the courtyard, led by a single guard, Kid, a white-haired youth. There was Clear, Cy, Claudia,

Beau, Tusk, Zale, Chuck (have we forgotten anyone?), except that Zale was dead already, shot, and being carried by Cy and Tusk.

"Had to make an example, old boy?" Dog asked the Kid.

"He's a lawyer." Kid still resented the foul luck in meeting one.

"Bravo," said Dog. "Any others?"

"What others?"

"They invariably move in pairs," Dog explained.

"I am a lawyer," Clear volunteered.

"Really?" said Dog. He moved his long rifle a little, and its roar enveloped the courtyard. Tusk was knocked over by the blast, and then they saw he was in pieces on the ground. The gun had been loaded with coins. "I hate them sagging and bumping in my pocket," said Dog. And the amused Kid pried a quarter from Tusk's ribs and tossed it in the wishing well.

"What did you wish for, sonny?" Dog called.

Kid turned to those left. His gray teeth grinned at Drew. "For her," he said, as if it was obvious.

A lunch was made from the kitchen, and it was apparent that only Dog, Breed and Kid were partaking. "Provisions in the desert are so scarce," Dog apologised.

Clear was loyal to his role of spokesman. "We also need to eat," he said.

Dog did not answer, and it was not clear whether this was because he was eating or because he had no answer.

"One has to feed one's prisoners," said Clear.

Now Dog laughed: "What utter rot! Do you think in the great crises of history – in war or revolution – people feed the prisoners and give them magazines to read? Sir," said Dog, "they off them. All modern ingenuity has been given over to the ways of offing them."

A little later, cooking slowly in the sun, Drew asked Clear, "So what do they do with us if we don't do anything?" No one had dared answer. The prisoners gazed away from their plight, like late riders on the subway trying to erase freaks and junkies.

"What *are* we waiting for?" Clear attempted in the middle of the afternoon.

"Well," drawled Dog, "we understand there is another survival group hereabouts – some fancy picture star. They come here to carouse."

As he drank more, Dog expounded on the philosophy of survivalism, its poetry – the raw desert ordeal and a new way of life, the good of the

389

community, the inspiration in stamping out danger, and the sublime fact of enemies.

"I was in bitter mid-life," said Dog. "Had this bistro in Malibu. Stupid place for stupid people. Smiling on their whims. But here!" He stood up and reached for the air. "I feel like Douglas Fairbanks. Senior," he added.

The shade of evening wiped the courtyard. Kid turned on Drew. "No," D whispered, asking his eyes not to notice.

He saw the amber light penetrating from the west. It honeyed all her hairs. He thought how ridiculous that it should be beautiful.

"Don't worry, my sweet," Drew told him. And then, out of breath or pleading, "Go away."

Must we say what happened? There should be a pause for looking away from the gaping screen and its placid rendering of such things. Description makes the writer and the reader more subject to dread. It went on and when it was over Drew was silent, cast down. Her great eagerness was gone and it was night. She was slumped next to D in the makeshift compound where the prisoners were tethered. Her blood shone like grease on an engine.

D did not know if she was asleep, dead or lost to talk. For hours he thought what to say to her. But he lacked the words. The desert had brought them to silence. Three days and they were savage and mute.

Then, quietly crazy, listening to what he might say, he thought he heard a whisper.

"Who's that?" he heard himself say. He wondered if Kid was back for more, more vicious in the dark.

"Who dya think at long last, kid?"

"Don't," D implored. "Not irony."

"What sort of welcome is that?" The voice was chipper and bantering, like a stand-up comic who had died over and over again, but would not go away.

"Who are you?" asked D. The husky voice was reviving him. He had to listen for its elusiveness.

"I have to spell it out?"

"Who?" D was at his limit.

"Tell you what," the voice was ready for another tack. "A man of many parts. Some missing maybe."

"Yes?" said D. "You're – "

"Hey, kiddo, be discreet, por favor. Did you hear the one about the man on a walking tour?"

"This is a joke?" D could not believe in such an approach.

"You be the judge. Anyway, this guy is out in wild country and the weather is looking bad. He comes to an isolated inn. He goes inside. It's warm and snug, and the landlord says, 'You're in luck, sir. We've just the one room left. Now, sit down by the fire, and warm yourself, and I'll bring you a supper. Will beef and oyster pie suffice?'"

"This is a long story?" asked D.

"At its best it is," the voice told him, a little vexed.

"We all of us here need to be rescued," said D. "This lady is close to death."

"I know that," said the voice. "I can very well see that." There was a pause as looking might have been going on. Yet in the dark, perhaps only touching could tell. "Anyway, the man is eating his supper, and the big storm breaks. He is on the coffee and brandy when the inn door opens and another traveler is nearly blown in by the gale, soaked and unsteady on his feet. Well, the first man watches the second man talking to the landlord. And, after a while and a few concerned glances, the landlord comes over and says, 'Sir, we have a little difficulty.'"

"This is Drew," said D. "Remember her?"

"I know," said the voice patiently. "Don't sound so serious."

"I let her down," said D.

"You did?"

"I wasn't good enough for her. But I took the bit I wanted."

The voice waited. It was not unkind. "You don't have to tell me. We've all done that. So the landlord says, 'This other gentleman needs a room, and we have only one. Yours. However, the bed in the room is very commodious. I wonder if, under these exceptional circumstances, you would be prepared to share. Of course, I'd make no charge.'

"What can the man say? He doesn't want to be uncooperative. He says, no problem. And the second man comes over and thanks him, and he seems a decent fellow. He has some of the same supper and they play a little dominoes together. And after a while, and another round of brandies – all on the house – they decide they'll go on up to bed."

"Can you get us out of here?" D asked. If he had to endure the story, he wanted certain assurances.

"Well, I tell you, I'm really not sure," admitted the voice. "That answer your question? Anyway, the two men get to the bedroom and the second man sits down on the bed and he unscrews his legs. Just like that. The first man is amazed. And the second man sees this and says, 'Oh, please don't be alarmed. I had a serious accident a few years ago.

Actually, I live alone now, so I can't often do this, but since you're here I wonder if you'd help me take my arms off? They're chafing tonight; it must be the damp.'

"And the first man says, 'Your arms too?'

"The second man nods and says, 'It was a terrible and unusual accident. The doctors agreed I was fortunate to survive.' So the first man helps him take off his arms, and there's just the trunk of the guy in bed. Looks like a piece of ginger.

"Well, they chat a little about hobbies and so on, and then they go off to sleep."

"Please!" hissed D.

"What is it?" asked the voice, hurt now. "You don't like the story?"

"I'm desperate."

"Well, of course you are. I was telling you the story to take your mind off it. Can't you make the effort to see that?"

"I suppose," grumbled D.

"Right. Well, in the middle of the night, the first man wakes up suddenly, and he can't place what it is that woke him. But the second man, he's awake too. And he says, 'Don't worry. A bird has flown in the window and it can't find its way out.' This is pitch dark, you understand?"

"Yes," sighed D.

"So the second man says, 'I have a way with wild creatures. Just screw my legs back on, if you will. I don't think I'll require the arms.'"

There came a great groan from Drew, as if she just realised she had heard this story before.

"The first man gets out of bed and, in the dark, as best he can, he has to put the second man's legs back on. This is not the simplest thing in the world. All the while the bird is flying around in panic, its wings beating."

"I think she's dead," said D.

"Yeah, she is," the voice agreed. "She was dead when I got here."

"She sighed."

"That was her body settling." There was silence. "She was a bit of terrific, wasn't she?"

"Better than we deserved," said D.

There was a silence, as if the voice was judging whether or not to say, "Don't be solemn", and decided against it.

"What happened then?" asked D. "In the story."

"Well, the second man sits up on the edge of the bed and he makes strange noises, sort of muttering, cooing sounds from inside his head. And the bird is slowly soothed or charmed by the sounds. It flies around less. And finally it lands on the second man's head. He was nearly bald, by the way."

"Yes," said D.

"And the second man gets up on his legs and, very slowly, so as not to disturb the trembling bird, he walks over to the open window."

"There was a storm," D remembered.

"It died away before they retired."

"Oh, well, OK, I suppose."

"And the man gets to the window and he leans his body forward so that his head and the bird are in fresh air. And he says very quietly to the bird. 'Away you go.' And the bird flew off with his head."

LIVING WITH REED

It is not easy making films. Nor is it pleasant. Anyone doing it looks forward to it being over. It is regularly perplexing to hear the remarks of lay friends who are sure it is delightful. But something about the enterprise smacks of hell – I do not mean just the exhaustion, the clash of boredom and sudden, savage crises, the aura of helpless, predestined waste and structural corruption, the ferment of egos all needing intimacy, reassurance and orders. Nor even the realisation at this or that stage that the film may not be worth making. No, the hardest thing of all to digest, if you are the film-maker, is the persistent sensation that the ordeal has become so ruinous, so toxic, you are prepared to sacrifice your precious intention, just to get the damn thing done. So you lose faith in yourself, just as you find ample evidence to dislike everyone else on the picture. You acquire the instincts and the capacity for vengeance, because you have felt so wretched. But if you once believed in such things as unique and precious intentions, you become disappointed most of all in film. You see that you are not as good as you wanted to be, but you discover something worse, that the very medium lacks the depth or faith you wanted. You feel you are on a train going in the wrong direction, and the effort it has all taken appears madness. Ironically, you end up rich and famous, as well as a natural murderer like Salieri.

Of course, you cannot stop the train, or get off, not if this is a large American picture, because there is a weight of money and contracts that cannot stop. You are not allowed to abandon the idea, and if, as the work proceeds, you see ways of changing it – because you have finally found the subject, as writers often discover what they should be doing in the act of writing – still, it is too late. A film is made according to its plan. Alter that along the way and you usually destroy the picture. You would need to begin again, as a painter might quickly paint over a deadlocked canvas, happy to have seen what the painting really is. In a film, you cannot paint over the first $15 million, or crumple it and toss it at the wastepaper bin until you get the throw right. You may have to drag your way on, just to finish it, knowing it is wrong and resenting it all the more because the strain is killing your joy and mugging your youth.

Warren decides to make *Reds*, and although it is a venture he has been nursing for longer than most people realise, when he decides to proceed with this huge picture there is something impulsive about it, like people who have lived all their lives in social discontent who realise one day in their early forties that this particular protest has gone a little further than others and that some arrangement of chance and history have made it such a cusp that something is astir which, by tomorrow maybe, will be called a revolution, and by the day after the hinge of epochs or the end of the world.

He has been intrigued by the life of John Reed, the Harvard boy, the writer, the impresario of political pageants, the middle-class red who went to Russia in 1917, who wrote *Ten Days That Shook the World* and was dead in 1920 at the age of thirty-three. He has himself been at the Widener Library at Harvard to study the many boxes of John Reed papers. He has hired research students, brilliant, pretty kids, who pore over the early history of the American Left and carry the digests to him in the Beverly Wilshire penthouse – blondes in suntops with small books on syndicalism and accounts of mining conditions in 1915. For years, being so rich, he is working on radicalism undercover.

As early as 1972, he films an interview with Manny Kamrov, a New York left-winger. He hears the first, vague words of tumbling memory. He sees an elderly face struggling to separate what was from the wishing. He realises how pleased the neglected old are to be talked to; they could talk for ever, especially those who claim they have nothing to say. This first interview will not appear in *Reds*: it does not have the visual style of the eventual witness scenes, but it is a beginning in which he discovers the need to decide how these scenes should look and how they might constitute a chorus. In 1976, he hires English playwright Trevor Griffiths to write a script for the project.

Griffiths is in America to attend Mike Nichols' wedding. He shares a car and a lot of talk with Warren from New York to Connecticut. A week later, Warren calls and asks what Griffiths knows about Reed. What do you want to know? the writer replies. "I don't want to know anything," says Beatty. "I've been looking at the guy's life for the last ten years." They talk for eight months on the trans-Atlantic phone – "He was finding out whether I could help him," says Griffiths. The script is commissioned and written; it is called *Comrades*.

Beatty reads the script, and considers. It is evidently huge, and not yet what Beatty wants. But he decides to show it in this form to begin to secure support. He sends it to Barry Diller at Paramount, who says he likes it and would want to make it. But it is so large and costly a venture that Charles Bluhdorn, the head of Gulf & Western, must give his approval too. Diller arranges a New York appointment with Bluhdorn for Beatty, and adds that the script should be a lot shorter by the time of that meeting.

And so, with only days to do it in, Beatty, Elaine May and a few others make a cutting circle. But in the time available they achieve only a mess, not a properly revised screenplay. Still, the working breakfast at the Carlyle Hotel cannot be denied. Beatty takes a copy of the script for *Heaven Can Wait* and puts it between *Reds* covers – his title. He can pat it and point to it, and it will look modest and manageable. He'll say, "I know you don't have time to *read* this, Charlie." Elaine May arranges to be demurely at another table in the Carlyle restaurant. If Bluhdorn does begin to examine the script, she will faint or have hysterics, or perhaps hurl scrambled eggs around the room. Can this be so? Is it real, or part of a comedy they think of making late one night? Paramount decides to go with *Reds*.

In time, Warren will ask Elaine May and Robert Towne – at least – to work on scenes for him. He will be reworking parts of the screenplay as the shooting takes place. He will tell actors on the day what they are to say. He will shape scenes at the moment of making them. Only Diane Keaton and Jack Nicholson among the other actors even have a script. Supporting actors, like Edward Herrmann, never see one. This is to allow improvements to be made at the last possible instant; it is to keep the huge enterprise "intimate" and secret; it also has the effect of dramatising Beatty's command and it lets the filmmaker delay making up his mind.

During the writing process, Coral Browne, the English actress, happens to stay with Lillian Hellman in New York. Late in the evening, when Ms Browne has retired, she hears someone come in the front door and go quietly upstairs to Lillian's bedroom, leaving much later. This happens on those nights when Hellman has ordained that they will not go out to dinner. Browne is so curious that on the next such night she lies in wait, manages to open the front door herself and finds a surprised Warren Beatty. "Oh yes," confirms a friend, "they sit upstairs drinking, and talking about radicals in the old days."

In March 1979, before he and she attend the Oscars ceremony, sitting so close to the TV cameras that they must smile patiently when Shirley

MacLaine wonders out loud about Warren's sexiness, Warren and Diane Keaton go with production designer Richard Sylbert to look for locations in Russia. Would the Soviets let *Reds*, or *Comrades*, be made in Leningrad? Would the shrewd Beatty really let them let him in? The Russians ask to see the script, and Warren declines. Alas, they say, the picture cannot therefore be shot in Russia. And so the makers settle on Helsinki for the revolutionary street scenes. After all, the same architect, long ago, had worked on the civic buildings in both Helsinki and St Petersburg.

Beatty is with Diane Keaton now. This does substantiate the observation of Leslie Caron that Warren is drawn to Oscar-winners – for Keaton wins for 1977 in *Annie Hall*. Equally, Beatty may see in Keaton not just the realisation of his sense of Louise Bryant, John Reed's wife, but the living woman. And Keaton is very far from just the best available actress for this central role: she is a shy but assertive woman, a good photographer (someone with her own work) who will display a cool ironic sensibility, in *Reservations* (a study of hotel lobbies) and *Still Life*, her droll collection of old Hollywood production stills. No other Beatty film contains so large or troubling a portrait of a woman, or is so concerned with sexual politics. And Diane Keaton deserves great credit for that, not simply as a performer but as a generating influence, the voice and independence Beatty hears the most. *Reds* has remarkable quarrels between Reed and Louise. It is not simply a film of seductions and betrayals, like *Shampoo*. It rages with the texture of everyday failure and company. A woman argues with Beatty on screen, silencing him again and again, and the tiredness in his face is not acting, but his age and the ordinary, unhideable dimming of romanticism.

The shooting takes place between August 1979 and July 1980 – there are some 240 days of actual filming, in Helsinki, in Spain (standing in for the Baku region of Russia), in New York, Washington and Los Angeles, but mostly in England. Some interiors are filmed at the Twickenham Studios, but the Reeds' Croton-on-Hudson house is found in Kent; Camber Sands, in Lincolnshire, is the location for the Provincetown beach scenes. There is also shooting in the Manchester area. In all, about 130 hours of film will be exposed, involving immense industry of costuming and art direction, large crowds, authentic period trains and cars – this is all the detail of film-making that the small army amasses and which the leader must check and approve.

There are key figures on the shoot – the Italian director of photography, Vittorio Storaro, Richard Sylbert, Shirley Russell, who does the costumes, the production manager Nigel Wooll and the assistant director, Simon Relph, and the associate producer, David MacLeod. But Beatty must be in charge of everything, and his is the mind that shapes the way the picture comes into being.

Sylbert, who has worked with Beatty on *Splendor in the Grass*, *Lilith*, *Bonnie and Clyde*, *Shampoo* and *The Fortune*, is impressed at his tact as director: "He's got an amazing brain, but he doesn't show off. He never says, 'Look at me directing.' He doesn't do phony stuff. He does story. He is never off on story. And while it was a big picture, a lot of the time it was really intimate and we were making it with only four or five people. And, you know, all the time we were learning – you couldn't figure out how to do this picture unless you just started doing it."

When the production goes to Spain, at Guadix, near Granada, Beatty lives in a small house with no hot water with Jerzy Kosinski, the novelist he has asked to play the Bolshevik leader, Zinoviev. For Kosinski, making a movie is rather a lark, something he will do just once, a kind of holiday. But he becomes fascinated by Beatty's deliberate, if not fanatical, absorption in detail and hardship, even at the cost of his health: "For me, as a novelist, I am living in a revolution. But I am also living with this pathetic American. I'm back into my past, like Zinoviev – hot days, cold nights. I'm enjoying it. But I'm living with John Reed, who is doing this ridiculous thing, and I'm annoyed by it. I'm very cynical. To me it's all a game. To him, it's an idea."

One day they are shooting in Seville, in 110 degree heat, a crowd scene with Reed addressing the throng. Warren has what is called the flu, or some collection of illnesses and fatigue that are asking him to stop and be sorry for himself. The Spanish extras are discontented. Storaro's crew begin to put the camera on a podium. Warren is discussing the scene with Kosinski when he breaks away, alarmed, because the podium may not take all the weight. He asks for the contractor for his opinion, but it is the Feast of Corpus Christi. A search goes on and the man is found. He looks and he says, why yes, of course, the podium must be made stronger. "You have to worry about such details yourself?" Kosinski asks in wonder. "Do you let anyone else check your manuscript?" Warren replies.

As the strengthening work goes on, Beatty speaks to the extras. He tells them the story of the film, of John Reed's life, and of the great issues it entailed. All of this has to be done through translation. It is a long speech, because Beatty wants the extras' upturned, listening faces to feel understanding and emotion, no matter that they are 1980s

Spaniards pretending to be Russians in 1920. The extras follow the stirring, but halting outline of socialism, and in the lunch break they come to Beatty with the case that in view of the noble principles of this picture they are really convinced they should be paid $90 a day each instead of $70. The deal is re-made and the scene is shot in the undiminished sunlight.

It all gets done – much more than all, in that only a fortieth of what is shot will be in the finished picture. The budget rises. And this is feared by Paramount, the company that will distribute the film and its largest source of financing. Barry Diller has been anxious at the speed with which shooting began and at the lack of pre-production. It is true that the availability of actors determined the starting date. While originally budgeted at $20 million, *Reds* soon takes on a size that will eclipse that figure. Diller grows angry and refuses to talk to Beatty because he feels that Paramount have been used, kept in the dark. The two men make up by the end of 1979 and resume talking and arguing. Yet, years later, Diller will admit that in long discussions with Beatty you realise later that you have given in, that you agreed, and yet you are not really much wiser about what he thinks. Somehow, he makes you explain yourself to him, as if you were anxious for him to like you.

What does the picture cost? The estimates range from $32.5 million to nearly $60 million. As the years go by, even the official estimate climbs to over $40 million. There is discretion in this, the deliberate downplaying of some costs, and the calculated inflation of others. It is also very hard to determine exactly what it costs. The picture has been a source of expense for years – the research, the script, Warren's time and his running costs. And now it is being made its deal is amazingly convoluted. Paramount are not the makers of the film. The copyright is with Barclay's Mercantile Industrial Finance Ltd, a British banking arrangement set up for this picture. But there is no readier subject for rumor, nor any greater need for imprecision, than spending a lot of money.

There is a lull in the second half of 1980, a rest, during which the editing begins, while Beatty and Storaro film the witnesses. They need a camera, a light and a black cloth, a microphone and a recorder, as well as the eagerness of all the veterans. There are thirty-two witnesses in the pictures, but many more are shot and some of the interviews are as long as two hours.

The editing is carried out at premises on West 54th Street in New York, with a crew headed by Dede Allen and Craig McKay. Beatty sometimes sleeps in the cutting room and tries out new solutions overnight. By the end of the summer, the picture is complete, at 199 minutes. It has been aimed at an early December release. In September, a long trailer – 4½ minutes – starts to play in theaters. The poster is planned – of the Reeds embracing in their last reunion. Not all of these things are exactly Beatty's ordering. He has had final cut on the film, and he ensures by contract and maneuver a major say in promotion. In the fall, he shows *Reds* to Paramount: Charles Bluhdorn and Barry Diller, and then Frank Mancuso and Gordon Weaver, the heads of distribution and marketing. When the picture gets an R rating, Beatty attends the appeal personally. He will not moderate the language or his lovemaking scenes, but he claims the picture merits a PG rating so that American school children may see this chapter of their history. He wins the appeal.

But there are murmurs against the film. Frank Mancuso fears the nation-wide response to its political radicalism and urges that the film be sold as a love story. Independently, Warren commissions political pollster Patrick Caddell (an acquaintance from Democrat campaigns) to survey advance attitudes to *Reds*. Caddell reports that the more people learn about the material of *Reds* the more intrigued they are to see it. But Beatty cannot prevail on Paramount to follow this line. He has a right of veto, but that is not the same as insisting that they accept his wishes. Paramount clings to the romance, but the disappointed Warren will consent to nothing more lyrical in imagery than the eventual poster. The result is a ruinous compromise, a poster in which the stars seem determined to hide.

Too many people in the Paramount organisation do not even see the film in the build-up. For those who do, of course, it is too late to take any action except the drastic. At exhibitors' screenings there are voices raised that had always been anticipated – that the picture will not play comfortably in rural and conservative areas; that it is too long.

Such feelings crystalise in the regret that Beatty is doing so little personally to promote the film. He does no interviews for it. The poster, it is argued, is perversely secretive or recessive – no one knows the woman is Diane Keaton, and the man has half his face buried in her shoulder. The trailer is confusing; it seems pretentious to some people. Out of fatigue and frustration with Paramount, Warren does not speak up for the film. If he ever thinks of what happened with *Bonnie and Clyde*, he may see that it is a young man's game.

Yet, his reticence is also the culmination of an old instinct. For years, he has believed films should speak for themselves, that art is denied or obscured if it needs to be explained. And he thinks that *Reds* is a great film. Those close to him stress his exhaustion and mention the fear that his own mixed reputation could hurt the marketing. He is attacked for doing so little by Rona Barrett. Yet he feels he has done so much.

The film will be a commercial failure, and of a kind that suggests no other promotion would have made a crucial difference. Still, the reticence here is curious. For it shies away at the last minute from an obvious duty, rich with material and potential. Think what might have been done to make a television documentary out of the witnesses, in which Beatty himself talked about the picture and American history. This is the kind of thing he says in spring 1982 when he accepts the Oscar for direction. But late in 1981 he is silent and withdrawn, as if to say love me without my wooing.

The huge effort to be seen and the final wish to be invisible are not out of character. They have been the odd pattern in all his acting, and maybe in much of his life. As Robert Towne has put it:

"I feel that Warren always has to be tougher than he thinks. He presents a peculiar problem as an actor because he is a man who is deeply embarrassed by acting . . . when you write scenes together, as Warren and I did in *Shampoo*, you've got to say, 'Look, you've got to be tough with yourself here, and not be afraid of yourself.'"

It is an odd life for such a man to have chosen, and *Reds* is probably the largest film ever made about hesitancy and shyness.

Lost parrot

Not long after dawn, when his loss had sunk in, Chuck shouted at D across their small prison yard, "You let her die!" D never answered, so Chuck turned to anyone else who would listen, "I knew not to trust him. He was never one of us."

"He seemed so nice," regretted Claudia Cannon, sure she knew him from somewhere.

"Let's not dispute among ourselves," urged Cy. "It hurts our chances."

"On our chances," Doc said to Chuck, "what would be your advice? You're hired for manliness, aren't you?"

"What does that mean?" Chuck was wary.

"Do we wait to die?"

"You think you're funny?" sneered Chuck. There was something abject in his eyes, lest the initiative, the lead, be dumped on him.

"I'm serious," said Doc. "What should we do?"

By the time Dog, Kid and Breed came out of the Castle for their morning promenade, Chuck had given much thought to this. And he made his stand by waiting until the three survivalists were close before getting up and kicking D swiftly in the side of the head, with a whoop of triumph to be sure it was noticed.

"I say, I say," Dog called out, his voice a flugelhorn in the morning air.

"He let her die," jeered Chuck, nodding at Drew's corpse, still propped against D.

"Rats," hissed Kid, who had only dragged himself out of bed at the absent-minded thought of more sport.

"That *is* careless," Dog pouted.

"It certainly is," said the panting Chuck. He was jumping up and down in panic.

"But, of course," Dog began.

"Yes, yes?" Chuck wanted to know.

"It's irrelevant."

Chuck was drained of energy by this attitude. He was like a bull now, sullen and backed up, opposed to having so many barbs inserted in his hide, too stupid to foresee the fishbone of a sword that would find a way between his ribs, however many thrusts it took.

"Pardon me," said a fresh voice, but one that D had heard lately. The voice spoke in a modest, off-handed way, no heavier than the sneaker tread that had brought its owner into the courtyard unheard.

"Good Lord," said Dog, assessing the slim figure in startling white shirt and slacks, burnished but unarmed. "Where did you spring from?"

"Have you seen my parrot?" asked the newcomer.

"Your what?" Dog was not sure whether to laugh.

"My parrot. I lost it yesterday."

"Did you, by Jove?"

"Green and gold, with a blue splash on its head. Is she dead?" The man in white had halted by Drew. He kneeled down beside her, and did what he could to calm her shocked hair. "What a pretty girl," he murmured to D.

"She is," D answered. "A very lovely face."

"A noble head," the visitor agreed.

"You know, I don't believe we have seen one parrot," Dog began, to break the spell.

"I did," said Doc. "I saw a parrot. Earlier. Big brute."

"There," said the man in white. "You see."

"It was red and blue," Doc added.

"Must have found a friend," said the man in white.

"What is this parrot stuff?" Kid asked Dog.

"Shut up," Dog told his junior, the pest, and to the man in white he said, "We're not the least interested in your bloody parrot."

"No? Well," the man in white reflected, "I imagine not – not if you're making a movie."

"Say again?" asked Dog.

"I get it," grinned the man in white. "You're keeping a low profile."

"A movie?" Dog wouldn't let go.

"That coat. Costume?"

Dog simpered. "More regalia, if you know what I mean."

"Uh-huh," the man in white was smiling through his narrowed, sceptical eyes. "So what's Eyes doing? I heard he didn't work much these days."

"Eyes?"

"Eyes the Star," said the man in white.

At which, Doc grimaced, "For God's sake!"

And D chimed in, "Now you've done it," with much fatalistic shaking of what was still a bruised head.

Dog was bewildered, but quick on the uptake. He could not fail to see how the respectful, sidelong and rather demure glances of this new fellow, and of D and Doc, were all directed at the one they called Chuck. Dog looked again. He wished he had his spectacles, but in a disaster there are things mislaid and survivors must soldier on. He took three grand strides towards Chuck. Could it be? Eyes hadn't worked since – when was it? Chuck's head drooped. By God, yes, it could be.

"You sly fox," said Dog to himself. And then, sticking out a large hand, "Mr Eyes, sir, an honor."

"Shake his hand," the man in white advised Chuck. "You can't pull that star thing in the desert where we're all men together."

"I'll say not," said Dog.

Chuck looked at the man in white. "What is this?" he said.

"It's your turn, kiddo," said the man in white.

"Mr Eyes deserves his privacy," protested Doc.

"Silence, cur!" said Dog.

Kid rammed Doc in the stomach with his booted foot. Doc collapsed and retched on the dry ground.

"You really didn't know?" the man in white asked Dog.

"Know? Why, sir, who ever knows in this life? I had a strong feeling. But one keeps an inborn reticence towards the great stars. They go their way."

"I suppose so," said the man in white. "And we go ours."

"Oh, assuredly. I'm grateful to you for the hint. Of course, it's been the word that he did live hereabouts."

"I heard that too."

"May I ask, sir, what you do?"

"Well," began the man in white, "I'm really something of a harmless old hermit. Had a shack, over in Marietta, but a family of jack rabbits moved in, so I drifted on, you know?"

"Yes, indeed," said Dog. "The great treasure of solitude."

"Exactly so," said the man in white. He was peering through the mounting glare of the day.

"What is it?" asked Dog.

"Well," said the man in white confidentially. "I lost my eye glasses years ago, but I could have sworn that was Claudia Cannon and Cy Lighthiser."

"The famous actress?" said Dog. "And her producer hubbie chappie?"

"The same," said the man in white. "You've got yourself a production here, I'd say."

"You would?"

"Oh, I would. I can even understand the fur coat."

"Yes?"

"It makes you a very big man in the desert."

"Ah!"

"To have Eyes and Claudia, and Cy to line-produce for you – "

"But equipment? Wouldn't we – ?"

"Bound to turn up," said the man in white. "With a deal like this in the palm of your hand," and he patted the buffalo gun, hot in the sun, "everything falls into place."

"A picture?" Dog surmised.

"And if you're short on stock, well, just remember that in Russia after the revolution they made pictures without film."

"Did they?"

"Just pretended, for the practice. Ran empty cameras."

"Cunning buggers."

The man in white considered. "I'd say you had a hit."

"Really?"

"There's not going to be much in the theaters."

"Are there theaters still?" asked Dog, recalling the devastation.

"Are we standing here?" asked the man in white.

"Definitely."

"It was night last night? Then we had morning?"

"The same as ever."

"An orange is still round?"

"I haven't seen one today, but – "

"Then there'll be theaters. By the time you're in post-production the clamor will build."

"This is exciting," said Dog. "I've always wanted to make movies."

"And you'll have Claudia Cannon as your property," the man in white did what he could to nudge Dog in the voluminous coat.

"Sir, I am a gentleman," said Dog.

"Don't think she won't be charmed by a gentleman."

"You think so?"

"Well," said the man in white, pausing, letting the momentum of their talk ebb away, "I'd imagine so. That's what I heard about the picture business. Lot of burying to do here."

Dog looked around. "Things mount up."

"Let me do it," said the man in white. "I know the best places to dig. I'll take these three to do the work." He indicated Doc, Clear and D, the three of them nodding like toy hounds on the back window ledge of family auto trips.

"They're poor material," Dog assured him.

"I can see," said the man in white. "We'll go off and find some bare spot in the desert."

"Back for lunch?" asked Dog.

"Well," said the man in white, looking up at the sun and estimating the labor. "Say high tea."

"That's the ticket," said Dog. "We'll have a roast."

"Oh, careful now," demurred the man in white. "I can't keep up with you showbiz jokesters."

Dog roared with laughter. He realised that he was happier than he had ever been.

And so the burial party fell in, and as they made their way out into the emptiness D was allowed to carry the still springy body of Drew. The man in white walked beside him, and they went along all together, too fond of the dead to speak, but quite sure a fine burial could be made.

REDS

As Richard Sylbert remembers it, *Reds* was sometimes made with only a handful of people present. But on other occasions there is a dead weight of a thousand expecting to be told what to do, resentful of indecision, a silent mass that prompts the nervous producer to recount the history of world revolution. And if you wish to rouse that mass to help you, to be alive and eager for the movie, you cannot very well complete your story by saying that John Reed died with less faith in the revolution or in Russia than he had ever had, overwhelmed and disappointed by ponderous size. You have to ignore that, and do all you can to smother the mood of dismay intrinsic to the story. You know you may kill yourself straining to lift up a proper dying fall and make a big finish of it. If you are Russian, and a Bolshevik, you bury Reed in the Kremlin, so that you can make sure the regret is kept out of sight.

Reds gets bigger as it is made: how can this not be the case? The total footage of exposed film mounts. The budget of the production goes up. The expectations and the anxieties at Paramount build so that more and more of the actor's time is spent in reassurance, no matter that he has to play a man running out of conviction and of the sense that he and history are one. For as the film expands so its maker discovers that his true subject is slight – nothing less than a love affair – and that the tone of his film is all to do with loss, failure and forgetting. If you are in the desert, it is like believing that the wind blows the sand into natural monuments, into epic achievements, only to realise that all the time the wind has been dispersing the sand.

No one as intelligent as Warren Beatty, or with a mind so open to doing so many things, can make *Reds* without some thought to its political consequences in his career. He does take the film and show it to America's President, Ronald Reagan, who says it's fine, but he wishes it had a happier ending. (There is all the market research Paramount needs, and the model of Reagan's success: he knows what America will buy.) *Reds* will be regarded as a picture about politics, and plainly its maker will be recognised for his interest in power. The Left will be touched by his generosity to their views. But the Left in America scarcely exists. There is much more danger, of course, that the main body of the country will be alarmed by undue compassion for reds and their doings. The picture does all it can to disarm that hostility. It says clearly that Russian revolution could not work in America; and it goes on to show that the revolution betrayed itself in Russia, too. What remains is nothing more threatening than the notion that hardship and suffering should be avoided; that the workers deserve fair wages and representation; that tyranny is odious and free love problematic.

No one in America has the heart or the nerve to dispute such views. Barry Diller, at Paramount, complains, "Not one media person, no liberal writer, has pointed out that this big American corporation supported a film that deals with a story that had been buried, a story never told, the absolutely hidden story of the IWW, the American Socialist Party, the American Communist Party. Not one has said, Gulf & Western may be rat bastards but at least they did that."

But this is not remarked upon because the film is so inoffensive and because shelves of dry books *have* told the story. It is a movie executive's fancy that nothing exists except the material of films; and perhaps a film-maker can fall for the same humbug. In fact, the "buried" story of *Reds* comes across as one that has been given up, gradually and naturally, over time. It is not a political picture. But like a few other American movies it makes vague but strident claims for itself. Gulf & Western deserve no credit for civic duty or courage. They have merely broadcast the limited, cautious political thinking of the film-maker, and been contractually confined by his confusions.

Reds, as the picture's terse press book puts it, "is the passionate love story of John Reed (Warren Beatty) and Louise Bryant (Diane Keaton), a couple whose love survived their conflicts over professional ambitions, personal goals and political ideals." Read that again, and then remember the inadvertent outburst of Zinoviev in the film, that truly politicised people do not have "personal goals". Not a word of that press book would be as it is without Warren Beatty's approval. The picture makes several large gestures towards history and accuracy. It has all the resources of well-funded art direction bent on making us believe we are seeing the years from 1915 to 1920. When Louise Bryant arrives in New York, a spanking old omnibus is so cleverly placed in the frame, shutting out more recent buildings, so that we can see the Flatiron Building as she would have seen it. Helsinki was chosen to be St Petersburg because it had mustard-colored buildings that looked like the real thing. There is a montage sequence in which still photographs of Lincoln Steffens, Margaret Sanger and so on are cut in with shots of Jack Nicholson as Eugene O'Neill and Edward Herrmann as Max Eastman. Above all, the thirty-two witnesses testify to the picture's interest in history and its fascination with myth and the turmoil of opinions.

But for *Reds* to be the 199-minute entertainment it wants to be, with two parts and an intermission, history has also been brutalised. The sentimental backbone of the film's second half is the separation of John Reed and Louise Bryant, the efforts she makes under great stress to cross the Atlantic, to trudge across the snowy wastes of northern Europe to find him, only to fail. All of this builds to the reunion – a very strong scene on the screen, despite every memory of other train station meetings – in Moscow, as the drained Reed returns from Baku on a shattered train. They embrace on the platform, and he begs her, "Please don't leave me." It is the moment of the picture's poster: in its vitality and its imagery it is as old-fashioned as pictures from the late 1930s. Like the closing of the first half, it reminds us of *Gone With the Wind*, the embodiment of Hollywood's faith that historical events rise to the occasion of exceptional human romance.

Louise Bryant did not make that thwarted trip in search of her husband. They did not miss one another, and wonder what was happening. She did go to Moscow in 1920 and was there on his return from the south, and for his death days later. It does not diminish the affection and love they felt, but Louise Bryant in America was having an affair with the painter Andrew Dasburg, just as Reed was dallying with a young Russian woman. The film omits these liaisons, though Dasburg is one of the witnesses and Beatty himself had an early inclination of playing John Reed when he met that Russian woman, probably during the trip taken with Natalie Wood.

The retriever of American history and the tactful companion to garrulous witnesses, as well as the endorser of a Reed who hated to be cut or misrepresented, is also a Hollywood picture-packager ready to go with whatever works on the screen. For without this looming obstacle to the romance, the agony of lovers reaching out for each other, the second half of *Reds* has no glue or character. There is little question but that the picture wallows in the detailed account of infighting on the American Left. For many, it founders. Not just hard to follow, and harder to sympathise with, it sinks into the pettiness and provincialism of dead and acrimonious meetings, and offers an inadvertent explanation of the failure of American radicalism. It is earnest of Beatty to pursue the tangle, but no part of the desire to make an epic romance. Still, in narrative terms, it is the pretext for Reed's second trip to Russia. The final twenty minutes of the picture seem hardly possible without some build-up and so we have tedious accuracy and flagrant fabrication to get us to the big finish.

But if there were no second half?. . . . Then there would be a modest romance, culminating almost by chance in the excitement of October 1917, and a superb portrait of turbulent love. For the first part of *Reds* is the best thing Warren Beatty has done yet, entirely faithful to period but alive with 1980's feeling for what film can do and for how a man and a woman should behave together. Beneath the rhetoric of international socialism, the first part of *Reds* is a crisp, challenging and very moving essay on sexual politics in which we see two people alike in so many things that they live together, but perplexed in that they both need to be the center of attention.

The film's subtlety has Reed wanting to back out of that central light while Louise squirms to get into it. Reed is a speaker, a writer, a known personality, a charismatic hero. Without ever meaning to, he over-shadows Louise's life and her efforts to become a writer and to be noticed for herself. In his company, she meets editors, writers and the best of Greenwich Village; but because she is just his girl she meets humiliation and failure that would be spared if she were on her own. They have idylls as a couple, but dissent and rows are their eventual mode. They stare at each other, seeing the pain of this ceaseless aggravation. They are fine and right lovers, but they may worry one another to death.

This relationship is set against the 1916 context of free love and suffragism, and the 1980 perspective of women's liberation. But the love story is timeless, too: it is just two people in love and argument. It could be the story of any ambitious people, of an actor and an actress endeavoring to make a marriage as well as their careers. Diane Keaton has never looked or acted better. She is the more arresting because we begin to suspect that this Louise Bryant is not an especially good writer, not a talent that destiny insists on putting on show. She is only a woman trying to write, caught up in the absolute solitude of that need, horrified by her own ego, but unable to still it or find any satisfaction.

We have seen other actresses work well with Beatty on screen (even if against his grain) – Natalie Wood, Jean Seberg, Faye Dunaway, Julie Christie – the chemistry of fiction igniting, whatever the real-life pitch of feeling. But nothing equals the complexity between Beatty and Keaton in *Reds*. In comparison, her Annie Hall is a flip kid, a surface skimmed for liveliness and flopped on the screen. Annie Hall is ordinary but magical – like most Hollywood heroines. Louise Bryant is of a different order: she is a very difficult human being, grappling with her difficulty and utterly without the advantage of magic or the peaceful cul-de-sac of being widely liked. She is only fit to be loved, and quite impossible. She is so good a character that the normal trappings of film fantasy burn off in her light. You do not get horny over her; but you tremble at the prospect of her company.

And Warren has made her the heart of his film. She is the rock, and Reed is the water, the volatility, that eddies around her. It is said in the movie that he was a great journalist. Henry Miller adds that he was just a busy-body whose political conscience came from empty-headedness or the need to suppress his deeper problems. *Ten Days That Shook the World* is mentioned, but not quoted. If you read it, you will find liveliness and interminable dullness. Reed was lucky: he found a "there" in its crucial moment. His book's success stems much more from that than from intrinsic virtues. It is now a nearly unreadable "literary event", just as Reed is more a curiosity than a lasting hero or achiever.

Beatty's Reed is a man striving to stay young, to be regarded as an energetic idealist, to affect the world while edging away from the center of vanity. He has a face that seems to live on light, twitching at it, flexing in and out from it, like an amoeba. There is an early scene, at a dinner table, when he and Louise look at one another and enjoy a flirting discourse, more glances than words, that must be the best available text on Warren Beatty's seductiveness. For while the face is clearly aging, its hope is growing younger.

It is Beatty's most energetic and beseeching performance, and the closest he has come to naked pain and comfortable sincerity. Yet he pales beside Nicholson's O'Neill just because Jack is by nature a movie actor, a gorgeous fake. He commands the picture effortlessly, peering between his curling brows and his kiss-me moustache. He is as strong and relaxed as Gable or Bogart. But Warren is still fidgeting to watch himself, doubting and growing querulous with himself at the advisability of the whole pretence. How can you pretend to be sincere? his wracked eyes ask. He is playing a man whose presence and immediacy are talked about by others, but who is really embarked on designing history, directing the show. He has the frantic, thin vitality of a flame about to go out. The face is twisted, trying to watch itself: at last, the seductiveness has reached its

411

proper task, to convince the man himself, to woo him and have him like himself.

I think he fails, and fails in such as way that he will never try as hard again. For the wish to be Reed, to be an artist and a politician, to be as fully "there" as Jack, is critically offset by the witnesses, pale, shaking humanity, and the film's stroke of genius.

This John Reed cannot be Rhett Butler or even Clyde Barrow because he is only a phantom remembered by others and recollected in so many contradictory ways that he is not a something but a question mark. The film as a whole, but the first half most actively, is given shape by the witnesses. They allow a fragmented structure, and they give us the constant stream of doubt and speculation that undermines the romantic monolith of the scenes. The witnesses rip the old-fashioned movie apart. They subject it to real, untidy life, and they constitute a pathos much greater than that of John and Louise.

For *Reds* becomes a film about old age, wayward memory, about being wrong – for everyone is wrong, that is how we are ourselves. The witnesses are white faces, proud of their ruin, eager still for attention and the very polite Mr Beatty to talk to. They are exposed on the slab of history, achingly lovely and distressed, decay and vibrance on the edge of expiration – several of them had died before the film opened. Together they say: we do not know, history is just the books, the slogans of the victors, and the stories, but do not trust it, for humans cannot comprehend what has happened to them. They tell stories. They think for most of the time that they lived life and were masters of their stories. But life only passed through them, like a wind, so slowly they did not notice it, so quickly it killed them. And at the end you feel the emptiness coming.

Toxic Flat

"What I had in mind," said Eyes. He was speaking slowly, like a far-sighted planner who could not always remember the point at hand. He was also stepping in loose tumbling sand, with Tusk draped across his shoulder. The four of them had walked for hours under Eyes' silent leadership. Clear wore the corpse of Zale like a collar. Doc was ruminating on how Look was his Cordelia, and D would not be parted from Drew's physical remains.

"We're building a golf course up there, up at Toxic," Eyes added, "and I pictured it how we might bury these four around the seventeenth green. It's bare still, without features. Maybe we could put the two ladies like hillocks on one edge of the green, and the lawyers on the other. We could call that hole the Devil and the Deep Blue Sea."

"With the green in between?" asked Clear, who was likely to get the supervisory role.

Eyes nodded wearily. He had just so much stamina for the detail. After that, he liked to settle to the sunsets, the quiet and the beauty of desolation.

"They would be the mounds for sand traps?" D wanted to know.

"Wouldn't you say?" said Eyes.

"Sand traps in the desert?"

"Kid, this is golf we're talking about here."

D nodded. "We'll have to bury them deep," he said.

"We want those little hills," Eyes pointed out. "Like the Scottish seaside links."

"There's a risk," D foresaw, "of the wind exposing the bodies."

"Ah," Eyes had it now. "Yeah, that wind can go like a bitch." He trudged on for another three minutes, and then he reasoned, "Can't we strike a balance?" His hands fluttered; he wanted to be rid of the issue.

"That'll do it," said Clear, cheering up to see how progress might be made in the desert.

"Think we can?" Doc asked D.

"I daresay," D told them. Even if he had to repair the erosion every day, putting the vanished grains of sand back in their proper places, a myriad silica mosaic on Drew's head, a soft shoulder for her to lie under, while dimpled balls could lift and drop on the no doubt astroturf green. He would honor her and replenish her tomb.

And so the sad but resilient cortège walked into Toxic Flat at dusk, ignoring the skull-and-crossbones signs along the way warning of the most hideous and irreversible damage done to the air, the land, and – if there was any – the water, not to mention human tissue, and making it clear that no known insurance plan would cover any idiot who went a step further.

"So long as the other people around here can read," Eyes surmised, "we'll be safe. But I wouldn't wonder if we didn't have to get a reading program going one day. Enlightenment is the watchdog of stability." His brow was pursed at the prospect – it was evident that the leader was looking far ahead for all of them. His pinched eyes were a little less here than there. "D," Eyes had decided, "I bet your good wife would be outstanding at that. It's something to see her teaching the little ones now, planting the salad vegetables, that kind of thing," he finished vaguely.

There was this tenuous produce patch in Toxic Flat, the golf course (still in its infancy), a small eating place, a number of shacks, the long, low manila experimental building and Eyes' place. It wasn't Bel Air, but it was another start, and you'd be surprised to realise how far Bel Air was just bald fields in 1900. There were a few paths defining Toxic Flat, marked out by rocks carefully gathered from the desert and graded for color so that any eye looking at the line saw the sweet, smooth fade of development.

As they arrived, Virginia looked up from one of the greens. There was a "17" on the plastic orange flag stuck in the hole. She was sweeping the green with a stiff broom.

"Hi," she called out. "Eyes, we have got to do something with this green. It's flatter than Faye Dunaway."

"I know, honey," said Eyes, putting Tusk down. "Got ourselves some mounding material here."

"What? Oh, yuk," said Virginia. "That's gruesome. Hi, Dad. Those poor guys."

"They can become their own memorial," Clear explained.

"I suppose," said Virginia. Then she recognised what D was holding, and her face fell in. "Oh, Dad, it's not . . ." They consoled each other as

414

best they could and put the four bodies by the green to wait for the morning's work.

"I'll stay with them," said D.

"Yeah?" said Eyes. "With the jackals, and so on?"

"I'll bring you a blanket, Dad," said Virginia. "And a bowl of chili. Chili OK?"

Time passed at Toxic Flat. D buried the bodies. At first he thought of them as lumps of feelings, there, in the ground, but little by little he saw Drew turning into the sands, fleeting and indeterminate, everywhere.

Doc and Clear were already in story conferences, with fresh yellow legal pads and sharpened pencils. D found lengths of heavy cable which he used to hold the bodies and then he built the mounds up with old tarpaulins and carefully graded the sand to make the hills. He saw a woman watching him work, standing a way away with a headscarf and a tanned face. She did not wave, but she seemed to believe in what he was doing.

"That's a real job you've done," said Eyes a few days later. He had come strolling by with Doc and a very elderly man, tall but stooped and with lugubrious strings of ashen hair hanging from his head. "Tell you what," said Eyes, "we'd better make you our construction man."

"He's good on dialogue, too," Doc added, and Eyes came to one of his dry, lovely but decidedly desert-paced bursts of laughter.

"Who's the old fellow?" D asked Doc when Eyes and the old man had sauntered on in their evening perambulation, the two of them using sand wedges as walking sticks.

"That's Howard," said Doc.

"Didn't he die? In a plane, in '76."

"Slipped away," Doc smiled. "I worked on that one, a pretty thing."

"Still alive?"

"Shot a ninety-five the week before we arrived."

"How did he 'slip away'?"

"Some out-of-the-way landing strip near Laredo. Another body waiting. The usual. The plane never turned off its engine. Howard had been looking to get out for a while."

"And he's been here ever since?"

"Healthy spot. Good air. Eyes has been looking after him. They're pretty close. Howard doesn't really talk to anyone but Eyes. But he's a nice old guy. Snickers if you tell him a good story and, every now and then, he'll just hover around one of Eyes' ladies."

"He was always prone to flight," said D.

415

D spent more nights out at the seventeenth, to be sure the hillocks persisted. The wind came up and it changed the shapes of the mounds, but their idea remained and D could always repair the form with his hands in the morning, pushing it backwards and forwards until he wondered if he really remembered its first form. He grew used to the slow life of Toxic Flat in which the emptiness was kept lively by the thought that Eyes might appear.

"Are we going to make pictures?" D asked Clear.

"Ah," said Clear. "The great enterprise. You should talk to Eyes. Better still, wait for him to raise the subject."

The days passed, and D found work on other parts of the golf course. It was not much more than a sketch of a course on the barren surface: There were years of work ahead. He might make a dogleg on the eleventh by encouraging the outcrop of mesquite; and there were rattlers in the swale on the fifth that could become a very testing natural hazard. He began to dream of water on the course, as pioneers and pirates in LA must once have looked to the Owens River, blue pools to keep the fairways honest. He often saw the same woman watching him, and he had worked out who it was. But no one wanted to hurry him.

"You know, D," Eyes told him, "one day we could have a Desert Classic here."

"If such things ever come again," said D.

"They will. They say LA's getting back in shape."

"Movies soon?" asked D. He had time on his solitary days to scheme out story after story.

"Maybe," said Eyes, stretching. "A new kind of movie."

"Ah," D sighed. That old promise.

"You see," said Eyes, "this desert air is all very well, but it's hell on the skin. I can't say I'm your ingénue any longer. More like Slim Pickens."

"Well," said D.

"Don't be kind."

"It's fine to be rugged, too," D pointed out.

"It is, isn't it? Anyway, I think George is going to have it licked soon."

"George?"

"You haven't met him? He's a mole, that one, He's in the experimental building all day long, with his gizmos. Sleeps there, too."

"What is he doing?"

Eyes looked at D and grinned once. "Well, old fellow," he began, "you won't shout this around?"

D had not shouted for so long. He smiled the thought away.

"George has this computer set-up. Generations of them. It comes out of animation and effects."

"Yes?" said D.

"Now, I'm not technical, but he thinks he's going to be able to program it, one day, soon, not far off, with all the old movies of any actor you like – some Walter Brennan or Wallace Beery, you know – "

"Yes?"

"And turn out new movies they never made."

"Walking and talking?" said D.

"An infinite archive. No actor need ever work again. You can program your plots, conversations and costumes, however you like. Just generate fresh likenesses till the end of time."

"But the stories?"

"You and Doc can plug 'em in, long as you like. And that Virginia of yours. She has a cute story mind, I can tell you."

"And you?" asked D.

"I can play golf," Eyes told him. "And I can be thirty-four for ever."

"A new life," D was enthralled.

"Not the half of it," said Eyes. "I can do appearances."

"How do you mean?"

"Once George has knocked the rough edges off the holograms, I could launch battleships, speak to both Houses of Congress, go on tours of Europe." He hesitated, for he was shy about the climax: "You see, I could be on TV, just walking around waving."

"And never have to leave the Flat," D saw it all.

Eyes was not exactly a young man anymore, but it was more doubt that had ravaged him than mere physical decline. D could see his determined, hopeful eyes still scanning the future, trying to project order there.

"I have to have some rest," Eyes told D suddenly, as if taking him into his confidence.

"Yes," said D.

"But how can you rest," Eyes explained, "if you see it all coming apart?"

"Will there be a world, you wonder, to take care of one's immortality?"

"God, yes!" said Eyes vehemently. He was close to tears.

"Well," said D. "I'll keep working on the golf course."

"Right," Eyes agreed. "That's the sine qua non."

"We might go on for ever," D proposed, his fancy trying to coax Drew's hologram to dance.

"Well," admitted Eyes, "George hasn't given up on that, either."

And so it happened that D earned his way into the settlement and the house where the tanned woman lived with all the children. She worked the land and instructed the young, her own and others springing up in the community. She seemed never to tire or soften with affection, yet everything she did was for others. And she got into the habit of giving D his dinners.

One evening, D was sitting outside the woman's hut. He had just eaten a stewed bean dish. He was thinking of a musical in which Eyes might play an amnesiac who discovers he has healing powers. It was still only a germ. On the golf course, Eyes and Howard were playing. They had dragged George out to caddy for them.

C set a pack of cards on the home-made table that was jammed into the sand. "You play hearts?"

"I think I remember," said D.

"I expect I can help you," C replied.

"Ah," he said.

She dealt. The cards were old and clammy, like slices of ham. There was the face of some pretty, nervous woman on the backs. Why was she afraid? D began to sort out his hand, the sorting remembering for him. He looked at the seventeenth green. He could see the smudge by the raised green that had been Drew, a bump in time. Eyes, Howard and George were standing there, looking down at their feet and at balls D could not see. They moved, they shifted, they turned. It was like a dance, the three men trying to vanish.

"Do you have the two of clubs?" asked C.

And D was pleased to see he did.

THESE DAYS

How does he know, late in 1981 and thereafter, whether he is simply tired in ways that cannot be repaired, afflicted by unequivocal failure, or untouchable? There is a wishful theory in show business that there are a very few people above and beyond the greedy reach of all common forms of mishap or failure. Such people rise above their own failures; they may not even need to work; they have so thorough and so richly alleged a pervasiveness that provable existence may even impair their aura. They have a there of their own, a special place, where the gods and luck live, and where "Fame! – I'm gonna live forever", is the lying muzak. Warren has to wonder whether or not he is there.

He fights long and hard in his own head to deny the disappointment of *Reds*. Industry analysts come to regard it as an example of marketing mistakes: the poster, the follow-up ads so dense with quotation that they are hurried over, the uncertainty that opens in 389 theaters and adds another 276 before Christmas (missing both the eminence of a début in just a few cities, with the picture building slowly, and the power of 1,000 screens), and the absence of Beatty himself. In April 1982, the annual round-up of grosses in *Film Comment* anticipates rentals between $25 and $30 million – "no disaster, but certainly a commercial failure". That is before the film fails to win the Oscar for best picture, or for best actor or actress. The award for direction is its one concession, and that does not affect the box office. A year later, the next round-up reports that *Reds* took in only $21 million – half of what it cost? – when surely it needed $100 million to be securely in profit.

Beatty never permits himself to be caught in a situation where he has to discuss this failure; perhaps he does not even admit it to himself. After all, the film is also a great success – there are many warm reviews, he is taken seriously, he is named best director. Beyond all that, *Reds* does contain some of his best work, so searching and so final that the true source of weariness may be less the time *Reds* took to make than its material and its dismay with both fame and accomplishment. Very soon

420

after *Reds*, he is offered an exciting project, and his quick answer speaks to special depths of depletion: "It's like I've been all night in the whorehouse, and I stagger out in the morning and I see Marilyn Monroe waiting."

Six months after the opening of *Reds*, Warren enlists Mike Mahern, a young man who has made a reputation in distributing exploitation pictures. He asks Mahern to research a way of re-releasing *Reds*, something that has never succeeded for so large a picture. Mahern discovers that the ideal Beatty audience is female, twenty-five and over, and upscale. He proposes a promotion that centers on John Reed as a man who set out to affect history, and Louise Bryant as the liberated woman who went with him. He senses that the film might always have been sold best on the issue of how does a smart, modern, independent woman fuck Warren Beatty and still keep her integrity? Of course, this is a question that interests Warren, too. Mahern devises a campaign and tests it, but the response is grim. *Reds* is now too well-known and too thoroughly written off to have a second chance. Mahern recommends against spending any more of Paramount's money.

But when the picture opens in Japan in 1982, Beatty goes with it. He spends several days with a few selected journalists and he speaks at a press conference for 200 members of the media. And when the picture is released on video cassette, the opening credits name the witnesses, who went unidentified in the first release. But nothing has yet been done with all the witness footage. The real body of history that Beatty recorded is waiting somewhere.

There are signs of him moving on. In the summer of 1982, he spends time with the lawyers who guard Howard Hughes' name, acquiring the rights to the life. He has himself written a first draft script for that project, and apparently it deals with Hughes' public years, with his time in movies and aircraft manufacture, before the great withdrawal. But when asked, Why Hughes?, Beatty's answer addresses the reasons for Hughes's retreat: "It has to do with becoming a victim of your own accumulated power," he says. Paul Schrader remarks that, of course, Warren's own life and career have far more in common with Howard Hughes than with John Reed. "And if he ever delves that subject," says Schrader, "it could be a truly great role for him. But in order to truly delve it, he would have to put himself in the hands of someone who could objectively observe his performance. And I don't think he is psychologically able to let someone else have that power over him. So that's why the Hughes thing persists, and in some way he knows it will be a great statement for him. And he knows that he can't do it. But on the other hand he knows that he can't let anybody else do it."

Other possibilities come and go as he tells himself he will "rest" and wait by merely hiring out as an actor. There is a picture Robert Towne wants to make, *Tequila Sunrise*, about old friends who meet again as a cop and a drug dealer. But Towne's career falters a little with his first direction, *Personal Best*, and with the disputes between him and his producer on that film, David Geffen. Then Towne writes another script, *Mermaid*, for producer Ray Stark. Arthur Penn will direct; Beatty will star. He will be paid $5 million for acting in a love story between a middle-aged man and a young sea creature. But it does not happen. There is a Dick Tracy project, with Beatty starring as the comic-book hero and Walter Hill directing. But it does not happen either. It is said that Beatty is becoming slower and more obsessively dedicated to negotiating his deals. Some others reckon it is a game, that he does not really want to work.

There is another Orson Welles venture in a Hollywood where the great man has managed nothing since *The Big Brass Ring*. He wants now to make a movie of *The Cradle Will Rock*, a play he mounted with the Mercury Theater in 1937. He approaches Beatty for introductions he needs in securing funding. The two men lunch at Ma Maison, a favorite haunt of Welles. Welles brings the script to the meal, and Beatty asks to see it at the lunch table. He begins to read it, and does not stop. It takes him three hours to read the script. In the meantime, the restaurant empties and closes. But the two men are left undisturbed. Then Beatty launches into a two-hour talk – about the script, the changes it requires, the need for further clarification. It is another humiliation for Welles.

It may be noticed that the picture business is changing. In the late 70s and the early 80s, the business gives up many old ghosts and attends instead to what kids want to see. The great empire of George Lucas and Steven Spielberg takes over, and that is the quality end of a product that reaches down to *Porky's*, and then lower. There are hosts of moviegoers who do not quite know who Warren Beatty is any longer. The very young did not bother with *Reds*, and they do not respond quickly to shy, middle-aged men. Legend can sleep a season now and awake to something close to anonymity.

Then there is the political campaign of 1984, a task that honestly beckons him, yet still an escape that he can convince himself he is bound to make. And he is on the telephone to Gary Hart day after day, and he attends parties and fund-raisers. He is a more important member of

Hart's campaign than the press realises. He is in San Francisco for the Democratic Convention, hobnobbing with George Lucas. At that time, he goes out with CBS television reporter Diane Sawyer. They go to see a movie, *Top Secret*, one night and play video games in the theater lobby. There he goes again, gossips murmur, escorting a new, bright young woman. But suppose now that the woman is the activator and that, on her way to *60 Minutes*, Sawyer is taking the opportunity to get acquainted with someone who might one day make an interesting, nostalgic segment on the Sunday show, puzzled witness to his own life?

On the evening of Monday, September 10, 1984, the Toronto Film Festival pays tribute to Warren Beatty – which is to say, they get him to attend and sit still for an hour or so. Roger Ebert and Gene Siskel are to host the tribute, interviewing Beatty on stage. But he is unwilling to contemplate many questions in advance, or even to confer with his future hosts. The arrangements are all being made through David MacLeod, his Canadian cousin.

But he does turn up, and for close to two hours clips of Beatty's films chosen by Warren (not by the festival) are interspersed with the appearance of guests who speak briefly about Beatty. The guests are Arthur Penn, Jack Nicholson, Robert Towne and Jerzy Kosinski.

Then Beatty appears, to be interviewed by Siskel and Ebert. They are tucked and pumped into tuxedoes, but Warren is more casual in a loose white suit. At the outset, he says, "When one has become a familiar face, it endows one with responsibilities to respond to questions. It's one of the things you have to go along with when you become a performer or a household word or a sex symbol." He can sometimes sound like someone or something heading slowly away from the known world.

Yet he is soon questioning Siskel and Ebert, to divert time and attention from himself. He teases them. He has always possessed a humor too elusive for the movies of his era. He mentions but does not read a speech he says he has written on the plane to Toronto, "The Crisis in Progressive Film-making and American Liberalism". Did he fly in from Sydney, or only LA? Reports say that his "charm and unaffected manner drew repeated bursts of applause". What cunning it is when celebrity himself can shape such occasions so that he looks like the only ordinary fellow in sight, an unsullied shaft of natural light amid all the flashbulbs.

So he has shown himself to the public, and given nothing away. He may have a little more reason to persuade himself that he is open and human. Yet the tribute is remarkable for the extent to which he has been not just its modest, nearly reluctant subject, but its producer. As Jack Nicholson confides at one moment in Toronto, indulging his grinning wickedness, "I don't usually tell stories about Warren – because you're not trained to . . ."

There are many women mentioned now, but no one who seems to grip his attention. He sees Jessica Savitch, another television commentator, but she is killed in an accident. The French press assert that he will marry actress Isabelle Adjani, but it does not happen. He is seen with models Dayle Haddon, Carol Alt and the Israeli Sippi Levine. (He is interested in Israel: he visits the country and talks to people at *The New Republic*.) He has Margaux Hemingway around sometimes at his house, and at the Toronto Film Festival tribute Diane Keaton is still there, but silent in the body of the audience, not on stage talking about, or to, him.

He begins to be a commonly mentioned personage in stories about other people – and these are often people of far less talent or distinction, no matter that he had the policy in public relations of never appearing or working with anyone beneath his level.

He has red letter days, but not always his. One is May 21, 1977 – Jerry Hall will never forget that date. She is the Texas model on her way to marrying Mick Jagger. And in the Memoirs she writes early in life, she recalls that day because at a New York restaurant she sits between Mick and Warren. "They were both being pretty keen. I'm sitting there and Warren starts to chat and then Mick leans over to talk and then he gets mad and says to Warren, 'She's with me,' because he had arrived first. And Warren looks at me and I say, 'I'm not with anyone. I'm engaged [to Bryan Ferry]. I just happen to be at this dinner.' And then Mick says, 'Now, Warren, listen, man . . .' and drags him off. And he takes him over to the telephone booth and starts calling up models, trying to fix Warren up with someone else." How long does this take? And what is the most profound definition of the word "model"?

Is this loneliness beginning, the life of John McCabe pressing through the seductive smile? He mixes more with the younger set in pictures, with actors like Timothy Hutton, Vincent Spano and Steve Bauer who seem to regard him as a model of success. He seems ready to give advice about this wicked, duplicitous world. Diane Lane is interviewed by *Interview*. Do you know Warren Beatty? she is asked. "Sure," she answers, "How can you not?" This is surely a testament to fame, yet it makes him sound like blue cheese dressing or the IRS. Lane says she "got some counselling from him". She met him with Spano and Steven

Porcaro, and Warren calls her afterwards and she says she is really uptight about a lot of things. And he says, "If you're going to talk to anyone please talk to me, you know I'm experienced."

How seldom a man really feels that about himself – perhaps it is still a part he is trying on. Lane feels secure about him – "I needed the comforting knowledge that I didn't have anything to worry about from him." But she does not "go out" with Warren: "I don't like being part of a harem."

But for every such instance of Warren with a night on his hands, there is a story that testifies to his authority still. Dominick Dunne is writing a profile on Diane Keaton for *Vanity Fair*. He gathers indirectly that he should not raise the matter of Warren with Diane. It is over, but there are regrets and confusions that remain. Dunne gets on well with Keaton, they talk a lot. And then one day, not long afterwards, Dunne is at a table at a hotel when Warren comes by like a waiter and says he hears that Dunne's been having very good talks with Keaton. But is there anything more fatiguing than to appear occasionally in public with that offhand mastery? How sweet to go away.

He is still – is he not? – a movie star and a filmmaker about to announce his next venture. He entertains many unlikely ideas. He talks to Wayne Wang, the Chinese-American director who has made *Chan is Missing* for $22,000. Warren admires the picture and its ingenuity. Moreover, Wang has a new script, written by Henry Bean, that intrigues Warren. But it worries him, too, because it is about a man who beats women. It is called *Who You Know*, and it is a reworking of *In a Lonely Place*, the Nicholas Ray picture in which Humphrey Bogart plays an embittered screenwriter suspected of murder. Beatty is drawn to the hostility in *Who You Know*, but he wonders if it could be there still, without the violence. Suppose the man drank or gambled? But Wang is determined to make more small, independent films, and Beatty insists that the medium needs big pictures. So they part company, with respect for one another.

As the election hopes of 1984 fade away, he moves back to pictures with what seems like fresh vigor and determination. He starts to develop several possibilities. There is the book *Edie*, a documentary about Edie Sedgwick, co-authored by George Plimpton, who has played a small part in *Reds*. Warren wonders if *Edie* could make a movie for the young actress Molly Ringwald. He is also sponsoring a script written by Elaine May, a vehicle perhaps for himself and Dustin Hoffman. There is renewed talk of *Dick Tracy*. That lapsed project comes back to life with

Diane Keaton

Isabelle Adjani

Beatty as star and producer, and perhaps with Martin Scorsese as its director.

And he is talking to James Toback again. He hires Toback to write a screenplay on the life of Bugsy Siegel, who walked out into the desert of Nevada and said let's make Las Vegas here. He is also ready, he says, to produce another Toback script, *The Pick-Up Artist*, which Toback wants to direct. He debates with Toback as to whether Timothy Hutton or Robert De Niro is most suited to the central part. He says he is going to set the picture up at a studio; he says this for months, during which Toback has no money. Toback asks when? And Warren says it won't be so long now.

In December 1984, Warren talks to Martin Scorsese about *Dick Tracy*: a picture with musical numbers, a lot of color, a good guy and bad guys, a big picture but fun. As they talk, Scorsese likes Warren more and more. They swap stories, and not a great deal gets done. The script – still problematic – is not reached in their pleasant evenings together. "The trouble is," says Warren, "you ask me a question and sometimes it takes me three days to think out the answer."

Of course, both men have other things on their mind. Beatty has his projects, while Scorsese is thinking about how to finance *The Last Temptation of Christ*, and about getting married again. But sometimes they do get to the Tracy script and Scorsese is impressed with Beatty's ideas on it. They do some research on cities with the proper 1930s look.

But gradually, Scorsese realises several things – that *Dick Tracy* can hardly help itself from becoming a bigger picture, not just $20 million, but at that point where budgets can magically double; he sees that Beatty does not yet have a firm studio deal on it, or even the urgent wish to proceed; and he is losing interest himself. Perhaps it has all been a chance for the two men to get to know one another.

They do haggle out a form of a deal, with final cut being a vexed issue. It ends up as "joint" final cut, with the last decision going to Scorsese in the event of an impasse. He signs the deal, but Warren never gets around to signing it. And so Scorsese marries, for the fourth time, and goes off to Italy on his honeymoon.

He has not mentioned this possibility to Warren. But Warren finds him at a hotel in Venice and calls him. "Well," he says, and pauses darkly. "Congratulations." "Yeah," says Scorsese. They agree to move on to other things.

When he's in Los Angeles, Warren lives at his house, now, on Mulholland Drive, just east of Benedict Canyon, built to his own design on a manufactured knoll, behind a ring of trees. It is modern, with white walls, wood floors and expanses of curved window. It has its own gym and a theater; it has a cook and a secretary. The walls are bare, there are no pictures. A visitor says, "It's a house where you know there's nothing to look at but whose house it is."

On the night of July 1, 1985, in an LA heatwave of over 100° F by day, he sits outside by the pool, oblivious to the temperature or the insects in the air. He has a speech that he is rewriting and rehearsing for a group of associates. It gets to be three in the morning, but he does not flag or settle for the current version of the speech. One of the friends goes back to his hotel, but an hour later Warren calls him to read the latest state of the speech.

The next day, July 2, he takes the speech to San Francisco, where he is to deliver it at a fundraiser on behalf of California Supreme Court Chief Justice Rose Bird, who is threatened by a forthcoming confirmation election. This event takes place at the Fairmont Hotel in front of 1200 people; it will raise $250,000 to help Rose Bird fight the campaign to oust her. The hotel ballroom is decorated with bunting and banners that proclaim "A rose for judicial independence".

For Beatty, this is unaccustomed in that it has the prominence not just of appearance, but of a featured address. It will be seen as a move; it is evidently a matter over which he has taken trouble. Anyone esteeming his shrewdness, therefore, might assume that the occasion has been carefully selected and that Warren and Rose are old friends likely to benefit one another.

Rose Bird is anxious to eliminate any hint that they are more than friends. It emerges that she and Warren have never met before. Beatty's speech is grand, far-reaching and dramatic. Everyone agrees that he has given it in fine style: "Those who are demanding 'Defeat Rose Bird', are the direct descendants of Joe McCarthy, the John Birch Society and the far Right that in the 1950s demanded the impeachment of Earl Warren. . . . Where we see constitutional rights, they see only demons."

The lady herself – seen as in a very delicate position in the polls, and not universally approved of by liberals or lawyers – says, "I think it's a little unfair to have a person who introduces you be better looking than you are." She glances at her keynote speaker. "I think how nice Mother Nature was to put such a nice mind on such a nice body. I hope you'll forgive me, Mr Beatty, for that sexist comment." Warren has to smile, whereas any of his movies would know how to squash such a remark.

If mixed impulses are any indication, this campaign is swaying from side to side. Beatty goes back to Los Angeles euphoric: he recalls a standing ovation and being interrupted three times by applause. He remembers that influential figures talked to him afterwards and said, well, if he was interested in running against Alan Cranston. . . . It was a move, and there was support. Now he has only to decide whether he has made the move or not.

The *San Francisco Chronicle* decides that the campaign got off to an "irresponsible and intemperate start". Beatty's speech is criticised as "outrageous, unfair and erroneous . . . It says little for Beatty's understanding of the democratic process and he can be excused only on grounds of vocation; the words were put in his mouth by others."

He moves arbitrarily and swiftly. He is everywhere – at the house on Mulholland, in LA hotels, at the Carlyle or the Ritz Carlton in New York. There are maybe a dozen projects to which he is attached; or there is only really Hughes. He is in Israel, in London, in Paris, in north Africa, in Deauville. He is on the phone, on the way, in the next room. So many places that he is seldom here, and always there.

Then he holds a press conference, but it concerns an old picture and his decision that it will not be seen on television. Arbitration has supported Beatty's claim that Paramount cannot sell *Reds* to ABC for network presentation if ABC elects to cut the picture for reasons of time. This has been a long drawn-out case, the continuation of a thirty-year struggle between film directors and television (first fought by George Stevens over *A Place in the Sun*). Beatty has had final cut on *Reds*, the contractual right to establish its length and form. Paramount has always dreaded 199 minutes, for it allows only one show every evening. Network television can cut a film on the grounds of standards and practices (for reasons of language, violence or sexual explicitness), but not for length. ABC wants to cut about ten minutes from *Reds* so that they can fit the movie into an evening schedule and finish by 11 p.m. in time for local news. Beatty will not budge and so the deal is off: ABC will not now pay Paramount the agreed $6.5 million for the rights.

Beatty describes this as a triumph of principle, and so it is in its belated way. But it is also madness when the movie can be seen intact on cassette and when it was always too long. As for Paramount – with Charles Bluhdorn dead and Barry Diller moved away to Twentieth Century-Fox what can they be thinking? Who else again would give Warren such a thorough final cut? And how would he work without it? Is his world moving towards stalemate, and is the principle here also an unconscious way of making work less likely?

Beatty gives a rare interview on this topic, he is so concerned about it. But the man emerging from the interview is more like a film-maker ready to give up the onerous business if it insists on being so small-minded. There is an air of retreat that the interview seems designed to illustrate.

He complains about seeing *Bonnie and Clyde* on television: "'I knew every cut and every gunshot and I knew were there for a reason,' said Beatty, sipping a diet soda on ice in a suite at New York's Ritz Carlton hotel. 'And then they were gone.'"

It is not that he really believes he can change the world; there is rather more sense of an urge to slip away from it: "'At a certain point, you feel a little silly about trying to retain nine minutes of a film. But then you remember when you were at a location trying to get something right. To think that this goes down the tube because someone in some town insists that the local news must start at 11 p.m. – it's bad enough it has to be interrupted by someone selling Roto-Rooter.

"'It all comes back to the same question.' He asks, 'Do we want to make an art form out of the movies, or do we want to just say they're made for distraction? What are we spending our time doing this for? Acting and directing movies are hard enough for me anyway. You feel foolish enough when you are trying to keep a 95,000-ton soufflé from falling, so we have to go through some rituals in order to keep our dignity in this work.'"

After several months of being on hold, *The Pick-Up Artist* moves forward. Beatty calls Toback out to Los Angeles, and every day for two weeks, from about six in the evening to three in the morning, they work on the script together at Beatty's house. They take it line by line, with Beatty always probing with what Toback calls "a good cruel sense of whether it plays". The script is improved commercially, and given an upbeat ending. It remains dark and funny, but it is more conventional and less dangerous than it was when only Toback's vision. Beatty sets the film up at Fox, and it is a script that could make a successful picture, about a young man's chronic appetite for women.

The casting changes. Timothy Hutton has been pencilled in for $1 million, but then Hutton elects to direct a Steven Spielberg *Amazing Stories* for television, and Beatty takes advantage of this to look elsewhere. Vincent Spano is now favored, and there is a chance of the film starting in September 1985, with Spano and Rebecca de Mornay. But then de Mornay says she will be in Sam Shepard's new play in the fall. Toback is very anxious to start quickly; there have been so many delays. But Beatty queries his impatience as being bad for the film. They consider Diane Lane and Jodie Foster, but judge neither will work well on screen with Spano.

Then Warren says, put it off until the spring of 1986. Do it then for sure, with Vincent Spano and Rebecca de Mornay. Then, as an after-thought, he suggests Toback keep looking at other people. You never know what you'll see. By the spring, he adds, he'll be able to look in on the shooting. He says there are people in the business telling him hair-raising stories about Toback. He lets the director gather that Beatty has been urged to watch him closely. Yet the virtue and character of Toback as a film-maker is his recklessness – it is as if Beatty is finding himself as the tamer to this frightening friend.

By the end of September 1985, Beatty is to depart for Morocco, there to make the film that Elaine May has written. It has a working title, *Ishtar*; it is a comedy about two stranded musical comedy men. The cast is Beatty, Dustin Hoffman and Isabelle Adjani, with May directing. The project has survived several pre-production worries – that Morocco is too close to the terroristic Middle East for the safety of stars; that the picture could prove too costly with two stars set for at least $6 million each; that Hoffman is more interested in other ventures; that he and Warren may engage in a destructive contest as to which is the greater perfectionist. Moreover, Columbia (putting up the money) flinches at an early budget of $30 million and talks it down to nearer $25 million, with Warren and Dustin required to put up some cash themselves. After all, a light romantic comedy having to take in $70 million, with a feeling of the *Road* pictures or *The Fortune*, may not be surefire. You have to wonder if this is another 95,000-ton soufflé.

As Warren is about to leave for the desert, Toback is still trying to tie down a cast for *The Pick-Up Artist*. It has now moved on, and centers on Steve Guttenberg and Rosanna Arquette.

This chapter could go on for ever, or for as long as it takes. This chapter is just keeping up with the present, mounting up as the days go by.

He returns from Morocco, and there is a holiday break, in January 1986, before filming of *Ishtar* resumes at the Astoria Studio. There are so many things to fill the pause. He has a little physical therapy for an injury from North Africa. He is being pressed to make a decision on whether or not, again, he will do *Dick Tracy*. He agrees to make a

personal presentation on behalf of the Russian poet Yevgeny Yev-
tushenko's film, *Kindergarden*, in New York. The PEN conference takes
place in that city and he is at a dinner party in a Central Park West
apartment that includes E. L. Doctorow, some South American writers
and Rosario Murillo, First Lady of Nicaragua, who has two young men
with her who have to be carrying (if not, why are they there?). The talk is
of Gary Hart and Edward Kennedy, of censorship and revolution, the
beef and the wine, and Warren says shyly, like a faded T-shirt, "Well, of
course, I'm the man who made *Reds*."

His mind may be somewhere else. He has had the first sixty pages of
Toback's Bugsy Siegel script. They are remarkable pages – full of
delirious talk, murder and sexual insolence. But only sixty pages.

A few days later they meet, to read the two new prospects for *The
Pick-Up Artist* (99 per cent sure to start in April) – Robert Downey and
Wendy Gazelle. After the reading, Beatty asks Toback:

"Where's the rest of my script?"

"Another forty pages by the weekend."

"What are you doing with it?"

"I could use some more of my expenses money."

"Tell you what, I'll dial the first digit of the Fox number, and for every
ten new pages you deliver I'll dial another digit."

"You like it then?"

"It's very interesting."

"By the way, you know I'd really like to direct it myself. Now I know
you like it."

"Uh-huh."

"What does that mean?"

"Finish the script. Then we'll talk about directors."

"Tell me I'll direct it, and that'll help me finish it."

"You know something? When you do *Pick-Up Artist*, you should not
have sex at all. You should be totally abstinent from the start of
pre-production."

"You're telling me that?"

"The film will be better if you never come."

"You're telling me that?"

"On *Bonnie and Clyde*, I never fucked once. It was important."

Ishtar finishes shooting on time, on March 16 1986. That leaves eight months for post-production if it is to make its appointed Thanksgiving opening. *The Pick-Up Artist* begins shooting on May 19. Susie Amos has been ready for the female lead until, four weeks before shooting, Toback is told that the part is re-cast. It will be Molly Ringwald. And Toback agrees, for, as he says, "There was nothing about it that did not make sense rationally."

In the summer of 1986, therefore, Beatty has much to look forward to. The Oscars for 1986 will be presented on March 30 1987, Warren's fiftieth birthday. *Ishtar* may bring him an extra present. Moreover, in the same span of time, he will have sponsored movies by two American directors, Elaine May and James Toback, known for their talent, independence and difficulty. What a producer he will appear as if he has enabled them to make their best films and their greatest hits.

The business wonders at how, or even whether, *Ishtar* will be promoted by its producer; and whether it will keep that title. There is no hint of what it will be except a double-page picture in the May 1986 *Life* of Beatty and Dustin Hoffman, in Morocco, on a camel – with Hoffman chuckling at a guarded Beatty, clad in blue robe and burnoose, eyes narrowed, as he gazes into the desert.

But then, in late August, as the picture is supposedly being mixed, Columbia take an ad in *Variety*, announcing the national release date for *Ishtar* – May 22 1987.

This delay is not quite as great as six months seems: it is only moving the picture from one peak season to another. Still, there are signs that Columbia has been caught by surprise. A ninety-second trailer for *Ishtar* has already been playing with *Armed and Dangerous*; and a six-month extension on what is said to be a $34 million picture can add $2 million in interest to the budget – or $5 million to the break-even rentals. One Columbia executive speaks of "grave disappointment."

There are reports of coolness between *Ishtar* and Columbia's new chairman, Englishman David Puttnam. Indeed, on the occasion of Oscars night in 1982 (when *Reds* won for direction, but Puttnam's *Chariots of Fire* took best picture), Puttnam has made open comments to the effect that Beatty is not as good a director as *Chariots'* Hugh Hudson. Puttnam's predecessor at Columbia, Guy McElwaine, had had responsibility for *Ishtar* as well as Beatty's fond regard. (In fact, we have met McElwaine already, in 1967: he was the Warner's press agent Rex Reed had to endure to get his interview with Beatty.)

There is no evidence, though, that Columbia has said *Ishtar* is not ready or good enough. Beatty gives a press interview to make it clear that he is protecting his and Elaine May's right to take the proper time and trouble with the picture:

> "Elaine is a meticulous director, and it seemed like a shame to force her into a rushed situation. When you're making a movie, you have to keep your eye on the ball and let someone work the way they work best."

As I write, it is the fall of 1986. There is no word of re-shooting on *Ishtar*, in Morocco or in some closer, less dangerous desert. The picture is being refined. And Warren is getting ready for 50. Both *Ishtar* and *The Pick-Up Artist* are scheduled to open in the spring of 1987, not long after the publication of this book.

DICKLESS DEMOCRACY

". . . a feature writer from the Associated Press asked Inez what she believed to be the 'major cost' of public life.

"'Memory, mainly,' Inez said . . . 'Things that might or might not be true get repeated in the clips until you can't tell the difference.'

"'But that's why I'm here. I'm not writing a piece from the clips. I'm writing a piece based on what you tell me.'

"'You might as well write it from the clips,' Inez said. Her voice was reasonable. 'Because I've lost track. Which is what I said in the first place.'"
    – Joan Didion, *Democracy* (1984)

I really think I'd prefer you not calling, Warren, if and when you read this book. Though I did consider writing such a call for this last chapter, as a way of covering a few things that need to be said. But I don't think I want to meet you, or get to know you, or have you play that game with me. The charm has been in the imagining.

I did ask you once to talk, and you were very doubtful, but you left me waiting for an answer, and so now, years later, you may reproach me for getting on and doing it without you; and you may wonder out loud in your lovely injured innocence how anyone could do such a book without knowing you. But I'm not sure the knowing is possible, and I have a hunch you offer it as a smokescreen, a way of concealing yourself. I suspect you believe you're unknowable because it helps you feel elusive. That's not a challenge or a criticism – I think it's probably vital in an actor and a public figure.

You can write your own book one day, if you will. There could be a dozen books about you and publishers' interest in your own memoirs would only mount. You know this very well, for you have always quietly urged others to write and think about you. And it has worked so well that you now need barely a public word to keep it going. So it's entirely up to you whether you write your book. I guess you won't, because you want to stay secret. I don't just mean you'd rather the public wondered; I think you're happier, freer, if you can go on wondering about it all yourself. The hard facts may be far too cold and blunt for comfort.

That's why I quoted that passage from *Democracy* at the head of this chapter. We can be angry or disturbed that public life dissolves memory. We can say that memory is history, integrity and responsibility. All true. Yet I'm not sure Joan Didion or her Inez are simply angry or devastated at the slippage, and not also a touch curious and enchanted by this slipperiness in public life. For public life digests all the facts and their helpless contradictions and turns them into an atmosphere – a mode that is impossible to recall or pin down accurately, but so hard to forget: it is not the butterfly, but our experience of its flight and its tiny, fragrant wind. That's how I think of you, Warren, not quite as a real man, but the idea of American beauty for men in this time. (Not that women don't think about you too.) And I wrote this book because I like the idea, and I wrote it in the way I did because I was trying to get the idea and the slipstream as well as you.

There's only one thing I'd ask. Don't ever run for any political office, please. It's not that you couldn't do the job, or wouldn't be more capable than many others. It's just that the routine is so actual and tedious, and so wearing; it's not even a true role, let alone a good script; it would bore you and leave you tired and bitter. Look at it this way. Do you really think in this time we're going to vote for a president, or any other public official, with a dick? No, we want the old-timers, the re-tread ghosts, the tepid smilers and those wishful, handsome guys whose eyes seem to have been put in by two different doll-makers.

We must get used to humdrum presidents and problems that are only solved in hand-outs and fireside chats. Before Reagan was elected, Gore Vidal warned of a man whose training had been to stand handsomely in the light and do as he was told. But the fact and the "numbers" of the Reagan years have only shown us how far our political impasses and lobbying interests not only require a stooge, but can hardly persist without one. A thinking leader could collapse or start assassinating his people. So the tedium and the intractability may make for many more actorly leaders ready to speak the tranquilising communiqués.

If you did get to be president now, there's not much to look forward to except those daily photo opportunities, and one day having your colon or your polyps spread across the evening news. So play parts like Bugsy Siegel instead, because, let's face it, if at fifty-plus you play that dashing

John Gutmann, *Face Behind Veil*, 1939

hood-killer-loudmouth-fucker, it wouldn't be a tactful run-in for election. America loves its killers and its cocksmen, but it likes them to know their place. (You know the deputy sheriff parts Reagan had to play; you should remember that the time America loved you best was when you started killing us, giving your shit-eating grin to all the sheriffs.)

Be dangerous and seductive – that's your thing. Be the great shy lady-killer of our time. And if the Smithsonian want to measure your dick, let them come to you. Get on with Siegel and all the other wild guys you could be, because you *are* nearly fifty, and I know you hurt your shoulder in Morocco filming *Ishtar*, and you're at an age when the hurt might not go away and you could wake up a year from now knowing you were old and . . .

You see, age is not kind to modern American magic. But the gorgeous young women go on for ever and they have backs like butter. You are already America's man, our most shady, elegant hero, and no one wants to know or see when you can't manage it any longer – not the new women, not America, and least of all you.

FUNLESS FILM

Ishtar opens; *Ishtar* closes. The picture is pulled forward a week, to May 15, to give it a chance against *Beverly Hills Cop II*. And it is the top picture for its opening week, grossing $4.3 million at just over 1,100 screens. This is not the performance of a winner, much less that of a confident summer comedy that has had a sandstorm of publicity, on television and in national magazines. Indeed, a small horror movie, *The Gate*, takes in only $100,000 less than *Ishtar* in as many theatres in the first week they share.

By June 3, Aljean Harmetz reports that, in 17 days, *Ishtar* has grossed only $11 million; that 'audiences are shrinking daily and the movie is losing theaters each week.' By the second half of July, it is virtually impossible to find *Ishtar* in American theaters. It has been dumped, to let more likely ventures have the screens. There is the overseas market to come (though not, presumably, that of Islam); there will be TV and video revenue down the line. This is Columbia, whistling in the dark, attempting to find the vantage from which things are not as dark as they seem. But the seeming cannot be denied.

Ishtar is a disaster: that hint of a cracked rhyme is only one of the merciless jokes made against the film. The deadpan vultures may be deemed the drollest touch in *Ishtar,* but gleeful birds of prey are out in the skies of showbiz. Columbia says as little as they can manage about the picture. The new regime there has only to shrug to let the blame settle on previous masters. It is a calamity, but not Columbia's fault: Warren has the only available shoulders for the load.

The picture's budget, too late in the day, becomes a subject for concern. Who ever said it was ever as little as $26 or $28 million? people now ask. It was always closer to $35 or $39 million. There are savage inside leaks that run as high as $51 million. Beatty himself is heard murmuring that a film should not be attacked just because it costs a lot. Yet, in the past, he has idealistically warned against the helpless swelling of movie budgets.

441

There are better reasons for regretting *Ishtar* than the loss of someone else's money. How shall we describe the film? Whatever the final cost, there is no disputing the overpowering time and deliberation that Beatty and Elaine May bring to *Ishtar*. Yet it feels like the movie that several bright, careless people might have sketched out at lunch—a parody of a situation, charismatic improvisation, something light and quick, like the desserts they play with—a scheme which, if they are lucky, no one ever mentions again. Tomorrow can be another phantom movie costing no more than the lunch. But this one drifts sadly into manufacture. It is the largest, emptiest dessert of all time, or it is that smothering soufflé Beatty has dreaded, settling on his boyish head.

Maybe there was a better picture lost in the traffic: the portrait of an odd friendship between two inept songwriters. As long as it is in New York, the film has a chance, and the wary fondness Beatty and Hoffman show for each other seems worth encouraging. Going to Africa is curtains. Elaine May is so uninterested in the intrigue, the chases and the "adventure" that sets in there. The view of Arabs is unexpectedly crude and old-fashioned. It is perverse to cast Isabelle Adjani, then wrap her in consuming clothes and give her so little to do. There is not even a love story, let alone a sexual contest. The obvious comparisons with Hope and Crosby reaffirm the wit, energy and instinct of the *Road* films. *Ishtar* is so obviously meant as a comedy, no one can ignore the lack of fun. Beatty is seldom as stunned or stricken as when required to be amusing.

Ironically, he has put himself out for *Ishtar*, even if cautiously, guardedly, with that disappearing grin that says, Why ask me silly questions? when he hopes it may deflect the naked ignominy by which he has put himself on the line, in a resplendent white suit, for the flimsiest of his movies. What spirals of suspicion let a man promote *Ishtar* and neglect *Reds*?

He does breakfast-show television interviews, and earns a good deal of amused comment for insisting on such control of these interviews that he edits them. He has also demanded they be done on film, not tape —for film is kinder to fading beauty. *Ishtar* itself shows how far Beatty's face is dissolving in indecision, lofty reticence and discreet soft focus. He has the presence of a stander-by, someone overlooked.

Above all it is evident that he has been away too long: the six-year gap between *Reds* and *Ishtar* has filled with kids who see only a stranger. At a fairly successful preview of the picture in Toronto, teenagers questioned in the lobby disclose with cheery innocence that they have not heard of Warren Beatty. The desert's capacity for oblivion begins to close in on fame.

It is a bad time in other ways. For just as *Ishtar* is about to open, Gary Hart falls in a furor of Washington townhouse logistics, *Monkey Business* snapshots and the dead-eyed prettiness of Donna Rice. The analyses that come in the next few days and months do not know or dare enough to pin it down, but they find a self-destructive recklessness in Hart that has been influenced by Beatty. Some say inspired. Mentioned in all such studies, Beatty begins to emerge as a laconic, rootless Mephistopheles. Two political careers are finished in one buzz of Bimini.

Then, in early August, while finishing *The Pick-Up Artist* for September release, he has his car stolen, from its parking place, as he dines at a Sunset Boulevard restaurant. There is a Hollywood joke, that he couldn't afford to pay the parking valet. No one believes that story, but the business now has many brave enough to be seen enjoying Warren's decline. This is a mood and a time in which such a star might easily withdraw—or find the courage and character to re-make triumph in the new state of middle age.

He will have to measure his own need and desire to discover which way to go—away, toward the desert of introspection, or back, into the center and its town, Hollywood, determined to re-take, and re-define the jittery place. The next ten years will decide whether he is artist and maker, or a great, enigmatic subject, real or just a legend.

Acknowledgments

I have to thank Warren Beatty for withholding himself. If you have been touched, amused or intrigued by this book, you are bound to honor Warren's exceptional refinement and reticence of presence and his Romantic calculation that there was more energy likely to be stirred here by his absence than his presence. Imagine the book that might have found itself having to transcribe his reveries, believe his confessions, and wait for his pauses. Imagine, too, a subsequent editorial process in which he would have had to ask himself if he had said what he meant; and, if he had, whether the book could be safely released.

Tactful and delicate, he left me hanging, and thinking. Perhaps he is inclined to believe that imagining still has more to offer a book than tape-recording. For example, the real Warren might have had to admit glumly, "Well, no, I've not read that." But in my speculations, I can shine up the possibility that he had known (all along) John Berger's book *A Seventh Man*, with its insight into all the lifelike imagery of our time:

> "A friend came to see me in a dream. From far away. And I asked in the dream: 'Did you come by photography or train?' All photographs are a form of transport and an expression of absence."

The presence of Warren Beatty, I believe, has a great deal to do with the melancholy of absence. That is why I have spent time in this book with the detail of the films, and with the suggestion of an unmade movie that might be fit for Warren. Such worlds have a place along with the real context measured by the IRS and *Variety*. This is a book about the way a movie star lives and wonders; and, as such, that involves him listening to us whistling up our imitation of him. If anything keeps Warren from doing something, it is his wondering about doing everything else. And if you care to understand a star and the mist of starriness, knowing them exactly, legally or biographically is not so much out of the question as a distraction from their heartfelt pursuit of metamorphosis.

This book has not talked to everyone alive who has touched Warren. It has sought and talked, here and there, but it has not wanted to be aggressive or intrusive. Actually, it has welcomed those who preferred not to talk. The one thing I have in common with Warren Beatty is shyness – and the worry that shyness is only the ingrowing flamboyance of those who would like to run the show, but cannot bear to be seen doing so.

But I am grateful to these people for varying amounts and degrees of talk and insight: Peter Bogdanovich, Raymond Carney, Helen Chaplin, Francis and Eleanor Coppola, Richard and Mary Corliss, Richmond Crinkley, Clint Eastwood, Roger Ebert, Jeannette Etheredge, Jeffrey Alan Fiskin, Sid Ganis, Frank Gilroy, Lee Goerner, Molly Haskell, Goldie Hawn, Buck Henry, Joe Hyams, Kevin Hyson, Henry Jaglom, Diane Johnson, Phil and Rose Kaufman, Jerzy Kosinski, Edith Kramer, Gavin Lambert, Tom Luddy, Arthur Mayer, Patrick McGilligan, David MacLeod, Mike Mahern, Daniel Melnick, Robin Menken, Monique Montgomery, Alan J. Pakula, Bob Rafelson, Maurice Rapf, Peter Scarlet, Paul Schrader, Martin Scorsese, Harry Dean Stanton, Tom Sternberg, Alan Surgal, Richard Sylbert, James Toback, Robert Towne, Wayne Wang and Debra Winger.

I owe a great deal to the initial instinct and support of Sam Vaughan at Doubleday, to the care and energy of Jim Moser and Heather Kilpatrick at the same house, and to the enthusiasm and insight of Laura Morris at Secker & Warburg, not just a publisher but a friend – always a portrait on the wall.

There have been several people at *California* magazine who have encouraged and assisted this project: Meredith White and Bill Broyles; Harold Hayes and, especially, Andy Olstein.

Then there are those who listen to me, and who had to try to live with me while I was wondering about Warren. Gratitude is such a small part of what they deserve – Kate, Mathew and Rachel Thomson and, above all, Lucy Gray, who has done her own research on living with the ghost of Warren Beatty.

Notes

All quotations from the dialogue in movies are transcribed from the films.

There are these other books on Warren Beatty:

Jim Burke, *Warren Beatty* (New York: Belmont Tower Books, 1976)

Suzanne Munshower, *Warren Beatty: His Life, His Loves, His Work* (New York: St Martin's Press, 1983)

Lawrence J. Quirk, *The Films of Warren Beatty* (Secaucus, N.J.: Citadel Press, 1979)

James Spada, *Shirley & Warren* (New York: Collier Books, 1985)

p.6   "The only way . . ." is from Barbara Leaming, *Orson Welles: A Biography* (New York: Viking, 1985), p.191.

p.7   "was so fascinated . . ." is Leaming, p.191.

p.17   ". . . this amazing business . . ." is F. Scott Fitzgerald to Max Perkins, April 23 1938, from *The Letters of F. Scott Fitzgerald*, ed. Andrew Turnbull (New York: Scribner, 1963), p.278.

p.17   background on Richmond, Virginia, is from Virginius Dabney, *The Last Review: The Confederate Reunion, Richmond, 1932* (Chapel Hill, N.C.: Algonquin Books, 1984).

p.17   "The competition was . . ." is from Shirley MacLaine, *Dancing in the Light* (New York: Bantam, 1985), p.32.

p.19   "My father was . . ." is from Shirley MacLaine, *Don't Fall Off the Mountain* (New York: Norton, 1970), p.2.

p.19   "He spent most . . ." is MacLaine, *Don't Fall*, p.3.

p.20   "He could see . . ." is MacLaine, *Don't Fall*, p.11.

p.21   "Why aren't these windows . . ." is MacLaine, *Don't Fall*, p.149.

p.26   "He'll do something . . ." is MacLaine, *Don't Fall*, p.17.

p.28   "I may be a prejudiced . . ." is quoted in Charles Higham, *Orson Welles: The Rise and Fall of an American Genius* (New York: St Martin's Press, 1985), pp.217–18.

p.29   "I never thought . . ." is Munshower, p.7.

p.30   "Warren would look . . ." is MacLaine, *Don't Fall*, p.4; "acting out his soul . . ." is p.16.

p.30   "I remember he . . ." is quoted in MacLaine, *Dancing in the Light*, p.70.

p.37   "My earliest childhood . . ." is an interview with Joe Hyams, *Show Business Illustrated*, March 1962.

p.39   "practice elocution . . ." is F. Scott Fitzgerald, *The Great Gatsby* (New York: Scribner, 1925).

p.40   "Maybe it has . . ." is Munshower, p.11.

p.40   "Mad Dog Beatty" is John Phillips, *Papa John* (New York: Doubleday, 1986), p.166.

p.40   "Warren would come . . ." is *People*, July 1 1985.

p.40   "a cheerful hypocrite . . ." is *Time*, September 1 1961.

p.49   "A guy actually . . ." is in Rex Reed, "Will the Real Warren Beatty Please Shut Up", *Esquire*, August 1967.

p.55   "I don't think . . ." is MacLaine, *Don't Fall*, p.17.

p.56   "You mean me . . ." is MacLaine, *Don't Fall*, p.21.

p.57   "It was a junk heap . . ." is in Tommy Thompson, "Warren Beatty, the Charmer", *Life*, April 26 1968.

p.61   "I was born tired . . ." is MacLaine, *Dancing in the Light*, p.145.

p.62   ". . . it's something I got . . ." is an interview with Jack Nicholson, *Rolling Stone*, March 29 1984.

p.64   "Alas, his college boy . . ." is Britt Ekland, *True Britt* (Englewood Cliffs, N.J.: Prentice-Hall, 1980), p.135.

p.70   "She equipped me . . ." is Quirk, p.34.

p.79   "I sent for him . . ." is Joshua Logan, *Movie Stars, Real People and Me* (New York: Delacorte Press, 1978), p.269.

p.79   "They worked very hard . . ." is Logan, p.270.

p.86   this and all quotations from *A Loss of Roses* are from the Dramatists Play Service edition, 1963.

p.88   "I have never . . ." is Inge, *A Loss of Roses*, p.5.

p.89   "I have to say . . ." is Spada, p.36.

p.89   "Warren won't listen . . ." is Reed, p.127.

p.89   "Warren is really . . ." is Munshower, p.19.

p.90   "Warren changed lines . . ." is Reed, p.127.

p.90   "sensual around . . ." is Kenneth Tynan, *The New Yorker*, December 12 1959.

p.97   "That boy . . ." is Joan Collins, *Past Imperfect* (New York: Simon & Schuster, 1984), p.159.

p.98   "He was about . . ." is Collins, pp.159–60.

p.100   "We became inseparable . . ." is Collins, p.164.

p.101   "Don't go, Butterfly . . ." is Collins, p.170.

p.101   "He was never happier . . ." is Collins, p.171.

p.102   "He was an excellent . . ." is Collins, p.170.

NOTES

p.110 "Butterfly, we *can't* . . ." is Collins, p.174.

p.111 "It's your engagement . . ." is Collins, p.181.

p.111 "There's a basic . . ." is Michel Ciment, *Kazan on Kazan* (London: Secker & Warburg, 1973), pp.40–1.

p.113 "I'm better with actresses . . ." is Ciment, p.42.

p.114 "I was in awe . . ." is Lana Wood, *Natalie: A Memoir by Her Sister* (New York: Putnam, 1984), p.61.

p.123 "As for Bud . . ." is Ciment, p.144.

p.136 "because she had squeezed . . ." is Wood, p.61.

p.137 "How to make a . . ." is Collins, pp.183–4.

p.138 "stubborn and aggressive . . ." is Collins, p.179.

p.138 military career: letter from Selective Service System, September 6 1985.

p.139 "expressing his misery . . ." is Collins, p.189.

p.139 "It's show biz . . ." is Collins, p.187.

p.139 "His hair . . ." is Collins, p.192.

p.147 "I walked up to him . . ." is Munshower, p.35.

p.147 "Go home to bed . . ." is Dotson Rader, *Tennessee: Cry of the Heart* (New York: Doubleday, 1985), p.46.

p.147 "the difficulty . . ." is letter from Gavin Lambert, December 26 1984.

p.149 "I found him charming . . ." is Susan Strasberg, *Bittersweet* (New York: Putnam, 1980), p.143.

p.149 "surrounded by . . ." is Strasberg, p.144.

p.150 "I wasn't quite sure . . ." is Strasberg, p.144.

p.158 "It was obvious . . ." is Collins, p.196.

p.158 "Two reasons . . ." is Collins, p.196.

p.164 "All gold . . ." is Wood, p.69.

p.165 "Together in public . . ." is Wood, p.62.

p.165 "Norman Mailer will . . ." is Mailer, *Marilyn* (New York: Grosset & Dunlap, 1973), p.237.

p.165 "They occasionally . . ." is Wood, p.64.

p.167 "He told me . . ." is Wood, p.66.

p.182 "everybody in the story . . ." is Bosley Crowther, *The New York Times*, April 12 1962.

p.183 "Almost against my will . . ." is John Houseman, *Final Dress* (New York: Simon & Schuster, 1983), p.204.

p.183 "In an astonishing . . ." is Houseman, p.204.

p.184 "From the start . . ." is Houseman, p.207.

p.184 "Physically, Beatty . . ." is Stanley Kauffmann, *The New Republic*, April 23 1962.

p.185 "To break another . . ." is Jon Whitcomb, *Cosmopolitan*, February 1962.

p.185 "This young man . . ." is Whitcomb.

p.192 "In the middle 60s . . ." is Michel Ciment, *Conversations with Losey*, (New York: Methuen, 1985), p.191.

p.194 "Actors today . . ." is Reed, p.127.

p.194 "I've given you . . ." is Joseph Laitin, *Saturday Evening Post*, July 14–21 1962.

p.195 "If Natalie knew . . ." is Laitin.

p.201 "that of comparing . . ." is an interview with Robert Rossen, *Cahiers du Cinéma in English*, no. 7, 1967.

p.203 "She's got that flawed . . ." is David Richards, *Played Out: The Jean Seberg Story* (New York: Random House, 1981), p.132.

p.203 "fraternal, very intimate . . ." is Jean Seberg, "Lilith and I", *Cahiers du Cinéma in English*, no. 7, 1967.

p.203 "Warren is a brilliant . . ." is in Richards, p.137.

p.206 "She has a kind of . . ." is J.R. Salamanca, *Lilith* (New York: Simon & Schuster, 1961), p.223.

p.214 "It's not a bad film . . ." is Mike Wilmington and Gerald Peary, Interview with Warren Beatty, *The Velvet Light Trap*, no. 7, winter 1972–3.

p.215 "I spent about . . ." is in William Lee Jackson, "Bye-Bye Beatty", *The Players*, Fall 1964.

p.217 "Beatty gives it . . ." is Archer Winston, *The New York Post*, September 28 1965.

p.222 "It was quite strong . . ." is in Aaron Latham, "Warren Beatty Seriously", *Rolling Stone*, April 1 1982.

p.225 "whenever she wants . . ." is Munshower, p.46.

p.225 "He was considered . . ." is in Latham.

p.231 "Warren was the most . . ." is Ekland, p.132.

p.233 "surrounded by young actresses . . ." is Roger Vadim, *Bardot Deneuve Fonda* (New York: Simon & Schuster, 1986), p.242.

p.233 "That's *Shampoo* . . ." is an interview with Martin Scorsese.

p.240 "Bonnie writes . . ." is David Newman in Dan Yakir, "The 401st Blow", *Film Comment*, February 1985.

p.240 "He likes and . . ." is an interview with Alan Surgal.

p.250 "What do you see . . ." is an interview with Robert Towne.

p.251 "The way he discarded me . . ." is Latham.

p.253 "You know how he is . . ." is in Kevin Thomas, *Los Angeles Times*, July 2 1968.

p.254 "Warren was truly . . ." is an interview with Towne.

p.261 "Back in New York . . ." is Reed.

p.261 "a tiny pink . . ." is Reed.

p.261 "the desperation to be liked . . ." is Reed.

p.261 "There is . . ." is Reed.

p.262 "I don't know . . ." is in Wilmington and Peary.

p.263 "What do you think . . ." is in Wilmington and Peary.

p.279 "a cheap piece of . . ." is Bosley Crowther, *The New York Times*, August 14 1967.

p.279 "the most gruesome carnage . . ." is Joseph Morgenstern, *Newsweek*, August 21 1967.

p.279 "Both Producer Beatty . . ." is *Time*, August 25 1967.

p.280 "is about two . . ." is Penelope Gilliatt, *The New Yorker*, August 19 1967.

p.280 box-office figures are *Variety*.

p.281 "grossly unfair . . ." is Morgenstern, *Newsweek*, August 28 1967.

p.282 "a totally irrelevant exercise . . ." is Stefan Kanfer, *Time*, December 8 1967.

p.282 ". . . in a number of roles . . ." is Pauline Kael, *The New Yorker*, October 18 1967.

p.283 "So I ran up . . ." is Beatty in the film, *George Stevens: A Filmmaker's Journey*, 1984, directed by George Stevens Jr.

p.287 "Duke, I know . . ." is an interview with Niven Busch, *Film Comment*, August 1985.

p.293 "I did my greatest . . ." is MacLaine, *Dancing in the Light*, p.159.

p.293 "He procrastinated . . ." is Roman Polanski, *Roman* (New York: Morrow, 1984), p.250.

p.293 "a stream of . . ." is Polanski, p.305.

p.294 "Like Papillon . . ." is Polanski, p.313; "You're absolutely . . ." is p.314; "I'm not going to . . ." is p.314.

p.295 "Oh, nothing . . ." is Burke, p.159.

p.297 "It was like . . ." is Henry Ehrlich, "Warren and Julie: Together at Last", *Life*, June 1 1971.

p.297 "It became very apparent . . ." is interview with Frank Gilroy.

p.307 "too simple . . ." is Pauline Kael, *The New Yorker*, July 3 1971.

p.308 "I like to play schmucks . . ." is Wilmington and Peary.

p.310 Vancouver: see Ehrlich, *Life*, June 1 1971.

p.311 "Well, actually . . ." is interview with Gore Vidal, *American Film*, April 1977.

p.316 "The American presidency . . ." is in Roland Flamini, *Harper's Bazaar*, November 1972.

p.316 "I don't do . . ." is in Richard Reeves, *Saturday Review*, July 8 1972.

p.316 "He is seldom . . ." is Tommy Thompson, *Life*, April 26 1968.

p.319 "Warren was a . . ." is Munshower, p.89.

p.319 "He took a year out . . ." is Joan Dew, "Warren Beatty: More Than Just a Lover", *Redbook*, May 1974.

p.319 "invented the political concert . . ." is Munshower, p.91

p.321 "A sound and reasonable . . ." is *San Francisco Chronicle*, July 7 1968.

p.322 "has a greater degree . . ." is an interview with Sally Quinn, *The Washington Post*, June 1972.

p.322 "Before Florida and Wisconsin . . ." is Chris Chase, *Life*, June 23 1972.

p.322 "The most desperate feeling . . ." is Ehrlich, *Life*, June 1 1971.

p.322 "I even tried to . . ." is Flamini, *Harper's Bazaar*, November 1972.

p.323 "You drop everything . . ." is Flamini.

p.326 "'Easygoing' is not . . ." is in Frank Rich, "Warren Beatty Strikes Again", *Time*, July 3 1978.

p.326 "What do you have . . ." is Dew, *Redbook*, May 1974.

p.341 "So who do you like . . ." is an interview with Alan J. Pakula.

p.348 "but is wasting . . ." is Gary Arnold, *Washington Post*, December 15 1971.

p.349 "As an artist . . ." is Burke, p.164.

p.349 "Warren's gaze . . ." is Ekland, p.133.

p.349 "I missed you . . ." is Ekland, p.134.

p.350 "Warren is a . . ." is Wood, p.190.

p.351 "He was very angry . . ." is an interview with Robert Towne.

p.364 "Not long after . . ." is an interview with Molly Haskell.

p.364 "There does seem . . ." is Patrick McGilligan, "Warren Beatty Smoother after 'Shampoo'", *Boston Globe*, March 30 1975.

p.370 "The truth is . . ." is Spada, p.170.

p.370 "He feels that . . ." is Spada, p.170.

p.371 "One way to describe . . ." is Spada, p.156.

p.371 "wanted the daughter . . ." is an interview with Paul Schrader.

p.371 "He will always win . . ." is an interview with Schrader.

p.372 "And apparently . . ." is an interview with Schrader.

p.373 "I've been working on it . . ." is *Los Angeles Times*, August 11 1976.

p.380 "wasting time waiting . . ." is in Martin Gottfried, *Jed Harris: The Curse of Genius* (Boston: Little, Brown, 1984), p.256.

p.380 "Warren, I'd like to . . ." is an interview with Peter Bogdanovich.

p.381 "He likes to work . . ." is an interview with Buck Henry.

p.383 gift: see *Time*, May 14 1984.

p.383 "There isn't a whisper . . ." is Pauline Kael, *The New Yorker*, September 25 1978.

p.384 "I've got to read . . ." is in Hollis Alpert, "James Toback: For Love and Money", *American Film*, May 1980.

p.384 "How did you get . . ." is an interview with James Toback.

p.395 "I don't want to . . ." is interview, *American Film*, December 1981.

p.398 "He's got an amazing . . ." is an interview with Richard Sylbert.

p.398 "For me, as a . . ." is Latham, *Rolling Stone*, April 1 1982.

p.398 "You have to worry . . ." is an interview with Jerzy Kosinski.

p.401 "I feel that Warren . . ." is in John Brady, *The Craft of the Screenwriter: Interviews with Six Celebrated Screenwriters* (New York: Simon & Schuster, 1981), p.401.

p.408 "Not one media . . ." is Latham, *Rolling Stone*, April 1 1982.

p.409 Louise Bryant: see Robert A. Rosenstone, *Romantic Revolutionary: A Biography of John Reed* (New York: Knopf, 1975); Elizabeth Hardwick, "A Bunch of Reds", *Bartleby in Manhattan and Other Essays* (New York: Random House, 1983).

p.420 "no disaster . . ." is *Film Comment*, April 1982.

p.420 "A year later" is *Film Comment*, April 1983.

p.421 "It has to do with . . ." is Munshower, p.145.

p.421 "And if he ever delves . . ." is interview with Paul Schrader.

p.423 "They go to see": Herb Caen, *San Francisco Chronicle*, July 25 1984.

p.423 Toronto Film Festival: see Martin Knelman, "Romantic Revolutionary: Mr Beatty Goes to Toronto", *Boston Phoenix*, October 24 1984; Judy Stone, *San Francisco Chronicle*, September 12 1984; Mary Corliss, *Film Comment*, February 1985.

p.424 "They were both . . ." is Jerry Hall, with Christopher Hemphill, "From Rags to Rio", *Vanity Fair*, March 1985.

p.425 "He gathers indirectly": in Dominick Dunne, "Hide-and-Seek with Diane Keaton", *Vanity Fair*, February 1985.

p.425 "It is called *Who* . . .": is an interview with Wayne Wang.

p.428 "The trouble is . . ." is an interview with Martin Scorsese.

p.429 "Those who are demanding . . ." is Larry Leibert, *San Francisco Chronicle*, July 3 1985.

p.430 "irresponsible and intemperate . . ." is editorial, *San Francisco Chronicle*, July 5 1985.

p.431 "I knew every cut . . ." is David T. Friendly, "Blood Lines Drawn on the Cutting-Room Floor", *Los Angeles Times*, June 9 1985.

p.431 "a good cruel sense . . ." is an interview with James Toback.

p.433 "Where's the rest . . ." is an interview with Toback.

p.435 "Elaine is a . . ." is from David T. Friendly, "No Ishtar This Year for Columbia," *Los Angeles Times*, September 4 1986.

p.436 ". . . a feature writer . . ." is Joan Didion, *Democracy* (New York: Simon & Schuster, 1984), pp.50–51.

Filmography

Splendor in the Grass. Produced and directed by Elia Kazan; screenplay by William Inge; photography by Boris Kaufman; music by David Amram; production design by Richard Sylbert; associate producers, William Inge and Charles H. McGuire; make-up by Robert Jiras. With Natalie Wood, WB, Pat Hingle, Audrey Christie, Barbara Loden, Fred Stewart, Zohra Lampert, Joanna Roos, Jan Norris, Gary Lockwood, Sandy Dennis, John McGovern, William Inge (Warner Brothers, 124 mins, opened October 10 1961)

The Roman Spring of Mrs Stone. Produced by Louis de Rochemont; directed by José Quintero; screenplay by Gavin Lambert, from the novel by Tennessee Williams; photography by Harry Waxman; music by Richard Addinsell; production design by Roger Furse. With Vivien Leigh, WB, Lotte Lenya, Coral Browne, Jill St John, Jeremy Spenser, Stella Bonheur, Josephine Brown, Peter Dyneley, Carl Jaffé, Harold Kasket, Viola Keats, Cleo Laine, Bessie Love, Warren Mitchell, Ernest Thesiger, Sarah Miles (Warner Brothers, 104 mins, opened December 28 1961)

All Fall Down. Produced by John Houseman; directed by John Frankenheimer; screenplay by William Inge, from the novel by James Leo Herlihy; photography by Lionel Lindon; music by Alex North; art direction by George W. Davis and Preston Ames. With Eva Marie Saint, WB, Karl Malden, Angela Lansbury, Brandon De Wilde, Constance Ford, Barbara Baxley, Evans Evans, Jennifer Howard, Madame Spivy, Albert Paulson (MGM, 111 mins, opened April 11 1962)

Lilith. Produced and directed by Robert Rossen; screenplay by Rossen from the novel by J. R. Salamanca; photography by Eugen Shufftan; music by Kenyon Hopkins; production design by Richard Sylbert. With WB, Jean Seberg, Peter Fonda, Kim Hunter, Anne Meacham, James Patterson, Jessica Walter, Gene Hackman, Robert Reilly, Rene Auberjonois, Lucy Smith (Columbia, 114 mins, opened September 20 1964)

Mickey One. Produced and directed by Arthur Penn; screenplay by Alan

455

Surgal; photography by Ghislain Cloquet; music by Eddie Sauter and Stan Getz; production design by George Jenkins; make-up by Robert Jiras. With WB, Alexandra Stewart, Hurd Hatfield, Franchot Tone, Teddy Hart, Jeff Corey, Kamatari Fujiwara, Donne Michelle, Ralph Froody, Norman Gottschalk, Dick Lucas, Benny Dunn (Columbia, 93 mins, opened September 27 1965)

Promise Her Anything. Produced by Stanley Rubin; directed by Arthur Hiller; screenplay by William Peter Blatty, from a story by Arne Sultan and Marvin Worth; photography by Douglas Slocombe; music by Lynn Murray; art direction by Wilfrid Shingleton. With WB, Leslie Caron, Bob Cummings, Hermione Gingold, Lionel Stander, Asa Maynor, Keenan Wynn, Cathleen Nesbitt, Michael Bradley, Bessie Love, Mavis Villiers, Warren Mitchell, Sydney Tafler (Warner Brothers, 98 mins, opened February 22 1966)

Kaleidoscope. Produced by Elliott Kastner; directed by Jack Smight; screenplay by Robert and Jane Howard Carrington; photography by Christopher Challis; music by Stanley Myers; art direction by Maurice Carter; assistant producer Peter Medak. With WB, Susannah York, Clive Revill, Eric Porter, Murray Melvin, George Sewell, Stanley Meadows, John Junkin, Larry Taylor, Yootha Joyce, Jane Birkin, George Murcell, Anthony Newlands (Warner Brothers, 103 mins, opened September 22 1966)

Bonnie and Clyde. Produced by WB; directed by Arthur Penn; screenplay by David Newman and Robert Benton; special consultant, Robert Towne; photography by Burnett Guffey; music by Charles Strouse; art direction by Dean Tavoularis; edited by Dede Allen; costumes by Theadora Van Runkle; make-up by Robert Jiras. With WB, Faye Dunaway, Michael J. Pollard, Gene Hackman, Estelle Parsons, Denver Pyle, Dub Taylor, Evans Evans, Gene Wilder, James Stiver (Warner Brothers, 111 mins, opened August 13 1967)

The Only Game in Town. Produced by Fred Kohlmar; directed by George Stevens; screenplay by Frank D. Gilroy, from his own play; photography by Henri Decaë; music by Maurice Jarre; art direction by Herman Blumenthal and Auguste Capelier. With Elizabeth Taylor, WB, Charles Braswell, Hank Henry (Fox, 113 mins, opened March 4 1970)

McCabe and Mrs Miller. Produced by David Foster and Mitchell Brower; directed by Robert Altman; screenplay by Altman and Brian McKay, from the novel *McCabe* by Edmund Naughton; photography by Vilmos Zsigmond; songs by Leonard Cohen; production design by Leon Ericksen; make-up by Robert Jiras. With WB, Julie Christie, Rene Auberjonois, John Schuck, Bert Remsen, Keith Carradine, William Devane, Corey Fischer, Shelley Duvall,

Michael Murphy, Anthony Holland, Hugh Millais, Manfred Schulz, Jace Vander Veen (Warner Brothers, 120 mins, opened June 24 1971)

$ (Dollars). Produced by Mike Frankovich; directed and written by Richard Brooks; photography by Petrus Schloemp; music by Quincy Jones; art direction by Guy Sheppard and Olaf Ivens; make-up by Ernest Schmekel and Robert Jiras. With WB, Goldie Hawn, Gert Frobe, Robert Webber, Scott Brady, Arthur Brauss, Robert Stiles, Wolfgang Kieling, Robert Herron, Christiane Maybach, Hans Hutter (Columbia, 119 mins, opened December 15 1971)

The Parallax View. Produced and directed by Alan J. Pakula; screenplay by David Giler and Lorenzo Semple Jr, from the novel by Loren Singer; photography by Gordon Willis; music by Michael Small; production design by George Jenkins. With WB, Hume Cronyn, William Daniels, Paula Prentiss, Kelly Thordsen, Earl Hindman, Kenneth Mars, Walter McGinn, Jim Davis, Bill Joyce, Bill McKinney, William Jordan (Paramount, 102 mins, opened June 19 1974)

Shampoo. Produced by WB; directed by Hal Ashby; screenplay by WB and Robert Towne; photography by Laszlo Kovacs; music by Paul Simon; production design by Richard Sylbert; edited by Robert C. Jones. With WB, Julie Christie, Goldie Hawn, Lee Grant, Jack Warden, Tony Bill, Carrie Fisher, Jay Robinson, George Furth, Brad Dexter, William Castle (Columbia, 112 mins, opened February 11 1975)

The Fortune. Produced by Mike Nichols and Don Devlin; directed by Nichols; screenplay by Adrien Joyce; photography by John Alonzo; music by David Shire; production design by Richard Sylbert. With WB, Jack Nicholson, Stockard Channing, Florence Stanley, Richard B. Shull, Tom Newman, John Fiedler, Scatman Crothers, Dub Taylor, Ian Wolfe, Rose Michtom, Brian Avery, Christopher Guest, Kathryn Grody (Columbia, 88 mins, opened May 20 1975)

Heaven Can Wait. Produced by WB; directed by WB and Buck Henry; screenplay by WB and Elaine May; photography by William A. Fraker; music by Dave Grusin; production design by Paul Sylbert; edited by Robert C. Jones and Don Zimmerman; costumes by Theadora Van Runkle, Richard Bruno, Mike Hoffman and Arlene Encell. With WB, Julie Christie, James Mason, Jack Warden, Charles Grodin, Dyan Cannon, Buck Henry, Vincent Gardenia, Joseph Maher, Dolph Sweet, R. G. Armstrong, John Randolph, William Sylvester (Paramount, 101 mins, opened June 28 1978)

Reds. Produced and directed by WB; executive producers, Simon Relph and

Dede Allen; associate producer, David MacLeod; screenplay by WB and Trevor Griffiths; photography by Vittorio Storaro; edited by Dede Allen and Craig McKay; production design by Richard Sylbert; music by Stephen Sondheim and Dave Grusin. With WB, Diane Keaton, Jack Nicholson, Edward Herrmann, Jerzy Kosinski, Paul Sorvino, Maureen Stapleton, Nicolas Coster, M. Emmet Walsh, Ian Wolfe, Bessie Love, MacIntyre Dixon, Pat Starr, Eleanor D. Wilson, Max Wright, George Plimpton, Harry Ditson, Leigh Curran, Kathryn Grody, Brenda Currin, Nancy Duiguid, Norman Chancer, Dolph Sweet, Ramon Bieri, Jack O'Leary, Gene Hackman, William Daniels, Dave King, Joseph Buloff, Josef Sommer, R. G. Armstrong (Paramount, 199 mins, opened December 3 1981)

Ishtar. Produced by WB; directed and written by Elaine May; associate producer, David MacLeod; photography by Vittorio Storaro; edited by Steve Rotter, Bill Reynolds and Richie Cirinzione; production design by Paul Sylbert; music by Dave Grusin; songs by Paul Williams. With WB, Dustin Hoffman, Isabelle Adjani, Charles Grodin, Carol Kane, Tess Harper, Jack Weston (Columbia, 103 mins, opened on May 15 1987)

As John Q McCabe

Index

461

Photo Credits

About the Author

David Thomson was born in London in 1941 and educated at Dulwich College and the London School of Film Technique. He has worked in publishing, and from 1977 to 1981 he was Director of Film Studies at Dartmouth College. He has been film critic for *The Real Paper* in Boston and for *California* magazine. He is the author of several books on film—*Movie Man; A Biographical Dictionary of Film; America in the Dark;* and *Overexposures*—as well as three novels, the most recent of which, *Suspects* (also in Vintage), is made up of characters from *film noir*. He is at present at work on a revised edition of *A Biographical Dictionary of Film*, the official biography of David O. Selznick, and several film scripts.